THE BEETHOVEN COMPANION

The
BEETHOVEN
Companion

Edited by

Thomas K. Scherman and

Louis Biancolli

Garden City, New York

Doubleday & Company, Inc.

1972

Grateful acknowledgment is made for permission to reprint excerpts from the following publications:

The Letters of Beethoven, Volumes I, II, and III, edited by Emily Anderson. Reprinted by permission of St. Martin's Press, Inc., Macmillan & Company, Ltd., and The Macmillan Company of Canada.

Masters of the Keyboard, by Willi Apel, copyright 1947 by the President and Fellows of Harvard College. Reprinted by permission of Harvard University Press.

The Analytical Concert Guide, edited by Louis Biancolli and William S. Mann. Reprinted by permission of the editors and Cassell and Company, Ltd.

Pleasures of Music, edited by Jacques Barzun. Reprinted by permission of Viking Press, Inc.

The Diaries of Tchaikovsky, translated from the Russian and annotated by Wladimir Lakond, copyright 1945 by Wladimir Lakond. Reprinted by permission of the author.

Vanguard VRS-1033 jacket notes by Abraham Veinus, copyright 1959 by Vanguard Recording Society, Inc. Reprinted by permission of the author and the publisher.

Vanguard VRS-1101 and VSD-71124 jacket notes by S. W. Bennett, copyright 1963 and copyright 1965 respectively, by Vanguard Recording Society, Inc.; Vanguard VRS-429 jacket notes by Sidney Finkelstein, copyright 1953 by Vanguard Recording Society, Inc. All reprinted by permission of the publisher.

A Critical Study of Beethoven's Nine Symphonies, by Hector Berlioz, translated by Edwin Evans; "The Tenth Symphony," by Ludwig Nohl, from *Beethoven's Symphonies: Their Idealized Meaning*, by Ernst Van Elterlein. Both reprinted by permission of William Reeves Bookseller, Ltd.

Beethoven's Sonatas Discussed, by Eric Blom. Reprinted by permission of J. M. Dent & Sons, Ltd.

Conversations with Casals, by J. Ma Corredor, translated by André Mangeot, copyright 1956 by E. P. Dutton & Company, Inc. Reprinted by permission of the publisher and Hutchinson & Company, Ltd.

Beethoven, by Walter Riezler. Reprinted by permission of E. P. Dutton & Company, Inc.

Angel COLH-66 jacket notes, by Eric Blom. Reprinted by permission of Gramophone Company, Ltd., and the author.

"The Immortal Beloved," by Max Unger. "Beethoven's Adelaïde," by Martial

Douel. "George Thompson, Publisher," by Richard Aldrich, Ludwig Van Beethoven, as quoted; all included in Vol. 13, 1927; "Erinnerungen aus meinem Leben," by Carl Czerny, Vol. 42, 1956; "Beethoven's Instrumental Music," by E. T. A. Hoffmann, translated by Arthur Ware Locke, Vol. 3, 1917; "Beethoven's Irische Lieder: Sources and Problems," by Alice Anderson Hufstader, Vol. 44, 1958. All articles above appeared in and were copyrighted by the *Musical Quarterly*. "Beethoven: Six Songs for High Voice," by H. E. Krehbiel, *Schirmer's Library of Musical Classics*, 1902, and Preface to Schirmer Edition of Opus 98, 1902, by H. E. Krehbiel; *Beethoven: Impressions by His Contemporaries*, edited by O. G. Sonneck, copyright 1926 and 1954 by G. Schirmer. All of the above reprinted by permission of G. Schirmer, Inc.

Beethoven's Last Sonata, by Philip T. Barford. Reprinted by permission of the author and Music and Letters, Ltd.

"The Choral Fantasia," by Edward J. Dent, "Beethoven and Goethe," by Scott Goddard, "Some Aspects of Beethoven's Art Forms" by Donald Francis Tovey, all included in *Music and Letters*, April 1927. Reprinted by permission of the publisher.

Composers on Music, edited by Sam Morgenstern. Reprinted by permission of Random House, Inc., and Faber and Faber, Ltd.

The Life and Works of Beethoven, by John N. Burk, copyright 1943 by Random House, Inc. Reprinted by permission of the publisher.

The Beethoven Quartets, by Joseph Kerman, copyright 1967 by Joseph Kerman; *Beethoven: His Spiritual Development*, by J. W. N. Sullivan, copyright 1927 by J. W. N. Sullivan and renewed 1955 by E. V. Sullivan; *Doctor Faustus*, by Thomas Mann, translated by H. T. Lowe-Porter, copyright 1948 by Alfred A. Knopf, Inc. All reprinted by permission of the publisher.

Program notes for the Boston Symphony Orchestra by John N. Burk and Philip Hale, copyright by the Boston Symphony Orchestra, Inc. Reprinted by permission of the copyright owner.

Nonesuch H-71025 jacket notes, by Edward Tatnall Canby. Reprinted by permission of the author and Nonesuch Records.

The Orchestra from Beethoven to Berlioz, by Adam Carse. Reprinted by permission of the original publisher, W. Heffer & Sons, Ltd., and Broude Brothers, Ltd.

"The Influence of Deafness on the Creative Instinct," by Terence Cawthorne, originally published in *The Laryngoscope* and later included in the bound *Transactions of the American Laryngological, Rhinological and Otological Society: 1960*. Reprinted by permision of the publisher.

"Disease—or Defamation," by Charles K. Carpenter, first published in *The Annals of Otology, Rhinology and Laryngology*, Vol. 45, No. 4, December 1936. Reprinted by permission of the publishers.

The Fugue in Beethoven's Piano Music, by J. V. Cockshoot. Reprinted by permission of Dover Publications, Inc., and Routledge & Kegan Paul, Ltd.

Monsieur Croche the Dilettante Hater, by Claude Debussy, copyright 1928 and 1956 by the Viking Press, Inc. Reprinted by permission of the Viking Press, Inc., and Ernest Benn, Ltd.

Beethoven, A Critical Biography by Vincent d'Indy. Reprinted by permission of the Boston Music Company.

The Musical Workshop, by Frederick Dorian, copyright 1947 by Harper & Row, Publishers, Inc. Reprinted by permission of the publisher.

Program notes by Edward Downes for the New York Philharmonic. Reprinted by permission of the Philharmonic-Symphony Society of New York, Inc.

Masterworks of the Orchestral Repertoire: 1954, Music as Metaphor: The Elements of Expression: 1960, and *Image and Structure in Chamber Music: 1964*, all by Donald N. Ferguson. Reprinted by permission of the University of Minnesota Press.

Beethoven's Pianoforte Sonatas, by Edwin Fischer. Reprinted by permission of Faber and Faber, Ltd.

In Chamber Music, by Roger Fiske, edited by Alec Robertson, and *Music Criticisms* by Eduard Hanslick, translated by Henry Pleasants. Both reprinted by permission of Penguin Books, Ltd.

Vol. I and II of *Thayer's Life of Beethoven*, revised and edited by Elliot Forbes, copyright 1969; Princeton Paperback, 1970. Reprinted by permission of Princeton University Press.

Concerning Music, by Wilhelm Furtwängler, translated by L. J. Lawrence, copyright 1949 by Atlantis Verlag, Zurich; English translation copyright 1953 by Boosey & Hawkes, Ltd. Reprinted by permission of the publishers.

Vox SVBX-545 and Vox FBX-53 jacket notes, by Harry Halbreich; Turnabout TV-34162 and Turnabout TV-4059 jacket notes. All reprinted by permission of Vox Productions, Inc.

The Art Song, by James Husst Hall, copyright 1953 by the University of Oklahoma Press; *Beethoven Studies*, by Ludwig Misch, copyright 1953 by the University of Oklahoma Press. Both reprinted by permission of the publisher.

Angel 35719 jacket notes, by Paul Hamburger. Reprinted by permission of the author.

"Beethovens Opferliedkompositionen," by Kurt Herbst, from *Neus Beethovenjahrbuch*, Vol. 5. Reprinted by permission of the original publisher, Edition Peters.

La Vie de Beethoven, by Edouard Herriot, copyright 1929 by Editions Gallimard. Reprinted by permission of the publisher.

Preface to *Szene Aus Vestas Feuer*, by Willy Hess, copyright 1953 by Bruckner Verlag, Wiesbaden, Germany. Reprinted by permission of Bruckner Verlag and C. F. Peters Corporation.

Mendelssohn, A Second Elijah, by Schima Kaufman, copyright 1934 and 1962 by Schima Kaufman. Reprinted by permission of Thomas Y. Crowell Company, Inc.

Das Werk Beethovens, compiled from *Thematisch-Bibliographischen Verzeichnis Aller Vollendeten Kompositionen Ludwig Van Beethovens*, by Georg Kinsky, edited by Hans Halm. Reprinted by permission of G. Henle Verlag.

The Complete Opera Book, by Gustave Kobbe, edited by the Earl of Harewood, copyright 1919 by Gustave Kobbe, copyright 1947 and 1951 by C. W. Kobbe. Reprinted by permission of G. P. Putnam's Sons and Putnam & Company, London.

The Study of Fugue, by Alfred Mann, copyright 1958 by Rutgers, the State University. Reprinted by permission of Rutgers University Press.

Angel 35509 and Angel 35843 jacket notes, by William S. Mann. Reprinted by permission of the author.

Beethoven: Biography of a Genius, by George R. Marek, copyright 1969 by George R. Marek. Reprinted by permission of Funk & Wagnalls and William Kimber & Company, Ltd.

Beethoven and His Forerunners, by Daniel Gregory Mason. Reprinted by permission of Scott Mason, Stamford Trust Company, Executor of the Estate of Daniel Gregory Mason.

The Quartets of Beethoven, by Daniel Gregory Mason, copyright 1947 by Oxford University Press. Reprinted by permission of the publisher.

Beethoven: The Piano Sonatas by A. F. Milne; *Some Thoughts on Beethoven's Choral Symphony*, by Ralph Vaughan Williams; *The Theories of Claude Debussy*, by L. Vallas, translated by M. O'Brien; *Beethoven*, by Donald Francis Tovey, edited by Hubert J. Foss; *Essays in Musical Analysis*, Vol. I, "Symphonies," Vol. II, "Symphonies, Variations and Orchestral Polyphony," Vol. III, "Concertos," Vol. IV, "Illustrative Music," Vol. V, "Vocal Music," Vol. VI, "Supplementary Essays," "Glossary and Index," and "Chamber Music," by Donald Francis Tovey; *The Main Stream of Music and Other Essays*, by Donald Francis Tovey. All published by Oxford University Press and reprinted with their permission.

Das Deutsche Lied Seit Mozart, by Hans Joachim Moser. Reprinted by permission of Atlantis Verlag.

Franz Grillparzer and the Austrian Drama, by Gustav Pollak. Reprinted by permission of Dodd, Mead & Company, Inc.

La Jeunesse de Beethoven, by J. G. Prod'homme, copyright 1927 by Librairie Delagrave; *Les Sonates pour piano de Beethoven*, by J. G. Prod'homme, copyright 1937 by Librairie Delagrave. Both reprinted by permission of the publisher.

Beethoven, by Alan Pryce-Jones, copyright 1957 by Gerald Duckworth & Company, Ltd. Reprinted by permission of the Macmillan Company and Gerald Duckworth & Company, Ltd.

Antonio Salieri—Beethovens Lärare, by Julius Rabe. Reprinted by permission of Svenska Samfundet för Musikforskning.

Beethoven, The Man Who Freed Music, by Robert Haven Schauffler, copyright 1929 by Doubleday & Company, Inc., copyright 1957 by Robert Haven Schauffler. Reprinted by permission of Holt, Rinehart and Winston, Inc., and the Estate of Robert Haven Schauffler.

The Great Pianists by Harold C. Schonberg, copyright 1963 by Harold C. Schonberg. Reprinted by permission of Simon & Schuster, Inc., and Max Wilkinson Associates.

Autobiography, by Johann Schenk as quoted in *Forgotten Musicians*, by Paul Nettl. Reprinted by permission of the Philosophic Library, Inc.

The Young Beethoven, by Ludwig Schiedermair, edited and translated by Thomas K. Scherman. First published in 1925 by Quelle & Meyer Verlag. Reprinted by permission of the Estate of Ludwig Schiedermair and the publisher.

Life of Beethoven, by Anton Schindler, Vol. 2 translated by Ignaz Moscheles. Reprinted by permission of Gamut Music Company.

Beethoven as I Knew Him, by A. F. Schindler, edited by Donald W. MacArdle and translated by C. S. Jolly. Reprinted by permission of the University of North Carolina Press and Faber and Faber, Ltd.

Beethoven, by Marion M. Scott, *Master Musicians Series*, first published in the United States in 1949. Reprinted by permission of Farrar, Straus & Giroux, Inc., and J. M. Dent & Sons, Ltd.

Preface by J. S. Shedlock to *Selection of Studies*, by Cramer. Reprinted by permission of Galliard, Ltd.

The Quartets of Ludwig Van Beethoven, by Arthur Shepherd, program notes for a memorial series of seven concerts by the Cleveland Quartet in Severance Hall, 1935. Reprinted by permission of Mrs. Arthur Shepherd.

Lexicon of Musical Invective, by Nicolas Slonimsky, copyright 1953 and 1965 by Charles Scribner's Sons. Reprinted by permission of the publisher.

The Ten Beethoven Sonatas for Piano and Violin, by Joseph Szigeti. Reprinted by permission of American String Teachers Asociation.

A Violinist's Notebook, by Joseph Szigeti. Reprinted by permission of Gerald Duckworth & Company, Ltd.

A Companion to Beethoven's Pianoforte Sonatas, by Donald F. Tovey, copyright 1931 and 1959 by the Associated Board of the Royal Schools of Music. Reprinted by permission of the Associated Board of the Royal Schools of Music and Belwin-Mills Publishing Corporation.

Rossini: A Study in Tragi-Comedy, by Francis Toye, copyright 1963 by Francis Toye. Reprinted by permission of W. W. Norton & Company, Inc.

Of Music and Music-Making, by Bruno Walter, translated by Paul Hamburger, copyright 1957 by Bruno Walter, English translation copyright 1961 by Faber and Faber, Ltd. Reprinted by permission of W. W. Norton & Company, Inc. and Faber and Faber, Ltd.

Beethoven: The Search for Reality, by W. J. Turner. Reprinted by permission of Ernest Benn, Ltd.

Ein Faust Opernplan Beethovens Und Goethes by Max Unger. Reprinted by permission of Gustav Bosse Verlag.

"Beethoven's F Major String Quartet, Opus 18, No. 1, in Its Original Version," by Carl Waack. First publihed in *Die Musik*, 1904. Reprinted by permission of Hans Schneider Musikverlag.

Richard Wagner's Prose Works, by Richard Wagner, translated by William Ashton Ellis. Reprinted by permission of Routledge & Kegan Paul, Ltd.

Notes by Herbert Weinstock, originally produced in programs of the Little Orchestra Society. Reprinted by permission of the Little Orchestra Society.

To Harry Scherman
Who loved music, books, and people
with his whole being

———♦———

ACKNOWLEDGMENT

———♦———

THIS book would never have materialized without the constant inspiration and prodding of Julius Kruskal, perhaps the greatest Beethoven buff of our time; the indefatigable assistance of Mary Lou Tuffin at the typewriter, at the library, and at the paste pot; and the equally indefatigable assistance of Jeanne Biancolli in matters of musical and literary advice not only to her husband but to her dear friend on the other side of the collaboration. Equally indispensable was the stimulation of Kenneth and Anne McCormick, as proud godparents of the *Companion*; and of Barbara Bikle, as witty and gracious editorial custodian. Above all we must betray the discreet anonymity of Frank Campbell, Chief of the Music Research Division of the Library of the Performing Arts of Lincoln Center, together with his select and highly trained staff, whose sedulous and perceptive aid was invaluable to the editors and, we hope, to the readers alike.

To all of these individuals whose imprints are felt on every page, we extend our heartfelt thanks.

L.B. AND T.K.S.

THIS is a "family Beethoven" in many respects. It measures up to what we have come to describe as "family size." It offers as comprehensive a view of Beethoven and his music as is possible in one volume, and it invites all members of a family of music lovers in the access and diversity of its material. Also, it is expected to serve such a family over a long period as a source of repeated reference to everything concerning Beethoven, and as a refreshing retreat for those who want to read beyond the immediate need. It is hoped that it will serve as a complete library in itself, making any further addition to the Beethoven shelf a matter of love rather than of pressing need. This Beethoven guide is for all Beethoven lovers, and who today, in some form or degree, is not one? The plan is an organic and evolutionary one. It takes the master period by period, development by development, one might say plateau by plateau, and examines him and his music from start to finish. Each of the sections summarizes the events of a given span of years. This is followed by the reminiscences of those who knew Beethoven, that in turn by the relevant letters, and finally a classified analysis of the compositions of those years, technical and lucid, for musician and layman alike.

For those interested in a particular composition, everything pertinent will be easy to locate, be it sonata, symphony, overture, or opera. From that point, whatever the place in the book, they may venture into the neighboring terrain of life, letters, and the social and artistic milieu within which the composition had its being. Some repetition could not be avoided, since the goal was to make each section a solid unit in itself, yet integral to the over-all scheme. The design of the book offers both a mine of easily found information and of incentives to go further.

Those who stay with the book long and frequently enough should find that Beethoven, *The greatest creative benefactor of all time*, bar none, comes fully alive through the succinct installments of his life, through the eyes and ears of his friends and contemporaries, and through the trained, fully attuned minds of the many scholars and musicians who have delved deeply into the fabulous continent that is the Beethoven that counts—his music.

LOUIS BIANCOLLI

I WOULD like to add a few explanatory notes in respect to the choice of analytical essays about Beethoven's music, which, as Louis Biancolli stated, make up the bulk of this book.

Because of publishing requirements, we have refrained from using actual musical texts or quotations. This, perforce, entailed two problems. In those essays which we felt were the most enlightening ones available about certain compositions, but which, in their original published form, included excerpts of musical texts as a necessary part of the author's explanation or analysis, we have substituted the much less adequate— but thoroughly necessary—short cut of describing the particular musical passage in prose. Those prose equivalents are indicated throughout the book by being included within square brackets: [ ]. We have tried, as well, to make them as clear as possible so that those readers who could not read music would be able to identify the passage to which the author was referring.

However, because of this imposed restriction, we have had to eliminate certain essays which we felt were indispensable to a complete understanding of Beethoven's compositions, because those musical quotations contained in them were so numerous and/or so involved that no other language *except music itself* could adequately reveal the author's intentions. Such works as Sir Donald Tovey's remarkable study of the Ninth Symphony; Heinrich Schenker's brilliant critical comments on the last five piano sonatas (included in his edition published by Universal in 1920, and now, unfortunately, out of print); Gustav Nottebohm's two volumes: *Beethoveniana* and *Zweite Beethoveniana* (Leipzig, 1872 and 1873), as well as his thoroughly annotated editions of two of the sketch-books from the years 1801 to 1803——together with discussions of them in English, by Paul Mies (*Two Sketch-Books by Beethoven*, London, 1929), and, in Russian, by N. L. Fuschmana (Moscow, 1962); and Allen Forte's *The Compositional Matrix* (based on the sketches of Beethoven's Opus

109), published by the Music Teachers' National Association in 1961—
these are but a few of the great analytical works about Beethoven's music
intended for the serious music student which, unfortunately, had to be
left out of this book.

For those readers who *can* read and understand musical notation, we
have included references to *measure numbers* in certain essays, such as
Sir Donald Tovey's fascinating essay comparing the Piano Sonata, Opus
28, and the String Quartet, Opus 131.

To summarize, we have tried to include those essays which, in our
judgment, represented the most illuminating analyses of Beethoven's
compositions, but which at the same time were intelligible and perspicuous
to the casual music reader, to the avid concertgoer or record-listener,
and to the serious and dedicated music student alike. In many cases we
have included more than one viewpoint about a particular work; we have
even gone so far as to include one musicologist's analysis of a particular
individual *movement* of a larger work *within* the over-all analysis by
another author.

Within the last three decades, the advent of long-playing records and
the infinitely more imaginative programing on the part of musical artists
and radio program directors have made the lesser-known, but often equally
fascinating, compositions of Beethoven much more readily available to
the average music listener. We have, therefore, included analytical essays
about *all* of Beethoven's instrumental works, as well as *all* the vocal compositions with orchestral accompaniments, obscure as many of these might
seem to the casual reader. Our philosophy was that, sooner or later, the
master's entire musical output would become known and familiar to an
ever-widening audience, and that an acquaintance with the background
and musical content of every Beethoven opus would become more of a
necessity. We have used as our schematic guide the comprehensive thematic and bibliographic catalogue of Beethoven's works by Georg Kinsky
(which was completed after Kinsky's death and thoroughly edited by Hans
Halm, and published in Munich by G. Henle Verlag in 1955). We have
identified those works which do not bear opus numbers in the same manner as is used in the Kinsky-Halm book—that is, with the letters "WoO"
(standing for "without opus number"), followed by the identifying
number.

Where our research has *not* been able to turn up a sufficiently illuminating essay, I myself have written short musical analyses. I have
also taken the liberty of adding my own editorial comments to certain
excerpts by other authors where I have felt that these would add to a
more complete musical comprehension of a particular composition.

There are, however, certain musical omissions which will be obvious
to even the most casual reader. One of the most important of these
omissions is the large body of Beethoven's vocal compositions with piano

accompaniment. We have attempted to cover those of his songs which appear most often on recital programs or are of distinct musical-historical interest. Many of the others have been covered in the over-all essays by J.-G. Prod'homme, extracted from his *La Jeunesse de Beethoven*, and the general survey of Beethoven's Lieder from Hugo Moser's *Das Deutsche Lied*, both of which are included. However, we definitely feel that a *thorough* analysis of the over one hundred songs by Beethoven, from a musicological, textual, and musically technical standpoint, demands a full volume of its own.

Another large area of Beethoven's creative output which we have taken the liberty of omitting is that of the fifty-odd canons, which appeared mainly in his letters or comments to his friends and the interest of which are, therefore, primarily biographical rather than musical.

To close, I would like to mention how privileged I feel to have been invited to undertake the selection of musical commentary for this book. In the first place, I was perforce required to restudy works which I had not thoroughly examined since my student days—a restudy which so often offered me startling new musical insights into passages which I had too frequently taken for granted. I also, at the same time, became acquainted with a great deal of Beethoven's vast musical output which I had not known up to the present. To be led through those fertile byways by such articulate and knowledgeable guides as Donald Tovey, Willy Hess, Donald MacArdle, Ludwig Misch, Jacques-Gabriel Prod'homme, Romain Rolland, Ludwig Schiedermair, and so many other equally stimulating authorities served to make that musical journey a high point in my professional life. I can only hope, along with Louis Biancolli, that the present book will partially convey that personal excitement to its readers.

THOMAS K. SCHERMAN

CONTENTS

PART TWO: 1792–1803

PART THREE: 1803–13

PART FOUR: 1813–27

PART FIVE

PART SIX

THE BEETHOVEN COMPANION

His Life

L UDWIG VAN BEETHOVEN was born at Bonn on the Rhine. His father, Johann van Beethoven, had married in 1767 Maria Magdalena Laym, daughter of the head cook at the palace of Ehrenbreitstein. Their first child died in infancy. Ludwig was the second. Of several others that followed only two lived to grow up, Caspar Anton Karl, born in 1774, and Nicholas Johann, born in 1776. The family was of Flemish origin; it was Ludwig's grandfather who had established the branch in Bonn.

In those days Bonn derived most of its importance from being the seat of Maximilian Friedrich, Archbishop-Elector of Cologne; and Johann van Beethoven earned his living as a singer in the electoral chapel. Johann, an easygoing man of weak character, was anything but an ideal parent, for he was intemperate, this weakness becoming more marked as he got older. Nevertheless it was he who first discovered Ludwig's unusual gifts, and with the memory of the young Mozart's triumphs fresh in his mind he hoped that his son might likewise win wealth and fame as a child prodigy. But the boy's genius was not of the kind that flowers prematurely and, when his disappointed father tried to drive him, he was met (we may guess) with a touch of Ludwig's characteristic obstinacy. And so we get our first glimpse of him as a tiny boy standing forlornly on a footstool in front of the keyboard, the tears streaming from his eyes.

With his music teachers during his early years we need not concern ourselves. They had little influence on his future development. One of them, a certain Tobias Pfeiffer, was a boon companion of Johann van Beethoven's. We hear of them returning late from the wineshop in a state of exaltation, rousing the little Ludwig from his bed and keeping him at the keyboard until dawn.

If he spent many such nights it is no wonder that he appeared unusually quiet in the morning. He was sent to an elementary school,

and there he is described as "a shy and taciturn boy, observing more
and pondering more than he spoke." We also hear without surprise
that he was unkempt and untidy. He learned to read and to write a
very fair hand (though in later life his letters grew more and more
illegible). He picked up enough French to write intelligibly though
atrociously in that language, and enough Latin to understand the texts
he set. Spelling, even in his native German, was always shaky, and
punctuation more shaky still: the mature Beethoven seldom ventured on
anything more decisive than a comma. Arithmetic was beyond him. He
might manage a little simple addition with the help of his ten fingers,
but the calculations involved in financial transactions always gave him
difficulty, and right at the end of his life the composer of the Ninth
Symphony was being instructed by his nephew in simple multiplication—
on his deathbed!

One must bear in mind that after the age of eleven he had no
regular schooling except in music. Yet it is curious that an intellect so
powerful in other directions should have failed so conspicuously in these
elementary matters. One can only regard it as an example of Beethoven's
general inability to adjust himself to the world around him. His intense
absorption in the rich spiritual and artistic world he created prevented
him from ever coming to terms with the life lived by ordinary mortals.
This characteristic remained with him to the end and showed itself in
other fields besides the intellectual. Physically he was clumsy: "In his
behavior," says Ries, who knew him well, "Beethoven was awkward
and helpless; his uncouth movements were often destitute of grace. He
seldom took anything into his hands without dropping and breaking
it. No piece of furniture was safe from him. He frequently knocked
his ink pot into the pianoforte. He could never learn to dance in time."
Socially he could never "fit in." He seemed incapable of realizing that
other people might quite honestly hold views different from his own,
and he was prone to attribute base motives even to his closest friends
whenever he found himself crossed. This curious limitation was generally
at the root of the violent quarrels in which he so often involved himself;
with his deafness it helps to account for the unworthy suspicion with
which he regarded almost everyone in his later years. In the whole of
history there are few things more pathetic than the spectacle of the old
lion, his brows wreathed with triumphant laurels and his sad eyes gazing
out perplexedly on a world that so inexplicably failed to conform to
his own fantastic conception of it.

In 1784 he secured the position of assistant organist in the electoral
chapel[1]—a proof that in his musical studies he had lacked neither diligence nor ability. Even before this date he had been taking some of

[1] In this year the old elector died and was succeeded by the Archduke Maximilian
Franz, youngest son of the Empress Maria Theresa. But this did not affect the position
of the Beethovens, father and son.

the organist's work in an unofficial sort of way, and by this means he had come into touch with Christian Gottlob Neefe, the court organist at Bonn since 1782. Neefe seems to have understood the boy and appreciated his gifts. Besides having his duties at the organ Ludwig was employed in the court theater, occupying the important position of "cembalist" at the stage rehearsals (which involved reading from score at the keyboard). In the intervals of this excellent practical work Neefe put him through a fairly systematic course of composition. Later on, when he began to compose in earnest and was developing into a pianist of unusual ability, Neefe's good will must have proved invaluable, especially in the matter of orchestral performances, and it was through Neefe again that the news of his youthful achievements became known in the larger musical world outside Bonn. When Ludwig migrated to Vienna he had still to learn counterpoint, but with this important exception, he had been well grounded in composition, he had a few respectable works already to his credit, and he was a virtuoso pianist of outstanding merit and some fame. The credit for all this is largely due, as Beethoven himself acknowledged, to Neefe.

His first visit to Vienna was a brief one made in 1787 and is chiefly remarkable for his meeting with Mozart, then at the height of his fame. Mozart was not much impressed by his playing—he had doubtless heard better pianists than this youth of sixteen—but when Beethoven started to improvise his attention was soon captured. Whether Beethoven actually took lessons from Mozart or not remains uncertain. In any event he could not have had many. He arrived in Vienna about May; in early July he was hastening home—to his mother's deathbed.

Of his mother Beethoven always spoke with respect and affection. From her he must have received the love and the kindness that he sought in vain from his father. The little that is known of her suggests a prudent, rather dim woman, struggling gallantly but ineffectually in a sea of difficulties that at last overwhelmed her, and without the strength of will to exercise a decisive influence over her unruly family. She had always been delicate, and now the frail, tired body could struggle no longer. Ludwig arrived in time and was with her when she died on July 17.

He was left with a heavy load of care. His father's drunkenness was getting steadily worse and on one occasion he had to be rescued by his son from the police. Every year he grew less able to manage the family affairs and bit by bit his authority passed to Ludwig. His voice, too, began to show signs of wear and in 1789 the elector "dispensed" with his services. Ludwig was eighteen, a tender age at which to assume the chief responsibility for such a household. But his duty was manifest and he undertook it without complaint. Fortunately he was now earning a rather large salary.

It is a relief to turn from the dark picture of the Beethoven home and to find that Ludwig had good friends outside the family circle. Chief among these were the Breunings, to whom he ever afterwards referred as his "guardian angels." He began by making the acquaintance of Stephan von Breuning, a lad somewhat younger than himself, in whom he found a friend for life. Stephan had a younger brother, Lorenz, and a sister, Eleonora, and he persuaded his mother, who was a widow, to call in Beethoven to teach the pianoforte to both of them. Ludwig soon became intimate with the whole family and was constantly in and out of the house. The Breunings were well-educated people, standing higher than the Beethovens in the social scale, and the influence of their culture was invaluable to the uncouth boy. With them he was happy. Frau von Breuning was one of the very few people who could manage him, and she did something to fill the ragged gap left by his mother's death. Lorenz died young. Eleonora was perhaps the only woman of approximately his own age for whom he entertained a deep affection quite untinged with sentimentality. In 1802 she married Dr. Wegeler, but this only served to draw Wegeler into the circle and made no difference to his wife's relations with Beethoven.

Another friend of these Bonn years was Ferdinand Ernst Gabriel, Count Waldstein. He arrived in Bonn in 1787 from the family seat at Dux[1] and soon made the acquaintance of the young musician. Waldstein was a rich nobleman, a few years senior to Beethoven. Dr. Wegeler, Eleonora's husband, calls him a "connoisseur and practitioner of music," and says, "We owe to this Maecenas Beethoven's later fame." Waldstein was well aware of Beethoven's poverty and helped him from time to time with gifts of money, which he described on each occasion as "a small gratuity from the elector," for fear of hurting his easily wounded pride. When, in November 1792, Beethoven set out once again for Vienna, turning his back forever, as it proved, on the city of his birth, he carried an encouraging letter in his pocket. It ran:

DEAR BEETHOVEN!
　　You are going to Vienna in fulfillment of your long-frustrated wishes. The genius of Mozart is mourning and weeping over the death of her pupil. She found a refuge but no occupation with the inexhaustible Haydn; through him she wishes to form a union with another. With the help of assiduous labor you shall receive Mozart's spirit from Haydn's hands.—Your true friend,

WALDSTEIN

A man of discernment, Count Waldstein!

—PETER LATHAM

[1] The household at Dux included at this time a remarkable librarian, brought there in 1785 by Count Ferdinand's elder brother. Count Ferdinand, who spent much of his time at Dux, must have met him often; but we do not hear that he spoke of him to Beethoven. Beethoven, who censured Mozart's *Don Giovanni* for the coarseness of its libretto, would hardly have approved of—Casanova!

The Place: Bonn

The nature of the country in which Beethoven spent the first twenty years of his life has been described in a fascinating manner by Victor Hugo. "As the dawn of a renascent civilization began to break over the Taunus Mountains there sprang up a delightful prattling of legends and fables; in every corner, brightened by this distant ray, a thousand supernatural and charming figures suddenly shone, while in the darker regions hideous shapes and dreadful specters struggled. An entire population of imaginary creatures in direct communication with beautiful ladies and handsome knights was scattered throughout the Rhine Valley: the oreads, who seized the mountains and forests; the undines, who took possession of the waters; the gnomes, who captured the inside of the earth; the spirit of the rocks; the spirit-rapper; the Black Hunter, who roamed the thickets mounted on a huge stag with sixteen antlers; the Maid of the Black Bog; the six Maids of the Red Bog. . . . In these valleys mythology grafts itself to the legends of the saints, and strange results are produced, fantastical flowers of the imagination. . . . In this period, immersed for us in a twilight where magic lights flash here and there, there is nothing in the woods, crags, and vales but apparitions, visions, stupendous combats, diabolical pursuits, infernal castles, sounds of harps in the thickets, melodious songs chanted by invisible singers, hideous laughter emitted by mysterious wayfarers."

The legends flourished along the entire length of the river. Even today the merciless realities of war, attested to by several monstrous symbols, have not succeeded in eradicating what remains of the fanciful imagination of mankind in this valley of intermingled races. Even in Coblenz, in the city scourged so severely by the armies of the Republic in 1794, in order to punish the Elector of Trier for his loyalty to the past, old fantasies survive. Near the fortress is the home of the electoral chancellor, where Goethe lived. The portico of the royal castle, its façades and its Ionic columns were conceived by French minds. An order issued from Rome disciplined the primitive barbarism of these forests. Reverie on the banks of this river transforms history into a poem. At the approach to Oberwesel, when the waters have subsided, the reefs, which imagination popularly styled the Seven Virgins in memory of the daughters of the Castle of Schönberg, emerge. Here is Heine's Lorelei, the rock of the enchantress who, after having seduced boatmen, herself succumbs to love. Religious relics around the old sanctuary of Remagen attract pilgrims. The story is related of how, when the Archbishop of Cologne had the relics of St. Apollinaris and the Magi Kings transported up the Rhine, the boat that bore them was stopped and held in place by a mysterious power until the exact moment when the precious cargo was safely deposited in a chapel. Paganism and Christianity live together here on familiar terms. Was not the castle of Rolandseck built by the Knight Errant? When the news spread abroad that he had been killed at Roncesvalles, his betrothed, the beautiful Hildegarde, took the veil and shut herself up in the convent of Nonnenwerth. Roland, returning from the war, learned that he had lost his beloved; he built a hermitage on the rocks for himself and lived there until one day upon hearing the chanting of the nuns coming from the island to his cell, he died of grief. And was it not on the Drachenfels that the dragon was killed by Seigfried, or at least that the monster was put to flight by the cross of St. Margaret?

Maurice Barrès, who gives due credit to Victor Hugo and even exalts him to the point of calling him a man of the Rhine Valley, has well noted the *human* qualities of the mythology of the river. "Mindful of the hazards that haunt their vigils, the good people grow compassionate in a *truly human* way, are moved together with the stricken, and never become accessories to forces loosed in nature and in man." These observations are important for those who seek to understand the role of the unconscious and of the milieu in the formation of Beethoven's genius. Similarly, Christianity, even if it seems not to have profoundly influenced the composer of the *Missa Solemnis*, has contributed more than a little to the spiritual life of the Rhenish people. One need but see the devoted throngs on a Saturday afternoon in the cathedral of Worms or of Spires, pressed against the door of the confessional, meditative, evidently very much attached to their creed.

From the quiet slope of Melheim the ruin of Drachenfels can be seen; it still dominates the mountain with its furred mantle of trees. The innumerable mansions—one, at least, is a monstrosity—the castles with their ruddy façades, and the railroad are somewhat out of harmony with the landscape, but one can easily reconstruct it as Beethoven knew it, with its vineyards descending to the gray waters of the river, the inns dedicated to Vater Rhein, the billowy clouds, the rough cracks in the rocks, and the specks of the purple beeches of Königswinter. And on a spring day this scenery reminds the visitor of that short page in the *Waldstein Sonata*, between the allegro and the rondo, that glistens like a brief shining of the sun between two thunderstorms. A suggestion of a boatman's song. The memory of the Rhine—EDOUARD HERRIOT

Family Background

One of the most fascinating, and at the same time the most baffling, problems of the biographer is to determine just what proportion of the characteristics of a great man are inherited from his ancestors, and what proportion take their origin in himself as an individual, to what degree his personality is merely a resultant or résumé of various qualities converging from many points into a fresh focus, and to what degree it is a unique creation, without traceable precedents or ascertainable causes. It is always possible to concoct a given character, however striking or unusual, by a judicious selection of ancestral traits; if we will but search far enough back, any man's ancestors will make up quite an adequate representation of the entire human race, so that each of his qualities need only be observed, noted, and traced to the particular great-grandfather or great-great-grandmother who happened to manifest it previously; and we can thus cleverly explain and label the oddest individual. The real difficulty is to explain how he happened to inherit just these qualities and no others, why he is, in a word, just this self instead of some other self, equally derivable but totally different. This difficulty has brought the whole subject of heredity into disfavor with some students; and it is certain that in the present state of our knowledge the study of the individual must precede and guide the study of his origins. Nevertheless, there are cases in which the essential qualities are so unmistakably inherited that the most illuminating way to approach an individual is through a study of his ancestors.

Such a case is Beethoven's. A French writer, M. Téodor de Wyzewa, in a book called *Beethoven et Wagner*, has made so masterly, so discriminating an analysis of Beethoven's parents and grandparents that no one can read it without a strong conviction of the important part played by heredity in the formation of this extraordinarily unique, peculiar, and well-defined character. No man ever existed who was more intensely individual than Beethoven; yet many of the traits which in him were so marvelously blended, and which in the blending produced so novel a flavor, were undoubtedly derived from earlier, and quite undistinguished, members of his family.

Beethoven's grandfather, Ludwig van Beethoven, born at Antwerp in 1712, was of an old Flemish family of marked national character. He early removed to Bonn, the seat of the Elector of Cologne, as a court musician, and in 1761 became court music director, a position which he held with zeal and ability until his death in 1773. "He was," says Monsieur de Wyzewa, "a man of middle stature, sinewy and thick-set, with strongly marked features, clear eyes, and an extreme vivacity of manner. Great energy and a high sense of duty were combined in him, with a practical good sense and a dignity of demeanor that earned for him, in the city he had entered poor and unknown, universal respect. His musical knowledge and ability were considerable; and although he was not an original composer, he had frequently to make arrangements of music for performance by his choir. He was a man of strong family and patriotic sentiment, and established in Bonn quite a colony of Flemish, his brothers and cousins."

Beethoven's grandmother, on the other hand, born Maria-Josepha Poll, developed early in her married life a passion for drink which finally obliged her husband to send her to a convent, where she remained, without contact with her family, until her death. It is probable that this unfortunate tendency was but a symptom of a morbid weakness of the nervous system, beyond the control of her will—a fact, as we shall see, interesting in its possible bearing on the interpretation of her grandson's idiosyncrasies.

In 1740 was born to this ill-assorted couple a son, Johann van Beethoven, the father of the composer. M. de Wyzewa treats him summarily: "His character, like his intelligence, can be described in one word—he was a perfect nullity"; adding, however, that he was not a bad man, as some of the anecdotes regarding his conduct toward his son seem to indicate: "He was merely idle, common, and foolish." For the rest, he was a tenor singer in the court chapel, and he passed his leisure in taverns and billiard rooms.

Beethoven's mother was a woman of tender sensibilities and affections, condemned to a life of unhappiness by the worthless character of her husband. Her whole life was devoted to the education of her son Ludwig, who wrote of her: "She has been to me a good and loving mother, and my best friend." She was of delicate health, and died of consumption when Beethoven was but seventeen.

This was the curiously assorted set of ancestors from which Beethoven seems to have drawn his more prominent traits. If, to begin with, we eliminate the father, who, as Monsieur de Wyzewa remarks, was an "absolute nullity," and "merely the intermediary between his son and his father, the Flemish music director," we shall find that from his grandfather Beethoven derived the foundation of his sturdy, self-respecting, and independent moral character, that from his mother he got the emotional sensibility that was so oddly mingled with it, and that from his afflicted grandmother, Maria-Josepha Poll, he inherited a weakness of the nervous system, an irritability and morbid sensitiveness, that gave to his intense individualism a tinge of the eccentric and the pathological. Without doubt the most important factor in this heredity was that which came from the grandfather; and although Monsieur de Wyzewa is perhaps led by his racial sympathies to assign an undue importance to this Flemish element, yet what he has to say of it is most suggestive. Pointing out the obvious fact that purely German composers, as well as poets and painters, are naturally disposed to vagueness, sentimentality, and cloudy symbolism, he remarks that nothing of the sort appears in Beethoven, "whose effort was constantly toward the most precise and positive expression"; that he eliminated all the artifices of mere ornament, in the interests of "a rigorous presentation of infinitely graduated emotions"; and that he "progressed steadily toward simplification of means combined with complication of effect." He shows how Beethoven owed to his Flemish blood, in the first place, his remarkable accuracy and delicacy of sensation; in the second place, his wisdom and solid common sense, his *"esprit lucide, raisonable, marchant toujours droit aux choses nécessaires"*; in the third place, his largeness of nature, grandeur of imagination, robust sanity, and heroic joy, justly likened to similar qualities in Rubens; and finally, his moral earnestness, that "energy of soul which in his youth sustained him in the midst of miseries and disappointments of all sorts, and which later enabled him to persist in his work in spite of sickness, neglect, and poverty."

Of Beethoven's mother Monsieur de Wyzewa says, "Poor Marie-Madeleine, with her pale complexion and her blond hair, was not in vain a woman *'souffrante et sensible,'* since from her came her son's faculty of living in the emotions, of seeing all the world colored with sentiment and passion." This emotional tendency, the writer thinks, the Flemish blood could not have given; and "it was to the unusual union of this profound German sensibility with the Flemish accuracy and keenness of mind that Beethoven owed his power to delineate with extraordinary precision the most intimate and tender sentiments." With a final suggestion, tentatively advanced, that the weaknesses of Beethoven's character, his changeable humor, his sudden fits of temper, his unaccountable alternations of gaiety and discouragement, may have been due to a nervous malady traceable to the grandmother, Maria-Josepha Poll, this masterly study of Beethoven's antecedents, from which, whether we entirely accept its conclusions or not, we cannot fail to gain illumination, comes to a close.[1]—DANIEL GREGORY MASON (1)

[1] "Beethoven et Wagner. Essais d'histoire et de critique musicales." Téodor de Wyzewa. Paris, 1898.

His Friends

—◆—

The Von Breuning Household

From 1783 on, young Beethoven acted as court organist for Duke Maximilian Franz. Despite his sometimes odd, shy manner, Beethoven had made friends and won sponsors among the colleagues of his father at the court and visitors to his home. The aura of his grandfather rested on him, and he could benefit from the feeling with which the renowned man was still regarded in Bonn. He carried with him the passport of his soul, which not only gained him Neefe's friendship, but also opened the doors of members of court circles with artistic interests. He became very close to the family of Councilor Joseph von Breuning.

The great ability of Councilor von Breuning had come to an untimely end in the palace fire of 1777. Paralyzed by fright, everybody stared at the terrible conflagration, which had suddenly broken out on that January night and destroyed countless treasures. There was universal confusion. Few remained calm. Breuning tried, with the help of some brave men, to rescue important documents and papers from the sea of flames. He had repeated success in this until a collapsing wall struck him and buried him under its ruins. At his deathbed stood his widow, only twenty-seven years old, with four little children. After the unexpected death of her thirty-six-year-old husband, Helene von Breuning, the daughter of the duke's physician and councilor, Stephan Kerich, had the difficult task of running the family and substituting for the children's father, which she managed to do since the economic situation of the family was reasonable and she was helped by her brother, Canon Abraham von Kerich, as well as by her two brothers-in-law, Canon Lorenz von Breuning, who immediately moved to Bonn, and Canon Philipp von Breuning. Of the children, Eleonore, who was to play an important part in young Beethoven's life, was six years old, Christoph, the renowned lawyer of later years, nearly four, Stephan, who was to become an adviser in the Viennese court during the war, was not yet three, while Lorenz had been born only a few months before his father's death. After the death of her husband, Helene von Breuning did not favor a quiet, shy mode of life. In her home near the square opposite the cathedral, there reigned a refreshing, lively spirit, in tune with Rhineland jollity and open to spiritual and artistic interests. The lady of the house, whose portrait shows a beautiful head, with a high forehead and aristocratic features, knew how to stave off distrust and anger, and how to arbitrate opposing views and arguments with kindliness and tact. Courtiers, artists, and intellectuals came and went in her home; she gave young people their due, and her children came into daily contact with others of their age and other friends. Undoubtedly the love of literature and fine art to be found in the palace was mirrored in the Breuning home. So the Breuning house soon became the focal point of a lively, spirited circle, in which "amid the youthful exuberance, there was also an easy, cultured atmosphere," in which the children displayed their poetic attempts, and "in which friends were able to mix usefulness with pleasure in pleasant conversation." In this circle there was also a poor, ambitious student, who came from an Alsatian immigrant family: Franz Gerhard Wegeler, who later became professor of medicine at the ducal university of Bonn, and the husband of Eleonore von Breuning, and whom we must thank for the very valuable biographical notes on Beethoven. After attending high school for five years, he entered the university on October 8, 1782, where he first completed two years of philosophy and then studied medicine from 1783. Wegeler had become acquainted with young Beethoven and introduced him in the Breuning home.

There were probably many reasons why young Beethoven was accepted in the Breuning home. The most likely reason is given by Gerhard von Breuning, a grandson of Frau von Breuning. The Breuning children, Eleonore and Lorenz (Lenz) needed a piano teacher, and with Wegeler's recommendation Beethoven was chosen. Since the cost of the lessons did not matter to her, Frau von Breuning could certainly have found an older, more experienced music teacher for her children. Therefore, besides Wegeler's recommendation, there must have been other weighty reasons why young Beethoven was chosen. The wise, sensitive lady may have seen the right musical companion for her children in the young court organist, who was proficient at the piano, and who could, as a contemporary, have a closer relationship with his pupils. Even if he had had a simple and insufficient upbringing, and sometimes gave evidence of strange moods, in her estimation he deserved, because of his talent, special treatment and suited her company as a pupil of Neefe who had not only technical skills in music. So young Beethoven was accepted in the Breuning house, with which he soon formed close ties. Here in the music room on the ground floor he not only taught and played half the night, but worked his way completely into the hearts of the company. Wegeler gives us some details: "When Beethoven was improvising one day in the Breuning house (on such occasions he frequently tried to display the character of somebody), a violin was forced on

Father Ries, to accompany him. After some hesitation, Ries agreed, and thus for the first time two artists may have improvised; a beautiful, very attractive melody . . ." Wegeler goes on to say: "Beethoven was soon treated as a child of the house; he not only spent a great part of the day there, but some nights as well. Here he felt unfettered and moved with ease; everything stimulated him and developed his spirit. I was five years older than Beethoven, and thus able to observe and judge this. . . . Whenever Beethoven, instead of giving lessons, flew to Mother von Breuning, who would watch him, she would shrug her shoulders and say 'Those are just the actions of a genius. . . .' Uncle von Breuning lived here (in Karpen), and each year he would be visited for five or six weeks during the holidays by his family and their friends. Beethoven too spent many happy weeks there, and he was often asked to play the organ in church." What this intimate relationship with the Breunings' circle meant to Beethoven cannot be stressed enough.
—LUDWIG SCHIEDERMAIR (TR. BY THOMAS K. SCHERMAN)

Count Waldstein

At that time, probably at the Breunings', Beethoven met another talented man, who was to be of great assistance to him, Count Ferdinand Ernst Waldstein und Wartenberg von Dux, who was a member of a very aristocratic family, in whom flowed a mixture of the greatest blood in the Austrian monarchy, but who, as a fourth son, could not inherit the entail, had determined to live in Germany under his German title. Since Duke Maximilian Franz was the head of the order to which he belonged, it is understandable that they became close. According to Wegeler he was "the favorite and constant companion of the young duke" and this leads us to believe that he moved into the palace soon after Maximilian Franz's accession. Wegeler states that "Beethoven's appointment as salaried organist in 1784, and his being sent to Vienna by the duke was because of the count's intervention." Count Waldstein was a clear-thinking man, with a leaning toward music; he was an accomplished pianist and a fair composer. According to his friend, Duke Ludwig Starhemberg, he was a lively, cultured knight. As a believer in enlightenment, he tried to bring education to young artists. Wegeler takes him to be not only the instigator of young Beethoven's appointment as salaried organist, and of his journey to Vienna, but also attributes to him financial support of his protégé and a spiritual influence which he had on Beethoven at this time. "Because of him, the young artist developed the talent of varying a theme extemporaneously and bringing it to its conclusion. . . . Beethoven must thank Count von Waldstein that his initial efforts to develop his genius were not suppressed; so we are also indebted to him for Beethoven's later fame."

The company at the Breunings' was attracted to young Beethoven because of his undeniable musical ability, to which was added a great liveliness of spirit. Besides his instruction of the Breuning children, he added considerably to the amusements of the company by his own musicianship. It is hardly likely that he hid his efforts at composition from his benefactors and friends, who treated him like a "child of the house." He would have played them his current works.—LUDWIG SCHIEDERMAIR (TR. BY THOMAS K. SCHERMAN)

Joseph Reicha

In 1785 a new artist entered the Bonn court music circle, which not only provided the ducal orchestra with an exceptional cellist, but enriched the local group of composers with the addition of a productive musician. Joseph Reicha came from Bohemia, and in 1774 had achieved a position with the court orchestra of the Duke of Ottingen-Wallerstein, which under the direction of Anton Rosetti "played the musical spectrum more exactly than any other orchestra, and obeyed the most delicate, almost unnoticeable variations in tone with pedantic thoroughness." He worked with renowned colleagues such as Anton Janitsch and played the works of the orchestras of Mannheim and Vienna. In 1778 and 1779 he and the violinist Janitsch undertook concert tours. We have letters from Leopold Mozart to his son about their stay in Salzburg, where in the Mozart house they learned and played works by young Wolfgang Amadeus, who was then on a journey to Mannheim and Paris: "Reicha, the cellist, who plays the piano quite well, said that [Mozart's Mannheim piano sonata] had been composed with thoroughness!" "They [Janitsch and Reicha] both play quite nicely; they are astonishingly accomplished and light-fingered in their bowing, and have a good tone and great expression. Reicha is quite a chap." "Reicha plays cantabile better than Janitsch. The concerto, as Reicha played it, was quite good; he injected new ideas, and played as you [Mozart] intended; [Michael] Haydn liked it too." On April 16, 1785, Reicha left Wallerstein and joined the Bonn court music circle, where he found an orchestra run by Mattioli on a basis similar to that in Wallerstein run by Rosetti. After his Wallerstein training, he could be regarded as a force to take over after Mattioli. In his new position he developed both as a soloist and as a conductor and brought both to the musical circles and to theatrical ones a broad, fruitful ability which suffered only occasional interruptions by bad attacks of gout. Also as a composer he was "quite a chap." Apart from large symphonic instrumental works which were printed in the 1790's and later, and the many cello pieces, which demanded no little skill, he is assured of a place in eighteenth-century divertimento and serenade music by the pieces he wrote (some of them in Wallerstein), the quintets, sextets, and octets for wind instruments, which by their joyful sound, their contrasts, and the combination of various types of tone give evidence of a singular talent. An earnest man, strict in the standard he expected from himself and from others in artistic endeavors, he won respect in the palace circles and was accepted by their members. According to Fischer, he came and went at the Beethovens'. A closer friendship with young Beethoven and a possible influence on his composition may have come about when his nephew, Anton Reicha, and young Beethoven became very close.—LUDWIG SCHIEDERMAIR (TR. BY THOMAS K. SCHERMAN)

Eleonore von Breuning

At Frau von Breuning's home on the Münsterplatz, young Beethoven met a girl who at first only attracted the attention of the piano teacher, but later was connected closely with his personal life; a simple crush changed to deep attraction.

Eleonore von Breuning, a little over a year younger than Beethoven (he thought they were the same age), was later described by her son as follows: "I never heard that my mother was ever particularly beautiful; rather, she had an interesting face. Moreover, she was well grown, slim, and athletic, and she had a lively spirit." Beethoven may have been attracted by her well-grown, athletic figure, as well as by her interest in literature and music, which had been awakened and fostered in her mother's house, and her natural, unpretentious demeanor. He met her often in the Breuning circle and may have noticed that she followed his musical ideas and plans and was attracted to him spiritually. Out of friendship and youthful affection grew a deeper, firmly rooted attraction.

Among Fischoff's effects there was Eleonore's letter to Beethoven on his twentieth birthday:

> For Beethoven's birthday from his pupil:
> Today I wish you good fortune and a long life, but I also wish something for myself. For your sake I wish for your approbation, for my sake I wish for patience for you.—From your friend and pupil
> Lorchen von Breuning.

Beethoven kept this letter, which had painted flower-wreathes around its border, in a wallet until his death. Whoever kept such a note, which contained nothing artistic and was written in the normal style of birthday greetings, with such care must have done so for reasons other than those of a simple childhood friendship. Eleonore's New Year's wishes to Beethoven, which may have been written around the same time, may be regarded similarly:

> Oh may you be so fortunate as I wish you to be! Your fortunes would then reach a peak this year.—These are the wishes of your friend,
> Lorchen Breuning.
> To Herr Ludwig van Beethoven.

The Wegeler family has kept two pages of an album which young Beethoven dedicated to Lorchen. One depicts a landscape to which a wreath of roses has been attached by a ribbon. In the wreath is the following verse:

> Take this gift, this rose, dear friend. It is a symbol of your good fortune. You deserve such fortune. Now let your glance also take in a forget-me-not.

On the ribbon Beethoven wrote: "To Fräulein Lorchen, from Beethoven, 1791." On the second page is a picture of a ship held fast by trees. Here we may read: "*Soyez aussi heureux qu'aimée.*"

Beethoven presumably changed "*heureux*" to "*heureuse.*"

This pleasant relationship between Lorchen and young Beethoven, such as is evidenced by these harmless pages, sometimes underwent an eclipse, which might last some time, or might quickly change to friendship again. An especially serious rift during his last years in Bonn, which according to Eleonore's entry in Beethoven's album had been cleared up at least superficially in Bonn, seems to have left definite traces in both of them; traces which Beethoven still showed after he had moved to Vienna. This is shown by letters, some of which are difficult to place as to the time they were written.

(1)

VIENNA, *November 2, 1793*

WORTHY ELEONORE!

MY DEAREST FRIEND:

Only now after I have been in the capital for nearly a full year are you to receive a letter from me, and yet your thought must frequently have turned to me. I often conversed with you and your dear family, but often not in the quiet atmosphere I would have liked. Discord still engulfed me, and my behavior seemed to me to be reprehensible, but it had occurred. How much I would give to be able to remove from my record my behavior, which was dishonorable and contrary to my character. Certainly there were some matters which always kept us apart, and I suspect our arguing about them was what prevented any agreement. We both thought in these cases that we spoke because of our convictions, and yet it was only spite, and we were both deceived. Because of your worthy and noble character, my dear friend, I am sure you have already forgiven me, but it is said that the best atonement is an admission of one's bad deeds, and this is what I wanted to do. And now let us draw a veil over the whole matter, and just retain its lesson: when friends argue, it is always better not to make use of a go-between, but for one friend to turn to the other.

I am sending you something I have dedicated to you.[1] I only wish the work were longer and more worthy of you. They were urging me here to finish this piece, and I used the opportunity to show my worthy E. proof of my regard and friendship for her and of a constant memory of her home. Accept this trifle, and remember that it comes from a friend who values you. If you like it, my wishes are fulfilled. Let it remind you of the time when I spent many happy hours in your home. Perhaps it will remind you of me until I return, which will of course not be very soon. Oh, how happy we shall then be, my dear friend! You will find me to be a happier man, the furrows of whose former reverses have been smoothed out by time.

If you happen to see B. Koch, please tell her that it is not nice of her not to write to me. I wrote to her twice. I wrote to Malchus three times; no reply. Tell her if she does not want to write, she should at least persuade Malchus to do so. To end with, I have to ask a favor. It is that I should be very pleased to have a sweater of hare fur, knitted by you, my dear friend. Secretly, I can tell you that it would also flatter my vanity to be able to say that I own something of the best, worthiest girl in Bonn. Admittedly, I still have the one you were kind enough to give me in Bonn, but its cut has gone out of style, and I can only keep this precious gift from you in my wardrobe.

---

[1] Kinsky identifies this as the violin and piano variations on *"Se vuol ballare,"* WoO 40, which are also mentioned in the following letter.—Ed.

You would make me very happy if you would soon send me a letter. If my letters please you, I promise to write as many as possible, since I gladly do anything to prove myself to be—Your adoring and true friend,

L. v. BEETHOVEN

(2)

I was very surprised by the scarf you made yourself. It made me feel very emotional, but I was delighted with it. It reminded me of times past, and made me ashamed when I thought of your generous behavior toward me. I really did not think myself worthy of your attention. Had you witnessed my emotion yesterday, you would not think it an exaggeration when I say that your memory makes me weep. I beg you, much as I do not deserve any grace in your sight, believe me, my friend (let me continue to call you this) that I suffered and still suffer now, through the loss of your friendship. I shall never forget you or your dear mother. You were so kind to me that your loss cannot soon be replaced. I know what I have lost, and what you were to me—but here I should have to speak of events which are unpleasant for you to hear, and for me to write.

In return for your kindness in remembering me, I am taking the liberty of sending you these variations[1] and a rondo for violin.[2] I have a lot to do, otherwise I would long ago have copied the sonata I promised you. In my manuscript it is only a rough draft, and it would be difficult for the scribe to read it. You can have the rondo copied and return the score to me. It is the only thing among those I am sending you that could be useful to you, and since you are about to travel to Karpen, I thought these little things might afford you some amusement.

Farewell, my friend; it is impossible for me to call you anything else, however little you may care for me. Believe me, I still honor you and your mother as much as ever. If I can contribute in any way to your amusement, please do not omit to tell me. This is the only way I can show my thanks for your friendship. Have a good trip, and bring your mother back in good health. Meanwhile, think of—Your ever adoring and true friend,

BEETHOVEN

P.S. The variations will be a little hard to play, especially the [eighth notes] in the coda, but this should not worry you. It is so arranged that you need play nothing but the [eighth notes]; leave out the other notes, because they also occur in the violin score. Normally I should not have written anything like that, but I have frequently noticed that now and again someone here in Vienna makes notes on my work while I play, and boasts of his knowledge. I

---

1 Variations on the theme "Se vuol ballare" from Mozart's La Nozze di Figaro for piano and violin, WoO 40.—Editor.
2 Rondo in G Major for piano and violin, WoO 41.—Editor.

realize that he may continue to make use of his notes, and I am forestalling him. Another reason is that I want to embarrass the local piano teachers, some of whom are my deadly enemies, and I want to have my revenge. I know that eventually someone will put the variations in front of them, and the gentlemen will make spectacles of themselves.

BEETHOVEN

to Fräulein von Breuning

Because of the repeated questions about the dates of these letters, discussions as to what they show of young Beethoven's relationship to Eleonore were often neglected. And on this matter they give us much information. First we notice that the style is more reticent and careful; Beethoven no longer writes to Lorchen, but to "worthy Eleonore." He has let "nearly a full year" pass by before he writes to her. But during this time she was continually in his thoughts; he "often" conversed with her in spirit, "yet frequently not so calmly as I should have wished." The reason for this lack of calm lay in the "unfortunate discord" in which he felt he had behaved so badly that he still said: "How much I would give to be able to remove from my record my behavior, which was dishonorable and contrary to my character." Some decades later, at the end of December 1825, Eleonore wrote to Beethoven: "Our Lorchen [Eleonore's daughter of her marriage to Wegeler] loves to hear about you. She knows all the details of our happy early years in Bonn; all about discord and forgiveness." Thus in Bonn the two of them frequently had differences, which were soon forgotten. Yet the "unfortunate discord" which arose at the end of the Bonn period and which moved Beethoven to such deep emotion cannot have been an insignificant matter. Even though Wegeler tells us that "Beethoven confessed more than he sinned," in this instance something must have happened concerning which Eleonore did not bear a grudge, but which did not rapidly fade from Beethoven's memory as had the other disagreements. Only when he notices that Eleonore has quite forgiven him is he calmed and drops the matter, although in the second letter he mentions a feeling "of shame because of his behavior." We are left uninformed as to the reasons of the "unfortunate discord," but Beethoven writes in the first letter that he believes that agreement was prevented by argument. He wants to mention the moral of this experience: "when friends argue, it is always better not to make use of a go-between, but for one friend to turn to the other." Perhaps the "unfortunate discord" arose from serious grounds, for it is noticeable that Beethoven had not forgotten it, although he had been away from Bonn for nearly a year. A young man away from home does not shed tears for months over a lost girl friend and an angry argument. Yet in the second letter we read no tender rhetoric, but a straightforward realization: "Had you witnessed my emotion yesterday, you would not think it an exaggeration when I say that your memory makes me weep." He who writes such words and painfully remembers an "unfortunate discord" for a long time and carries her notes until his death was not connected to Eleonore by a mere passing friendship. When Beethoven thinks about "the many, happy hours in your home" and asks for a sweater "knitted by you, my dear friend," and bolsters this plea with "Secretly, I can tell you that it would also flatter my vanity to be able to say that I own something of the best, worthiest girl in Bonn," we realize that more than a simple friendship is intended. Beethoven starts the first letter with "Worthy Eleonore! My dearest friend"; in the second, the words "my dear friend" are underscored and emphasized by "let me continue to call you this." But after the "unfortunate discord" he does not return to "beloved Lorchen." As if he wished to persuade himself that the opposite was true, he wrote "as indifferent as you may feel toward me."

It appears that Beethoven's first deep love was Eleonore von Breuning.
—LUDWIG SCHIEDERMAIR (TR. BY THOMAS K. SCHERMAN)

Last Years in Bonn

We are fairly well informed about Beethoven's public life from 1789 until the end of 1792 (his last years in Bonn). Wegeler has briefly mentioned the camaraderie in the Zehrgarten, in which young Beethoven took part. The owner of this house near the market place, a Widow Koch, had opened a pleasant drinking parlor in which gentlemen of higher circles, councilors, professors, and even young artists could converse. The house's main attraction was the beautiful daughter Barbara (Babette), who later became the second wife of Count Anton Belderbusch. She was "a close friend of E. von Breuning, a lady who approached the ideal for women closer than any other I met during my rather full life." This opinion was supported by all who had the good fortune to know her. She was surrounded not only by young artists like Beethoven, both Rombergs, and Reicha, but by mature men of all walks and ages." There were many connections between the Breuning house and Barbara Koch, and in his letter of November 2, 1793, from Vienna, Beethoven wrote: "If you should see B. Koch, please tell her that it is not nice of her not to write to me. I have written her twice." A picture in which Beethoven appears not only as a member of a party at table, but as an artist, is painted by Wurzer,[1] who later worked in Marburg: "In the summer of 1790 or 1791 I was shopping near the Godesberg well. After dinner Beethoven and some young men approached. I told him that the Marienferst church had been repaired and cleaned, and that this applied also to the organ there, which was either quite new or had been overhauled. The company begged him to do them the favor of playing it. He very agreeably acquiesced. The church was locked, but the priest was agreeable and opened it. Beethoven began to play variations on themes which the company gave him, and we were entranced. But what was more, and what gave evidence of this new Orpheus, was the fact that some common laborers, who were cleaning the church after its repairs, laid aside their tools and listened with amazement and evident satisfaction." In Godesberg the memorable meeting between Beethoven and Haydn is supposed to have taken place, as Wegeler writes: "When Haydn first returned from England, he was given a breakfast by the ducal orchestra in the village of Godesberg, near Bonn. On this occasion Beethoven gave him a cantata, which Haydn admired, and for which Beethoven had studied continuously. This cantata was to be performed later in Mergentheim, but many parts were so difficult for the wind instruments that some musicians said they could not play them, and so the performance was canceled." This cantata is undoubtedly the "Cantata for the Death of Joseph II" and perhaps also its sequal, "Cantata for the Coronation of Leopold II," both of which Beethoven wrote after the death of the emperor in February 1790.

We have considerable evidence of the Bonn court orchestra's stay in Mergentheim (which was from the beginning of September until the end of October 1791, according to Deiters) and the part played there by young Beethoven. In a Mergentheim journal recently discovered by Adolf Sandberger there are news items about participating guests, knights and dignitaries, and about artists, events, and performances in theaters, concerts, and churches. There were headlines about the lavish receptions and banquets. The knights, among them Count Waldstein, were dressed in white cloaks, and Georg Joseph von Breuning, Helene's brother-in-law, acted as secretary. The following events were scheduled: on Mondays, a ball; Tuesdays, an operetta; Wednesdays, a big concert; Thursdays, a play (Häussler's Theater Troupe); Fridays, a conference; and Saturdays, an operetta. Solemn requiems were said for the head of the order. The following Bonn artists were present: the Willmann family, Simonetti, Ries, both Rombergs, Müller, Mändell, Spizeter, Lux, Beethoven, Pfau, Goldberg, Göpfert, Battus, and "the eight harmonic wind instrumentalists." On the duke's saint's day the court was given one thousand ducats.

[1] Electoral councilor at Bonn and later president of the Landgericht. He was a contemporary and school-fellow of Beethoven's.—Editor.

Young Beethoven received about forty guilders. The journey to Mergentheim is described by Wegeler: "This journey, made by the orchestra in
two yachts up the Rhine and the Main at the best time of the year,
provided Beethoven with a fruitful source of pleasant memories. Among
other roles which he assigned, the singer and comedian Lux appointed
Beethoven and Bernhard Romberg scullery boys, and put them to work.
A diploma giving evidence of his promotion was given to him. I saw it in
his possession in 1796. A big, pitch seal, tied down by some unraveled
twine, made the diploma look important." The happy band, filled with
Rhineland mirth, stopped in Aschaffenburg. Of this time Wegeler writes:
"On a journey from Bonn to Mergentheim, the residence of the duke
in his role of Grand Master of the Order, he stopped with the orchestra
in Aschaffenburg, where he was brought by Ries, Simrock, and the two
Rombergs, to Sterkel,[1] who gave in to their pleas and sat down to play.
Sterkel played very lightly and pleasantly and, as Ries put it, in a rather
effeminate manner. Beethoven stood next to him, all agog. He was to
play too, but did so only after Sterkel had told him that he doubted
whether the composer of the variations could play them perfectly himself.
Now Beethoven played as many of these variations as he could remember
(more than Sterkel was able to do), and also a number of others no less
difficult; he played these, to the great astonishment of the audience, in the
style he had seen Sterkel just use. It was so easy for him to copy someone
else's style."

A more complete description of Beethoven's playing on this journey is
given us by Chaplain Junker. In this eulogy by Junker, we hear not only
of the great impression made at that time by Beethoven's playing, and
by the high standard of his piano technique, but also of the "unique
manner of playing" which he had developed. We also find warm praise for
Beethoven as a person. One matter is demonstrated by these reports,
namely that young Beethoven's playing differed from the mundane methods of southern Germany. Beethoven himself blamed his coarse playing
on his frequent organ playing. Schindler feels that another equally important reason was the absence of a good teacher. Actually the reasons
were probably not so much excessive organ playing and insufficient
acquaintance with first-class pianists as his own impulsive method of
playing, which he knew differed from contemporary techniques and which
Neefe encouraged rather than suppressed.—LUDWIG SCHIEDERMAIR (TR. BY
THOMAS K. SCHERMAN)

[1] Abbe Sterkel, one of the finest pianists in Germany.—Editor.

His Teachers

—◆—

Tobias Friedrich Pfeiffer

Johann van Beethoven, who was primarily a singing instructor, and a successful one at that, began to have doubts as to whether he could help his son in the light of his own limited knowledge of the piano and the violin. He turned, therefore, to his colleagues at court, with whom he was acquainted and whom he thought to be able to further his son's musical education. According to the cellist Mäurer, who was active as a court musician in Bonn until 1780, an old friend of the family, van den Eeden, now instructed young Beethoven at the piano and possibly combined with it occasional organ and bass lessons. Toward the end of 1779 he was replaced by Tobias Friedrich Pfeiffer, a member of the Grossman Theater. Pfeiffer left Bonn again at Easter 1780, thus ending musical instruction in the Beethoven household. Pfeiffer, a smart young man from the Weimar region, had only recently joined the theater, and had become a lodger at Johann van Beethoven's house. From his bearing and from his connections with the Beethoven family, [Gottfried] Fischer [, son of the Bonn baker Theodor Fischer, who owned the Rheingasse house in Bonn where Beethoven's family lived for many years,] tells the following:

"Music teacher Pfeiffer had odd moods. He often walked to and fro in his room half the night, wearing the heavy boots that were then in fashion, possibly thinking about music. Herr Fischer, who slept underneath that room, asked Herr Pfeiffer to kindly remove his boots and wear slippers, since his sleep was being interrupted. Pfeiffer let Herr Fischer know that he would remove one boot and continue to wear the other. Fischer made no reply. One morning some time later he threw his barber, Triputt, down the whole staircase, and it was feared that he had sustained multiple fractures. Fischer asked what should be done. Barber Triputt screamed at him that he was a real musical idiot. In future they could all have their hair cut elsewhere. He had always said that one can do one's best and someone will still complain. Triputt was a coarse man. Who knows what he may have done to make Pfeiffer lose his temper. Beethoven made no sound, but employed another barber, named Henseler.

"Once Pfeiffer asked Cäcilia whether she would accompany them upstairs. She replied that if her mother allowed it, and if he then played the flute, she would come. 'Oh the flute,' said Pfeiffer. 'That instrument doesn't interest me; you waste your breath for other people, and I don't like that.' Pfeiffer seldom played the flute, and he had to be begged to do so then. But when he did play, and Ludwig accompanied him on the piano, people stopped to listen in the street and praised the beautiful music. Once Herr Pfeiffer became ill in that house. The Beethovens provided him with all sorts of assistance and care and did whatever they could to please him. They thought a lot of him, and he was worth it. Normally he was a good person about whom one could not complain. The Beethovens' maid complained that Herr Pfeiffer had given her a lot of work during his illness, and she would not forget that. She said that before and since his illness Herr Pfeiffer often ordered, late in the evening when others were retiring, coffee, wine, beer, and brandy, and in her opinion he mixed these up when he drank them. This left no mark on him, and one never sees him drunk, but always in a respectable state.

"When these three collaborated, Ludwig played the piano, Pfeiffer the flute, and Ruffangtini [Rovantini] the violin. They made beautiful music, which people outside stopped to listen to and to praise, and say that they could listen to such a thing day and night. When Ruffangtini [consented,] Ludwig would play the violin, which he liked, since he played it well.

"At length Herr Pfeiffer took his leave of Herr Johann van Beethoven and Madame van Beethoven, at which time they and Ludwig expressed great gratitude to him for being such a good instructor; Ludwig had learned all his skill from him."

In the records of Pfeiffer's artistic accomplishments we find mention of his later years, and Wegeler attributes to him the character of a "fair artist and a very congenial person." That Pfeiffer was a clever musician and a skilled pianist, yet had strange traits as a person, is certain. His method of instruction may also have been odd. Mäurer writes: "Pfeiffer was at that time employed in the theater by Grossman as a tenor, pianist, and oboe player. He was asked to teach Louis [Ludwig]. Yet no regular time was agreed on. Often when Pfeiffer and Beethoven's father had been drinking in a wineshop until eleven or twelve o'clock, they would return home, where Louis was asleep in bed. His father would shake him awake and the crying child would go to the piano, where Pfeiffer would sit with him until morning, because he could see that he was talented. After a year Pfeiffer had to leave Bonn and Louis was able to sleep peacefully. In view of Pfeiffer's strange character, it is possible that young Beethoven's instruction really did not follow normal lines, that the teacher did recognize his pupil's extraordinary talent, and that the youth was really able to learn something from Pfeiffer.

Christian Gottlob Neefe

This man, praised by his contemporaries but quickly forgotten after his death, has been studied by researchers time and again, and for some time he has been called the most noteworthy teacher of young Beethoven. One cannot do justice to his labors and products if one compares his musical work with the masterpieces of his great pupil, instead of comparing them with the works of Johann Adam Hiller, Georg Benda, or Christian Felix Weisse (the generally accepted cultural leaders of his day).

Neefe came from a large Protestant family (his father was a tailor) from Chemnitz in Saxony. He was a child during the Seven Years' War, which left its mark of devastation on the city. His home was poor yet decent, and the lad was especially close to his ailing father. The city school provided a reasonable musical education, and a very thorough one for boys in the choir, in preparation for further studies. The boy's musical development was greatly assisted by Christian Gotthilf Tag, who had shared a desk with Johann Adam Hiller at the Kreuz school in Dresden, and who was then acting as cantor in the nearby town of Hohenstein. His father wanted to teach him his own trade, but finally he agreed that the boy should finish school and enter the University of Leipzig as a law student. During his seven years at Leipzig young Neefe finished his legal studies with a public dissertation on the legality of a father disinheriting his actor son, and changed to the field of music. By giving instruction and participating in weekly concerts he obtained his day-to-day needs, while his thoughts and feelings dwelled entirely in the sphere of art which had been brought into existence by Gottsched and Keller on the one hand, and by Sebastian Bach on the other. Gellert's lectures on moral philosophy had a profound effect on him, and while he shied away from Gellert's apparent hypocrisy, the latter's precept "Try to achieve a completely clear and thorough knowledge of your duties" became the guiding light of his life. Later he stressed the feeling of gratitude he felt toward Gellert with the words: "My heart will bless his memory forever."

In conversation with the students of Bach at Leipzig he came into contact with the art of Sebastian Bach, which was not being ignored despite changed musical trends of that time. He looked up to Sebastian's elder son, Philipp Emanuel, with honor and amazement, and dedicated his twelve piano sonatas of 1773 to him. Nevertheless, Johann Adam Hiller had a pronounced influence on his musical development. He had found his way to Hiller, whom he later called the "musical Gellert," already as a student in Chemnitz, and it was thanks to Hiller that, in his early years, he was able to bring to the public his smaller instrumental and vocal works. This helpful man, who established a dynamic interest for German music in Leipzig, became his keen exhorter and stimulator. His influence on Neefe was especially powerful since he was very cultured. He taught Neefe about the budding German operetta, but also drew his attention to literary works such as Sulzer's *Theory of Fine Art* and Homes's *Fundamentals of Criticism.* Under Hiller's influence the operettas *The Chemist's Shop, Love's Peepshow,* and *The Protest* came into being, and these were followed by *Heinrich and Lydia* and *Zermire and Azor.* These quickly conquered important operetta stages and made his name well known. And just as with the German operetta, we see Neefe at that time working on the German lied, to which he added several volumes, many of which were some Freemason's songs. These Freemason's songs confirm that he, like other intellectuals and artists of that time, had influence with the lodges, and for some time belonged to an order. Furthermore he liked to move among people with similar leanings and avoided the company of uneducated actors and singers.

Neefe's works drew the attention not only of the Rhineland public, but also of the court circles in Bonn. He had admirers in Bonn's literary circles, since he was sympathetic to north and central German culture. In these court circles, and among the families of officials, he found sponsors and friends who helped him achieve the position of court organist. The fact that he was a Protestant did not prevent him from obtaining this position in a liberal-minded court.

As his professional duties increased, he endeavored to broaden his knowledge of music. Besides Philipp Emanuel Bach, Gluck and Mozart, Benda and Schweitzer, he also included Italian and French masters. The many-sidedness of his cultural interests and his spiritual flexibility matched the many-sidedness of his professional ability and the uncommon ease with which he attacked and conquered the most divers tasks. The operatic performances in Bonn allowed him to choose and study the presentations as well as to direct them, since the responsibility during Lucchesi's absence and Reicha's attacks of gout was his alone. He also acted as court organist and harpsichord player during court concerts, and as piano teacher in Bonn society. He had an assistant organist (young Beethoven) at his disposal, and during the change of government in 1784 there were schemes to replace him with his assistant. He also did fairly comprehensive work as an interpreter of Italian and French operas (among them Mozart's *Don Giovanni* in 1788), and later in arranging piano pieces, mainly for Simrock's publishing house. Yet this was not the whole of

Neefe's artistic ability. He excelled as a poet, as the biographer of Grossmann's late wife Karoline, as contributor to reputable publications, and not least as a composer.

Neefe was no artistic genius, yet in certain ways he was far above average as a musician, who could be classed with Hiller and Benda. He was no common figure because of his general education, his many interests, and his social position. The musical and dramatic circles in the Bonn court could claim this man as their own, yet they repaid him with some spite and little gratitude. His Saxon origin and non-Catholic faith seemed a blemish to his detractors, and his manner of avoiding releases of Rhineland spirits and tensions seemed to narrow-minded townspeople to be haughty and uncaring of their local customs. They denied his art and did not accept him as a person, but demanded that he exchange his idea of life for theirs. Johann van Beethoven took no part in these unfriendly acts, yet it was the musician in Neefe, rather than the man, that he prized and wished to acquire for his son after Pfeiffer's departure. Whether Duke Maximilian Friedrich was the cause, or whether Father Johann had already reached a decision for practical reasons, it is unclear as to the exact time when young Beethoven became Neefe's pupil. Perhaps we may put the start of the instruction in 1780 and assume that he immediately continued Pfeiffer's teaching. It is certain that in June 1782 Neefe mentioned his assistant court organist (young Beethoven) and tried to direct general attention to his pupil in Cramer's magazine in March 1783.

When young Beethoven met his new teacher, he was ten or eleven years old. He was nearing the end of his schooling and had received a musical education from his father, van den Eeden,[1] and Pfeiffer,[2] to which he added with the aid of the city organists by his own efforts. An inner force freed within him the first urges of creative ability. It was of decisive importance how the further education and development of the young man were to proceed. The more so since he had an unusually complicated nature which demanded careful observation and loving understanding. The spirit of the youth, which absorbed all experiences and impressions, needed not only a good music instructor, but also a helpful, conscientious leader and mentor who could carefully channel his thoughts and would not gruffly shrug off his plans and inclinations. Neefe had the virtues of such an educator. He did not try to win the young scholar by excessive indulgence, nor by weak permissiveness; he demanded neither submissiveness nor surrender of his personality, but only a stark sense of duty like his own, and unceasing hard work. In his view a clever artist had also to be a clever man, and this held true in the education of the artistic youth. The intensive study of examples was natural for him, and he

[1] Heinrich van den Eeden, court organist at Bonn until Neefe succeeded him.—Ed.
[2] Tobias Friedrich Pfeiffer, tenor singer with Grossman's theatrical company.—Ed.

undertook youthful composition in full knowledge that it would undergo criticism. Young Beethoven's work and studies did not decrease or become easier than they had been under his father's and Pfeiffer's mismanagement, but Neefe handled his pupil more gently, even if he did judge his early compositions harshly; he had an understanding for the boy's feelings, he could give him more artistically, he could stimulate the pupil's spirit with technical instruction, and feed him from musical and literary sources. The master eventually became a friend, and Thayer correctly writes that young Beethoven "never had a closer, kinder or more valuable friend, who remained such for his whole stay in Bonn."

Neefe's instruction extended to the piano, and certainly afterward to the organ. Even if Neefe could not be classed with the important virtuosos of his day, he had, as the Hotha Theater Journal pointed out in 1778, definite ability on the piano. That he was also proficient as an organist is proved by his appointment as court organist in Cologne, a position in which he was reappointed by Maximilian Franz. Young Beethoven could improve and broaden his abilities as pianist and organist with the help of this teacher. His attempts at composition during these years, which after all made claims on his ability as a pianist, show how his piano technique had developed. His instrument was as heretofore the old clavichord, but later on the pianoforte as well. In his younger years, Neefe was prejudiced against this modern "hammerklavier" and thought it hardly suitable for "various modifications of tone," but during his stay in Bonn, he became fond of it and learned the necessary new technique for playing it. The material certainly included the piano pieces then popular on the Rhine, as reported in a Bonn journal, also Neefe's own compositions and Philipp Emanuel Bach's piano works, which the great admirer of this master certainly did not keep from his pupil, and some works of Sebastian Bach. Young Beethoven learned now, as he had partly learned before, also in Bonn's musical circles, north and south German piano music, large and small samples of the sonata, fantasy, and variation in many forms. This was common piano music, but there were also the *Sturm und Drang* of the early romantic movements. Something extraordinary in piano instruction at that time was provided by Sebastian Bach's work, which opened for young Beethoven a wonderful world of preludes and fugues hidden from most contemporary musicians. If the son of the court musician had so far taken part in the performances of dramatic, symphonic, and church works in Bonn, he now had an insight into Bonn's contemporary opera, which his theater-loving teacher demonstrated with piano extracts or even with scores; by his instigation, the student was eventually used as prompter during rehearsals. Practical and theoretical instruction was intermingled. General instruction was carried out with the aid of books by Sorge, Marpurg, Kirnberger, and Philipp Emanuel Bach, and by "exercises in composition," i.e., studies with additions. Even if we do not, as in the case of young Mozart, possess Beethoven's exercise books to show us his progress in theory, his Bonn compositions in the '8o's show that together with a study of Bach's works, he gained some knowledge from his studies, even if Neefe's reserve in regard to the complicated forms of counterpoint did not let him achieve complete freedom and fulfillment, and later led him to intensive efforts in Vienna.

Practical and theoretical instruction was not the limit for a teacher of Neefe's caliber. The general spiritual education of a young artist seemed essential to him, and even though it was not a normal course of study, in many unforced conversations with his pupil, sometimes only in a passing word, he touched philosophical and aesthetic questions which concerned art and life. As he had developed versatility and purpose in his own artistic and spiritual development, he similarly demanded it of a student who was to go beyond the stages of "music lover" and simple musician. In his opinion, anyone with a natural ability had no right to be idle, but had the duty to bring the gift to maturity by unceasing work. Beethoven did not resent these efforts by his teacher as he had those of his father and Pfeiffer, but he allowed himself to be led into a strange and disturbing world of knowledge and art. It became clear to him what was lacking in his home, and what it could therefore not give him. All the human and artistic views of his teacher became his; he viewed all human and artistic problems through the eyes of his leader, and he overcame them with his help. Thayer has quoted Beethoven's own words written to Neefe in 1793: "I thank you for your advice, which you very often gave me as I advanced in my heavenly art." And that Neefe realized the trust his pupil placed in his own ideals, and became aware in 1783 of the extraordinary talent that had been entrusted to him, is shown in his report from Bonn in Cramer's magazine.—LUDWIG SCHIEDERMAIR (TR. BY THOMAS K. SCHERMAN)

Contemporary Reminiscences

Christian Gottlob Neefe (1783)

At the tender age of twelve Beethoven had begun to assist his teacher at the organ and as cembalist in the opera orchestra, when Christian Gottlob Neefe (1748–98), court organist at Bonn to the Elector of Cologne and a composer of once popular *Singspiele*, contributed on March 2, 1783, to "Cramer's Magazine" the following prophetic communication (the translation here used is that of Thayer).

Louis van Beethoven, son of the tenor singer mentioned, a boy of eleven years and of most promising talent. He plays the clavier very skillfully and with power, reads at sight very well, and—to put it in a nutshell—he plays chiefly "The Well-Tempered Clavichord" of Sebastian Bach, which Herr Neefe put into his hands. Whoever knows this collection of preludes and fugues in all the keys—which might almost be called the *non plus ultra* of our art—will know what this means. So far as his duties permitted, Herr Neefe has also given him instruction in thorough-bass. He is now training him in composition and for his encouragement has had nine variations for the pianoforte, written by him on a march [by Ernst Christoph Dressler] engraved at Mannheim. This youthful genius is deserving of help to enable him to travel. He would surely become a second Wolfgang Amadeus Mozart were he to continue as he has begun.

Carl Ludwig Junker (1791)

In the autumn of 1791 the elector, the music-loving Maximilian Francis, took with him to Mergentheim, the capital of the Teutonic Order, his court musicians for the entertainment of the assembled Commanders and Knights of the order. Junker, better known as a writer on music than as a composer, visited the musicians at Mergentheim. In his letter to Bossler's "Correspondenz" on November 23, 1791 he overflowed with admiration for his "friend Bethofen" in these enthusiastic terms:

Here I was also an eye-witness to the esteem and respect in which this chapel stands with the Elector. Just as the rehearsal was to begin Ries was sent for by the Prince, and upon his return brought a bag of gold. "Gentlemen," said he, "this being the Elector's name-day he sends you a present of a thousand thalers." And again, I was eye-witness of this orchestra's surpassing excellence. Herr Winneberger, Kapellmeister at Wallenstein, laid before it a symphony of his own composition, which was by no means easy of execution, especially for the wind-instruments, which had several solos *concertante*. It went finely, however, at the first trial, to the great surprise of the composer. An hour after the dinner-music the concert began. It was opened with a symphony of Mozart; then followed a recitative and air sung by Simonetti; next, a violoncello concerto played by Herr Romberger [Bernhard Romberg]; fourthly, a symphony by Pleyel; fifthly, an air by Righini, sung by Simonetti; sixthly, a double concerto for violin and violoncello played by the two Rombergs; and the closing piece was the symphony of Winneberger, which had very many brilliant passages. The opinion already expressed as to the performance of this orchestra was confirmed. It was not possible to attain a higher degree of exactness. Such perfection in the pianos, fortes, rinforzandos—such a swelling and gradual increase of tone and then such an almost imperceptible dying away, from the most powerful to the lightest accents—all this was formerly to be heard only in Mannheim. It would be difficult to find another orchestra in which the violins and basses are throughout in such excellent hands. . . . The members of the chapel, almost without exception, are in their best years, glowing with health, men of culture and fine personal appearance. They form truly a fine sight, when one adds the splendid uniform in which the Elector has clothed them—red, and richly trimmed with gold.

I heard also one of the greatest of pianists—the dear, good Bethofen, some compositions by whom appeared in the Spires' "Blumenlese" in 1783, written in his eleventh year. True, he did not perform in public, probably the instrument here was not to his mind. It is one of Spath's make, and at Bonn he plays upon one by Steiner. But, what was infinitely preferable to me, I heard him extemporize in private; yes, I was even invited to propose a theme for him to vary. The greatness of this amiable, light-hearted man, as a virtuoso, may in my opinion be safely estimated from his almost inexhaustible wealth of ideas, the altogether characteristic style of expression in his playing, and the great execution which he displays. I know, therefore, no one thing which he lacks, that conduces to the greatness of an artist. I have heard Vogler upon the pianoforte— of his organ playing I say nothing, not having heard him upon that instrument—have often heard him, heard him by the hour together, and never failed to wonder at his astonishing execution; but Bethofen, in addition to the execution, has greater clearness and weight of idea, and more expression—in short, he is more for the heart—equally great, therefore, as an *adagio* or *allegro* player. Even the members of this remarkable orchestra are, without exception, his admirers, and all ears when he plays. Yet he is exceedingly modest and free from all pretension. He, however, acknowledged to me, that, upon the journeys which the Elector had enabled him to make, he had seldom found in the playing of the most distinguished virtuosos that excellence which he supposed he had a right to expect. His style of treating his instrument is so different from that usually adopted, that it impresses one with the idea, that by a path of his own discovery he has attained that height of excellence whereon he now stands.

Had I acceded to the pressing entreaties of my friend Bethofen, to which Herr Winneberger added his own, and remained another day in Mergentheim, I have no doubt he would have played to me for hours; and the day, thus spent in the society of these two great artists, would have been transformed into a day of the highest bliss.—O. G. SONNECK (1)

His Letters

—————◆—————

To Dr. Joseph Wilhelm von Schaden, Augsburg[1]

[Autograph in the Beethovenhaus, Bonn]

BONN, September 15, 1787

MOST NOBLY BORN AND ESPECIALLY BELOVED FRIEND!

I can easily imagine what you must think of me. That you have well founded reasons not to think favorably of me I cannot deny. However, before apologizing I will first mention the reasons which lead me to hope that my apologies will be accepted. I must confess that as soon as I left Augsburg my good spirits and my health too began to decline. For the nearer I came to my native town, the more frequently did I receive from my father letters urging me to travel more quickly than usual, because my mother was not in very good health. So I made

[1] Dr. Joseph Wilhelm von Schaden was a lawyer at Augsburg, where Beethoven stopped on his return journey from his first short visit to Vienna (c. April to June, 1787). Schaden's wife was an accomplished pianist and singer. During his stay at Augsburg, Beethoven presumably met the family of Johann Andreas Stein (1728-92), the famous organ builder and improver of the fortepiano, whose daughter Nanette was later to become one of his staunchest friends in Vienna.

as much haste as I could, the more so as I myself began to feel ill. My yearning to see my ailing mother once more swept all obstacles aside so far as I was concerned, and enabled me to overcome the greatest difficulties. I found my mother still alive, but in the most wretched condition. She was suffering from consumption and in the end she died about seven weeks ago after enduring great pain and agony.[1] She was such a good, kind mother to me and indeed my best friend. Oh! who was happier than I, when I could still utter the sweet name of mother and it was heard and answered; and to whom can I say it now? To the dumb likenesses of her which my imagination fashions for me? Since my return to Bonn I have as yet enjoyed very few happy hours. For the whole time I have been plagued with asthma; and I am inclined to fear that this malady may even turn to consumption. Furthermore, I have been suffering from melancholia, which in my case is almost as great a torture as my illness. Well, just put yourself in my place; It was extraordinarily kind and friendly of you to lend me three carolins[2] when I was at Augsburg. But I must beg you to bear with me a little longer. For my journey has cost me a good deal and I cannot hope for any compensation here, not even in the smallest way. Fortune does not favor me here at Bonn.

You must forgive me for taking up so much of your time with my chatter, but it has all been very necessary for the purpose of my apology.

I beg you not to refuse from now on your esteemed friendship to me whose most earnest desire is to deserve it, if only to a small extent.

With the greatest respect I remain—your most obedient servant and friend

L. v. BEETHOVEN
Court Organist to the Elector of Cologne[3]

(EMILY ANDERSON)

[1] Beethoven's mother, Maria Magdalena, née Keverich (1746–87), died on July 17. Beethoven, born shortly before December 17, 1770, the date of his baptismal register, was not yet 17.
[2] One carolin, a gold coin used chiefly in southern Germany, was worth nine gulden, about eighteen shillings.
[3] Beethoven, who since June 1782 had been assistant to the court organist C. G. Neefe, was appointed deputy court organist in June 1784 at a yearly salary of 150 gulden.

The Music

—•—

Orchestra

I. PIANO CONCERTO IN E FLAT, WoO 4

The boy Beethoven was no prodigy. He could not have competed with the precocious Mozart. Some effort was made for him to appear such a prodigy when he made his first appearance as a pianist in Cologne in 1778—he was billed as a "six-year-old." The *Concerto in E Flat*, written in 1784, was supposedly the work of a boy of twelve, according to the handwriting on the original manuscript. The falsification of two years was of course an effort on the part of his father to make him out to be a prodigy. The composer was not aware of the hoax until he was nearly forty.

When Beethoven wrote what could perhaps be called his first piano concerto, he was undoubtedly influenced by Neefe, who was not only his first significant teacher but also a real friend. Like most of his early works he repudiated it. Although known to have been written, in the course of time the original orchestral parts were lost and only a piano condensation remained. In its present form the Concerto is a restoration by Professor Willy Hess, who was able to work out the score from cues in the piano manuscript.

The restoration was worked backwards with the final rondo done first. This was performed in 1934 over the Oslo Radio by the pianist, Walter Frey. The other two movements were restored in 1943 when the complete work was published. It has fallen to the pianist, Orazio Frugoni, to champion its cause. How close the restored version is to the original in sound can only be conjectured. Professor Hess has somewhat modernized the scoring and treated the cadenzas in his own special way while using Beethoven's material; nevertheless, the simplicity of the harmonies and the orchestration sufficiently preserve the atmosphere to give the work its proper profile. As such the Concerto is probably of definite historical interest.—MILES KASTENDIECK

II. *Konzertstück* FOR VIOLIN SOLO AND ORCHESTRA, WoO 5

In 1787 Beethoven, then seventeen years old, made his first trip to Vienna, where he played for Mozart, who realized the young man's rare talent and said to his friends, "Here is someone that the world will talk about."

Beethoven stayed only a short time in Vienna, but we may conclude that he took lessons from Mozart and had an opportunity of learning his works, including the violin concertos. After returning to Bonn, Beethoven started three compositions: a quintet, a concerto for piano, and a violin concerto, of which the present *"Konzertstück"* formed a part.

It is natural that Mozart's influence should be felt in these three works, and in the *"Konzerstück"* this can be seen at the end of the second section for the solo instrument; the influence of the concertos K. 207 and 213 is evident.

Eighteen years later, when Beethoven, free from all influences, wrote his Violin Concerto in D major, it still retained some memories of that first effort. In Beethoven, as in all the great masters, the characteristic procedures are repeated, as are the musical ideas.

Beethoven often resumed an idea and reworked it until he found its definitive and complete expression. One example that can be cited is the Finale of the Fantasia with Choruses Opus 80 (1803), an idea that is taken up again in the Chorus of the Ninth Symphony (1823). It is not surprising, therefore, that the two violin concerti present similar musical ideas. The attentive violinist will find many parallels not only between the two violin concerti, but also between the *"Konzertstück"* and the first two piano concerti.

If the score, which is preserved in a celebrated European musical museum, written in Beethoven's hand on Bonn ruled paper, were not adequate and irrefutable proof of authenticity, the most rudimentary acquaintance with Beethoven's style would suffice for the affirmation. Only Beethoven, in all the periods of his production, has phrases with a passion and purity like the answer to the theme of the second section of the *"Konzertstück."*

The concerto was not limited to an unfinished portion of the first movement. After thorough study of all the sketches that have been found, and knowing the absolute logic of Beethoven's style, it was possible to form an idea of its completion. It was only necessary to refrain from putting into the simple style of the young Beethoven elements that were still foreign to him. The piano quartets [WoO 36], the sextet,[1] and the two *"Kaiser-Kantaten"* are obvious evidences of this. This is not a

[1] For two clarinets, two horns, and two bassoons, Opus 71.—Editor.

first effort at a concerto, as is proved by thorough and sure-footed working-up of the thematic material.[1] He makes full use of the singing quality of the violin; but his propensity to excessively severe counterpoint in the orchestration sometimes interferes with the melodic line. Evidently, Beethoven at that time did not yet know all the resources of the orchestral apparatus. Under these circumstances, however, nothing more was needed than slight retouches which did not in any way disturb either the original sonority nor the melodic texture. In the handling of the violas, which often double the bass, Beethoven follows the example of Gluck and Mozart. The change in style that Beethoven later adopted, with the violas used independently, was not in keeping with the spirit of the work. Conformably to the style that he indicated himself at the beginning of the work, the horns have been almost always limited to open sounds. Finally, the woodwinds region, which is situated too high, had to be moderated in order to avoid stridencies that Beethoven himself would have eliminated if he could have heard his work. In making these touches, all that was needed was to follow the example of other works, such as [WoO 36][2], of about the same period as this concerto.—JUAN MARÉN (TR. BY THOMAS K. SCHERMAN)

III. Ritterballet, WoO 1

A "chivalrous ballet" (Ritterballet), presented in 1791 under the patronage of Count Waldstein by the ballet master, Habich, from Cologne, is only a divertissement, and is of secondary importance, but it turned out to be the only orchestral work of Beethoven's that his contemporaries in Bonn heard. The two other orchestral compositions (the Imperial Cantatas) are of much more importance—in fact, they are the most important compositions of Beethoven's adolescence. What is significant, however, about the Ritterballet is that Beethoven, barely twenty years old, had such complete mastery of the orchestra.

The ballet organized by Waldstein and danced in Bonn on March 6, 1791, was made up of eight short pieces, most of them with repeats or da capo. A march in D major served as the introduction, followed by a German Song (Deutscher Gesang) in the same key, two phrases of eight measures, which were repeated after each piece. This was followed by a hunting air in D, repeated four times (129 measures in all) which permitted, and justly so, the horns and clarinets to show off their virtuosity. A Romanze Andantino in 3/8 follows in B minor, accompanied by the pizzicati of the strings. This romance or "Minnelied" (love song) is

[1] In 1785, when Beethoven was appointed court organist, he started a piano concerto in C minor, which likewise remained unfinished.—Editor.
[2] The three piano quartets, written in 1785.—Editor.

followed by a boisterous *Song of War* in which the horns, trumpets, and tympani resound. A *Drinking Song*, two phrases of eight measures, for flutes, clarinets, horns, trumpets, tympani, and strings, follows, then a *Trio* in C for piccolo and violins, leading to a repetition of the initial theme, completes No. 6.

No. 7 is a *German Dance* in 3/8 for clarinet, horn, and strings. A "D" which is obstinately repeated by the bass makes the waltz somewhat of a musette. An *allegro vivace* coda, intersected by an *andantino*, where for the fifth and last time the *German Song* is heard, makes a brilliant finale for the entire spectacle.—J.-G. PROD'HOMME (1) (TR. BY THOMAS K. SCHERMAN)

Chamber Music with Piano

I. PIANO TRIO, WoO 38; VARIATIONS FOR PIANO TRIO, OPUS 44; TRIO FOR PIANO, FLUTE, AND BASSOON, WoO 37; VARIATIONS FOR PIANO AND VIOLIN, WoO 40

A Trio in E flat for Pianoforte, Violin, and Violoncello, found among Beethoven's posthumous papers, was published in 1830 by Dunst in Frankfurt-am-Main. On the original publication its authenticity was certified to by Diabelli, Czerny, and Ferdinand Ries, and it was stated that the original manuscript was in the possession of Schindler; Wegeler verified the handwriting as that of Beethoven. There is a remark in Gräffer's written catalogue of Beethoven's works: "Composed *anno* 1791, and originally intended for the three trios, Op. 1, but omitted as too weak by Beethoven." Whether or not this observation rests on an authentic source is not stated.

Dr. Deiters points out as characteristics of the trio the freedom in invention and development, the large dimensions of the free fantasia portion, its almost imperceptible return to the principal theme, and the introduction of a coda in the first movement. These indicate that it was not written by Beethoven at the age of fifteen, as Schindler states, but long after the pianoforte quartets. Thematic motives from this movement recur in later works, for instance, the Sonata in F minor, Opus 2, and the Pianoforte Concerto in C major. Beethoven seems to have used the designation "Scherzo" in it for the first time.

The Variations in E flat for Pianoforte, Violin, and Violoncello, which were published in 1804 by Hoffmeister in Leipzig as Opus 44, may belong to the last year of Beethoven's life in Bonn. Nottebohm found a sketch of the work alongside one of the song *"Feuerfarbe,"* which fact points to the year 1792; Beethoven in a letter to the publisher appears not to have laid particular store by it, a circumstance easily understood in view of the great works which had followed the youthful effort.

Besides these compositions there is a Trio for Pianoforte, Flute, and Bassoon. On the autograph, preserved in Berlin, the title, placed at the end, is *"Trio concertant a clavicembalo, flauto, fagotto, composto da Ludovici van Beethoven organista di S. S. Electeur de cologne."* The designation of the composer as organist, etc., fixes the place of its origin, and the handwriting indicates an early date. The combination of instruments in the piece leads one to conjecture that it may have been composed for the family von Westerholt. Count von Westerholt played the bassoon, his son the flute, and his daughter the pianoforte. Moreover, their descendants have affirmed that the trio was written for their family.

It is more than likely that the variations for Pianoforte and Violin on Mozart's *"Se vuol ballare"* ought to be assigned to the latter part of the Bonn period. They were published in July 1793 by Artaria with a dedication to Eleonore von Breuning, to whom Beethoven sent the composition with a letter in 1794. The dedication leads to the presumption that the work was carried to Vienna in a finished state and there subjected only to the final polish. The postscript of the letter to Fräulein von Breuning betrays the reason for the hurried publication: Beethoven wanted to checkmate certain Viennese pianists whom he had detected copying peculiarities of his playing in improvisation which he suspected they would publish as their own devices.[1]—ALEXANDER WHEELOCK THAYER (1), EDITED BY ELLIOT FORBES

II. 3 Piano Quartets, WoO 36

The three quartets for piano and strings,[2] composed at Bonn in 1785, are not only remarkable as witnesses of [Beethoven's] earliest stage of development, but also as examples of an instrumental combination (piano, violin, viola, and cello) which was scarcely known at that time. It is even possible that they antedate Mozart's two masterworks in g minor (K. 478) and E flat major (K. 493) by a few months! Thus, they stand at the very beginning of an evolution that ultimately led to the few great piano

[1] See Schiedermair's account of the musical and social relationship between Beethoven and Eleonore von Breuning on pages 14–19. The letter by Beethoven about these variations is quoted in full.—Editor.
[2] WoO 36.—Editor.

quartets in music history, by Schumann, Brahms, Dvořák, Fauré, and Martinu.

Though Beethoven's essays sometimes show some clumsiness in their part writing, they are by all means interesting music, and the composer thought well enough of No. 3 in C major to borrow two of its tunes for his first published set of piano sonatas: the second subject of the first movement reappears at the same place in Opus 2, No. 3, whereas the slow movement's opening is to be found in Opus 2, No. 1.

All three quartets are cast in three movements. The first, in E flat major, which shows the influence of the Mannheim school, consists of an introductory "Adagio assai," a passionate "Allegro con spirito" in sonata form and in E flat minor (!), and a cantabile theme with six variations, followed by an energetic Coda.

Whereas the second quartet, in D major, is rather less interesting, the third, in C major, offers plenty of enjoyable music. The lively "Allegro vivace" in sonata form, the "Adagio con espressione," and the charming "Rondo-Allegro" are definitely worth knowing!—HARRY HALBREICH (1)

III. RONDO FOR PIANO AND VIOLIN IN G, WoO 41

In a letter of 1794 to Eleonore von Breuning from Vienna, fraught with pangs of bad conscience, Beethoven offered her as a "slight return for your kind remembrance of me" both the Variations for Violin and Piano on *"Se vuol ballare"* from Mozart's *Nozze di Figaro* (WoO 40) and this rondo. He does go on to suggest that she have the rondo copied and send the score back to him.

He adds modestly that "these trifles might perhaps give you some pleasure." Indeed, like most of the works that he wrote for Countess von Breuning, the piano part is not demanding, but it is attractive and likely to please a gifted amateur pianist such as herself. The delightful little piece is in 6/8 with a main theme which is truly in the rhythm of an allemande, such as those which were being played in the Viennese ballrooms at the time. When Kreisler used that theme as the basis for his Variations for Violin and Piano on a Theme of Beethoven, he changed the 6/8 to 3/4 and doubled the time value of the notes, making Beethoven's eighth notes into quarters. He also slowed the tempo to andante from the implied allegretto which is characteristic of the allemande. Kreisler's piece is sweet and nostalgic, Beethoven's original is gay and pert, but both are purely Viennese in spirit; the bittersweet Vienna of the early twentieth century compared to the confident Vienna of the end of the eighteenth century.—THOMAS K. SCHERMAN

Chamber Music Without Piano

I. OCTET FOR WINDS, OPUS 103
I—Allegro; II—Andante; III—Menuetto; IV—*Finale* (Presto)

Just prior to his phenomenal rise as a piano virtuoso, during the first half of the 1790's Beethoven not only entertained but indulged what the biographer A. W. Thayer calls a "particular predilection" for the wind instruments.

Just as any practical contemporary composer might score a piece for a specific group which would ensure him performance and enhance his reputation, so the young Beethoven scored his Wind Octet in E Flat for the dinner orchestra of Max Franz, the Elector of Bonn. This ensemble comprised two oboes, two clarinets, two bassoons, and two horns.

When, a few years later, Beethoven removed from Bonn, his birthplace, to Vienna, he rescored the composition for string quintet and published it as Opus 4. The original was brought out posthumously as Opus 103. The arrangement varies considerably from the original and is a more mature piece. [However, the] very key in which Beethoven placed the composition, E flat, is one in which the winds are most comfortable, and which brings out their best points.

In the first movement, the oboe spins out an utterly charming theme, the rhythm of which permeates, in one instrument or another, the entire movement. It is really woodwind, and sounds as native to the clarinet and bassoon as to the oboe, which announced it. The second theme in the bassoon finishes with a curt little bow from the clarinets. With this simple material, happy and vigorous, Beethoven worked out the movement in classical sonata form. The lush melody with which the oboe opens the second movement might be an arioso out of an early Italian opera. When the bassoon repeats the theme, the operatic feeling is intensified. The solo oboe carries on its *bel canto* in the second section of the movement in a minor key, accompanied in a guitar-like staccato by the second oboe. It is all completely vocal, even to the graceful cadenza with which the oboe closes the section. In the last section of this three-part song form the entire ensemble joins to bring the movement to a lovely pianissimo close. The *menuetto* is a preview of the later Beethoven scherzo. Even more, it is a foreshadowing of the scherzo in the Ninth

Symphony, both rhythmically and melodically. In its trio there is a charming dialogue between the clarinet and the horns in which the characteristic color of these instruments is beautifully contrasted. The last movement, witty, gay, and mischievous, has more than a hint of *Till Eulenspiegel*. The instruments tumble over each other in sprightly runs, arpeggios, and syncopated chords. The second theme has the outline of the Hymn to Joy. The entire movement is brimming over with humor and good feeling.—JACKET NOTES FOR WESTMINSTER S-9008

II. RONDINO IN E FLAT FOR WINDS, WoO 25

When Beethoven's Rondino in E Flat for Winds was first published in 1829, two years after the composer's death, it was given no opus number. It is now designated as his Opus 146 because Sir George Grove gave it that number when listing Beethoven's works for his Dictionary of Music and Musicians. The date of its original composition is not known, but internal evidence—its musical style and its handling of instruments—suggests that it was written early in Beethoven's active life as a composer. It was in all likelihood contemporary with his only other piece for the same eight wind instruments, the octet now known as Opus 103. Indeed, the brevity of the rondino and the fact that it is (like the octet) in E flat major suggest that it may have been composed as a movement for the octet.

A rondino is a brief rondo—in which a leading melody, presented several times, alternates with contrasting, secondary thematic material ("couplets" or "episodes"). Beethoven scored the present rondino for two oboes, two clarinets, two French horns, and two bassoons. The full score takes up only eight pages; its playing time is, of course, lengthened by repeats. The principal melody is introduced in the opening measures by a horn. Thereafter, the evolution of the musical ideas is clarity itself, the special sort of clarity which belonged to the era in which Beethoven was born, the high noon of late-eighteenth-century chamber music.[1]— HERBERT WEINSTOCK

III. TRIO FOR STRINGS, OPUS 3

I—Allegro con brio; II—Andante; III—*Menuetto* (Allegretto); IV —Adagio; V—*Menuetto* (Moderato); VI—*Finale* (Allegro)

With the Trio for Strings, Opus 3, in E flat begins the series of chamber works without piano which terminated with the Septet, Opus 20,

---

[1] A remarkable innovation, instrumentally, for a young apprentice composer is the passage between the two solo horns, twenty measures from the end, in which Beethoven creates echo effects by muting the horns in every other measure. This foreshadows the dramatic symphonic composer who was to emerge.—Ed.

and the first six string quartets, Opus 18. From the point of view of form this work is to be compared with Mozart's Divertimento composed in 1788, also in the key of E flat, which was so often employed by Beethoven. He did not give this trio the usual three or four movements of a sonata, but rather six, as adopted by Mozart—an allegro, an andante, two menuets separated by an adagio, and a final allegro. Mozart's imprint can be seen in many places, such as in one particular thematic motif [a simple turn played to the rhythm of an eighth note, two sixteenth notes and two eighth notes, it forms the basis of the second theme of the first movement]. Beethoven later used this same motif almost to a saturation point in the first quartet, Opus 18, No. 1. However, Mozart's inspiration is certainly not to be credited to the complete work, and Beethoven is most recognizable on his own throughout the composition.

The first theme with its syncopated rhythm immediately draws one's attention. The second subject, which is more peaceful, follows, and makes considerable use of the Mozartean motif. Beethoven combines these two elements in the development. At the end of the development he introduces the recapitulation in a way which was very much his own style [after an agitated section, where the violin and viola play vigorous phrases over a syncopated pedal point on the dominant played by the cello, the motion of the two upper instruments suddenly subsides (the syncopation, however, continuing in the cello); gradually the three instruments fade to a pianissimo as the violin and viola play block chords which form a perfect cadence leading smoothly to the recapitulation]. The ensemble, in which each of the instruments plays an equally important role, is lacking neither in grace nor humor. If this work, which certainly does not reveal the inexperience of a first work, was conceived before his arrival in Vienna, it is [equally] evident that it had been worked over after the composition of Opus 1, which would make it around 1796. This is indicated by a stranger's hand on the autograph.

The andante, in B flat, repeats a group of four notes with much insistence—a motif which was to become, but with what a different mood, the "prophetic" motif of the Symphony in C minor. In the present andante it is presented in an almost continuous staccato with piquant contrasting dynamics. Sudden sforzandi arise violently out of the predominantly gray texture which forms the basic color of this agreeable tableau.

Between the menuets—about which there is little to say—the motif of the adagio in A flat, over the dolce and piano accompaniment of the viola, is restricted at first to the violin. It again makes use of the Mozartean rhythm of the first movement. This tender melody is developed and passed to the viola and cello together, but returns to the violin, which finishes the phrase. The entire movement resembles a broad cantilena which is now and then interrupted by violent outbursts before being sung for the last time.[1]

Quick and alert, the finale in 2/4 unfolds in the form of a rondo. The main motif, which starts shyly, almost tentatively, has a more lyrical second part that passes from the violin to the viola and then to the cello. A tender second subject soon contrasts with this one. In the middle section, which is in minor, there is a tumultuous race in which the three instruments share in rapid triplets, underlined by incessant sforzandi on the offbeat of the measure; there is a short-lived lull before its conclusion in a fortissimo. The third section of the movement is a replica of the first except that the tender second theme is in the tonic, with a reversal of the roles among the instruments. The coda brings back fragments of the two principal themes, in a brilliant and rapid peroration which is interrupted just before the end by an adagio of three measures— a typical Beethoven technique.[2]—J.-G. PROD'HOMME (1) (TR. BY THOMAS K. SCHERMAN)

IV. Allegro and Minuet for Two Flutes in G, WoO 26

The autograph manuscript of this work has been preserved. It is dated August 23, 1792, and it reads: "To my friend Degenhart, a souvenir of my coming departure." This is, in fact, the last piece composed by Beethoven in Bonn before he left for Vienna. Degenhart, a law student, was a close enough friend of the young musician to write in his notebook on October 30, shortly before Beethoven was to leave, a few lines of poetry commemorating their friendship. No doubt the two young men played this short and pleasant piece together. The allegro is in sonata form without the usual recapitulation, and the development is mostly in the minor key. In the development, the longer notes of the first flute are contrasted with the far more playful nature of the rest. In the minuet, one's attention is especially drawn to the ending, in e minor, of the first phrase.—JACKET NOTES FOR TURNABOUT TV 4059

[1] Thayer-Deiters compares certain passages of this movement, and not without reason, with passages of a similar inspiration in the first trio, Opus 1, the piano sonata, Opus 10, No. 1, and the concerto, Opus 15.

[2] See "Beethoven's Opus 3, An 'Envoi de Vienne.'" This is a fascinating article by Carl Engel in *Musical Quarterly*, Vol. XIII, No. 2 (April 1927), in which the author refutes Thayer's and Schiedermair's contention that Opus 3 dates from 1792 in Beethoven's Bonn years. His argument is based on well-authenticated research of the reminiscences of the contemporaneous English author W. H. Gardiner, which refer to hearing a "trio by the young composer L. Beethoven." These reminiscences, the author points out, refer to a composition written in 1794 or 1795, when Beethoven was well established in the musical life of Vienna.—Editor.

V. 3 Duets for Clarinet and Bassoon, WoO 27

The year 1792 saw the composition of three duos, in C, F, and B flat, for clarinet and bassoon. By their nature these works, like the flute duet, are but rarely performed, which is a pity, for though slender they contain attractive music. The B flat duo consists of a full sonata-form movement and a set of variations. It could hardly be expected that the writing for the instruments would be generous in the matter of rests, but Beethoven contrives to make the works playable and well worth the effort.—JOHN WARRACK

Piano Music

I. 9 Variations on a March by Dressler, WoO 63; 3 Sonatas (E Flat, F Minor, and D), WoO 47; Praeludium in F Minor, WoO 55; Rondo in A, WoO 49

We know on Beethoven's own authority that his first compositions were a set of Variations on a March by Dressler and three sonatas for clavier dedicated to the Elector Maximilian Friedrich. Thus the boy attacked at once two musical forms he was to make especially his own.

It is also significant that these Dressler variations and the sonatas were for clavier. Paul Bekker, one of the most Beethoven-minded of critics, says: "Beethoven's work is based on the piano: therein lie its roots and there it first bore perfect fruit." The powerful tone qualities offered him an adequate vehicle for his boldest harmonic and melodic designs, and, being himself a magnificent pianist, he expanded the scope of piano music till it is hard to apportion the debt between instrument and player.

The nine Variations on a March by Dressler, in C minor, were composed in 1783[1]—or perhaps earlier, as that was the year of publication. On their own merits they are neat, discreet music, superior to the theme on which they are spun. But for us (who from the distance of more than a century can see Beethoven's career in the map-like manner enjoyed by the Intelligences in Hardy's *Dynasts*) the real excitement is that the Dressler variations are a kind of child's sketch for the mighty thirty-two variations on an original theme composed by Beethoven in 1806. Original theme? Yes, in that it is wholly Beethoven's; but all the

[1] Kinsky-Halm sets the composition date as 1782.—Editor.

same it is like the ghost of Dressler's march, transformed into a chaconne and translated to an Olympian grandeur.[1] Continuing the comparison between the two works, one sees they run a not dissimilar course, allowing for the infinitely grander scale and richer decoration of the later work. At the end they diverge. In the short early variations Beethoven modulates to C major for the last variation, thus making it an apotheosis of the old *tierce de Picardie* (the major chord which by ancient custom closed all works in a minor key), while in the thirty-two variations he places a group of C major variations in the middle, flanking them by minor sections before and after in an organized design that approximated to aria form.

The three Max Friedrich sonatas for clavier belong to nearly the same date (1783) as the Dressler variations and are much more interesting. The first, in E flat major, cautiously follows the old type of binary (not triune) sonata form for its first movement, but already Beethoven showed his instinct for the psychologically sensitive spot in sonata form, viz., the return to the principal key after the development. In later works his imagination and inspiration often rose to their highest at this point. In this boyish movement he was not content to slide back by the routine reversal of the outward journey, so preceded the return by some arpeggios that queerly forecast his figure for the finale of his "Moonlight" Sonata. The second sonata, in F minor, is a still more remarkable presentiment of a later work—his Sonate Pathétique of 1797. One opens with a short, pathetic larghetto, the other with a grave, preparing an allegro in which the slow section recurs with strong emotional effect. There is even kinship of phrase between the two allegros. The other movements of the F minor, well contrasted as to material, are wonderfully "in the picture." "A knowledge of suffering, appalling in a twelve-year-old boy, trembles through the quiet *andante*, and rages through the excited, urgent, *unisono* passages of the *presto*," says Bekker.

The third sonata, in D major, is rather Haydn-like in its tunefulness.

The Praeludium in F Minor[2] is simply a handy little piece for clavier or organ with which to fill a gap.

[1] Besides the similarity of keys there is the coincidence that both themes start with the tonic (C) in the bass, which slides to B natural in the second measure. However, the relative simplicity of the earlier work shows that B natural returning comfortably to C (and the tonic harmony) once more. In the much more sophisticated WoO 47, the B natural continues to slide to B flat, thus introducing the new relationship with the subdominant harmony and all the possible tone relationships which that harmony involves.—Editor.

[2] It is obviously a study in the keyboard style of J. S. Bach and as such is probably a composition exercise. The voice leading is remarkably adroit for a student of seventeen, and the bold modulations would be even more noteworthy (the shift from B flat minor through E flat major, A minor, F minor to the dominant seventh on G and hence to a cadence in C minor all within six measures) if they did not display the awkwardness of an apprentice-composer showing off.—Editor.

The Rondo in A Major is clean, neat, and tuneful, with just one modulation which—simple as it seems—is, I think, Beethoven's earliest example of a pivot modulation, i.e., a note or notes approached as belonging to one key and quitted as in another, the music being *swung* over on a pivot. The device may mean nothing with a commonplace composer, but in the hands of Beethoven and Schubert it can be magical. [In the rondo, Beethoven ends a section in A minor on the dominant with an E in the bass and an E in the treble. In the next measure *without modulation* he starts a brilliant fortissimo passage in C major allowing the E in the treble to remain constant.] One looks with reverence at the little change here from A minor to C major, catching in it the first glimpse of things to be—for example, the superb passage in the Kyrie of the *Missa Solemnis* where (as Professor Tovey says) the "*Christe eleison* dies away on an incomplete minor chord, which, by a method of modulation typical in Beethoven's works, becomes part of the original major tonic chord of the Kyrie."

The remaining works for piano during Beethoven's Bonn period were a rondo,[1] a concerto in E flat major, a minuet[2] (not published till 1805), a sonatina[3] written for Wegeler, and twenty-four variations on Righini's arietta *Venni Amore* (1790). These variations show many authentic Beethovenisms, and, besides being valuable as a portrait of Beethoven the pianist in his last year or two at Bonn, they figured in his famous contest with Sterkel, and later at Vienna. Dr. Ernest Walker, in his admirable study of Beethoven, describes these Variations as of unusual technical difficulty and mentions their forecasts of much later music.—MARION M. SCOTT

II. RONDO IN C, WoO 48

This virtually unknown rondo in C was composed by Beethoven when he was about thirteen years of age. It was printed in a German weekly musical publication of 1783, entitled:

Blumenlese für Klavierliebhaber. Eine musikalische Wochenschrift. Zweiter Theil. Herausgegeben von H. P. Bossler, Hochf. Brandenb. Rath. Speier, 1783

where the composer is described as "Hrn: Ludw: van Beethoven alt eilf Jahr" (Mr. Ludwig van Beethoven, aged eleven years). It is contemporaneous with Beethoven's three earliest sonatas for piano (in E flat major, D major, and F minor), which were issued later that year

---

[1] In C major, WoO 48.—Editor.
[2] WoO 82.—Editor.
[3] In F major, WoO 50.—Editor.

by the same publisher. Doubtless the underestimation of the youthful composer's age was due to an understandable desire on his proud father's part to enhance his son's precocity.[1]

This early composition contains a number of interesting and characteristic features. Of particular note are bars 79–80, in which the sudden dynamic contrasts show, even at that early age, Beethoven's characteristic sense of humor. Bars 33–36[2] are strongly reminiscent of the style of his Piano Trio movement Allegretto, in E flat, written at about the same period, and indeed the rather fussy original phrasing, which is typical of Beethoven's early compositions, is more characteristic of strings than of the piano.[3]—JACK WERNER

III. MENUETT FOR PIANO IN E FLAT, WoO 82

Thayer places the composition of this little piano piece in 1785, because the words "dans l'âge de 13 ans" are written on the original edition (which appeared later) in an unknown hand. (Beethoven's father lied about his son's age by two years, to cash in on the "child prodigy" market.)

It is a simple minuet with a trio. Its key, as well as its highly sophisticated voice leading (in the second half of the minuet) and the echo effects in different octaves, suggests to me that it might well have been a sketch for a minuet movement in some larger work for wind ensemble, which interested Beethoven considerably at that time.[4] There is a fascinating premonition of a later work in the trio: a small three-note figure is repeated in two voices and overlaps twice, causing a momentary discord. Beethoven used this same device twenty-five years later in the Piano Sonata ("Les Adieux"), Opus 81a, and, coincidentally, in the same key!—THOMAS K. SCHERMAN

[1] In a letter to his friend Wegeler, dated May 2, 1810, Beethoven wrote: "I have lived for a long time without, unfortunately, knowing myself how old I am."
[2] Directly before the first episode.—Editor.
[3] The work is in a fast 3/8 tempo typical of many early Haydn finales. It is in the simplest rondo form, A-B-A-C-A. The theme is a straightforward eight-measure phrase, repeated. The first episode (B) is in the key of the dominant; the second episode (C) is in the tonic minor. Aside from the interesting features mentioned by the author is the fact that the transitional passage from B back to A is based thematically on the A theme (appearing twice in the key of the dominant minor and the tonic minor). The sudden dynamic contrast mentioned by the author is a fortissimo upbeat to the recapitulation of the main theme which appears, piano, after this episode.—Editor.
[4] Duets for Clarinet and Bassoon, WoO 27; Octet, Opus 103, for Winds; and Rondino, WoO 25.—Editor.

IV. 24 Piano Variations on *"Vieni Amore"* of Righini, WoO 65

Ludwig van Beethoven, as might have been expected, follows Mozart completely in his first variations. This is all the less surprising in view of the fact that his first works in this form stem from his Bonn period, and Beethoven took much longer than Mozart to secure his own artistic individuality. But as early as in his twenty-four variations on the arietta *"Vieni Amore"* of V. Righini (1790) his freer approach, his broader view, and his bolder attack in the structure of the variations are unmistakably visible. Even the large number of the variations (Mozart never goes beyond twelve), which he himself exceeded only twice thereafter, is significant in this respect, and still more so are the richness and many-sidedness of the variations; the principle of adorning and embellishing the thematic melody, which is still predominant in Mozart, is now put into the background by the modifications of the theme, treated as a motif. In general Mozart tries to preserve the most significant melodic peaks of the theme in his variations as points of recognition; Beethoven, even in this early work, was able to fuse the free figure work of his immediate predecessor with the predominantly contrapuntal procedure of J. S. Bach and thereby achieve structures that not only modify the character on the surface but, delving deeper into its organism, give it a basically lateral illumination. The link between the theme and its variations is then to be found only in its harmonic structure, which too on occasion is subjected to considerable rebuilding. In the light of what has been said, one might compare, for example, Nos. 1, 4, 6, 7, and 21 of the variations in question, to form a conception of the new idea of the entire variation form that was emerging in Beethoven. No. 14 is very original; it is a double variation, in which every four bars of the sixteen-bar theme occur twice in succession, once as allegretto, then as adagio. No. 23 is notably different in character, in which the gently swinging arietta theme (2/4 time) goes over into a broad adagio sostenuto (3/4 time) strongly reminiscent of the slow movement of the Trio Opus 97. The Coda is less satisfactory; its sequence of modulations presents many authentically Beethoven features, but it seems too externally put together to fulfill its purpose as a finale vigorously driving to a close. There can be no doubt that the Righini Variations, with which Beethoven made his debut as a pianist in Vienna (a proof that he must have thought highly of them), are the best of the twelve works he wrote in this form up to 1800, not only in that they are the earliest comprehensive proof of his mastery, which appears so vividly in this form, but especially in that they are the type of the specific advance that the form was

to make in the creative, innovating hands of Beethoven.—OTTO KLAU-
WELL (TR. BY THOMAS K. SCHERMAN)

V. 13 PIANO VARIATIONS ON THE THEME "*Es war einmal ein alter Mann*," FROM THE OPERA *Das rothe Käppchen*, BY DITTERSDORF, WoO 66

Dittersdorf's comic opera, written to a libretto by Gottlieb Stephanie,
who also provided the text for Mozart's *Entführung*, was a big success
in Vienna in 1788, and when it appeared in Bonn in 1792, it was
such a smash that it was repeated for several seasons. The songs from
it were so popular that the publishing firm of Simrock issued an album
of six small excerpts from the opera for piano, four hands, which also
included Beethoven's set of variations on the "hit tune."

The theme is unusually long (thirty-seven measures) for a theme
to be varied. Its harmonies are very simple. However, it has one feature
which obviously intrigued the young Beethoven. There is an interrupted
cadence at the end of the second phrase followed by a bar of silence,
and then five measures which lead back from the key of the dominant
to its repetition, followed by *another* bar of silence just when the
audience is expecting the final cadence, ending with another repetition
of the concluding phrase but varied in an entirely new tempo and
mood (again andante 6/8), which dies off to a whisper.

These innovations alone show how far the young Beethoven had
progressed in variation form from the style set by Mozart. It is no
wonder that his teacher, Neefe, was extremely complimentary about this
set of variations.—THOMAS K. SCHERMAN

VI. 6 EASY VARIATIONS ON A SWISS SONG FOR HARP (OR PIANOFORTE), WoO 64

The simplicity of this theme (eight measures long) and its harmonic
structure (simple two-voice writing), coupled with the rather naïve figuration in the variations (even for the young twenty-year-old student
Beethoven in 1790), would relegate this small work to an insignificant
footnote in musical history were it not the first time that we know in
which Beethoven composed for the harp. The only other time when he
used the harp as a solo instrument was in the beautiful fifth movement
of the music for the ballet *Prometheus*, Opus 43, where it is used as
one of three concertante instruments.—THOMAS K. SCHERMAN

VII. 8 Variations for Piano, For Hands, on a Theme of Count Waldstein, WoO 67

The Duet Variations, written when about sixteen or seventeen (1787)[1] and based on a theme of Count Waldstein's, are noteworthy. This was the Count Waldstein who proved such a friend in need in Bonn, and whom afterwards [Beethoven] immortalized in the "Waldstein" Sonata.

With regard to the Waldstein Duet Variations, we must not forget that all along Beethoven had been writing various compositions for strings and orchestral instruments, and there is no doubt that the diction used for these got largely into his piano style, and indeed the individual and dialogue manner of writing for them accounted a good deal for the closely woven thematic style typical of his works in sonata form.

Hence, you may trace, so to speak, the staccato flute in the first variation, the scintillating violin in the second, the interjected mournful clarinet or flute phrase in the third, a tutti, a full orchestra in the fourth, and so on.

The variations are in the melodic style and, though not very ingenious, are interesting and well contrasted.—HERBERT WESTERBY

VIII. 2 Preludes Through the Major Keys for [Piano or] Organ, Opus 39

The two preludes Opus 39 were singled out by Beethoven in that he allotted an opus number to them. He wrote them in 1789. The original autograph is lost, but an authenticated copy bears Beethoven's own signature and the date 1789.

The preludes were written for either piano or organ performance. A piano edition is contained in Peters Edition No. 297. Up to now these interesting works have been woefully neglected. Pianists are not likely to perform Opus 39 too eagerly, in view of the incomparable grandeur and size of Beethoven's other piano music. Organists, on the other hand, have far stronger reasons to use these works, considering the slim output of original organ literature of that time. What speaks even more in favor of organ performance is the obvious advantage of colorful organ registration to enhance and to build up these works.

Beethoven was not the first composer to base a composition on modulating meanderings through all the keys. Among others, Caldara (1670-1736), Locatelli (1695-1764), and Bach (1685-1750)—the last

[1] Kinsky-Halm sets the probable time of composition as 1791-92 in Bonn.—Editor.

mentioned in "A Short Harmonical Labyrinthus," contained in Vol. IX of the *Complete Organ Works of Bach* (P.E. No. 2067)—have preceded him.

Architecturally speaking, the first prelude is built on the pyramid principle, with a brilliant climax in the middle section. Looking at the score of the second prelude, the music seems to have a rather academic character, yet judicious use of its antiphonal architecture by alternating two contrasting registrations makes the work surprisingly impressive.— LUDWIG ALTMANN

IX. Organ Fugue in D, WoO 31

The fugue in D major was written in 1783. Beethoven probably used the work for the examination for the position as assistant court organist in February 1784 in Bonn.

The short work has the earmarks of a study and it would be futile to try to find indications of Beethoven's own, personal style in it.[1] But it is an effective work just the same if played in a brisk tempo, with bright, brilliant stops and good contrast of sonority between great and swell.—LUDWIG ALTMANN

X. 2 Movements of a Piano Sonatina in F, WoO 50

The fragmentary adagio in F major of the sonata [written for Eleonore von Breuning] bears a distinct resemblance to the likewise slow sonata movement in F which his friend Wegeler possessed. The manuscript of the latter contains the inscription: "Written and [sic!] especially fingered for me by Beethoven." This slight sonata movement written for Wegeler (and published in 1787 [!] by Schubart and Sons along with the sketch of an allegretto movement) is interesting not only as an insight into the unique and very practical fingering employed by the young Beethoven, but above all for a melodic germ used later in the *Trauerkantate*.[2]—LUDWIG SCHIEDERMAIR

The autograph which is reproduced in Leopold Schmidt's edition of Beethoven's letters to Simrock, Wegeler, etc. (Berlin, 1909), reveals a lovely Mozartean cantilena movement in 4/4 with the left hand alternating between a simple Alberti bass in sixteenth notes, and slow repeated

[1] However, the musical tension created by the long pedal point toward the close, with the moving voices recapitulating the theme and its several countersubjects, is definitely worthy of note—how thoroughly Beethoven learned from his great baroque predecessors. —Editor.
[2] Cantata on the Death of Joseph II, WoO 87.

chords. The suspensions in the inner voices of this bass are remarkable in the high degree of sophistication.—Editor.

XI. Sonata Facile in C, WoO 51 (Dedicated to Eleonore von Breuning)

This little sonata appeared after the three sonatinas dedicated to the Elector of Cologne (WoO 47). [It was probably written in 1791 or 1792 in Bonn.]

It has come down to us without the third movement, which was probably a rondo; all that remains today are the first two movements, allegro [4/4 in C] and adagio [3/4 in F], and even the latter is incomplete. Ferdinand Ries has finished the last eleven measures.

In this sonatina, which Lenz described as "without interest," one can easily see, with Riemann, a definite progress over the preceding sonatas and sonatinas, if only in the manner in which the exposition closes in the key of the dominant with the development of entirely new motives. It is certain that the young Beethoven strove to imitate the models that were available to him. The opening figure [of an upbeat trill on the dominant, followed by a descending arpeggio in the right hand and an ascending arpeggio in the left hand], which exists in many of the Mannheim symphonies, and in Mozart, was also used in the 1785 Piano Quartet in C, upon which Beethoven borrowed so heavily later while composing his first sonatas [Opus 2] in Vienna.

One can observe the frequency of modulations and the importance given to the bass in the second theme. But probably the most remarkable feature of the allegro is the brusque manner (truly Beethovenian) with which the young composer, after the close of the exposition, establishes the relatively distant key of E flat without modulation. It is managed in an analogous way, but less brutally, in the Sonata in A major, Opus 2, No. 2, where the development section begins in C major, and in the F major Sonata, Opus 10, No. 2, where the recapitulation after a long preparation commences in D major instead of F.

The one youthful weakness it betrays, alongside the progress over his earlier works, is the clumsiness of the initial passage toward the dominant key in the exposition.—J.-G. PROD'HOMME (3) (TR. BY THOMAS K. SCHERMAN)

The incomplete second movement, which was rounded out later by Ries, is in simple three-part song form. It is noteworthy because of the skillful decorative variations which occur on each reappearance of the theme. Also the tender suspensions in the second part are harbingers of his graceful first period style.—Editor.

Vocal Music

I. CANTATAS

a. "On the Death of Joseph II," WoO 87

The cantata opens with an orchestral prelude, whose first four measures, alternating between strings and woodwinds, are to be found again at the beginning of the prison scene from *Fidelio*. At the close of the prelude, where the oboe is heard in a plaintive cry, sustained by the woodwinds, the choir deplores the death of the emperor: "Death, groan through the gloomy night; may the rocks shed tears and you, the sea, roar and toss in your deepness. Joseph the Great, the father of immortal action, is dead!" From this emphatic and banal poetry the composer was able to paint a moving and lugubrious tableau by the mixture of voices (chorus and soloists) and instruments and the employing of ingenious rhythms and dynamics. After the voices have proclaimed their distress, there is a sudden piano at the words, "Cry again," pronounced by the soloists, which is very effective. It is a harbinger of the constant contrasts of dynamics which were later to become a Beethoven trademark. The orchestra then paints a picture of the waves in the howling seas as indicated by the "poet" Averdonck. The exclamation "Joseph is dead!" marks the zenith of this lamentation.

And this cry, repeated by the soloists and the choir, is then repeated pianissimo after the entrance of the first violins. The last syllable ("dead") is held for five measures, and, from the choir, this cry starts out piano and builds anew to a powerful crescendo. Finally the resonance decreases, little by little.

After this pathetic instrumental and vocal introduction, the second piece (recitativo presto), for baritone, seems to imitate Handel. The text cannot be considered to be very inspiring to the composer. Nonetheless, the orchestration has its happy moments with its many nuances, particularly to the following text: "A monster by the name of fanaticism rises from the depths of hell and grows larger between the earth and the sun—its name is night."

The aria which follows is composed to the words: "And then Joseph appears; with a divine force he terrorizes the menacing beast between heaven and earth, and crushes its head." It is in the form of a cavatina, is developed at length, and is not lacking in dramatic intensity or vocal difficulties; it is, however, eminently "singable" provided one possesses a voice of the required range and intensity.

The aria with chorus (No. 4, andante molto), "And then the men will move toward the light and the happy earth will revolve 'bout the sun and the sun will warm it with divine rays," is introduced by the oboe; its melody is the same one, note for note, which Beethoven was to employ fifteen years later in *Fidelio*. In the opera he was to apply the following words: "To you, O noble woman, alone, is reserved the right to deliver him to full liberty!" The soprano soloist resumes the lyrics, and, after a short prelude by the strings, the voices of the soprano and the tenor form a tender dialogue. After this Andante in F there follows a Largo in D minor for the soprano: "He sleeps . . . he sleeps." At this point the composer produced a lugubrious effect analogous to the text by an accompanying instrumentation of first violins pianissimo with the flutes. The aria which follows this recitative unfortunately is not up to the high standard of the mournful beginning. It is but a commonplace imitation of Mozart and one searches in vain for traces of originality. And yet certain words, most expressively stressed, tend to relieve the insignificance. The finale, which is almost a complete textual repetition of the first piece, quickly erases this impression. And suddenly, instead of remaining in the key of E flat, Beethoven shifts into C minor with an augmented instrumentation, più largo, quasi molto adagio, and impressively terminates the work.—J.-G. PROD'HOMME (1) (TR. BY THOMAS K. SCHERMAN)

LETTER OF BRAHMS TO EDWARD HANSLICK, VIENNA, MAY 1884

Naturally the cantata on the death of Joseph II interests us chiefly. For such a historical event one doesn't write merely a *pièce d'occasion!* Were we to commemorate this unforgettable, irreplaceable man today, we would be as impassioned about it as Beethoven and everyone else at the time. Nor did Beethoven merely write a *pièce d'occasion*. We have only to observe how this artist never fails to fashion artistically, to exert his greatest efforts, and this is more easily seen in a young man than in the master. In the very first mourning chorus, we get the picture of Joseph himself. Not a word or note would leave you in doubt. A recitative, uncommonly vigorous, follows: "A mighty one, his name, Fanaticism, rose from the depths of Hell" (later crushed by Joseph, in an aria). I cannot help thinking back on that time when—as the vehement words demonstrate—the entire world understood what it had lost in Joseph. The young Beethoven also understood that he had something great to say and, as was right, said it forcefully right at the start, in the powerful Overture. To the words: "The people came forth into the light," we hear the magnificent F major movement from the finale of *Fidelio*. Here, as there, the beautiful, moving melody in the oboe. We find many examples where the great masters use the same thought in several places. I find it particularly good here. How deeply Beethoven must have felt the melody in the cantata, as deeply and beautifully as later, when he sang the noble song of the love of a woman—a song of liberation as well—to its conclusion. After further arias and recitatives, the work closes with a repetition of the opening chorus.

—SAM MORGENSTERN

b. "On the Coronation of Leopold II," WoO 88

The second cantata, written six months after the first (March 1790) to celebrate the accession of Leopold II, is the one which Beethoven presented to Haydn during the latter's stay at Bonn. Composed after a text by the same poet, Averdonck, as a complementary elegy to the first one, it is made up of six pieces in which the composer attempted to give more movement and variety than in his first cantata:

I. A recitative for solo soprano without orchestral introduction which begins exactly like the narrative, largo, of the preceding cantata, with the chorus becoming more and more animated. This blends directly into:

II. An aria andante con moto for soprano, which is preceded by a long instrumental preamble. This aria is developed at considerable length and is followed by:

III. A recitative of several measures for bass, accompanied solely by the cello and the figured bass.

IV. Another recitative, for tenor accompanied by strings.

V. A terzetto (soprano, tenor, and bass) reminds one happily of the late Emperor Joseph. This trio leads directly into the final chorus, accompanied by the full orchestra.

In these different pieces Beethoven showed as much strength and ability as in the funeral cantata, although he was more inspired by the graveness of the latter. One notices the attention and care with which he attempted to translate the text into music, and the *"Sturzet neider, Millionen"* by the full chorus in the finale (allegro maestoso) appears already as a distant forerunner of the majestic *"Seidumschlungen, Millionen!"* by Schiller, in the finale of the Ninth Symphony.

In these two cantatas Beethoven had already found his own distinctive orchestral palette, with tones exaggeratedly violent or overly pathetic. One observes, among other individualities, his preponderance to use wind instruments, for which the critics were to take him to task after his First Symphony. From the Mannheimers he had learned about contrasting dynamics, but only his own genius and inspiration could raise these orchestral techniques from mere vehicles of display to an intensely expressive plane. Also one observes here his penchant for clearly defined characteristic rhythms. The solo parts of the second cantata especially present some difficulties for the singers. Through Salieri's advice Beethoven would later make much progress in vocal composition, but as for chorus he was destined never to really master the human instrument.—J.-G. PROD'HOMME (1) (TR. BY THOMAS K. SCHERMAN)

II. Songs

In song writing Beethoven had no great models. His own works are the bridge between the ingenuous songlets of the eighteenth century, written for domestic performance and the exquisite *lieder* of Franz Schubert. At the outset Beethoven relied largely on instinct. Indeed, looking at his songs composed during the Bonn period, there are moments when I wish he had never studied under Salieri. The jolly bass arias with orchestra (1790), *Prüfung des Küssens*[1] and *Mit Mädeln sich vertragen,*[2] have a youthful sing-yourself zest that is most attractive, and the simplicity and pathos of *Elegie auf den Tod eines Pudels* (1792)[3] still go straight to the heart. It is true many of the early songs show weak spots in the workmanship and even a vein of sentimentality, but they have lyric impulse and that young man's freshness which can never be recaptured in mature composition. With Beethoven it vanished—so far as his songs were concerned—under the ministrations of Haydn and Salieri in Vienna. Haydn simply confirmed Beethoven in the convention of doubling the vocal line with the top part in the accompaniment, a bad habit that, under guise of supporting the voice, trammelled it, and Salieri led him back to Italian models which, excellent in themselves, were alien to Beethoven's genius.—MARION M. SCOTT

Beethoven's compositions for the voice were not very numerous up to 1792. At the most about a dozen works. A first attempt appears in the form of an innocent little air in 6/8 which appeared in 1783 in the *"Blumenlese"* of the Councillor Bossler, with the following inscription: *"von Hrn. Ludw. van Beethoven alt eif Jahr."* It is "The Portrait of a Young Girl" (*Schilderung eines Mädchens*)[4] and the poet is not acknowledged in any way. A little later we find an arioso in 3/4 entitled "To an Infant" (*An einem Säugling*),[5] which proved

[1] WoO 89.—Editor.
[2] WoO 90.—Editor.
[3] Kinsky-Halm sets the date of composition as 1787 and designates it as WoO 110.
[4] WoO 107.—Editor.
[5] WoO 108.—Editor.

to be equally uninteresting. It serves to show with what awkwardness the fledgling composer, less familiar with prosody than with his own art, strove to adapt the poetry to his musical composition. Certain other attempts must have been lost, as we do not come upon another vocal work for two or three years, and this time it is a drinking song (*Trinklied*), allegretto in C, "to be sung at a farewell"[1] in which the piano accompanies the five stanzas with simple harmonies followed by a chorus. Each stanza is followed by a chorus singing a refrain.

"Elegy on the Death of a Water Spaniel,"[2] composed about 1787, is a more important work—a 2/4 in F minor modulating to an A flat, divided into two movements: an andante in thirty-six measures for the first three couplets, followed by an andante ma non troppo in forty-one measures, where the melody of the preceding stanzas is reproduced in a somewhat modified fashion but with a new and less intimate accompaniment. This little poem concerning the death of a water spaniel, which brought out certain philosophical thoughts, can be considered as Beethoven's first appreciable work for the voice. The melancholy mood which runs through these four couplets is certainly in keeping with the mood of the young composer, and it is very likely that it was composed following his return from Vienna and the death of his mother.

After having composed two very different versions, Beethoven entered the following in his collection of songs, Opus 52: "*Im Arm der Liebe*" after verses by Ueltzen, published in the Goettingen "*Musenalmanch*" of 1788.[3] In 1789 he composed another drinking song, "*Punschlied*"[4] for a reunion of friends (it remains unedited), and, from Goethe's *Faust*, a melody which was to be later marked as Opus 75 [No. 3], in 1810, with an added chorus. It is Mephistopheles' "Song of the Flea": the first line is "*Es war einmal ein Koening . . .*"

In the collection of Eight Songs, which appear as Opus 52 in 1805, we find several melodies of that period. The first, "*Urian's Reise*" (Urian's trip around the world, with words by Claudius), was, according to Wegeler, the first "romance" of Beethoven. The second is "*Feuerfarbe*" (Color of Fire), which Fischenich, a friend of Schiller, sent to Charlotte von Schiller with the accompanying note:

I am sending you a composition entitled "Feuerfarbe" and would like to have your opinion concerning it. It is the work of a young man here whose musical talent will become universally acknowledged and whom the prince elect has sent to Vienna to be with Haydn. He will set Schiller's "Ode to Joy" to music—all the stanzas. I expect something wonderful will be the result for he seems to me to be

[1] WoO 109.—Editor.
[2] WoO 110.—Editor.
[3] Opus 52, No. 3.—Editor.
[4] WoO 111.—Editor.

very drawn to, and capable of, the grand and the sublime sort of music. Haydn has written that he will pass on to this musician operas to compose which he himself must abandon. In the meantime he occupies himself with smaller works, so small in fact that the attached is the result of a request from a woman. (January 26, 1793)

Charlotte von Schiller replied as follows on February 11:

"The work entitled 'Feuerfarbe' is very fine; I expect much from this artist and I am pleased that he will set the 'Ode to Joy' to music."

Thus Beethoven, at the age of twenty, was already thinking of putting the Schiller Ode to music, an idea which bore fruit thirty-four years later as the final movement of his Ninth Symphony. Even the musical idea was born around this period or very little after, as one sees it in a song which appeared in 1796, "Seufzer eines Ungeliebten"[1] (Sighs from One Unloved).

From this same collection, Opus 52, the fourth number, "Maigesang," became a new melody for "La Belle Cordonnière," of Umlauf; and the penultimate number, "Marmotte" (from Goethe), the refrain of which is in French Avec que sa Marmotte, borrows its first measures from "Urian's Voyage." It is possible that the other numbers also date from the same period: "Molly's Abschied," by Burger, Lessing's "Ohne Liebe lebe wer er kann," and Burger's "Das Blümchen Wunderhold." One thing is certain, and that is that this collection was received with very little enthusiasm by the "Bulls of Leipzig," who reviewed it at the time when Beethoven was presenting Fidelio. The following is an example of the criticism:

Is it possible that these eight songs could be the work of this remarkable artist, so often admirable, even when not at his best? Reality forces us to accept this as so. His imprinted name appears over the title. The name of the publisher is clearly shown and the songs appeared in Vienna, the composer's residence. They even bear the number of his most recent opus. It is difficult to understand that such a common, poor, worthless work could come from such a man; it is even worse to realize that it could be offered to the public! (from Allgem. musik. Zeitung, August 28, 1805)

These works of such a fledgling composer certainly deserved neither excessive praise nor the indignities leveled at them. But we will discover that Beethoven was not on the best of terms with the Leipzig publishers. Toward 1790 Beethoven again wrote "Die Klage"[2] (The Moan), a melody in 2/4 in E major at the head of which he made this indication: "From the beginning to the end the motives should be drawn and

1 WoO 118.—Editor.
2 WoO 113.—Editor.

bound together as much as possible." The melody is in two parts, of which the second part, in the minor key (fifteen measures) is followed by a nine-measure postlude.

In a completely different mood is *Der Freie Mann*[1] (The Free Man) to words by Goethe, given by Beethoven to Wegeler some time later, who turned it into a Masonic chant for the lodge at Bonn. The vigorous rhythm of this song, based on a simple melody, and written for several voices, admirably reflects the mood of the words of the poet: "What is a free man?, etc." On the occasion of a presentation of *Claudine de Villabella*, also by Goethe, Beethoven wrote two happy melodies for bass voice with humorous orchestral accompaniment: *"Prüfung des Küssens"* (Proof of the Kiss) and *"Mit Mädeln sich vertragen"*[2] (To Get Along Well with Young Girls).—J.-G. PROD'HOMME (1) (TR. BY THOMAS K. SCHERMAN)

[1] WoO 89.—Editor.
[2] WoO 90.—Editor.

His Life

A PART from the project of taking lessons in counterpoint from Haydn, to which Count Waldstein alludes in his letter, it is very unlikely that Beethoven had any fixed plans when he reached Vienna toward the end of 1792. A young man not quite twenty-two, he had come to the most musical city of Europe, the chosen home of Mozart and Haydn, to test himself by the severe standards he would find there. His future course must depend on the result of that test. Meanwhile, there was the counterpoint.

Haydn knew something of him. The old man had passed through Bonn in 1790 and, quite apart from that, he could hardly be ignorant of Beethoven's growing reputation as a pianist. The lessons began almost at once and continued for about a year. They were not a great success. Kind, easygoing "Papa" Haydn hardly knew what to make of this outlandish youth from the provinces with his bad manners and boorish ways, who would never take any rule on trust, but must always know the "why" as well as the "how." Beethoven on his side felt that he was getting nowhere and attributed his slow progress to Haydn's preoccupation with matters outside the lessons, and it certainly appears that the master, with many diverse calls upon his time, was sometimes a little careless in correcting his pupil's exercises. At the root of their failure to appreciate one another was a profound temperamental divergence, and it was perhaps a consciousness of this that made Beethoven refuse to describe himself as a pupil of Haydn in the dedication of the pianoforte sonatas Opus 2. Yet they never quarreled. Haydn watched the young man go his own tempestuous way, witnessed his triumphant progress as a virtuoso, gently reproved his overbearing manners by nicknaming him the "Great Mogul," but forbore to break with him, although there was much in Beethoven's music, even his early music, with which he could not sympathize. As to Beethoven, with all his ignorance of the world, he realized the value of Haydn's good will and was careful not to offend him. For his counterpoint he went to Johann Schenk and then to Albrechtsberger, the strictest teacher of them all. The story that when working with Albrechtsberger he filled the margins of his exercises with sarcastic remarks is pure fiction. Everything goes to show that from these lessons he got exactly what he wanted. Not even Albrechtsberger could make him a smooth and impeccable contrapuntist; but he took him as far as double fugue and triple counterpoint and he gave to his musical thought a contrapuntal turn, the healthy influence of which is everywhere apparent in the works composed after the conclusion of the lessons in 1795.

But the essential business of consolidating his technique and thus preparing for his future triumphs occupied only a small part of the young Beethoven's time and energies. Outside his study lay the whole city of Vienna with its manifold musical activities, and into these he threw himself heart and soul.

Vienna's reputation as a musical center was due, first and foremost, to the enlightened patronage of the Austrian nobility. Many of them were connoisseurs of the art, nearly all of them enthusiasts. A few, like Prince Esterházy, Haydn's old patron, could afford a private orchestra. For the less wealthy this was out of the question, but even they could hire a string quartet now and again or, failing that, a pianist. As a consequence there was an enormous demand for chamber music and instrumental players. Other branches of the art were comparatively neglected: there was an opera, but it was Italian; church music, Thayer tells us, was "at a very low point" in 1793; and a public concert was a rarity.

With the Viennese aristocracy Beethoven's success was immediate and overwhelming. He had introductions from Count Waldstein, and it probably went for something that he came from the elector at Bonn, who was the emperor's uncle, and that he was a pupil of the great Haydn. His music and his personality did the rest, and he soon made a reputation for himself both as pianist and teacher. He was in constant demand at the houses of the rich and for several years he had rooms of his own at Prince Carl Lichnowsky's. A glance at the dedications of the first half of the piano sonatas gives one an idea of the class of people he mixed with. There is no need here to copy that list of sonorous titles.

Beethoven refused from the first to adopt the subservient attitude that the patrons of music had been wont to expect from its practitioners. He would meet them as an equal or not at all. Even on that footing he was not an easy guest to entertain. Arrogant, sensitive, afraid of ridicule, and quite unable to hold his own in a battle of words, he often flew into a passion on the most trifling provocation and rewarded the kindness of his hosts with the grossest rudeness. The conditions of his early life had made him uncontrolled, emotional, self-willed, and with the coming of success the flaws in his character became apparent. We must distinguish carefully between character and personality. Even in these early years no one could fail to be impressed with the force of Beethoven's personality. But his character lacked firmness. Unlike those ancient worthies whose stoical constancy he so much admired in Plutarch's account of them, he was easily exalted by good fortune and as easily cast down by failure. Just now his star was in the ascendant and he was becoming more and more conscious of unusual power within him, with the result that his head was turned and his manners suffered.

Yet the Viennese aristocracy would never have tolerated him had they not discerned qualities that more than counterbalanced his insolence and conceit. His genius, his magnetic personality were acknowledged by all, and there was besides a gaiety and animation about the young Beethoven that people found immensely attractive. The troubles of his boyhood were behind him: his father had died very shortly after his departure from Bonn, and by 1795 both his brothers were established in Vienna, Caspar Karl as a musician, Johann as an apothecary. During his first few months in the capital he had indeed been desperately poor, depending as he did very largely on the small salary allowed him by the elector. But all that was over now. He had no responsibilities and his music was bringing in enough to keep him in something like affluence. He had a servant, for a short time he even had a horse; he bought smart clothes, he learned to dance (though not with much success), and there is mention of his wearing a wig! We must not allow our picture of the later Beethoven to throw its dark colors over these years of his early triumphs. He was a young giant exulting in his strength and his success, and youthful confidence gave him a bouyancy that was both attractive and infectious. Even in 1791, before he left Bonn, Carl Junker could describe him as "this amiable, lighthearted man." And in Vienna he had much to raise his spirits and nothing (at first) to depress them.

Within a comparatively short time after his arrival Beethoven had become, after Haydn, the most eminent musician in the city. As a pianist he took Vienna by storm. More finished, more elegant playing his audience had perhaps heard, but never such power, such fire, above all, such improvising. He made his first appearances before a public audience at two charity concerts in March 1795, and the very fact of his engagement on these important occasions bears witness to his growing reputation. Soon he was the unquestioned king of Viennese pianists—"the giant among pianoforte players," one admirer calls him. Whenever a traveling virtuoso visited the city it was with Beethoven that he was inevitably compared, and in this way he had to measure himself against the greatest masters in Europe. Joseph Wölffl was in

Vienna in 1798, J. B. Cramer a year or two later; if Beethoven could maintain his supremacy against such competition as theirs he must indeed have been a remarkable pianist. It is pleasant to record that he established excellent relations with both Wölffl and Cramer; in spite of his "somewhat haughty pose" he could respect and appreciate a great rival. His pupils included such notable performers as Ferdinand Ries and Carl Czerny, besides a number of young ladies of title, many of whom played excellently.

He himself made more than one concert tour during the period under consideration. Prague was visited twice, Berlin once and possibly Dresden, Nuremberg and other places. At times he thought of leaving Vienna permanently, of moving to Paris, perhaps, or London. But his characteristic irresolution kept him from any decisive step,[1] and in the end Vienna held him. Every summer, however, he would pay a long visit to the country, taking rooms in Mödling, Heiligenstadt, Teplitz, or some other pleasant resort, or staying with his friends the Brunswicks in Hungary or the Lichnowskys in Silesia. There he would take long walks, for he loved the country passionately and drew from the beautiful works of nature his clearest intimations of the divine Artist. This habit of walking, so good for body and mind alike, remained with him through life. In his pocket he would carry the inevitable scrap of music paper on which to jot down any ideas that came to him, and often he would ensconce himself in the fork of a tree or some other convenient resting-place to consider, or even to work out on paper, the great lines of some new masterpiece.

In 1800 Beethoven brought out his eleventh piano sonata (in B flat, Opus 22). His works at that time included the piano trios, Opus 1, the string trios, Opus 9, the cello sonatas, Opus 5, and the violin sonatas, Opus 12. He had written two piano concertos and the third (in C minor, Opus 37) appeared in 1800, as did also the septet, Opus 20, the first six string quartets, Opus 18, and the first symphony, Opus 21. Most of these, it will be noticed, are chamber compositions, and their dedications generally indicate the patron for whom they were written. A dedication by Beethoven was usually a matter of business. Some rich nobleman would commission a work from him and pay for it. In return for this he would receive the manuscript with a dedication and have the exclusive use of it for an agreed period—six months as a rule. After that the autograph reverted to Beethoven, who was then free to make his own arrangements concerning publication. There were

[1] Certain reviewers of the first edition of "Lives of the Great Composers" have taken me to task for saying that Beethoven's character lacked resolution. They have a right to their opinions. But they should have been aware (as apparently they are not) that this is not an original judgment of my own. Thayer expresses the same view, which was also shared by Stephan von Breuning (as is shown by a letter of von Breuning's which Thayer quotes). If I err I am in good company.

exceptions, of course: Beethoven was very angry when his lifelong friend, Nicolaus Zmeskall, tried to give him a present in return for the dedication of the F minor quartet, Opus 95. But these disinterested dedications are rare, and we must be on our guard against reading any romantic significance into his numerous dedications to ladies with charming names and impressive titles. They were generally in return for cash down.

On the other hand we have abundant testimony that Beethoven was constantly in love. Indeed he was seldom out of it. Already in Bonn he had afforded more than one instance of his susceptibility, and in Vienna the list of ladies he had loved and lost soon grew really imposing. Few women could hold him for long; on one occasion he laughingly boasted of his constancy because he had worshiped at the shrine of the same divinity for the unprecedented period of seven months. How many of these episodes were serious, how many mere diversions, it is impossible to say. He proposed marriage to Magdalena Willman in 1794 and probably to Therese Malfatti in 1810; and very likely he entertained serious thoughts of matrimony with two other ladies, the Countess Giulietta Guicciardi and the Countess Therese von Brunswick. Undoubtedly he longed to get married, to settle his vagabond life on a regular basis, and to have children; a sidelight is thrown on his conception of the married state by his refusal ever to flirt with a married woman. Yet he never found a wife. It was not that he was unattractive to women; though clumsy and by no means handsome,[1] he was continually surprising his friends by the difficult and unexpected conquests he made. Many of these ladies were far above him in station, and the difference in rank, combined with his reputation for eccentricity, must often have imposed an insurmountable barrier against matrimony. But equally often, one is inclined to think, the obstacle lay in himself: he idealized women, idealized them romantically without any reference to realities; and one after another the girls on whom he cast his eyes were discarded because they failed to live up to his impossible standards.

He remained celibate; but in spite of his high-mindedness he was not quite untouched by the moral laxity of his times. Thayer makes the unqualified assertion that he was not chaste and although he suppresses the evidence Thayer was far too conscientious a biographer to make a positive statement of that kind without being sure of his facts. Did Beethoven in these years of early manhood commit some foolish indiscretion for which he had to pay a terrible penalty? There is strong reason to believe he did, though in my opinion the case is not con-

[1] Beethoven was not more than five feet five inches in height, but his frame was muscular and well knit, and the splendid head was set on magnificent shoulders. Like many of his contemporaries he was pockmarked, the result of an attack of smallpox in his childhood. The grim line of the mouth, which contributes so much to the tragic effect of the later portraits, was not nearly so noticeable in his early years, when his expression was much more animated.—Editor.

clusively proved. If indeed it were, it would not only account for his celibacy, but provide us at last with a plausible theory of the appalling calamity that was so soon to darken his horizon and turn the story of his life to tragedy.—PETER LATHAM

The Place: Vienna

Beethoven settled in Vienna at the beginning of the winter of 1790, several months after the brilliant coronation at Frankfort of the stern and harsh Francis II, who was to reign over the submissive Austrians for forty-three years. In the same way that in the classical sonata the second theme provides new resources for the development of the piece, so the Viennese milieu offered its wealth of inspiration to the young Rhenish musician.

The engravings exhibited at the Rathaus during the Centenary Festival enable us to reconstruct the appearance of the city and the character of the times. With its narrow and twisting streets graced by occasional Florentine palaces, in spite of its statues and mausoleums, Vienna was not yet the brilliant capital with broad streets that it became in the second half of the nineteenth century, particularly through the construction of the famous Ring. Ten years after Beethoven's arrival, Madame de Staël visited the city and described it. She accused the Danube of "losing its majesty" in its too numerous detours, like certain men and women. For a half century through the generosity of Joseph II, the Prater with its cafés and continuous country fair had offered its avenues to a clamorous public that beset the worldly Corso; Corinne heard the rutting deer bell on the meadows. People were fond of walking there in the Italian manner, slowly and peacefully. The emperor and his brothers, if they went by carriage, fell into line. At the entrance to the Augarten, Joseph II had an inscription placed, the epitome of his good nature: "A place for recreation, dedicated to all men by their friend." Rousseauesque. People gathered there particularly on Thursdays between six and eight in the morning near the Seufzerallee to listen to the music. Fashionable men, in blue riding coats and white trousers, hats under their arms, promenaded with fashionable women, their hair arranged like butterfly wings under their little parasols so like peach tree blossoms. Vendors of Italian oranges and salami circled in and out among the tables at which people sat drinking. There was also a promenade very elegantly designed; it was a garden between the Ballhaus-Platz, the tennis court, and the court stables, with a row of poplar trees encircling a neo-Greek temple. With similar nicety the grenadiers in white uniforms maneuvered in serried ranks in front of the barracks.

Fashion decreed that in the morning one betake oneself to the Augarten; in the evening good breeding demanded that one have a turn around the music pavilion, on the Bastion and on the empress's terrace. Poles, Bosnians, and Turks in native costume contributed an exotic note to this scene arranged for the pleasure of society and for amorous intrigues. Sometimes a gypsy melody, fierce, impassioned, nostalgic, quivered in the distance.

There were many theaters in Vienna. Joseph II established the National-theater, which failed, by virtue of that special privilege conceded to all the plans of this ill-fated sovereign. Opera was given at the Kärntner-thortheater, and at the Theater an der Wien. There were also playhouses in the suburbs, In der Rossau, Beim Fasan. Emanuel Johann Schikaneder, author of the libretto of *Die Zauberflöte*, for a long time simply a vagrant musician, directed the *Theater im Starhembergischen Freihause auf der Wieden*, and on occasion botched Mozart. Music everywhere, concerts for the dilettanti, barrel organs for the man in the street. Also, there was dancing at the ridottos where one saw, according to Madame de Staël, "men and women, facing each other, gravely executing the steps of the minuet, which they chose to call amusement." The Emperor Francis played the violin; the Empress Maria Theresa sang to her own accompaniment at the harpsichord, organized concerts, arranged for the presentation of Italian operas at Schönbrunn; Joseph Haydn dedicated a mass, and Beethoven his Septet to her. As for the rest, delightful, agreeable manners, a correct and cordial civility, a taste for social visits and clubs. This was the society in which Beethoven was henceforth to live.

By good fortune in the glorious Vienna of this period, there were abundant resources for a musician twenty-two years of age, who felt that his education was not yet complete. Let us consider for a moment all that spiritual grandeur that the city contained about 1792. It had scarcely been five years since Ritter von Gluck had died, after having completed a splendid career which covered with glory the son of Prince Lobkowitz's little gamekeeper.

Gluck had completely dominated his period; through his efforts music ceased to be treated as a diversion, and established itself as a perfect and sovereign art.

Mozart after piteous suffering died on December 5, 1791, at the age of thirty-five years and ten months; no one followed his poor body, thrown unwitnessed into a poor-pit; no one knows where his coffin is hidden.

The men with Mozart in his last hours were those who were to welcome the young Beethoven: Albrechtsberger and van Swieten. Vienna mourned, but less tenderly than Prague; more grateful than others, and without doubt, more moved by this tragic end, the newcomer was to give him several phrases of his Quartet in A as a splendid shroud.

The history of Austrian music toward the end of the eighteenth century is a dazzling succession of luminaries. Younger than Beethoven by eight years, Johann Nepomuk Hummel, son of the Kapellmeister of Schikaneder's theater, pupil of Mozart and Albrechtsberger, Haydn's successor with Prince Esterházy, also lived in Vienna pursuing evasive resources; we shall find him in mourning near the deathbed of the Master. Thus an incomparable family was completed, united by the common bonds of race, modest beginnings, perseverance in work, and genius. Salieri, who ought not to be undervalued, struggled a little lower, nearer the valley; one must acknowledge in him a flexible and clever talent; overshadowed by Gluck, he won for himself an honorable name, and after 1787 he directed the court orchestra. Signor Bonbonieri, as he was called, taught Beethoven how to set Italian texts.

In so small a region, and in so short a space of time, such coincidence is astonishing. Unless one refuses to music, on the ground that it is altogether insubstantial, the same considerations granted to belles-lettres or painting, isn't one tempted to say that the history of the arts offers few such confluences? A miracle of mankind similar to that given us by the period of Leo X or that of Louis XIV, to use academic labels. Joseph II contributed only through his good-natured protection. However, the geographical position of Vienna facilitated this concentration on music. What better place was there in which to collect the Slavic melodies which we hear frisking in the Beethoven quartets in the form of Russian themes? Here was the gateway to Italy. Domenico Cimarosa, who went to Russia, following Paisiello's example, but who was unable to endure the climate of the country, stopped in Vienna on his return; there he wrote Il Matrimonio segreto, about 1792, which won a tremendous success, and with which Beethoven was enchanted. Ferdinando Paër left the theater of Venice, where he directed the orchestra, to settle in Vienna, and Mozart's influence on his style is noticeable from this time on. Cherubini was to be exalted here. The social conditions of Austria favored this prolific blossoming. Musicians were as necessary to Prince Esterházy as were cooks; it was necessary that the Bishop of Salzburg have a good organist. Gluck, Haydn, Mozart, Beethoven, Schubert, as children, breathed an air saturated with music. But from where did their genius come? And why did this genius select sons of the lower classes from all the others who had only talent?

In the city of Vienna, which war had not yet disturbed, in the midst of a society in which only a select few had a taste for pure music, far removed from the theaters that played very little except an Italian repertoire, the new Mozart, careless with money, enthusiastic, eager to observe and to learn, in great demand as a virtuoso but firmly determined not to be satisfied with his first success, associated with princely families not yet affected by hard times, freed himself from the state of servility which had burdened the musicians of the preceding period, took part in the soirées which the intelligent Baron van Swieten held, tried his new compositions at Prince Lichnowsky's morning musicales, and had himself presented to the generous Count Rasoumowsky. And the dilettanti, Haydn's friends, the admirers of *Don Giovanni*, had no trouble in discerning in this red-faced young man with the disheveled hair and the unconventional behavior, who improvised in so brilliant a manner, the rival or the heir of the Masters of Music. Haydn and Mozart, confirmed Josephists, were affiliated with the Freemasons, the former with the lodge Zur wahren Eintracht, the latter with the lodge Zur gekrönten Hoffnung. According to all probability Beethoven imitated them: evidence can be found in examining the manuscripts of the Seventh Quartet. In the salons, enlivened by charming and beautiful women, and frequented by silk-stockinged musicians, he apparently took great pride in preserving a provincial manner, an almost slovenly attire, a coarse voice, and a blunt humor. But those who already knew him, who had listened to him, were charmed by his genius, and whereas Prince Esterházy made Haydn wait in his antechamber, the Countess von Thun begged Beethoven's favor on her knees.—EDOUARD HERRIOT

His Teachers

Antonio Salieri

Among Beethoven's teachers in Vienna, the old conductor of the royal orchestra, Antonio Salieri is always mentioned together with Haydn and Albrechtsberger. It is usually said that Beethoven studied vocal composition, especially in Italian, or dramatic music with this famous opera composer, and it is only Hugo Riemann who provides us with any more detailed information about these studies in the latest edition of Thayer's book, which he revised. The studies are said to have concerned stress and the expression of individual words, the rhythm and the metric grouping of the verses, the logical breakdown of thought, the atmosphere of the text, and its musical equivalence. Riemann also says that Salieri's instruction was not regular and systematic, and that Beethoven learned the method of how to recite a text in a correct manner from him. But he rejects any deeper influence by Salieri on Beethoven's style or personality as an artist, and in so far as the author of this article has been able to find out, the relationship between Beethoven and Salieri has never been the object of a thorough analysis. The sole purpose of this article is to set forth a few viewpoints indicating that this problem should not be wholly without interest for Beethoven researchers who aim at explaining the conditions for Beethoven's new and brave symphonic style, the aesthetic meaning of which is certainly as important as its purely musical merits.

Everyone who has to some extent studied the history of Beethoven's life knows that Beethoven's relationship with Salieri was of a more personal nature than that of any of his other teachers. The differences in age between the student and his three main teachers condition this situation. It is true that Salieri was twenty years older than Beethoven, but Haydn and Albrechtsberger were thirty-eight and thirty-four years older than their student. Salieri belonged to Beethoven's circle of friends. Although they did not see each other often, the completion of Beethoven's actual studies during his first years in Vienna—about 1795—did not bring about a breach in their relationship. Beethoven dedicated his three violin sonatas Opus 12 published in 1799 to Salieri, and Moscheles relates that, once in 1809, he had found on Salieri's desk a piece of paper where Beethoven had written in big letters: *"Der Schüler Beethoven war da!"* (Your student Beethoven was here!) And at Beethoven's great concerts in December 1813 when *"Wellingtons Sieg"* was performed, Salieri was among the musicians who honored Beethoven by participating, and conducted "the cannonade" from the side of the podium.

Salieri's friendship with and admiration for Gluck took him to Paris in 1784. Mosel relates that the Paris Opera called upon Gluck to name a young musician *"der fähig wäre, für das erwähnte Theater eine französische Oper nach den Grundsätzen jener Kunst-Philosophie zu schreiben, welche Gluck durch Wort und That gelehrt hatte, und mit deren Befolgung allein eine wahrhaft dramatische Musik hervorgebracht werden kann."* (who was capable of writing a French opera according to the principles of the Art Philosophy for the mentioned theater which Gluck had taught in word and deed, and only when followed, was it possible to create truly dramatic music.) Gluck proposed Salieri, and thus Salieri wrote according to his own words *"unter Gluck Leitung"* (under Gluck's leadership), his first French opera *Les Danaïdes*. The text was by Calsabigi, well known from Gluck's opera reform, and the music was said to be by Gluck and Salieri. It was only after the twelfth performance, when one no longer had to doubt about the success of the piece, that Gluck revealed the true situation. Salieri then remained a great name in Paris for several decades, and his foremost operas were among the greatest successes at the opera house.

After his return to Vienna, he was appointed conductor of the royal orchestra, and thus Salieri came to hold a central position in the life of art in the imperial city, although already in 1790 he was freed from the obligation of conducting at the theater. We can hardly find an account of the life of music in Vienna concerning the time from about 1800 to up about 1820 where Salieri is not shown as the great personality. A great many students were attracted to him, he was highly cherished at the court, and foreigners came to see him from near and far.

Mosel's description of Salieri as a person gives the reader a very favorable impression. He was cheerful and kind, maybe a somewhat weak man who, on several occasions, showed concern about and helpfulness toward his fellow human beings. Like Beethoven, Salieri also worshiped the beauty of Nature and he was fond of the surroundings of Vienna where he had his favorite places, even special trees which he loved and visited in order to rest in peaceful reverie from work and vexations. He also possessed a fine sense of humor and charming self-irony of which the following words of his witness: *"Wie sollte ich die deutsche Sprache gut gelernt haben, da ich erst fünfzig Jahre in Deutschland lebe?"* (How could I have learned the German language well when I have only lived in Germany for fifty years?) Like Gluck, whose mother tongue was Czech, Salieri never learned to speak German fluently.

There seems to exist some uncertainty about the type of Salieri's instruction. Partly he taught singing; partly he taught composition. As concerns the latter, it is usually said that it consisted of *"italienische Gesangskomposition und dramatische Musik"* (Italian song composition and dramatic music). Furthermore, we know that most of the time there were no organized lessons or a methodical course but that his teaching was rather informal. It is also known that Salieri in this way taught young musicians free who were less well off. Mentioned as his students, except for Beethoven and Franz Schubert whose talent Salieri was among those to discover, are a great number of the *dei minores* of that time: Joseph Weighl, Nepomuk Hummel, Ignaz Moscheles, Giacome Meyerbeer, Friedrich Himmel, and others.

Ignaz von Seyfried in his famous edition of *"Beethovens Studien im Generalbass etc."* (Beethoven's studies of figured bass, etc.) characterizes the relationship between the teacher Salieri and his students as *"lehr-reicher Umgang,"* instructive togetherness. At this point, we would like to draw your attention to another until now seemingly ignored source, which gives us more detailed information about the matters Salieri discussed with his students during their informal "lessons." This source is a letter from Nepomuk Hummel to Ignaz von Sonnleithner.[1] Here Hummel gives us an account of his career, and as concerns his teachers he relates about counterpoint studies for Albrechtsberger and about his studies for Salieri, who gave him instruction *"in der Gesangskomposition, in den ästhetischen Ansichten und der musikalischen Philosophie überhaupt"* (in song composition, in aesthetic aspects and in music philosophy in general).

This statement about the contents of Salieri's instruction is wholly commensurate with what is known about the form of his teaching activity. It is not possible to teach *"Die ästhetischen Ansichten"* (the aesthetic aspects) during lessons, and the informal, "instructive togetherness" is the forum best suited for discussing *"die musikalische Philosophie überhaupt"* (music philosophy in general). There is no reason not to consider Hummel as an entirely competent witness, and there is as little reason to believe that Beethoven did not enjoy the same kind of instruction from Salieri as Hummel. It is easy to imagine that a student's composition of the music for a given Italian aria text was the starting point for a discussion of anything mortal or immortal that possibly related to music, and it is then clear that the teacher's aesthetic principles and viewpoints concerning individual questions of art were of greatest importance for shaping the student's ideas about music. In other words, it may be important to become familiar with Salieri's manner of viewing music, for it is certain that Beethoven was not able to avoid being influenced by it. It is true, Beethoven was not an immature youth when he came to Salieri. On the contrary, we have to picture him possessing such a degree of maturity that he was not subjected to his teacher's influence without resistance. The fact that Beethoven maintained a personal relationship with Salieri for such a long period of time does, however, indicate that he did not show resistance, and that he did not too much criticize or reject his teacher's way of viewing art.

Music being the servant of the word is Salieri's as well as Gluck's musical principle. It is said about Gluck that when composing an opera he first of all tried to forget that he was a musician, and Mosel relates a small anecdote from the work on *Les Danaïdes* in Paris which is at the same time characteristic and funny. When Salieri had finished his opera, he looked it over together with Gluck. In doing so they came upon a

[1] Obviously meant to be a part of the archives of Gesellschaft der Musikfreunde; first published in the "Neue Zeitschrift für Musik" in 1838. Later reprinted by La Mara, and others.

passage in an aria which Salieri was not quite satisfied with. Gluck looked at the score and asked Salieri to sing the aria once more. "You are right, my dear friend," Gluck then said after he had heard the aria the second time, "the aria as a whole is good, but the part which you are not satisfied with does not please me either, although I cannot tell you what is wrong. Sing the aria once more and once more again." When Salieri then came to the discussed part the last time, Gluck suddenly interrupted him, exclaiming: "Now I have it! The part *smells of music!*"

This hegemony of the word over the tone did, however, not make instrumental music preposterous, neither in the opinion of Gluck nor in that of Salieri. Behind their search for letting the word and its meaning appear to advantage there was—and there always is—a firm belief in the suggestive power of expression of the music. It is not as much from the *word* sung that the music needs support as from its meaning, its idea. Thus, in his overtures, Salieri like Gluck also tries to picture a character, a situation or a "poetic idea," using a recent aesthetic term. Already the overture to Salieri's *Armida* (1771), written before Gluck's *Iphigenia in Aulis*, forms a prologue to the opera or rather relates the background. While working on this opera, Salieri constantly read Tasso's *Gerusalemme liberata*, from where the action of the opera is taken. This gave him the idea of composing the overture as a kind of pantomime performed by the orchestra. Through the textbook, the audience got a hint about the intention of the piece and received it with lively applause. The motive for this depiction is Ubaldo's landing on Armida's enchanted island. The island is concealed by heavy fog through which Ubaldo penetrates. Then he is attacked by the dragons which he defeats, climbs the steep rock, and reaches then the peaceful and lovely valley which is shown on the stage when the curtain rises.

There are many opera overtures where Salieri describes the outer course of action in similar manners, but there are also examples of overtures rendering the personalities of the main characters and their differences. That is the case in the opera *Eraclito e Democrito*. The text is about the two well-known Greek philosophers Heraclitus and Democritus, and the overture depicts the characters of the two men. But, Mosel says, the contrast between the gloomy one and the cheerful one has not become a unity. The connecting idea is missing, and that is why one only hears "*heterogene Elemente*" (heterogeneous elements).

What has been brought up here may suffice to create an idea about Salieri's aesthetic viewing of music. And nobody can say that Beethoven, as he appears in his works, has been completely unfamiliar with this "*musikalische Philosophie*" (music philosophy). On the contrary, we dare to believe that it was nothing new for him when he came to Salieri. He had learned about it in Bonn, where he had received practical acquaintance with it sitting in the elector's royal orchestra playing in

Benda's melodramas, Salieri's *Trifonio*, Mozart's *Don Giovanni*, *Le Nozze di Figaro*, and *Die Entführung aus dem Serail*, or Grétry's operas. There the belief in the connection of music to characters and situations was maintained, and from there he also obtained strong musical impressions, as shown by reminiscences pointed out by Sandberger. In his conversations with Salieri, Beethoven can only have received a completely clear picture of what he already knew, that is that music could be set in direct and conscious relation to feelings, situations, and characters.

It should, however, be possible to deduce from this little exposé that there were very strong forces that drove Beethoven in the direction toward what Paul Bekker calls the "poetic idea." Salieri has certainly not exerted any deeper influence on Beethoven's musical style, on his way of writing. In order to do that, *"caro Gluckino,"* as he is called by a French author, has too insignificant specific gravity as a musician. His tones have hopelessly faded compared to Gluck's, and his disciple Beethoven was certainly a far deeper musical personality. But Beethoven's young belief in the power of expression of music has been elucidated and has been confirmed through his instruction by Salieri.

That is the reason why there is an unintended symbol in Beethoven's words, when he one day in 1809—after the "Eroica," the fifth and the sixth symphonies, after the "Kreutzer" sonata, the "Appassionata" and the Rasumowsky quartets, after the choral Phantasy—leaves his card at Salieri's house and writes: *"der Schüler Beethoven war da"* (your student Beethoven was here).—JULIUS RABE (TR. BY THOMAS K. SCHERMAN)

Josef Haydn

Haydn visited Bonn on December 25, 1790, on his way to London, and the next evening he was guest of honor for a dinner for "the most capable musicians."[1] There is no indication that Beethoven was one of those chosen to attend this dinner, but all the members of the chapel had been introduced to Haydn that day after the church service. Nohl says that it is most improbable that Beethoven had met Haydn in 1787 during the few weeks that he spent in Vienna with Mozart, but whether or not the older master and the youth had met in 1787 or in 1790 there can be no doubt that Beethoven heard much discussion of Haydn during his Bonn visit.

Wegeler reports that, on his way back from London to Vienna (i.e.,

[1] Initialed source references omitted.—Editor.

in July 1792), Haydn stopped at Bonn again. "The electoral orchestra gave him a breakfast at Godesberg, and there Beethoven laid before him a cantata 'which received the particular attention of Haydn, who encouraged its author to continue study.' It is not improbable that the arrangements were in part now made under which the young composer became a few months later the pupil of the veteran," though any arrangements then made could have been only tentative, since the Elector was not present. Schiedermair, however, is not convinced that this second Bonn visit ever took place. Wegeler's account is the only contemporary record of such a visit, if an account written more than forty-five years after the event can be called "contemporary"; there are discrepancies and improbabilities in Wegeler's narrative that lead Schiedermair to the conclusion (to which Deiters also leans) that in all probability the "Cantata on the Death of Joseph II" was laid before Haydn at the time of his only visit to Bonn in December 1790.

The thought that induced Elector Maximilian Franz to send Beethoven to study with Haydn may well have been to give his talented court organist an opportunity to attain fame as a composer and virtuoso so that, brought back to Bonn as Kapellmeister, he would reflect glory on the court and its prince. Musicians of promise or accomplishment like Anton Kraft, Pleyel, and Wranitzky had been pupils of Haydn, and Beethoven would gain in standing as well as in knowledge by similar association with the great man. Nohl suggests that a prior discussion of this plan for the future between Haydn and the Elector may have explained Haydn's passing thought of taking Beethoven to England with him at the end of 1793.

Beethoven started work with Haydn within a few days after his arrival in Vienna early in November 1792. The statement that Zmeskal brought Beethoven to Haydn, as given in the Fischhof manuscript, can be true only in the sense that he guided the stranger from Bonn around the city. Note that this statement would indicate that Beethoven made Zmeskal's acquaintance within his first few days in Vienna.

Haydn had prepared for the use of his pupils an abstract of Fux's "Gradus ad Parnassum," modified somewhat in accordance with his own ideas. A copy of this abstract (now lost) was given to Beethoven; its scope is indicated in considerable detail in Nottebohm's "Beethovens Studien." Haydn's problem in teaching Beethoven was not an easy one. The Bonn compositions strongly indicate that with Neefe Beethoven had studied more than merely the rudiments of harmony. "The fact seems to be that Beethoven, conscious of the disadvantages attending the want of thorough systematic instruction, . . . had determined to accomplish a complete course of contrapuntal study, and thus renew, revise, and reduce to order and system the great mass of his previous scientific acquirements."

Haydn's task, then, was to adapt his course of instruction to the needs of his pupil: to skip where he could, to drill where he must. His pupil was a strong-willed young man whose accomplishments as a composer and whose growing recognition as a virtuoso in the salons of Vienna could not have made him any the easier to work with. Haydn, past sixty, was universally and properly recognized as the greatest living composer; for much of the year that Beethoven worked with him he was preparing for a second London season, and working on the six new symphonies that his contract with Salomon called for. It was not within reason to expect that he would take docilely to correcting exercises in strict counterpoint; as Jacob put it: "At this particular time he would have been a bad teacher for any pupil."

Beethoven soon discovered that he was not receiving from Haydn the quality of instruction that he felt he had a right to expect. From August 1793 until after Haydn's departure for London on January 19, 1794, Beethoven also worked in secret with Johann Schenk, though the exact way in which he worked simultaneously with his two teachers is not clear. It is much to Beethoven's credit, and to Haydn's as well, that no open break took place between the two men. Throughout the year in which they played at a pupil-teacher relationship, and indeed for the fifteen years of life that remained thereafter for Haydn, their relations were friendly if not cordial. It seems probable that some time during 1793 Haydn presented his young pupil to the Esterházys, at either Eisenstadt or Vienna. Beethoven's status as a pupil of Haydn was undoubtedly of assistance in gaining for him admission to the salons of the nobility.

The Dutch flautist Drouet gives a circumstantial account by an unidentified English lady of a conversation that is supposed to have taken place between Haydn and Beethoven, in which the older man praised Beethoven's gifts very highly but criticized the erratic nature of his works, as a result of which Beethoven destroyed much of his earlier music and revised the rest. While it is most unlikely that the conversation as reported by Drouet ever took place, the words attributed to Haydn probably represent his actual opinion, and the effects on Beethoven's Bonn compositions of Haydn's advice and comments would probably have been as the anecdote indicates. On January 26, 1793, Fischenich of Bonn wrote to Charlotte Schiller about Beethoven: "Haydn has written here that he would put him to work on great operas, and then he himself would soon be forced to cease composing." The good-natured irony of these words of Haydn, who at the time of the letter could have had Beethoven as a pupil for only a few weeks, was apparently lost on Fischenich.

In "Beethovens Studien" (1873) Nottebohm has made a careful study of the 245 of Beethoven's exercises for Haydn that were still extant.

Corrections by Haydn appeared in only 42 of them, and in the others there were at least as many mistakes, on the average, as in those that had been corrected. "Here and there Haydn had changed notes; he marked many places with an 'X' or a 'NB'; but nowhere had he added a single explanatory word." Nottebohm concludes that this disregard of mistakes in the elements of musical grammar "can be explained only by the assumption that Haydn did not take the time to look through Beethoven's exercises carefully. . . . Haydn was not a systematic, thorough, or careful teacher." However, "we cannot agree with Beethoven's statement as quoted by Ries that he had learned nothing from Haydn. He had certainly learned something, even though it was more from the course of study than from the teacher, and the teacher cannot be wholly separated from his course of study . . . Schenk's statement that Beethoven had advanced to double counterpoint in the octave with Haydn is certainly incorrect."

When Beethoven's first year in Vienna had come to an end, Haydn wrote on November 23, 1793, to the Elector, sending five works of Beethoven's composition to indicate what he had accomplished during his year of study, and expressing his belief: "Expert and amateur alike must perceive from these works that as time progresses Beethoven will take his place with the greatest composers of Europe. I shall be proud to be known as his teacher, and hope that he may be allowed to remain with me for a considerable time." With this letter went one from Beethoven to the Elector, in which Beethoven says that during the year just past he has "applied all the powers of my mind to the general principles of music," thus substantiating the conclusion by Unger that "in Beethoven's first year in Vienna no important compositions came from his workshop." The Elector's reply was very unenthusiastic, since four of the five works that Beethoven sent had, at least in preliminary form, been heard before he left Bonn.

Nottebohm says that on a sheet on which Beethoven had sketched a part of the first movement of Opus 2 No. 1, he had written, "Another half-year of counterpoint and you can do whatever you want to." Nottebohm adds, "This remark sounds as though it had come from the mouth of Joseph Haydn." That is quite possible: the three sonatas of Opus 2, though published only in March 1796, had become known in Vienna through manuscript copies as early as the spring of 1795, so that what is clearly an early study for the first movement of the first of the sonatas might well date from 1793.

Probably in December 1793 or early January 1794, Beethoven introduced his Trios Opus 1 to the artistic world at a *soirée* at Prince Lichnowsky's, to general acclaim. "Haydn also said many complimentary things about them, but advised Beethoven not to publish the third Trio, in C minor." Later, when Ries asked Haydn why he had made this recommendation, his reply was "that he had not believed that this Trio would be so quickly and easily understood and so favorably received by the public." There can be no doubt, however, that Beethoven felt rebuffed by Haydn's comment: his statement that while he had taken some lessons from Haydn he had learned nothing from him may have been due not so much to the inadequacy of the instruction as to pique at his master's cool reception of what Beethoven undoubtedly considered one of his best works. It was this same sense of injured self-esteem that led Beethoven to refuse Haydn's wish that on the title-page of his first works he named himself "pupil of Haydn." Any irritation that the older man might have felt was put aside when, for the concert on December 18, 1795, to celebrate his second triumphant return from London, Haydn invited Beethoven to play one of his own concertos. This was a compliment to Beethoven's ability and to his acceptance by the music lovers of Vienna, but no less a public recognition by Haydn of Beethoven's status as an artist. A few months later Beethoven responded gracefully by dedicating to Haydn his first set of piano sonatas, Opus 2.—D. W. MACARDLE

Johann Albrechtsberger

Johann Georg Albrechtsberger's *Gründliche Anweisung zur Komposition* appeared in 1790—two years before Beethoven arrived in Vienna to study with Haydn. It is one of the ironic facts of the history of music that this association of Haydn and Beethoven proved unsuccessful. Beethoven felt that his work was not given enough attention and correction and eventually turned to Haydn's friend and colleague Albrechtsberger for instruction. Thus, very shortly after its publication, Albrechtsberger's *Anweisung* found its historic mission: It was used as the basis for Beethoven's studies.

Beethoven's choice is all the more interesting because it stresses the fact that a particular need for didactic aid arose toward the end of the eighteenth century. There is no question that a feeling of great mutual respect existed between Beethoven and Haydn. Beethoven's dedication of his trios Opus 1 shows his regard for the older friend and master, and it was a particular satisfaction to Haydn to be able to hear the first public performance of these works before he made his second journey to London—the journey which, according to original plans, Beethoven was to have undertaken with him. What Beethoven missed in Haydn's teaching was a methodical treatment of the basic laws of composition understandable in terms of his generation and its widened scope of musical ideas. Haydn used for the lessons with Beethoven his own abstract of Fux's *Gradus*,[1] which could not sufficiently serve this purpose.

Martini had stressed twenty years earlier that the greatest obstacle confronting the young composer was the growing number of different styles of composition. The necessity of dealing with this enlarged musical practice brought about a stronger distinction between the tasks of the composer and those of the teaching theorist than the first half of the century had known.

Albrechtsberger's writing shows that he assumed his role as one of the first modern theorists with understanding and competence. No longer concerned with the establishment of a method or the defense of a system, he based his work on the experience that eighteenth-century theory had gathered, and applied it to the needs of his own era with a sense for the important and for the practical and with many expressions of musical and aesthetic judgment which lend a refreshing quality to his style.

Fux, who had occupied the post of chapelmaster at St. Stephan's in Vienna almost a century before Albrechtsberger, was his chief guide. Following the general plan and substance of the *Gradus ad Parnassum* as "his oracle,"[2] he adapted Fux's teaching to major and minor tonalities. He added a chapter on the chorale fugue, the combination of fugue and cantus firmus setting, which Fux mentions only briefly, and a chapter on the canon, which is not treated in Fux's *Gradus*, and in which Albrechtsberger refers to Marpurg rather than Fux. These two chapters are the portions with which Albrechtsberger's writing is here represented.

Beethoven's notes in the course of studies he followed under Albrechtsberger have been preserved. Along with the musical examples we find copious comments, often presenting digressions which arrested Beethoven's attention; for example: "Albrechtsberger told me today that there are some works by the old master Froberger in which the use of the fourth, even that occurring by inversion of the triad, is completely avoided. This was done because the perfect triad, as symbol of the Holy Trinity, was to be maintained with absolute purity." The examples lead from simple cantus firmus settings to fugal studies and finally to a combination of both in the chorale fugue.

After giving Beethoven a cantus firmus, Albrechtsberger derives from it a fugal theme and shows how this theme might be set in a stretto passage.

Beethoven begins the chorale fugue—probably in Albrechtsberger's

---

[1] "Elementarbuch der verschiedenen Gattungen des Contrapunkts, aus dem grösseren Werke des Kapellmeisters Fux von Joseph Haydn zusammengezogen" (cf. C. F. Pohl, *Joseph Haydn*, I, 176 f.).
[2] *J. G. Albrechtsberger's sämtliche Schriften*, ed. by I. Ritter von Seyfried, p. viii.

presence. He writes an exposition of the theme in three parts, introducing the cantus firmus with the fourth entrance, according to Albrechtsberger's instructions.

After the cantus firmus is completed, Beethoven begins a new exposition which leads to a tenor entrance of the cantus firmus at the tonic.

The first problems in Beethoven's work arise here because of the necessity of reconciling a four-part fugal texture to the cantus firmus setting. Albrechtsberger suggests various changes which gradually grow into an independent continuation of the work. But once he feels his points have been illustrated sufficiently, he again turns it over to Beethoven, who completes the fugue. The entire work was finally copied once more by Beethoven, with all of Albrechtsberger's variants.

In another case, Albrechtsberger's corrections lend poignancy to the harmonic changes suggested in the outer parts, while avoiding a tritone progression and an entrance without reference to thematic material in the inner parts.

The spirit of strict discipline which speaks from these pages stands in strong contrast to the popular image of the composer's unfettered genius. Yet this spirit never left Beethoven's working procedure. We can recognize it in the ever-changing versions of his sketches and in his exhaustive use of thematic material. An essential part of Beethoven's nature emerges from this conscientious account of his studies, which he concludes with the words: *"Omnia ad majorem Dei gloriam*/Patience, diligence, persistence, and sincerity will lead to success."—ALFRED MANN

Johann Schenk

In 1792, His Highness Archduke Maximilian, *Kurfuerst* of Cologne, graciously sent his protégé Louis van Beethoven to Vienna to study musical composition with Josef Haydn. Toward the end of July of the same year Abbé Gellinek told me of his acquaintance with a young man, who showed such great virtuosity on the piano as he had not heard since Mozart. In the course of our conversation he also mentioned that Beethoven had begun to study counterpoint with Haydn more than 6 months previously and was still working on the first exercise; also His Excellency Baron von Swieten seriously recommended to him the study of counterpoint and often inquired how far he had advanced in his studies. The fact that he had to hear these frequent inquiries and that he was still in the early stages of his studies aroused displeasure in this anxious student of which he often spoke to his friend. Gellinek, who took Beethoven's suffering and bad moods to heart, asked me whether I would be inclined to help his friend in the study of counterpoint. After all I had heard about him, I desired to make his acquaintance soon. A day was fixed on which I was supposed to meet Beethoven in Gellinek's living quarters and to hear him play the piano.

On that day I saw and heard for the first time that now so famous composer. After the usual polite phrases were exchanged, he expressed a desire to play a fantasy on the piano and asked me to listen to it. After a few chords and somewhat casual figures which he produced nonchalantly, this creative genius gradually unveiled the profound and sensitive image of his soul. The beauty of the manifold motifs, interwoven so clearly with utter loveliness, compelled my attention and I let myself be carried away by this delightful impression. Surrendering himself completely to his imagination, he gradually departed from the magic of his sounds and, to express violent passion, he threw himself into discordant scales with the glowing fire of youth. I was entirely overcome by this agitation and excitement. Now he began to grope his way to heavenly melodies with many a turn and with pleasant modulations, to those great ideas so often found in his works. After the artist had thus masterfully proven his virtuosity, he changed the sweet sounds into sad and woeful ones, then he went from tender and touching effects to gaiety and merry playfulness. Each of these figures was characteristic of their kind and had all the earmarks of the expression of his own passionate feelings. There were nowhere any feeble repetitions, nor any empty considerations of many incoherent thoughts; on the other hand there were no impotent decompositions through constantly interspersed arpeggios which usually give the listeners the feeling of encroaching sleep. This fantasy was throughout correct in its execution.

It was a clear day, full of light. More than half an hour had elapsed, when the master of sound left the piano. This unforgettable fantasy with which he enchained ear and heart and tickled the musical palate is still fully alive in my soul.

The first thing I did next day was to pay a visit to this still unknown artist who had proved his mastership so well. I found a few phrases of his first contrapuntal exercises lying around on his desk. After a short examination I realized that there were some mistakes in every key (however short the exercise may have been). This proved Gellinek's contention. As I was now certain that my student was not familiar with the rules of counterpoint, I gave him the well-known textbook by Josef Fux, Gradus ad Parnassum, for his further exercises.

Josef Haydn, who had returned from the country to Vienna at the end of that year, was anxious to use all his time for the composition of new masterworks. In consideration of this laudable endeavor of his it was understandable that Haydn had little time left to teach the musical alphabet. This made me decide to help Beethoven who was so eager to learn. But before I began to help him I made him understand that our combined efforts must always be kept secret. I therefore recommended that he copy each phrase which I had corrected so that Haydn should never be able to recognize another person's handwriting. After a year's time Beethoven and Gellinek had some kind of quarrel, the cause of which I no longer remember, but it seems to me that both were to blame. Because of this strife, Gellinek was furious and divulged our secret. From then on Beethoven and his brother made no secret of it any longer.

I began to teach my dear Louis in the first days of August 1792 and, without interruption, continued to hold this honorable post until the end of May 1793, when he finished learning the double counterpoint and prepared to go to Eisenstadt. Had His Royal Highness placed his protégé under Albrechtsberger's guidance, his studies would have never been interrupted and been entirely completed. . . .

In the middle of May he informed me that he was about to leave for Eisenstadt with Haydn and that he would stay there until the following winter. The day of departure was not yet set. One day in the beginning of June I came to give him his lesson as usual—but my good Louis was no longer there. He had left me the following note which I copy word for word:

"DEAR SCHENK,

I wish I had not been compelled to leave for Eisenstadt today. I would have liked to talk to you before I left. But meanwhile be assured of my gratitude for all the kindness you have shown to me. I shall try to make good for it as best as I can. I hope I'll see you soon again and have the pleasure of your company. Farewell and do not entirely forget your

BEETHOVEN"

——JOHANN SCHENK

Contemporary Reminiscences

Franz Gerhard Wegeler (1794–1796)

In the literature about Beethoven the "Biographical Notices" (1838) by
Franz Gerhard Wegeler and Ferdinand Ries occupy a prominent position.
Wegeler, five years older than Beethoven, was one of Beethoven's most
intimate friends at Bonn. When the victorious French army occupied the
Rhineland in 1794, Wegeler, then the Rector of the University of Bonn,
though only twenty-nine years old, fled to Vienna where he renewed his
intimate friendship with Beethoven during the next two years. The following reminiscences of Wegeler (Thayer, I, 180–81) relate to the years 1794–
1796, when Beethoven's financial affairs had taken a turn for the better.

Carl, Prince of Lichnowsky, Count Werdenberg, Dynast Granson, was
a very great patron, yes, a friend of Beethoven's, who took him into
his house as a guest, where he remained at least a few years. I found
him there toward the end of the year 1794, and left him there in the
middle of 1796. Meanwhile, however, Beethoven had almost always a
home in the country.

The Prince was a great lover and connoisseur of music. He played
the pianoforte, and by studying Beethoven's pieces and playing them
more or less well, sought to convince him that there was no need of
changing anything in his style of composition, though the composer's
attention was often called to the difficulties of his works. There were
performances at his house every Friday morning, participated in by four
hired musicians—Schuppanzigh, Weiss, Kraft and another (Link?), besides our friend; generally also an amateur, Zmeskall. Beethoven always
listened with pleasure to the observations of these gentlemen. Thus, to
cite a single instance, the famous violoncellist Kraft in my presence
called his attention to a passage in the finale of the Trio, Opus 1, No. 3,
to the fact that it ought to be marked "sulla corda G," and the indication
4-4 time which Beethoven had marked in the finale of the second
Trio, changed to 2-4. Here the new compositions of Beethoven, so far as
was feasible, were first performed. Here there were generally present
several great musicians and music-lovers. I, too, as long as I lived in Vienna,
was present, if not every time, at least most of the time.

Here a Hungarian count once placed a difficult composition by Bach
in manuscript before him which he played *a vista* exactly as Bach would

have played it, according to the testimony of the owner. Here the Viennese author Förster once brought him a quartet of which he had made a clean copy only that morning. In the second portion of the first movement the violoncello got out. Beethoven stood up, and still playing his own part sang the bass accompaniment. When I spoke about it to him as a proof of acquirements, he replied with a smile: "The bass part had to be so, else the author would have known nothing about composition." To the remark that he had played a *presto* which he had never seen before so rapidly that it must have been impossible to see the individual notes, he answered: "Nor is that necessary; if you read rapidly there may be a multitude of typographical errors, but you neither see nor give heed to them, so long as the language is a familiar one."

After the concert the musicians generally stayed to dine. Here there gathered, in addition, artists and savants without regard to social position. The Princess Christiane was the highly cultivated daughter of Count Franz Joseph von Thun, who, a very philanthropic and respectable gentleman, was disposed to extravagant enthusiasm by his intercourse with Lavater, and believed himself capable of healing diseases through the power of his right hand.

Beethoven, brought up in the most straitened circumstances and always, so to say, under tutelage, even though it might only be that of his friends, had no idea of the value of money and was anything but economical. Thus, to cite an instance, four o'clock was the dinner hour in Prince Lichnowsky's palace. "And so," said Beethoven, "I must get home every day at three-thirty, put on a better suit, shave, and so on. . . . I can't stand that." For this reason he often went to the taverns, where incidentally, as in all matters economic, he fared the worse because, as already said, he knew nothing of the value of things themselves or of money. The Prince, who had a loud, metallic voice, once commmanded one of his servants that should he and Beethoven ring at the same time, the latter was first to be served. Beethoven overheard him and hired a servant of his own the very next day. In the same way, though the Prince placed his stables at his disposal, he bought a horse for himself when seized by a passing fancy for learning how to ride.

Among the biographical notices with which Ignaz, Ritter von Seyfried, has provided his study of Beethoven, we find the following sentence, on p. 13: "Beethoven never married nor, strange to say, did he ever have a love affair." The truth of the matter, as my brother-in-law, Stephen von Breuning, Ferdinand Ries, Bernhard Romberg and I myself came to know it, is that Beethoven never was out of love, and usually was much affected by the love he was in at the time. . . . In Vienna Beethoven, at least so long as I was living there, always had some love affair in hand, and on occasion he made conquests which many an Adonis would have found it difficult, if not impossible, to encompass.

Johann Wenzel Tomaschek (1798)

This excellent Bohemian organist, teacher and composer (1774–1850) published his autobiography in the "Libussa" year-book of 1845. It contained the following independent and valuable discussion of Beethoven's powers and characteristics as a pianoforte virtuoso. Thayer, in quoting most of it, reminds his readers that Tomaschek down to 1840 had heard all the greatest virtuosos from Mozart on, and calls attention to Beethoven's own claim three years later that he had greatly perfected his playing.

In the year 1798, in which I continued my juridical studies, Beethoven, the giant among pianoforte players, came to Prague. He gave a largely attended concert in the Konviktssaal, at which he played his Concerto in C major, Opus 15, and the Adagio and graceful Rondo in A major from Opus 2, and concluded with an improvisation on a theme given him by Countess Sch . . . [Schlick?], "Ah tu fosti il primo oggetto," from Mozart's "Titus" (duet No. 7). Beethoven's magnificent playing and particularly the daring flights in his improvisation stirred me strangely to the depths of my soul; indeed I found myself so profoundly bowed down that I did not touch my pianoforte for several days. . . . I heard Beethoven at his second concert, which neither in performance nor in composition renewed again the first powerful impression. This time he played the Concerto in B flat which he had just composed in Prague. Then I heard him a third time at the home of Count C., where he played, besides the graceful Rondo from the A major Sonata, an improvisation on the theme: "Ah! vous dirai-je, Maman." This time I listened to Beethoven's artistic work with more composure. I admired his powerful and brilliant playing, but his frequent daring deviations from one motive to another, whereby the organic connection, the gradual development of idea was put aside, did not escape me. Evils of this nature frequently weaken his greatest compositions, those which sprang from a too exuberant conception. It is not seldom that the unbiased listener is rudely awakened from his transport. The singular and original seemed to be his chief aim in composition, as is confirmed by the answer which he made to a lady who asked him if he often attended Mozart's operas. "I do not know them," he replied, "and do not care to hear the music of others lest I forfeit some of my originality." As a composer I am competent enough here to express my opinion of Beethoven's artistic career without hesitation.

I consider him one of the most gifted composers, but only for instrumental music, not for vocal music, in which he did not fare very happily. Harmony, counterpoint, eurhythm, and particularly musical aesthetics, he did not seem to have overly much at heart; hence his larger works are defaced by occasional trivialities.

Countess Therese Brunswick

When we were in Vienna, my mother wished to secure for her daughters Therese and Josephine the priceless advantage of Beethoven's piano tuition. Beethoven, so Adalbert Rosti, one of my brother's schoolmates declared, could not be induced to accept a hapchance invitation; yet should Her Excellency so far discommode herself as to climb his three flights of winding stairs in St. Peter's Place and visit him, he could vouch for her success. This was done. Like a schoolgirl on her way to school, my copy of Beethoven's Sonata with violin and cello accompaniment under my arm, we entered. And dear, immortal Louis van Beethoven was very amiable and as polite as possible. After we had exchanged some conventional remarks he had me sit down at his piano, which was out of tune, and I at once led off by singing the violin and cello accompaniments, while I played quite decently. This so delighted him that he promised to come every day, to the Archduke Karl Hotel, then known as the Golden Dragon. It was in May, and the last year of the century just past.

He came assiduously, but instead of remaining for an hour, from 12 o'clock on, he would often stay until 4 or 5 and never wearied of holding down and bending my fingers, which I had learned to stretch up and hold flatly. The great man must have been well content; for sixteen days in succession he did not once fail to appear. Until it grew to be 5 o'clock we did not feel hungry; and my dear mother, though hungry, did not complain—to the great indignation of the innfolk, for at that time it had not yet become the custom to eat dinner at 5 o'clock in the evening.

It was at this time that I formed the warm, intimate friendship with Beethoven which endured to the end of his life. He came to Ofen; he came to Martonwásár; he was accepted by the circle of chosen spirits who formed our social republic. A circular place in the open was planted with tall linden-trees; each tree bore the name of a member of the society. Even when we mourned their absence we spoke with their symbols, conversed with them and let them teach us. Very often, after bidding the tree good-morning, I would question it regarding this and that, whatever I wished to know, and it never failed to make reply!

Ignaz von Seyfried (1799–1806)

When Ignatz von Seyfried in March, 1797, at the age of twenty-one, assumed the responsible position of one of Schikaneder's opera conductors, he had already attracted attention as a promising composer. His intimacy with Beethoven seems to have begun in 1800 and to have lasted until about 1806. Many years later (1832) he issued under the title of "Beethoven's Studien" a book which is under a cloud among Beethoven scholars because of its arbitrary and unreliable statements about Beethoven's studies in the theory of composition. On the other hand, his personal reminiscences and impressions of Beethoven at the end of the book are accepted as authentic, though savoring somewhat of exaggerated self-esteem.

The first quotation printed below refers to the meeting in 1799 between Beethoven and his rival Josef Wölffl (1772–1812) which, according to Thayer whose translation of that episode is used, bears all the marks of being a faithful transcript of the writer's own memories. The absence of jealousy between the two rivals was proved on Wölffl's part by the dedication of his Pianoforte Sonatas, Opus 7, to Beethoven.

Beethoven had already attracted attention to himself by several compositions and was rated a first-class pianist in Vienna when he was confronted by a rival in the closing years of the last century. Thereupon there was, in a way, a revival of the old Parisian feud of the Gluckists and Piccinists, and the many friends of art in the Imperial City arrayed themselves in two parties. At the head of Beethoven's admirers stood the amiable Prince Lichnowsky; among the most zealous patrons of Wölffl was the broadly cultured Baron Raymond von Wetzlar, whose delightful villa (on the Grünberg near the Emperor's recreation-castle) offered to all artists, native and foreign, an asylum in the summer months, as pleasing as it was desirable, with true British loyalty. There the interesting combats of the two athletes not infrequently offered an indescribable artistic treat to the numerous and thoroughly select gathering. Each brought forward the latest product of his mind. Now one and anon the other gave free rein to its glowing fancy; sometimes they would seat themselves at two pianofortes and improvise alternately on themes which they gave each other, and thus created many a four-hand Capriccio which if it could have been put upon paper at the moment would surely have bidden defiance to time. It would have been difficult, perhaps impossible, to award the palm of victory to either one of the gladiators in respect of technical skill. Nature had been a particularly kind mother to Wölffl in bestowing upon him a gigantic hand which could span a tenth as easily as other hands compass an octave, and permitted him to play passages of double notes in these intervals with the rapidity of lightning. In his improvisations even then Beethoven did not deny his tendency toward the mysterious and gloomy. When once he began to revel in the infinite world of tones, he was transported also above all earthly things;—his spirit had burst all restricting bonds, shaken off the yokes of servitude, and soared triumphantly and jubilantly into the luminous spaces of the higher aether. Now his playing tore along like a wildly foaming cataract, and the conjurer constrained his instrument to an utterance so forceful that the stoutest structure was scarcely able to withstand it; and anon he sank down, exhausted, exhaling gentle plaints, dissolving in melancholy. Again the spirit would soar aloft, triumphing over transitory terrestrial sufferings, turn its glance upward in reverent sounds and find rest and comfort on the innocent bosom of holy nature. But who shall sound the depths of the sea? It was the mystical Sanscrit language whose hieroglyphs can be read only by the initiated. Wölffl, on the contrary, trained in the school of Mozart, was always equable; never superficial but always clear and thus more accessible to the multitude. He used art only as a means to an end, never to exhibit his acquirements. He always enlisted the interest of his hearers and inevitably compelled them to follow the progression of his well-ordered ideas. Whoever has heard Hummel will know what is meant by this. . . .

But for this (the attitude of their patrons) the protégés cared very little. They respected each other because they knew best how to appreciate each other, and as straightforward honest Germans followed the principle that the roadway of art is broad enough for many, and that it is not necessary to lose one's self in envy in pushing forward for the goal of fame!

Every year Beethoven spent the summer months in the country, where under skies of azure blue he liked best to compose, and composed most successfully. Once he took lodgings in romantic Mödling, in order to be able to enjoy the Lower Austrian Switzerland, the picturesque [Brühl], to his heart's content. So a four-horse wagon was freighted with a few articles of furniture and a tremendous load of music; the tower-like machine slowly got under way, and the owner of its treasures marched along ahead of it as happy as could be, *per pedes Apostolorum*. No sooner did he cross the city boundary and find himself among blossoming fields, where gentle zephyrs set the green corn swaying like waves, amid the jubilant song of fluttering larks, celebrating the longed-for coming of lovely spring with trills of raptured greeting, than his genius awoke; thoughts began to traverse his mind, were spun out, ranged in order, noted down in lead-pencil—and the aim and goal of his migration was entirely forgotten. The gods alone know whither our Master strayed during the whole long period which elapsed, but suffice to say it was not until dusk was falling that dripping with sweat, covered with dust, hungry, thirsty and tired to death, he arrived in his chosen Tusculum. Yet, heaven be merciful, what a horrible spectacle awaited him there! The driver had made his snail-like way to his destination without mis-adventure, but had waited two full hours for the patron who had hired and already had paid him in advance. Since he did not know his name it was impossible to make inquiries; and in any event the cart-horse tamer wished to sleep at home. So he made short work of it, unloaded the whole contents of his wagon in the marketplace and drove off without futher ado. Beethoven was at first very angry; then he broke into uproarious laughter, after a brief reflection hired half-a-dozen gaping street boys, and had all he could do before the cries of the watchmen an-nouncing the midnight hour rang out on the air, to get the children of his brain safely under the shelter of a roof by the light of Luna's silver ray.

The more his hearing failed, and those intestinal troubles which in the last years of his life also afflicted him gained the upper hand, the more rapidly there also developed the ominous symptoms of a torturing hypochondria. He commenced to complain about a world which was all evil, intent only on delusion and deceit; about malice, betrayal and treachery. He insisted that there were no longer any honest men, saw the darkest side of everything, and at length even began to suspect his housekeeper, who had proven herself by many years of service. He suddenly decided to be quite independent, and this fantastic idea, like every other which took firm root in his mind, he at once proceeded to realize. He visited the market in person, chose, chaffered and bought, undoubtedly at anything but the most reasonable prices, and undertook to prepare his food with his own hands. This he continued to do for some little time, and when the few friends whom he still suffered about him made the most serious representations to him, he became quite angry and, as a valid proof of his own notable knowledge of the noble art of cooking, invited them to eat dinner with him the following day. There was nothing left for those invited but to appear punctually, full of expectation as to what would happen. They found their host in a short evening jacket, a stately nightcap on his bristly shock of hair, and his loins girded with a blue kitchen apron, very busily engaged at the hearth.

After waiting patiently for an hour and a half, while the turbulent demands of their stomachs were with increasing difficulty assuaged by cordial dialogue, the dinner was finally served. The soup recalled those charitable leavings distributed to beggars in the taverns; the beef was but half done and calculated to gratify only an ostrich; the vegetables floated in a mixture of water and grease; and the roast seemed to have been smoked in the chimney. Nevertheless the giver of the feast did

full justice to every dish. And the applause which he anticipated put him
in so rosy a humor that he called himself "Cook Mehlschoberl," after a
character in the burlesque, "The Merry Nuptials," and tried by his own
example and by extravagant praise of the dainties which still remained
to animate his continent guests. They, however, found it barely possible
to choke down a few morsels, and stuck to good bread, fresh fruit, sweet
pastry and the unadulterated juice of the grape. Soon after this memorable banquet, fortunately, the master of tones grew weary of ruling the
kitchen. Of his own free will he resigned the scepter; his housekeeper once
more entered upon her former honors and dignities, and her resigned
Master returned to his writing-desk, which he was now not allowed to
leave so frequently in order to procure himself an indigestion by means of
his own culinary mixtures.

As a conductor our Master could in no wise be called a model, and
the orchestra had to pay heed lest it be misled by its mentor, for he
thought only of his tone-poems, and was ceaselessly engaged in calling
attention to their authentic expression by means of the most manifold
gesticulations. Thus he often struck *down* with his baton at a strong
dynamic point, though it might occur on the weak beat of the measure.
He was accustomed to indicate a *diminuendo* by trying to make himself
smaller and smaller, and at the *pianissimo* slipped under the conductor's
desk, so to say. As the tonal masses increased in volume, he too seemed
to swell, as though out of a contraction, and with the entrance of the
entire body of instrumental tone he rose on the tips of his toes, grew
to well-nigh giant size, and swaying in the air with his arms, seemed
to be trying to float up into the clouds. He was all active movement,
no organic part of himself was idle, and the whole man might be
compared to a *perpetuum mobile*. With increasing deafness, it is true,
a rude disagreement often took place when the *maestro* was beating
in arsis and the orchestra was accompanying him in thesis; then the
conductor who had strayed from the path found his way back most easily
in the soft movements, while the most powerful *forte* meant nothing
to him. In these cases his eye also came to his assistance: he could
observe the bow-stroke of the string instruments, guess from it the figure
they were playing, and soon find his place again.

While Beethoven was not as yet burdened with his chronic infirmities
he took pleasure in repeatedly attending opera performances, especially
those given at the then splendidly flourishing *Theater an der Wien*,
at times, no doubt, because he could do so in all comfort, since he practically had but to step out of his room to find himself in the parterre.
There he was especially captivated by the creations of Cherubini and
Méhul, which at that time had just begun to rouse the enthusiasm of all
Vienna. There Beethoven would plant himself directly behind the orches-
tra-rail and remain, seemingly dumfounded, to the very last bow-stroke.

And this was the only visible sign he gave of being interested in the art-work. When, on the contrary, it did not appeal to him, he turned right about face at the end of the first act and made off. In general it was difficult and well-nigh impossible to read in his face any indication of approval or distaste; he remained ever the same, apparently unmoved, and was equally reticent in passing judgment on his artistic colleagues; his soul alone toiled unweariedly within him, its bodily covering seemed a soulless marble statue. Strangely enough, listening to wretched, execrable music appeared to cause him the utmost joy, which he at times proclaimed with roars of laughter. All who were better acquainted with him knew that in the art of laughter he also was a virtuoso of the first rank; it was a pity, however, that even those nearest him seldom learned the why and wherefore of an explosion of the kind, since as a rule he laughed at his own secret thoughts and imaginings without condescending to explain them.

Our Beethoven was by no means one of those pigheaded composers whom no orchestra in the world can satisfy; at times he was all too considerate, and did not even have passages which had gone amiss during first rehearsals repeated, saying: "The next time it will go as it should." He was very meticulous with regard to expression, the more delicate shadings, an equalized distribution of light and shade, and an effective *tempo rubato*, and without betraying the slightest impatience always took pleasure in discussing them individually with the various musicians. And then, when he saw that the musicians had grasped his ideas, and moved, carried away and filled with enthusiasm by the magic charm of his tonal creations, were playing together with increasing fervor, his face would be illumined with joy, all his features would radiate happiness and content, a satisfied smile would wreathe his lips, and a thundering *Bravi tutti!* would reward the successful artistic achievement. It was the first and the most beautiful moment of triumph for this lofty genius, compared with which, as he himself admitted without reserve, even the stormy applause of a great receptive public was cast into the shade. When it was a matter of playing at first sight, the players often were obliged to stop to make corrections, and the thread of continuity was severed: even then, however, he was patient. But when, especially in the Scherzos of his symphonies, sudden, unexpected changes of tempo threw all into confusion, he would laugh tremendously, assure the men he had looked for nothing else, that he had been waiting for it to happen, and would take almost childish pleasure in the thought that he had been successful in unhorsing such routined orchestral knights.

Among his favorite dishes was a kind of bread-soup, cooked like mush, to which he looked forward with pleasure every Thursday. Together with it ten sizable eggs had to be presented to him on a plate. Before they were stirred into the soup fluid he first separated and tested them by holding them against the light, then decapitated them with his own hand and anxiously sniffed them to see whether they were fresh. When fate decreed that some among them scented their straw, so to speak, the storm broke. In a voice of thunder the housekeeper was cited to court. She, however, well knowing what this meant, and between two fires, lent only half an ear to his raging and scolding, and held herself in readiness to beat a quick retreat before, as was customary, the cannonade was about to begin, and the decapitate batteries would begin to play upon her back and pour out their yellow-white, sticky intestines over her in veritable lava streams.

Beethoven never was seen in the street without a little notebook in which he jotted down his ideas of the moment. When by chance this was mentioned, he would parody the words of Joan of Arc: "I may not come unless I bear my flag!" With a steadiness without compare he stuck to this law he had laid down for himself, although in other respects a truly admirable confusion ruled in his household. Books and music were strewn about in every corner; here the fragments of a cold snack, there bottles, still sealed or half-emptied; on his standing desk was the hurried sketch of a new quartet; elsewhere were the débris of his breakfast; here on the piano, in the shape of scribbled-over pages, lay the material for a magnificent symphony, still slumbering as an embryo; there drooped a corrected proof waiting for release. The floor was covered with business and personal letters; between the windows stood a respectable loaf of *Strachino*, beside it the still notable ruins of a genuine Verona salami—and despite all this higgledy-piggledy our Master, quite contrary to the actual facts, had the habit of calling attention to his accuracy and love of order with Ciceronian eloquence on all occasions. Only when something he wanted had to be hunted for hours, days and even weeks, and all endeavors to find it remained fruitless, would he strike a new note as he looked about for a victim to blame: "Yes, yes," he would wail pitifully, "it is my misfortune! Nothing is left in the place where I put it; everything is moved about; everything is done to play me a trick. O these humans, these humans!" The servants, however, knew the good-natured growler; they let him grumble to his heart's content and—after a few minutes had passed—all was forgotten until a similar cause called forth a similar scene.

He himself often poked fun at his actually almost indecipherable handwriting and would add in extenuation: "Life is too short to paint letters or notes, and more beautiful notes would not help me out of my 'Nöten'" (troubles).

The whole forenoon, from the first ray of dawn up to dinnertime, was devoted to mechanical work, to actual note-writing; the remainder of the day was dedicated to thought and to the arrangement of his ideas. No sooner had Beethoven swallowed his last mouthful than, unless he had some extended excursion in mind, he would set forth on his customary promenade, that is to say, he would twice make the circuit of the city in double-quick step, as though something had stung him. Did it rain, snow or hail, did the thermometer stand at sixteen degrees below zero, did Boreas blow with icy breath from puffed cheeks from across the Bohemian border, did thunders roar, lightnings zigzag through the air, winds howl or Phoebus' torrid rays fall vertically on his head as in Lybia's seas of sand? How could any of these things trouble this man filled with a sacred fire, who bore his God in his heart, and in whose soul, perhaps, there blossomed forth a springtime of paradisiacal mildness amid all this uproar of the elements.

Even in the presence of his intimate friends Beethoven seldom permitted himself to judge any of his artistic colleagues. What he thought of the following four masters, however, his own words may testify:

"Among all living opera composers Cherubini is for me the most deserving of respect. I am furthermore entirely in accordance with his conception of the Requiem, and, should I ever decide to write one myself, shall take much from him as it stands.

"Karl Maria von Weber began to study too late; his art could never develop in an altogether natural manner, and it is evident he strove only to be recognized as a genius.

"Mozart's greatest work remains 'The Magic Flute'; for therein he for the first time reveals himself as a German master. 'Don Juan' still is fashioned altogether in the Italian style and, besides, art, which is sacred, should never be degraded to serve as a pretext for so scandalous a subject.

"Handel is the unattained master of all masters. Go to him and learn how to produce great effects with scant deploy of means."

When he did not really feel in the mood, one had to ask him repeatedly in order to get him to sit down at the piano at all. Before he commenced to play he was in the habit of striking the keys with the palm of his hand, of running a finger along their length, in short, of indulging in all sorts of nonsense, laughing heartily at himself the while.

Once, while visiting at a patron's country estate in the summer, he was so importuned to play for the foreign visitors present, that he grew positively angry and firmly refused to perform what he scornfully termed a hireling's task. The threat to confine him to the house—it was, of course, not seriously meant—resulted in Beethoven running away in the dark and the dew to the nearest town, a distance of an hour, and thence hurrying to Vienna as though on the wings of the wind by extra post. His patron's bust supplied the expiatory victim for the insult offered him, and was cast from the closet on which it stood to smash on the floor.

One of Beethoven's curious manias was his passion for changing his lodgings, although moving with all his possessions always greatly discommoded him, and always was accompanied by a loss of belongings. No sooner had he taken possession of a new dwelling-place than he would find something objectionable about it, and then would run his feet sore trying to discover another. As a result it sometimes happened that he rented various lodgings at the same time and then, a second Hercules at the crossroads, found himself not a little embarrassed regarding their rights of priority in accordance with the claims of justice and cheapness.

Beethoven, in the truest sense of the word, was a real German, body and soul. Entirely at home in the Latin, French and Italian languages, he used by preference and whenever at all possible his native tongue. Had he been able to have his own way in the matter, all his works would have appeared in print with German title-pages. He even tried to delete the exotic word "pianoforte," and chose in its stead the expressive term *Hammerklavier* ("hammerpiano") as a suitable and appropriate substitute. As a relief from strenuous work, aside from poetry, for which he had a spiritual affinity, he turned to the study of universal history. Among German poets Goethe was and remained his favorite.

With regard to the other arts and sciences he also possessed, without making any show of it, a fund of more than surface knowledge; and took especial pleasure in discussing political matters with intimate friends. His summaries were so apt, his conceptions so correct, and his viewpoints so clear that none ever would have credited this diplomatic neophyte, who lived only in and for his art, with having formulated them.

Justice, personal decency, the moral code, a devout mind and religious purity meant more to him than all else; these virtues were enthroned in him and he demanded that others cultivate them. "A man is as good as his word" was his motto, and nothing angered him more than an unkept promise. He took pleasure in helping others out of pure love for his neighbor, only too often making considerable sacrifices, greatly to his own disadvantage. Anyone who turned to him in free and full confidence always could count upon certain, actual aid. He was neither avaricious nor yet extravagant; yet neither had he any idea of the real value of money, which he regrded merely as a means of procuring unavoidably required necessities. Only during his last years did he show signs of a worried thriftiness without, however, ever allowing it to interfere with his inborn propensity for doing good. While half the world re-echoed the illuminate singer's praises, only a few were capable of estimating his lofty human values to their full extent. Why was this? Because the majority were rebuffed by the rough outward shell and never even guessed at its noble inner kernel. Yet is not the most costly, well-nigh priceless diamond often concealed in a pallid, dull, colorless and unpolished wrapper?—

O. G. SONNECK (1)

His Letters

———◆———

To the Elector Maximilian Franz, Bonn[1]

[Autograph not traced][2]

*[*VIENNA, *shortly before May 3, 1793]*[3]

MOST WORTHY AND MOST EXCELLENT ELECTOR!

MOST GRACIOUS LORD!

A few years ago Your Electoral Excellency was pleased to retire my father, the Court tenor van Beethoven, and by a most gracious decree to allow me out of his salary 100 Rheinthalers so as to enable me to have my two younger brothers clothed, fed and educated and also to discharge the debts which our father had incurred.

I was about to present this decree to Your Excellency's Landrent-meisterei[4] when my father earnestly besought me not to do this lest he should be publicly regarded as incapable of supporting his family by his own efforts. He added that he himself would pay me the 25 Rheinthalers every quarter; and this was always punctually done.

After his death, which took place in December of last year,[5] I wanted to avail myself of your most precious favor by presenting the aforementioned most gracious decree. I was horrified, however, to find that my father had done away with it.

Hence with the most dutiful reverence I beg Your Excellency graciously to renew this decree and also to instruct Your Excellency's Landrentmeisterei to send me the previous quarterly amount which fell due at the beginning of February.[6]

Your Electoral Excellency's most humble and most faithfully obedient

LUDWIG VAN BEETHOVEN,
Court Organist

[1] Maximilian Franz (1756–1801), the youngest son of the Austrian Empress Maria Theresa, was Elector of Cologne from 1784 until 1794, when Napoleon's armies invaded the Rhineland. For a full account of this Elector's interest in the musical life of Bonn see Thayer.

[2] According to Nohl who first published this letter, the original document was then in the Rhenish Archives, Düsseldorf.

[3] The reply of the Elector's Privy Council acceding to Beethoven's petition is dated May 3, 1793.

[4] I.e. the Elector's Inland Revenue Office and Exchequer.

[5] Beethoven's father, Johann van Beethoven (c. 1740–92), had died on December 18, 1792.

[6] According to Thayer, Beethoven continued to draw a quarterly salary of 50 thalers until March, 1794.

To A. Vocke[1]

[Autograph not traced][2]

VIENNA, *May* 22, 1793

I am not wicked—Hot blood is my fault—my crime is that I am young. I am not wicked, truly not wicked. Even though wildly surging emotions may betray my heart, yet my heart is good—[3]

Precepts. To do good whenever one can, to love liberty above all else, never to deny the truth, even though it be before the throne.

Continue to think now and then of your friend who esteems you.

LUDWIG BEETHOVEN
from Bonn near Cologne.

To Johann van Beethoven, Vienna[4]

[Autograph in the possession of Kommerzialrat Otto Reichert][5]

DEAR BROTHER! PRAGUE, *February* 19, [1796]

So that you may know at any rate where I am and what I am doing, I really must write to you. First of all, I am well, very well. My art is winning me friends and renown, and what more do I

---

[1] Nothing is known of A. Vocke, who was a merchant at Nuremberg.

[2] Beethoven's letter was written in Vocke's album.

[3] This paragraph is quoted from Schiller's "Don Carlos," Act II, sc. 2.

[4] Nikolaus Johann (1776–1848), Beethoven's youngest brother, was first apprenticed to a pharmaceutical chemist at Bonn, then came to Vienna in 1795 and, after qualifying at the University, was employed in a chemist's shop. In 1808 he acquired a business of his own at Linz, which he exchanged in 1816 for one at Urfahr. Meanwhile he had married in 1812 Therese Obermayr who already had a daughter Amalie, born in 1807. Since 1809, when he had been a successful war profiteer, Johann had been accumulating considerable wealth. So in 1819 he retired from business and bought a large estate at Gneixendorf, near Krems. For an excellent account of Johann's life and character see Dr. Otto Zekert, *Apotheker Johann van Beethoven* (Vienna, 1928).

[5] On the verso of the autograph are these additional remarks in Beethoven's hand:

"To my brother Nikolaus Beethoven to be delivered at the chemist's shop near the Kärntnertor."

"Will Herr von Z. be so kind as to give this letter to the wigmaker who will arrange for its delivery."

The Herr von Z. may be Zmeskall, one of Beethoven's first friends in Vienna.

want? And this time I shall make a good deal of money. I shall remain here for a few weeks longer and then travel to *Dresden, Leipzig and Berlin*.[1] So it will certainly be six weeks at least before I return—

I hope that you will enjoy living in Vienna more and more. But do be on your guard against the whole tribe of bad women. Have you been to see *Cousin Elss*[2] yet? You might write to me here if you care to, and have time to do so.

P[rince] Lichnowsky[3] will soon be on his way back to Vienna. He has already left Prague. Should you need any money, you may make bold to go to him, for he still owes me some. And now I hope that your life will become more and more pleasant and I trust that I shall be able to contribute to your happiness. All good wishes, dear brother, and think sometimes of your true and faithful brother

L. BEETHOVEN

My greetings to our brother Caspar.[4]

My address is: Im goldene Einhorn auf der Kleinseite.[5]

To Christine Gerhardi[6]

[Autograph in the Beethovenhaus, Bonn]

MY DEAR FRÄULEIN G[ERHARDI],

I should be lying if I did not tell you that the verses you sent me have caused me some embarrassment. It is a peculiar feeling to see and to hear oneself praised and at the same time to realize one's own inferiority as fully as I do. I always treat such occasions as ad-

---

1 Very little is known about Beethoven's tour to Prague, Dresden, Leipzig and Berlin.

2 Not identified.

3 Prince Karl Lichnowsky (1756–1814) had been a pupil and a patron of Mozart whom he took to Prague, Dresden, Leipzig and Berlin in 1789. He married in 1788 Maria Christiane, one of the three beautiful daughters of the Countess Wilhelmine von Thun-Hohenstein. Like his younger brother, Count Moritz, he was a devoted lover of music and an enthusiastic admirer of Beethoven's works. Moreover, during his early years in Vienna the composer lived in the same house as Lichnowsky in the Alserstrasse; and to this patron he dedicated Opus 1, 13, 26, 36 and WoO 69.

4 In the autograph Caspar Carl's name is heavily crossed out, but the obliterated word has a wavy line underneath to indicate *stet*.

5 "Das goldene Einhorn" was then one of the largest inns at Prague. In April, 1789, Mozart and Lichnowsky had stayed there.

6 Christine Gerhardi, a gifted soprano of Italian extraction, was an enthusiastic admirer of Beethoven's compositions. She was married on August 20, 1798 to Dr. Joseph Frank (1771–1842), who, like his distinguished father Johann Peter Frank (1745–1821), was a Viennese physician. In 1804 she and her husband left Vienna and settled in Vilna, where Frank became a famous doctor and his wife continued to sing in public.

monishments to strive toward the inaccessible goal which art and
nature have set us.—These verses are really beautiful save for the
sole fault that in regard to their subject they are far from truthful, a
fault which admittedly one is accustomed to find in poets whose imagination induces them really *to hear and to see what they want to,*
even if the reality is sometimes far beneath their ideal—You may
well believe that I should like to meet *the poet or the poetess.* And
now I thank you too for the kindness you are showing to

L. v. BEETHOVEN who admires you.

To Christine Gerhardi

[*Autograph in the Koch Collection*]

DEAR CHR[ISTINE], [VIENNA, 1797]
You said something yesterday about that likeness of me.—I do
wish that in this matter you would proceed rather circumspectly. For
I fear that if we choose F. to return it, perhaps that wretched B. or
that extremely stupid Joseph[1] will interfere and, in that case, the affair
may then become a trick to be played upon me; and that would be
really deplorable. I should have to revenge myself again; and surely the
whole populace[2] don't deserve that.—Try to get hold of the thing, if
it is at all possible to do so. I assure you that after this experience I
will appeal in the Press to all painters not to paint me again without
my knowledge. I really did not think that this face of mine would
ever cause me embarrassment. As for Sara[3] and taking off my hat,
why, that is really too stupid and, what is more, too discourteous for
me to exact retribution for anything of the kind. Please expound to
her the rights of anybody who is taking a walk—Adie,[4] the devil
take you.—

To Breitkopf & Härtel, Leipzig[5]

[1] The persons indicated by F. and B. have not been identified. But the third name may
be a reference to Dr. Joseph Frank.
[2] In the autograph the word used is "populasse."
[3] Not identified.
[4] A very colloquial form of "adieu." The autograph is not signed.
[5] This famous firm of music publishers at Leipzig was founded in 1719 by Bernhard
Christoph Breitkopf (1695–1777), who was a printer. His great-grandson, Christoph
Gottlob Breitkopf (1750–1800), who had inherited the business from his father, was
joined in 1795 by Gottfried Christoph Härtel (1763–1827). Thereafter the firm was
always known as Breitkopf & Härtel.

[*Autograph in the Beethovenhaus, Bonn,*
H. C. Bodmer Collection]

VIENNA, *April* 22, 1801[1]

P.P.[2]

You must forgive my delay in replying to your letter to me. For a while I was continually indisposed and at the same time overwhelmed with work; and, since in any case I am not a very regular letter-writer, let this fact also serve to excuse me.—In regard to your proposal about some of my compositions, I am very sorry not to be able to accept it at the moment. But please be so kind just to inform me what types of composition you would like to have from me, namely, symphonies, quartets, sonatas and so forth, so that I may be guided by your wishes and, should I happen to have the works you require or desire, be able to supply them.—*Mollo*[3] here is going to publish, with my consent, seven or eight works; and *Hoffmeister* in Leipzig is also publishing four works.—In this connection I merely point out that *Hoffmeister* is publishing one *of my first concertos,*[4] which, of course, is not *one of my best compositions.* Mollo is also publishing *a concerto which was written later,* it is true, but which also is *not one of my best compositions of that type.*[5] Let this serve merely as a hint to your Musikalische Zeitung[6] about reviewing these works, though indeed, if one can hear them and, I should add, well performed—one can then best form an opinion—Musical policy demands that one should keep one's finest concertos to oneself for a time— Advise your reviewers to be more circumspect and intelligent, particularly in regard to the productions of younger composers. For many a one, who perhaps might go far, may take fright. As for myself, far be it from me to think that I have achieved a perfection which suffers no adverse criticism. But your reviewer's outcry against me was at first very mortifying. Yet when I began to compare myself with other composers, I could hardly bring myself to pay any attention to it but remained quite calm and said to myself: "They don't know anything about music." And indeed what made it easier for me to keep calm was that I noticed how certain people were being praised

---

1 This is the first known letter to Härtel, with whom Beethoven continued to correspond until 1816. The firm published a large number of his compositions.
2 P[raemissis] P[raemittendis], i.e. with the necessary introduction. In his business letters Beethoven occasionally used this form of address. In the autograph he has written by mistake P.S.
3 Tranquillo Mollo, a Viennese music publisher, was from 1793 to 1798 a partner in the firm of Artaria & Co. He then founded his own firm in which Domenico Artaria was his partner until 1804. In 1832 Mollo sold his firm to relations. Between 1799 and 1802 he published eleven works of Beethoven. See Kinsky-Halm, p. 773.
4 Opus 19.
5 Opus 15.
6 The *Allgemeine Musikalische Zeitung*, published by Breitkopf & Härtel from 1798 to 1849, was founded at Leipzig by Johann Friedrich Rochlitz (1769–1842), theologian and writer, who was its editor until 1818.

to the skies who in Vienna had very little standing among the best local composers—practically none at all, whatever other excellent qualities they might possess—However, pax vobiscum—Peace between you and me—I should never have mentioned a syllable of all this, if you yourself had not raised the point—

I recently visited a good friend of mine who mentioned the *sum that had been collected for the daughter of the immortal god of harmony*,[1] and I was amazed at the small amount which Germany, and especially *your Germany*,[2] had contributed to this person whom I revere for the sake of her father. And that has made me hit on the following idea; how would it be if I were to publish some work by subscription for the benefit of this person and, in order to protect myself against all attacks, to inform the public of the sum collected and of the yearly profit from the work?—You could do most for this object. Let me know quickly how it could best be arranged, so that it may be done before *this brook* dies or, rather, before this brook has dried up and we can no longer supply it with water[3]—It is clearly understood, of course, that you would publish the work.[4]

With kindest regards I remain your devoted

LUDWIG VAN BEETHOVEN

To Franz Gerhard Wegeler, Bonn

[*Autograph in the possession of Julius Wegeler*]

MY DEAR KIND WEGELER,   VIENNA, *June 29,* [1801]

I do thank you most warmly for your remembrance of me of which I have so little deserved or even endeavored to deserve where you are concerned. Yet you are so very good; you allow nothing, not even my unpardonable carelessness, to put you off; and you are still the same faithful, kind and loyal friend—But you must never think that I could ever forget yourself and all of you[5] who were once so dear and precious to me. There are moments when I myself long for you and, what is more, would like to spend some time with you—For my fatherland, the beautiful country where I first opened my eyes

---

[1] Regine Susanna Bach (1742–1809), the only surviving child of Johann Sebastian Bach, was living in great poverty. In May, 1800, Rochlitz had published in the *Allgemeine Musikalische Zeitung* an appeal for funds to assist her.

[2] By "Germany" Beethoven means the German-speaking countries. By "your Germany" he means Germany proper.

[3] Beethoven is punning on the word "Bach," which means "brook."

[4] There is no evidence that this plan was ever carried out.

[5] Beethoven is referring, of course, to the von Breuning family.

to the light, still seems to me as lovely and as clearly before my eyes as it was when I left you. In short, the day on which I can meet you again and greet our Father Rhine I shall regard as one of the happiest of my life—When that will be I cannot yet tell you. But indeed I can assure you that when we meet you will certainly see that I have become a first-rate fellow; not only as an artist but also as a man you will find me better and more fully developed. And if our Father-land is then in a more prosperous condition, my art will be exercised only for the benefit of the poor. Oh blissful moment, how happy do I count myself that I can help to produce you, that I myself can create you—You want to know something about my present situation. Well, on the whole it is not at all bad. For since last year Lichnowsky who, although you may find it hard to believe what I say, was always, and still is, my warmest friend (of course we have had some slight mis-understandings, but these have only strengthened our friendship), has disbursed for my benefit a fixed sum of 600 gulden, on which I can draw until I obtain a suitable appointment.[1] My compositions bring me in a good deal; and I may say that I am offered more commissions than it is possible for me to carry out. Moreover for every composition I can count on six or seven publishers, and even more, if I want them; people no longer come to an arrangement with me, I state my price and they pay. So you see how pleasantly situated I am. For in-stance, I see a friend in need and it so happens that the state of my purse does not allow me to help him immediately; well then, I have only to sit down and compose and in a short time I can come to his aid—Moreover, I live more economically than I used to; and if I remain in Vienna for good, no doubt I shall contrive to obtain one day for a concert every year. I have given a few concerts.[2] But that jealous demon, my wretched health, has put a nasty spoke in my wheel; and it amounts to this, that for the last three years my hearing has become weaker and weaker. The trouble is supposed to have been caused by the condition of my abdomen which, as you know, was wretched even before I left Bonn, but has become worse in Vienna where I have been constantly afflicted with diarrhea and have been suffering in consequence from an extraordinary debility. Frank[3] tried to *tone up* my constitution with strengthening medi-cines and my hearing with almond oil, but much good did it do me! His treatment had no effect, my abdomen continued to be in the same state as before. Such was my condition until the autumn of last year; and sometimes I gave way to despair. Then a medical asinus ad-vised me to take cold baths to improve my condition. A more sensible doctor, however, prescribed the usual tepid baths in the Danube. The

---

[1] It is not known for how many years Prince Karl Lichnowsky gave Beethoven this financial assistance, which he first granted in 1800.

[2] Beethoven had given concerts in Vienna since 1795, including ten important ones. For particulars of these concerts see an article by Hermann Reuther in Alfred Orel, *Ein Wiener Beethovenbuch* (Vienna, 1921), pp. 72-107.

[3] Probably Johann Peter Frank, Director of the General Hospital and Professor of Medicine at Vienna University.

result was miraculous; and my inside improved. But my deafness persisted or, I should say, became even worse. During the last winter I was truly wretched, for I had really dreadful attacks of colic and again relapsed completely into my former condition. And thus I remained until about four weeks ago when I went to see Vering[1] For I began to think that my condition demanded the attention of a surgeon as well; and in any case I had confidence in him. Well, he succeeded in checking almost completely this violent diarrhea. He prescribed tepid baths in the Danube, to which I had always to add a bottle of strengthening ingredients. He ordered no medicines until about four days ago when he prescribed pills for my stomach and an infusion for my ear. As a result I have been feeling, I may say, stronger and better; but my ears continue to hum and buzz day and night. I must confess that I lead a miserable life. For almost two years I have ceased to attend any social functions, just because I find it impossible to say to people: I am deaf. If I had any other profession I might be able to cope with my infirmity; but in my profession it is a terrible handicap. And if my enemies, of whom I have a fair number, were to hear about it, what would they say?—In order to give you some idea of this strange deafness, let me tell you that in the theater I have to place myself quite close to the orchestra in order to understand what the actor is saying, and that at a distance I cannot hear the high notes of instruments or voices. As for the spoken voice it is surprising that some people have never noticed my deafness; but since I have always been liable to fits of absent-mindedness, they attribute my hardness of hearing to that. Sometimes too I can scarcely hear a person who speaks softly; I can hear sounds, it is true, but cannot make out the words. But if anyone shouts, I can't bear it. Heaven alone knows what is to become of me. Vering *tells me that my hearing will certainly improve, although my deafness may not be completely cured*[2]—Already I have often cursed my Creator and my existence. *Plutarch* has shown me *the path of resignation*. If it is at all possible, I will bid defiance to my fate, though I feel that as long as I live there will be moments when I shall be God's most unhappy creature—I beg you not to say anything about my condition to anyone, not even to *Lorchen*;[3] I am only telling you this as a secret; but I should like you to correspond with Vering about it. If my trouble persists, I will visit you next spring. You will rent a house for me in some beautiful part of the country and then for six months I will lead the life of a peasant. Perhaps that will make a difference. Resignation, what a wretched resource! Yet it is all that is left to me—

---

[1] Gerhard von Vering (1755–1823) was a distinguished surgeon in Vienna. His daughter Julie (1791–1809), who was an excellent pianist, married Stephan von Breuning in April, 1808, but died the following year. Beethoven dedicated to her his own arrangement of his violin concerto, Opus 61, as a pianoforte concerto, published in August, 1808, by the Bureau des Arts et d'Industrie. See Kinsky-Halm, pp. 148–49.
[2] For an excellent and comprehensive study of Beethoven's many illnesses see Walther Forster, *Beethovens Krankheiten und ihre Beurteilung* (Wiesbaden, 1956).
[3] Eleonore von Breuning.

You will forgive me, I know, for asking you, who are already facing so much sorrow, to take an interest in the troubles of your friend—
Steffen Breuning is now in Vienna and we meet almost every day. It
does me good to revive the old feelings of friendship. He has really
become an excellent, splendid fellow, who is well-informed and who,
like all of us more or less, has his heart in the right place. I now
have very fine rooms overlooking the Bastei, which, moreover, are
extremely beneficial to my health.[1] I am almost certain that I shall
be able to arrange for B[reuning] to join me.[2]—I will send you your
Antioch[3] and also a great many of my compositions, provided you
do not think that the postage for them will cost you too much.
Frankly, your love of art still gives me the greatest pleasure. If you
let me know how to set about it, I will send you all my works, which,
I must admit, now amount to quite a fair number, a number which
is daily increasing—In return for my grandfather's portrait,[4] which
I beg you to send me by the mail coach as soon as possible, I am
sending you the portrait *of his grandson*, of your ever loyal and
warmhearted Beethoven.[5] This portrait is being published here by
Artaria who like many other art dealers in foreign countries too has
often asked me for one.—I will soon write to Stoffel[6] and blow
him up a bit about his peevishness; I will thoroughly drum our old
friendship into his ears and insist on receiving from him a solemn
promise not to cause more trouble to you who, as it is, are facing a
great deal of sorrow—I will write also to our kindhearted Lorchen.
Even though I have never sent you news of myself, I have never
forgotten a single one of all you dear ones; but, as you know,
writing was never my strong point. Even my best friends have had
no letters from me for years. I live entirely in my music; and hardly
have I completed one composition when I have already begun another. At my present rate of composing, I often produce three or
four works at the same time—Now do write to me more often
and I will make a point of finding time to write to you occasionally.
Give my greetings to all and, in particular, to our kind Frau Hofrä-
tin,[7] and tell her that 'I still have now and then a raptus.[8] As for
the Kochs I am not at all surprised at their change of luck.[9] Fortune

[1] In the spring of 1801 Beethoven took rooms in the Hambergisches Haus in the
Seilerstätte with a fine view over the ramparts of Vienna.
[2] So far as is known, Beethoven and Breuning did not live together until the winter of
1803–1804.
[3] According to Wegeler and Ries (*Biographische Notizen über Ludwig van Beethoven*,
Coblenz, 1838) this was a picture by Füger, Director of the Vienna Academy of Art.
[4] This oil portrait of his grandfather, Ludwig van Beethoven (1712–1773), which
Beethoven always hung up in his rooms, was painted by Radoux, the Electoral Court
painter at Bonn.
[5] A drawing by Gandolf Stainhauser engraved by Johann Joseph Neidl.
[6] Christoph von Bruening (1771–1841), the eldest son of the family, studied law,
settled at Bonn and spent the rest of his life in the Rhineland. He retired in 1838.
[7] Frau Helene von Breuning, the widowed mother of the family.
[8] I.e. a fit of mental abstraction.
[9] Barbara Koch, the daughter, had become engaged to be married to Graf Anton von
Belderbusch.

is shaped like a sphere and therefore, I need hardly add, does not always fall on the best and noblest people—As for Ries, to whom I send cordial greetings, I will write to you more fully about his son, although I think that he could make his fortune more easily in *Paris* than in *Vienna*.[1] Viena is flooded with musicians and thus even the most deserving find it difficult to make a living—But in the autumn or the winter when people are hurrying back to town I will see what I can do for him—All good wishes, kind and faithful Wegeler; and rest assured of the affection and friendship of your

BEETHOVEN

——EMILY ANDERSON

The Pianist

[Joseph] Gelinek, a Bohemian pianist who had also studied for the priesthood and who had been ordained in 1786, is remembered largely because of his encounter with Beethoven. Until the rash young man from Bonn came along, Gelinek was the most popular pianist in Vienna and also a composer of variations that enjoyed a great vogue. Then Beethoven stormed into town. One day Gelinek told the father of the young Carl Czerny that he, Gelinek, was going to have a pianistic duel that night with an unknown pianist. "I'll fix him!" Next day the elder Czerny asked Gelinek how it had turned out. But let Carl Czerny tell the story:

> Gelinek looked quite crestfallen and sad. "Yesterday was a day I'll remember. That young fellow must be in league with the devil. I've never heard anybody play like that. I gave him a theme to improvise on, and I assure you that I've never heard anybody improvise so admirably. Then he played some of his own compositions, which are marvelous, really wonderful, and he manages difficulties and effects at the keyboard that one never dreamed of."
>
> "I say, what's his name?" asked my father, with some astonishment.
>
> "He is a small, ugly, swarthy fellow and seems to have a willful disposition," answered Gelinek. "Prince Lichnowsky brought him from Germany to Vienna to let him study composition with Haydn, Albrechtsberger and Salieri, and his name is Beethoven."

In many things, Beethoven was ahead of his time, and so was his piano playing. It had unprecedented power, personality and emotional appeal. In many respects he can be considered the first romantic pianist: the one

[1] Ferdinand Ries, a son of Franz Anton Ries, who had taught Beethoven the violin, came to Vienna probably during the winter 1801–2.

who broke all of the laws in the name of expression (for in the nineteenth century the word "expression" was to take the place of the eighteenth-century "taste"); the one who thought orchestrally and achieved orchestral effects on the piano. In that he was alone in his day, and his like was not to be seen until the maturity of Franz Liszt.

But it was piano playing that raises a few questions. Why, for instance, is Beethoven's own piano music so relatively conservative, not to say often old-fashioned, in its layout? Clementi, Dussek, even Steibelt added more to piano technique on the printed page than almost anything to be found in the Beethoven sonatas, incomparably greater musically as the latter are. One answer would be, of course, that with Beethoven the idea counted more than its execution. His sonatas are not necessarily conceived in terms of the piano per se, but in terms of idea expressed in form. Some of his piano writing can be frightfully difficult, but it is not "pianistic." There is a great difference. (Much the same can be said about Beethoven's contemporary, Franz Schubert; but where Beethoven was a brilliant pianist himself, Schubert was not, although he could get around the piano well enough.)

Another answer might lie in the fact that Beethoven was, in many respects, a self-taught pianist. His instructors, when he was a child, were not professional pianists. Professionals, when they teach, generally instill into their pupils the proper regard and respect (not to say reverence) for their instrument, and in ninety-nine cases out of a hundred the instrument ends up being more important than the music. Quite the reverse was the case with Beethoven, who turned out to be a musician first, a pianist second. His tenor-singing father, who wanted to put him on display as a second Mozart, might have been aghast had he been musician enough to know where the child's training was leading. Around 1781, Beethoven's teacher was Christian Gottlob Neefe, court organist at Bonn, and he was the best Beethoven ever had. Neefe turned out to be not only a sympathetic mentor but a friend, and in 1793 Beethoven was writing to him: "I thank you for the counsel which you gave me so often in the progress of my divine art. If I ever become a great man, yours shall be a share of the credit."

Instead of starting Beethoven with flashy "technical" music, Neefe put Beethoven on the *Well-Tempered Clavier* and also instructed him in organ, theory and composition. Beethoven made giant strides, and Neefe hastened to let the world know what he had developed. In his news letter of March, 1783, he wrote about his twelve-year-old pupil: "He plays the clavier very skillfully, with power, and (to put it in a nutshell) he plays chiefly the *Well-Tempered Clavier* of Sebastian Bach, which Herr Neefe put into his hands. Whoever knows this collection of preludes and fugues in all the keys, which might almost be called the *ne plus ultra* of our art, will know what this means."

Young Beethoven in addition was a formidable improviser and sight reader, and at twelve he was cembalist and violinist in the Bonn orchestra. It was this kind of training that led to such feats of pure musicianship as playing the rehearsal of his C major Concerto in B major because the piano was a half-tone out of tune.

It was in 1792 that the short, homely Beethoven exploded over Vienna. His playing—and it was as a pianist, not as a composer, that he made his initial impact—was overwhelming. And it was overwhelming not so much because Beethoven was a great virtuoso (which he probably wasn't) but because he had an ocean-like surge and depth that made all other playing sound like the trickle of a rivulet. Certainly Vienna had heard pianists who had a more polished delivery—Mozart, Clementi, Wölffl, and Cramer, to mention but four. Beethoven's playing probably was rough in comparison. But a pianist with Beethoven's elemental force and conception was entirely unknown up to that time: a shellburst among the bows and arrows of his contemporaries. The well-known story of his playing for Mozart, and of Mozart saying, "Keep an eye on this young man. He will make a great splash in the world," is said to be apocryphal. But, then again, nobody has really proved it never took place. Anyway, all Vienna realized it was up against something new, something elemental, a primal, impolite force that, with unparalleled harmonic daring and disrespect for the niceties, would swarm all over the piano with complete confidence and freedom, storming the most distant keys, swinging through the most abstruse modulations.

His originality was hailed from the very beginning. Carl Ludwig Junker in 1791 pointed out that Beethoven's playing "differs greatly from the usual method of treating the piano, that it seems as if he had struck out an entirely new path for himself." The critic commented on Beethoven's "fiery expression." Everybody was struck by Beethoven's fiery expression. When Tomaschek first heard Beethoven, he was so disheartened by the young pianist's splendor that he could not touch the piano for several days. (Then, reasonably, he decided to return to practicing with ever-increased industry, Beethoven's sound always in his inner ear.)

Where Beethoven especially shone was in his improvisations. His improvisations, indeed, were better than his performances of published pieces, for after coming to Vienna, Beethoven had little time, or inclination, to practice. How much Beethoven prepared his improvisations we do not know. Most pianists did prepare, knowing full well that sooner or later they would be called upon to study an improvisation on "*Batti, batti*" or a similar well-known tune. And all pianists had at their command a thorough supply of passagework by the yard, which they could snip off and use for any possible contingency. But when Beethoven improvised, prepared passagework or no, it was evident to his hearers that after a while he was on his own, idea pouring after idea. Then he would get carried away, pound the piano, and the strings of the delicate Viennese instruments would pop, or hammers would break. No piano was safe with Beethoven. Czerny says that Beethoven's bearing, while playing, was "masterfully quiet," but that does not quite jibe with the impressions of most others who saw him in action. A quiet player does not snap strings and break hammers. Almost every pianist of the day kept his hands close to the keys, but there is plenty of evidence that Beethoven was a most lively figure at the keyboard, just as he was on the podium. Ignaz von Seyfried told Spohr that once, at a public concert, Beethoven got into a rage about something and, at the first chords of his solo, broke half a dozen strings. And Anton Reicha relates that one evening, when Beethoven was playing a Mozart concerto at court, "He asked me to turn pages for him. But I was mostly occupied in wrenching the strings of the pianoforte which snapped, while the hammers stuck among the broken strings. Beethoven insisted on finishing the concerto, and so back and forth I leaped, jerking out a string, disentangling a hammer, turning a page, and I worked harder than Beethoven." (This would have been about 1795 or 1796. Beethoven for the most part played only his own music in public, and only two exceptions are known. On March 31, 1795, he played a Mozart concerto at a benefit concert for Mozart's widow, and he repeated it on January 8, 1796. At home, of course, he would play or read through a variety of music by other composers.) Beethoven broke more pianos than anybody in Vienna. Czerny, who hailed Beethoven's "titanic execution," apologizes for his messiness by saying that he demanded far too much from the pianos then being made. Which is very true; and which also is a polite way of saying that Beethoven banged the hell out of the piano.

It is impossible to describe a Beethoven improvisation, though the opening of the *Choral Fantasy* is supposed to give an idea. J. B. Cramer told his pupils that nobody could say he had ever heard improvisation had he not heard Beethoven. Carl Czerny said that Beethoven's improvisations were so brilliant and amazing that often the eyes of his listeners filled with tears, while some members of the audience would sob loudly, "for apart from the beauty and originality of his ideas, and his ingenious manner of expressing them, there was something magical about his playing." Czerny describes the hands that caused such magic; he says that they were densely covered with hair; that the fingers, especially at the tips, were very broad; that the stretch was not large, hardly capable of a tenth. Those hands may have wrenched tears from many eyes, but to some conservatives Beethoven's harmonies were uncontrolled. Tomaschek, who so admired Beethoven's playing in 1798, never could get used to his "frequent daring deviations from one motive to another. . . . Evils of this nature frequently weaken his greatest compositions." But to Ignaz von Seyfried, Beethoven's improvisations were "a cataract, elemental, a force of nature." Woe be to the pianist who crossed Beethoven in competition when the latter was in a combative mood. The insufferable Steibelt once felt the full force of Beethoven's fury.

Steibelt had come to Vienna in 1800, fresh from his glories in Paris (and his precipitate retreat therefrom). Beethoven's friends were worried that the visitor would be too much for him, especially as Steibelt was not particularly bashful about advertising his own virtues. He beat his drum much louder than his wife the tambourine. Naturally Steibelt did not take the trouble to visit Beethoven. That would have been beneath his dignity. They finally met at the house of Count Fries, where Beethoven played the piano part in his new Trio in B flat. Steibelt listened with condescension and apparently gave Beethoven a few compliments of a not-bad-old-boy variety, one great composer to another. Then Steibelt sat down to play *his* music, making a great effect with his specialty, the tremolo passages, at that time something quite new. Beethoven listened but could not be induced to play a solo. A week later the two met once more at Fries's house. This time Steibelt had prepared a brilliant fantasy for piano and strings, the theme coming from the Beethoven trio he had heard the previous week. Steibelt's admirers were in raptures. Now the issue was joined, and Beethoven *had* to show his strength. He walked to the piano, grasped the cello part of the Steibelt work en route, put it upside down on the piano and insultingly drummed out a theme with one finger. Then he improvised, and—angry, excited, on his mettle—how he must have improvised! Before Beethoven had finished, Steibelt stole from the room. He never again would meet Beethoven, and made it a condition before going anywhere in Vienna that Beethoven not be invited.

In that he produced new effects, broke all the rules, used an extraordinarily wide dynamic palette, and was highly expressive in his playing, Beethoven was the direct link to the romantic pianists. Unlike the disciplined Mozart or Cramer, he played as he felt, unclassically, wrong notes and all. The chances are that he never, even at his best, was an accurate pianist, and his work at times must have been distressingly sloppy, even before deafness set in. He "played like a composer." The hero-worshiping Schindler was forced to admit that his performances left much to be desired "on the score of pure execution." But, Schindler hastens to add, "all music performed by his hands appeared to undergo a new creation. These wonderful effects were, in a great degree, produced by his uniform legato style, which was one of the most remarkable peculiarities of his playing." Nobody seemed to mind Beethoven's technical roughness except purists like Moscheles. But Moscheles, who complained of the lack of precision and clarity in Beethoven's playing, did not hear him until 1814, by which time Beethoven's hearing was all but gone. And enough evidence of Beethoven's playing until 1805, when deafness caused him to curtail the number of his professional appearances, is available to reconstruct his style with fair certainty.

At the beginning he had a good enough technique. Czerny points out that nobody equaled Beethoven in the rapidity of his scales, double trills, skips and such like matters—not even Hummel. Schindler discusses Beethoven's combinations of distant intervals and keys, heightened by idiosyncrasies of rhythm and staccatos, and set off by a smooth legato. "Unlike Steibelt, Dussek and some of their contemporaries in their effort to *draw* out the tone, Beethoven would often throw it out in detached notes, thus producing the effect of a fountain gushing forth and darting its spray on all sides, well contrasting with the melodious episodes which he still preserved." Nobody ever referred to Beethoven's "singing style," a description often applied to other pianists. He was far too dynamic. He also made far greater use of the pedal than was customary. Czerny says that in 1803 (when Beethoven could still hear, and was in practice) he held the pedal through *the entire slow movement* of his C minor Concerto. Granted that Beethoven was using a light Viennese piano, in which the sustaining tones quickly dissipated, this still sounds like an incredible statement. Could Beethoven have forgotten his pianistic ABCs under the stress of public performance and left his foot on the pedal? But we do know he was lavish in the use of it, as witness his own pedal markings at the opening of the D minor Sonata (Opus 31, No. 2). Czerny says that Beethoven used the pedal "far more than is indicated in his works." (How could Artur Schnabel ever have written, in the preface to his edition of the Beethoven sonatas: ". . . the fact being that the pedal is very seldom used in the classic piano literature as a means of coloring"?)

One of the most fascinating sections in the Schindler biography concerns Ferdinand Ries's observations on how Beethoven played his own music. Ries was a piano student of Beethoven's from 1801 to 1804, later settling in London. Whether or not Ries himself was a good pianist—he had a high reputation, as any Beethoven pupil would, but von Lenz called him a woodchopper and most experts agreed—he at any rate was a trained observer. And he has some fascinating things to say about Beethoven's style at the piano:

> In general he played his own compositions in a very capricious manner, but he nevertheless kept strictly accurate time, occasionally, but very seldom, accelerating the tempo. On the other hand, in the performance of a crescendo passage, he would introduce a ritard [so much for present-day purists], which produced a beautiful and highly striking effect. Sometimes, in the performance of specific passages, he would infuse into them an exquisite but altogether inimitable expression. He seldom introduced notes or ornaments not set down in the composition.

To which Schindler adds that all the pieces he himself heard Beethoven play were, with hardly any exceptions, thoroughly free and flexible. "He adopted a tempo rubato in the proper sense of the term, according as subject and situation might demand, without the slightest approach to caricature." Schindler likens it to "the most distinct and intelligible declamation."

Schindler goes into a detailed analysis of how Beethoven played the E major and G major Sonatas (Opus 14, Nos. 1 and 2). The Schindler biography is not hard to come by, but most pianists today seem unaware of this very important analysis and its implications. If Schindler is accurate (and there is no reason why he should be distrusted) the difference between Beethoven's own conception of his music and how we today approach it in the name of "fidelity" becomes apparent.*

I will now, as far as verbal description may permit, endeavor to convey an idea of the manner in which Beethoven himself used to play the two sonatas contained in Op. 14. His wonderful perform- ance of these two compositions was a sort of musical declamation, in which the two principles [the contrasting principles of sonata design] were as distinctly separated as the two parts of a dialogue when re- cited by the flexible voice of a good speaker.

He commenced the opening allego [of the G major sonata Op. 14, No. 2] with vigor and spirit, relaxing these qualities at the sixth bar, and in following [two measures which contain the syncopated leaps in the right hand leading to the cadence of the phrase] a slight ritar- dando made preparation for gently introducing the entreating princi- ple. The performance of the [two-measure] phrase [measures 7 and 8 which contain motive of the repeated D's and the falling figure from E to D] was exquisitely shaded; and to the [four] bars, [measures 14 through 17 which starts the rising sequence] Beethoven's manner of holding down particular notes, combined with a kind of soft, gliding touch, imparted such a vivid coloring, that the hearer could fancy he actually beheld the lover in his living form, and heard him apostro- phizing his obdurate mistress. In the groups of [six rising and falling sixteenth notes in measures 22 and 23] he strongly accented the fourth note of each group, and gave a joyous expression to the whole passage; and, at the succeeding chromatic run [measure 24], he re- sumed the original tempo, and continued it [throughout the second theme] until he arrived at [the closing theme, measures 45 ff. with its thirds in the right hand and the moving bass in every other measure of the left hand] which he gave in *tempo andantino*, beautifully ac- centing the bass, and the upper part of the harmony [after each tied note in the right hand], thereby rendering distinct to the ear the sep-

---

* In the following quotation from Schindler, there are several references to passages from the sonatas which are printed in musical notation. For the sake of clarity for the readers who cannot interpret musical notation, we have substituted prose descrip- tions for these passages. We have also supplied measure numbers for interested music students who can easily follow the score.—THE EDITORS.

aration of the two principles. On arriving at [measure 56, where the bass rises in eighth notes A, A sharp, B, and C natural], he made the bass stand out prominently, and closed the succeeding cadence on the dominant in the original tempo, which he maintained without deviation to the end of the first part [i.e., to the double bar, measure 63].

In the second part, Beethoven introduced the phrase in A flat major [from measure 81 on, where the main theme is in the bass], by a *ritardando* of the two preceding bars. He attacked this [A flat major] phrase vigorously, thus diffusing a glow of color over the picture. He gave a charming expression to the phrase [starting with the rising octave jump as upbeat to measure 103, followed by three measures of descending scale with the characteristic rhythm of a dotted eighth and five sixteenth notes in each bar. He did this] by strongly accenting and holding down longer than the prescribed time the first note in each bar, while the bass was played with gradually increasing softness, and with a sort of creeping motion of the hand.

The passage next in succession [commencing at measure 107 with thirty-second notes in the right hand over a pedal-note D in the bass], was touched off brilliantly; and in its closing bars [measures 113 and 114], the *decrescendo* was accompanied by a *ritardando*. The following phrase [commencing at measure 115 with the triplet broken chords in the left hand and the sixteenth-note figure of the opening theme alternating in the low and high registers] was started in andante tempo. At the fifth bar, [where the sixteenth-note figure alternates at closer time intervals], there was a slight *accelerando*, and an increase of tone. At the sixth bar, [measure 120, the bar before the *fortissimo* climax], the original tempo was resumed. Throughout the remainder of the first movement, Beethoven observed the same tempo as that which he had taken in the opening bars.

Various as were the tempi which Beethoven introduced in this movement, yet they were all beautifully prepared, and, if I may so express myself, the colors were delicately blended with one another. There were none of those abrupt changes which the composer frequently admitted in some of his other works with the view of giving a loftier flight to the declamation. Those who truly enter into the spirit of this fine movement will find it advisable not to repeat the first part; by this allowable abridgment, the gratification of the hearer will be unquestionably increased, while it may possibly be diminished by frequent repetitions of the same phrases. . . .

With regard to the second Sonata in E major (Op. 14 No. 1), the subject of which is similar to that of the first, I shall confine myself to the description of Beethoven's manner of performing a few passages. In the seventh bar of the first *allegro movement*, [where the lyrical passage in eighth notes commences in the right hand], as well as in the following bar, he retarded the tempo, touching the keys more forte, and holding down the fifth note. By these means he imparted to the passage an indescribable earnestness and dignity of character.

In the ninth bar, [where the melody descends from the high B], the original tempo was resumed, the powerful expression still being maintained. The tenth bar [where the inner voices descend in quarter notes] was *diminuendo* and somewhat lingering. The eleventh and twelfth bars were played in the same manner as the two foregoing.

On the introduction of the middle movement [i.e., second subject of first movement at measure 22 commencing with four descending eighth notes], the dialogue became sentimental. The prevailing tempo was *andante*, but not regularly maintained; for every time that [the descending eighth notes were] introduced, a little pause was made on the first note. At the [second portion of the second subject, commencing at measure 39 with the *gruppetto* in the soprano voice], a joyous character was expressed. The original tempo was taken, and not changed until the close of the first part.

The second part, from [measure 67, the eighth note octave melody] forward was characterized by an increased breadth of rhythm, and augmented power of tone, which, however, was further on shaded into an exquisitely delicate *pianissimo;* so that the apparent meaning of the dialogue became more perceptible without any over-strained effort of imagination.

The second movement *allegretto* was, as performed by Beethoven, more like an *allegro furioso;* and until he arrived at the single [D minor seventh] chord, [at measure 43 tied over to measure 44], on which he made a very long pause, he kept up the same tempo.

In the *maggiore,* [of the second movement] the tempo was taken more moderately, and played by Beethoven in a beautifully expressive style. He added not a single note; but he gave to many an accentuation which would not have suggested itself to any other player. On the subject of accentuation, I may state, as a general remark, that Beethoven gave prominent force to all appoggiaturas, particularly the minor second, even in running passages; and, in slow movements, his transition to the principal note [preceded by an *appogiatura*] was as delicately managed as it could have been by the voice of a singer.

In the rondo of the sonata to which I am here referring, Beethoven maintained the tempo as marked until he arrived at the bars introducing the first and third pauses. These bars he made *ritardando.*

The two sonatas in Op. 14; the first sonata (F minor) in Op. 2; the first sonata (C minor), Op. 10; the *Sonate pathétique* (C minor), Op. 13; the *Sonata quasi Fantasia* in C sharp minor, Op. 27, and some others, all are pictures of feeling; and, in every movement, *Beethoven varied the tempo according as the feelings changed* [italics added].

Well! Schindler's remarks indicate something that could have been guessed without them: that Beethoven was no metronome. But there is only one thing wrong with playing those sonatas that way [today]. The pianist who tried it would be laughed off the stage as an incompetent, a stylistic idiot who knew nothing about the Beethoven style, and as a bungler who was incapable of adhering to a basic tempo. Ries's remark about Beethoven keeping "strictly accurate time" must be taken relatively. By the standards of Beethoven's own day, the metrical pulse was strict; by present-day standards it would be intolerable. Twentieth-century pianists know as much about Beethoven's pianistic style as he knew about ours. We would consider his performances sheer anarchism if he returned today, while he would listen to current Beethoven specialists and consider them dry, unmusical and anything but expressive.

Free as Beethoven was in his own playing, he tried hard to train his pupils according to classical ideals. Do as I say, don't do as I do. "Place the hands over the keyboard in such a position that the fingers need not be raised more than necessary. That is the only method by which the player can learn to *generate* tone." He did follow Clementi by insisting on legato playing, terming the old-fashioned Mozart style "finger-dancing" or "manual air-sawing." One pupil Beethoven did not take was his nephew Carl. He turned him over to Czerny, but kept close watch on his progress. Beethoven was constantly telling Czerny how to teach his nephew. Carl, he said, should first be taught to concentrate on fingering; then rhythm; then the notes "with tolerable correctness." And, Beethoven insisted, "do not stop his playing on account of minor little mistakes, but only point them out at the end of a piece."

Beethoven even wrote out a series of suggested exercises for the boy. In his early years Beethoven constantly recommended C. P. E. Bach's piano-instruction books; later he turned to Clementi. But at all times he was particular about correct hand position, about students working on scales in all the keys, and especially the use of the thumb. As he grew older he, like many people, grew more conservative (though not in his own music!). He told Tomaschek in 1814 that "it has been known that the greatest piano players were the greatest composers; but how did they play? Not like the pianists of today, who only run up and down the keyboard with long-practiced passagework, *putsch, putsch, putsch!* What does that mean? When the true piano virtuosos played," continued Beethoven, warming up, "it was something integrated, something whole. One could regard it as a work written in good continuity. That is real piano playing. The rest is nothing." Thus spoke the master of form.

Then who were the pianists Beethoven admired? For the Steibelts and Voglers of the world he had nothing but contempt. Mozart he considered old-fashioned, and he had some slighting things to say about Moscheles. His opinion of Cramer, however, was very high, and he had great respect for Clementi. Several women pianists interested him: whether because they were pianists or because they were women is hard to say. Unfortunately he did not, in his letters, write much about other musicians and performers, as Mozart had done. But he did, in 1817, write to Marie Pachler-Koschak in more than extravagant terms. "I am delighted that you are sparing us another day. We will make a great deal more music. Surely you will play for me the Sonatas in F major and C minor [probably Opus 54 and the *Pathétique*], won't you? I have not found anybody who performs my compositions as well as you do, and I am not excluding the great pianists, who often have merely mechanical ability or affectation. You are the true fosterer of my spiritual children."

Marie Bigot de Morogues was another lady whom Beethoven held in high regard. She may have been good. When Haydn first heard her, he folded her in his arms and is reported to have said: "My dear child, that music is not mine; it is yours." And Beethoven, hearing her, was impelled to say, after she played one of his sonatas, "That is not exactly myself, it is something better." Marie in 1814 had played the *Appassionata* Sonata from manuscript. A woman who could do that could do anything. It is very likely that Beethoven had a crush on Marie. A letter to her, written in 1807, makes clumsy advances—at least, so it might indicate to a suspicious mind:

MY DEAR AND MUCH ADMIRED MARIE!
    The weather is so divinely beautiful—and who knows what it will be like tomorrow?—So I propose to fetch you about noon today and take you for a drive.—As Bigot [Marie's husband] has presumably gone out already, we cannot take him with us, of course—but for that reason to abandon my plan altogether, why, Bigot himself would surely not want this—Only the morning is now the most lovely part of the day—why not seize the moment, seeing that it flies so quickly?—

It so happened that Bigot had a suspicious mind, and Beethoven had to write several long letters to Herr and Frau Bigot, apologizing and making all kinds of lame excuses for his proposal to gather his rosebuds. He put on a wounded air: "How can our kind Marie put such an evil construction on my actions?" Beethoven was not cut out to be a Don Juan.

Marie Bigot was not the only woman who specialized in Beethoven's music. So did Dorothea von Ertmann, to whom Beethoven dedicated the most subtle of his sonatas—the A major (Opus 101). Beethoven was constantly calling upon her to help him in his concerts. The relationship between them was close; she had studied with him since 1803, and was always available when he needed a pianist. Clementi called her a great master. She was married to an army officer, Baron Stephan von Ertmann, and Beethoven was never anything but polite to *her.*

Piano problems constantly plagued Beethoven. For most of his life he used Viennese pianos, at first with a five-plus octave range, then—starting with the *Waldstein* Sonata—a six-octave instrument. But he was never happy with them, and kept urging the manufacturers for a more rugged, sonorous product. He wrote the piano-manufacturer Johann

Streicher a bitter letter as early as 1796: "There is no doubt that as far as the manner of playing it is concerned, the pianoforte is still the least studied and least developed of all instruments: often one thinks that one is merely listening to a harp. And I am delighted, my dear fellow, that you are one of the few who realize and perceive that, providing one can feel the music, one can also make the pianoforte sing. I hope that the time will come when the harp and the pianoforte will be treated as entirely different instruments." The day did not come soon enough for Beethoven to take advantage of it. In 1818 John Broadwood sent Beethoven a magnificent grand piano, with a range of over six octaves—a sonorous giant, as unharp-like as any piano at that time could be. Beethoven was ecstatic, and kept the instrument the rest of his life.

But by 1818 Beethoven's hearing was about gone. The deaf, chaotic composer would sit at his Broadwood with a wild look on his face, banging out wrong notes that he could not hear. And soon his beloved Broadwood became a tangle of wires. At his best, Beethoven could never keep a piano in decent condition. Ries said that he seldom laid his hand upon anything without breaking it, and he had the habit, just fine for a piano, of emptying the inkwell in it. Toward the end of Beethoven's life he was visited by an instrument-maker named Johann Andreas Stumpff, who was taken directly to the Broadwood. Stumpff recollected the scene in horror. "Quite a sight confronted me," he later wrote, cut to the quick. "The upper registers were mute, and the broken strings in a tangle, like a thorn bush whipped by a storm." Yet Beethoven could once in a while coax music out of it, deaf as he was, battered as the instrument was. When Friedrich Wieck visited him, Wieck—who was the father and teacher of Clara Schumann and knew what he was talking about —said that Beethoven played "in a flowing, genial manner, for the most part orchestrally, and was still quite adept in the passing over of the right and left hands (a few times he missed the mark), weaving in the clearest and most charming melodies." But these moments were atypical. For a picture of the pity and the terror of the old Beethoven, one turns to Sir John Russell's account of the pianist who had once been the *enfant terrible* of Vienna, the great interpretive artist who had brought tears to the eyes of his listeners:

The moment he is seated at the piano he is evidently unconscious that there is anything else in existence. . . . The muscles of his face swell and its veins stand out; the wild eye rolls doubly wild; the mouth quivers; and Beethoven looks like a wizard overpowered by the demons he has called up. . . . And considering how very deaf he is, it seems impossible that he should hear all he plays. Accordingly, when playing softly, he does not bring out a single note. He hears it himself in his "mind's ear," while his eye, and the almost imperceptible motion of his fingers, shows that he is following out the strain in his own soul through all its dying gradations. The instrument is actually as dumb as the musician is deaf. . . .—HAROLD C. SCHONBERG

The Conductor

Beethoven should not really figure in any survey of conductors, and the only justification for including him in this instance is that the bad conducting of a great man is always more interesting than the good conducting of a small man.

Beethoven held no appointment as *Kapellmeister* either at Bonn or at Vienna. He took charge occasionally of performances of his own works, but had no qualifications as a conductor, no routine-experience as such, and he never traveled far afield to hear orchestras outside of Vienna.

Schindler explained the situation in these words: "At the time when his hearing was yet perfect, he had not often occasion to come in contact with the orchestra, and especially to acquire practice in the conducting department at the theater, which is the best school for that purpose. In the concertroom the talent most fitted for this difficult function is never fully developed, and remains one-sided and awkward. Thus we see composers of eminence incapable of conducting the orchestra in the performance of their own works, if they have not previously acquired the necessary routine, in listening to, and in superintending numerous bands."[1]

In 1808 Beethoven was invited to become *Kapellmeister* at Cassel. That he did not occupy that position was, no doubt, all for the best, whether regarded from his own point of view or from that of the music at Cassel. Beethoven had enough music in him to have made scores of conductors, but he had neither the necessary experience, the temperament, or the right personality for such work; added to which, his growing deafness would in any case have been enough to prevent him from every becoming proficient as a conductor.

When we read of Beethoven "conducting" this or that work of his own, it should not be assumed that he took complete control of the playing of the orchestra as a conductor now does. We have already seen that he sometimes sat at the piano and supervised the performance in the manner of the eighteenth century keyboard-conductor, leaving the actual control

[1] Moscheles' translation of Schindler, in *Life of Beethoven*, I, p. 112.

to the violinist-leader. But there are also contemporary descriptions of Beethoven standing up in the orchestra and making movements with his arms which might easily be mistaken for conducting in the modern sense of the word. Descriptions by Moscheles, Seyfried, Czerny, Franz Wild, Ries, Reichardt, Spohr, Schindler and Atterbohm, all tally in that they make it quite clear that even if Beethoven did sometimes give a time-beat, his main concern was to indicate the expression, the dynamics, and the style of the performance in general by means of gesticulations.

Beethoven's method of indicating the expression appears to have been quite his own, as the following extracts will show:

"He had ears only for his composition and was ceaselessly occupied by manifold gesticulations to indicate the desired expression. He used to suggest a *diminuendo* by crouching down more and more, and at a *pianissimo* he would almost creep under the desk. When the volume of sound grew he rose up also as if out of a stage-trap, and with the entrance of the power of the band he would stand upon the tips of his toes almost as big as a giant, and waving his arms, seemed about to soar upwards to the skies. Everything about him was active, not a bit of his organism idle, and the man was comparable to a *perpetuum mobile*."[1]

"For scarcely had the music begun before its creator offered a bewildering spectacle. At the *piano* passages he sank upon his knee, at the *forte* he leaped up so that his figure, now shrivelling to that of a dwarf, disappeared under the desk, and anon stretched up far above it like a giant, his hands and arms working as if with the beginning of the music a thousand lives had entered every member. At first this happened without disturbance of the effect of the composition, for the disappearance and appearance of his body was synchronous with the dying away and the swelling of the music; but all at once the genius ran ahead of his orchestra and the master disappeared at the *forte* passages and appeared at the *piano*."[2]

"Beethoven had accustomed himself to give the signs of expression to his orchestra by all manner of extraordinary motions of his body. So often a *sforzando* occurred, he tore his arms which he had previously crossed upon his breast, with great vehemence asunder. At a *piano*, he bent himself down, and the lower, the softer he wished to have it. Then when a *crescendo* came, he raised himself again by degrees, and upon the commencement of the *forte*, sprang bolt upright. To increase the *forte* yet more, he would sometimes, also, join in with a shout to the orchestra, without being aware of it."[3]

"At last he (Moscheles) amuses his hearers exceedingly by imitating Beethoven's movements as a conductor; his stooping down more and

1 Thayer, *Studien*, p. 94.
2 From Franz Wild's *Autobiography*.
3 Sophr, *Autob.*, I, p. 186.

more until he almost disappeared at the 'piano' passages, the gradual rising up at the 'crescendo,' and standing tiptoe and bounding up at the 'fortissimo.' Moscheles does not forget to add: 'Inasmuch, however, as I cannot emulate that great man in his works, I abstain from copying him in his attitudes; with him it was all originality, with me it would be caricature.' "[1]

"At a *pianissimo* he knelt down and stretched his arms towards the floor; at a *fortissimo*, like an arrow from the bow, he bounced up, appearing to have suddenly grown tall, and thrust his arms wide asunder; between these two extremes he was constantly swaying up and down."[2]

These are the words of eye-witnesses. Even if Beethoven thought that he was controlling the orchestra, it is fairly clear that he was not really doing so; in fact, he was hampering it, and steps had to be taken to provide some guidance which the players could understand and on which they could depend. Seyfried told us that "the orchestra had to have a care in order not to be led astray by its master,"[3] and at the revival of *Fidelio* in 1814 when "Beethoven conducted, his ardour often rushed him out of time, but Chapelmaster Umlauf, behind his back, guided everything to success with eye and hand."[4]

But it is, at any rate, open to question whether Beethoven ever thought that he was actually conducting at these performances. It is difficult to believe that he would have tolerated the presence of another active conductor if he had imagined that he was himself in control of the performance.

A translated extract from a Viennese journal which appeared in the *Harmonicon*,[5] referring to the first performance of the Choral Symphony, suggests that Beethoven's share in the performance was not that of conductor, but rather that of one who supervised the rendering, without actually controlling it: "The leaders of the music were Kapellmeister Umlauf and M. Schupanzigh, and the great Composer himself assisted on that occasion. He took his place at the side of the principal leader (Umlauf), and, with his original score before him, indicated the different movements and determined the precise manner in which they were to be given; for, unfortunately, the state of his hearing prevented him from doing more."

There are stories of misunderstandings and breakdowns, and the more deaf Beethoven became, the more distracting were his efforts to direct and influence the performance of his works, Throughout the whole story there is no evidence that he ever held a baton or any other implement in his hand.

[1] *Life of Moscheles*, II, p. 140.
[2] From Atterbohm, Hanslick, p. 276, f.n.
[3] Thayer, *Studien*, p. 94.
[4] Thayer, *Treitschke*, p. 278.
[5] Oct., 1824, p. 180.

The picture is rather confused, and it is certainly unique. The tragedy of Beethoven's deafness hangs over it all and gives a sad tinge to what might otherwise appear to have been rather grotesque. Nature has played some queer tricks, but none more capricious than giving Beethoven the power to conceive the nine great symphonies, the overtures and concertos, *Fidelio*, and the great Mass in D, and then taking away his hearing and letting him stand in the orchestra behaving like a mountebank while the leader and another conductor behind his back did their best to rescue the performance from the effects of his strange conducting.

It seems that Beethoven was also unreliable regarding the *tempi* of his own works. He changed his mind about the metronome speeds, and Schindler told how he gave the *tempi* for the Choral Symphony to Umlauf at his house, and then altered them again at the rehearsal.— ADAM CARSE

The Music

———◆———

Orchestra

I. SYMPHONIES
  a. Symphony No. 1 in C, Opus 21
    i. Adagio molto; Allegro con brio
    ii. Andante cantabile con moto
    iii. Menuetto: Allegro molto e vivace; Trio
    iv. Adagio; Allegro molto e vivace

i. The first movement opens with a short introduction (*Adagio molto*, C major, 4/4 time) of thoughtful, dignified character; it well sounds the note of preparation for what is to follow. The opening measures, for strings, woodwind, and horns, are a notable stroke of originality in the matter of tonality for Beethoven's day: if there was any one key to which young composers were warned against modulating until near the end of a composition, this key was the subdominant; yet Beethoven begins this symphony in C major immediately with the chord of the dominant seventh of F major (subdominant of the principal key). In fact, the symphony may be said to begin at once with a "modulation to the subdominant."

The main body of the movement (*Allegro con brio*, C major, 2/2) opens with a strong statement of the first theme in the strings, the woodwind and horns coming in with sustained modulating chords between the phrases. In this announcement of the theme we find the application of a time-honored principle: making the second phrase a note-for-note repetition of the first, only a whole-tone higher—that is, in the relative minor of the subdominant. The first phrase is thus in C major, the second in D minor; this paves the way for a modulation to the dominant, through which the tonic is reached, to round off the period. The opening measures of the Overture to "Prometheus" are based upon essentially the same harmony, as are also those of Bach's first prelude in the "Well-Tempered Clavichord." 'A brilliant first subsidiary, consisting mostly of passage work, follows (most of the figures are taken from the first theme), and leads to an elaborate *fortissimo* cadence in the dominant. One sees that Beethoven had not yet got beyond the old Mozart plan of rounding off each section of his first part with a very definite and long-prepared cadence—the sort of cadence which Wagner once compared to the noise of changing the plates and knives and forks between the courses of a dinner. Nor is this the only Mozartish trait in the movement; the bright and cheery second theme, with its light play between oboe and flute, is quite on the Mozart plan and wholly different from that more cantabile "*Adagio* in the midst of an *Allegro*" which we find in most of the second themes of Beethoven's later symphonies. It is followed in its turn by a strong second subsidiary and some vivacious passage work on figures from the first and second themes, leading to a very brief conclusion theme, with which the first part of the movement ends on the dominant. This first part is repeated.

The free fantasia is comparatively short, but none the less elaborate. Toward the end it works up strongly and steadily to the third part of the movement; there is no hint at that dramatic "moment of exhaustion" which we find near the close of the free fantasia of the "Eroica" Symphony. The third part stands in quite regular relations to the first, and there is a rather long coda.

II. The second movement (*Andante cantabile con moto*, F major, 3/8) is also strictly in the sonata form. It opens with the graceful first theme exposed as a fugato, although this imitative contrapuntal style of treatment soon ceases.[1] This is followed by a half-playful, half-tender

[1] The first nineteen measures of this *Andante* might well stand for the exposition of a tonal fugue, were it not for some irregularity in the management of subject and response. The subject first enters in the second violins, passing immediately from the dominant to the tonic; the response first enters in the violas and cellos; it is strictly tonal, passing immediately from the tonic to the dominant, the tonal mutation coming at the beginning. This entry, however, gives only half of the response. The third entry is in the double basses and bassoons; it gives only half of the subject, transposed to the key of the dominant. The fourth, and last, entry gives the whole of the subject in the tonic, in the first violins, flute, and oboe.

second theme in the dominant (C major), which in turn makes way for a severer, more contrapuntal subsidiary idea. A lightly tripping coda in triplets for first violins and flute, accompanied by alternate chords in the other strings and woodwind and horns, closes the first part of the movement in the dominant. This first part is then repeated. There is a short development and a regular recapitulation, in which the fugal entrances of subject and answer are now accompanied by a countersubject in running figures. The movement closes with a coda, in which one finds at least a premonition of the wonderful development Beethoven afterwards gave to the coda in the first movement of the "Eroica."

III. The third movement (*Allegro molto e vivace*, C major, 3/4) may be regarded as standing on the boundary line between the old Haydn symphonic minuet and the Beethoven scherzo. It is marked "Menuetto" in the score; but the dotted minim strives so successfully to assert itself as the metrical unit—instead of the crochet—that it might equally well have been marked "Scherzo." It is, moreover, full of the capricious, ingenious character of the scherzo. It is quite regular in construction, save that the delicate, fairy-like little trio is in the tonic C major, and concise in form. There is more of bold and unexpected modulation within its brief compass than in all the rest of the symphony put together.

IV. The fourth movement begins with six bars of *Adagio*, 2/4, in which, after a long-held G by the full orchestra, the first violins give out playful little introductory scale passages, full of expectancy. Then they rush softly and nimbly into the main body of the movement (*Allegro molto e vivace*, C major, 2/4), being joined by the other strings in the bright, cheery first theme. The character of this theme is entirely that of one of those vivacious country-dance tunes that Haydn was so fond of taking for his final rondos, and this character is kept up by the principal and subsidiary themes that follow it. For some time one takes the movement to be a real rondo. Neither does the repeat of the first part undeceive one, for it might well mean nothing more than the return of the principal theme according to the true rondo pattern. The brief, but by no means unelaborate, development section that comes next might equally well be an episode of working out in the midst of a rondo. It is only when the third part of the movement comes, with its regular reproduction of the scheme of the first, that one sees clearly that the movement is after all strictly in sonata form. But, when the first theme reappears in its entirety (and in the tonic, too) at the beginning of the coda, the rondo character of the movement is still further emphasized. Upon the whole this finale might not ineptly be called a rondo in sonata form.—WILLIAM FOSTER APTHORP

The symphony is scored for two flutes, two oboes, two clarinets, two bassoons, two horns, two trumpets, timpani, and the usual strings.

This work is wholly different in form, melodic style, harmonic sobriety, and instrumentation from the compositions of Beethoven that follow it. When the composer wrote it, he was evidently under the sway of Mozartian ideas. These he sometimes enlarged, but he has imitated them ingeniously everywhere. Especially in the first two movements do we find springing up occasionally certain rhythms used by the composer of "Don Giovanni"; but these occasions are rare and far less striking. The first *Allegro* has for a theme a phrase of six measures, which is not distinguished in itself but becomes interesting through the artistic treatment. An episodic melody follows, but it has little distinction of style. By means of a half-cadence, repeated three or four times, we come to a figure in imitation for wind instruments; and we are the more surprised to find it here, because it has been so often employed in several overtures to French operas. The *Andante* contains an accompaniment of drums, *piano*, which appears today rather ordinary, yet we recognize in it a hint at striking effects produced later by Beethoven with the aid of this instrument, which is seldom or badly employed as a rule by his predecessors. This movement is full of charm; the theme is graceful and lends itself easily to fugued development, by means of which the composer has succeeded in being ingenious and piquant. The scherzo is the first-born of the family of charming badinages or scherzos, of which Beethoven invented the form, and determined the pace, which he substituted in nearly all of his instrumental works for the minuet of Mozart and Haydn with a pace doubly less rapid and with a wholly different character. This scherzo is of exquisite freshness, lightness, and grace. It is the one truly original thing in this symphony in which the poetic idea, so great and rich in the majority of his succeeding works, is wholly wanting. It is music admirably made, clear, alert, but slightly accentuated, cold, and sometimes mean and shabby, as in the final rondo, which is musically childish. In a word, this is not Beethoven.—HECTOR BERLIOZ

Beethoven's first symphony, produced in 1800, is a fitting farewell to the eighteenth century. It has more of the true nineteenth-century Beethoven in its depths than he allows to appear upon the surface. Its style is that of the Comedy of Manners, as translated by Mozart into the music of his operas and of his most lighthearted works of symphonic and chamber music. The fact that it is comedy from beginning to end is prophetic of changes in music no less profound than those which the French Revolution brought about in the social organism. But Beethoven was the most conservative of revolutionists; a Revolutionist without the R; and in his first symphony he shows, as has often been remarked, a characteristic caution in handling sonata form for the first time with a full orchestra. But the caution which seems so obvious to us was not noticed by his contemporary critics. Carl Philipp Emanuel Bach, who, much more than his father, was at that time regarded as a founder of modern music by persons who considered the lately deceased Mozart a dangerous person, had gone very much farther in this matter of opening in a foreign key than Beethoven ever went in the whole course of his career. Where the contemporary critics showed intelligent observation was in marking, though with mild censure, the fact that Beethoven's first symphony is written so heavily for the wind band that it seems almost more like a "Harmoniemusik" than a proper orchestral piece. This observation was technically correct. Beethoven had at that time a young composer's interest in wind instruments, which he handled with a mastery stimulated by the wind-band ("Harmonie") masterpieces of Mozart. His handling of the strings was not less masterly, though his interest in their possibilities developed mightily in later works.

The position then is this: that in his first symphony Beethoven overwhelmed his listeners with a scoring for the full wind band almost as highly developed as it was ever destined to be (except that he did not as yet appreciate the possibilities of the clarinet as an instrument for the foreground). The scale of the work as a whole gave no scope for an equivalent development of the strings. Even today there is an appreciable difficulty in accommodating the wind band of Beethoven's first symphony to a small body of strings.

The introduction, made famous by pedantic contemporary objections to its mixed tonality, has in later times been sharply criticized by so great a Beethoven worshiper as Sir George Grove for its ineffectual scoring. With all respect to that pioneer of English musical culture, such a criticism is evidently traceable to the effect of pianoforte arrangements, which often suggest that a chord which is loud for the individual players of the orchestra is meant to be as loud as a full orchestral passage. When two pianists play these *forte-piano* chords in a duet, they naturally make as much noise as they can get out of their instrument. This sets up an impression in early life which many conductors and critics fail to get rid of. Hence the complaint that the pizzicato chords of the strings are feeble, a complaint that assumes that it is their business to be forcible.—DONALD FRANCIS TOVEY (2)

    b. Symphony No. 2 in D, Opus 36
        I. *Adagio molto—Allegro con brio*
        II. *Larghetto*
        III. *Scherzo, Allegro*
        IV. *Allegro molto*

The works that produce the most traceable effects in the sub-sequent history of an art are not always those which come to be re-garded as epoch-making. The epoch-making works are, more often than not, merely shocking to just those contemporaries best qualified to ap-preciate them; and by the time they become acceptable they are ac-cepted as inimitable. Even their general types of form are chronicled in history as the "inventor's" contribution to the progress of his art, only to be the more conspicuously avoided by later artists. Thus Beethoven "invented" the scherzo; and no art-form has been laid down more precisely and even rigorously than that of his dozen most typical examples. Yet the scherzos of Schubert, Schumann, Mendelssohn, and Brahms differ as widely from Beethoven's, and from each other, as Beethoven's differ from Mozart's minuets. The nearest approach to a use of Beethoven's model is to be found where we least expect it, in the grim and almost macabre scherzos of Chopin.

Far otherwise is it with certain works which immediately impressed contemporaries as marking a startling advance in the art without a dis-concerting change in its language. Beethoven's Second Symphony was evidently larger and more brilliant than any that had been heard up to 1801; and people who could understand the three great symphonies that Mozart had poured out in the six weeks between the end of June and the 10th of August 1788, would find Beethoven's language less abstruse, though the brilliance and breadth of his design and the dramatic vigor of his style were so exciting that it was thought advisable to warn young persons against so "subversive" (*sittenverderblich*) a work. What the effect of such warnings might be is a bootless inquiry; but Beethoven's Second Symphony and his next opus, the Concerto in C minor (Opus 37), have produced a greater number of definite echoes from later composers than any other of his works before the Ninth Symphony. And the echoes are by no means confined to imitative or classicist efforts: they are to be found in things like Schubert's Grand Duo and Schumann's Fourth Symphony, works written at high noontide of their composers' powers and quite unrestrained in the urgency of important new develop-ments. Indeed, Beethoven's Second Symphony itself seems almost clas-sicist in the neighborhood of such works as his profoundly dramatic Sonata in D minor, Opus 31, no. 2; while we can go back as far as the C minor Trio, Opus 1, no. 3, and find Beethoven already both as mature and as *sittenverderblich*[1] in style and matter. . . .—DONALD FRAN-CIS TOVEY (2)

1. *Adagio molto*, D major, 3/4. Like most of the early symphonies, this one begins with an introduction, the material of which opens,

[1] "Morally corrupting," used by Tovey with poetic license.—Editor.

after a *fortissimo* D, in the oboes and bassoons. The main movement (*Allegro con brio*, D major, 4/4) begins with its principal subject in the cellos and basses. There is a transitional passage leading to the second theme which, somewhat marchlike in character, appears in A major in the clarinets, answered, *fortissimo*, by the strings. The working out begins with development of the first theme, later the second subject is brought forward, a new triplet figure making its appearance in the strings. The recapitulation is ushered in with a sudden modulation to the original key of D, the first subject opening as at the beginning of the movement. The second theme, now in D major, is heard, given out by the oboes, clarinets and horns. There is an extensive coda, based for the most part upon the principal subject.

II. *Larghetto*, A major, 3/8. The principal theme is announced at once by the strings, the woodwind and horns taking it up at the eighth measure. A second section follows in the strings, the winds again repeating it. The transitional passage leading to the second subject employs new material which is set forth by the clarinet and bassoon. The second theme is announced in E major by the first violins. Another section of it, presented by the cellos and second violins in octaves, is to be noticed. Development now follows, in its turn succeeded by a recapitulation in which the first theme is presented as at the opening of the movement. The second subject, scored as before, is now in A major. There is a short coda based upon the first theme.

III. Scherzo. *Allegro*, D major, 3/4. This movement is cast in the three-part form peculiar to most—but not all—scherzos. It begins with a subject characteristically alternating *forte* and *piano*, the greater part of the first division making use of it. The trio does not change key. It begins with a simple subject played by the oboes and bassoons. The strings enter, *forte*, and the theme of the trio recurs. At the end the whole first part of the scherzo is repeated without alteration.

IV. *Allegro molto*, D major, 2/2. The finale begins with a spirited subject, in which a motive for the strings and woodwind, *forte*, alternates with a *piano* passage for the strings alone. A new theme is employed for the transitional passage. The second subject begins in the strings in D major, but soon modulates to the orthodox tonality—in this case A major. There is another section of it, which makes its appearance in the woodwind, lightly accompanied by the strings. A coda, of the conventional description of early nineteenth-century music, leads to a return of the principal theme. Development begins with a working out of the first subject. The recapitulation opens with the first theme, scored as at the beginning of the movement, and the second theme, too, is scored as at its first appearance. There is a final repetition of the principal subject. Following a pause there comes a new idea, *pianissimo*, and a coda brings the movement to a conclusion with final suggestions of its opening theme.—FELIX BOROWSKY

The symphony is scored for two flutes, two oboes, two clarinets, two bassoons, two horns, two trumpets, timpani, and strings.

In this symphony everything is noble, energetic, proud. The introduction (*largo*) is a masterpiece. The most beautiful effects follow one another without confusion and always in an unexpected manner. The song is of a touching solemnity, and it at once commands respect and puts the hearer in an emotional mood. The rhythm is already bolder, the instrumentation is richer, more sonorous, more varied. An *Allegro con brio* of enchanting dash is joined to this admirable *Adagio*. The gruppetto which is found in the first measure of the theme, given at first to the violas and cellos in unison, is taken up again in an isolated form, to establish either progressions in a *crescendo* or imitative passages between wind instruments and the strings. All these forms have a new and animated physiognomy. A melody enters, the first section of which is played by clarinets, horns, and bassoons. It is complete en tutti by the rest of the orchestra, and the manly energy is enhanced by the happy choice of accompanying chords.

The *Andante*[1] is not treated after the manner of that of the First Symphony: it is not composed of a theme worked out in canonic imitations, but it is a pure and frank song, which at first is sung simply by the strings, and then embroidered with a rare elegance by means of light and fluent figures whose character is never far removed from the sentiment of tenderness which forms the distinctive character of the principal idea. It is a ravishing picture of innocent pleasure which is scarcely shadowed by a few melancholy accents.

The scherzo is as frankly gay in its fantastic capriciousness as the andante has been wholly and serenely happy; for this symphony is smiling throughout; the warlike bursts of the first *Allegro* are wholly free from violence; there is only the youthful ardor of the noble heart in which the most beautiful illusions of life are preserved untainted. The composer still believes in immortal glory, in love, in devotion. What abandon in his gaiety! What wit! What sallies! Hearing these various instruments disputing over fragments of a theme which no one of them plays in its complete form, hearing each fragment thus colored with a thousand nuances as it passes from one to the other, it is as though you were watching the fairy sports of Oberon's graceful spirits.

The finale is of like nature. It is a second scherzo in two time, and its playfulness has perhaps something still more delicate, more piquant.—
HECTOR BERLIOZ

[1] Berlioz here refers, of course, to the *Larghetto*. In a sketchbook of Beethoven, dated 1801–2, the theme of the *Larghetto* is given to the horns, not to the strings.—Editor.

"Beethoven's Second Symphony is a crass monster, a hideously writhing wounded dragon, that refuses to expire, and though bleeding in the Finale, furiously beats about with its tail erect." (*Zeitung für die Elegante Welt*, Vienna, May 1804)—NICOLAS SLONIMSKY

II. MISCELLANEOUS WORKS FOR ORCHESTRA
a. Music for the Ballet "The Creatures of Prometheus," Opus 43

OVERTURE—Adagio; Allegro molto con brio

Act I
INTRODUCTION—Allegro non troppo
No. 1—Poco Adagio; Allegro con brio
No. 2—Adagio; Allegro con brio
No. 3—Allegro vivace

Act II
No. 4—Maestoso; Andante
No. 5—Adagio; Andante quasi allegretto
No. 6—Un poco adagio; Allegro
No. 7—Grave
No. 8—Allegro con brio; Presto
No. 9—Adagio; Allegro molto
No. 10—Pastorale; Allegro
No. 11—Andante
No. 12—Maestoso; Adagio; Allegro
No. 13—Allegro
No. 14—Andante; Allegro
No. 15—Andantino; Adagio; Allegro
No. 16—Finale, Allegretto

In June 1801, Artaria published a piano arrangement of the score [of the ballet music for *The Creatures of Prometheus*] (giving it the Opus 24, later transferred to a violin sonata) and in 1804 Hoffmeister published the orchestral parts, giving the work its present Opus 43. With the passage of time, however, and the changing tastes in ballet which finally consigned Viganò's[1] choreography to limbo, the music was also forgotten. The one exception was the overture, which was performed frequently during Beethoven's lifetime.

Beethoven was attached to his score, and while he never again wrote a ballet, many ideas from the *Prometheus* music reappeared in later works. Two themes in the finale of the ballet were turned by him into ballroom dances, as No. 7 and No. 11 of his 12 German Dances or *Contretänze*

[1] Salvatore Viganò, the choreographer, lived from 1769 to 1821 and was prominent in Viennese theatrical circles from 1793 on.—Editor.

of 1802.[1] Also in 1802, he gave the first of these, No. 7 [of the 1802 German Dances, and the main theme of the finale, No. 16, of the *Prometheus* music], a profound and exalted elaboration as the theme of his Grand Variations and Fugue for Piano, Opus 35. In a letter to the publishers Breitkopf and Härtel, Beethoven demanded that the title page of this work be altered, at his expense if necessary, to include the information that the theme was taken from his "allegorical ballet" *Prometheus*. However, we now call this work the "Eroica" Variations, due to the fact that in 1804, this same rustic dance melody found its apotheosis as the theme of the great set of variations which close the Third ("Eroica") Symphony. Furthermore in the beautiful slow movement of the Second Symphony of 1802, which itself could be called a "dance rhapsody," we can sense the presence of *Prometheus* elements (the first bars of the Adagio melody of the overture, for example, or the chain of melodies in No. 5). And reminiscences of the ballet music carry as far as the Sixth "Pastoral" Symphony of 1807-8.

In writing the *Prometheus* score, Beethoven had to adhere to the conventions of ballet music. It had to proceed as a chain of relatively short pieces, the rhythmic patterns of which had to be a translation of dance steps and gestures. The music had to enhance and seem to be inspiring the movement on the stage, but it could not absorb the listener in following extended thematic development or other structural patterns that might draw attention away from the stage. But to Beethoven, necessity was the "mother of invention," and he created a flow of winsome, graceful, and even stirring melodies. As a ballet by a major composer, it stands alone in the nineteenth century (but for ballet interludes in operas) until, in 1875, Tchaikowsky would compose *Swan Lake.*—S. W. BENNETT (1)

To subject musical expression to the exigencies of the stage, to impose an auxiliary function upon it, is a constraint to which Beethoven, truthfully speaking, in spite of *Fidelio* could never submit. An overture like the one by Egmont recapitulates the pathetic or naïve themes of the drama to the point of integrating within it the breadth of human emotion. In another sense, the musical introduction is synonymous with the piece rather than illustrating it. When the overture has culminated in the final apotheosis, there is no need for the curtain to rise: all has been said. Sufficient unto itself, such music paradoxically compromises the theater performance to which it was meant to add, and assumes its independence.

This was not the case with the dance music that Beethoven composed for the theater. The ballet of *The Creatures of Prometheus*, although it did not suffer a failure similar to that of *Fidelio*, enjoyed rather an indifferent success, remaining most often marginal in Beethovian studies.

[1] WoO 14, Kinsky-Halm.—Editor.

This episode, neglected by scholarship, is intriguing to the historian of the dance because the execution of this ballet put Beethoven in contact with the greatest choreographer of his time, the man of whom Stendhal could say: "His is an imagination in the style of Shakespeare, there is both the genius of the painter and the musician in his head." It is on a scenario by Salvatore Viganò, a Neapolitan, nephew of Boccherini, that Beethoven composed his *Prometheus* and it was this same master of ballet who directed its setting and dances.

Viganò is at this time at the height of his glory as a virtuoso, but he has not yet given his all as a choreographer, in spite of a training period of some ten years. He is still only the continuator of his father and the imitator of Dauberval, student of the great Noverre. We are still far from his mature works; those even which made Stendhal cry out at the miracle: the *Vestal*, the *Titans*, and this new *Prometheus*, staged in 1813 at la Scala in Milan and of which the one of 1801 is only a sketch. It is important for us to study this work because the "comments" by Viganò's first biographer, Carlo Ritorni, only touch upon his two sojourns in Vienna.

Under Leopold's reign, according to the poet Heinrich von Collin (author of *Regulus*, applauded at the Burgtheater), the ballets, which since the time of Noverre drew the court and the town, again came into vogue. The rivalry between Muzzarelli, the acknowledged master of ballet, and the "intruding" Salvatore Viganò brought the ferment to a head. The quarrel became so bitter that Viganò's wife, the Spanish Maria Medina "developed before the astonished spectators an art until then unheard of; the bursts of applause drowned the voices of the purists who cried 'indecency!'" The witness quoted above speaks with ecstasy about this natural, gay, free dance, about these charming and expressive gestures of the head and contrasts the "simple forms of nature" to the lifeless and worn out artifices of the Italian ballet. He also makes us conjecture about the distinguished beauty of Medina, who almost became the Lola Montez de Schoenbrunn. The liberty (if not license) of its improvisations brought out the "very classical quality of the masculine dance" of her spouse. The Viennese public was infatuated with this dangerous and fickle beauty. Beethoven was not unaware of this general infatuation. Prod'homme notes of him a minuet à la Viganò (in the style of Viganò).[1]

Nothing is clear about the manner of collaboration between Viganò and Beethoven. Ordinarily, the musical scores of Viganò's ballets are mosaics, rather dissimilar, of freely linked *morceaux* (musical compositions) in which pages from Mozart, Haydn, Grétry, or Spontini adjoin "padding" from Weigl, Lichtental, Gullemberg, and other subordinates, somewhat in the manner of modern film technique. When necessary, Viganò, musician of talent and knowledge, put his own hand to the palette.

[1] Danced, besides, not by the very beautiful Medina but by Venturini et Cecchi.

Prunières published some rather good music by him. Whatever the case may be, the idea of musical *unity* of a ballet was foreign to the master, who unscrupulously often adapted famous or obscure works, whether or not appropriate, to his subject. The case of *Prometheus*, which is entirely Beethoven's work, is thus exceptional. How did this come about?

Beethoven, who at the age of twenty had sketched a *Ballet of Chivalry* (remaining in his portfolio), composed, since 1794, certain variations on the Russian dance, interpreted by Miss Cassentini in the ballet *Das Waldmaedchen*. Knowingly, Kalischer had Cassentini appear in what he calls the "feminine entourage" of Beethoven. *The men of Prometheus* was created on March 28, 1801, at a benefit performance by Cassentini. The musical score by Beethoven could thus be an homage to an admired beauty.

All that is known leads one to believe that the performance was improvised in haste. Announced for March 21 by a sign that we find in the second posthumous *Beethoveniana*, by Nottebohm, the ballet was set forward by a week; its title was slightly modified. The program entitles it "*The Creatures of Prometheus*, a heroic ballet, allegorical in two acts, from the ingenuity and interpretation of Mr. Salvatore Viganò." It is only after the synopsis that we find the musician mentioned, who is none other than *Herr* von Beethoven, and the scene painter, *Herr* Platzer, a painter of the Imperial and Royal Chamber and theatrical decorator of the court.

It is fitting to interpret this argument *in extenso*, since no printed program of the work exists. Beethoven worked on two distinct schemas (one Italian, the other German), traces of which one finds in his notebooks. Finally, Ritorni's résumé completes his fragmentary and hasty information. Here, thus, is the text, written in a slightly macaronic German.

"The foundation of this allegorical ballet is the fable of Prometheus. The philosophers from Greece who know it expained it in this way: that he was a sublime character who, in his time, found men in a state of ignorance, refined them through the sciences and arts and impressed morals upon them.

"According to these interpretations, in the present ballet, two animated statues were represented who, by the power of harmony, are opened to all passions of human life. Prometheus leads them to Parnassus, to have Apollo, God of Beaux Arts, teach them. Apollo orders Amfione, Arione and Orpheus to teach them musical art and orders Melpomene and Thalie to reveal tragedy and comedy to them; he makes them initiate the pastoral dance invented by both Terpsichore and Pan; and the heroic dance which is the ingenuity of Bacchus."

We are far, with this shabby text, from the vast philosophical concepts that Viganò realized in Milan; it is not the great choreographical oratorio of the *Prometheus* of 1813; it is simply a cantata or divertissement to which the myth of Prometheus serves as a pretext. The true subject is an allegory of the "power of music and dance"; the entirety imagined as an homage to the protectress of the arts, Marie-Thérèse, second wife of the Emperor François. The immense success of the *Creation* by Joseph Haydn, "doctor ès music," will not have been unknown at the choice of the theme.

The manuscript of *Creatures* is not preserved for us. But a copy reviewed by the master himself exists which is at the basis of the "Canonical" edition by Breitkopf & Härtel.

The musical score includes the overture linked with the introduction and sixteen dance "numbers," isolated *morceaux*, assuming fixed, symmetrical forms without continuity in the themes; they are less the parts of a coherent whole than musical episodes juxtaposed and contrasted. Some of Beethoven's annotations, completing Ritorni's biography, allow us, as best they can, to connect the musical text to the action. The overture, very Mozartian in aspect, offers the parallel and contrasted development of two abstract themes, difficult to interpret in terms of a program. On the contrary, the introduction (containing the oldest reduction for piano entitled *Tempesta*) paints with evidence by heavy accents and punctuating bursts of eighth notes, the raging of the elements and peals of thunder. The curtain rises and we see, reads one of Beethoven's notes, "the two statues (Viganò and Cassentini) who, coming from the back-scene, slowly cross the stage. Prometheus recovers consciousness slowly . . . he was overtaken by rapture seeing that his project had been so successful and delighted about this, he gets up and signals the children to stop." According to Ritorni and the reviews of the gazettes of the time, we would have at first seen Prometheus running, pursued by the furies of the heavens, holding his torch in his hand and inflaming the hearts of the clay statues with it. Some changes of tempo express the incertitude of the situation; the lamentation of the adagio alternates with the exultation of the allegro. The second *morceau* rests on the same contrast. It begins with this lamentation by Prometheus, who does not succeed in making the statues listen to reason "and finishes by threatening them without making himself understood"; he is on the verge of destroying his work when an inner voice warns him to do nothing. Once more the allegro supersedes the adagio and it is in the same rapid movement that the finale of the tableau (which is only a prologue) unfolds; Prometheus, comforted, has conceived a new plan; he takes the statues with him.

The second act opens with a *living tableau* on Parnassus, staged without music, which, like the dance, has not yet been invented. Prometheus' entrance is emphasized by a subdued accompaniment. We see him "talking, praying." Then, from a sign of God, the animation of the statues begins. It begins by an ode to Music without words. After three chords of the harp, the flute sets forth the theme that makes the violoncello sing

powerfully. Euterpe, Amphion, Arion, Orpheus, and Delian himself participate in this concerto, without, however, characterizing the motives for
their successive interventions. "While listening to their tunes," a note explains, "the two young beings begin to show signs of reason amd reflection."
Ritorni, more explicit, shows the "candidates" at first obscurely moved,
running here and there, then awakening to more human feelings and
falling into the arms of their reputed father. Whatever may be the case,
the pantomime does not rely on any discernible reference mark in the
musical score, which is no more than an unmarked musical background.
However, the saltatorial themes already permeate the action; it is in a
polonaise movement that the animated statues, filled with admiration,
cross the stage.

However, it is only with the grand entrance of Terpsichore and Bacchus
(whose warlike character is very unforeseen in such circumstances and
poorly explained) that the so-called dance takes possession of the stage.
The corps de ballet of graces and bacchantes appears on the scene with
a grave, heavy, and spontaneous melody. The Pyrrhic dance which they
perform with the support of the bass drum has the air of a marked combat.
The tempo picks up and ends in a breathless presto. The statues, carried
away by this heroic dance, seize arms and join to take part in the feigned
battle.

Then Melpomene appears and performs a kind of mute recitative manifested by the tremolo of the chords. She finishes (we know through
Ritorni because the musical text does not lend itself to any conjecture on
this order) by striking Prometheus with her fist. Thalie comes to console
the two weeping "orphans" and places, in turn, his comic mask on each
of their faces; the gay and amusing "pastorella" of the muse is followed
by the half-solemn, half-burlesque episode of Pan, who visits Prometheus.
It becomes more and more difficult to join the musical developments to
the insufficient data of the arguments. The maestoso of the twelfth movement does not apply to anything plausible. After a flute adagio, a grotesque
"terzettino" surges between the two sequences, bounding and reminding
one of a faun, so to speak and especially if one knows what it is about.
Furthermore, there is so much pure music which we can only very
arbitrarily join to the program. One would anticipate a spectacular grand
finale by Prometheus. But what Ritorni calls the "Little Prometheus," by
contrasting it to the version of 1813, will only have been a divertissement
created at little cost and resisting the use of a complicated "technique."
In fact, these are simple dance soli which crown the denouement; that of
Cassenti on a dialogue between the flute and the horn and "choro" of
the protagonist, Salvatore Viganò, whose clarinet and bassoon vigorously
interpret the motif. Only the finale of this "little composition" (of which
Ritorni avoids naming the author) drew the attention of musicographers
to this sacrificed work. It is the theme expressing, according to scholars,

the great satisfactions of a heroic pride which Beethoven used again, in the second *contredanse* for piano, which dominates the finale of the "Eroica" Symphony; and finally in the piano variations [Opus 35], composed in 1804. The "Little Prometheus" held the stage rather well; it did not have less than sixteen performances throughout the year and thirteen others in 1802; a rather good average.

However, the *Zeitung für die Elegante Welt* states that the work "failed to please on the whole." The critic complains about the unpleasing spectacle of the fixed Parnassus, or the muses behaving like inanimate statues (until it was their turn to dance). He ironically ridicules Cassenti, who could have compensated the public the four thousand florins of receipts with a little effort and avoided the indifference which she constantly displayed toward what occurred on the stage. As for Beethoven, he was criticized for having shown himself "too learned, conforming too little to the requirements of the dance," even for a "*ballo serio*." His music, in spite of its "uncommon merits," does not answer to expectations. It was found to be uniform, indeed monotonous; he was reproached for having seen too great and exaggerated a scale for a simple *divertissement*. The critic went even so far as to insinuate plagiarism concerning Pan's entrance.

Prometheus was never, however, returned to its original form. In the version of 1813, of which Stendhal was supposed to have admired the grandiose flight still while admitting its absurdities, Viganò used a part of Beethoven's music while reinforcing it with excerpts from Haydn's *Creation*. We have tried to demonstrate, from the beginning of this article, to what point the servitude of the theater musician was incompatible with Beethoven's temperament, incapable of alienating his personality and conforming his inspiration and thought to an imposed task. Whatever his illusions may have been about this subject, deception must have been cruel, and he holds Viganò responsible. "In order to still say something about me," he writes on April 22, 1801, to Hofmeister, the musical editor in Leipzig, "I have made a ballet, but the master of ballet has not exactly executed it for the best." This disavowal serves as a conclusion to the reports, fortuitous if not forced, between the two great men: a short-lived truce arrived at between Orpheus and Terpsichore for the duration of the court spectacle and perhaps meant mostly for the beautiful eyes of a pretty dancer.—ANDRE LEVINSON (TR. BY THOMAS K. SCHERMAN)

The overture opens with an introduction (Adagio, C major, 3/4) sixteen bars long. After four fortissimo bars an expressive theme is given out by the woodwinds, horns, and strings. The main movement (Allegro molto con brio, C major, 2/2) has its principal subject given out in a rapidly moving figure by the first violins. This is repeated, fortissimo, by the full orchestra. The second theme, in G major, is given to the flutes and oboes. The development section is concerned principally with the opening subject. In the recapitulation the first theme is set forth by the first violins as in the exposition, and the second subject, now in C major, is allotted to the flutes and oboes as before. There is a lengthy coda, in which further development is given to the principal theme.—FELIX BOROWSKY

The introduction is perfect theater music, with its mysterious tremolos and hints of drama to come, capturing exactly the expectant mood of an audience when the curtain rises. No. 1, with its hesitant figures and alternating happy outbursts, and No. 2 with its dramatic contrasts, would seem to have accompanied the bringing of the clay figures to life; a kind of jolly reference to the opening of Haydn's *Creation*, which had been first heard in Vienna two years earlier. No. 3 is the most lilting of toe-dancing music and also rings down the curtain on Act I.

No. 4 is an appropriately theatrical curtain raiser to Act II, and it introduces one of the loveliest sections of the score—No. 5, perhaps a *pas de deux*, starting with harp arpeggios and a flute solo over pizzicato strings, then moving into touching modulations in a trio of bassoon, clarinet, and flute, followed by a captivating interplay of cello solo and woodwinds.

No. 6 is a sprightly dance (Allegro, 3/4) which undoubtedly por-trayed the two "creatures" of Prometheus running excitedly about in re-action to the beautiful music which has just been played by Euterpe and Amphion (No. 5). It is in a simple A-B-A form. However, the recapitula-tion of the main theme is compressed and, instead of the expected final cadence, there are three measures of portentous chords, fortissimo, which lead without interruption to the following movement, No. 7. This is marked "Grave" and starts with a pompous Handelian passage in the unison strings followed by a lyrical answering phrase in the winds. The whole movement is a subtly worked-out piece which seems to follow the pattern of one of Beethoven's slow movements in modified sonata form. There are surprise key changes and ingenious contrasts between the Han-delian character of the strings and the lyric character of the winds. Again, instead of a final cadence there is a grandiose transitional passage leading to a final impressive chord which is held suspensefully.

The tension is resolved by the opening of the next number (8), a heroic dance (Allegro con brio, 4/4) which is very martial in character. It starts with the solo timpani, playing a characteristic dotted rhythm, piano, and a short dramatic crescendo in the full orchestra leading to the main theme, which alternates a loud strident opening with a soft perky theme played pianissimo. The entire movement is a well-worked-out rondo with three contrasting episodes, the last of which ends with a suspenseful chord of the dominant in the key of the relative minor. But, without modulation, the music returns immediately to the tonic key and seems to be starting the fourth appearance of the main theme. But with dramatic surprise, typical of Beethoven's composition at this period, we hear not *the main theme but music based on it, thematically, and interrupted constantly with impressive fermatas. The last fermata is followed by four measures of alternating string and wind chords on the tonic and dominant leading into a flashy presto coda with many fanfares of the brass and drums.—Editor.*

In No. 9, which might have been devoted to Melpomene, we have another high point of the score, an introduction, followed by a poignant oboe solo over throbbing strings, which inaugurates the most somber and close-to-tragic music of the evening. Then comes a jolly Pastorale, a chain of rustic dances beginning with a bagpipe drone. Could this have been the Bacchus episode? It also hints at the coming "Pastoral" Symphony. Beethoven is here working on a broader scale than in the first act.

No. 11 is nothing but a short eight-measure introduction, typical of classical ballets, to accompany the entrance of a solo dancer (in this case Thalia) who takes her place for the next big number. Her solo (No. 12) is a comic dance in which a mock-serious introduction is followed by a beautiful Adagio flute solo in triple time. This, however, is cut short by a pause on a fortissimo dominant seventh chord. The Allegro which succeeds it is a joyful dance in 4/4 contrasting soft, sprightly phrases in the winds with impressive fortissimo passages in the strings and brass. No. 13 is a typical lighthearted contredanse which might easily be played in the Viennese ballrooms of the time. It is a succession of eight- or sixteen-bar dance themes, each coming to a distinct close and proceeding, without benefit of modulatory or transitional passages, to the following one. It holds no musical surprises, except for an occasional unexpected pause, which probably had choreographic significance.—Editor.

No. 14 is a beautiful Haydnesque Sinfonia concertante for basset horn (its only appearance in Beethoven's works) and [oboe], like a folksy slow movement and rondo. No. 15 is a lively, melodious little three-movement Sinfonia or Serenade (Andantino; Adagio; Allegro) that sounds positively Schubertian. (Could Schubert have studied this score before he wrote the *Rosamunde* music?) No. 16 is the grand finale, starting with the now famous "Eroica" dance theme, and developing it, along with its companion country-dance theme, in a blaze of hilarity and high spirits.— S. W. BENNETT (1)

The overture and the ballet music are scored for two flutes, two oboes, two clarinets, two bassoons, basset horn, two horns, two trumpets, timpani, harp, and strings.

b. 12 *Minuets for Orchestra,* WoO 7;
    12 *German Dances for Orchestra,* WoO 8

Both of these sets of "popular" dances were written for the yearly benefit masked ball given by the Pension Society for Viennese Painters in November 1795. The society evidently could afford prominent composers as well as conductors, for in previous years such eminent musical figures as Haydn, Koželuch, and Dittersdorf had provided the original music—each time thirteen minuets and twelve German dances or allemandes. The announcement of this particular occasion read in part: "The music for the Minuets and Allemandes for this ball is again entirely new . . . For the big hall [the Redoutensaal], the compositions have been especially created by the 'Meisterhand' [in the sense of master craftsman] of Ludwig van Beethoven out of the love for the Artistic Community."

Because of other monumental compositions for orchestra by Beethoven, audiences have a tendency to ignore these unpretentious but thoroughly enchanting popular pieces. However, there are many signs of the "Meisterhand" both in the harmony, the voice writing, and particularly in the orchestration.

The minuets are all in standard dance form—a two-part first section of eight or sixteen bars (each part repeated) and a two-part trio (each part also repeated) and a reprise of the main section. Evidently Beethoven reverted to the baroque meaning of the "trio," so-called in French classical dances because this middle section was customarily played by three solo winds (two oboes or flutes and a bassoon) in contrast to the strings or full orchestra, which played the main section of the minuet. There is exceptional solo wind writing in the trios of Nos. 1, 2, and 3, a brilliant clarinet solo in the trio of No. 4 and a prominent independent flute part in No. 12. The solo horns are used very effectively in Nos. 3 and 10.

Other Beethovian touches are the echo effects in the second half of the trio of No. 3, the scherzolike pizzicato string writing in the trio of No. 5, the subtle canonic writing in Nos. 6 and 12, the odd phrase length in the second half of No. 10, the surprise offbeat accents in No. 9, and the very military use of the trumpets and drums in Nos. 4, 7, and 11.

The German dance is also in triple time but is less formal than the minuet. It was originally a peasant dance in which the dancers placed their hands firmly on the backs of their partners and turned back and forth. A later derivative (undoubtedly danced around this time by aristocrats as well as commoners) was the ländler, a strictly Austrian product, which was more gliding than its German peasant predecessor, and included a love pantomime and the kissing of one's partner. Both the

German dance and the ländler are direct forerunners of the waltz—the ländler especially so because it was the first popular dance in which the partners put their arms around one another.

There are many more craftsmanlike subleties in this group than in the minuets. There is highly subtle polyphonic writing in the second half of No. 3. The trio of No. 4 has typical Beethovian syncopated writing. The trumpets and drums are used in a very symphonic manner in No. 5 and there are lovely solos for the clarinets and horns in its trio. The trio of No. 6 is a typical ländler with its smooth, sinuous string writing and its peasantlike drone bass. It is very reminiscent of the trio of Mozart's "Linz" Symphony and Symphony No. 39. The offbeat accents and the great downward leaps are surprising foreshadows of the Scherzo of the great string quartet, Opus 132. Beethoven makes very characteristic use of the piccolo in the trio of No. 10 and for the only time in either set makes use of the so-called *militar-musik*—the triangle, snare drum, tambourine, and bass drum—a self-conscious extramusical effect used frequently by serious composers in the war-torn Vienna of the 1770's and '80's.

The most fascinating feature of these dances, musically, is the fact that there is an extended coda to the group symphonic in its proportions. It starts like the trio of the last dance (No. 12), so to the unaware listener it seems like a second appearance of that trio after the recapitulation of the main section. However, the simple thematic material is immediately developed and after a dramatic held chord on the dominant seventh harmony there is an enchanting solo for posthorn—a signal for the dancers that the ball is over and that they should go home. It is repeated after a long dramatic crescendo which is the trademark of the mature Beethoven. The piece ends with a massive fanfare of trumpets, horns, and drums, far more suitable to an opera or symphony than to the close of this simple but elegant group of popular dances.—THOMAS K. SCHERMAN

Both groups of dances are scored for piccolo, two flutes, two oboes, two clarinets, two bassoons, two horns, two trumpets, timpani, and strings (without violas). The German dances also call for triangle, tambourine, snare drum, bass drum, and a solo posthorn.

c. 6 Gesellschafts-Menuette for Two Violins and Bass, WoO 9

This group of minuets, written around the same time as the minuets (WoO 7) and the German dances (WoO 8) for the November 1795 Benefit Ball, are on a smaller scale, being just for strings. Incidentally the lack of a separate part for violas (true in all of these sets of popular dances) is not surprising—unsophisticated orchestras of the time had few or no accomplished violists, and those that they did have merely doubled the bass line. The bass line, however, was played by both violon-

cellos and string basses and in several instances Beethoven indicates a
separate part for the cellos. Although the themes are mentioned in
Thayer's 1865 catalogue of Beethoven's works, they were not published
until 1933, when they were resurrected by Georg Kinsky, the famous
Beethoven scholar and author of the most authoritative thematic and
bibliographical catalogue of the complete musical output of Beethoven.

There is little of musical sophistication in the works. One might point
out the marcato pizzicato chords in the trio of No. 3, alternating with
gentle ländlerlike arco writing. In No. 5 there is a subtle alternation of
unison passages and harmonized melodies. The light staccato triplet accompaniment in the second violins in the trio of No. 5 is particularly
delightful. The distinguishing characteristic of No. 6, in G major, is the
fact that the last repetition of the main theme starts in A minor instead of
the expected G major, but Beethoven quickly shifts the harmonies, ending comfortably in the tonic.—THOMAS K. SCHERMAN

d. 6 Minuets for Orchestra, WoO 10

Time of Composition: 1795, like WoO 7–9[1] (the appearance of the piano
arrangement: 1796). In Thayer's chronological catalogue (No. 292, page
170) he quotes the following observation by Dr. Sonnleithner:[2] "These
six minuets have survived only in the piano transcription prepared by
Beethoven for publication by Artaria and Co. in 1796; but considering
their content and the indication '2nd Part,' it is highly probable that
they were composed for orchestra." Nottebohm (in his thematic catalogue,
page 150) also holds this view.

W. Hess surmises that this group of six minuets along with the preceding
six (WoO 9) were conceived as a complete cycle of twelve minuets.
"These six minuets which appear in Edition of the Complete Works
[as No. 194] are consequently a piano arrangement of the second part
of a group of twelve minuets for two violins and bass, of which the score
is lost and of which the first part has come down to us only in the individual instrumental parts." To this, however, may be added that the
manner of instrumental setting [voice leading, etc.] suggests more a full
orchestra than a string trio (notice especially the thick texture of No. 6).
Also the title "2nd part" printed in the piano transcription is similar to
that of the previous piano transcription of the twelve minuets for orchestra, WoO 7, which appeared in December 1795.—GEORG KINSKY,
EDITED BY HANS HALM (TR. BY THOMAS K. SCHERMAN)

[1] See essays on 12 Minuets for Orchestra, WoO 7; 12 German Dances for Orchestra,
WoO 8; and 6 Minuets for 2 Violins and Bass, WoO 9.—Editor.
[2] Dr. Joseph von Sonnleithner, 1766–1835, intendant of the court theaters in Vienna
from 1804–14 and translator of Beethoven's "Leonore" from the French of Bouilly.
—Editor.

Each of the six minuets is in two parts, each repeated, plus a trio, also in two repeated parts, which in all but one case is more lyrical than the minuet proper, which is usually of a robust nature. Harmonically and thematically they are quite a bit more sophisticated than the earlier set of six, WoO 9. The second minuet is the famous "Minuet in G." The trio of the fourth minuet in B flat exhibits a unique manner of overlapping leading voice that definitely indicates that it was originally conceived for orchestra with each phrase played on a different instrument. Likewise the delicate trio of No. 5, in D major, certainly suggests pizzicato strings. The most instrumental of all, however, is the trio of No. 6, in C major. Its dotted rhythm and its imitative phrases in different registers are indicative of brass fanfares answered by lighter strings or winds.—Editor.

e. 7 "Ländlerische Tänze," WoO 11

Thayer lists these unpretentious dances as being written "before 1799." They appear in the Breitkopf and Härtel Complete Edition as piano works, but Kinsky says they were probably originally written for two violins and bass (violoncello). Willy Hess, in an article in the *Schweitzerische Musikzeitung und Sängerblatt* (Vol. 70, 1930, page 886) gives credence to Kinsky's supposition by pointing out that the set of six "*Ländlerische Tänze*" for pianoforte that appears in the complete edition as a piano set is actually a piano transcription by the composer of the six orchestral dances, WoO 15, according to the title page of the first edition (Artaria and Company, 1802), with the only difference being that the order of the first two dances is reversed.

All seven of the WoO 11 set are in D major, suggesting they were played as a continuous group. As has been mentioned before, they are harmonically and thematically quite unsophisticated. However, the drone bass of No. 3, the supple broken-chord writing in the second part of No. 4, as well as the clever dominant pedal point in No. 5, lift the set out of the realm of the banal. A coda which follows No. 7 with the most subtle references to thematic material drawn from several of the dances is a very definite Beethoven touch. By this device he showed that he was thinking symphonically and that, far from being a group of individual dances joined together merely by key, the set was conceived as a whole. This delightful coda ends with a prolonged diminuendo very reminiscent of the Piano Sonata Opus 28 (the "Pastoral"), which was written three years later. Probably in creating the latter Beethoven was unconsciously thinking of the simple dance which he wrote for the enjoyment of the patrons of the Redoutensaal.—THOMAS K. SCHERMAN *f. 12 Minuets for Orchestra, WoO 12; 12 German Dances with Coda, for Orchestra, WoO 13*

In May 1872, the archivist of the *Wiener Pensionsgesellschaft*, Anton Perger, discovered a file with twelve minuets by Beethoven that were not similar to those which he wrote in 1795[1] for the same society. They were given by Perger to the National Library. [Perger's] supposition that these minuets were written in 1799 was corroborated by the inscription on the only existing bass part: "*Dal Signor Luigi de Beethoven, 1799.*" He also surmised that they were not performed at the Artists' Ball in that year because twelve minuets by Anton Teyber and twelve German dances by Count Wilhelm Lichnowsky had been given in the large ballroom, and twelve minuets were composed for the smaller hall by the treasury officer Josef Lipavsky, where, also, twelve German dances by Franz Teyber were repeated on November 24, 1799. Now it is hard to believe that Beethoven would have written these minuets without specific invitation by the Pension Society, or that the *"Meister"* of the years 1795–99 would be treated so offhandedly that the dances requested of him would not be performed. However, the fact remains that they were found in the archives of the society and that the file which contained them resembled an earlier one, which somewhat justified Perger's supposition.

It is noteworthy that Beethoven's new minuets were copied out for the smaller hall—there exist sixteen parts but no director's score—and yet that he, as composer, was supplanted by one of the two dilettantes of the year, namely, Lipavsky.

They have been published in a piano arrangement by Jean Chantavoine (1903), and later (1906) reconstructed for orchestra by him. He also filled in the missing viola part for the latter edition.

Of the twelve minuets in varying keys, most noteworthy are No. 10, which thematically resembles the Andante of the Septet, Opus 20, and No. 11, which makes conspicuous use of the solo horns. The first minuet is more like a military fanfare than a piece of music to be danced to. Its use of the horns, trumpets, and drums is a harbinger of the music for band which appeared ten years later in 1809.—Editor.

The [twelve] German dances must have been written around the same time as these puzzling minuets. Whereas with the latter their origin (the Pension Society) and the date on the bass part (1799) supply a reference point, the title page of the German dances clearly testifies to their original appearance at the small hall of the Pension Society. [The title page reads: "*XII Deutsche Tänze mit Koda fur den K. k. kleinen Redouten-Saale in*

[1] WoO 7.—Editor.

Wein/Komponier von Ludwig van Beethoven."] Certainly it is to be concluded that these dances were definitely performed.

The original orchestral setting, which is lost, was undoubtedly for the normal small dance orchestra—two violins, two flutes, two oboes, two clarinets, two bassoons, two horns, two trumpets, timpani, and bass. They are examples of practical dance music typical of the time, but replete with typical Beethovian modifications. The second part of the eleventh dance is very similar to the second movement of the A minor Quartet, Opus 132, as has been pointed out by Riemann.—OTTO ERICH DEUTSCH (TR. BY THOMAS K. SCHERMAN

Equally noteworthy are the scherzo-like theme of No. 2, which is definitely related to the Minuet of the First Symphony, and the dramatic fall of two octaves from the upbeat to the downbeat of No. 4 as well as its drone bass, both of which are reminiscent of the D major Sonata (the "Pastoral"), Opus 28. The thematic motive of a simple mordent in the Trio of No. 4 is used as the basis of an extended coda which is replete with bold modulations and very sophisticated thematic development.— Editor.

g. 12 Country Dances, WoO 14

The giants who brought the great music of sonata form and symphony into being—men like Haydn, Mozart, Beethoven and Schubert—were anything but one-sided. In addition to their epic achievements they provided the people of their time with some of the most enchanting dance music to which anyone ever lifted a toe. And what they wrote in this form was genuine popular dance music, made of the musical common coin of their time, intended to be played in ballrooms and beer gardens, even in village streets. The listeners of the late eighteenth or early nineteenth century could recognize the rhythms and turns of phrase of their popular music even in the most serious works of the great masters.

Ludwig van Beethoven differed greatly from Haydn and Schubert in the way in which he used this popular material. The latter two would frequently bring a popular-style song or dance melody directly into a large-scale work and then proceed to vary or develop it. In Beethoven's art the process is more complicated. His symphonies are rich in material taken from dance, and from its close kin, the march. Beethoven has put the popular material he knew and loved through an additional process of distillation and reworking, before introducing it into a larger work. And so those who know only the symphonies and chamber works will find in these twelve country dances a different Beethoven, even a surprising one. Yet there are close connections to his big works.

The country dance originated in England, then spread to France as the

Contredanse, and finally arrived in Germany as the *Contratänz*. It is a generic term, not referring to a specific dance step, but to a style of dance and music which, in Rousseau's description, "should have marked rhythms and be brilliant and gay, yet with much simplicity." Such dances were welcomed in ballrooms as a refreshing change from the more stately minuet. Beethoven's *Contratänze* are mostly in two-part form, and in 2/4 time.

The set of twelve country dances was probably written in the fall of 1801 or in 1802, and intended for the Vienna balls. It was published, without opus number, in 1803.[1] In 1801 Beethoven was still a young and "promising" composer. Few major works of his were known to the broad Vienna public. And so, while writing these gay dances, Beethoven seized the occasion to spread further the music from a work on which he pinned great hopes, the ballet *The Creatures of Prometheus*. And indeed this ballet became one of his great early successes, being performed sixteen times in 1802 and thirteen in 1803.

The melody which Beethoven took from his *Prometheus* ballet and made into a country dance, the third dance [of the group],[2] is the same one which the composer was to use again in his piano variations, Opus 35, and finally in the last movement of his "Eroica" Symphony. In the bass of the seventh dance [of the group] we can find a suggestion of the *menuetto* of the Eighth Symphony. The eleventh again has a hint of the *Prometheus* theme.—SIDNEY FINKELSTEIN

The original score called for strings (without viola) and "wind instruments: ad libitum." Beethoven filled in the following wind parts: one flute, two oboes, two clarinets, two bassoons, and two horns.

h. 6 German Dances for Two Violins and Bass, WoO 15

These dances were conceived during the period of Beethoven's work on the Second Symphony, which is perhaps one of the reasons why the predominant key of the dances is D major, as is that of the symphony. Other similarities exist between the symphony and the dances, such as the chromatic inner-voice harmonies of the sixth dance, which are so much more dramatic when they (the chromatics) appear in the bass of the codas of the first and last movements of the symphony, albeit the resulting harmonic scheme is the same in all three places; likewise the offbeat accents of the symphony's scherzo are very noticeably anticipated

[1] The set is identified as WoO 14 in the Kinsky-Halm catalogue.—Editor.
[2] Actually, No. 7, according to Kinsky-Halm.—Editor.

in the first and fifth dances, and there is a decided thematic similarity between the dramatic descending leap of a tenth which characterizes the melodic scheme of the fifth dance and the similar melodic scheme of the scherzo of the symphony. The gradual and dramatic crescendo in the second half of the second dance is a precursor of the equally dramatic but much longer crescendos in the codas of the first and fourth movements of the symphony. It is also interesting to note that there is a long coda to the dances (forty-five measures long, as compared with the sixteen measures of each of the six dances) which is symphonic in conception: it takes up the thematic scheme of the last (the sixth dance) and *develops* it both melodically and harmonically; after an excursion into the relative minor key (which was anticipated in the third dance) it is pursued downward to the subdominant in the coda, after which the tonic key is proudly reinstated, fortissimo, preparing the thoroughly grand and symphonic close.

Other interesting musical features of the dances are the key relationship between Nos. 3 and 4 (the latter being the only one of the six in the tonic minor rather than major); the mazurka-type rhythm in the fourth dance; and, above all, the subtle offbeat accents on the second as well as the third beats of certain measure groups in the fifth dance resulting in a "hemiolia"—that is, a 3/2 measure made up of two 3/4 measures with offbeats accents—which is so predominant in many of Brahms's chamber works. Also there is a rather innocent (for Beethoven) voice imitation between the two upper voices in the second half of the sixth dance which, however, is given distinct subtlety by the daring pedal which underpins it and the clashing harmonies which result thereby.

All in all, the dancing couples for whom WoO 15 was written were unwittingly treated to music which was a foretaste of the great Second Symphony, which was so much to mystify and titillate the audiences at a symphonic concert six months later.—THOMAS K. SCHERMAN

III. CONCERTI
    a. Piano Concerto No. 1 in C, Opus 15
      I. Allegro con brio; II. Largo; III. Rondo: Allegro

The first three pianoforte concertos of Beethoven show, in the opening tuttis of their first movements, a phenomenon almost unique in his works. In other branches of music we may find signs of a struggle with stubborn material, and Beethoven himself sometimes admitted that for this or that problem of vocal and dramatic music he had "not studied enough." But in the first two pianoforte concertos all is facile and spacious, while in the third, in C minor, which he declared, before he wrote it, "will be the best of the three," he not only made a great stride in the direction of his "second style," but set the model for the orthodox concerto form of his younger contemporaries and later theorists. Yet in all three concertos the nature of the opening tutti is radically misconceived; and that of the C minor Concerto executes a charmingly dramatic *volte-face* in mid-career, as if to say "But no!—I must not be the beginning of a symphony." In his later concertos Beethoven realized and carried out the purpose of Mozart's opening tutti, one of the subtlest and grandest art-forms ever devised; but no sooner was he able to do this than he was able to transcend Mozart in every line of instrumental and harmonic form, so that contemporary and later orthodoxy blundered far more grossly about his concerto form than any early failure of his to see the purport of Mozart's.

The composer or theorist may imagine that because Mozart's tutti is voluminous and flowing it is also discursive and can indulge in passages of development. Or he may imagine that it can be throughout like the exposition of a symphony, and that it should accordingly display its first subject, transition, and second subject, so that the listener knows beforehand exactly what the solo instrument is going to do. The first misapprehension is shown by Beethoven in his first two concertos; the second appears in the C minor Concerto and is instantly corrected, but not until its impression has been made with such force that, until Brahms came to the rescue, the opening tutti of the classical concerto remained a mystery to composers and theorists alike.

Now the C major Concerto (which is later than the B flat Concerto published second to it as Opus 19) seems to have been an object of more interest to Beethoven than he admitted. At all events he wrote no less than three cadenzas to its first movement, and the third of these cadenzas is one of his most splendid successes in recording the style of an extemporization. It is fully in his "second manner," and the compass given to the pianoforte shows that it must have been written at least as late as the published score of the C minor Concerto, that is to say, later than the Kreutzer Sonata, and not much earlier than the Waldstein Sonata, which it closely resembles in pianoforte technique. It affords a noble pretext for reviving a neglected early master-piece which it harmoniously lifts to a higher plane of musical thought.

The C major Concerto begins with quiet and martial energy. A forte counterstatement leads to a grand pause on the dominant, upon which a fragment of the second subject appears in a remote key, and is carried through other keys in rising sequence.

This is very beautiful; but processions (or concerto tuttis) will get into difficulties if they often thus digress in search of the picturesque; and it is this passage which Beethoven worked up bodily into his, unfortunately incomplete, first cadenza. The next passage, founded on [the opening theme], is also discursive and forms the opening text for all the three cadenzas.

At last the orchestra settles down to a cadence theme in Beethoven's most British grenadiers style, and with a final paragraph [based] on [the octave jump of the opening theme], the orchestra comes to a formal close. Not until the G major Concerto did Beethoven follow the example, twice set by Mozart, of letting the solo enter on the dominant chord with an introductory passage. On the other hand he follows several examples of Mozart in beginning with an entirely new theme, though, unlike Mozart, he omits to develop it later, not even finding room for it in any of his cadenzas. The orchestra intervenes with [the octave jump of the opening theme of the orchestral tutti], and the dialogue now follows the orthodox course of a concerto, the pianoforte working out a broad transition to G major, where [the lyrical theme, originally stated by the orchestra, now] appears as a regular and complete melody by way of second subject. After a short digression, [the "grenadiers" cadence theme] follows, and brilliant passages then run an easy course.

The development is, as usual in concertos, largely episodic, the pianoforte beginning grandly with another entirely new theme. Perhaps one reason why Beethoven abandoned his first cadenza was a feeling that if he once began to pick up loose threads there would be no end to the task; and that the true course was to accept the pleasure that the Mozartean Angel of All Art-Forms allows to those who Really Can Extemporize.

The return to the recapitulation is gravely dramatic in Beethoven's best "first style"; the pianoforte taking its final plunge thereinto by an octave-glissando; at which the modern pianoforte jibs. The recapitulation itself is adroitly curtailed as to the first subject and unaltered as to the second.

And now comes the pause for the cadenza. Beethoven's third cadenza storms away in magnificent Waldstein-sonata style, at first apropos of [the development of the octave jump of the opening theme], which starts on a voyage round the solar system. The second subject appears at last in vastly remote keys, and drifts sublimely from the style of *La Clemenza di Tito* to the style of *Fidelio*. Thunderous further developments of [the octave jump] burst forth, and at last the usual final trill is heard; but surely rather too much on the dominant of G? Quite so; we have something to say in G major about [the cadence theme]; please don't interrupt! This being said, the trill arrives again and develops with great excitement—while the orchestra waits for the final turn. Instead of which the trill trails off into runs. And at last the cadenza ends without any trill at all.

The difficulties of the classical concerto form are almost entirely confined to the first movement, and especially to its ritornello. In slow movements and rondos Beethoven was from the outset as great a master in concertos as in other instrumental forms; and [an examination] of themes is all the commentary required for the rest of this unjustly neglected work. The largo begins with a three-strain melody (A, B, A), of which [a sweeping eight-bar lyric and diatonic melody makes up] the first clause.

A broadly designed transition to the dominant gives an impression that the whole may be developed into full sonata form with [a second subject based on a theme curiously reminiscent of the piano's entrance in the first movement]. But Beethoven prefers to keep space for a less crowded scheme, and he brings back his whole first melody with rich ornamentation and new scoring (in all his early orchestral works there is no other example showing such appreciation of the clarinet), and, without any allusion to the middle portion, concludes with a long-drawn coda full of solemn new ideas.

Beethoven never wrote a wittier paragraph with more Haydnesque irregularity of rhythm than the main theme of the rondo of this concerto. The first episode, which is treated (as in all full-sized concerto-rondos) like a second subject, gives rise to a romantic digression in E flat and G minor, such as has made the second subject of the first movement of Beethoven's First Symphony famous; and it is remarkable in how many points the First Symphony follows cautiously the steps this rondo had already taken firmly and boldly.

The returns to the main theme are effected by [a] Schubertesque transformation [of the second subject].

The middle episode alternates two superb themes in contrast, the one spirited and the other quiet, chromatic, and polyphonic.

The rest of the movement arises naturally out of these materials, and the coda is full of Haydn-Beethoven surprises, being (with the addition of several small underdeveloped cadenzas) a glorified version of the later and less elaborate comic windup of the First Symphony.— DONALD FRANCIS TOVEY (4)

Besides piano, the score calls for one flute, two oboes, two clarinets, two bassoons, two horns, two trumpets, timpani, and strings.—Editor

b. Piano Concerto No. 2 in B Flat, Opus 19
I. Allegro con brio; II. Adagio; III. Rondo: Molto allegro

In 1795 Beethoven published his *Opus 1*, three trios for piano, violin, and cello. During that same year he made his first public appearance in Vienna, of which he had become a resident shortly before. The chief item of interest in that program of March 29, 1795, was his own performance of the solo part in his *Piano Concerto in B flat major*, the earliest of his works employing orchestra which he acknowledged by publication. Although he had certainly written it as a vehicle for his own performance, the *Concerto* did not please him. He tampered and fussed at it, effecting a final revision of the entire piece during 1800. By the time he permitted its publication in 1801 he had already published the *Piano Concerto in C major, opus 15*. This required him to label the *B flat major* "No. 2," though its original composition had preceded that of No. 1. [It] is dedicated to "Carl Nikl, Noble of Nikelsberg."

The intensely romantic, stormy, and fearlessly original Beethoven of later years is only suggested by the *Second Piano Concerto*. He is present in its notes, but concealed—and to listen for him is probably to miss the classical charm and eighteenth-century polish that mark it so definitely with the manners of Haydn and Mozart.

I. [The concerto] opens with an *allegro con brio* in which the solo piano is largely reserved for comment on what the orchestra has already stated, most of the important melodic material being given first to the orchestra.[1]

[1] For Beethoven's writing-out of the cadenzas to his own piano concerti and their stylistic discrepancies from the movements for which they were written, see the footnote to the Piano Concerto No. 3, Opus 37, on page 149.

Beethoven's cadenza (1809–10) to the first movement of Opus 19 (1795–96) bears a similar relationship to the movement for which it was written, as the New York edition (1908) of Henry James' *Daisy Miller* does to its original publication (1878), or Verdi's reworking in 1881 (between *Aïda* and *Otello*) of his 1857 *Simon Boccanegra*. It was not, as in James and Verdi, an attempt to reproduce or re-edit or recompose a complete work of the past from beginning to end, and to make out of its best features a new, completely reoriented creation approached from the new point of view of the creator's own maturity. Beethoven's was, let us say, the easier way out, an interpolated comment on an earlier work—a footnote, as it were—showing how he would have approached the thematic material if he had had his present felicity at that time. It is no more an integrated part of the first movement than was Patti's rendition of Variations on "Home Sweet Home" or "Comin' Through the Rye" in the lesson scene of Rossini's *Barber of Seville* compatible with the music of the rest of the opera. It is, on the other hand, a complete and fascinating composition within itself, and is, therefore, revealing and exciting for us, as well as for the audiences of 1809–10, to listen to. (After all, the taste of the highly aware audience of *that* time must have changed considerably in the intervening fourteen years.)

After the pregnant 6/4 chord in the orchestra, Beethoven does not attempt to resolve it through a 5/7 chord or some other related progression. Instead he commences a completely worked out fugue ("con alcuna licenza," as he was to compose for the Opus 106 Piano Sonata) based, more or less, on the virile opening theme. As Tovey remarks, fugues or fugatos *within* a composition in sonata form (as opposed to separate compositions in fugal form) are dangerous, because they harmonically progress nowhere —for the moment the over-all tonal picture stands still. Beethoven obviously was aware of this, because his plan of the cadenza is not the usual progression of chords from tonic 6/4, through a succession of interrelated and preferably highly extraneous chords, to the final trill on the dominant seventh harmony, leading into the final entrance of the orchestra. Instead his cadenza is a complete short separate fugal composition within itself, beginning *and* ending in the tonic.

In some of the episodes within the fugue he recalls the lyric second theme and some of the sixteenth-note passage work that occurred during the movement. However

II. The middle movement, an *adagio*, is not one of those ecstatic, hushed slow movements which Beethoven made into magic in later years, but a successful essay in decoration. The contours of its melodic matter are often wreathed in figurations and arabesques. As it nears its close the solo piano alternates with the orchestra, a seemingly conversational or argumentative device of which Beethoven was very fond, and of which he made much.

III. The finale of the *B flat major Concerto* is a *rondo*. It neatly reverses the construction of the opening movement, allowing the piano to set forth melodic and other ideas on which the orchestral ensemble makes comment. It is a fittingly eighteenth-century conclusion to the first composed of the pieces Beethoven published, the trios of *opus* 1 possibly excepted. It is music-making for music's own self-sufficient sake, quite devoid both of the darker inklings of tragedy which marked Mozart's maturity and of the autobiographical urgency of some of the music that Beethoven himself would shortly be composing.—HERBERT WEIN- STOCK

The piano is accompanied by flute, two oboes, two clarinets, two bassoons, two horns, two trumpets, timpani, and strings.

c. Piano Concerto No. 3 in C Minor, Opus 37
I. Allegro con brio; II. Largo; III. Rondo: Allegro vivace, Presto

Beethoven's third concerto was projected at the same time as his first and second; neither of which, as he openly avowed, was so important as this, for which he was reserving his best efforts. It is one of the works in which we most clearly see the style of his first period preparing to develop into that of his second. The main theme is a group of pregnant figures which nobody but Beethoven could have invented. They would rank as important themes in his latest works; but he here states them, quite successfully and unselfconsciously, in the tonic-and-dominant symmetries that still interested him for their own sake in

the emphasis is on the fugue "theme" constructed upon the opening theme of the movement.

Beethoven dispenses with the usual and expected ultimate trill on the dominant seventh chord by the soloist. He closes his busy "fugue" on three repetitions of the tonic chord played pianissimo in the low register of the piano. Instead of the usual trill, he substitutes a spectacular scale passage up and down the keyboard in unison, thirds, and sixths, from the lowest B flat to the B flat in altissimo. And there is a crescendo throughout the passage from pianissimo to fortissimo.

As every conductor knows, the soft entrance of the orchestra for its last six measures of comment after this exciting interpolated composition is, at the very best, the most embarrassing of anticlimaxes. On the other hand, I feel Beethoven's own backward look at the child of his youth is worth the dramatic consequences!—Editor.

his first period. With the transition theme he emphasizes the barest harmonic formulas with a youthful sententiousness peculiar to an artist who has grown conscious that these formulas are still necessary but no longer interesting, and that until some totally new light can be shed on them they are best left undecorated. (Two other works in the same key, the C minor Quartet, opus 18, No. 4, and the C minor Violin Sonata, show the same drastic simplicity at this juncture.)

Now comes a turning-point in the history of the classical concerto.[1] The opening orchestral ritornello of the first movement in the concerto form had been developed by Mozart on a scale that has not to this day been surpassed; with the result that the entry of the solo instrument must, if it means anything at all, mean an event impressive because long delayed. If, then, long delayed, it must be long expected; and the expectation must be roused by the music and not merely by the title of the item on the program. Mozart's opening tuttis are among the highest triumphs of art in their command of expectant exposition; no two examples are identical in their own plan, or in relation to the solo. Nor can Mozart's forms be correctly said to have a restraining influence on Beethoven's early work. *To him these forms were no more orthodox than the forms of Richard Strauss were to the young composers of 1900.*[2]

At all events Beethoven had something better to do than to consult textbooks on the subject of concerto form. He did not immediately achieve Mozart's solution of the problem of the opening tutti; indeed it is arguable that he did not at first grasp what the problem really was. In the C minor Concerto [the transition theme] takes direct dramatic action and leads to a long passage of preparation for the second subject in its destined new key. This is sheer symphonic exposition; it rouses no expectation of the entry of a solo instrument, and, as we shall find, leaves nothing essential for the pianoforte to add when its time comes. The second subject [consists of] a cantabile midway between a Mozart heroine and the heroine of Beethoven's *Coriolanus* overture. Suddenly the orchestra seems to realize that it has no right to take the drama into its own hands; that its function is not drama but chorus-like narrative; and with a modulation in itself dramatic, the melody calmly turns round to C major and is followed by a series of cadence-phrases in the tonic minor (including derivatives of [the opening theme]) which bring this, the longest of all Beethoven's concerto tuttis, to a massive formal close.

The works of Beethoven that have had the most influence on later composers are rather such transitional compositions than the compositions which Beethoven himself based on the experience he gained therein. It is the C minor Concerto that has ever since been taken as the

[1] Italics by the editor.
[2] Italics by the editor.

normal classical example, and not the G major and E flat Concertos, which are supposed to introduce bold innovations. *Yet it is only in these later works that Beethoven achieves Mozart's methods of handling the opening tutti*[1] plus his own methods of setting the solo free. Spohr, Hummel, Chopin (in his F minor Concerto), and even Joachim in his Hungarian Concerto, all took Beethoven's C minor Concerto as their model for concerto form; and they all regarded as an inimitable and individual stroke of genius the one feature (the sudden shift back to the tonic during the announcement of the second subject) by which Beethoven rectifies something that dangerously resembled a mistake. This stroke being thus regarded as unorthodox, the "classical" opening tutti henceforth became accepted as an ordinary symphonic exposition, prefixed, for reasons impious to inquire, to a sonata for a solo instrument with orchestral accompaniment. *No wonder the easy common sense of Mendelssohn abolished this convention.*[2] Until Brahms tackled the true problem again, the vitality of concerto forms was becoming the vitality of undesirable things.

Beethoven, then, has in this C minor opening tutti recognized and saved a dangerous situation in the nick of time. The pianoforte can now enter and restate the exposition that the orchestra has given. Beyond two introductory bars of scales, dramatically useful in later entries, and a slight expansion of the passage of preparation for the second subject, the pianoforte follows the opening tutti, bar for bar, until the second subject [the *cantabile*] has arrived. Here there is of course no need for the *volte-face* made in the original tutti: the pianoforte is now at last free to expand the material into a brilliant group of new phrases. These consist mainly of developments of [rhythmic jumps of tonic and dominant, which make up the third and fourth measures of the opening theme; these appear] with running accompaniments, culminating in a long [trill], below which clarinets and horns enter with a triumphant version of the whole theme. Then the full orchestra bursts out with its cadence phrases, and soon proceeds to shed new light on the long passage of preparation for the second subject by giving it in G minor.

This is a genuine and important innovation, which Beethoven uses with powerful effect in the E flat Concerto, and in the Violin Concerto. Mozart never lets his second tutti modulate, and always brings it to a full close. Beethoven's new experiment goes far to set his form free. The pianoforte enters with its introductory scales, not as a formula on a tonic, but as a dramatic intervention on a dominant. It then settles down to a pathetic cantabile development of [the opening theme, the rhythmic jumps of which unify] the whole design by persisting as

[1] Italics by the editor.
[2] Italics by editor.

an accompaniment. In broad and distinct steps the threshold of C minor is reached, and, after suitable preparation, the first subject begins the recapitulation fortissimo. After the close of the second subject (the triumphant clarinets beneath the final [trill] now becoming trumpets), the orchestra enters in the minor and soon leads to the usual pause for a cadenza,[1] which Beethoven leaves to the player to compose or extemporize. After the cadenza it was usual for the orchestra to conclude the movement formally with the last few bars of the opening tutti: but Mozart had already found ways of using the solo instrument in the coda, notably in his C minor Concerto, a work which influenced Beethoven profoundly and conspicuously both as a whole and in detail. And so here the final trill of the cadenza leads to an unexpected turn

[1] Beethoven's cadenza for the first movement of his Opus 37 was written down in 1809, nine years after the composition of the concerto, at the behest of his pupil Archduke Rudolf. Therefore, stylistically, it is somewhat more mature than the movement for which it was written. This should not deter present-day players from using it. There is naturally a major difference in Beethoven's compositions—including, naturally, his improvisations—between his first period and his second period. This roughly covers at least a dozen years in the most fertile period of his creative life and obviously his mind did not stand still. When he revived, for one reason or another, one of his earlier works, he would naturally (especially for publication) give it the imprint of the knowledge and know-how that he had acquired in the interim. Major difference as this might be, it is the same creator *as well as the same pianist* at work; and whatever discrepancy between the style of the movement proper and its candenza, it will, I feel certain, seem less jarring than the justaposition of the former with the compositional and keyboard style of a Thalberg, a Leschetisky, a Brahms, a Godowsky, or a Rachmaninoff (to name a few later composer-pianists who have published cadenzas to the concerto). This is not at all to detract from the value of those subsequent artists' creative approach to Beethoven's music, which in each case was, artistically, entirely valid considering the times in which they lived, the audiences for whom they performed, and their own creative-interpretive approach to Beethoven's music. After all, each generation should and must have its own approach to the interpretation of the great masterpieces of the past.

Beethoven's 1809 cadenza to the first movement of his C minor Concerto (1800) begins with the soloist re-echoing the two final bars of the orchestra ending on a 6/4 chord. Instead of resolving this suspense-laden harmony he immediately launches into a canon based on the first theme in octaves in both hands. Then for a few bars he concentrates on the descending portion of that theme leading to the remote key of D flat. Five repetitions of the three rising half notes of the theme ornamented with progressively more complex arpeggios up and down the keyboard (in the keys of D flat, B flat minor, G flat, A dominant seventh, and D major) ultimately bring into focus the key of G major. In this key the mood gets quieter and he announces dolce the second theme. After a short development of the first portion of this theme, the quiet is shattered by a presto passage which alternates brilliant triplets in the right hand with rough chords hammered in the left hand, which then plays a progression of measures based on the opening theme in diminution. A succession of descending arpeggios and descending and ascending chromatic scales in thirds and sixths leads to the trill on the G dominant seventh chord which most listeners would expect to be the end of the cadenza. But Beethoven extends the trill enormously, announcing the opening theme above *and below* it, ending in a series of falling chords leading to the trill on D-E flat once more. But this trill being in the *minor* key Beethoven extends it again by three more trills, D-E natural, D sharp-E natural, and finally E natural-F, resolving pianissimo into the C seventh chord which begins the mysterious coda as the orchestra enters.—Editor.

of harmony which, together with the quiet entry of the drums with [the rhythmic jumps of the opening theme], is one of Beethoven's most typical strokes of genius. The pianoforte retains the whole conduct of the coda, and ends the movement with scales recalling its first entry.

The largo is the most highly developed slow movement in all Beethoven's concertos, and *a fortiori* in any concerto. In his later concertos the slow movements lead into the finales; gaining thereby various dramatic subtleties and depths by release from the necessity of completing their own design. But in the C minor Concerto we have one of the great independent symphonic slow movements, reaching the climax of Beethoven's powers of solemn expression in his first period, and indeed quite in keeping with all that he found to say in his second. The shock of the first chord [of E major], in its remoteness from the C minor of the rest of the work is in itself a feature of Beethoven's second period, though his earlier works show some preoccupation with things of the kind.

An ornate transition theme leads to a well-defined second subject in the dominant.

This is followed in due course by a somber episode in dark keys, with cloudy pianoforte arpeggios accompanying a slow dialogue in the winds. The episode, which has the function of a development, drifts steadily toward the tonic, E major, and so returns in its own good time to the first subject. Instead of recapitulating the transition and the second subject, Beethoven makes a broad coda out of the orchestral pendants to the first subject, having already redistributed the dialogue as between solo and orchestra.

The shock of E major after C minor is chiefly concentrated in one note, G sharp, the major third of E. This is so near in pitch to A flat that on keyed instruments the same note has to serve for both. Haydn, in the last and greatest of his pianoforte sonatas, had ventured upon this shock in a still more paradoxical form, as between the keys of E flat and E natural (equivalent in this case to F flat); he accordingly began his finale with a theme which first taps rhythmically at G natural, and, having duly explained this as third of E flat, proceeds to show that the next step is A flat.

The first two notes of Beethoven's finale are a more immediate and drastic summary of a similar process. Like Haydn, Beethoven has taken care that the last chord of the slow movement shall display his Berkeleyan G sharp. [In a Dr. Johnson frame of mind, Beethoven] refutes [the G sharp with an upbeat of G (F double sharp) and a downbeat of A flat (G sharp).] This great rondo is an admirable study in temper, worthy of the wisdom that inspired the tragic style of the other movements. Among the works with which this concerto is always provoking comparison by reason of its singularly direct influence on later composers.

three finales are conspicuous—those of Joachim's Hungarian Concerto, Brahm's First Pianoforte Concerto, and Mendelssohn's C minor Trio. It is astonishing how closely both Brahms and Joachim have followed the scheme of this finale, even in such details as the structure of the transition passages and the fugue passage of development after the second episode. The interest in comparing Mendelssohn's C minor Trio finale is different; it is a warning against giving tragic weight to emotions which in real life relieve themselves in a gust of temper. Mendelssohn's first theme is in much the same temper as Beethoven's, and promises a not less spirited career. His second theme is in an enthusiastic mood which would be rather shocked by an apparent lack of moral indignation in Beethoven's energetic second theme [which starts with a descending scale punctuated with flippant appoggiaturas].

And for the consolatory middle episode and triumphant end of his finale Mendelssohn unfortunately bursts into tears and a chorale. Beethoven's way of sounding the depths [in the similar place] is more religiously consistent with his opening. [His middle episode is a lyrical theme incorporating the little sixteenth-note turn of the second measure of the main theme.]

This comfortable and leisurely tune is followed by a little fugue on the main theme, beginning in F minor. The pianoforte intervenes dramatically and carries us to a remote key which is the more impressive in that it happens to be that of the slow movement. From this the steps back to C minor are broad and firm, and the anticipation of the return to the rondo theme is duly exciting. The recapitulation of both main theme and second subject is complete and regular.

But the coda is utterly unexpected. In the tuttis of the main theme the oboe had already made a splendid point by appearing with the theme in the major, transforming its initial G–A♭ into G♯–A♮. Now the pianoforte, entering after an ornamental cadenza, takes up this idea in the new tempo [of 6/8]. The rest of this presto is a brilliant series of fresh cadential phrases, the last of which is a transformation of [the energetic second theme].—DONALD FRANCIS TOVEY (4)

Besides piano, the concerto is scored for two flutes, two oboes, two clarinets, two bassoons, two horns, two trumpets, timpani, and strings.

d. Rondo in B Flat for Piano and Orchestra, WoO 6

The only facts about this work that were known up to the present[1] are that it was found in an unfinished form in the estate of Beethoven and that it was completed by Carl Czerny and published in that arrangement in 1829. Its character and contents indicate its conception

[1] January 1900.—Editor.

as being before 1800, and Otto Jahn surmised that it was probably originally intended as the final movement of the Piano Concerto No. 2 in B flat, Opus 19. Closer information can only be drawn from Beethoven's handwriting, which research remains unpursued up to the present time. That reward has been gained amid the confusion of old music which has been brought again to light through the efforts of Herr Carl Roulard, the present choir director of the parish church of St. Peter in Vienna, whose circumspection also was responsible for saving one of the most valuable manuscripts of Franz Schubert from destruction. Beethoven's manuscript of the Rondo in B flat had passed over into the possession of the *Gesellschaft der Musikfreunde,* in Vienna. This manuscript gives a new insight into the form in which Beethoven left the work and shows (in comparison with the printed version) how far Czerny was responsible for the completion of the work.

When one compares the manuscript with the published version, which appears in the Breitkopf & Härtel edition of the complete works of Beethoven as No. 72 in Volume 9, one discovers the following discrepancies:

[Mandyczewski quotes measures 6 through 16 of page 4 of the published version (the passage for piano solo leading to the appearance of the second theme in F major in the orchestra). He shows that the sixteenth-note figuration is merely indicated in the manuscript by eighth notes outlining the melodic and harmonic structure. The printed version also is an octave higher than the original.] . . . Initially (as the manuscript indicates) this approach to the second theme sounded entirely different: [a simple outlining of the dominant seventh chord in eighth notes, followed by a scale of two octaves from the high B flat to the low C in the right hand, a passage of merely eight measures]. Beethoven was obviously concerned with the expansion of this transition passage [to eleven measures]; however, its external form remains unfinished.

Also [the brilliant sixteenth-note passage which closes the F major section] is merely indicated in the manuscript. Here Czerny's judgment is worthy of note. [Mandyczewski points out how much more elaborate the printed version is than the original manuscript.]

The left hand is missing from the following passage—in the manuscript the lower system remains entirely empty—but since no rests appear it is obvious that Beethoven did not intend the left hand to remain unoccupied. . . . In the approach to the first repetition of the main theme a fermata appears in each part of the accompanying wind parts in the last measure, although the high E flat in the solo part is merely held for a half bar in the manuscript. This is a clear indication that Beethoven intended the soloist to fill out this bar with a cadenza.

In the manuscript this first repetition of the main theme is written out entirely simply as it appeared at the beginning of the piece. [In the published version the theme appears in octaves.]

In the E flat andante section at the close of its main theme [when it appears in the piano after its announcement in the orchestra] Beethoven cuts off the solo part without accompaniment. [In the printed version this last phrase is repeated in the orchestra.] This results in making the passage two measures longer. This small but characteristic shortening was made by Beethoven himself during the working-out of the score.

[Mandyczewski proceeds to point out other discrepancies between the manuscript and the printed form. Some of them, he points out, were made by Beethoven himself during the original working-out of the score, others were elaborations by the editor. The article closes with these comments:]

The piano part in all other cases is identical with the printed version. The orchestra parts of the manuscript correspond with those of the printed version identically from beginning to end, in every detail.

It becomes clear from all of the above that the Rondo in B flat is written entirely by Beethoven and that Czerny only wrote out the cadenzas and filled out the passage work, which Beethoven, in the hurry of composition, only sketched. These external discrepancies were such that Beethoven, as player as well as composer, would have improvised. Czerny, who in his youth was a pupil of Beethoven's and later a devoted and highly esteemed friend, was thoroughly familiar not only with Beethoven's piano technique but also with his compositional style. The piece could hardly have been treated by better hands in reconstructing Beethoven's obvious intentions. The manner in which Czerny restored those passages which were left out of the manuscript point not only his artistic talent but also his honest diffidence [to the master]. The outward trimmings which he gave to the work in no way altered the composition. He changed not a single note of the orchestra accompaniment; he merely added an external luster to the piano part.

. . . The supposition that the work was composed before 1800 is supported by the appearance of the handwriting throughout. It however bears no date or any signature of Beethoven. Externally the probabilities are great that it was not conceived as a separate work but that it was thought of as part of a multimovement composition, probably the third movement of the Piano Concerto No. 2 in B flat. This becomes clearer when one compares it musically with that work. . . . Form, tempo, and rhythm are similar in both works. In both the piano solo begins with an eight-measure phrase; in both the transition to the second theme follows a complete close in the tonic and an outlining of the B flat major triad in unison in the orchestra; the short motive [of a falling interval of a third] which appears in the rondo [as a sort of appendage to the second theme in F] is reflected in [the third movement of the concerto] in the similar place; also in the coda of both movements the passages in thirds differ only in the respect that in the rondo they are diatonic and in the concerto they are chromatic.

These inner similarities bear out Otto Jahn's contention that the rondo was conceived as the last movement of the B flat concerto.— EUSEBIUS MANDYCZEWSKI (TR. BY THOMAS K. SCHERMAN)

e. Romance in G for Violin and Orchestra, Opus 40

The Romance in G [Opus 40] begins with a principal theme [of two parallel four-bar phrases, played by] solo violin in double stops, which are anything but easy to play, instead of with the more customary exposition of the theme by the orchestra. The title of the composition sufficiently indicates the composer's intentions: *Romanze* is synonymous with *Lied*, i.e., "song" in German, hence the composition is a song from beginning to end. Beethoven indicates the tempo as Adagio cantabile. After the orchestra has repeated the two violin solos, [the solo violin] introduces the secondary theme [with orchestral accompaniment].

The entire composition [is] like a tender dialogue, here and there interrupted, and in keeping with this colloquial style should be played with unaffected beauty of tone and expression. [The secondary theme is developed and leads to a second appearance of the two phrases of the principal theme, again announced first by solo violin (with more elaborate double stops) and repeated by the orchestra. Then appears a third] theme in E minor which, [because of] its energetic character, offers a contrast to the preceding lyric theme. It calls for a tempo somewhat more movemented than that of the principal theme. The sixteenth-note figure [which appears four measures later] is *not* an ordinary passage, but a variant of the E minor theme. [The E minor theme is also developed, ending with a descending diatonic scale and a rising chromatic scale in even sixteenth notes which] call for the greatest rhythmic and dynamic control on the part of the soloist. The scales lead to the last appearance of the principal theme, this time played by the solo violin in the brilliant upper register with a much richer orchestral accompaniment. The figured variants are most delicate. The Coda starts with a delicate trill, piano [underneath which the orchestra performs a very beautiful modulation which increases in intensity until the solo violin reaches a high E]. From this climactic point it carries on more and more quietly, until the two closing chords —which Beethoven has provided with the indications "a tempo" and "ff"—have been reached.—LEOPOLD AUER

Besides the solo violin, the romance is scored for one flute, two oboes, two bassoons, two horns, and strings.

f. Romance in F for Violin and Orchestra, Opus 50

The second romance, Opus 50, in F major, as regards both its form and its mood, shows a great resemblance to the romance in G major. Here, too, it is the solo violin which presents the principal theme, this time with the accompaniment of the orchestra, however; whereupon the latter repeats the eight measures which resume the motive.[1] Until [the second appearance of the solo violin] the character of the composition is somewhat contemplative; but subsequent to this the melody grows a little more agitated, supported by the sonorous passages which end [after a brilliant scale ascending to C in altissimo] on two trills. At [this point] an exchange of contrasts in the melody commences between the orchestra and the solo violin; the former forte, rough and decisive, and the latter delicate and intimate, growing gradually brighter in tone and leading over to the principal theme by means of a cadenza two measures long. [After the orchestra again repeats the eight-measure phrase with its short Codetta] the mood grows a trifle more agitated in [a new theme] in F minor [played by the solo violin with a turbulent orchestral accompaniment], and retains this character until [the chord of the dominant] has been reached. Here begins the preparation[2] for the return of the principal theme in the solo violin. [At the close of this third and last appearance of the principal theme, the four-bar Codetta is repeated by the orchestra alone. Then, as an ornamental filigree to support a repetition in the orchestra of the material of the codetta] a chromatic scale commences [in the solo violin] in sixteenth notes and moves in a steady crescendo, interrupted by a sudden piano, [at which point] the violin commences to play thirty-second notes. The passage reaches a climax with the same two trills which closed the first subsidiary section. [The orchestra starts the concluding phrase, after which] the violin enters, dolce, and, growing softer and softer, delicately brings the composition to a close with a ritenuto on the F major scale.[3]—
LEOPOLD AUER

Besides the solo violin, the score calls for one flute, two oboes, two bassoons, two horns, and strings.

[1] The orchestra also adds a little four-measure codetta to the eight-measure phrase.
—Editor.
[2] A dialogue between the orchestra in unison and the solo violin, both playing arpeggios on the chord of C major played staccato and martellaro.—Editor.
[3] Notice the subtle way in which Beethoven imitates the last three notes of the solo part, in the different sections of the orchestra (playing in unison) and in three different registers. This close is, I feel, a masterpiece of orchestration.—Editor.

Chamber Music with Piano

I. QUINTET FOR PIANO, OBOE, CLARINET, BASSOON, AND HORN, OPUS 16;
QUARTET FOR PIANO, VIOLIN, VIOLA, AND VIOLONCELLO, OPUS 16
I. Grave, Allegro ma non troppo; II. Andante cantabile; III. Rondo
(Allegro ma non troppo)

In the direct line of descent from Mozart's piano and wind quintet
is Beethoven's work for the same combination, also in E flat (as is
most of his wind music). It is an inferior work to its begetter, but
its neglect is certainly not justified. Like the more enterprising septet,
it dates from his first period, treading carefully though with ambition
the paths of classical form. There is no feeling that the music calls
for these five instruments and these only, as there is in Mozart's work;
indeed, a quartet version by the composer for piano, violin, viola, and
cello appeared simultaneously, with the same Opus number (16) in
1796. It tends in style much more toward a solo piano work with
wind accompaniment, especially as the themes are invariably stated in
full by the piano and answered by concerted wind. This opposition
of forces persists, though to a lesser degree in the Andante, throughout
the work. Mozart solved the problem of texture by knitting his instruments together in the themes; Beethoven sets them in contrast to each
other, piano against wind, with the piano *primus inter pares*. This is
basically a less satisfactory plot, and *there is evidence that Beethoven
himself felt this, for his string version includes passages accompanying
the piano that do not appear in the original*.[1]

The work opens with a fanfare in unison on the notes of the tonic
chord for all instruments, answered gracefully by the piano, and then
repeated with a wind reply. Thereafter the instruments are each given
a hearing; the forces are displayed, the winds weaving patterns over
accompanying figures on the piano. The contrast of winds versus [piano]
is then reemphasized, and over a dominant pedal on the piano the
introduction pauses, and plunges into the first subject of the Allegro.
The winds, led by the clarinet,[2] answer literally, over a skeleton piano
accompaniment which turns to triplets as the winds one by one declare
a three-bar phrase based on the opening of the first subject.[3] They

[1] Italics by the editor.
[2] The violin, in the piano quartet version.—Editor.
[3] In the string version the order is viola, cello, and violin.—Editor.

then relapse into chords, and the piano leads into the cantabile second subject.

As before, the clarinet[1] leads the wind answer, and after a very similar working the exposition closes over a long insistence on the dominant by the piano.

The cadence figure with which this ends is repeated at the start of the development and thereafter the winds are given a freer individual hand than formerly. The piano's fondness for unisons in its accompanying role is maintained, and the turn into the recapitulation is long heralded, as at the end of the exposition, by an emphasis on the dominant.

The recapitulation is straightforward apart from an embryo cadenza for the piano. Beethoven yet again imitates Mozart in gay arpeggios for the horn near the end,[2] but differs in adding a graceful nineteen-bar coda based on the opening of the first subject.

The Andante cantabile might be described as a developing rondo. The theme is given out at once by the piano and answered, as in the Allegro, by the winds with the clarinet stating the tune.[3] The first episode exploits the oboe, in a four-bar phrase, and the bassoon, in a more elaborate eight-bar one, and as the four wind instruments enter at the end of these exchanges in a canonic figure, the simple chordal accompaniment grows richer, and eventually the piano emerges on its own and leads back into the theme, now decorated. The winds reply as at first. The second episode is in the minor, and is a horn solo over piano accompaniment, divided in the middle by a wind passage derived from the first four notes of the theme. The third statement of the theme is the most florid, and gives the piano a chance of brilliant display while the winds answer over its filigree with the same theme again. A brief coda features scale passages.

The last movement is also a rondo, based on a Mozartean hunting theme. As usual, the piano gives it out and is answered by the winds. The first episode is in two halves, the first featuring piano arpeggios and a wind figure taken from the sixth measure of the theme, the second using a wind arpeggio. Both play important parts in subsequent episodes.—JOHN WARRACK

[1] Violin in the string arrangement.—Editor.

[2] In the wind version there are two descending arpeggio figures for the horn, the first in eighth notes, the second in triplets, each answered by a rising ascending passage in the piano. In the string version the two horn solos are replaced by descending scales in the violin, also in eighth notes and triplets, the second one supported by the viola and cello.—Editor.

[3] In the string version, the violin takes the lead in the first answer, as well as dominating the first episode (substituting for the oboe); the cello substitutes for the bassoon in the eight-bar reply; in the second episode, in B flat minor, the viola substitutes for the horn solo.—Editor.

Before the return to the first theme, there is a solo cadenza by the piano. The second episode commences with all instruments announcing the main theme, fortissimo and in minor. It proceeds with brilliant piano figurations under solo announcements of snatches from that theme by winds (strings) one by one. The return to the last reprise of the theme is ushered in by a rising chromatic scale in the piano in sixteenth notes from the low B flat in the bass to the high F, from which it descends in nonchalant eighth notes while the winds (strings) over a pedal point rise in dignified whole steps, two to a bar. The last appearance of the main theme has one distinct Beethovian touch. The second and third measures of the theme, announced by the piano solo, as before, are echoed immediately by the other instruments. But the piano does not wait for each reply but continues unconcerned, thus causing a tonic-dominant discord clash. However, after this momentary confusion everything else proceeds smoothly through the theme, a repetition of the first episode (now in the tonic key) to the Coda, which features a long trill by the piano on the high B flat while two characteristic hunting-horn arpeggios (sounding less impressive in the string version when they are played on the cello) usher in a pert, joyous close.—Editor.

It is interesting and important to note that almost the majority of Beethoven's early works show a nervous abruptness which is as different from the humor of Haydn as it is from the Olympic suavity of Mozart. There are, indeed, early works which are Mozartean, notably the most brilliant success of Beethoven's first period, the septet, which is perhaps the only work of Beethoven's which earned Haydn's unqualified and enthusiastic praise; but the Mozartean Beethoven imitates only the lighter side of Mozart. In the quintet for pianoforte and wind instruments, Opus 16, Beethoven is, indeed, obviously setting himself in rivalry with Mozart's quintet for the same combination; but, if you want to realize the difference between the highest art of classical composition and the easygoing, safety-first product of a silver age, you cannot find a better illustration than these two works, and here it is Mozart who is the classic and Beethoven who is something less.—DONALD FRANCIS TOVEY (1)

II. TRIOS FOR PIANO, VIOLIN, AND VIOLONCELLO, OPUS 1

The instant and striking success of Beethoven as virtuoso by no means filled up the measure of his ambition. He aspired to the higher position of composer, and in order to obtain this more was needed than the performance of variations, however excellent. To this end he selected the three trios afterwards published as Opus 1, and brought them to performance at the house of Prince Lichnowsky, to whom they were dedicated. Happily for us, Beethoven related some particulars concerning this first performance of these compositions in Vienna to his pupil Ries, who gives us the substance of the story thus (*Notizen*, p. 84): "It was planned to introduce the first three trios of Beethoven, which were about to be published as Opus 1, to the artistic world at a soirée at Prince Lichnowsky's. Most of the artists and music-lovers were invited, especially Haydn, for whose opinion all were eager. The trios were played and at once commanded extraordinary attention. Haydn also said many pretty things about them, but advised Beethoven not to publish the third, in C minor. This astonished Beethoven, in as much as he considered the third the best of the trios, as it is still the one which gives the greatest pleasure and makes the greatest effect. Consequently, Haydn's remark left a bad impression on Beethoven and led him to think that Haydn was envious, jealous and ill-disposed toward him. I confess that when Beethoven told me of this I gave it little credence. I therefore took occasion to ask Haydn himself about it. His answer, however, confirmed Beethoven's statement; he said he had not believed that this trio would be so quickly and easily understood and so favorably received by the public."

The Fischoff manuscript[1] says: "The three trios for pianoforte, violin, and violoncello, Opus 1 (the pearls of all sonatas), which are in fact his sixth work, justly excited admiration, though they were performed in only a few circles. Wherever this was done, however, connoisseurs and music lovers bestowed upon them undivided applause, which grew with the succeeding works as the hearers not only accustomed themselves to the striking and original qualities of the master but grasped his spirit and strove for the high privilege of understanding him."

More than two years passed by, however, before the composer thought fit to send these trios to the press; perhaps restrained by a feeling of modesty, since he was still a student, perhaps by a doubt as to the success of compositions so new in style, or by prudence, choosing to delay their publication until they had been so often performed from the manuscript as to secure their comprehension and appreciation, and thus an adequate number of subscribers.

. . . The author is disposed to place [the] origin [of the trios] in the Bonn period. . . . Argument in favor of this view can be found in the fact of their early performance in Vienna, for there can be no reasonable

---

[1] A collection of some sixty pages of miscellaneous recollections of Beethoveniana, which ended up in the National Library in Berlin in 1859, having arrived there by way of Karl, the nephew; his guardian, Jacob Hotscheuar; and Joseph Fischoff, professor at the Vienna Conservatory. Thayer, during his research, urged caution in using any of the material as biographical fact, as most of the information was second- or third-hand. That he did see fit to mention it in this instance adds weight to the contents quoted.—Editor.

question of the correctness of Ries's story, for which Beethoven himself was authority, that they were played at the house of Prince Lichnowsky in the presence of Haydn. This performance must have taken place before January 19, 1794, because on that day Haydn started for England. Now, Beethoven's sketches show that he was still working on at least the second and third of the trios after 1794, and that they were not ready for the printer before the end of that year. Further explanation is offered by the following little circumstances: since Haydn was present, the performance at Prince Lichnowsky's must have been from manuscript. In the morning meeting which probably took place before the soirée, Beethoven's attention was called to the desirability of changing in the last movement of the second trio the time signature from 4/4 to 2/4. Beethoven made the change. From these facts it may be concluded that after a first there was a final revision of these trios, and that the former version disappeared or was destroyed after the latter was made. It has been intimated that the author believes that the rewriting of compositions completed in Beethoven's early period is more far-reaching than is generally assumed. The case therefore seems to present itself as follows: Haydn heard the trios at Lichnowsky's in their first state; Beethoven then took them up for revision and in the course of 1794 and the beginning of 1795 brought them to the state in which we now know them.—ALEXANDER WHEELOCK THAYER, EDITED BY ELLIOT FORBES

a. Trio in E Flat for Piano, Violin, and Violoncello, Opus 1, No. 1
I. Allegro; II. Adagio cantable; III. Scherzo (Allegro assai); IV.
Finale (Presto)

The Trio of Opus 1, in E flat major, starts with a vigorous Allegro, whose main theme surprisingly makes a venture into the subdominant as soon as the third bar (a venture similar to the one taken by Haydn at the start of his big E flat Piano Sonata No. 52). Although the material itself is still largely influenced by Haydn and Mozart, the will to *oppose* both themes is illustrated by the appearance of the second one in the dominant's relative minor, the key of G minor, rather than in B flat itself, and further by the existence of a prominent "conclusive" element, which plays a conspicuous part in the central development. The following Adagio cantabile in A flat is even more striking, for it too contains a true development—an unusual feature for a slow movement—culminating in an impressive C major climax. Next comes a very individual Scherzo— which even at this early stage Beethoven chooses as a substitute for the customary minuet. Starting with a mysterious unison in C minor, it reaches the main key of E flat only through F minor and B flat major, a decidedly adventurous procedure! The trio ends with a dashing and

humorous Presto, which for all its high spirit and witticism, is in full
keeping with the consistent high level of the preceding movements.—
HARRY HALBREICH (2)

    b. *Trio in G for Piano, Violin, and Violoncello, Opus 1, No. 2*
    I. *Adagio, Allegro vivace*; II. *Largo con espressione*; III. *Scherzo*
    (*Allegro*); IV. *Finale* (*Presto*)

The second Trio, in G major, remains more "galant" and divertimento-
like for three of its four movements [than the other trios of Opus 1]. The
Allegro vivace is preceded by an extended slow introduction, in the
character of an improvisatory recitative, foretelling the Allegro's main
theme, which lightheartedly hops along in the dominant key before
reaching the tonic. Several subsidiary ideas join in, confirming the delightful, entertaining quality of an otherwise not peculiarly striking piece.
The Scherzo (Allegro), with its folk-song-like Trio in B minor, belongs
to the same category. But there remains the second, slow movement, the
crown of the work, one of Beethoven's first truly personal, subjective
utterances, all the more remarkable for its amiable surroundings. By
setting this great Largo con espressione in the remote key of E major,
the young composer follows Haydn's footsteps. The very extended and
elaborate piece, sometimes forecasting Schubert's magic lyricism, plumbs
impressive depths in the course of a tight polyphonic development leading to a powerful climax and then peaceful recession.—HARRY HALBREICH
(2)

Among other things, Beethoven must surely have learned from Haydn,
during those lessons, a sense of adventure where keys are concerned.
Mozart was not adventurous over keys; he nearly always put his slow
movements in the subdominant. Beethoven put the slow movement
of his G Major Piano Trio (Opus 1, No. 2) in the unexpected
key of E, which is precisely what Haydn was doing that same year in
his "Gypsy Rondo" Trio, also in G. We may guess that Beethoven did
this on his master's advice, or as a compliment to his taste. Perhaps he
also learned from Haydn how to disguise the start of his recapitulation.
At the very start of the finale of this G Major Trio the violin tune [is]
accompanied by rather unenterprising chords on the piano, one or two
to the bar; [at the return the same tune] slips in so quietly that one
scarcely notices it. Haydn himself had a liking for that particular trick.
But it must have been Beethoven's own idea to write *scherzi* instead of
minuets for the E Flat and G Major Trios. The minuet had long been
out of fashion as a dance, and after the revolution it must have seemed
as dead as the dodo. The six quartets Haydn wrote in 1781 (Opus 33) have

scherzi (not very characteristic examples), but elsewhere he does not use the title and it did not strike him as absurd that, in his last eight string quartets, four of the minuets are marked *allegro* and four *presto*. To Beethoven the minuet was never a reality, and he seldom used the title except when he was writing a consciously old-fashioned dance movement. In other words, he wrote a quick dance at this point much as Haydn did, but used the more up-to-date title.—ROGER FISKE

c. Trio No. 3 in C Minor, for Piano, Violin, and Violoncello, Opus 1, No. 3
I. Allegro con brio; II. Andante con variazioni;
III. Menuetto; IV. Finale (Prestissimo)

The third Trio [Opus 1, No. 3, in C minor] is by common consent the most significant of the three [piano trios, Opus 1]. (Beethoven's C minor mood is always portentous.) The pregnant [first subject] (Allegro con brio, C minor, 3/4), unharmonized until its cadence, is no mere assertion of the tonic key. Its impact is heightened by the fermata, so that it needs no repetition. The continuing phrases have patent relativity and the whole progression to the [second subject] until the flowing 6/4 chords (measure 57) open the door for the gracious theme. But even this is darkened (measure 80) so that the close, made of already established matter, intensifies the dominant mood. Clearly, this is music with more than a purely musical purpose.

The Andante con Variazione (E flat, 2/4) has a theme somewhat lighter than one might anticipate after the first movement. The variations, however, are no mere ornaments of the theme, but are imaginative transformations of it, whether of its actual line or of its harmonic substratum. They indicate a fact which will become more apparent and will be vividly illustrated in the last trio[s][1]—that Beethoven is the most imaginative variationist of the great composers.

The Menuetto (C minor) does not exceed the conventional dimension of that dance. Neither is it at all in the character of a scherzo. But it does effectively re-establish the C minor mood; and the downward scale that delicately begins the Trio becomes (measure 69) a significant recall of that same design which was so vividly interjected at the close of the first movement.

The Finale (Prestissimo, C minor, 2/2), in sonata form, emphatically opposes the convention of the happy ending. It first presents an incisive arpeggio figure[2] that sternly establishes the key, and then finds a rhyth-

---

[1] Opus 97 (the "Archduke") and Opus 121b ("Kakadu" Variations).—Editor.
[2] Like the contemporaneous dramatic "Mannheim rocket," which was also used by Beethoven in the opening theme of the E flat Trio, Opus 1, No. 1.—Editor.

mically obsessed continuation that is wholly in character. As in the first movement, the [second subject] (measure 69) is made to enter almost unannounced, and the [first subject] yields, most pertinently, the substance of the [closing subject]. The development, which is mostly [based] upon [the second subject], thus gains a heightened significance. The *pp* ending, in the perspective of the whole trio, is an imaginative stroke of the highest order.—DONALD N. FERGUSON (3)

III. TRIO IN B FLAT FOR CLARINET, VIOLONCELLO, AND PIANO, OPUS 11
I. Allegro con brio; II. Adagio; III. Allegretto

This work, probably composed in 1798, has many characteristics in common with the trios of Opus 1. However, the part given to the clarinet imposed limitations which make the work seem somewhat simpler than the earlier trios. This difference pleased contemporary critics, who, for the most part, found Beethoven's early works too scholarly and difficult. "This trio," says the *Allgemeine Musikalische Zeitung* in 1799, "is by no means easy in parts, but it runs more flowingly than much of the composer's other work and produces an excellent *ensemble* effect without piano-forte and clavier accompaniment. If the composer, with his unusual grasp of harmony, his love of the graver movements, would aim at natural rather than strained and *recherché* composition, he would set good work before the public, such as would throw into the shade the stale, hurdy-gurdy tunes of many a more talked-of musician."

In the first movement, Allegro con brio, there are indeed surprising harmonic changes, such as the opening of the second subject in D major, following immediately upon the strong F major close of the preceding section. The abrupt alteration of one-measure phrases in A minor and F major in the course of the second subjects also represents a harmonic adventurousness.

The second movement, Adagio, is built on two expressive figures, the first echoing the theme of the minuet from the Sonatina, Opus 49, and hinting at the yet-to-be-written Septet. The key of the movement is E Flat major.

The last movement, Allegretto, is a highly interesting set of nine variations based on a rather everyday sort of theme from Weigl's opera *The Corsair*.[1] The first variation is for piano solo, the second for clarinet and cello, and the third combines the three instruments. Variation IV introduces the tonic (B flat) minor while the fifth returns to a forceful

[1] This two-act comic opera was produced for the first time on October 15, 1797, at the Vienna Hoftheater. The theme Beethoven uses comes from the final trio, which became very popular. Among other composers who created variations on it was Paganini, who in 1828 produced a Grand Sonata and Variations for violin and orchestra based upon it.—Editor.

reiteration of the major. Variation VI employs echo effects between piano and clarinet with cello, while Variation VII again employs the minor, this time in more dramatic fashion. Variation VIII utilizes lyrical statements of clarinet and cello over more agitated triplet figurations in the piano, again in the tonic major. Variation IX is, fittingly enough, the most elaborate of the lot, employing imitative development and trills in the piano. A final Allegro in 6/8 is followed by a brief coda.—JACKET NOTES FOR DECCA DL 9543

IV. 14 VARIATIONS IN E FLAT FOR PIANO, VIOLIN, AND VIOLONCELLO, OPUS 44

It is not clear in what year these variations were composed. Thayer attributes them to the period of the Septet, Opus 20 (1800) because of a note by Otto Jahn that there were sketches of them on some pages that were missing from a sketchbook of that period. Riemann places them a year *later* than the *Prometheus* music, Opus 43, because the theme is so similar to the music which opens the second act of that ballet (No. 4). This would place them in 1801 or 1802. Nottebohm, who is usually so reliable on questions of the dates of the sketches in the notebooks, places the composition during the last years of the Bonn period (1792–93). Whichever of these authorities is correct, the music itself attests to the fact that it was a work of the early period but written with enough mastery to qualify it as a "serious" effort and not as what Beethoven himself regarded as "bread and butter" music.

The theme is made up of stealthy disconnected notes traveling up and down the E flat arpeggio and sneaking as unobtrusively into the key of B flat (the dominant). The Beethovian surprise, of which he makes masterful use throughout the variations, is that a continuation in the same pattern seeming to be returning to a reprise of the first four-bar (arpeggio) phrase halts on the B flat, which is held. Instead of the expected disconnected-note reprise there is a legato continuation which for the first time is harmonized.

Variation I features the piano ornamenting notes of the theme with a figure of one eighth and two sixteenth notes identical to the figure of one of the variants in the finale of the little Sonata in G minor, Opus 49, No. 1 (1795–96: another possible clue to the year of the composition of the trio).

Variation II features the piano alone in smooth eighth notes; Variation III, the violin in eighth-note triplets; Variation IV, the cello in smooth eighth notes similar to the piano's solo variation; Variation V, the piano in triplets identical to the violin's variation. Each of these variations makes a point of the fermata before the return of the reprise. Variation

VI "connects" the bare notes of the arpeggio of the theme by scale figures in eighth notes played in unison by the three instruments. Variation VII in minor is an expressive largo in 6/8 in which the arpeggio theme takes on a completely new character as played alternately by the cello and the violin with a somber accompaniment in the piano similar in mood to the funeral march of the Piano Sonata, Opus 26. For the first time in this variation the fermata on the dominant is *not* featured.

Variation VIII is perhaps the most fascinating: in major in a fairly slow tempo, the bass of the piano plays the theme absolutely unchanged; the violin and cello add to this an accompaniment of soft repeated notes in triplets; above this combined background the right hand of the piano plays a gorgeous cantabile florid melody worthy of Bellini! Even the fermata is graced with a purely vocal cadenza, written out. This is a little gem!

The following four variations, all fast, feature the theme in progressively more complex figurations. Variation XIII is again in adagio and in minor; however, the harmonic setting is much more complex than the earlier minor variation, so it does not seem to be a repetition of the same mood. The last variation is in a fast 6/8 and acts not only as a variation but as a developed coda. After it has concluded its ornamentation of the theme, its concluding phrase is developed and leads suddenly to a false cadence in C minor. After a typical Beethoven silence full of anticipation the meter changes back to 2/2 and the tempo to andante. It appears as if Variation XIII were to be repeated once more but in C minor (instead of E flat minor). But Beethoven subtly leads the harmonies back to the area of E flat and to a most expressive trill in the right hand of the piano, descending dramatically over a period of seven bars, from E flat to C, on which note there is another pause and an even more florid cadenza than before. This leads us to the last appearance of the arpeggio notes of the theme divided among the three instruments, which gain speed and propulsion and then burst into the final Presto peroration.—
THOMAS K. SCHERMAN

V. TRIO FOR PIANO, CLARINET OR VIOLIN, AND VIOLONCELLO, OPUS 38
  (AFTER THE SEPTET, OPUS 20)

The septet, for four strings and three wind instruments, dedicated to the Empress Maria Theresa . . . was offered to Hoffmeister[1] and was pub-

1 Franz Anton Hoffmeister, a prolific and popular composer in Vienna at the time of Beethoven's arrival. Although he was considerably older than Beethoven, he extended the young genius a helping hand. In the 1780's he established a music-publishing firm in Vienna. In 1800 he moved to Leipzig and formed a new firm there in partnership with Ambrosius Kühnel. The latter firm later became known as C. F. Peters and is still in existence.—Editor.

lished by him in 1802. The septet speedily won great popularity and was frequently transcribed. Hoffmeister had an arrangement for string quintet which he advertised on August 18, 1802. Ries thought that Beethoven had made it, but he was in error; nevertheless . . . Beethoven gave Hoffmeister permission to publish an arrangement in which strings were substituted for the wind instruments. Later Beethoven did transcribe it as a pianoforte trio with violin or clarinet ad lib (Opus 38) as a tribute of gratitude from the composer to his new physician, Dr. Johann Schmidt. The doctor played the violin and his daughter the pianoforte, both fairly well, and Beethoven arranged his popular piece for family use and, as was customary at the time, gave Dr. Schmidt the exclusive possession of the music for one year.—ALEXANDER WHEELOCK THAYER, EDITED BY ELLIOT FORBES

The clarinet was probably chosen because it carries the main theme of the first movement of the original (Opus 20) and the glorious lyric theme of the Adagio cantabile. In the trio arrangement Beethoven writes characteristically for the piano, substituting sixteenth-note accompaniments in the bass for the simpler syncopated figure originally in the strings in the coda of the first movement, and octave writing in the second half of the theme and variations instead of the simpler voicing of the original string parts.

However, the cello is a poor substitute for the typical horn figure in the trio of the Minuet, although it is a worthy substitute for the bassoon solo in the middle of the slow movement. And giving the famous violin cadenza of the last movement to the piano instead of the original violin does it a great injustice as far as brilliance is concerned. On the other hand the triplet arpeggios of the coda are more suited to the piano than to the original violin, and bring the trio to an exciting conclusion.—Editor.

VI. VIOLIN AND PIANO SONATAS

If we examine the status of Beethoven's Ten Sonatas for Piano and Violin without preconceived ideas, we come to some rather unexpected conclusions. (By the status of a body of works such as Beethoven's Quartets, or Mozart's Piano Concerti, or Scriabin's Sonatas, or Handel's Concerti Grossi and so on—we mean the degree of wholehearted acceptance of these large segments of a composer's entire oeuvre; we also mean the degree of conviction and devotion that the "conveyers," the executants of these works have shown toward them.)

When the three Sonatas Opus 12 appeared in 1799, the critic of the *Leipziger Allgemeine Musikalische Zeitung* censured the composer for "hankering after bizarre modulations, despising the natural harmonic links." Although we have come a long way from such narrowmindedness and misrepresentation, one finds in as recently as 1924, traces of this quibbling attitude in a highly scholastic theoretical analysis of the Sonatas by a German musicologist. He speaks of one of the telling touches of Beethovenian genius (an unexpected willful detour from D major to E flat major, in the Finale of Opus 12, No. 1, 39 bars from the end) in the following terms: "One of those capricious vagaries which often come over him in human intercourse, but that he generally rarely indulged in when it came to creative activity."

Beethoven's piano playing was the talk of musical Vienna during those early years, but it is less generally known that he took his violin playing seriously enough to ask his favorite Quartet leader Ignaz Schuppantzigh (some years his junior) to give him regular lessons at a time when he had already reached the relatively ripe age of twenty-four. (Beethoven had already played the violin in his early Bonn days.)

Every one of the thirty-three movements shows his preoccupation with the potentialities of the violin. We find in them challenges even now, some hundred and fifty years after they were composed, even though the technique and the teaching of the instrument have made such immense strides since the turn of the century.

These challenges are technical ones only in the sense that musical and expressive demands like Beethoven's are more difficult to realize than the mere stunts of Paganini, Ernst, Wieniawski, Vieuxtemps, et al. A Beethoven expression mark may look deceptively simple until one tries to bring it to life. Violin chords that are played softly and short *"non arpeggiando"* and are a reply to the identical soft and short chords of the piano (Sonata Opus 30, No. 1, Finale, Variation IV) can be a bigger technical problem than anything in Ravel's Tzigane! A simple accompaniment figure such as in the first movement of Opus 12, No. 3 (accompanying the second theme) and likewise in the third movement (also in the second theme) can become quite a problem. But more surprisingly still Beethoven gives the violinist the hardest nut to crack when he is at his simplest. For instance, when in the Adagio of this same Sonata he "commands" the violinist to accompany the piano's eloquent phrase with [repeated eighth-note G's, five or six to the bow, at the beginning of the coda] a figure that must be perfectly controlled, and not disfigured by a portamento, but blend with the piano phrase as if it were played by the pianist's left hand. In the Adagio cantabile of Opus 30, No. 2, we encounter the similar problem of doing justice to the pianissimo staccato (and non-portamento) figure [of repeated C's in triplets in the coda] which has to be integrated into the pianist's identical chordal figure if it is to give the listener the "Time stands still" feeling that this bridge passage implies. And what is one to say about the countless sforzandi in which these scores abound and about the crescendi that lead to a piano or pianissimo? Or about the third variation of the First Sonata with its stormy crescendi and sustained sforzando chords and moments when the violin has the well-nigh impossible task of competing with the turbulence of the piano? The reluctance of contemporary violinists to use a vigorous martele bowing at the nut puts them to great disadvantage in this variation with its fortissimo scales in triplets. What can one say except: not to give these touches their full due is to impoverish their expressive content and significance. These are just a few examples among many that show that the composer disregarded the hopes of his violin playing dedicatees, be they patrons or virtuosi like Rodolphe Kreutzer (1766–1831) or Pierre Rode (1774–1830) (Rode was the dedicatee of the Sonata Opus 96 and one of the two Romances) in the same way that he ignored the remonstrances of the—sometimes outraged—Quartet leaders. (Kreutzer, by the way, refused to play the great Opus 47 dedicated to him and accused Beethoven of being "outrageously unintelligible!" His walking out during a Paris performance of the Second Symphony while stopping his ears demonstratively, is another instance of his complete lack of understanding of Beethoven's music.)

Czerny wrote about Beethoven's playing: ". . . as his playing, his compositions, were far ahead of his time, the pianofortes of the period (until 1810) still extremely weak and imperfect, could not endure his gigantic style of performance."

The Opus 47 was played by the mulatto violinist George Bridgetower, who earned the composer's praise in this most popular and in certain respects most demanding Sonata, which he titled "*Sonata per il Pianoforte ed uno Violino obligato in uno stile molto concertante come d'un Concerto.*" (It is obvious that he wished to emphasize the difference between this Sonata and its predecessors; a note by Bridgetower tells of his having improvised "at the repetition of the first part of the Presto," the flight at the 18th bar of the piano (the C major arpeggio passage) and that Beethoven jumped up, embraced him saying: "Noch einmal, mein lieber Bursch!" ("Once again, my dear boy!"), and Beethoven held the open pedal during this flight, says Bridgetower. One wonders what would happen to the violinist who would repeat Bridgetower's exploit in our Urtext snobbery days! Not only Beethoven's contemporaries but even the recent past had less inhibited feelings about the performance of his works than we have in our "antiseptic" age (as one critic calls it).

When one tries to see the *Ten* from a bird's-eye view, instead of as a series of occasional works, the three of Opus 12, the three Emperor Alexander I Sonatas, Opus 30, and so on, and when one compares the different solutions of identical problems, such as first movement, slow movement, Variation, Scherzo, Finale, one cannot help but marvel at Beethoven's protean capacity for approaching problems from a new point of view every time, and solving them in an equally new manner. How different is the variation theme in Opus 12, No. 1 (A major), from that in Opus 30, No. 1, also in A major (or the minore variations in these superficially similar movements), and how worlds apart are the variation theme of the "Kreutzer" from the bucolic, earthy one in Opus 96. There is a certain family resemblance in the Adagios but how many individual touches abound in them, that give them their own profile!

Can contrast be greater than between the first movements of, say, the first and sixth Sonatas (the latter of quartet-like linear texture)?

One could go on pointing out ever renewed approaches to the problem called Scherzo or the unmistakable tempo in which he cast those elusive middle movements which are neither "slow movements" nor Allegrettos and are *piu tosto* this, that or the other.

The instrumental layout too, the "orchestration" as it were of the Ten Sonatas, shows the same march away from the more expected, tradition-based procedure of the first Sonata to the rarefied heights of the later ones. While Opus 12, No. 1 opens with a unison fanfare by violin and piano, five of the set, Opus 12, No. 2, No. 3, and the Fourth Sonata, Opus 23, the Sixth, Opus 30, No. 1, the Seventh, Opus 30, No. 2 give the first statement of the first movement to the *piano*, using the violin only as an accompanying instrument. (True, in the sixth the violin does spin one of the essential three voices of this linear movement.)

Beethoven returns to the three part unison statement of Opus 12, No. 1, only once more, in the opening of Opus 30, No. 3.

In the "Spring" Sonata, Opus 24, the "Kreutzer" Sonata, Opus 47, it is the violin that first exposes the principal theme, a crucial change from the instrumental planning of the bulk of the set. Surely this is something of real significance and should give us food for thought.

But what is to my mind more revealing than the actual scoring choices is the fact that the set opens with a youthful swagger, almost a clarion call in D major, and closes with the self-questioning motif [of the opening measure of Opus 96, with its graceful, trilled upbeat. This latter motif is] in G major, an affirmative key too, but affirmative in what a different sense! Here we have a symbol of the road to maturity the young titan traversed between the end of the century and now; 1812— so much in so few years! As if the short span of life allotted to him had determined the tempo of his creative life and as if this timetable had been ever present in his mind.

In every such cycle (as the Ten) there are works that are tacitly accepted as "favorites" and others that have remained comparatively stepchildren both from the point of view of critical evaluation, audience appreciation and interpreter-sponsorship.

It seems to me that here enters a question of artistic ethics on the part of the performer. It is enough to hear one of the "even-numbered"

Beethoven symphonies, say the Fourth, under one of the, alas, now so rare type of conductors who at every performance starts afresh, who re-evaluates the work as if it had no "past" of a century and a half behind it, who proceeds entirely from the score and not from tradition with its many accretions; one realizes then what immense responsibility the performer, the "conveyer" has in respect to those less than fully appreciated and popularly accepted works. How they shine in their original purity and plasticity and eloquence under such a conductor!

These present lines are an attempt to persuade students and young performers to give those of the *Ten* which seem to me not to have had the full share of "limelight" (to use a vulgar word!), like the early four and the Sixth the kind of re-evaluation, restudying "in depth" that opera houses under a musical director worth his salt give to repertoire operas when they plan a "Neue-instudierung," a "Neu-inszenierung." They will then see how wrong the habit of classifying certain works with a cliché transmitted from earlier times, really is. They will then realize that what is considered the "naïve," metrical regularity of a tune like the middle movement's of the Second (A major) Sonata does not take into account such sophistications of writing as for instance the canonic imitation at the recapitulation of the theme and more particularly the way [the four] simple cadential bars [of the main theme (measures 21–24 in the piano and measures 29–32 in the violin)] are made to yield new thematic material by a "splitting" process to which Beethoven submits them. By an eloquent crescendo on the first of these bars, and a dramatic stop, he starts this process of elaboration of the [first measure and the downbeat of the second measure of that cadential figure] and then plays around with the second bar, which he repeats either entirely or in part six times. [This device serves to] usher in the final statement of the theme (that is, the coda). One is also apt to "take for granted" an original twist like the one he uses in the first movement of the same Sonata just before the coda, [34 measures before the end] where the leading voice is at first in the right hand of the piano part, while violin and bass complete this motif in contrary motion (for four bars): then the procedure is changed and violin and bass take the "leading" voices with the piano (right hand) completing the three part pattern.

The early piano sonatas have—as one writer has aptly put it—"simple but by no means unsubtle beauties" and we should look out for these when re-evaluating the early violin sonatas. *The erroneous idea that Beethoven, before the Eroica, was simply writing in the idiom of Haydn and Mozart was brilliantly refuted by Donald Francis Tovey among others.*[1]

The somewhat patronizing attitude toward the first three Sonatas does not take into account the known self-criticism of young Beethoven either.

[1] Italics by the editor.

He would not have presented this bouquet of three early works—some of which (or some parts of which) quite possibly belong to his Bonn days—if he had not had full faith in them. After all, he had to compete with such works of his as the C minor Piano Trio, Opus 1, No. 3, the C minor String Trio, Opus 9, No. 3, and the early Piano Sonatas. The fact that the middle movements are so different in their planning: the Andante con variazioni, the ingratiating, nostalgic songlike Andante-Allegretto of No. 2 with its *balladesque* character, and the only true arioso Adagio con molto espressione of the third of the set show that the twenty-six-year-old master was fully conscious that stern self-criticism must determine the choice (among many early works) when making his first offerings to the publisher. (It is surmised that the Andante piu tosto Allegretto, that jewel which graces the second Sonata, may have been added to movements that belong to his Bonn days.)

This "patronizing" attitude stems perhaps from the confusion and the preconceived ideas which divide Beethoven's "oeuvre" into three styles, three periods. This arbitrary division does not take into account facts such as the use of the theme of the Finale of the Opus 23 (A minor) Violin Sonata in the "in Gloria Dei Patris" movement in the Missa Solemnis, Opus 123, where it is turned into a major key [and becomes the theme of the great concluding fugue].

Contrast seems to have been uppermost in the composer's mind when deciding the alternation of the three works and the character of their respective movements. Just as the middle movements are as far as imaginable apart from each other, so are the others: the humor and light texture of the opening of No. 2 is as far as possible removed from the stern brio and stormy passage work of the first movement of the E flat No. 3. The quasi Landler-Scherzo lilt of the third movement of the A major sets it quite apart from the D and Eb major Sonatas.

A word about Opus 23 and 24 which were written for Count Moritz von Fries after a voyage in Italy in 1799. They were composed at around the same time and should be given together; this is never done. They complement each other—the flowing melody of the "Spring" was to provide a release from the tenseness and terseness of the first and last movement of the A minor (especially of that concentrated first movement). No greater contrast can be imagined than between the peremptory [Presto theme in A minor, an almost casually dictatorial utterance,] and the ingratiating long line of Opus 24. The presentation of the two Sonatas Opus 23 and 24, which belong together, is only one of the "opportunities" that are habitually missed in performances of this set of Ten Sonatas.

Much has been said and written about the incompatibility of violin and piano Sonatas written for this combination. Bartók in the first movement of his Second Sonata deliberately avoids using the same thematic materials for both instruments. He did this—as he told me—out of a profound conviction, and it is significant that he never wrote another sonata for violin and piano after 1923.

Beethoven's stubborn will made him attempt the practically impossible in chain passages like [the one 16 measures before the end of the Adagio of Opus 12, No. 3,] where the right hand piano part has to be blended with the violin against the part for the left hand; or in the Andante of Opus 23, [just before the recapitulation where the continuous eighth-note melody is divided between the piano and the violin in the same register].

Of course such writing presupposes great sensitivity on the part of the executants, who have to be worthy of the well-nigh impossible demands of the composer in dividing these rising or falling lines between the two [performers] so that the linear and thematic continuity is perceived by the listener in spite of the essential difference (the incompatibility) of the two instruments.

The question of coloristic enhancement of accompaniment figures that are apt to sound somewhat lame when played with the obvious conventional fingering should exercise our violinistic ingenuity.

In the earthy folk-dance Finale of the Eighth Sonata (Opus 30, No. 3) where the piano growls in the bass and the violin responds with [two repeated eighth notes, preceded by the characteristic appoggiatura], playing it on two strings in the third and later in the fourth position will—I think—not only match the pianist's passage better, but bring out the appoggiatura dissonance latent in this folksy dance.

After these performance hints, it might be enlightening to compare the closing bars of the slow movements and try to group them into different categories. The endings of the "Kreutzer" variation and of the Tempo di Menuetto of Opus 30, No. 3 seem to present a somewhat similar approach to the use of the [dotted rhythm as an upbeat and a longer note as a downbeat. This characteristic close] for want of a better tag of identification I will call the "Lebewohl" motif. In both cases violin and piano exchange the fragment several times: in Opus 30, No. 3, six times, ending with an identical and simultaneous curtsy, as it were. We find this "figure of speech" in the first movement of the Sixth Sonata (before the repeat sign), in the F major Romance and elsewhere too.

Thomas Mann in his *Doktor Faustus* rhapsodizes in Chapter VIII about the "Lebewohl" motif in the Arietta of Opus 111 with an eloquence that remains unforgettable for anyone who has read the book. This passage culminates in the interpretation that the author gives of the hidden meaning of this particular leave-taking: leave-taking also from the *Sonata form as such* which "has arrived at its consummation, fulfilled its destiny, reached its goal, beyond which it cannot go." (I give only an approximate translation.)

But it is these endings which are the cruelest tests of the instrumental mastery of both players: to make clear to the listener that the pianist's [upper voice, the C and A flat] is the salient voice in the C minor Sonata, in these seven-part chords; to do justice to the exchange between the two instruments of the six leave-taking phrases in the last four bars of the Adagio of Opus 24; such moments belong to the highest goals in ensemble playing.

Detailed "appreciation" of the felicities of the works we attempt to play seems to me to be one of the prerequisites of our task. (I put the word "appreciation" advisedly in quotes because the words "music appreciation" have in our time apparently taken on a different meaning from what I have in mind . . .) That is the reason why I have been discussing seemingly secondary matters too, and expressing admiration in a manner that some may think redundant. But I feel that the "appreciation" of these fine points, these not immediately obvious intentions of the composer is as much a tool of the performer as instrumental technique, musical talent, memory, "perfect pitch," muscles, a good instrument and what have you. . . .

When we come to the group of "true" Adagios: those of Opus 24 ("Spring"), of the Seventh (C minor) and of Opus 12, No. 3, we are in the region of the characteristically lofty Beethovian utterance where the concluding bars quite naturally and inevitably fall into place.

Look at the last variation in Opus 12, No. 1. This ending with the triplet figure [(10 measures before the end), which is] derived from the second bar of the theme and which the composer repeats no less than nine times, represents to my mind a sophistication which belies its place as the first of this "early" Beethoven set. By stretching the point somewhat we can establish a relation between the seventh and eighth bars of the first movement and this motif too. An analytical look at the various details forces us to admit that the closing bars of the Variation movement of the most famous of the "middle period" sonatas: the "Kreutzer" Opus 47 are less delicately wrought and less original than this corresponding coda of Opus 12, No. 1. In the "Kreutzer" Variation, Beethoven simply repeats the motive derived from the seventh bar of the theme with [the] slight rhythmic variant [of making the upbeat a dotted rhythm, instead of two even notes. This little motif is repeated] five times in dialogue between violin and piano. Or take the Andante piu tosto Allegretto of the Second Sonata. This plaintive-nostalgic "Maiden's Song" (as it has come to stand for me)—(these nebulous identifications with a "program" are of course always intensely personal!), [bears] a faint family resemblance to the middle movement of the Sixth Sonata's (Opus 30, No. 1) tune in B minor [starting at measure 17 of the Adagio,] and to the third and fourth bars of the [slow movement of the] String Trio, Opus 9, No. 3. [These three examples (all in minor) have the same melodic contour—a rise from the fifth step of the scale, up a minor sixth to the third step of the scale, and a lazy fall back to the tonic. They are also to be appreciated in the context of another "A minor" piece like the third "Rasoumowsky" Quartet's (Opus 59, No. 3) Andante con molto quasi Allegretto. This confrontation cannot fail to shed light on our "A minor" movement! (It may not even be farfetched to remember in this connection another "A minor" piece, though so vastly different in tempo, passionate drive and general style; the Allegro appassionato of the late Quartet Opus 132 (written in 1825, that is, some twenty-six years after the Opus 12, No. 2).

For in the case of Beethoven, coming events *do* cast their shadows decades before.

Appreciation means—at least to me—appreciation not only of the "what" but also of the "how." Not only "what" the composer has transmitted to us, but also "how" the master fashioned his message and how he came to find just this formulation, elaboration, development (call it by whatever name you will!).

Take the deceptively simple Second Sonata about which I already spoke. Can anything be simpler than the cadential bars 15 and 16 of the third movement? But see what use Beethoven makes of it in the further "events" of this movement: Six bars before the second subject in D major it serves him as a modulatory bridge; then in [the] waltzlike second subject it becomes a self-sufficient countermotive in the bass of the piano. All in all we find this apparently "inconsequential" motive not less than thirty-six times in this comparatively short movement and there is never the feeling of obsessive repetition or surfeit!

At the change to D minor and later to F major, he operates with this fragment still more surprisingly, [the decrescendo passage starting 18 measures before the second change of key signature]. And how dramatic is the ninefold repetition of this motive utilizing the enharmonic change from [G, B flat, A flat, G to F double sharp, A sharp, G sharp, F double sharp. How masterfully he uses these minute enharmonic changes to effect a subtle modulation from F major to the far distant key of B minor!] And consider how bars 13 and 14 gave him new chromatic material 34 bars before the end (at the crucial point of the coda).

How true are the words of the Hungarian poet and aesthetic "arbiter" of a whole generation of poets (and artists generally)—Milan Füst, when he says: "Beethoven shows us almost palpably how he improves, develops; he allows us to witness how he experiments and prepares us for the triumphant consummation of the work before our very eyes. And thus, he makes it easier for us to participate in the sudden 'changes of fortune' (like in a drama) of his themes, motives, fragments . . ."

[Gabriel Fauré's preface to the posthumously published book on Bee-

thoven's Quartets by the dedicated amateur violinist Joseph de Marliave]
concludes in this touching tribute: "Il aimait avant de réfléchir; il
sentait avant d'essayer de comprendre." (He loved before reflecting; he
felt before trying to understand!)

In concluding this volume, I would like to give this as an injunction
to my readers, lest they are led to false conclusions by the tone and the
procedure of these pages.

Although I stressed the necessity of appreciating, analyzing, although
I warned against the habit of "taking for granted" and accepting clichés
of evaluation, I, too, consider that the primary motive force in taking
possession of a body of works like the Beethoven Sonatas, must be—love
and feeling.[1]—JOSEPH SZIGETI (1)

a. Sonata No. 1 in D, Opus 12, No. 1
I. Allegretto con brio; II. Tema (Andante con moto) con
variazioni; III. Rondo (Allegro)

The subject matter of the first movement is unimportant, and the
portion between the exposition and the restatement so slight that it
hardly deserves the name of "working-out section," although it is wholly
evolved out of motives derived from the first subject. But if we miss
thoughts of deep significance, wonderful evolutions, and striking reflections, compensation may be found in the truly delightful natural flow,
brightness, and joyousness. Form and style seem to have been prompted
by the duality of the executive forces, which are in constant amicable
contention, manifested now by alternation, now by united or opposing
combination. Playfulness is, so to speak, the keynote of every part of
the movement. True, the "working-out section" assumes a somewhat
serious appearance, but the seriousness is as little seriously meant as the
working out. As the structure is both obvious and orthodox, we may
safely shirk the trouble of a detailed analysis. The first subject, followed
by a second subject in the dominant key, and their recurrence in the
principal key after an intervening section need neither be pointed out
nor commented upon.

Now we come to the second movement. The theme of the variations is
full of simple feeling, not passionate, but warm. And then, in the first two
variations, how tenderly the composer fondles the lovely thing! After this

[1] Violinists, professional as well as amateur, would be strongly advised to purchase
this invaluable little book by one of the outstanding interpreters of Beethoven of our
generation. Because of the general character of the present volume the editor has
purposely condensed Szigeti's comments to those nontechnical ones which he felt would
be of interest to the general music lover and give him an idea of the *creative* genius
inherent in such outstanding interpreters as Joseph Szigeti. The editor particularly
recommends study of the ten-page Appendix, subtitled "Some Practical Hints to the
Performer" (pages 46–55).

serenity and happiness, the aspect of matters changes in the third variation (A minor), where passion and strife supervene. Happiness returns in the fourth: happiness after passion and strife, however, can never be the same as it was before; it may be more intense, but must also be tinged with sadness and fear. Examining the form of the variations, we find that the first two adhere strictly to the harmony and remain more or less faithful to the melody of the theme, the faithfulness of the first being inferior to that of the second, the violin part of which may be described as a highly ornamental version of the original melody. The third variation, on the other hand, is less a variation in the orthodox fashion than a fantasia on a motive of the theme. The last variation shows itself loyal to the original melody and harmony up to the last four bars of the model, when it takes its own course and draws slowly (thirteen bars) to the close of the variation, which is also that of the movement. This dying away—but no! it is not that; I should have said, this passing away into the silent world of dreams—is very beautiful, and so is likewise the climax of interest which the series of variations exhibits.[1]

The skeleton of the Rondo can be drawn as follows:

    1. a (D major)
       b (A major, modulates to D major)
       a (D major, modulates to F major)
    2. c (F major, modulates to D major)
    3. a (D major)
       b (D major)
       a, b, c, a (D major, with modulations; motives from
                different sections are utilized)

Of course this does not give the slightest idea of the frank gaiety, the youthful animation, the unrestrained frolicsomeness, and irresistible rush of the movement, least of all, of the topsy-turvy medley of motives in the wild winding up, this madness with a method. We have not here the heroic Beethoven, but nevertheless we have Beethoven truly and unmistakably.

Most hearers will no doubt be reminded of Mozart in the sonata under discussion; they will be reminded of him in the first movement, more strongly in the variations, and most strongly in some parts of the Rondo—and not without good cause. Yet, on closer inspection the similarity is found to be considerably less than one thought it. In fact, Beethoven, although under the influence, was not under the dominion of his predecessors. They could not at any time neutralize his individuality. Mozart's ideal was absolute beauty, Beethoven's characteristic beauty. With the former, euphony and harmoniousness had a greater importance than with the latter, who thought more of the intellectual and emotional element.

[1] Szigeti in his general article on the ten violin sonatas points out the enormous sophistication of the last variation, where a tiny triplet figure is repeated no less than nine times.—Editor.

The beauty followed by Mozart was soft-outlined and fair-complexioned, that followed by Beethoven, strongly marked and dark. Mozart loved the kindred moods of tenderness, sweet melancholy, and serene joyousness, Beethoven freely used a more extensive emotional scale.—FREDERICH NIECKS (1)

b. Sonata No. 2 in A, Opus 12, No. 2
I. Allegro vivace; II. Andante più tosto allegretto; III. Allegro piacevole

The second of the three sonatas Opus 12 (A major) is pervaded by lightheartedness and suffused with sunshine. The few thin clouds that pass by only subdue temporarily the brightness of the scene but cannot darken it. All through the first movement (A major, 6/8)—with the exception of the solemn, mysterious bars in the conclusion of the first and second parts[1]—there is frisking and whisking, tripping and skipping, again and again interrupted and accompanied by jubilant caroling. Who does not hear and feel those quickened pulses and pantings of joy! Neatness, agility, and spiritedness are the qualities demanded of the players for the execution of this work. The form presents neither obscurities nor remarkable novelties. After the first subject, in A major (thirty bars), comes a cantabile modulating passage (call it a transition, or regard it as a complementary first, or part of the second subject; please yourself), which leads to a second subject in E major, followed by a coda that ultimately concludes triumphantly. The working-out section, in consonance with the spirit of the composition, is light and short. As to the restatement of the matter of the exposition, it proceeds on the orthodox lines.

The second movement, an Andante più tosto allegretto (A minor, 2/4), consists of three sections, of which the third is a repetition of the first in a modified and extended form. The charm of the movement lies in its simplicity and naïveness, and in the truth of its tender, plaintive accents. In the middle section (F major) Beethoven carries simplicity and naïveness to their extremes; opinions will differ as to whether he thereby attained sublimity or the reverse.

The keynote of the last movement, allegro piacevole (A major, 3/4), is struck by the adjective piacevole; indeed, nothing can be more "pleasing than that flow of delicious suave and cheerful melody that extends

---

[1] The passage starting twenty measures before the first double bar, where the constant eighth-note and sixteenth-note motion ceases and the two instruments play a chorale-like passage in unison spanning three octaves.—Editor.

from one end of the piece to the other."[1] The form is that of a rondo.
Here is the scheme:

1. a (A major, modulating to)
   b (E minor, modulating to)
   a (A major)
2. c (D major; followed by a transition of considerable
        extent based on motives from a)
3. a (A major)
   b (A minor)
   a (A major; not a repetition, but constructed out of
        motives derived from the principal subject)

FREDERICH NIECKS (1)

[The first movement of Sonata No. 2] in A major offers so good an
example of Beethoven's part placing that it will serve as well as any later
work to show his master craftsman's cunning. The first subject opens with
the theme in the piano, the accompaniment in the violin part; [the
theme consists of a falling arpeggio embellished by the lower neighbor
note on each step of the descent; the accompaniment consisting of a
simple "um-pah-pah" on the lowest strings of the violin]. When this
is repeated the parts are reversed, yet not exactly, because Beethoven's
perception told him that, while it was quite satisfactory for the piano to
carry the melody notes across the low, jog-trotting accompaniment of the
violin, it would not sound well if the violin, when charged with the
melody, got mixed up with the middle of the piano chords. Beethoven
not only solved the problem but strengthened the musical interest by
his solution. [It was by the ingenious device of starting the descending
arpeggios on the violin and continuing them with the piano.]—MARION
M. SCOTT

I think this sonata deserved as well to be called the "Spring" as No. 5;
or perhaps, while in No. 5 spring is at its height, No. 2 is more like
the very first messages of spring. The opening theme is like the first
intoxicating breeze with the scent of spring.

As for the andante, it has the most touching and wonderful dialogue.
I can only imagine that St. Francis and St. Clara spoke of things like
that when they met at Assisi, and Beethoven alone could put it into
music, as he did so many conversations, each lovelier than the other.—
YELLI D'ARANYI

[1] Szigeti in the same essay discusses in detail the thematic interrelationship of this last
movement.—Editor.

c. *Sonata No. 3 in E Flat, Opus 12, No. 3*
I. Allegro con spirito; II. Adagio con molto espressione; III. Rondo (Allegro molto)

The first movement of this sonata is by no means of an exalting or enrapturing kind. Its subject matter consists of current phrases and figures, and the working out of these amounts to little more than a pretty sporting with commonplaces. But if Beethoven falls short of his better self, he does not fall short of the standard by which inferior mortals are measured. A man of genius puts his stamp on all he does. A commonplace uttered by him seems no longer a commonplace, and whatever he sets forth impresses us somehow with the idea of the eternal fitness of the thing. Hence we find also in this movement an opportunity for admiration and enjoyment. First there is the exhilarating "go" that distinguishes it generally, and further a number of beautiful details. We reach higher ground in the second movement. It is one of the early examples of his grand, long-breathed slow movements, in which the composer remains still unrivaled. Sublimity of feeling and a noble simplicity reign here supreme. The *con molto espressione* in the superscription is superfluous; every line, bar, and note call for it loudly. The form may be indicated by the letters *a, b, a,* the second *a* standing for the recurrence of the principal subject greatly modified and largely extended, after an intervening section (F minor, A flat major, etc.) Of course, such an indication is wholly inadequate for the appreciation of the beauty of the form which can only be realized by a detailed analysis.

With this calm and profound *Adagio*, the last movement, a Rondo overflowing with fun and merriment, contrasts effectively. No questionings here about "to be or not to be," or the why and wherefore of things. He who is not carried away by the spirits that are at play in this rondo must be dead to joy. Let me give you the program of their games:—

1. a (E flat major).
   b (B flat major).
   a (E flat major).
2. c (E flat minor, modulations).
   a (E flat, modified).
3. b (E flat major).
   a (E flat major, modified and extended).

—FREDERICH NIECKS (1)

d. Sonata No. 4 in A Minor, Opus 23
I. Presto; II. Andante scherzoso, più allegretto; III. Allegro molto

Opus 23, the A minor sonata, the first two movements of which were composed in 1800, was in print on October 28th, 1801. It appeared along with the sonata in F, afterwards published as Opus 24 under this title: *Deux Sonates pour le Piano-Forte avec un Violon composées et dédiées à Monsieur le Comte Maurice de Fries, Chambellan de S. M. I. et R. Par Louis van Beethoven Oeuvre 23, à Vienne chez T. Moll et Comp.* This sonata is a real gem, and marks an immense advance on its three predecessors. It might be called an idyl, so sweet and lovely is its character. Nowhere in it grandeur, charm everywhere. We cannot but marvel at the giant Beethoven's lightness of touch. But no less marvelous is the conciseness and exquisite perfection of form.

A swift and soft-footed *Presto* (A minor, 6/8) opens the work. In following its charming motions, mostly winding but sometimes tripping, do not overlook the humorous element. From the first subject (A minor) a transition (C major to E minor) leads to the second subject (E minor), followed by a coda. The working-out section, chiefly based on the first subject, partly also on the coda, introduces a new subject before the entrance of the next section. In the restatement the second subject begins in C major and modulates at once. An extended coda, in which the new subject and a motive from the first subject are resumed, brings the movement to a close.

Nothing can be more delightful than the playful [second movement in A major, 2/4]—note, please, the mock-heroic strut of the second half of the first subject. It has the first-movement form: the first subject of two parts (A major), the second subject (E major), a short working-out section discussing motives of the two halves of the first subject, and a restatement appears tricked out with [trills] twirls, and other ornaments,[1] and the second subject in its original form, but of course transposed to A major.

The restless, longing last movement, although not so named, is a rondo, but differs in form from those we have already considered. The following hints will sufficiently point out where the differences lie. I only premise that the section d is at least three times as long as the longest of the episodical sections that alternate with the principal subject (a).

[1] In the same essay Szigeti points out the difficulty of balance and blending of the two instruments just before the recapitulation, where the continuous melody is divided between the piano and violin, *in the same register.*—Editor.

1. a (A minor).
   b (modulating passage, C major—A minor, with E minor as chief key).
   a (A minor).
   c (A major).
   a (A minor).
2. d (F major).
3. a, b, c, d, a (A minor chief key—d in B flat major).

—FREDERICH NIECKS (1)

e. Sonata No. 5 in F, Opus 24
I. Allegro; II. Adagio molto espressivo; III. Scherzo (Allegro molto); IV. Rondo (Allegro ma non troppo)

The structure of the opening movement scarcely differs from that of the first period sonatas, with one reservation, namely, that there is always a double exposition of the subjects, the melody being first given to the violin, and then repeated in the piano part, an arrangement employed by Beethoven exclusively in his sonatas for two instruments, and this almost without exception. The "terminal development," anticipated in certain movements of the first period, can hardly be said to exist in this first movement and is suddenly curtailed by a somewhat commonplace coda.

The Adagio molto espressivo, whose initial theme seems to have escaped from some opera by Mozart, is an aria (lied) in five sections, the fourth of which is a finely expressive modulatory development, while the fifth is merely a conclusion with no definite return of the theme.—
WALTER WILLSON COBBETT

The Scherzo in F major is a gem, the charm and humor of which cover a multitude of musical subtleties. Unlike the usual practice of the eighteenth-century minuet or scherzo movements, the first half is not repeated in toto (Beethoven makes doubly sure by placing the following cautionary note over the music: "La prima parte senza repetizione."). His reason is that in actuality the short eight-bar phrase announced originally by the piano, ending in a half-cadence in the key of the dominant (C) is, in actuality, repeated, but with clever "reinstrumentation": the piano merely repeats its eight measures, but the violin plays along with it an octave higher, and delays the melody in some measures by one beat so that a delicious canon effect is achieved. In his typical brusque harmonic style of the period, he starts the second half (also only eight measures long) in the seemingly distant key of A major (after the previous cadence in C), without the benefit of a modulation; and equally without a transition returns abruptly to the original phrase in F. After a repetition of this minute but harmonically very adventurous second half of the Scherzo there is a delightfully tongue-in-check coda of four bars in which the last cadence is repeated three times but with the echoes of the violin getting twice as slow the third time.

The Trio (also in C) starts off with the violin and piano in thirds and sixths rather than in octaves as in the main portion of the Scherzo. (Note the enormous subtlety and care with which Beethoven changes the parallel scales of the violin and piano from thirds to sixths in the fifth measure in order to stress the dominant-seventh harmony rather than the tonic harmony which would have occurred if the previous relationship between the instruments had continued.) With this master stroke he was able to achieve an implied cadence: V_7–$I_6/_4$–II_7–V without seeming to change the even flight of the two instruments.—Editor.

The finale is assuredly the most original movement in the work. Constructed according to the very distinctive Beethoven rondo form, it proceeds as follows:

> *1st refrain*, in F.
> > 1st couplet: bridge and second theme, in C.
> *2nd refrain*, in F.
> > 2nd couplet, founded on fresh material.
> *3rd refrain*, in F.
> > 3rd couplet: bridge and second theme, in different keys.
> *4th refrain*, which concludes.

Everything goes as usual until the third couplet, which, far from proceeding in the manner of its first period relatives, leads the second theme away into unexpected and distant tonalities (A flat, E flat minor, E flat major), from which the latter extricates itself with much difficulty in order to find its way back to the fourth refrain. This last, presented under the guise of an *ornamental variation*, soon gives place to one of those endings of which Beethoven possessed the secret. This secret consists in introducing an entirely new element, but one so near akin, in its very essence, to the movement itself that it could not appear in any other sonata without doing violence to the work.—FREDERICH NIECKS (1)

f. Sonata No. 6 in A, Opus 30, No. 1
  I. Allegro; II. Adagio; III. Allegretto con variazioni

The three sonatas Opus 30 (A major, C minor, and G major) were composed in 1802, and first advertised as printed on May 28th, 1803, under the title *Trois Sonates pour le Pianoforte avec l'Accompagnement d'un Violon, composées et dédiées à Sa Majesté Alexandre I. Empereur de toutes les Russies par Louis van Beethoven. Oeuvre XXX. À Vienne au Bureau d'Arts et d'Industrie.* Now Beethoven is quite Beethoven:

he has parted company with his predecessors, and thrown off all visible ties that connected him with them. This we perceive at once on hearing the sonata in A major, and become more and more convinced of it as we proceed. We are transported into a poetic atmosphere, an atmosphere different from that enveloping the earlier works we have discussed. As to the two instruments, they form now an organic unity. The subject-matter of the first movement (*Allegro*, A major, 3/4) cannot be called important, but must be allowed to be charming. Nothing, however, shows more distinctly the change that has come over the composer than the working-out section, although the whole style and texture of the composition, notwithstanding their lightness, show it distinctly enough. Who will henceforth be reminded of Mozart or of any other predecessor? If I were asked to say what chiefly characterized Beethoven's style, my answer would be: its logicalness—the way in which every thought is developed, and the several thoughts connected.

The second movement (*Adagio, molto espressivo*, D major, 2/4) has the rondo-form.

a (D major).
b (B minor).
a (D major, followed by a transition through various keys—E flat major, and etc., to D minor).
c (D minor).
a (D major.—With a long coda in which new and old matter is worked up).

I take great pleasure in quoting approvingly [Lenz's][1] remarks in connection with this movement, of which he says that it belongs to the most effective and lovely music for violin and piano; that it is based on a *cantilena* whose impassioned expression is Italian in character; that, finally, it is a real violin declamation and contains in it a breath of the "Adelaide" (27th bar from the end, etc.).

The last movement of the sonata consists of a theme with variations (*Allegretto con variazioni*, A major, ¢). The broad *cantabile* nature of the theme, no less than more than one passage in the *Adagio*, calls to one's mind Beethoven's heavenly setting of Matthisson's "Adelaide." In the variations the contrapuntal element is very prominent (2nd, 3rd, and 5th), and throughout the several parts move with a wonderful ease, freedom, and buoyancy. A transition leads from the fifth to the sixth variation (*Allegro ma non tanto*, 6/8). There is nothing forced about this change of rhythm, as is often the case in the works of the older composers. The concluding *Allegro* comprises besides the variation proper a coda,

[1] Wilhelm von Lenz, 1808–83, Russian councilor at St. Petersburg, and, if not the originator, certainly the first outspoken proponent of the theory that Beethoven's works may be divided into three separate epochs each displaying a unique stylistic trend. —Editor.

which may be described as a fantasia on the theme. Whatever may be said against the last 18 bars, their liveliness cannot be questioned.— FREDERICH NIECKS (1)

Sometimes I wish when Beethoven was in such a hurry to finish the Kreutzer[1] for its first performance, he had taken the Adagio as well as the last movement out of the No. 6 sonata.[2] The Adagio of No. 6 is a great favorite of mine. The blend of the two instruments is so perfect a thing; that by itself is a joy, and besides the ethereal beauty of the theme every note of the accompaniment is full of expression and movement and quite as lovely to play as the theme itself. The whole movement has such a feeling of tenderness and sorrow it reminds me, if I am allowed the comparison, of Michelangelo's *Pietà*, and his unfinished marvel, the *Descent of the Cross*. I do not want to suggest that this adagio could be called religious music, I am only thinking in both cases of the expression of infinite tenderness and sorrow, whether put into sound or carved in stone.—YELLI D'ARANYI

g. Sonata No. 7 in C Minor, Opus 30, No. 2
I. Allegro con brio; II. Adagio cantabile; III. Scherzo (Allegro); IV. Finale (Allegro)

When we come to the seventh sonata we find ourselves on holy ground; there may be mutterings and thunderings, but they are the voice of divine vengeance, or the laying down of the law. The whole sonata is a master-piece.

After eight bars given to the piano, the violin continues the first subject [a virile theme which though commencing softly is like a taut spring about to snap—a theme based on the rhythm of one dotted half note, four sixteenth notes, and one quarter note followed by a silence of three beats, only gathering momentum in its fifth measure]. A strenuous but brief modulation leads to the second subject [announced by the violin, and featuring an almost military cast with its constant rhythm of dotted eighth and sixteenth notes and a pert staccato] to which the piano adds substance. A more stormy episode follows in which are some big climaxes. The fine [closing] section starts with a new [legato] idea [in the violin] to which the bass contributes the first six notes of [the opening theme] for foundation. [It] leads imperceptibly into the development section, where there is a working out of the [military second theme] first in octaves, then as the groundwork for a stormy

---

[1] It was never actually played by Kreutzer, for he thought it too outrageously unintelligible.
[2] The last movement of the "Kreutzer" Sonata, Opus 47, was originally intended as the finale of Opus 30, No. 1.—Editor.

dialogue. This having subsided gradually, the [first theme] returns in a mighty fortissimo, and then, after ten bars of quiet chords (a kind of rest or breathing place after the turbulence of the [development] section), we [continue with] the recapitulation. The Coda is as fine and passionate as any portion of the sonata.

The Adagio cantabile is solemn in tone, but charged with a beauty and attractiveness which make it ever welcome; it is "sacred" music in the truest sense of that much abused word. Its main theme [is] a diatonic sostenuto, noble and serene in character. A second strophe of equal charm follows, and then a more plaintive tone steals in, the violin having a long drawn out melody [of half notes] to which the piano adds a staccato accompaniment [of sixteenth-note arpeggios]. At the ninth measure the piano takes up the theme and the accompaniment is divided between the violin and the [bass of the] piano. Then the [suave opening theme] returns with a new accompaniment [made up of the sixteenth-note arpeggios and later thirty-second-note scales up and down. This] is followed by an extended Coda, which is most interesting. It starts with a new phrase [of eighth-note triplets] and mixes with it snatches of [the opening theme], now treated quite differently from heretofore, and brilliant little scale passages [now in sixty-fourth notes]. Unexpected modulations help to complete the charm of this "linked sweetness" long drawn out.

A bright tuneful Scherzo follows founded on a piquant [staccato] phrase [with unexpected offbeat accents and playful use of the dotted upbeat as accompaniment]. The busy little Trio is notable for its imitative passages.

The Finale is another busy movement but more serious than the Scherzo, its business being not to amuse but to stimulate one's moral faculties to higher and loftier purposes. Curiously enough it starts off with a sputter [of eighth-note upbeats, repeated staccato quarter notes, tentative short chords followed by silences, and sudden rough changes of dynamics]. Almost before we realize it the passage has been played twice, the second time more fully scored. The legato [continuation] is more staid, but [the opening sputter] dominates the movement. A pattering little phrase [in E flat] starts the first episode, and develops into a fine swinging melody. The [second episode] is taken up with a fugal treatment of the [legato theme which acted as a continuation of the main theme]. There is a masterly Coda in which a short phrase [of whole notes] plays an important part. Of this Coda we may say *finis coronat opus*, for it is indeed a really lofty and eloquent peroration, worthily concluding a sonata which has few, if any, superiors.—SAMUEL MIDGLEY

The Sonata in C minor offers an astounding contrast to anything that had been composed before in this genre. The four movements follow an almost symphonic plan. Beethoven's abolition of the customary repeat mark in the first movement was a bold course dictated by the urgent nature of the music. The impression of a "poetic idea" behind the work is insistent. Five or six years later he would have made his meaning so clear that no one could miss it—as in the "Appassionata" Sonata—but there is no gainsaying that the C minor [violin] Sonata has a protean quality that provokes opposite views. [It has been called] one of the great masterpieces and [said] of the first and last movements that "their wonderfully strong, sombre energy and passion strike a note hitherto unheard in Beethoven's music." Beethoven experienced no vacillation over the first and last movements, but was less certain about the Adagio cantabile and the Scherzo. As originally planned, the Adagio stood in G major. Its opening theme would have sounded heavenly on the violin in that key. But Beethoven transposed it into A flat major, perhaps thinking that key better for the piano, or that the *barbaresco* (his own word) nature of A flat was more suitable in this stormy sonata. One cannot feel convinced by Beethoven's afterthought. The key finally chosen did not afford enough change from the note C, which persists throughout the sonata with almost Russian monotony. Moreover, A flat, a closed key on the violin, muffles its capacity for cantabile. The Scherzo is a most piquant movement. Later on Beethoven talked of it as out of keeping with the rest and wanted to remove it; he even wanted to reduce all his four-movement sonatas for piano and violin to three. Fortunately he was dissuaded.—MARION M. SCOTT

The grandeur and symphonic scope of the Sonata in C minor has already been touched upon. It is the power of the dramatic message that seems to lead Beethoven to these utterly new instrumental formulas, these torrential scales, staccato-martellato passages, the superimposition of long, plaintive lines into subterranean rumblings in the bass (in the coda of the first movement). These formulas (the percussive and the declamatory aspects of the "Kreutzer" also come to mind) have given the violin-piano sonata a new dimension. This new approach permeates everything that follows: there is that "time stands still" moment in the moving, contemplative song of the Adagio [at the twenty-seventh and twenty-eighth measures before the end, and again eight measures later, where] it is interrupted by the fortissimo summons of the piano just before the theme turns for a brief moment to the consoling key of F major. The sforzando cross rhythms of the Scherzo, the symphonic proportions of the Finale with its relentless drive, with its dissonances (see seventeenth bar before the end), they all open up new vistas and it is difficult for us to visualize the impact such a work must have made at the time of its appearance.

This is the place to mention [an interesting sidelight on] the canonic interplay after the first sixteen bars of the C major tune [in the Finale. The theme starts at measure 107. It is noteworthy that] the following eleven bars (in C major) [measures 123 to 133] were an *afterthought* on Beethoven's part. These eleven bars were clumsily sewn with white thread onto the final manuscript, which I had the privilege of seeing in Zurich at Dr. Bodmer's house, before it was deposited at the Beethoven House in Bonn. (These interpolated eleven bars precede the return of the C minor working-out section and they afford us a precious glimpse into the workings of a great mind, intent on enriching and improving up to the very last moment.—JOSEPH SZIGETI (1)

h. Sonata No. 8 in G, Opus 30, No. 3
I. Allegro assai; II. Tempo di menuetto (ma molto moderato e grazioso); III. Allegro vivace

The eighth sonata, although not on the same level as the seventh and the ninth, is yet a sonata we would not willingly dispense with. The first and last movements are bright, jovial, and merry, but the middle movement is a bit tedious.[1]

The opening Allegro assai has a somewhat frisky subject [alternating a measure of sixteenth-note scale-based figures with pert arpeggios of staccato eighth notes]. The continuation, however, is quieter and more staid. A rollicking modulation leads to the second [group made up of many thematic elements: a theme starting with pianissimo chords in the piano in B minor followed by the sixteenth-note passages of the opening theme, then a flowing legato passage in very supple three-part polyphonic writing transposing to a vigorous theme in D minor of quarter and eighth notes whose melody is later played at twice the speed, finally cadencing in D major, where another theme with rhythmic upbeats and a sighing figure on each downbeat appears]. The listener will be continually charmed by the ever-varying moods.

The Tempo di menuetto has a simple yet graceful first subject [in which the theme is first played in the piano with smooth quarter-note countermelodies in both the violin (*below the piano*[2]) and the bass of the piano. The continuation is full of subtle phrase groups of 2/4 in an over-all 3/4 pulse]. The Trio is based on a broader, more sustained melody [first announced by the violin with a simple accompaniment in the piano punctuated by accents on the weak second beat of each measure]. Judging by the number of times the subjects are repeated [and the variety of accompanying figures], it would appear that Beethoven was fond of them, since, not content with writing out the repeats

---

[1] A viewpoint to which I take vigorous exception. Its gentleness conceals many remarkable musical and structural subtleties.—Editor.
[2] Italics by the editor.

in full, he actually repeats *both* sections of the minuet *after the Trio*,[1] and in addition writes an unusually long Coda, which is based primarily on the theme of the Trio. [It is as if he were going to follow the scheme of repeating the Trio a second time, as in the Seventh Symphony, but he very adroitly cuts off the Trio material and closes the Trio with thematic material from the first part.]

Most welcome is the Finale with its artless and genial flow. Before the entry of the violin the piano plays a [sixteenth-note] figure on which the violin superimposes a [scherzolike] little [eighth-note figure] in the fifth measure. This engaging amiability and gaiety characterize the whole of the Finale, a movement perfectly simple in subject matter, most of its passages springing naturally from [the sixteenth-note figure and its eighth-note counter-subject]. The construction, however, is very free, the episodes being extremely short and containing scarcely any new subject matter. There are some delightful modulations and the whole bubbles over and sparkles along in the most charming manner. It might almost be incorporated in Mozart's *Figaro* with its lightheartedness and effervescence.—SAMUEL MIDGLEY

i. Sonata No. 9 in A, Opus 47 ("Kreutzer")
I. Adagio sostenuto, Presto; II. Andante con variazioni; III. Finale (Presto)

So popular a classic as the "Kreutzer" Sonata needs either no analysis or else a very detailed one. It is not, like the Schumann Quintet, a work in which certain minute points can be made to throw light on some special peculiarity of artistic method, for it is thoroughly in touch with the early classical conceptions.

For the present it must suffice to mention a few respects in which the "Kreutzer" Sonata is more unusual than disproportionate familiarity disposes us to recognize.

The first of such points that occurs to me is that it was, and still is, a very unusual thing that a work introduced so broadly in a major key should proceed to a stormy and passionate first movement in the minor. I am aware of only two instances before the "Kreutzer" Sonata, the first being Mozart's G major Violin Sonata (K. 379), where, however, the opening adagio is felt as something much more independent than an introduction, and the second being a very early pianoforte quartet on precisely the same lines as the Mozart sonata, by Beethoven himself—a work which he afterwards carefully disowned.

It is, again, perhaps interesting from a dramatic point of view to note that in the introduction to the "Kreutzer" Sonata it is only the first four

[1] Italics by the editor.

bars (for the unsupported violin) that are really in A major, though their breadth is such that the seal of A major seems at once set upon the work. But the entry of the pianoforte casts a most dramatic cloud over the opening and sets the tone for that wonderfully wistful, yet terse anticipatory expression that makes this introduction one of the landmarks in musical history.

As to the following presto it is, perhaps, well to guard oneself against a misconception that has misled not only a certain great novelist[1] but also many less nervous music-lovers into underrating the rest of the work. The mood of the first movement is very fiery and passionate, but it is the passion of Homeric fighting, not that of Aeschylean tragedy: and the rich set of ornate variations follows with exactly the right contrast of tone; while the happy and witty finale (though originally intended for a smaller and earlier work, which it would most certainly have overbalanced) is the one possible outcome of the other two movements that is neither trivial nor sententious.

The type of form shown in the first movements of sonatas contains all the elements of Beethoven's art in its highest state of organization. In taking advantage of this, we must beware lest it lead us into the common error of estimating our musical value simply by counting up their obvious intellectual assets. How foolish this is with passages taken out of their context! It is not less foolish, and it is a much more likely error, in the case of whole movements and whole art-forms.

The commonest form of this error is that which invariably criticizes a small, or lighthearted, finale as the weak point of a work. [Naturally,] we need not suppose that Beethoven is infallible. He often changed his mind in the earlier stages of a composition, and in two important instances he wrote a new finale, transferring the original brilliant finale of the Violin Sonata, Opus 30, No. 1, to the "Kreutzer" Sonata, partly because it was too brilliant for the earlier work, and partly because he had arranged for a public performance of the "Kreutzer" Sonata and had no time to write any other finale. The first movement of the "Kreutzer" Sonata is immeasurably finer than the rest of the work, but the criticism that despises the rest of the work is based on the assumption that, in works that proceed in time, the best should be reserved for the end. And this is simply not true. In the first place, as the eminent painter asked of the brainless athlete who said he could not keep fit on less than so many hours' exercise a day, "Fit for what?"—best for what? *That finale is best which is the most refreshing after what has gone before.*[2]—DONALD FRANCIS TOVEY (8)

[1] See Leo Tolstoy's novella *Kreutzer Sonata*, which melodramatically pictures a husband murdering his wife due in part to passions aroused by Beethoven's sonata.—Editor.
[2] Italics by the editor.

While Beethoven's piano works generally reflect his own keyboard virtuosity, he was on less familiar grounds in his violin compositions. His collaboration with Viennese violinists like Franz Clement, Ignaz Schuppanzigh, and Joseph Boehm was useful though he was inclined to scoff at advice. More casual was Beethoven's contact with visiting virtuosos, yet he may have gathered some valuable information about the French violin style through the visits of Kreutzer, Rode, and Baillot. Beethoven's interest in the French violin school was primarily concerned with the technical aspects of the instrument.

Kreutzer came to Vienna in 1798, accompanying the French ambassador, General Bernadotte. Beethoven, who at that time was a frequent visitor at the French legation, may have met and heard Kreutzer there. In 1804 Beethoven remembered Kreutzer as "a good, amiable man who during his stay here gave me much pleasure. His unaffectedness and natural manner are more to my taste than all *extérieur* or *intérieur* of most virtuosos." Beethoven also thought highly of Kreutzer's musical ability, for he decided to dedicate his Violin Sonata Opus 47 to him. "Since the sonata is written for a first-rate player, the dedication is all the more fitting."[1] The work was originally composed for the violinist George Bridgetower; the dedication to Kreutzer was an afterthought, planned as a surprise to the recipient. Possibly Kreutzer resented this sequence of events; at any rate, he did not acknowledge the dedication or play the sonata in public. Obviously Beethoven misjudged his "good friend," for Kreutzer continued to show hostility toward Beethoven's works when the conductor François Habeneck tried to introduce the Second Symphony to the Parisian public. According to Berlioz, Kreutzer found Beethoven's Sonata Opus 47 "outrageously unintelligible."[2] The whole concept of equal partnership may have struck him as absurd; in those days, the virtuoso expected preferential treatment even in chamber music. On the other hand, this sonata certainly did not lack brilliance; in fact, Beethoven had planned it "in a very *concertante* style, in the manner of a concerto."[3] While the second and third movements show an idiomatic treatment of the violin, the first movement is "outrageously" awkward; furthermore, the piano tends to overpower the violin, which is often held in too low a register.—BORIS SCHWARZ

[1] Both quotations from letter to Simrock, Oct. 4, 1804.
[2] H. Berlioz, *Voyage musical en Allemagne et en Italie*, Paris, 1844, p. 263 f.
[3] *In un stilo molto concertato, quasi come d'un Concerto*, wrote Beethoven on the inside of his sketchbook of 1803 (described by G. Nottebohm).

VII. 6 Deutsche Tänze (Allemandes) for Violin and Piano, WoO 42

These six simple dances are much more primitive than the orchestral German Dances, WoO 8, etc. They are all constructed on a two-part scheme (two eight-measure phrases each repeated). In almost all of them the first, as well as the second part, ends in the tonic, so there is not even the variety of modulation. Only Nos. 3 in F and 6 in G have trios, and only in the last do the harmonies deviate from the tonic, dominant, and dominant-seventh chords. The violin writing is extremely crude, mostly doubling the right hand of the piano or adding simple accompanying figures.—THOMAS K. SCHERMAN

VIII. Sonata No. 1 in F for Violoncello and Piano, Opus 5, No. 1
    I. Adagio sostenuto, Allegro; II. Rondo (Allegro vivace)

> "Music is the true element from which all poetry arises and to which it all returns."
> —GOETHE

It was in 1795 that Beethoven appeared for the first time before the Viennese public. [The appearance] must have been a great success, because in the following year he was invited to give concerts in Prague, Nürnberg, Dresden, and Berlin, where he made the acquaintance of King Frederick William II. At the court he was much admired as a pianist, composer, and improviser. Since the king was a passionate devotee of the cello, Beethoven got the idea during his stay in Berlin of writing and dedicating to him the two sonatas in F major and G minor for piano and cello.[1] The dedication brought him a magnificent snuffbox "like those given to ambassadors," full of louis d'or.

The appearance of the Sonata, Opus 5, No. 1, marks a memorable date in the history of the violoncello sonata, because before it there had been no "duets" in which the piano part was so thoroughly worked out as to assume the same importance as the stringed instrument. And how splendidly Beethoven met this first test! With a most fortunate selection of themes, he was able to maintain the sonata character from the beginning to the end, and if in the finale he felt like using the rondo form, it cannot be said, as Bekker[2] ventures to assert, that it was

---

[1] At the court of the same Frederick William II a cordial reception was also given to Boccherini and to Mozart, who dedicated to the sovereign his quartets with the cello "soli" in the highest positions. Haydn had also dedicated six quartets to him.
[2] Paul Bekker, *Beethoven*, Schuster and Leoffler, Berlin-Leipzig, 1911.

only for the sake of giving the performers a pleasing change from the austerity of the preceding movements.

[It] begins with a short Adagio, profound and full of feeling. While the theme is developed between the cello and piano, suddenly the latter goes into an elegant virtuoso passage leading majestically to a crescendo, which ends (in typical Beethoven fashion) piano and then pianissimo to bring to an end the beautiful prelude. The pause is very brief, and the piano attacks the theme of the Allegro, a noble, tranquil theme of pure Beethoven style. It is taken up by the cello, taking on a very special charm. [The music] alternates again between the two instruments and develops in the most interesting way, swelling in controlled joy, passing to tender sentimentality [with a subtly syncopated theme starting in A flat but cadencing in the key of the dominant C. After brilliant scale figures echoed between the two instruments another extended concluding theme ends the exposition with passages of true transport].

The first theme appears again [after the exposition], with slight variants, in the tonality of A major, prepared by two solemn sonorous chords, and then goes into D minor; and while the parts go forward, now tranquilly, now with accents of passion, the theme returns triumphantly in F major. But perhaps the supreme moment of the movement appears toward the end, when the piano, in an elegant passage in sixteenth notes, diminuendo e rallentando, brings us to a six-measure adagio that gives the violoncello a superb chance to display itself in its finest notes on the second and third strings. This short, mysterious, totally unexpected adagio perplexes the hearer, who asks himself, "What is this?" The answer comes from the piano, which starts the Presto and makes it clear that the ending is being prepared. In its turn the cello makes a surprising entry, and the two instruments break into a long and stirring trill on the chord of the dominant seventh, on which they come back to the main theme.[1] The cello sings, the piano accompanies it, and after a few measures the movement closes in a wealth of sound and joy.

The Allegro vivace has a joyfully tripping theme. The parts interweave and chase each other in the most fascinating contrapuntal play and combine in triumphal sonority. This leads us to a second theme [starting in B flat minor], which derives from the first one: we are in the midst of "dance music," music of full folk flavor, fresh, smooth, delightful, recalling the theme of one of the figures of the lancers, the celebrated international dance form. Here Beethoven enjoys himself by

[1] Actually this is all part of a written-out cadenza a duo commencing after the typical fermata over the 6/4 chord (fifteen measures before the Adagio) and concluding with the triple trill which leads back to the Tempo I, which acts as a short coda. —Editor.

creating all sorts of effects of accent and contrast, then returning to the first theme in masterly fashion. At the outset it appears only faintly in the figuration, but in the end, after being prepared by a brilliant, impetuous passage on the piano, it re-enters decisively, sung pianissimo in thirds by the two instruments [under a long trill by the pianist's right hand]. Then it suddenly varies again in forte and fortissimo and arrives at a fermata, after which Beethoven, with one of his famous rallentandos, prepares [the listener for] the final measures of the movement. After two delightful adagio measures, the F major chord returns, full and strong, the Tempo I is taken up again, and the last eight measures frame off the beautiful and exciting sonata.—EUGENIO ALBINI (TR. BY THOMAS K. SCHERMAN)

IX. SONATA No. 2 IN G MINOR FOR VIOLONCELLO AND PIANO, OPUS 5, No. 2

    I. Adagio sostenuto ed espressivo, Allegro molto più tosto presto; II. Rondo (Allegro)

It must be noted that Beethoven's violoncello sonatas display a particular structure which is not to be met with in the violin sonatas, still less in those for piano. It would seem that the composer, attracted by the tenor voice of the instrument, has done his best to bring out this singing quality by means of broad, slow phrases, and to give it more importance than the element of virtuosity. This tendency explains why [the first two] sonatas open with a long and often pathetic introduction, and also why the second subjects of the quick movements—the expressive subjects—are treated at much greater length than in the other sonatas.

[The opening of] Opus 5, No. 2 [consists of] a broad Adagio, developed at some length. In the Allegro, which follows, while twenty-six bars suffice for the statement of the first theme, the second, not content with spreading itself—at a length of ninety-five bars—over three phrases differing in character, sees fit to take to itself a further complementary Coda, by way of [an] ending to the expository section. We notice, in the transition passage between [these] two themes (the technical term for which is the "bridge"), a rhythmic figure, employed by Beethoven eight years later, for the same reason, in the first movement of the Third Symphony ("Eroica").[1] After the development, which calls for no particular notice, and the recapitulation, which is the usual repetition of the exposition, there appears, for the first time in the history of music, a modification introduced by Beethoven into the regular scheme

[1] This is the motive starting at measure 50 of the Allegro of Opus 5, No. 2, and at measure 45 of the first movement of the "Eroica." It is also interesting to note that both these transition passages lead to a second group in the key of B flat.—Editor.

of the sonata. The movement proper is concluded, but the composer is anxious to emphasize the several constituents in order to drive them home, and he here introduces a fresh system of development which we call a "terminal development," in the course of which the first theme reappears, hesitating and in broken rhythm, before he finally concludes. This arrangement, unknown to Haydn and Mozart, is regularly employed by Beethoven in his remaining works.—WALTER WILLSON COBBETT

After the melancholy character of the G minor, the passage is made to the Rondo, whose laughing theme is in great contrast with the preceding movements.

The main element in the development of this movement lies in the figuration and the virtuosity of the two instruments.

The themes, always beautiful and brilliant, go from cello to piano and back, or are given to one or to the other, depending on their character. What a delightful surprise is the theme in C on the piano accompanied by arpeggios on the cello, "sempre piu piano e leggiero," as Beethoven directs! The episode is repeated, each time more agreeably.[1] And what shall we say of the point at which the piano makes its re-entry from a modulation in A flat to the main theme, while the cello sings those marvelous eight bars of the second theme! The entire Rondo enchants performers and listeners with its brilliance, its freshness, and its unexpected dynamic effects.[2]—EUGENIO ALBINI (TR. BY THOMAS K. SCHERMAN)

X. 12 VARIATIONS FOR PIANO AND VIOLONCELLO ON THE THEME "*Ein Mädchen oder Weibchen*," FROM MOZART'S *Zauberflöte*, OPUS 66

These variations were written in 1799, two years after the two sonatas for piano and cello, Opus 5, that were written for King Frederick William of Prussia. Since the cello part in the variations is not as spectacular as in the sonatas, it is likely that they were written for a cellist who was not quite as accomplished as the great French soloist Duport, for whom he conceived the two sonatas.

The unique feature of Papageno's aria in the opera is that the first phrase of each strophe is in a moderately paced 2/4 with a full cadence in

[1] Prod'homme in *La Jeunesse de Beethoven* points out that the second phrase of this C major episode is lifted bodily from Beethoven's early setting of Lessing's "Lied" for voice and piano, published as No. 6 of Opus 52.—Editor.

[2] A pleasant anecdote is told about this sonata (*Die Musik*, 3. Beethoven-Heft, 1903–4). Domenico Dragonetti (1773–1846), the celebrated Venetian double-bass player, came to Vienna in 1799 and soon became a great friend of Beethoven. One day they decided to play the cello sonata in G minor and Dragonetti played it so well that Beethoven was enraptured. At the arpeggios of the finale, he was so moved that as soon as the final chord had sounded he sprang up to embrace Dragonetti, along with his double bass.—Editor.

the tonic which is followed after a short pause by the second phrase in a sprightly 6/8 which starts in the dominant. Then by the introduction of the flatted seventh in the melody, the dominant harmony becomes a dominant seventh and the strophe ends with two repeated cadences. This variety of tempo and the shift from dominant to dominant seventh give this delightful aria its unique feeling of jauntiness and its somewhat kittenish flavor.

Beethoven, in adapting the arietta as a theme for an independent set of variations, very wisely simplified the structure in order to save the variety of tempi for the later variations. There are still the two phrases, but the second is set in the same allegretto 2/4 as the first. The feature that Beethoven does emphasize in the theme is the point in the second phrase where the dominant harmony shifts to dominant seventh. He has a crescendo to a sforzando at the change of chord, which is further stressed by a fermata. This fermata is a feature of all the variations.

Among the most interesting variations is No. II, in which the harmonies are changed vitally by a chromatic bass and shifting inner voices. The cello part in this variation is the most brilliant in the entire set with the exception of the final variation.

Variation V contains very clever melodic imitations among the three voices. Variation VII changes the dominant seventh in the second phrase to a dominant ninth, and the fermata is filled out by a series of trills on a descending chromatic scale. In the first minor variation (X), which is an adagio, the same dominant seventh is changed to a diminished seventh chord. This variation is followed surprisingly enough by another adagio variation, also in minor, in which a noble legato theme in quarters played on the lower strings of the cello is backed by an accompaniment of repeated chords in triplets in the piano. Beethoven very subtly changes the role of the two instruments as the piano triplets get more melodic and take over the lead while the deep quarters in the cello become the bass. The fermata is now decked out with a florid cadenza, leading to the two-measure cadence figure which is repeated three times, the last time incompletely. This leads to the last variation (XII), an allegro 3/4 which is highly developed. Each phrase of the theme is repeated and has an extended Coda in which the motion is continued shifting the harmonies through D minor to the remote but very bright key of D major, in which key the cello repeats the theme. Two casual measures bring the music back to F major, where the piano has the last word in the ornamentatation of the theme. The end is a Beethoven surprise: after brilliant scales in the cello and the piano the dynamic suddenly changes to pianissimo and the whole piece ends lyrically.—

THOMAS K. SCHERMAN

XI. 12 VARIATIONS FOR PIANO AND VIOLONCELLO ON A THEME FROM HANDEL'S ORATORIO *Judas Maccabeus*, WoO 45

The three sets of variations for piano and cello represent an art form which Beethoven cultivated enthusiastically all through his career. The twelve variations on a march from Handel's oratorio *Judas Maccabeus* are close both in period and in style to the Sonatas Opus 5, so that they belong to the time when Beethoven derived inspiration from the playing of the virtuoso Duport.[1] The highly popular melody "See, the Conquering Hero Comes" by Handel, whom Beethoven revered, undergoes a succession of mainly figural variations, in which the basic tonality of G major darkens into G minor only in the fourth and eighth variations. In general this potent, optimistic theme is presented in a variety of ways to illustrate different musical features derived from it (cantilena phrases, chains of triplets, staccato passages).—KARL SCHUMANN

XII. 7 VARIATIONS FOR PIANO AND VIOLONCELLO ON THE THEME "*Bei Männern, welche Liebe fühlen,*" FROM MOZART's *Zauberflöte*, WoO 46

The seven variations on the duet "Bei Männern, welche Liebe fühlen," from "The Magic Flute," largely adhere to the six-eight rhythm of the melody, but they are more free, brilliant and expansive than the previous set. The piano and cello parts are equally virtuistic in conception. There are abundant rhythmical and harmonic contrasts. The true variation of character (this work was written in 1801 at the time of the 2nd Symphony) comes into its own especially in the Allegro Finale, which anticipates the joyous élan of certain middle period piano sonatas.— KARL SCHUMANN

XIII. SONATA FOR FRENCH HORN AND PIANO IN F, OPUS 17
I. Allegro moderato; II. Poco adagio, quasi andante; III. Rondo (Allegro moderato)

Horn players are intrepid people, for the horn has the reputation of being the most difficult of all instruments—after painful acquisition of the technique, music itself may conceivably be produced. Jan Václav

---

[1] The celebrated French cellist Jean Pierre Duport, about whom Voltaire remarked, "*Vous avez fait d'un boeuf un rossignol!*" Duport was living in Berlin at the time Beethoven visited the court of King Frederick William II, for whom the two sonatas Opus 5 were dedicated. As the king's cellist, he was the first interpreter of those works.—Editor.

Stich (1746–1803), better known under his Italianized stage name of Giovanni Punto, fled a serf's life in Bohemia to become, in his early twenties, the most accomplished horn player of the second half of the eighteenth century. Mozart was very impressed by him, Beethoven even more so, for Punto revealed the possibilities of the horn more than anyone he had previously heard. Thayer says that this kind of revelation "delighted" Beethoven: "Nothing more natural, therefore, than his readiness to compose a sonata for himself and Punto to be played at the latter's concert" (April 18, 1800). According to Ries: "Beethoven began the work the day before the performance, and it was ready for the concert."

Opus 17 is quite unabashedly a showpiece made of Beethoven's delight, and is one of those generous gestures which were not untypical of him. The Rondo is particularly effective, allowing the horn a pleasant series of exuberant gambols. It is not profound music, nor is there any reason that it should be: it was written to entertain, though the Adagio is meditative. The Beethoven signature is nevertheless easy to discern, and the work betrays certain characteristics of this phase in Beethoven's development.—WALLACE BROCKWAY

XIV. THEME AND VARIATIONS FOR MANDOLIN AND PIANO, WoO 43; SONATINE FOR MANDOLIN AND PIANO, WoO 44

This title will not seem surprising if its recalled how popular the mandolin was at the end of the eighteenth century, at the time when Sor and Carulli were on every music stand, when Hummel, Weber, and Mozart himself were not above writing for one of the last representatives of the lute family. By Mozart, there are two melodies with mandolin accompaniment, "Was frag' ich viel" and "Komm, liebe Zither, komm." And everyone remembers Don Giovanni's serenade. It is definitely for the mandolin and not for any similar instrument. Berlioz, in his Traité d'orchestration, took the trouble to say so, with his usual sharpness.

Although with a few days of study a guitarist or even an ordinary violinist can become familiar with the neck of the mandolin, people in general have so little respect for the intentions of the great masters, they allow themselves to play the mandolin part of Don Giovanni on pizzicato violins or guitars. The timber of these instruments does not have the mordant finesse of the one they are replacing, and Mozart knew very well what he was doing when he chose the mandolin to accompany his hero's erotic song.

Accordingly, Beethoven could have written for this instrument; he must have done so. And as a matter of fact, in 1888, in the Supplement to the great Breitkopf edition, Dr. Mandyczewski published two compositions by the Master, one entitled Sonatine, the other Adagio, which show that the composer of the Ninth Symphony was no exception to the fashion of his time.

For my part, I recently had the good fortune of discovering a series of pieces for mandolin and piano, whose attribution is beyond any question. They had been buried in the library of the Counts von Clam-Gallas in Prague. Among them is the adagio that Mandyczewski published, but in its completed form, not in the rough draft of the manuscript that was used for the Breitkopf edition. And moreover—and this is very important—the autograph version in the collection of the Counts von Clam has the dedication "*Pour la belle J. par L.V.B.*" (For the fair J. by L.V.B.). Finally, along with these two pieces, already known, there are three others, still for mandolin and piano, which have remained completely unknown down to the present. It is one of these that is discussed here.

The "*belle J.*" here is the Countess Josephine Clary, who later became Countess von Clam-Gallas. It was to her that Beethoven dedicated the great concert air "*Ah perfido.*"

It is known that Beethoven stayed in the capital of Bohemia in 1796, drawn there, as Mozart had been seven years earlier, by the munificent patronage of Prince Lichnowsky. He lived, as he says in a letter to his brother Nicholas, in the house of the "*goldenen Eichorn*" and had a very good time in the City of a Hundred Towers. He was well received by Prague society. In the forefront of that society [was] the Count [Christian Philip] von Clam [a noted patron of the arts, especially music].

Count Christopher (1771–1838), eldest son of Count Philip, was one of the founders of the Prague Conservatory, which is still in existence at this time. On November 30, 1797, he married Josepha, Countess Clary.

Beethoven was a frequent guest at the house of the Counts von Clam. We have a proof of this in a curious passage in the memoirs of the musician and teacher W. J. Tomaschek:

I heard Beethoven for the third time at the house of the Count von C. . . . . The original and the singular seem to have been the core of composition for Beethoven. And thus, when a lady asked him whether he often went to hear Mozart's operas, he replied: "I don't know them, and don't care to hear the music of others, for I want to keep my own originality."

Such was the young and spirited Beethoven whose muse the Countess Clary had inspired. The "Ah perfido," Opus 65, is dedicated to her, as we have said.

[The] sketch [for this scene and aria] brings us back to our subject, for it is followed by a few bars which are note for note in the Allegro for Mandolin [Sonatine]. This last confirmation, added to what we have seen up to the present, seems decisive to us. The work found in the papers of the Counts von Clam, dedicated to Countess Clary, is one of the series of compositions by the author of *Fidelio*, in the course of a visit to Prague, which must be dated 1796. And so the Beethoven literature is enriched by a new work.

The reader will judge the value of the work. That value is the same as that of many other compositions of the master's youth. It is music for entertainment, amiable, elegant, and well suited to an instrument for pleasing the tastes of a dilettante aristocracy.—ARTHUR CHITZ

Chamber Music Without Piano

I. SEPTET FOR CLARINET, BASSOON, HORN, VIOLIN, VIOLA, VIOLONCELLO, AND BASS, OPUS 20
I. Adagio, Allegro con brio; II. Adagio cantabile; III. Tempo di menuetto; IV. Andante con variazioni; V. Scherzo (Allegro molto e vivace); VI. Andante con moto alla marcia, Presto

The Septet for string quartet (violin, viola, violoncello, and bass), clarinet, bassoon, and horn, Opus 20, is contemporaneous with the First Symphony and is the high point of [the] early cycle of chamber works of Beethoven. Drafted during the same period as the quartets, Opus 18 (1799), it is a perfect example of the genre so happily cultivated by Mozart—*divertimenti*, cassations, and serenades. It is dedicated to the empress and was publicly performed on April 2, 1800, but it had undoubtedly been played previously in a private concert at the home of Prince Schwarzenberg. Its publication, in July 1802, was followed almost immediately by arrangements for quartet and also for piano, published under Beethoven's supervision. Also Beethoven later made an arrangement which he entitled "Grand Trio for Pianoforte with Clarinet or Violin and Violoncello, after the Septetto arranged by the same author," [which] appeared as Opus 38.

Eighteen measures of adagio in 3/4 precede the first allegro con brio. The violin dominates it like a messenger about to announce the action to follow. It does so in long (and slightly mannered) arabesques which are interrupted, at first, by the heavy chords of the other instruments marking each beat of the measure, but then retiring to the role of accompaniment. The strings, minus the bass fiddle, announce the first theme, which is in 2/2 (ten measures). This is taken up almost immediately by the clarinet. It is a brisk theme which is not dissimilar to that of the Sonata in F for Violoncello (Opus 5, No. 1). By means of two other episodic ideas it is linked to a second theme in B flat. Here, the clarinet and the bassoon, separately and then together, answer the phrases of the strings. The exposition closes, fortissimo, and the development section opens, equally loudly, with all the instruments presenting the opening theme in unison in C minor. That theme then reappears, changing key as each instrument, in turn, has its chance to play it. After a recapitulation, which is almost textually identical to the exposition, there is a surprisingly long coda, in which the closing theme is expanded into a broad mellow phrase, played first by the horn, and then taken up by the other instruments.

The lyrical theme of the Adagio cantabile in A flat, 9/8, is played first by the clarinet with string accompaniment, and then taken up by the violin. It lends itself to short rhythmic variations where the fioratura passages of the violin predominate. Beethoven was to use a similar technique twenty years later in the Adagio of the Ninth Symphony. It is as if this particular theme [of the septet] were a very distant anticipation of that great movement.

The divertimento usually contained two minuets preceded and followed by a slow movement. Beethoven conformed to this, but he replaced the second minuet by a scherzo. After the long Adagio he obviously does not wish to lay too much stress upon the Tempo di minuetto. He satisfies himself by orchestrating, in a light and happy manner, a minuet from the as yet unpublished Sonata, Opus 49, No. 2.[1] To its two foursquare phrases, he adds a fast and spirited trio which leads directly to the da capo.

The Andante is based on a popular Rheinish theme[2] commenced by the violin and viola and completed symmetrically by all of the instruments. These eight measures are repeated and followed by a second phrase of eight measures, which balances the first phrase. This very calm theme has the style and allure of the old pilgrims' songs. It is followed by five variations in which the ingeniousness of the composer is revealed, having at his command, as he does, almost the entire gamut of the orchestral timbre. In the first variation, the viola and violoncello pass the

[1] The same theme was used earlier in the slow movement of the Trio, Opus 11. —Editor.

[2] "Ach, Schiffer, lieber Schiffer!" which Andreas Kretzchmer published in his German Folk Songs (1838). But the editor seems to have provided the words to Beethoven's music, although he gives as his source "according to a widely known street-singer, Frau Luetzenkirchen." It is actually, therefore, not known whether this tune existed before Beethoven's Septet, or whether, on the contrary, it was derived from the latter. —Editor.

theme from one to another, to a quiet, almost indefinite, accompaniment of the violin. But in the second variation, the violin sparkles with arpeggios and rapid passages while the other strings, strengthened by little touches of the clarinet and bassoon, serve their turn as accompaniment. The first part of the third variation is played by the clarinet and bassoon restating, in their own manner, the theme in canon. The strings do likewise for the second part of that variation. The fourth variation, in minor, gives the main role to the horn, which plays a slow but brief melody over a fast, light accompaniment in triplets by the violin. The horn phrase is repeated by the two other wind instruments while the bass instruments of the quartet stress each beat, pizzicato. The contrast among the three groups of instruments is marvelous. With the fifth (and last) variation the theme returns quite simply, harmonized at first by the quartet (four measures) and then by the complete ensemble. As is often the case with Beethoven, the Coda, this time of twenty-five measures, alluding lightly to the theme, presents many sudden dynamic changes which, here in the septet, are made even more piquant by the variety of timbres.

The horn, somewhat neglected until now, sounds the fanfare in E flat which opens the Scherzo. This movement is in a joyous and free mood. As mentioned earlier, it takes the place of a second minuet. It is in the form of a scherzo followed by a trio, each having two phrases which are repeated. Beethoven did not compose as pithy a scherzo until that of the Third Symphony. While the latter is more dramatic and mysterious, here all is light and serene, as proclaimed by the simple, almost banal theme of the Trio, which is sung by the violin.

Next comes the finale, preceded by an andante con moto alla marcia in E flat minor (sixteen measures), the gravity of which contains nothing of passion or of melancholy. Its slow gait serves more to stress the bounce of the main theme of the final Presto. That theme is announced first by the strings and repeated, in a spirit of gaiety, by the clarinet and the bassoon. The first part of the movement is repeated and it is between that repetition and the final recapitulation that we hear the wind chorale which was borrowed from the Sextet, Opus 71.[1] That foursquare chorale, melodically and in its stately tempo, is not unlike the theme of the variations which preceded the Scherzo. After this momentary repose which the chorale provides, a violin cadenza (considered rather banal by today's standards) leads into the last appearance of the main theme in the recapitulation. The Coda, in which the violin dominates the six other instruments with its rapid arpeggios, forms a

[1] Prod'homme in his discussion of the Sextet, Opus 71, points out that, in its rondo, which has a brisk fast-moving main theme, Beethoven inserts for contrast a slow chorale-like theme. The melody of that theme (A flat, B flat, A flat, G, A flat, B flat, G, A flat) is almost identical to the chorale theme which appears in the middle of the rondo of the septet.—Editor.

brilliant conclusion to the movement and to the entire work—a fitting end for an eighteenth-century serenade.—J.-G. PROD'HOMME (1) (TR. BY THOMAS K. SCHERMAN)

II. SEXTET IN E FLAT FOR 2 CLARINETS, 2 BASSOONS, AND 2 HORNS, OPUS 71
I. Adagio; II. Adagio; III. Menuetto (Quasi allegretto); IV. Rondo (Allegro)

The Sextet in E Flat, Opus 71, for pairs of clarinets, bassoons, and horns, dates from 1796, though its first two movements may perhaps come from earlier composition, possibly out of the many suppressed works of the Bonn period which Beethoven brought with him to Vienna. (This large body of early music until recently was not even known to have existed.) The work is a forerunner of the immensely popular Septet, Opus 20, of a few years later, the best known of all Beethoven's early works. The septet, though not so named, was a true divertimento (more properly, a serenade), with six movements and both a minuet and a scherzo; the sextet, like many of Mozart's, is an abbreviated divertimento with only four movements. Though these terms were somewhat old-fashioned in Beethoven's day, the tradition was still strong and Beethoven had studied it closely. The typically relaxed, outdoor quality of the divertimento style is very much apparent in the sextet as is the traditional wind sound, so long associated with easy entertainment music, and the characteristic wind key of E flat. After 1800, Beethoven wrote no more music in this manner.

The opening movement of the sextet is its longest by far, a body wagging the tail of its three other movements (somewhat as the overture in the baroque suite dominated its "tail" of short dance movements). A brief introduction, adagio in the manner of Haydn, leads to the relaxed, minuetlike allegro, more nearly moderato, led off by the perky clarinet. Attuned to the Austrian wind tradition, the music is full of brilliant solo scales and mellow arpeggios for each of the three types of instruments. But the prevailing mood is lyric, a long, leisurely string of melodic ideas, bound together by a relaxed harmony. Indeed, here we have a direct ancestor of the later "Eroica" Symphony, in the same key and in the same triple time. There are interesting (but never very tense) modulations in the short development section, which ends with one of Beethoven's favorite indulgences in later music, the long-drawn-out dominant-seventh chord before the return of the opening idea. There is even an almost-cadenza near the end—an explosion in the horn, no more. That is enough. The music is precisely calculated in its chosen degree of relaxation-with-coherence.

The short slow movement, not particularly contrasted, continues the lyric quality of the first movement in a slower tempo. Bassoon and clarinet are featured in many lovely melodic excursions; the harmony moves gently to the dominant, B flat, and goes no further; the opening bassoon melody reappears without an intervening development. Again, a calculated simplicity. The minuet is virtually a scherzo, though still with the characteristic horn passages of earlier and slower minuets; Beethoven knew the tradition. (By the time of the "Eroica," the horns had taken refuge in the central Trio—they could not play fast enough for the high-speed scherzo.) The final movement is a brilliantly casual rondo; for all its masculine vigor it once more avoids expressive complications in favor of relaxed simplicity. The pattern is a simple A B A C A with an energetic B in the minor and a predictably gentle C section in the subdominant major,[1] sandwiched between expositions of the Rondo A section. Even the traditional pattern for this section is observed knowingly; the first and last A are played out complete with repeats, whereas the central A is a shortened one. So did Mozart write on a hundred occasions. So also, later, did Schubert.

It is interesting that the theme of this finale has close relatives in a number of other Viennese works of the day. A wind divertimento of Mozart uses virtually the same tune, minus the dotted rhythm.[2] The slow movement of Schubert's Second Symphony, composed eighteen years later, is a charmingly feminine echo of the very same idea—in the same key.

In 1809, submitting the sextet at last for publication, Beethoven wrote his publisher that it was one of his earlier works, "written in a single night." It was a typically quixotic remark, for in fact he had worked on it, intermittently, during some fifteen years before it was brought to its ultimate and publishable form. So Beethoven's sketches tell us. The man was an incredible perfectionist in his music, the embodiment of that "infinite capacity for taking pains" that is one aspect of genius. It would be a mistake to think of [this composition] as in any way immature or superficial. Beneath [its] deliberate suavity is the work of a master of musical architecture.—EDWARD TATNALL CANBY

III. SEXTET FOR STRINGS AND 2 HORNS, OPUS 81B
   I. Allegro; II. Adagio; III. Rondo (Allegro)

This Sextet belongs to Beethoven's early chamber music period and illustrates the development of the younger Beethoven as he proceeds

---

[1] It is this section which has a choralelike flavor that Prod'homme points out is echoed stylistically in the Septet, Opus 20.—Editor.
[2] Divertimento, No. 12, K.V. 252, written in 1776, twenty years before the Beethoven sextet.—Editor.

from movement to movement. The last movement, Rondo, is one of his most beautiful compositions: A vigorous and rhythmical first subject foretells the magnificent Rondo of the Violin Concerto, and a haunting second subject gives it great profundity. The first movement is less expressive, being limited to a pattern of conversation between Horns and Strings, though it contains some beautiful Horn passages. The second movement already reveals some of that passionate "Weltschmerz" which in later years characterized all Beethoven's slow movements.

Especially noteworthy is Beethoven's treatment of the Horn. At the time of composing the Sextet, the valves were not yet introduced. Beethoven, however, must have anticipated this development, as he demands a degree of virtuosity from the player which was far in advance of his time.

Composed between 1794 and 1795, the Sextet was first published by N. Simrock, Bonn, the parts in 1810, the first score in 1846.—ALEXANDER VOGEL

IV. STRING QUINTET, OPUS 4 (AFTER THE OCTET, OPUS 103)
    I. Allegro con brio; II. Andante; III. Menuetto (Allegretto); IV. Finale (Presto)

In the *Wiener Zeitung* of the 8th February, 1797, the following was advertised as just published: *Grand Quintetto per due Violini, due Viole, e Violoncello del Sgr. Luigi van Beethoven. Opera IV. In Vienna presso Artaria & Comp.* While during the last fifty years one has occasionally encountered in concerts the younger brother of this quintet, the Opus 29 so popular among amateurs, Opus 4 has hardly ever been performed. Also the amateurs, who happily enough have not died out altogether, usually refuse to play this Opus 4 and give as their reason that it is only an adaptation of the wind octet published in 1834 as one of Beethoven's posthumous works, with the misleading Opus number 103, a composition which certainly reaches back to Beethoven's stay in Bonn.

It seems impossible to eradicate this prejudice. Notwithstanding I have already in the 1st volume (1901-2) of the periodical *Die Musik*—which is not intended for music scholars but for the large circle of music friends—given proof of the fact that this string quintet is by no means a mere arrangement of the wind octet but a complete revision and augmentation was inspired to this investigation, in which the varying number of bars in which the original second themes have been replaced by others. I was inspired to this investigation, in which the varying number of bars of the respective works are also quoted, by the note of Hermann Deiters in the 1st volume of the 2nd edition of his version of A. W. Thayer's "Life of Beethoven," p. 288 (published 1901) which reads: "In regarding the octet one must free oneself entirely of the reminiscence of the quintet Opus 4 of which it is the original version. The latter is not merely . . . an arrangement, but an entirely new and frequently augmented revision." I also pointed out that Beethoven evidently knew that Mozart had converted a wind octet (Koechel 388) into a string quintet, however without thematic changes and augmentations, a thing Beethoven also avoided when in 1817 he created from his Trio Opus 1 No. 3 the string quintet Opus 104.

Deiters, and his successor Hugo Riemann, thoroughly agreed with me in the 2nd volume of the above mentioned Beethoven book (1910) p. 33 and continued as follows: "Superficial inspection, it is true, shows that the themes in Opus 4 are the same as those in Opus 103; but careful comparison goes to prove that the quintet, utilizing those themes, is an entirely new work. Not only have the string instruments been given their due with regard to sound quality and efficiency, involving changes of pitch, rearrangement of themes, etc.; the structure has undergone decisive changes. Already in the first movement we find the first countertheme entering in a different key; the end of the first part, the development, the return to the theme, the conclusion, all are entirely remodeled. Similarly the charming Andante has become an entirely new movement through the addition of new themes and richer employment of the existing ones; the Scherzo has retained its character but undergone many changes; in the first Trio the violin has been given an opportunity for elaboration, and a second Trio, charmingly polyphonic and with interesting modulations, has been added. In the last movement the time has been changed (2/4 instead of 4/4) in accordance with the easier rendering by the instruments; cutting out a passage of the original a new second theme has been found, and the figurations, adapted to the character of the string instruments, are far richer, especially rich toward the end, nothing of which is found in the octet. Only the wonderful, soaring and hope-inspiring intermediary theme in A flat . . . has been retained but is then developed independently. Naturally the beautiful sound of the horn could not be upheld and has been replaced by appropriate passages in the violins. Everything is greater, also more artistic; in compass and content the composition oversteps the character of light entertainment or table music." Evidently it was for this purpose that the octet was created, following the model of others and the custom that royalty and the nobility retained eight wind musicians for their table music (as did Don Giovanni in the second finale of Mozart's opera). This is also indicated by the heading *parthia* (meaning *partita*) of the original manuscript which must have been in the hands of the Electoral hornist and music publisher Nikolaus Simrock in Bonn not later than August, 1794.

In the 3rd volume of the *Zeitschrift für Musikwissenschaft* (1920–21), pp. 159–79, Alfred Orel once more investigated very thoroughly the relations between the quintet and the octet, he emphasized that the former had been divested of the character of entertainment music.[1]

Let us hope that at last Beethoven's Opus 4 will receive full recognition as a string quintet and will no longer be set aside as a mere arrangement.— WILHELM ALTMANN (1)

V. String Quintet, Opus 29

I. Allegro; II. Adagio molto espressione; III. Scherzo (Allegro); IV. Presto

A string quintet in C major was begun about 1800 and published in 1802 as Opus 29. Even though it was written after the string quartets of Opus 18 were well on the way to completion and was indeed published after the quartets, the quintet retains certain of Beethoven's early characteristics. But it also quite definitely points to the future and gives an indication of what is to come after 1802. This is one of the transitional works which lies squarely across style boundaries.

Few of Beethoven's works flow as smoothly and easily as the quintet's first movement; its melodies move from cadence to cadence with a quality of repose that is delightful. The lyric, florid adagio, with its recitative-like middle section and its wealth of contrapuntal detail, is a charming inspiration worthy of comparison with the best works of Mozart. These two movements, taken together, are probably as closely akin to the mature Salzburg master as anything Beethoven wrote. But these beauties are echoes of the past.

Then the picture changes; at once we enter a new tonal world. The third movement, a pungent and concentrated scherzo, is generations removed from Beethoven's immediate predecessors. Its dominant feature is a one-measure motive, repeated ceaselessly in every instrument and on every scale step. This is a late Beethoven characteristic: the reiteration of a single figure. The scherzo moves forward relentlessly, and clearly anticipates certain of the great scherzos of later decades. And the finale is a

---

[1] The article mentioned is highly recommended and bears the most detailed study by anyone interested in Beethoven's "arrangements" of his own works and his extraordinary sensitivity to the differences in the media for which he is writing. Its length and musical detail unfortunately preclude it from inclusion in this book. Orel's conclusions are that in the short space of years between the octet (1792) and the quintet (1796) the great London symphonies of Haydn had appeared and, by osmosis if not actual study, Beethoven felt this change of emphasis in his larger forms. Whereas the octet looks backward to the divertimenti and serenades of the past, the quintet expresses the more serious expression and intent of the great Viennese symphonic works. That Beethoven not only felt able to, but *clearly obliged to,* make this major revision, while still keeping the essential thematic structure intact, shows how far the court composer at Bonn had developed into the great symphonist of the future. —Editor.

surging, restless piece containing probably the most advanced contrapuntal passages Beethoven had composed up to that time. The form
itself is enlarged; it includes three complete themes plus a codetta, and, in
the development section, an entirely new theme which prepares for and
justifies the final coda. Transitional details and modulations in this finale
deserve careful study; the whole movement is a masterwork. In this
fragmentary description of the third and fourth movements we see the
Beethoven of the future.

In what respects, then, is the C major quintet a transitional work?
In what sense is it merely anticipatory of second-period works and not
one of them? The question cannot be answered fully until Beethoven
reveals his later characteristics in the string quartets. But a phrase comes
to mind, one that indicates in which direction the answer will lie:
the generating power of the individual motive. Beethoven, in his post-
1802 compositions, became able to endow his motives with life of their
own. An organic growth, logical and controlled, and virtually unknown
in music previous to that date, is disclosed. In Opus 29 that organic
growth was not attained, even though other characteristics of the second
period were. Thus, the quintet came to the very border of the new
style without crossing it. With all its qualities, it is essentially a first-period
work.—HOMER ULRICH

VI. STRING QUARTETS
a. String Quartet No. 1 in F, Opus 18, No. 1
I. Allegro con brio; II. Adagio affetuoso ed appassionato;
III. Scherzo—Allegro molto; IV. Allegro

It is difficult to believe that so blithe and naïve a theme as that which
launches this first quartet is one of those laboriously wrought ideas that
found its definite form only after much hesitant experimentation. It is a
matter of record on the evidence of the composer's sketchbooks that not
even the "Joy" motive of the Ninth Symphony gave Beethoven so much
trouble in bringing about a satisfactory form. J. de Marliave[1] records that
five complete pages of one notebook and eleven of another are devoted
to experimentation on this theme.

[Nottebohm cites several tentative forms, most of which are in 4/4
instead of the final 3/4. In all of them the first five notes are the same
as the final form but the last two notes are quarter notes, instead of
eighth notes, to accommodate the rhythmic change. In all of them he
repeats the significant turn: F, G, F, E, F in various registers. Only in the
final tentative form is this turn followed by the important note C, which
distinguishes the final form.]

[1] Joseph de Marliave, author of *Essai sur les quatuors de Beethoven*, and *Études
musicales* (1917).

Once the idea was satisfactorily hammered into shape, Beethoven literally worked it for all it was worth; it became all-pervading throughout the first movement. Even the subordinate theme is subservient to the tyrannical little turn of the initial *motif*.

In the pursuit of his artistic ideals Beethoven's intuitions never played him false. The youthful composer, as revealed in this work, seems to be doggedly set upon achieving a perfect clarity of texture and a maximum of euphony. The seeming superficiality of thematic material of the first movement may well have been a deliberate means to this end. If the pattern is somewhat too obvious, the total effect is a simple integrity of style within self-imposed limits and a brilliancy of sonority that might have been lessened with more self-sufficient thematic material.

The second movement, *Adagio affetuoso ed appassionata*, is at every turn a frank avowal of a romantic impulse. It is, however, the romanticism of Beethoven's early period which becomes entangled with obvious Italianisms that were accumulated, in all probability, during the composer's apprenticeship as cembalist in the opera house at Bonn.

For the comfort of those who crave the *extra* illumination of verbal interpretation, there is Amenda's[1] story that it was the tomb scene in Shakespeare's "Romeo and Juliet" that inspired this movement. A measure of credence attaches to this interpretation on account of a sketch dated 1799 which bears the words, "*Les derniers soupirs,*" at the end of the movement.

The Scherzo *Allegro molto*, shows more affinity with Haydn than with Mozart by reason of its high-spirited humor and its capricious syntax. Sir Donald Tovey[2] is authority for the statement that Beethoven never made specific use of the term *scherzo* unless the movement to which it was attached showed humorous implications.

We cannot agree with M. de Marliave that this movement is "*but a hint* at the sparkling tonal audacities that the artist is later to mould into his form." On the evidence of the rhythmic treatment alone, the twenty-nine-year-old composer has gone far to indicate his own inimitable style.

The Finale, *Allegro*, maintains, to a remarkable degree, a sense of cumulative verve and vitality. It reveals at many points a greater resourcefulness and spontaneity than the first movement. This sense of vigor may be perceived through the finely contrasted rhythmical structure of the prevailing ideas.

The first is a distinctive run in sixteenth-note triplets, starting with

[1] Karl Ferdinand Amenda, young friend and companion of Beethoven, to whom the composer gave the manuscript of the F major quartet.
[2] Sir Donald Francis Tovey (recently knighted for distinguished achievements in musicology), Reid Professor of Music, Edinburgh.

*the characteristic turn F, E, F, G, F of the first movement and followed
by a descending scale to the low E. The E is repeated twice and jumps to
the third above. This, incidentally, is close to the composer's first sketch
for the first movement which was cited by Nottebohm.*

*The movement is in the form of a rondo, and the bridge section to the
first interlude is characterized by an ascending scale (in the relative minor
key of D minor) but this is in staccato eighth notes rather than legato
sixteenth-note triplets. The scale ascends from low A to a high F which is
held momentarily and then descends, still in eighth notes but this time
legato instead of staccato and characterized by mordents on every other
step of the scale.*

*The second interlude, which appears after the second appearance of the
original theme, is a lyrical passage in an entirely new rhythm—a dotted
quarter followed by an eighth note and in the remote key of D flat.
—Editor.*

It seems that César Franck must have remembered well the above D flat
major theme, which found its analogy in the second theme of the finale of
his own splendid quartet.—ARTHUR SHEPHERD

It was in the spring of last year when I was invited to participate in
a chamber music evening at the home of a family that I knew, that I
played Beethoven's Quartet, Opus 18, No. 1, in its *initial setting*.[1] Beethoven's F major quartet in its first version! Who would not be intrigued
by the possibility. The present lucky owner of the rarity is Frau Anna
Kawall, whose maiden name was von Amenda, the granddaughter of
Karl Ferdinand Amenda. That Amenda, during his approximately one
year's sojourn in Vienna in 1798–99, struck up an intimate friendship
with Beethoven and often played music with him, and had the questionable privilege of being the confidant of the innermost spiritual troubles
of the great man, is well known to any student of Beethoven's life and
works. Amenda was probably one of the first to know of Beethoven's
disastrous hearing malady, for the letter to Amenda of June 1, 1801,
unveils the deeply hidden secret of Beethoven's heart, and in tender
words he reveals to his "fondly beloved" friend his apprehension and
inner struggle. In this letter we also find that Beethoven requested
Amenda, in reference to the aforementioned quartet, which he had
probably presented to him at their separation, "not to show it to anyone
for it has been very much changed. I have only just learned how
properly to write quartets."

At the head of the first violin part, in as clean a hand as that of the
carefully written copy, Beethoven inscribed the following dedication:

[1] Italics by editor.

BELOVED AMENDA!

Accept this quartet as a slight remembrance of our friendship. As often as you[1] play it for yourself, please remember our days together, how sincerely good you were, and always shall be.

Your true and warm friend,

LUDWIG VAN BEETHOVEN

Vienna, June 25, 1799

The composition which was published in the year 1801 as Opus 18, No. 1, has the words "Quartetto II" on the first violin part and is therefore actually the second of the first six quartets.

Through the kindness of the owner I am in the position to make first movement of the quartet.[2] It will certainly be welcome to all Beethoven enthusiasts to have a comparative glance into the workshop of the mighty Titan and see what he meant by "just now learning to write quartets properly."

In every measure of the later version, as opposed to the original, we find that Beethoven has arrived at more conciseness, and more concentration of form and structure, without altering the strength of the voice leading. For example, we discover that the passage from measures 15 to 35, up to the appearance of the main theme in B flat minor, is two measures shorter. This cut is, on the whole, one of the most trenchant alterations of the first version to be shown. The first four measures of the realization remain unchanged. Then already in the fifth bar of the later version there emerges a reconstruction of the composition formula, which introduces the important tonality in the modulation to B flat minor, which does not appear in the original version until ten bars later. This produces a more and more gradual change in the physiognomy of the passage so that the new key is well established in the listener's ear. The rhythmic transformation, the homogeneous treatment, and the imitative changes among the various instruments, as well as the symmetrical interlocking of the thematic threads, endow this passage not only with a fully new tone color but in retrospect ensures it a significant place in the over-all symmetry and dramatic keenness of a well-formed structure. One has only to examine the B flat minor entrance itself and observe the leadership of the violoncello as a substitute for the bass voice; the yielding toward F minor; and particularly the passage toward C major and the iridescent intensification of that key up to the repetition of the main theme in its own tonic, where as a result of the countermovement of the main motivic figure between the cello and the second violin, sup-

[1] Beethoven uses the familiar "Du" and "Dir" throughout the dedication.—Editor.
[2] In the appendix to the issue of "Die Musik" (Volume 12, March 2, 1904) which contains this article, Waack collated the two versions of the quartet in parallel staves.—Editor.

ported by the syncopated exploitation of the middle voice and the first violin, everything works toward a heightening of the pull toward the resumption of the fundamental idea—and one can easily understand the energetic polishing which Beethoven undertook for the benefit of the definitive publication. Also a comparison of the dynamic differences is highly interesting, such as the sforzandi in measures 19 and 20, 25 and 26, 31 to 34, and so forth.[1]

Beethoven, as has been proved, set to work in putting forward his compositions with painstaking precision and care, and this first version of the quartet acts as an extremely worth-while example to witness this creative process in action.—CARL WAACK (TR. BY THOMAS K. SCHERMAN)

b. String Quartet No. 2 in G, Opus 18, No. 2
I. Allegro; II. Adagio cantabile; III. Scherzo—Allegro; IV. Allegro molto quasi presto

A study of Beethoven's melodic style, as manifested throughout his amazing artistic evolution, will reveal many fascinating details which focus the attention on his creative processes.

D'Indy, Mies,[2] Nottebohm,[3] Bekker,[4] and other Beethoven students, have pointed out many characteristics which, as they carry over from one work to another, seem to represent an expansion or development of the same train of thought.

The vernal freshness of the opening theme of the second quartet finds a certain analogy in the theme of the violin sonata in F major Opus 24, familiarly known as the "Spring" sonata. But a gratuitous German christening, presided over by Theodor Otto Helm[5] has encumbered this work with the name "Compliments Quartet." "The principal subject," declares this commentator, "brings before one's imagination a brilliant scene in some eighteenth-century *salon*, with all the ceremonious display and flourish of courtesy typical of the period. The doors of the drawing-room swing open to usher in the arriving guests, met with bows and gracious words of greeting.[6] The master of ceremonies, the host of the

[1] In the comparative collation of the two versions by Carl Waack the measures are numbered from the beginning of the development section at measure 135 of the first movement. Readers who wish to study the two versions should therefore adjust the measure numbers accordingly.—Editor.

[2] Paul Mies (1889–   ), author of *Beethoven's Sketches: an analysis of his style.*

[3] M. G. Nottebohm (1817–1882). Noted chiefly for his Beethoveniana.

[4] Paul Bekker (1882–   ), author of "The Story of Music," "Beethoven," and other historical writings.

[5] Theodore Otto Helm, Ph.D. (1833–1920). Distinguished music critic and aesthetician.

[6] The contrast of rhythmic and melodic ideas among the first eight measures undoubtedly gave rise to the author's pictorial description: the first two measures are characterized by a quarter note, an elaborate rising flourish in thirty-second

evening, looks upon the gaiety with a smoldering passion in his eyes, felt in the theme in D major, a theme characterized by two soft staccato chords followed by a sudden sforzando and then more staccato chords played twice as fast, but he cannot resist the impulse of the moment. . . ."

The stylistic affinity with Haydn and the peruked elegance may easily be conceded, but one can hardly be expected to endorse the rest of Helm's fantastic "hifalutin."

In the *Adagio cantabile*, the Haydnesque manner is again in evidence. De Marliave points to the interruption of the slow tempo and the ensuing *Allegro* section as an innovation on the part of Beethoven, but here again Haydn had already broken the ground in the final movement of his *C major quartet, Opus 54, No. 2*, wherein there is a similar slow-fast-slow alternation. Note also the elaborate variation in Haydn's movement and Beethoven's similar procedure.

It is a constant surprise to learn from Beethoven's sketches how often his original or tentative thematic ideas were transformed from a binary to a ternary measure. One of the early forms of the *Adagio* theme of the second quartet [was in 4/4 time with the original descending C major arpeggio appearing as four even quarter notes instead of the more subtle dotted quarter and three eighth-notes of the final form. The first sketch has two phrases of two measures each, whereas the uneven three-bar phrases of the present form are far more pungent. The melodic outline, however, is fairly identical in both the sketch and the finished product. This raw sketch of the first six measures of the theme] eventually achieved far greater lyrical beauty in its final perfected contour.

The *Scherzo* (here again Beethoven makes specific use of the title) is replete with capriciousness, gaiety and wit. The wit ran to the extent of making the *Scherzo* theme play a disguised secondary role as variant of the theme of the preceding *Adagio* movement, [that is, the rhythmically pert first six measures of the *Scherzo* theme follow remarkably closely to the melodic outline of the beginning of the *Adagio*—the falling arpeggio and the poignant descending second of each three-measure phrase].

The correspondence between the two themes may be a pure coincidence, but it is also highly indicative of Beethoven's mental or subconscious processes working toward a unification of his materials beyond the formal boundaries of the individual movements.

The spirit of gaiety is maintained in the Finale, *Allegro molto, quasi presto*. Helm, giving further reign to his fancy, remarks: "The cham-

---

notes, and a return to the original note; the second two measures are made up of a staccato descending arpeggio in the very jerky rhythm of a double-dotted eighth note followed by a thirty-second note; the last four measures are legato and lyrical, ending comfortably on the tonic.—Editor.

pagne has been round. . . ." But here the commentator is in safer ground, for Beethoven himself described this movement as *"aufgeknopft"* (unbuttoned).—ARTHUR SHEPHERD

c. String Quartet No. 3 in D, Opus 18, No. 3
I. Allegro; II. Andante con moto; III. Allegro; IV. Presto

No authentic reason is given by Beethoven's biographers for the composer's numbering out of order these three quartets. There is, to be sure, his urgent request to Amenda to suppress the original draft of the F major quartet (the second in actual order of composition) in favor of a much improved revision. One may indulge in a bit of guesswork on the basis of internal evidence of the printed pages. With regard to inner expressiveness and freedom from what was aptly called "Zopf (pigtailed) Musik," the first movement of the D major quartet (the first of the set in actual order of composition) is distinctly superior to that of the quartet in F major. There is, in the D major, less subservience to stereotyped pattern and figure. Externally there are, to be sure, many points of adherence to the Haydn-Mozart formulae: an insistent emphasis on symmetry in phrase balance; the inclusion of a quasi *scherzo* movement that harks back to the Minuet style; the predominance of the first violin through many pages of each movement. On the other hand, one has not far to look to discover bold strikes betokening the individuality that was predestined to enlarge the potentialities of the quartet medium.

It is in the harmonic procedures and the ordering of tonalities that Beethoven's native independence is most strikingly demonstrated. Unexpected modulatory digressions provide an admirable foil for the more conventional structural features. Note, for instance, the emphasis on the key of C major in the second element of the subordinate theme, affording a happy palliative for a too insistent A major (key of the dominant). It was in such matters that Beethoven became the true tonal logician.

Serenity, contemplativeness and nobility pervade the slow movement, *Andante con moto*, which pursues its course with impressive deliberateness. In breadth of design and true internal development, it goes ahead of the typical Haydn or Mozart slow movement, and gives intimations of one of Beethoven's most important innovations: making the slow movement the expressive apex of an entire work.

The formal design of this movement is that of the Sonata-Rondo and in style it conforms to what d'Indy designates as the *"Lied developpé."*

There is a certain ambiguity in the usual classification of the third movement as a scherzo. Some call it a minuet. Beethoven called it neither and was satisfied to append only the tempo indication—*Allegro*.

It is clearly of minuet lineage, and in style it harks back to Mozart rather than to Haydn.

Here again, it is well to look beneath the surface, for while the texture is as simple and transparent as that of Mozart, the composer achieves a unique purity of sonority through a stark economy of means and sheer perfection of part-writing.

The final movement, *Presto*, reveals the thirty-year-old master at his jolliest. It is a veritable *tour de force* of gay badinage, yet there are indications in the sketchbooks that the thematic material did not spring forth whole and radiant like Minerva from the brain of Jove. The first draft of the theme [is in 6/8 time, but with the upbeat slurred to the first two eighth-notes, followed by a succession of similarly phrased three-note motives in which the three notes each form descending steps of the tonic arpeggio. However, the first note of each group is the upper note of the particular arpeggio, and always appears as an upbeat, resulting in] a figure which automatically displaces the natural accent in accordance with the highest note. How much more pungent and fluent the idea became in its perfected form [where the stressed note, the highest note, is always on the main beat].—ARTHUR SHEPHERD

d. String Quartet No. 4 in C Minor, Opus 18, No. 4
I. Allegro ma non tanto; II. Scherzo—Andante scherzoso quasi allegretto; III. Menuetto—Allegretto; IV. Allegro

With dramatic suddenness the first movement of this quartet confronts us with the Beethoven of tragic portents. Coming in the midst of the five other works of this set—all in major tonalities—the C minor of the fourth brings us in touch with the fateful reverberations that became more and more resonant with the onrushing years.

Paul Bekker, d'Indy and others have expounded at length regarding the esoteric significance attaching to Beethoven's choice of tonalities as affecting his own particular psychologic and poetic schemata. Bekker asserts that "it is quite justifiable to speak of a 'C minor problem' dominating the tragic works of Beethoven's youth and early manhood which later gives way to 'F minor and D minor problems.'"

Thus Bekker senses in this C minor quartet "a gnawing inner dissatisfaction; a desire to meet and overcome difficulties; the spur of ambition and the longing for victory." It is at any rate an abrupt contrast to those "magnificent lies" of smiling visage with which the tone-poet defiantly confronted a cruel fate as he came to a realization that his noblest faculty (his hearing) was subject to permanent impairment.

From the fact that no preliminary sketches of this work have been found, it is surmised that it was written rapidly, in the heat of inspiration. This observation seems to find a measure of confirmation in the close organic relationship between the principal and subordinate themes in which the figure [of an upward leap of a sixth, answered by a gentle downward glide of a second,] plays such an important role as unifying element.

In the second movement the designation "scherzo" is somewhat arbitrary. Its tempo indication: *Andante scherzoso quasi allegretto*, modifies the characteristic rapid tempo of the usual scherzo. It is, moreover, cast entirely in fugal style, which, in turn, is adapted to the Sonata design with regulation "bridge" passages, development and recapitulation. What more impressive evidence of technical mastery could one look for? But it may be remembered that mastery was already in evidence in Beethoven's Opus I.

In the following *Menuetto—Allegretto*, the profile of Mozart is once more discernible; the *sforzandi* on alternating notes of the first phrase being reminiscent of the Menuetto of the older master's G major quartet (the first of the set of six dedicated to Haydn).

If Beethoven pays deference to Mozart in the third movement, just as definitely does he doff the hat to Haydn in the finale. Some commentators seem called upon to explain or justify the nonchalant style of this movement with reference to the weightier content of the first movement. D'Indy finds comfort in pointing an analogy with the rondo movement of the piano sonata Opus 13 in C minor (the *"Pathétique"*).

There is a lively anecdote concerning a detail of the finale of the C minor quartet. The story comes from Ries[1] in reference to a passage in the second phrase, which he interpreted as "forbidden" fifths: "One day as I was walking with him (Beethoven) I mentioned the instance in one of the first quartets (that in C minor) where two perfect fifths are used with striking beauty and effect. Beethoven did not remember the passage, and thought that I was wrong, and that they could not have been fifths. As he usually carried ruled paper with him, I asked him for some, and noted down the phrase in four parts. Realizing that I was right after all, Beethoven remarked: 'Ah! well! Who is it who says that perfect fifths are wrong?' I was not sure how to take the question, but he insisted, until I replied at length, quite disconcerted, 'They are forbidden by the first fundamental rules of harmony.' The question was repeated again, and I added, 'It is Marpurg, Kirnberger, Fuchs, and all the theorists, who forbid the use of consecutive fifths . . .' 'Very well,' replied Beethoven, 'I allow the use of them, thus!'" It seems, almost, that Beethoven was making sport of Ries, for the fifths in question move in contrary direction and are apparent to the eye only, and certainly not to the ear.—ARTHUR SHEPHERD

[1] Ferdinand Ries (1784–1834), noted pianist; pupil of Beethoven and Albrechtsberger.

The occasional displays of counterpoint in Beethoven's early works are far more than merely competent. They are, unquestionably, brilliant. They are not as unostentatious as Mozart's, and they are not meant to be, for Beethoven never released himself from his task of increasing his dramatic range; but take the triple counterpoint that adorns the recapitulation of the *Andante scherzoso quasi allegretto* in the C minor Quartet, Opus 18, No. 4. If our masters of counterpoint have any criteria according to which that is not masterly, their criteria must lie outside anything we want to know about classical music. Further discussion of Beethoven's counterpoint as such belongs to a later chapter, but we must already beware of confusing the question of its intrinsic qualities as counterpoint with the general musical and dramatic question of the limits to the use of contrapuntal devices in sonata style and of explicit philosophic argument in drama. This parallel between music and drama is exact. The danger of a passage of fugue in a sonata is that it stops the action, just as a philosophic discussion may stop the action of a drama.— DONALD FRANCIS TOVEY (1)

e. String Quartet No. 5 in A, Opus 18, No. 5
I. Allegro; II. Menuetto; III. Andante cantabile; IV. Allegro

The division of [Opus 18] into two *cahiers* could have been occasioned by nothing more than a publishing convenience, but there is a certain sense to the separation, whether accidental or not, that strikes deeply into the quality of the works. For all their great variety and their even greater invention, the first three quartets of Opus 18 hold in principle to the standard design; they are serious, intense works in a more or less conventional dynamic. With the later three quartets, in A major, C minor, and B flat, Beethoven seems suddenly to have thrown the classical framework in doubt. These pieces all entertain experiments with different types and arrangements of movements. They show signs of perfunctory composition, of odd retrospective tendencies, even (it has been surmised, with a good show of reason) of the reuse of quite ancient material. Disruptive forces of all kinds are at work in these quartets, and from the standpoint of final aesthetic coherence the results leave a good deal to be desired.

That the later three quartets also incorporate the most interesting proleptic flashes will scarcely come as a surprise. The *Eroica* Symphony, that great turning point in Beethoven's career, and in the history of modern music, was conceived in 1802–3. From 1800 on, the compositions of each new month show his imagination racing in more and more extraordinary fashion. The road from Beethoven's so-called "first period" to his second is not altogether simple to trace—since, after all, the very concept of such periodization has been hewn roughly from the rich forest of an artist's creative activity. But the last three quartets of Opus 18 mark an important stage on this road, even though it may be one that is obscured by a certain amount of dead wood.

The most palpable general novelty in the three quartets has to do with interrelationship and balance among the movements, a matter to which Beethoven will in later years direct very searching attention. He begins to tamper with the accepted weight, role, and style of each of the movements in the conventional cyclic form. Of the four movements, doubtless the first was the one to suffer the least radically—for the moment. Nevertheless, changes in the aspect of the first movement should not be overlooked. They amount to a rather new conception of the opening statement of the quartet form.

Evidently the general idea was to lighten this opening statement. Previous first movements had been intellectual and dense, staking much on a considerable adventure in the development and a consequent new ascendancy over old material in the recapitulation and coda. This stems explicitly from the work of Haydn and Mozart.

All the changes in the formal plan of the first movements [of Opus 18, Nos. 4, 5, and 6] tend in a single direction: they stress the symmetrical or architectural aspects of sonata form at the expense of the progressive or dramatic aspects. Beethoven was trying to write an easygoing opening, and succeeding only too well, perhaps: he is likely to strike us as perfunctory. Much of the time, these movements are content to cover space.

All in all, there is just less stuff in these movements than in the earlier ones. Not only is a characteristic bridge omitted from the expositions; all the other sections are composed less densely, more like Förster than Haydn, more like Mozart in the "Prussian" Quartets than in the six quartets dedicated to Haydn (but less densely than the "Prussian" Quartets). The Quartet in A is also one of the very few Beethoven compositions that can be said to admit a vacuous development section. Almost a third of it is taken up by the final dominant preparation, and almost another quarter by a literal restatement of the theme, twelve bars in the most placid possible key, the subdominant. The conclusion of this development on a 6/4=5/3 progression—highly formal, curiously archaic in sound—would be hard to find duplicated in the work of Haydn or Mozart later than the 1770's. Such genuine development as this movement allows itself is of an elementary, unexciting sort.

Grace and ease the movement does possess; in places it betrays a strongly Mozartian flavor. The principal theme itself, save for tiny details, could have been written by Mozart, who would have come upon the soaring subdominant in bars 5 and 9 more naturally than Beethoven. But a run-through of Mozart's themes in the Köchel Catalogue does not suggest any model so close as Beethoven's own [in his] Violin Sonata,

Opus 12, No. 2, in the same key and in the same 6/8 time signature. (This had just been published, in January 1799.) For Beethoven, as for Mozart, the violin sonata was never a very solemn form, certainly nothing comparable to the quartet.

Whitening the opening movement of this quartet was probably planned in relation to the placement of the minuet second in order, rather than third, after the slow movement, the traditional position. Perhaps this placement was promoted, in turn, by the choice of an especially lengthy, cumulative form for the slow movement, a theme and variation. In any case, the whole arrangement followed Mozart's Quartet in A major, K. 464, Beethoven's immediate model. The reversal of the two inner movements was not uncommon in the chamber music of Mozart and Haydn.

Again: the minuet is starkly simple, by comparison with the scherzos of the earlier quartets. But it would be a mistake to equate its fragility with innocence, crudity, or anything elementary in conception. This is a pensive essay in classic grace, with a sophistication of its own, and most astonishing of all, with a delicacy that matches Mozart without at all following him in spirit. Reminiscences of the *Teutsche*—Beethoven's favorite dance alla Tedesca, forefather of the ländler and the waltz— creep into the second section, as does also a touch of iron in a strongly reiterated fortissimo C sharp. The return of the original melody branches into a charming three-part canon in the subdominant—another instance of the use of formal counterpoint in the quartets, this one lightly worn. The canon is far from strict, but the countersubject makes up for this by multiplying itself elegantly in the viola.

Then the trio, with its positively Schubertian lilt, is the most mature and individual trio in the Opus 18 quartets. It is also the simplest, once again.

This movement derives nothing from the Minuet of Mozart's Quartet in A, unless one chooses to see kinship in the fact that both minuets are completely out of the ordinary—in different ways. It is the third and fourth movements of Opus 18, No. 5, which borrow directly from the corresponding movements of Mozart's composition, movements which Beethoven is known to have copied out in full.

Now the fact of this Mozart imitation has been well known since at least the time of Theodor Helm's book of 1885, but it seems never to have astonished commentators sufficiently. That Beethoven copied Mozart at the age of fifteen, writing his childish piano quartets, is one thing; it is quite another to find him so interrupting the preparation of a set of string quartets featuring movements like *La Malinconia*, and the first and second movements of the Quartet in F. The man was no timid beginner; he was, however, facing a really serious artistic problem—perhaps for the first time in his career. I take this Mozart imitation as the most dramatic sign of his uncertainty and sense of disruption at this particular stage of the quartet project. *Beethoven, who was capable of filling page after page of a notebook with compulsive sketches of a single melody, was also capable of threshing around at Mozart, in an inchoate effort to find some way out of a momentary impasse.*[1]

Why this particular quartet of Mozart's? Beethoven seems to have made it a special favorite, to judge from a report by Carl Czerny: "Once Beethoven came across the score of Mozart's six quartets in my house. He opened the fifth, in A [K. 464], and said: 'That's what I call a work! In it, Mozart was telling the world: "Look what I could do if you were ready for it!"'" A patrician choice: the Quartet in A is Mozart's most serious and troubled composition in the genre, less "available" and more learned than the others. It stands out as one of Mozart's most chromatic compositions, though this aspect of the matter did not interest Beethoven at this point. Of the six quartets dedicated to Haydn, this one probably owes him the most.

Back of his interest in the slow movement, furthermore, may have been a feeling of circumspection in planning a serious theme and variations as the center of gravity in a quartet. With late Beethoven in our ears, we tend to feel it quite natural for a piece in this weighty form to belong in a quartet or a sonata. But the Beethoven of 1800 would have felt rather differently. Though he had written and improvised many such pieces for piano, within larger works he had placed only the innocent variations in the Piano Trio in C minor and the Violin Sonata in D; the stupid ones in the Piano Sonata in G; and the brilliant variations on somebody else's tune in the finale of the Clarinet Trio, Opus 11 (a distant and, I am afraid, a rather contemptuous nod to Mozart's Clarinet Quintet). Only occasionally had Mozart and Haydn built slow movements of real weight in variation form. The idea was a fairly novel one, novel anyhow to Beethoven. He could scarcely have looked to a finer model than the third movement of Mozart's Quartet in A.

Mozart's variations are in the major mode. His form is large and [surprisingly] varied: six variations, the fourth of them an expanded minore paying due attention to the flat VI degree, B flat. The concluding passage or coda reaches a passionate climax in a plunge down to B flat, and this leads at once to a ten-bar compressed return of the original theme. This provides Mozart with a rounding effect. A new idea is the ostinato figure in the finale variation, which continues well into Mozart's concluding section, pulsing up from the cello into all the other instruments.

Beethoven has five variations, and no minore, though Variation 4 grows chromatic and touches upon strange (indeed, clumsy) minor harmonies. B flat is just barely indicated. But when Variation 5 is done, a sudden modulation occurs to this key. Only after an intervening episode in the subdominant (G major) may the piece return to its tonic key, D major;

modulation was Beethoven's personal contribution to the formal plan laid down by Mozart. Very much like Mozart, Beethoven concludes with a fragment of his theme, in variation—preceded by an analogous, but less successful rhetorical plunge involving (once again) the B flat. From Mozart he also took the idea of linking the conclusion back to the final variation proper by means of a striking low ostinato rhythm. This is more self-consciously handled than in Mozart, and soon drops out. Among his variations, the first is notable for its contrapuntal try, and the last for an unprecedented driving orchestral style which forecasts a late variation in the Quartet in C sharp minor, Opus 131.

That Beethoven would go out of his way to modulate, even in variations, one could perhaps have predicted, just knowing the man. One could certainly have predicted it on the basis of his other essays in the form. In another set of D major variations, for example, a favorite old piano showpiece on Righini's *Vieni Amore*,[1] which he was rewriting around this time, the coda moves to the same flat VI and IV (but also to flat V) before coming home triumphantly with a half variation in the tonic. The inconsequential D-major variation movement in the Serenade-Trio, Opus 8, pulls B flat out of the air for an analogous conclusion, which is very like the quaint contrapuntal [excursion] which diverted the composer in the modulatory passages of the coda [of this set of variations].[2]

It is well known that Beethoven loved a drastically simple variation theme—well known from the '*Appassionata*' Sonata, the Violin Concerto, and the Sonata in G, Opus 14, No. 2, not to speak of the "Diabelli" Variations. There is no more naïve outcome of this love than the present piece. Rhythmically, the theme slices its sixteen bars with machinelike rigor. Harmonically, it clings to four and only four chords, I, IV, V, and V of V. Melodically, it marches up and down the scale like the noble Duke of York. Mozart's [theme in his A major Quartet is] an impressive, subtle melodic invention; Beethoven's is not a tune at all, but an abstract construction.[3] The idea does shed some light on the contrapuntal [excursion] of the conclusion: the scale spawning a mirror image of itself in double time. It does not much warm the movement as a whole, however, which for all its points of interest certainly stands inferior to

[1] Written as early as 1792.—Editor.
[2] The deceptive cadence of the conclusion of the boisterous fifth variation lands us in B flat. The second violin timidly states the first two measures of the theme, in B flat accompanied by the viola's countersubject, described by Daniel Gregory Mason as "a funny little variant on itself, taken twice as fast and turned upside down."—Editor.
[3] Tovey describes it thus: "The ostentatious naïveté of the tonic dominant bass is in keeping with the wit of the melody which goes down and up [the scale] with a nursery-rhyme kind of wit. Meanwhile the viola has its own opinions, which it tells sleepily, like the tale of the Dormouse . . . in *Alice in Wonderland*." —Editor.

the variations of Mozart in practically every way. If Beethoven had been quite sure how to write as good a variation movement as Mozart, there would presumably have been less need to model on him.

Beethoven's need to model in the finale is more obscure—because his success is so much clearer. But the impulse was strong enough to have him lift one of Mozart's themes, only superficially modified, as well as the scale idea for its development. Mozart's theme first appears toward the end of the development[1]—a great surprise. Beethoven's is simply the second subject, though it does return with an analogous function at the end of his development too. Probably it was the change of pace that attracted him; and in Mozart's principal theme, he was probably attracted by the quality of swift, highly articulate simplicity. In the whole matter of plotting a last movement, I believe, Beethoven found himself faced with a problem similar to that of the first movement. He wanted to lighten the finale; his earlier ones had made a good effect, but only by means of frantic effort, by working too hard and showing it. In the present quartet he still clung to the idea of brilliance in conjunction with some measure of density, but [with] a glossy, easy, relaxed brilliance. And this, Beethoven may have thought, could be learned from Mozart.

Effortlessness—that is a key term, maybe, for Beethoven's most imponderable and unruffled quartet. It must also be counted the least personal of the quartets: pursuing again and again the will-o'-the-wisp of Mozart, Beethoven blunders into blankness in the first movement and (just as bad!) happens upon Mozart in the finale. The minuet, only, is a small gem. As for the slow movement, look at it as the starting point of a journey leading through the *Appassionata* Sonata and the "Archduke" Trio to the Ninth Symphony and the last piano sonatas and quartets, to Opus 127 and Opus 131. As a work in its own right, this theme and variations has had too much claimed for it, by Helm and Marliave, D'Indy and Mason. But it would take hard insensitivity toward the adventure of musical history to remain altogether unmoved by its earnest, rather stolid tentative effort.—JOSEPH KERMAN

f. String Quartet No. 6 in B Flat, Opus 18, No. 6
I. Allegro con brio; II. Adagio ma non troppo; III. Scherzo (Allegro); IV. La Malinconia (Adagio), Allegretto quasi allegro

The sixth quartet presents such a curious commingling of styles as to suggest a doubt whether it was not put together from pieces of divers dates that Beethoven happened to have on hand; only its final Adagio

---

[1] A quiet theme, in whole notes and half notes in D major after a long, energetic forte passage ending on C sharp.—Editor.

and Allegretto look forward to more dramatic methods to come. Such methods are foreshadowed in the specific title given to the Adagio (*La Malinconia*: "Melancholy") and in the definiteness of the direction that heads it: "This piece to be played with the utmost delicacy." More intrinsically, qualities of the music itself point toward the trenchant contrasts, closely juxtaposed, of the second and third periods [of Beethoven's style. It is true that the Adagio is regarded by some writers, among them d'Indy and Marliave, as a separate movement; and we cannot deny that there are between it and the Allegretto no easily recognizable metric relations such as we shall find bridging the most extreme expressive contrasts in the last quartets. On the other hand, however, the first and longest of the four Adagios leaves us in suspense as upon a question the ensuing Allegretto seems to answer; the alternations of the two opposed tempos become, as the movement proceeds, more frequent, suggesting closer bonds between them; and in its last pages the association is intimate enough to seem almost if not quite organic.

So surprising a forward look as the finale thus makes, both in expression and in structure, is little prepared by the earlier three movements. The first two, with their frequent formal cadences dividing them into compartments, and their highly flowered eighteenth-century type of melody, not to speak of certain quasi-operatic touches in both melody and harmony, seem to look more backward than forward. Even the Scherzo, with its complicated syncopations imposed on a metrical basis none too clear, is one of those semifailures described by Stevenson as "*pierres perdues* of successes," an experiment significant more for its promise than its achievement.

In mood the opening Allegro con brio is of a buoyant *bonhomie*, touched with humor delicate and neat rather than boisterous. The "rising rhythm" of its motives gives it a gay irresponsibility, the leaping staccatos of each of them clearing by their momentum a bar-line as if it were a negligible hurdle, to land square on the "heavy" of the next two-measure group. In the cello answer, this goal-note is divided into the two of a feminine cadence, tempering its energy with easy good humor. The flavor of drollery thus imparted is later to permeate much of the development section. At the bridge [between the first theme (in the tonic) and the second theme (in the dominant)] is introduced almost surreptitiously a second motive, also gay, a long rising scale culminating in a Mozartian formal half cadence. Theme II, also, closes with a tuneful fall that might have been borrowed from a Mozart opera.[1] Operatic in a less happy vein are some of its harmonies, notably the Neapolitan sixth,

---

[1] I feel that Professor Mason has somewhat overlooked the subtlety of this Theme II with its bold alternating of major and minor. Far from being banal, I feel the surprise excursion into the distant key of A flat, pianissimo, is quite as advanced as similar equally sudden and startling harmonic changes toward the close of the slow movement of the quartet, Opus 74, written over ten years later, when Beethoven was already tentatively experimenting in his ultimate "third" style.—Editor.

described by d'Indy as *très banale*, but redeemed just in time by a truly imaginative change from minor to major, followed by some witty variants.

It is enlightening to contrast the manipulation and consequent effect of the two empty measures used in the development. The first [, toward the beginning of the section, falls] metrically [on] the heavy of a pair where we least expect silence, and [cuts] off unceremoniously some busy self-important violin figures; [it] is a prank, whimsical, abrupt, teasing. It obliges us to "sit up and take notice," thus sensitizing us afresh for the new and charming treatment of the upward-scale motive that is to provide most of the further development. Not all, however; for after a good deal of fun the mood softens to a tenderer one, introducing one of those leisurely dialogues between upper and lower instruments on a thematic fragment that Beethoven is later to enjoy so often. This in turn leads to a brief series of echoes of its last two notes from upper instruments to lower, and so to two slower chords, poising as if to suggest that re-capitulation is due. It is at this point that our second silent measure supervenes, the polar antithesis of [the first:] light instead of heavy, tranquil rather than abrupt, calming rather than exciting. The next pair of measures, its light prolonged by a hold, further lengthens the moment of repose, thanks to which the return of activity, in the now sometime expected reappearance of the theme, becomes most welcome.

The Adagio has a lovely purity, a sort of childlike innocence, all its own. Its form, to begin with, is about the simplest possible: a theme in E flat, its statement followed at the ninth measure by a poignantly expressive contrast and a brief flowered restatement; then an almost equally simple second theme, in B flat minor; finally Theme 1 again, more flowered and slightly extended—the whole completed by a short coda on both themes.

The harmonic scheme, too, is delightfully "eighteenth-century," albeit Beethoven already knows how to make one of the commonest of all chords, the dominant seventh, deeply moving in the contrast section (measure 9, and even more on its second appearance). This has an eloquence almost as profound as that of the similar contrast section in the great variation theme of Opus 127. The coda, for all its trans-parence, uses C major shrewdly, with rich double stops, to foil and re-fresh the color of E flat for the naïve close.

Finally, childlike is the candid joy the composer takes in flowering his main theme a little more ingeniously each time it appears. (Compare [the first restatement,] where he takes pains to direct the viola and the cello to mark each note distinctly, with [the second restatement,] where the violin fragments begin to hover like spray over a wave, and again with [its third and last restatement,] where the wave itself be-comes, as it were, iridescent.) All such highly flowered passages require for satisfactory interpretation the complete technical control that alone gives players repose, together with an elastic yet fundamentally just sense of the space of detail within mass. The least hurrying will confuse the main stresses, and thus ruin the combination of continuity with contrast by which their grace should enhance the leisurely charm of the return of the theme. Unfortunately the performances and recordings of even the best-known quartets differ almost unbelievably in this capital matter of justice in meter and rhythm spacing. Accordingly, to whatever group we listen, it is always worth while to ask ourselves questions like these: Are the main pillars of the harmony (which synchronize with the rhythm) so justly presented that we grasp at once their place in the whole scheme? Are the *fioriture* made to lighten without distorting the chief masses? Or, on the contrary, are the players allowing themselves to be tempted by the legerity of intermediate tone-clusters into hurrying the main pulses (as if the carving on some noble temple were to pull the columns into zigzags)? By asking oneself such questions one exercises and develops one's power of discrimination, the essence of taste.

In the Scherzo our listener's share in setting the meter becomes tantalizingly difficult, possibly at first baffling. What is the basic measure of this amusing piece? Of course we realize from the start that Beethoven is playing with many daring syncopations, seldom letting important notes of the tune coincide with downbeats of the measures, almost always tying them back to preceding normally unaccented ones, and often adding *sforzandos* further to emphasize these dislocations. But this helps us little to savor the full whimsicality of the tune until we have answered the prior question: Just where *are* those down-beats? What are the locations that by their opposition give these dislocations their effect, what the regularities against which alone these irregularities tell? In a word, what meter controls all these vagaries of rhythm?

Looking at the opening phrase of the tune, we see that most of its four measures divide themselves into six eighth notes. Beethoven tells us in his signature (3/4) that these make three quarter notes, that is to say, three groups of two eighths each, counted "ONE and, two-and, three-and," stressing the "ONE," as we indicate by capitals. But we find (to our sorrow) that it is just as easy, if not easier, to hear them as two groups of three eighths each (6/8), counted "ONE-two-three, four-five-six," stressing "ONE," and "four" slightly less. Thus we are dealing here not alone with the two elements of all measured music: rhythm and its underlying meter, but with three: rhythm and *two* opposed meters, on either of which we may choose to base it, and which differ profoundly in their aesthetic effect. For if we count for our tune "-and three-and, ONE-and two," etc., we get a syncopation that is complex, tense, exciting. If on the other hand we count, as the author humbly confesses he could not help doing until after many hearings and long study, "four-five-six, ONE-two-three," etc., there results only a flat and disappointing sing-song.

Who is to blame for this unfortunate ambiguity? Can it possibly be Beethoven himself? His initial accompanying groups [of three eighth notes] in the cello and the viola rather encourage our false start "four-five-six." By the time the cello gives us a clear "ONE-and two" [not until the second phrase of the second part], followed soon by three actual quarter notes in inner voices, we find it rather late to reset our apperceptions. Only in the charmingly fresh and headlong trio do we get unequivocal quarters. . . .

It is not too much to say that the forty-four measures entitled *La Malinconia*, for all their unprecedented conciseness, in part perhaps because of it, carry us into new regions of musical expression. In this strange half-light, this mystical atmosphere of trance and the suggestion of something unknown impending, we are far indeed from the gay sunlight of eighteenth-century finales. Likely to come to mind is only one prototype, the equally remote introduction to Mozart's C major quartet, Köchel 465, also followed like this by a quick movement that shakes us almost rudely out of our contemplation. But Mozart makes no further use of his introduction, while Beethoven's *Malinconia*, seeming at first only to usher in its incongruous partner the easygoing Allegretto, ends in close partnership with it.

Brief as it is, the little piece already presents within itself almost a compendium of the methods eventually to produce the transformation into Beethoven's second period. In so striking a change even the superficialities are of interest. Such, for instance, are the effective opposition, in the opening measures, of middle and low-register sonorities; in the third phrase the famous Beethoven crescendo culminating not in loud but in soft; the later bold oppositions of *pianissimo* and *forte* in successive chords, with unconventional placing of instruments in the interchange of melody notes between the first and second violins; in the E minor section [which follows] the color range from palest *pianissimo* to the full-blooded chord on the cello open C string; and at the end, the long-sustained progression up from low to high register and from softest to loudest utterance.

Greatly as all these momentary effects contribute to the final impression, they remain superficial in comparison with deeper-lying innovations, both rhythmic and tonal. In rhythm, most basic of all the elements of music, Beethoven is feeling out toward wider spans. Thus while the first two phrases, of four measure each, balance with the neatness of a couplet of Pope, the third, preparing us for bolder flight by its taking off from an already mysterious and suspensive diminished seventh chord, soars to twice their length, maintaining the suspense through a series of further diminished sevenths, to poise at last, rather than alight. So too with the phrases that follow: they also achieve, either by imitative entrances of voices at uneven distances (in the E minor section) or through a steady movement of all voices in one direction but with no definite melody (near the end) a sort of freely balanced festooning of uneven rhythms reminding us less of eighteenth-century precision than of the romantically wayward versification of Keats.

Rhythmic and tonal structure are so intimately related, indeed so mutually dependent, that this new flexibility of phrase would have been unattainable by Beethoven had he not been long experimenting toward new methods of tonal organizations. Tovey has shown[1] that a passage in one of his childish piano quartets, composed at fifteen and not published until after his death, already "embodies one of his most epoch-making discoveries, namely, the art of organizing a long series of apparently free modulations by means of a systematic progression in the bass." Of that passage, as Tovey goes on to show, Beethoven himself thought well enough to lift it bodily for later use in [the first movement] of his third piano sonata. Sonata, and if one compares those measures with the last eight of *La Malinconia*, one sees that while in the first the bass moves downward, in the other upward, in both it is the bass that by its regular progression holds together the whole phrase. Thus does harmonic logic make feasible a hitherto unattained rhythmic span. A systematic bass taking in its stride many modulations:—is not this the structural pattern that is broached with the unconsciousness of genius in the childish quartet, improved in the three most striking progressions of *La Malinconia*, and later perfected (as Tovey also suggests) in the ineffable introduction to the C major Quartet, Opus 59, No. 3?[2] Still further, since most modern tentatives can be found in germ in Beethoven, is it not also the pattern of many of Wagner's, Chopin's, and Cesar Franck's greatest inspirations?

When at last, eventually surmounting all the problematic hesitations of the introduction, after one last pause, the music finally plunges into the Allegretto, B flat major, lilting 3/8 time, like a long dammed-up brook at length finding free channel, we may like to tell ourselves that at this point all the composer's problems vanished as easily as do ours. In point of fact, as Mies' analysis in his *Beethoven's Sketches* clearly shows, they only changed their conditions; and while, as the saying reminds us, "easy writing makes hard reading," such fascinating spontaneity as Beethoven here achieves arrived only after he had solved some tough problems. To suggest them briefly: he had to plan for nearly three hundred measures of sixteenth-note motion, in which his main theme, according to rondo plan, was to "come around" many times, and to be each time increasingly welcome. Had he accepted the first try at it—or the second or third—that occurred to him (and that Mies prints), such frequent repetitions of a flowing but ingenuous melody, harmonized in unrelieved tonic and dominant, would have grown intolerable. It was only by a persistent trial-and-error process that he gradually achieved this sweetly amiable tune, meandering through its diversified harmonies to its widely spaced cadences.

[1] Article "Beethoven," in Encyclopaedia Brittanica.
[2] And in the coda of the first and last movements of the Second Symphony, Opus 36, written three years after the Opus 18 quartets.—Editor.

A glance at one or two of its returns will show us how richly his art is rewarded. [At the bridge section before the first reprise of the main theme,] for instance, suspended on the dominant, intensifying the suspense by slowly rising in pitch, and after reaching its high point poising a moment as if in uncertainty, it finally more than satisfies our expectations with new delights. [Further on in the movement, what appears at first like the *third* appearance of the main theme] uses a different means to the same end. A "systematic progression of the bass," to use Tovey's term, here builds more than a dozen measures into a single climax culminating in [a] dramatic *fortissimo* diminished seventh chord and cello recitative. What is coming? The return of the main theme we expect is *interrompu*, as d'Indy puts it, by what, in this context, is a surprise. It is *La Malinconia* that supervenes, arresting the momentum and transforming the mood. Yet, after but two phrases, this too is broken off, and we hear an equally brief fragment of the Allegretto theme, now in A minor. It stops as suddenly as it began, there is a whole measure of uneasy silence, and once more *La Malinconia* asserts its domination, reduced now to its lowest terms—two measures—four notes. Then, at last, the main theme resumes supremacy, stealing in at first in a false entrance in G major, but working quickly back to the central key and final statement.

In the coda, the theme dissolves into fragments, tossed from player to player, but all of them in B flat, tonic and dominant, to apprise us that the end approaches. [When these fragments are reduced to the mere three-note upbeat over a constant tonic-dominant bass, the melodic idea reaches] the ultimate quintessential form, to bid farewell. Threatening in the Poco adagio to lose for a moment its long and gay momentum, it proves to be only taking breath and pulling itself together for the final glorious rush of the Prestissimo.—DANIEL GREGORY MASON (2)

g. *String Quartet in F (from the Piano Sonata in E, Opus 14, No. 1)*
I. Allegro; II. Allegretto; III. Rondo (Allegro commodo)

"The unnatural craze," Beethoven writes to Breitkopf & Härtel on July 13, 1802, "for transferring even piano music to fiddle instruments that are in all respects so contrary might well stop. I assert firmly, only Mozart could transfer himself from the piano to other instruments, and Haydn as well; and although not comparing myself with these two great men, I assert the same of my piano sonatas. Not only must full passages be effaced or altered, but one has to add new passages and this amounts to so many stumbling blocks which one has either to be the master to overcome or at least the same adroitness and invention that went into the original piano sonata.—I have transformed only one of my Sonatas into a string quartet, for which I had urgently been asked, and I am sure that nobody else could easily have done it."

The "Thematic Catalogue of All Printed Works by Beethoven," the second edition of which, carefully revised by Gust. Nottebohm and issued in 1868, mentions already this [arrangement of his own Sonata, Opus 14, No. 2] as published by the Bureau des Arts et d'Industrie, Vienna, in 1802, and reprinted in the same year by Simrock, Bonn.

[Gustav Nottebohm in] his book *Zweite Beethoveniana* (1887, p. 47) remarks: "Beethoven has arranged this Sonata for 4 instruments, and it is not impossible that this version was already envisaged at the conception of the work."

I found the original edition in the Musiksammlung der kgl. Bibliothek, Berlin. A superficial comparison of the parts with the piano version showed me [so many] important deviations that I hastened to compile a score of the quartet. This led me to a full confirmation of Beethoven's above cited words.

[Comparing] the score with an original piano part [gives] an idea in particular to young musicians, how a master of the musical art has transformed an original piano setting for string instruments.—WILHELM ALTMANN (2)

VII. SERENADE FOR VIOLIN, VIOLA, AND VIOLONCELLO, OPUS 8
  I. Marcia (Allegro); II. Adagio; III. Menuetto (Allegretto);
  IV. Adagio; V. Scherzo (Allegro molto); VI. Allegretto alla Polacca;
  VII. Tema (Andante quasi allegretto) con variazione; VIII. Marcia
  (Allegro)

The Serenade Trio, Opus 8, appeared in October 1797. Divided into six parts like the preceding one [Opus 3], it enters the category of the earlier divertissements and cassations which were popular during Mozart's time, but which had ceased to be by the end of the eighteenth century. As Wasielewski so well explains: "The luxury of the Austrian nobility in maintaining the chapels had all but disappeared, and at the same time the occasions for such entertainments as divertissements for the lords. Beethoven had, no doubt, little inclination to devoting himself to this type of composition; and since we do not really know of the circumstances relative to the composition of this 'serenade' one can imagine that he wrote it to give the impression of the spontaneous artistic spirit. It is that which this work reflects perfectly. It is an ephemeral *pièce d'occasion*, but a small, finely worked tableau—one might almost say an idealized serenade. Here Beethoven had no pretext to deepen the musical expression and he therefore guarded himself against the use of strict contrapuntal forms. A sense of humor is the center of gravity in this work."[1]

[1] Joseph W. von Wasielewski, *Beethoven*, Vol. I, pp. 127–28.—Editor.

The work is composed of seven movements of small dimensions: first a march in D major with two phrases, each of which is repeated. This is followed by an Adagio in 3/4 in the same key. In it, the violin plays the first half of the main theme, which is answered by the viola accompanied by the cello. This latter instrument, playing in a very high register, introduces a second subject, which is repeated and developed by the violin. After the entire first half of the movement is repeated, the violin introduces a new motif in a minor key. The agitation of this latter section gradually subsides as the violin leads delicately into the recapitulation of the first part.

A minuet in D, with a trio in G, has a brief and humorous coda. It serves as an interlude between the first Adagio and a second Adagio in D minor. This [movement] has three reprises (the two first ones are repeated textually). Between each appearance of the Adagio theme there appears an Allegro molto in major. These brisk sections make, with their staccatos, a piquant contrast to the dominating mood.[1]

A polonaise in F major follows and forms the nucleus of the composition. The three reprises are like so many variations for the violin. Finally an Andante with variations permits the other two instruments to come into their own. The first variation is given to the violin, the second to the viola playing a light staccato; but after the third variation in minor, with its syncopated rhythm, the cello dominates up until the moment when, in a 6/8 rhythm, sempre staccato, the violin and the viola interrupt and force the cello into the role of accompanist. After this brief interlude the cello again attempts to recover the theme, in B flat major, but the violin barely allows it to finish. Finally, after a brief coda, the opening march is repeated, as was usual in the divertimenti and cassations, making up the seventh and last movement of this delightful serenade.—J.-G. PROD'HOMME (1) (TR. BY THOMAS K. SCHERMAN)

VIII. String Trio in G, Opus 9, No. 1
I. Adagio, Allegro con brio; II. Adagio, ma non tanto e cantabile; III. Scherzo (Allegro); IV. Presto

Opus 9 is the first important work for three stringed instruments written by Beethoven. He himself designated it, without prevarication, in his dedication to "the first Mecene of the Muse," Count Browne, as the "best of his works" in a medium which he did not often cultivate. Published in July 1798, the Opus 9, it seemed, existed as a project at least a year beforehand. Certain sketches are known (the end of the first movement of the first trio in G major and the scherzo of the third

---

[1] Note the subtle way in which Beethoven compresses the second appearance of the Allegro, interrupting it with several brilliant chords, then leading back in a choralelike fashion to the last appearance of the Adagio. It is a harbinger of the composer's mature style.—Editor.

in C minor) which are contemporaneous with those of the first sonata, Opus 49 (first movement) and of the Rondo of the "Pathétique" Sonata. We find, still, formulas inherited from Mozart. But here it is Beethoven who looms large. He had very clearly profited from the studies which he had just terminated with Albrechtsberger.

In the first trio in G major, an Adagio introduction precedes an Allegro con brio; the first measures of the Allegro, which are carried by the violin, seem to be a continuation of the introduction rather than a new theme. However, we realize that we are in the main body of the work when, a few bars later, another vigorous subject of four measures is announced by the violoncello, and then taken up by the violin. This new subject is developed in a spirited way, and closes fortissimo on the dominant of D major. Another new motive, calm, pianissimo, in D minor, acts as contrast. Before the end of the exposition there appears a new rhythmic figure in D major. This is the motive of a simple mordant in the rhythm of one eighth note, two sixteenth notes and two eighth notes, which already appeared in the Opus 3 trio—a decidedly Mozartean rhythm and motive, which later was to dominate the entire first movement of the first Quartet, Opus 18, No. 1. The exposition is repeated, and there follows a development section which is dominated by the tonalities of B flat major and G minor, a common procedure of Beethoven's. This allows the tone D, the dominant of G major, to appear quite naturally in preparation for the recapitulation. The recapitulation is repeated, followed by a coda which starts off quite normally in the key of G. But suddenly the violoncello repeats its original theme in E flat major, but shortly the tonic key is re-established and the movement ends with a spirited ensemble.

In the Adagio [in E major] each beat of the 3/4 measure is continually subdivided into triplets. The violin, which from the first measure establishes this persistent rhythm, generally retains the prime role. After a second appearance of the theme in the middle of the movement, Beethoven effects a brusque modulation to G major, in which key the violoncello takes over the lead. The triplets of each beat become sextuplets, and the mood becomes considerably more agitated. However, the sense of calm returns when the key of E major is re-established. By its tonality, as well as by the lightness with which it is developed, this Adagio, on the whole, retains the same atmosphere of serenity as the first movement—this, despite the brusque sixteenth note figurations which momentarily interrupt the lulling "berceuse" rhythm and the delicate arabesques of the violin.

The Scherzo in G major is composed of two brief phrases, both of which are repeated, and followed by a middle section (a trio) in C major. The first sixteen measures of this trio are repeated. But the second phrase just trails off, after a few bars, followed by a measure of silence. It is again repeated in a new key, but again trails off into silence. Its third repetition, in still another key, leads us back directly to the repetition of the first part of the Scherzo. This da capo is written out, rather than just marked d.c., because Beethoven introduces some slight variations which add spice to this delightful movement. On the whole the witty badinage among the three players makes the Scherzo a frothy transition between the Adagio and the finale.

This finale is the first truly Beethovenian presto which is *not*[1] written in the form of a rondo. It is characterized by the rapid staccato of the opening violin passage. Without warning, a new theme of an entirely different character appears in the key of B flat major, which rapidly modulates to D, where the busy staccato resumes until the end of the exposition in that key. The exposition is repeated in its entirety. After the repetition this D becomes not the bass of the tonic chord but the potent part of the dominant seventh chord of E flat major, in which key the development section commences with a repetition of the first theme. With a truly novel skill in the variety of his handling of the instruments, Beethoven, in this development section, increases their sonority by means suggested, less by the lessons of his teachers, than by his own sense of humor. That sense of humor is also prevalent in the subtle way he alters the recapitulation, in order to present the second theme in E flat and the closing theme in G, making of this a true sonata-allegro movement.—J.-G. PROD'HOMME (1) (TR. BY THOMAS K. SCHERMAN)

IX. STRING TRIO IN D, OPUS 9, No. 2
I. Allegretto; II. Andante quasi allegretto; III. Menuetto (Allegro); IV. Rondo (Allegro)

The second trio in D major starts *in medias res* with a 2/4 Allegretto in which the violin plays the first theme pianissimo.[2] There then intervenes, forte, a characteristic grupetto which, passing among all the instruments, is heard throughout the movement. In answer to the agitation it engenders, there appears a more measured theme played, dolce, by the violin and the viola in harmony. The first part of the movement terminates in the dominant key of A. The development section opens with an allusion to the initial theme, but appearing this time in D minor instead of D major. This section utilizes elements of all three themes of the exposition. Toward its close the violoncello ascends to its highest register, even sounding *above*[3] the violin part—a frequent procedure in the Opus 9 trios. The first appearance of the high A in the violoncello ushers

[1] Italics by the editor.
[2] One can compare the measures which follow (measure 19 ff.) with the very first ones of the Allegro con brio of the preceding trio Opus 9, No. 1; the same rhythmic elements can be found in both.
[3] Italics by the editor.

in a delightfully disguised version of the initial theme—disguised so subtly with syncopations and staccato accompaniment that we do not realize we have arrived at the recapitulation until the reappearance of the grupetti. After this point the recapitulation of the first part of the movement is quite regular and it is followed by a brief, humorous coda.

The Andante quasi allegretto in 6/8 offers a capricious motive in D minor, which continues the mood created by the first movement. Over an arpeggio accompaniment of the viola, the violoncello announces a second theme in A minor, which the violin repeats at once in G minor. After a varied reprise of the first part, the violin and the viola in unison repeat the second motive. In the coda, after a few measures played coll'arco during a powerful crescendo, we again hear the pizzicati which are associated with the first theme, and which, throughout, give a slightly severe character to this entire movement.

The Menuetto, in two parts, each one subdivided into one small and one large phrase, would seem, by the allegro tempo indication, to play the role of a scherzo rather than a tempo da menuetto. The second part, the trio, definitely gives that impression. It amounts to nothing but a mysterious rhythm, a buzzing that vibrates with a certain monotony. It has an other-worldly quality, with its incessant pianissimo and light staccato. But the da capo, with its more marked accents, reminds the listener that this movement is still a minuet.

The Rondo is an allegro in D major. Its theme, which is announced three times by the violoncello in a high register, and then repeated by the violin, is a fairly ordinary, almost banal tune, which is given more sophistication by a syncopated accompaniment on the viola. After the appearance of this main theme, the three instruments offer, as contrast, comments upon various aspects of it—in the manner of the development section of a sonata-allegro movement. Also they develop another lyrical theme, which appears in A major for the first time and later in G major. That new lyrical theme leads, upon its last apperance, to a recapitulation of the rondo theme, but this time, in the surprising key of B flat major. The violoncello here takes on the role of the viola (the syncopated accompaniment), while the viola reciprocates. Then all three interchange the running figure of the last measures of the theme, after which the viola and violoncello alternate with the syncopated accompaniment, while the violin performs a brilliant florid passage which, in effect, is derived from the main theme. As a conclusion to the movement the violin has the last word in recapitulating the jolly main theme.—J.-G. PROD'HOMME (1) (TR. BY THOMAS K. SCHERMAN)

X. String Trio in C Minor, Opus 9, No. 3
    I. Allegro con spirito; II. Adagio con espressione; III. Scherzo (Allegro molto e vivace); IV. Finale (Presto)

The last trio, in C minor, is conceived on a completely different scale from either of the others. "This is really Beethovenian pathos," says A. B. Marx, "a sustained passion which is built up powerfully and majestically with inevitable logic." The key of C minor, as used by Beethoven, always inferred a sense of grandeur and heroism. The division into four movements (Allegro, Adagio, Scherzo, Presto) is symphonic in its concept.

The tonality, and with it the Beethoven mood, commands attention from the very outset of the Allegro con spirito (6/8), where the three instruments in unison outline the first four downward steps of the scale. The first part of the movement, the exposition, which ends in E flat major, is like a spiritual and humorous bantering among the three instruments, with scrupulously "democratic" division of labor, so that none of the three dominates the scene more than either of the others. The development commences with the initial four-note scale motive, but transforms it this time into a series of vigorous sforzando chords that now establish the tonality of F minor. Fast and light, but chopped up by incessantly contrasting dynamics, the development resembles, at times, a pitched battle among the three participants, but at other times the most harmonious of accords. Little by little, the key of C minor re-emerges, and with it, the imposing four-note scale motive in its original form, proclaiming the beginning of the recapitulation. The entire second part of the movement, the development and the recapitulation, is repeated, and is followed by a coda which starts with a return of the paramount four-note theme. The music gradually becomes more and more animated, keeping up its relentless drive right up until the last fortissimo chord.

The Adagio con espressione in C major is built upon a six-measure phrase, announced by the violin and then by the viola. Some rapid scales of the violin serve as an introduction to the second theme, which is very calm and intimate. Its succession of even eighth notes is punctuated by sudden sforzandi which give to it a certain air of sadness. The middle section of the movement commences in the key of E flat major, in which key the three instruments alternately vary the first theme. After a powerful crescendo there occurs a dolorous struggle, interspersed with some loud cries and heart-rending lamentations. The main theme then reappears, piano, again in C major, followed by the return of the second theme in the same key. This time, the second theme is played, not by the viola together with the violin, but by the violin and the violoncello in its highest register. There is a quiet conclusion after the animation created (as before) in preparation for the return of the second theme.

The Scherzo vivace is made up of a first section of twenty-six measures (two times thirteen) and a second section of thirty-two measures (two times sixteen). The basic key is C minor. The violin announces its nervous theme. There follows a trio in C major which, because of its calmness and repose, forms a perfect contrast to the Scherzo. The da capo of the Scherzo is followed by a short coda which gradually gets softer and softer and ends with a breathless pianissimo. The whole movement forms a brief tormented interlude between the sad Adagio and the final intense Presto, where at last the key of C minor manages to attain a certain lightness.

The first theme of the Presto is somewhat analogous, on the exterior, to the final rondo of Opus 22 (the piano sonata dedicated to Countess von Browne in 1800), but it is not developed with the same grace. Riemann sees in it a certain restlessness, also a certain sad resignation. The similar impression of trouble, of struggle, which was felt in the Adagio and in the tormented motive of the Scherzo, here is felt in the shattering tumult which occurs in the middle of the exposition, and in the theme in E flat minor which precedes that outburst. The development section opens with the last measures of the original theme played in major instead of in minor, which gives to them an entirely different character. The rapid scales of the opening theme are also tossed playfully from one instrument to another, as is the little triplet which formed the upbeat to the theme. In a surprisingly mature way, considering the date of the composition, Beethoven approaches the recapitulation in a completely unobtrusive way. It actually sounds as if it were a continuation of the development section. The coda is equally ingenious with its pungent conclusion, pianissimo, in C major.—J.-G. PROD'HOMME (1) (TR. BY THOMAS K. SCHERMAN)

XI. SERENADE IN D FOR FLUTE, VIOLIN, AND VIOLA, OPUS 25
I. Entrata (Allegro); II. Tempo ordinario d'un menuetto; III. Allegro molto; IV. Andante con variazioni; V. Allegro scherzando e vivace; VI. Adagio; VII. Allegro vivace

Beethoven fairly wallowed in E flat at that time.[1] But there was method in his monotony. E flat was by far the best key in which to draw together his disparate teams of wind instruments. He emerged from it to compose the delicious Serenade in D major, Opus 25, for flute, violin, and viola in 1797—a work fit for a fairy. Yet its fairylikeness in no way interfered with its practicability. It could be played in the streets by players as mobile as any for whom Haydn had written *Gassadenmusik* forty

[1] 1796–97.—Editor.

years before, and it followed the old plan of grouping together a number of short movements, such as had served Haydn in his notturni and cassations. Beethoven wrote here for the flute with real understanding of its nature and an enchanting humor. Just think of the Entrata, where the tiny flute prances [to the foreground] first, all alone with a fanfare that might come from a fairy turned gamin; or look at that lovely Variation III in the Andante, where the viola sings a solo to an accompaniment that uses with consummate skill the violin's capacity for flowing sostenuto and the flute's dexterity in skipping.—MARION M. SCOTT

XII. TRIO IN C FOR 2 OBOES AND ENGLISH HORN, OPUS 87
    I. Allegro; II. Adagio cantabile; III. Menuetto, Allegro molto, Scherzo; IV. Finale (Presto)

The trio in C, Opus 87, for two oboes and English horn, dates from 1794, two years after Beethoven's permanent move to Vienna. Publication was delayed a dozen years, until 1806. Many of the works of the First Period were withheld from publication by Beethoven until well into his Second Period, when financial problems made the sale of new works important. In the later years he unearthed many a prudently held-over work, to be used as "petty cash" to pay for rent and food; but, true to his own artistic conscience, he seldom released the music *without a thorough going-over and revision,*[1] unless the work was already outstanding. (Paradoxically, Beethoven's "potboilers" were invariably of current production.)

The trio [is imbued] with an intensity that belies its youthfulness. It is quick and incisive, its ideas rapidly enunciated and strongly developed, its harmonies flashing and poignant. It is a work of strength beneath its beautifully polished eighteenth-century exterior. And in this, notably in the first movement, it comes straight out of Mozart—as we now know Mozart. It is out of Haydn, too, particularly in the last movement. Not the mere styles of these masters, but the most profound principles of their composition, are absorbed here. Beethoven had learned well. With deliberately limited resources he makes music of virtuosic intensity.

As in Mozart's intense works we find a deceptive casualness in the opening movement, which moves only moderately fast. It is in the eloquence of the melody, the richness, the sudden drama of the harmonies that we infer the inner tension. The sonata form is of the most eloquent sort with a proliferation of successive ideas, a dramatic transition section from tonic to dominant (the English horn introduces the strangely altered harmonies) and a considerable development, ending on a long high oboe G, before the return, that suggests the same moment in the later Fifth Symphony in the same key (though in the minor). All this is

[1] Italics by the editor.

completed via a lavishly rewritten recapitulation (the strange harmonies even more dramatic) and an added coda, foreshadowing many such in later works.

The slow movement, as befits this intense sort of music, is eloquent, in unusually slow tempo—hallmark of later Beethoven slow movements —the three instruments intertwined in a sustained legato, scarcely seeming to breathe at all. A tour de force of writing and of performance. The third movement is a true scherzo, though ambiguously marked, rushing at dazzling speed in the new Beethoven manner. How it must have astonished its first hearers! The Finale is a brilliant sleight-of-hand play upon the familiar rondo forms of the day, full of Haydnesque false leads and musical *double-entendres* piled pell-mell one upon the other, leaving the initiated listener positively breathless. The whirlwind little rondo theme at the beginning, straight from Haydn, is quickly followed by a minor-key episode, presumably the contrasting section of the usual fast rondo; it gives way quickly to a "return" to the opening key which, because of its position, seems irresistibly a variation upon the main tune, in fast oboe triplets, though it is nothing of the sort. Two false leads. Again the minor-key interlude and then, at last, the true return of the rondo theme. The center of the movement is a long contrasting lyric section in the subdominant; the rondo theme returns predictably—and is instantly followed by its "variation," the triplet oboe figure, omitting the minor-key episode entirely. The final return of the rondo theme is drawn out into a brilliant coda ending.—EDWARD TATNALL CANBY

XIII. 8 VARIATIONS ON THE THEME *"La ci darem la mano,"* FROM MOZART's *Don Giovanni,* FOR 2 OBOES AND ENGLISH HORN, WoO 28

These delightful variations are among Beethoven's most adroit settings for winds. They feature each of the three instruments soloistically and yet there is never a sense of sparseness in the harmony. The problem of compositions for three winds is that any chord of over three notes must be *implied,* either by shifts in the melody or in one or the other of the lower voices. Beethoven had fully explored the pitfalls and the possible solutions in the little C major Trio, Opus 87, for the same instrumental combination, written two years earlier in 1794. However, nowhere in that trio is there such clever voice leading as in Variation IV or Variation VI (*Lento espressivo, minore*). Particularly clever is the setting of the last variation (VIII), in which the melody of the familiar theme is passed back and forth between the first oboe and the English horn while the second oboe plays broken chord figures in thirty-second notes, thus filling out the harmonic texture.

The coda which follows Variation VIII without a pause is a clever little fugato based on a scherzolike version of the theme in a fast 6/8. However Beethoven returns to the more staid tempo of the theme toward the end, and the little gem gradually gets softer and softer as if the two protagonists in the opera were walking off-stage.—THOMAS K. SCHERMAN

XIV. DUO FOR VIOLA AND VIOLONCELLO ("WITH TWO OBBLIGATO EYE-GLASSES"), WoO 32

The sonata movement for viola and cello solo is designated by Beethoven himself as a "Duet with two obbligato eyeglasses." The epigraph would suggest that it was intended for two definite players, to whose shortsightedness Beethoven jestingly referred by the "obbligato eyeglasses."

In the second edition of Thayer's biography of Beethoven, Hugo Riemann gives a brief description of the duet, pointing out in particular its striking thematic relationship to the first movement of the C minor quartet in Opus 18, suggesting that the two movements were written at about the same time. Judging from internal evidence, this should have been about 1795–98.

The manuscript is rapidly written and in some places all but undecipherable; it gives only the notes. There are no dynamic indications of any kind, and the bowing is indicated only in three places [two slurs in the cello voice as well as staccato wedges (′′′) which Beethoven always used to] indicate a sharp short casting off of the tone, clearly distinguished from the dots (...) indicating a less brief staccato. Also in the original are the directions *pizz.* and *col arco* in the viola voice, bars 105–6, and the Adagio in bar 108.—FRITZ STEIN (TR. BY THOMAS K. SCHERMAN)

XV. WORKS FOR THE *Spieluhr* ("*Flötenuhr*"), WoO 33

Among the original manuscripts auctioned off after Beethoven's death, No. 184 of the sales catalogue, was a notebook of horizontal music paper, sixteen manuscript pages designated in the catalogue under the title "Pianoforte pieces, partly with accompaniment, partly indeterminate."

This manuscript later came into the Grasnick Collection and passed, with that collection, to the Berlin Royal Library, which later became the German State Library, labeled "Gr. 23." It contains Nos. 1, 3, 5 and 6 of the variations for piano, four hands, on "*Ich denke dein,*" composed for the Countesses Giuseppina and Teresa Brunswick. These four variations date from 1799, as can be shown, while variations II and IV were only composed in 1803–4. This dates the manuscript and hence the other pieces it contains.

For a long time it was not possible to decide what instruments those other pieces were composed for. There is an Adagio[1] of great musical beauty, developed at length, in F major, written on four lines, and a Scherzo and Allegro in A major, written on two lines. They cannot have been for the piano or for string instruments; the harp too is out of the question. Albert Kopfermann argued convincingly that these three pieces were almost certainly written for a mechanical organ, the so-called Flötenuhr or Spielühr. The Adagio's notation is precisely the same as that of the Fantasia, K. 608, of Mozart, the manuscript of which was in the Beethoven "estate" and which was intended for the Flötenuhr of Müller's "*Gabinetto d'arte.*" Count Giuseppe Deym, who was managing an "Art Cabinet" under the bourgeois name of Müller (he had been forced to give up his title because of a duel), knew Beethoven and later married Countess Giuseppina Brunswick. One would hardly go wrong in supposing that Beethoven wrote these three pieces out of friendship for Count Deym and his Flötenuhr. How much interest Beethoven had taken in performing this task is shown not only by the high musical level of the works but also by the fact that he wrote similar compositions subsequently.—WILLY HESS (1)

Piano Sonatas

I. SONATA NO. 1 IN F MINOR, OPUS 2, NO. 1
  I. Allegro; II. Adagio; III. Menuetto (Allegretto); IV. Prestissimo

We do not know what Haydn thought of Beethoven's sonatas. No such enthusiastic testimony to the young genius came from him as that which he so spontaneously offered to Leopold Mozart about the greatness of his son. On the other hand, no such affectionate and respectful preface as Mozart addressed to Haydn is prefixed to Beethoven's sonatas; but if no love was lost between the hotheaded young man and the older master, they respected each other in spite of the fact that the former had very quickly discontinued his lessons. The Sonatas, Opus 2, are Beethoven's very convincing expression of that respect, and there can be no doubt that Haydn must have been impressed by the assurance of their mastery,

---

[1] Ludwig Altman in an edition of Beethoven's organ works has the following to say about the Adagio: "[It] is not just a marginal work [or] a casual oddity— it is on a level with many achievements of [Beethoven's] 'middle period.' This is perhaps best borne out by the telling resemblance of the opening theme to the mood and the melody of the Romance for Violin [and Orchestra] Op. 50, which Beethoven wrote about the same time. The second theme anticipates by six years the music of Marzelline's Aria from *Fidelio*. And finally, there is a six-note motif in the 8th measure of the piece which is identical to a phrase in the 'Egmont' Overture."—Editor.

even if he found them here and there too subversive in method and violent in expression for his taste.

Allegro.—The first-subject group of the Sonata No. 1 opens at once with the [first] theme, [consisting of a] rising figure which is identical (except for the difference of key) with the opening of the finale in Mozart's G minor Symphony (K. 550), [followed by a falling cadential figure]. It cannot be often enough emphasized that the music of Beethoven, even at its earliest stages, is anything but Mozartean, and that it is no tribute to either master to pretend to find any traces of such an influence in the younger one's work. That Beethoven learned a great deal from Mozart in the matter of the sheer management of the *materia* of music is too evident to be talked about, and the talking becomes futile directly it is recognized that temperamentally the two composers have so little in common that, even had Beethoven by accident worked with Mozart's own themes without being aware of the fact, the music he would have constructed on them could not have failed to be entirely different in spirit from what their owner made of them. When two composers are spiritually so utterly unlike each other as these two, there is simply no possibility of their meeting on common ground in their works, which are carriers of messages from their disparate worlds of the spirit.

[That two-measure theme] is continued by means of harmonic changes, the [falling] figure being insistently drawn together three times. After a pause [the rising figure] starts in the dominant (minor) and in the bass, rather as though Beethoven, who was brought up on Bach's *Well-tempered Clavier,* had subconsciously thought of a fugal answer and then, very properly in a work in sonata form, resisted the impulse to carry out the idea.

A new sequential treatment provides the modulations necessary to lead to the new key (A flat major) for the second-subject group, which is approached very early and with scarcely any transitional material. It is for some time poised firmly on a dominant bass, and the minor ninth (F flat) gives it a darker coloring than the second subject in works in minor keys generally took on in the exposition at that time, although the custom was to set it definitely in the tonic minor in the recapitulation.

Another theme follows in which a descending figure akin to that [of the second subject] appears in the bass, and then an expressive phrase, into which, although it is still in A flat major, a minor third repeatedly introduces its plaintive note, concludes the exposition.

The working-out begins with [the opening two-measure theme] in A flat major, but very soon passes on to [the second subject], which before long is heard modulating in the left hand. The music then becomes thematically more featureless, but the interest is sustained by a series of emphatic syncopations and later by broken figures that keep up the tension by suggesting some tentative approach to a new event. What happens is that [the falling figure of the first theme] returns in a new succession of sequences and suddenly brings the music back to F minor, leading it the more unexpectedly into the recapitulation because the up-beat of [its opening rising figure] is omitted. The recapitulation proceeds normally, with an interesting new modulation provided where the transition to the second subject has now to be so managed that everything continues to be heard in the tonic key of F minor. The few clinching bars at the end are perhaps hardly enough to be called a coda in the full Beethovian sense of the term, but already they show how well aware the composer is that this feature of the sonata form is going to be of the utmost signif-icance to him later on. Nothing in this movement, which has both the elegance and the passion of youthful genius, is more telling than the sudden divergence of the plaintive clinching theme into an unexpected cadence, which makes the addition of a few extra bars imperatively necessary before the final tonic chord can be reached.

Adagio.—The slow movement, in F major, is so simple in expression and form as to need no detailed analysis. At the same time it will not do to let our knowledge that it is a much earlier composition than the rest of the sonata mislead us into listening to it patronizingly. It may not be especially interesting; but it is certainly filled with a truly Beethovian melodic nobility, and [is] a highly finished piece of craftsmanship, in spite of its somewhat rudimentary form. This defect, if it be a defect, is easily explicable: Beethoven sets out to write an adagio in sonata form, with two groups of subjects, which inevitably means excessive length compared with the size of a fast first movement in that form. Thus he discovers that he must give up the idea of inserting a working-out section of any sort, and he accordingly proceeds straight from the exposition to the re-capitulation. However, he feels that there should be some sort of develop-ment, and so hits upon the notion of varying his themes as they come round again. The result is a sonata movement which is incomplete in form, but for compensation has an interestingly elaborated layout of its ma-terial. Another evidence of how keenly Beethoven's sense of balance was developed, even at the very early age at which he wrote this movement, is his cutting out from the recapitulation of the transitional theme between the two subject groups and then making up for his omission by adding a few bars, partly derivative and partly new, by way of a coda.

Minuetto: Allegretto.—This is not a dancing minuet like that in *Don Giovanni*, for example. The minuet in classical sonata form music came, even before Beethoven's days, much nearer to the scherzo which he was to evolve out of it than musicians usually choose to remember. It is not surprising, therefore, that this early sonata minuet of Beethoven's should approach his later scherzo manner, for all that its pace is still too leisurely for a real scherzo. There is a touch of the spleen about it already, as will be gathered from the opening bars, and it will become more and more evident as the music proceeds to an irascible outburst of octave unison passages and several explosive accents, some of them off the place where the strong beat would naturally be expected.

The trio section, in the major, runs on quite smoothly by way of contrast. The hands exchange their figures in a way that seems to have been suggested to Beethoven by some exercise in double counterpoint, but here the principle of that device is not carried out strictly. The impulse to yield to free musical invention is too strong for a young composer who has not yet discovered the secret of finding inspiration in rigorous discipline.

The minuet, needless to say, is repeated.—ERIC BLOM (1)

Menuetto: Allegretto. F minor: with Trio in Tonic Major.

If we imagine the first accent to fall on bar 2, the whole Minuet and Trio will be in 4-bar and 2-bar groups with all the cadences closing on to strong bars; until we reach the last 8 bars of the Trio, where we shall find that the melody has changed step though the total amount remains even. Meanwhile, there are so many cross-currents, and Beethoven's *sforzandos* in bars 31 and 33 are so explicit, to say nothing of the positions of his sudden *fortes* and *fortissimos*, that our interpretation of bar 1 as preliminary will survive only for listeners who conscientiously support it with sniffs. After all, what sort of abstraction can an accent be if it is *never* the loudest note of a passage? There is, then, no sufficient evidence that Beethoven is not conceiving this music in the sense which will reach the naïve listener who apprehends that it begins at the beginning. A *sforzando* on the third beat is a mere cross accent; but the *sforzandos* on the first beat once in two bars will keep us in step. Meanwhile, what does it matter that the cadences are weak? The long penultimate note in bars 39–40 almost suffices to suggest a weak cadence. A short chord in its place would have been much less amenable. You can shift your step if you like; but then, whichever way you take the Trio it will turn round upon you at the end. It seems simpler to suppose that the ear is right in accepting an irregularity than to suppose that Beethoven is addressing himself to Prout and Riemann as the only worthy recipients of his message.—DONALD FRANCIS TOVEY (9)

Prestissimo.—The precipitous finale is in sonata form. The first-subject figure is the most important feature in the structure, [with its agitated triplet accompaniment in the left hand and the alternating loud and soft staccato chords in the right hand]. It has the curious effect of shifting the accent which would seem most obvious to the ear by beginning its accompaniment on the first beat of the bar, for the three chords in the right hand look very much as though they were a half-bar upbeat followed by a strong accent on the third chord. Thus a certain ambiguity of accentuation

prevails throughout the first-subject group, which includes a more melodious episode.

The first idea of the second subject is laid out in triplets throughout
and frequently combines two [eighth-notes] in the left hand with the three
in the right. There is another strain later that also belongs to the second
subject, a descending melodic phrase played by the right hand in octaves
on various degrees of the scale of C minor—the key in which the whole
of this group stands, with incidental modulations, of course.

The exposition is repeated. Upon it follows a working-out section with
a distinctly Mozartean feature, though it is not in the least like Mozart
in character. The earlier master often begins a working-out with an
entirely new thematic notion, generally purely melodic, as though he were
much too innocent to know what to do with the themes he has
brought forward in the exposition. That is, of course, only his sly way of
deceiving his hearers and suddenly surprising them by tying up his
material in such intricate knots of development that he and they
enjoy the ingenuity all the more for the teasing in which he has indulged
for a while. This is more or less what Beethoven does in this finale of his,
except that the knots later on are not going to be forbiddingly Gordian.
He introduces a surprisingly long independent episode in A flat major,
which almost necessitates a kind of development of its own. At last the
rhythmic beat of [the opening theme] returns stealthily and makes itself
heard almost continuously for the rest of the working-out section, which
thus merges naturally into a recapitulation that is perfectly regular and has
a few bars of brilliant triplet arpeggios tacked onto it as a coda.—
ERIC BLOM (1)

II. SONATA No. 2 IN A, OPUS 2, No. 2
    I. Allegro vivace; II. Largo appassionato; III. Scherzo (Allegretto);
    IV. Rondo (Grazioso)

Allegro vivace.—With a characteristic gesture of defiance Beethoven
at once falls to one of the brief thematic snatches that group themselves
together as his first subject [i.e., the falling fourth, the eighth-note rest,
and the thirty-second-note scale figure which brings us back to the tonic].
It is played by both hands in unison and leads through a descending
chord of the dominant seventh back again to the tonic, in which [an-
other] more extended phrase appears. The easily woven polyphonic texture of this passage should be noticed: such things came naturally to the
young composer and were as readily abandoned again for a different
layout. The studies with Albrechtsberger had borne fruit, but none of
his pedantry had passed to the pupil of genius.

A third idea, still in A major, because still belonging to the first-subject
group, appears a little later. [It consists of a rising scale figure in

sixteenth-note triplets followed by a descending scale figure in staccato eighth-notes.]

The approach to the second subject is made with great subtlety, emphasized by a slight retarding of the pace for an instant. The orthodox key for the second subject was, of course, E major in a movement in A major, but Beethoven boldly makes for E minor. Not only that, but his subject passes through a series of extremely daring modulations that take it to G major and B flat major.

At that time a subject in a sonata or symphony was supposed, not only to start in its proper key, but to remain in it for at least a reasonable time. To make it do neither was a drastic new departure. Beethoven had spent his youth in a period that witnessed a tremendous political revolution, and it was he who expressed its tendencies most openly in music, as far as that art can reflect outward events. But his time was not ripe for artistic insurrections of the most rabid kind. Note that in the bass of [this extraordinary passage] there was a glorious opportunity to defy the authorities by writing consecutive triads—a chance which Debussy or Puccini or dozens of other composers of a century later would have welcomed. But Beethoven is seen [at the beginning of every other bar] to go out of his way to avoid what would then have been an unpardonable solecism [by delaying the rise of the upper note of the triad].

In the end the second-subject group does arrive at E major, in which key it asserts itself triumphantly. A peroration to the expository section of the movement is made up from the theme of which [the motive combining sixteenth-note rising scales and eighth-note falling scales] is a fragment, and there is a very quiet close in E major. This whole section is repeated.

A link from the exposition to the working-out is made by a suggestion of E minor, from which, with the fifth of the chord left out, it is only a step into C major. In that key the opening theme at first asserts itself vigorously, and it passes through the dominant of C major as it had previously gone through that of A major. But it jerks with dramatic suddenness into A flat major, and the theme now alternately presents itself below and above a regularly moving sixteenth-note accompaniment, returning by way of F minor to C major. This, however, soon reveals itself as being merely the dominant of F major this time, and it is in F major that the second strain of the first subject now presents itself. Having insisted on that tonality just long enough for us to fancy that it was meant to be more than episodic, there is a sudden contraction of the rhythmic periods, which now go through a variety of keys, with D minor tending to be uppermost, producing an effect of restlessness, as though the composer were anxious to resume the main argument. But there are digressions of some length, loosely based on the main material.

When the recapitulation comes, it is as normal as possible. Scarcely anything is modified but the turn into the second subject, which, of course, now begins in A minor, ending in A major, and the peroration, which has to remain in the latter key. Some octave displacements in the second subject are due merely to the shortness of Beethoven's keyboard, which would not allow of upward transposition. There is not even a coda— at any rate so the schools would say. This is not due to immaturity, for in Beethoven's first sonata there is, at the corresponding place, a coda which, for all its brevity, is astonishingly eloquent. The absence of this feature here is due rather to the fact that there has already been enough concluding matter in the exposition, with its counterpart at the end of the movement. It might thus be more to the point, though less academic, to say that, so far from there being no coda to this movement, it has already been included in the exposition.—ERIC BLOM (1)

One of the most powerful passages in Beethoven's early works is that which begins the second group of the first movement of the A major Sonata, Opus 2, No. 2. After sixteen very thoughtful bars of dominant preparation, the second group begins in the dominant minor at bar 58, and then, instead of illustrating that key, continues with a series of startling modulations which reach the extreme distance of B flat in their course before they restore any hope of a return to E minor. Yet this remote key of B flat is the merest incident in the whole passage, and you will not have completed the harmonic sense of Beethoven's device until you have reached bar 87, nor the rhythmic sense until you have added the supplementary four bars closing into bar 92. On the lines of the old-fashioned harmony-books the passage can be explained as a series of enharmonic modulations with details not uninteresting to those who care for such things. The explanation is correct as far as it goes. It is quite true that the D sharp in bar 60 really turns to E flat in bar 61, and the F sharp in bar 64 to G flat in bar 65. The only trouble about the grammatical explanation of these enharmonic affairs is, first, that for general readers, and also for experienced composers, grammar is a dull subject when the study of it does not happen to be a painful necessity; and secondly—a far more serious objection—that the grammatical sense of this passage could not only be kept inviolate, but made much clearer, by simple alterations in the bass that would literally knock the bottom out of the whole plot.

Now in this passage of Beethoven's there are two unprecedented facts: the first is that, at a cardinal point in the exposition of a movement— that is to say, just where the composer or dramatist must be careful that his discursive license helps instead of hindering him to display all his data to the listener—Beethoven indulges in enharmonic modulations the very nature of which makes it impossible for us to know where we are. How can you trace a key-relation through a chord that had changed its meaning before it resolves? Alice, when in Wonderland, may have been very dull in not seeing for herself that one of the masters in the

Mock-Turtle's school was called Tortoise "because he taught us," but we are not all as clever as mock-turtles.

The second paradox about Beethoven's passage is that, after all, it sounds anything but discursive and aimless. On the contrary, it is one of the most solid and cogent affairs of dramatic destiny to be found in any music. And the secret is ridiculously simple. It is that the bass is rising steadily by tones and semitones from E up to the F sharp a ninth above. At this point it pauses with dramatic questionings, and the following eight bars (4+4) complete the remaining steps to the dominant of E; for it does not matter through what octaves you distribute the G sharp, A, A sharp, and B; the harmonic sense of rising ignores the octave, just as your ear will ignore a change of octave when a soprano voice hands over the continuation of a melody to a bass voice.

[Beethoven's] use of the gradually rising bass is neither decorative nor mysterious. Its purpose is to give the most solid dramatic reasons for modulations which would otherwise be mere accidents. In the Sonata, Opus 2, No. 2, he has even shown that not only the utmost remoteness of key, but the deliberate concealment of such key-relationships as are present, can be perfectly reconciled with the duties of dramatic exposition. —DONALD FRANCIS TOVEY (1)

Largo appassionato.—The principle of the slow movement is the very emphatic statement of one important theme with comparatively little modification, its solidity being thus insisted upon while at the same time monotony is avoided by a variety of episodes. The theme lasts for eighteen and a half bars of very deliberate time. It is in D major, with an A major middle section and a return to the tonic. The muffled staccato bass under the sustained upper notes is characteristic and was novel in its time. The A major section is written in parts, like a string quartet, details repeating themselves above and below.

There has been little change of key in the theme. For compensation Beethoven modulates very freely in the first episode, which begins in B minor.

The first restatement of the theme is substantially unaltered; but the hearer who does not read music—which is understandable—or who, doing so, does not happen to have a copy of Beethoven's piano sonatas—which is inexcusable—would do well to memorize the first statement of the theme from a gramophone record for comparison with the second. The small changes which occur will serve as well as anything to give him an insight into a great composer's carefully weighed procedures.

For the second episode, which is quite short, Beethoven never departs from the key of D major. This may seem contrary to an original intention to throw variety of key mainly into the episodes. But we shall discover in a moment that it is precisely an astonishing sense of balance that made the composer so reticent here. For now it is at the third return of the theme that he chooses to go in for vigorous modulation. With a startling loudness the theme suddenly bursts in, not as before, but in D minor, whence it makes an even more surprising excursion into B flat major. The former A major section is cut out to make way for a bridge passage that leads back to D major, in which the theme is concluded over a new inner accompaniment figure of gently purling semiquavers. There is a short coda—nothing more than two slightly extended and decorated cadences, but quite enough to round off a movement that has contained so much significance.

Allegretto.—After a movement built on extended melodic phrases comes a Scherzo that depends for its pouncing effect upon short figures. [There are] three scraps from which a tasty dish is made with remarkable economy: [The first is a sprightly arpeggio figure of sixteenth-notes which reaches the high note on the main beat of the bar, which is answered pertly by a staccato chord in the left hand on the second beat. The second tiny motive is a simple V-I cadence played forte. The third is a lyrical melody whose characteristic is the repetition of its high note three times.]

The hearer who does not seek the assistance of the printed page may amuse himself by trying to trace by ear the derivatives they engender. In this way the music may piece itself together in his mind much as it did in Beethoven's when it was composed, one phrase giving rise to another until the pattern is complete. Note, for instance, how the third of the fragments [the one with the three repeated notes] at first opens a short melodic phrase in G sharp minor, the only sustained melody in this section of the Scherzo, and how it afterward makes up the modulatory bridge [which ends with a surprise measure of silence]. This leads to the return of the opening themelet.

The trio, by way of a change, is a smoothly flowing piece in A minor, distinctly melodic in character, without however producing a memorable tune. This again, whether instinctive or deliberate, is a wonderfully ingenious contrivance: what was wanted here was a mild contrast, not an arresting one. To provide that is the function of the preceding and following movements.

The scherzo is restated without repeats.

Grazioso.—This Rondo has already been described as perhaps the most Mozartean movement in Beethoven's sonatas, though with a warning not to regard even this as anything but characteristically Beethovian, with that "impatient gesture" at the beginning, which grows more emphatic with each repetition.

The opening of the piece at once states the main rondo theme. [It consists of an arpeggio rising over three octaves from the low A in the bass to the high E in the treble, followed in the next measure by an equally precipitous jump from that high E over an octave to the G sharp in the middle register.]

To us, who have Wagnerian thunderstorms and Straussian fretfulness behind us, this sounds mild enough, and we must remember that after all the *grazioso* direction was uppermost in Beethoven's mind. All the same, things are smoldering in this music of which the eighteenth century had no notion. Not only that upward arpeggio in the first bar, but the leap in the second and the *sforzando* in the fourth are symptomatic of Beethoven's later manner—and also, we may say, of his manners. There is a certain gruffness even about a piece of his in which he sets out to be gracious.

After the first eight bars of the rondo theme, which is a melody—a distinctly instrumental melody—with an Alberti bass accompaniment, come another four bars containing a contrasting strain with some polyphonic imitations that make for a pleasing variety of the musical fabric. The four concluding bars are based on the four opening ones.

The first episode, which occurs after some subsidiary matter of a mainly ornamental character, is in the nature of a second sonata-movement subject, for it is in the key of the dominant and held in reserve for another appearance later. It spins itself out with perfect naturalness into another transition, which leads to the first restatement of the main theme. The opening arpeggio now spreads itself over four and a half octaves instead of three and a half, as before, and the figuration is slightly altered later on.

The next episode is entirely different in key (A minor) and character, so much so, in fact, as to have almost the effect of an intrusion. It is true that such independent incidents were exactly what was expected in a rondo, but it is impossible not to feel that the young Beethoven, with his exuberant faculty of developing any thematic idea at length and without loss of interest, was here in danger of letting his chief topic out of sight and writing a piece complete in itself.

When at last the rondo theme reappears, it is preceded by an up-rushing scale instead of an arpeggio, and again the pianistic figures are changed, those of the intermediate strain being converted into sixteenth notes, still treated in contrapuntal imitation. The bridge passage leading to what has been described as the second subject then recurs, followed by that subject itself, now of course in the tonic key. This enables the main theme to glide back quite unostentatiously. But it makes an interesting display after a few bars of simply varied restatement by suddenly modulating into the remote key of F major and back again, by a short cut, to A major, where the opening figure becomes unexpectedly active in a dialogue between bass and treble. Then, just as we expect to have heard the last of it in this intensified form, which seems to forecast the end, the music takes another surprising turn and makes, of all things, a reference to the long A minor episode which has seemed before

as though it could have no possible organic connection with the structure
of the rondo. Beethoven's instinct for form after all gets the better of his
inventive exuberance; he cannot forbear to make his earlier digression
relevant to the whole on the last page but one. The rondo concludes with
a final statement of the principal theme, which is pleasantly diverted into
a short closing period.—ERIC BLOM (1)

III. SONATA NO. 3 IN C, OPUS 2, NO. 3
   I. Allegro con brio; II. Adagio; III. Scherzo (Allegro); IV. Allegro
   assai

Allegro con brio.—The first movement shows a sonata-form scheme of
the greatest clarity: two immediately distinguishable groups of subjects,
including one feature that is interchangeable between them. The opening
theme is structurally important. [Its first two measures contain the
elements which will be developed at length throughout the movement—
the tonic half-note, followed by a sixteenth-note and eighth-note flourish,
ending with two quarter-note chords of the dominant at the beginning
of the second measure, followed by a half-measure of silence. The
sixteenth-note] groups at once assert their significance by taking part in
the development, appearing very soon in the bass. It is all very demure at
first and kept strictly in four parts, like a string quartet; but suddenly
the music breaks loudly into a passage that could not be anything but
keyboard music [made up of broken octaves and arpeggios rising and
falling]. This is the incident which is to return in the second-subject
group. It is extended by modulation toward G major and followed by a
brief new idea ending with an emphatic insistence on that key, thus clinching the first subject in the manner of the eighteenth century, which liked
to have the formal landmarks of a sonata or symphony movement clearly
pointed out. Very ingeniously, however, Beethoven does not wholly
dispel the impression that G here is still the dominant of C major,
for reasons that will reveal themselves later.
   The second subject, however, has to be definitely in the key of the
dominant, and it begins with a strain in G minor, a relic from the piano
quartet written at Bonn at the age of fifteen, which had already yielded
him the slow movement of the Sonata, Opus 2, No. 1. It modulates
smoothly to D minor and A minor, a new notion with a descending
scale appearing in the latter key. Further modulations lead at last to what
is a more normal key for the second subject in a C major sonata—G
major, in which a beautiful melody arises, treated in imitation, one
phrase acting as an accompaniment for the other.
   After some extension of this, [the brilliant pianistic passage] returns,
slightly modified but in its original key of C major at first. It reverts
to G, however, and leads into a descending passage of syncopations in

which Beethoven shows that disregard for harmonic clashes of which there is a familiar and notorious example in the *Leonore* Overture No. 3 (bars 360–77, if anyone wishes to look it up). Three rising arpeggios that follow include an augmented triad—a considerable audacity for the end of the eighteenth century, and [the] concluding phrase is important: [it alternates repeated staccato octaves, a trill, and a peaceful V-I cadence]. The actual close of the exposition, though, is made by unharmonized broken octaves, more akin to [the brilliant pianistic passage]. This whole section is repeated from the beginning.

The long and interesting working-out section begins with a development of [the concluding phrase], modulating successively into C minor, F minor, and the dominant of E flat major. At that point all thematic allusion disappears for a while to give way to sharp, glittering chords, broken into sixteenth notes. They are played by the right hand to patternless basses with gradually changing harmony in the left. Thus, over a sudden diminuendo, we arrive at D major, in which key the opening strain of the first subject returns. Its two initial phrases are almost unchanged, save that the key has risen by a whole tone. But now two of its figures [the sixteenth-note and eighth-note flourish and the staccato quarter-note chords] detach themselves, to be independently developed at some length, the former unaccompanied, the latter in bold octave formations in which fierce clashes of semitones are conspicuous. After three alternations in various keys, these two elements are brought together again, but still spun out in new ways, and then a chain formed of [the flourish] and descending over dominant harmony leads back to [the opening theme] in its original form and key: in other words to the recapitulation.

This is remarkable for its ruthless omission of [the brilliant pianistic figure], made perhaps because this incident has already been twice used in the exposition. A new thematic formation based on the concluding cadence of [the opening theme] is substituted, and then the music proceeds straight to the theme previously used to clinch the first-subject group. This is done in exactly the same way as before, and again the impression is created that the key of G reached here is really still the dominant of C. The reason for this now becomes perfectly clear: the second subject is, of course, not to be allowed to turn to G again, but must remain in the principal key of the sonata. The first theme of the second-subject group accordingly turns up in C minor, and [the tender melody with the alternating imitated phrases] is led up to without any other change than that of tonality, to reappear in C major.

When the concluding figure has been reached and the movement appears to come to its inevitable end, Beethoven springs his surprise: for the first time in a piano sonata he ventures on a large coda. It is approached in the most original manner. There is a sudden leap of an interrupted cadence from C major into A flat major, a tonal region the composer has so far avoided, and here a free fantasy begins which eschews every thematic reference and confines itself solely to broken chords—mainly diminished sevenths. When the music is arrested on a conventional 6/4 chord, we cannot fail to gather, from the experience of countless musical precedents, that we are in for a cadenza. And so it proves. This ornamental feature is for a moment concerned with [the sixteenth-note flourish of the opening measure of the movement] but dissolves into a [trill] and, with a rapid chromatic descent, comes back to [the complete opening theme] again, with which the coda continues. There is still some new development to come, but eventually the music turns back to the broken octave figures with which the exposition had concluded.—ERIC BLOM (1)

In a loosely constructed work, Beethoven is not above using an old Italian practical joke which Mozart often used in his slighter works. The joke consists in letting the exposition reach a pause on the home dominant, and then, like Mr. Wemmick in *Great Expectations*, saying: "Hulloa, here's a church! Let's go in! . . . Let's have a wedding!"— in other words, treating this home dominant as a real key and continuing in it. Probably Nature, having been driven out with a pitchfork, will assert herself by introducing the necessary enhanced dominant at a later stage, just as Mr. Wemmick was certainly able to produce the necessary documents in time for the wedding to proceed.

In the Sonata Opus 2, No. 3, the practical joke is followed by the remarkable passage which Beethoven resurrected from one of his juvenile pianoforte quartets, a passage which, starting in the dominant major, roams through several keys on a systematically falling bass.[1]

If Beethoven's early works had been mostly in the style of Opus 2, No. 3, and he had died before producing anything more characteristic, it would have been possible to argue that here was an ambitious composer who evidently aspired to be greater than either Mozart or Haydn, but who already showed the tendency to inflation that leads through the style of Hummel to the degenerate styles of the virtuoso pianoforte writers. We could even point to the cadenza in the first movement of Opus 2, No. 3, as [an] illustration of a license which was beneath the dignity of Haydn and Mozart. In the light of Beethoven's actual record, we need not view [this] lapse so severely as Beethoven doubtless viewed [it] himself. The mature Beethoven had seen the folly of [it]. As a matter of fact, cadenza-writing is a very good exercise in composition, and [this is a] good cadenza. Still, it is not for these things that we need to study Beethoven's early works.

[1] The passage from measure 27 to measure 38, which Tovey elsewhere points out as far more advanced harmonically than anything Haydn or Mozart anticipated.—Editor.

One of the most illuminating ways of listening to classical music is to ignore all your previous information and to let the music tell you step by step whether it is the work of a master; or, if that be a question-begging term, whether it is meant to be a sustained effort of composition. Any provocative young man can throw at your head a formula, an epigram, or a paradox. Epigrammatists are much less rare than dramatists. A young artist who is capable of drama is almost certainly capable of epigram, and his dramatic instincts must be powerful if he is to resist the temptation of sacrificing them to the easier art of epigram. There is an opposite source of dramatic weakness, and that is what is shown in certain features of the Sonatas, Opus 2, No. 3. Luxurious and loosely constructed as [this work is, it] might have led to a degeneration into something like the master of the well-constructed play. Here, again, my own private conviction is that it is ungrateful to spend much of one's critical life in grumbling at things which give refined pleasure. Only professional critics are obliged to take an overdose of them, and if the epigrammatist succeeds in distending himself into a writer of well-constructed plays, we may pity the hard fate of the forcibly fed critic without being ungrateful to the eupeptic dramatist who gives us as much pleasure as we choose to accept at his hands.—DONALD FRANCIS TOVEY (1)

Adagio.—The slow movement is in E major—a long way from the main key of the sonata. If we choose to think of Schubert on seeing such a bold departure, we are entitled to some astonishment at Beethoven's making it before that master was born, and very early in his own career; but it is worth remembering that Haydn had already been partial to such enterprising key distributions between a group of movements within one single work.

There is a recurrent theme with intervening episodes, which are themselves recurrent; in other words, we have here a slow rondo with strong leanings toward sonata form.

The principal theme [is a lyrical ten-measure outpouring made up of two-measure groups. It has a certain tentative quality produced by the silence at the end of each bar. Particularly arresting are the syncopated upbeats in the seventh and ninth measures]. Very soon the key changes to E minor, and the right hand plays continuous murmuring figures with the break of a pause on each beat. There is much crossing of hands.

The music has arrived at the first restatement of the main theme, which recurs at first without any modification. The reason is an exceedingly subtle one, and none the less so if one likes to consider the result due to unconscious promptings rather than to deliberation. Beethoven, by refraining from developing his theme at once, makes a change the more dramatic when it does come, quite unexpectedly. It is nothing less than a sudden explosive restatement of the initial thematic figure in a new key, or rather in an old and almost forgotten key, for the sonata remembers all at once its distant home tonality of C major and drops into it without the slightest preparation. But the flowing right-hand figures return and quickly lead back to E major, in which key, instead of G major, the crossed-hand figures return.

At its final appearance the main theme is beautifully elaborated and kept for the most part higher up on the keyboard. An extension in which its predominant melodic motif is played quietly in the bass, as though on two discreet bassoons, under a single repeated B in the treble, is exquisitely poetical, and so is the questioning pause that follows and finds its answer in one of the most curious and characteristically pianistic final cadences Beethoven ever devised.

Allegro.—[In place of a minuet movement, we now have] a real scherzo, explicitly so called by the composer. It begins in [a] lightly polyphonic, gracefully imitative manner. There are two sections, each repeated, and the second one is more than three times as long as the first. Almost the whole is based strictly on [the polyphonic opening theme], but with great resourcefulness of development. The only extraneous feature is [a characteristic rhythm of an accented upbeat followed by a cadential figure on the downbeat]. It is this which provides the concluding bars, which are rounded off by an abrupt drop of Cs in bare octaves.

The trio, in A minor, consists entirely of rapid arpeggios for the right hand which let no distinct thematic material arise—itself a contrast to the sharp-featured music from which it provides relief. It leads back, over a descending dominant-seventh arpeggio of C major, to the Scherzo, which is played right through again. More than right through, in fact, for this time the octave drop does not conclude it: there is a short coda. The octaves are twice repeated, each time a minor third lower (A and F sharp), and then chords in the right hand are accompanied by rigid basses with a semitonal growl, based on the Scherzo theme. Once more Beethoven contrives a most original conclusion.—ERIC BLOM (1)

However you pair the bars in the movement, you will find yourself out of step in the middle of the Scherzo, and again at the end of the trio; unless you consent to listen naïvely and allow Beethoven's *sforzandos* and changes of pitch to push and pull you wherever he chooses. You will get into mere confusion if you try to make the cadences in the first strain fall on to strong bars by taking your time from bar 2, for you can maintain this only by supposing that the sudden *fortes* fall on weak bars; and if you can retain an "accentuation" so violently against the actual sounds, you will not be able to perceive any irregularity of rhythm that can prevent the theme from returning at bar 39/40 on the basis of weak cadences. On the other hand, this reversal cannot be supposed to be an intentional subtlety, so long as rhythm concerns the human ear at all. The plain facts that reach the ear are that none of the cadences in the Scherzo is strong, and that the rhythm is sometimes displaced. The ear will probably take bars 33/34-36 as a 3-bar group echoed by bars 36/37-39. And the coda is intelligible only when bars 60/61-64 are taken as a 4-bar clause entry on the 4th bar. The Trio begins on a main bar, but changes its step by the *sforzandos* in its second strain—an admirable illustration of Beethoven's way of appealing to human ears.—DONALD FRANCIS TOVEY (9)

Allegro assai.—The finale is a rondo in very rapid 6/8 time. The chief thematic landmark [a brilliant rising scale in sixths] is exposed at once. Having driven toward the dominant, it is repeated in that position, only to turn back to the tonic—in the naïvely spontaneous manner that is common to innumerable classical themes and derives, of course, ultimately from the people's songs and dances. (Which may or may not be accepted as a hint not to take the classics more seriously than they took themselves.) There is a not very clearly thematic continuation in [sixteenth notes], making for a return of [the opening theme], this time with a modulatory twist that brings us to the first episode, in G major, a strongly accentuated melody over a broken-chord accompaniment and a bass descending in three consecutive steps. When it is repeated an octave higher it soon turns into G minor, and its attendant figures are much extended until detached upward runs in the manner of the chief theme herald its return.

The subject remains unaltered at first, but presently the runs are transferred to the bass, and in this way the music modulates three times. Broken figures in contrary motion then act as a transition to the new key of F major, in which the second episode, a gentle, sustained melody laid out in right-hand chords, rises and falls. It passes into bass octaves accompanied by fluttering treble groups of two notes that come in off the beat, and after a brief subsidiary idea these are given to the left hand while the right resumes the chord treatment of the melody. This kind of development is carried on for a surprisingly long time, with the subsidiary theme returning twice, ingeniously turned the second time into another display of rising detached notes.

The second return of the main theme is thus prepared, and we now find ourselves in a regular sonata recapitulation, with the second rondo episode returning, in the key of the tonic, as a definite second subject. A new approach is made to yet another appearance of the main rondo theme, which actually comes back to form an important coda. It begins where a high trill becomes conspicuous, below which [the rising scale theme] is played by the left hand. A free development of it follows which is in the nature of a cadenza rather than in that of a coda closely worked to form a structural climax. For some thirty or forty bars we seem to be listening to a concerto at a moment when the orchestra happens to be silent rather than to a sonata. But thoughtfulness returns when the subject, once more in the bass, is heard slowly and softly just before the end, which comes with a last outburst of energy.—ERIC BLOM (1)

IV. SONATA NO. 4 IN E FLAT, OPUS 7
   I. Allegro molto e con brio; II. Largo, con gran espressione;
   III. Allegro; IV. Rondo (Poco allegretto e grazioso)

This is certainly the richest, most mature, and most original of the early sonatas. The first movement (Allegro molto e con brio) displays an overflowing wealth of motifs, which already have the method of expression so characteristic of Beethoven's style, based on sharp contrasts, almost dramatic picturesqueness, and expressive dialogues. The songlike second theme, which is instinct with the most intimate sentiment, affords a strong contrast to the easy flow of the first theme, which in its turn has striking shorter episodes of contrast. The exposition runs its course in a broad stream of tone and hastens to its close in extremely effective tension. In the conspicuously short development section drastic expression replaces length. The peak of the movement is not reached till after the reprise in the powerful coda, in which a second development is worked up to a greatly impressive close.—HUGO LEICHTENTRITT

Do not be surprised, or, if you enjoy the surprise, do not try to minimize it, by discovering clever logical [connections] when Beethoven makes an exposition of several disconnected ideas thrown at you with Mozartean abruptness, as at the beginning of the E flat Sonata, Opus 7. Clever people tell us that in Opus 7 the rhythmic figure of bars 1–4 is latent in the bass of bars 5–10. If you are as clever as all that, you may be far too clever to see that the right hand of bars 5–12 is not a single voice, but is in dialogue; that the C at the end of bar 6 goes down to the following B flat in the left hand, while a new voice answers the figure above; and that there is a similar new entry at the join of bars 8–9. These facts are not evident to the eye, but they are evident to the ear, unless the player has no natural instinct for phrasing. A composer who has written over a hundred works in sonata form cannot fail to have procedures that can be classified; yet there is little use in attempting the classification of Beethoven's expositions.—DONALD FRANCIS TOVEY (1)

The second movement (Largo) is one of those sublime hymnlike monologues of a depth and power of expression such as no later composer has achieved. With its fear and sorrow, its ejaculations, its defiant desire, and ghostly visions, it is the deeply moving and uplifting confession of a great soul, and its strains are also eloquent of conquest of self, humility, and submission to inevitable fate. The devotional, serene first theme is the fixed point of this deeply moving fantasy. The music roams far afield from it and returns to it, and there at last finds peace and resignation.— HUGO LEICHTENTRITT

In the recent, but now moribund, reaction against Romanticism, some of our cleverest writers achieve their best effects of unconscious comedy by casting doubts upon its sincerity. They should know better than to mistake for insincerity that early phase of technique in which the artist has recourse to carefully measured pauses that are dangerous rhetorical gestures, or stage effects. The occasion for such effects is adequate, and their danger is nothing compared with that of filling up their spaces with explanations. They [certainly do not] overstrain the suggestive powers of the pianoforte and the listener's capacity to integrate slow broken rhythms, as happens in the slow movement of the Sonata, Opus 7, where Beethoven is evidently working at high emotional pressure. If such things are defects, they are signs of excitement, not of insincerity. Even in his early works, Beethoven indulges in rhetorical gestures and pauses less often than Haydn, and then only for Haydn's reasons—that it is better to break off than to explain.—DONALD FRANCIS TOVEY (1)

In the third movement (Allegro) Beethoven creates a new type for himself, which is neither minuet nor scherzo, but a lyrical intermezzo. The floating grace of Mozart illuminates the first theme, which nevertheless is mingled with Beethoven's manly strength. The middle section, marked "minore," leads us into regions of romance which are prophetic of Schumann and Chopin. It is a somber muttering among the low notes with which a greatly expressive melody emerges like a plaint in the night. The principal theme of the finale, a rondo, expressive of many moods, full of enchanting grace, sets the skill of the player many grateful tasks, and fascinates the expert with the beauty of its craftsmanship. A vigorous, agitated episode in C minor is, so to speak, the manly counterpart of the feminine charm of the theme of the Rondo. Shortly before the end we have a surprise which is a foreboding of romanticism. The principal key, E flat major, unexpectedly turns to the remote B major, till in a gracious harmonious curve the chords find their way back to E flat major with assured elegance.—HUGO LEICHTENTRITT

V. SONATA NO. 5 IN C MINOR, OPUS 10, NO. 1
   I. Allegro molto e con brio; II. Adagio molto; III. Finale (Prestissimo)

The three Sonatas, Opus 10, published in 1798, are dedicated to
the Countess von Browne, to whose husband Beethoven had already
inscribed the three string Trios, Opus 9, with the following words, at
once grateful and self-congratulatory: "*Au premier Mécène de sa Muse la
meilleure de ses oeuvres.*" It is clear that already at this time Beethoven
had a very good notion of his own worth, and if he thought his Opus 9
his best work up to the time of its dedication, it by no means follows
that he did not soon afterward regard Opus 10 as better still. Indeed he
had good reason to be proud of it. The passionate first sonata of the
set, in C minor, was a considerable advance in personal expressiveness.

The epithet "passionate" applies most obviously to the first movement,
with its far-flung opening gesture, its melodic suspensions, suggestive of
suppressed agitation, and its dramatic, breathless pauses; but passion is
also disclosed by some of the quick, almost violent figuration in the slow
movement and by the abrupt, short-tempered first subject of the finale.

Allegro molto e con brio.—The opening gesture referred to above
[is a precipitously rising dotted rhythmic figure outlining the C minor
triad]. It is followed by that gentle answer which is so characteristic of
Beethoven's first subjects: they are a kind of reflection in miniature of
the thematic duality that is, on the larger scale of a whole movement,
the guiding principle of the classical sonata form. The theme repeats
the same procedure in dominant harmony, and then comes a second
strain of the first-subject group [—a haunting, falling phrase of two measures, repeated three times, each time with] subtle changes. The melodic
suspensions already mentioned extend it the third time. Next come
[several of the dramatic, breathless pauses referred to above], intersecting
a small triplet figure which at its third recurrence leads back to [the
opening upward gesture]. But now only the energetic dotted figures are
heard—again three times—and the gentle answering chords are omitted.
A character has left the stage and a dialogue has become a soliloquy, if
we like to give a dramatic interpretation to a movement that is quite
histrionic enough to warrant such an expedient.

Now comes a very striking rhetorical device: three abrupt ejaculations,
a moment's pause for reflection, and then an entirely new thought,
[tender rather than gruff, sad rather than tragic]. Technically (for one
must abandon metaphor before it gets out of hand) Beethoven operates
in a very curious manner here. He uses in fact the effective trick of first
doing the expected and then following it up with a complete surprise.
The three [abrupt ejaculations just mentioned] conclude the first subject
in no uncertain manner. It is not only dispatched, but three nails are

very emphatically knocked into its coffin, which is perfectly in keeping with the habits of the eighteenth century, when the sonata was a new toy and composers made a point of showing its inner workings as clearly as possible. But the eighteenth-century mind would now have expected the contrasting second subject to follow immediately, and of course in the key of the relative major in a work cast in a minor key. Here we have [a lyrical theme which] sounds ideally like a second subject, at any rate in relation to our particular first-subject material. But it is in A flat major, the wrong key for the purpose, and moreover it repeats itself immediately in F minor and in D flat major. Only when this last key has been traversed does the music settle on the dominant of E flat major. (The right-hand figures [of three repeated notes and the fall to the next note of the scale, like elaborate sighs,] afterwards have an ornamental variant. [They] are structurally more important than they look at the moment, as we shall see presently.) And now the second subject is at last ready to appear in its orthodox key [—a lyrical diatonic melody over a single eighth-note accompaniment]. It too has a more elaborate extension and it diverges to other matter with dramatic accents off the first beat, until the [eighth-note] accompaniment affects the right hand, which for four bars plays in unison with the left in a powerful crescendo. Then the [precipitous gesture that opened the movement] is used as an approach to a last-moment idea that is in a way new, yet has a strong rhythmic affinity with the right-hand motif [which was used to usher in the second subject]. Thus the exposition ends in E flat major.

The working-out can be so called only because it begins with a new version of [the opening theme,] which, with its C major and diminished-seventh harmony, leads to [an entirely] new theme in F minor. From here onward none of the material is, properly speaking, "worked out," so that this section might more aptly be called a "working toward" the recapitulation. But though not thematically allusive, it is certainly thematically relevant. The music passes through keys that have not been touched by the exposition and eventually turns on the dominant of C minor, in which key the recapitulation begins in the normal way.

It does not remain normal for long. The restatement of what we may call the sham second subject surprisingly follows immediately after the triplet figures intersected by pauses, the earlier resumption [of the opening dotted rhythm] being omitted. But even more unexpected than this elision is the fact that the transitional theme enters in the key of G flat major, for which the close of the triplets in C major has left us quite unprepared. The immediate effect of this is that the true second subject is now brought into the key of F major, whereas according to the rules it ought to stand in the tonic minor. Beethoven's way out of this unusual situation, which he has of course purposely created in order to show both his independence and his unabashed resourcefulness, is to modulate to

C minor next (which is easy enough, since F is the subdominant) and to reiterate the second subject, at full length and with some changes of figuration, in the proper key. After that he has simply to transpose the whole material of his previous E flat close into C minor, including the allusions to the dotted rhythm and the right-hand figures of repeated notes and the sighing fall of a second. A coda would, he may have felt, have overweighted this section of the movement in view of the F major interpolation; at any rate he dispenses with that feature.

Molto adagio.—The slow movement has the first and second subjects and the coda of a sonata, but no working-out section, which is omitted no doubt partly to avoid excessive length and partly because three movements in regular sonata form in a single work would have been too much—for the finale is also in that form. But Beethoven does not deprive a highly organized movement of an important structural feature without making some sort of compensation. We have just seen this in the first movement, where a redundant section was in retrospect made to appear justified by the omission of a coda. Here the compensation for the missing development is made by letting the principle of variation assume an important function. The opening strain of the first subject [is a broad eight-measure melody that rises with tremendous inner tension to the high octave poised over a subdominant chord, and then gently falls back again to the dominant. It undergoes many changes through the course of the movement.] It is in fact heard in a modified form as soon as the passage has been completed.

A bridge to the second subject is formed by violent arpeggio figures, followed by a sharply rhythmic formation of chords. This occurs three times. [The third time the arpeggio is in the bass, and the rhythmic chords result in a suspension leading to the B flat dominant-seventh chord followed by an almost operatic cadenza.]

The second subject, in E flat major, follows immediately [—a haunting, almost tentative melody over repeated chords in the left hand]. This too is varied, in turn by precipitately rapid, by jerky, and by restless broken figuration which discloses the passionate feeling that was said to underlie even the slow movement of this sonata.

The return to the first subject is made in the simplest way, by a detached dominant chord of A flat major following on the tonic of E flat. There is on the face of it no more art in this than in the change from one section to the next in a Johann Strauss waltz or an operatic potpourri; but as we know that Beethoven was capable of effecting the most cunning modulations when he chose, we realize that here his art reveals itself precisely in the decision not to use a complex device when a simple one happens to be perfectly suitable. The variants of the first subject should now be noted by comparison with [its original form], and they need no detailed explanation; but I will show why I have [earlier pointed out] an incident from the bridge passage, a conjunction which has now to lead to A flat major instead of E flat. [On the third repetition of the arpeggio, the rhythmic chords result in a suspension, not over a B flat dominant seventh [as it originally did] but over a C flat dominant seventh.]

Here we have a striking example of that Beethovian ingenuity in modulation to which I have just referred. The bass behaves at first almost exactly as before, except that the E flat in the arpeggio has become F flat. The bass C flat remains static for a moment: it refuses to sink down as before, as though it were waiting for the raised top harmony to descend with it. What happens is that the top harmony comes down first, which is just the opposite of what occurred earlier, and now the bass decides that it may as well follow, whereupon the harmonic situation is exactly as before. But that would bring the second subject back in E flat again, which is what must on no account happen; so the top harmony sinks down yet another degree of the scale, from which the next natural step is for treble and bass to converge together on a dominant seventh of A flat.

The way is now open for the second subject to re-enter in that key, and so to lead to a conclusion. But something else than the second subject is wanted to round off the movement, and this is done by a coda based on yet another variant of the first theme. This, however, would only seem to lead the music into a kind of endless pendulum swing between first and second subject if it took the same turn as before, and Beethoven now drastically alters not only the figuration of the theme, but, after the first four bars, its whole melodic deportment. It loses its distinction as a tune and becomes more and more purely harmonic, thus making an admirable peroration suggestive of a gradual vanishing.—ERIC BLOM (1)

The Adagio of this little C minor sonata shows that Beethoven [does not] yet feel ready to attempt a powerful design in a slow tempo. It is melodious; but [it] does [not] attempt to be more than sectional in its total effect, except perhaps at the end, where the coda, with the evident attempt at an effect of breadth, becomes dangerously thin. It was not long before Beethoven found out that what such a coda needed was, not to expand itself, but to make the rest of the movement seem gigantic by introducing a human detail in the foreground.—DONALD FRANCIS TOVEY (1)

Prestissimo.—It has already been said that the finale, like the other movements, is in sonata form. As is to be expected of Beethoven, however, he guards against a feeling of monotony not only by producing great contrasts of character, pace and mood between the movements, but by contriving a structural climax to compensate for sameness of shape. As usual, he hits on a surprisingly simple expedient. He has had no coda in the first movement and no working-out in the second. Very well, there shall be both a coda and a working-out in the finale, and behold, short as the movement is, especially in view of its extremely fast tempo, the impression of a heightening in constructive power is most convincingly made, more especially as the working-out really is a thematic development this time. The fact that it is extremely condensed only seems to give it a more forceful structural function.

The first subject begins [with a characteristic six-note motif repeated three times, the first two played] in octave unison, [the third time expanded and harmonized]. The second [subject] opens like [a march theme with a rising scale figure in eighth notes answered by a descending figure in quarter notes—all extremely delicate because it is played softly and staccato]. Its continuation is delightfully underpainted by a bass derived from [the rising eighth-note scale figure]. But [the characteristic six-note motif of the opening theme] almost at once reasserts itself in the left hand and then, rising for one single flash into the right, calls forth a succession of small themes which, in the highest of spirits and with the nimblest wit, bring about the close of the exposition in E flat major.

When that section has been repeated, the very concise working-out makes use exclusively of [the opening six-note motif], which eventually comes to a halt, with the comic effect of some disgruntled character in an *opera buffa*, on a series of dropping diminished sevenths. The recapitulation is regular, with the second subject in the tonic major. The close seems to come quite naturally in C minor, but the bass suddenly falls a major third to A flat, which reveals itself as the dominant of D flat major. In that key the second subject is once more alluded to, but in a halting, timid manner that seems to belie the boisterous character of the whole piece and to introduce a touch of sentiment. But that character reasserts itself in a few closing bars based on the main theme, [very subtly combined with the rising eighth-note scale figure of the second theme, the whole texture getting softer and softer, and ending breathlessly in C major instead of C minor].—ERIC BLOM (1)

The finale of Opus 10, No. 1, is violently compressed. Properly played, it sounds broader than one might expect. This finale is the first of two occasions on which Beethoven used the direction "prestissimo" for a whole movement, the other case being in the second movement of the Sonata, Opus 109. In both cases the direction is unfortunate. A player experienced in Beethoven's style will soon find that in the effort to be clear in the details of these highly compressed and highly charged movements one is apt to drag. As a warning against this tendency, the direction "prestissimo" is natural enough, but as a positive direction to players whose ideas of classical style are vague, it is very misleading. When such music is played as fast as possible, it gives no more impression of pace than a sewing-machine. If it is really to sound fast, you must hear what it says.—DONALD FRANCIS TOVEY (1)

VI. SONATA NO. 6 IN F, OPUS 10, NO. 2
I. Allegro; II. Allegretto; III. Presto

The F major Sonata is the least considerable of the Opus 10, though it was much favored by the composer himself. The prevalent mood is humor—the typically Beethovenian humor which shows itself in abrupt statements of short sentences and in a habit of twisting and turning them, very much as he twisted words into puns and nonsense rhymes in his letters. In the F minor middle movement there are moments of suppressed anger which alternate with bouts of tenderness and little outbursts of temper. Emotionally this is the maturest of the three movements; it foreshadows the splenetic mood of many of Beethoven's later scherzos.

Allegro.—The first movement opens with a pithy remark [alternating two rising chords with seemingly insignificant Italian *opera buffa* turns in sixteenth-note triplets. The significance of the triplet figure in the working out of the movement will only be realized later]. A syncopated, [lyric] melody follows, which quickly leads back to the opening motif, still in F major, but immediately turned by means of a cadence suggested by the triplet figure into the dominant of A. Having led us to wonder whether A major or A minor will ensue, Beethoven, with comic abruptness, goes to C major, the proper key for the second-subject group in a movement in F major. He has thus reached this feature quite unexpectedly and much earlier than his normal procedure of spinning out a first subject would suggest.

The theme with which the second-subject group begins [has a grandeur with its rising arpeggio outlined nobly in quarter notes]. Compared with the first, it is disproportionately long, but although C major prevails to the end of the exposition, with several new thematic ideas remaining in that key, Beethoven astutely guards against letting it predominate unduly over the main tonality of F major, which he has so far curiously neglected, by inflecting his harmony heavily toward other keys. Thus a subsidiary theme appears poised on the dominant of C major after a cadence verging on G major. [This subsidiary theme is characterized also by an Italianate mordent at the end of its first two measures and by three falling staccato chords halting comfortably in C major]. Immediately afterwards, having been restated in a varied way, [fortissimo,] and in the minor, it abuts momentarily on A flat major by means of an interrupted cadence. A little later C major is confirmed again by yet another theme, led up to by a cadence formed from the triplets of [the opening phrase. This concluding theme begins with a Haydnesque repeated-note upbeat] and ends, [peremptorily, with the falling I-V-I in C major, played fortissimo in double octaves].

After the repeat of the exposition, the clinching figure, [the I-V-I,] is used for the opening of the working-out. It is merely due to a useful convention that this section can be so named in this case, for in actual fact it works out next to nothing. Neither the first nor the second subject is once referred to, unless the triplet motion is to be regarded as coming from [the opening triplet figure] in spite of the fact that the figuration is different. All that Beethoven develops here is the concluding phrase of the exposition, and even that development is interrupted by a lengthy and wholly independent episode in the middle, which is thematically rather featureless and passes through the keys of D minor, G minor and B flat major. It should be noticed that F major is still studiously avoided, though once the music comes as near it as the tonic minor.

When a pause indicates the place at which the recapitulation is to be reached, a very curious thing happens. Here, if anywhere, we feel that the main key should at last assert itself. It does nothing of the kind, however. Beethoven has the astounding audacity to reintroduce his first subject in the alien key of D major. It takes a moment's reflection to explain his procedure, which is in fact extraordinarily subtle. We have seen that his working-out contained the permissible minimum of thematic development; but we may now regard the odd behavior of the re-capitulation as a compensation. By turning his first subject into D major and thus compelling himself to give it a new modulatory curve before it can be made to return to the principal key, Beethoven makes this juncture in his musical discourse partake in some measure of a working-out as well as a recapitulation. Small differences in the presentation are worth attentive study. It is important to note that the triplet figure in the D major restatement does not descend a step with the change to the dominant harmony as at first [but remains poised on A, the fifth note of the scale of D major. This] point fails to become clear until an instant later we find that this new formation serves the composer for his long-delayed return to F major in this way [—by raising the A to B flat and changing the harmonies under that B flat to G minor and C, which, of course, is the dominant of F major]. It is one of the evidences of his mastery that he cannot only find such means of giving point to a transition, but that he also knows the art of hinting at it before it actually turns up.

The second strain of the first-subject group, which has already come up in that false start in D major, now returns in the main key, and from here to the end F major remains predominant, exactly as C major had done in the greater part of the exposition. The movement ends in the same way as that section, there being no coda.

Allegretto.—The second movement is a scherzo, though not so named by the composer, perhaps because of his irregular expedient of varying the return of the main theme after the contrasting trio section. The piece is in F minor, but during the stealthy first strain of eight bars it modulates quickly into the relative (A flat) major. This passage is repeated. Then comes a new idea which is imitated in canon at the fifth. Strong accents on the third beat lend the music a capricious, quick-tempered character. The opening phrase is then repeated two octaves higher up the key-board, in the right hand alone, and when the left joins there is another brief suggestion of canon. Its [last six notes—C, D flat, B flat, E, F, C—are] then used as accompaniment to a cadence that leads to the concluding strains.

The trio section, in D flat major, is calm and consolatory at first. As a modulation to A flat major is approached, we come upon another instance of Beethoven's subtlety in preparing the hearer for a point that is about to arise: [the upbeat of two rising eighth notes leading to the A flat (the fifth scale-note in the key of D flat) would presumably be F, G flat, A flat].

The interesting factor here is the G natural in the upbeat, which gives an A flat major implication to the passage from the start, although the next two bars are still quite distinctly in D flat major and would not by themselves indicate any impending modulation. As the opening tune of the trio is restated, the left hand adds a new figure which cuts rhythmically across it and is like the sting of angry words thrust into a suave conversation. The two contrasting ideas are then developed at considerable length.

A drop of a semitone from the concluding tonic (D flat) brings us to the dominant of F minor, in which key the first section is now repeated with a different pianistic lay-out. The first eight bars are no longer written down with repeat signs, but twice newly set forth, the second time in syncopation. From this point on the syncopated motion continues almost throughout, save where the little theme in canon returns in an inverted form.

Presto.—We have not done with formal curiosities yet. The humorously blustering opening theme of the finale suggests a rondo. (The concluding F is the implied ending of the phrase, but it rarely arises in that form, being as a rule dovetailed with the beginning of the next statement.) When the right hand enters with the same figure while the left continues a contrapuntal course, the rondo theory may be abandoned and the development of a fugue suspected. Only by those, however, who do not know that the second entry of a fugue subject cannot, like the first, be in the tonic, as it is here. The third appears in the dominant, but by this time Beethoven has abandoned polyphony, so that the texture is no longer even suggestively fugal. Now, as we do not yet know that there is going to be no real second subject, we may decide for sonata form; and indeed, for all that such a subject fails to arise, sonata form it is—of a kind. As far as the exposition goes, Beethoven may be said to have reverted here to the form of the old Italian harpsichord sonata or, if we like, to something like that of the very first sonatas actually written for the pianoforte by Lodovico Giustini of Pistoia, though it is inconceivable that Beethoven can have known his work. The mock-fugal opening reminds one strongly of Domenico Scarlatti. In feeling, as distinct from form, the piece is, of course, thoroughly Beethovenian.

A new development of the theme toward the end of the exposition, with the tune in the bass, faintly suggests a second subject, but only because it is in the key of the dominant, for it does not assume a sufficiently independent character. In any case we soon discover that it comes too near the close of the exposition and has been set into the dominant merely because that section must end in the neighboring key (C major).

After the repeat of the exposition the music plunges unexpectedly into A flat major, with a variant of [the opening blustering theme] which soon resumes its normal form over a flowing sixteenth-note accompaniment. Beethoven then begins to develop the tune and fragments of it with a good deal of contrapuntal elaboration, so that now we have the curious experience of a closely thematic working-out section allied to an exposition and recapitulation in a rudimentary sonata form, the exact opposite of what happened in the first movement. Here again Beethoven seems to have acted on a principle of, or more likely an instinct for, compensation, thus miraculously achieving a satisfactory balance even where he is apparently most erratic in his treatment of form. The climax of the development of his theme comes where he brings in the bass tune, [which ended the mock-exposition,] in contrary motion.

He uses this [device] again, in F major, for a brief coda; but first he deals with his material in a section that by reason of its position must be regarded as a recapitulation, though in reality it makes such free modulatory excursions and indulges in so many new elaborations as to be more in the nature of an improvisation. But Beethoven keeps to the point just as logically as if he merely repeated with the conventional modifications what had gone before, with the result that this finale of his, for all its humorous exploits, *is structurally as satisfying as the most strictly formal of his sonata movements.*[1]—ERIC BLOM (1)

[1] Editor's italics.

VII. SONATA NO. 7 IN D, OPUS 10, NO. 3
I. Presto; II. Largo e mesto; III. Menuetto (Allegro); IV. Rondo
(Allegro)

The opening of the first movement seems to spring out at us like a
panther. Beethoven, however, is an experienced sportsman with a camera
instead of a gun. He has had to move his tripod too quickly to take a
very continuous film, and we also had better abandon our metaphor and,
descending to the musical plane, remark that Beethoven, after a pause
for breath if not for safety, answers his first four bars with six bars,
in themselves an expansion, but cut off with a full close. This still
leaves his opening in the condition of the novel which begins with the
famous objurgation of the otherwise retiring Duchess; and Beethoven
sees that it would be futile to make anything else of the situation. He
begins a counterstatement in which the panther springs just one step
farther and knocks us into the middle of the next day. We might almost
as well have said "next week," for the next key is the so-called "relative
minor," and Beethoven needs a very long and flowing paragraph, passing
through several keys, before he can arrive at his objective, the orthodox
dominant; but this paragraph flows gloriously. Even apart from its context, it would be evidently the work of an artist with unlimited
talent for composition, and in its context it justifies Beethoven for having
begun his story with such alarming abruptness.

In [this sonata] Beethoven's power appears with an intensity which
must have come more as a shock than as a revelation to his contemporaries.
It is doubtful whether any part of it except the exquisite minuet can
have been acceptable to orthodox musicans in 1798. The slow movement
is not only Beethoven's first essay in tragedy, but is by far the most
tragic piece of music that had ever been written up to that time.[1]
—DONALD FRANCIS TOVEY (1)

It is in the monumental Largo e mesto of the sonata in D major
(Opus 10, No. 3), that the full grandeur of Beethoven's soul is for
the first time revealed. (The work is contemporaneous with the first
attacks of the malady that ruined his life: 1798.) From the opening
chords, in that majestic 6/8 whose august swing so often, in Bee-

[1] Tovey calls attention to a comparison between this largo and two other slow
movements (also in D minor), where Beethoven has used the same device of
silence (or nonmovement) at the point in the movement where he returns to the home
tonic after the so-called "development." Each example is different, but the silences are
all intensely dramatic.—Editor.

thoven, give the temples of his melancholy their rhythm,[1] the soul
of the listener yields to the hand of the master. The sadness that speaks
through the music is so full of his strength and of the laws of his
destiny that it no longer seems, as in the preceding sonatas, the confidence of a single being: it is the Chorus of an antique tragedy. The
personal pain here becomes the good of all; and by its very plenitude the
elegy of a man expands to the epic of a race or of an epoch.

The movement falls into three great divisions. The motive of Grief once
posed on the slow epic rhythm, the arms raised to heaven, a melodious
lamento blends with the tender accents that have come from Mozart
the violent contrasts that are Beethoven's own, his pathetic declamation,
his Ajax sighs, the exasperation of his intolerable suffering, that finds its
outlet at last in noble tears that might accompany a funeral cortège.

In conformity with the plan of the future Funeral Marches, the second
part opens with a calmly elegiac motive.

But grief breaks in upon it once more: destiny strikes; the tears
flow forth; broken sobs are rhythmed by the inexorable tread of the
march.

They die away—*smorzando*—*pianissimo*; a final resurgence, *f*, *sf*, is followed by a *decrescendo* of the sobs, bringing with it a return of the
majestic first theme.

In the second ascent of the third part the mighty march of the bass,
with its *sforzando* accents on the second and fifth beats expresses the
implacable force of the Destiny that subdues the shudders of the revolting
soul, suddenly smitten to its knees and subsiding from cries to silent
tears. Finally, the vast sad resignation of exhaustion, the knell-like sighs,
the expiring breath.

An immense tragedy, having for its substance the soul of a people
incarnating itself in its Corypheus. The royal picture of Melancholy.[2] We
are reminded of the Aeschylean choruses—Envy (in *Saul*), Jealousy (in
Hercules)—dedicated by Handel to the Great Goddesses, the Eumen-
ides. Never until this work had Beethoven realized the classic plenitude
of a lyric form in which the exigencies of his Ego and the majesty
of impersonal law are fused into one. And it was long before he realized
it again.—ROMAIN ROLLAND (2)

*The Menuetto (Allegro) is, as Tovey remarked, the only movement
of this sonata which might possibly have been acceptable to the orthodox
musicians of 1798. However, its exquisite grace hides multitudes of
craftsman-like subtleties: the syncopated upbeat to its main theme (an-*

[1] See the celebrated Adagio of Opus 106.
[2] "Each one," said Beethoven to Schindler in 1823, "perceived in this *Largo* the
state of mind of a melancholic, together with all the many degrees of light and
shade there are in the picture of Melancholy."

swered, retrospectively, by another accented syncopated upbeat at the end of its first phrase); the smooth fugato writing in the second half of the Minuet proper, which drifts unnoticed into the recapitulation of the first theme, however now appearing in an inner voice below an extended trill on the dominant; the extension of the opening phrase by sequences on rising notes of the scale, which prepares it for a close in the tonic major; the wistful pianissimo cadenza, so simple and yet so poignant; the unfinished recapitulation of the first part of the trio to make ready for the da capo of the Minuet. These are as sure signs of a master as the more grandiose first movement and the fantastically romantic devices of the Largo.—Editor.

The Finale of the Sonata is in a peculiar case. We seem to have got over the antiromantic reaction against Beethoven's slow movements, but fashionable criticism does not yet seem to have discovered Beethoven's sense of humor. I have already, almost unnecessarily, pointed out that critics are to be pitied, rather than reviled, for this omisison, in as much as to describe Beethoven's humor adds to the horrors of all verbal description of music the hideous ineptitude of analyzing jokes. Fortunately, as has been often pointed out, there is nothing which we fear so intensely as the accusation of not seeing the humor of this or that; so I shall confidently assert that Beethoven is humorous wherever I think that he is, and the reader may doubt me at his peril. The finale of Opus 10, No. 3, is one of the funniest things Beethoven ever wrote, and differs from later and larger manifestations of his humor in the fact that it is not yet stated, like, for instance, the Finale of the Eighth Symphony, on an Olympian architectural scale.—DONALD FRANCIS TOVEY (1)

VIII. SONATA No. 8 IN C MINOR, OPUS 13 (*"Pathétique"*)
    I. Grave—Allegro di molto e con brio; II. Adagio cantabile;
    III. Rondo (Allegro)

The *Grande Sonate pathétique*, Opus 13, stands with the "Moonlight," "Waldstein," and "Appassionata" among Beethoven's most beloved sonatas. Its conspicuous popularity was shown in Beethoven's own day by the numerous ensemble arrangements that were published of this work and seems to have started right with its publication in 1799. Thus, the pianist Moscheles recalled that as early as 1801, in Prague, "Although but seven years old, I actually ventured upon Beethoven's Sonate pathétique. Imagine if you can how I played it; imagine also the Beethoven fever, to which I fell a victim in those days. . . ." Quite as today, the emotional drama of this music must have had an immediate appeal for all pianists. The authentic title, calling the noble passions to mind, must have helped to distinguish this work at once too.[1] The review in [the *Allegemeine Musikalische Zeitung*] (by Rochlitz?), which appeared this time only a few months after publication (February 1800), begins, "Not incorrectly is this well-written sonata called pathetic, for it has a truly distinct emotional character." In a Conversation Book from June and July of 1823 Schindler asked Beethoven about the "two principles"—i.e., dualism or conflict of ideas—in the second movement of Opus 13 (as well as Opus 14/2/i), which "thousands [of people] don't understand." Schindler says that in reply Beethoven went so far as to describe a dialogue of conflict between a man and a woman. The idea of a personified conflict continued to be read into this "pathetic" music throughout the romantic era. Thus, Mathis Lussy's book on Opus 13 (published posthumously in 1912) still was "an attempt to interpret the sonata as a dialogue, 'a contest between an unhappy man and fate.'" It will be recalled that as recently as 1935-36 Arnold Schering chose this work as one of the earliest of Beethoven's sonatas to be interpreted symbolically, finding its inspiration and poetic meaning in Musäus's version of the Hero and Leander story.

The influence of [the powerful opening of] Mozart's Sonata in C, K.V. 457, on Opus 13 [is noteworthy]. Numerous other derivations have also been suggested, including Dussek's Sonata in C, Opus 35/3 (ca. 1796)[2] and works by J. B. Cramer, Cherubini, and Grétry. Furthermore, the Rondo finale of Opus 13, generally conceded to be the least strong of the three movements, was probably anticipated by Beethoven himself in sketches for piano and violin of about 1797 and other sketches that may date back to 1785. In the light of these derivations, the only reservation made in that same review is interesting—that is, to the effect that the thematic material seemed to have been heard before, though just where could not be said. From what Ries tells us about Beethoven's own performance of the finale, the originality may have been partly in the manner of playing it.—WILLIAM S. NEWMAN

The fascination which this sonata has always exercised over lovers of music, and even over people who care more for the romantic in all its forms than for music as such, is accounted for by Miss Scott in a few lines of penetrating criticism which are well worth quoting:

> In poetic content Beethoven's *Pathétique* is tragedy as the young feel it, with the glamour, urgency, even exaltation, of a *Romeo and Juliet*. And few southern love-scenes could be more softly glowing than Beethoven's slow movement with its almost unbelievable melodic loveliness and velvety tone.

[1] Beethoven himself regretted this distinction in later years, especially as he regarded all his works as "pathetic."
[2] Dussek's second movement is called "Adagio patetico ed espressivo."

The sonata is dedicated to Prince Carl von Lichnowsky, Beethoven's friend and patron from the early Vienna days onward. The composer, aged twenty-three and almost unknown when he first lodged under the roof of Lichnowsky's house, as any poor person might in those days live in the attics of the Viennese nobles' town residences, so long as he had some respectable recommendation, was very soon discovered by his music-loving landlord to be worth cultivating, and before long he was taken into the princely household.

Grave—Allegro di molto e con brio.—The optional slow introduction of the classical symphony and sonata form occurs remarkably rarely in Beethoven's piano sonatas. In his symphonies he followed the precedent of Haydn and Mozart, more or less, so far as the frequency of such introductions went. Four symphonies out of his nine have them. But among the thirty-two sonatas only three have introductions prefixed to them, the present work, Opus 81a, and Opus 111.

As regards the treatment of the introduction in the "Pathetic" Sonata, it is very curious, for Beethoven not only uses it as a preface to his quick-paced first movement, but inserts two reminiscences of it into that movement itself—between the exposition and the working-out and again between the recapitulation and coda. The intention is quite plainly a dramatic one. These interruptions of the impassioned Allegro are not merely pathetic; they hint at some tragedy that may well have been actually before Beethoven in a concrete form, so unbridled does this movement seem in its urgent expressiveness. The ordinary lover of Beethoven who has no farfetched theories to impose on an ungratefully skeptical world will be content to use his own imagination about the possible sources of inspiration which may have caused the composer to regard this sonata as more pathetic than others.

The opening figure [starts with a powerful C minor chord played forte-piano (a distinctly orchestral dynamic indication) followed by the dotted rhythm outlining the melody C-D-E flat and the quarter-note answer E flat-D. It] dominates the introduction at first. In the third bar it is crowded together with an effect of heightening the eloquence, and two bars later, after an ornamental incident, it appears softly in E flat major, only to be rudely interrupted and tossed from one key into another. Restless and broken, it resigns itself to being lost in the freer passages that follow. A descending chromatic scale is like a ruthless tearing up of this introductory page, and after a moment's hesitation the music is precipitated into the fiery Allegro.

Sonata form now asserts itself. The main theme of the first-subject group is [dominated by a tautly rising figure in quarter-note chords punctuated by an offbeat sforzando halfway up. The first four measures swing us daringly from middle C to the C two octaves higher. The next four measures in half-note chords lead us down again, while the tension is retained by the rising bass. If this is the main theme] another motif must be [noted], as it is important that it should be recognized in the later development. It occurs after the opening eight-measure theme has been repeated, leading to the harmony of the dominant. It is a compression of the tautly rising figure of the main theme reduced from four measures to two. Using this motif as the thematic basis of a bridge, the music glides gently into the second subject, the chief melody of which is first stated in E flat minor.[1]

The usual classical procedure in a sonata movement in a minor key was to make the first statement of the second subject in the relative major. But Beethoven is here obviously intent on avoiding a major contrast in so conspicuous a position. Only in the course of letting the second subject modulate through various keys does he allow it to appear in a brighter key (D flat major), and later he lets a subsidiary theme, beginning with a treble note repeated in syncopation, appear in the orthodox second-subject key of the relative (E flat) major. Another idea, distinguished by running passages in the right hand, also appears in that key, but where the first subject is again alluded to at the end of the exposition, the tonality verges once again toward C minor. The whole of the Allegro heard so far is then repeated, and it is worth noticing how Beethoven alters the final harmony the second time in order to lead, not again into C minor, but into G minor for the working-out section.[2]

It is here that the slow introduction interposes itself, though only for the length of four bars, and here also that a drastic modulation to as remote a key as E minor is compressed into a very small space with remarkable effect. It is in E minor, surprisingly enough, that the Allegro is resumed for the working-out. This section ignores both the main subjects and draws entirely on material previously treated as side issues. The effect, in some curious way that is more easily felt than explained, is overwhelmingly dramatic, mainly, no doubt, because the hearer is kept in suspense all through this section as to what is going to happen next, since he can hardly fail to expect the principal actors to enter at any moment and to wonder why they never do. The stage meanwhile is held by [the short motif originally used for the bridge from the first to the

---

[1] The rising opening B flat-E flat-F-G flat is thematically important in the working-out of the movement and is also alluded to in the finale.—Editor.

[2] Professor Blom points out in an earlier essay the utmost simplicity with which Beethoven effects this change. Both times the three repeated falling octaves E flat to E flat are combined with the bass descending stepwise from E flat to G. Both times also this leads to a dominant seventh chord of G minor with F sharp in the bass and high D as the upper note. The first time this high D jumps down two octaves and the bass rises a half step to G, thus landing us in the chord of the dominant seventh of C minor, and the repeat of the exposition follows quite normally in that key. The second time Beethoven also jumps from the high D to the low D, *but* the F sharp in the bass does not change. We are still in the harmony of D⁷, the dominant seventh of G minor, and the working-out section begins easily in that key.—Editor.

second subjects. It is also held] by the transformation of [the rising and falling motif of the first measure of the slow introduction, now appearing in two measures of Allegro. The bridge motif] passes into the left hand for a time, and later it is expanded in the treble.

At last [the main Allegro theme] returns for the recapitulation, and a new, striking use is made of its [falling half-note chords. These appear] in three rising sequences. Beautiful as this new development is, it also has a structural reason, which gives an opportunity to say that in formal music, as in architecture, the features which are the finest in appearance are generally those which at the same time have a practical application, although needless to say this view must not be carried too far in connection with an art in which practical considerations can only serve ideal ends.

This transition makes a modulation to F minor, in which the second subject now appears, again rather irregularly, the key being that of the subdominant minor, whereas normally the second subject, having first been in the relative major, would in the recapitulation stand in the tonic minor. It passes into that, however, and not into a major key as before, the whole section being in a darker set of tonalities than the corresponding one in the exposition. The peroration, made of the matter auxiliary to the second subject, then remains in C minor. Finally the first subject returns for the coda, to be intersected once more by an allusion to the introduction. It now appears broken by silences on the first beats (i.e., with the [forte-piano chords at the beginning of each measure] cut out). The movement then ends abruptly with a last outburst of [the main Allegro theme].

Adagio cantabile.—The slow movement needs very little description. It is filled with a flood of lyrical melody that is best responded to purely emotionally, though it may be worth attention that the form is that of a simple rondo with two episodes. The subject is a lovely eight-bar melody played without any introduction in the middle register of the keyboard and restated an octave higher with a fuller accompaniment (two moving inner parts instead of only one). The first episode is a new melody in F minor, appearing in the right hand over a simple accompaniment of evenly repeated chords. It is songful, but too ornamental and too widely spread to be sung—an ideal tune for a violin and needing the warmest sort of imitation of violin tone and phrasing a modern piano can produce. In other words Beethoven is here a long way from the harpsichord style, and it is mere pedantry to pretend, as has been done recently, that he was quite satisfied with the thin tone of the early pianoforte, or would still be if he could hear a more recent instrument. A rather gloomier second strain concludes this episode, and the main theme is then restated exactly as at first, but without the modified repetition.

The second episode, beginning in A flat minor, is like a duet between a mezzo-soprano and a baritone, the former having a tender phrase, the latter a more lively reply. After an intersecting passage, the duet is repeated in the remote tonality of E major. An interesting modulatory bridge quickly leads back to A flat major for the second return of the chief theme, now enriched by a triplet accompaniment and again fully given out twice, the second time in the higher position, as before. A short coda for which Beethoven's inexhaustible invention finds new ideas at the last moment, but ideas by no means irrelevant to what has gone before, then brings the movement to its conclusion.

Allegro.—The finale is a more fully developed rondo. The principal theme opens [with an upbeat of three eighth notes which outline the same melodic shape (G-C-D-E flat) that was outlined in the opening of the second subject of the first movement. The first four measures fall gently from E flat to C and then rise more ornamentally to G, the fifth note of the scale, which is repeated three times to stress its melodic significance. The theme] continues for another four bars and then begins to develop, closing with an emphatic C minor cadence. The first episode goes by sequential modulations into E flat major, in which key it presents its first, suavely flowing melodic idea, as also a passage with [a motif in which five notes of eighth-note triplets in the right hand leading to a poised half note are answered by a similar rhythmic and melodic passage in the left hand. These figures dovetail very adroitly and the motif] will be seen to assume some importance as a binding substance. It may be regarded as the mortar used by the composer in his structure, the themes themselves being the bricks, or rather blocks of stone. Another of these, still belonging to the first episode, is a main feature. [It is chorale-like in its four-part harmonization.] It will be used again, like a second sonata subject, in a later episode. The dovetailing triplet motif then provides the transition to the first return of the main theme, which reappears exactly as before, but is attended by a new episode made of two melodies proceeding by fourths and fifths in contrary motion between the two hands. They are afterwards separated, the top one being used in double counterpoint against running scale passages. A new bridge of broken chords leads to the second return, where the theme is modified by a restatement in the left hand. The suave melody then turns up in C major for the third episode, and [the dovetailing triplet motif] is again used for a transition to [the chorale-like theme], also in C major, but with an F major inflection; [it] is then restated in [C minor] but considerably extended by a series of wonderful modulations, which lead to the last return of [the principal theme]. An extended coda follows in which [the triplet figure] is drawn upon to a considerable extent, and the Rondo closes with shy allusions to the main theme, followed by an energetic descending scale.—ERIC BLOM (1)

In Beethoven's earlier works, we find [a] kind of rondo, related to the old *rondeau en couplets*. Its characteristics are: first, that its theme is a single strain, with or without a couple of echoing tags; secondly, that its episodes at first tend to be definitely sectional, though, later on, the movement may become more highly organized; and thirdly, that there is probably an episode, or even more than one episode, in the home tonic at the end, so as to provide a large and expanding coda. There is also nothing to prevent the influence of sonata form on such a rondo, by making the first episode recur later on in the home tonic. This is very clearly seen in the finale of Opus 13, the *Sonata Pathétique*. This kind of rondo, which is more or less typical of Haydn, Beethoven also uses in some of his early slow movements, Opus 2, No. 2, and the Violin Sonata, Opus 30, No. 1.—DONALD FRANCIS TOVEY (1)

IX. SONATA No. 9 IN E, OPUS 14, No. 1
I. Allegro; II. Allegretto; III. Rondo (Allegro comodo)

The date 1799, assigned to this work, is not that of composition, but that of its publication, which occurred on December 21 of that year. It is not certain when the sonata was written. Beethoven's sketches for it are found close together with those for the Piano Concerto in B flat major, which he completed early in 1795; but from internal evidence one would be inclined to judge that the sonata was probably not finished until nearer its date of publication, as it shows a good deal more maturity, both technical and spiritual. Both the sonatas of Opus 14 are purged of all external effect, and No. 1 in particular turns every pianistic device to an expressive purpose. Though it may contain technical difficulties, nothing in its whole course has the appearance of being written for the sake of display. The performer's problem now is that of penetrating into the emotional significance of the music rather than that of solving digital problems.

The Sonatas, Opus 14, are dedicated to the Baroness von Braun, the wife of Baron Peter von Braun, a wealthy manufacturer raised to the rank of a nobleman, who was for a time manager of the opera in Vienna.

Allegro.—This mere tempo indication hardly meets the case. One cannot help feeling that, had Beethoven written this movement but a very little later, he would have qualified his "allegro" with "ma sempre con sentimento," or something else indicative of the profound feeling the music so restrainedly yet so penetratingly suggests. No previous sonata of his begins with so utterly unrhetorical, so immediately expres-

sive a theme, [with its tenderly rising half notes in the right hand accompanied, deceptively simply, by repeated chords in the left hand. The upper
notes of these left-hand chords also outline a melody rising from B to E.
This] is the first subject, or rather the principal strain of a first-subject
group, for it is attended by other ideas that make for variety without
destroying the unity of the composer's scheme, which consists mainly
in keeping the whole of this material in the key of E major. First we
have a [sixteenth-note] passage repeated four times, at each appearance
an octave lower, then a twofold phrase the second statement of which is
an octave higher, and lastly a cadence with chromatic inner parts, which
is also twice stated in different octaves, the second recurrence being the
lower. This merges into a new development of [the first subject], with
changing harmonies in the accompanying [eighth notes] and a new
melodic development at the third bar leading to an episode built over
a repeated pedal on [F sharp] that serves to establish the dominant of
B major, the key—itself the dominant of the main tonality—in which
the second subject is to make its appearance. Before it does so, there
is an energetic half-close on three chords of F sharp major.

The second subject [starts with an upbeat of four eighth-notes falling
scalewise from F sharp to B. These are followed by three measures, full
of tension, in which by quarter notes Beethoven ascends chromatically
from B to F sharp and then beyond to G sharp where the melody is
harmonized for the first time. The G sharp descends through F sharp to
E and the harmony relaxes into C sharp minor. These four measures have]
a sequential continuation a degree of the scale lower by which [the
theme] returns to B major from its temporary sideslip into C sharp
minor. It then coils itself into passages of imitation between treble and
bass, the beginning of which [is] an interesting example of the asperities
from which Beethoven did not shrink when they happened to do for
him what he wanted. If in his later years he had written anything like
that cluster of semitones (B sharp, C sharp, C double sharp, D sharp)
that cross each other so harshly, it would be universally explained as an
instance of how his deafness made him insensitive to such rough places;
but at the time this sonata was written, his hearing, if not perfect, was
still intact. It is much more to the point to say that he did not mind
occasional harshnesses, that he even deliberately sought them now and
again as—shall we say?—a relief to his tenderer feelings, just as he would
storm and curse and be rude to people in order to avoid making an
exhibition of the love he bore the brotherhood of man—one of his great
artistic themes, when all is said and done.

An entrancing melody at once compensates us the moment this short
dispute between two exponents of the same idea is over. But note that
after the suave phrase there is an interruption by a passage with angry

displaced accents, which in turn is followed by another conciliatory, delicate reply.

Beethoven himself gives us a clue to this interpretation. He told Schindler, in a conversation regarding the desirability or otherwise of giving the public indications as to the poetic content of his music, that when he wrote his sonatas "people were more poetical and such indications were superfluous. . . . Every one saw that the two Sonatas, Opus 14, represented a struggle between two opposing principles, an agrument between two persons."

The exposition of the movement ends with a brief reference to the main theme, which now appears in the bass, very softly, with the broken [eighth-note] accompaniment above it. This leads to the repeat of the exposition. When it has been heard again, the music seems once more to be taking the same turn, but now Beethoven leads it into a different channel by the simple process of depressing the C sharp, F sharp figure shown in the second bar of [the main theme] to C natural, F natural. This takes him into his working-out section, if one may use that term merely geographically, as it were. For although the music has reached the place at which the working-out ought to begin, Beethoven actually develops nothing. That this remarkable suppression of his extraordinary gift of thematic exploitation is entirely deliberate is proved, as Sir Donald Tovey reminds us, by a note in the composer's sketch for this work: "*ohne das Thema durchzuführen.*" To which Sir Donald adds in his dryly witty manner: "Accordingly, critics who disapprove of episodic developments are not entitled to suppose that Beethoven was episodic by inadvertence."

An entirely new tune—a melody as distinct from a theme—fills almost the whole of this section. It is played in octaves by the right hand and accompanied by chords broken into [sixteenth-notes]. Beethoven evidently does not intend the episode to thrill us especially: he keeps it of set purpose on a low level of interest and restricts its eventfulness to a series of modulations which take us, with slowly shifting basses, through keys as remote from the main tonality as A minor and C major. With a sudden jerk into E minor we again come near it, however, and then, in the dominant of E major, we have once more a brief allusion to [the rising half notes of the main theme], alternating between bass and treble.

This leads into the recapitulation, which begins, surprisingly, with a new version of [the main theme], the right-hand figures being now laid out in full chords and the left accompanying with ascending E major scales. The three auxiliary ideas, however, remain as before; but at the place where the first subject is due to return another surprise awaits us in the shape of an interrupted cadence that leads, not back into E major, but into C major. The transition receives a slightly different treatment and the half-close before the second subject is in B major as the dominant of the principal key, in which that subject reappears this time, according to classical precedent. Beethoven never defies an established principle for the mere fun of doing so: whenever he flouts traditions it is with a definite artistic purpose; otherwise they are good enough for him. The rest of the movement, up to the coda, also proceeds perfectly normally, with one single exception, and even that dictated by an external circumstance. It will be observed that through the transposition of the second-subject group into E major the suave phrase which followed the second subject now lies a fourth higher, with the result that, as the piano was constructed in Beethoven's time, the phrase, repeated as it stood before, would have exceeded the range of its keyboard. It is therefore turned down [in its third measure, instead of rising].

The brief coda of fifteen bars is, again, built on the main theme, which first appears in the bass, then in the treble, and is quite freely treated though always with the characteristic figures of accompaniment with which it was associated from the first. The whole passage is of a stillness that would be perfect but for the fourfold repetition of a groaning bass that falls alternatingly by semitones and whole tones, [causing two semitonal clashes]. To the last the unquiet Beethoven must needs utter a faint note of apprehension. It is just like him.

Allegretto.—The restlessness continues. The second movement is a scherzo in motion and form, but one of those pieces filled with the hollow kind of mirth we find in Beethoven's work again and again. This is the first time that this mordant humor comes to its full expression in a piano sonata. All the same, it is, remarkably enough, already in evidence to some extent in the scherzo movements of the earlier sonatas and elsewhere in his preceding works. It is curiously noticeable that his later manner, with its characteristic touch of grimness and its almost defiant avoidance of eighteenth-century mannerliness, comes into prominence much earlier in his scherzos than in any other type of movement. One may thus fairly say that the scherzo brings out the very core of his individuality almost from the start.

The Allegretto, which is in E minor, begins with [an eight-measure sentence ending on the dominant harmony. Several of its elements are important for the future expansion of the movement, particularly the melodic outline of measures 2 and 3 (E-D sharp-E-G) and the eighth-note ornament in measure 4. The entire sentence] is then repeated, preceded by an upbeat this time, an octave higher. Then Beethoven, with great thematic economy, carries on the discourse mainly with new presentations of [the melodic element E-D sharp-E-G of the first phrase;] but fertile as well as economical, he quickly finds a new aspect for discussion in this fragment. After a slight hesitation, he returns to the theme in its first form, emphasizes [the eighth-note figure of measure 4] by repetition, twists [it] into a flowing cadence, and ends his first part by turning that figure upside down and heightening the capricious character of his music by creating a major-minor ambiguity and confusing the rhythm by cross-accents.

A trio section in C major follows, more suave, but still with a suspicion of unrest. It is all one continuous melodic formation. Formally this episode remains attached to the old dance forms, with a repeated first half ending in the key of the dominant and a second returning to the tonic. The only departure is a kind of tailpiece of six bars that leads back to the scherzo by means of a half close on the dominant of E minor.

The whole scherzo is restated note for note, and then the melody of the trio begins again. But we are cheated of an expectation to hear it all over once more, aroused in us, perhaps, by our experience of the scherzo in the Seventh Symphony. Beethoven here uses merely the final statement of the tune by way of a coda, with the tailpiece leading once more into the dominant of E minor. But that key is no longer insisted upon: the piece ends with a bare threefold repetition of the note E in octaves.[1]

Allegro comodo.—The finale is a rondo with the feature of a second subject borrowed from the sonata form—in other words, a rondo with episodes highly organized. More than that, the principal subject [, which consists of a lyrical eight-measure theme, whose first four measures are accompanied in the left hand by descending chords of the sixth broken up into eighth-note triplets,] contains a feature—a phrase beginning with the rapid descending scale—which also lends itself to what might almost be called a symphonic development. The theme is at once stated without preliminaries.

It will be of interest to consider this passage for a moment as another instance of Beethoven's frequent disregard of the mere amenities of sound. To begin with, those descending [broken] chords rather low down in the bass are not particularly agreeable, though their hardness is mitigated by the device of breaking them up into triplets; but much more noticeable are the ruthless semitional clashes on the last beats of the first and second bars [where the descending bass line of broken chords clashes harmonically with the repeated quarter notes in the melody]. In the first place we have E against D sharp, in the second A against G sharp. Beethoven, as already pointed out, was not deaf when he wrote this sonata, so that, quite apart from the extraordinary faculty of aural

---

[1] One interesting detail, often overlooked, is more obvious to the eye than the ear. At the end of the coda Beethoven prints a measure of silence with a fermata over the full-bar rest. This has a twofold reason, I feel. Firstly, it completes the four-bar phrase which has been prevalent throughout both scherzo and trio. But, secondly, it emphasizes that the audience is not to be allowed to relax after the final pianissimo E's; rather the tension is to be retained through this silent measure until it is relieved by the lyrical opening theme of the Rondo in E major. Beethoven knew, as well as Haydn did, the dramatic musical effect of silence.—Editor.

imagination he must have possessed, he actually heard these clashes on playing his music. The inference is that, if he did not write them with a purpose, he at least obviously tolerated them. It is time someone made an exhaustive study of all the roughnesses of this sort to be found in his early music in order that the critical habit of making his deafness alone the explanation of his later awkwardnesses—if one likes to call them so —may be repudiated once and for all.

The [two-measure phrase starting with the rapid descending scale] having set the movement going, [it] may be called the key phrase of the whole structure. [It] is at once restated an octave lower. Then comes a repetition of the whole procedure, with the one difference that the second appearance of the descending scale is now an octave and a fourth lower, so that its further elaboration is displaced into the key of the dominant (B major). This prepares the field for the first episode, which is later to reveal itself as a true subject of the sonata type. It is a short, sustained melody in B major with a final turn and a staccato bass resembling that of plucked strings. After a slightly modified repetition, the final tonic chord of B major is transformed, by the addition of A natural in the bass, into the dominant seventh of the principal key, E major, in which the main theme returns, at first unchanged, then veering toward G major, in which key the descending scales lead to the second episode.

This is a long, independent passage, beginning in G major and traversing a variety of keys, made only of broken triplet chords and arpeggios, with simple, conventional basses and without any clear thematic outline. The intention is doubtless to do without anything of special interest in order to heighten the contrast.

The next return of the main theme again transposes the falling scales, so that now they establish A major, in which key the second subject is brought back. In the regular sonata form this return is, of course, made in the tonic key; its resumption in that of the subdominant is unusual. Even more so, in this particular case, is the sudden modulation to F major, attended by a fascinating turn back to E major within the space of two bars. The final recurrence of the principal theme in the form of a coda shows considerable changes. It is in fact restated twice over in different forms, the first time running away, so to speak, to permit itself a little virtuosic excursion before it is finally dismissed with another variant. But even here it is to be observed that, as I pointed out at the beginning of this sketch, Beethoven in this sonata always subordinates effect to an expressive aim. Here virtuosity is all very well, but the point is that a climax was wanted and that the technical display happens to supply it perfectly. The final bars, which lead to a sudden energetic close, are built on [the key phrase, but with the rapid scale passages going up as well as down].—ERIC BLOM (1)

The first thing the general reader needs to know about tonality is that the names of keys do not represent important aesthetic facts. This statement is in evident conflict with various attractive and fantastic utterances by Beethoven himself and by other composers. Beethoven, for instance, when setting Scottish melodies, wrote to his Edinburgh publisher, Thomson, that the key of A flat did not fit a certain tune that was sent him, in as much as that tune was marked *amoroso*, whereas the key of A flat should be called *barbaresco*. Curiously enough, all Beethoven's compositions in A flat are remarkably suave. The main reason why his fairly numerous movements in A flat have not the *barbaresco* character that he imputes to that key is that it comes in relation to C minor; and, it is not keys in themselves, but key-relations, that have character, and, moreover, a character that is deeply rooted and the same for all listeners. The slightest practical convenience will override Beethoven's most clearly stated notions of a key as having a character of its own. I have no more idea why F major seems pale pink to me than why E major seems grass-green. Nor have I either any recollection that Beethoven said anything about the character of these keys, or the slightest means of guessing what he would have said about them. But we do know that when he arranged his Pianoforte Sonata, Opus 14, No. 1, as a string quartet, he transposed it from E major to F major for reasons solely concerning the technique of the instruments. Gevaert, one of the most learned authorities on ancient music and the author of two monumental treatises on orchestration, considered that such a transposition would be equivalent to altering all the colors of a picture. He did not know this remarkable quartet-arrangement of Beethoven's, which was not published until some time after Gevaert's death, but his remarks on classical tonality are a favorable example of the kind of fantasy which many learned musicians still fail to confine to its proper place among psychological obscurities. In other words, he talks sad nonsense about tonality.

The character of keys in themeselves is, then, a psychological vagary about which no two persons need trouble to agree. Key-relationship, on the other hand, is the source of an enormous proportion of Beethoven's harmonic color effects, and is one of the primary elements in his form. You see that I am already driven to use metaphors, and I shall continue to speak of key-relations as "dark" or "bright" and "high" or "dull" in color. These metaphors will not be fancies, but verifiable musical experience. They are quite unaffected by transposition; and you need not have a sense of "absolute pitch" to enjoy them. In the little E major Sonata, Opus 14, No. 1, the C major key of the trio of the middle Allegretto brings with it a pleasant darkness and warmth in relation to E minor, which is exactly the same as the D flat which it becomes in relation to the F minor of that movement as arranged for string quartet, and, incidentally, exactly the same as the "barbarous" key of A flat in relation to the C minor with which Beethoven almost always brings it into contact.—DONALD FRANCIS TOVEY (1)

X. SONATA No. 10 IN G, OPUS 14, No. 2
I. Allegro; II. Andante; III. Scherzo (Allegro assai)

The first movement (Allegro) is an idyll of spring. At first there are light floating rhythms in the principal theme. Later we hear the twittering of birds and then a song blossoms forth, at first steadily in the higher octaves (the second theme), then fuller and deeper (closing theme). The development section contains some curious intertwining of the motifs, complications of rhythm and part-writing. In the middle section the opposition of the sixteenth notes in the bass to the triple sixteenth notes in the higher voice produces tension moving to a climax of sound, which is then relaxed in far-flung descending melodic lines.

The Andante consists of a simple songlike theme in C major, followed by three simply constructed variations, full of lovely sound effects. In the first variation the theme is given to two voices in the left hand, and in the right there is a new upper part which begins like the song of a bird in nature. The second variation conceals the theme in the accompanying chords while the right hand follows, and the new middle part strikes the ear as the principal subject. In the middle section the tone glows with a romantic glamour. The third variation makes the original bass the principal melody, as though it were expressively sung by the cello, while dainty figures play round about it in the right hand.

The finale, entitled Scherzo, is at once a scherzo and a rondo finale— a cheerful piece of delicate humor, slim and dainty in its outlines and agile in its movement. The spasmodic principal theme darts hastily hither and thither like a lizard. In the episodes there are fuller, warmer sounds, a broader melody turning near the end to a rougher jollity. —HUGO LEICHTENTRITT

XI. SONATA No. 11 IN B FLAT, OPUS 22
I. Allegro con brio; II. Adagio con molto espressione; III. Menuetto; IV. Rondo (Allegretto)

I propose to base a survey of Beethoven's art forms on [a] specimen chosen as the closest approximation, by Beethoven or any composer, to "normal" sonata form.

The "normal" example is the first movement of the Pianoforte Sonata in B flat, Opus 22. This sonata is neglected by pianists and despised by the superior person. But Beethoven set great store by it, though he had already written such impressive and original works as the sonatas Opus 2, No. 2, Opus 7, Opus 10, No. 3, the wonderful string trios, Opus 9; and was at the time occupied with the string quartets, Opus 18. "Die Sonate hat sich gewaschen," he wrote to his publisher; an expression fairly equivalent to R. L. Stevenson's claim that *The Master of Ballantrae* is a howling cheese." Beethoven felt that while dramatic force and surprising originality were all very well, it was a fine thing to achieve smoothness also and to show that he was no longer inferior to Mozart in Mozart's own line. Hitherto his works were never less Mozartian than when they resembled Mozart externally. You have but to compare Beethoven's quintet for pianoforte and wind instruments, Opus 16, with the Mozart work which it emulates, to see that point for point Beethoven is doing something slight, diffuse and yet rigid, where Mozart's quintet is important, concentrated and supple. Beethoven could not master Mozart's technique by imitating Mozart or by restricting his own ambition; and in Opus 22 he first achieved an entire work in which mastery of Mozart's forms is attained without either the timidity of the works with wind instruments or the self-assertive boldness and abruptness which in many of Beethoven's other early works is the characteristic mask of that timidity when he has something unusual to say.

Let us now go through the first movement of the Pianoforte Sonata, Opus 22, mentioning other works as they serve for illustration. The first movement begins abruptly with three bars all on the tonic chord of B flat, containing a figure in a pregnant rhythm, of which the [sixteenth-notes in the inner-voice] group will be constantly used. The continuation is a cantabile which in four bars closes into a passage in which [the sixteenth-note motif] is worked up on the tonic and dominant, ending in a half-close on the dominant (bar 11). Thus far we have a statement which, by ending on the dominant, and by its energetic business-like manner, strongly suggests that it will be followed by a counterstatement, that is to say, by a restatement of the same material with a different outlook. A single bar (plus preliminary beat) with an uprush of [the sixteenth-note motif] from the bass, is all that does duty for this counterstatement. It leads to three bars of sustained harmony in quite a different style, drifting down to the dominant of F. On this dominant, C, six bars of a tremolando figure follow, with the sole purpose of impressing upon us that we have left the key of B flat and are intending to settle in F, not as by way of going from one part of a decorative design to another, nor as a necessary variety of key in an argumentative work such as a fugue, but as a dramatic event, the first turning point in the action. Students are far too often allowed to think that these passages of "dominant preparation" owe their existence to an unsophisticated style of harmony, and that with greater harmonic wisdom they disappear. With

greater harmonic wisdom they may be very much modified; and indeed
nobody has ever gone further to modify them than Beethoven in earlier
works than Opus 22 (*e.g.*, Opus 10, No. 3); but, modified or plain,
they are as necessary to Brahms as they are to Mozart. Indeed, we must
recognize their function in Wagner and Strauss before we can fully
appreciate Mozart's and Beethoven's power in the handling of them.

At bar 22 the section misnamed "Second Subject" begins. First, there
is an eight bar phrase closing into another theme. The running bass
which supports these eight bars arises out of a scale at the end of the
preceding "dominant preparation." This fact is a mere ornament of style,
and if the sonata were to swarm with such facts the "logic" of the music
would still depend on principles deeper and radically different. The next
theme, beginning at bar 29, is a new melody of great distinction, built on
rising sequences and closing, after eight bars, into itself, with the obvious
purpose of being repeated. We have, then, reached a point where the action of the music is at leisure for melodies to behave like lyrics with a regular stanza-form. But we shall always find that in masterpieces of sonata
style this behavior is not allowed to interfere with the dramatic action. A
phrase of this length will repeat itself, perhaps (as here) with ornamental
variation, as far as half or three-quarters of its length, but then it will
take a new turn and will expand into something unpredictable. In
the rare cases where a broad theme is repeated entirely (as in the E
major theme of the first movement of the Waldstein sonata) the theme
will be austerely simple and the passage which follows its repetition will
be enormously expanded. Here, in Opus 22, the repetition of the melody
diverges at the seventh bar, with an unexpected modulation and an outpouring of rapid motion on the surface (bar 44). Below the surface the
harmony moves slowly, veering back to F in the course of four bars. With
this a climax is reached, and the rapid [sixteenth-note] movement forms itself in a brilliant four-bar phrase on chords expressive of a full close in F.
This closes into another four bars which repeat the same cadential matter
in another position. Then (bar 56), on tonic pedal, we have a quiet two-
bar phrase closing into its repetition in a higher position.[1] In this repetition the supertonic is flattened (G flat) which gives a special point to the
device of repeating the last bar twice, first with the natural, then with the
flattened note. The device of breaking off and reiterating the last bar
of a cadential phrase clearly means that a stage of the action is coming
to an end. You will not find this device in Bach or Handel, for they
have no dramatic interest in thus marking the sections of their designs.
Their contemporary, Domenico Scarlatti, uses it constantly, "hammering
in his points," as Parry says, "like a mob orator." Bach's son, Johann
Christian, the London Bach of the Bach and Abel concerts, uses it

---

[1] With the music before him the reader will understand that I speak of one
phrase as "closing into" the next when the closing chord is not within the rhythmic
period but on the beginning of the next period.

typically, and Mozart caught it from him, though he would have undoubtedly arrived at it in any case. Here again, we are not masters of
its meaning until we can trace the principle in Brahms and in the music
dramas of Wagner and Strauss. In Opus 22 this quiet cadence theme is,
however, not the end of the exposition of the first movement. A new
theme, going straight up the scale and down again in a strong rhythm,
enters with drastic force, and closes into three bars of tonic-and-dominant
cadence which allude to [the sixteenth-note motif of the opening theme.
This is] the only piece of thematic "logic" since the detail of the bass
[at the beginning of the second subject, which, as we saw, was derived from the scale-figure which preceded it].

Before discussing the development section let us review this exposition
in the light of general principles and classical precedents. No one who has
analyzed the movement of a drama, or of a great piece of prose, can fail to
recognize that our analysis has depended on two things: First, the assertion of key and key relation, which is, so to speak, the topography
of music, and, secondly, the lengths of the phrases. What themes these
phrases contain, and whether one phrase alludes to another not in immediate juxtaposition, whether, in short, the whole composition is written on
one theme or on a dozen, are questions entirely secondary to the proportions and contrasted movements of the phrases. In the present case, even if
we ignore the [sixteenth-note] digression [following the close of the
broad eight-measure melody which served as the second element of the
"second subject group"] (a digression which has no discoverable connection in theme with what has gone before) we cannot account for the
second subject with less than four totally distinct themes. The quiet
penultimate theme on a tonic pedal has indeed [an eighth-note] figure
which might be regarded as an augmentation of [the inner-voice sixteenth-
note figure of the opening], but Beethoven gives no evidence that he
so regards it or expects it to be recognized. What reaches the ear in
the first movement of Opus 22 is a pair of distinct themes, [the opening
group of tonic chords with its pregnant sixteenth-note element in the inner
voice], and a cantabile before the key of B flat is left; and four other
distinct themes in F, besides an independent passage of preparation on the
dominant of F, and a spacious digression before the cadence themes.
The result is obviously very different from the scheme of two subjects
or themes, of which the second is to be a cantabile, while the intervening spaces are to be filled up with "Hi diddle diddle the Cat and
the Fiddle" by way of "brilliant passages" which, according to Spohr,
must end with a trill. It so happens that in the present instance both the
cantabile and the brilliant passages are there; but their place among
the other ideas gives no support to the theory that they come there by rule.
To ask which of the four themes in F is the "real" second subject is as

futile as to ask who are the hero and heroine of A *Midsummer Night's Dream*.

We come now to the development of this movement. The function of the exposition has been to assert two keys, the tonic and (in this case, as usual) the dominant. Other keys occur, if at all, only as purple patches, and here the only suggestion of the kind is the modulation which started the brilliant digression from the cantabile theme.

The function of the development is to travel through a wider harmonic range and to make the known themes of the exposition break up into new combinations. Actually new themes will give a development a lighter and more episodic character, unless, as in the Eroica Symphony, the design is on an enormous scale which leaves room for highly organized use of the old material as well. Any passage that stays long in one key will almost certainly be in a key not heard in the exposition (the exceptions are extremely interesting and do not produce the impression that the key is already familiar), and will probably be on the dominant of that key, thus arousing expectation and in no way reproducing the manner of an exposition, except in so far as concerns the bridge between first and second subject.

The development of Opus 22 begins with two bars of dialogue on [the important sixteenth-note figure] in F, which is just as likely to be a dominant as a tonic. The strong scale-theme breaks in, treating it as a dominant and leading in four bars to the note D, on which bass we have the whole six bars of the quiet tonic-pedal theme [that appeared as the third of the four "second subjects." It appears at this point in the development section, complete] with its doubts as to whether the supertonic should be flat or natural. Now here we have a typical instance of the subtlety of classical tonality, for though this is an exact transposition (except in position of parts) of the passage which we accepted as on the tonic of F, half major and half minor, nobody can possibly mistake it for D major in its present context. It is unquestionably the dominant of G, and it arouses anticipation of some event in that key. But the scale-figure, now in three-part and four-part polyphony, angrily drives us from dominant to dominant, two bars of scale-figure alternating with two of [the opening sixteenth-note figure] as a continuous run. Three of these four-bar steps, then, drive us from the dominant of G minor to that of C minor and thence to that of F minor. [The sixteenth-note motif] with an arpeggio pendant then moves alone in no less than seven two-bar steps, the bass moving still more slowly by tones and semitones so that it descends from C to E flat [over a period of fourteen bars]. The whole fourteen bars thus constitute a dramatic decrescendo, not less unmistakable in its effect though the actual drop of tone is confined to the single [last bar] which Beethoven requires to fall from fortissimo to piano. We are now on the dominant of A flat, of all keys the most unlikely to lead to our tonic. The scale theme stirs in the bass in four-bar phrases. The harmony changes to a dominant of F with a minor ninth which even in pianissimo presses severely on the D natural of the scale theme below. Thence it drops to the dominant of B flat (our tonic) also with its harsh minor ninth, which does not yield until the latter half of the fourth bar. The tension of expectation is great, and is kept up for fifteen bars, ending with a pause.

And so we are at home again and the recapitulation begins. The whole phenomenon of recapitulation is one of the most subtle things in music, and is usually dismissed by critics, and by some composers, as merely the part of a design which may be mechanically copied from a previous part. And it would be idle to deny that in the physical process of writing a large composition the recapitulatory portions are a more mechanical task than the rest, and may well be deferred until matters of greater difficulty are settled. But we must not confuse between the practical technique of writing and the function of the imagination. No great composer making full use of his mature powers ever thought of a recapitulation merely as a part which is the transposition or copy of another part. It is his profoundest instinct to think of recapitulations as things colored by the first statements and all that has happened between. One of the first conditions of musical invention is the capacity to conceive the effect of a statement not only in its first context but in the possible ways in which it may return.

In the recapitulation of a classical sonata-movement the first thing [for the listener] to notice is, obviously, any point which differs from the original statement. In well-conceived works you will not find that such points are mere digressions introduced for the sake of variety. If there is to be a recapitulation at all (and Haydn was far from thinking this necessary, nor did Beethoven disagree with him) the composer will not be afraid to make it exact. But there will always be some difference, possibly very slight, but of the kind that makes "all the difference." It will be as if the original matter were something you had seen with one eye, and the recapitulation were something you saw with both. One point where there must be some change is at the moment of transition to the key of the second subject. As the second subject is to be recapitulated in the tonic, the passage which changed the key cannot remain unaltered. But even at this juncture a change in the recapitulation is not to be ascribed to mere practical necessity: and in the Sonata Opus 22 we have a beautifully typical case of a great master's procedure. The opening had been perfunctory to the verge of insolence; and, as we have seen, its counterstatement had been reduced to a single bar and a quarter. Now [in the corresponding place in the recapitulation] the two new bars of vigorous dialogue on [the sixteenth-note motif] make the whole retrospect stand out in relief. Then comes the uprush corresponding to bar 12 [of the exposition]. It reaches a higher note, and five bars are required instead of three, for the drift down to the dominant, which is now our own dominant of B flat, not that of F. From this point the passage of "dominant preparation" and the whole of the second subject are recapitulated in the tonic with no alteration except occasional shifts of octave, not always necessitated by the limited compass of Beethoven's pianoforte at that date. There is no coda; the movement ends in the tonic exactly as its exposition ended in the dominant.

Perhaps we are wise after the event; but the perfunctory first subject is almost a sufficient indication that the weight of the movement is so poised upon a luxurious second subject that the recapitulation of the second subject is the inevitable and sufficient end of the story. Such is the case with most of the sonatas of Domenico Scarlatti that were known to Beethoven. The openings are drastically bald assertions of a tonic from which the elvish Domenico bounces off into a dominant or some remoter key, there to pour out a number of ideas, some sentimental, but most of them rattling away with a fantastic keyboard technique, and always ending with a cadence phrase broken up into smaller and smaller fragments.

Certainly Beethoven had no feeling that he had done an easy thing in shaping this movement without [a] coda—rather he felt like a sculler who has got his boat to a difficult landing-place without changing his stroke. *Die Sonate hat sich gewaschen.* Codas and other grand and clever features he had already often achieved. His triumph here is to achieve noble proportions without any startling features. The perfunctoriness of the first subject is, as we have seen, essential to the scheme. This "normal" movement is in the paradoxical position of being quite unlike any other movement in Beethoven, Mozart or Haydn. So are all the other mature movements of these composers. An analysis that does not detect this is no nearer to the truth than a child's scrawl that represents the human face by a circle containing two dots for eyes, a line for the mouth (curved upward for joy and downward for grief) and a nose in profile. Shorter first subjects Beethoven had written before, and was to write later. But the early ones such as in the sonatas, Opus 2, No. 1, and Opus 10, No. 2, were in works on as small a scale as the opening indicates, and, by the way, the same absence of coda is to be noticed. And the later ones are associated with much more rapid and powerful dramatic action.—DONALD FRANCIS TOVEY (11)

Adagio con molto espressione.—It has been observed (by Paul Bekker) that this slow movement points forward directly to the nocturnes of the romantic period, and it is true that Beethoven's emphasis on singing melody, which was none too congenial to the early piano and far from usual in its music, is one of those prophetic touches which show a great genius guessing future achievements and insisting on them before their time. If we take John Field as a middle link, we may without extravagance see a direct connection with Chopin in this *adagio*. Chopin would have dissolved the rigid accompaniment into more fluid, more congenially pianistic figurations, but it was Field who showed him how to do it, though he would himself, standing halfway between two worlds, still occasionally be content with accompaniments less exclusively suited to the keyboard. As for Beethoven, the left-hand chords with which this movement opens are merely music that happened to be set down for the piano; they are not music of necessity imagined in pianistic terms. Beethoven did not say: "Here is a piano, let's write something for it"; he said: "I must write this music: the piano will do very well for it."

The first subject—for the movement is in a quite regular sonata form—[is a *cantilena* with many *fioratura* passages connecting the keynotes of the melody].

Now this melody is, in spite of its ornamental richness, essentially a vocal tune, transformed into instrumental terms by an elaboration very similar to that which Chopin applied to his recollection of familiar vocal music, sometimes Polish folk songs and sometimes operatic arias, the most inspiring of which he found in Bellini. Field, too, transformed vocal types of melody into true keyboard music (one of his nocturnes[1] is in the shape not only of an operatic air, but of a whole operatic scena), and he might very well be imagined to have written the melody just quoted, if we happened to be ignorant of the fact that Beethoven did so. However, while Field *could* have set it over an accompaniment similar to Beethoven's [(simple chords repeated monotonously in eighth notes)] it is not likely that he *would*. But play Beethoven's tune over [an accompaniment of broken chords covering two octaves,] and a Fieldish, indeed, almost a Chopinesque nocturne stands before you.

The first subject is exceptionally long for a continuous melodic formation. It covers nine bars of slow 9/8 time, not counting the repetition of the final cadence and two extra bars of peroration. A transitional subject in the same key follows, leading over a purposely ambiguous modulation to B flat major for the second subject. This is rounded off first by an ornamental [thirty-second-note] passage which, but for its regular metrical division into two 9/8 bars, might be one of Chopin's cadenza-like *fioriture*, and by an expressive passage distinguished by a rising bass figure and a melodic cadence with a strong accent off the beat.

The working-out begins here. It is free development of the first subject melodic phrases. Three times the opening figure of [the first subject] is heard over the dominant of C minor, with discordant sus-

[1] C major, No. 14, in Breitkopf & Härtel's edition.—Editor.

pensions on the stressed beats. This is followed by a duet based on [the fourth bar of that subject], with the phrases overlapping, as though played, let us say, by an oboe and a clarinet. A sequence of dominant sevenths modulates as far afield as A flat minor, in which key the figuration changes, the repeated [eighth-notes] in the bass becoming flowing [sixteenth-notes]. The music is now strictly in three parts, all of them melodic, much as if a bassoon had joined the oboe and clarinet. When the trio has become a quartet, a second bassoon coming in with a low B flat, the music finds itself on the dominant of E flat major, ready for recapitulation. This is formally quite normal, but the passage-work in the right hand is frequently elaborated, very much as it might be in a Chopin nocturne.

Menuetto.—This movement is particularly interesting—small as it is, it shows Beethoven in the twofold act of looking back upon the music of the eighteenth century and predicting that of the nineteenth. Broadly speaking, the minuet itself is music of the past, the trio music of the future, though there is an episode in the middle of the former which may be said to stand for the present—the very urgent present Beethoven was so determined to face.

The bland opening strain is akin in character to the well-known minuet in the Septet, Opus 20, of which a pianistic version appears in the little Sonata Opus 49, No. 2.[1] In none of the preceding ten sonatas had Beethoven written so conventional a dance movement as this appears to be for the first eight bars. He had, in fact, described only two movements as minuets at all, one in Opus 2, No. 1 and another in Opus 10, No. 2, neither of which was much of a minuet in anything but name. Both are typical early Beethovenian scherzos, not in the least like dance movements of the suite or divertimento sort, as is the minuet in the Septet, a work that is very much of a divertimento or serenade.

The episode that hints at a break with the past will be easily recognized by the undulating passage which swells like a wave and breaks into an emphatic cadence. The first strain is then charmingly varied—again in a kind of concerted wind-instrument style—and the minuet closes with a quiet afterthought.

The stormy trio in G minor, with its angry rumblings in the continuous [sixteenth-note] left-hand passages and the cutting accents off the beat in the right-hand chords, is like a gathering of revolutionary forces. In a musical sense, it certainly is subversive: a violent overthrow of the placid courtliness of the minuet.

Allegretto.—The finale is a last farewell to convention, with here and there a sign of straining at the leash. Its principal theme is suave and elegant; the episodes show some audacity and impatience. On the whole,

[1] It appears also in the slow movement of the Trio, Opus 11, for piano, clarinet, and violoncello.—Editor.

though, formality wins, and the piece is cut to a regular rondo pattern. The theme is, again, very extended. [It starts with an eight-measure phrase whose first measure is preceded by an upbeat of three sixteenth-notes which make the descending scale figure in sixteenth notes seem like a continuation rather than a beginning. The whole eight-measure phrase] is repeated in octaves and has a long, ornamental final cadence. New material leads gradually to the first episode, the main features of which are [thirty-second-note] arpeggios and modulations by whole-tone steps from G to D flat in the bass. A bridge-passage is then constructed from the opening phrase [of the main theme with its characteristic upbeat of three sixteenth-notes followed by a descending scale also in sixteenth-notes. Used in dialogues, this short motif] makes for the first return of the subject by means of an unaccompanied right-hand passage which curiously anticipates a very similar incident in the third "Leonora" Overture—the famous and very difficult rush of strings in the coda.[1]

[The main theme follows] slightly modified by details of figuration. The next episode begins with an energetic, strongly rhythmic theme, continued with brilliant [thirty-second-note] work, treats the rhythmic theme contrapuntally with a figure of different pattern, and returns by way of the [thirty-second notes] and a charmingly modulated transition to the main theme once more. This now appears in the left hand at first, with a broken dominant pedal note in the right, but reverts later to something like its original presentation, though rather more lavishly decorated. The first episode returns in the tonic key, in other words as a second sonata subject. After one more restatement of the rondo theme, with new variations, there is a coda based mainly on the rhythmic theme of the second episode. The passing of the subject into the bass at the end was not so much of a novelty in Beethoven's time as might appear. The device is found in Mozart's piano sonatas.—ERIC BLOM (1)

XII. SONATA No. 12 IN A FLAT, OPUS 26
I. Andante con variazioni; II. Scherzo (Allegro molto); III. Marcia funebre sulla morte d'un eroe; IV. Allegro

The work was published on 3rd March 1802, by Cappi of Vienna, with a dedication to Prince Carl von Lichnowsky. It is in a way, as we have seen, the most significant composition written by Beethoven in 1801, a year not very fruitful in great music for other media than the pianoforte, and although the two sonatas in fantasia form that followed it are at least as interesting, they obviously owe much of their new

---

1 Professor Blom quotes measures 46 through 49 of the movement, which, with the diminution in time value of the scale figure, are indeed prophetic of the scale figures which lead to the final Presto in the "Leonora" Overture No. 3.—Editor.

boldness and freedom to the experience gained with the work now under notice.

But if no other work composed in 1801 meant a greater advance in Beethoven's development than this Opus 26, it is interesting to recall here one written the preceding year, the first performance of which took place nearly a year before this sonata was published. This was the ballet, *Die Geschöpfe des Prometheus*, produced at the Burgtheater in Vienna on 28th March 1801. Its connection with the sonata is obvious, if indirect: it contains the theme Beethoven used in 1804 for the finale of the *Eroica* Symphony, and the funeral march in that symphony has often been regarded as the second outcome of Beethoven's playful threat to Paer to "compose that," the march in the sonata being the first. At any rate, the slow movement in the sonata may justifiably be regarded as a kind of sketch or exercise for the greater one in the symphony.

The earlier funeral march was orchestrated by the composer in 1814 for use as incidental music in a drama by one Duncker, entitled *Leonora Prohaska*,[1] which was never produced, the censor having banned it on account of its subversive glorification of political freedom. Not having a scheme of tonalities between different movements to consider, Beethoven transposed the march a tone and a half up, into B minor, in order to write in keys more convenient to orchestral instruments.

Andante con variazioni.—The five variations are built on an extended theme in three sections of which the first strain [is eight measures long. Any description in words of its classical symmetry or of its subtle voicing (which eliminates the doubling of the melody in the tenor after the second measure) would be an unnecessary intrusion on our aesthetic sensitivity. Suffice it to say that the phrase ends on the dominant]. It is repeated with a very slight elaboration and a full close in place of the half close at the end. A middle section modulating by way of a descending sequence makes a contrast both of melody and of key—a turn of phrase of a kind that is easily memorable and therefore readily identifiable when it occurs again in varied form. The theme is rounded off by a return of the first section, stated only once this time and with the harmony of the full close laid out in a slightly different form.

Structurally the variations keep so close to the theme that it could hardly escape the least attentive of listeners even when the decorations grow as exuberant as in the second variation or when the harmony changes, as it does in the third. Variation I intersperses the melody with little arpeggios on the first beat and spreads it more widely over the keyboard.

The second variation looks as modern on paper as one of Schumann's *Variations symphoniques*, and indeed as far as the instrumental treatment goes it is ahead of anything that could have been effectively played on

[1] See the essay on the incidental music for *Leonora Prohaska* in Part III.—Editor.

the earliest pianofortes, not to mention the harpsichord or clavichord. The syncopated right-hand chords and octaves are very modern—relatively speaking—and the wide intervals in [certain] passages daring in the way they display the strain shown in the second half of [the first phrase] in disguise in the middle of the keyboard. [Actually] the notes are repeated exactly as before, but for octave and time displacements, and this is in fact what happens throughout the present variation.

The third variation, in A flat minor, is very interesting. As it comes halfway through the movement, it is taken farthest away from the original form of the theme, thus giving the impression of a central peak we have been gradually climbing to gain a new view, and from which we are as gradually to descend again. It is in the middle section that the fresh outlook becomes especially fascinating. In the first statement of the theme [a two-bar phrase in the closely associated tonality of B flat minor was introduced by a tied-over upbeat in the bass voice] with a downward sequence following, [bringing the tonality back to A flat major. In the present variation in A flat *minor*, there is obviously no surprise effect of a minor mode at this point in the scheme of things. Beethoven thus eschews B flat minor as a tonality (which would have been awkward in the over-all tonality of A flat minor) and achieves his surprise by introducing his two-bar phrase in D flat minor and placing the tied-over upbeat in the tenor voice instead of in the bass]. The sequence is thus transformed into a wider modulatory step that gives the music a wholly new turn. The variants of the chief strain of the melody are syncopated in the right hand throughout.

In Variation IV, where the music returns to the major, everything is curiously broken up by rhythmic displacements and by constant capricious moves up and down the keyboard. The gradual tightening of the accompanying rhythm is a peculiarly attractive feature. The middle section, though it returns to its former sequential presentation, is found to have remained under the influence of its harmonic complications in the preceding variation. But all through the harmony has become greatly subtilized by chromatic passing notes.

The fifth and last variation is found to have descended to the level of the first again. Except for its more elaborate figuration [in sixteenth-note triplets and (upon the repetition of the first phrase) in thirty-second notes] it resumes the harmonic and rhythmic simplicity of the earlier statements of the theme. But when Beethoven is so deliberately intent on keeping our attention comparatively disengaged, we may be pretty certain that he has a surprise up his sleeve. Sure enough, the surprise comes just when he seems to have arrived at the end of his theme for the last time, and when apparently there is nothing more to be said. What he does say, in fact, and not at all *zum Überfluss* (by way of superfluity), like Schumann's "Eusebius," is something quite new and unexpected. He tacks a coda of fifteen bars on to the end of the last variation, just to clinch matters conclusively, since there is no reason why one ordinary straightforward variation should be final rather than another, and since this one, without any particular qualifications for it, happens to have been chosen to act as conclusion.

The theme of the coda [seems at first to be made up of completely new material]. It is not nearly as independent as it appears at first. Apart from balancing the composer's whole design wonderfully by being itself in the form of a tiny variation (for [its opening] melody is immediately repeated in a more decorated form), it may be regarded as being [somewhat] derived from a telescoped version of the main theme.[1]

Molto allegro.—The scherzo opens, very curiously, not in its own key, A flat major, but in that of the dominant, E flat major, and even then the first chord (F minor) is one outside that key. We may thus safely assume that Beethoven meant to play one of his favorite games—that of momentarily confusing the ear as to harmonic issues. The pace being rapid, the witty point is made in a flash, and as the movement is explicitly called a scherzo, we need have no compunction in letting it amuse us.

At the fourth bar the right key establishes itself, and at the sixth it becomes clear. The [first two four-bar] phrases are restated with variants, which is doubtless the reason why the first section remains unrepeated. The second, on the other hand, is given repeat signs, although it is three times as long even as written. But as it contains new variants of [the opening two phrases] after a statement of matter that is episodic rather than strictly thematic, the proportions are perfectly kept. Much of the new material, having begun by promising some striking features, turns out to be merely transitional. The main theme then returns in the left hand, with evenly running [eighth-note] passages above it. Afterwards the process is reversed, the theme being transferred to the top and the runs to the bass. This cannot be called a case of double counterpoint, however, the [eighth-note] passages not being reproduced with absolute fidelity after the exchange.

The trio section, in D flat major, is built wholly on trochaic figures in single bars (a [half note] followed by a [quarter note]), and its interest is harmonic rather than melodic. There is a beautiful final cadence set into relief by a sforzando. Each of the two short sections is repeated, and at the close there is a transitional passage referring to the scherzo theme[2] and in fact forming a bridge for the return of the main section. The long repeat is not made this time.

Maestoso andante (*Marcia funebre sulla morte d'un eroe*).—The fu-

---

[1] Professor Blom quotes the first two measures and the last two measures of the theme and compares them with the first four measures of the coda.—Editor.
[2] In the tenor voice.—Editor.

neral march for Beethoven's unknown or purely imaginary hero begins [with a dotted rhythm in the right hand, almost unrelieved, and a completely unrelieved insistence on the top note, E flat, in much the same way that he was later to employ (for different dramatic purposes) in the second movement of the Seventh Symphony, written ten years later]. A comparison with Paer's march will at once reveal Beethoven's weightier and more significant manner, and his harmonic daring will strike the hearer a few bars later, when a drastic turn occurs, surprisingly early in the movement.

The cadence at the end of the eighth measure is in C flat major. To the ear alone the impression of what follows is simply a transition to C flat minor; but as that key would require seven flats and three double flats, Beethoven transforms it into B minor, which on the piano is the same thing, and he is in any case intent on finding somewhere in the course of the transition a short cut to the sharp side of the circle of keys. We discover in the course of a very few bars that he uses B minor as a steppingstone to its nearest relative, D major, which is however very far from his original key. Arrived there, he at once turns toward the flat regions again, this time by way of a chord of the diminished seventh [in which the D natural becomes the bass of the chord instead of the top voice]. The first strain returns, exactly as at first, but with a change in the bass (note the trill [on the C flat at the beginning of the third measure]) and a harmonic extension of the final cadence.

The trio, in A flat major, is quite short and simple. If we like to hear the "salutes fired over the grave," and rolling drums into the bargain, it will be quite easy to identify them—as easy as such things almost invariably are in music, once they have been pointed out by commentators. There are two sections of four bars, each of which is repeated.

The main section of the march returns exactly as before, but it is rounded off by a short coda this time. A curiously ambiguous tone prevails here, very far removed from any suggestion of mere official mourning, but hinting with great subtlety at the complex mixture of feelings attending a personal grief. The harmony clears serenely into an A flat major, but at the same time it is clouded by inflections of minor ninths, all of which may, if we like, convey to us an impression that although sorrow has become outwardly calm, it secretly stings the mourner all the more poignantly.

Perhaps such interpretations are farfetched, but it is at any rate as legitimate to try to discover psychological subtleties in the art of Beethoven as to make it an excuse for the kind of picturesque illustration that has been attempted in the case of the trio section of this march. One thing is certain: although we know that Paer wrote funeral music to express the grief of Achilles over the death of Patroclus and have no information as to what personal emotions Beethoven may or may not express, a comparison of the two marches [will show] that the greater composer had a far richer store of imagination and poetry to draw upon, whether his inspiration was due to some particular "situation" or sufficed of itself to engender great music. Beethoven was no doubt well aware of this, and that is what makes his remark about having to "compose that" understandable and even excusable.

Allegro.—The finale is in rondo form—Beethoven's highly organized rondo form, which brings back the first episode like the second subject of a sonata-form movement. Apart from its formal construction, this movement is particularly interesting by reason of its texture. Two principles are at work almost throughout: inversion and interchange. This can be shown at once by [listening to] the first dozen bars. [The main subject appears at once unaccompanied in the right hand. It outlines, in sixteenth-notes, a descending harmonic progression from the tonic to the dominant. When the latter is reached the left hand enters and accompanies the right-hand sixteenths with an eighth-note tenor melody. This is followed by an] inversion, where the left-hand part is an exact reproduction of the opening, except that it stands an octave lower, while the top part presents the same figures turned upside down and inside out. The interchange of parts [continues in the next two measures]. Save for the fact that the tune first heard from the left hand now appears in octaves in the right, and that the harmony in the last bar is differently distributed, this is a case of strict double counterpoint. The music [proceeds] with another specimen of the same kind, complicated this time by the displacement of the two interchanging parts by means of a sequence, [the eighth-note motion starting off in the left hand and being echoed in the right].

The music continues for a while with [this sequence as a thematic basis, along with] a fragment of [the opening phrase]. Then comes the first episode, an undistinguished theme in itself, perhaps, but admirably suited to the composer's scheme because it enables him to refine still further upon his ingenious arrangement of parts. For here the principles of inversion and interchange are actually applied simultaneously.[1]

This episode, being treated as a second sonata subject, stands in the key of the dominant, E flat major. The main theme is then repeated exactly as before, the only difference being that the final E flat of the episode still lingers on in the bass when [the opening phrase] returns, a point of great interest, a complete break between the episode and the return of the subject being thus avoided in the simplest possible way.

The second episode [consists] of two sections in C minor and G minor, strikingly new in character. The next return of the theme is

[1] Professor Blom quotes the first, second, fourth, and fifth measures of this episode, pointing out that whereas the syncopated eighth-notes which start out in the left hand remain intact when they appear two bars later in the right hand, the sixteenth-note broken-chord figure is inverted upon its second appearance.—Editor.

again unaltered, except for a new transition to the third episode at the end, necessitated by the fact that this takes the form of a second subject, and is therefore in the key of the tonic this time. A short coda, based on the opening figures of the main theme and gradually sinking down to pianissimo, brings the sonata to a close.—ERIC BLOM (1)

XIII. SONATA No. 13 IN E FLAT, OPUS 27, No. 1
    I. Andante, Allegro, Andante; II. Allegro molto e vivace; III. Adagio con espressione; IV. Allegro vivace

The exact date of composition of this sonata is uncertain, but it may with reasonable accuracy be placed in the year 1801, since it was published on 3rd March 1802. It is dedicated to the Princess Josephine Sophie von Liechtenstein, née von Fürstenberg, wife of General Field Marshal Prince von Liechtenstein. Beethoven first met her at Prince Lichnowsky's, and she became his pupil and one of his patrons. He must have been on as friendly terms with her as their respective positions would allow, for when his pupil Ries was conscripted in 1805 and found himself obliged to leave Vienna penniless, Beethoven wrote a letter to the princess asking her to assist the young musician.

The two Sonatas Opus 27, the second of which is the so-called "Moonlight" Sonata, are the first works of Beethoven's to bear the significant title of *Sonata quasi una fantasia*. They show the composer emancipating himself from the classical sonata pattern and doing it as drastically as possible by substituting pieces in a freely chosen form for the traditional first movement that was always the most important part of a sonata, though not invariably in what we now call sonata form. In the first sonata of Opus 27 Beethoven may be said to be looking back, in his opening movement, to the old suite form, in the second forward to that of the Schubertian impromptu or even the Mendelssohnian song without words.

The first definite break with the established first-movement form was, in fact, made by him in the sonata preceding the present one, Opus 26, in A flat major; but that was not by any means an original departure on Beethoven's part. He uses the variation form for a first movement much as Mozart did before him. What he does contribute to the evolution of the sonata with absolute independence, however, is his way of transferring the most vital part of his musical discourse into the finale. Even this did not flash upon him suddenly: the last movement of the Opus 26 Sonata fails to compensate for the absence of a strict form in the first, for it is above all a brilliant virtuoso piece. But with Opus 27, No. 1 the second step is made toward a goal it would have been too much of a miraculous achievement to reach in a single stride even for so bold an artistic rebel. The finale of this sonata, as we shall presently see, is at once the support and the chief aesthetic feature of its structure.—ERIC BLOM (1)

The opening of [the] very remarkable sonata, the *Sonata Quasi una Fantasia*, Opus 27, No. 1, [deserves attention—more attention than it is likely to receive by those who give it but a cursory glance]. Bülow considered the first movement of this E flat sonata unworthy of Beethoven; but, humorist as Bülow himself was, his formidable cleverness was not always a match for Beethoven's still more formidable skill in the cruel sport of prig-sticking. Edward Fitzgerald, in the intervals of polishing his *Omar Khayyám*, said that "people will not believe Mozart to be powerful because he is so beautiful." It would be idle to pretend that the beginning of Opus 27, No. 1, is powerful. Persons who find it childish may be rebuked with the correction that it is childlike. If, on the other hand, any one should plead that the first eight bars are in double counterpoint which is afterwards inverted in bars 67–70 and 75–78, and that this is a highly intellectual procedure, Beethoven himself would uproariously laugh the belief out of court. The real intellectual values of this ostentatiously ridiculous movement depend on the following facts.

The opening nursery rhyme, with its bass, or, to speak learnedly, its counterpoint, running like a kitten in pursuit of its tail, has nothing but the most ordinary harmonies of the key of E flat. It has not even a half-close on the dominant. Its cadences are tonic, and so is that of the very sentimental new four-bar strain that follows without change of key; but this new strain, like the first one, needs a second strain, and the second strain begins with a bright chord of C major. As a mere point of color, the effect is [powerful]. But the chord does not turn out to be a key at all, but is mere leading-note to our next-door neighbor, the supertonic, and the tune, having left its message next door, finishes itself at home as if nothing had happened. Nothing, in fact, has happened. Further, after this burst of energy, the first tune returns in both its strains with their repeats. The repeats are varied by the following highly intellectual process. The original rhythm being *Dum-dum-dum*, the variation is at first *Dum-dum-dum-dum-dum*, which, in the repetition of the second strain is, however, developed into *Diddle-diddle-diddle-diddle-dum*; after which, something really does happen. An energetic movement begins in the key of C major. There is no process of modulating to C major. There need not be. We have already heard its chord explained away as mere leading-note to the supertonic. The only novelty is that we are now transported to the real key of C major, existing in its own right. This episode is worked out as a complete symmetrical section, but the repetition of its second strain diverts the harmony through C minor to the home dominant of E flat. The passing through C minor establishes the indirect relation of C major to E flat, and, by dwelling on the home dominant, Beethoven makes us take the return to E flat seriously as a reasoned process and not as a mere juxtaposition. The final *da capo* of the opening theme is only slightly more intellectual with its double counterpoint than the former rhythmic variation. Then, with an appropriate touch of the subdominant, hitherto unheard, there is a line of coda which, if played simply and gravely enough, with a sense of beauty in pianoforte tone, faintly hints at more serious things. And the rest of the sonata has an energy which deserves to be called powerful as well as serious.

Any novel-reader whose tastes are not bounded by the average bestseller will understand that a witty writer must be careful neither to make his characters talk too cleverly for their place in his world, nor to fall into the trick of abusing his own creative authority by bullying them. There is no doubt that the first movement of Opus 27, No. 1, is "fooling." Tastes may differ whether the fooling is excellent or not, but there is no fooling in the handling of that chord of C major, first as an illusion that fades into the common light of the home supertonic, and, secondly, as a key in its own right; and there is no fooling in the rest of the sonata. Probably we shall be wise to be not less unkind than our gruff and grim Beethoven to such aristocratic fooling.—DONALD FRANCIS TOVEY (1)

Allegro molto e vivace.—In the C minor scherzo Beethoven seems to be deliberately restricting his music to a purely harmonic and rhythmic interest, for throughout the piece, including the trio, there is nothing that could be called a melody. The scherzo itself consists of a succession of groups of three [quarter notes], laid out in single notes (occasionally in octaves) for each hand and generally in contrary motion. Each measure represents the unfolding of a simple triad. They suggest two-measure groups of which the first is weak, the second strong.

It will be [observed] that there is nothing more than two-part harmony at any point; but the motion is so rapid that for the ear the effect is that of listening to a series of complete chords. The notes pass as quickly as the shells and stones and bits of colored glass in a kaleidoscope, and the result is that we do not perceive these fragments separately, but fused into a rich pattern. Needless to say, the effect of harmonic amplitude can be very easily heightened by means of the sustaining pedal; but it is questionable whether this ought to be used at all during this portion of the sonata, for it modifies the peculiar artistic result of these illusory chords by substituting an actual harmonic fullness.

The trio section, in A flat major, again predominantly harmonic and rhythmic, nevertheless introduces some fragmentary, tentative melodic features. But to say that there was a tune would be going much too far: Beethoven keeps very consistently to his scheme of holding songfulness in reserve, for what purpose will appear as soon as the recapitulation of the scherzo is over. It is resumed at first exactly as it stood before, but at the repeat of the first portion the right-hand part is delayed for the value of [an eighth note] by syncopation. It is played *legato* while the left hand anticipates it *staccato*. The second portion, instead of being repeated, is briefly supplemented by a coda that ends in C major. This, however, has not the effect of a lighting up of the prevalent minor tonality by a major tonic chord at the end, for the harmony immediately preceding indicates that this C major chord is to be felt as the dominant of F minor. It thus makes a connecting link with the next movement, which follows without a break and is in A flat, the relative major of F minor.

Adagio con espressione.—The tunelessness of the scherzo now explains itself. Beethoven at once opens his slow movement with one of those great emotional melodies to which an *adagio* was so apt to inspire him, and it is, of course, all the more telling for the melodic aridity that had been purposely maintained before. [The movement is one continuous song, the broad melody falling vaguely into four-bar groups. However the connecting links between these groups are so suave that it is difficult to tell where one melodic sentence ends and the next begins. We are aware that about halfway through the piece the opening bars of the melody are] resumed an octave higher with a different accompaniment and, as it were, in a more luminous setting. However, only half of it is thus restated, and suddenly a rapid upward run, culminating on two [trills,] marks the end of this brief lyrical interlude. There is only a short cadenza by way of conclusion, and once again the music flows straight into the next movement.

Allegro vivace.—We have now reached the movement into which Beethoven chose, in the *quasi una fantasia* form, to throw the greatest intellectual weight. It is both the longest and the most highly wrought as regards thematic workmanship and form. The rondo form, always a rich field for exploration in Beethoven's eyes, appears here in an uncommon shape and with some interesting special features. The principal theme begins [with a four-bar phrase which] is repeated an octave higher and comes to a full close in E flat major. There is a second strain, played in octaves by the right hand to a persistent [sixteenth-note] accompaniment for the left. [This melody is characterized by triads unfolded upward with an offbeat accent on each high note and then a scalewise descent over the next two measures.] This at first takes twice as much space as the first strain, which, however, returns in a new guise, with a small fragment of it [(actually its first two measures)] scattered up and down the keyboard. The first episode, in B flat major, then begins with [a characteristic] figure, which it continues for some time.

[This figure is an eighth-note melody in sixths in the right hand and a repeat note in the left hand. What makes it unique is that each chord of the right-hand melody is broken into two sixteenth notes, the lower note being played first; also the repeated note in the left hand, which ought to act as a pedal-tone in the bass, actually is played in the same register as the melody and thus sounds as an inner voice.]

One may here see a lingering influence of the harpsichord style of the preceding century. To play a single repeated left-hand note in the middle of a right-hand figuration was, of course, very much easier on the harpsichord with two keyboards. That, however, does not detract from its novelty as an effect on the early pianoforte, where, in fact, it was a daring enough thing to attempt precisely because it must have been thought of in Beethoven's day as essentially a two-keyboard device.

The second half of the episode makes use of entirely new material, beginning with striding arpeggios on the triad of B flat and continuing with a theme in octave figures for the right hand, the left being again busy with [sixteenth notes].

The return of the principal theme is modified toward the end, where the second strain [that of the rising and descending octaves] goes into the minor and thus leads to G flat major. Now Beethoven indulges unexpectedly in a development of his material that approximates to the working-out section of a sonata. After so much mere diversion and lyrical expansion in the first three movements, he evidently feels an imperative need to strengthen his edifice by some solid constructive feature. This may not be the only way of writing a fantasia, but it is for him one of the countless varieties of the only procedure of composing what is, after all, still a sonata. At any rate, it is *his* way, perfectly logical and, it follows, aesthetically satisfying.

The development begins with a quasi-fugal transformation of three notes of the main theme, with running figures in double counterpoint against it (i.e., sometimes above and sometimes below). This way of handling a brief motif of this sort already foreshadows the fugal treatment of the principal theme in the last Sonata, Opus 111, in C minor, dating from 1822. The three notes in question [are followed by an eighth-note tag to form a three-measure theme suitable for a double counterpoint fugato. This tag is] used in a variety of ways as the development proceeds. Next comes a new treatment of the first episode, the theme now taking [on a new form: the repeated notes are now in the treble and the chords of the melody (now in the left hand) are no longer broken, thus achieving a smooth rhythm of eighth notes, uncluttered by the sixteenths which had been so prevalent up to this point in the movement. The melody,] gradually broken up as though losing its way, is at last cut off by an energetic [trill] in the bass that heralds the next return of the principal theme. It begins as before, but presently the second strain is transferred to the bass. The version [in which small fragments of the first theme were scattered up and down the keyboard] again follows and leads as before, though in a different key, to a restatement of the first episode. Here again we have a feature of the sonata form, for this idea now reveals itself as a second subject and is accordingly reintroduced in the orthodox manner in the principal key. But Beethoven, by no means content to let tradition sway him, has a surprise in store yet. The whole of the first episode having turned up again as a regular second sonata subject, he suddenly makes his music come to a standstill on a dominant-seventh chord and then brings back the broad melody of the slow movement, this time in E flat major and with minute but significant changes. This brief quotation, like the movement from which it is taken, ends with a free cadential passage, similar to the first, yet altered with astonishing subtlety. It leads into a final presto of twenty bars based mainly on the first two notes of [the first strain of the rondo].—ERIC BLOM (1)

XIV. SONATA No. 14 IN C SHARP MINOR, OPUS 27, No. 2 ("MOONLIGHT")
I. Adagio sostenuto; II. Allegretto; III. Presto agitato

Scarcely any sonata has had so much written about it as Opus 27, No. 2, though it lasts only sixteen minutes. In Beethoven's own time it was called the *Laube* (Arbor) sonata because it was thought to have been composed in an arbor. The nickname "Moonlight" Sonata came from the poet Rellstab, who was inspired to call it that by a moonlit night on the Lake of Lucerne.

From various facts that have come to my knowledge I have conceived a different theory of the origin of the work which I should like to mention here without claiming any historical authenticity for it.

There is in Vienna a manuscript of Beethoven's which contains a few lines from Mozart's *Don Giovanni* in Beethoven's undoubted hand: the passage after Don Giovanni has killed the Commendatore. Underneath Beethoven has transposed the passage into C sharp minor, and the absolute similarity of this with the first movement of Opus 27, No. 2, is quite unmistakable. In particular the postlude is note for note as in Mozart.

At the time one of Beethoven's aristocratic friends died and was laid out in state in his palace. One night Beethoven is said to have improvised as he sat by the corpse of his friend; is it so unlikely that Beethoven was reminded of the similar scene in *Don Giovanni* and that this was the reason for the striking similarity which we have mentioned? In any case, there is no romantic moonlight in this movement: it is rather a solemn dirge.—EDWIN FISCHER

The two Sonatas, Opus 27, were published in 1802, and it is more than probable that both were written in 1801, to which year Beethoven's famous letter to the "Immortal Beloved" is also conjectured to belong. The dedication of the present sonata to the young Countess Giulietta Guicciardi is one of the reasons why it was for a long time taken for granted that this letter was addressed to her, sentimental commentators insisting on seeing in it a musical counterpart to the love letter. That view, however, is now no longer favored, though it has never been definitely decided who the woman may have been to whom Beethoven addressed this passionate message.

[There is a] curious story of the dedication of the C sharp minor sonata to Giulietta. It is pleasantly romantic to think that he addressed this work, which is so popular a favorite, to the "Immortal Beloved." Unfortunately he did not himself very particularly care for this sonata, and he did not mind saying so on one occasion. What is more, we have it from Giulietta herself that he at first intended to inscribe the Rondo in G major, Opus 51, No. 2, to her, but, having to dedicate something to the Princess Lichnowsky, changed his mind and assigned to Giulietta the C sharp minor sonata instead. Not only would it thus appear that he preferred the rather slight rondo to the sonata, and perhaps the Princess Lichnowsky to the Countess Guicciardi; it is certain that the idea of finding romantic dreams of a beloved woman in the first movement of the sonata is all moonshine—the only "moonlight," in fact, that may legitimately be sought in connection with the work.

As a new depature in sonata form the work is one of extreme interest. The big sonata movement, instead of coming at the beginning, is placed at the end and the slow movement comes first. It is a peculiar slow movement, too, not unlike some of the nonpolyphonic preludes in Bach's *Well-tempered Clavier*. At the same time it was, for its period, distinctly modern. It looks forward in some respects to the impromptus of Schubert and to the songs without words of Mendelssohn. Like the former, it is in the nature of a free improvisation, without a great deal of detail, and unconventional from the sonata-form point of view; like the latter, it sets songful phrases of a distinctly vocal character over figures of accompaniment that keep to the same pattern throughout. One might add that this movement also anticipates the type of Chopin's nocturne in some ways, though the direct approach to that was made by the line of specialist pianist-composers through John Field and by way of the operatic aria through Bellini.

Allegretto.—Here for once those who do not look at the printed page are at a slight advantage. They are in no danger of being startled by an apparently violent change of tonality at the sight of the key signatures of the first two movements—four sharps for the Adagio, five flats for the Allegretto. To the ear there is nothing abrupt in the change, for it represents in reality nothing more than a passing from minor to major by the enharmonic sidetrack. This scherzolike second movement is in effect in C sharp major, Beethoven writing it enharmonically in D flat major merely for the player's convenience. It is easier to read a piece with five flats than with seven sharps—that is all.

Anything less like moonlight than this piece could hardly be imagined. It is sunny music, the clear and blithe melody of bright daylight. The whole of the first section has a large melodic sweep that is exhilarating, and what makes it curious that it should produce this effect is the fact that it is made up entirely of short two-bar figures. This sectional treatment is at first accentuated by the device of making the phrases alternately tied and detached. Afterwards this process is abandoned, perhaps because it is no longer required; the hearer has been made sufficiently aware of this periodicity by a slight initial exaggeration to keep it in his consciousness as the prevalent rhythmic pulse of the piece.

In the trio a similar procedure is to be noticed. In the first part strong accents off the beat are marked by the composer, while in the second they are omitted, though the rhythmic scheme remains the same. It is surely not too fanciful to imagine that Beethoven knew that they would be felt without being actually played, once the ear had caught the intention. The art of musical innuendo need not be put past him.

It is hardly necessary to say that there is a repeat of the first part of this scherzolike movement.

Presto agitato.—We have now arrived at the true sonata movement—the most important section, into which Beethoven throws all his ardor and constructive skill, going out of his way to crown it all with a very spacious coda that contains moreover the concertolike feature of a cadenza. Clearly brilliance as well as eloquence and action is the intention here; moonshine and the Lake of Lucerne have vanished wholly out of sight, and so, no doubt, has the Countess Guicciardi, whom such towering passion must have terrified, if she could have understood it. As she evidently had a hankering after the G major Rondo and considered herself treated second-best with this sonata, we may take it for granted that she did nothing of the sort. On artistic grounds it is surely the Princess Lichnowsky who ought to have been offended; but then, again, she might have felt this movement to be too indecorous an offering for one of her rank. The probability is that few of Beethoven's contemporaries grasped such music as this, stuck fast as they still were in eighteenth-century conventions. The wonder is that the Viennese aristo-crats of the time were enlightened enough to tolerate his musical revolts and his incredibly boorish behavior for the sake of his genius.

In the finale of the C sharp minor sonata all pretense at courtly formality of demeanor, at which the composer still aimed to some extent in that of Opus 22, is ruthlessly abandoned, though mastery of musical form is maintained as firmly as ever. The music plunges at once wildly into the first subject, which is not a tune, but merely a reckless sweeping of the keyboard with frenzied arpeggios, punctuated by an explosive accent at the end of each. The effect of the accents is the greater because the rest is kept in a suppressed tone until the next feature presents itself, a long passage poised on the dominant and ending with a pause on a bare G sharp. The initial process is then repeated with varied harmony, modulating into G sharp minor, in which key the second subject presents itself. Here at last the music is given a melodic feature.

This is followed by some remarkable scale passages with crashing ac-cents and breathless syncopations in the accompaniment, and another extensive theme, also in G sharp minor and thus belonging to the second-subject group, succeeds to this. It is characterized by repeated notes and little broken phrases. The exposition closes with an allusion to [the melodic opening of the second subject], still in the same key. It is re-peated. When it is heard again, the music is carried over into the work-ing-out by a conversion of [the opening theme] into C sharp major. It then modulates to F sharp minor for an almost immediate return of the second subject, the melody of which soon passes into the left hand and is developed at some length. The material that serves as a bridge to the recapitulation is new.

The working-out [is] very concise, no doubt because some develop-ment of the thematic matter is still in store for the extended coda, which follows after a perfectly normal recapitulation. It (the coda) begins with a contraction of the arpeggios of [the opening] into a dif-ferent, more convulsive rhythmic grouping and then reintroduces the second subject, first in the left hand and afterwards in the right. Next comes [a] cadenza, beginning with arpeggios kept strictly in time and later, after a [trill], introducing a freely ornamental figure that falls rapidly into the bass, which is arrested by two bars of adagio, containing merely a cadence of bare bass octaves. The coda is rounded off by a reference to the afterthought to the second subject already heard at the end of the exposition and recapitulation.—ERIC BLOM (1)

XV. Sonata No. 15 in D, Opus 28
I. Allegro; II. Andante; III. Allegro vivace; IV. Allegro ma non troppo

This work was written in 1801 and published, by the Bureau des Arts et d'Industrie in Vienna, on 14th August 1802. It is dedicated to Joseph, Edler von Sonnenfels. The period is a rather uneventful one, productively if not biographically. Outwardly, at any rate, Beethoven's life ran on without any great disturbance, though it was only the following year that the so-called Heiligenstadt Testament, that suicidal document, was wrung from him by adversities which at least momentarily seemed to him no longer bearable. The major calamity, so far as we can tell, was his approaching deafness.

There are certainly no heated passions displaying themselves in the four paino sonatas Beethoven wrote in 1801, except in the finale of the "Moonlight" Sonata, and Opus 28 is the calmest of them all. Hence, no doubt, the title of "Pastoral" Sonata given to it later by the Hamburg publisher Cranz, which, though it is doubtful whether Beethoven would have countenanced it,[1] is at least less inappropriate than many other sobriquets of the kind. The movement it fits best is the last.

It is in form rather than in subjective expression that Beethoven advanced at this time. The first two works he called by the name of *Sonata quasi una fantasia*, Opus 27, are greater departures in the matter of shape than in that of content. Beethoven found a new mold first, while the new thought that was destined to fill it did not at once pour itself out very freely. Perfect adjustment of the new outlook to the new manner of presentation was to come later. It is rare enough for both to manifest themselves in one and the same composer, as they did in the maturer Beethoven; to have appeared together at a single moment in the career of one of them would have been too much of a miracle even for so great a creator.

The present sonata reverts to the classical form—a regular sonata movement, a piece in a moderate tempo based on the song form, a scherzo and a final rondo. It may be noted that Beethoven here for the last time uses this normal four-movement form in a piano sonata. Three movements predominate thereafter and as he goes on there is a tendency toward two, a compression compensated for by greater enlargement within each piece.—ERIC BLOM (1)

Unlike the "Moonlight" title, the "Pastorale" title could well have been known by Beethoven, since Opus 28 was already so entitled

1 See Newman's remark on this point.—Editor.

in an English edition (Broderip & Wilkinson) published about three years after the original edition (or about thirty-five years before the Cranz edition heretofore given as the first use of this title). Czerny said that the Andante was long a favorite of Beethoven, who played it often.[1]—
WILLIAM S. NEWMAN

No less interesting than a study of Beethoven's themes is a study of how they are used during the course of the movement, particularly in the development section. It was inevitable that Beethoven, the unrivaled master of musical strategy, should give the greatest attention to this section, much more so than did Haydn and Mozart, who only in some of their latest symphonies approximated what Beethoven achieved. In Beethoven's development sections the technical devices of modulation, fragmentation, reiteration, combination, and so on, are vested with a new significance. They are used in such a way as to bring about a feeling of evolution and growth, of increased intensity and higher temperature, of dynamic stress and climax, of a battlefield where the musical forces come to grips. Particularly frequent and effective is a technique which, for the purpose of short reference, may be called segmentation. This means that a theme, instead of being presented in full, is cut into halves, and that only the second half is used for the continuation. The development sections of Beethoven's sonatas show numerous examples of this technique, applied deliberately and profusely. Particularly interesting in this respect is the first movement of the sonata in D major, Opus 28. The first theme of this movement—by the way, one of the few themes of Beethoven in which descending motion prevails—[is built over a constant pedal point on the tonic, repeated quarter notes. It is ten measures long (of which the first measure is a silent one)]. At the beginning of the development section this theme appears twice in its full shape, first in major, then in minor. After this there starts an extended process of successive segmentation in which the theme is reduced to its second half, which is played [four] times in alternation between the right and the left hand. [Then] the four-measure motive is reduced to one of two measures, and this is used again in alternation of high and low. Finally this is cut down to a one-measure motive which is repeated over and over again, like incessant strokes of a hammer.[2]—WILLI APEL

[1] Cf. Jacques-Gabriel Prod'homme, *Les Sonates pour piano de Beethoven*, Paris: Delagrave, 1937, p. 133. The over-all unity of Opus 28 is discussed in Ludwig Misch, *Die Faktoren der Einheit in der Mehrsätzigkeit der Werke Beethovens*, Munich: G. Henle, 1958, pp. 72–78.
[2] The first theme comes to a complete cadence in the tonic. A bridge section starts with a four-bar phrase repeated four times (featuring a new characteristic rhythmic and melodic turn in its third and fourth bars). The bass descends in scale steps from D to A and then from A to E, ending on the dominant of

Andante.—The slow movement (not very slow) may be said, though with some qualifications, to be in the form of a da capo aria. It is at any rate formed on the plan of A B A, the chief irregularity being a coda that may be represented by the formula C(A+B), being a new idea shaped out of the elements of both principal sections of the movement itself.

The music begins [with a four measure phrase—a choralelike melody], in D minor, [over a pert staccato bass in sixteenth notes. It ends with a half cadence on the dominant]. The clause that immediately succeeds [this] is a corresponding phrase beginning in F major and ending in A minor. The whole section is repeated and then comes a new strain in the dominant of D minor, followed by a modified restatement of [the opening phrase]. That is, so to speak, the main section of the aria.

The key changes to D major for the middle section, which is entirely independent of what has gone before. [In each measure it alternates simple chords repeated in a scherzo-like dotted rhythm with a lively passage in triplets, unaccompanied—the effect is of four horns alternating with a solo flute. The music maintains this pattern] almost throughout. There are two sections, each of which is repeated.

The opening portion of the movement is resumed, at first exactly as before; but instead of being merely indicated, the repeats are now fully written out, for Beethoven, in order to introduce variety, sets them out in [thirty-second-note] figuration. It may be objected that the comparison with the form of the da capo aria breaks down here, since the old composers who handled it merely indicated the repeat and did not write it out with varied ornamentation. This, however, is to reckon without the continuo player, who, always free to fill in the figured bass as he chose, so long as he kept to the harmonic directions, must in the case of da capo arias have frequently, if not generally, introduced new patterns of accompaniment at the recurrence of the first section. Indeed, one may very well hold the view that it was this factor which made this form of song, often regarded as so tedious nowadays, not only tolerable, but actually extremely interesting to its contemporaries.

In the coda Beethoven at first gives us a bare outline of [the opening chorale-like melody] in two different harmonic versions, each time ar-

---

the dominant. However the second-theme group starts, not as would be expected, in A major (the dominant), but in the key of F sharp minor, but its first phrase ends in A major. In contrast to the first theme, it is rising instead of falling. Its second portion is a long sustained legato passage with a broken chord accompaniment in the inner voices. The closing theme is a syncopated theme in which the melodic note appears not on the downbeat but on the upbeat. It is an eight-measure phrase, whose last measures are again descending scale steps, which leads to the repeat of the exposition by modulating back from the dominant to the tonic. The second time around that tonic becomes the dominant of the key of the subdominant in which the development section begins.—Editor.

rested on a pause; then he alludes three times to [the rhythmic design of the middle section] with a dramatic tension that culminates in the chord of the dominant minor ninth, and he concludes with a broken cadence that resolves itself into a chord of D minor from a discordant mixture of dominant and tonic.

Allegro vivace.—The whole of the scherzo—apart from the trio section —is built on or derived from the two figures which are at once presented at the opening. [They are, first, a single-note falling over four octaves— one note to a bar; and second, a pert answer with a falling broken chord on the first two beats of each bar with a significant silence on the third beat.] The notes descending in four octaves are especially important. They recur again and again, sometimes unharmonized, sometimes in chords, cartwheeling humorously down into the bass; but when the left hand sets them against a kind of waltz accompaniment in the right they turn upwards on the last note, thus effecting short-cut modulations.

The trio is entirely different, a short four-bar tune in B minor alternately turning back into that key and away into D major. It is heard eight times over: variety, apart from the two different turns of the cadence, is left entirely to the accompaniment to provide, which it does with the readiest resourcefulness. The scherzo proper is, of course, repeated.

Allegro ma non troppo.—The final rondo has a principal subject which will at once show that this must have been the movement which led Cranz to call the sonata a "pastoral" work. [The bass, starting alone, is like a drone, but is given variety by an upbeat to each pedal tone. The rhythm is 6/8. The right hand comes in on the eighth-note upbeat to the third measure with a simple eighth-note melody which is given significance by its syncopated opening and by the harmonies in the inner voice. That melody] has continuing figures [of short one-bar phrases always starting on the upbeat and always jumping up to the same high note (the dominant) at the end of each phrase. A repetition of these phrases is varied by adding groups of three sixteenth notes to the motion.] A series of arpeggios, which deliberately withholds any thematic interest for a moment, leads to the first episode, also of a distinctly bucolic nature and [immediately] varied in much the same way as [before—by adding groups of three sixteenth notes to the melodic outline].

Brilliant broken octave passages lead to the first restatement of the main theme, now slightly modified by a new embroidery. To this succeeds another long episode, or rather an episodic group of three distinct incidents, which make for variety at once of tune and of key. The connecting octaves are then used again, but in a reversed form and followed by descending scales which had not previously appeared. These are arrested on the dominant and bring back the theme a second time, with the embroidery amplified a little. The arpeggios are then used to lead to a return of the first episode, now in the principal key, and again the broken octaves follow, leading to G major this time.

The coda opens in that key, with the bass of the main theme, deprived of its melody, but with syncopated chords added [in the right hand]. A delightful harmonic transition takes us back, still with the same rhythmic beat, to the dominant of D major, in which the bass persists for some time while the treble at first strains back toward G major. The dominant-seventh chord is consolidated at last by a rising arpeggio, four times repeated with diminishing emphasis, to which succeeds, più allegro quasi presto, a short and dazzling peroration, still making use of the [opening bass pattern] and breaking up its melody into rapid [sixteenth-note] figures which to the eye obliterate its outline but still let the ear remain conscious of it. No art but music is capable of thus making things appear the same and yet not the same, and Beethoven is among the musicians who best understand the secret of such subtle transformations.
—ERIC BLOM (1)

XVI. SONATA No. 16 IN G, OPUS 31, No. 1
I. Allegro vivace; II. Adagio grazioso; III. Allegretto

First movement: after a dashing start, the main characteristic of the movement appears: the anticipation of the left hand by the right. The same pattern is repeated in F major. After the dominant, D major, has been reached, the pattern appears again in G, and modulates to F sharp, the dominant of B, in which key the second subject is introduced. A short codetta with a melancholy alternation of major and minor is reminiscent of Schubert. The development and recapitulation are normal; the extended coda is particularly charming. Its humor and delightful little surprises show us clearly just how Beethoven wished the whole movement to be conceived. Beethoven maintained his sense of humor, though it sometimes took a rather grim turn, to the very end.

It is doubtful whether the *piano* at the beginning of the movement is correct. I play it forte; at any rate, Beethoven wanted the third bar to be a contrast, as is shown by his direction *piano*.

The second movement: Have you ever come across an old country-house in the middle of an old-world park with a murmuring fountain? When the great venetian blinds are opened the light floods into a world long since vanished—a world of faded carpets, furniture of all periods, with an old spinet and a smell of withered rose-leaves. The atmosphere of such an old house fills one with nostalgia for a past in which there was still time to exchange sweet secrets with the flowers and listen to bird-song at eventide.

This is the kind of feeling I get in the second movement, with its ornaments, trills and its *adagio grazioso*—may Beethoven not have been looking back to the past quite deliberately for once? The form is A B A, A being in three sections. B, with its [sixteenth-note] staccatos, introduces rather more movement. It is important to play the ornaments of the main subject very fluently and without too strict a metrical division, while the bass keeps to strict time. When the opening theme, which is reminiscent of Haydn's *Mit Würd' und Hoheit angetan*, appears in the bass it must be played softly and transparently, not clumsily.

The third movement is a cheerful rondo—the episodes are the D major section which flows along in triplets, and the section in the minor which is characterized by a series of modulations. The whole movement may be conceived as in sonata form with the contrapuntal passages in the flat keys being the development. In the coda, one must be careful not to take the bars marked adagio too slowly—all that the composer intended was an improvisatory freedom such as often occurs, later on, in Schubert.
—EDWIN FISCHER

When Beethoven wishes to give remoter keys important functions in the organization of continuous movements, these immediate juxtapositions will not be to the purpose, for their effect is to disjoin sections, not to emphasize continuity. It is true that the remoter keys establish themselves just because they are not directly related. You may dwell in a directly related key for a long time without becoming sure that it is not merely part of a melody that begins and ends in the tonic, and the only way to make the tonic sink out of sight is to harp upon the dominant of the new key with so much emphasis and accessory harmony that it becomes the enhanced dominant. One chord can no more make a remote key than one swallow can make a summer: the remote key must establish itself by displaying its own retinue of chords. But it can so establish itself without any preparation. It needs preparation only when we are to be convinced that it is not a detached episode but part of a continuous action. The dominant preparation—that is to say, preparation on its own dominant—remains the simplest and most obvious kind. If the composer is handling his new resources as paradoxes to be put forward in a provocative manner, he may establish his remote key in quite a short passage of dominant preparation. Thus, in the G major Sonata, Opus 31, No. 1, twelve bars are all that he needs by way of dominant preparation from the first shock of the F major chord at the join of bar 53/54 until the B major second group begins in bar 66. Most of the rest of the group, by the way, is in B minor, the ordinary mediant; but this does not wipe out the impression made by the B major of its eight-bar main theme.

The clearest of all lessons in the development of Beethoven's style can be obtained by comparing the G major Sonata, Opus 31, No. 1, with the "Waldstein" Sonata, Opus 53, adding thereto the Andante in F, which at first belonged to the "Waldstein" Sonata, but for excellent reasons was extruded from it and published separately. In the "Waldstein" Sonata, Beethoven's wider range of key is no longer either a paradox or an affair to be confined to display in sections. Not only in the choice of the mediant major for the second group, but also in the bold harmonic lay-out of the opening, the "Waldstein" Sonata develops the harmonic idea of Opus 31, No. 1. Moreover, Opus 31, No. 1, has a slow movement which is definitely reactionary in its florid elegance; and the sonata ends with a graceful and brilliant rondo of which the coda pauses, rather rhetorically, to reflect, with the fatal consequence that it bursts into a *fou rire* and ends the sonata as a joke. Tastes may differ whether the whole result is convincing. If you can really enjoy the company of that provocative young man, the first movement, for nearly seven minutes, you will need all your politeness to save yourself from a yawn while you give your attention for ten minutes to that dear old lady the Adagio grazioso, who would certainly dread the irruption into her drawing-room of the young man with his muddy boots. All the same, there is good comedy in the contrast, though, on the small scale of sonata-time, ten minutes' restriction to grandmotherly company-manners is a high price to pay for it.

In the interesting and perhaps unconscious study for the "Waldstein" Sonata, the G major Sonata, Opus 31, No. 1, there is a highly organized quasi-fugal cadenza toward the end of the finale, bar 206 onward. As befits the style of the work, it fails to keep up its countenance, and relapses into excellent fooling *à la* Haydn, causing the pretty main theme to dress up its alternate phrases as a solemn adagio, and eventually running away with an uncontrollable attack of giggling.—DONALD FRANCIS TOVEY (1)

XVII. SONATA No. 17 IN D MINOR, OPUS 31, No. 2
I. Largo, Allegro; II. Adagio; III. Allegretto

The inquirer who asked Beethoven what his music "meant" usually received an answer according to his folly. Hence the yellowhammer with a compass of two octaves in the *Pastoral Symphony*, and hence the lack of time to finish the Sonata Opus 111 with a triumphant finale. There is more illumination in Beethoven's advice to "read Shakespear's *Tempest*" in connection with the D minor Sonata, though the two works have not a single course of events on any parallel lines and though each contains much that would be violently out of place in the other. But there is a mood that is common to both. Beethoven would never have posed as a Shakespeare-scholar; but neither would he have been misled by the fairy-tale element in Shakespeare's last plays into regarding them as consisting only of mellow sunset and milk of human kindness. With all the tragic power of its first movement the D minor Sonata is, like Prospero, almost as far beyond tragedy as it is beyond mere foul weather. It will do you no harm to think of Miranda at bars 31–38 of the slow movement; but people who want to identify Ariel and Caliban and the castaways, good and villainous, may as well confine their attention to the exploits of the Scarlet Pimpernel when the *Eroica* of the C minor Symphony is being played.—DONALD FRANCIS TOVEY (9)

In view of Beethoven's wonderful firmness of purpose in shaping his creative vision, the assumption is justified that the form of a Beethoven work will be "problematical" only so long as one fails to recognize, or misunderstands, the structural principle. Which fully justifies a new endeavor to fathom the much-discussed "problem" of the first movement of [the Sonata, Opus 31, No. 2] in order to discover the principle underlying this independent form; that is, to find a point of view wherein the "anomalies" remarked hitherto appear as the logical effect of a homogeneous structural principal.

Since the movement, in the total layout in sonata form, does not begin with a principal theme of ordinary structure but with the contraposition of two sharply contrasting motifs underlined by a change in tempo, which are to undergo a broader development later, at the first glance one obviously takes the opening Largo, Allegro part (along with its intensified repetition) for an introduction and assumes that the actual exposition starts at bar 21. Here, at the return of the tonic, a new allegro melody begins, which is developed from the largo motif and in so far as its shaping and its inner content are concerned, might well be taken for a "principal theme."

But this interpretation, which is also held by Leichtentritt,[1] proves to be untenable. It is chiefly invalidated by the fact that the presumably principal theme does not reappear in the recapitulation. The absence of the principal theme in the recapitulation would be just as incompatible with the sense of the "recapitulation" as with the idea of the "principal theme" according to the classical concept. For the "resumption" of the thematic idea of the exposition is not based on considerations of symmetry alone. Its real, structural significance rests rather on the changed relationship between the thematic parts, which—apart from the influence of the development—is the result of assimilating the tonality of material which was first introduced in contrasting keys.

For this very reason the part in question (from bar 21) cannot be the

[1] Hugo Leichtentritt, *Musical Form*, Cambridge, 1951.

principal theme.[1] Furthermore it also lacks one decisive characteristic of a principal theme. The principal theme of a Beethoven sonata movement regularly represents and circumscribes the principal key, no matter how extensive the scope of the tonality may be. But in this case it is a question of a pattern, the development of which leads in thematic elaboration from the principal key to the dominant of the dominant, that is, of a section having the typical structure of the usual transition from the first to the second theme.

The "problem" of the first movement of the D minor sonata becomes very much simpler the moment we see that the complex of the first six bars (in spite of the two-tempi structure, which is misleading at first glance) may well be a "theme." For as soon as we recognize the first statement of the Largo, Allegro as theme, we find a completely normal layout of the recapitulation. First of all it begins with the same "theme" as the exposition, which is then followed by the C major repetition of the largo (by dispensing with the second allegro answer). The theme thereby undergoes an intensification through the *recitative* growing out of the largo, as always happens with the themes in Beethoven's recapitulations one way or another. As far as form is concerned, this *recitative* and its pendant after the second largo are naturally no longer puzzling, since Riemann[2] recognized it as a constituent part embedded between the original members of the theme. After this partly expanded, partly curtailed, but unmistakable repetition of the *Hauptsatz* (as we may now call this part) the recapitulation does not perchance "skip" a substantial part of the exposition but, in keeping with the expositon, bring a "transition" leading to the *Seitensatz*. Since this part has to fulfill a different function in the third section of the sonata form than in the first (connecting two parts of a movement that are of identical rather than contrasting tonality), in the recapitulation it differs regularly from the exposition. However much we may marvel at an inventive power which here gives the recurrent "transition" an entirely new character, there is essentially nothing strange about this deviation from the corresponding portion of the exposition. Even a casual glance will show that in other respects the recapitulation then progresses in a thoroughly analogous manner. So it need only be mentioned for the sake of completeness.

This would prove first of all that no part of the movement ever breaks through the logic of the sonata idea or even deviates from the usual movement plan of the sonata form.

[1] Leichtentritt assumes that the principal theme has been "skipped" in the recapitulation "since it has been very thoroughly treated in the development section and if it were repeated again in the recapitulation it would lose its impressiveness." That means either that Beethoven is guilty of a structural error or that one supposes a treatment of form appropriate to the romantic mode of thinking but not to Beethoven's structural and compositional methods.

[2] Hugo Riemann, *Analyse der Beethoven Klaviersonaten mit historischen Notizen aesthetische und formaltechische Analyze*, Berlin, 1920.

The section that follows the "transition" like a "second theme"—which we must view as the thematic core of the *Seitensatz* (bars 42–55)— unmistakably derives its motivic characteristics (the upbeat eighth-note movement with feminine ending as well as tonal repetitions so characteristic of the melody) from the first allegro. Therefore even Marx recognized that the *Seitensatz* had its origin "in the *allegro* entering after the first and second *largos*." And the recent investigations of Eugen Schmitz have, in the same sense, led to the conclusion that the group of bars in question "is not original, but derivative."

If our analysis is to rest on a firm foundation, we must not fail to prove our claim regarding the origin of bars 42–55.

Unclarity or doubt with respect to the given relationship can only be due to the fact that the primordial form of the motif introduced in the first allegro does not reappear in the second theme. But does it not undergo a metamorphosis right after the second largo? No one will deny that these bars (8 ff.) represent an intensified resumption and further continuation of the first allegro. Furthermore, a sketch, cited by Nottebohm, which has the second allegro begin as an exact transposition of the first, confirms this analogy. If we now consider the nature of the change that takes place in the motif of the first allegro in the process of the harmonic and metrical expansion to the second largo, we then recognize that the deviation from the primordial form rests on augmentation and change of direction of the interval steps, whereby the note repetitions, which result originally from suspensions, now appear partly in the form of auxiliary notes and anticipations. But the same principle of the motivic development that operates in the second allegro (in itself "the most usual transformation of a motif because the least menacing as regards its recognition"[1]) leads logically from the motivic configuration of the second allegro to the motivic figures from which the "great period" of the second theme is formed. It is only necessary to compare the opening bars of the two passages to convince oneself of this. Thus the main portion of the *Seitensatz* is the result of a gradually progressive developmental process which extends not only to the motivic material itself but also to the metrical units formed therefrom (and increasing from step to step at that).

We must now learn to grasp the underlying sense of this peculiar structure. The first assumption is that the movement plan incorporates a structural idea of earlier days. Does not the motivic origin of the beginning of the *Seitensatz* remind one of the pre- and early-classical sonata form in which the first and second themes derive from a common root? The type of movement in question from the early period of the "classical sonata form" is directly characteristic of the change in style

[1] Hugo Riemann, *Grundriss der Kompositionslehre*, Leipzig, 1910.

which the two-theme principle (current later on) achieved only gradually as against the still popular idea of the "unity of the theme."

Such considerations raise a question that in turn resolves for us the structural idea of the first movement of the D minor sonata. Can the aforesaid portion of the *Seitensatz*, which is nothing but a new developmental stage of the first allegro idea, lay any claim whatever to the designation of a "second theme"? If a Philipp Emanuel Bach or a Haydn develops from the motivic material of the principal theme a theme expressly destined for the *Seitensatz*, then this refashioning of the material is apparently intended to provide a contrasting idea to the first theme, or at least something new, something different. But in Beethoven's D minor sonata there can be no question of such a relationship between the *Seitensatz* and the initial theme. Here the *Seitensatz* does not proceed from a transformation of thematic material for the sake of contrast, but from the further development of a thematic idea which in its original version is already effective as a contrasting principle. In this case the purpose of the *Seitensatz* is not to introduce a new factor of contrast, but *to carry out an already existing one*.[1] How could its themelike core—however much it may resemble a theme—be considered a new, second "theme" when it lacks not only motivic independence but also the property of contrasting with the theme from which it develops? While the real second theme of the classical sonata exposition is in the contrasting key, the presumable second theme in the first movement of the D minor sonata represents merely a fragment thereof—a gigantic dominant that awaits tonal completion. True, its last note brings it just within the range of the tonic, but how could this one quarter note, which is already the beginning of a new motivic section, be of any importance in the face of a fourteen-bar organ point that rivets the whole complex into the harmonic unity of a dominant?[2] And especially, since this dominant component of the key of the *Seitensatz* proceeds directly and unnoticeably from the modulatory section in such a way that the harmony attained from the main key, as dominant of the dominant, changes into a dominant of the contrasting key without intervention of the new tonic.

The mighty dominant block at the entry of the *Seitensatz* postulates a correspondingly broad establishment of the tonic; the tremendous piling up of the harmony demands a broad expansion of the tonality. But this supplement, which is harmonically and metrically necessary and rounds out the key, is effected with new material.

For this reason we could not simply call the motivic unified section

[1] Italics added by the editor.
[2] In a seemingly related case (the second theme of the first movement of the F minor sonata of Opus 2) the situation is really entirely different, since here the organ point already clears the way for a cadence in the first period.

(the special subject of our examination) a *Seitensatz*. We had to resort rather to more specialized designations. One will not do justice to this peculiar structure by trying to apply to it schematically the ordinary technical terminology.[1]

The second part of the exposition (calculated from the beginning of the organ point, bar 41) shows, it is true, two sections of different motivic material; but the harmonic progression disregards this structure (*Gliederung*). The second complex beginning with the tonic of A minor (bar 55)—thematically a unity of inseparable, interlocking, motivic members riveted together and growing one out of the other—is, as cadence, indissolubly connected with the first, the "pseudo second theme." It could be taken for an "epilogue" if, before its entry, a second theme were present, or if the *Seitensatz* were already completed as a unified whole, in the tonality sense. But the tonality of a *Seitensatz* only results from the union of the "pseudo closing group" and the "pseudo second theme." Therefore the sections *Seitensatz* and "closing group" are fused here into an inseparable unity.

The statement that the second part of the exposition contains no theme of its own, that the principal thematic idea of the *Seitensatz* neither plays the role of a contrasting "second" theme nor evidences in any way the formulation of a "theme," provides a definite answer to the earlier question as to the relationship existing between the antithesis Largo-Allegro and the movement as a whole. This answer, which removes every vestige of the "problematical" and lets the structural idea of the movement come out clearly and completely, can only be: the antithesis Largo-Allegro at the beginning of the movement is really "theme" and not (as it might seem before examining the *Seitensatz*) a questionable "first" theme, one half of which might belong to the *Hauptsatz* and the other half to the *Seitensatz*. But it is *the* theme pure and simple, the *only* theme of the entire movement.

In this one theme, the contrast, which we otherwise usually find in the relationship between the two themes, is anticipated *in nuce*. Therefore in accordance with the logic and economy of Beethoven's structural methods, it is neither necessary nor possible to introduce a second theme. The idea behind the further progress of the exposition is to develop the theme according to its individual nature, that is, to "intensify" the contrast presented at the beginning, to carry out the dualism of the theme. Beginning with a simple contraposing of the contrasting motifs within the narrow space of a six-bar theme, the "battle of two principles," which is the underlying idea of this highly dramatic composition, constantly increases in intensity and scope. In this respect the *Seitensatz* bears the same relationship to the "modulatory section" as the first and

[1] This is also true of the attempts of Riemann and Nagel to subdivide it, with contradictory results.

second allegro to the first and second largo. In the development section (note the triple statement of the largo motif), this thoroughgoing intensification principle reaches a climax (with the result that the conflict, which has been pressing for a decision, is finally decided: after the last onrush of the "largo motif," the presence of the "allegro motif" is only still revealed in the undulation of its accompanying figures). We have already spoken of the thoroughly regular treatment of the recapitulation as compared with the exposition.

According to a much quoted and commented statement by Czerny, Beethoven while at work on Sonata Opus 31 is supposed to have said that he "wanted to take a new path." If our interpretation of the form is convincing, then Beethoven's structural idea for the first movement of the D minor sonata is far more novel and simple, more daring and logical at the same time, than all the former analyses led one to suppose.—
LUDWIG MISCH

When the inexperienced composer fails in a slow movement, it is not so often because he tries to be learned and interesting; every critic has warned him against that. But nobody warns him against the fact that slowness takes time, which is the chief dimension of music, and so he is apt to proceed without the slightest notion of the physical size of his own ideas.

One of the best and most vivid illustrations on this point is accessible with a pianoforte and a volume of Beethoven's Pianoforte Sonatas, and I have often had occasion to quote it. In the Adagio of the D minor Sonata, Opus 31, No. 2, the main theme is a sixteen-bar, four-square melody closing into the seventeenth bar. With an elementary knowledge of those misleading terms "binary" and "ternary" form, the instructed reader recognizes the symmetry of this object at a glance, usually with the fatal result that, though he knows that it ought to be played very slowly, he does not imaginatively realize that at its proper tempo (M. about 96 to the [eighth]) it takes exactly a minute. He thinks of it as he might think of a letter-weight designed in the shape of the Great Pyramid. Macaulay knew better, for, though he was no art critic and is only once recorded to have recognized a tune, he did remark that absolute size was an important element in architecture, and illustrated this profound aesthetic observation by the Great Pyramid, for "what," said he, "could be more vile than a pyramid thirty feet high?" The Finale of the D minor Sonata is usually taken too fast. It is only marked *allegretto*, and a good tempo for it would be M. 72 to a bar. Thus, seventy-two bars of this *allegretto* will take exactly as long as that sixteen-bar affair in the slow movement. And just see where this brings you—nearly to the end of the exposition, after a course of events in which melodies have repeated their later portions in diminishing fragments, a broad transition has organized itself on a large scale, and we have had, expanded by emphatic repetitions, two of the three distinct themes of the second group. I have found that to some naïve listeners all this sounds actually shorter than the single main theme of the slow movement. This will happen if they enjoy a sense of muscular activity more than a sense of solemn contemplation. But to most people who think of music in terms of phrase-length the fact that seventy-two bars of this Finale are equal to sixteen of the slow movement comes as a complete surprise. Of course, we are not to suppose that the listener is meant to have a mere clock-sense of time identical for the slow movement and for the Finale. The art of the composer tells us "who time ambles withal, who time trots withal, who time gallops withal, and who he stands still withal." The opening of this slow movement would seem to be meant for those who time "stands still withal." But it has an august momentum of its own. The reader will see at a glance that that immense four-square, sixteen-bar paragraph is followed by shorter phrases; and, now that he has been duly warned of the danger of seeing musical facts at a glance instead of letting them take their time, he may be allowed to save his own time in this way. But now turn to the beautiful melody that constitutes the second group of the movement—the eight-bar tune in F major that consists of four bars repeating themselves with the difference that the first cadence is medial and is answered by a more final cadence overlapping into the next phrase (bars 31–38). Now, at the join of bar 34/35, the bass moves down to F through the three quavers A, B flat, G. Substitute for this, three quavers, C, A, F, leading down to the dominant C, and continue the melody, not with self-repetition, but with a parallel phrase beginning on the dominant. The mischief is already done. We know that we shall have to go round another musical quadrangle of the same size as the opening theme. We have lost our variety of proportion, and all other kinds of external beauty will be powerless to restore it. The form of the whole movement involves a recapitulation of both themes. Beethoven himself, when he came to recapitulate his first theme, adorned the third and fourth sides of its quadrangle with glorious festoons of arpeggio. Even these would still leave the recapitulation almost as disastrous after our sixteen-bar version of the second theme, and the recapitulation of the expanded second theme would be the worst disaster of all. Beethoven's self-repeated eight bars are as refreshing in their recapitulation as they were on their first appearance.

Now turn to the last six bars of the movement (108–113). Do not put any strain on your conscience by trying to believe that this is not an entirely new theme. Clever people may see some subtle connection between its curves and the ornamental details of the main theme, but it is a mistake to suppose that the logic of music consists in any such notions. The logic of these six bars is that they reveal the whole rhythmic scale of the movement by bringing us down to human proportions, [that they demonstrate to the listener] the vastness of the whole. Beethoven effects this with a new theme for two reasons. Perhaps his main reason (for he worked by thinking and sketching in music, not by theorizing in words) was that an absolutely new theme would be even more refreshing than Rudyard Kipling's early device of hinting at untold volumes by the phrase, "But that is another story"; but his practical reason is that he had no previous material that could be broken up into shorter units at all.— DONALD FRANCIS TOVEY (1)

Allegretto.—The finale is a practically unbroken *moto perpetuo* of [sixteenth notes, starting with an upbeat on the fourth sixteenth of a 3/8 bar, thus giving a feeling of a duple rhythm (6/16) instead of the intended triple[1] pulse. Harmonically, however, there is no doubt about the tonality of the first theme with its I-V-I emphasis in D minor]. The D minor flow, after turning into the dominant, reverts to the tonic through a Neapolitan inflection of E flat. When this has happened twice the figure [of the three sixteenth-note upbeat] of the first subject passes into the bass and the music turns, by way of C major, into A minor for the second subject, which by a cross-rhythm creates the momentary illusion that the 3/8 motion has been replaced by 2/8.[2]

A new concluding theme brings the exposition to a close in the key of the dominant (A minor), with a figure which again divides the bar into 2/8 groups. But Beethoven is careful here to mark accents on each first beat: he has already safeguarded himself against the danger of rhythmic monotony by relieving the continuous [movement in sixteenth notes] by [two] incidents of metrical ambiguity and is now content with a similar device in a much milder form. Four connecting bars lead to the repeat of the exposition, which includes the connecting passage at the end. This, by a diminished-seventh turn of a harmony, opens the working-out section, sustained wholly by the rhythmic life of [the opening theme,] and, although spun out for a very long time, full of an interest that is mainly modulatory, but depends also upon such variety as change of position, inversion, and density can impart to the unchanging figuration.

By way of an extended run of unaccompanied right-hand [sixteenth notes] the recapitulation is at last approached. It proceeds normally, though, of course, with the necessary change of key for the second subject's appearance in the tonic and the new transitional procedure which this involves. When [the mildly offbeat close of the concluding theme]

[1] Similar examples of this duple, triple ambiguity appear in the Scherzo of the String Quartet in B flat, Opus 18, No. 6 (1799–1800) and the piano piece "Für Elise," WoO 59 (*as late as* 1810!).—Editor.
[2] Still another rhythmical ambiguity entirely different but quite as subtle as the first.—Editor.

has been played again, this time in D minor, the connecting passage already heard at the end of the exposition paves the way for a long coda based on material that has by now become familiar. The whole concluding section is, in fact, an extension of the first-subject group, made structurally important by its persistent emphasis of the key of D minor.
—ERIC BLOM (1)

XVIII. SONATA No. 18 IN E FLAT, OPUS 31, No. 3
      I. Allegro; II. Scherzo (Allegretto vivace); III. Menuetto (Moderato e grazioso); IV. Presto con fuoco

Although the composition of the three Sonatas Opus 31 dates from 1802, the present work did not appear until three years later. It was published without opus number in the *Répertoire des Clavecinistes*, by Nägeli of Zürich, in which Nos. 1 and 2, G major and D minor, had already been issued in 1803.

With the exception of Opus 106 this is the last of the piano sonatas to contain more than three movements and quite the last to include a formal minuet. That movement, indeed, points back to the eighteenth century. On the other hand there is a scherzo which makes a daring departure from the usual 3–4 time and is in other ways the most unconventional section of this on the whole fairly sedate work. The greatest enterprise shown in it by Beethoven is seen not so much in his musical idiom, always excepting the scherzo, as in his curious array of four almost violently contrasted sections. What makes this contrast still more remarkable is that not one of the four movements goes at a slow pace.

Allegro.—The opening of the first movement is magical: "a wonderful soft call to attention—as if the Evening Star tapped on the casement," to quote Marion Scott. Beethoven, usually so fond of constructing symphony and sonata themes from the common chord, here begins in an ambiguous harmony, which clearly reveals itself as poised on the subdominant of E flat major only when the chords have glided chromatically into the dominant. The sforzando and pause [on the 6/4 chord in the sixth measure] go out of their way to emphasize that dominant, as though to make up for the initial indecision. On the other hand the tonic is hinted at only fleetingly [in the following two measures where an ornamented melody closes off the phrase in the tonic but continues after that chord is reached, transforming itself into a simple rising major scale in triplets. That] scale again leads to the subdominant position, with the falling motif [of the opening phrase] descending by octaves. After a second appearance of the [ornamented cadence melody] a tonic pedal asserts itself, without however establishing the actual tonic harmony (E flat major triad) much more firmly. The whole first-subject group, in fact, fights curiously shy of it. The entire exposition, it might be said, is not so much *in* E flat major as *roundabout* E flat major, which is not to imply that Beethoven is undecided about the use of keys, but on the contrary that his grasp of the distribution of tonality allows him to play with them in exceedingly subtle and varied ways.

A transition produces interesting developments of [the falling fifths and the repeated chords of the first six measures,] beginning with the falling figure in the minor and then cutting it out in order to modulate through [the repeated chords] to B flat major for the second subject. This is a treble melody with a long, lyrical flow interrupted by little stuttering figures. It is set over broken chords in the left hand which revert frankly to the eighteenth-century Alberti bass.

An interesting point arises in the passage which connects the first statement of the new subject with its more ornamental repetition. [The whole passage is a florid bravura display of fast notes (mostly sixteenth notes) running up and down the B flat major scale, seemingly at random. The first measure of this passage is of particular interest. Beethoven writes a group of four sixteenth notes covering the first beat of the measure, a sixteenth-note quintuplet covering the second beat, climaxed by a group of twelve (!) thirty-second notes in the third beat.] It is quite impossible to play the group of twelve notes on a single beat of so rapid a tempo, with the result that the third beat of this bar, provided that the passage is correctly played, inevitably becomes retarded. Pianists who wish to keep up the pace at all costs may resort to the expedient of distributing the whole twenty-one notes more evenly over the bar, in which case it becomes just possible to fill it at the prescribed pace. But it is obvious that Beethoven could himself have so distributed them had he wished to do so, and therefore equally obvious that he meant the twelve [thirty-second notes] to take up the third beat only. And if this cannot be done without retarding that beat, it follows that he wanted it retarded. In other words, he forces the player to make a particular rhetorical point without seeing the necessity of insisting upon it by any specific direction, since it is bound to produce itself automatically if the performer plays what is written. If there is anything wrong about Beethoven's notation, it is merely that, like other great composers, he was innocent enough to take it for granted that all pianists play what they see before them on paper.

The exposition closes with an ingenious expansion of the cadence that concludes the second subject, a longish ornamental passage with an extended [trill] in the right hand and a short new melody so constructed as to melt easily into the opening figure of the first-subject group. Thus the exposition is repeated without any apparent break in the musical continuity. In the same way the composer approaches the working-out section, which begins with the first two bars of [the opening theme, the falling fifths]. The section which now follows is literally a working-out. Every scrap of it is derived from the material that has gone before, mainly from the first-subject group, but also from the auxiliary material used to round off the exposition.

After a normal recapitulation there is a coda, short but laden with significance. The chief strains of the first subject make up the bulk of it, but one of the subsidiary motifs of the group, alternating in the player's two hands, supplies the concluding bars.—ERIC BLOM (1)

If the main theme should happen to begin with some other chord than that of the tonic, there will always be a dramatic subtlety in its return, for the composer is unlikely to lose the opportunity of preparing a return to the chord itself, without telling us too much about its key. At all events, one can hardly imagine a composer showing so little sense of his opportunities as to prepare for an ordinary return to the home tonic with the purpose of closing therein and starting again. Thus, for instance, in the E flat Sonata, Opus 31, No. 3, the first chord of the main theme is that known as an added sixth: a very good name, inasmuch as, if you take a triad upon the subdominant and add a sixth to it, this chord will result. When theorists tell us that it is really a chord of the dominant eleventh which has happened to omit the dominant and the third they are evidently saying "the thing that is not," especially at the opening of this sonata, where the whole point is that the bass starts on the subdominant and gradually moves up toward the dominant. The chord is this or that, according to the way in which it happens. Why should it not be a chord of the added fifth—that is to say, a sixth into which a fifth has crept? That is what happens at the end of the development. Beethoven finds himself on a sixth in the key of F minor. Its top note happens to be the right note for the main theme. Beethoven plays about with the chord, sings the figure of the theme on it, and, at the third bar of the recapitulation thus begun, inserts the missing fifth.—DONALD FRANCIS TOVEY (1)

Allegretto vivace.—Nobody would have dreamed of calling this movement a scherzo if Beethoven had not explicitly done so. Such labels in music stick to particular forms, irrespective of mood; a scherzo is expected to be in triple time and to have a contrasting trio. As this piece is in 2–4 time and in sonata form, it could not have mattered to pundits that it has all the characteristics of a typically Beethovenian scherzo except the formal ones: they would not have dared to give it the composer's own title, and we ought therefore to be glad that he, perhaps foreseeing their difficulty, did so himself.

The principal subject might be an amiable rondo theme, if it were not for those cross-accents off the second beat which give the impression of "crossness" in another sense. The strongly rhythmic rappings in octave unison which follow soon after are positively sinister. The whole dynamic scheme of the scherzo should be carefully noticed, for it is that rather than the melodic formation of the themes which gives it such a restless character. Harmony, however, also has a good deal to do with it. The sudden outburst of F major, like the crack of a whip, where the transition to the second subject begins, as well as the dominant minor ninths which delay its appearance, are quite in keeping with the irascible mood in which this piece seems to have been written. The second subject itself, in E flat major, tries to be more amiable, but is too jumpy and too short quite to achieve such a contrast.

The working-out manipulates the main theme in new keys (F major, C major) and also makes use of the minor-ninth preparation. Toward the end it goes off into little flickering, nonthematic figures, like angry flashes of distant summer lightning, and by way of descending *staccato* scales approaches the recapitulation, which shows the usual redistribution of keys. There is a very brief coda, ingeniously made from a perfectly natural continuation of the second subject and humorously clinched by bare dominant and tonic octaves.—ERIC BLOM (1)

Menuetto: Moderato e grazioso.—Those who attach the wrong kind of importance to the function of thematic figure-work in the "logical development" of music may learn a useful lesson from this movement. As Sir Henry Hadow pointed out long ago, the melody of this minuet is remarkable for taking beautiful shape without clearly recapitulating any of its figures. Self-repetition on the spot, as in bars 8–9, contributes nothing but its length to the symmetry of the whole; and the appoggiaturas that are distributed in a symmetrical way are little essential to that purpose [as will be shown in the da capo. Incidentally, Beethoven has written out the] da capo of the Minuet in full for two reasons: first [he] insists on both repeats; and secondly [he wishes] to prepare for a coda by the following slight but careful changes in the last bar. At the first time the [eighth-note] movement is stopped [in the bass]; at the second time a plain note replaces the original appoggiatura [in the treble] without making too abrupt a change of manner. The result draws attention to the second beat in the bass, which sets up a resultant rhythm of its own in the following coda. Apart from this, the main purport of the whole movement is the vivid contrast between a flowing melody and the melodic form of the trio built "logically" (more or less) out of detachable figures.

[In the coda, which we have pointed out has been so carefully yet subtly prepared by Beethoven], the pathetic ninth of bars 9–10 [of the Minuet] finds its yet more pathetic answer in two bars giving the same figure on the tonic with [the flattened supertonic]. The two bars are repeated and the second bar twice echoed, closing into two tonic bars, with the last melodic inflection spinning down to a final chord.—DONALD FRANCIS TOVEY (9)

Presto con fuoco.—It is owing to the finale that this sonata is sometimes called *La Chasse* or *Jagd-Sonate*; but fortunately this fancy name, which is at least as inappropriate to the work as a whole as "Moonlight" or "Pastoral" is to others, has not spread disastrously far. But however unsuited it may have been, there was no escaping it. Was there not 6/8 time? Was there not a theme like a hunting signal? And was not the favorite horn key of E flat major employed? All this coming together was too much for the conventionalists, who could scarcely be expected to come across even one of these features without thinking of the only sport that had so long provided a fashionable musical theme.

But let us abandon the chase and keep to music. The finale, which is again in sonata form, is a study in continuous rhythmic patterns, two of which are almost unceasingly used. The first, heard at the opening, is a figure of accompaniment [whose steady eighth-note motion is thrown off balance by the fact that it starts on the fifth eighth of the 6/8 bar, a decidedly weak beat. The ear does not completely adjust itself until the right-hand melody enters in the third bar with a distinct accent on the downbeat]. The second is the "horn" theme, if we like to call it so, made of broken sextolets in a saltarello rhythm. Bekker calls the movement "a kind of German tarantella," which is at any rate descriptive if ethnologically farfetched, and he too is unable to resist speaking of [the second rhythmic pattern] as "a simple hunting song." With this material and a third theme, the first-subject group scurries along. The accompaniment continues the even triplet motion when the chief strain of the second-subject group appears, which will be recognized by the much-repeated note of its opening. The rhythm of [the "horn" theme], which is also that of the third strain, reasserts itself in the rising and falling theme with which the exposition ends, with a pause on a dominant-seventh chord.

After the repeat the passage leading to that chord is restated in another key, thus bringing the music abruptly to G flat major. In that key [the "horn" theme] returns, and it is developed in the course of the working-out section with a new, forcible theme in descending octaves, again accompanied by triplets. Other interesting new applications of the thematic material follow, and the turn into the recapitulation is effected in a most unexpected and fascinating way. Only a broken triplet is left, many times repeated and gradually dying away. Then suddenly [the lop-sided accompaniment figure] bursts out again emphatically. The music is by no means recapitulated without further changes, though the modified themes appear in their proper places. The coda begins by scrapping all melodic features and leaving only accompanying figures. But it is the short melodic snatch [of the original right-hand figure] which is the chief character to bring down the curtain, and Beethoven shows an inexhaustible fertility and imagination in the handling of it.—ERIC BLOM (1)

XIX. SONATA No. 19 IN G MINOR, OPUS 49, No. 1
I. Andante; II. Rondo—Allegro

It was Beethoven's brother Caspar who sent the Opus 49 to the Bureau des Arts et d'Industrie for publication, and he did so without the composer's sanction. This meant trouble for him and annoyance for his famous brother, but, as Sir Donald Tovey suggests, good fortune for posterity, "as we might otherwise have been deprived of the two most beautiful sonatinas within the range of small hands and young players." This is by no means the first time that these two small works have been called sonatinas: they have often been published under that title, and the fact is that it fits them perfectly. They are easy music in a compressed sonata form. As a curiosity it may be noted that Beethoven in both cases restricted himself to two movements, an economy he did not practice again until he reached the sonatas of a later period, beginning with Opus 54.

Andante.—The structure of the first movement is extraordinarily simple —sonata form reduced to its elements. The exposition contains merely first- and second-subject groups, with scarcely any elaboration or extraneous incidents. The first subject is, of course, in the reigning key of G minor, [with an upbeat D leading to the B flat above as the all-important, key-implying downbeat of the first measure].

The second [subject group] appears in the relative major (B flat) [with a characteristic turn of sixteenth notes encompassing the dominant upbeat. The eighth-note] F is the implied thematic feature, which is seen to establish itself an octave higher. The exposition closes in B flat major and is repeated.

The working-out begins with a very simple but nonetheless ingenious use of [the second theme], modulating to E flat major, in which key some episodic material appears. But it is [that theme] which continues to dominate, although a definite connection with it is to be felt rather than traced in a bridge passage leading to the recapitulation.

This begins exactly like the exposition, except that the opening note after the upbeat is now D instead of B flat, this being the logical response to the leading C sharp that precedes it by way of a link. Even in so early a work Beethoven knew how to refine the organization of a movement by smoothing the corners round which the music turns from one division into the next. No less masterly is his new transition to the second-subject group, which has now to remain in the tonic key. He cunningly draws attention to this point of interest by varying not only the modulation but also the pianistic texture; the theme is transferred to the left hand and new figuration appears in the right. An almost dramatic cadence that traverses a chord of the diminished seventh opens a brief coda in which [the main theme] appears with gentle insistence in the bass, as though reluctant to be dismissed. But the right-hand figures dissolve themselves into a mere accompaniment, under which a low G pedal becomes fixed, and this very softly turns the music into an unexpected close in G major.

Allegro.—The finale is a rondo in the key which has been cleverly prepared by the close of the first movement. Having restricted himself to two movements, Beethoven obtains variety by casting the second in the tonic major; but, as we shall see in a moment, he is careful not to make the change too drastic. The chief subject [starts with a four eighth-note upbeat, unusual for a movement in 6/8 meter. The third and fourth measures contain a descending scale figure of six notes, appearing for the first of many times]. As soon as it has been fully stated, the composer remembers that this work was after all begun as a sonata in G minor, and he restores the balance by returning to that key for an episode that is approached by [a] connecting passage [whose flattened third and sixth steps imply the minor mode. This four-bar connecting passage] is the germ cell from which not only the G minor incident springs, but also the following [theme], in B flat major, which is later perceived to be in the nature of a second subject.

A modulating passage, still making use of the [descending scale figure of the opening theme, and the characteristic upbeat to the four-bar connecting passage], leads to a modified restatement of [the second theme]; then back to the first episode, and so to the return of the chief theme. There are some slight changes, including a more conspicuous use of the [descending scale] figure (canon and contrary motion), and then [the second theme] recurs in G major, thus revealing itself as a true second subject, restated, according to classical usage, in the fundamental key. Instead of going once again to the first episode, Beethoven dismisses it and lets [the opening theme] follow on immediately. After a pause on a dominant seventh, a short coda closes the movement with free allusions to the basic material.—ERIC BLOM (1)

XX. SONATA No. 20 IN G, OPUS 49, No. 2
   I. Allegro ma non troppo; II. Tempo di menuetto

Scholars are generally agreed that the minuet movement in the second
of the Opus 49 sonatas is earlier than the minuet, based on the same
melody, in the Septet, Opus 20, which was published in 1802. As Grove
gives the date of composition for the septet as "before 2nd April 1800,"
it is not easy to see why he should put 1802 as the latest possible date
for the sonatas. But a very similar theme occurs also in the slow movement of the Trio for Clarinet, Cello, and Piano, Opus 11, written in
1797, and if Bekker is right in considering that this too is later than
Opus 49, one may also accept his date for the sonatas (1796) as fairly
safe. What is certain is that they are by no means more mature in style
and manner than the first three piano sonatas, Opus 2, published that
year and known to have been composed in 1795. That Sir Donald Tovey
even goes so far as to regard Opus 49 as anterior to Opus 2 is shown
by a sentence in his *Companion to Beethoven's Pianoforte Sonatas*,
where he speaks of the Rondo of No. 1 as being "in a peculiar form,
only once partially adopted by Beethoven later on in the slow movement
of Opus 2 No. 3."

Allegro, ma non troppo.—It would seem at first sight that sonata form
could not be demonstrated more clearly than by the present example.
All redundancies and inessentials are dispensed with, and only the bare
elements of the traditional pattern retained in what is in reality a sonatina.
Yet it must be said that the demonstration would result rather in a
piece of evidence proving that Beethoven uses sonata form just as freely
as the exigencies of the moment dictate. He works logically according to
rules only so long as their modification does not seem expedient to him.
If it does, he will not hesitate to bend or even break them. Here, for
example, nothing could be more orthodox than his exposition and
working-out, for even if the latter is very brief, it is not unusually so
once we have accepted this work as a sonatina. But he does not scruple
to extend his recapitulation in a startlingly drastic way, having once
chosen to bring about the culmination of his third act, so to speak,
by the particular order in which he wishes his characters to reappear.

Here are his four chief actors, as it were. The first subject [is
characterized by the triplets in the second half of its first measure].
Its companion [is a series of broken chords in the right hand outlining the
harmonic scheme I-IV-I in the dominant key]. The second subject [is
conspicuously gentle, its smooth quarter-note melody being introduced by
an upbeat of three repeated eighth notes]. The companion of the second
subject [is more brilliant, commencing with a descending scale in triplets

answered two bars later by an ascending scale]. They will be seen entering in that order, accompanied by some minor figures added for the sake of conversational flow and picturesqueness. [The companion to the first subject] has the last word in the opening act—the exposition—which closes in D major.

The second act (working-out) is episodic and extremely short, a mere interlude with only a fleeting appearance of the second subject, and that in a costume which almost completely disguises it. In fourteen bars all is over, and the third act (recapitulation) is reached without a break, by a descending scale that overlaps into the opening [bars of the main theme]. This duly returns, but instead of being followed by its own attendant, this is very surprisingly displaced by that of the second subject, now in a C major mood. However, [the closing broken-chord companion to the first subject] follows as soon as the key has changed to G major, in which the second subject comes in last of all. But now the regular course of the first act is followed to the end, though one had expected that [the broken chord motive] would be allowed no further say. It does enter again, also in G major, which is now maintained to the end, though with some deceptive inflections tending toward C major. It is obvious now that [its] irregular intrusion was not intended to deprive it of its proper place later on, but to compensate for the surprising lack of events in the second act. It was simply an incident of development which by rights should have taken place in the working-out, but was delayed until the recapitulation was in full swing. It is thus that genius adjusts accepted forms to the inspiration of the moment without spoiling their symmetry. On the contrary, Beethoven here achieves a remarkable feat of formal balance by taking something away from his thickening of the plot in order to add it to his denouement.

Tempo di Menuetto.—This movement is so simple that to elucidate it would be to insist on the obvious, much as that famous sentence did in a certain Spanish conversation book: "Look, our postilion has been struck by lightning." Moreover, there is not even any lightning here: the music is exceedingly mild, and its beautiful shape is as clear to the ear as it could possibly be made to the understanding by analysis.

Instead of that, it will therefore be preferable to supply a brief comparison with the similar movement in the septet, a work scored for clarinet, bassoon, horn, violin, viola, cello, and double bass. It is in E flat major, a convenient key for wind instruments. The likeness of the two movements in question is confined to the first strain.

It will be seen—to begin with a small difference—that the melody in the septet version is made more incisive by double dots. Beethoven, it seems, wanted to make sure of a snappy rhythm where more lyrical instruments than the comparatively dry piano were to interpret this precise little movement. On the other hand he simplifies it formally there by merely marking a note-for-note repeat of this first strain, whereas in the piano version the restatements are not only treated differently, but intersected by an auxiliary idea of four bars.

After that the music takes an entirely different turn in the two pieces. In the septet the texture is finer, the part writing more sophisticated; in the sonata, on the other hand, the section that comes between the first and second complete statement of the principal theme is very much more extensive (27 bars as against 12). It seems to be a sort of multiplication of the four-bar incident already mentioned, everything being proportionately enlarged. To continue the analogy, the septet movement may be said to be built up only by addition.

The fact is that in the sonata the material is dealt with as in a rondo, not a minuet proper, as it is in the septet. There we have a well-developed trio, which incidentally gives brilliant opportunities to clarinet and horn, whereas a section in the subdominant (C) major, which appears in the sonata as though it were in the nature of a trio, proves to be simply a second rondo episode. For, unlike the septet version, the keyboard piece does not revert to the first section by a da capo repeat: the opening strain is written out again in full, with the addition of a coda. This was not the classic way of dealing with the simple dance forms inherited from the suite. It is true that Beethoven was often given to a minuet-scherzo type that did restate the first section exactly as played and was rounded off by a freshly devised coda (e.g., Sonata, Opus 10, No. 2, where, after the trio, we find the indication *scherzo da capo e poi la coda*); but where the feature of a coda is found together with a section that can be regarded as at most a rudimentary trio, as in this sonata, one must really decide for the rondo form, even if that too, with only two episodes of very unequal size, must be looked upon as elementary.— ERIC BLOM (1)

Piano Variations

I. 12 VARIATIONS ON THE MINUET A *la* Viganò, WoO 68

The 12 Variations on the Minuet A *la* Viganò, [are] notable for [the] freedom of resources and boldness of idea displayed in the variations, without being farfetched in any way. The canon in octaves in the twelfth variation is interesting and is good for practice.—HERBERT WES-TERBY

Variation XI.—This variation opens canonically, following the outlines of the theme quite closely. Only the rhythm is strictly imitated, and this breaks off at 3^3. When the imitation is resumed at 12^3, the effect is of three parts in *stretto*, though the music is confined to a play on the opening motif.

Variation XII, Bars 4^2–8^3, 12^2–16^2.—At 4^2 the music of this variation breaks into a short canon in octaves at two [beats'] distance. The two motifs used are the rising scale and the descending thirds, which are heard from the beginning of the variation. These motifs are of course heard in the Theme. Inspection shows that the canon, which begins at the octave, cannot be continued throughout at that interval because of consecutive fifths at $6^{2/3}$. The position is soon restored. In making this deviation Beethoven is able to use all the material of the first three bars of the variation.

At the resumption of the canon at 12^2, it is reduced to one crotchet's distance, with the upper part leading. Again, the canon is not kept at the octave throughout, as the music follows more closely the course of the Theme at this point.—JOHN V. COCKSHOOT

II. 9 VARIATIONS ON THE THEME *"Quant' è più bello,"* FROM THE OPERA *La Molinara,* BY GIOVANNI PAISIELLO, WoO 69

These variations are constructed on the principle of ornamentation of the original theme progressing from the simple to the more complex and showy. They were written in 1795 and dedicated to Prince Lichnowsky, Beethoven's patron, who was also the recipient of the dedications of such infinitely more ambitious works as the three trios, Opus 1, the *"Pathétique"* Sonata, the A flat Sonata, Opus 26, and the Second Symphony.

The only distinguishing feature about the theme is that its second strain is repeated. Beethoven in the variations takes advantage of this and instead of an exact repetition always alters the register, the ornamentation, or the accompaniment. In the fourth variation in minor, he even goes so far as to present that phrase in different keys, the first time in C major, the second time in A minor. There is some very supple chromatic writing in the melody as well as the harmony in that variation. There is some adroit canonic writing in Variation 6, and in the eighth variation some imitations foreshadowing the last movement of the First Symphony. The last variation is an extended Tempo di menuetto in which both strains of the theme are repeated and very brilliantly ornamented on their second appearance. The second phrase ending, of course, on the tonic, is followed abruptly by a short coda based on the main theme but starting in F sharp minor and proceeding through C sharp minor before its last forte appearance in the tonic (A major). The figurations get softer and softer and the piece ends pianissimo with a last allusion to the theme played by the right hand in the lowest register, crossing over the left hand, which plays the simple accompaniment.—THOMAS K. SCHERMAN

III. 6 VARIATIONS ON THE DUET *"Nel cor più non mi sento,"* FROM THE OPERA *La Molinara,* BY GIOVANNI PAISIELLO, WoO 70

Beethoven was seated in a box at the opera with a lady of whom he thought much at a performance of *La Molinara*.[1] When the familiar *"Nel cor più non mi sento"* was reached, the lady remarked that she had possessed some variations on the theme but had lost them.[2] In the same night Beethoven wrote the six variations on the melody and the next morning sent them to the lady with the inscription: "Variazioni, etc. Perduto par la—ritrovata par Luigi van Beethoven." They are so easy that Beethoven wished that she should be able to play them at sight.— FRANZ WEGELER

The simplicity of the piano writing is matched by the simple invention of the separate variations. The only noteworthy aspects are the supple chromatic harmonies in the minor variation (No. 4) and the flashy coda to No. 6, where the left hand crosses the right echoing wisps of the original theme, first in the low register and then in the high register.—Editor.

IV. 12 VARIATIONS ON A RUSSIAN DANCE, WoO 71

Beethoven's variations on the Russian dance from the ballet *Das Waldmädchen* (1796) are of interest for the manifold ways in which, in the course of the variations, the composer avoids the harmonic monotony of the continual oscillation of the theme between tonic and dominant. Obviously, this could be done only at the cost of the given course of modulation. But what took place here out of stringent necessity[3] later slipped into the inventory of the tools of the variation; and since Beethoven a thoroughgoing alteration of the modulatory sequence of the theme, on occasion, is no longer an uncommon formal principle of the variation form.[4]—OTTO KLAUWELL (TR. BY THOMAS K. SCHERMAN)

[1] In the second half of the year 1795.—Editor.
[2] Variations on the theme had also been composed by Abbe Gelinek, J. N. Hummel, and others.—Editor.
[3] Mozart provides an instance of a major alteration in the modulation, due to similar reasons, in the Variation VIII on "Come un agnello."
[4] Johannes Brahms once said to the author that where the theme modulated, the variations must modulate too, without however putting any constriction on the mode in which these modulations were derived from the theme.

V. 8 Variations on the Theme *"Une fièvre brûlante,"* from Grétry's
Opera *Richard, Coeur de Lion,* WoO 72

1798 is probably the date of the 8 Variations on the Theme *"Une
fièvre brûlante,"* be Grétry. They follow the Mozartean pattern on the
whole and would not call for special mention except for the fact that
in Variation 4 they contain a fine example of the new kind of variation,
in which mode, rhythm, melody, modulation, and tempo all take an equal
part in the re-forming process.—otto klauwell (tr. by thomas k. scherman)

VI. 10 Variations on the Theme *"La stessa, la stessissima,"* from the
Opera *Falstaff,* by Salieri, WoO 73
8 Variations on the Trio *"Tändeln und Scherzen,"* from the Opera
Soliman II, by Süssmayer, WoO 76

A new means of giving structure, one that was to be of importance
for the further development of the variation form, appears when we consider the F major Variations on Süssmayer's trio *"Tändeln und Scherzen"*
and the B flat major variations on Salieri's *"La stessa, la stessissima."*
Both these works were written in 1799 and their pattern of variation
does not rise above previous ideas, any more than the set just mentioned.
What makes them significant links in the chain of development of the
variation form is the principle, here first consistently carried out (neglecting some isolated earlier efforts), of a clearly arranged form of motion
running through all the variations. The individual variations do not
follow one another haphazard, but are members inserted according to a
plan into a definite pulsation of rising and falling movement. To attain
this goal, Beethoven changes the rhythm or the tempo, and frequently
both at the same time. It is true that no external proof can be brought
for the differences in the tempi of the various variations, since with
virtually no exceptions the composer has given no indications of changes
in tempi, but internal factors make it almost impossible to doubt their
existence, once the nature of the several numbers is considered with
care. The F major variations present a picture of heightened movement
from the flowing figures in sixteenths of the first variation through the
triplets in sixteenths of the second and the broken rhythm in thirty-
seconds of the third to the triplets in thirty-seconds of the fourth. From
this point on the movement slows down through the fifth and sixth
variations to the Molto adagio ed espressivo of the seventh, a tempo
expressly given by the composer, after which, in sudden contrast, comes
the bold entry, with a short fugato in 2/4 time, of the final variation

in Allegro vivace. Graphically, this movement would give the following image:

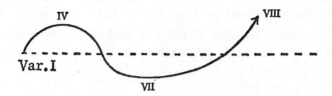

The B flat major variations have an essentially different development. After a similar rising trend at the beginning, there is a sudden reaction in the fifth variation. An equally sudden new upswing through the sixth and seventh leads to a second, but smaller, reaction in the eighth variation, from which the movement goes through a slight quickening in the ninth and then in the finale pursues its course unchanged in a moderate Allegretto, finally leading back to the initial tempo of the theme:

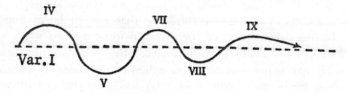

It is clear that such a planned grouping of the individual pieces could not but give the totality of the work a solid backbone and an interest going beyond the attractiveness of the process of variation, and that here one of the principal means has been found for realizing the organic connection among the several variations, something that had previously been lacking.

Further testimony concerning Beethoven's conception of the variation form as an organic whole is provided by the care taken in both the works in question to insure the external and internal continuation of the coda. It is true that in Mozart we already [find] the coda to have considerable extension; but on closer examination we see the absence of the inner connection and logical structure, which this composer does not seem even to have aimed at. Clearly, Mozart envisaged the coda only as the virtuoso peak of the whole work, and so treated it in the same way as what are called the cadenzas in the concerti. Almost never is the six-four chord of tension absent, with its fermata, nor the brilliant passage and stereotyped closing trill, while the development of the theme recedes into the background. Beethoven, on the contrary, in the concluding portions of his variations, as in those of his sonata movements, sought to make room for a new development and continuation of his themes in order to bring the tone organism evoked out of the theme to a fully satisfying conclusion, at pleasing length and in a freer form liberated from previous constraints on the variation procedure. The coda of the F major variations begins with a fugato on the first four bars of the theme, quite unaltered melodically but rhythmically entirely changed; to this, after an organ point on the dominant, a free version of the motifs of its second part is annexed. The keys of A flat major, B major, D major, D minor, B flat major, and G minor are traversed in natural flow, followed by a return to the original F major, which is maintained for some time; then come some measures in adagio tempo, in which we recognize once more a free rhythmic reworking of the four last bars of the theme. In other words, the coda is itself a variation, in a much broadened sense. The beginning, middle, and end of the theme form the beginning, middle, and end of the coda; only, the frontiers of the theme are expanded outward, and its various parts are used for long free developments. With this in mind, Beethoven entitled the coda Variation VIII, thereby solving the problem that had not been faced up to before him, the problem of bringing a set of variations not so much to an external end as to a termination arising out of its own internal motive force, while still remaining within the framework of the form laid down once and for all as the basis. The concluding number of the B flat major variations is still more demonstrative of the final character; actually, it is a group of variations whose several parts are interconnected by flowing passages, sometimes strongly modulating, concluding with a reminiscent fragment of the theme in its original form.—OTTO KLAUWELL (TR. BY THOMAS K. SCHERMAN)

Variation VIII of WoO 76.—This variation opens in the style of a fugue and for a little way continues as one. It is for three voices, and the Subject follows the theme quite closely. The first bar is converted into a syncopation, possibly a development of the opening of Variation VII. The rhythm of 2 reverses that of bar 2 of the Theme, so that the [sixteenth notes] come at the end. The [eighth notes] in 3 derive clearly from the Theme and 4 acts as a codetta. The three principal bars of the Subject are thus given different rhythms.

A tonal Answer enters in the alto at 5, but Beethoven cleverly avoids introducing the E flat at 7^1, which would have given too much weight to the key of B flat, and made the return to F for the third entry more difficult. One must assume that the "mistakes" in the Answer result from a deliberate subordination of it to the needs of the soprano, because 15 and 18 show that Beethoven knew the correct form of the Answer.

Consecutive sixths between the upper parts in 11 ff. foreshadow the nature of this fugato which is not highly contrapuntal. The bass uses the last part of the Subject in sequence through a short Episode leading to a short Middle Section at 16. Here the soprano has the Subject, which appears over a free bass, derived from 4.

In the Episode in 19 ff., the alto echoes the end of the Subject, followed by the soprano (21^2 f.), which elides a bar. This makes the cadential approach to the dominant pedal in 23 ff. more tidy. Over this pedal the upper parts alternate the rhythm of 1 f. in a recognizable melodic shape to 31, where the fugal writing ends.—JOHN V. COCKSHOOT

VII. 7 VARIATIONS ON THE QUARTET "Kind, willst du ruhig schlafen," FROM THE OPERA Das unterbrochene Opferfest, BY PETER WINTER, WoO 75

Winter's opera was produced in Vienna in 1796.[1] We may be sure that Beethoven did not choose this naïve theme *of forty-nine bars*[2] because he was particularly attracted by it, nor did he compose these pretty, cheerful, but for the most part insignificant variations just to please himself. No doubt he had an ulterior object in view—the replenishing of his purse, or the gratification of some friend or patron.[3] The fifth variation [with its double counterpoint] is the most important; and the seventh (Allegro, 3/4) with an [extended] coda (first in the same movement and tempo, afterwards in Allegro molto, 2/4 [where Beethoven alludes again to the original theme]) has its *beaux moments.*—FREDERICH NIECKS (2)

VIII. 6 EASY VARIATIONS ON AN ORIGINAL THEME, WoO 77

This work, composed about 1800,[4] was published in December 1801. The piece owes its success to the really charming theme [in 2/4, Andante quasi allegretto, starting with an upbeat of a half bar and consisting of two parallel eight-bar phrases, each repeated]. We may say that the variations derive thence their sweetness and gracefulness, which are inherited qualities. Do not look for learned ingenuities or flashes of genius! All is plain sailing in the smooth waters of melodic decorativeness. These variations conjure up for us the golden age of childhood, with its simple and innocent pleasures.

[1] It was repeated many times during the following seasons, six times in the year 1799, the year of Beethoven's variations.—Editor.
[2] Italics by the editor.
[3] There is no dedication.—Editor.
[4] It was composed at the same time as the Sonata, Opus 22, and a working sketch appears next to sketches for the finale of the String Quartet, Opus 18, No. 2.—Editor.

The most interesting variation is perhaps the fourth, with its threatening gloom in the first part, and the brightening view in the second. We must call truly delightful the coda with its variously turned snatches from the theme.[1]—FREDERICH NIECKS (2)

IX. 7 VARIATIONS ON AN ORIGINAL THEME (IN F), OPUS 34

If we survey the variations written by Beethoven after 1800, we note among them several in which he relapses into the earlier external variation manner, despite the deepening of the form that he had achieved in the meantime. Obviously, Beethoven himself was aware of the difference in worth between this sort of work and those created out of an inner urge; it can be seen explicitly in a letter dated December 26, 1802, sent with two sets of variations done in the same year, Opus 34 and Opus 35, to the Leipzig firm of music publishers Breitkopf and Härtel. "Since these variations," he says, "differ considerably from my earlier ones, I have included them in the actual number of my larger musical works, instead of designating them with a number, and especially so since the themes are also by me." In point of fact, the considerable difference makes its characteristic appearance first in the 7 Variations in F major, Opus 34. Even the theme is an eloquent piece of evidence for this. If we disregard the unimportant Variations in G major (2/4 time), which were obviously written only for purposes of instruction, this is the first theme composed by the master himself; in contrast to the thin, often sketchy earlier themes, it has the form of a carefully developed broad three-part Adagio movement, most expressive in character and of great beauty. It was precisely the formal completeness and integration of this little movement, combined with its careful melodic, rhythmic, and harmonic development, affording complete aesthetic satisfaction, that would make it seem not too well suited to being the thematic basis of a set of variations; at least, it would not seem to create a need for being treated by varying it. This may have been Beethoven's reason for departing entirely from the more or less rigorous adherence to the theme that had previously been his practice and replacing it by a freedom of treatment that carried the variation process almost beyond the limits of its definition. In the first five of the seven variations we have a sequence of freely conceived fantasies, completely different in character from one another. And it is the individual independence of the characters of these pieces, combined with their unmistakable dependence on the theme, that, along with their absolute beauty, constitutes the tremendous charm of this set of variations, incomparable in its kind. A feature that is

[1] The supple three-voice writing with its florid inner voices of Variation V are also noteworthy.—Editor.

quite unique in the literature is the fact that here Beethoven felt that the independence of the content of each piece should be further supported from the outside, by choosing ever different keys, rhythms, and tempi. While Variation I is still close to the theme in tempo and rhythm, but almost ostentatiously leaves the former track by shifting to the key of D major, No. II is in B flat major, Allegro ma non troppo, 6/8; No. III in G major, Allegretto, 4/4; No. 4 in E flat major, Tempo di minuetto, 3/4; No. 5 in C minor, Marcia, 2/4. The key of C minor, which, as we see, is gradually reached in a series of thirds downwards, changes by a modulation to major into the dominant of the fundamental key of the theme and leads, by way of a six-measure transition, into Variation VI, once more in F major 6/8, which once again, and more clearly, exhibits similarity with the theme. Variation VII really does not deserve the name, since it is only the theme, which to be sure is richly ornamented. A cadenzalike run by the right hand on the basis of the tonic 6/4 chord and an expressive prolongation of the last bars of the theme close this uniquely beautiful work.—OTTO KLAUWELL (TR. BY THOMAS K. SCHERMAN)

X. 15 VARIATIONS AND FUGUE ON A THEME FROM *Prometheus*, OPUS 35

The Variations (Opus 35) are a very complete and perfect work, eminently characteristic of the pianoforte and marking an epoch in the history of the variation form. The finale of the Eroica is the finale of a symphony, and, while it contains the principal ideas of these earlier Variations and Fugue transformed into an orchestral style unusually rich and free even for Beethoven, it leaves an immense amount unsaid for which the Pianoforte Variations have abundant scope. The Variations are in the position of the epic poem with its almost unlimited room for description and rhetoric. The finale of the symphony has all the heightened and direct effect of drama, with all its stern practical and aesthetic necessity for compression and immediate action. The difference between the two works is thus no mere question of Beethoven's progress in musical thought. For instance, it is right for the symphonic finale to begin abruptly with an outburst in a foreign key; but it is right for the Pianoforte Variations as an independent work to begin simply with an introductory tonic chord, which, by the way, is in the same position as the first chords of the whole Eroica Symphony.

Then Beethoven proceeds to build up his work as in the symphonic finale, with the grotesque bare bass of his theme. Speaking strictly from the point of view of the work in itself, this absurd bass is the real theme, and Beethoven might perhaps have called it so if the fully harmonized tune had not existed years before in the Prometheus Ballet.

On the other hand, much of the point of this bare bass lies in its extreme grotesqueness, which in the second part amounts to a sheer practical joke; and even the counterpoints with which it is gradually clothed in the three sections marked à 2, à 3, à 4 (i.e. duet, trio, and quartet) are all of the nature of formulas; so that there is no doubt that when the Tune (which I spell with a capital T) sails in on the top with a dance-rhythm accompaniment it is what we have been waiting for all the time.

Now we come to the variations officially recognized as such.

Var. I ornaments the Tune with brilliant arabesques.

Var. II retains much of the outline of the Tune in still more brilliant passage writing.

Var. III. In Variation III only the harmonic scheme is preserved, and the bold pianoforte writing remarkably anticipates the keyboard technique of a later generation of pianists with whose tendencies Beethoven was by no means wholly in sympathy. On the strength of this variation a very plausible case might be made for Beethoven's claim to have invented some of the features of the virtuoso technique of Thalberg and even of Henselt.

Var. IV is a running étude for the left hand, very quiet.

Var. V is a graceful cantabile in the lightest open part writing, with much of the melody in the bass as well as on the surface.

Var. VI. In Variation VI the bass is abandoned and the Tune is ingeniously put into C minor by mere alteration of the harmonies without transposition. Just in the last two bars the harmony is screwed back again into the tonic so as to lead to

Var. VII, which is mostly in two-part canon in the octave. Like all Beethoven's canons, this is a humorously crude performance; but let no one be misled by some otherwise excellent authorities to suppose that it expresses nothing but an inability to handle the technique of such forms. It expresses the spirit of caricature in which an archaic form may most effectively enter into a work which is eminently brilliant and full of allusive wit. For this very reason there is now a call for a deeper note; and

Var. VIII begins quietly with one of the great romantic moments in this work.

Var. IX reacts from this in very brilliant and sonorous pianoforte style which can only fill one with astonishment that contemporaries should have thought even Weber, to say nothing of Hummel, Beethoven's equal in the treatment of the instrument.

Var. X is brilliant in another way, entirely pianissimo until the second part, where a harmonic stroke of genius lifts the whole conception to a higher intellectual plane, or rather shows the real nature of Beethoven's interest in brilliant technique. Throughout these variations, as also in the

Eroica finale, you may expect the beginning of the second part of the theme to be the place in which strange things may happen; and what happens here is that the pitch is suddenly screwed up from B flat to C flat.

Var. XI is graceful and playful with an entirely new melody (by the way, the original Tune has hardly been recognizable since Var. VI, except in very faint outline in Var. X; while the Bass has long refrained from obtruding itself at all). The second part of this 11th Variation again contains a beautiful harmonic feature, though not one which radically changes the key.

Var. XII is another interesting pianoforte étude in humorous dialogue between the right hand and the left; while Var. XIII brings the bravura aspect of the work to a very original climax with a device extremely troublesome to the player (so that, like almost all Beethoven's brilliancies, it has never been imitated since) but hilariously effective.

The natural reaction from this is the sad sobriety of Var. XIV, in the minor mode. The long-lost bass does duty as a tune with a new melody below it. In the repetitions the Bass resumes its proper position below, and another new melody is given above. When this variation has reached its despondent end, a melodious run leads back to the major mode, and Var. XV begins in extremely slow 6/8 time with a highly ornamental version of the Tune. Though nothing has been added to the framework, the Tune has become enormously expanded by the slow time [and intricate ornamentation]. The whole theme, stated in this style with repeats, lasts fully a couple of minutes and fills several pages. The ornamentation becomes more and more brilliant, especially in that musical blank check, the second part of the theme; until some listeners might almost think it an open question whether Beethoven is taking quite seriously these great ladies whom he is portraying with such a bold technique. But Beethoven is too great a portrait painter to be unsympathetic even in satire; and there is no fundamental change of tone when in the coda [starting at measure 31 of this variation] he reverts harmonically to the plaintive rewriting of his Tune in C minor (as in Var. VI) while transforming it rhythmically [so that] he gets the whole of the first part of the theme easily into the space of two bars. He hesitates for a long time on the dominant of this new key and strikes a solemn dramatic pause there.

Then the fugue begins quietly.[1] Although it is on quite different lines from the fugue passages in the Eroica finale, it foreshadows many salient features in the later work, being of course founded on the first four notes of the bass [followed by two measures of sixteenth notes which at once with the entrance of the second voice transform themselves into a regular countersubject]. It also brings, as in the Eroica finale, the first

[1] There is a brilliant analysis of the fugue of Opus 35 in J. V. Cockshoot's book *The Fugue in Beethoven's Piano Music*, Routledge and Kegan Paul, London, 1959. —Editor.

phrase of the Tune into effective combination, reversing its accents in just the same surprising way as in the later work. [Also, as in the Eroica, the first four notes of the theme are inverted.]

But, being exclusively a fugue, it has no room for those glorious episodes and complete variations which constitute half the bulk of the Eroica finale. However, it very clearly embodies the most glorious part of the whole scheme, in the culminating pause on the dominant followed by the final return of the Tune in slower time (andante) with its repeats varied and crowned with a last triumphant complete variation. After this the pianoforte work has little more to say. It concludes with the first notes of the Tune repeated in more and more rapid versions, like the last rotations of a spinning top. That is the way this great set of Pianoforte Variations ought to end.—DONALD FRANCIS TOVEY (7)

The significance of this work does not consist in any new principle of variation coming to light in it, but, in the magnitude of its plan, going beyond the bounds of the previously known variation form, and the exhaustive utilization of its thematic values. In both these directions together it is unmatched among the variations of Beethoven and his predecessors; in the second one alone, it is surpassed only by the master's later C minor and C major variations [1806].[1]—OTTO KLAUWELL (TR. BY THOMAS K. SCHERMAN)

Miscellaneous Compositions for Piano

I. 7 BAGATELLES, OPUS 33
   No. 1 in E flat major.—Andante grazioso, quasi allegretto
   No. 2 in C major.—Scherzo (Allegro) with two trios and a coda
   No. 3 in F major.—Allegretto with two trios and a coda
   No. 4 in A major.—Andante
   No. 5 in C major.—Allegro ma non troppo
   No. 6 in D major.—Allegretto quasi andante
   No. 7 in A flat major.—Presto

Inevitably the word "mere" goes with "bagatelle," and just as inevitably it seems a word singularly inept to use in connection with Beethoven. He called his bagatelles "Kleinigkeiten," which may be translated as "trivialities"; but since, in common usage, this carries with it

[1] WoO 80 and the "Diabelli" Variations, Opus 120 (1819–23), respectively.—Editor.

connotations unnecessarily derogatory, the literal rendering "little pieces" seems preferable. Since *"Kleinigkeiten"* seem incompatible with the stature of so mighty a master, an air of embarrassment and a posture of apology have sometimes characterized the attitude of some Beethoven admirers toward these works. Many of these little pieces are evidently quite lovely, and all of them evidently quite characteristically Beethoven.

The essence of the bagatelles lies in their brevity and in their variety, each bagatelle a facet of a complex personality. They are intimacies as unmonitored as a craftsman like Beethoven could allow them to be. As transient pieces, they traverse the vast ranges of his personality, recording indelibly the strange polarities of his tenderness and his rudeness, his fantasy and his gentleness, his irritation and his good humor. They are precious to the musician, for they are not only characteristically but also profoundly Beethoven.

Of the Bagatelles, Opus 33, those that have most struck the fancy of pianists are No. 2 in C major, a sweet and nicely pianistic Scherzo, with two trios and a coda; the lilting No. 3 in F major, which likewise has two trios and a coda,[1] and No. 6 in D, which Beethoven marked to be played "Con una certa espressione parlante"—"with a certain expression as if speaking."—ABRAHAM VEINUS

The Bagatelles, Opus 33, were published in 1802, and Beethoven had certainly by that time polished them to perfection. It is, therefore, unfortunate for their reputation that the autograph bears, in a scrawl indistinguishable from Beethoven's, the date 1783. At that date Beethoven could never have come within dreaming distance of their style, all the more because they are exactly the bagatelles that he calls them; but the underlying ideas very probably did date from 1783. They are full of precisely the kind of wit and fancy that children can originate and enjoy, and that men of genius can retain throughout their lives. One of the wittiest is No. 3, which begins with as straightforward a line as "Three children sliding on the ice."

[Think of all the F's in measures 5 to 8 as F naturals. The effect would naturally be] dull. Melodic modulations from a major tonic to its unchanged mediant or submediant have no very definite character. A modulation to the dominant would be commonplace, and therefore less dull to tastes who find dullness more dull when it is vague than when it is obvious; but the three children were sliding on the ice "all on a summer's day." [But with F sharps in bars 5 to 7, thereby creating a sudden and unexplained D major tonality,] you at once have an authentic word of power from Beethoven.

Note the way in which Beethoven returns to his key. He shows how

---

[1] See Tovey's interesting comments on No. 3.—Editor.

the summer's day originated. The F sharp merely changes to F natural, [in the tenor voice during measure 8,] and so we find ourselves at home.

The critic who values a work of art according to the number of epigrams it contains will despise the rest of this bagatelle for containing no other interesting harmonies at all, but the rest is exactly right. Beethoven's D major is not quite parallel to the "all on a summer's day" of the rhyme, for the rhyme is meant to be nonsense, and is continued with similar contradictions to the bitter end; but Beethoven's bright flash of D major is perfectly sensible, and the rest of the bagatelle very rightly shows no sense that anything shocking has happened.—DONALD FRANCIS TOVEY (1)

II. 2 RONDOS, OPUS 51

The two rondos, Opus 51, are founded on Mozartean themes, and it is only in the characteristic workmanship that we discern Beethoven's hand. Both are quite in the florid ornamented violin style. As is known, rondos have a chief theme which appears at least three times with intervening episodes. With Mozart and Beethoven the first episode assumes the more important form of a second subject in a contrasted key and at the close is often brought back into the tonic, as in a sonata. This happens in the rondo in G. The theme in both also gets more elaborate with repetition.

The main features of the Rondo in C are the unusual transposition of the theme into A flat and the later episode in the remote key of A flat.

In the Rondo in G it is the unusual allegretto episode in four sharps and altered rhythm which attracts our attention. Apart from these facts, the rondos are neither characteristic nor specially noteworthy.—HERBERT WESTERBY

III. "RAGE OVER THE LOST PENNY," OPUS 129[1]

It would be difficult to find anything merrier than this whim; I laughed heartily about it the other day when I played it over. But how amused was I when, playing it through for the second time, I read the following remark on its contents: "This capriccio, found among Beethoven's posthumous works, is entitled in the manuscript, 'Rage over the Lost Penny, Released in a Capriccio.'" It is the most amiable, harmless anger, similar to that felt when one cannot pull a shoe from off the foot and perspires and stamps while the shoe very phlegmatically looks up at

[1] According to Kinsky-Halm, this piano composition was composed between 1795 and 1798 but was not published until January 1828.—Editor.

its owner. Now I have you, Beethovians! I could be angry with you in quite another way when you gush with enthusiasm and cast your eyes to heaven and rave about Beethoven's freedom from earthliness, his transcendental flight from star to star. "Today I feel altogether unbuttoned," was his favorite expression when he was inwardly merry. And then he laughed like a lion and beat about him, for he was always untamable! "But with this capriccio I'll get you!" You will think it common, unworthy of a Beethoven, like the melody to *Freude, schöner Götterfunken* in the D minor Symphony; you will hide it far, far beneath the *Eroica!* And should we have a new renaissance of art—the genius of truth holding the balance with this comic capriccio on one side and ten of the newest pathetic overtures on the other—the overtures would rise as high as heaven. Young and old composers, there is one thing you may learn from it of which, above all things, it is necessary to remind you—Nature, Nature, Nature!—ROBERT SCHUMANN

Beethoven's *Rondo à Capriccio* for piano (better known as *The Rage over the Lost Penny*) has been popular for decades—the *pièce de résistance*, in fact, on the program of many a young pianist. But little attention has ever been paid to the fact that no autograph of it was known. The manuscript has recently turned up, not in the showcase of a public library or a museum, but more surprisingly as a personal possession treasured by the owner and a small circle of friends and connoisseurs.

The existence of the autograph was first disclosed in an article by Otto E. Albrecht.[1] The autograph is owned by Mrs. Eugene Allen Noble of Providence, R.I., to whom I am greatly indebted for letting me examine the precious manuscript.

The Noble manuscript reveals important facts previously unknown about the composition. A minute comparison between the autograph and the printed editions, which are all based on Anton Diabelli's first publication (1828), shows numerous discrepancies, such as the omission of whole measures, the supplying of accompaniments wherever missing, and false readings and misinterpretations of the musical text. Worst of all, Diabelli concealed the fact that the composition was unfinished, and deceived the public with the remark: "This *Capriccio*, which was found completed in L. v. Beethoven's estate, has in the manuscript the following title, *The Rage over the Lost Penny, Vented in a Caprice*."[2] All evidence proves beyond doubt that the Diabelli publication of the *Rondo à Capriccio* is an arrangement prepared after the composer's

[1] *Adventures and Discoveries of a Manuscript Hunter* in *The Musical Quarterly*, XXXI (1945), 495. Concerning this manuscript, Dr. Albrecht recorded little more than its existence.
[2] Footnote in the first edition.

death—moreover, an arrangement made by someone not painstaking enough to preserve Beethoven's intentions.

In addition, the autograph settles the problem of the date of the composition. Beethoven scholars, in heated controversies, assigned the work to various periods between the composer's youth and his last years, although a critical study of the form and style of the piece could by itself have answered that question perfectly well. Thanks to the newly discovered holograph, I find that the style of the handwriting as well as the sketches on its last page make possible a more exact dating. In fact, this question can be settled once and for all. The span of more than thirty years within which Beethoven scholars variously dated the composition can now be reduced to three.

The manuscript contains four single leaves, size 25×32 cm, which may have originally formed two double leaves. It is not unlikely that it was at one time part of a notebook, from which these leaves were torn. In its present state it is badly trimmed on the left-hand side and at the top of the pages. Because of the trimmed edges the leaves are loose, and are now held together by two stitched-in threads. Otherwise the autograph is well preserved. One of the leaves has the watermark "RFM" or possibly "RFA." Each page contains sixteen staves. Of the eight pages of the manuscript the *Rondo à Capriccio* itself is found on pages 2 to 7, while page 1 contains sketches for the Rondo and page 8 extraneous sketch material.

The ink shades range from a dark to a light brown, the lighter shades being perhaps caused by dipping the pen only when dry.[1] As a rule the main melodic line, obviously written first, appears more regularly in darker ink, whereas the accompaniment figures and later corrections have a fainter coloring. Most interesting is the correction—to be exact, the double version—of the last rondo return: the composer superimposed on the chordal variation of the theme in dark ink a figurated variation in fainter ink, unfortunately without making it clear which one of the two should be used.[2]

Apart from occasional blurs—due to ink spots or corrections by Beethoven—the handwriting offers comparatively little difficulty in reading. Much of the manuscript is so neatly written that some observers believed it a forgery. There is, however, no doubt that this is an authentic holograph of Beethoven, even though it is not signed by him.

The general appearance of the handwriting is convincing proof that the *Rondo à Capriccio* is a work of Beethoven's youth.[3] Here are all

[1] I am indebted to Mr. Robert Hill, a manuscript expert of the New York Public Library for this information.
[2] The way Beethoven crammed the sixteenth notes into too small a space lends support to the assumption that the figurated variation was the later version.
[3] Little research has been done on the changes Beethoven's handwriting underwent during his lifetime. Gustav Nottebohm, the greatest authority in this field, never

the peculiarities characteristic of his writing between his arrival in Vienna (1792) and the turn of the century. First, there is the way he marked the braces for the system: a double stroke through the two staves with little dashes pointing in opposite directions from the upper and lower staves. To my knowledge he discarded this habit of bracing the staves about 1800 and substituted a single line curling at the top and bottom.[1] Very characteristic, too, are the figures in the time signature, which are identical with those pointed out by Max Unger as samples of Beethoven's early writing.[2]

Other youthful idiosyncrasies appear—for example, his peculiar way of writing the clefs and flat and sharp signs. Most characteristic is the vigorous curve of the beams that connect eighth- and sixteenth-notes, particularly when the stems point upward; in the later years the beams became thinner and straighter. All these observations leave no doubt that the Noble manuscript stems from before 1800. On the other hand, it cannot have been written during his Bonn period, i.e. before 1792—as is obvious to anyone who has ever seen autographs, or reproductions of them, from that period.[3]

These conclusions regarding the time of composition are confirmed by an examination of the sketches on the last page. The material on this page—including, as it does, ideas related to the finale of the First Symphony and the first movement of the C major Piano Concerto—makes it possible to narrow down still further the period in which the work must have been written. Sketches with similar material[4] were published by Nottebohm[5] and J. S. Shedlock.[6]

---

published his observations in comprehensive form, although he gave important hints throughout his diverse writings. The best monograph on Beethoven's handwriting in general is Max Unger's *Beethovens Handschrift* (Vol. 4 of *Veröffenlichungen des Beethovenhauses in Bonn*, Bonn, 1926). I am confident that a detailed comparative study of the Beethoven autographs that are at present inaccessible, will facilitate a more exact dating of his works.

[1] *Cf.* the facsimile edition of the Piano Sonata Opus 26, published by E. Prieger, Bonn, 1895.

[2] Unger, *op. cit.,* p. 13.

[3] *Cf.* the facsimile pages of the *Ritterballett* in *Der Junge Beethoven* by Ludwig Schiedermair, Leipzig, 1925, between pp. 388–89, or those in *La Jeunesse de Beethoven* by J.-G. Prod'homme, Paris, 1927, between pp. 208–9.

[4] Other sketches of the same subject matter can be found in the famous Kofka *Notirungsbuch* (London British Museum, Add. 29,801), which contains on detached leaves—the fact that they are detached makes it difficult to draw conclusions regarding chronology—most interesting material pertaining to works written between 1785 and 1800. J. S. Shedlock gave a summary account of its contents (with numerous excerpts) in a series of articles published under the title *Beethoven's Sketch Books* in *The Musical Times*, Vols. XXXIII–XXXV (1892–94).

[5] Nottebohm, *Beethoven's Studien*, Leipzig and Winterthur, 1873, pp. 202–3; *Zweite Beethoveniana*, Leipzig, 1887, 228–29.

[6] *The Musical Times*, XXXIII (1892), 331. Since Nottebohm was the first to discover sketches with this material and since the Shedlock examples are mere supplements, I shall call all these sketches **Nottebohm Sketches**.

The Nottebohm sketches, showing attempts to formulate the symphonic theme with the initial run, were found on the same page with the most advanced counterpoint exercises written under the direction of Albrechtsberger. Since Beethoven stopped taking lessons with Albrechtsberger in the middle of 1795, these sketches cannot have been made after, nor much before, that date. The Noble manuscript, however, contains a plan for a whole movement based on the theme as already formulated in the Nottebohm sketches. Therefore, the Noble sketches must have been written after, or at the same time as, the Nottebohm sketches. This line of reasoning leads to the conclusion that the *Rondo à Capriccio* was written between 1795 and 1798.

Why did many Beethoven experts believe that the Rondo came from the composer's late period? Only the older writers considered it an early work. Of Beethoven's personal friends Carl Czerny alone mentioned it: in his memoirs[1] he called it a "Jugendarbeit." Wilhelm von Lenz never missed an occasion to speak of the Rondo in deprecatory terms: ". . . from the earliest period and without interest"; or ". . . as to style, if style there be, it belongs not quite to Beethoven's first, not quite to his second manner of composition."[2] Without commenting further on the work Adolf B. Marx said, ". . . from an early period."[3]

Curiously, all later writers insist that the piece is a work of Beethoven's maturity. Whereas Nottebohm and Thayer in their catalogues refused to date the composition, Hans von Bülow, their contemporary, stated flatly in 1872 that it came from Beethoven's "latest creative period."[4] Carried away by his enthusiasm for the piece, he saw in it certain style characteristics which he thought supported his argument, but which actually point unmistakably to an early phase in the composer's development. All Bülow's ammunition can be turned against him.

"The choice of the major mode of the relative minor key" in the third rondo episode, referred to by Bülow in support of his thesis, can be found in the first movement of Opus 10, No. 2, where a false reprise of the theme in D major precedes the recapitulation proper in F major. The harmonic shift from E major to E flat major before the last return of the rondo theme, considered by Bülow characteristic of Beethoven's late period, has its perfect counterpart in the last return of the rondo finale of Opus 7, with a rather romantic effect in both cases. "The independence of the several parts of these melodic and rhythmic imitations" can hardly have been much of a problem for a composer who had

---

[1] Czerny's Memoirs were published in the *Jahresberichte der Gesellschaft der Musikfreunde*, 1869–70.
[2] Wilhelm von Lenz, *Critischer Catalog sämmtlicher Werke Ludwig van Beethovens*, Hamburg, 1860, III, 301. Id. *Beethoven et ses trois styles*, St. Petersburg, 1852, p. 191.
[3] Adolf Bernhard Marx, *L. van Beethoven*, Berlin, 1863 (2nd ed.), II, 378.
[4] Hans von Bülow's edition of the Rondo in *Beethovens Werke für Pianoforte solo von op. 53 an*, Stuttgart, 1872, II, 222 ff.

gone through Albrechtsberger's course of strict counterpoint. As a matter of fact, there are examples of polyphonic writing in Beethoven's early works that are even more striking, such as the finale of Opus 10, No. 2.

Beethoven scholars have respected the awe-inspiring authority of the great pianist.

The inclination to place the Rondo in Beethoven's late period may be explained by its having been found in his estate; it was thus one of those posthumous works that are likely to be considered examples of a composer's most mature style. To be sure, the "proof" always rests on so-called "stylistic considerations," but it often turns out to be a rationalization of a point of view preconditioned by the very fact of posthumous publication.

We are quite well informed about the auction of Beethoven's effects on November 5 and 6, 1827. In a report in the *Allgemeine Musikalische Zeitung* (Leipzig)[1] its Vienna correspondent mentioned that most of the forty unknown works then auctioned stemmed from Beethoven's youth. He said in particular: "Herr Diabelli's partner bought, among other items, at a relatively high price Beethoven's last work . . . futhermore a solo caprice, and a rondo for piano and orchestra."

Music historians who studied the structure of the work were at a loss to account for its curious organization.[2] Maybe the title Beethoven gave it can throw some light on its peculiarity. The penciled inscription *Leichte Kaprice* was not its original title. It was an afterthought, probably added many years later, to judge by the handwriting. Beethoven's original title was *Alla ingharese. quasi un capriccio.*[3]

Alla ingharese stands for *Rondo all' ongarese,* one of the favorite forms of composition in the late eighteenth century. Haydn, Dittersdorf, Pleyel, and Hummel wrote pieces in the Hungarian gypsy fashion. The two best known are the finale of the pianoforte concerto in D (1784) and the finale of the G major Trio (1795), both by Haydn. Just at the time when the *Rondo à Capriccio* must have been written, Beethoven made several trips to Hungary. In 1794 he accompanied Haydn to Eszterháza. In 1796 he visited Pozsony (now Bratislava), then a Hungarian city. It is not accidental, then, that several Beethoven works of that period show Hungarian influence. The rondo finale of the C major Concerto is a perfect example, particularly the A minor episode.

Compared with this concerto, Beethoven's *Rondo à Capriccio* shows

---

[1] XXX (1828), cols. 27–30.
[2] Carl Pieper (*Musikalische Analyse,* Cologne, 1925, p. 157) considered it a "little sonata form." Rudolf von Tobel (*Die Formenwelt der Klassischen Instrumentalmusik,* Bern and Leipzig, 1938, p. 128) interpreted it in the light of a bona fide rondo. He even speaks of a fourth and fifth *couplet.*
[3] The word *ingharese,* of course, does not exist. Haydn's String Quartet Opus 33, No. 2, contains an *Allegretto alla zingarese.* Perhaps Beethoven fused *ongarese* with *zingarese* and thus came out with *ingharese.*

few Hungarian characteristics. But, curiously enough, it is related to Haydn's *Rondo all' ongarese*, the finale of the popular G major Trio of 1795, which did make use of original Hungarian dances. The figuration as well as the rhythmic distribution in the accompaniment is similar. The periodicity of phrases in both pieces follows the pattern of Hungarian dances, i.e. eight-measure phrases often dynamically contrasted by a regular alternation of *piano* and *forte*. True, such a contrast was not indicated by Beethoven, who gave no dynamic signs at all. But dynamic contrast is implied in the nature of the theme and also in its accompaniment, which Beethoven changed from three-note chords to four-note chords at two-bar intervals. Played with alternations of two measures *piano* and two measures *forte*, the theme sounds less monotonous and takes on a more Hungarian flavor.

The first part of the work (through m. 133 [125]) is modeled after the finale of Haydn's Trio.[1] Each of the episodes, like Haydn's, is made up of eight-measure periods, sometimes with repeat marks. Graph No. 1 shows a simplicity of structure that is rather rare in Beethoven.[2] He

Graph No. I[3]

			THEME (24)												24 [24] "fine"	
	A 8				A′ 8					A 8						
a	b	a	b′	a′	b	a′	c		a	b	a	b′				
	V		I		V					V		I				
G_____				e_____			V of G_____									

E MINOR EPISODE (16) ([8])			40 [32]		THEME (24)			64 [56]
[8]		8			A	A′	A	
	V	I	⟶ V of (G)		G	e	G	
e_____								

G MINOR EPISODE (24)			88 [80]		THEME (24)			112 [104]
‖: 8 :‖: 8 :‖ 8					A	A′	A	
	a b a b theme preparation					slightly varied		
g B♭	B♭ g	E♭ ⟶ V of (G)			G	e	G	

	E MAJOR EPISODE (21)		133 [125]	134 [126]
	‖: 8 :‖: 8 :‖		5 bridge	
	V	I		
		⟶ V of (G)		
E_____				

---

[1] The fact that Haydn's Trio was not written before 1795 may be additional evidence that Beethoven did not write his Rondo before 1795.

[2] The finale of the Trio for 2 Oboes and English Horn, Opus 87 (1794), has such a simple structure.

[3] Capital letters mean major mode, small letters minor mode.

obviously intended to write a simple *rondo all' ongarese* of the type of the Haydn Trio, or, for that matter, one even simpler; he went so far as to write *"fine"* at the end of the theme to save himself the trouble of writing out the last return.[1] One looks in vain for the *da capo* sign which would justify the *fine*; evidently Beethoven changed his mind.

Beginning with m. 134 [126], the piece ceases to be a simple rondo. Here the technique of composition changes completely. Instead of the originally intended *da capo* there is a new version of the theme which ushers in a long and elaborate development section constantly concerned with the initial motive. At the end of this development section (m. 259 [251]) Beethoven starts a second development section, as long and as elaborate as the first, again introduced by a variation of the theme. The formal relationship of the two developments can be seen in Graph No. II. Even the coda is another development, similarly introduced by a varied presentation of the theme, and this third development again concentrates on the initial motive.

GRAPH No. II

THEME(24) 157 [149]			FIRST DEVELOPMENT (102)						259 [251]
A	A'	A	12	20	22	10	24	6	8
new accompaniment			b developed	A A' $\frac{A}{2}$ theme in A♭	a developed	cadenza	A A' A theme in B♭ varied	a developed	cadenza
G	e	G	G——→A♭ f A♭ A♭——→V of—B♭ g B♭——→V of (G)——						

THEME(24) 283 [275]			SECOND DEVELOPMENT (94) [92]					377 [367]
A	A'	A	12	20	24	4	34 [32]	
	varied		b developed	free figuration	a developed	cadenza	$\frac{a}{2}$ developed	
							chromatic	
G	e	G	G——→ V of A♭ ——→V of (G)					

THEME (24) 401 [391]			DEVELOPMENTAL CODA (47)				448 [438]
A	A'	A	10	8	12	17	
	varied		A' developed	cadenza preparation based on $\frac{a}{2}$	cadenza $\frac{A}{2}$ in stretto	b over pedal point	
G	e	G	G				

[1] The only examples of *da capo* rondos I could find in Beethoven are the finales of two Duos for Clarinet and Bassoon which, although not dated, must be very early works.

The composition as a whole thus falls into two parts, the simple rondo and the development sections. Such a break in the piece probably gave Beethoven the idea of adding to the title *quasi un capriccio* in order to explain the second half. It looks as though he made the addition as an afterthought, when he saw how things were going with the piece. And this may account for the strange punctuation in the title: *Alla ingharese* is followed by a period.

Why did Beethoven think that *quasi un capriccio* would explain the curious construction of this composition? Obviously, there was no better name for such a free, informal structure; the term *capriccio* as well as *fantasia* had been used for centuries as a convenient title for any such experimental work.

Unlike the *Fantasias* of C. P. E. Bach, Beethoven's "capriccio," as well as Haydn's, was the proving ground for developmental experiments. The procedure of hounding a motive to death, found in all three developments (including the coda), obsessed Beethoven in most of his works of the later '90's. In his Opus 18, No. 1, Beethoven repeated the main motive of the first movement 104 times. In the first version of this movement he used it 130 times. This technique of making the most of a single musical idea by different lightings, by tossing it from one voice to another, by exhausting all its possibilities, was exactly the technique he later developed to such perfection in his Fifth Symphony. The second part of the *Rondo à Capriccio* was an early experimental study in this very technique.

By adding this study in developmental techniques to a piece originally designed as a simple rondo, Beethoven ended up with a hybrid which he hoped to justify in part by the title *Alla ingharese. quasi un capriccio.* But he must have been aware of the inconsistency in the form. That he intended at one time to revise it seems to be indicated by a set of sketches written on the front page of the Noble manuscript.

Apparently Beethoven realized that the *Rondo à Capriccio*, in the version of the Noble manuscript, was not beyond the stage of revision. But the sketches show changes only in details. Now there must have been some reason why Beethoven did not tackle the larger problem of working over the whole into a more convincing form, as he did in other instances, for example the above-mentioned string quartet Opus 18, No. 1. While he took pains to improve the quartet he never bothered to shape the Rondo into a more balanced form.

Why did Beethoven neglect to do so? I should like to offer a hypothesis to explain this seeming carelessness on his part. In the '90's Beethoven could not make a living out of his works alone. He had to earn a livelihood as a pianist, and soon became one of the outstanding pianists of his time. At first he achieved a reputation in the musical circles of Viennese aristocracy. He played at musicales in the homes of Baron van Swieten, Prince Lichnowsky, Court Councilor Klüpfell, and Baron Browne, before he gave public performances in 1795. After that he even made concert tours. Not everyone liked his playing, but all agreed that his improvisations surpassed those of all other pianists, including Mozart. The audiences were spellbound. Reports from the '90's are numerous and extravagant in their praise of his *"freie Phantasie."*

Carl Czerny, in his memoirs, has given more detailed information about these improvisations. He distinguished three types. Two of them, a "free variation form" and a "mixed genre—*à la potpourri*," he disposed of briefly. A third type, based on the "form of the first movement or rondo finale of a sonata," he discussed at some length:

After the introduction of a second theme [*Mittelmelodie*] in a related key, etc., Beethoven brought the first section to a close. In the second section he abandoned himself freely, using however the main motive all the time and in all sorts of combinations. In allegro movements the whole performance was enlivened by bravura passages which were even more difficult than those to be found in his printed works.

Most of this description fits our *Rondo à Capriccio* amazingly well. In the second part of the composition Beethoven does nothing but elaborate his main motive in exactly the fashion Czerny described. The "bravura passages" are there too in the cadenzas which, as they stand, are probably mere approximations of what Beethoven actually played. (Free improvisation of cadenzas was still at that time expected of any virtuoso pianist.) For Beethoven must have played this composition. He could not, however, play it as it stands; but it did serve as a useful framework. On the other hand, since it answers Czerny's description, it is logical to assume that we have here an example of Beethoven's improvisations.

If this is an improvisation—which, as such, would fit into Czerny's third category—why did Beethoven take the trouble to write it down at all? He once made a personal memorandum in a sketchbook: "Strictly speaking, you improvise only when you pay no attention to what you play. That is also the best and truest way to improvise in public—to abandon yourself to whatever comes into your head." Is this not an indirect admission that, whenever he could, Beethoven carefully planned his famed *freie Phantasien?* For when Beethoven writes "strictly speaking" (*eigentlich*), he usually implies that what follows should be done but isn't. The *Rondo à Capriccio* may have been a provisional notation on which he based improvisations.

Even the sketches afford more corroborative evidence for the hypothesis that Beethoven used the piece for improvisations. The alternate versions found in the sketches are not noticeable improvements, but may have been useful variants for *ex tempore* performances. One of the sketches, as a matter of fact, contains a modulatory plan with only the bass given. The rest was left perhaps to the inspiration of the moment.

As long as Beethoven was the acclaimed improviser-pianist he was not interested in getting the Rondo into shape for publication. Quite the contrary: he was probably interested in withholding it from publication. He even withheld finished piano compositions while he was making a living as a pianist, because he wanted to retain the sole rights of performance.

After he had arrived at a more mature style he became dissatisfied with compositions of the '90's. His anxiety about the first version of the quartet and his disparagement of the first and second piano concertos have already been mentioned. In the case of his song *Adelaïde*, he expressed himself even more strongly in a letter of 1800 to the poet, Friedrich von Matthison: "I send you the Adelaïde with diffidence. You yourself know what a change a few years produce in an artist who is constantly advancing. The greater the progress he makes in his art, the less do his older works satisfy him." His dislike for the Septet, Opus 20, led him to the devastating statement, "In those days I did not know how to compose."[1]

The *Rondo à Capriccio* cannot have pleased Beethoven after he attained maturity. The form must have seemed a misconstruction to him who, even in his earlier works, had shown such a keen sense of proportion and formal design. The style, a manifestation of his *Sturm und Drang* period, had become obsolete for the composer of the *Eroica* and the *Waldstein Sonata*. With so many greater tasks ahead of him Beethoven was no longer interested in the little rondo—the *"Leichte Kaprice"* as he later slightingly called it. For all we know, he even concealed its manuscript from the eyes of his later friends and kept it locked up in his drawer, where the administrators of his will found it. To succeeding generations *The Rage over the Lost Penny* has always had an immediate appeal as an effective, entertaining, and not too difficult show piece. It will undoubtedly continue to appear on programs— in a form, I hope, more faithful to the intentions of the composer.[2]
—ERICH HERTZMANN

IV. INTERMEZZO FOR PIANOFORTE IN C MINOR, WoO 52
   ALLEGRETTO FOR PIANOFORTE IN C, WoO 53

These two short pieces have their origin in 1797. The sketches are associated by Nottebohm with those of the Piano Sonata in C minor, Opus 10, No. 1, and from this he concludes (in his *Second Beethoveniana*,

---

[1] A remark Beethoven made to C. Potter in 1817.
[2] A new edition of the work based on the Noble manuscript has been prepared by Hertzmann and published by G. Schirmer in 1949.—Editor.

p. 31) that they were to be a part of that sonata. It is known that after that sonata was composed Beethoven wished to insert in it an Intermezzo in C major but never carried out that intention.

The intermezzo is a presto in 3/4 time, a true scherzo with a trio in C major. It has the impetuous abandon that characterizes the first and third movements of Opus 10, No. 1. It starts with four repeated G's and a low C in the bass answered by a short motive with eighth-note ornaments in the treble register (which is very much akin to a motive in the equally passionate scherzo of the F major sonata, Opus 10, No. 2, written around the same time). The scherzo is in two parts, each repeated. The first part, ending in E flat major, consciously develops the opening bass motive of the four repeated notes, overlapping ingenuously in the two-voice writing. The second half concentrates on the motive with the eighth-note ornament leading back from E flat through G minor to C minor, where the opening section is reprised. There is an ingenuous compositional device at this juncture. The right hand has a transitional passage of two measures leading scalewise down from G to C. However, before it arrives there the bass has already started its motive of the repeated notes, and the right hand arrives at the C just in time to announce its short answer. This is a very mature device and looks forward to some of the masterful voice writing in the Opus 18 quartets.

The trio is more lyrical in vein, being based on a legato descending scale in thirds later followed by an ascending scale in thirds in the treble hand played simultaneously with a descending scale also in thirds in the bass. This again anticipates the string-quartet writing.

The Allegretto in C major, WoO 53, is much shorter but equally facile in its voice writing. The trio seems to commence in A minor, but after a few measures reveals itself to be also in C major. It is characterized by a smooth running bass line in eighth notes. The second half starts out with bold octave jumps similar to those in the D major Sonata, Opus 10, No. 3. After the da capo of the first part of the allegretto there is a short coda which is remarkable in that it starts with the last four measures of the allegretto (including its syncopated cadence) but with its voices reversed—Beethoven had learned his exercises in double counterpoint with Albrechtsberger very well!—THOMAS K. SCHERMAN

V. 2 CADENZAS TO MOZART'S CONCERTO IN D MINOR, WoO 58

On March 31, 1795, Mozart's widow, Constanza, arranged a performance of *La Clemenza di Tito* at the Hofburgtheater in Vienna, in which her sister, Aloysia Lange, sang the role of Sextus. "After the first intermission," it stated in the announcement, "Herr Ludwig van Beethoven will play a piano concerto of Mozart's composition." Probably this was Beethoven's beloved D minor Concerto (K. 466), and both of the necessary cadenzas for it were composed by Beethoven for this occasion. At least this is implied in the announcement. Autographs pertaining to the writing out of these are presumed to be of a later time.—GEORG KINSKY (TR. BY THOMAS K. SCHERMAN)

The cadenza for the first movement surprisingly starts out immediately with the trill on the dominant instead of reserving it for the close. But by shifting the trill through three rising notes of the diminished seventh chord and moving the bass in contrary motion, Beethoven already establishes the key of E flat major. After a short development of the main subject of the movement, he shifts this to E flat minor and, by an enharmonic change, to the distant key of B major (C flat major). This is just the first few of myriad key surprises in this tightly packed cadenza. The second theme is treated first in B major, then in B minor. A further development of the opening theme commences in G minor and progresses to A major, which is first treated as a key in its own right and then as the dominant of D minor. The cadenza closes with brilliant sixteenth-note scales in octaves and an extended trill supported in the bass by the rising triplet figure which dominated the orchestra's first few measures.

The cadenza to the last movement is clever in its treatment of two germs from the first theme: the vehement rising arpeggio upbeat (the Mannheim rocket) and the more reposed quarter notes which follow it. He treats these, unlike Mozart, in counterpoint against each other. The harmonic scheme is not as bold as Beethoven's first-movement cadenza, sticking to closely related keys. But the closing extended trill (or trills) display a virtuosity justifying the young Beethoven's reputation as a brilliant keyboard artist as well as a master improviser. Trills on different notes, starting on A followed by the C sharp a sixth below, then the A followed by the D below, get progressively faster as the intervals decrease in size. There is a trill on each note of a rising chromatic scale. When the decisive penultimate note is reached, the trill is embellished by the arpeggio motive, then becomes a double trill, and finally reaches its climax as a three-voice trill.—Editor.

VI. ALLEMANDE IN A, WoO 81

This entire little piece is in its artistic content very modest but not without charm. Its subtleties will not be perceived if one makes the mistake of confusing Beethoven's allemandes with Bach's. Beethoven, as is well known, in the various different periods of his creative life, composed a whole series of allemandes (also known as "Deutsche Tänze" or just *"Deutsche"*) for orchestra, for piano and violin, and for piano alone. Beethoven's and Bach's allemandes have basically nothing in common except the name. Their stylistic origin is entirely different. The older allemandes, especially the musically highly developed piano allemandes of Bach, were "the last stylized form of an early German round dance that was reimported into Germany by a long detour through France and Italy." Paul Nettl (in his *"Zur Vorgeschichte des Tänzes,"* Hague, 1923) sketches the development of the new allemande:

"In the middle of the eighteenth century this dance, which originated in Southern Germany and was perfected by the simple country folk, was transformed into the counterdance, or *"Contratänze."* On its detour through France it became a community dance. From purely sociopsychological reasons, the "allemande," as it was called in France, gained such wide popularity (the couples all circling at the same time was something new and fascinating to a people newly elevated in the social structure) that a series of counterdances were developed out of it, each with its own individuality and named for its geographical origin, such as *"Tyrolienne," "Strassbourger," "Alsacienne,"* etc. At first, these dances were in the even meter of the bourée, subdivided into 3/8 or 6/8. They were not, however, transformed over into the final and exclusive 3/4 meter until the end of the century."

The new allemande (or *"Deutsche"*) is the immediate forerunner of the Viennese waltz. Beethoven's allemandes must be thought of in this context. Schindler once made the following interesting comment on Beethoven's dance compositions: "He even experimented in Austrian dance music; however, he added little of individuality to the typical ballroom music of the day." We must agree with Riemann that these comments concern mainly the earlier dances of Beethoven up to about the year 1795. The present A major allemande reveals a certain inclination toward elegance and sophistication, especially in the second half of the main section. One can see this also in the flexible bass line. (The *"Deutsche Tanz"* from the Ritterblitt [1790] and also for the majority of the "Six Deutsche for Piano and Violin" [1795] are much more solid and heavy in comparison.) The little A minor trio section of the allemande has an almost pantomimic quality. [It is characterized by sharply staccato eighth notes separated by two sixteenth notes.] The style of the new allemande can be heard throughout the work in the heavily accented upbeats.—ARNOLD SCHMITZ (TR. BY THOMAS K. SCHERMAN)

Compositions for Piano, Four-Hands

I. SONATA FOR PIANO, FOUR HANDS, OPUS 6

The little sonata for four hands in D, composed simply of an allegro molto and a rondo, resembles, according to Marx, the little sonatas for four hands in D and in B flat by Mozart, both in form and content. At least it is closer in spirit to those than to the Bonn sonatas. Published by Artaria in October 1797, it was probably composed just a little prior to that date. One notices from the beginning of the first part in 3/4 the "prophetic" rhythm of the Symphony in C minor, which recurs often at the reprise and recurs again in the last measures.— J.-G. PROD'HOMME (1) (TR. BY THOMAS K. SCHERMAN)

II. 3 MARCHES (C, E FLAT, D) FOR PIANO, FOUR HANDS, OPUS 45

An engagement which Beethoven had obtained from Count Browne[1] for Ries was one that gave the student leisure to pursue his studies, and he often came to Vienna and Heiligenstadt for that purpose. Two interesting anecdotes from Ries's *Notizen* (pp. 90–92) may be introduced here:

"Count Browne made a rather long sojourn about this time in Baden near Vienna, where I was called upon frequently to play Beethoven's music in the evening in the presence of enthusiastic Beethovenians, sometimes from notes, sometimes by heart. Here I had an opportunity to learn how in the majority of cases a *name* alone is sufficient to characterize everything in a composition as beautiful and excellent, or mediocre and bad. One day, weary of playing without notes, I improvised a march without a thought as to its merit or any ulterior purpose. An old countess who actually tormented Beethoven with her devotion went into ecstasies over it, thinking it was a new composition of his, which I, in order to make sport of her and the other enthusiasts, affirmed only too quickly. Unhappily Beethoven came to Baden the next day. He had scarcely entered Count Browne's room in the evening when the old countess began to speak of his most admirable and glorious march. Imagine my embarrassment! Knowing well that Beethoven could not tolerate the old countess, I hurriedly drew him aside and whispered to him that I had merely meant to make sport of her foolish-

---

[1] Count Johann Georg Browne, 1767–1827, a nobleman from an old Irish family, employed by Empress Catherine II of Russia, in her imperial service.—Editor.

ness. To my good fortune he accepted the explanation in good part, but my embarrassment grew when I was called upon to repeat the march, which turned out worse since Beethoven stood at my side. He was overwhelmed with praise on all sides and his genius lauded; he listening in a perturbed manner and with growing rage until he found relief in a roar of laughter. Later he remarked to me: 'You see, my dear Ries, those are the great cognoscenti, who wish to judge every composition so correctly and severely. Only give them the name of their favorite; they will need nothing more.'

"This march, however, led to one good result: Count Browne immediately commissioned Beethoven to compose three Marches for Pianoforte, four hands, which were dedicated to Princess Esterházy [Opus 45].

"Beethoven composed part of the second march while giving me a lesson on a sonata—a thing which still seems incomprehensible to me—which I had to play that evening in a little concert at the house of the count mentioned above. I was also to play the marches with him on the same occasion.

"While the latter was taking place, young Count P . . . , sitting in the doorway leading to the next room, spoke so loud and so continuously to a pretty woman that Beethoven, after several efforts had been made to secure quiet, suddenly took my hands from the keys in the middle of the music, jumped up and said very loudly, 'I will not play for such swine!'

"All efforts to get him to return to the pianoforte were in vain; he would not even allow me to play the sonata. So the music came to an end in the midst of a general ill humor."

According to Jahn's papers, the following came from Czerny: "In composing, Beethoven tested his pieces at the pianoforte until he found them to his liking, and sang the while. His voice in singing was hideous. It was thus that Czerny heard him at work on one of the four-hand marches while waiting in a side room."

In an unaddressed letter, presumably to Ries, Beethoven asked if "Count Browne had already given the two marches to be engraved." The first two were written together at this time, and Kinsky-Halm dates the third as completed in 1803. They were published all together as Opus 45 in 1804.—ALEXANDER WHEELOCK THAYER, EDITED BY ELLIOT FORBES

These three marches are surprisingly advanced for music composed for piano, four hands—they are no longer in the category of salon music to delight the spirits of two amateur pianists. These marches approach the seriousness of the Sonata in F for piano duet by Mozart and his two late fantasias, and the great compositions of Schubert such as the Grand Duo in C, the Hungarian Fantasy, and the F minor Fantasy.

They are symphonic in their conception, using many imitations in different registers of the piano and sudden dynamic changes reminding

*one of the differences in texture between tutti orchestral passages and
those for solo wind instruments. The harmonic scheme is also on a par
with the best works of Beethoven's middle period. Of particular note is
the canonic writing in the trio of the first march; the sudden shift from
E flat to D flat in the second march, the humorously accented bass in
its trio, like an allusion to the popular drum and cymbals in the militar-
musik of the period; the very adroit bridge from the B flat middle section
to the D major reprise of the main theme in the third march playing the
triplet descending scales in various registers of the paino against the dotted
rhythm of the main section; and finally the very advanced harmonic
structure of the trio of the third march.—Editor.*

III. 6 DUET VARIATIONS ON *"Ich denke dein,"* WoO 74

The Six Duet Variations on a song theme, *"Ich denke dein,"* are
unassuming, mostly melodic in style, and of no particular merit. Beethoven's duet works are indeed, as compared with Mozart and Clementi,
somewhat disappointing. It is apparent that he did not give serious
attention to this branch of the art.

Possibly the duets of Beethoven were more or less educational in intent
and sketched out at an early date.—HERBERT WESTERBY

Music for Voice with Piano Accompaniment

I. *"Adelaïde,"* OPUS 46

Of all the lieder of Beethoven, not one has been accorded more
contradictory verdicts than has the "Adelaïde." Between the appreciation
of Reichardt, who regards this famous song as nothing less than an image
of life, and that of Vincent d'Indy, to whom it is "merely one more
romance and nothing more," there is such disparity of opinion that we
should find it an extremely difficult task to discover which of the two is
right, were not the song itself available, successively extolled and repudiated
according to the fashion of the moment. In its ingenuousness, it has
for more than a century pleased or displeased according to circumstances
or waves of opinion, but in its humanity and truth it has equally overcome
the influence of time, and none can say that we do not experience its
surpassing beauty even now, as it was appreciated when it first appeared in
Vienna.

Besides—these are affirmations from which there is no escape after an interval of a century—the young Beethoven needed all the might of his genius and the illusion of an admiration which, after all, he shared with the times in which he lived, to feel moved to such a degree by so trifling a work as that of the too famous elegist Matthisson—and to find in it the wherewithal to feed the flame of his own inspiration. Nothing indeed, could be more tame than this short poem to which the musician must have devoted the whole of himself, producing a work of art far surpassing the inspiration of the poet:

Slowly wanders thy friend in lovely garden, Spangled o'er with glittering drops of dew, Which on every swelling rosebud tremble,
    Adelaïde, Adelaïde!

In the crystal stream, in Alpine snow, In the setting sun's departing ray, In the star brightly twinkling, Beams thine image.
    Adelaïde!

Leafy boughs in the evening wind are fluttering, May flowers whisper softly through the dell, Streamlets murmur, the nightingale complaineth,
    Adelaïde!

When I slumber beneath the silent grave, From my ashes a wondrous flower shall rise, Still revealing on every purple blossom,
    "Adelaïde! Adelaïde!"

Doubtless Matthisson labored under no self-delusion when he declared that no musician had improved upon his poetic effort as Beethoven had done, nor of the opinion of Beethoven himself, when he spoke of the "perfect happiness" which Matthisson's poetry had "always given" him and "would still give him."

Assuredly these were not simply polite phrases, and we feel certain that Beethoven was sincere in his appreciation. Still, we are left guessing how such poetry should come to deserve such a meed of admiration, and how much of himself was put into it by a creator who, however young, and, the acknowledged author of the early trios, appears to have devoted the best of his genius and his inspiration to this cantata, working at it and improving it again and again between the years 1795 and 1797!

Both text and music—especially the music—of "Adelaïde" are indebted for the success which permits us still to speak of it, to that element of tender though profound passion, which so vitally inspires it; it would be quite paradoxical for such a love song not to owe its original inspiration to some love crisis, especially as we are dealing with a Beethoven in whom the blended influences of life and inspiration were so manifest and whose entire work—pehaps for the first time in the history of modern music—offers so certain and so pathetic an element of autobiography.

What then is it that "Adelaïde" represents in this work of his, and with which circumstances of Beethoven's emotional life must it be connected?

Beethoven's early loves do not appear to have been less fruitful than his latter ones in the development of his genius and the inspiration of his work; it may be that she who inspired the "Adelaïde," if we can discover her, will enlighten us.

Beethoven, who was never without a love affair, met in Vienna, in 1794, the year when the first sketches of the "Adelaïde" appeared, the singer Magdalena Willmann, a comrade of his youthful years at Bonn, who, like himself, had belonged to the musical company of the Elector of Cologne, the Archduke Maximilian, and for whom he certainly, at the time, expressed the tenderest feelings. This young lady, of practically the same age as himself, and whom he had known at least during the latter years of his adolescence, was actually, in 1790, one of the most highly esteemed artists of his native town. It is certain that he was greatly moved by his somewhat unexpected meeting with her in Vienna. During the four years' interval, a transformation had taken place in the singer; her artistic progress had won for her a reputation extending beyond Bonn, and when Peter Winter, one of the impresarios of the time, had been summoned from Munich to Vienna to organize a carnival season of *opera-seria* and *opera-semi-seria,* he had engaged as prima donna Magdalena, who then left Bonn with the whole of her family, in July 1793. As a matter of fact, this unforeseen carnival season enabled her to obtain an immediate engagement at the Schikaneder Theatre in Vienna, where she sang on the following April 27 at the reprise of Umlauf's *Gilded Shoes,* a popular score to which Beethoven had just added a couple of airs,[1] one of them intended for his former comrade. What happened between the two artists? We are reduced to conjectures, yet conjectures, indeed, fairly evident.

Magdalena was a beautiful woman, of acknowledged artistic reputation. At Bonn, Beethoven must already have come under the sway of that voice "so wonderfully deep and of rarest charm," and of that remarkable presence which made of her—as her contemporary Gerber affirmed—"a lyric artist who left nothing to be desired." Beethoven was sufficient of a connoisseur to appreciate her at her worth. There is but little doubt that he was not blind to so many combined attractions and that his heart was not long in coming under the spell.

If we reflect that this meeting, and the intimacy—so easy in a theater —that must have followed, coincided rather exactly with the first at-

---

[1] An aria for tenor: "*O welch ein Leben! ein ganzes Meer*" (actually a strophic song) and an aria for soprano: "*Soll ein Schuh nicht drükken,*" which was written especially for the popular diva Anna Maria Weiss, who sang the title role in the first performances, but reworked for the revival in which Magdalena Willmann was the star. Both songs are grouped as WoO 91. (The tenor air turned up later as the melody which Beethoven used for the setting of Goethe's *Mailied.*)—Editor.

tempts at writing the "Adelaïde," then one of the circumstances casts
a singular light upon the other, and the role of Magdalena Willmann
both in the life and in the work of our composer is correspondingly
manifest; for this inspiration, owing its origin to a first great passion,
expands into a whole series of profound reverberations and controls an
entire period of his productive activity.

At this stage, in default of precise biographical documents, memoirs
or letters dealing with this period of his emotional life, we shall have
to rely upon the musician's work itself.

Begun a few months after the singer's arrival in Vienna, "Adelaïde"
occupied his mind during the whole of 1796, and was finished and
published only in February 1797. At the same time, Beethoven was
engaged upon that other melody, a posthumous publication entitled
Seufzer eines Ungeliebten, the second part of which, *Gegenliebe,* constitutes the first version of a theme which was to accompany him throughout his life, on to the final expression which he gave to it in the Chorus
of his Ninth Symphony: the theme of Joy. Is this a mere coincidence?
It seems very difficult to imagine that this dual inspiration, that of the
ineffable and sorrowful tenderness of the "Adelaïde," and that which
was about to convey to the World the revelation of his Joy, thus encountered each other by chance in his notebooks, and had no connection with the circumstances of his life.

Magdalena Willmann lived in Vienna with her father and a sister-
in-law. Beethoven must have had every facility for meeting her, both
at her home and at the theater. Deeply in love, the youth must have
indulged in dreams of a future marriage with the object of his affections.
After a period of unassuming tenderness, his heart secretly aflame with
a passion he may not have had the courage to declare, the lover one day
declared himself with a suddenness which must have startled her and
opened her eyes to the state of things. To the demand in marriage
of which she was the object, and which after all could not long be
postponed, the coquette in all probability did not immediately reply
by the scornful refusal of which, more than sixty years afterwards, her
sister spoke to Thayer, who states that Magdalena rejected the suit of
Beethoven "because he was too ugly and half demented." Without
discouraging him so outrageously, she must have kept him on tenterhooks for a considerable period—no doubt she had other ambitions than
the company of this poor little musician, of whose genius she had no
conception.

Nevertheless, in all probability, it was Magdalena who was the first
to sing "Adelaïde" in public. At a concert given on April 7, 1797, Magdalena Willmann sang an air of Beethoven, the exact title of which has
not been handed down, though it can scarcely have been any other
than the cantata which had appeared a few weeks previously; this,

moreover, proves that the young lady had not yet dismissed her inamorato, which she did less than two years afterwards, either directly or by the public announcement of her marriage in 1799 to a certain Galvani. She would appear to have been able to reconcile Beethoven, and the rejected composer, plunged back into the bitter solitude of a deceived resignation, must have found consolation in his art—and, perhaps, also soon afterwards, in a new love. Apparently, "Adelaïde" was forgotten.

Was this really so? On this point also Beethoven's work throws a singular and expressive light; it enables us to glimpse faintly the deep wound which veiled his renunciation, the regrets of frustrated love caused by the downfall of his hopes.

Though to all outward appearance he forgot his trouble, and showed nothing of it to the one whose thoughtless egotism was unable to gauge how profoundly she had been worshiped, at least he frequently unburdened his heart in music, and during the following period he was conscious of a regret to which, in Matthisson's lied, he had given an expression that, to him, was more than musical. It is probable that the influence of Magdalena upon the composer increased rather than diminished after their rupture; in any case, the theme of "Adelaïde," or at least the larghetto at the beginning, only very slowly disappeared from his mind. It obsessed him for a considerable period. At the time of his love for Magdalena, the theme in which he expressed it to her, consciously or unconsciously, supplied him with abundant material for inspiration, as we see in some of his works of this time. . . . Mention may be made of the largo of the First Concerto in C Major (Opus 15), played in Vienna in 1795. The theme, in F minor, is very closely related to that of "Adelaïde," and measures 102–3 are a literal reproduction of the final measures of the short prelude to the song itself.

The Adagio of the first pianoforte sonata (F Minor, Opus 2, No. 1) published in 1796, is manifestly of contemporary inspiration; it also interprets in almost identical fashion the same effusion—it may be remembered that in Vienna, in Beethoven's days, this sonata generally was referred to as the *"amoureuse."*

Thus, we have three works, certainly belonging to the same period and inspirational influence, which reproduce, with scarcely perceptible differences of form, a theme into which Beethoven assuredly put the best and purest of himself. And its influence was continuous. In 1797, when the published cantata was being interpreted by the lady who in all probability inspired it, Beethoven brought out his Fourth Pianoforte Sonata in E Flat (Opus 7), dedicated to his youthful pupil Babette Keglevicz, subsequently Countess Odescalchi, and the Rondo still showed tender traces of "Adelaïde," especially in the development of the final reprise: see particularly measures 157–75.

Nor was this inspiration dead even three years afterwards. The deception of a vanished love must then have considerably diminished, and yet there is still in his mind the obsessing cantilena, almost note for note, as he writes his Third Concerto in C Minor (Opus 37), where the Allegro con brio is little more than a long paraphrase of the theme, though expanded and developed with considerable power.

Is it not in such pages as these that we must seek the very essence of Beethoven's genius, both in its first and in its second manner? A virile soul, profoundly stirred by tenderness and the urge of self-sacrifice, using the most thread-bare theme to express its longings. Take the adagios of the youthful Beethoven in all the ardent flush of his twenty-fifth year and his love for Magdalena, his ever unappeased passion creating musical inspiration and passing it on to generations of listeners. In this sense most certainly "Adelaïde" remains at the very heart of his work, as it remained, in all that was noblest and purest of his life, the theme of that "eternal womanly" to which he related his successive affections, through experiences with which, so ardently and ingenuously right on to the end of his life, he sought to illumine the sombre path his rugged genius was to traverse along the awful solitudes of deafness and abandonment.

Besides, does not this favorite theme of Beethoven's adagios, inspired by the youthful singer of Bonn, bring out the tender and adoring side of a genius that was so essentially human? Outpourings of love, tender desire and gloomy melancholy express but one of its aspects. The other aspect, that of triumph, of victorious moments, of lofty flights which entrust the empire of the world to triumphant love, remained with Beethoven for many a year to come.

It may be remembered that his notebooks—about the same time as his early sketches of "Adelaïde"—contain the *ébauche* of a lied[1]—the second part of which, the *"Gegenliebe,"* is nothing less than the first inspiration of the theme upon which, in 1823–24, he was to write the choruses on the "Ode to Joy." When we reflect upon the tardiness of such an evolution, the potency of a like obsession, may we not expect to find its origin in the same events [and people] that have thrown light upon the "Adelaïde," [especially] Magdalena Willmann, whom he ardently longed to marry in 1795, when jotting down pell-mell in the same notebook all the tenderness of the "Adelaïde" and all the joy of the *"Gegenliebe"*?—MARTIAL DOUEL (TR. BY FRED ROTHWELL)

II. "Seufzer eines Ungeliebten," WoO 118

The last five years of the century brought forth less than a dozen vocal works [from Beethoven], of which only two or three merit much

1 *"Seufzer eines Ungeliebten,"* WoO 118.—Editor.

attention. [One of these is] *"Seufzer eines Ungeliebten,"* [which] is an important work. It is based on words by Burger and is contemporaneous with "Adelaïde" (1794–95) and the Sextet, Opus [81b].[1] As in the aria "*Ah! Perfido*" and "Adelaïde," a recitative (nine measures) precedes the initial Andantino in 3/4, which reminds one of Mozart. "In the forest, over the prairies, the wind and the sea, where can one go who has never been loved? Everything is loved, except me!" On the last words, "Does he exist? If only I knew . . . if only I knew!" the melody remains suspended on the dominant-seventh chord. The Allegretto in 2/4 in C major, which follows the Andantino, begins with the same words. Its theme reappears later in the Fantasy with Chorus,[2] and still later, greatly magnified and enlarged, in the "Ode to Joy" of the Ninth Symphony. But here, still in the embryonic stage, he intermingles little *ritournelles*, which are far from solemn.[3]—J.-G. PROD'HOMME (1) (TR. BY THOMAS K. SCHERMAN)

III. *"La Tiranna,"* WoO 125

The following piece by Beethoven seems to have escaped the notice of researchers and musicians entirely, up to the present: at any rate, it is not in the Breitkopf & Härtel *Gesamtausgabe*, nor, to my knowledge, is there any mention of it in any of the numerous bibliographies or other reference works dealing with Beethoven.

It is a printed work, copies of which are in the British Museum and the Bodleian Library at Oxford. The title runs:

A favourite / Canzonetta / for the Pianoforte,/ composed by / L. vn Beethoven,/ of Vienna,/ The poetry by Wm. Wennington,/ and by him / most respectfully dedicated to / Mrs. Tschoffen. / Published in Vienna, by the Principal Music Shops,/ and in London, by Messrs. Broderip & Wilkinson,/ Hodsoll, & Astor & Co.

The inside of the cover bears the caption: "*Canzonetta. La Tiranna.*" There is no indication of date, but the names of the publishers indicate that the piece must have appeared some time between 1799 and 1808;

---

1 Prod'homme mistakenly wrote "Sextet, Opus 71," which was not composed until a year and a half later.—Editor.

2 Opus 80.—Editor.

3 One should certainly not minimize the importance of these coincidences or the repetition of a certain same theme after such a long period of time—there is a period of thirty years between the lied "*Seufzer eines Ungeliebten*" and the symphony in question—when one realizes that Beethoven had been thinking about setting to music the "Ode to Joy" since 1792. Only if one studies the great number of sketches, spaced out during months and years in which Beethoven searched out the definitive thoughts of his major works, can one appreciate what incessant work, what marvelous unity of thought, governed his artistic and creative life, and what profound harmony controlled the strength of his soul, to borrow a phrase from Nottebohm.

and there is another piece of probable evidence which, as we shall see, points rather to the earlier limit. The music, it must be admitted, is not Beethoven's most inspired. But in as much as no other piece of Beethoven's music was published in England before 1805, it can hardly be supposed that anybody thought it worth his while to forge the name of the composer before he was well known. Furthermore, the style resembles some of Beethoven's early works (e.g., the turn B flat B natural C A flat G occurs in the piano Trio, Opus 1, No. 1), and elsewhere there is more than one trait that suggests the real Beethoven, in particular at "I mark'd the vivid lightnings roll." Actually, the piano part is quite expressive and so difficult in some passages that it calls for a skilled performer. One also has the feeling that the balance of the interest as between the vocal and the piano parts is very much in favor of the instrumental, and the curious wording of the title page seems quite justified from this point of view.

The text, as the subtitle *"La Tiranna"* seems to suggest, [is undoubtedly] a translation from the Italian; and, so far as we can get an over-all view of his life, Wennington must have been a trained translator. He seems to have started out as a musical entertainer. He went abroad [around 1797], and in 1799 there appeared in the bookstores of London and Vienna *The Man of Nature, or Nature and Love, from the German of Miltenberg by Wilm. Wennington.* The book turns out to be, in point of fact, a translation of La Fontaine's novel *Der Naturmensch.* It seems that Wennington lived in Vienna at [the] time [and] also made something of a name for himself in society and acquired some influential connections. For the book begins with a list of almost two hundred subscribers, the most important and most interesting of which is, for us, the name of "M. The Prince Linhouski," presumably none other than Prince Carl Lichnowsky, Beethoven's friend and patron. It is a reasonable supposition that Wennington met Beethoven in Lichnowsky's house and that our canzonetta was heard there. We know nothing more of him thereafter except that in 1811 he published another translation from the German. In any event, his claim to fame is justified if we grant that in all probability he was the first man to import Beethoven into England.—J. H. BLAXLAND (TR. BY THOMAS K. SCHERMAN)

IV. "Opferlied," WoO 126

V. "Der Wachtelschlag," WoO 129

The song entitled "Wachtelschlag" ("The cry of the quail") composed around 1799–1800 and offered to the editors Breitkopf & Härtel on

October 22, 1803, appeared [for the first time as late as] March 1804, that is to say a little after the *"Geistliche Lieder"* of Gellert, Opus 48—the year that first heard the "Eroica" Symphony. The words were by a provincial school master, Samuel Friedrich Sauter.

This little piece, sort of a spiritual song with a popular appeal, was written by Sauter in 1796 and published in 1798 in the *Taschenbuch* of Carl Lang, where Beethoven must have seen it.

Beethoven did not treat it as a *chant à couplets* [a song with repeated music for each verse], but *durchkomponiert* [treated it as an over-all composition]. He even went so far as to point this out to Breitkopf. The work consisted of five movements: Larghetto, Allegro molto, Adagio, Allegro, and Allegretto finale (107 measures in all). From the very beginning (F major, 2/4) one hears the lively motive of the quail, which appears in each of the strophes, but in different guises: fearful, God-loving, forgiving, praising—each guise dramatized musically by the composer.

The Allegro (5 measures for piano alone) which precedes the final Allegretto is distinguished by an iambic rhythm, in a fast tempo which, as well as the "cry of the quail," is found in the piano Sonata Opus 31, No. 3. Other similarities exist between the two works: for example, the accompaniment in triplets in the left hand on the words *"traue Gott"* around the middle of the final Allegretto, and the shrill notes in the right hand which again recall the cry of the bird, and which appear throughout the end of the song, the same as the last movement of the sonata.

This latter, in E flat, dates from 1802, the year in which Beethoven thought of presenting his song for publication. Its first and fourth movements, only, appear to us to recall formally the *"Wachtelschlag."*

In a different meter (3/4 allegro instead of 2/4 larghetto) and in a similar notation (dotted sixteenth note followed by a thirty-second note in the song, an eighth note followed by a sixteenth note in the sonata), the leading motive—where Riemann saw a mannerism (the *Seufzer* [sighing motive] of the Mannheim school)—is merely the song, the over-all cry, of the bird. This cry, stylized, permeates the entire first movement of the sonata.

The finale, which M. Chantavoine[1] compares to a hunt, is not without its similarity to certain parts of the song. The triplets, in the left hand, are echoes of the song, while the right hand recalls the iambic rhythm which, since the twelfth measure, was dominant: it recalls note for note the Allegro which, for piano alone, precedes the final Allegretto

---

[1] Jean François Henri Chantavoine (1877–1952), noted French musicologist. Besides many musicological treatises he is also known for an adaptation of Beethoven's *Prometheus* ballet.—Editor.

of the song, punctuated by the shrill notes which are like the pipings of the bird.

This sonata which, over-all, in the first movement and in the finale, appears to us to be suggested by the song—its senior by two or three years—may also be considered (as well as so many other pages of Beethoven) as a pastorale for piano, a harbinger of the Sixth Symphony, in which the master expressed still one more time, with the full magnificence of his orchestra and with the full maturity of his genius, his profound and intense love of nature.—J.-G. PROD'HOMME (2) (TR. BY THOMAS K. SCHERMAN)

VI. "Erlkönig," SKETCH TO GOETHE'S BALLAD, WoO 131

Not only Franz Schubert and J. K. G. Löwe have set Goethe's "Erlkönig" to music. There also exists a sketch by Beethoven for a musical setting of "Erlkönig," which, however, remains unworked out. It is the property of the Society of the Friends of Music in Vienna and was studied by Nottebohm, who established its date as between 1800 and 1810 (in his Beethoveniana, Vol. I, pp. 100 f.), which I believe is a little too early. A strange working-out of the sketch[1] was published by J. B. Schuberth, music publishers, in Leipzig in 1897 and was highly praised. Beethoven did not take the sketch up after its inception. Probably Schubert's "Erlkönig" came to his attention, or at least he received information of the great enthusiasm with which that setting (written in 1815) was received when it was presented at a concert on January 25, 1821. A few weeks thereafter the Schubert "Erlkönig" was engraved by the music firm of Diabelli.

Beethoven's approach to the words was, for its time of composition, highly dramatic, although not fully matured.—THEODOR FRIMMEL (2) (TR. BY THOMAS K. SCHERMAN)

An examination of the sketch and its deciphering by Nottebohm, both of which appear in the J. Schuberth publication of 1897, show that Reinhold Becker, who arranged the song from the sketch, had very little to do.

The agitated sixteenth-note scheme of the ritornello and its dying out in the postlude are fully indicated, as is the flowing accompaniment of the tender words of the Erlkönig as he describes his daughter, which becomes more agitated as the Erlkönig's impatience mounts.

There is also an indication of "unisona" (sic!) over the words of the father, "Mein sohn, was birgst du so bang dein Gesicht." (It is interesting to note that at the identical place in Schubert's setting the piano accompaniment follows the vocal line exactly.)

[1] By Reinhold Becker.—Editor.

The vocal line of the first stanza is completely written out, as is that of the terrified words of the boy (full of dramatic silences and a fortissimo climax over repeated diminished-seventh chords) as he relays to his father the fact that the cold hand of the Erlkönig has already touched him.

What makes this vocal line thoroughly advanced for its time is that, in a song with a steady 6/8 rhythm, there is a 9/8 bar at the end of each stanza, a detail which throws the rhythmic pulse off momentarily and adds considerably to the restless character of the whole work.

The accompanying figure of groups of six sixteenth notes with a silence on the all-important downbeat of each group also conveys the spirit of agitation, and the repetition of the chords in each group evokes the wild galloping hoofs of the horse in, to my mind, a more subtle manner than the repeated empty octave triplets of Schubert's accompaniment.

All in all, I feel that Becker's reconstruction of Beethoven's song is a brilliant addition to the early-nineteenth-century song literature.—Editor.

Music for Voice with Orchestral Accompaniment

I. "Ah, Perfido!" OPUS 65

This famous concert aria was written in Prague, in 1796, probably for the well-known singer Josepha Duschek, for whom Mozart, on the occasion of the Prague *première* of *Don Giovanni*, had written one of his finest concert arias, *Bella mia fiamma* (K. 528), which served as a model for Beethoven's work. The aria was first performed by Mme. Duschek in Leipzig, on November 21, 1796, and published there in 1805, as Opus 65. Cast in the customary eighteenth-century form of the *aria monumentale*, the piece is notoriously difficult, and it is reported of one early interpreter that she was "overcome by terrific stage fright, almost suffered a heart attack, and completely ruined the piece."

Although there are many truly Beethovenian moments, particularly in the development of the *Allegro* section, the text and ground plan of the piece depend to a large extent on the conventions of the contemporary Italian stage. Writing in 1808, when his "middle period" style was in full flower, Beethoven realized this: "The aria is in the dramatic style and written for the theater, and can't make any effect in the concert-room.

All its meaning is lost without a curtain, or something of the kind—lost—lost—all to the devil . . . a curtain, or the air will be lost!"

The scene depicts the conflict raging in the breast of the heroine after she has been betrayed by her lover. In a forceful recitative she calls down the wrath of the gods on the head of the faithless one, but relents in the recitative's final slow section, and begs fate to spare him. In the extended first part of the aria proper, *Adagio*, she utters the hope that she may not be forsaken forever, or else she would die of grief. In the succeeding *Allegro* she rages once more against her fate, and in the gentler section marked *Più lento*, asks for mercy. The slow section shortly before the end and the brief resumption of the *Allegro* are a surprising, and rather personal, touch on the part of Beethoven.

Ah, perfido! spergiuro, barbaro traditor, tu parti?
e son questi gl'ultimi tuoi congedi?
Ove s'intese tirannia più crudel?
Va, scellerato, va, pur fuggi da me!
L'Ira de' Numi non fuggirai!
Se v'è giustizia in Ciel, se v'è pietà,
congiureranno a gara tutti a punirti!
Ombra seguace, presente, ovunque vai,
vedrò le mie vendette;
io già le godo immaginando;
i fulmini ti veggo già balenar d'intorno.
Ah! no! fermate, vindici Dei!
risparmiate quel cor, ferite il mio!
S'ei non è più qual era, son io qual fui;
per lui vivea, voglio morir per lui!

Aria (Adagio)
Per pietà, non dirmi addio,
di te priva che farò?
Tu lo sai, bell' idol mio,
io d'affanno morirò.

(Allegro assai)
Ah crudel! tu vuoi ch'io mora!
Tu non hai pietà di me?
Perchè rendi a chi t'adora
corsì barbara mercè?
Dite voi, se in tanto affanno
non son degna di pietà?

Ah, faithless liar, vile deceiver, thou leavest me?
and are these thy last words of parting?
Can any cruelty be harsher than thine?
Go hence, villain, flee from me!
The wrath of the gods thou wilt not escape!
If there is justice in Heaven, if there is mercy,
everything will conspire to punish thee!

As a fleeting shadow pursuing thy path
will I see vengeance wrought;
I savor it already in my thoughts,
seeing vengeful lightnings flash around thee.
But no, stay your wrath, ye gods!
spare his heart and strike mine!
Though he no longer is what he was, I am unchanged;
I have lived for him—let me die for him!

For pity's sake, do not leave me;
parted from thee, how shall I live?
Thou knowest it, my beloved,
that I shall die of grief.

Ah, cruel one! thou wantest me to die!
Hast thou no pity for me?
Why dost thou reward so cruelly
my adoring love?
In this affliction,
am I not worthy of compassion?

PHILIP HAMBURGER

II. "*Tremate, empi, tremate!*" (TRIO FOR SOPRANO, TENOR, AND BASSO), OPUS 116

[Early in 1814, Beethoven wrote the following letter] to Archduke Rudolph.

YOUR IMPERIAL HIGHNESS!

I hope for pardon for my nonattendance. Your displeasure would punish me when I am innocent. In a few days I will make it all up . . . For my second concert the arrangements have been made in part, and I must compose something new for *Milder* for it.—Meanwhile I hear, and it is comforting to me, that Your Imperial Highness is in better health,[1] I hope, unless I am flattering myself too much, soon again to contribute to it. . . .

Your Imperial Highness's very obedient servant

LUDWIG VAN BEETHOVEN

The *Wiener Zeitung* of February 24 contains the advertisement of the "Akademie, next Sunday, the 27th inst. in the large Redoutensaal," announcing "a new symphony not yet heard and an entirely new as yet unheard terzetto" as novelties.

The report in the *Allgemeine Musikalische Zeitung* contains the program in full with a few short and pertinent observations [including the following:]

[1] The archduke was so troubled with gout in his hands that he had to abandon pianoforte playing.

1. The new symphony (A major) which was received with so much applause, again. The reception was as animated as at the first time; the Andante (A minor) the crown of modern instrumental music, as at the first performance had to be repeated.

2. An entirely new Italian terzetto (B flat major) beautifully sung by Mad. Milder-Hauptmann, Hr. Siboni and Hr. Weinmüller, is conceived at the outset wholly in the Italian style, but ends with a fiery allegro in Beethoven's individual style. It was applauded.

The "something new for *Milder*" resulted in something rather old; for the terzetto in which she sang was the "*Tremate, empi, tremate!*" fully sketched in 1801–02 but now first written out and completed in its present form.—ALEXANDER WHEELOCK THAYER, EDITED BY ELLIOT FORBES

This dramatic trio for soprano, tenor, and bass, possibly contemplated for some opera, is based on a cliché-filled text by the composer-poet Bettoni. An irate bass cries: "Tremble lest my severe wrath fall on your haughty heads!" The soprano responds: "O gods, spare me such blood!" The tenor intervenes: "Let your wrath fall solely on me!" The two together plead: "Have mercy on an innocent love!" The bass is implacable: "My heart is hard as stone!" Upon such nonsense Beethoven constructed a thoroughly convincing ensemble based musically on the operatic traditions of the day. Orchestrally it is far more ingenious even than some of the arias and ensembles from Fidelio. The solo winds play a thoroughly integrated role with respect to the singers' lines, proudly taking up a melody as a singer leaves off, falling discreetly into the background when the singer has a brilliant show passage. The vocal writing is very adroit, especially in the final portion, where both the soprano and tenor have brilliant florid lines overlapping in the most supple manner and punctuated harmonically by periodic outbursts of the bass. Such a showpiece for all three soloists as well as for the orchestra does not deserve its present neglect.—Editor.

III. SCENE AND ARIA "*No, non turbati,*" FOR SOPRANO AND STRING ORCHESTRA, WoO 92a

[The scene and aria "*No, non turbati*"] was noted as early as 1864. Otto Jahn, the perceptive biographer of Mozart, mentioned it in his study, *Beethoven and the Editions of his Works*, which is still worth reading today. One year later A. W. Thayer's *Chronologisches Verzeichnis der Werke Beethovens* (Chronological Index of Beethoven's Works) appeared (F. Schneider, Berlin), which lists thirty-two Italian songs, including the scene and aria "*No, non turbati!*" as the twenty-third. Finally, Gustav Nottebohm, in his fundamental book, *Beethovens*

Studien, erster Band: Beethovens Unterricht bei Haydn, Albrechtsberger und Salieri (Beethoven's Studies, First Volume: Beethoven's Instruction under Haydn, Albrechtsberger and Salieri) (Leipzig and Winterthur, 1873), published the entire recitative in melody and figured bass, giving a penetrating analysis of Salieri's corrections and of Beethoven's treatment of Italian declamation.

We have no information as to performance of the work during Beethoven's life, and it is hardly likely there was any. Beethoven himself seems to have considered it as part of his studies in the composition of Italian song, since the manuscript bears the caption, *"Esercicii—da Beethoven."* We should not regard these studies of his with Antonio Salieri as instruction in the strict sense of the term. Gustav Nottebohm remarks (op. cit., p. 207): "There is every reason to believe that Beethoven took advantage of Salieri's affability and willingness to give needy musicians free instruction at certain hours, and that he visited him from time to time to get advice on song composition."

Beethoven's studies of this kind came in the years from 1793 to 1802. The scene and aria *"No, non turbati"* was written at the end of 1801 or the beginning of 1802, according to Nottebohm. This is not the place for a critical discussion of Beethoven's way of treating the Italian language and Salieri's corrections in this respect.[1] All these questions have been treated by Gustav Nottebohm in his thoroughgoing and exhaustive way. We should like to make some fundamental observations, however. Examination of the three versions of Beethoven's opera *Fidelio* for the musical treatment of the text will show full-blown, there, what we find here in germ: The instrumental composer takes pains to bring his purely musical inspirations into line with a singable declamation of the text. The masterly final versions of such cries as *"Töt' erst sein Weib!"* or *"Ja, sieh hier Leonore"* were arrived at only after endless laborious trials, and the entire reworking of *Fidelio* was guided not only by a quest for brevity but also by a thorough check on the musical treatment of the text. That was the nature of Salieri's corrections too in these *early works*: he tries to bring the declamatory flow of language into correspondence with the musical flow, making corrections where Beethoven leaves musically unaccented syllables that are accented in the meter of the verse, and improving faulty elisions, etc. Anyone who compares the two versions carefully cannot help noticing that the absolute musical beauty often is seriously impaired: For example, [the setting of the words *"ne' d'amor ti parlerò"*] is definitely lovelier and more exciting in its original version; the wildly moving rhythmic pulse corresponds to an immediate impression, and its effect is seriously cut down in Salieri's simplification. Further,

---

[1] The text of the work comes from Metastasio's *La tempesta.*—Editor.

Salieri's cuts are not at all in line with Beethoven's [melodic] idea even though they eliminate some repetitions of the text (still another problem in the original version of *Fidelio*).

In order to show interested composers and musicologists the way in which the Italian maestro corrected a work of Beethoven's, the two versions are shown alongside one another with the notes exactly reproduced.[1]

The simple and technically easy accompaniment should make this hitherto unknown work by Beethoven a welcome gift to the many small orchestral groups that have good strings but lack trained winds.
—WILLY HESS (2) (TR. BY THOMAS K. SCHERMAN)

[1] As an example of one of Salieri's "corrections" in the recitative: Beethoven has set the words *"io non ritorno a parlati d'amor"* to the rhythm quarter note, two eighth notes, quarter note (the downbeat of the bar receiving the heaviest accent—it comes on the syllable *"tor"* of *"ritorno"*), two eighths (of which the first elides with the last syllable of *"ritorno"* with *"a"*), quarter note (on the second syllable of *"parlati"* and on the third beat of the measure—a heavily accented beat), two eighths, and a quarter. Salieri evidently felt that a quarter and an eighth on the second and third syllables of *"ritorno"* stressed the second syllable too much. He gives two eighth notes to *"-torno,"* then eliminates the elision by inserting an eighth rest, and substitutes the rhythm of two sixteenth notes to the *"a par-."* To summarize, Beethoven's setting is more smooth musically, but Salieri's is much more sensitive to the rhythm of the words. Another place in the recitative where Salieri appears not only as a good teacher but as an anticipator of one of the trademarks of his "pupil's" future output occurs a few bars later. An orchestral crescendo ends with a sudden piano—a dramatic device which Beethoven was to develop a thousandfold in the next two and a half decades. It is especially appropriate to the dramatic situation at this point: the poet's description of his resignation at the acceptance of an unkind fate is followed immediately by his personal physical reaction to the menacing sight of an approaching storm. The orchestral crescendo depicts this sudden change of mood and the sudden piano at its close reinforces the approaching menace. Beethoven unfortunately spoiled the effect by having the singer sing the word *"vedi!"* ("look!") at the very moment of the orchestra's sudden change in dynamics, so its dramatic force is weakened. Salieri, the experienced opera writer, merely inserted a half bar's rest at that point so the mood change would "sink in" to the listener, creating automatically a sense of anticipation. Then, when one hears the words *"vedi! che il ciel minaccia,"* they have much more power.

Such corrections by Salieri in dramatic intensity and in the prosody of the Italian language are numerous in the recitative. However, as Willy Hess points out, even the young Beethoven is more deft with melodic line and harmonic scheme than his older and more experienced colleague when it comes to the aria proper. As far as I am concerned, Salieri's only improvement in the latter is the elimination of one measure at each appearance of the words *"Nice ingrata io partiro,"* which come, musically, at a cadence phrase. Beethoven's melodic line makes it necessary to repeat the words three times at each cadence. By a slight adjustment of the harmonic pattern, Salieri's cut dispenses with one of these awkward repetitions and has the added advantage of varying the rhythmic scheme—Beethoven had not yet acquired in his vocal writing the ability that Haydn and Mozart had perfected of escaping from the four-square rhythm of the words. His notebooks, as Hess also points out, show his particular concern with this in his setting and resetting of the libretto of *Fidelio*, seven and fourteen years after these very valuable examples of advice from Salieri, undoubtedly his peer in these matters.—Editor.

IV. 2 ARIAS FROM THE SINGSPIEL *Die schöne Schusterin,* WoO 91

At the time of the classical Viennese school, it was customary that well-known and respected composers would write original musical selections for already existing operas, Singspiels, and dramas, if a work in the repertoire would by this means get a new lease on life, or if a certain soloist would take pleasure in performing such an alternative number.

Beethoven was no exception. As early as the Bonn years he composed two arias, *"Prüfung des Küssens"* and *"Mit Mädeln sich vertragen"* [WoO 89 and WoO 90], probably for the leading bass of the Court Theater, Joseph Lux. The text of the second aria is from Goethe's *Claudine von Villabella.* It is not known in what production Lux sang these two special arias. It could not have been (as Prod'homme suggests in *La Jeunesse de Beethoven*) in an actual production of the Goethe play because the text of the first aria is not by Goethe. It is possible that the well-known Goethe text, as well as the aria by the unknown author, was interpolated in some *Schauspiel* or drama in which Lux was appearing at the Court Theater.

On the contrary, the two arias Beethoven composed in 1796, as part of Ignaz Umlauf's Singspiel *Die schöne Schusterin (The beautiful cobbler),* have their definite and unequivocal places in that well-known musical play. The Singspiel is a German adaptation by Gottlieb Stephanie the younger, from a French *opéra comique* originally produced in Paris on January 11, 1776, with music by Alexander Frizer.

In the season 1782–83, an earlier German adaptation of the original French was on the boards of the Bonn National Theater, and it is highly possible that Beethoven already knew this delightful and inoffensive work from that time.

The story is about a practical joke played by the hero, Baron Piccourt, a French officer stationed in an Alsatian border town, with the help of his servant Michael, on Lene, the charming wife of the town shoemaker, Sock. The practical joke backfires, but all ends well.

The German adaptation by Stephanie the younger, with music by Ignaz Umlauf, was presented for the first time in Vienna on June 22, 1779, at the Hoftheater. Thayer says: "The [Singspiel] appears to have remained unproduced until 1795. On May 30, 1795, it was revived at the Kärntnertör-Theater. Mademoiselle Willmann took the role of Frau Sock [Lene] for the first time and the [Singspiel] was presented six times in that year, three times in 1796, and four times in later years."

Both of Beethoven's arias were composed for the performances in 1796. Of them the text of Lene's aria (*"Soll ein Schuh nicht drücken,"* first act, second scene) appears in the original textbook; Beethoven simply wrote a new composition on the words [substituting for Umlauf's original music]. On the other hand, both the text and the music are new for the baron's aria in the second scene of the first act. Undoubtedly, the new text [set by Beethoven] is more worth while than the [original]; the rather primitive extolling of pleasure as such appears again in an apotheosis as a true, deeply felt joy of living when Beethoven used the same melody to his *"Mailied"* (Opus 52, No. 4) [as a setting of words by Goethe]. The instrumental accompaniment is executed with great finesse and the simple original *Strophelied* is transformed into a varied *Strophelied*: in each verse the accompaniment is different, in the first verse simple eighth notes, in the second triplets, in the third introducing the winds for the first time, which up to then had only appeared in the ritornellos. Thus after two appearances of the melody accompanied by strings alone, the last verse is crowned by the full orchestra. As a background for Goethe's words [*"Mailied"*] singers might be wise to use this instrumental accompaniment [rather than the original piano accompaniment of Opus 52, No. 4] and thereby gain themselves a true *Orchestralied* by Beethoven.

Also the soprano aria of Lene, despite some charming coloratura passages, remains within the model of a song form. Both works very beautifully portray the essential character and meaning of the poet's words: the baron's noble lightheartedness is as successfully drawn in music as the harmless and innocent beauty of the young shoemaker's wife.— WILLY HESS (3)

V. SCENE AND ARIA *"Primo Amore,"* FOR SOPRANO AND ORCHESTRA, WoO 92

Elliot Forbes, in his revision of Thayer's biography of Beethoven, mentions that in 1798 Beethoven wrote two arias for soprano and orchestra. One is the well-known *"Ah, perfido!,"* Opus 65. The other is *"Primo amore,"* which is published in the supplemnet to Breitkopf & Härtel's collected works of Beethoven. He adds, "Nothing is known about the work beyond the fact that a copy of the song exists in the Artaria Collection marked 'Dal L.v.B.' Presumably it was written during the period in which Beethoven was studying with Salieri," with the express purpose, as we know, of perfecting the technique of dramatic vocal composition, of which Salieri was a master.

The text by an unknown poet is undistinguished. It describes the feelings of the singer's first love and the misery which follows when it is discovered that the object of that love has fled to the arms of another sweetheart.

Beethoven has constructed the scene and aria musically in much the same manner as he treated the text by Metastasio for "Ah, *perfido!*" However, since the text is dramatically less absorbing than Metastasio's, Beethoven's music was bound to be less impressive. However, what little drama appeared in the poet's words was highlighted by Beethoven.

The over-all form of the work falls roughly into four sections. There is a slow 3/8 section in A major in which, after an extended orchestral introduction which highlights the solo winds and is replete with subtle imitations, the singer enters with a long, supple melody interrupted only by dramatic and unexpected pauses in typical Beethoven manner. The postlude to this section is full of offbeat sforzandi and sudden pianos which depict the agitation of the abandoned loved one. It ends in the tonic key.

There follows immediately an Allegro orchestral introduction in the subdominant key of D major to a recitative passage in which the singer describes the disillusionment of being abandoned by her love for another sweetheart. The quick key changes and the orchestral comments on the vocal line make this recitative section the highlight of the work.

The slow rhythm of 3/8 and the cantabile vocal line return after a conventional operatic close to the recitative. However, here Beethoven has a surprise in store for the listener, for the return of the passage is in A minor instead of the expected A major. In this section there are some highly melodramatic tremoli and startling dotted rhythms in the orchestral accompaniment. The music quiets down and closes with a fermata on the dominant chord, where undoubtedly, in the tradition of the time, the soloist interpolated a cadenza.

The concluding portion is an Allegro con brio in alla breve rhythm in the basic key of A major. It contains all the traditional fioratura and brilliant high notes of the typical dramatic opera arias of the period. There are two musical distinctions: the first is the announcement of the main theme of the section by various solo winds while the singer is introducing new material; the other is the interpolation of two measures of the opening adagio just before the final cadence.—THOMAS K. SCHERMAN

His Life

UP TO THE YEAR 1800 Beethoven's Viennese public regarded him first and foremost as a virtuoso of the pianoforte. Of course he was a composer as well—most pianists composed in those days—and there was a boldness and originality about his works which made them unusually interesting. But had he died in 1800 it is as a pianist that they would have mourned him. By the end of the next decade all this was altered: as a pianist he had ceased to count, but he had become incomparably the greatest composer of his day. The change in his orientation was the result of a catastrophe. Beethoven lost his hearing.

He himself indicates 1798 as the year in which he first noticed signs of this dreadful affliction. He did not take it very seriously to begin with. He had been suffering a good deal from a kind of dysentery and he thought the weakness in his ears was very likely associated with the weakness in his stomach. It would soon pass! But instead of passing it became worse, till in 1800 Thayer describes it as a "chronic and increasing evil." By this time Beethoven was really anxious. He did not yet anticipate that he would become completely deaf, but he was already wondering whether his ears would ever regain their original acuteness. He abandoned his plans of travel, took medical advice, and tried various treatments. His friends had not yet noticed his misfortune, and for the present he keeps his secret jealously guarded. If they are struck by anything unusual they will attribute it, he knows, to his absent-mindedness. This policy of concealment was suggested in part by his natural sensitiveness, but in part also by fears for his professional prospects. What hope was there for a musician who was deaf? And it succeeded so well that even his pupil, Ferdinand Ries, who was with him constantly, dates his malady from 1802. Earlier than that he had noticed nothing.

But the doctors could do little to check the steady onward march of his complaint, and in 1801 his distress is such that he can keep silence no longer. In two poignant letters of June of that year,[1] one to his dear friend, Karl Amenda, the other to Dr. Wegeler, he opens his heart, lays bare his misery, and begs for sympathy and advice. In the fullness of his pride and strength the young genius has been struck down by an enemy against whom neither pride nor strength avails him. He had looked forward to a brilliant and glorious career. Now he sees in front of him—nothing! "My hearing has grown steadily worse for three years," he writes to Wegeler. "My ears whistle and buzz continually night and day. Heaven knows what will become of me!" He withdraws from society, avoids the brilliant gatherings wherein he had been wont to shine, because he cannot bring himself to the confession "I am deaf!"

But now came a short idyll to bring temporary relief. On November 16, in another letter to Wegeler, he says that he is being coaxed out of his retirement "by a dear, fascinating girl who loves me and whom I love." This was the Countess Giulietta Guicciardi, a near relation of his friends the Brunswicks, and to her he dedicated the sonata in C sharp minor, Opus 27, No. 2, the work that will probably always be known as the *Moonlight Sonata*.[2] He was certainly in love with her for a while and probably she with him, though, as usual with Beethoven, the affair came to nothing. The romantic qualities of the sonata have induced some writers to regard it almost as an autobiographical document. Actually, the work that Beethoven originally sent to the Countess was the *Rondo in G*, Opus 51, No. 2, a graceful but not particularly significant piece. Desiring later to present the *Rondo* to someone else, he recalled it and gave Giulietta the sonata in its place. Its origin, so far as it had an origin outside the world of tone, is probably to be found in a poem by Seume, *Die Beterin*. In 1803 the Countess Giulietta Guicciardi married Count Gallenberg, but by that time Beethoven was busy with the *Eroica*.

We may therefore reject the romantic legend that makes of Giulietta the supreme, unique love of Beethoven's life. Yet there is reason to believe that the impression she made on him was no light one. A medallion portrait of her was found among his effects after his death, and in a secret drawer of his desk was a letter, the most passionate love-letter Beethoven ever wrote. But there are difficulties about this letter. In dating it Beethoven has omitted the year, and though he gives the day of the week and the day of the month we have cause to suspect that either or both these dates may be wrong—he was notoriously careless about such things. We do not know from where it was sent—there is no ad-

---

[1] Or just possibly of June 1800: in this instance, as in many others, we cannot be quite sure when the letters were written.

[2] Beethoven never gave it this title; nor did he call the F minor *Appassionata*. He is responsible for the title *Les Adieux, l'Absence et le Retour*, of the sonata in E flat, Opus 81A, and he at least acquiesced in calling the early C minor, Opus 13, *Sonata Pathétique*. All the other fancy names for sonatas were given without his sanction.

dress—nor even whether it was actually sent at all. And lastly no name is mentioned: the object of his adoration is called only the "Immortal Beloved." The weight of opinion inclines to Giulietta as the recipient of this mysterious letter; but Thayer votes for Therese von Brunswick, and Magdalena Willmann, Therese Malfatti and Amalie Sebald has each her champion. A truly singular uncertainty!

By 1802 most of Beethoven's intimates were aware of his deafness, but as he still withheld his confidence they dared not show their sympathy. His love affair was over now and he was left more and more alone to brood. That summer he went to Heiligenstadt, and there things reached a climax. In deep seclusion, remote from his friends, he fought his battle, and the echoes of it only come down to us through that strange document known as the Heiligenstadt Will. He never seriously contemplated suicide, but he does seem at this period to have anticipated an early death, and so he writes the "Will" and addresses it to his two brothers. Testamentary dispositions occupy but a small part; the bulk of it is concerned with an account of his illness, laments over his lot, invocations to himself to be patient, to endure (since nothing else now remains), and an exhortation to his brothers that they train their children in virtue. The whole document is too long to transcribe, but the postscript with its passionate cry of despair may be quoted:

> Heiligenstadt, October 10th, 1802, thus do I take my farewell of thee—and indeed sadly—yes, that beloved hope—which I brought with me when I came here to be cured at least in a degree—I must wholly abandon, as the leaves of Autumn fall and are withered so hope has been blighted, almost as I came—I go away—even the high courage—which often inspired me in the beautiful days of summer—has disappeared—O Providence—grant me at last but one day of pure *joy*—it is so long since real joy echoed in my heart—O when—O when—, O Divine One—shall I feel it again in the temple of nature or of men—Never? no—O that would be too hard.

This is the very climax of his agony. At the internal struggles which followed we can only guess, but we know that he emerged victorious. To suffering, to renunciation, he resigned himself since he must. But he could still compose and in his compositions he would fulfill himself! How magnificently he rose to his destiny is shown by the works that followed. From Heiligenstadt he returned with the sunny second symphony, the most lighthearted of them all!—a warning to those who insist on reading a composer's life into his work. In 1803 he embarked on an even vaster project, the *Eroica*. This was finished in 1804, and during that year and the next he was busy with his opera, *Fidelio*. In 1806 comes the fourth symphony, in 1807 the fifth (which was actually begun before the fourth). 1808 brought the *Pastoral*, 1812 the seventh and eighth symphonies. Was there ever such a flood of masterpieces? And our list takes no account of the *Mass in C*, the two last pianoforte concertos, the violin concerto, the *Coriolan* and *Egmont* overtures, the Rasoumovsky quartets, and a whole sheaf of sonatas, including the most famous of all, for piano solo or for piano and violin—though all these works and others besides belong to the same overwhelming period. Yet all the while the composer was growing deafer and deafer, till in 1810 Bettina Brentano had to write her share of her conversations with him on paper.

The piano he continued to play as long as he could. Early in this epoch Czerny could still speak of him as a virtuoso and say, "Nobody equaled him in the rapidity of his scales, double trills, skips, etc.—not even Hummel." Even much later, in 1811, when Czerny took piano lessons from him, he found that he still "corrected with the greatest exactitude." But by that time he had ceased to be a soloist. His last public appearance as a virtuoso was in 1808, though he still continued to play in chamber music and his improvisations remained impressive till a much later date. Conducting too he found quite practicable, and most of the masterpieces of the period were performed for the first time under his direction.

As his malady got worse Beethoven abandoned his pathetic efforts to conceal it. Among the sketches for the Rasoumovsky quartets he writes: "Let your deafness no longer remain a secret—not even in art!" He mingled once again in society, laughed, flirted as before. Life had played him a sorry trick, but he would triumph in spite of it—he would even be happy! Thanks to the success of his work he was comfortably off, and as he sat talking and jesting with his friends he was often cheerful, even gay—although by 1804 it was already becoming an effort to converse with him. Yet the crisis had left its mark, and in the same year (1804) Stephan von Breuning, writing to Wegeler, speaks of the "indescribable, I might say fearful effect of the gradual loss of hearing," and mentions "reserve, mistrust" among the qualities that he now observes in his old friend. The deaf often become mistrustful, and Beethoven's keen sensibilities combined with his loss of hearing to produce what may almost be called suspicion-mania. He suspected his household, his business associates, even his friends, in the most unwarrantable way and thereby added much to his own sufferings. Accounts of quarrels grow more frequent and he is continually changing his servants or his lodgings.

It will have been noticed that the portion of Beethoven's life we are now considering coincided roughly with the great victories of Napoleon Bonaparte. Beethoven always regarded himself as a democrat, though his opinions were never of the violent kind and matured eventually into a steady if rather unexpected admiration of the English people and their constitution. The startling rise of Napoleon he watched with deep interest. To him the great Corsican appeared as the champion of an ideal

Freedom, and it was in his honor that the *Eroica* symphony was composed. Early in the spring of 1804 the score was ready for dispatch to Paris, with Napoleon's name on the title-page, when the news arrived that the First Consul had proclaimed himself Emperor. In an access of rage and disappointment that his hero should prove so false to his conception of him, Beethoven tore out his dedication and substituted a new one, to Prince Lobkowitz. Some years later, in 1809, the artillery of Napoleon was battering at the gates of Vienna—and the composer lay in a cellar, his head smothered in pillows, desperately endeavoring to preserve the poor remnants of his hearing from the shattering effects of the bombardment.

Another light is thrown on Beethoven's democratic principles by an incident that occurred during the few days that he spent in the company of the poet Goethe. It was in Teplitz during the summer of 1812. Not long before Beethoven had written his music to Goethe's *Egmont*, and Goethe's interest in Beethoven had been aroused by the enthusiastic accounts he had received from their mutual friend, Bettina Brentano. For a week or so in June they saw a good deal of each other. They went for walks together, and on one occasion, Bettina tells us, they met the Empress and the whole Court. Goethe stood aside, bowing obsequiously. Beethoven made straight through the throng, merely acknowledging to right and left the greetings of his acquaintances. The difference between democratic independence and mere bad manners was not, apparently, very clear to him.—PETER LATHAM

Beethoven at Thirty

The man whom I am studying in this [essay] is the Ego of the period of combat. And I must sketch his portrait in the rough. For if it is easy enough to see at a glance, after the lapse of a century,[1] in what respect this mountain is part of the range of a distant epoch, it is necessary also to distinguish the respects in which it dominates the range, and the declivities, the precipices, the escarpments that separate it from its attendant peaks. True, the Ego of Beethoven is not that of the Romantics; it would be absurd to confuse these neo-Gothics or impressionists with the Roman builder. Everything that was characteristic of them would have been repugnant to him—their sentimentality, their lack of logic, their disordered imagination. He is the most virile of

[1] Rolland wrote this essay in 1927.—Editor.

musicians; there is nothing—if you prefer it, not enough—of the feminine about him. Nothing, again, of the open-eyed innocence of the child for whom art and life are just a play of soap-bubbles. I wish to speak no ill of those eyes, which I love, for I too find that it is beautiful to see the world reflected in iridescent bubbles. But it is still more beautiful to take it to you with open arms and make it yours, as Beethoven did. He is the masculine sculptor who dominates his matter and bends it to his hand; the master-builder, with Nature for his yard. For anyone who can survey these campaigns of the soul from which stand out the victories of the *Eroica* and the *Appassionata,* the most striking thing is not the vastness of the armies, the floods of tone, the masses flung into the assault, but the spirit in command, the imperial reason.

But before we speak of the work, let us consider the workman. And first of all let us reconstitute the carpenter's framework—the body.

He is built of solid stuff well cemented; the mind of Beethoven has strength for its base. The musculature is powerful, the body athletic; we see the short stocky body with its great shoulders, the swarthy red face, tanned by sun and wind, the stiff black mane, the bushy eyebrows, the beard running up to the eyes, the broad and lofty forehead and cranium, "like the vault of a temple," powerful jaws "that can grind nuts," the muzzle and the voice of a lion.[1] Everyone of his acquaintance was astonished at his physical vigor.[2] "He was strength personified," said the poet Castelli. "A picture of energy," wrote Seyfried. And so he remained to the last years,—until that pistol shot of the nephew that struck him to the heart. Reichardt and Benedict describe him as "cyclopean"; others invoke Hercules. He is one of the hard, knotty, pitted fruits of the age that produced a Mirabeau, a Danton, a Napoleon. He sustains this strength of his by means of vigorous ablutions with cold water, a scrupulous regard for personal cleanliness, and daily walks immediately after the midday meal, walks that lasted the entire afternoon and often extended into the night; then a sleep so sound and long that he thanklessly complained against it.[3] His way of living is substantial but simple. Nothing to excess; he is no glutton, no drinker (in the evil sense of the word) as some have wrongfully described him.[4] Like a good

---

[1] "*Löwenstimme . . . Die Nase viereckig wie die eines Löwen . . . Das Haar dick, in die Höhe stehend . . . Stirne und Schädel wunderbar breit gewölbt und hoch wie ein Tempel . . . Bis an die Augen ging sein erschrecklich starker Bart . . .*" For all these details see Ries, Röckel, and particularly Benedict, who, seeing Beethoven with Weber, was struck by the contrast between the two men.

[2] Röckel (1806), Reichardt (1808), Müller (1820), Benedict (1823), Stumpff (1824).

[3] "Unfortunately I have to give up too much time to it!" (Letter to Wegeler, November 1801.)

[4] Nothing hurt him so much as this, for these evil reports came even to his ears. On his deathbed he heard that some people attributed his dropsy to over-

Rhinelander he loved wine, but he never abused it—except for a short period (1825-26) with Holz, when he was badly shaken. He was fonder of fish than of meat; fish was his great treat. But his fare was rough and countrified: delicate stomachs could not endure it.

As he grows older, the demon that possesses him brings more and more disorder into his way of living. He needs a woman to look after him, or he will forget to eat; he has no hearth of his own. But there is to be found no woman who will devote herself absolutely to him; and perhaps his independence would revolt in advance against the rights that devotion of this kind would establish over him.

Yet he likes women, and has need of them; they occupied a greater place in his life than in that, I will not say of a Bach or a Handel, but of any other musician. I will come back to this point. But though his avid nature cries out for love, and though love fled from him less than has been supposed (as we shall see later, he fascinated women, and more than one offered herself to him), he is on his guard against them, on his guard against himself. His sexual continence has been exaggerated. Certain entries of the year 1816 in his journal[1] testifying to his disgust, testify also that he has had experience of the light-o'-love. But his conception of love is too lofty for him to be able, without a sense of shame, to degrade it in these—to use his own word—bestial (*viehisch*) unions. He ended by banishing the sensual from his own passional life; and when Guilietta Guicciardi, the beloved of the old time, still beautiful, comes to him in tears and offers herself to him, he repulses her with disdain. He guards the sanctity of his memories against her, and he guards his art, his deity, against contamination: "If I had been willing thus to sacrifice my vital force," he said to Schindler, "what would have remained for the nobler, the better thing?"

This governance of the flesh by the spirit, this strength of constitution, both moral and physical, this life without excess, ought to have assured him an unassailable health: Röckel, who in 1806 saw him nude, splashing

---

indulgence in drink; and the poor man begged Breuning and Schindler to defend his memory against the charge. Let me quote some moving passages from a little-known letter from Schindler to Wegeler of the 6th July, 1827: "Beethoven, in the last weeks of his illness, often spoke to Breuning and myself of the vexatious talk there would be about his moral character if he died of this malady. . . . It grieved him exceedingly, all the more because these calumnies were spread abroad by men whom he had received at his table. He implored us to preserve for him after his death the love and friendship we had shown him during his life, and to see that at any rate his moral life was not besmirched" (*und zu wachen, das wenigstens sein moralisches Leben nicht befleckt wurde*).

[1] Also a discreet allusion of his doctor Bertolini, to whom his weaknesses were known. (When Bertolini was ill with cholera, in 1831, and believed himself to be dying, he ordered all the intimate Beethoven papers in his possession to be burned.)

about in the water like a triton, said that "you would have predicted he would live to the age of Methuselah."

But his heredity was flawed. It is more than likely that he derived from his mother a predisposition toward tuberculosis; while the alcoholism of his father and his grandmother, against which he fought morally, must have left its mark on his system. From early days he suffered from a violent enteritis; also, perhaps, from syphilis[1]; his eyes were weak, and there was the deafness. He died of none of these, however, but of cirrhosis of the liver. Moreover, in his last illness there were fortuitous circumstances that brought about the fatal result,—first of all pleurisy, the result of the furious return from the country to Vienna in an ice-cold December in a milkman's cart, without any winter clothing; then, when this first trouble seemed to have been stemmed, a fresh outburst of anger that brought on a relapse. Of all these cracks in the building, the only one that affected the soul—and that terribly—was, as we know, the deafness.

But at the point of departure of about the year 1800—for other men it would have been a point of arrival—when, in his thirtieth year, he has already won the foremost place for himself by the side of the venerable Haydn, his strength appears intact, and he is proudly conscious of it. He who has freed himself from the bonds and the gags of an old rotting world, freed himself from its masters, its gods, must show himself to be worthy of his new liberty, capable of bearing it; otherwise, let him remain in chains! The prime condition for the free man is strength. Beethoven exalts it; he is even inclined to overesteem it. *Kraft über alles!* There is something in him of Nietzsche's superman, long before Nietzsche. If he can be fierily generous, it is because such is his nature and because it pleases him to distribute royally, to "friends in need," largesse from the booty he has won. But he can also be pitiless, lacking in all consideration, as, indeed, he sometimes is. I refer not to those furious outbursts of rage in which he respects no one, not even his inferiors; he professes at times a morality of the stronger,—*Faustrecht*: "Strength is the morality of the men who stand out from the others, and it is mine."[2]

He is rich in scorn—scorn for the feeble, the ignorant, the common people, equally so for the aristocracy, and even for the good souls who

---

[1] An excess of scrupulosity prevents the publication of certain documents that exist in a Berlin collection,—sketches sent by Beethoven to his doctor, that had to do with a malady that must have dated from the first years of his residence in Vienna, the nature of which Beethoven himself did not understand exactly. See the articles of Dr. Leo Jacobssohn, head physician of the Städl. Krankenhaus Moabit-Berlin, in the *Deutsche Medizinische Wochenschrift* (Sonderabdruck, No. 27), and in the Berlin *Der Tag*, No. 276, 1919.

[2] "*Kraft ist die Moral der Menschen, die sich vor Anderen auszeichnen, und sie ist auch die meinige.*" (Letter to Zmeskall, about 1800.)

love and admire him; a scorn of all men, terrible in itself, of which he never quite succeeded in purging himself. As late as 1825, for instance, he says: "Our epoch has need of powerful spirits to lash these wretched, small-minded, perfidious scoundrels of humanity." In a letter of 1801 to his friend Amenda he speaks thus insultingly of a man (Zmeskall) who will remain faithful to him to his last breath, and who, to share with him the terrors of his last days, has his own sick body carried to a house near that in which Beethoven is undergoing the final agony: "I rate him and those of his species only according to what they bring me; I regard them purely and simply as instruments on which I play when I please."

This bragging cynicism, that he displays ostentatiously before the eyes of the most religious of his friends, bursts out more than once in his life, and his enemies fasten upon it. When Holz, about 1825, is about to become intimate with him, the publisher Steiner lets him know that it is very good of him to do anything for Beethoven, who will cast him aside, when he has made use of him, as he does all his *famuli*; and Holz repeats the remark to Beethoven.

Imputations of this kind are belied, at every period of his life, by the torrent of his warm humanity.[1] But we must recognize that the two currents, vast love, vast scorn, often came to a clash in him, and that in the full flush of his youth, when victory broke down all the floodgates, the scorn poured out in torrents.

May gentle souls forgive me! I do not idealize the man: I describe him as I see him.

But it is here we become conscious of the antique sublimity of the destiny that smites him, like Oedipus, in his pride, his strength, just where he is most sensitive—in his hearing, the very instrument of his superiority. We remember the words of Hamlet:

> . . . and that should teach us
> There's a divinity that shapes our ends,
> Rough-hew them how we will.

We who, at a century's distance, can see that tragedy for what it was, let us prostrate ourselves and say, "Holy! holy! Blessed is the misfortune that has come upon thee! Blessed the sealing-up of thine ears!"

The hammer is not all: the anvil also is necessary. Had destiny descended only upon some weakling, or on an imitation great man, and bent his back under this burden, there would have been no tragedy in it, only an everyday affair. But here destiny meets one of its own stature,

---

[1] "Never since my childhood has my zeal to serve poor suffering humanity relaxed. . . . Never have I accepted any reward for this; I need no other than the feeling of well-being that always accompanies a good action." (December 1811.) This passion for charity increases later, after the man has known suffering—notably in the period 1811–1812. For the moment it is in the shade.

who "seizes it by the throat,"[1] who is at savage grips with it all the night till the dawn—the last dawn of all—and who, dead at last, lies with his two shoulders touching the earth, but in his death is carried victorious on his shield; one who out of his wretchedness has created a richness, out of his infirmity the magic wand that opens the rock.

Let us return to the portrait of him in this decisive hour when destiny is about to enter; let us savor deliberately the cruel joy of the combat in the arena between the Force without a name and the man with the muzzle of a lion!

This superman over whose head the storm is gathering (for the peaks attract the thunderbolt) is marked, as with smallpox, with the moral characteristics of his time—the spirit of revolt, the torch of the Revolution. They declare themselves already in the Bonn period. The youthful Beethoven has attended at the University the lectures of Eulogius Schneider, the future public prosecutor for the department of the Lower Rhine. When the news of the taking of the Bastille comes to Bonn, Schneider reads from his pulpit an ardent poem that arouses the enthusiasm of his pupils. In the following year the *Hofmusicus* Beethoven subscribes to the collection of revolutionary poems in which Schneider hurls in the face of the old world the heroic defiance of the democracy that is on the way:

"To despise fanaticism, to break the sceptre of stupidity, to fight for the rights of humanity, ah! no valet of princes can do that! It needs free souls that prefer death to flattery, poverty to servitude. . . . And know that of such souls mine will not be the last!"[2]

Who is it that is speaking? Is it Beethoven already? The words are Schneider's; but it is Beethoven who clothes them with flesh. This proud profession of republican faith is arrogantly carried by the young Jacobin—whose political convictions will indeed change in time, but never his moral convictions—into the upper-class salons of Vienna, in which, from the days of his first successes, he behaves without ceremony toward the aristocrats who entertain him.

The elegance of a world that is nearing its end has never been finer, more delicate, more worthy of love (in default of esteem) than on this the eve of the last day, when the cannon of Wagram were to arrive. It recalls Trianon. But these grand seigneurs of Vienna on the threshold of the nineteenth century, how superior they are, in taste and culture, to

[1] *"Ich will dem Schicksal in den Rachen greifen"*: Beethoven to Wegeler, 16th November, 1801.

[2] Karl Nef, *Beethovens Beziehungen zur Politik* (*Sonntagsblatt der Basler Nachrichten*, 1st, 8th, and 15th July, 1923). In this same year 1790 the first big work of Beethoven, the cantata on the death of Joseph II, for solo, chorus and orchestra celebrates, in the melodramatic style of the Revolution but still not without grandeur, the herculean struggle of the man who brought "the monster Fanaticism" to the ground.

their princess in exile, the daughter of their Maria Theresa! Never has an aristocracy loved the beauty of music with a passion more complete, or shown more respect for those who bring down the blessings of it to mortals. It is as if they would win pardon for their neglect of Mozart, who had been thrown into a common grave. In the years between the death of poor Wolfgang and that of Haydn the Viennese aristocracy bends the knee before art, pays court to artists: its pride is to treat them as equals.

The 27th March, 1808, marks the apogee of this consecration, the royal coronation of music. On that date Vienna celebrates the seventy-sixth birthday of Haydn. At the door of the University the highest aristocracy, accompanied by the musicians, awaits the son of the Rohrau wheelwright, who is coming in Prince Esterhazy's carriage. He is conducted into the hall with acclamations, to the sound of trumpets and of drums. Prince Lobkowitz, Salieri, and Beethoven come to kiss his hand. Princess Esterhazy and two great ladies take off their cloaks and wrap them round the feet of the old man, who is shaken with emotion. The frenzy, the cries, the tears of enthusiasm, are more than the composer of the *Creation* can bear. He leaves in tears in the middle of his oratorio, and as he goes out he blesses Vienna from the threshold of the hall.

A year later, the eagles of Napoleon swoop down on Vienna; and Haydn, dying in the occupied city, carries the old world to the tomb with him. But the young Beethoven has known the affectionate smile of this old world that so nobly throws the mantle of its aristocracy under the feet of the artist, and he despises it; he tramples the mantle under-foot. He is not the first of these peasants of the Danube and the Rhone (the first two of them were Gluck and Rousseau) to see the proud nobility anxious to please them, and who revenge themselves on it for the affronts that generations of their own class have had to endure. But whereas the "Chevalier Gluck" (a forester's son), who is artful by nature, knows how to blend the permitted violences with what he owes to the great, and even how to make these violences an advertisement for himself, and whereas the timid Jean-Jacques bows and stammers and does not remember until he is descending the stairs all the bold things he should have said, Beethoven blurts out straight to their faces, in the crowded salon, the contempt or the insult that he has on his tongue for this world. And when the mother of Princess Lichnowsky, the Countess von Thun, the noble woman who had been the friend of Gluck and the protectress of Mozart, falls on her knees before him and begs him to play, he refuses without even rising from his sofa.

How kind this princely house of Lichnowsky is to him! They have adopted this little savage from Bonn as a son, patiently set themselves to hewing him into shape, all the while taking infinite pains to avoid rousing his susceptibilities. The princess shows him the affection of a grandmother (the word is Beethoven's own); "she would put him under a glass so that no unworthy breath should touch him"; and later we have the story of that soirée at the Lichnowsky palace in December 1805, at which some of his intimates are trying to save *Fidelio*, which Beethoven, after the first failure, has refused to revise, and the princess, who is already mortally ill, appeals to the memory of his mother and conjures him "not to let his great work perish." Yet only a few months after that it will need only a word that seems to him to be directed against his independence for Beethoven to smash the prince's bust, run out of the house, and bang the door behind him, vowing that he will never see the Lichnowskys again.[1] "Prince," he writes to him on separating from him, "what you are you are by the accident of birth; what I am, I am of myself. There are and there will be thousands of princes. There is only one Beethoven."[2]

This spirit of proud revolt breaks out not only against the people of another class but against those of his own, against other musicians, against the masters of his own art, against the rules: "The rules forbid this succession of chords: very well, I allow it."[3]

He refuses to take for granted the edicts of the classroom; he will believe only what he has himself experienced and tested. He will yield only to the direct lesson of life. His two teachers, Albrechtsberger and Salieri, confess that he owes nothing to them, for he has never been willing to admit that they taught him anything; his real master was his own hard personal experience. He is the rebellious archangel: according to Czerny, the astounded and dismayed Gelinek said, "There is Satan in this young man!"

[1] Yet he loved them; and some words of his show that in his heart he preserved his gratitude to them. But this gratitude gave no one whatever rights over his liberty. Let me add that he paid his protectors royally: to Prince Lichnowsky he dedicated the three Trios (Opus 1), the *Pathétique* sonata (Opus 13), the Funeral March sonata (Opus 26), and the second symphony; to Princess Lichnowsky the piano arrangement of the *Prometheus* ballet; to the princess's mother, Countess von Thun, the B flat trio (Opus 11), etc.

[2] See the account of the prince's physician, Dr. Weiser, in Frimmel, *Beethoven* (1903); also Thayer. The scene was much more violent than the accounts indicate; but Beethoven's friends tried to hush the affair up. In an intimate letter of the 28th December, 1837, from Ries to Wegeler, contained in the Wegeler archives (*Beethoven als Freund der Familie Wegeler-Breuning*) we find the following: "Had it not been for Count Oppersdorf and a few others there would have been a brutal scuffle, for Beethoven had picked up a chair and was about to break it over the head of Prince Lichnowsky, who had had the door forced of the room in which Beethoven had bolted himself. Fortunately Oppersdorf threw himself between them." The cause of the quarrel was Beethoven's refusal to play for the French officers who were Lichnowsky's guests at dinner.

[3] Thus Ries. But Czerny tells us that when Anton Halm, showing Beethoven a sonata in 1815, excused certain irregularities with the remark that "Beethoven also has permitted himself many infractions of the rules," the composer replied, "I can do so, but not you." He knows exactly what he can do; he ventures with open eyes. And, after all, we must admit, the "harmonists" of today find him very prudent.

But patience! The spear of St. Michael will bring forth the God concealed in him. It is not from a vain pride that he refuses to bow before the judgments of authority. In his day, people thought it monstrous that this young man should regard himself as the equal of a Goethe and a Handel. But he was.

If he is proud before others, he has no pride before himself. Speaking to Czerny of his faults and his imperfect education, he says, "And yet I had some talent for music!" No one has ever worked harder, more patiently, more tenaciously, from his first days to his last. The theoreticians whom he rejected at twenty he returns to and re-reads at forty; he makes extracts from Kirnberger, Fux, Albrechtsberger, Türk, Philipp Emanuel Bach,—and this in 1809, after he has written the *Pastoral* and the C minor![1] His intellectual curiosity is enormous. Near the end of his life he says, "Now I am beginning to learn." Patience! already the iron is emerging from the fusing ores. The jealous passion for glory, that is nourished by the rivalries of the virtuosi and the exciting contact with the public, is only, as it were, an infantine skin eruption. When his friends, says Czerny, speak to him of his youthful renown, he replies: "Ah! nonsense! I have never thought of writing for renown and glory. What I have in my heart must out: that is why I write." Everything is subordinated to the imperious voice of his interior life.

Every true artist has within himself, diffuse and intermittent, this dream-life that flows in great streams in the subterranean world of him. But in Beethoven it attains to a unique intensity; and that long before the closing of the doors of his hearing blockade him from the rest of the universe. Think, for example, of the magnificent Largo e mesto in D minor in the sonata Opus 10, No. 3,—that sovereign meditation that dominates the vast plain of life and its shadows! It is the work of a young man of twenty-six (1796). And the whole of Beethoven is already there. What maturity of soul! If not so precocious as Mozart in the art of smooth harmonious speech, how much more precocious he was in his interior life, in knowledge and mastery of himself, of his passions and his dreams! His hard childhood, his premature experiences developed these aptitudes early. I see Beethoven as a child as his neighbor the baker used to see him, at the window of that garret of his that looked out over the Rhine, his head in his hands, lost in his "beautiful, profound thoughts." Perhaps there is singing within him that melodious lament, the poetic adagio of his first pianoforte sonata.[2] Even as a child he is a

[1] But observe that it is for his pupil, the Archduke Rudolph, that he accumulates these copies, these *Materialien zum Contrapunkt.* (See Nottebohm, *Beethoveniana,* pp. 154 ff.) And this fact elucidates the tart rejoinder to Halm, quoted on the preceding page. Crutches are good for the weakly!

[2] This fine adagio, before becoming part of the sonata Opus 2, No. 1 (Vienna, 1795), had figured in the quartet in C major, written at Bonn in 1785, when

prey to melancholy; in the poignant letter with which his correspondence begins we read, "Melancholy, that for me is an evil almost as great as illness itself. . . ."[1] But even in the early days he has the magic power to win free of it by fixing it in tones.[2]

But conqueror or conquered, he is always alone. From his infancy, wherever he may be, in the street or in the salons, he isolates himself with a peculiar strength. Frau von Breuning used to say, when he was thus lost in the distance, oblivious of everything, that he had his *raptus*. Later this becomes a gulf in which his soul disappears from the sight of men for hours and days. Do not try to recall him! That would be dangerous: the somnambulist would never forgive you.[3]

Music develops in its own elect that power of concentration on an idea, that form of *yoga*, that is purely European, having the traits of action and domination that are characteristic of the West: for music is an edifice in motion, all the parts of which have to be sensed simultaneously. It demands of the soul a vertiginous movement in the immobile, the eye clear, the will taut, the spirit flying high and free over the whole field of dreams. In no other musician has the embrace of thought been more violent, more continuous, more superhuman.[4]

Once Beethoven takes hold upon an idea, he never lets it go until he possesses it wholly. Nothing can distract him from the pursuit. It is not for nothing that his piano playing is characterized by its legato, contrasting in this respect with the Mozart touch,[5] that was delicate, pointed, clean-cut, as well as from that of all the pianists of his own time. In Beethoven's thought, everything is connected, and yet it appears to gush out in torrents. He controls the thought, and he controls himself.

Beethoven was fourteen. He himself regarded it as a lament, and Wegeler, with his consent, brought it out as a melody with the title *Die Klage*. This is to be found in the appendices to Wegeler and Ries's *Biographische Notizen*.

[1] Letter of 15th September, 1787, to von Schaden. It is translated in full in Prod'homme's *La Jeunesse de Beethoven*.

[2] In this very Largo e mesto from the sonata Opus 10, No. 3, of which I have just spoken, Beethoven, according to his own avowal, has described "the state of mind of a melancholic." The adagio of the sixth quartet, Op. 18 (published before 1800), bears the title *La Malinconia*.

[3] The painter Kloeber, who made a fine portrait of him in 1818, which he has supplemented in his notes, says: "I often met him on his walks. It was most interesting to see him stop, seem to be listening, look up, then down, and begin writing. I had been warned never to speak to him when he was like this, for if I did he would make himself extremely unpleasant."

[4] I would venture to say, *more inhuman*. Let us be careful: here is the key to the Beethoven enigma, to his genius, and perhaps even—yes, so I believe! —to his tragedy. Nature cannot with impunity be violated by the soul. If the latter tears from it secrets it has withheld from everything else, it will have to pay for them.

[5] Beethoven, who had heard Mozart, told Czerny that he had "a fine but broken way of playing, no ligato." Czerny adds that Beethoven was especially admirable in legato, and that he treated the piano like an organ.

He appears to be delivered up to the world by his passions; but in fact no one can read the thought that is moving in the depths of him. In these early years of the nineteenth century, Seyfried, who studies him at close quarters both in drawing rooms and at home (they live in the same building), is struck not so much by the traces of emotion in his face as by its impassiveness: "It was difficult, even impossible," he says, "to read either approbation or dissatisfaction on his face [when he was listening to music]; he remained always the same, to outward appearance cold and reserved in his judgments. Within him the mind was working without respite; the fleshly envelope was like a marble without a soul."

This is a different Beethoven from the ordinary conception of him as looking like King Lear in the storm! But who really knows him? One is always inclined to accept the impression of the moment.

In his thirtieth year his mind is a formidable equilibrium of opposing elements. If in the outer world he gives free rein to his passions, in his art he holds their mouth in with a bit controlled by a wrist of steel.

He rejoices in improvisation; it is then that he comes to grips with the element of the unforeseen in genius; the subconscious forces are unchained, and he must subdue them. Many of the great musicians have been masterly improvisers, especially in the eighteenth century, when music, its joints still supple, cultivated the faculty of free invention. But this public of connoisseurs, that only yesterday had been spoiled by Mozart, unanimously vows that in this field no one can compare with Beethoven. They agree also that in the whole art of Beethoven itself there is nothing to compare with the unheard-of power of his improvisation.[1] It is difficult for us to form an idea of it,[2] in spite of the fact that expert pianists like Ries and Czerny have described for us its inexhaustible wealth of ideas, its bewildering posing and solving of difficulties, its unexpected sallies, its swirl of passion. These professionals, on their guard as they are, fall as easy victims to the conqueror as the others. Wherever he happens to be playing, says Czerny, there is no resisting him; the public is staggered. "Apart from the beauty and originality of the ideas, there was something extraordinary in the expression." Aloys Schlösser speaks of his "poetic fury." Beethoven is like Prospero: he calls up spirits from the very depths to the very heights. The listeners break into sobs: Reichardt weeps bitterly: there is not a dry eye anywhere. And then, when he has finished, when he sees these fountains of tears, he shrugs his shoulders and laughs noisily

---

[1] "Whoever has not heard Beethoven improvise," said Baron de Trémont, "has no idea of the depth and the total power of his genius." Someone who heard him about 1790 or 1791 declared that "his playing is different from the ordinary way of treating the piano."

[2] Except, perhaps, by means of the Choral Fantasia, Opus 77, if we are to believe Moscheles, who could never listen to it without being reminded of Beethoven's improvisations.

in their faces: "The fools! . . . They are not artists. Artists are made of fire: they do not weep."[1]

This aspect of Beethoven—his contempt for sentimentality—is hardly known.[2] They have turned this oak into a weeping willow. It was his listeners who wept; he himself has his emotion under control. "No emotion!" he says to his friend Schlösser at parting: "man must be strong and brave in all things."

If he ignores in his art the torments that ravage his inner life, it is because he wills it so. The artist remains master of them; never do they sweep him away. Has he been their plaything? Well, it is his turn now! He takes them in hand, and looks at them, and laughs.

I have been describing so far the man of 1800, the genius as he was at thirty—with the big, repellent traits that indicate an abuse of strength, but strength indubitably, an immense interior sea that does not know its own boundaries. But there are grave risks that it may lose itself in the sands of pride and success. This God whom he bears within himself, will he prove to be a Lucifer?

I do not use the word "God" as a mere figure of speech. When we speak of Beethoven we have to speak of God: God to him is the first reality, the most real of realities; we shall meet with him throughout all his thinking. He can treat him as an equal, or behave as his master. He can regard him as a companion to be treated roughly, as a tyrant to be cursed,[3] as a fragment of his own Ego, or as a rough friend, a severe father *qui bene castigat*. (The son of Johann van Beethoven had learned as a child the value of this treatment.) But whatever this Being may be that is at issue with Beethoven, he is at issue with him at every hour of the day: he is of his household, and dwells with him; never does he leave him. Other friends come and go: he alone is always there. And Beethoven importunes him with his complaints, his reproaches, his questions. The inward monologue is constantly *à deux*. In all Beethoven's work, from the very earliest, we find these dialogues of the soul,[4] of the two souls in one, wedded and opposed, discussing, warring, body locked

---

[1] "*Aha! die meisten Menschen sind gerührt über etwas gutes; das sind aber keine Künstlernaturen, Künstler sind feurig, sie weinen nicht.*" Yet immediately after saying this he plays for Bettina his immortal setting of Goethe's immortal lyric, "*Trocknet nicht, Thränen der ewigen Liebe!*" ("Dry not, tears of eternal love.")

[2] This man who is so hard with himself, so scornful of the feminine in man and its effusions, in his private life is extremely reserved,—so much so that even his intimate friends knew next to nothing of his love affairs, and chance alone has preserved for us the solitary letter "to the Immortal Beloved." Nor is he any more prodigal of confidences on the subject of his art; and when his art betrays him too openly he feels resentment against it. I will speak later of the hostile silence he preserves with regard to his *Moonlight* sonata.

[3] "Often I have cursed the Creator." (To Wegeler, June 1810.)

[4] The allegro of the Trio, Opus 9, No. 3 (1796–1798), the superb first movement of the quartet Opus 18, No. 4 (1799–1800) (which foreshadows the *Coriolan* overture), and the *Pathétique* sonata (1798) are striking types of these Beethovenian dialogues, veritable dramas of the passions.

with body, whether for war or in an embrace who can say? But one of them is the voice of the Master: no one can mistake it.

Toward 1800 Beethoven, while still recognizing it, contends with it. The struggle goes on again without intermission. Each time the Master imprints his burning seal on the soul. And he waits and watches for the fire. As yet comes only the first flame, kindled by the feeble breath of Beethoven's religious friend Amenda.[1] But the flame and the pyre are ready. Only the wind is wanting!

It comes!

The misfortune that descends on him between 1800 and 1802,[2] like the storm in the *Pastoral*—though in his case the sky never clears again—smites him in all his being at once; in his social life, in love, in art. Everything is attacked: nothing escapes.

First of all, his social life; and that is no small matter for the Beethoven of 1800! Imagine the brilliant position of an artist who has given to the world in five years the first ten pianoforte sonatas (among them the *Pathétique*), the first five sonatas for piano and violin, the first eight trios, the first six quartets (thrown at Prince Lobkowitz's feet in a single sheaf), the first two piano concertos, the septet, the serenade! And these are merely the most famous of the works, those whose fires are still unpaled after a century. Conceive to yourself the treasures of poetry and of passion that this young genius has poured into them—the melodic grace of them, the humor and the fantasy, the unleashed furies, the somber dreams! A whole new world, as, indeed, his contemporaries, especially the younger of them, immediately perceived; as Louis Schlösser put it, "the musical hero whose genius has unchained the interior infinite and created a new era in art."

This piano music and chamber music (for the impetuous genius has had the rare patience not to attempt the conquest[3] of the symphony until after he has made himself master of the whole domain of *Kammermusik*), enjoys an unprecedented popularity. Before he is thirty years of age he is recognized as the greatest of all clavier composers; and as regards other music, only Mozart and Haydn are regarded as his equals. From the first years of the century he is performed all over Germany,

---

[1] A young Courland theologian, one of the two or three friends whom Beethoven, by his own account, loved most. They lived together in 1798/9.

[2] Until the epoch at which we have now arrived, Beethoven's hearing had been excellent. He prided himself on the extraordinary fineness and precision of it— "a sense that I had in complete perfection," he writes in the despairing Heiligenstadt Testament of 6th October, 1802; "a perfection possessed by few musicians at any time." Dr. Aloys Weissenbach confirms this claim: "Until the accident that caused the deafness, his hearing was incomparably fine and delicate" (*unübertrefflich zart und feinhörig*). He adds that even as late as 1814 Beethoven suffered greatly under the least false note (*Auch jetzt noch allen Uebellaut schmerzlich empfindet.*)

[3] That is to say, the public conquest; for we know now that the youthful Beethoven had been secretly experimenting with all the forms of his art for ten or fifteen years before he gave the public his first symphony.

in Switzerland, in Scotland, in Paris (1803). At thirty he is already the conqueror of the future.

Take now a look at this conqueror, this Beethoven of thirty, the great virtuoso, the brilliant artist, the lion of the salons, who fascinates youth, kindles transports, and thinks little of this elegant, vibrant, refined world, though he has need of it—(he has always lived in it, from the time when, as a child, he became a little *Hofmusicus;* when he emerges from his father's poor hearth, or now, at Vienna, from his untidy bachelor's rooms, it is always to breathe the most aristocratic atmosphere in Europe and taste the intoxication of it)—this Beethoven whose bad manners the good Princess Lichnowsky has patiently polished, and who affects to despise fashion but for all that carries his chin well up over his fine white three-deep cravat, and out of the corner of his eye looks proudly and with satisfaction (though at heart a little uneasy) at the effect he is creating on the company, this Beethoven who dances (but how?), this Beethoven who rides a horse (unhappy animal!), this Beethoven, whose charming humor, whose hearty laugh, whose delight in life, whose concealed grace and elegance (very much concealed, and yet there!) find expression in ravishing works like the Bonn *Ritterballet* (1791), the *Serenade* of 1796, the exquisite Variations on *Vieni amore* (1791), on a Russian dance tune (1795–97), on an air from *La Molinara* (1795), the frisky German dances (1795–97), the youthfully happy waltzes and *Ländler*. Do not fall into the error of regarding this man as unsociable. He may clash with this society, but he cannot do without it. And that fact gives us the measure of what it must have cost him later to be deprived of it.

But for the moment he is enjoying it. He is its favorite. Yet the poor plebeian young man knows how precarious is this favor, this attachment, how much of irony, benevolent or malevolent, there is blended with it— the suspicious young bumpkin believes in his heart that it is so, and he is right; he knows that these noble admirers are on the lookout for his gaucheries, his absurdities, his weaknesses, and that (we know this sort of friend!), however much they may like him, tomorrow they would not mind throwing him over. Observe that he has not troubled to conciliate them: he conciliates no one; that is a natural impossibility with him; he would rather die than mince the truth. If he has many a devoted Maecenas, he has also, it goes without saying, enemies, jealous rivals whom he has mortally offended, virtuosi whom he has discomfited, embittered colleagues,[1] fools whom he had deflated, and even young artists whom he has not gone out of his way to flatter. He is rough

---

[1] See, for example, in the recollections of Ries, the story of the comical duel of virtuosity between Beethoven and Steibelt. A quintet by the latter has just been performed. Beethoven, on his way to the piano, takes the cello part from one of the desks, turns it upside-down, picks out with one finger a nonsensical theme from the opening bars, and begins improvising on it. Steibelt goes out in a temper and never forgives him.

with people who show him their insipid works; and he lacks the address
to build round himself a clientele of obsequious disciples (all he has,
at the most, is one or two professional pupils). Never was anyone less
the "dear Master" than he.

He is alone on his tightrope; below is the gaping crowd awaiting the
false step. He gave them no thought so long as he was sure his body was
whole. To be one against them all rejoiced him; he sported with vertigo.
. . . But today, now that destiny has dealt him a grievous wound? Imagine
the man on the tightrope suddenly becoming dizzy. What must he do?
Confess that he can no longer see clearly? He clenches his teeth: so long
as there is a glimmer of light for his eyes he will go forward.

The imminence of the night that is about to descend on him increases
the fury of creation in him.

And it increases love.

Beethoven is a man possessed with love. The fire burns unceasingly,
from his adolescence to the shadows of his last days. "He was never
without a love affair," one of his intimates tells us. Sensitive to beauty,
he can never see a pretty face without being smitten, as we learn from
Ries. It is true that none of these flames lasts very long: one expels the
other. (He is coxcomb enough to boast that the most serious of them
lasted only seven months.) But this is only the outer zone of love. Within
it there are sacred passions, of the kind that leave forever in the soul
the Wonne der Wehmut, the wound that never ceases to bleed. There
are the "little friends"; there are the women he has been in love with;
and there is the "Immortal Beloved." Between the one kind and the
other it is often difficult, where a Beethoven is concerned, to draw a
dividing line: more than one of these little affairs commences in jest
and ends by being serious.

Every variety of passion and of love is contained in these first years
of the century, just when his malady is about to immure him. There is
not a day when he is not surrounded in some Vienna salon or other by a
swarm of young girls, several of whom are his pupils—that kind of
pupil he never refused!—while all pay him court. Let us insist on this
fact, which at first sight is astonishing! He is the fashion; it is he who
writes for Vigano and la Casentini the new ballet, Die Geshöpfe des
Prometheus (The Creations of Prometheus) given at the Court Theater
on the 26th March, 1801.

In every epoch the virtuoso, the artist who is in the public eye, has
attracted women. Beethoven has always exercised a fascination over
them.[1] Ugly and common as he appears at first sight, unpleasant as

[1] His confidant and lifelong friend Stephan von Breuning said to his wife,
who could not understand how Beethoven could attract, "And yet he has always
been successful with women!" (Gerhard von Breuning: Aus dem Schwarzspanierhause,
1874.)

the first approach to him may be, hardly has he begun to speak
or smile when all of them, the frivolous and the serious, the romantic
and the quizzical, are at his feet. They notice then that he has
a fine mouth,[1] dazzling teeth, and "beautiful speaking eyes that mirror
the changing expression of the moment, by turns gracious, agreeable, wild,
angry, menacing."[2] No doubt they laugh at him,[3] and are delighted
to find ridiculous things in him that they can quiz him about: these indeed
are their defense, for without them he would be dangerous; in this little
duel of hearts they assure their advantage over him. And of course there
can be no question of these young girls, beautiful, rich, titled, letting
the adventure go any further than a drawing-room flirtation. No one will
blame them for that! What surprises us rather is that the heart of more
than one of them is touched. The women's letters published by La Mara
and M. A. de Hevesy often mention Beethoven, "who is an angel!"
And even while they are making fun of him their imagination is sometimes a trifle too occupied with him. They take him about with them
in their castles in Hungary; and behind the thickets, at night, sweet
words pass, kisses are exchanged—perhaps promises too, that are only
thistledown on the wind. (But we hear the wind blowing hot and
furious through the presto agitato of the finale of the *Moonlight*
sonata.)

These years 1799–1801 see the beginning of the intimacy with the two
related families of the Brunsviks and the Guicciardi. He loves the three
cousins, Tesi (Therese), Pepi (Josephine), and Giulietta by turn and all
together. (They are aged respectively twenty-five, twenty-one and sixteen.) And his feelings are reciprocated, as well as they can be by these
volatile creatures, intoxicated with their spring,—the beautiful and coquettish Giulietta, the fascinating Josephine, who is tender and proud
(the one of the three who most truly loved him at this time), and the
serious (though not so serious then as later!) Therese Brunsvik, who
remained so long uncertain of herself and unhappy. Giulietta carries the
day over her rivals; she unchains a tempest of passion in Beethoven.
It is not to her, however, that the letter of eleven years later to "the

[1] *Zierlich*, says Müller in 1820. Benedict, in 1823, speaks of his "gentle and
nobly shaped mouth." The attractive mouth, set in the tormented face, was also
one of the secrets of the charm of Mirabeau, to whom I have already compared Beethoven.
[2] Thus Müller. The young Charlotte von Brunsvik, Countess Teleki, writing to
her sisters in March 1807, tells them of a little Hungarian boy of ten years old
whose lovely eyes and precocious intelligence have fascinated her; and she makes
the following unexpected comparison, "His physiognomy is just like that of Beethoven,
he has the same expressive and lively glance; you can see the genius in his
eyes." (La Mara, *Beethoven und die Brunsviks.*)
[3] Not, however, the Brunsvik sisters. I cannot find in their letters or intimate
journals a single ironic or unkind word about Beethoven; a fact that has struck
me forcibly, knowing how easily his appearance lent itself to derision or, more
wounding still, to commiseration.

Immortal Beloved" is addressed[1] but in November 1801 she is "this dear girl, this enchantress" (*ein liebes, zauberisches Mädchen*), who has captured Beethoven's heart, and by whom he believes himself to be loved. She alone dissipates the clouds of melancholy and misanthropy that have gathered about him since he became haunted by the "specter of deafness,"[2] only to let them descend again, alas, more crushingly than before!

Precisely because he feels the trouble approaching—that mortal infirmity that soon he will no longer be able to conceal!—he feels the need to fly to a woman for refuge. And now it is not a question merely of love, but of marriage.[3] From now until 1816 this will be his constant hope—and his constant deception. The poor man sees the light going out, and he searches for the faithful hand that will guide him. But who will reach him that hand? It will not be any of the women who then attract him. Apart from their pride of caste—and if they themselves have none, their families see to that for them—what means of existence has he to offer them?[4] Until the first onset of his malady he has lived without thought for the morrow. At present his compositions bring him in little, he does not see to getting paid for the lessons he gives, he exists on provisional pensions that are always wounding to his susceptibilities. To lay anything by he would have had to tour Germany and Europe as a virtuoso. The idea occurs to him.[5] But the deafness comes on so swiftly that already the project makes him uneasy. In any case it would be years before he could amass sufficient to marry on.

Giulietta does not wait for him. She marries—a double affront, this!—a

[1] It appears to be proved today that these famous letters belong to the year 1812, at which time there was no longer any question, so far as Beethoven was concerned, of Giulietta. (See my article on *La Lettre à l'Immortelle Aimée*, in the *Revue Musicale*, October 1927.) I will return to the matter when we reach the Teplitz period, during which the seventh symphony was written.

[2] "You can hardly believe how sad my life has been, what a desert, for the last two years; everywhere my wretched hearing appeared to me like a specter" (*Wie ein Gespenst ist mir mein schwaches Gehör überall erschienen*), he writes to Wegeler on the 16th November, 1801.

[3] "For the first time I feel that marriage could make me happy." (To Wegeler, 16th November, 1801.) He had thought of it as early as 1798, in which year he asked the hand of Grétry's "Zémire," the beautiful Bonn singer Magdalene Willmann, who was then engaged at the Vienna Court Opera. But she refused him because "he was so ugly, and half cracked" (*weil er so hässlich war, und halbverrück*). In the following year she married another admirer, who was more satisfactory both to her aesthetic sense and to her common sense.

[4] Neither the Brunsviks nor the Guicciardi were free of money cares. Giulietta struggles all her life under a growing load of embarrassments, and has to live by her wits. The Brunsviks have vast domains, the revenues from which, however, are uncertain. And anyhow the girls do not benefit by them. They remain until marriage (Therese never marries) dependent on their mother, who sacrifices them to their brother. Josephine, who was the first to marry, loses her fortune in wretched lawsuits.

[5] "Had it not been for my hearing, I would by now have gone over half the world. I ought to do so." (Letter to Wegeler, cited above.)

musician (and what a musician!), a man of the world, an amateur, a handsome fellow, one of those dandies who play at being the great artist, without having the faintest idea of the gulf there is between insipidities like theirs and a work of genius. This little Count Gallenberg, a cub of twenty, will have the impertinence, at the orchestral concerts of the winter of 1803, to put side by side with the symphonies of Beethoven his own overtures, pieced together out of Mozart and Cherubini; and Giulietta is no more conscious of the difference than he is. She marries him on the 3rd November, 1803, a year and a half after Beethoven had dedicated *alla Damigella Contessa* the sorrowful *Sonata quasi una fantasia*, Opus 27, No. 2 (the *Moonlight*). The illusion had been short-lived; and already the sonata showed more suffering and wrath than love. Six months after this immortal ode, Beethoven, in despair, writes the Heiligenstadt Testament (6th October, 1802).

Beethoven would not be Beethoven if he were not *too much* of whatever he was. I do not praise him; I do not blame him; I am trying to paint him *whole*. Whoever would understand him must be able to embrace the excess of his contrasts, that brings about his mighty equilibrium. Yes, Beethoven is capable—at any rate in his youth—of feeling joy and sorrow almost simultaneously. The one does not exclude the other; they are the two poles of his "electrical genius"[1]; it is by means of these that he discharges and recharges his formidable vitality. The most extraordinary thing about him is not his enormous capacity for suffering and loving but the elasticity of his nature. Of this the crisis of 1802 is the most magnificent example.

Beethoven is felled to the ground; never has a more heart-rending cry of despair than this testamentary letter (which was never dispatched) been torn from a human breast. He measures his length on the ground,— but, like the Titan of the fable, only to raise himself again at a bound, his strength multiplied by ten. "No, I will not endure it!" . . . He seizes destiny by the throat. . . . "You will not succeed in bowing me utterly down."

In natures such as this, the excess of suffering determines the salutary reaction; the strength increases with that of the enemy. And when the prostrated one finds himself on his feet again he is no longer merely one man: he is the army of the *Eroica* on the march.[2]—ROMAIN ROLLAND (2)

[1] He so describes it himself to Bettina, who repeats his remarks in a letter of 28th May, 1810 [to Goethe]. The word "electricity" is frequently used there to explain the subconscious of the spirit and the explosions of genius.
[2] The Heiligenstadt agony is in October. In November his letters show him taking up with life once more, almost sprightly, indulging in his usual rough talk, his peasant humor.

The Place: Heiligenstadt

The frequency of pastoral inspiration [in Beethoven's works composed just after the turn of the century] has often been pointed out. In order to understand [them] we shall follow Beethoven to Heiligenstadt, where he went in the warm seasons.

This is one of the places in which we can become most intimately acquainted with him. It is a little village, today belonging to the district of Döbling, not far from the gray waters of the Danube, to the north of Vienna, and at the foot of Kahlenberg and Leopoldsberg. Beethoven was fond of walking in the woods when, at the end of winter, they were just beginning to bud. A little higher up is the formidable Augustinian Abbey of Klosterneuburg, the wealthiest and oldest in Austria, crumbling under its own weight, built during the eighteenth century, from whose terrace the mountains may be seen and, lost in the fog, the Schloss Kreuzenstein.

A good wine comes from the Abbey vineyards. As evidence thereof, a huge cask is fêted like an idol and is more renowned than the altar at Verdun with its niellos. But to the moderate imbiber, Heiligenstadt offers quieter charms. The vineyards, arranged like checkerboards on the little hills, receive the morning sunlight and warmth. The main street ascends gradually like those in our villages, between little shops which the advertisements of modern soap and sugar magnates have not succeeded in defacing. Low houses, looking as if they had been crushed together, are carried on the shoulders of robust arches. The street is surveyed by inns ornamented with the symbolic fir tree, where on festival days violins and guitars strum quick and sharp little melodies with a sort of breathlessness like Basque songs. A man with a checkered vest and a green hat enters one bearing this inscription:

> Grüss Gott, ihr lieben Leute,
> Kommet öften, nicht nur Heute.

> God be with you, good people;
> Come often, not just today.

This is the inn *Zum Nussberg*. It is adjacent to one of Beethoven's lodging houses. We enter: at the end of a small court is a flight of stairs, a gate flanked by two black fir trees, an orchard in the bloom of spring,

filled with some woman's snowy washing. It is an unpretentious setting
with its festive cherry trees.

At the upper end of the main street, which, like a canal, glides along
between the little houses on its banks, the Eroicagasse leads to the Pfarr-
platz dwelling. One imagines Beethoven as Grillparzer saw him, the white
scarf which he held in his right hand trailing to the ground, stopping
in front of a gate to admire a beautiful peasant girl climbing into her
haycart. The frame becomes larger. Above a greater court set off by
laurel bushes in pots, is the loft under a high sloping roof, with simple
dormer windows, in which Beethoven is said to have written the *Eroica*.
Long vines, climbing over the wall from a trellis, twist their withered arms
in the face of a little rural distillery, in which *Slibowitz*, the liquor of
the district, is made. Near by, a wooden statue of St. Michael in a
plumed helmet, lance in hand, guards the niche of an angel. The church
of the hamlet, just like those of Champagne, hides, in the shadows of
its gallery, an unassuming altar, lighted by two red candles. Nothing of
the heroic here, save the wind, which stirs the draperies of the patron
saint, surrounded by four feeble trees, and bends the branches, each
bearing a white chalice. A landscape in which a meditative soul is liberated, but on the condition that it give its uttermost. No noise other than
that of the heavy wooden carts, or of the children on their way to school.

The house in which the Testament[1] was written presents still more
humble charms. This dwelling with its wooden staircases is indeed the
very abode of poverty; near a linden tree, a very slender linden, a decrepit
dial surmounts a postern; a balcony decorated with clusters of box leads
to the two rooms that the master filled with his harmonies. Artisans, the
family of a plumber who offers to do any little odd job, a baker, half
naked, live there all packed together. The old woman who today[2] occupies
the two rooms at which the meanest of our hotels would blush, performs
the honors of these few square feet with great delight. All the possessions
of a hard-working woman are scattered about on the furniture. And
she apologizes for her straitened condition. Beethoven, she tells us, was so
modest. *So bescheiden!* The view takes in several small fields formerly
planted with vineyards, today reduced in size and menaced by the invasion of villas. The composer of the *Eroica* was content with this
environment. In the same way Rousseau, when he wished to refresh himself in the country, gained, through the boulevards and the rue du Chemin
Vert, the heights of Ménilmontant, the fields of Charonne; the pleasant
country that separates these two villages, a halt at the *Galant Jardinier*,
sufficed to inspire his touching *Reveries*.

Here in October 1802, Beethoven wrote the letter to his brothers which

[1] Beethoven's will—often referred to as the Heiligenstadt Testament—in which he
reveals the depths of his despondency.
[2] Early 1930's.—Editor.

is so often referred to as the Heiligenstadt Testament. It suggests Jean-Jacques from the very beginning. "O you men who believe or declare me to be vindictive, stubborn, or misanthropic, what injustice you do me! You do not know the secret cause for my seeming so. My heart and mind were ever inclined from childhood to a tender feeling of benevolence." One recalls the first pages of the *Confessions*: "I feel before thinking. . . . I have conceived nothing; I have felt everything." With both of them there was an innate love of music. I think of the little Jean-Jacques seated near his aunt Suzon while she embroidered and sang, listening to her endearing chatter, watching the two black lovelocks arranged, in the style of the period, over her temples, and learning from her songs, which she hummed in a soft, sweet voice, repeating the words which he could never recall without weeping:

> *Tircis, je n'ose*
> *écouter ton chalumeau*
> *sous l'ormeau.*

Thyris, I dare not listen to your shawm, under the elm tree.

Rousseau also experienced early an "infirmity that increased with time." We can understand now why the two sonatas *quasi una fantasia* move us so deeply. Novalis—Friedrich von Hardenberg, who died in 1801 on the threshold of his twenty-ninth year—has acquainted us with the forms German expression assumed during this period. Novalis, a dark-eyed youth, well represented the idealistic generation that was maturing in Germany. Love—a love timid and naïve—completed the influence that a kind of religious mysticism, philosophic prattling, and the cult of legends exercised on these dreaming spirits. But lyricism colored everything, transformed everything; the pages written by Novalis the day after [the death of his beloved Sophie] bear a great resemblance to the Heiligenstadt Testament, at least by virtue of that desire to live which prevails over suffering and pain. The novel *Heinrich von Ofterdingen* was written as a reaction against *Wilhelm Meister* and as a defense of poetry, *das Gemüth*, and *die Sehnsucht*. With a singular devotion a young man consecrates himself to the discovery of the *blue flower* which will reveal to him the meaning of the universe, and to this search he bends all his efforts; in a dream he reclines on the greensward among some rather bluish rocks or plunges into an enchanted pool from whose surface a host of young maidens emerge and vanish. The Romanticism that French writers were to express later is already present in this work; Novalis defines it. The poems *Hymnen an die Nacht* are the best commentary on the two sonatas *quasi una fantasia:* in both, the same ecstasy, the same serenity. In listening to the adagio of the work dedicated to Giulietta, I recall the end of the first poem: "Hast thou, O somber night, a

heart like ours . . . A precious balm is discharged from the poppies thou
holdest in thy hand . . . Thou freest the weighted wings of the soul . . .
More celestial than the stars appear those infinite eyes that Night opens in
us . . . Needing no light, they penetrate the depths of a loving heart."—
EDOUARD HERRIOT

Patrons and Friends

Of the princely persons who had a decisive influence on Beethoven's
life in Vienna, those who were in closest contact with him were Prince
Carl Lichnowsky, and his fragile, sickly wife, his intellectual brother,
Count Moritz, Prince Lobkowitz and Prince Kinsky, and afterward the
Archduke Rudolph. Later others were added to the list: his lady confessor, the Countess Erdödy; his sympathetic interpreter, Baroness Ertmann and Prince Rasumovsky, whose name shares his immortality because
of the dedication of the imperishable Quartets which are now called after
him, the Counts Browne, Fries and lastly Count Brunswick, whose sister
was linked to him by such a fervent though silent affection that most
people believe her to have been "the Immortal Beloved." We have already
mentioned Count Ferdinand Waldstein, who as long ago as in the Bonn
days had been his understanding patron and had received a right royal
meed of thanks by the dedication of the Waldstein Sonata in C major,
Opus 53. They all pass before us like characters in a shadow play, and of
only a few of them can silhouettes be sketched.

Among all the men of this high-born band, the two brothers Prince
Carl and Count Moritz Lichnowsky were probably the most attractive.
It was certainly they who meant most to Beethoven by reason of their
human understanding and their friendship not for his person alone but
for his music.

The former was an imposing gracious gentleman, very fond of the
pleasures of this life. A massive expansive man with booming voice. He
wore his scanty dark hair parted. He was handsome with a slightly
ruddy face, which was almost too large for his thick white stock or
cravat, a low forehead and somewhat sleepy eyes, and a fleshy well-shaped
nose. His full sensual lips and a strong chin radiated a good-natured
joy of life. So well disposed was he to Beethoven that he overlooked
all his eccentricities—perhaps did not even notice them—up to the day
of the often mentioned quarrel about the French officers, when Beethoven's incredible pigheadedness put an end to the cordial freedom and

absence of restraint which had marked their intercourse. Thenceforth anything but cool and purely formal relations become impossible. In spite of this, Lichnowsky and his family did not change in their kindly feelings to the difficult Master, and the family kept up the tradition after his death.

In 1824 the name of the young Prince Carl Lichnowsky was the first on the petition, in which many of the foremost men in Vienna begged him to arrange a performance of his latest great compositions and to write a new operatic work. They knew him and his greatness too well to take offense at his rough ways, his touchiness and his unruly temperament, which tolerated neither consideration nor any favors.

An incident which occurred at Gratz, due to the resounding voice of the old Prince, is a striking proof of his distaste for consideration which he thought had been carried too far. From his room Beethoven heard the Prince outside giving the order in too loud a voice to his personal servant (Kammerjäger) to the effect that if he himself and Beethoven were to ring the bell at the same time, Beethoven must be attended to first and he himself kept waiting. On the very next day Beethoven engaged a footman for his own personal service. He had felt oppressed by such excessive attention on the part of his host. He was not touched by the friendliness which had prompted all the attempts to spoil him, and only regarded them as irksome. He simply would not submit to petting, and it was perhaps not due only to his supreme contempt for all formality in social intercourse, that the deference paid him in Prince Lichnowsky's household often goaded him to perverse impatience.

Perhaps in spite of his great, unconcealed pleasure at such a sign of true friendship, he may sometimes have felt angry and embarrassed when shortly after the beginning of their acquaintance, the Prince settled an annuity of 600 gulden on him, to be drawn as long as he lived or until he had been secured by an adequate post (which by the way he never found). It was intolerable to his love of liberty to be obliged to stay so often in the Prince's palace, and to submit to the rules of the household, and appear at the dinner table punctually at four o'clock and comply with the rules of good manners. "Now I suppose I shall have to get home by half past three every day, put on proper clothes and shave my beard, and so on. I cannot stand it."

Hear what he said to Princess Christiane, Lichnowsky's delicately refined, always somewhat invalidish and fervently enthusiastic wife. One day he exclaimed bitterly: "Her Highness would have preferred always to keep me under a glass case, so that no common person could touch me or breathe on me." We may imagine with what painfully subdued impatience the Great Mogul, as Haydn was fond of calling him in jest, would brush aside her exaggerated anxiety and cosseting. She loved

Beethoven with all a mother's love for a son who is her pride, but whose lofty flights alarm her.

This noble lady, who led a somewhat solitary life by the side of the rough, jovial, sporting, sensual Nimrod of a husband, had had both of her breasts removed because of threatened cancer. Her physical condition, which demanded every care, debarred her from the pleasures of the nobility, such as the Spanish Riding School, the chase, routs and balls, and thus she had to look to music for everything that life had denied her. When she crouched shivering in one of the deep brocaded armchairs at one of her weekly concerts, and especially when a piece of Beethoven's was being played, she might well have served as a model for a painting to be called "A Listening Soul." At such moments a ray of transfiguring beauty seemed to light up her narrow, otherwise not remarkable but expressive face, half hidden beneath a wealth of dark ringlets and the mass of twisted veils which towered like a turban above her head, the slightly arched eyebrows, the large dreamy eyes, the thin nervously quivering nostrils and the wide mouth with its bitter sweet smile.

At that time there can have been but few who could penetrate into Beethoven's genius with such intimate understanding, and perhaps no one who could, as successfully as she, tame his rebellious spirit and force him to submission. It was in her drawing-room that the memorable scene was enacted after the failure of "Fidelio" at its first performance in the year 1804, which is described by Joseph Röckel, the tenor, then a young man, who later was famous in the part of Florestan.

The company tried to induce Beethoven to make several cuts, and more particularly to compress into one the first two of the opera's three acts. Several of the singers of the Court Opera who had taken part in the work and some friends had assembled at the house of the Princess to meet the refractory Master, who was in a state of great agitation, for the purpose of going through the work and discussing the proposed cuts. But the longer the meeting lasted, the more stiff-necked grew Beethoven's refusal to make any alteration. "He defended every bar," wrote Röckel, "with such majesty and artistic dignity that I wanted to fall at his feet."

When the important question was reached—that of the omission of an exposition section and the welding of two acts into one—he lost all control of himself and "perpetually shouted 'not a note' and wanted to rush off with his score." But the Princess cast a speaking look at him, and sat with her hands folded over the music, till he regained control over himself and sat down again at the piano. They sang, disputed and repeated many passages, till it was midnight when they came to the last bar. The pale, weak woman who had kept silent till then, now turned to the obstinate composer with an imploring look: "And the revision, the shortening?" He refused: "Do not ask it of me. Not one note must go."

She appealed to him once more: "And so, Beethoven, your great work must still be misunderstood and be condemned?" Still he answered evasively: "My dear Princess, it has reward enough in your approbation."

Then she rose. If was as if a stronger spirit had entered into the delicate woman's body, and half-kneeling and clasping him in her arms, she cried with enthusiasm: "No! Beethoven, your great work, you yourself, must not perish thus! God, who breathed into your soul these sounds of the purest beauty, will not permit it. The spirit of your mother, who at this moment is praying to you and warning you through me, forbids it. It must be. Beethoven, give way. Do it for the sake of your mother's memory. Do it for me, your only, your truest friend."

Beethoven stood before her deeply moved, fighting with himself. Then he burst into sobs: "I will do it—I will do everything for you and for my mother." Then he reverently lifted her up and gave his hand to the Prince, as if to seal the compact.

It is certainly a mistake to consider this description of the remarkable evening to be an emotional exaggeration in the style of the period. The story is certainly true and accurate. The men and women of those years were like that and spoke like that, and Beethoven not less than the others: a glance at his Letters proves it.

We stand deeply moved before the spectacle of the usually so unsentimental and irritable Master thus allowing himself to be guided by noble womanliness and by nothing else in the world. He realized that a woman with her clear vision can decide more rightly and more morally than any man in his obstinacy. Today we know that the Princess was right: we know the matchless masterpiece in its definite shape, which we owe to her alone. The world has forgotten the first version, so memorable, so beautiful in some parts, but all too incoherent and unbalanced. And in the last years of his life Beethoven placed his hallmark on it in a final version. "Fidelio" had to be rejected before it could become immortal.

Beethoven's relations with Count Moritz Lichnowsky, the Prince's brother, were quite different from those which subsisted between him and the princely couple. Beautiful and human as that friendship was, there was an invisible barrier which prevented too close a union.

In the case of the Count, on the other hand, we have not only an admiring Maecenas on the one hand, and on the other a great Master, who by reason of his greatness was at home in quite other worlds. It was an intimate union as between two brothers, or between two friends in the highest sense of the word, who had much in common, whose trust in each other was unshakable.

The refined, slimly built nobleman seemed not only mentally but even physically to be of a different race from his more robust brother. Rubens or Jordaens would have painted the best portrait of the Prince: the Count would have been a more fitting subject for Van Dyck or better still for one of the nobly restrained Englishmen of the period like Sir Joshua Reynolds, or Gainsborough. His carelessly lissom figure makes the impression of being animated less by overflowing vitality than by a graceful intellect and a highly disciplined will. Nor does his face bear any relationship to that of his brother. His forehead was high and open, above thick arched brows: the large dark eyes looked thoughtfully and with serene kindliness from under somewhat heavy lids. His nose was slightly hooked, not small but finely formed. His opulent, epicurean lips, curiously drawn down at the corners, gave his face a look of irony. The whole was framed in hair slightly grizzled at the roots and curling at the ends. Nor was he in the least like any of the nobles of that circle. They looked what they were: swashbuckling cavaliers, arrogant Grands Seigneurs, reckless libertines, swaggering bravos, jovial topers or shrewd diplomatists; nor were suggestions of degeneracy and stupid conceit lacking.

If any unbiased spectator were asked which of all these aristocratic patrons best deserved the title of true nobleman—not in virtue of blue blood only, but of character—he would unhesitatingly point to Count Moritz von Lichnowsky with the air of distinction of his slightly fatigued, overindulged, yet delicate and spiritualized features, and would perhaps even have detected in him a certain resemblance to Mendelssohn. At any rate he certainly looked the most musical of them all.

It is enough to know his relations with Beethoven to realize his whole character, his steadfast loyalty, his conscientiousness in counsel, his zeal in carrying out many a delicate task. His ever ready concessions to the most incalculable caprices of the Master bespeak a high-souled man wholly free from vanity, in complete self-forgetfulness, susceptible to beauty in all its forms, and able to bow before genius.

It is surely no accident that Beethoven dedicated to him the Sonata in E minor, Opus 90, one of his most delicately soulful and intimate works, with its endless flow of passionate fervor. No one who appreciates the ever wakeful suspiciousness of the Master and his abruptly varying moods, need be surprised that even he, the truest of the true, had more than once to endure the thunders of Beethoven's wrath. More than this, there was never once any question of his taking offense, and no reconciliation between the two was necessary because the Count instantly forgot any slight, for he completely understood: yet he was neither a thick-skinned flunky, nor a brainless snob. Beethoven understood this perfectly and knew how to draw the distinctions. He simply despised others who outwardly acted in the same way, but he loved the Count to the end. This, however, did not prevent him occasionally from misunderstanding his friend and wounding him deeply.

The best illustration is that memorable first performance of the Ninth Symphony, when the Count concocted a little scheme with Schindler, Beethoven's dry-as-dust amanuensis, and Schuppanzigh, the corpulent violinist, the "Falstafferl" of the Master. It really must have been like a scene from Shakespeare's "Henry IV"—when they tried to pin down the composer, who could not make up his mind about details of this concert, and delayed everything over and over again by upsetting all the arrangements for the program. As they wanted something definite, they persuaded him to sign the notes of the results of various meetings. But as soon as they had left the house, Beethoven became suspicious, and when he got wind of their kindly-meant scheming, naturally thought he had been hoodwinked and sent furious ultimatums to all three, the worst to Lichnowsky: "Deceit I despise. Visit me no more. The Concert does not take place. Beethoven."

This time it certainly lasted longer than usual before the Master saw how wrong he had been. But this time too the first sign of his repentance sufficed to bring his faithful friend back at once to his side, for he knew but too well that Beethoven himself suffered more than the objects of his rage from his own irritability and his often unjust outbursts.

The lofty nature of this friendship between the two men is sufficiently proved by the very style of his letters, in which he avoided all his usual slovenliness, his students' slang and his dreadful plays on words. It is shown also by the way in which he took and accepted favors, which is the unfailing standard of the value of a man. Here, in contrast to the common run of men who are servile in giving and impudent or cringing and at the same time really insatiable in taking, we had two men who could give each other presents without loss of dignity, without humiliation or disillusion on either side.

The beautiful letter of Beethoven which accompanied the already mentioned Dedication of the E minor Sonata is a welcome testimony of the feelings of both. "I see that you always heap favors on me," wrote the Master in his usual somewhat heavy-handed style:

"As I do not wish you to believe that anything I do may appear to be prompted by new self-interest, or anything of the kind, I say to you that a Sonata of mine will soon appear which I have dedicated to you. I wished to surprise you, for this dedication was destined for you long ago, but your letter of yesterday induces me to make it known to you now. It needed no inducement to make me publicly display my appreciation of your friendship and acquaintance, but with anything that might have the least semblance of a gift you would cause me pain, for thus you would completely misunderstand my intention, and I can only refuse anything of the kind. I kiss the hand of the Princess for her remembrance and kind disposition toward myself. I have never forgotten the many debts I owe you, which I cannot show as I should have wished."

Beethoven could nevertheless have accepted without a qualm the present which the Count intended for him. He would still have remained the giver. But his feelings do equal credit both to him and the other: the blameless knight in whose quiet, high-bred, restrained, harmonious and gentle character we think we may see reflected the spirit of Mozart, and not only because he had been his pupil.

The nobles of that period must altogether have been gifted with more munificence, a clearer understanding of the soul and more appreciation of true worth than we find in later times. And when we consider how sensitive and fastidious they were, how they were always on their guard against anything that savored of middle-class manners, how they feared all tactlessness, which of itself embarrassed them, and drove them to stand aloof, then we must find in the attitude of these Viennese aristocrats to this Beethoven, who was in every way so difficult, so splendid from the purely human point of view, a significant proof of homage to command-ing genius, such as surely even they rarely paid.

This is true above all things of the three men whose generosity finally bound the Master to Vienna, who showed an incomparable nobility of mind in spite of Beethoven's readiness to take offense, his intractability and his obstinate insistence always and in all circumstances on the show of deference. Two of them never failed him, even when their personal relations with him had been broken off because of his senseless and often offensive behavior. It would have been much, had they understood Bee-thoven's untamable self-esteem. He took as a tribute due to him every understanding of his ideas, all the admiration and all the material favors that were offered to him, and resented as an injustice everything that was kept from him or given him in a diminished degree. Perhaps several of them felt at the back of their minds how little the Master appreciated their love of art. The greater therefore is the value of their loyalty. Whether or no Beethoven was right in his underestimation of them is another story. In this respect he had some really curious experiences.

Ferdinand Ries, one of his very few pupils, for whom he had secured a post as pianist with Count Browne, tells us of an entertaining episode of this kind. One evening, tired of playing so much by heart, he improvised a March. An old Countess, an undiscriminating Beethoven worshiper, who had often irritated the Master by her hysterical enthusiasm, thought the March was a new composition by Beethoven, and could not be loud enough in her expressions of delight, and Ries in a mischievous mood confirmed her in her belief. Unfortunately Beethoven went to Baden the next day to pay a visit to the Count. At once the old Countess attacked him with expressions of her boundless enthusiasm for the splen-did new work of genius. Ries could think of no way out of his em-barrassment but to explain the state of affairs to the Master, who was at first astonished and then amused. Finally Ries had to play the March again "which now turned out much worse, as Beethoven was standing near him." Beethoven now had to listen again to the most extravagant eulogies of his genius. This made him confused and angry, until relief came in loud laughter. Later on he said to Ries: "Look, my dear Ries, these are the great connoisseurs who pose as infallible and keen judges of all music. All they want is the name of their favorite."

This expression of opinion may apply to most lovers of music of this (and all other) epochs, and to two of the above-named three men, the Prince Lobkowitz and Count Kinsky, but certainly not to the third and the best of them all, the Archduke Rudolph, who until he was enthroned as Archbishop of Olmütz in the year 1819 was Beethoven's pupil, and one who showed himself worthy of his teacher.

There were always among the Austrian Archdukes, so to speak, some sports, to whom life at the Imperial Court with its brainless rigidity, its strict ceremonial and the exactions of an unintellectual hothouse existence, became intolerable. Some rebelled openly against this marionette existence and earned disfavor in the highest quarters when they broke out and, at the cost of all their dignities and emoluments, decided to lead their own lives. The others gained their object more quietly and sought refuge in dilettantism or in the serious study of science or art, and thus in a very special sense secured their existence, which otherwise would have been shipwrecked in brilliant emptiness.

The young Archduke Rudolph belonged to the latter class of Princes who protested in silence and retained their independence and spiritual freedom. He was born about eighteen years later than Beethoven and was almost a lad when he made the acquaintance of the composer, which from that hour became his most highly cherished spiritual possession. The very goodhearted simple-minded youth in his appearance unmistakably embodied the Habsburg family type. But he was a sympathetic Habsburg. The somewhat childlike face, the pouting mouth, the powerful long nose, the questioning dark eyes, the smooth high forehead and the fair hair falling in curls over the ears and parted in the middle, seemed, in spite of his serious mien, almost to be inconsistent with the pomp of the Cardinal's robes. He seems to express joy in the beautiful things of this world and in the lofty manifestations of the spirit and of art.

The young Prince must have had many a tragic experience to be driven to cut himself adrift from the Court and also from his artistic pursuits, and to be inspired with the determination to escape into high spiritual dignity. Up to his twenty-fifth year he probably hardly thought of such an escape. He was a passionate musician and undoubtedly gifted as a composer, and it is beautiful to contemplate with what a feeling of happiness and also with what reverent friendship he carried on his intercourse with Beethoven and embarked on his training as a patient and grateful pupil.

The lessons were both a trouble and a pleasure to Beethoven. He was always forced to observe at least a minimum of formal etiquette and could not indulge his moods of frank playfulness and his rough humor as much as usual. He had to swallow the dictates of court behavior, even if in homeopathic doses. Though he did not indeed put too severe a restraint on himself in his fear of lapsing into any unseemly behavior toward his Imperial pupil, he never lost his dignity or degenerated into a flunky. Yet he never flattered, and ordered his coming and going as and when it seemed good to him, and often he did not come at all.

One day when the Archduke kept him waiting an unusually long time in the antechamber, he immediately gave him a double lesson. He trounced his pupil as never before, scolded him, even often swept his fingers from the keyboard, and when the puzzled Prince asked him what was the matter with him that day, he said harshly that he had lost so much time in waiting that he was now impatient and had to make it up. The lesson, probably the only one that he had to give to this sensitive young man, bore fruit.

The Archduke's attendants received strict orders to introduce the Master to him without delay, and it proved also this time—and incidents with his other noble friends prove it also—that it was just those men who were so used to venal servility and unquestioning agreement, who were, so to speak, almost educated into the habit of kicking their fellow men, that had the greatest respect for the frankness of a true man and artist. The more offensively the lies and contemptible incense strewn before them by their lackeys poisoned the air, the better they knew how to honor him.

But these lessons were really a pleasure to the Master, because after a time his original, and in principle not unjustifiable, suspicions of the true musical gifts of the Archduke soon yielded to the conviction that he was not dealing with one of the many insufferable artistic dilettanti, to whose misshapen bantlings he was expected to give artistic form, so that the high-born gentlemen might gracefully put their names to the finished work and satisfy their vanity as authors.

With the Archduke Rudolph there was nothing of the kind, for he was a thoroughly serious musician and pursued his studies with Beethoven with more thoroughgoing zeal and a more fruitful talent than many a member of the craft. We know that with all his failings, untruthfulness was not one of Beethoven's vices, and that, as far as art was concerned, he would never have been capable of any insincere praise, even though he might sometimes have judged his Imperial pupil by a lower standard than anyone else. But surely he would never have used the epithet "masterly" of the Archduke's Forty Variations on a Theme he had given him, if they had been rubbish, or even an inadequate production. Though today they seem somewhat moth-eaten, they are really a very capable piece of work, and would have done credit to any honest musician of the craft, and indeed even more than that.

Moreover the reading of Beethoven's letters to the Archduke Rudolph gives special pleasure: they are a testimony both to him who wrote them and to him to whom they were written. He always addressed him, if the paradox may be allowed, most submissively from above. He never hid his face behind the mask of the devoted servant, but always, so to speak, held it in his hand, thus emphasizing his clear understanding of the necessary distance between them, to which, however, he did not pay much attention. He talked to his "Imperial Highness" always in the third person and yet through all his formal correct phrases we can always read an almost condescending heartiness which expressed itself not only in his sincere interest in the well-being and the delicate health of the Prince, but was also damped down into a consciously restrained fatherly affection, the expression of which was over and over again muffled by self-esteem, which was always ready to spring into action, and was angered by even the semblance of any claim to superiority.

It was as if he were always ready to withdraw himself as in fear of possible misinterpretation, when by chance he had become too cordial. In this he did an injustice to the Archduke, who always remained un-affectedly friendly and amiable, always carefully avoiding any courtly formalities and all false intimacy, which might wound the bourgeois as being heedlessness or hidden gracious condescension, of which he would have been quite incapable. It was not only tactfulness which prompted him, but also the thoroughly sincere feelings of a youth who looks up to a great man, while his higher nature deems the accident of his own high birth as ridiculous and of no account. It is just this quality which gives his letters to Beethoven an unspeakable charm, which is the more fascinating the less he seems to realize how subtle his own emotions are.

Nor did he change when he became a Prince of the Church; in all that he wrote to the Master, we always see the same undertone of the grateful admiration of a modest acolyte for the unapproachable Chief of the Mysteries. It would scarcely have surprised us if the Archbishop of Olmütz had asked the composer for his blessing. It was never the other way round. Beethoven's mind was far too unecclesiastical and undogmatic to think of such things.

But he has in the truest and most real sense of the word given his blessing to the Cardinal with the Missa Solemnis, which he had not begun on a commission from his patron, but had written under the impulse of his sincere affection for the pure and serious youth, whom he thus consecrated at the beginning of his religious office. Perhaps it would be more correct to say "would have consecrated," had the gigantic work, which on its pinions wafted him to ever greater heights, been completed in time. But the work was of slow growth.

What was meant to be a Mass like his earlier ones, and was to have made the first High Mass of the young Archbishop into a celebration of unique solemnity, a gift, a festal greeting and music worthy of the moment, became a song of God and Mankind, such as had never been heard before. Certainly, the Archduke Rudolph had no part in the creation of this Mass, perhaps the most magnificent in all musical art, save that he was what he was. On the one hand nothing in him has any-thing in common with this music so eloquent of violent struggles, so secular yet so devout, so impersonal yet springing from the inmost depths of Beethoven's soul. On the other hand it must have been a lovable being, far above all that is common, that could call into being this music, at first so angrily questioning, so directly accusing, lashed into such fearful passion, and then becoming so other-worldly, so full of tidings of hope from the Beyond, such a heart-throb of consoled humanity.

But who knows? Who knows whether this soul had not had to fight battles equally obstinate and hard-won, whether it had not passed through phases of confusion, disillusion, revolt and doubt, before it could resign itself to the decision to turn away from the world and find refuge in the bosom of the Church? Or is the truth that the Archbishop was part of this work only as an external stimulus, and influenced only its first plan. However this may be, the Missa Solemnis would not have been created without the Archduke Rudolph, and for this reason alone he shares the immortality of Beethoven.

It was this Prince of the Imperial House who became the first Patron of the newly founded Society of the Friends of Music (Gesellschaft der Musikfreunde) to whose energetic initiative we owe the Master's stay in Vienna.

In the year 1809, seventeen years after the Master had settled there, without being able to obtain a permanent position, or even the title of a "Hofkapellmeister," which his ambition desired, a tempting proposal was made to him. Napoleon's brother Jerôme, known as "König Lustig" (The Merry Monarch), the frivolous, pleasure-seeking ruler of Westphalia, caused the Master to be summoned to him, offered him 600 gold ducats as yearly salary, and 150 ducats as traveling expenses, if he would come to his Court occasionally to play to him and direct the few concerts of Chamber Music in the Palace of Kassel. No doubt the offer was flattering and seductive. It seemed to guarantee a certainty, which, as history teaches us, would have turned out to be deceptive. What was demanded was not exacting and in no way detracted from the dignity of an artist.

Beethoven weighed it very seriously and after some hesitation was inclined to accept it. When the Archduke heard of it, he was shocked and alarmed. He implored Beethoven not to be overhasty. He must not leave the haunts hallowed by Haydn and Mozart. Nowhere else would he find a second Vienna, and he promised he would confer at once with his Imperial brother and all Beethoven's noble patrons in order to secure for him an appropriate salary, which would save him from all further anxiety. Whether he did actually speak with the Emperor is not certain.

Presumably Beethoven thought it over. He knew only too well that the good Emperor Francis was a niggard especially where such luxury articles as music or a great composer were concerned, even if he were a hundred times the pride of the capital and became one of its strongest attractions for the foreigner. Anyhow the Emperor did not support his brother's action to the extent of a single penny. Also the other noblemen to whom the Archduke wished to apply—Liechtenstein, Eszterházy, Palffy and Károly—seem to have failed him, even if they were approached. Only two noblemen agreed and made possible the conclusion of the already mentioned agreement which secured to Beethoven a total yearly income of 4000 gulden.

Again, if anyone had been shown a collection of the portraits of the noble patrons of that time, and had been asked to guess from their features which were the two generous gentlemen who could be thought capable of endowing Beethoven in this manner, it would have been a hundred to one against his selecting the right persons. Prince Lobkowitz, with his puffy childish face, with the vulgar snub-nose, and the friendly shrewdly smiling mouth, the pair of merry boy's eyes looking with cheerful questionings into the world, who could be roused to any interest in music only by Beethoven's flowing mane, might, to judge from his whole appearance, have been rather a guzzling epicure than a man of artistic nature.

The unkempt Prince Kinsky, with his flying curly hair, his whiskers, his full mouth under the short mustache, his soft sensual chin, and his widely open, ruminating eyes, surely resembled a figure of Lenau's imagination and still more an elegant, melancholy Hussar of the Honved, rather than a man able to penetrate into Beethoven's spiritual world. Perhaps he preferred gypsy music to the Ninth Symphony, and one would hardly do these two gentlemen an injustice if one were to ascribe their noble gesture and their further conduct rather to the wish to please the Archduke than to a burning desire to keep Beethoven in Vienna.

Lobkowitz indeed did not make too great an effort. It is unlikely that the 700 gulden which he added to the Prince's 1500 had any great share in the ruin which soon befell him.

Kinsky went further than either of them. He signed for 1800 gulden, and this completed the projected sum of 4000 gulden. Unfortunately soon afterwards he fell from his horse, and the executors of his Will could think of nothing better to do than to suspend the payment of his share to Beethoven's annuity. The tremendous fall in the value of money which occurred after the Napoleonic wars and the financial disasters of Prince Lobkowitz, who had been severely affected, further contributed to the reduction of the composer's income to one-half.

Beethoven's fury knew no bounds. He raged, he went to law; he secretly, and not only secretly, accused the Archduke of having prevented him from accepting the offer from Kassel and having forced him into this hopelessly precarious position. Yet he was the only one who produced his share, and thus held Beethoven indemnified as far as he was concerned.

It was only after endless urgent letters from Beethoven that Princess Karoline Kinsky attacked the Trustee Courts and the Prince's obstinate chief cashier and ordered payment in full.

Prince Lobkowitz was the only one who refused to keep his word in these changed circumstances and relied on his shattered fortune as excuse.

These painful negotiations dragged on till the year 1813. The incensed Master spoke only in words of abuse of the Prince who from a patron became "a Princely rogue," and it must be confessed that in his morbid terror of want, Beethoven adopted a quite unseemly tone and behaved in a way unworthy of himself. Finally the action was decided against him.

Then an amazing thing happened, with which one would never have credited that rosy-cheeked baby face. Prince Lobkowitz, as soon as he had won his case against the effervescing, abusive Master, made up his mind to pay his contribution to Beethoven's allowance in full and made arrangements for its continuation after his death. But he refused ever to see the humiliated composer again. Beethoven tried in vain to approach him to explain and to make it up. He tried to make good what he had done, dedicated a Cantata to the Prince for his birthday, but all in vain. The Prince contemplated Beethoven's successes from afar, and wrote to the Archduke, who tried to act as mediator: "As a passionate lover of music I am glad that people are really beginning to appreciate his certainly great works." But he had been too deeply wounded and irritated by the inconsiderate and ungrateful behavior of Beethoven, from whom one never knew what to expect, to bring himself to resume intercourse with him.

It is easy to understand and therefore to honor the noble magnanimity with which Lobkowitz had ended a troublesome affair and given evidence of the nobility of his nature and his reverent understanding of Beethoven.

The failure of the Master's humanity and the proved superiority of his aristocratic patron are lamentable, and can only be explained by Beethoven's childishness in all the practical affairs of life, and the specter of want which always haunted him. His ever-recurring feeble plays on words about the "scores" which only add to the "scores" which are chalked up against him are a significant symptom.

Another series of representatives of Vienna of that time were cast for parts in the drama of Beethoven's life. But they appear in other acts, or at least in other scenes, and the list of persons must be given elsewhere. They are mostly men and women belonging rather to the bourgeoisie who bore the outward tokens of nobility in their names rather than in their manners however clearly the hallmark was impressed on their real natures.

A good example is the Baron von Gleichenstein, a colorless man, who was truly devoted to the Master. Then there was Nikolaus von Zmeskall, Beethoven's "Mudlark" and "Count Guzzle," the fussy, always slightly worried, serviceable adherent, who was magnificent only in the pleasures of the table, and who was a close companion of many often difficult years. And there were many others who will, as these two did, come to the fore in another section of this dance of life.

There is, however, one figure which must be sketched, that of a man indissolubly connected with Beethoven's Chamber Music, whose name shines for all times through the dedication of three immortal Quartets, Count and later Prince Andreas Cyrillovitch Rasumovsky, who for nearly a quarter of a century was *persona grata* as Russian Ambassador at the Court of Vienna. He was elevated to the rank of Prince on the ashes of his beautiful home in Vienna by the Czar Alexander I, who happened to be present.

His palace on the Landstrasse soon became the center of the artistic life of the city. The extensive building, half in the Empire style and half in that of the Renaissance, with the projecting roof garden, supported by six beautiful Ionic columns, stood at that time isolated on hilly meadow land. Now it is hemmed in by houses of all kinds, and the trees which surrounded it have long since been felled. It now serves Science, for it is the seat of the Imperial Geological Institute.

At that time, however, light and music flooded the splendid palace, the interior of which was famous already for the Canova Hall, full of the choicest statues of the much-admired sculptor, who had already gained fame as the creator of the noble Christina monument. But the wonderful library, the valuable picture gallery and the collection of other works of art, spoke more eloquently of the artistic culture of the Rasumovskys, of which still more striking proofs were the musical evenings in the noble marble hall, which had become historic through the first hearing of many of the Chamber Works of Haydn and Beethoven and the presence of their creators.

The Prince himself had the reputation of being an admirable violinist, and had been initiated into the mysteries of his quartet style by Papa Haydn himself, and was looked on as the guardian of the true tradition of performance of these masterpieces. That he had a real knowledge of all that was great in the art of music and that Beethoven highly esteemed him as such could be proved—even if we did not know it by hearsay—by the sure evidence of Beethoven's imperishable three Quartets, Opus 59, which he dedicated to the Prince. Under the name of Rasumovsky Quartets their name has long since been synonymous with virile strength, with inspiration and a wonderful homogeneity of whole movements, the splendid flowers of which are the blossomings of one single seed.

Whoever credits this patron and employer with a true understanding of these magical worlds of sound confined within the four corners of one narrow tone-picture, must feel true respect for him. From Prince Rasumovsky's appearance no one could guess that Goethe's epigram: "Sometimes they are cold, sometimes coarse" did not apply to him as it did to other patrons.

The tall, slight, spare gentleman looked more like a Russian Chief of Police than a generous supporter of the best Chamber Music. The face, over which his dark hair curled tightly like a cap, the suspicious, watchful eyes, set far apart, the squat nose, the mouth pressed together till the lips had almost disappeared, and the brutally projecting chin, give the whole, strikingly small head an expression of such cold malevolence, that one would rather expect to see the knout in his small, well-cared-for hand than a violin bow. Perhaps he was fighting with passionate anxiety against his own character, against hereditary cruelty and atavistic contempt of mankind, and sought and found refuge for himself in art. He seems to have intoxicated himself with music—more even when he was listening, than when he himself sat at the first or second violin desk and was playing one of the Haydn Quartets, for which he had such boundless affection.

At first Chamber Music was played alternately in his palace and in that of his brother-in-law, Lichnowsky. Then he engaged Ignaz Schuppanzigh and his three colleagues, Sina, Weiss and Linke, for life as his private Quartet. These four artists became world-famous under the name of Rasumovsky Quartet as unsurpassed models for the interpretations of the works of the Vienna Master. Above all, Beethoven set the seal on their fame by acknowledging them as the authentic mouthpiece of his intentions and the best heralds of his Chamber Music.

No wonder: Prince Rasumovsky, who was one of the first to recognize the demonic audacity of Beethoven's idiom, placed the Quartet entirely at the service of the Master. He was free to have a rehearsal at any time. Immediately after he had conceived any passage, he could satisfy himself how it sounded, and whether or no it were playable. He made full use of the opportunity of learning and teaching, with all the joy which can be known only by an insatiable artist who is consumed by the flames of his genius.

In this princely house Beethoven was quite himself. He felt he was understood, was not obliged to keep a tight rein on himself, and was free both actually and metaphorically to enjoy himself in shirt-sleeves, as he certainly often did during rehearsals. It is perhaps the only case in the whole of Beethoven's relations with his aristocratic friends of which no strained relations, no disturbing incidents have to be reported. Unfortunately the fire mentioned above, which destroyed the Prince's palace, his collections and all the sculptures and pictures, also disturbed the external relationship of the Master to Rasumovsky.

This time, however, the Master was blameless. The Prince buried the secrets of his inner life under the ruins. At the beginning of the nineteenth century all that he had built up, all the ultimate refinements of the pleasures of sight and hearing, all that he, like one of the Medici, had created for himself by the force of his personality and confined within his four walls, had become unique in Vienna.

It was all laid in ruins on one night, on New Year's Eve of 1814, and Rasumovsky, who had seen his life's work, the focus and the content of his existence in such service of art, and not in his (so-called "eminent") diplomatic work, grew more and more indifferent to life, till he lapsed into deplorable melancholia. For two years longer he attempted to find comfort and cheerful peace of mind in his beloved music, but in vain. It was no longer a palliative for him; it only stirred up his suffering to greater hopelessness. Not even in the ineffable spirituality of the Adagio in E major of the second Rasumovsky Quartet, in which we seem to hear voices from above, the movement of all the three Quartets commissioned by him for which he had the most enthusiastic fondness—the movement, too, of which Beethoven was wont to say that it came to him as he was contemplating the star-studded sky and thinking of the harmonies of the spheres—could the unhappy Prince find relief from his ever growing dejection and misanthropic feelings.

He dismissed the Schuppanzigh Quartet, the members of which were scattered to Russia, to Paris and to the four winds of heaven. He showed his fine sense of responsibility, however, to the four musicians who had believed that they were provided for with him for all time, by settling pensions for life on them. It is but one more feature in the portrait of this curiously contradictory greathearted man.

It was a fateful decision for Beethoven. He had been vitally stimulated by constant contact with his interpreters, who had influenced his own creative work, not only by giving him a chance of testing all the possibilities of technique and tone-color, but also by setting up a tradition for the correct playing of his works. The vital, perfect performances of his Chamber Music which he was enabled to hear gave him the assurance that he was progressing in safety over the most perilous heights that loomed above his uncharted way. Now he had to depend only on his inner hearing, and always marched on with wildest self-will by sidetracks and into the unknown.

At the time of this event his deafness had increased with relentless certainty. Small wonder then that he withdrew more and more into his own world, where importunate curiosity could not follow him.

Possibly he looked on the conflagration in which he had lost so much as a warning from fate, which had to impose renunciation after renunciation on him, so that he might learn to rely on himself alone and be released ever more and more from the brutal realities of life. Certain it is that those flames burned away one of his last ties with the outer world of Vienna.—RICHARD SPECHT (TR. BY ALFRED KALISCH)

Beethoven as a Piano Teacher

The utility and importance of Cramer's Etudes have been recognized by all pianists and especially by those who are not only players but also teachers. Let us quote a passage from Schindler's biography of [Beethoven]. On pages 182 and 183 of the second volume (third edition) we find the following:

> Further to hand were the two books of John Cramer's Etudes, all that had been published up to that time. Our master declared that these Etudes were the chief basis of all genuine playing. If he had ever carried out his own intention of writing a Pianoforte-School, these Etudes would have formed in it the most important part of the practical examples, for on account of the polyphony predominant in many of them, he looked upon them as the most fitting preparation for his own works. That he regarded them from this point of view, and didactically prepared twenty numbers for his nephew to study from—everywhere indicating the manifold means of expression by accentuation of various kinds, all, *however, in conformity to one fixed rule so as to accomplish the chief aim*—must be considered one of the most precious inheritances to hand.

It need scarcely be said that these remarks of Schindler are of very great interest. Many regard music on a "poetical basis" as if it were a thing of quite modern times; but to no music is the term more applicable than to the pianoforte sonatas of Beethoven. And Beethoven, it is known, had, at one time, serious thoughts of revealing the poetical basis of his sonatas. The reference to the technique tendency sounds as if it were written in our day. There is, however, reason to believe that this complaint of attention being given to technique rather than to the inward spiritual meaning of music will apply to almost any period.

I have duly considered the solemn request to choose the right moment for making known Beethoven's method of treating pianoforte music, and am persuaded that in these days, when the meaning of instrumental music is so eagerly discussed, no hint from the greatest of musicians, helping us toward a proper understanding of his works, will run any danger of being neglected.

A word in conclusion respecting Beethoven's own comments. Schindler, it must be remembered, distinguishes between his master's comments and those which he drew up himself in imitation: he calls attention to this distinction in his prefatory remarks, and further gives Beethoven's name after some, but his own initials after the others. We imagine no one can read these "Beethoven" comments without coming to the conclusion that at any rate they emanate from Beethoven. Their boldness and originality speak in favor of their genuineness. It may be that in the matter of definiteness a few of them are not all that could be desired; but all of them were probably only written down as texts which the master expounded fully by word of mouth when he taught his nephew. In one respect Beethoven's mode of treating the Cramer Etudes becomes clear after reading the comments; he regarded the mere notes in the music as an incomplete revelation of the composer's intentions; they were the letter into which the interpreter had to infuse the spirit. But though in relation to the Cramer Etudes these declarations are of extreme interest, in their application to Beethoven's pianoforte works they become of the highest importance. But these Cramer-Beethoven comments are, as it were, a bombshell thrown into the camp of the purists—the sticklers for the exact text. Genius knows no law, and it is easy to understand that having felt the spirit of his music he was comparatively indifferent to its letter-form. But interpreters have to arrive at the spirit through this letter, and must, therefore, deal reverently with it. But all may derive incalculable advantage from these comments if the general principle which they teach be taken seriously to heart, and that principle is to regard the notes MERELY AS AN INDEX to the composer's thoughts and feelings.

Beethoven's comments at the foot of each study

Ex. 1.—The rhythmical accent is the same on all beats of the bar. In this way it appears in scalelike progressions. In order to obtain the necessary binding the finger must not be lifted off the first note of each group until the fourth note is to be struck. With pupils, this study must naturally be practiced at first in very slow time.—BEETHOVEN.

Ex. 2.—In like manner the rhythmical accent must be uniformly placed on the first note of each triplet. In the four introductory bars the thumb adheres firmly to the fundamental note, so that the broken triads, and in a similar manner all broken chords, may be made clear. In order to obtain binding, the triplet figure in the left hand must be dealt with in the same way.—BEETHOVEN.

Against the 16th bar is written—The melody in the third note of the triplet.

Ex. 3.—The melody is nearly always to be found in the third note of each group; but the rhythmical accent must be given uniformly on the first note. On account of binding, the finger should dwell on this accented note.—BEETHOVEN.

Ex. 4.—Here the longs and shorts must be attended to throughout, *i.e.,* the first note long (—), the second short (⌣), the third in its turn long, and the fourth in its turn short: the same as in scanning trochaic measure. At first, the first, also third note is to be intentionally lengthened so that long may be perceptibly distinguished from short, but without prolonging the first and third notes as if they were dotted. The movement should only be increased later on, and then the sharp edges will easily be smoothed down. The intelligence of the pupil becoming gradually more formed will help, and proper binding will be obtained. The hands to be somewhat spread out.—BEETHOVEN.

Ex. 5.—The movement is written throughout in four voices. The melody lies in the upper voice, as is shown by the mode of writing. Were, however, [all of the sixteenth notes connected in one brace,] still the first note of each group would have to be uniformly accentuated and held down. The middle voice *ec. fc. gc.*, etc., must not be given out with the same strength as that of the upper voice. The measure shows itself as trochaic.—BEETHOVEN.

Ex. 6.—The rhythmical accent on the first note of each triplet. But here the rhythmical articulations, now long, now short, must be attended to, for without this a false rhythmical progression would become perceptible in the melody. The study up to the fifteenth bar is in four voices.—BEETHOVEN.

Ex. 7.—Here the first and third notes of each group carry the melody (in trochaic measure). The finger continues to dwell, for the space of two [eighth notes], on the long syllable (first note). The tenor seconds the soprano; therefore alto and bass should not be given out with equal strength.—BEETHOVEN.

Ex. 8.—The melody is to be found in the highest tailed notes. The rhythmical accents are unequally distributed; in the first bar they occur on the first and third beats, in the second bar, however on the first note of each group. The position of the right hand must be broad and firm on the accented beats (first and third), but in the second, fourth, sixth, eighth and tenth bars on the first (note) of every group, otherwise the hand loses its equilibrium.—BEETHOVEN.

Against the eleventh bar is written—The touch here uniformly broad.

In bars 16 and 17—On account of binding the first note must always be held on.

And in bar 19—The rhythmical accent uniformly on each group.

Ex. 9.—The triplets in the bass constitute a melody-bearing figure. The accent falls throughout on the first note of each triplet which almost always supports the middle voices. This study must be practiced at first with firm touch, also in slow time. Since the character of the melody demands a certain breadth, it should never be played quickly; even in moderate movement it is, and remains difficult, because the player's attention is always on the stretch.—BEETHOVEN.

Ex. 12.—The melody throughout lies in the second note of each group, the rhythmical accent falls on each first of the group. This should be given *at first* in very moderate *tempo* and with pretty strong, though not short blows. In proportion as the *tempo* is afterwards increased, the sharp blows will decrease, and the melody and character of the study will stand out in clearer light.—BEETHOVEN.

Ex. 13.—The study of longs and shorts in passages is here the aim. The rhythmical accent occurs on almost all beats of the bar, for instance, from the second to the fifth bar inclusive—from the seventh to the eleventh bar inclusive, longs and shorts, the first of which I mark V, placing it under the note which has to be accented. By paying heed to these longs and shorts the melodic movement stands out in the passages; without so doing, every passage loses its meaning.—BEETHOVEN.

Ex. 15.—Longs and shorts alternately in both hands. The principal accent rests on the first note of each group; hence the finger holds firmly on to it, except in those groups in which there is a progression of a second, as for instance, already in the second bar in the bass. From the thirteenth to the sixteenth bar inclusive the melody lies in the highest notes; the accentuation here resembles Iambic measure. Further when the motive is taken up again from the ninth and twelfth bars, attention must be paid to the accent in the middle voice which I mark thus V.—BEETHOVEN.

Ex. 16.—The aim here is the study of the bass figures which progress, for the most part, in longs and shorts: a delicate and difficult matter. In some places I again mark a V: all *nuances* cannot be indicated, neither can they in other pieces. These studies provide counsel and help for all cases.—BEETHOVEN.

Ex. 18.—The aim is proper treatment of the longs and shorts in passages in which groups rise or fall in thirds, fourths, etc. The first and third of each group are long, the second and fourth short; the accentuation uniform.—BEETHOVEN.

Ex. 21.—Attention must be paid to the accent of the fifth note of each group which mostly appears as (the first note of a) minor second. Trochaic measure forms the basis of each group: the first note accented and long, but less so the fifth.—BEETHOVEN.

Ex. 23.—The first note of each group bears the melody in closest connection, hence the finger ought not to leave the key until the next melody-note is to be struck. Only thus will proper binding be achieved.—BEETHOVEN.

Ex. 24.—In the first five bars the first note of the first triplet and the third note of the second triplet must be connected together in the best possible manner, so that the melody may stand out. The finger, therefore, must remain on the long note. For the rest, the rule for the rendering of the triplet holds good; but here the second triplet must be less strongly accentuated.—BEETHOVEN.

Ex. 27.—The melody, which is unequally distributed, must first be sought out; it begins with e♭, a♭, c, a♭. Further, the whole must be rendered with longs and shorts, which, in fact, follow one another. The hand must lie more firmly than usual over the keys, almost press on them.—BEETHOVEN.

Ex. 29.—The aim is to learn to withdraw the hand lightly: this will be accomplished if it is placed firmly on the first of the two connected notes, moving almost perpendicularly upward as the second note is struck.—BEETHOVEN.

Ex. 41.—The aim is the management of the second voice in the four-part writing, with due attention to all the longs and shorts. This study is one of the most difficult and most important. Strict binding throughout.—BEETHOVEN.

Rhythm, or the proper grouping of notes according to their importance, was for Beethoven a matter of the highest import; and, according to the testimony of those who heard him, wonderful accentuation appears to have been a striking feature of his pianoforte playing. Of Czerny he is said to have often complained because "he has no binding, and accentuates falsely." Beethoven evidently meant the binding or connecting together of notes with regard to their power in a musical phrase or period. In the comments on the Cramer studies we seem to perceive a struggle going on in Beethoven's mind between the letter which killeth and the spirit which giveth life. By letter we mean the accent which is the result of a certain meter or measure, or natural grouping and, to use a happy phrase of Hauptmann's, "the kind of motion in that measure." For Beethoven the expressive meaning of a melody often determined its rhythm and rhythmical accents.

London, 1893

J. S. SHEDLOCK (1)

A Pupil: Carl Czerny

(This manuscript sketch, entitled *Erinnerungen aus meinem Leben,*
now in the possession of the Vienna Gesellschaft der Musikfreunde,
was written by Czerny in 1842. The complete text was first printed
by the Musical Quarterly, July 1956.)

From my earliest days I was surrounded with music, since my father
used to practice a great deal (especially works by Clementi, Mozart,
Kozeluch, etc.) and received the visits of many fellow countrymen whom
he knew professionally, e.g., Wandhall,[1] Gelinek,[2] Lipavsky,[3] etc. I was
approximately six months old when he took a job as piano teacher at a
Polish estate. We promptly moved to Poland, which is the scene of my
first childhood memories. I am supposed to have been a very lively
child and to have played a few little pieces on the piano when I was
three. Originally, my parents were to have remained in Poland for
twelve years, but since the last Polish partition brought with it unrest
and unsettled conditions, which would have made a continued stay very
disagreeable, my father decided to forgo the advantages of his contract
and c. 1795 moved back to Vienna, where he remained for the rest
of his life. His study of Bach's works and others like them had helped
my father to develop a good technique and a proper approach to the
fortepiano, and this circumstance had a beneficial influence on me. My
father had no intention whatever of making a superficial virtuoso out of
me; rather, he strove to develop my sight-reading ability through continuous study of new works and thus to develop my musicianship. When I
was barely ten I was already able to play cleanly and fluently nearly everything by Mozart, Clementi, and the other piano composers of the time;
owing to my excellent musical memory I mostly performed without the
music. Whatever money my father could set aside from the scant pay
for his lessons was spent on music for me, and since I was carefully
isolated from other children and thus was under my parents' constant
supervision, diligence became a habit. Without my father's special en-

[1] J. B. Wandhall, a Bohemian pianist who appeared in Vienna as early as 1760,
and who composed much key board music and quite a few Symphonies.—Editor.
[2] Joseph Gelinek (Abbé), 1758–1825, of Czech origin, settled in Vienna in the
early 1790's. He was much appreciated by Mozart, who knew him in Prague.
Gelinek was on good terms with the young Beethoven, and it was he who is
supposed to have arranged for Beethoven's studies with Johann Schenk. In later
years the much-sought-after piano teacher became estranged from Beethoven.
[3] Joseph Lipavsky (1772–1810), a Bohemian pianist and composer active in Vienna.

couragement I began, when I was only seven, to put down some ideas of my own; I should add that they were at least written correctly enough that in later years when I received instruction in thorough-bass I found little occasion to change anything.

At this time—during the last years of the past century—the following were the most famous pianists in Vienna:

Wölfi,[1] renowned for his virtuosity;

Gelinek, a general favorite because of the dazzling elegance of his technique as well as for his variations;

Lipavsky, a fine sight-reader and celebrated for his performances of Bach fugues.

I still remember how one day Gelinek told my father that he was invited to a party that evening where he was to oppose a foreign virtuoso in a pianistic duel. "I'll fix him," Gelinek added. Next day my father asked Gelinek about the outcome of the battle. Gelinek looked quite crestfallen and said: "Yesterday was a day I'll remember! That young fellow must be in league with the devil. I've never heard anybody play like that! I gave him a theme to improvise on, and I assure you I've never even heard Mozart improvise so admirably. Then he played some of his own compositions, which are marvelous—really wonderful—and he manages difficulties and effects at the keyboard that we never even dreamed of." "I say, what's his name?" asked my father with some astonishment. "He is a small, ugly, swarthy young fellow, and seems to have a willful disposition," answered Gelinek; "Prince Lichnowsky brought him to Vienna from Germany to let him study composition with Haydn, Albrechtsberger, and Salieri, and his name is Beethoven."

That was the first time I heard that name, and I immediately besought my father to get Beethoven's compositions. Soon I had everything by him that was then available—the first three trios and sonatas, some variations, his *Adelaïde*, etc.; and since I already knew so many fine works by other composers, I soon learned, within the limitations of my age, to appreciate the beauty and originality of Beethoven's compositions. I must add that my understanding was furthered by another circumstance. At that time an older man by the name of Krumpholz,[2] who was the brother of the inventor of the pedal harp, came to see us almost every day. He was a violinist and member of the court opera orchestra; at the same time he had the greatest enthusiasm for music, which was so extreme that it knew no bounds. Nature had given him a high degree of true

[1] Joseph Wölfi, 1773–1812, a student of the two Mozarts and the two Haydns, had such a reputation for improvisation that his skill was compared to Mozart's and Beethoven's.
[2] Wenzel Krumpholz, c. 1750–1817, brother of the famous harpist, Johann Baptist, was one of Beethoven's oldest friends. Besides teaching him the violin, he hovered over the composer like an adoring uncle.

and subtle perceptivity for the beautiful in music so that even without great technical knowledge he was able to evaluate any composition with considerable acumen and thus to anticipate the judgment of the connoisseurs. As soon as the young Beethoven had appeared on the scene, Krumpholz attached himself to him with such worshipful tenacity that he quickly became his friend, spending almost the whole day with him, and that Beethoven, who usually was very secretive about his musical projects, told him about all his ideas, asked him to listen to every new composition, and improvised daily for him. And although Beethoven often made fun of the ingenuous ecstasy that would seize Krumpholz on such occasions and called him his fool, he was nonetheless moved by the loyalty with which he defended Beethoven's cause against his numerous enemies regardless of the many bitter feuds this involved. (At that time the general public completely condemned Beethoven's works, and all the followers of the old Mozart-Haydn school opposed him bitterly.) It was this man, then, for whom I had to play Beethoven's works every day, and, although he knew absolutely nothing about piano-playing, he was obviously able to tell me a good bit about such matters as tempo, manner of performance, intended effect, character, etc., since he had often heard them performed by Beethoven himself and had in most cases witnessed the process of composition. His enthusiasm soon proved infectious and I soon became a Beethoven worshiper like him, memorized all his works, and, considering my age, played them with as much proficiency as enthusiasm. Krumpholz also used to tell me what new compositions Beethoven was working on and he would sing or play on his violin the themes he had heard there in the morning. In this way I always found out much earlier than anyone else what Beethoven was working on and thus was amazed to learn later how long Beethoven would labor over his compositions, how it often took him *several years* before he would publish them, and how in composing new works he would utilize motifs that had come to him many years before. I might add that our friendship with Krumpholz lasted many years, until his death in 1817.

My father was not wealthy enough to engage teachers for me, but several of my father's pupils were young students and apprentices who were too poor to pay for their lessons and instead contributed to my education as part-time tutors. One of them taught me Italian, which I spoke fluently when I was only ten. Another gave me lessons in French, a third in German (my parents had spoken Bohemian with me), a fourth guided my great penchant for literature, etc. Most of these young men later achieved good careers as civil servants; some of them are still living, e.g., the mayor of Neustadt. Thus it happened that I did not even think about the kind of things children ordinarily do, never missed the friendship of other boys, and never went out without my father.

At that age (ten—twelve) I got all the usual children's illnesses (small-pox, measles, etc.). Each time I was so violently ill that my health, which had been robust up till then, remained considerably impaired for many years thereafter, a state that was not improved by my domestic activity.

I was about ten when Krumpholz introduced me to Beethoven. With what a mixture of fear and elation I looked forward to the day on which I was to see the admired master! Even today that moment stands out vividly in my memory. It was a wintry day when my father, Krumpholz, and I walked from Leopoldstadt (where we were still living) into the city, to the so-called Tiefen Graben (a street), and there climbed stairs to the dizzy heights of the fifth or sixth floor. A far from clean-looking servant announced our visit to Beethoven and then admitted us. We entered a very slovenly-looking room—pieces of paper, articles of clothing, and a few suitcases scattered all over the place, bare walls, hardly a chair except the rickety one for the Walter piano (the best ones made then), and in that room a group of six to eight people, including the two Wranitzky brothers,[1] Süssmayr,[2] Schuppanzigh,[3] and one of Beethoven's brothers. Beethoven himself was wearing a jacket and trousers made of some dark gray material of furry texture and he immediately reminded me of the picture of Campe's Robinson Crusoe, which I happened to be reading at that time. His jet-black hair, cut à la Titus, made him look shaggy the way it stood off from his head. Since his beard had not been shaved for several days, the lower part of his swarthy face looked even darker. I also noticed immediately with the power of observation so typical of children that both his ears were stuffed with cotton which seemed to have been dipped in a yellow liquid. But at that time he certainly appeared to be not the least bit hard of hearing. I had to play something right away, and since I was too bashful to start with one of his works, I played the great C-major concerto by Mozart (the one that starts with chords).[4] Beethoven soon took notice, moved close to my chair, and played the orchestral melody with his left hand whenever I had purely accompanying passages. His hands were very hairy, and his fingers very broad, especially at the tips. When he expressed satisfaction I felt encouraged enough to play his recently published *Sonate Pathé-*

---

[1] Anton Wranitsky, 1761–1820, was a good violinist, but of the two brothers it was Paul, 1756–1808, who became famous. A member of Haydn's orchestra at Eszterház, where he was much appreciated by his conductor, he was the author of innumerable symphonies and concertos, though it was his *Singspiele* that made him a well-liked composer.

[2] Franz Xaver Süssmayr, 1766–1803, Mozart's pupil, who completed the latter's Requiem.

[3] Ignaz Schuppanzigh, 1776–1830, the first violinist to organize a string quartet for public performances, a devoted admirer of Beethoven and first interpreter of his chamber music.

[4] K. 503.

tique and finally the *Adelaïde,* which my father sang with his very respectable tenor voice. When I had finished, Beethoven turned to my father and said, "The boy is talented, I myself want to teach him, and I accept him as my pupil. Let him come several times a week. But most important, get him Emanuel Bach's book on the true art of clavier-playing, which he must have by the time he comes to see me again." Everybody present congratulated my father on Beethoven's favorable judgment, and especially Krumpholz was ecstatic. My father left immediately to get Bach's book.

During the first lessons Beethoven made me work solely on the scales in all keys and showed me many technical fundamentals, which were as yet unknown to most pianists, e.g., the proper position of the hands and fingers and particularly the use of the thumb; only much later did I recognize fully the usefulness of these rules. He then went through the various keyboard studies in Bach's book and especially insisted on legato technique, which was one of the unforgettable features of his playing; at that time all other pianists considered that kind of legato unattainable; since the *hammered,* detached staccato technique of Mozart's time was still *fashionable.* (Some years later Beethoven told me that he had heard Mozart play on several occasions and that, since at that time the forte-piano was still in its infancy, Mozart, more accustomed to the then still prevalent *Flügel,* used a technique entirely unsuited for the fortepiano. I, too, subsequently made the acquaintance of several persons who had studied with Mozart, and found that Beethoven's observation was confirmed by their manner of playing.)

Since my father would never let me take the long walk into the city alone, he always took me to Beethoven himself with the result that he lost many lessons, especially since it often happened that Beethoven was in the midst of composing and therefore excused himself. So it came that after a while the lessons were interrupted for a rather long period and I was again on my own.

At that time (1802 ff.) I made the very useful acquaintance of Government Councillor Hess (a friend of Mozart's and Clementi's), who not only owned a valuable library of music by the old classical composers, but allowed me to copy from it anything I wanted. In this way I acquired Sebastian Bach's fugues, Scarlatti's sonatas, and many another work that was hard to get at that time. In 1802 Beethoven gave his first public concert in the theater, where he played his First Concerto in C major, had his first two symphonies performed, which received tremendous applause, and finally improvised on the theme *Gott erhalte Franze den Kaiser.* I was especially interested in the symphonies and I was so curious to find out how such orchestral works are written that I conceived the notion of making my own scores of these works from the parts, so that pretty early in my life I got a fairly correct concept of instrumentation.

I enjoyed this type of work so much that I applied the same procedure
to several Haydn and Mozart symphonies (something far more useful
for the student than to study a ready-made score). At the same time
this activity endowed me with great skill in speedy writing of musical
notation, a skill that came in very handy later on.

For several years (c. 1801–04) my father and I visited Mozart's widow;
every Saturday there were musical soirées at her house, where Mozart's
younger son (a pupil of Streicher's)[1] gave very skillful performances.
On one occasion the party was a good bit larger than usual, and among
the many elegant persons I was especially fascinated by a very striking
young man. His unpleasant, common-looking face, which twitched constantly, and his utterly tasteless clothing (a light-gray coat, a long scarlet
vest, and blue trousers) seemed to indicate that he was some village
schoolmaster. But the many valuable diamond rings he wore on almost
all fingers provided a most peculiar contrast. As usual there was music,
and finally this young man (he might have been somewhat older than
twenty) was asked to play. And what an accomplished pianist he turned
out to be! Even though I had already had so many opportunities to hear
Gelinek, Lipavsky, Wölfl, and even Beethoven, the playing of this
homely fellow seemed like a revelation. Never before had I heard such
novel and dazzling difficulties, such cleanness and elegance in performance, nor such intimate and tender expression, nor even so much good
taste in improvisation; when later he performed a few of Mozart's sonatas
with violin (he was accompanied by Krommer)[2] these compositions,
which I had known for a long time, seemed like a completely new world.
The information soon got around that this was the young Hummel, once
Mozart's pupil and now returned from London, where for a long time he
had been Clementi's student. Even at that time Hummel had reached
the pianistic proficiency—within the limits of the instruments of that
time—for which he became so famous later. While Beethoven's playing
was remarkable for his enormous power, characteristic expression, and his
unheard-of-virtuosity and passage work, Hummel's performance was a
model of cleanness, clarity, and of the most graceful elegance and tenderness; all difficulties were calculated for the greatest and most stunning
effect, which he achieved by combining Clementi's manner of playing,
so wisely gauged for the instrument, with that of Mozart. It was quite
natural, therefore, that the general public preferred him as pianist, and

[1] Johann Andreas Streicher, 1761–1833, a friend of Schiller, was a pianist, composer, and teacher. After marrying Nanette Stein, daughter of the famous Augsburg piano maker, he established a branch of the Augsburg firm in Vienna and
gradually devoted all his time to the manufacture of pianos.
[2] Franz Krommer, 1760–1831, was one of those jack-of-all-trades that characterize
Viennese music of the Mozart-Beethoven era. Violinist, organist, composer, conductor, etc., he could do a little of everything and well enough to move about
in excellent company.

soon the two masters formed parties, which opposed one another with
bitter enmity. Hummel's partisans accused Beethoven of mistreating the
piano, of lacking all cleanness and clarity, of creating nothing but confused noise the way he used the pedal, and finally of writing willful,
unnatural, unmelodic compositions, which were irregular besides. On the
other hand, the Beethovenites maintained that Hummel lacked all
genuine imagination, that his playing was as monotonous as a hurdy-
gurdy, that the position of his fingers reminded them of spiders, and that
his compositions were nothing more than arrangements of motifs by
Mozart and Haydn. I myself was influenced by Hummel's manner of
playing to the extent that it kindled in me a desire for greater cleanness
and clarity.

In 1804 Krumpholz introduced me to Prince Lichnowsky, Beethoven's
friend and one of his most zealous supporters. The prince and his
brother Count Moritz had been pupils of Mozart and later of Beethoven;
both were gracious and humanitarian men as well as true connoisseurs of
art. It was Prince Lichnowsky who brought the young Beethoven to
Vienna, had him study with Haydn, Salieri, and Albrechtsberger, treated
him as a friend and brother, and induced the entire nobility to support
him. I was fortunate enough to possess so good a musical memory that
I played all of Beethoven's piano compositions (quite apart from
other composers' works) completely and precisely from memory—a natural talent that I have preserved to this day. After he had listened to
my playing for the first time, the prince was so favorably impressed that
almost every morning I had to spend a few hours with him during
which I had to play from memory anything he happened to want to hear.
Every month he made me a present which was a welcome benefaction
for my good but poor parents. On one such morning Beethoven, too,
was at the prince's house and seemed quite satisfied with my progress.
(Beethoven had not seen me during the past two years and was angry
with my father for having interrupted the lessons.) "I said right away,"
he said, "that the boy was talented, but," he added with a smile,
"his father was not strict enough with him." "Ach, Herr von Beethoven,"
replied my father good-naturedly, "it's just that he is our only child."
He was pleased with my sight-reading too, after he had asked me to play
the C-major Sonata Opus 53 from manuscript. From that time on Beethoven was well disposed toward me and until his last days he treated me
like a friend. I had to proofread all his newly published works, and
when in 1805 his opera *Leonore* was produced he let me make the piano
reduction of the score. It is owing to the suggestions he made while I
was working on this project that I acquired my skill as an arranger,
which became very useful to me in later years. At that time his relative,
Ferdinand Ries [sic], stayed with him as his pupil. Ries played with great
dexterity and had acquired a good deal of his master's offhand, humoristic

style; yet, on the whole, his playing was unexciting, and Beethoven, too, was not altogether satisfied with him.

Especially noteworthy among Beethoven's friends was Schuppanzigh. One would never have expected that this small, stout man, so full of love of life that Beethoven always called him his Falstaff, actually was a very subtle and inspired artist. One of the best violinists of the time, he was an unexcelled quartetist, a very respectable soloist, and the best conductor of his time. Since he himself did not compose, no egotistic motives ever interfered with his unshakable fidelity to Beethoven, and thus in his performances he employed all his artistry to show the public the greatness and beauty of Beethoven's works. And indeed there was no one better qualified than Schuppanzigh to penetrate to the core and spirit of these compositions, and his friendship was very useful for Beethoven.— CARL CZERNY

His Love of Nature

My decree: to live only in the country. How easily that is fulfilled in any spot! My ill-fated hearing does not plague me here. It is, indeed, as if every tree spoke to me in the country: holy, holy! Delight in the forests! . . . Sweet stillness of the woods! The wind, which hastens to make his appearance on any second beautiful day, drives me from Vienna, since he is my enemy.

Almighty in the forests! I am filled with bliss and happiness in forests: every tree through Thee. O God! what sublimity! In such a wooded region, on the heights is Silence, Rest to serve Him.

A farm; then you will escape from your misery. (*On leaves of sketches*, *1815*.)

How glad I am to be able to wander among bushes and forests, amid trees, herbs, rocks! No man can love the country as I do. Forests, trees, cliffs echo what Man desires. (*To Theresa von Malfatti, probably May, 1810*.)

L. VAN BEETHOVEN

For Beethoven, Nature was not merely a consoler in his sorrows and his disenchantments, but a friend with whom he delighted to hold intimate converse—the sole intercourse to which his deafness raised no obstacle.

How did the author of the Pastoral Symphony see and conceive Nature? Not, assuredly, in the dry theoretical fashion of Rousseau, whose writings on the natural education were nonetheless one of the sensations of the time; what point of contact could subsist between the Genevan Calvinist and the effusions of a Beethoven, Catholic by birth and culture? Neither was it at all after the manner in which the Romanticists had already begun to treat the fields, forests and plains. Beethoven never looked upon Nature as "immense, impenetrable and proud," in the way of Berlioz (speaking through the mouth of his Faust). A little nook in a valley, a meadow, a tree, sufficed for Beethoven; so thoroughly could he penetrate natural beauties that, for more than twelve years, all his music was as if impregnated with them; as for pride, there could be no question of that beside this indulgent friend, this discreet confidante of his woes and his joys. Yes, indeed, Beethoven loves Nature ardently, and can show her to us through the prism of an artist-heart, a heart full of tenderness and kindness, aiming at a single end—to elevate himself and, through his love for Creation, penetrate to the Creator: "In the fields I seem to hear every tree repeating 'Holy! Holy! Holy!'"

Shortly after the terrible crisis caused by his love for Giulietta Guicciardi, there might have been seen on Beethoven's table a book which, during twelve years, was his favorite volume, the *Lehr-und Erbauungs-Buch*, of Sturm. The underscored passages in this work, so well thumbed that he was obliged to procure a second copy, permit of no doubt with respect to the assertion just put forward. Still better, he himself copied, that it might be ever-present to sight and thought, the following passage from the book in question: "One might rightly denominate Nature the school of the heart; she clearly shows us our duties toward God and our neighbor. Hence, I wish to become a disciple of this school and to offer Him my heart. Desirous of instruction, I would seek after that wisdom which no disillusionment can confute; I would gain a knowledge of God, and through this knowledge I shall obtain a foretaste of celestial felicity."

Now, precisely what may have been this Nature beloved of Beethoven, the moving cause of so many masterworks, this countryside which evoked such lofty inspirations? Why, nothing more nor less than the Nature of his immediate neighborhood, the open country through which he could ramble familiarly on his daily walks. While Beethoven was an indefatigable pedestrian, to the point of sometimes harshly rejecting offers to accompany him, he was never what is nowadays termed an excursionist. The tourist "fad," this mania of modern Germany, which has reached the pitch (with the concurrent instinct for militarization) of investing itself in a uniform (a grayish green sack-coat with staghorn buttons, and an ugly little hat with tufted tassel), this tourist fad, we repeat, did not exist at the beginning of the nineteenth century. When one undertook a long journey, it was for business, not recreation; but short excursions afoot were in great vogue.

At that period—and still at the present time—the small hamlets in the vicinity of the larger German towns were dotted with cheery *Wirth-schaften* (taverns), not as yet ticketted with the pompous barbarism *Restauration*. These inviting publics opened their friendly doors in fine weather to the crowd of burghers from the towns, who, famishing for a breath of fresh country air, had the satisfaction of encountering on the wooden tables the habitual sausage escorted by the traditional *Schoppen* of beer. Each hospitable cabaret found its completion in a dance-hall wherein a very limited orchestra regulated the prancing of ruddy-cheeked *Burschen* and sentimental *Mägdlein*, while a discreet garden offered, between dances, its perfumed walks for amorous effusions. Out beyond the suburban village stretched the real country; cultivated fields, narrow valleys, with streams issuing tranquilly from nearby heights, and almost everywhere, quite near at hand, a real forest of century-old trees whose shadows invited revery. Here one left the domain of the holiday-making citizen to enter that of the peasant, who similarly celebrated his rest days in drinking, dancing and singing. But songs and dances took on a far ruder and more characteristic aspect beneath this open sky than in the tepid atmosphere of the suburban tavern.

Whether in the immediate environs of Vienna—at Döbling, at Heiligen-stadt, at Penzing, Mödling, Hetzendorf—or in the vicinity of the towns whose sulfurous or alkaline waters invited him when in ill health, and only excepting the parks *à la française* of certain princely mansions, such was the landscape which everywhere met Beethoven's eye during his rambles, now north or west of Vienna, now in the plain watered by the Wien, or skirting the rocks of Baden, or beneath the great fir-trees of Teplitz.

But among all these rural nooks, the one most fertile in inspiration is, incontestably, that extending northward from the Austrian capital to the slopes of the Kahlenberg and Leopoldsberg. When he hired for the summer a cottage in Döbling or Grinzing or Heiligenstadt (as yet not promoted to the grade of official suburbs), the Master had to walk but a short distance to find himself in the open country. Turning to the right, just after passing the last houses in Heiligenstadt, he descended into the Wildgrube (a narrow, green valley) by a footpath which is still called the *Beethovengang* (Beethoven Path), and stayed his steps beside the brook of the Sixth Symphony, the placid and shady Schreiberbach. Here he found himself about midway between the burgher waltzes and the peasant songs, and in several of his works he notes this bizarre antithesis. Would he push on yet further? He crossed the brook at a bound or, in the season of freshets, on a shaky plank, and ascended the sloping hillside through an unbroken forest. After pausing, perhaps, halfway up for re-freshment at the sign of the Iron Hand, he sought out the villagers on their native heath, in the hamlet of Kahlenberg, and sometimes strolled even a league farther, to the rustic town of Weidling. So it must have been within the narrow limits of some eight or ten miles either to the north of Vienna, or at Baden or Hetzendorf, that were conceived and written (or, at least, sketched) not a single "Pastoral Symphony" but ten pastoral symphonies, that is to say, ten great works, at the fewest, telling of Beethoven's impressions face to face with Nature.

First of all, according to date, the charming sonata for piano Opus 28 (entitled "pastoral" in some editions). This work (antedating, despite the number, his Opus 27) seems like the avowal to fields and forests of a moment of calm happiness, at the dawn of his love for "la Damigella Contessa Giulietta di Guicciardi." Then come the sonatas Opus 30, No. 3 (for violin, to Emperor Alexander) and Opus 31, No. 3 (for piano, 1802-1803); the admirable sonata in C major, Opus 53, which the Germans call the Waldstein-Sonate, and the French "l'Aurore," contemporary with and, so to speak, consolatory for the tortures of Opus 57; then three movements out of four in the seventh quartet (1806), and the Sixth, Seventh and Eighth Symphonies; finally, the superb tenth sonata for violin, Opus 96, in its entirety (1812); without taking account of the rustic dances, the finales of the trios Opus 70, No. 2, and Opus 97, or the pastoral entr'acte in *Egmont*.

While an analysis of each of these genial productions will hardly be expected here, it will be to the reader's advantage to observe that it was never a material impression, the realistic reproduction of sounds tuneful or noisy of the countryside, which Beethoven sought to express in his music, but solely the spirit of the country as it penetrated the heart of the artist and was transmuted into sonorous forms by his intelligence.

Let us rapidly trace the genesis of the Sixth Symphony. How does Beethoven succeed in suggesting to us the calm of the fields, the soul's tranquillity in contact with Nature? By means of harmonic agglomerations ingeniously arranged, which may satisfy curiosity, but do not touch the heart? Oh, far from it! He will seek, and seeking will find, a simple melody; and the compass of the melodic design, limited to excess (for it embraces only the interval of a sixth, from F to D)[1], will suffice to induce within us a feeling of calm both by its comparative immobility and by the duration of this immobility. In fact, the exposition of this melody founded on the interval of a sixth fills fifty-two measures of uninterrupted repetitions in different timbres, but musically identical. Wagner will utilize later an analogous procedure to portray the monotonous majesty of the river, in the introduction to *Das Rheingold*. The second idea in this first movement of the Pastoral Symphony is duplex. We

[1] In his "Essais de technique et d'esthétique musicales" (1902, pp. 380-383) M. Élie Poirée has already remarked on the pastoral character of this interval in the tonality of F major, which he explains, through a very plausible phenomenon of "color-audition," as corresponding to the color green.

might liken it to the appearance, in the heretofore inanimate landscape, of two human beings, a man and a woman, strength and tenderness. This second idea forms the thematic base of the whole work. In
the Scherzo, the effect of a sudden cessation of motion produced by
the tune on the strolling musician's bagpipe (the solo for oboe, then for
horn), and overcoming the noisy merriment of the peasants, is due to the
cause stated above; though in the present case the melody, save for one
note, proceeds within the range of a fifth.

The storm which interrupts the villagers' assembly makes no pretense
of frightening us. Far from letting loose all the known instruments of
percussion, and inventing new ones at need, Beethoven contents himself
with the insufficient kettledrums to reproduce the rolling of the thunder;
but, after all, he does better. Have you noticed, that in four pieces out of
the five of which the symphony is composed, there is not a passage, not
a fragment of development, established in a minor tonality? That is why
this key of F minor, held in reserve for the gloom overspreading the
landscape until then flooded with sunshine and gaiety, produces, in
every soul poetically endowed, the inevitable sense of oppression, of
distressful uneasiness, which accompanies the approach of a thunderstorm. Then, too, what a burst of light, how freely one breathes when the
blue sky reappears with the theme that preceded the storm, in the same
ambitus of a sixth whose tranquil significance was revealed to us in the
commencement of the symphony! Now a shepherd's song is heard, ushering in an explosion of joy; and these two themes are nothing more nor
less than the two elements, masculine and feminine, developed in the
first movement.

We have intentionally withheld, for the close of this succinct analysis,
the Andante, the most admirable expression of genuine nature in existence; there are only a few passages in Wagner's *Siegfried* and *Parsifal*
that may be compared with it.—Conductors generally err by taking this
Andante too slowly, thereby impairing its alert poetic spirit; and yet the
composer wrote the careful direction "Molto moto, quasi allegretto." It is
a veritable model of construction in sonata form. While the flow of the
stream provides a plastic foundation for the entire movement, lovely
melodies expressively rise up out of it, and the feminine theme of the
initial Allegro re-emerges alone, as though uneasy at its companion's
absence. Each section in the movement is completed by the entrance of
a theme of a few notes, pure as a prayer. It is the artist who speaks,
who prays, who loves, and who takes delight in crowning the divisions
of his work with a sort of Alleluia. This expressive theme terminates the
expositions, twines about the steps of the development, in the midst of
which the obscure tonalities cause a shadow to pass over the land; then,
following the somewhat puerile episodes of the bird songs, it is again
thrice repeated, to conclude the whole with a touching affirmation.

Space forbids our speaking of the sonata Opus 53—eminently *pastoral* in the sense which Beethoven attached to the word. Curiously enough, the theme of the finale of this sonata, which seems so perfectly simple, is one of those whole definitive shaping required the greatest efforts; Beethoven's sketchbooks present its final form only after six sketches very different in rhythm and even in melody.

The symphony in A, which the musicologists (following Wagner) have baptized "the apotheosis of the dance," is a pastoral symphony pure and simple. In the rhythm of the first movement there is certainly nothing dancelike; it seems rather as if inspired by the song of a bird.[1] The trio in the Scherzo reproduces, it is said, the melody of a pilgrims' chant heard at Teplitz in 1812; and the finale is a village festival aptly characterized.

The Eighth Symphony also evidently retraces impressions received from Nature. The trio of the pompous Minuet, where clarinet, violoncello and horn carry on an almost grotesque passage at arms, does it not represent a peasants' band? And the Hungarian theme—the hymn of Hunyadi—which appears periodically in the finale, does it not imitate the arrival of itinerant musicians, Gypsies, in the midst of a festival?

But the work which, together with the Sixth Symphony, most vividly awakens in our soul a sensation as of the smiling Austrian countryside, is the sonata for piano and violin in G major, Opus 96. In the first movement one already feels the caresses of a soft breeze; and although troops twice march by in the distance, one speedily forgets the panoply of war in the fair dream-landscape evoked by the music. The Adagio, in song-form, is a real masterpiece of penetrating melody, a reverie on a wooded slope which would be a fitting pendant to that "on the bank of a brook." It does not reach completion; a peasant festival, serving as a Scherzo, suddenly breaks in upon the reverie. And there is nothing more curious than this Scherzo. In it Beethoven, perhaps for the first time, becomes descriptive. Lying in a meadow, or maybe perched in a tree, the poet at first notes a dance of countryfolk in rough, almost barbarous rhythms—the Scherzo; then from another quarter there come to his ear, now louder, now fainter, as if borne on gusts of wind, the echoes of a burgher dance—a *valse noble*, as Schumann would have said—which soon give way in turn, as befits a good classic trio, to the Scherzo *redivivus*. And this little descriptive tableau for two opposites is not unique among Beethoven's works; the same form, though less completely expressed, will be met with in the finale to Opus 53, in the trios Opus 70 and 97, and, lastly, in the Minuet of the Eighth Symphony, mentioned before. This admirable sonata for violin, the last written by Beethoven for that instrument, and too often played in a style subversive

---

[1] Beethoven himself mentioned the twittering of swallows in connection with the first movement of the symphony.—Editor.

of its true sense, is like a résumé of the trio in B flat, likewise dedicated to the Archduke. We do not hesitate to place this famous trio also among those of Beethoven's works which were inspired by his ardent love of Nature—almost equal in its productivity of masterworks, during this second period of his creative life, to his love of Woman.— VINCENT D'INDY (1)

His Love of Women

The "Immortal Beloved"

I. THEORIES

The death of Beethoven left musicological research heir to a riddle which remains unsolved to this day. Among the deceased tone poet's posthumous papers was found an ardent effusion, written in pencil by his own hand, the only veritable love letter he is known to have penned. In it the name of the addressee is missing, as well as the date; and those who have busied themselves with the study of Beethoven's life story have racked their brains not a little in order to classify the epistle with regard to place and date of writing, for all that its contents offer a whole series of external indications. Time and place, however, were finally, not quite twenty years ago, positively fixed by Wolfgang Thomas-San-Galli, in his treatise *Beethoven's "Immortal Beloved": Amalie Sebald* (Halle u. S., O. Hendel 1909). The writer himself in a small subsequent book entitled *On the Track of Beethoven's "Immortal Beloved"* (Langensalza, 1910) was able to supply further evidence to support him. Thomas-San-Galli's contention that the lady to be identified was Amalie Sebald of Berlin, however, he feels obliged to reject. The name of the actual addressee, in fact, remains unknown to this day, and it is also most uncertain whether it ever can be discovered. On the other hand, the proof as to when and where the letter was composed has been settled beyond all doubt.

In the following pages we will essay first of all to make clear, as concisely as possible, the status of the matter; in addition we will also endeavor to present some new data, in which connection two new proofs as to the correctness of the dates discovered, in particular, will attract attention.

What are the actual facts that may be deduced from this letter in three parts? Let us examine it in order to establish them. Beethoven, on the morning of July 5, arrived at a certain spa at four o'clock in the morning. Evidently he had promised his beloved to write her his address at once, but he spent the first day after his arrival in a fruitless search for lodgings. Nor had he as yet discovered a permanent place of abode on the day when he began his letter, though he at least hopes to have secured one the very next day. (Evidently it is in view of this beginning of the letter and several other passages that Alexander W. Thayer, in his *Life of Beethoven*, takes for granted the probability that the latter had enjoyed a conversation with his "Immortal Beloved" prior to his setting out on his journey.) Because of the bottomless roads the four-horse post chaise in which the tone poet traveled broke a wheel, the identical fate which overtook a certain Esterházy posting to the same destination along the other, more commonly used road, in an eight-horse equipage. Beethoven's letter is addressed to a certain specific place—"K"—distant approximately some two days' journey from the place where the letter was mailed. The post went every day from Teplitz to "K," yet Beethoven at first thought that it went only Mondays and Thursdays. The indication that the sixth of July was a Monday is of special importance in this connection.

As stands to reason, all the years of Beethoven's middle and later life in which the sixth of July falls on a Monday were first of all most closely examined against the possibility that they might be taken into consideration in this particular matter. It was trouble taken in vain: it was impossible to squeeze the letter into a single one of them. As has been mentioned, it was due to Thomas-San-Galli that the correct year was finally discovered. At the beginning of a letter which he wrote in July 1812 to Breitkopf & Härtel in Leipzig, Beethoven expressly states that since July he had been stopping in Teplitz, the well-known Bohemian spa. Before this two circumstances invariably have misled Beethoven investigators: the fact that the Master's name is entered in the visitors' list at the spa as having arrived on July 7; and the additional one that the friend of Beethoven's later years and his first biographer, Schindler, had stated that the famous letter had been written at a *Hungarian* springs. Both of these original objections to the year 1812 dissolve into thin air once we are convinced they are negligible—and proof to this effect is easily supplied by the text—and that, first of all, the visitors' list, even at that time, was not very accurately kept, and that Beethoven evidently was entered as arriving on the later date because, as he says at the start of his letter, it was not until beginning with July 7 that he had a fixed dwelling place in the town. In second instance, it was impossible for Schindler to have known anything at all about the letter, for he himself saw it for the first time only after the Master's death. His assertions in this matter, so open to question, are one of the innumerable incorrect presentations of fact in which his book abounds. The mere mention of Esterházy in the letter was evidently quite sufficient to lead Schindler to transfer the whole affair to Hungary.

The letter unquestionably dates from a year whose July 6 fell on a Monday. The proofs that Beethoven actually wrote the letter on July 6 and 7, during the year 1812, and at Teplitz are of quite conclusive gravity. To those furnished by Thomas-San Galli and again summarized by the writer, the two new ones which follow may be added: first, that, according to his own testimony, it is positive that the tone poet arrived in Teplitz, the Bohemian spa, on July 5, 1812; secondly, that the weather, as we know from the diary of Goethe, who stopped at that time in Karlsbad and in Teplitz, was extraordinarily bad, so that it premises the conditions of Beethoven's accident.

Without any further circumlocution, Karlsbad may be accepted as the letter's place of destination. It took two days to send a letter from Teplitz to Karlsbad—as is mentioned in one place in the letter—so that it came to the addressee's hand on the third day. Furthermore, as the writer was able to prove, from Prague, the direction from which Beethoven and Esterházy traveled, there were two roads which led to Teplitz. Beethoven had taken the shorter but more difficult road, traveling by post; Esterházy had come by the longer road, probably traveling in his own coach. More especially convincing, however, is the verification which the author (p. 23 of his monograph) was able to make, how, namely, the master of tone came to fall into the error with regard to the times of departure of the post for Karlsbad. The writer was able to refer to a postal route schedule of the year 1815, which, in first instance, gave the information that the post took the road in the direction of Karlsbad and Eger only on Mondays and Thursdays, at eight o'clock in the morning. At the end of the schedule, however, was printed the following annotation: "From May 15 to September 15, the post arrives daily from all the Imperial-Royal Austrian Hereditary Domains, early in the morning, and leaves daily in the forenoon, at eleven o'clock, for these same."

What held good for 1815 or, perhaps better said, the year preceding, for it was then, in all probability, that the schedule cited by the author was written, surely must have held good for the year 1812; it is certain that in those days post-route schedules were not altered with each passing year.

Whosoever, however, after all this data corroborating Beethoven's own letter still may entertain doubts regarding the correctness of the year 1812, and might feel inclined to claim that the tone poet may have made a mistake in the day of date of his letter to Breitkopf & Härtel, to him we may here reveal that the date of Beethoven's departure from Prague can be established by documentary evidence. According to the

Prager Post-Zeitung of the year 1812, he left Prague on the forenoon of July 4 and took the post to Teplitz. Ordinarily the journey to Teplitz took until the evening of the day of departure. But if the post coach, in consequence of the bottomless road, broke a wheel, it is evident that it would not reach its destination until early in the morning the following day. And, at last, the writer is in position to produce an Esterházy who also traveled from Prague to Teplitz during those same days in July. Yet it was not Paul Esterházy, that member of the princely family with whom the tone poet was most closely connected, but Prince Moritz Esterházy, imperial and royal Austrian ambassador at the Saxon court in Dresden. A couple of official documents, still preserved in the Saxon State Archives, prove that Prince Moritz *made the trip from Prague to Teplitz at the same time that Beethoven did*; and that after a short stay there he left to resume his journey to Dresden. In the Teplitz visitors' list we read: "Prince Esterházy, Chamberlain and Imperial and Royal Ambassador at the Royal Saxon Court, together with his lady, from Dresden," but the entry does not appear until July 23, the reason for this late entry not calling for explanation at this point. Once more it is made evident how unreliable these lists are. Goethe, incidentally, when he in turn arrived at Teplitz on July 14 of the same year, entered "Prince Lichnowsky, Prince Esterházy" in his diary as being the first two individuals whom he met there. This last Esterházy is obviously identical with the Esterházy whose previous arrival, in any event, is already guaranteed by a letter dated July 8.

The writer is convinced that under the circumstances there will remain no reader, no matter how prejudiced in favor of another date, who will still question the correctness of the year 1812 and that of the town of Teplitz as date and place of the letter's writing. And his only wish—as the editor of a new, collective edition of Beethoven's letters—is that he might lay hand on only a part of the many confirmations of a definite year date existing for this letter in the interests of other undated writings.

Yet who was the "Immortal Beloved" herself? Unfortunately, as matters now stand, this question cannot be answered. No answer, however, is to be preferred to an erroneous one. We may, nevertheless, in order to establish what negative proof exists, look into the tone poet's relations with all the women who ever have been mentioned as candidates for the honor. In this case the singer Willmann, to whom the tone poet is supposed to have offered his hand in marriage while still in Bonn, may first of all be counted out, since at so late a date as the one with which we have to deal she no longer calls for consideration.

But the love affair with Countess Giulietta Guicciardi, for whom Schindler, Nohl, and Kalischer have entered the lists, also occurs at too early a date to make her candidacy for the post a possibility. In addition, Giulietta, ever since 1803, had been the wife of Count Wenzel

Gallenberg, had gone with him to Italy shortly after her marriage, and did not return to Vienna until toward (or after) the year 1820. The entries which Beethoven, in the course of a conversation with Schindler in 1823, made in his *Konversationsheft* are sufficiently well known, yet it may not be [superfluous] once more to refer to the fact that, when laid on the jeweler's scale, they refuse altogether to jibe with the famous love letter. To convince ourselves, let us once more read the words as they appear in Beethoven's awkward original French:

> *Jétois bien aimé d'elle et plus que jamais son epoux—il étoit pourtant plutôt son amant que moi, mais pour elle j'apprenois de son misère et je trouvois un homme de bien, qui me donnoit la some (somme) de 500 fl. pour le soulanger. Il étoit toujours mon ennemi, et c'étois justement la raison que je fusse tout le bien possible. Elle est née Guicciardi. Elle s'étoit l'épouse de lui avant son voyage en Italie—[arrivée à Vienne], elle cherchoit moi pleurant, mais je la méprisois. . . .*

She loved me very much indeed, and more than ever she did her husband—he [Gallenberg] nevertheless, loved her far more than I did, but from her I learned of his necessitous condition and found a philanthropist, who gave me the sum of 500 gulden for his support. He always was my enemy and it was for that reason that I did him every possible favor. She was a Guicciardi born. She married him before his journey to Italy. [When she again arrived in Vienna] she sought me out, weeping, but I scorned her.

This, when compared with the love letter, sounds relatively cool. It might be objected that Beethoven, twenty years later, may have viewed his love affair with the Guicciardi more dispassionately. Yet the letter written his friend Wegeler on November 16, 1801, which probably refers to the lady in question, already indicates that his affair with her was a passing flirtation rather than a great passion: "I am again living somewhat comfortably, seeing that I go about more among people. . . . This change is due to a dear, enchanting girl who loves me and whom I love; after two years I once more enjoy some moments of bliss and for the first time I feel that marriage might make me happy. Unfortunately, she is not on my social plane—and now—to tell the truth, I could not marry; I must still bravely knock about a bit. . . ." These confessions, too, fail to harmonize with the one uniquely great love symphony contained in the letter under consideration.

With regard to the candidacy of Therese Brunsvik, the sister of Beethoven's friend Count Franz Brunsvik, the writer had taken occasion to express himself, and as he believes with sufficient warrant, in the Berlin *Allgemeine Zeitung*, of the year 1810. Thayer, without pretending to set up absolute contentions, had proposed this lady, distinguished by her lofty gifts of character, for discussion; others took up his proposal and raised the mere assumption of Beethoven's betrothal to Therese Brunsvik to the status of a positive engagement; La Mara (Marie Lipsius) finally, in particular. She did so, despite the fact that in the recollections of the countess published by her there is not to be found the least little word pertaining to such things. About twelve years ago La Mara at last was moved to change her opinion; unfortunately this change of mind did not represent an improvement. In her last monograph: *"Beethoven und die Brunsviks"* (Leipzig, C. F. Siegel, 1920), however, she was obliged to overturn the whole house of cards which she herself had erected on her fallacy. An examination of the family papers left by Therese Brunsvik had proven the utter impossibility of what La Mara had claimed. Since La Mara herself has made this confession, no further reference to her previous combinations is necessary. We shall allude only to the coincidence that Therese, it is true, not until the year 1815, when she was forty, was in love—if only in the sense of feeling a purely romantic inclination for him—with a man whose first name was Louis. Yet the object of her affection was not our great tone poet, but a certain Count Louis Wilhelm Migazzi, occupying an official position under the Hungarian government.

Yet what does the writer now go on to do in her last book? Without offering any evidence at all, and ignoring the dates established by the most exact investigation, she simply puts the Countess Josephine Deÿm, Therese Brunsvik's younger sister, in the place which Therese's removal left unoccupied. And this for the sole reason that in the new letters on which she has drawn there occurs one or another allusion to what is quite obviously a harmless flirtation between Beethoven and the handsome young woman in question.

Josephine Brunsvik, like Therese, one of Beethoven's piano pupils, in 1799, married a Count Deÿm, who died, however, toward the end of the year 1803. La Mara, since the year 1812 by no means answers her purposes, prefers to transfer the alleged love affair between Beethoven and Josephine Deÿm to the year 1807. Unfortunately, in so doing her psychology goes utterly to the dogs. It is precisely during this latter period that nothing at all exists to testify to any reciprocal attachment on Beethoven's part for Josephine Deÿm or vice versa. On the contrary, it seems as though toward the middle of the year 1806 some sort of an affair was getting under way between the countess and a certain Baron Wolkenstein (see on p. 70 of La Mara's book the baron's letter to Therese Brunsvik). Incidentally, we get the impression that chance was trying to make a fool of musicology, for it was during the very summer of 1807—a year whose July 6 falls on a Monday—that Therese Brunsvik and Josephine Deÿm traveled together with their mother to Karlsbad and Franzenbad. The somewhat delicate Therese, who was suffering from curvature of the spine, had been advised that a strengthening "cure" was necessary. Now it would be quite possible to contend that the whole love-letter affair might have occurred in Teplitz in 1807. Yet there is nothing to this supposition, for even La Mara does not venture to assert that Beethoven might already have been in Teplitz at that time. Besides, a journey on the part of the tone poet undertaken at this time practically must have duplicated that made in 1812. Yet what does La Mara do? She insists on the possibility that the whole thing took place in July 1807 in the interior of Hungary. We now know, however, that the tone poet was established in Vienna or in Baden, nearby, during the summer of 1807. Hence La Mara's entire new edifice again appears as a reconstruction expressly designed to keep the "Immortal Beloved" in the Brunsvik family.

Nor could the love letter, if written shortly before the journey of the Brunsviks, have been intended for the youthful Therese Malfatti, the object of Beethoven's matrimonial plan of the year 1810. The matrimonial project suffered shipwreck that same spring, probably because the young lady felt no more serious reciprocal attachment, and her parents were opposed to the match. Probably no musicologist has even attempted to see the "Immortal Beloved" in Therese Malfatti. Nevertheless she should not be entirely passed over in this processional of women whom the Master loved, or even merely thought he loved.

The case of Amalie Sebald, on the contrary, would here have to be taken more carefully into consideration had not the writer already done so in his aforementioned article, for the period of Beethoven's relations with this charming Berlin singer, as a matter of fact, coincides with that of the love letter. This conclusion is supported by the following data: The tone poet had made Amalie Sebald's acquaintance in the summer of 1811, during his *first* visit to Teplitz, and again met her there the following summer. Yet both a surface reason and one inwardly more valid, the latter in particular, argue against the acceptance of Thomas-San-Galli's conclusion. In the first place, at the beginning of July the young lady was not in Karlsbad at all, and Beethoven, as would appear from his letter of July 17 of the same year to Breitkopf & Härtel, took for granted that she was still in Berlin. Secondly, the notes addressed to her in the second half of September 1812—that is to say, some two months and a half after his document of passion aflame—bear witness to what at the most might be a flirtation and in no sense betray a love able to move mountains. If one reads these charming *billets* after reading the great love letter, one need not be much of a psychologist to determine the great contrasts of feeling. And how, after all, is the consistent *"Sie"* [the polite, less intimate form of the German "you"] in the various notes to Amalie Sebald, contrasted with the consistent *"Du"* [familiar] and extravagance of phrase in the letter to the "Immortal Beloved" to be explained?

We might also make incidental mention of the fact that Carl Maria von Weber, albeit only for a short time, corresponded with Amalie Sebald, and only two years ago two letters by this early master of the romantic opera turned up in the possession of the Berlin antiquary Poseck. He had written the Berlin sisters, Auguste and Amalie Sebald, during his trip to Berlin in the year 1812, motivated by the performance of his *Silvana*. We will quote but a single passage from his letter of February 18, 1814; which bears witness to certain musical interests the writer and the recipient of his letter had in common:

It is very kind on your part to continue to show such a preference for my works, to cherish and cultivate them. At times I no longer have any faith in my creative powers. Herewith, at last you have the Tieck song as I have reacted to his poem. You know that for a long time I held back, did not even want to attempt it at all; I had often read it and reread it, again and again, and then once more laid it aside with a sigh, since my inspiration refused to grasp it. Once, finally, when I had well nigh forgotten it, it fell into my hands while going through some of my papers, and it stood clearly revealed to my soul. It is full of passion and ardor and I let it carry me away. I need not tell you, by way of a bribe, that Tieck was very much affected by it. I found no opportunity to have certain other songs copied, yet they shall soon follow and that, in fact, even before they appear in print.

The latter probably deals with the setting of a poem by the romanticist Ludwig Tieck, the song "*Sind es Schmerzen, sind es Freuden*," which in any event is already supposed to have been written on January 29, 1813, in Prague, and together with others was not published by Schlesinger in Berlin before the beginning of 1814.

And now to return to our subject after this brief digression. The writer, not long after Thomas-San-Galli had published the correct year date, in the *Musikalische Wochenblatt* (Leipzig, 1909), himself had drawn attention to Bettina von Arnim as the possible addressee of Beethoven's letter.

Yet he had withdrawn his supposition, for in the first place Bettina von Arnim had been the wife of the poet Achim von Arnim since the year 1811; secondly, she was not staying in Karlsbad at the beginning of July 1812—though she did, for a fact, together with her husband, arrive in Teplitz on July 24, or shortly before—and thirdly, Beethoven's only known letter to her, written on August 11, 1810, does not quite fit in with the love letter in question. The two other letters which the Master is supposed to have written her, as well as the sonnet he is supposed to have addressed to her on the occasion of her wedding, and which the author reprinted in his book, must be included in the circle of those poetic inventions of which she was so fond.

Is it so strange, we might ask ourselves, that the name of Beethoven's "Immortal Beloved" has remained a secret from his day to our own? Those who are best acquainted with the Master's whole nature and character will at once be ready to answer, "No," for they know that, communicative as he was in so many respects, he was just as uncommunicative in others. One should also remember that good friends of his are authority for the statement that, "he was never without a love!" This may be somewhat exaggerated, yet without any question the names of a whole series of ladies for whom his heart once beat amorously, and including that very woman for whom it probably glowed most ardently, and for whom that letter addressed to Karlsbad was intended, have not been handed down to us.

That the Karlsbad postilion was the object of his quite special attention, incidentally, we may deduce from something else written by the tone poet; something which has not yet been taken into consideration in connection with the matter in question. In the middle of his sketches for the Eighth Symphony, Beethoven at that time jotted down the fanfare which the Karlsbad postilion had blown on his horn (Comp. Nottebohm, *Zweite Beethoveniana*, p. 290).[1] Did the sound of the little melody, perhaps, sometimes rouse in his heart hopes of the arrival of a letter from his "Beloved"?—MAX UNGER (1) (TR. BY FREDERICK H. MARTENS)

II. TEXT OF "THE LETTER,"[2] ADDRESSEE UNKNOWN

[1] Professor Unger quotes a three-measure trumpet fanfare which, with its juxtaposition of eighth notes with eighth-note triplets on the one hand and sixteenth notes on the other, presents an intriguing little rhythmic picture which might well have titillated Beethoven's creative mind.—Editor.

[2] Immediately after Beethoven's death on March 26, 1827 this famous letter was found together with other documents, such as the Heiligenstadt Testament and a portrait of Therese Brunsvik in a secret drawer in his wardrobe. It was discovered by Karl Holz, who at Breuning's request was searching for seven bank shares which had been bequeathed by Beethoven to his nephew. The letter, which consists of three separate parts, was probably never dispatched. Anton Schindler, Beethoven's friend, amanuensis and first biographer, published it in his life of the composer, which appeared in 1840.

The mystery surrounding the unknown recipient has been set forth by all Beethoven's biographers with widely differing solutions. From the dating, Monday, July 6, of the second portion of the letter (assuming, of course, that Beethoven dated it correctly) it could have been written in the years 1795, 1801, 1807 or 1812. But now that Beethoven's residences and movements during those years have been established to a reasonable degree of certainty, the only possible year is 1812; and the inference is that he wrote the letter at Teplitz immediately after his arrival there on July 5th from Prague, where he had spent two or, at most, three days.

According to Schindler who first published it in 1840, the letter was written in 1801 from a Hungarian spa to the Countess Giulietta Guicciardi, then aged 17. According to A. W. Thayer it was written in 1806 (an impossible year, which was altered in later editions of Thayer to 1812) to the Countess Therese Brunsvik. According to W. A. Thomas-San-Galli in his biography of Beethoven, published

[Autograph in the Deutsche Staatsbibliothek, Berlin]

[TEPLITZ], *July 6 and 7, [1812]*

July 6th, in the morning

My angel, my all, my very self.— Only a few words today, and, what is more, written in pencil (and with your pencil)— I shan't be certain of my rooms here until tomorrow; what an unnecessary waste of time is all this— Why this profound sorrow, when necessity speaks—can our love endure without sacrifices, without our demanding everything from one another; can you alter the fact that you are not wholly mine, that I am not wholly yours?— Dear God, look at Nature in all her beauty and set your heart at rest about what must be— Love demands all, and rightly so, and thus it is for *me with you, for you with me*— But you forget so easily that I must live *for me and for you*; if we were completely united, you would feel this painful necessity just as little as I do— My journey was dreadful and I did not arrive here until yesterday at four o'clock in the morning. As there were few horses the mail coach chose another route, but what a dreadful road it was; at the last stage but one I was warned not to travel by night; attempts were made to frighten me about a forest, but all this only spurred me on to proceed—and it was wrong of me to do so. The coach broke down, of course, owing to the dreadful road which had not been made up and was nothing but a country track. If I hadn't had those two postilions I should have been left stranded on the way— On the other ordinary road Esterházy[1] with eight horses met with the same fate as I did with four—Yet I felt to a certain extent the pleasure I always feel when I have overcome some difficulty successfully— Well, let me turn quickly from outer to inner experiences. No doubt we shall meet soon; and today also time fails me to tell you of the thoughts which during these last few days I have been revolving about my life— If our hearts were always

in 1913, the letter was written from Teplitz to Amalie Sebald. According to La Mara (Marie Lipsius) in her book *Beethoven und die Brunsviks*, Leipzig, 1920, it was written in 1812 to the Countess Josephine Stackelberg, *née* Brunsvik.

The supposition most recently put forward in an elaborately documented volume by Siegmund Kaznelson, *Beethovens ferne und unsterbliche Geliebte* (Zürich, 1954), is that the letter was written to the Countess Josephine Stackelberg (née Brunsvik) and that Beethoven was the father of the third child of her second marriage, Minona, a daughter born on April 9, 1813. Many facts serve to disprove this quite untenable theory, notably the recent discovery of the thirteen letters written by Beethoven to Josephine during the years 1804–1807, the last of which obviously points to the termination of their friendship. Moreover, in all these letters to her Beethoven uses the Sie form of address, whereas the intimate Du-form is used in this very passionate three-part letter to an unknown recipient. It is very doubtful whether the identity of the woman for whom this letter was intended will ever be established.

[1] Prince Paul Anton Esterházy (1786–1866), son of Prince Nikolaus Esterházy, was then Austrian Envoy to the Saxon Court at Dresden. According to documentary evidence provided by S. Kanznelson, Paul Esterházy was at Prague at the same time as Beethoven and wrote a letter to Metternich from Teplitz dated July 8, 1812.

closely united, I would certainly entertain no such thoughts. My heart overflows with a longing to tell you so many things— Oh— there are moments when I find that speech is quite inadequate— Be cheerful—and be for ever my faithful, my only sweetheart, my all, as I am yours. The gods must send us everything else, whatever must and shall be our fate— Your faithful

LUDWIG

Monday evening, July 6th

You are suffering, you, my most precious one— I have noticed this very moment that letters have to be handed in very early, on Monday—or on Thursday—the only days when the mail coach goes from here to K.[1]— You are suffering— Oh, where I am, you are with me— I will see to it that you and I, that I can live with you. What a life!!!! as it is now!!!! without you—pursued by the kindness of people here and there, a kindness that I think—that I wish to deserve just as little as I deserve it—man's homage to man—that pains me—and when I consider myself in the setting of the universe, what am I and what is that man—whom one calls the greatest of men—and yet—on the other hand therein lies the divine element in man— I weep when I think that probably you will not receive the first news of me until Saturday— However much you love me —my love for you is even greater—but never conceal yourself from me—good night— Since I am taking the baths I must get off to sleep— Dear God—so near! so far! Is not our love truly founded in heaven—and, what is more, as strongly cemented as the firmament of Heaven?—

Good morning, on *July 7th*

Even when I am in bed my thoughts rush to you, my eternally beloved,[2] now and then joyfully, then again sadly, waiting to know whether Fate will hear our prayer— To face life I must live altogether with you or never see you. Yes, I am resolved to be a wanderer abroad until I can fly to your arms and say that I have found my true home with you and enfolded in your arms can let my soul be wafted to the realm of blessed spirits—alas, unfortunately it must be so— You will become composed, the more so as you know that I am faithful to you; no other woman can ever possess my heart— never—never— Oh God, why must one be separated from her who is so dear. Yet my life in V[ienna] at present is a miserable life— Your love has made me both the happiest and the unhappiest of mortals— At my age I now need stability and regularity in my life— can this coexist with our relationship?— Angel, I have just heard that the post goes every day—and therefore I must close, so that you may

---

[1] Probably Carlsbad.
[2] In the original the words used are "Unsterbliche Geliebte" (immortal beloved), and this phrase has been adopted by all biographers and commentators as a title for the letter. It obviously means "eternally beloved".

receive the letter immediately— Be calm; for only by calmly considering our lives can we achieve our purpose to live together— Be calm
—love me— Today—yesterday—what tearful longing for you—for you
—you—my life—my all—all good wishes to you Oh, do continue to
love me—never misjudge your lover's most faithful heart.
ever yours
ever mine   L.
ever ours

—EMILY ANDERSON

The Brunsvik Sisters and Cousin Giulietta

At the end of 1800 Giulietta Guicciardi appears on the scene. She
came from Italy. She was hardly any older than Shakespeare's Juliet, and
no less seductive. But she was not fitted by nature for the tragic, for
the proof of which we have only to look at the charming miniature of
her of this date, with the mischievous little face, the animated eyes, so
sure of their power, the lovely, avid mouth, the delicately plump figure
that she holds so straight. She knows she has only to show herself in the
Vienna salons to create a sensation. Certain little remarks, not devoid of
malice, of her cousins Brunsvik lead us to think that "la belle Guicciardi," as she is called from the beginning in Vienna, is putting them
in the shade. Beethoven takes fire at once. The ardent stage of this
passion seems to extend from the spring to the autumn of 1801; it no
doubt came to its climax, and to a confession, at Korompa during the
summer of that year, in the house of her uncle Brunsvik, who had
gathered around him and his daughters his young and pretty Brunsvik
and Guicciardi nieces.[1]

That the passion was encouraged we can hardly doubt, even though
in after years Giulietta and her family denied that they had ever been
aware of it. But a drawing by Giulietta herself[2] betrays the *Vergognosa*
who conceals herself in order to see better: it represents Beethoven—
young, fashionable, bewhiskered, in an elegant frock-coat pinched in at
the waist—leaning on his elbow, his chin in his hand, on the garden
balustrade and devouring with his eyes Giulietta's window on the ground-
floor; while she, hiding behind the curtains, peeps out on this odd Romeo.

[1] The tradition of the neighborhood is that Beethoven wrote the *Moonlight* sonata in
the park at Korompa.
[2] Reproduced in La Mara's *Beethovens unsterbliche Geliebte*.

In any case Beethoven had no doubt that she returned his affection; his letter of November 1801 to Wegeler says explicitly, "She loves me and I love her." And in 1823, talking with Schindler, he writes in his Conversation Book these categorical words: "I was greatly loved by her and more than ever her husband was" ("J'étais bien aimé d'elle et plus que jamais son époux")[1] He even accused her of having in later days taken advantage of her passion for him and exploited it. She was the *Primavera*; she does not love, but she is loved; and it is justly so, and one should be grateful to her. Beethoven, like every deceived lover, was unjust; and the bitterness of his rancor in later years only proves the depth of his wound. A further testimony to it is the fact that until his death he preserved, in his secret sanctuary, the portrait of *La Giovinetta*.

For the moment, in 1801, he is giving her lessons; and as he refuses to take money from her she makes him a present of a dozen shirts sewn by her own lovely hand. She was a good musician, though perhaps not so truly an artist as Therese, for Beethoven often gets angry, throws the pages on the ground, and stamps about in his rage. But she is clever enough to play very prettily, and the Guicciardi pride themselves on having the master at their soirées. It is during the winter of 1801/2 that he dedicates to the "*Damigella Contessa*" the *Moonlight* sonata, which is published at the beginning of March 1802.

Disillusionment has already come. From the first months of 1802 Giulietta openly shows her preference for the young Count Gallenberg, who was hardly a year older than herself, and had been an intimate friend of hers since her arrival in Vienna.

He had not failed to see the difficulties, if not the impossibility, of a marriage with Giulietta, even in the days when he believed himself to be loved by her.[2] The revelation that she preferred Gallenberg to him, bitter as it was, could not be, for a man still young and overflowing with energy, such a catastrophe as the forced renunciation, ten or twelve years later, of the "Immortal Beloved,"—his last harbor of refuge. He was sufficiently master of his feelings not to break off social relations with Giulietta; the decisive proof of this is a letter of Giulietta to Therese, dated 2nd August, 1803, in which we see Beethoven visiting Giulietta in the year after the Heiligenstadt Testament, and the little coquette, too sure of her charms, boasting that she has given him a scolding.[3] Beethoven's visits to the Guicciardi house probably lasted almost until the eve

---

[1] In French in the text. But Beethoven adds: "*Il* [Gallenberg] *était pourtant plutôt son amant que moi.*"

[2] "For the first time I believe that marriage might bring happiness. Unfortunately she is not of my class; and in any case I could not marry; so I must extricate myself gallantly" ("*ich muss mich nun noch wacker herum tummeln*"). (Letter to Wegeler, 16th November, 1801.)

[3] "I have spoken to Beethoven. . . . I have scolded him about it ["*ich zankte ihn darüber aus*"], and he promised me everything."

of the marriage with Gallenberg (3rd November, 1803) and the departure of the couple for Rome.

Pepi (Josephine) regained for a time the place in Beethoven's heart of which Giulietta had for a moment deprived her. "*Der göttliche Beethoven*," as she called him, enchanted her with his music, his quartets, his septet, his sonatas, his "divine variations." Each of the new sonatas that at this time "opened a new path," as Beethoven himself had said,—after the two sonatas *quasi una fantasia*, the *Pastoral*,[1] and the first two of Opus 31 (that appeared in August 1802)—were taken at once to Josephine, who read them with delight and wrote to Therese: "These works annul everything he has written until now."[2]

We can understand Beethoven being more and more attracted by this woman who understood him so well,—this good, beautiful, intelligent, artistic creature, full of grace and wit, whose charm had conquered Vienna. Her seductive power was all the more irresistible because of its innocence; according to one of her passionate admirers, "She had not the least idea of it!"[3]

Beethoven's correspondence shows him eager for her society, exigent, imperious. As yet there is no question of anything but music; or at all events music is the pretext.

But at the end of 1803 the husband Deym disappears from the scene; a pneumonia, contracted on a journey to Prague, carries him off in a few days. He leaves his young wife with four children; his financial affairs are in disorder, and she can make nothing of them. From this date Josephine's health is broken; she suffers from nervous fevers of which she never gets rid.[4] Grief at her husband's death and the confusion of his affairs, and the aristocratic fragility of this hothouse plant that a rough breath can kill, deliver her over to the hazards of feeling; and Beethoven, from whom she is no longer separated by the barrier of conjugal honor, at once sees

---

[1] Opus 28.—Editor.

[2] "*Welche alle vorhergehenden vernichten.*"

[3] Therese draws a ravishing portrait of her in 1809, in which she humbly depreciates herself in comparison with her, and says: "There are certain persons who, by means of a strong will, have succeeded in attaining to a height on which they can afterwards let themselves go without risk; they stay there without ever being in danger of becoming common or mean; in characters of this kind everything, even indifference, is ennobled. I have an example under my own eyes: never will Josephine be common, however freely and unconcernedly she may give herself. She is always gracious and distinguished; she has acquired a perfect tact, perfect fineness of taste; and everything that lacks this is repugnant to her. . . . And the purity of her taste for what is and what is not beautiful!" (Her unpublished *Journal*: in French in the original.)

[4] The whole Brunsvik stock, so refined in mind and heart, had fragile nerves. Josephine died of a nervous consumption (*Nervenschwindsucht*). Of her six children, five died young. Her mother suffered from nervous fevers. Her brother Franz was ailing until maturity, and mentally not quite normal. Therese, the weakest in her youth, had most resisting power, and survived them all. But she was in constant warfare with her own nature.

the door of hope swing open. His passion increases. In the summer of 1804 he is Pepi's neighbor in the country, and he sees her frequently.[1] But it is during the winter that his assiduity becomes so ardent that it disquiets Pepi's sisters; and they occupy themselves with the problem not of how to put an end to it—for everyone in the Brunsvik family loves him—but of how to keep it within bounds. The danger is not only in the excitement of Beethoven, whom the Brunsviks know, but in the weakness of Pepi, who, as the future was to show, was of the type that is the victim less of its own heart than of that of others, for it knows not how to say No.

It is easy to follow this romantic story by means of Charlotte's letters to Therese and Franz in November–December 1804—

"Beethoven is extraordinarily amiable (*äusserst liebenswürdig*); he comes every other day, and stays with Pepi for hours" (20th November). Pepi is the first to become aware of his most secret thoughts, the first to whom he plays "several magnificent numbers" from the opera he is writing; and it is not a matter of indifference to us to learn that this feminine image was associated with the first inspirations of *Leonora*.

A month later "this is becoming a little dangerous."[2] On the 24th December Charlotte writes to Franz: "Beethoven is here almost every day: he gives Pipschen lessons—*you understand me, my dear!*" At the commencement of January 1805, again: "He comes almost every day, and is infinitely amiable (*unendlich liebenswürdig*). He has written a song for Pepi." But Pepi insists that no one else shall see it: it is a secret!

On the 20th January Therese can no longer conceal her apprehension:

"But tell me, what is going to happen with Pepi and Beethoven? (*Was soll daraus werden?*) She must look out. (*Sie soll auf ihrer Hut sein!*) I suppose it is with reference to her that you have underlined these words in the score you send me: '*Ihr Herz muss die Kraft haben nein zu sagen.*' ('Your heart must have the strength to say No.') A sad duty, if not the saddest of all!"

[1] Josephine, who was ill, had had to rent a country house at Hietzing; and Therese, who was with her, writes in June 1804: "We have visited Beethoven, who looks very well [*sehr gut aussieht*]; he has promised to come to see us. He does not mean to travel this summer; and perhaps he will stay at Hütteldorf, so that we shall be near each other."

It is noticeable that the account given by Therese, Charlotte and Pepi of Beethoven's moral and physical condition that year (the summer of the *Appassionata*) does not agree with that of his faithful companion Breuning. While the latter is disturbed about Beethoven's nervous fever and his gloomy mood, Beethoven is always laughing and radiant when he is with the three sisters. But perhaps it was they who brought the sun to him.

[2] "Beethoven comes very often. . . . It is a little dangerous, I confess. ("*Das ist etwas gefährlich gestehe ich dir. . . .*") (19th December.) Already at the end of the preceding month we find Therese, who is away from Vienna but has been kept informed by Charlotte, writing cautiously to Pepi not to make so much music, out of regard for her health; and the passage I have cited from one of Charlotte's letters show that Therese had expressed her apprehensions to her.

It is impossible to be more explicit. There is no need to search for reasons why Therese and Charlotte should regard a marriage as impossible. They were plentiful enough—class feeling in the first place, but above everything, incompatibility of temper. The Brunsviks knew Beethoven too well not to be aware of the intractable character of their great intimate, and of the crushing menace of that developing deafness the cloud of which already cast its shadow over his future. Pepi's two sisters had the best of reasons for warning her against such a union. A fragile work of art like the exquisite Josephine, elegant and invalid, rising from her sofa only to receive company or to play the piano, unskilled in practical life,—could one imagine her in the hands of a Beethoven? These two different worlds, these two sick beings,—what would they have made of each other?

Later, however, Therese reproaches herself for having helped to separate them. In her unpublished *Journal*, which Mlle. Dr. Marianne de Czeke has been good enough to allow me to see, she gives voice forty years later to a moving expression of regret that sounds like remorse. Long after both Josephine and Beethoven are dead, in March 1847, she writes: "Beethoven . . . he who was so very like her in spirit! . . . Josephine's friend in house and heart! They were born for each other, *und lebten beiden noch, hätten sie sich vereint!*" This phrase would be striking enough if we were to translate it: "If they were still living, they would be united." But in the opinion of Mlle. de Czeke and certain linguistic authorities whom I have consulted, Therese's general style and the Viennese idiom of the day (in which the "*und*" carries a hypothetical meaning), would authorise us to read: "Had they been united, they would be living now!"

The sisters, then, had their part in the responsibility for Josephine's decision; but in any case this decision could not be condemned; we can imagine that Josephine herself believed it to be necessary; and "her heart had the strength to say No." I will not go so far as to believe that it cost her a great deal; but even if her inclination had not been strong, her natural goodness of heart must have made her suffer by the thought that she was causing suffering. And these inward questionings and uncertainties were a torment to her. Her health gave way under them; we see her, in January, a prey once more to her nervous crises, to cruel headaches, to a profound melancholy from which music alone could rouse her. I fancy that, in the months that followed, Beethoven was warned in some way or other; for when, in September 1805, the song that had been written for Pepi and was dedicated to her appeared,[1] the dedication was suppressed.

If there was any explanation between them it was affectionate, without the least hint of a quarrel. At the end of March, Josephine still speaks

[1] *An die Hoffnung (To Hope)* [Opus 32]; the words are taken from Tiedge's *Urania*.

with the old warm interest of "the good Beethoven." During the summer of 1805 they are neighbors again at Hetzendorf; then they become separated, and meet again only at rare intervals. In the winter of 1805/6 Josephine, at her mother's house in Ofen, is a queen of beauty and wit in the festivities arranged by the Grand Duke of Tuscany: she kindles ardent passions among the aristocracy. After that time her life drifts away from that of Beethoven; and in the summer of 1808 she comes under the sway of Baron Stackelberg, whom she marries in February 1810. Soon she is overwhelmed with domestic and financial anxieties; and when, in 1811, Therese speaks to her of Beethoven and asks of her a little service in connection with her old friend, Josephine does not reply. The past is dead: the painful present occupies all her thoughts.

As yet I have spoken only incidentally of Therese; during this period she occupies only a secondary place in Beethoven's life. For one thing, she has much fewer opportunities than her sisters of meeting him. She is the least favored; she is generally living far from Vienna, at Martonvásár or at Ofen, with her mother, from whose domineering character and narrowness of mind she suffers a good deal. Further, at this period she is apt to be isolated by her extremely delicate health. All these circumstances undoubtedly contributed to the formation of her strongly-marked individuality.[1]

---

[1] She was isolated in spirit, certainly, but not detached from the world, in which she had some brilliant triumphs. She did not lack admirers in aristocratic circles. [Besides] her "Toni," who loved her and was loved in return, we shall see, later on, *blasé* great gentlemen like the Grand Duke of Tuscany in her court; and even after she is forty Baron Podmaniczky will weary her with his pursuits and his proposals of marriage, which she will refuse for four years. We know her features only from a solitary portrait of her in her youth, a bad copy of which, probably by her own hand, is in the Beethoven House at Bonn. A description of a bust of her, in a letter of 1808, speaks of "her ardent and yet veiled glance, and the charming smile that never leaves her" (*"Ihr lebendiger und doch umschleierter Blick, das liebenswürdige Lächeln, das Sie nie verlässt . . ."*). Do we not seem to recognize these characteristics in the intimate sonata, Opus 78, that Beethoven dedicated to her?

She had a fault of figure of which we should never have known had not she, and she alone, referred to it in her *Memoirs* and in her *Journal*—a proof that it was not very noticeable and that she succeeded in disguising it. What precisely was it?

She speaks of *"einem gekrümmten Rückgrat"* ("a curved spine"), and of the "bandage for the shoulders," that she put on only in the morning. Perhaps her sedentary life at one period in her youth, when she read and dreamed too much, may have given her a tendency to slight curvature of the spine. In a note of 1809 she prescribes for herself: "I must straighten my figure by extreme vigilance, and, if possible, appear quite erect." (29th March.)

Two seasons at Karlsbad (1807–1808) and the simple and healthy open-air life she led after 1809 seem to have entirely restored and strengthened her. In the half-century that remained to her she showed extraordinary powers of resistance, for she never took care of herself. Nor was she spared crushing fatigues and trials of all sorts, ruin, mourning. "My whole life," she writes at a later date, "is like a battle-field" (*"Einem Schlachtgemetzl gleicht Dein ganzes Leben"*). She preserved an invincible energy to the end.

Her intimate jottings, which I have been privileged to read, tear away the veils that hid the "hard combat" of her heart, and the crises that wholly transformed her.

The first revelation brought us by the *Journal* is the absolute sincerity of this soul. Many men and women in the France and Germany of the bygone time have gazed into their mirror and described themselves courageously. But it is rarely that self-esteem has not played its part in the description; and, as with the Impenitent of Geneva, certain ugly features are only avowed out of a pride in the public confession of them. There is nothing of this kind in Therese. She writes neither for the public nor for her own vanity; she is making her confession in the true sense of the term, the religious examination of her conscience[1]; and she does not spare herself, for she is alone with God. She pardons herself nothing; she overlooks nothing in herself.

And this lucidity of gaze, that penetrates without the least weakness into the crevices of her thought, is allied with an inward flame, an unbridled imagination, that seems incompatible with this absolute need for truth. It is because she knows the weakness and the perils of them that, when alone with herself, she furiously pursues and denounces them. But warned though she may be, again and again she falls, and these descents to earth, these combats, these revolts give to the interior life of this young girl, a hidden pathos that will later attain to grandeur, and, by flashes, to the sublime. This frail girl (yet with such powers of resistance! she survived all her family and lived to be eighty-six!), this chaste woman who knew no other little arms around her neck than those of the children of other women, the thousands of little orphans whom she adopted, was and always ran the risk of being the prey of the powers of the unknown in the soul, and being delivered over to the hazards of their gales. And she knew it, knew it in shame and terror. She was built to understand the tragedy of the *Appassionata*, that had been dedicated to her brother, and that she was the first to hear and perhaps to play.

[1] Some of the most moving "Reflections on myself" (with which her *Journal* opens) were written at Pisa, during a sad journey in which she was quite alone, abandoned by those she loved: in her hotel room she had no other company than the tic-tac of her little watch. It was the 12th April, 1809, the Wednesday of the week after Easter. A fortnight earlier, in Florence, on Wednesday in Holy Week, she had had that celestial illumination the whole secret of which she does not communicate to us, but the profound vibrations of which endured throughout her life, so that Wednesday was always a holy day, to be consecrated to absorption in God. We breathe again with her the atmosphere of those days,—the bells of Florence, the mourning in the churches, the contagion of regrets, nostalgic memories and self-collection. From the bottom of these Christian hearts there rises, with the tears evoked by the Passion, all the melancholy of their sins committed, of the bruises inflicted by life. They say their *mea culpa*. Therese does not fail in this duty of loyal and lucid humility. And when, after the unrolling of the veils of Holy Week, after the sunlit sleep of Easter Week, the monotony of ordinary days returns, increased, for Therese, by the solitude of Pisa, and by the abandonment of her by her family, she takes up her pen and opens the door to a Confession that will continue for half a century.

For the rest, she had a sound intelligence, and a taste that guided her by instinct to the loftiest and most beautiful. When, in January 1805, she is sending her sisters Schiller's *William Tell*, which she has just discovered, she writes: "Truly, as long as Schiller and Beethoven are creating one ought not to wish to die!" And this remark of the young girl about Beethoven links up, after more than half a century, with that of the old woman evoking the memory of the great vanished friend and comparing him with Christ.[1] In spirit she was of the secret company of genius, and she knew it when, in the same year 1805, she wrote, not without a pride for which she reproached herself harshly later: "Immediately after the geniuses come those who know how to prize them."

Her musical talent was considerable. A friend who used to go to the best concerts said in 1805 that he would give them all "to hear Therese play a single Beethoven sonata." Another letter, in 1808, speaks of her "charming fingers, that play Beethoven's sonatas in a style that turns the master's and his disciples' heads." She was not only a pianist; before taking lessons from Beethoven she had studied harmony and counterpoint with an organist; and in 1805/6, during the musical festival organized at Ofen for the Grand Duke of Tuscany, Therese's knowledge and authority were sufficient to enable her to assume for several months the co-direction of the symphony concerts with the composer Spech, besides taking a contralto part excellently. Her chief successes were in poetic and lyric declamation. She drew and painted. Her intelligence was equally attracted by the sciences, and in later years she urged the claim of women to study these.

The richness of her nature is thus sufficiently indicated. And yet, without the rude shocks and the moral crises that, between her thirty-third and fortieth years, plowed up her very soul and brought about in her a second, a veritable birth, she might have lost herself, like the majority of aristocratic women, in the thousand futilities of a life of happy and useless idleness.

This painful birth to a high destiny is shown without the least concealment in her *Journal*. I have not found in it a line, a confession, that does not increase one's respect for the memory of Therese. I can understand perfectly the mistrust of the depositaries of these papers of the section of the public that leaves its finger-marks on the secrets of the heart. I will therefore confine myself to a sketch of the moral evolution of this feminine soul during the early years of the century.

The brilliant young girl who found Beethoven in the spring of 1799 was careless enough of the future; existence seemed to her a happy dream.

---

[1] "*Hat Beethoven seine order unsere Zeit erquicket? Seine Zeit hat ihn nicht verstanden. Christus, sans comparaison*" ("Has Beethoven quickened his time or ours? His own time did not understand him. Christ, *sans comparaison*": i.e., "without comparison being intended"). Therese's *Journal* in the last years: cf. La Mara: *Beethoven und die Brunsviks*, p. 93.)

Life began by separating the three sisters who were so passionately devoted to each other. After Josephine's marriage Therese remained isolated in her mother's castle. She was of a lively sensibility, with an excess of imagination that was fed by her reading and her dreams. She was a great dreamer: her retired and idle life, that alternated for several years with spells of fashionable and empty pleasures, encouraged at the same time this fever of the spirit and a tendency to fly from anything like regular activity or even physical effort. Her health suffered by it,—all the more because the tendency was contrary to her true nature. This becomes plainly evident later: the heroism of action was her normal temperature; and the damming of this need threatened to pervert her whole being. In the exaltation of this delicious somnambulism she formed, as she herself confesses, too high an opinion of herself, and conceived a wounding disdain of others. This attitude was not calculated to win her sympathy; and her character became bitter in consequence. She showed herself domineering, of a rough and crushing frankness that brought her into conflict with the rest of the family, even with Josephine, whom she adored. And here we can detect, under the pen of Therese, the curious ascendancy of the younger girl. Pepi, a widow with four children at the age of twenty-five, dominated the elder sister by means of the superiority of her experience and the certitude that she was loved. Therese became passionate only over Josephine, and could not refrain from falling foul of her; into everything she brought disquiet and tempest. Josephine, who had just lost her husband and was shaken to the depths, had need of all her strength to maintain her moral equilibrium; she showed no indulgence and cut herself off from this tormented and tormenting sister of hers. "I still feel," Therese writes, "all the bitterness, the pain and the despair that took possession of me, when, after several attempts [to live together], she told me for the last time that she could not keep me with her, that I dragged her down, that I hindered her from advancing, and that, in her sick state, with four children and a big house to look after, it was impossible for her to have the influence on me that she would have liked. . . . I went away, and thought I was separated from her for ever."

This was during the summer of 1804, at the very time when Beethoven, their neighbor in the country, was listening to the thunder in him of the tempest of the *Appassionata*.

Another tempest was devasting Therese's heart. She had the feeling that she had lost everything,—both friendship and love. It was complete night within her: she lived through months of despair, during which she could not help comparing her own total abandonment with the happiness of others—Josephine surrounded by children, admired, flattered by society, courted by Beethoven; the youngest sister, Charlotte, betrothed and soon afterwards married. After having consumed herself in solitude for months, her energy revolted; she would at all costs regain the esteem and the love she could not do without. But into the achievement of her purpose she put the old violence. First of all, from November 1804 to November 1805, there is a passion, for a young officer (Toni) whom, it seems, she loved; but the others opposed the union. Then, in the winter of 1805/6, at Ofen, she is seized with a mania for amusements and fetes in which she wants to play, and does play, the leading part,—a striking illustration of the demoniac force that is engendering in this abrupt, wild creature, taciturn, violent and just a little deformed. She is determined to make herself loved, admired, sought after, courted. She succeeds magnificently. She is, and becomes still more so, beautiful, gay, witty, lively, amusing; she has every talent; she is an admirable musician, "queen of declamation," dramatic and lyric, "frivolous of speech, with a thousand trinkets and an infinite number of dresses" that bring her "incredible successes." She is the princess of the salons, sought after and loved; even the Grand Duke of Tuscany is smitten with her. Happiness transfigures her; and, with its coming, there return to her serenity, sweetness, affectionate thoughts. She dreams of marriage; but, as she says, to this apparent victory there corresponded no victory within herself. An ordinary woman would have been content; but in Therese, as in her sister Josephine, there was a foundation of moral seriousness and above all (much more in Therese than in Josephine) of intrepid truth, that permitted of no illusion as to the emptiness of the soul and could not remain satisfied with that.

This was in 1807. Josephine, who had long been separated from Therese, wrote to ask her to return and help her in the education of her girls. Therese, proud of this change of heart in the sister she loved, burning with desire to run and throw herself in her arms, still cannot rid herself of all the rancor the offense of old had bred in her; and her new successes in the social world make her shrink from accepting the life of humble affection and domestic devotion that Pepi offers her. She replies evasively, postpones her decision, and goes to Karlsbad. Later she regrets bitterly having let go by this last chance to attach the heart of Josephine to her forever; for Josephine, who once more draws away from her, meets in the following year the man whom she is to marry and who is to prove the misfortune of her life. And Therese, without explaining herself in her confession of 1809, lets us see that for her also "the misfortune of my whole life" was decided in those two years.

What had happened between 1807 and 1809?

Without trying to elucidate the mystery here, and without seeing any connection between these unknown troubles and the presence of Beethoven, it can be shown that it is at this moment he becomes part of Therese's most intimate circle. She had never ceased to feel an interest in him as an artist; and Beethoven, when he saw Josephine or Charlotte, never failed to wish Therese, through her, *"alles Schöne und Liebe"* ("all loveliness and love"). But these amiabilities did not go beyond the formulas of ordinary courtesy. They take on a more intimate tone in 1807, when Beethoven asks Franz to embrace his sister Therese for him, and teasingly reminds her that she had promised to paint his portrait.

Franz was the intermediary: the brother and the eldest sister had been drawn closer together by the fact that neither of them had married. And Franz was a passionate admirer of Beethoven's music. It might even be said that music was his sole passion; for until his forties, when love took its revenge, this weak and ailing, gifted and inactive young man showed an indifference toward women that laid him open to pleasantries. His sisters called him "the ice-cold Knight" (*"der eiskalte Ritter"*). There is something comical in the fact that this piece of frigidity should have had the honor of the dedication of the *Appassionata* (or was it really dedicated to him, or only to others through him?). But for the one and only Beethoven he was and remained enthusiastic. Beethoven sent him the manuscripts of his works as soon as they were finished.[1] He took refuge with him in Hungary; and it was in Franz's castle that he seems to have completed the *Appassionata* during the summer of 1806. He was treated by the young Count as one of the family; and between 1807 and 1812 their friendship took on quite a fraternal character. . . . "Brother! dear brother!" wrote Beethoven, who, indeed, in a letter of 1802, vowed that Franz was his only brother,—more brother to him than those of his own blood.

We can believe, then, that a stream of affectionate interest circulated regularly, by way of Franz, between Beethoven and Therese; and the jovial commission of the 11th May, 1807, reached its address. We shall see later that Beethoven received from Therese not only "his fine portrait" but an allegorical drawing in which she represented him under the form of an eagle gazing at the sun. This, however, belongs to a later period.

During the period with which we are at present occupied, Beethoven and Therese discover themselves to each other only slowly. Therese, indeed, has hardly begun to discover her own self. The years 1807 and 1808, the summers of which she passed at Karlsbad, are for her a period of fashionable pleasures and agitations. Her health has been restored; and her mother, in order to assure her a way of life that shall be independent and worthy of her name, has had built for her a house at Egra. She sees Beethoven often enough in these years; but it would seem that the memory of Josephine's affection for him is still uppermost in

[1] Notably the Rasoumovsky quartets, which Franz was in no hurry to return to him. (16th November, 1807.)

him. The name of the one sister calls up in his mind that of the other.[1]

Everything changes in the course of the year 1808,—not only Josephine's life but that of Therese and the direction of her thought. During the summer Josephine comes to Karlsbad to take her sister to Switzerland. They visit Pestalozzi, at Yverdon. Josephine is preoccupied with the education of her children; but it is Therese who receives the moral radiance of the apostle. Pestalozzi kindles in her a spark of the divine flame[2] that, after having developed in silence for some years, will now consume her utterly; she becomes the passionate genius of that work of education and social action the magnificent creation of which—the love of poor and abandoned children, a sort of universal maternity—Hungary celebrated in 1928.

Josephine contributes to this evolution,—not without a certain egoism, for she shifts to Therese's shoulders the heavy burden of the education of her many children. For at Pestalozzi's she has met Baron Stackelberg, to whom she has taken a fancy and who will become her second husband. Her preoccupations enclose her within the circle of her own house and people; and into the service of these she draws and sacrifices the devotion of Therese. The latter's grandeur consists in the fact that she will love the sacrifice to the point of converting it into a source of new life and happiness, though not without passing through a period of passionate meditation to which the *Journal* bears witness: she was not free from doubts and sorrows. I should say that it is psychologically possible and natural that at this time, more than at any other, Beethoven and Therese should have come near to understanding each other and uniting their destinies; though I do not venture to say that it was so. Let it suffice here to say that these years (1809–1813) are for each of them the period of the great crisis, of trials, deceptions, and inward unsettlement. The true Therese is born: the young Beethoven dies.

My opinion at present—so far as I have been able to study the documents that have been communicated to me—is that, if it be not at all impossible that Therese may have met Beethoven at the indicated place and time, and that she may have provoked in him, in one of her moments of exaltation and passionate weakness, the crisis testified to in the famous letter to "The Immortal Beloved," it is practically certain that in that case Therese would afterwards master herself and return the letter to him.

---

[1] In a letter that belongs to the summer of 1808, Therese writes: "*Beethoven sah ich die letzten Tage sehr viel . . .*" ("I have seen Beethoven very often these last days"). And she asks that a portrait of him just painted by a certain Neigart shall be sent to Pepi. In March 1807 again, when the younger sister Charlotte sees a child whose glance and expression remind her of Beethoven, the first thought that occurs to her is, "How I wish Pepi could have seen him!"

[2] "It was there [at Yverdon] that he transplanted his fire of love into my bosom. There I learned what it was my spirit needed—action for the people. The word was found. From that time there was an end of my egoistic self-culture; we dedicated ourselves to the Fatherland, as educators of the masses. To them our strength, our time! To the future generations our love!" (The *Memoirs*.)

For she no longer belonged to herself, she could no longer dispose of herself for a life of matrimony: she was now caught up in a whirlwind of duties, the most pressing of which was not her religious and social mission (that still needed some years to develop in her) but the ruin of her sister Josephine, the domestic catastrophe that had befallen her family, in these very months that exacted of her a complete devotion to them and their salvation—an absolute sacrifice.—ROMAIN ROLLAND (2)

The Others

It was not only in the presence of women of great worth that his wonted imperious, regal heedlessness so utterly failed him. He had nothing of the ascetic in him. His senses were fully alive, and he had powerful impulses. His health was robust in spite of his oversensitive nerves. This showed itself in a certain irritation and obstinacy of his digestive organs, which indeed he maltreated roughly and cruelly enough until they became chronically deranged. His full-blooded body craved satisfaction no less than his mind. Only hypocrites will be astonished or offended at the thought that he, who so loathed all physical enjoyment and subdued all his physical instincts with an impatience which had in it something sublimely contemptuous, now and then looked with pleasure on—let us say—a beauty of the people.

Grillparzer, in his reminiscences of Beethoven, relates a curious episode of this kind. While he was staying in Heiligenstadt, the youthful Master had been struck during a walk by the pretty daughter of a decayed farmer called Flohberger, who, by the way, had a somewhat doubtful reputation. From that day he made a point of passing the neglected farm every day. He would stop at the gate to contemplate the buxom young woman hard at work at a hay or manure cart, plying her pitchfork, obviously with a liberal exhibition of her undeniable charms. But he never addressed her. He only stopped and looked with the curious, almost sneering expression, that he had when his feelings were aroused. When Fräulein Liese, who, by the way, would have found a strapping farm lad more to her taste than this strange admirer who gazed at her without a word, scared him away with a light jest or a saucy laugh, he would take to his heels, muttering strangely. But he returned punctually the next day and stared through his lorgnette, in rapt contemplation, at all the attractive outlines of this Dulcinea of Döbling, without daring to approach her.

Nevertheless, it is certain that the eccentric Master, who even here was too embarrassed, must have felt an interest in the certainly not unapproachable beauty, which far exceeded mere pleasure of the eye, for when her dissolute father had been put into the village lockup for drunkenness and brawling, Beethoven himself went to the Village Council and appealed for the liberation of Herr Flohberger so energetically and withal so uncivilly that the worthies of the Döbling Council almost sent him to prison too. What a curious lofty soul, which was incapable even of a passing movement of the senses without combining it with human sympathy and thus ennobling it.

It really seems as if Beethoven was incapable of using an unseemly, still less a ribald, expression to any woman. Even in the company of men, he could bring no indecent word over his lips, even in talk about the forward or the venal.

In the first volume of the Conversation Books (which unfortunately for the present remains the last), issued by Wilhelm Nohl, we read how Beethoven was twitted again and again about a Frau Janick, with whom he would often gladly retire into solitude. Her husband, by the way, was notoriously indulgent, not to say complaisant. He does not seem to have denied that her kisses were not at all unpleasing to him; but the moment that the conversation threatened to become doubtful, he interposed; certainly it was immediately broken off. How terribly ashamed he was of himself when he was once induced to visit a woman of the town we have already told.

We almost see his ready blush and the painful blinking of his eyes when he—this is told us by the Conversation Book—was caught by a friend in one of the narrow alleys into which he had after all been sometimes driven by the needs of his body. "Where were you going today about seven o'clock near the Bauernmarket?" he was once asked by an indiscreet visitor, and he received only the hasty angrily written answer in bad Latin, "*Culpam trans genitalium.*"

He needs must deliver himself as quickly as possible from all physical needs. He dared not risk distraction by anything which could remind him of his body and hamper his mind in its free untrammeled flight.

A pleasing little incident is related by Ferdinand Ries who tells us how susceptible Beethoven was to feminine beauty and how quickly he succumbed to such charms, even those of a completely unknown woman. The youth came to Baden for a lesson, but found a beautiful young woman sitting next to Beethoven on the sofa. Not wishing to disturb the Master, he wanted to disappear, but Beethoven called him back: "Just you play for a few minutes." He obeyed. The Master and the lady remained sitting behind him and seemed every now and then to whisper to one another. "I had been playing for quite a long time when Beethoven suddenly called out: 'Ries, play something love-sick,' and shortly afterwards 'Something melancholy'; then 'Something passionate!' Suddenly Beethoven jumped up saying, 'But all this is music of mine,'" obviously in pretended astonishment, but secretly pleased that he was able to say to the pretty creature next to him something beautiful not in words only but in music also, and could own that he was the creator of so much beauty. Shortly afterwards the lady left, and it appears that Beethoven had not the smallest notion what her name was, or who she was. She had simply come to make his acquaintance, and he had made no objection. An older woman would certainly not have been admitted. He and Ries even followed her in the hope of finding out where she lived, but she got away from the pair in the doubtful light of the moon, and Ries learned only later that she was the mistress of a foreign prince. He brought the news to Beethoven, who took no notice and never again mentioned the episode. Either what the pupil told him drove her from his mind, or he had not thought of her for a long time before that.

In contrast with the real passions which sometimes dominated him for years, such tiny flames never burned for long. He caught fire as quickly as he soon grew cold and indifferent, and he was surprised at himself when such an amorous interlude lasted longer than a few days. When Ries once dared to tease him about the conquest of a certain beautiful woman, he confessed she had attracted him for a longer time and more strongly than any other, namely a full seven months. Even in the case of serious loves, which were begun in tragedy, his constancy did not last beyond their duration. He was not one of those who love only once in a lifetime and then cannot forget. He never mourned a shadow that had passed.

It is not evidence to the contrary that he treasured till the day of his death the letter to the "Immortal Beloved" which he never sent or received back. There were certainly two or three women in his life who for a time meant everything to him; the goal of longing and the fulfillment of his earthly existence, from whom he was separated not by disillusion, but by Fate and the exclusive domination of his work. It is certain that he was not starved of love by necessity. It was he who elbowed aside many women who offered themselves to him. It was almost always the result of his own inner conflict and his own free self-determination. It was perhaps only once that circumstances forced him to renounce a woman whom he had wooed in suffering. Equally certain is it that his lofty morality, his manly dignity, the irresistible nobility of his self-respect, his absolute sacrifice of himself to his art, are proved as convincingly by his shuddering disgust at all that is merely physical, as by his passing fancies, which he knew could have no sequel, wholly and deeply as he was absorbed by them for the moment. The host of chosen women who offered him their hearts is but another proof.

Had it been otherwise, this affection would not have lived on even after a separation which was not always caused by their fickleness. It was always his terror lest a definite union might mean the loss of his individuality and make him untrue to his higher mission, that brought about the end of Beethoven's love episodes. Later he himself always deplored it bitterly and yet thanked heaven for it, knowing the reason. He knew full well the inevitable and inalterable Tables of the Law, which ruled his life and forbade him to taste any happiness in divided allegiance.

Beethoven never, as we have already said, desired a woman whom he really loved otherwise than as his wife. The fact that, especially as a young man, he was obliged to choke down such desires with clenched teeth, is due in the first line to his character, as it then was, in which timidity was not counterbalanced by vehement self-will and assured consciousness of worth as in later years. But doubtless these feelings were already awake then.

Did Leonore von Breuning suspect that she was the first of whom the defiant fervent youth dreamed as his wife? Perhaps it was a half-unconscious dream which haunted him, but certainly not when his "Raptus" was on him. That was the name which Frau von Breuning, his motherly friend, half in earnest, indulgently gave to his cheerful, riotous or furious outbreaks of feeling. No, shy and solitary, he forced back his dream into the half-light of his boy's soul, which longed for intimacy and warmth. Assuredly then it came nearer to communion with an equal when it longed for the lissom, austere, high-bred young woman, who somewhere in the depths of her sisterly being knew what she was to him and what he might have become for her.

But it probably was in a "Raptus" that the young Beethoven made an ill-considered offer of marriage to the singer, Magdalena Willmann. We know little of this affair of the heart, but we shall scarcely go wrong if we look upon it as one of the impetuous, thoughtless acts of the rash young composer. He must have been wild with delight when he escaped from this entanglement, and afterwards realized at what a price he would have bound himself to a woman who knew so little of him. His inner power and the majesty of his music meant nothing to her in comparison with his unpleasing person. She rejected him because he was too little of an Adonis for her. She was not attracted by the undersized, sturdy figure, the pock-marked, reddish-brown face with its mop of wiry dark hair, his black fiery eyes, the chin with its double dimple. Not even his magnificent forehead and his refined proud mouth with his dazzling white, sound teeth, could reveal to her his high-minded sensitive manliness and the demonic spirit which had impressed its authentic hallmark on his face. Report even says that she was content, if not too happy, with a certan better-groomed M. Galvani, and she died at an early age. We may suppose that she was terrified of Beethoven and his elemental superiority. And she was right. At his side she would not have been able to breathe; at her side he would have been suffocated.

There was only one other woman in his life, whom he desired as wife, and who, though even more fascinating to look upon, was as superficial as she. She was the beautiful, volatile, Therese Malfatti, the niece of his doctor. It was he who was so embittered against the Master, presumably by this love affair, that he at first refused to come to his deathbed and finally obeyed his importunate call so late that even his vaunted skill could no longer delay the end. It is said that otherwise he might have been able to save, or at least to prolong, his threatened life for a considerable time. Thus the purest of all artists died, perhaps prematurely, owing to the coquetry of a heartless woman. She was the only one among all the women whom Beethoven desired, who not only rejected him but played with him, who now apparently yielding, now suddenly cold, with a promising eye and a refusing mouth, always kept him hovering between high-hearted hope and painful disenchantment, and often reduced him to despair by her unscupulous levity. So little could he learn from experience. The good Baron Gleichenstein, who was in love with Therese's morally superior sister and married her soon afterwards, had at that time to play the intermediary and messenger for the distracted lover, and he must have suffered greatly from his untamable impatience, his outbreaks of discouragement, his quivering hopes, his angry questions, and his wrath at her puzzling and evasive answers. A letter which Beethoven wrote in the year 1811 to her, who loved admiration above all things, seems to reveal to us his trembling heart, his fears, his inner solitude and his touching efforts to lay bare his world to the fickle, fascinating creature, and in this way to bring her nearer to it.

"It would probably be hoping too much of you or putting my value too high, if I were to ascribe to you the saying: 'It is not only when they are side by side that two people are together: even at a distance they can be alive for us.' Who would ascribe anything of the kind to the flighty Therese, who takes all life so lightly?"

He implored her to make music: "You have such a pretty talent for it, why not cultivate it seriously?"

He sent her the working out of a theme on which he had recently improvised and begged her to find out the difference between the two versions. "But please do not call punch to your aid." It would appear as if the reckless creature was sometimes not averse to raising her spirits by taking a little too much, and it is curious that it obviously annoyed him, the lover, while he was ready to offer sweet wine to the two "Witches," Caroline Unger and Henriette Sontag, and enjoyed the spectacle of their slight elation. He wanted to send her *Wilhelm Meister* and Schlegel's translation of Shakespeare; he wished her to share his pious delight in Nature: "Do not forests, trees and rocks give man the echo of his feelings that he longs for?" And in conclusion: "I wish you everything good and beautiful in life. Remember me and with pleasure—forget my madness—and never doubt me, even if you have no further interest in your most devoted servant and friend, Beethoven." It is not without pain that we reflect what kind of creature it was on whom so high-minded a man as Beethoven was lavished all that was best and purest in him, and spoke to empty air. Happily for him it did not take him long to realize it. The episode was soon over but the disenchantment and humiliation rankled in his mind for a long time.

Nevertheless for all the intensity with which he flung himself into it, it is not necessary to take such a passion too tragically. The real tragedy is in the fact that such loves and the constantly recurring cycle of irresistible ardor and weary renunciation were typical of him.

It was not without intention that I named the year 1811. A short year before Beethoven had been completely bewitched by the capricious spell of Bettina von Brentano. A year later he wrote one of the most beautiful love letters of all time to the "Immortal Beloved." But even to this day we do not know whether it was addressed to the Countess Thérèse Brunswick or to the singer Amalie Sebald. There is evidence in favor of both possibilities. This does not mean that Beethoven was fickle or faithless. He had suffered too much from both of these passions and their hopelessness. But it shows how fierce was his craving for the woman in whose company he could at long last taste at once the happiness of this life and the joys of creation, and how in every woman he sought not a Helen of Troy but a Penelope.

Above all, however, we are here concerned with a quite different and a purer type of womanhood—true kindred souls—than were those who meant in Beethoven's life only a passing relief to his overcharged blood, or at best a perhaps necessary and salutary relaxation from the super-human concentration in his work.

Here we are concerned with women who were worthy of him—if indeed the woman who was worthy of Beethoven could ever have existed.

I must confess that it seems to me to be completely unimportant which of these two women—both solitary, but widely contrasted, and both distinguished by charm of character and alertness of mind—was the one to whom Beethoven addressed his imperishable love letter.

With the words "Immortal Beloved" he might have conferred the patent of nobility on any one of the women who had been consecrated by his choice, and it is mere chance that while most written testimonies of his passionate tenderness have been destroyed or lost, just this one has been preserved, which like a halo adorns the brow of the one woman of his choice. I must admit that I was for a long time convinced that no other than Bettina von Arnim could have been the Chosen One, who could have inspired the fervent ecstasy which is poured forth so feverishly in the romantic triptych of that letter.

Bettina von Brentano was rarely fascinating, fantastically overwrought, vivacious, effervescing, incalculable, in whom Peer Gynt-like elements, wit and humor, sibylline enigmas, ingenuous girlishness, fascinating fictions, fantasies of genius and exotic elfishness were fused into an irresistibly magnetic whole. She it was who created those brilliant pictures of Beethoven and Goethe which seem to be more genuine than the real men. All this served to convince me that Beethoven could not have escaped. Her glamour, her childlike, appealing yet shrewdly discriminating sympathy, her inconsequent, but also caressing, now frothy and amusing, now soulful and affectionate chatter, her capricious, abruptly variable temperament, now hectic now dreamy, then again in a moment hiding beneath a mask of playfulness, must have singled her out from the host of others who could only languish, who could only be serious, who were only ready to yield, or could only hesitate and shed tears.

And last, not least, there was the sweet, refined, pale face with the dark questioning eyes, the tender, serious, smiling Mona Lisa mouth, the daintily chiseled nose, the thin cheeks, and the reflections of her dark hair, which flowed down in soft ringlets to the swanlike neck, with a few rebellious locks escaping from the narrow parting. Could Beethoven have resisted?

Above all, however, the tone of the letter is vastly different from that of all the others which Beethoven addressed to the women he loved—at least as far as we have knowledge of them. Unhappily Thérèse von Brunswick caused the whole correspondence to be destroyed, and it would certainly have been the most enlightening of all, and not in this respect only. There is an authentic note of Bettina in the onrush of these uncontrollable outpourings, a real echo of the same melody of high romance which she sang in her Epistles.

We hear it also in the Beethoven letters, which have long been suspect as inventions, or at least as reconstructions from memory, published by her long after Beethoven's death together with one that was genuine. The melody runs through those letters too which she sent from Vienna to Goethe, in which she describes her meetings with Beethoven in her usual slightly eccentric way, while occasionally hitting the mark triumphantly with a few lifelike pen strokes. It is almost as if in this diary of a love affair of three days, which is undoubtedly authentic and was found in his desk after his death, his speech had become one with hers.

The bewitching, exciting young woman, who one day suddenly burst into his room unannounced, at once so fascinated him that he remained in her company till the evening, played for her, and sang his Goethe Songs for her, in his rough voice, till the rafters rang. He tried many times, both by letter or personally, to be with her again. He felt he owed her a debt for bringing about his personal acquaintance with Goethe, for with vehement insistence she had almost wrung from the reluctant poet, in spite of his usual insistence on etiquette, his consent to a meeting, which had resulted in a slowly growing but inevitable mutual admiration and also in some disillusionment. We know all about this meeting at Teplitz and its less pleasant episodes. Certain it is, however, that by her efforts on Beethoven's behalf she had raised herself in his esteem, and that he never forgot them.

Beethoven had from his youth upwards felt an unmeasured admiration for Goethe and had expressed his gratitude in his own way by his music to "Egmont," and by setting many of his poems. Thus the days he spent with Goethe remained to the end of his life a precious and proudly cherished memory.

But there remains one fatal objection to this view. The letter to the Immortal Beloved would have had to be written in the year 1810, if it had been addressed to Bettina von Arnim, and the date on it, "Monday, the 6th July," does not fit that year. It was not till 1812 that the 6th July fell on a Monday. There are also other certain grounds for holding 1810 to be the only year in which these lines could possibly have been written, which with their winged, deep-breathed, rhythmical prose are worthy to rank with the great love lyrics of the world.

But in 1812 Bettina von Brentano had already become the wife of Achim von Arnim—a fact which cannot be ignored; for we know what was Beethoven's conception of marriage. We know it meant for him a divine sacrament against which it would be sacrilege to offend. We know he would have torn out his tongue rather than suffer it to utter words of such glowing passion and regret to another's wife or to a woman dear to him as Bettina was and always remained in his mind.

Is it then idle to speculate whether, failing her, the letter to the Immortal Beloved was not addressed to the fiery and emotional Countess Thérèse von Brunswick or to Amalie Sebald?

Amalie Sebald, the singer, was a graceful woman in the flower of youth, slender, virginal, with dark deep eyes, a slightly hard mouth, tightly wound plaits of chestnut hair above the smooth parting which ended in a triple row of curls, a delicately formed low forehead of pale ivory; and the oval of her small face was perfection.

Is it not essentially unimportant whether it was the rising or the setting star to which he called in this other Trilogy of Passion? Are not after all the only things that matter the document itself, and the insight it gives us into Beethoven's tempestuous love, his ecstasies and his emotional experiences? Thérèse or Amalie—in favor of each of them there is weighty evidence.

Should no further records come to light to solve the riddle once for all—Romain Rolland hints at some such possibility—the question will in all probability never be definitely answered. At this moment the balance inclines neither to one side nor the other: but at any moment something may be thrown into the scale to make one side or the other kick the beam. It would in any case be strange if Amalie Sebald had been crowned by Beethoven as the Immortal Beloved, for it would have happened all too soon after his farewell to Thérèse after years of disquiet and conflict, of battling for a love which should have led to a union in marriage. The parting had to be, not because of craven misgivings lest Society should refuse to recognise the mésalliance or because of concession to objections—which, moreover, were never raised—from the lady's family. To judge by all appearances, the end was brought about by the scruples of the brave young Countess, who was ready for any sacrifice, but yet shrank from taking her place by the side of the giant as his unquestioned equal and worthy mate. Their farewell, when they were together for the last time as hopeless lovers on the journey to Teplitz by way of Karlsbad, must have been heart-rending indeed.

Then at Teplitz, four days later, Beethoven saw the girlish Amalie Sebald for the first time after a passing acquaintance in the previous year, and at once succumbed to her bitter-sweet charm. The man was captivated by her demure beauty, the musician by the penetrating warmth of her voice.

It is a curious characteristic of the masterminds of music, even that of the deaf Beethoven, that they are always ready to succumb to the mediating power exercised by music, by the spell of a speaking voice, or even by the mere appreciation of a composition. Thus Beethoven succeeded in persuading himself into an admiring friendship for the arid Tietge, the author of the "Urania" epic, once the terror of schoolboys, only because he was always in the company of Amalie. How she won the admiration of Beethoven immediately after their first meeting is shown by his sending to her in a letter to "Tiedsche"—that was how he always pronounced the name—soon afterwards, in the autumn of 1811, half in jest, a "fiery kiss as long as nobody sees it." He wrote her civil notes and letters, and a year later he announced himself, on the very day of her arrival, with the lines in her album:

Ludwig van Beethoven
Who in your memory should dwell
Though to forget him you'd like well.

Then he wrote her eight times from his sickbed, and asked her to come to him.

But all this passed without storms, in rather an atmosphere of dead calm, peace and satisfaction, in contrast with that fiery declaration of love, which one could hardly imagine in this case. Yet we might imagine even that to have been addressed to the timid young singer, who did not feel herself worthy of him, had not Beethoven just previously torn himself away from Thérèse and had his wounds not been still unhealed.

If, however, we question the music which was created at the time, it will give the eloquent answer that Amalie Sebald really had poured balm on his wounded heart, that with her modest freshly blossoming youth she meant for him fresh hope and tender appeasement, not untinged with melancholy regrets.

In the Eighth Symphony—especially when we contemplate it after the bacchantic mysteries of the Seventh, we find him no longer in turmoil, no longer wrapt in dreams. His soul's wounds had closed. He had steeled himself to new effort. With a magical cheerfulness he pressed bravely on. With an all-conquering humor he only snapped his fingers at the things of this life.

The very words of the songs he wrote at this time and certainly addressed in his mind to the beloved singer, tell the same story. "To the Beloved," "What a wondrous life" and "Spring is blooming"—are they not so many declarations of love? It is uncertain whether the marvellously beautiful Cycle "An die ferne Geliebte" (To the distant beloved), this astounding anticipation of Robert Schumann, was meant for Amalie. That it is not improbable may be inferred from what he said later (in 1816) when he poured out his troubled heart to a friend. "He has an unhappy love. Five years ago he became acquainted with a woman. He would have deemed it the highest happiness of his life to form a closer union with her. It was unthinkable, almost impossible, a will o' the wisp, but yet his feeling was still as on the first day. This harmony, he added, he had not yet found. He had not, however, got as far as a declaration: his mind would not yet consent."

It is a fact that he met the delightful, simple-minded and affectionate young woman with the jubilant bird voice for the first time five years before, in 1811; and as at that time he had known Thérèse von Brunswick about ten years, these words and probably that moving Song Cycle referred to Amalie.

But this love, which was gentler, more equable, quieter than the Master's earlier tempestuous passions also ended in renunciation, like all the others. Even if there was no violent abrupt separation, it faded, so to speak, into the twilight and left behind it no wild grief, only a sad smile of resignation.

We shall understand his enduring affection in the light of the letter which Amalie wrote long afterwards when she had for years been the wife of Justizrath Krause in Berlin. She speaks of Beethoven in terms of deepest affection. Even if we do not read in the letter any reference to Beethoven, every line gives proof of a mind richly gifted and kindly, of a lively understanding, keenly interested in all the important happenings of the life of the moment. So delightful, ironical, roguish was her chatter, so free from any hint of scandalmongering, that we can feel how enduring—even till those later years—was the spell which she had exercised as a girl, whose modesty forbade her even to dream that she could ever mean anything to the Master who was drawn to her by an affection, more peaceful perhaps, but tenderer than that which he felt for any other woman who had crossed his path.

There is also a considerable number of female figures who crossed Beethoven's path, to whom his work united him in friendship. And if a passing wave of fancy might bring them nearer to him for a time, it was always only an ephemeral period of sensuous pleasure which need not be taken too seriously.

This was the case with the Master's first Leonore, the imposing Anna Hauptmann-Milder, who was at the time one of the most popular ornaments of the Vienna Opera, and also the idol of the connoisseurs of Berlin. She was always one of the most eloquent propagandists of Beethoven's art, and it was the same in the case of the piquant Mademoiselle Christine Gerardi, the excellent and charming singer who never made use of her art for profit, but only appeared in public on carefully chosen occasions for charity, and that but rarely. So distinguished and perfect was her vital singing that it is said that Haydn wrote the part of Eve in his "Creation" for her. She had been so carried away by Beethoven's earlier works that she sent fiery enthusiastic verses to the Master, who was then twenty-eight years old. They obviously gave him keen pleasure, and he always answered them with a proud modesty all his own: "It is a peculiar feeling to see and hear oneself praised, and then to be conscious of one's own weakness as I am. I always look upon such occasions as a command to approach nearer, however difficult it is, to the unattainable goal which Art and Nature set before us."

In any case his acquaintance with the writer ripened into intimacy, and his letters tell us that she occasionally enchanted him as much by her peculiar, butterfly ways as she puzzled and annoyed him by her parade of her friendship with him. They went no further than lovers usually do, and what his view was of such things is proved to us by his manly words: "Nature herself gave us the weaknesses of Nature.

. . . Reason, the Ruler, should strive by her strength to guide and cure us of them."

Two other women must be mentioned, whose cordial friendships for the Master were enduring because no erotic feeling intruded to confuse them. Both were exceptional beings in their soulful womanliness. They were large-hearted human beings and musical to their finger tips. Both were absorbed in Beethoven's music and both were his insistent apostles on the piano. But here it was not music only which wound its indissoluble bonds round them and him. Their womanly charm always attracted him to them.

One is the Countess Maria Erdödy, who, although she was not older than he was, played the mother to him, his confessor from whom he had no secrets. It was to her that he brought all good and all tragic tidings, all his joys, his sorrows and his failings. This lady, who was early left a widow, and was always surrounded by a host of young children, was exceptionally frail and of an almost incorporeal thinness. It almost seemed as if angina and the influence of its streptococci had weakened the heart. Though she was partly disabled by paralysis of the lower limbs, this noble lady overcame all physical ills by mental and moral strength and her indomitable will. She could hardly walk, was forced to drag herself toilfully from chair to chair, leaning on the furniture at every step, or had to be helped. She was not beautiful, but the speaking expression of her soft melancholy eyes gave her face a peculiar charm. A perfect cataract of reddish-brown piled-up hair fell over her narrow childlike shoulders. Her slender throat seemed hardly able to support her small head. Her nose was slightly aquiline and longish, and her cheeks were thin. She was not free from freckles, and her figure was quite incredibly slim, but the patient, hardly perceptible smile which played round her weary mouth and her kindly questioning look told of the patience of a heart inured to sorrow. Beethoven loved and esteemed her highly as a friend. He confided everything to her and obtained absolution from her for all the sins of his domineering anger, even when she had suffered from them. There were often misunderstandings which had to be cleared up. Once or twice their relationship was seriously disturbed by his explosive roughness; but at such times his beautiful quality of realizing the wrong he had done never failed him, and he was always ready to make amends. He would, with exaggerated self-reproach, plead for pardon from his friend, whose fragile and delicately sensitive soul suffered more than any other from the sudden outbursts of his "Raptus," till peace was restored. With Maria von Erdödy, he forgot his obstinacy, his suspicious vigilance, and his perpetual attitude of defense against possible slights to his sensitive honor. With her he felt no constraint and knew that he was understood, even on the occasions when he had stayed away for a few days, quite without reason, or when his choleric nerves got the better of him. He could come and go when he liked. His friend was always ready to receive him equably, calmly, ready to cope with his greatness and his caprices alike. He was glad to make music with her and for her. He loved to hear her play and sympathized sincerely with her joys and sorrows. In short, she was a real value in his life.

The other is his Dorothea-Cecilia, Baroness Ertmann, who lived, as the authentic interpreter of Beethoven, long enough to visit Felix Mendelssohn in Italy, who learned something from her virile, fiery and plastic playing.

At that time she was already an old lady and very much out of practice (it was a strange meeting; does not the principal theme of the Sonata Opus 101, which was dedicated to her, point prophetically to Mendelssohn?) "In every finger tip a singing soul," Reichardt said of her, "and in the two equally nimble hands, what vigor and power over the whole instrument when it plays, sings and speaks, voicing all that is great and beautiful in art." Beethoven had acted most correctly when he first made the acquaintance of this unusual, externally somewhat stiff and aggressive lady, with her opulent black hair, which was almost like a periwig. As she writes herself:

"At first there was a great deal of opposition to the great Master and the trend of his music. Most people thought it unintelligible and dull. Being anxious to make the acquaintance of his new Sonatas I went one day to the music shop of Mr. Haslinger, had some of them shown to me and immediately played them on one of the pianos which were there. In my excitement I had not noticed a young man who was standing shyly in a corner, and then gradually came nearer to me. What was my astonishment when he suddenly seized my hand and thanked me in the warmest terms for the successful interpretation of his Sonatas. It was Beethoven. From that moment we were friends."

They became real friends. Her playing could never have satisfied the Master so completely if the man Beethoven had not spoken to her from his works, or if on the other hand his music had not been revealed to her by his cyclopean, naïvely humorous, rebellious character. For this reason she was never offended by him when in childishly rough jest or sudden anger he kicked over the traces. She understood the grounds of his irritability and the deaf man's suspicions, and thanks to this understanding of him, both as man and artist, their friendship had a quality of permanence and a freedom from any unpleasant episodes which few others had in his life. But his Dorothea-Cecilia had no need to "calculate" about him. His music had no secrets from her and so she knew him to the very depths of his soul.

It was only Maria Pachler-Koschak from Gratz who could bring his work home to him as fully as this lady. For that reason she was of great significance to him, as was her playing, which completely expressed his wishes and therefore held up to him the mirror of his self.

There was a touching incident which proved how sincerely he was attached to her, what true sympathy he showed in every incident of her life, but it also tells how it was only through his music he could ever enter into full communion with his friends and reveal his thoughts, which were too deep for words. Dorothea von Ertmann had buried a dearly loved child, but no word came from Beethoven, no sign of his sympathy. For the first time she did not understand her friend, who had always shown the most lively and the warmest interest in her and hers. She could not understand that he was forced into silence because all the words he could have said to her appeared to him but poor, and everything merely conventional was intolerable to him. Finally, after several weeks he appeared at her house, took her hand without a word and silently went to the piano and played for hours. Later she said: "Who could describe this music? we seemed to hear choruses of angels greeting the entrance of my poor child into the realms of light." Then when he had finished he sorrowfully pressed her hand and went away as he had come, without a word.

He had spoken to her through his music, which was the highest he had to give. That was Beethoven's way of offering comfort to a mourning mother and showing her his reverence for her grief.

When the whole procession of women whom Beethoven loved passes before us, we might think he had been frivolous and fickle, always too ready to welcome change and only too easily comforted. This is the reverse of the truth. In reality he had always loved only the same woman —the phantom image created by his longing for the right soul-mate, whom he thought he had found in every one of these women. By its side each separate figure became almost secondary, just as the theme which he found for one of his symphonies after much searching became secondary by the side of the total structure of the movement. As in his works he did not simply set one idea in its place after another, but took a theme from the molten mass of elemental music and poured it into his own peculiar mold, and then seized from thence each separate idea, so somewhat similarly he delved in the mines of love, and bestowed the ore he had won as a gift on each one who resembled the image he bore in his soul.

He "was" love, as he "was" music. This he also proved because, though he could renounce, he could never forget. To all whom he loved he remained to the end faithful in the highest sense. He would not blot out of his memory even the most superficial and the most frivolous one of all, Therese Malfatti, the dark beauty who even when she was Baroness Drosdick could not abandon her dangerous coquetries. Even when he was fifty years old, he was drawn to her. He went to the house of the Malfattis, found no one at home, tore a sheet from his sketchbook and wrote down a melody to the words of Matthisson, whose verses had inspired his unforgettable "Adelaïde," and scribbled at the head the words, "To my dear Therese . . ."

He hoarded all the tokens of past tenderness. After his death the letter to the Immortal Beloved and a miniature medallion of Giulietta Guicciardi were found in his desk. Never did his warmth cool, never was his longing for love satisfied.

In the summer of 1818 he went for a walk in Baden deep in his dreams of sound. A carriage passed and he recognized one of the women who had been dear to him, no matter which one it was. The initial with which he indicates her is hard to read, it might equally well be an "M" or an "R," or the two letters intertwined. When he came home, the Master, who had been stirred to his depths, flung some words on to paper, which sound like a prayer of his unsatisfied longing, "Only love— it is love alone that can give you a happy life. O God, let me find her— at least her who will fortify me in virture, whom Thou wilt suffer to be mine." And he added the words, "Baden, 27th July after M. [?] had driven past me, and I thought she had given me a look." He was still in an inward fever.

Thoughts of love and marriage were always in his mind: he could not think of one without the other. Happiness always passed him by: he always stood by the roadside and looked after the woman whom he had recognized too late, who always beckoned to him as she was disappearing.

Which of these was really the Immortal Beloved? Perhaps none and in the last instance every one whom his live had touched. He bore all of them away into his Eternity. In this sense the Song Cycle "To the Distant Beloved" was not destined for Amalie Sebald alone. It belongs to the band of loved ones who from afar gathered round the songs which they had inspired.—RICHARD SPECHT

His Deafness

On April 26, 1966, I was introduced socially to the charming Mrs. Samuel Rosen. In the course of the delightful afternoon, I happened to mention the fact that I was, at the time, compiling a cross-section of the multifarious words that have been written about Beethoven from 1780 on, and attempting, as far as possible, to weed them out. Mrs. Rosen, with considerable humility, mentioned the fact that her husband, Dr. Rosen, the great ear specialist, had once been cited at an international meeting of authorities on ear maladies, as the only person who *could* have cured Beethoven, had the two of them been alive at the same time. Naturally, the many "ifs" of the proposition included the possibility that Dr. Rosen, *while* Beethoven were alive, would have had the resources of the two centuries of research which had led up to his epoch-making development of the operation known in medical terms as the "mobilization of the stapes." Not being medically informed, nor having any special theory to develop about Beethoven's deafness, I asked Mrs. Rosen whether I might presumé to "pick the brains" of her husband about his feelings on the *strictly medical* aspects of Beethoven's case—a case that has been clouded and misrepresented since long before 1827 by well-meaning personal friends, glory-seekers, historians, musicians and musicologists, romantics, poets, and biographers of all kinds, idol-smashing or otherwise. The net result of this confusion about the case has been that the poor uninformed public was forced to rely upon so-called "informed" literature and to make up its own mind as to the validity of the information contained, based upon the *accepted* accreditation of the author.

Dr. Rosen, it turned out, is an avid music lover himself and was more than glad to talk to me about one of his heroes. He was kind enough to give me several hours of his time (actually, it turned out to be on the very eve of his departure with his wife, who is also his medical assistant, to one of the highest and most inaccessible reaches of the Caucasus Mountains to do some research on the effects of extreme altitude and extreme old age upon the sense of hearing).

He was, he said, convinced by all the available evidence he had seen, that the cause of Beethoven's deafness must have been otosclerosis—a nonhereditary disease, he explained, that can fortunately now (incidentally due to his discovery) be cured in most cases. He also was kind enough to point out to me the following paper by Dr. Terence Cawthorne, which was presented a few years back at an international meeting of the American Laryngological, Rhinological and Otological Society. The very name of the society scared me, but Dr. Rosen was patient enough to explain to me (in language I could understand) some of the multisyllable medical terms, and also the relative significance of certain hypotheses.

I am not including this essay as, in my judgment, the *truest* of the many opinions about Beethoven's malady. I am including it because, in the eyes of one of this century's greatest authorities on ear maladies, it presented the facts with very little prejudice—that is, as little prejudice *as is possible* when discussing a great human being such as Beethoven, who has had such a shattering influence on the thinking and culture of his generation and all succeeding generations. I am personally convinced that no person living, doctor or not, can be *completely* objective about Jesus or Gandhi, Michelangelo or Picasso, Julius Caesar or Napoleon, Homer or Tolstoy, Shakespeare or Shaw. Or Beethoven!

To me, Dr. Cawthorne's article was especially meaningful because of his comparison among three creative and highly sensitive human beings, of the terrible effect *on their creativity*, of the loss of a vital sense. As a musician, *not a doctor*, I find that the only passage in the article to which I take exception is the summary that "the supreme tragedy was that he [Beethoven] could not hear what he had composed." Any educated musician, I know, can "hear" notes on a piece of paper as clearly as when the same notes are actually played—*sometimes more clearly*. A great genius like Beethoven must, then, have had this faculty developed to the highest degree. Therefore, he was not, I would judge, in any way cut off from the musical world. I feel that the *real* tragedy for him was, more probably, the lack of ability, of such a highly gregarious individual, to communicate with his fellow man.

Incidentally, Dr. and Mrs. Rosen in describing to me some of the characteristics of many deaf people, including their own patients, mentioned: bitterness, rudeness, slyness, vacillation, dishonesty in small matters, lack of trust in others—all characteristics, according to contemporaneous records, that were common also to Beethoven, one of the greatest creative geniuses the world has ever known. Actually, just because of this very greatness, those unpleasant characteristics, which are customary it seems in some degree to practically all deaf patients, have been misjudged, misinterpreted, masked, or explained away by a century and a half of well-intentioned historians. It is, therefore, refreshing at this point to re-examine them in the unprejudiced light of medical knowledge. Whatever slight irritation those personal idiosyncrasies may have caused his contemporaries (or the blind hero worshipers who came after him), they can do nothing to take away from the incomparable contribution he left to the whole human race!—THOMAS K. SCHERMAN

The Influence of Deafness
On the Creative Instinct

It has been said of the creative artist that his work, be it prose or poetry, painting or sculpture, music or drama, is the product of an inner compulsion whose only standard is of his own making; and that the desire to please others in no way influences or even stimulates his compositions, which, no doubt, accounts for the fact that many creative artists never live to see their work appreciated.

My purpose here is to show how deafness may be said to have influenced the creative instinct of artists in three quite different fields: a writer, a painter, and a composer. In each I believe the cause of the deafness was different; in two it must surely have left its effect on their work, but it may well be disputed whether it had any effect on the output of the third; but as I shall hope to show you there may well be a good reason for this.

Here then are two great creative artists, Jonathan Swift and Francisco José de Goya,[1] each gregarious and each shut off from his fellow creatures by a severe form of perceptive deafness. In each the artistic output was tinged with pessimism and even despair; and I suggest that it was their deafness that played a large part in their gloomier outpourings.

Now we come to our third patient, the composer Beethoven, who was born in 1770 and who, despite his deafness, must surely be the greatest composer the world has known.

Our first knowledge of his affliction comes from the Heiligenstadt Testament, which was in fact his will and was opened and read only after his death.

During the summer of 1802, Beethoven was in the small village of Heiligenstadt, not very far from Vienna, engaged in composing his Second Symphony. He was thirty-two years of age at the time and his will and testament, which he wrote during this summer, included the following remarks about his deafness:

> "But only think that during the last six years I have been in a wretched condition; rendered more by unintelligent Physicians, decreased from year to year with hopes of improvement, and then finally forced to the prospect of lasting infirmity."

Here then is the patient's own account of his deafness, which he had noticed for at least six years—at the age of twenty-six—and no doubt it had been coming on slowly before that.

Is there any wonder that Beethoven was a difficult man; one who could claim to be the very Prince of Sound and yet he could not hear himself?

All the deaf are sensitive about their affliction, but how much more sensitive a musician must be to the sly laugh or grin that his defect would be bound to evoke from the less charitable of his acquaintances; yet despite this great and progressive handicap he composed a hundred

[1] The author describes in some detail the effect upon the creative output of Swift, who gradually became deaf over a period of twenty-five years due to what is known as Ménière's disease; and Goya, who suddenly became deaf at the age of forty-seven, due not to syphilis, as some authorities suggest, but to the so-called Vogt-Koyanagi syndrome—a little known affliction of the pigments of the skin.—Editor.

more works after writing this Heiligenstadt Testament. After his death in 1827 his skull and temporal bones were examined but nothing definite was found, though as usual that etiological whipping boy of those days, syphilis, was evoked.

Like Swift, and possibly for the same reason, Beethoven was unmarried; though there is ample evidence to show that he was attracted to women. I think that he too preferred not to share his affliction with someone else, though I also think that both he and Swift would have been happier men if they had.

As regards the cause of Beethoven's deafness, I cannot help agreeing with my friend Dr. Tremble and many others, that the most likely cause of a progressive deafness starting in early adult life is otosclerosis.

Another point in favor of this is that as he became more deaf he used to listen to the piano as he was playing by holding one end of a short stick between his teeth, the other end being applied to the piano top. Surely this is evidence of good bone conduction such as one would expect with otosclerosis. He also used hearing aids, though of course in those days they were nonelectrical; but the mere fact that he even tried hearing aids suggests that he had a conductive deafness which, in the absence of any history of evidence of suppuration, was almost certainly due to otosclerosis.

Why then, it may be asked, did not Beethoven's deafness have any noticeable effect on his artistic output? Why was his music, if the argument is to be logical, not gloomy or even macabre?

So far as his everyday life is concerned it seems that he behaved in the conventional way of the hard of hearing. He was difficult, quarrelsome, suspicious, and withdrawn, but his artistic output does not appear in any way to have been influenced by his deafness. His Eighth Symphony is as gay and light as his Second, and it is difficult, nay impossible, to believe that any of his compositions could have been improved upon.

I think that one reason that his deafness did not affect him more seriously is that his was a conductive deafness. He did not have to suffer the *distortion and discord* of the *fluctuating deafness* of Ménière's disease, *in which the very sound of music can be intolerable;* moreover, he was not, like Goya, *suddenly* cut off from all outside sounds. His was a gradually increasing deafness which did not become profound until the pattern of musical expression was well established in his mind. After that, what was important was what he created in his mind and what he could write down; not what he heard. For him the supreme tragedy was that he could not hear what he had composed. Though he knew it was right, he did not have what must be the consummation of musical experience, the ability to hear his own work played back to him by a full orchestra.

No doubt many other examples of the influence of mental and physical disorders can be adduced, but equally there can be no doubt that in all three patients I have mentioned deafness was a great burden, and that in at least two of them it affected their artistic output, *while in the third it robbed him of the fullest appreciation of his own genius.*[1]—TERENCE CAWTHORNE

Theories of Cause

Was Beethoven syphilitic? Or is he, as Carl Engel suggests, the victim of those who have tried to fasten on him a disease he never had? An important question—so its increasing discussion seems to indicate. This paper naturally does not attempt to answer it as a physician might, but, with a prefatory statement of the sicknesses which he really had, it does attempt to show the flimsy foundation of the charge; the extent, despite that flimsiness, in which biographers have repeated it, and in brief compass the published opinion of the medical profession. On this basis an answer can be and is arrived at.

For only a short period did Beethoven enjoy the health which with his great natural strength he should have had. For the remainder— from the chills of his childhood trip to Holland, to that moment when the stricken giant shook his fist at the storm and fell back dead—there was a succession of ailments. Smallpox was one of them, for all descriptions include the pockmarks on his face; probably typhus was another. Digestive troubles and chest affections began early in his life at Vienna. In 1798 came the first sign of the deafness which almost drove him to suicide.

By 1810 his hearing, which had been unusually keen, was largely gone and within another half dozen years a silence that was almost complete had closed in upon him. Aggravated by irregular habits, other troubles had in the meantime developed. In roughly chronologic sequence, there came increased digestive troubles with colic; enteritis, bronchitis, followed by chronic catarrh, rheumatism, asthma, pleurisy, eye troubles, intense and long-continued headaches, gout, cirrhosis of the liver (which killed him) with dropsy, and perhaps pneumonia from exposure on that fatal ride from Gneixendorf. The story of the four months' attack that marked the end is too well known to need restatement. In 1817, he had written: "I consider myself doomed. . . . Thank God, I shall soon have finished my part in the play. . . . May God help me." The finish was an appalling struggle for life.

[1] Italics by the editor.

Biographers, not content with this, now quite generally add syphilis. Whether Beethoven had that disease or not is in itself of little consequence—he had begged that the truth about him, whatever it might be, be told—but it is of consequence whether or not those biographers have without sufficient warrant attributed it to him. Alexander Wheelock Thayer, the great authority on the facts of Beethoven's life, started the theory, strangely enough, through the very vagueness of his statements. What and all that he said in print appears in the following citations—and he said nothing about venereal disease. The inference was easily drawn, however, that Thayer was concealing something and that that something was detrimental or even disgraceful. Syphilis may cause deafness, and Beethoven was deaf; it may contribute to cirrhosis of the liver, and from that disease he died; and Thayer kept something up his sleeve. Therefore, Beethoven had syphilis. To this choice bit of reasoning was added what Thayer was said to have said in letters or orally, what a surgeon of Vienna was said to have said was "probable," and the rumors of two prescriptions.

The charge first got into print in 1879, in Sir George Grove's article on the composer in his "Dictionary of Music and Musicians." Having written, "One thing is certain . . . that he (Beethoven) had no taste for immorality," he says, five pages later: "The whole of these appearances (in the postmortem examination) are most probably the result of syphilitic affections at an early period of his life." The shock comes not from the text but from the footnote:

"This diagnosis, which I owe to the kindness of my friend, Dr. Lauder Brunton, is confirmed by the existence of two prescriptions of which, since the passage in the text was written, I have been told by Mr. Thayer, who heard of them from Dr. Bertolini."

Thus were these famous but elusive prescriptions started on their biographical career. Some thirty years after Grove, Theodore von Frimmel wrote that, in addition to certain possible causes of Beethoven's deafness, there was another "about which I must not keep silence, since many years ago Thayer gave me by letter definite information about this other malady of Beethoven's." The malady was not named nor the text of the letter given. Then Dr. Leo Jacobsohn said: "After Frimmel's communication I do not feel I am committing any indiscretion when I say that in the private possession of a man of culture there is an as yet unpublished note in Beethoven's own hand referring to a cure that leaves no doubt as to the specific nature of his malady." Hevesy's "Beethoven, the Man" puts it: "In 1819 he (Beethoven) notes: 'L. V. Legunan. L'art de connaître et de guérir toutes les contagions veneriennes'"—a memorandum that he must get the book, says Ernest Newman in quoting Hevesy. Specht's still more recent "Beethoven as He Lived" (1933) makes it an order for the book, and gives the price. Friederich Schultze (1928) holds to the original story of the two prescriptions privately held and not to be published.

And now for the beginning of it all, Thayer's statements, here quoted as given in the Krehbiel edition of his "Life of Beethoven." At Volume I, page 253:

> "After spending his whole life in a state of society in which the vow of celibacy was by no means a vow of chastity; in which the parentage of a cardinal's or archbishop's children was neither a secret nor a disgrace; in which the illegitimate offspring of princes and magnates were proud of their descent and formed upon it well-grounded hopes of advancement and success in life; in which the moderate gratification of the sexual was no more discountenanced than the satisfying of any other natural appetite—it is nonsense to suppose that under such circumstances Beethoven could have puritanic scruples on that point. Those who have had occasion to ascertain the facts know that he had not, and are also aware that he did not always escape the common penalties of transgressing the laws of strict purity."

And in Volume II, page 294, after quoting from the eulogy written by Dr. Aloys Weissenbach in 1814:

> "Remarks follow upon Beethoven's ignorance of the value of money, of the absolute purity of his morals (which unfortunately is not true) and of the irregularity of his life."

And in Volume II, page 87, referring to Dr. Bertolini, Beethoven's physician from 1806 to 1815:

> "In 1831 he gave a singular proof of his delicate regard for Beethoven's reputation; supposing himself to be at the point of death from cholera, and being too feeble to examine his large collection of the composer's letters and notes to him, he ordered them all to be burned, because a few were not of a nature to be risked in careless hands."

So stands the whole of the main indictment. Thayer asserts that Beethoven did not always escape the common penalties of transgression, that the reference to the absolute purity of his morals is not well founded, and that a physician had destroyed his correspondence lest some of it fall into careless hands. That is a slim foundation, but it covers all that Thayer committed to print. Not even in discussing the composer's deafness or cirrhosis does he make an intimation of a syphilitic origin. All the rest of the so-called evidence cited by later biographers is at second or third hand, and refers to documents which are not produced and which cannot be published, though the implied existence of the disease is trumpeted to the world! Hevesy and Specht give at least partial specification, but Ernest

Closson cleans the slate by saying that the documentary evidence must have been destroyed.

Testimony so indefinite would merit scant attention were it not that other writers have accepted it. That documents which are not produced have no value as evidence is a point which needs little urging. Even if Hevesy's reference to a memorandum and Specht's to an order were to be accepted, they would only put Beethoven in the position of seeking a book on the symptoms and cure of venereal disease twenty-one years after his deafness had begun and, significantly, at the very time that he was worried to death by a nephew who was given to dissipation but whom Beethoven loved and tried in his groping, unhappy way to protect and educate. This is no attempt to shove disease off onto the nephew, but only to show conditions that should be taken into account. Newman had them in mind, though without acknowledging their import, when he wrote of Beethoven's having "an agonized vision of the pleasure-loving and easily led Carl coming to moral and physical shipwreck in the stews of Vienna."

Ernest Newman, in his book, "The Unconscious Beethoven" (1927), is the most positive of the later writers. "It is matter of common knowledge that Thayer had in his possession evidence which he could not bring himself to make public." "For about half a century it has been known—or confidently assumed—that some time in his early manhood Beethoven had contracted syphilis, and the further confident assumption was made that this was the ultimate cause of his deafness." He cites Grove, Thayer, von Frimmel, Jacobsohn and Hevesy; brushes aside Dr. Waldemar Schweisheimer who, in 1922, made, as he admits, a "searching examination" of the subject; adds a citation that Beethoven was given to flirtations "from which he did not always emerge happily"—and starts his next chapter, quite unwarrantedly it would seem, with these words of finality: "The fact of Beethoven's malady seems then to be beyond dispute."

Having, without the production of the evidence, established Beethoven's guilt to his own satisfaction, Mr. Newman seeks to sustain the verdict by inferences drawn from incidents of his life—these inferences, however, being manifestly the outgrowth of the syphilitic theory and not its proof. Beethoven's malady, he says, will "account for his venomous hatred of unchaste women and for his desire to protect his brothers from them"; will explain the "excessive restrictions upon the goings and comings, the companions and the amusements" of the nephew, the "unwarrantable interference" with the lives of his brothers and the "hatred of their women-folk that passed the bounds of reason."

Upon the appearance of Newman's book, an English musician with some medical training, William Wallace, jumped to his support in *The Musical Times*, of June 1, 1927, with evidence which, he asserted, "clinched the diagnosis." As early as 1914, Wallace had pronounced upon Beethoven's illnesses. "The cause .was syphilis," he said in his book, "The Musical Faculty," and proceeded: "From first to last, Beethoven's clinical history illustrates the usual course that his malady takes." In 1927 came his "clinching" proof, a "certified photograph" of Beethoven's skull taken at the exhumation of the body in 1863, showing the bone in the region of the right ear to be "enormously thickened." A photograph is a skittish thing, at best, but there is here also the question of what it was that was photographed. At the autopsy the organs of hearing were dissected, and Dr. Frank says they "were preserved in the Anatomical Museum in Vienna, but when, many years later, Politzer desired to examine them for study, they had disappeared." This is confirmed by a letter from Dr. Politzer to Dr. Cabanes, February 12, 1901. It is further recorded that at the exhumation, in 1863, the skull was found to be in nine pieces, and Gerhard von Breuning, who as a lad had waited at Beethoven's death-bed and was now a leading surgeon in Vienna, had the sad duty of reconstructing it. "The skull was completely distorted by the dampness of the grave," says Paul Bekker, and Ernest Closson adds that certain parts proved to be missing. Of the photograph taken by Rottmayer and preserved in at the Beethoven Museum in Bonn, Dr. Sorsby says:

> "No such bulge is shown in the masks of Beethoven taken during life and on his death. The postmortem reports speaks of the uniform thickness of the vault of the skull. The careful description of the fragments disinterred in 1888, when they were in very much the same condition as in 1863, makes no mention of any irregularity in the bones, and Choulant's drawings do not show it. The bulge in the Rottmayer photography—and enlargements based on it—is there-fore regarded as an artifact; probably a piece of clay attached to the bones."

Dr. Choulant's drawings were made upon the second exhumation, at which time there was a second reconstruction of the skull, and Dr. Georges Canuyt, in a discussion of Beethoven's deafness (*Le Medecine International Illustrée*, March, 1934), asserts that Drs. Weisbach, Fold and Meinert took exact measurements of the skull and did not report any thickening of the bone. Mr. Wallace's confident pronouncements seem to have been without foundation.

The influence of Mr. Newman's skillful writing upon other commen-tators has been marked. Daniel Gregory Mason, distinguished musicolo-gist and composer, while refusing to accept the picture "more like a caricature than a portrait," presented by the "more aggressively 'modern' writers" ("Beethoven and His Forerunners," 1930), takes Newman at face value, and refers to Beethoven's "well known hatred of loose women, . . . a phobia due to his unconscious association of sexual irregularities with the venereal disease which in his case they had led to, and with the terrible affliction of deafness which that had brought in its train" ("Essays," 1928). Former Premier Edouard Herriot ("La vie de Beethoven" 1928) puts a query: "One must ask oneself if he did not also suffer from another malady very widely distributed in the Vienna of that epoch, as we are told, and less easily treated then than today." Romain Rolland ("Beethoven the Creator," 1928) says "perhaps from syphilis" and refers to "an excess of scrupulosity" which "prevents the publication of certain documents that exist in a Berlin collection." W. J. Turner ("Beethoven: The Search for Reality," 1927) is in opposition to the extent of citing the composer's ability to hear through bone conduction as against a syphilitic origin of his deafness. Marion M. Scott ("Beethoven," 1934) asks, apropos of the injunction to Johann to beware of the whole tribe of bad women, "Had Beethoven become the burnt child who dreads the fire?" and again, as to the Heiligenstadt Testament: "The disaster was as complete as any in a Greek tragedy, and if biographers are right who believe that Beethoven's deafness resulted from a syphilitic trouble, then it also fulfilled the Greek doctrine of Nemesis." J. H. Elliot ("Music and Letters," January, 1934) refers to the "unsavory explanation of Beethoven's ultimate deafness." René Fauchois, in his often unpleasant and imaginative "La Vie d'Amour de Beethoven" (Paris, 1928), asks: "Was Beethoven affected by syphilis? Was it for that that he was denied experience of all that comprises the ordinary happiness of mankind? . . . Certain documents exist, it appears, in a collection in Berlin, details which Beethoven transmitted to a physician who was treating him." Pryce-Jones says: "A high proportion of the great has been syphilitic, and although his deafness gave no evidence of syphilis, Beethoven may well have been among them." Then he gets a bit stronger: "His behavior to his sisters-in-law is probably rightly diagnosed by Mr. Newman as the result of a sexual complex due to his own disease." Robert Haven Schauffler ("Beethoven, the Man Who Freed Music," 1929) concludes that Beethoven probably suffered from a venereal disease, that the cirrhosis may have been so caused, that the deafness was not, and that the "hatred of the sisters-in-law had at times the blind intensity of a sexual obsession." Chotzinoff ("Eroica," 1930) has syphilis running as an undercurrent— not named—in his romance on the composer's life. Hevesy ("Beethoven the Man," 1927) darkly questions, "or from some still more formidable malady?" and puts in a footnote: "The poison which was undermining his body was day by day destroying his hearing." Ernest Closson ("L'élément Flammand dans Beethoven," 1928) disposes of the missing papers: "It is generally admitted today that the musician suffered from a secret malady, not hereditary but directly contracted, upon which the piety of his friends and his biographers has drawn a veil and the documentary evidence of which must have been destroyed." Finally, a writer in *The Musical Times* refers almost casually to the "usually accepted" cause of the deafness.

These subsequent writers in the main follow or agree with Newman; Newman relies upon Thayer—"A biographer of Thayer's exceptionally judicial habit of mind would not have said all he did say on such a matter unless he had been absolutely sure of his facts." He quotes Grove's statement above given with the footnote regarding Dr. Brunton, discusses Dr. Schweisheimer who opposed the syphilis theory, refers in a footnote to Dr. Jacobsohn on the cause of the deafness—and so far as concerns medical authority he stops right there. Succeeding writers in general make no references whatever to medical diagnosis. In other words, the new school of biography rests its case upon Thayer's cryptic utterances and the alleged incriminating documents which have not been produced in the fifty-seven years that have elapsed since Grove's article was published. Without medical support for its assertions, the conclusion would seem inevitable that, whatever virus coursed through Beethoven's body, the virus of an inadequately supported charge is poisoning his biography.

The medical profession in the meantime has shown a constantly increasing interest in Beethoven's case, with especial reference to his deafness. Dr. Beverley R. Tucker ("The Gift of Genius," 1930) diagnosed it as due to infection of the middle ear, but the infection was not syphilitic. The author says:

> "It has been hinted that Beethoven's deafness and idiosyncrasies were probably due to syphilis, but no evidence, clinically or from the autopsy of his brain, can be adduced of the disease. From all descriptions he had middle ear deafness, cirrhosis of the liver and ascites (dropsy), and in all probability the whole vicious circle was inaugurated by nasopharyngeal infection early in life. Again, Beethoven's mental or rather temperamental aberrations were not those of paresis (syphilis) but in reality those of congenital emotional instability aggravated by circumstance and by deafness."

In the book written by Dr. G. Bilancioni ("La Sordità di Beethoven," 1921) syphilis as a cause is not suggested, and Dr. Schweisheimer is quoted to the effect that is it not mentioned in connection with Beethoven by any authority. Dr. Bilancioni's conclusion was this:

> "Beethoven's deafness was caused by otosclerosis, that is, by a disease intimately connected with disturbances in the calcium metabolism which occur in serious organic changes found in people with alcoholic and tuberculous antecedents."

Dr. Schweisheimer (1922) denied that the autopsy showed any condition probably referable to syphilis, and rejected the contentions based upon the alleged thickening of the skull. Dr. Marage, of Paris, in an address to the Academie des Sciences, in 1928, and in subsequent correspondence with Rolland, also eliminated syphilis, a disease which "produces an absolutely different order and development of deafness." Raoul Blondel ("The Deafness of Beethoven," London Quarterly Review, January, 1931) commends Dr. Marage as especially qualified and cites his researches as leading to a diagnosis of inflammation of the inner ear caused by a grave pathologic heredity, abuse of alcohol and liver trouble. Dr. Maurice Sorsby, of London, (*Journal of Laryngology and Otology*, August, 1930), finds no indication that syphilis was the cause either of the deafness or the cirrhosis. The alleged circumstantial evidence that Beethoven had the disease, he adds, "is hardly deserving of serious attention." That otosclerosis is commonly caused by syphilis, as Jacobsohn contended, Dr. Sorsby declares is "an exploded fallacy," and he adds: "Cirrhosis of the liver of syphilitic origin is as questionable an entity as otosclerosis of syphilitic origin. There are quite enough causes in Beethoven's life for cirrhosis without having to call in a problematic syphilitic infection." Dr. Henry L. F. A. Boyle, of Paris, also rejected the syphilis theory ("Beethoven vu par les Medicins," 1928).

Dr. Thomas J. Harris, in a paper read at the New York Academy of Medicine (1936) reached the conclusion that "syphilis involving the ear is not characterized by such symptoms as Beethoven had," and that the cause was otosclerosis. Dr. Jacobsohn (1910) had also said otosclerosis—probably the result of typhoid fever but possibly of syphilis—this latter on the basis of the alleged thickening of the right parietal bone: "A very feeble argument," said Canuyt, "since every infectious disease may cause the same lesion and produce a like result." Jacobsohn's reference to the alleged note mentioning a remedy "the use and purpose of which are not doubtful," met a similar fate in Canuyt's article: "This is of little consequence. Beethoven had consulted so many physicians and taken so much medicine that even if there should be found a prescription directing the use of mercury, it would be nothing extraordinary." Canuyt attaches no value to unpublished documents, but seems to follow Professor Escat in the opinion that the disease may have existed in hereditary form, and he is "inclined to hold" that the deafness was of labyrinthine type, and of syphilitic origin, whether inherited or acquired.

Of medical authorities, Dr. Ira Frank cites Klotz-Forest (whose diagnosis is catarrh of the eustachian tube developing into otitis media); Baratoux and Natier (progressive labyrinthine spongification with ankylosis of the stapes); Garnault (atrophy of the nerves due to inflammation); Bonnier (a common tympanolabyrinthine sclerosis); Marage (labyrinthitis from cerebral and intestinal causes); and Bilancioni (otosclerosis). He adds: "All the evidence appears to favor Bilancioni's opinion and with it one is forced, in the absence of more decisive proof of any other condition, to be in agreement."

"It is indeed on slight grounds that the attribution of syphilis has been made," said Dr. J. F. Rogers (*Popular Science Monthly*, March, 1914). Perhaps Mr. Newman has after all hit upon the proper characterization. "*Beethoven's supposititious syphilis*," he calls it on page 39 of his book—and the supposititious is by definition the counterfeit, the spurious, or, even at its best, the hypothetical—a thing assumed without proof.—
CHARLES K. CARPENTER

The Conversation Books

Beethoven's Conversation Books (*Konversationshefte*) are bound memorandum pads. After he became deaf, he kept a supply of them always handy, carrying one with him when he left the house. Offering a pencil to his conversational partner—sometimes more than one at the same time—he invited him or her to write his remarks or questions. Thus, these books were the chief means of communication used by Beethoven's relatives, friends, publishers, callers, etc. (Other means were writing on a slate, scribbling on loose sheets of paper, or merely gesturing.)

After Beethoven's death Stephan von Breuning inherited the Conversation Books. There were more than four hundred of them. When Anton Schindler began his project of writing the biography of the composer, Breuning gave him the books as a gift. After some years Schindler sold the collection to the Royal Prussian Library in Berlin. He told S. W. Dehn, then the custodian of the library, that Beethoven himself had expressed the wish "to have these original documents, as well as the major part of his mental legacy, deposited as a whole in a suitable public place, so that they could be available to everybody" (1846). But what arrived at the library was not four hundred books: there were only 136 (or 137 if one counted two small, incomplete volumes separately). Where were the missing 264? Schindler told Dehn that he had destroyed some of them. He justified his action by stating that the missing books were of small importance and that they contained compromising political remarks. Two books particularly, said Schindler, contained uncouth and unbridled invectives against the emperor, the crown prince, and other high members of the imperial family. He wrote to Dehn: "I am convinced that if Your Excellency had had knowledge of the contents of these writings, you yourself would at once have ordered them burned, so that the Royal Library could not be regarded as a repository of licentious assaults against persons in highest places." It is generally agreed that there is little truth in these statements and that Schindler willfully detroyed these books because they may have contained facts about or allusions to Beethoven's private life detrimental to the image of the master he was trying to create; or, equally probably, that they contained unflattering remarks about Schindler himself.

The Conversation Books were examined by Thayer, who quotes from them in the *Life of Beethoven,* and by several other scholars. Walter Nohl, nephew of the Beethoven scholar Ludwig Nohl, began a critical edition in 1923, but got only as far as half a volume. His work was taken up by George Schünemann. Between 1941 and 1943 he published three volumes. His work too was unfinished: he only got as far as the Conversation Book of July 1823. A French scholar, Jacques-Gabriel Prod-'homme, penetrated a little further, publishing further excerpts at random (*Les Cahiers de Conversation de Beethoven,* Paris, 1946).

Amazing as it seems, no complete edition of these important documents—ranging from 1818, when Beethoven was forty-eight years old, to three weeks before his death in 1827—has ever been published.

In the division of Berlin, the Royal Prussian Library, now renamed the *Deutsche Stadsbibliothek,* was ceded to the Eastern Zone. Dr. Karl-Heinz Köhler, director of the Music Division of the library, with his staff of assistants, has now embarked on the task of editing and publishing all the Conversation Books. The work is progressing very slowly, since he is attempting to clear up every single name and reference mentioned. The first volume under his editorship, beginning where Schünemann left off, has been published in 1968. It will be many years before all the books will be ready for publication. Fortunately, Dr. Köhler is a young man and in good health.

The deciphering of the Conversation Books entails such problems as these: parts have almost completely faded and now need to be brought back to legibility; this is being accomplished through a special photographic process developed by the Institute for Criminology of the Humboldt University, Berlin. Some curious signs were discovered which, on being submitted to an expert, turned out to be stenographic marks. The system of shorthand used was one developed around 1823 and is now obsolete.

Through the courtesy of Dr. Köhler I have been able to gain access to all the Conversation Books in their unedited stage, and to quote from them at will. I journeyed to the library in East Berlin: there I sat and read extensively, using, at Dr. Köhler's suggestion, a handwritten transcript. When a point seemed doubtful, when, for example, I wasn't sure who was writing, I was able to consult the original books. Dr. Köhler unlocked a huge safe; I must say it was quite a thrill to hold in my hand these unretouched testimonies of life as it was lived in Beethoven's room. The force of his personality, which exercised so magic an effect on his friends, transpires through the lines.

Only rarely did Beethoven himself write in the books. He usually replied *viva voce*. He talked and, according to the testimony of his friends, he talked vivaciously and forcefully until his final illness. Therefore, what you read is dialogue in which the voices of the main actor is absent. Yet one can reconstruct some of Beethoven's remarks and imagine others. When he did write, it was usually when he was afraid of being overheard, or when he wanted to jot down a reminder, or, as happened once or twice, when he spoke to another deaf person.

The Conversation Books have had a curious recent history. In the early 1950's they were stolen by an expert thief, specializing in the purloining of valuable documents. This Arsène Lupin, who made away with papers instead of jewels, spirited the Conversation Books away from the Eastern Zone into West Germany and offered them for sale, posing as a German patriot who had "saved this important legacy from the Russians." He was eventually caught and tried. The court took a negative view of his supposedly patriotic gesture and restored the books to the library.

The subjects covered in the Conversation Books range from the lofty to the most trivial. Musical discussions occur rarely. Beethoven thought about music while he was alone and noted his thoughts in a shorthand of his own in his Sketchbooks. In the Conversation Books we have political, philosophic, and literary exchanges with his friends, many discussions of a business nature—prices to be asked for compositions, arrangements to be made for concerts, evaluations of one publisher against another—and no end of evidence of the minutiae of existence, proving that a great man was as subject to indigestion or as receptive to praise as all of us are. The Conversation Books show Beethoven at his most human. For example:

He is in a restaurant. Beethoven writes: "To charge 1 florin 20 for fried chicken is monstrous! He [the proprietor of the restaurant] makes a profit of at least 40 kr. . . ." His companion: "I have had enough. I only empty the bottle so that the innkeeper won't make too great a profit . . ." B: "I do not think we will come here again very often."

Nephew Karl interviews a servant who says that in the past, when she was placed in more "fortunate circumstances," she spoke French like a native French girl and Italian like an Italian. Thereupon Karl spoke in French with her but discovered that "her French was no better than her German spelling." He finds her unsatisfactory.

Karl, probably chiming in with Beethoven's brother Johann: "Don't give your original manuscripts away. They can always be sold for a good sum. Some day they will be worth more. You can tell that by the autographs of famous men. For example, Schiller—his letters are worth a lot." (Beethoven did not heed this advice.)

A note by Beethoven: "Woolens and flannels are to be washed in water as hot as possible. As soon as they are clean, dip them quickly in cold water and then hang them up to dry. To remove snails and worms from vegetables and plants, soak them in salt water. That will kill them." One can only guess that Beethoven read these household hints somewhere and wanted to make a note of them; having at that moment no paper conveniently handy, he used a Conversation Book. Why should Beethoven have been interested in such domestic details? Was it to instruct a servant?

Karl: At the Wilden Mann [an inn] you are known among the waiters as Baron Beethoven. The other day a waiter said to his assistant, "Quick, a plate for Baron Beethoven."

A friend of Holz: All the churches of Vienna have their eye on you. You will simply *have* to become pious [*gottesfürchtig*].

Beethoven's deep interest in history and his reading tastes are documented here. I discuss the substance of his reading in Chapter IX, but the books reveal further literary notations. For example, a year before his death he talks with Holz about Aeschylus and calls him "the greatest" of the tragic poets, preferring his *Oresteia* to the plays of Sophocles and Euripides. Beethoven writes that he wants a six-volume work of *Explanatory Comments on Homer* and he makes a memorandum of the address of a dealer in rare books (*Antiquar*) who has Xenophon's *Speeches and Deeds of Socrates* in stock. The poet August Kanne borrows Beethoven's copy of Goethe's *Theory of Color*.

"Schiller and Goethe are two names worthy to stand side by side,"[1] writes Dr. Bach, Beethoven's friend and lawyer, and urges him to turn Schiller's *Fiesco* into an opera. Beethoven inquires about an edition of Sir Walter Scott—in thirty volumes!

As to history—some of the works noted in the Conversation Books are: *History of the Hellenic Tribes and Cities*, by Otfried Müller; *Universal History*, by Johannes Müller (who was a follower of Rousseau) in twenty-four volumes; M. I. Wikosch's *Outline of Universal History*, which Karl mentions; and *History of the Germans*, by J. H. Voss, the translator of Homer. Beethoven's interest in the cultures of the past extends to Egypt, and he makes a memorandum of a collection of Egyptian antiquities in Vienna, with the times at which it can be seen and the price of admission. He plans to inspect a mummy from Thebes in the possession of a member of the Hungarian Legation.

[1] The question of who was the greater was endlessly discussed by Beethoven's contemporaries. Goethe said to Eckermann: "Now the public is fighting as to who is greater, Schiller or I. They ought to be glad that there exist in the world a few fellows worth fighting about."

Kuffner, the poet, writes: ". . . the lightning rod, the invention of which is attributed to Franklin, was most certainly known to the Egyptians and the Etruscans." Beethoven's interest in painting is slight, but friend Peters does report that a Heinrich Seelig, innkeeper of the "City of Triest," owns "an exceptionally beautiful Leonardo da Vinci" (most probably a spurious one). Seelig himself calls on Beethoven, brings him a bottle of fine Hungarian wine, and asks "for the honor of a visit any morning."

Karl tells his uncle what he has learned in school. The housekeeper suggests menus. Beethoven scribbles financial calculations, trying to convert old currency into new or foreign currency into Austrian.

It is just this mixture of the transitory and the revelatory, of the requirements of a minute and the requirements of a mind, that makes these books moving and instructive to the biographer. Eventually their contents will become accessible to everybody. In the meantime, I am glad to have had the opportunity to turn their pages.—GEORGE R. MAREK

The Text of the Heiligenstadt Testament

[Autograph in the Stadtbibliothek, Hamburg][1]

Heiligenstadt, October 6, 1802

"For my Brothers Carl and [Johann] Beethoven[2]

O my fellow men, who consider me, or describe me as, unfriendly, peevish or even misanthropic, how greatly do you wrong me. For you do not know the secret reason why I appear to you to be so. Ever since my childhood my heart and soul have been imbued with the tender feeling of good will; and I have always been ready to perform even great actions. But just think, for the last six years I have been afflicted with an incurable complaint which has been made worse by incompetent doctors. From year to year my hopes of being cured have

---

[1] This famous document was found among Beethoven's papers after his death by Schindler, who sent copies of it to Rochlitz at Leipzig and Moscheles in London. Rochlitz published it in the Leipzig Allgemeine Musikalische Zeitung of October 17, 1827. After many wanderings the autograph was eventually sent to its present repository in 1888. It has been reproduced in facsimile many times, recently again in a monograph by Hedwig M. von Asow (Vienna and Wiesbaden, 1957).

[2] In the autograph the name of Beethoven's youngest brother, Johann, is omitted both in the letter and in the postscript dated October 10.

gradually been shattered and finally I have been forced to accept the prospect of a *permanent infirmity* (the curing of which may perhaps take years or may even prove to be impossible). Though endowed with a passionate and lively temperament and even fond of the distractions offered by society I was soon obliged to seclude myself and live in solitude. If at times I decided just to ignore my infirmity, alas! how cruelly was I then driven back by the intensified sad experience of my poor hearing. Yet I could not bring myself to say to people: 'Speak up, shout, for I am deaf.' Alas! how could I possibly refer to the impairing *of a sense* which in me should be more perfectly developed than in other people, a sense which at one time I possessed in the greatest perfection, even to a degree of perfection such as assuredly few in my profession possess or have ever possessed—Oh, I cannot do it; so forgive me, if you ever see me withdrawing from your company which I used to enjoy. Moreover my misfortune pains me doubly, in as much as it leads to my being misjudged. For me there can be no relaxation in human society, no refined conversations, no mutual confidences. I must live quite alone and may creep into society only as often as sheer necessity demands; I must live like an outcast. If I appear in company I am overcome by a burning anxiety, a fear that I am running the risk of letting people notice my condition—And that has been my experience during the last six months which I have spent in the country.[1] My sensible doctor by suggesting that I should spare my hearing as much as possible has more or less encouraged my present natural inclination, though indeed when carried away now and then by my instinctive desire for human society, I have let myself be tempted to seek it. But how humiliated I have felt if somebody standing beside me heard the sound of a flute in the distance and *I heard nothing*, or if somebody heard *a shepherd sing* and again I heard nothing—Such experiences almost made me despair, and I was on the point of putting an end to my life—The only thing that held me back was *my art*. For indeed it seemed to me impossible to leave this world before I had produced all the works that I felt the urge to compose; and thus I have dragged on this miserable existence—a truly miserable existence, seeing that I have such a sensitive body that any fairly sudden change can plunge me from the best spirits into the worst of humors—*Patience*— that is the virtue, I am told, which I must now choose for my guide; and I now possess it—I hope that I shall persist in my resolve to endure to the end, until it pleases the inexorable Parcae to cut the thread; perhaps my condition will improve, perhaps not; at any rate I am now resigned—At the early age of 28 I was obliged to become a philosopher,

---

[1] Evidently Beethoven had moved to Heiligenstadt early in April. In his day it was a small village with sulphur springs. He stayed there also during the summers of 1807, 1808, and 1817.

though this was not easy; for indeed this is more difficult for an artist than for anyone else—Almighty God, who looks down into my innermost soul, you see into my heart and you know that it is filled with love for humanity and a desire to do good. O my fellow men, when someday you read this statement, remember that you have done me wrong; and let some unfortunate man derive comfort from the thought that he has found another equally unfortunate who, notwithstanding all the obstacles imposed by nature, yet did everything in his power to be raised to the rank of noble artists and human beings.—And you, my brothers Carl and Johann, when I am dead, request on my behalf Professor Schmidt,[1] if he is still living, to describe my disease, and attach this written document to his record, so that after my death at any rate the world and I may be reconciled as far as possible—At the same time I herewith nominate you both heirs to my small property (if I may so describe it)—Divide it honestly, live in harmony and help one another. You know that you have long ago been forgiven for the harm you did me. I again thank you, my brother Carl, in particular, for the affection you have shown me of late years. My wish is that you should have a better and more carefree existence than I have had. Urge your children to be *virtuous*, for virtue alone can make a man happy. Money cannot do this. I speak from experience. It was virtue that sustained me in my misery. It was thanks to virtue and also to my art that I did not put an end to my life by suicide— Farewell and love one another—I thank all my friends, and especially *Prince Lichnowsky* and *Professor Schmidt*. I would like Prince L[ichnowsky]'s instruments to be preserved by one of you, provided this does not lead to a quarrel between you.[2] But as soon as they can serve a more useful purpose, just sell them; and how glad I shall be if in my grave I can still be of some use to you both—Well, that is all—Joyfully I go to meet Death—should it come before I have had an opportunity of developing all my artistic gifts, then in spite of my hard fate it would still come too soon, and no doubt I would like it to postpone its coming—Yet even so I should be content, for would it not free me from a condition of continual suffering? Come then, Death, *whenever* you like, and with courage I will go to meet you—Farewell; and when I am dead, do not wholly forget me. I deserve to be remembered by you, since during my lifetime I have often thought of you and tried to make you happy—Be happy—

                                                    LUDWIG VAN BEETHOVEN

[1] Joseph Adam Schmidt (1759–1808), a physician of great repute and professor of anatomy at the [Army] Medical School in Vienna. He and his family were devoted to music [and] Beethoven dedicated to him his [Trio] Opus 38.

[2] The instruments given to Beethoven by Prince Karl Lichnowsky were a violin and a cello by Guarnieri, an Amati violin, and a viola dated 1690. These are now in the Beethovenhaus, Bonn.

For my brothers Carl and Johann
To be read and executed after my death[1]—
Heiligenstadt, October 10, 1802—Thus I take leave of you—and, what
is more, rather sadly—yes, the hope I cherished—the hope I brought
with me here of being cured to a certain extent at any rate—that hope
I must now abandon completely. As the autumn leaves fall and wither,
likewise—that hope has faded for me. I am leaving here—almost in the
same condition as I arrived—Even that high courage—which has often
inspired me on fine summer days—has vanished—Oh Providence—do but
grant me one day *of pure joy*—For so long now the inner echo of
real joy has been unknown to me—Oh when—oh when, Almighty God—
shall I be able to hear and feel this echo again in the temple of
Nature and in contact with humanity—Never?—No!—Oh, that would
be too hard.—EMILY ANDERSON

His Work Habits

It is one of the fortunate facts in the study of the creative process
that a very substantial number of Beethoven's sketches have been preserved. Many of these sketches have come down to us in the form of
notebooks which contain not only drafts of initial suddenly occurring
thoughts but also the elaborate development of ideas. The credit for
having made these sketches available to the musical world goes to a
poverty-stricken scholar, Gustav Nottebohm, a friend of Brahms, who
probably had a hand in this important enterprise. The first of these
Skizzenbücher were published in 1865. These sketchbooks were Beethoven's permanent companions: "I always carry around a sketchbook
like this, and if an idea occurs to me, I make a note of it instantly.
Even during the night I get up when something occurs to me, lest
I forget the idea."[2] And a contemporary witness, Anschütz, describes
him during the throes of creation as follows: "I saw a man lying in
the field, rather disheveled, leaning his head on his left hand—a head
heavy with thought, very spiritual and beautiful in a wild sort of way.
His eyes stared at a sheet of note paper, on this he wrote with his
right hand heavy mystical figures, meanwhile tapping with his fingers."

[1] These two directions are added at the left side of the postscript, which is written
on the fourth page of the autograph and dated four days later than the letter.
Furthermore, in both cases Beethoven spells his country resort Heiglnstadt.
[2] Schindler, *Biographie Ludwig van Beethoven*, Münster, 1845.

We have only to look at these sketches to see what sort of scribbling went on. The mute signs on the paper eloquently bespeak excitement, reflection, vacillation, stormy pushing onward. Every stroke is the sign of an inner struggle. Countless motifs come, are caught in hurried script, whirling through each other. All this is only raw material, mined rapidly from the subconscious. Arduous work is required to polish the crude material into beautiful, shining stones. But the way from the first flash to the elaborated idea is long in space and time. The main theme of the first movement in the Seventh Symphony is found only after six pages of untiring efforts. Six pages of trying, rejecting, testing. For other solutions, Beethoven required weeks, months, years of inspired labor before his music finally reached the form dictated by his inner vision.

This was the way Beethoven created from youth on. Rapidly he jotted down and sketched the sounds which raged within him. In the creative excitement, it made little difference what sort of paper he used. The special notebooks (as Nottebohm published them), or regular loose sheets, were not always at hand. And so Beethoven resorted to any kind of paper he could grab: bills and correspondence, individual pages in almost any size, papers which had piled up on his piano or desk. He snatched household notes of which one side had been left empty, free pages from his calendar, and all possible and impossible sorts of loose leafs which he folded together and carried around with him in his pocket on walks.

In these books and notes of Beethoven, various types of sketching can be discerned. One type aims at the conquest of motifs, themes, melodies. Another type tests the usefulness of a theme which has already been chosen for the later development of a movement. Sketches for the second movement of the Ninth Symphony leave the theme unchanged and deal only with the development of this scherzo. In the sketchbook of the year 1803, a theme of the Eroica appears with its finished profile. Beethoven explores with it the further development, and possible contrasts, in a most extensive web of sketches. This is the type of sketching which Beethoven himself describes as "changing, reflecting and testing."

In other cases, Beethoven aims specifically at form—accepting and rejecting thoughts with a final blueprint clearly in view. For the sake of the form of a movement, or of a whole cycle, themes are exchanged, one thought is substituted for another. Here not the shaping of motifs, but the formation of a unified ground plan appears as the purpose of sketching. Different parts are weighed against each other; their inner balance is sought. Sometimes a certain detail is the focal point around which all sketches rotate. Along with the primary elements, dynamics and tone color also have a part in these experiments. The envisioned orchestration is often made evident by such directions as "violin," "bassoon," "oboe," or "with blowing instruments." In the sketches for the *Missa Solemnis* Beethoven notes the instrumentation: "The Kyrie of my new Mass only with blowing instruments and organ."

In the Agnus Dei of the Mass, Beethoven reminds himself of the stylistic attitude: "Utmost simplicity, please, please, please." It is in the drafts for this final movement that we note the intimate tie-up between Beethoven's aesthetic speculation and the tonal vision. Beethoven first jots down a melody and reminds himself of its harmonization with a few figures. Below he writes the following words: "Dona nobis pacem noch in moll denn man bittet ja um den Frieden darum der Frieden allein behandelt als wäre er schon da." (Dona nobis pacem, still in minor, since one prays for peace and therefore treats peace as though it were already granted.) This remark is an important psychological clue to Beethoven's approach. Originally he had planned two contrasting sections in major and minor respectively. He pursued the tonal idea in the immediately following pencil sketch. The idea is derived from aesthetic thinking which is further in evidence on another leaf on which Beethoven notated: "Es kann auch Stärke der Gesinnungen des innern Frieden über alles sein (Sirach!)." (Strength of the convictions of inner peace can be above everything.) Beethoven, the intense student of philosophy and ethics, apparently thought here of the book, *Ecclesiasticus* or *The Wisdom of Jesus, the Son of Sirach*, a work teaching humility and love of peace. The allegretto vivace of this movement in the *Missa Solemnis* bears the motto: "Prayer for outer and inner peace." The tonal figuration which builds its music is already visible in the sketch.

In general, Beethoven's various types of sketches freely overlap. His approach is always different, not subordinated to any pre-established scheme. Once the seeds are planted, Beethoven searches for melodic lines, counterpoints and forms. The draft might pertain to an exposition, a development, a whole movement, a cycle. Throughout the sketches, we realize how, from a mere skeleton, from sporadic notes and remarks, the work is gradually built and finally reaches its superb synthesis. We witness that amazing and tireless "elaboration in the broadness, in the narrowness, in the height or depth," as Beethoven himself describes his approach. The stupendous spiritual effort does not cease until the last creative possibility is reached, until the onrushing flood of ideas is conquered and the distant goal is reached. This is usually a process consuming a great deal of time. As already mentioned, years may pass before a work emerges from such elaborate search in its final shape. The growth may also occur in installments—broken up by other creative experiences interrupted by new enterprises.

Certain observers have claimed that this titanic struggle in Beethoven's work is nothing more than an indication of intrinsic difficulties which blocked an orderly and direct approach to the execution of his material. This "difficulty," in turn, has frequently been contrasted with the prodigious facility apparent in the work of Mozart or Schubert. The difference is undeniable. But it lies not so much in a difference in the method of procedure as in the composer's final goal. Beethoven could produce with great facility, too: in one single night a complete work such as the Sextet, Opus 71, or the *Fidelio* overture originated. His thoughts streamed in infinite waves to him just as thoughts did to Haydn, Mozart or Schubert. But Beethoven's very nature was one of strife. As he struggled for inner and outer peace (as indicated by the motto of the Agnus Dei in the *Missa Solemnis*), so his creations, too, reflect the constant self-imposed struggle for artistic truth, the right, the good.

Beethoven's notebooks frequently show new thoughts occurring in an environment of sketches with which they have no external connection whatsoever. On June 29, 1800, Beethoven writes to Wegeler: "I live only in my notes, no sooner is one here than the next one is already started. The way I am working now, I frequently do three or four things simultaneously." Instances of such simultaneous work on different scores are the string quartets, Opus 59, 130, 131 and 133. And even when working on one single score, Beethoven did not necessarily take up the composition in its finished order. The first sketches for the Sonata Pathétique, Opus 13, occur during work on the finale of the Trio in G major, Opus 9, No. 1, and on the scherzo of the Trio in C minor, Opus 9, No. 3. Sketches for the Sonata, Opus 14, No. 1, occur at several places: for instance on the last pages of a leaf which already contained music for the second and third movements of the Piano Concerto in B-flat. Working on the Seventh Symphony, Beethoven sketched the scherzo movement while also writing the two preceding movements. Preparing the Ninth Symphony, Beethoven tackled the second and third movements simultaneously. In fact, the genesis of the Ninth Symphony shows a yearlong—no, a lifelong pursuit of that tonal vision of a choral scene with orchestra which haunted the master since his youth and remained unsolved until the last years of his searching life. In consequence of such a method of work, where different tasks are started at the same time, the sketches overlap each other. But Beethoven's mind, equipped with the uncanny memory that is one of the marks of genius, was well able to cope with such seeming irregularities of notation.

Nottebohm justifiably divided Beethoven's sketches into one group in which the total form appears as the aim from the beginning, and another, in which thematic work predominates, with the form only distantly in mind. Psychologically, however, the origin of ideas is closely related, no matter how Beethoven elaborated upon them. A flash occurs and brings a motif, a harmony, or suggests an idea pertaining to form. Nevertheless, the various examples show the different function which such inspirational occurrences have in reference to the architecture of the finished music. The differences lie in the composer's evaluation of his tonal substance—where and how the various thoughts fit into the plan of a specific work.

The drafts for Beethoven's Fifth Piano Concerto in E-flat Major are stamped from their very beginning by a conception of form rather than by a pursuit of melodic and other tectonic elements. Already in the initial sketches, the form idea unfolds itself. The piano introduces the concerto with a brilliant passage, without a pronouncement of the main theme. Along with this unusual opening, and likewise clear from the inception of the music, we observe its familiar harmonies. Yet the main theme of the concerto is not evident at all at this early stage of composition. Motifs come and go; they are accepted, rejected and newly cast. Obviously, they are of lesser importance for it was not a theme or rhythm which untied the flow of Beethoven's imagination. It was rather a definite idea of a form, given a priori, which inspired and remained the decisive factor throughout all stages in the composition of this movement.

An analogous procedure is shown in the sketches to the first movement of the Piano Sonata in D Minor, Opus 31, No. 2. Again, Beethoven is primarily concerned with the form. He envisions a recitative to be interpolated in the blueprint of the sonata movement at the recapitulation of its main thought. As in the case of the Fifth Piano Concerto, the melodic lines as such are only of secondary importance in relation to the pattern of form. In the early sketches, in which the usual form of this movement is already established, the thematic material itself is still in a problematic stage and shows little resemblance to its final shape. Without any decisions as to main or secondary themes, the form alone lives clearly in Beethoven's mind. He seeks and finds the blueprint first. In the piano concerto as well as in the sonata, the composition does not originate from thematic flashes. Waves of form decide their course.

"The way I am accustomed to write, I always have the whole thing before my eyes. I carry my thoughts a long time, often very long before I write them down. Therein my memory remains loyal to me, since I am sure not to forget a theme even after years, once I have conceived it. Some things I change, reject, try all over again until I am satisfied."[1]

From these words of Beethoven, the total pursuit of work clearly emerges. The total idea of the planned work, then, gives direction to the creative imagination. With the specific goal and definite blueprint in mind, the composer has a selective attitude toward all the products of his

[1] Wegeler and Ries, *Notizen über Beethoven.*

tonal fantasy. He rejects as well as accepts. Censoring, he chooses those ideas which fit specifically into the framework of his plan, or he transforms earlier thoughts which he might originally have chosen for a different score.

Even if the artist envisions a great form in its totality, ideas pertaining to details naturally occur. At times, such work on smaller sections occupies the composer's full attention. This happened, for instance, in Beethoven's work on the first movement of the Eroica. Of all the passages in Beethoven's works, few caused so much bewilderment and stirred such heated arguments as the horn call in the first movement, four measures before the recapitulation. When the symphony was first heard following its completion, contemporary listeners thought this passage absurd—either an obvious error of notation, or the idea of an altogether mad musician.

Even when Ferdinand Ries, Beethoven's associate and disciple, heard the entry of the horn at the first rehearsal, he flew into a rage, upon which (as witnesses assert) the dumbfounded apprentice barely escaped a box on the ears from his master. Time passed, but brought no progress in the understanding of this perplexing passage. To make matters worse, J. J. Fétis, the esteemed professor of theory of the Paris Conservatory, actually changed in his Beethoven edition the tonic form of the horn passage to a dominant form. The ultraconservative theorist rationalized for his willful correction by pretending that Beethoven, in his hasty score writing, must have committed an error and put the part in the wrong clef.

No doubt, Beethoven's conception was revolutionary. These measures, bridging the development and the recapitulation with a most original superimposition of the dominant and tonic harmonies, were something unheard of in 1804. Turning to the true meaning of this passage of trials, the sketches established the fact that Beethoven had the quoted horn call firmly in mind while working on the rest of the great movement. He considered the audacious transition at an early stage of planning. The development section was far from finished when he concentrated his attention on this particular problem. Soon after the end of the exposition, it apparently became clear to Beethoven that the main motif ought to be reintroduced in a specifically daring way. And the sketches show how he planned first to bring the horn call in the remote key of D major. This would have been a sharp contrast to the E-flat tonality of the approaching recapitulation. Still another draft establishes that such a combination of dissonant tonalities was by no means a passing flash. Adhering stubbornly to this unusual conception, Beethoven finally arrived at the desired solution. The terrific excitement and fury of the development gradually calms down. With overlapping tonalities as its harmonic background—and four measures before it would have entered "normally"—the horn motif sounds. At this point, most of the instruments have already become silent, the dynamics have decreased from fortissimo to pianissimo. Only the violins remain in softest tremolo, in the B and A flats of the suggested dominant harmony. Now playing unexpectedly the main theme in the tonic, the horn calls like a voice from real life into the depths of a dream. The E-flat major motif restores the daylight of the oncoming recapitulation. This stroke of genius, so much ahead of its time and therefore so incomprehensible to contemporaries, might have been "heaven-sent." Its elaboration was certainly earthly: the result of human toil.

Generalizing, we can assume that nowhere in the development of great music can the tie-up between the total work plan and the details be ignored. In fact with many of Beethoven's scores, the first movements are commentaries on what happens in the first measures. No motif in any score in history incites the entire cyclic motion of an extended symphony as does the opening of Beethoven's Fifth. Like a turbine, the famous four notes generate the motion of the music. The structure of the inciting theme is one of utmost simplicity. It uses a design which is the favorite of all classical composers, consisting of tonic and dominant forms, reductions and cadential condensation. Yet as this scheme unfolds, we become aware of the unshakable logic of Beethoven's symphonic architecture.

As to the andante of the Fifth Symphony, we have traced the reasons which led to Beethoven's intense reworking of the theme: the one-time minuet had to be fused into the symphonic ground plan in its entirety. Even seemingly isolated ideas—striking modulations and unusual instrumentation in the Eighth Symphony, the various bird calls interpreting the voice of nature, the bubbling of the brook, lightning and thunder in the Pastoral—are all associatively inspired by the total idea. All these ideas are unthinkable detached from the fundamental plan.—FREDERICK DORIAN

Beethoven and Goethe

Among the contemporaries of Beethoven one is pre-eminent. Goethe (who was twenty-one when Beethoven was born, and lived five years after his death) stands supreme in the history of art in eighteenth-century Germany and after. During Beethoven's lifetime the writer enjoyed an honorable reputation and a far-reaching fame such as the musician never attained. Now the case is altered, and of a thousand to whom the name Beethoven is at least not empty of meaning there are probably but ten in whom Goethe awakens response. But during their lives there was no question as to which of the two played the greater part in the popular imagination. Goethe with his wide interests sustained by phenomenal powers of comprehension and expression was looked upon as though he were the possessor of divine attributes, and his opinion was sought with an almost Delphic reverence. His acquisitive mind had taken on, by the time he reached the middle years, a marvelous flexibility. There seemed to be nothing in which he was not willing to interest himself, and most things he comprehended with a fullness that showed his extraordinary depth of insight. He alone is worthy to be compared with men of the Italian Renaissance like Leon Battista Alberti and Leonardo da Vinci, men whose minds were laid open to all the currents of knowledge, men irresistibly curious as to the nature of things and the ways of mankind. More surely than any of his contemporaries Goethe was able to keep under survey the whole field of human knowledge, immensely extended since the days of Leonardo. It is only when we endeavor to determine the degree of his appreciation of music in general and of Beethoven's music in particular that our admiration for the high power of his intellect suffers a check and is changed to a feeling of astonishment that in this direction the admirable law which guided that great mind should have ceased to function. For there is no doubt that Goethe had little knowledge of Beethoven's work, and that what he did know failed to move him. Neither did he succeed in gauging the importance of Beethoven in the development of art, though he was not alone there, and few people of that time would have been anything but surprised to hear the verdict of history that places the two men on the same plane.

It may be well to digress for a moment in order to attempt some diagnosis of Goethe's musical constitution. In his early years he was taught the pianoforte but does not appear to have made sufficient headway to make it possible for him to play even passably or to become interested, through the pianoforte, in instrumental music.

When a young man he took lessons at Strassburg on the violoncello with no more lasting result. For him music implied the voice. This tendency was strengthened by this gradual severence from the ideas implicit in the phrase "Sturm und Drang" (in which abstract instrumental music with its increased freedom of expression found a place), and by the journey to Italy (1786), where he seems to have heard a large amount of vocal music. (In the "Italienische Reise" it is more often a question of that kind of music, and only seldom of instrumental compositions or performances.) The song and the aria were his chief delight, and his powers of appreciation stopped short at opera. In these genres he showed his usual lively critical sense. Speaking, for instance, to Eckermann of Beethoven's setting of "Kennst du das Land" he said: "I cannot comprehend how it is that Beethoven and Spohr so misunderstand the nature of a song while they are at work on it. . . . Surely they could have realized that in this case they had to do with a simple song. . . . Being what she is, Mignon may justifiably be made to sing a song—but not an aria!" Goethe's inclinations tended more and more, as the years went on, toward purely vocal and away from abstract instrumental music. He could appreciate Mozart, whom he had heard in 1763 perform at a concert at Frankfurt, when they were both small children. "Mozart died in his thirty-sixth year, Raphael the same, Byron but a little older. All these had fulfilled their mission perfectly and it was high time that they departed, so that other men should still find something left for them to do in this long-lived world." And again: "How can people talk of Mozart *composing* 'Don Juan'! Composition! As though it were a piece of biscuit made up of egg, flour and sugar! It is a creation of the spirit, the part as well as the whole coming from one source, at one burst, filled with the breath of life; so that it cannot be said that the creative artist tried first this thing or cut that one into a certain shape or disposed of anything as he himself willed it; the divine spirit of his genius so overpowered him that he was forced to carry out its commands."

The musicians that Goethe counted among his friends were, with one exception, unimportant figures whose name and work are now forgotten. The exception is Mendelssohn, who came to Goethe when the latter was already an old man and was the first to interest him in Beethoven's instrumental music.[1] Zelter is the most interesting, both for his published correspondence with Goethe (with its rather complacent talk about Beethoven) and because he was Mendelssohn's master and introduced the young Felix to Weimar. Of Ph. Chr. Kayser, who went to Italy to stay with Goethe and whom Goethe helped, sending him to study in Vienna under Gluck, and commissioning him to write music for "Egmont," Goethe's own words are sufficient comment: "Foolish, passionate bestowal of favor upon questionable talent was a fault of my early years, one from which I never have quite been able to escape." Kayser was the first cultured musician to enter the Goethe circle. Further there was Joh. Ferd. Reichardt, executant and critic, an estimable musician, whose correspondence with Goethe may still be studied. And there was von Seckendorff, composer of the music to Goethe's "Lila." None of these men were of first rank and none were able by their example to stir Goethe from his conception of music as being a thing that a cultured

[1] Mendelssohn's description of the effect on Goethe of hearing the first movement of the C minor Symphony played on the pianoforte is of great interest as showing the narrow extent of his acquaintance with Beethoven's work. "He said solemnly: 'Ah, but that doesn't move so much as astound one; it's immense.' Then he muttered on to himself and after some time said: 'That magnificent stuff, quite crazy! One might well be afraid of the roof's falling in! And to think of what it must be like when they all play it together!' And later at table, in the midst of other conversation, he returned to it again."

person should know something of, in order that he might be able to talk
about it. Goethe with his passion for knowledge of everything took music
en passant. Music retaliated by withdrawing herself from such treatment.

The case is a curious one. It is as though Goethe's mind was unable to
project upon music that searching light of the intellect that seemed always able, in other cases, to pierce the outward appearance of things
and lay bare their hidden spirituality. Goethe may be said to have lived
in a visible world whose reflection he revealed in poetry and the most
poetic prose. Beethoven on the other hand, moved—it is the common
experience of all writers of music—in an invisible world whose messages
he translated into sounds. Herr Gundolf, writing of the two men and
their mutual reactions, puts it in this manner: "For him (Goethe)
music was little more than a means of providing adornment, ease, dignity,
charm to life, and in no way did he feel for it as being that expression
of universal principles that Beethoven both saw in his imagination and
realized in his works." This insensibility on Goethe's part to any but
the more superficial appeal of music—differing signally from his approach
and reaction to the other arts—was the direct result of the changed
outlook on life that he underwent when, after "Götz von Berlichingen"
(1773) and "Werther" (1774), works which reflect the ideas of "Sturm
und Drang," he came under the influence of the hellenist Winckelmann,
and eventually (1786) journeyed to Italy. From then onward the character of his work changed, tending toward a classicism that was to strike
what Walter Pater called a "note of revolt against the eighteenth century." But it was to be a species of revolt very different from that
which fired Beethoven's imagination. With him the break with eighteenth-century convention was to lead, via the French Revolution, to
the brotherhood of man. To Goethe, Napoleon, the man who had
disappointed Beethoven, was always a type of hero. As late as 1813,
just after Moscow, he could write to the German patriots Körner and
Arndt: "Rattle away at your chains! This man is too big for you, you'll
never be able to shatter him!" The revolt against the eighteenth century
that Goethe indulged in was in another direction than that which
Beethoven took. It led him to a purely aristocratic view of life wherein
everything was to be invested with the balanced grace of a Grecian
mode of life. This change of front came as a surprise to those of his
contemporaries who had fallen under the spell of the unrestrained romanticism of "Werther," and was not understood, not even realized by the
majority. It is certain that Beethoven failed to take it into account. To
him Goethe was still the author of the "Sturm und Drang" works. His
imagination was fired by "Egmont," a work pertaining to that earlier
period, which Goethe finished, with some feeling of a duty performed,
in Rome as late as 1787, the last sign he gave of interest in the romantic

feelings of his youth. That Beethoven was strongly under the influence of the early romantic works of Goethe is probable, and there is much to be said for Kögel's observation that it is in "Werther" that one must look for the counterpart of that particular turn of thought and manner of expression which colors the pianoforte sonatas, Opus 13, 27 (2) and 57, and the C minor and D minor symphonies. There is no doubt that the young Beethoven, like the young Mendelssohn of later years, was attracted to Goethe by "Werther." The passionate unreason of the book seems to have impressed itself as strongly upon his imagination as it did upon that of all the other young people of that day. So far Beethoven could go with Goethe, finding in the early writings an echo of his own youthful turbulence, seeking for a solution of his insistent difficulties.

In 1810 he finished the "Egmont" music, but not until 1812 did this finally reach Goethe's hands. In the meantime Beethoven had met the man whose work he had known since long and for whom he had come to have feelings of veneration. "When you mention me in your letters to Goethe," he writes to Bettina von Arnim, "search out all those words that are expressive of my deepest reverence and admiration." And again: "How can one ever adequately thank that most precious jewel of a nation, a great Poet!"

Here we may for a moment digress in order to review the actual circumstances of the meeting between Beethoven and Goethe. The most popular authority for a description of the meeting is Bettina Brentano (von Arnim, as she later became). Her reputation for veracity has of late had a severe strain put upon it, and it is no longer possible to accept her tale absolutely. The piquancy of her best story—that of the meeting of Beethoven and Goethe with a group of royalty in the streets of Teplitz—has been taken away by recent research; though what still remains true of the intimate dealings between this delightful young literary lady and the two great men has even now all the charm of the finest ingenious, yet ingenuous, tuft-hunting. It is evident that the discrepancies which are to be found between the facts as they are now known and as they were depicted by Bettina von Arnim arise, not so much from a deliberate attempt at falsification on her part, but simply from an unrestrained delight in writing a good, but not necessarily literal, tale. And it must be owned that Bettina von Arnim had enough discernment to recognize a big lion when she saw him. The situation was easy for her to deal with. Goethe had heard of Beethoven from Zelter, but his music still remained practically unknown to him. Beethoven was, in this case, better informed. We have seen that he knew Goethe through the early works. But it must be remembered that he had remained under their influence and was unaware of the change in the writer's outlook. Both men, in varying degrees, were pleased to deal with the resourceful and amusing Bettina. It is only necessary to read her description of her unexpectedly appearing at a large dinner-party accompanied by the great Beethoven to realize that the character of *dea ex machina* was not displeasing to her. Beethoven and Goethe were both willing to help toward a meeting, Beethoven eager to express the reverence and admiration he felt for the author of "Werther," Goethe by that time in the full tide of popular esteem, "Werther" and all such youthful ebullitions well behind him, his reputation as statesman and man of letters by now unshakable, having no real knowledge of Beethoven as an artist to cause him to look to the meeting with more than a mild interest, a favor he could grant to Bettina. They met and talked once or twice at Teplitz, in July, 1812, where they were both taking a cure. Beethoven's deafness was already firmly enough ingrained to be a hindrance to intercourse, especially in this case, where Beethoven's sense of reverence may well have had the effect of making his sentences unwieldy, a misfortune when dealing with Goethe, who was a master of the well-turned phrase and the well-modulated expression. Goethe, too, was not in the habit of shouting his fine conversation. But Beethoven played to him and thus expressed himself more completely than he could through speech. The encounter, nonetheless, resulted in no lasting friendship, and the two men were not to meet again.

Their first recorded utterances about each other after the Teplitz meeting show the impressions that remained. Beethoven, writing to Breitkopf & Härtel on Aug. 9th, 1812, says: "Goethe is more fond of the atmosphere of courts than is becoming in a poet. No call, therefore, to talk of the absurd behavior of *virtuosi* when poets, who should be looked up to as being the foremost teachers of the nation, forget all else for the sake of such outward show." And Goethe, writing to Zelter from Karlsbad, on Sept. 2nd of the same year, says: "I made Beethoven's acquaintance in Teplitz. His talent amazed me; unfortunately he is an utterly untamed personality, not altogether in the wrong in holding the world detestable, but he does not make it any more enjoyable either for himself or others by his attitude. He is, however, to be excused, and much to be pitied, as his hearing is leaving him, which, perhaps, mars the musical part of him less than the social. He is of a laconic nature and will become doubly so because of this lack." On Feb. 8, 1823, eleven years after the Teplitz meeting, Beethoven wrote to Goethe to ask for a subscription for the edition of the "Missa Solemnis" from the Weimar court. The letter was badly put together, turgid and redundant, the very thing to puzzle and annoy Goethe, himself careful of his words and delicate in his letter-writing. He is said to have been ill at the time the letter came. At any rate the plea remained without attention. It is of interest to see how Beethoven, cognizant, at last, of the change in Goethe's mental outlook, tries to enlist his sympathy by touching on a subject that to the musician meant nothing, but to the writer much: ". . . for years I have been a father to the son of a deceased brother—a promising youth—wholly devoted to science and already at home in the *rich lore of Hellenism.*"

He is reported by Rochlitz to have said (in 1822): "I became acquainted with him (Goethe) in Karlsbad (Teplitz). . . . I was not so deaf then as I am now, but hard of hearing. How patient the great man was with me! . . . How happy he made me then! I would have gone to my death for him; yes, ten times!" Goethe might be expected to have been the one man among Beethoven's contemporaries to understand and value the greatness of his genius. But as Ambros says: "Goethe . . . seems to have been moved but little by the spiritual grandeur of this apparition (Beethoven). We must take it that, without in any way realising Beethoven's greatness, he saw in him little more than a person unfitted for society through his deafness and rendered difficult of approach because of his rough exterior and caustic temperament."[1]

The failure lay with Goethe. Beethoven at least knew Goethe through his works, a step that Goethe had never felt able to take with regard to Beethoven's compositions. Beethoven's notebooks are filled with quotations from Goethe, and it was he who said this to Rochlitz: "He has killed Klopstock for me. . . . You smile that I should ever have read Klopstock! I gave myself up to him many years, when I took my walks and at other times. . . . But Goethe, he lives and wants us all to live with him. That's the reason he can be set to music. Nobody else can be set to music so easily as he." (Thayer [Krehbiel] III, 75). And in conversation with Bühler (1823) he said: "Because of money, which is necessary to me, I cannot write only what I like the most. By that I do not mean that I write simply for money. As soon as this stage is passed, I hope at last to write that which for Art and for me is the highest thing—'Faust.'"—SCOTT GODDARD

[1] Ambros: "Beethoven, Goethe and Michelangelo," quoted by Frimmel, "Beethoven und Goethe," Vienna, 1883.

Contemporary Reminiscences

———◆———

Ferdinand Ries (1801–05)

The following impressions are quoted from the "Biographical Notices" of Wegeler and Ries (1838), to which reference has already been made. Ferdinand Ries (1784–1838), son of Franz Ries in Bonn, to whose family Beethoven owed a debt of gratitude, studied with Beethoven from 1801 to 1805. After very successful concert tours as pianist through practically all of Europe, Ries in 1813 settled for several years in London. There he used all his influence to foster the art of his admired and beloved master, though his correspondence with Beethoven proves that it was not always easy to do so to Beethoven's satisfaction. As a composer Ferdinand Ries showed in his more than two hundred works skillful industry rather than originality and they are today practically forgotten.

My father gave me my first instruction in piano playing and in music in general, instruction which, fortunately for my future career, was thorough in the highest degree. When he decided, for Bonn had suffered deeply owing to the war, that it was time for me to continue my musical education elsewhere, I was sent at the age of fifteen, first to Munich and then to Vienna.

The friendly relations which my father had maintained uninterruptedly with Beethoven as a boy and as a youth, justified his expectation that the Master would receive me kindly. I carried a letter of recommendation with me. When I handed it over to Beethoven upon my arrival in Vienna, in 1800, he was extremely busy completing his oratorio "Christ on the Mount of Olives," since it was to be presented for his benefit under favorable auspices for the first time at a great *Academie* (concert) in the Vienna Theater. He read the letter and said: "I cannot answer your father now; but tell him that I have not forgotten how my mother died; that will content him." Later I discovered that when the Beethoven family had been in great want my father had helped them materially in every way.

In the course of the first few days Beethoven discovered that he could use me, and hence I often was sent for as early as five o'clock, something which also happened on the day the oratorio was to be given. I found him in bed, writing on single sheets of paper, and when I asked what they were, he answered: "Trombones." At the performance the trombones blew from these manuscript parts.

Among all composers Beethoven thought most of Mozart and Handel, and next came Bach. When I found him with music in his hand or saw some lying on his desk, it was sure to be a composition by one of these heroes. Haydn seldom escaped without a few digs in the ribs, for Beethoven cherished a grudge against him from earlier days.

It was Haydn's wish that Beethoven place on his earlier works: "Pupil of Haydn." This Beethoven refused to do because, as he said, though he had taken a few lessons from Haydn, he never had learned anything from him. Beethoven also had studied counterpoint with Albrechtsberger and dramatic music with Salieri. I knew all of them well; but though all three had the highest esteem for Beethoven, they were agreed with regard to their opinion of him as a student. Each said that Beethoven was so obstinate and so bent on having his own way, that he had to learn much which he refused to accept as a matter for study through bitter personal experience. Albrechtsberger and Salieri, in particular, dwelt on this; the former's pedantic rules and the latter's unimportant ones with regard to dramatic composition (according to the older Italian school) did not appeal to Beethoven.

What follows may serve to corroborate the above: Once, while out walking with him, I mentioned two perfect fifths, which stand out by their beauty of sound in one of his earlier violin quartets, in C minor.[1] Beethoven did not know of them and insisted it was wrong to call them fifths. Since he was in the habit of always carrying music paper about him, I asked for some and set down the passage in all four parts. Then when he saw I was right he said: "Well, and who has forbidden them?" Since I did not know how I was to take his question, he repeated it several times until, much astonished, I replied: "It is one of the fundamental rules." Again he repeated his question, whereupon I said: "Marburg, Kirnberger, Fuchs, etc., etc., all the theoreticians!" And *so I allow them!*" was his answer.

Beethoven had promised to give the three solo sonatas, Opus 31, to Nägeli in Zurich, while his brother Karl (Kaspar) who—the more's the pity!—always meddled in Beethoven's affairs, wanted to sell them to a Leipzig publisher. The brothers often argued about the matter, since Beethoven wished to keep his promise, once he had made it. When the sonatas were about to be sent away Beethoven was living in Heiligenstadt. During a walk the brothers quarreled again, and even passed from words to blows. The next day Beethoven gave me the sonatas, to send to Zurich at once, together with a letter to his brother, enclosed in another from Stephan von Bruening, for Kaspar to read. No one could have expounded a nobler moral in a more kindhearted way than Bee-

[1] Opus 18, No. 4.—Editor.

thoven in writing his brother anent the latter's behavior on the preceding day. First he showed its real contemptibility, then he forgave him completely; though he foretold a wretched future for him unless he completely mended his life and ways.

These same sonatas [Opus 31] were responsible for a curious occurrence. When proofs of them arrived I found Beethoven busy writing. "Run over the sonatas for me," he said, and remained sitting at his writing-desk. There were an uncommon number of mistakes in the proofs, which in itself made Beethoven very impatient. At the end of the first Allegro in the G major Sonata, moreover, Nägeli had even written in four measures of his own composition.[1]

When I played them Beethoven leaped up in a rage, came running over to me and half-pushing me away from the piano, shouted: "Where the devil did you find that?" His astonishment and anger when he saw that the music was so printed were inconceivable. I was told to draw up a list of all the errors, and send back the sonatas to Simrock in Bonn at once. He was to have them re-engraved with the addition: *Edition très correcte*. And to this day the phrase is printed on the title-page. The four spurious measures, however, may still be found in some other reprint editions.

When Steibelt (1765–1823), the famous piano virtuoso, came from Paris to Vienna, in all the glory of his fame, several of Beethoven's friends were afraid the latter's reputation would be injured by the newcomer.

Steibelt did not visit Beethoven; they met for the first time in the home of Count Fries, where Beethoven gave his new Trio in B-flat major, Opus 11, for piano, clarinet and violoncello, its initial performance. It does not give the pianist much of an opportunity. Steibelt listened to it with a certain condescension, paid Beethoven a few compliments, and felt assured of his own victory. He played a quintet he had composed, and improvised; and his *tremulandos*, at that time an absolute novelty, made a great impression. Beethoven could not be induced to play again. Eight days later there was another concert at Count Fries' home. Steibelt again played a quintet with much success and besides (as was quite evident), had practiced a brilliant fantasy for which he had chosen the identical theme developed in the variations of Beethoven's trio. This roused the indignation of Beethoven and his admirers; he had to seat himself at the piano to improvise, which he did in his usual, I might say unmannerly, fashion, flinging himself down at the instrument as though half-pushed. As he moved toward it he took up the violoncello part of Steibelt's quintet, purposely put it on the piano-rack upside-down, and drummed out a theme from its first measures with his fingers. Then,

[1] He had inserted four measures of the tonic to parallel the already existing measures on the dominant.—Editor.

now that he had been definitely insulted and enraged, Beethoven improvised in such a way that Steibelt left the room before he had concluded, refused ever to meet him again, and even made it a condition that Beethoven was not to be invited where his own company was desired.

When Beethoven gave me a lesson he was, I might almost say, unnaturally patient. This, as well as his friendly treatment of me, which very seldom varied, I must ascribe principally to his attachment and love for my father. Thus he often would have me repeat a single number ten or more times. In the Variations in F major, Opus 34, dedicated to Princess Oldescalchi, I was obliged to repeat almost the entire final Adagio variation seventeen times; and even then he was not satisfied with the expression in the small cadenza, though I thought I played it as well as he did. That day I had well-nigh a two hour lesson. When I left out something in a passage, a note or a skip, which in many cases he wished to have specially emphasized, or struck a wrong key, he seldom said anything; yet when I was at fault with regard to the expression, the *crescendi* or matters of that kind, or in the character of the piece, he would grow angry. Mistakes of the other kind, he said, were due to chance; but these last resulted from want of knowledge, feeling or attention. He himself often made mistakes of the first kind, even when playing in public.

Once we were taking a walk and lost our way so completely that we did not get back to Döblingen, where Beethoven lived, until eight o'clock. Throughout our walk he had hummed and, in part, howled, up and down the scale as we went along, without singing any individual notes. When I asked him what it was he replied: "The theme for the final Allegro of the Sonata (in F major, Opus 57) has occurred to me." When we entered the room he ran to the piano without taking off his hat. I sat down in a corner and soon he had forgotten me. Then he raged on the keys for at least an hour, developing the new Finale of this Sonata (which appeared in 1807) in the beautiful form we know. At last he rose, was surprised to see me still there and said: "I cannot give you a lesson today; I still have work to do."

In the year 1802 Beethoven composed his Third Symphony (now known under the title of *Sinfonia eroica*) in Heiligenstadt, a village an hour and a half distant from Vienna. In writing his compositions Beethoven often had some special object in mind, though he often laughed and scolded about musical tone-paintings, especially those of a more trifling nature. In this connection Haydn's "Creation" and his "Seasons" sometimes served him as a text, for all he did not contest the composer's great merits, and gave the most deserved praise to many of his choruses and other compositions. In his Symphony Beethoven had thought of Bonaparte, but Bonaparte when he still was First Consul. At that time Beethoven held him in the highest esteem and compared him to the great consuls of ancient Rome. I myself, as well as other intimate friends of his have seen this symphony, already scored, lying on his table, with the name "Bonaparte" at the very top of the title-page, and at the very bottom "Luigi van Beethoven," without another word. How and wherewith the gap was to be filled in I do not know. I was the first to announce to him the news that Napoleon had declared himself emperor, whereupon he flew into a rage and cried: "Then he, too, is nothing but an ordinary mortal! Now he also will tread all human rights underfoot, will gratify only his own ambition, will raise himself up above all others and become a tyrant!" Beethoven went to the table, took hold of the top of the title-page, tore it off and flung it on the ground. This first page was rewritten, and not until then was the symphony entitled *Sinfonia eroica*. Later Prince Lobkowitz bought the right to use this composition for a few years from Beethoven and it was several times performed in his palace. It was there it chanced that Beethoven, who was himself conducting it, in the second section of the first Allegro where such a long series of half-notes moves against the beat, so completely put out the orchestra that it had to begin again from the beginning.

In the same Allegro Beethoven plays the horn a shabby trick. A few measures before the theme again appears in its complete form in the second section, Beethoven has the horn announce it, while the two violins are still holding a chord on the second. One who does not know the score inevitably feels that the horn-player has miscounted and come in at the wrong time. At the first rehearsal of the symphony, which was horrible, but in which the horn-player entered at the right time, I was standing beside Beethoven; and thinking he had made a mistake, said: "That damned horn-player! Can't he count! This sounds atrociously false!" I think I came very near getting a box on the ear, and Beethoven did not forgive me for a long time.

Beethoven liked to see women, especially lovely, youthful faces and usually, when he passed some girl who could boast of her share of charm, he would turn around, gaze keenly at her through his glasses, and then laugh or grin when he saw I had noticed him. He was very often in love, but as a rule only for a short time. When I once teased him about his conquest of a certain beautiful lady he admitted that she had captivated him more potently and for a longer period of time—seven whole months—than any other.

One evening I went to him in Baden to continue my lessons. There I found a beautiful young lady sitting on the sofa beside him. Feeling that I had come at an inopportune time, I was about to retire when Beethoven held me back and said:

"First play me something!"

He remained seated behind me with the lady. I already had been playing a long time when Beethoven suddenly cried: "Now play something sentimental," then, not long after, "Something melancholy," then, "Something passionate"; and so on. From what came to my ears I could take for granted that he had in some way offended the lady, and was trying to smooth it over with these whimseys. At last he jumped up and cried: "Why, those are all things I have written!" I had, in fact, played nothing but movements from his own works, connecting one with the other by short modulations, and this seemed to have pleased him. The lady now left, and, to my great surprise, Beethoven did not know who she was. I only heard that she had entered shortly before I came, in order to make Beethoven's acquaintance. We soon followed her to find out where she lived and, later, what her social position might be. We could see her in the distance—it was a clear, moonlit night—but suddenly she disappeared. Talking of one thing and another we walked about for an hour and a half in the adjacent beautiful valley. When I left Beethoven, however, he said: "I must find out who she is and you must help me." A long time afterwards I met her in Vienna and discovered that she was the mistress of a foreign prince. I informed Beethoven of what I had learned; but neither from him nor from any other person did I ever hear anything more about her.

Beethoven never visited me more frequently than when I was lodging in the house of a tailor who had three very beautiful but absolutely reputable daughters. To them he refers in the conclusion of his letter of June 24, 1804, in which he says: "Do not do too much tailoring, remember me to the fairest of the fair, and send me half a dozen needles."

Beethoven suffered repeatedly, and as early as 1802, [indeed, even earlier than 1800, as appears from his first letters to Dr. Wegeler] from defective hearing, but the trouble soon disappeared again. He was so sensitive about his incipient deafness that one had to be very careful about calling his attention to his deficiency by talking loudly. When he did not understand something he usually blamed the absent-mindedness to which he really was subject in the highest degree. He lived much of the time in the country, where I often went to take a lesson. Sometimes, in the morning, around eight o'clock, after breakfast, he would say to me: "First let us take a little walk." We would start out, but several times we did not return until three or four o'clock, after we had eaten something in a village. On one of these excursions Beethoven gave me the first startling proof of his increasing deafness, which Stephan von Breuning already had mentioned to me. I had called his attention to a shepherd who was blowing his syringa-wood flute very passably in the forest. For a whole half-hour Beethoven heard absolutely nothing at all, and though I repeatedly assured him (which was not the case), that I myself heard nothing either he grew extremely quiet and glum. . . . When, on occasion, he did seem in good spirits, though this was not often the case, he usually went to extremes.

Beethoven was extremely good-natured, but just as easily inclined to anger or suspicion, motived by his deafness, but even more by the conduct of his brothers. Any unknown could easily defame his most proven friends; for he was all too quick and unquestioning in crediting their lies. He would then neither reproach the person suspected nor yet ask him for an explanation, but his manner toward him would immediately show the greatest haughtiness and the most supreme contempt. Since he was extraordinarily violent in all he did, he would also try to find his supposed enemy's most vulnerable spot, in order to indulge his rage. Hence it often was impossible to tell how one stood with him until the matter was cleared up, in most cases by merest chance. Then, however, he would try to atone for the wrong he had done as quickly and effectually as possible.

Etiquette, and all that etiquette implies, was something Beethoven never knew and never wanted to know. As a result, his behavior when he first began to frequent the palace of the Archduke Rudolph often caused the greatest embarrassment to the latter's entourage. An attempt was made to coerce Beethoven into the deference he was supposed to observe. This, however, Beethoven found unendurable. He promised betterment, it is true, but—that was the end of it. One day, finally, when he was again, as he termed it, being "sermonized on court manners," he very angrily pushed his way up to the Archduke, and said quite frankly that though he had the greatest possible reverence for his person, a strict observance of all the regulations to which his attention was called every day was beyond him. The Archduke laughed good-humoredly over the occurrence, and commanded that in the future Beethoven be allowed to go his way unhindered; he must be taken as he was.

Beethoven attached no importance to his autograph compositions. In most cases, once they had been engraved, they lay about in an adjoining room or in the middle of his workroom scattered over the floor among other music. I often have put his music in order, yet when Beethoven was looking for something, everything was turned upside down again. I could at that time have carried off all those original autograph compositions of his which already had been engraved, and had I asked him for them, I am sure he would have given them to me without a moment's hesitation.

In Vienna Beethoven already had taken violin lessons from Krumpholz and at first, when I was there, we occasionally played his sonatas for violin together. But it really was awful music, for in his enthusiastic zeal his ear did not tell him when he had attacked a passage with the wrong fingering (even then Beethoven did not hear well).

In his manner Beethoven was very awkward and helpless; and his clumsy movements lacked all grace. He seldom picked up anything with his hand without dropping or breaking it. Thus, on several occasions, he upset his inkwell into the piano which stood beside his writing-desk. No furniture was safe from him; least of all a valuable piece; all was overturned, dirtied and destroyed. How he ever managed to shave himself is hard to understand, even making all allowance for the many cuts on his cheeks. And he never learned to dance in time to the music.

At times Beethoven was extremely violent. One day, at noon, we were eating dinner in the "Swan" tavern when the waiter brought him the wrong dish. No sooner had Beethoven remarked about it and received a somewhat uncivil reply, than he took up the platter—it was calf's lights with an abundance of gravy—and flung it at the waiter's head. The poor fellow was carrying a whole slew of other portions, intended for other guests, on his arm—an art in which Viennese waiters are very adept—and was quite helpless. The gravy ran down his face, and he and Beethoven shouted and abused each other, while all the other guests burst into laughter. Finally Beethoven, looking at the waiter—who, licking up the gravy trickling down his face with his tongue, would attempt to curse, then have to return to his licking while he cut a most comical phiz, worthy of Hogarth—burst out laughing himself.

Beethoven hardly knew what money was, which frequently gave rise to disagreeable incidents; for suspicious by nature, he often thought he was being cheated when this was not the case. Easily excited, he would call people cheats to their faces and, where waiters were concerned, often had to make up for it with a tip. Finally, in the taverns which he was most accustomed to frequent, all came to know his oddities and his absent-mindedness, and let him say and do what he wished, even permitting him to leave without paying his bill.

In many matters Beethoven was very forgetful. Once he had received from Count Browne a handsome saddle horse, in return for the dedication of the Variations in A major, No. 5, on a Russian song. He rode it a few times, but soon forgot it, and, what was worse, forgot about its feed. His servant, who quickly noticed this, began to hire out the horse for money which he slipped into his own pocket, and, in order not to arouse Beethoven's suspicions, put off handing in the feed bill for a long time. Finally, to Beethoven's great surprise, a very large feed bill was presented to him which suddenly recalled to him his horse, as well as his negligence with regard to it.

Beethoven took great pleasure in recalling his early youth and his Bonn friends, although in reality those had been hard times for him. He frequently spoke of his mother, in particular, with love and emotion, and often called her a fine, kindhearted woman. Of his father, who was chiefly to blame for their domestic difficulties, he spoke seldom and with reluctance; but any harsh word let fall by a third person made him angry. All in all, he was a dear, good fellow; only his variable humor and his violence where others were concerned, often did him disservice. And no matter what insult or injustice had been done him by anyone, Beethoven would have forgiven him on the spot, had he met him when crushed by misfortune.

Josef August Röckel (1806)

The tenor Josef August Röckel (1783–1870) was entrusted with the *Florestan* role in the second version of Beethoven's opera "Fidelio," performed on April 10, 1806. After the *première* of the opera on November 20, 1805, followed by two repetitions, Beethoven's friends saw clearly the necessity for changes and cuts, if "Leonore," as the original version was called, was not to remain a failure. Röckel's vivid narrative of the memorable meeting in December, 1805, at the palace of Prince Lichnowsky, when Beethoven finally agreed to changes in his opera, follows.

It was not until we were on our way to the Prince's palace that Mayer [bass-singer; brother-in-law of Mozart] informed me that we would find Beethoven there among his most intimate friends, and that together with the other opera artists who had taken part in the fiasco of his opera "Leonore," we would once more give a critical performance of the work in order to convince the Master himself of the necessity of a revision. Since Beethoven held the former tenor uniquely responsible for the failure of the opera, I myself, in whose voice he placed more confidence, was to sing the role of Florestan at sight, in this solo performance. At the same time, together with Mayer and the other artists, I was continually to present to the Master, using the most urgent pleas, the need of cuts and changes and, finally, the fusion of the first two acts.

I shuddered at the thought of having to sing the difficult part of Florestan at first sight, for the composer, a composer as hard to satisfy as he was given to outbursts of passion; though I frequently had heard it sung by my former teacher and present rival, and, in part, had studied it with him. I dreaded quite as much the stage intrigues of the offended tenor, whose successor the present step would make me. I should have liked best of all to turn back again, and would have done so had not Mayer clung to my arm and literally dragged me along with him. Thus we entered the Prince's *hôtel* and ascended the brilliantly lighted stairs down which several lackeys in livery, carrying empty tea-trays, came to meet us. My companion, familiar with the customs of the house, looked much annoyed and murmured: "Tea is over. I am afraid your hesitation has created a very delicate situation for our stomachs."

We were led into a music-room with silken draperies, fitted out with chandeliers lavishly supplied with candles. On its walls rich, splendidly colorful oil paintings by the greatest masters, in broad, glittering golden frames bespoke the lofty artistic instincts as well as the wealth of the princely family owning them. We seemed to have been expected; for Mayer had told the truth: tea was over, and all was in readiness for the musical performance to begin. The Princess, an elderly lady of winning amiability and indescribable gentleness, yet as a result of great physical suffering (both her breasts had been removed in former years) pale and fragile, already was sitting at the piano. Opposite her, carelessly re-clining in an armchair, the fat Pandora-score of his unfortunate opera across his knees, sat Beethoven. At his right we recognized the author of the tragedy "Coriolan," Court Secretary Heinrich von Collin, who was chatting with Court Counsellor Breuning of Bonn, the most in-timate friend of the composer's youth. My colleagues from the opera, men and women, their parts in hand, had gathered in a half-circle not far from the piano. As before, Milder was Fidelio; Mlle. Müller sang Marzelline; Weinmüller, Rocco; Caché the doorkeeper Jaquino; and Steinkopf the Minister of State. After I had been presented to the Prince and Princess, and Beethoven had acknowledged our respectful greetings, he placed his score on the music-desk for the Princess and—the performance began.

The two initial acts, in which I played no part, were sung from the first to the last note. Eyes sought the clock, and Beethoven was importuned to drop some of the long-drawn sections of secondary importance. Yet he defended every measure, and did so with such nobility and artistic dignity that I was ready to kneel at his feet. But when he came to the chief point at issue itself, the notable cuts in the exposition which would make it possible to fuse the two acts into one, he was beside himself, shouted uninterruptedly "Not a note!" and tried to run off with his score. But the Princess laid her hands, folded as though in prayer, on the sacred score entrusted to her, looked up with indescribable mildness at the angry genius and behold—his rage melted at her glance, and he once more resignedly resumed his place. The noble lady gave the order to continue, and played the prelude to the great aria: *In des Lebens Frühlingstagen*. So I asked Beethoven to hand me the part of Florestan. My unfortunate predecessor, however, in spite of repeated requests had not been induced to yield it up, and hence I was told to sing from the score, from which the Princess was accompanying at the piano. I knew that this great aria meant as much to Beethoven as the entire opera, and handled it from that point of view. Again and again he insisted on hearing it—the exertion well-nigh overtaxed my powers—but I sang it, for I was overjoyed to see that my presentation made it possible for the great Master to reconcile himself to his misunderstood work.

Midnight had passed before the performance—drawn out by reason of many repetitions—at last came to an end. "And the revision, the curtailments?" the Princess asked the Master with a pleading look.

"Do not insist on them," Beethoven answered somberly, "not a single note must be missing."

"Beethoven," she cried with a deep sigh, "must your great work then continue to be misunderstood and condemned?"

"It is sufficiently rewarded with your approval, your Ladyship," said the Master and his hand trembled slightly as it glided over her own.

Then suddenly it seemed as though a stronger, more potent spirit entered into this delicate woman. Half kneeling and seizing his knees she cried to him as though inspired: "Beethoven! No—your greatest work, you yourself shall not cease to exist in this way! God who has implanted those tones of purest beauty in your soul forbids it, your mother's spirit, which at this moment pleads and warns you with my voice, forbids it! Beethoven, it must be! Give in! Do so in memory of your mother! Do so for me, who am only your best friend!"

The great man, with his head suggestive of Olympian sublimity, stood for many moments before the worshiper of his Muse, then brushed his long, falling curls from his face, as though an enchanting dream were passing through his soul, and, his glance turned heavenward full of emotion, cried amid sobs: "I will—yes, all—I will do all, for you—for my your—for my mother's sake!" And so saying he reverently raised the Princess and offered the Prince his hand as though to confirm a vow. Deeply moved we surrounded the little group, for even then we all felt the importance of this supreme moment.

From that time onward not another word was said regarding the opera. All were exhausted, and I am free to confess that I exchanged a look of relief not hard to interpret with Mayer when servants flung open the folding-doors of the dining-room, and the company at last sat down to supper at plentiously covered tables. It was probably not altogether due to chance that I was placed opposite Beethoven who, in spirit no doubt still with his opera, ate noticeably little; while I, tormented by the most ravenous hunger, devoured the first course with a speed bordering on the ludicrous. He smiled as he pointed to my empty plate: "You have swallowed your food like a wolf—what have you eaten?" "I was so famished," I replied, "that to tell the truth, I never noticed what it was I ate."

"That is why, before we sat down, you sang the part of Florestan, the man starving in the dungeon, in so masterly and so natural a manner. Neither your voice nor your head deserves credit, but your stomach alone.

Well, always see to it that you starve bravely before the performance and then we will be sure of success."

All those at the table laughed, and probably took more pleasure in the thought that Beethoven had at last plucked up heart to joke at all, rather than at his joke itself.

When we left the Prince's palace Beethoven spoke to me again: "I have the fewest changes to make in your part; so come to my house in the course of the next few days to get it; I will write it out for you myself."

A few days later I presented myself in the anteroom where an elderly servant did not know what to do with me, since his master was bathing at the moment. This I knew because I heard the splashing of the water which the noble eccentric poured out over himself in veritable cascades while giving vent to bellowing groans, which in his case, it seemed, were outbursts of content. On the old servant's unfriendly countenance I read the words: "Annouce or dismiss?" in grumpy, wrinkled letters, but suddenly he asked: "Whom have I the honor—?"

I gave my name: "Joseph Röckel."

"Well, that's all right," said the Viennese, "I was told to let you in."

He went and immediately afterward opened the door. I entered the place consecrated to supreme genius. It was almost frugally simple and a sense of order appeared never to have visited it. In one corner was an open piano, loaded with music in the wildest confusion. Here, on a chair, reposed a fragment of the *Eroica*. The individual parts of the opera with which he was busy lay, some on other chairs, others on and under the table which stood in the middle of the room. And, amid chamber music compositions, piano trios and symphonic sketches, was placed the mighty bathing apparatus in which the Master was laving his powerful chest with the cold flood. He received me without any fuss, and I had an opportunity of admiring his muscular system and his sturdy bodily construction. To judge by the latter the composer might look forward to growing as old as Methusaleh, and it must have taken a most powerful inimical influence to bring this strong column to so untimely a fall.

Beethoven greeted me affably, gave me a contented smile, and while he was dressing told me what pains he had taken to write out my voice part from the illegible score with his own hand, so that I might receive it as soon as possible and in an absolutely correct form.

A few weeks later the other members of the opera cast also had their parts in the new version. We were all astonished at Beethoven's capacity for hard work, and that in so short a time he had completed the reshaping of his genial score, which we once more performed in the *Theater an der Wien*, no later than March 29, 1806, that is to say, hardly more than four months after its first short stage appearance; but this time we had a comfortable "Viennese" audience.

The management had guaranteed the composer a percentage and I, since I had so willingly taken over the great role which really lay outside the range of those I habitually sang, had been promised an additional honorarium. Beethoven quarreled violently with the director before the beginning of the opera because his work, which he had expressly named "Fidelio," was once more, for commercial reasons, presented on the play-bills under its old title of "Leonore," familiar owing to Paër's opera. We spared no possible effort to make the opera triumph, and though we were not completely successful the first time, the theater was much better filled for the second and third performances, and even the critics did some if not all justice to the work.

Yes, it pleased more, yet did not please as much as an art-work rising so high above the level of anything before heard should please. This was evident to us when we glanced at the house, still not quite full; and to Beethoven when he got his percentage, regarding the small amount of which he was complaining to Court Banker Braun, when I sought out the latter the day after the third performance (of the new version), to receive my stipend from him. While I accidentally chanced to be waiting in the anteroom to the Baron's business office, I heard a violent altercation which the financier was carrying on with the enraged composer in the adjoining room. Beethoven was suspicious, and thought that his percentage of the net proceeds was greater than the amount which the Court Banker, who was at the same time director of the *Theater an der Wien*, had paid him. The latter remarked that Beethoven was the first composer with whom the management, in view of his extraordinary merits, had been willing to share profits, and explained the paucity of the box-office returns by the fact that the boxes and front row seats all had been taken, but that the seats in which the thickly crowded mass of the people would have yielded a return as when Mozart's operas were given, were empty. And he emphasized that hitherto Beethoven's music had been accepted only by the more cultured classes, while Mozart with his operas invariably had roused enthusiasm in the multitude, the people as a whole. Beethoven hurried up and down the room in agitation, shouting loudly: "I do not write for the multitude—I write for the cultured!"

"But the cultured alone do not fill our theater," replied the Baron with the greatest calmness, "we need the multitude to bring in money, and since in your music you have refused to make any concessions to it, you yourself are to blame for your diminished percentage of return. If we had given Mozart the same interest in the receipts of his operas he would have grown rich."

This disadvantageous comparison with his famous predecessor seemed to wound Beethoven's tenderest susceptibilities. Without replying to it with a single word, he leaped up and shouted in the greatest rage: "Give me back my score!"

The Baron hesitated and stared as though struck by lightning at the enraged composer's glowing face, while the latter, in an accent of the most strenuous passion repeated: "I want my score—my score, at once!"

The Baron pulled the bell-rope; a servant entered.

"Bring the score of yesterday's opera for this gentleman," said the Baron with an air; and the servant hastened to return with it. "I am sorry," the aristocrat continued, "But I believe that on calmer reflection—." Yet Beethoven no longer heard what he was saying. He had torn the gigantic volume of the score from the servant's hand and, without even seeing me in his eagerness, ran through the anteroom and down the stairs.

When the Baron received me for a few minuts later this composed gentleman was unable to conceal a slight apprehension; he appeared to realize the value of the treasure with which he had parted. Out of sorts, he remarked to me: "Beethoven was excited and overhasty; you have some influence with him; try everything—promise him anything in my name, so that we can save his work for our stage."

I excused myself and hastened to follow the angry Master to his Tusculum. All was in vain, however, he would not allow himself to be soothed. The revision of "Fidelio" already had been put away in the manuscript closet, whence not until seventeen years later did the Sleeping Beauty of the new world of opera, the youthful Schröder-Devrient, conjure it forth from oblivion's spider-webs like a Phoenix newly risen.

Ignaz Moscheles (1810–14)

If Moscheles (1794–1870) in his reminiscences of Beethoven, as appended by him to his English translation (1841) of Schindler's biography of the master, gives 1809 as the year in which he finished his studies under Weber (Dionys, not Carl Maria von Weber), this was a lapse of memory: actually he had left Weber to study with Albrechtsberger, ertswhile teacher of Beethoven, in the previous year. Moscheles began his long, honorable and fruitful career as pianist and composer in Prague at the age of fourteen, when he performed a pianoforte concerto of his own composition. That Beethoven thought highly of Moscheles is evidenced by the fact that he entrusted in 1814 to his young admirer the task of making the vocal score of "Fidelio."

In the year 1809,[1] my studies with my master, Weber, closed; and being then also fatherless, I chose Vienna for my residence to work out my future musical career. Above all, I longed to see and become acquainted with *that man* who had exercised so powerful an influence over

[1] It should be 1808.

my whole being; whom, though I scarcely understood, I blindly worshiped. I learned that Beethoven was most difficult of access, and would
admit no pupil but Ries; and, for a long time, my anxiety to see him
remained ungratified. In the year 1810, however, the longed-for opportunity presented itself. I happened to be one morning in the music-shop
of Domenico Artaria, who had just been publishing some of my early
attempts at composition, when a man entered with short and hasty
steps, and gliding through the circle of ladies and professors assembled
on business or talking over musical matters, without looking up, as though
he wished to pass unnoticed, made his way direct for Artaria's private
office at the bottom of the shop. Presently Artaria called me in, and said,
"This is Beethoven!" and, to the composer, "This is the youth of whom
I have just been speaking to you." Beethoven gave me a friendly nod,
and said he had just heard a favorable account of me. To somewhat
modest and humble expressions which I stammered forth he made no
reply, and seemed to wish to break off the conversation. I stole away with
a greater longing for that which I had sought than I had felt before
this meeting, thinking to myself—"Am I then indeed such a nobody that
he could not put one musical question to me?—nor express one wish
to know who had been my master, or whether I had any acquaintance
with his works?" My only satisfactory mode of explaining the matter and
comforting myself for this omission was in Beethoven's tendency to
deafness, for I had seen Artaria speaking close to his ear.

But I made up my mind that the more I was excluded from the
private intercourse which I so earnestly coveted, the closer I would follow
Beethoven in all the productions of his mind. I never missed the
Schuppanzigh Quartets, at which he was often present, or the delightful
Concerts at the Augarten, where he conducted his own symphonies. I also
heard him play several times, which however he did but rarely, either in
public or private. The productions which made the most lasting impression upon me, were his Fantasia with orchestral accompaniments and
chorus, and his Concerto in C minor. I also used to meet him at the
houses of MM. Zmeskall and Zizius, two of his friends, through whose
musical meetings Beethoven works first made their way to public attention: but, in place of better acquaintance with the great man, I had
mostly to content myself on his part with a distant salute.

It was in the year 1814, when Artaria undertook to publish a pianoforte
arrangement of Beethoven's "Fidelio," that he asked the composer whether
I might be permitted to make it: Beethoven assented, upon condition
that he should see my arrangement of each of the pieces, before it was
given into the engraver's hands. Nothing could be more welcome to me,
since I looked upon this as the long wished-for opportunity to approach
nearer to the great man, and to profit by his remarks and corrections.
During my frequent visits, the number of which I tried to multiply by

all possible excuses, he treated me with the kindest indulgence. Although his increasing deafness was a considerable hindrance to our conversation, yet he gave me many instructive hints, and even played to me such parts as he wished to have arranged in a particular manner for the pianoforte. I thought it, however, my duty not to put his kindness to the test by robbing him of his valuable time by any subsequent visits; but I often saw him at Maelzel's, where he used to discuss the different plans and models of a Metronome which the latter was going to manufacture, and to talk over the "Battle of Vittoria," which he wrote at Maelzel's suggestion. Although I knew Mr. Schindler, and was aware that he was much with Beethoven at that time, I did not avail myself of my acquaintance with him for the purpose of intruding myself upon the composer. I mention these circumstances to show how very difficult of access this extraordinary man was, and how he avoided all musical discussion; for even with his only pupil, Ries, it was very seldom that he would enter into any explanations. In my later intercourse with him, he gave me but laconic answers on questions of art; and on the character of his own works, made only such condensed remarks as required all my imagination and fancy to develop what he meant to convey. The impatience naturally accompanying his infirmity of deafness, no doubt greatly increased his constitutional reserve in the latter part of his life.

During one of my visits to Vienna, my brother, who is a resident of Prague, made a journey expressly to see me; and one morning, finding I had an appointment with Beethoven, was exceedingly anxious to get a sight of a man of such celebrity, whom he had never yet had an opportunity of seeing. It was very natural that I should wish to gratify his curiosity, but I told him, that although he was my own brother, yet I knew the peculiarities of the man so well, that nothing could induce me to commit the indiscretion of an introduction. He was, however, too intent upon his wish to let the opportunity escape without a further endeavor, and said that, surely, I might allow him to call, as if in furtherance of another appointment which we had mutually made. To this I consented, and off we went to Beethoven's, where I left my brother in the passage below to wait the issue of our arrangement. I remained with Beethoven about half an hour, when taking out my watch and looking at it, I hastily wrote in his conversation-book that I had a particular appointment at that hour, and that I apprehended my brother was still waiting below to accompany me. Beethoven, who was sitting at the table in his shirt-sleeves, instantly started from his seat, and quitting the room with precipitation, left me in no little embarrassment, wondering what was to follow. In a minute afterwards back he came, dragging in my brother by the arm, and in a hurried manner forced him into a seat. "And is it possible," said he, "that you, too, could think me such a bear as not to receive your brother with kindness?" My brother, who had before received some vague insinuations that the renowned composer was not at all times in his sober senses, looked as pale as ashes, and only began to regain his self-possession on hearing the question which Beethoven so kindly, yet so reproachfully, asked me; for it appeared that the latter had rushed precipitately down the stairs, and, without saying a word, seized my brother by the arm and dragged him upstairs as if he had caught hold of a criminal. No sooner was my brother fairly seated than he behaved in the most kind and obliging manner toward him, pressing him to take wine and other refreshments. This simple but abrupt act clearly shows, that however strange his manners were, he had at heart that kindly and good feeling which ever accompanies genius. If we were to take the external manner for the internal man, what egregious mistakes should we often make!

1808. It goes without saying that Beethoven, that great man, was the object of my most profound veneration. In view of my own high opinion of him I could not comprehend where the Vienna society ladies found the courage to invite him to their musical performances and play him his compositions. He must have liked it, however, for he often was to be met at these evening entertainments. It is possible that even then his wretched deafness may have made him loath to play himself, and that hence he entrusted his new compositions to these feminine hands.

1814. When I came early in the morning to Beethoven, he was still lying in bed; he happened to be in remarkably good spirits, jumped up immediately, and placed himself, just as he was, at the window looking out on the Schottenbastei, with the view of examining the "Fidelio" numbers which I had arranged. Naturally, a crowd of street boys collected under the window, when he roared out, "Now what do these confounded boys want?" I laughed, and pointed to his own figure. "Yes, yes; you are quite right," he said, and hastily put on a dressing-gown.

When we came to the last grand duet, "Namenlose Freude," and I had written the words of the text—"Ret-terin des Gat-ten," he struck them out and altered them to "Rett-erin des Gatt-en"; "for no one," said he, "can sing upon *t*." Under the last number I had written "*Fine* mit Gottes Hülfe" (the end with the help of God). He was not at home when I brought it to him; and on returning my manuscript, the words were added, "O, Mensch, hilf dir selber!" (Oh, man, help thyself!).

Louis Spohr (1812–16)

The impressions of Beethoven which Spohr recorded in his autography belong to the most vivid we possess. Louis Spohr (1784–1859) frankly confessed his inability to comprehend Beethoven's music of the last period. He attributed Beethoven's "aesthetic aberrations" to his deafness, but apparently it never occurred to Spohr that his own ears might have been at fault. Considered in his time either the equal of Paganini as a violinist or second only to him, Louis Spohr laid much greater stress on his importance and fame as a composer. As such, his popularity generations ago certainly was not inferior to that of Beethoven. His music was much more chromatic and much more "romantic" than Beethoven's. Hence, in a way, more "modern," but such externals of style do not determine the longevity of music—the music of Beethoven, by far the greater genius, lives, including the (in Spohr's opinion "monstrous," "tasteless" and "trivial") Ninth Symphony, and that of Spohr, apart from his ever-valuable violin concertos, is dead. That this should have been the fate of his remarkably beautiful opera "Jessonda," too, is a pity.

Upon my arrival in Vienna I immediately paid a visit to Beethoven; I did not find him at home, and therefore left my card. I now hoped to meet him at some of the musical parties, to which he was frequently invited, but was soon informed that Beethoven, since his deafness had so much increased that he could no longer hear music connectedly, had withdrawn himself from all musical parties, and had become very shy of all society. I made trial therefore of another visit; but again without success. At length I met him quite unexpectedly at the eating-house where I was in the habit of going with my wife every day at the dinner hour. I had already given concerts, and twice performed my oratorio. The Vienna papers had noticed them favorably. Beethoven had therefore heard of me when I introduced myself to him, and he received me with an unusual friendliness of manner. We sat down at the same table, and Beethoven became very chatty, which much surprised the company, as he was generally taciturn, and sat gazing listlessly before him. But it was an unpleasant task to make him hear me, and I was obliged to speak so loud as to be heard in the third room off. Beethoven now came frequently to these dining-rooms, and visited me also at my house. We thus soon became well acquainted: Beethoven was a little blunt, not to say uncouth; but a truthful eye beamed from under his bushy eyebrows. After my return from Gotha I met him now and then at the theater "an der Wien," close behind the orchestra, where Count Palffy had given him a free seat.

After the opera he generally accompanied me to my house, and passed the rest of the evening with me. He could then be very friendly with Dorette and the children. He spoke of music but very seldom. When he did, his opinions were very sternly expressed, and so decided as would admit of no contradiction whatever. In the works of others, he took not the least interest; I therefore had not the courage to show him mine. His favorite topic of conversation at that time was a sharp criticism of the management of both theaters by Prince Lobkowitz and Count Palffy. He frequently abused the latter in so loud a tone of voice, while we were yet even within the walls of his theater, that not only the public leaving it, but the Count himself could hear it in his office. This used to embarrass me greatly, and I then always endeavored to turn the conversation upon some other subject.

Beethoven's rough and even repulsive manners at that time, arose partly from his deafness, which he had not learned to bear with resignation, and partly from the dilapidated condition of his pecuniary circumstances. He was a bad housekeeper, and had besides the misfortune to be plundered by those about him. He was thus frequently in want of common necessaries. In the early part of our acquaintance, I once asked, after he had absented himself for several days from the dining-rooms: "You were not ill, I hope?"—"My boot was, and as I have only one pair, I had house-arrest," was his reply.

But some time afterward he was extricated from this depressing position by the exertions of his friends. The proceeding was as follows:

Beethoven's "Fidelio," which in 1804 (or 1805) under very unfavorable circumstances (during the occupation of Vienna by the French), had met with very little success, was now brought forward again by the director of the Kärnthnerthor-Theater and performed for his benefit. Beethoven had allowed himself to be persuaded to write a new overture for it (in E), a song for the jailer, and the grand air for Fidelio (with horns-obbligati) as also to make some alterations. In this new form the Opera had now great success, and kept its place during a long succession of crowded performances. On the first night, the composer was called forward several times, and now became again the object of general attention. His friends availed themselves of this favorable opportunity to make arrangements for a concert in his behalf in the great "Redouten Saal" at which the most recent compositions of Beethoven were to be performed. All who could fiddle, blow, or sing were invited to assist, and not one of the most celebrated artists of Vienna failed to appear. I and my orchestra had of course also joined, and for the first time I saw Beethoven direct. Although I had heard much of his leading, yet it surprised me in a high degree. Beethoven had accustomed himself to give the signs of expression to his orchestra by all manner of extraordinary motions of his body. So often as a *sforzando* occurred, he tore his arms, which he had previously crossed upon his breast, with great vehemence asunder. At a *piano*, he bent himself down, bent the lower the softer he wished to have it. Then when a *crescendo* came, he raised himself again by degrees, and upon the commencement of the *forte*, sprang bolt upright. To increase the *forte* yet more, he would sometimes, also, join in with a shout to the orchestra, without being aware of it.

Upon my expressing my astonishment to Seyfried, at this extraordinary method of directing, he related to me a tragicomical circumstance that had occurred at Beethoven's last concert at the theater "an der Wien."

Beethoven was playing a new Pianoforte Concerto of his, but forgot at the first *tutti* that he was a solo-player, and springing up, began to direct in his usual way. At the first *sforzando* he threw out his arms so wide asunder that he knocked both the lights off the piano upon the ground. The audience laughed, and Beethoven was so incensed at this disturbance that he made the orchestra cease playing, and begin anew. Seyfried, fearing that a repetition of the accident would occur at the same passage, bade two boys of the chorus place themselves on either side of Beethoven, and hold the lights in their hands. One of the boys innocently approached nearer, and was reading also in the notes of the piano-part. When therefore the fatal *sforzando* came, he received from Beethoven's outthrown right hand so smart a blow on the mouth, that the poor boy let fall the light from terror. The other boy, more cautious, had followed with anxious eyes every motion of Beethoven, and by stooping suddenly at the eventful movement he avoided the slap on the mouth. If the public were unable to restrain their laughter before, they could now much less, and broke out into a regular bacchanalian roar. Beethoven got into such a rage, that at the first chords of the solo, half a dozen strings broke. Every endeavor of the real lovers of music to restore calm and attention were for the moment fruitless. The first *allegro* of the Concerto was therefore lost to the public. From that fatal evening on Beethoven would not give another concert.

But the one got up by his friends was attended with the most brilliant success. The new compositions of Beethoven pleased extremely, particularly the Symphony in A-Major (the seventh); the wonderful second movement was *encored* and also made upon me a deep and lasting impression. The execution was a complete masterpiece, in spite of the uncertain and frequently laughable direction of Beethoven.

It was easy to see that the poor deaf *Maestro* of the piano could no longer hear his own music. This was particularly remarkable in a passage in the second part of the first *allegro* of the symphony. At that part there are two pauses in quick succession, the second of which is *pianissimo*. This Beethoven had probably overlooked, for he again began to give the time before the orchestra had executed this second pause. Without knowing it, therefore, he was already from ten to twelve bars in advance of the orchestra when it began the *pianissimo*. Beethoven, to signify this in his own way, had crept completely under the desk. Upon the now ensuing *crescendo*, he again made his appearance, raised himself continually more and more, and then sprang up high from the ground, when according to his calculation the moment for the *forte* should begin. As this did not take place, he looked around him in affright, stared with astonishment at the orchestra, that it should still be playing *pianissimo*, and only recovered himself when at length the long expected *forte* began, and was audible to himself.

Fortunately this scene did not take place at the public performance, otherwise the audience would certainly have laughed again.

As the salon was crowded to overflowing and the applause enthusiastic, the friends of Beethoven made arrangements for a repetition of the concert, which brought in an almost equally large amount. For some time, therefore, Beethoven was extricated from his pecuniary difficulties; but, arising from the same causes, these recurred to him more than once before his death.

Up to this period, there was no visible falling off in Beethoven's creative powers. But as from this time, owing to his constantly increasing deafness, he could no longer hear any music, this of necessity must have had a prejudicial influence upon his fancy. His constant endeavor to be original and to open new paths could no longer, as formerly, be preserved from error by the guidance of the ear. Was it then to be wondered at that his works became more and more eccentric, unconnected, and incomprehensible? It is true there are people who imagine they can understand them, and in their pleasure at that, rank them far above his earlier masterpieces. But I am not of the number, and freely confess that, I have never been able to relish those last works of Beethoven Yes! I must even reckon the much admired Ninth Symphony among them, the three first movements of which, in spite of some solitary flashes of genius, are to me worse than all of the eight previous symphonies, the fourth movement of which is in my opinion so monstrous and tasteless, and in its grasp of Schiller's "Ode" so trivial, that I cannot even now understand how a genius like Beethoven's could have written it. I find in it another proof of what I already remarked in Vienna, that Beethoven was wanting in aesthetical feeling and in a sense of the beautiful.

And at the time I made Beethoven's acquaintance, he had already discontinued playing both in public and at private parties; I had therefore but one opportunity to hear him, when I casually came to the rehearsal of a new Trio (D major 3/4 time) at Beethoven's house. It was by no means an enjoyment; for in the first place the pianoforte was woefully out of tune which, however, troubled Beethoven little, since he could hear nothing of it and, secondly, of the former so admired excellence of the virtuoso scarcely anything was left, in consequence of his total deafness. In the *forte,* the poor deaf man hammered in such a way upon the keys that entire groups of notes were inaudible, so that one lost all intelligence of the subject unless the eye followed the score at the same time. I felt moved with the deepest sorrow at so hard a destiny. It is sad misfortune for anyone to be deaf; how then should a musician endure it without despair? Beethoven's almost continual melancholy was no longer a riddle to me now.

The Baron de Trémont (1809)

Under the title of "The Baron de Trémont. Souvenirs of Beethoven and Other Contemporaries," J. G. Prod'homme contributed a number of the latter to "The Musical Quarterly," July, 1920. They are preserved at the National Library in Paris in six bulky manuscript volumes, apparently compiled by the Baron de Trémont from 1840 to 1850, and containing in a more or less reminiscent form the biographies of 257 of his contemporaries. Louis-Philippe-Joseph-Girod de Vienney (1799-1852) was created a Baron of the Empire in 1810 in recognition of his services as Auditor of the Council of State. He met Beethoven in the previous year, while on a diplomatic mission to Vienna. The Baron de Trémont continued to be a musical enthusiast and *maecenas* for the remainder of his life. He prided himself on having had for fifty years (1798-1849), except during forced absences from Paris, musical *réunions* at his home "at which all the celebrated musicians, either French or foreign, were pleased to display their talents."

Does not our vanity count for something in all that makes us feel flattered by being well received and giving pleasure to some person of bad character, churlish and eccentric, rather than by one possessing all the qualities that amiability and amenity of manner are capable of suggesting? To carry out the comparison still further, if a dog belonging to someone else is vicious and prone to bite, and yet fawns on us, we think more of him for this than we do of a good beast that rushes eagerly to crouch at our feet.

Such was the impression produced on me by Beethoven. I admired his genius and knew his works by heart when, in 1809, as Auditor to the Council of State while Napoleon was making war on Austria, I was made the bearer of the Council's dispatches to him. Although my departure was hurried, I made up my mind that in case the army should take Vienna I must not neglect the opportunity to see Beethoven. I asked Cherubini to give me a letter to him. "I will give you one to Haydn," he replied, "and that excellent man will make you welcome; but I will not write to

Beethoven; I should have to reproach myself that he refused to receive someone recommended by me; he is an unlicked bear!"

Thereupon I addressed myself to Reicha. "I imagine," said he, "that my letter will be of no use to you. Since the establishment of the Empire in France, Beethoven has detested the Emperor and the French to such a degree that Rode, the finest violinist in Europe, while passing through Vienna on his way to Russia, remained a week in that city without succeeding in obtaining admission to him. He is morose, ironical, misanthropic; to give you an idea of how careless he is of convention it will suffice to tell you that the Empress [princess of Bavaria, the second wife of Francis II] sent him a request to visit her one morning; he responded that he would be occupied all that day, but would try to come the day after."

This information convinced me that any efforts to approach Beethoven would be vain. I had no reputation, nor any qualification which might impress him; a repulse seemed all the more certain because I entered Vienna after its second bombardment by the French army, and besides, was a member of Napoleon's Council. However, I intended to try.

I wended my way to the inapproachable composer's home, and at the door it struck me that I had chosen the day ill, for, having to make an official visit thereafter, I was wearing the everyday habiliments of the Council of State. To make matters worse, his lodging was next the city wall, and as Napoleon had ordered its destruction, blasts had just been set off under his windows.

The neighbors showed me where he lived: "He is at home (they said), but he has no servant at present, for he is always getting a new one, and it is doubtful whether he will open."

I rang three times, and was about to go away, when a very ugly man of ill-humored mien opened the door and asked what I wanted.

"Have I the honor of addressing M. de Beethoven?"—"Yes, Sir! But I must tell you," he said to me in German, "that I am on very bad terms with French!"—"My acquaintance with German is no better, Sir, but my message is limited to bringing you a letter from M. Reicha in Paris."— He looked me over, took the letter, and let me in. His lodging, I believe, consisted of only two rooms, the first one having an alcove containing the bed, but small and dark, for which reason he made his toilet in the second room, or salon. Picture to yourself the dirtiest, most disorderly place imaginable—blotches of moisture covered the ceiling; an oldish grand piano, on which the dust disputed the place with various pieces of engraved and manuscript music; under the piano (I do not exaggerate) an unemptied *pot de nuit*; beside it, a small walnut table accustomed to the frequent overturning of the secretary placed upon it; a quantity of pens encrusted with ink, compared wherewith the proverbial tavern-pens would shine; then more music. The chairs, mostly cane-seated, were covered

with plates bearing the remains of last night's supper, and with wearing apparel, etc. Balzac or Dickens would continue this description
for two pages, and then would they fill as many more with a description of the dress of this illustrious composer; but, being neither Balzac
nor Dickens, I shall merely say, I was in Beethoven's abode.

I spoke German only as a traveler on the highways, but understood it
somewhat better. His skill in French was no greater. I expected that, after
reading my letter, he would dismiss me, and that our acquaintance
would end then and there. I had seen the bear in his cage; that was
more than I had dared hope for. So I was greatly surprised when he
again inspected me, laid the letter unopened on the table, and offered
me a chair; still more surprised, when he started a conversation. He
wanted to know what uniform I wore, my age, my office, the aim of my
journey; if I were a musician, if I intended to stay in Vienna. I
answered, that Reicha's letter would explain all that much better than I
could.

"No, no, tell me," he insisted, "only speak slowly, because I am very
hard of hearing, and I shall understand you."

I made incredible conversational efforts, which he seconded with good
will; it was a most singular medley of bad German on my part and bad
French on his. But we managed to understand each other; the visit
lasted nearly three-quarters of an hour, and he made me promise to
come again. I took my leave, feeling prouder than Napoleon when he
entered Vienna. I had made the conquest of Beethoven!

Do not ask how I did it. What could I answer? The reason can be
sought only in the *bizarrerie* of his character. I was young, conciliatory
and polite, and a stranger to him; I contrasted with him; for some unaccountable reason he took a fancy to me, and, as these sudden likings are
seldom passive, he arranged several meetings with me during my stay in
Vienna, and would improvise an hour or two for me alone. When he
happened to have a servant he told her not to open when the bell rang,
or (if the would-be visitor heard the piano) to say that he was composing
and could not receive company.

Some musicians with whom I became acquainted were slow to believe
it. "Will you believe me," I told them, "if I show you a letter he has
written me in French?"—"In French? that's impossible! he hardly knows
any, and he doesn't even write German legibly. He is incapable of such an
effort!"—I showed them my proof. "Well, he must be madly in love with
you," they said; "what an inexplicable man!"

This letter—so precious an object to me—I have had framed. Call
to mind the reflection which heads this article; my vanity would scarcely
have moved me to do as much for Papa Haydn.

I fancy that to these improvisations of Beethoven's I owe my most
vivid musical impressions. I maintain that unless one has heard him

improvise well and quite at ease, one can but imperfectly appreciate the vast scope of his genius. Swayed wholly by the impulse of the moment, he sometimes said to me, after striking a few chords: "Nothing comes into my head; let's put it off till——." Then we would talk philosophy, religion, politics, and especially of Shakespeare, his idol, and always in a language that would have provoked the laughter of any hearers.

Beethoven was not a man of *esprit*, if we mean by that term one who makes keen and witty remarks. He was by nature too taciturn to be an animated conversationalist. His thoughts were thrown out by fits and starts, but they were lofty and generous, though often rather illogical. Between him and Jean-Jacques Rousseau there was a bond of erroneous opinion springing from the creation, by their common misanthropic disposition, of a fanciful world bearing no positive relation to human nature and social conditions. But Beethoven was well read. The isolation of celibacy, his deafness, and his sojournings in the country, had led him to make a study of the Greek and Latin authors and, enthusiastically, of Shakespeare. Taking this in conjunction with the kind of singular, though genuine, interest which results from wrong notions set forth and maintained in all good faith, his conversation was, if not specially magnetic, at least original and curious. And, as he was well affected toward me, by a whimsey of his atrabilious character he preferred that I should sometimes contradict him rather than agree with him on every point.

When he felt inclined to improvisation on the day appointed, he was sublime. His tempestuous inspiration poured forth lovely melodies, and harmonies unsought because, mastered by musical emotion, he gave no thought to the search after effects that might have occurred to him with pen in hand; they were produced spontaneously without divagation.

As a pianist, his playing was incorrect and his mode of fingering often faulty, whence it came that the quality of tone was neglected. But who could think of the pianist? He was absorbed in his thoughts, and his hands had to express them as best they might.

I asked him if he would not like to become acquainted with France. "I greatly desired to do so," he replied, "before she gave herself a master. Now, my desire has passed. For all that, I should like to hear Mozart's symphonies—(he mentioned neither his own nor those of Haydn) —in Paris; I am told that they are played better at the Conservatoire than anywhere else. Besides, I am too poor to take a journey out of pure curiosity and probably requiring great speed."—"Come with me, I will take you along."—"What an idea! I could not think of allowing you to go to such expense on my account."—"Don't worry about that, there's no expense; all my charges for the post are defrayed, and I am alone in my carriage. If you would be satisfied with a single small room, I have one at your disposal. Only say yes. It's well worth your while to spend a fortnight in Paris; your sole expense will be for the return journey, and less than fifty florins will bring you home again."—"You tempt me; I shall think it over."

Several times I pressed him to make a decision. His hesitation was always a result of his morose humor. "I shall be overrun by visitors!"—"You will not receive them."—"Overwhelmed by invitations!"—"Which you will not accept."—"They will insist that I play, that I compose!"—"You will answer that you have no time."—"Your Parisians will say that I am a bear."—"What does that matter to you? It is evident that you do not know them. Paris is the home of liberty, of freedom from social conventions. Distinguished men are accepted there exactly as they please to show themselves, and should one such, especially a stranger, be a trifle eccentric, that contributes to his success."

Finally, he gave me his hand one day and said that he would come with me. I was delighted—again from vanity, no doubt. To take Beethoven to Paris, to have him in my own lodgings, to introduce him to the musical world, what a triumph was there!—but, to punish me for my pleasurable anticipations, the realization was not to follow them.

The armistice of Znaim caused us to occupy Moravia, whither I was sent as intendant. I remained there four months; the Treaty of Vienna having given this province to Austria, I returned to Vienna, where I found Beethoven still of the same mind; I was expecting to receive the order for my return to Paris, when I received one to betake myself immediately to Croatia as intendant. After spending a year there, I received my appointment to the prefecture of l'Aveyron, together with an order to wind up an affair at Agram with which I had also been charged, and then to travel in all haste to Paris to render an account of my mission before proceeding to my new destination. So I could neither pass through Vienna nor revisit Beethoven.

His mind was much occupied with the greatness of Napoleon, and he often spoke to me about it. Through all his resentment I could see that he admired his rise from such obscure beginnings; his democratic ideas were flattered by it. One day he remarked, "If I go to Paris, shall I be obliged to salute your emperor?" I assured him that he would not, unless commanded for an audience, "And do you think he would command me?"—"I do not doubt that he would, if he appreciated your importance; but you have seen in Cherubini's case that he does not know much about music."—This question made me think that, despite his opinions, he would have felt flattered by any mark of distinction from Napoleon. Thus does human pride bow down before that which flatters it. . . .

When Napoleon took possession of Vienna for the second time, his brother Jerome, then King of Westphalia, proposed to Beethoven that he should become his *maître de chapelle*, at a salary of 7000 francs. As I was then at Vienna, he asked my advice, in confidence. I think I did well in advising him not to accept the offer, but to observe his agreement with regard to the stipulated pension [from Archduke Rudolph and Princes Kinsky and Lobkowitz]; not that I could already foresee the fall of the royalty, but Beethoven would not have stayed six months at Jerome's court. . . .—O. G. SONNECK (1)

His Letters

To Friedrich Sebastian Mayer

[*Autograph not traced*][1]

DEAR MAYER! [VIENNA, *probably April 8, 1806*]

Please request Herr von Seyfried to conduct my opera today. I want to see and hear it myself today at a distance. At all events my patience will not then be so severely tried as it would be if I were near the orchestra and had to listen to the murdering of my music!—I cannot but think that this is being done on purpose. I shall not say anything about the wind-instruments but—that all the *pianissimos* and crescendos, all the decrescendos and all fortes and *fortissimos* should have been deleted from my opera! In any case they are not all observed. All desire to compose anything more ceases completely if I have to hear my work performed *like that!*—

Tomorrow or the day after I shall fetch you for dinner. Today I am rather ill again. Your friend

BEETHOVEN

PS. If the opera is to be performed the day after tomorrow,[2] then we must have another rehearsal in the room *tomorrow*—If not, things will be worse every day!

[1] From a copy made by Aloys Fuchs (1799–1853), the distinguished musicologist and enthusiastic collector of musical MSS and autograph letters of musicians. The copy is now in the Benedictine Abbey, Göttweig.
[2] I.e. on April 10th.

To Breitkopf & Härtel, Leipzig

[*Autograph in the Beethovenhaus, Bonn, H. C. Bodmer collection*]

VIENNA, *January* 7, 1809

You will say there is this one and that one and that one and this one —True enough, a more unusual letter-writer than myself it would be hard to find—Surely you have received the trios[1]—You know, of course, that one of them was already completed before your departure.[2] But I wanted to wait and send it with the second one—The latter was finished too a couple of months ago, but I forgot all about sending them to you—In the end our W[agener][3] pounced on me—You would be doing me a very great kindness, and I most earnestly beg you to do it, if you would postpone *until Easter* the publication of all the compositions you have received from me, for I shall certainly be with you *during Lent;* and until then do not let any of the new symphonies[4] be performed in public—For if I go to Leipzig it will indeed be a real treat to have them performed by the Leipzig musicians, of whose excellence and goodwill I have been told—Besides I will deal there with the proof-reading at once—

At last owing to intrigues and cabals and meannesses of all kinds I am compelled to leave my German fatherland which is still in its way unique. For I have accepted an offer from His Royal Majesty of Westphalia to settle there as Kapellmeister at a yearly salary of 600 gold ducats— I have just sent off by today's post my assurance that I will go, and am only waiting my certificate of appointment; whereupon I shall make my preparations for the journey, which will take me through *Leipzig—* Therefore, so that the journey may be all the more glorious for me, I request you, provided that this is not too much to your disadvantage, not to make any of my compositions known to the public *until Easter*—In the case of the sonata which is dedicated to Baron Gleichenstein,[5] kindly omit the description of him as Imperial and Royal Secretary, for he doesn't like it—Abusive articles about my latest concert will perhaps be sent again from here to the Musikalische Zeitung. I certainly don't want everything that is written against me to be suppressed. But people should bear in mind that nobody in Vienna has more private enemies than I have. This is the more

[1] Opus 70.
[2] Härtell had visited Vienna in September, 1808.
[3] Härtel's business correspondent in Vienna.
[4] The fifth and sixth symphonies, Opus 67 and 68.
[5] Opus 69.

understandable since the state of music here is becoming worse and worse
—We have Kapellmeisters who not only do not know how to conduct but
also can hardly read a score—Conditions are worst of all, of course, at the
Theater auf der Wieden—I had to give my concert there and on that occasion obstacles were placed in my way by all the circles connected with
music[1]—The promoters of the concert for the widows, out of hatred for
me, Herr Salieri being my most active opponent,[2] played me a horrible
trick. They threatened to expel any musician belonging to their company
who would play for my benefit—In spite of the fact that various mistakes
were made, which I could not prevent, the public nevertheless applauded
the whole performance with enthusiasm—Yet scribblers in Vienna will certainly not fail to send again to the Musikalische Zeitung some wretched
stuff directed against me—The musicians, in particular, were enraged that,
when from sheer carelessness, a mistake had been made in the simplest and
most straightforward passage in the world, I suddenly made them stop
playing and called out in a loud voice: *"Once more."*—Such a thing had
never happened to them before. The public, however, expressed its pleasure at this—But every day things are getting worse. On the day before my
concert in the short and easy opera "Milton",[3] which was performed at
the Theater in der Stadt,[4] the orchestra so went to pieces that the
Kapellmeister and the leader and the orchestra really suffered shipwreck
—for the Kapellmeister, instead of giving the beat in advance, gave it
later, and then only did the leader come in—Let me have an immediate
reply, my dear fellow.

    With kindest regards, your most devoted servant

BEETHOVEN

    Please do not make public anything definite about my appointment
in Westphalia until I let you know that I have received my certificate
—Accept my good wishes and write to me soon—We shall discuss the
question of new works at Leipzig—Of course, a few hints about my leaving
Vienna might be inserted in the Musikalische Zeitung—and with the
addition of a few digs, seeing that people here would never do anything
worth mentioning for me[5]—

[1] A concert consisting entirely of Beethoven's compositions had been given on December 22, 1808, in the Theater an der Wien. Beethoven conducted his fifth and
sixth symphonies, was the soloist in his G major pianoforte concerto and extemporized
on the pianoforte.
[2] Salieri, who was intensely anti-German, certainly intrigued against Mozart and may
have worked against Beethoven too.
[3] A short one-act opera by Gasparo Spontini (1774–1851), first performed in Paris
on November 27, 1804. It was produced on September 24, 1805 at the Burgtheater,
Vienna, in a German translation by G. F. Treitschke, and was subsequently revived
from time to time at other theaters in the city.
[4] I.e. in the Innere Stadt, the city, not the suburbs.
[5] This postscript is written inside the cover. On the cover itself below the address
in Beethoven's hand is a remark in another hand, probably made by the firm:
"Oh, how very interesting."

To Breitkopf & Härtel, Leipzig

[*Autograph in the Beethovenhaus, Bonn, H. C. Bodmer collection*]

My DEAR SIR,   VIENNA, *July* 26, 1809

You are indeed mistaken in supposing that I have been very well. For in the meantime we have been sufferirng misery in a most concentrated form. Let me tell you that since May 4th I have produced very little coherent work, at most a fragment here and there.[1] The whole course of events has in my case affected both body and soul. I cannot yet give myself up to the enjoyment of country life, which is so indispensable to me—The existence I had built up only a short time ago rests on shaky foundations—and even during this last short period I have not yet seen the promises made to me completely fulfilled—So far I have not received a farthing from Prince Kinsky, who is one of my patrons—and this happens just at a time when money is most needed—Heaven knows what is going to happen—Normally I should now be having a change of scene and air—The levies are beginning this very day—What a destructive, disorderly life I see and hear around me, nothing but drums, cannons, and human misery in every form—My present condition now compels me to be stingy with you again. Hence I am inclined to think that you could surely send me 250 gulden A.C. for the three major works—Indeed I consider that this is by no means an excessive sum; and just now I do need it—For at the moment I cannot count on receiving all that was granted to me in my certificate of appointment—So let me know if you will accept this offer. Why, I could have obtained a fee of 100 gulden A.C. for the Mass alone[2]—You know that in matters of this kind I am always frank with you—

Here is a good plateful of misprints, to which, since I care not a jot about what I have already composed, my attention has been drawn by a good friend of mine. (They are in the violoncello sonata.[3]) I am having this list copied or printed here and inserted in a newspaper, so that all those who have already bought the sonata may obtain a copy of the list—And that reminds me of the confirmation of my experience that the most correct engravings have been made of those compositions of mine which were written out in my own handwriting—No doubt you will find

[1] Vienna surrendered to the French on May 12th and a general armistice was signed two months later.
[2] Opus 86.
[3] Opus 69, which had been published by Breitkopf & Härtel in April, 1809.

several mistakes in the copy which you possess. For when he *looks over his own work* the composer really *does overlook* the mistakes[1]—You will soon receive the song 'Ich denke dein'.[2] It was to have been included in *Prometheus which came to grief*[3] and which, if you had not reminded me, I should have entirely forgotten—Accept it as a small present—Only now am I thanking you for the really beautifully translated tragedies of Euripides[4]; among the poems intended for me I have marked a few from "Kallirhoe" which I propose to set to notes or tones—But I should like to know the name *of the author or the translator of this tragedy*[5]—At Traeg's office I took away *the Messiah*, using a privilege which you had already granted me here in a somewhat pressing manner (namely, when you were in Vienna[6]); and for that very reason, I must confess, I have extended the privilege still further. I had begun to have a little singing party at my rooms every week—but that accursed war put a stop to everything—With this in view and in any case for many other reasons I should be delighted if you would send me by degrees most of the scores which you possess, such as, for instance, Mozart's Requiem and so forth, Haydn's Masses, in short, all the scores you have, I mean, those of Haydn, Mozart, Johann Sebastian Bach, Emanuel Bach and so forth—I have only a few samples of Emanuel Bach's compositions for the clavier; and yet some of them should certainly be in the possession of every true artist, not only for the sake of real enjoyment but also for the purpose of study. And my greatest pleasure is to play at the homes of some true friends of music works which I have *never* or seldom seen—You may rest assured that I shall arrange for you to be compensated in a way that will satisfy you—I hear that *the first trio is now in Vienna.*[7] I have not received a copy, so I am asking you to send me one. I should be glad too if you would send me for correction the proofs of the other works which are to be published. In future you will receive all the scores in my own handwriting, unless I send you the written out parts which have

[1] Beethoven is punning on the verb "übersehen" which can mean "look over" or "check," and "overlook."

[2] This song, WoO 136, a setting by Beethoven of a poem "Ich denke dein" by Matthisson, was published with the title "Andenken" by Breitkopf & Härtel in March, 1810.

[3] *Prometheus* was a periodical founded in 1808 by Leo von Seckendorf and the poet J. L. Stoll. It ran for only one year. Beethoven's four songs "Sehnsucht," WoO 134, were published in its third number.

[4] No doubt Friedrich Heinrich Bothe's translation of Euripides, published in Berlin, 1800–3.

[5] A tragedy by Johann August Apel (1771–1816), a well-known writer living at Leipzig. It had been published in 1807. The libretto of Weber's opera "Der Freischütz," produced in Berlin in 1821, was based on a story in the *Gespensterbuch*, of which Apel was part-author.

[6] Härtel had visited Vienna in September, 1808.

[7] The first trio of Opus 70 had appeared in June, 1809. The second trio was published in August.

been used by performers—If I change my address, I will let you know
immediately—But, if you write at once, your reply will certainly find
me still in Vienna—Perhaps Heaven may grant that after all I shall not
have to abandon the idea of regarding Vienna as my permanent home—
All good wishes. Indeed I wish you all that is good and beautiful, that
is to say, as much as our tempestuous age permits. Do remember your
most devoted servant and friend

BEETHOVEN

To Breitkopf & Härtel, Leipzig

[*Autograph in the Beethovenhaus, Bonn, H. C. Bodmer collection*]

VIENNA, August 8, 1809

I have left with Herr Kunz & Co. a sextet for two clarinets, two
bassoons and two horns,[1] and two German Lieder or songs,[2] with the
request that they be forwarded to you as soon as possible—You must
regard them as gifts in return for all the works *which I have requested you
to send me as presents*—moreover I have forgotten the *Musik-Zeitung*
and therefore wish to remind you of it in a friendly way—Perhaps you
could arrange for me to receive editions of Goethe's and Schiller's
complete works—*Such works flow into your literary coffers as a matter
of course;* and then in return for several works of that kind I will send
you *something which will flow out into the whole world*—These two
poets are my favorites, as are also Ossian and Homer, though unfortunately I can read the latter only *in translations*—Since all you have to do
is to hand out these two poets—Goethe and Schiller[3]—from your literary
treasury, you will afford me the greatest pleasure—NB. If you will let
me have them soon[4]—the more so as I am hoping to spend the rest
of the summer at some pleasant country spot[5]—

The sextet is one of my early works and, what is more, was composed in one night[6]—All that one can really say about it is that it was
written by a composer who has produced at any rate a few better works—
Yet some people think that works of that type are the best—

---

[1] Opus 71.
[2] WoO 136 and 137.
[3] In the autograph these three words are added at the foot of the page.
[4] In the autograph this short NB. is added at the foot of the page.
[5] It is doubtful whether during that disturbed year Beethoven did go into the country
for an appreciable time.
[6] Opus 71 was composed in 1796 or possibly earlier, but was not performed until
April, 1805. See Kinsky-Halm, p. 169.

Accept my good wishes and let me hear from you very soon. Your most devoted

BEETHOVEN

I should like to have a few more copies of the violoncello sonata[1]; and, in general, please send me always half a dozen copies—I never sell any—but here and there I come across poor musici, to whom I cannot refuse copies of my works.

To the Archduke Rudolph, Vienna[2]

[Autograph in the Gesellschaft der Musikfreunde, Vienna]

[BADEN, August, 1810][3]

I see that Your Imperial Highness wants to have the effects of my music tried on horses as well. All right. But I must see whether the riders will thereby be enabled to make a few skillful somersaults—Well, well, I cannot help laughing at the idea of Your Imperial Highness's thinking of me on this occasion as well. And for that favor I shall remain as long as I live your most willing servant

LUDWIG VAN BEETHOVEN

NB. The music for horses which you have asked for will be brought to Your Imperial Highness at the fastest gallop.[4]

---

[1] Opus 69.

[2] The Archduke Rudolph (1788–1831) was the youngest son of the late Emperor Leopold II and a half-brother of the reigning Emperor Francis I. Born at Florence he was brought to Vienna in 1790 and since 1803 had his own court personnel which in 1814 consisted of the two Counts von Troyer, Baron von Schweiger and Baumeister, who was first his tutor and later his librarian. So far as is known the Archduke began to take lessons from Beethoven in 1803 or 1804 and soon formed a close friendship with his teacher. At times Beethoven felt irked by his constant attendance on the Archduke, but there is no doubt that he cherished a real affection for him. Moreover his pupil was certainly gifted, not only as a pianist but also as a composer. He was rather delicate and liable to attacks of epilepsy.

[3] In all the *Gesamtausgaben*, beginning with Nohl II, no. 107 (Nohl follows Köchel's edition of 83 letters to the Archduke Rudolph, Vienna, 1865), this letter is dated November, 1814, and no composition is suggested. But the autograph and copies of WoO 18, which are discussed in Kinsky-Halm, pp. 456–58, clearly point to the Horse Show held at Laxenburg, the Imperial summer residence, on August 24, 1810, in honor of the Archduke's mother, Maria Ludovica.

[4] Probably not only the march WoO 18 but also WoO 19 and others in the same numerical series.

To Breitkopf & Härtel, Leipzig

[*Autograph in the Library of Congress*]

MOST HONORED SIR!   VIENNA, *January* 16, 1811

Scream at—curse—that B(eethoven) who hasn't written to you—
For God's sake publish the Mass just as you have it, without waiting
for the organ part.[1] It would be better for the work to appear as it is
than to be kept back any longer for what is after all an immaterial
reason—But I hope that it will be published in score—The translation
of the Gloria I consider very suitable, but that of the Kyrie not so good.
Although the beginning "tief im Staub anbeten wir" is very appropriate,
yet several expressions, such as "ew'gen Weltenherrscher" and "Allgewal-
tigen" seem to fit the Gloria better. The general character of the
Kyrie (I consider that in a translation of this kind only the general
character of each movement should be indicated) is heartfelt resignation,
deep sincerity of religious feeling, "Gott erbarme dich unser," yet without
on that account being sad. Gentleness is the fundamental characteristic
of the whole work. And here the expressions "Allgewaltiger" and so forth
do not seem to convey the meaning of the whole work. Apart from "Eleison erbarme dich unser"—cheerfulness pervades this Mass. The Catholic
goes to church on Sunday in his best clothes and in a joyful and
festive mood. Besides the Kyrie Eleison is the introduction to the whole
work. If such strong expressions were used here, few would be left for
those portions where really strong expressions are required.—The three
missing songs[2]—are on the way—I cannot promise to compose and add
another song to the five Italian ones. In any case four ariettas and a duet
ought to be acceptable[3]—but I don't absolutely reject your request—As
soon as I have received everything I will send you the certificate of
ownership. But indeed I hope that you do not distrust me. Or has that
scoundrel of a captain[4] been able to achieve this? In a few days Herr
Kühnel[5] will receive from me a letter which he has been told to show
you as well—in regard to this matter—Well, Herr Riotte,[6] who came

---

[1] The Mass in C, Opus 86.
[2] Opus 83.
[3] Opus 82.
[4] Christian Ludwig Reissig.
[5] Ambros Kühnel, who was F. A. Hoffmeister's partner in charge of the Bureau
de Musique at Leipzig.
[6] Philipp Jakob Riotte (1776–1856), born at Trier, settled in Vienna in 1809. He
became a successful conductor and composer and wrote an immense number of works
for the theater. In 1818 he was appointed conductor at the Theater an der Wien.

to see me the other day, informed me that you had asked him for his opinion of my latest works and, incidentally, whether you ought to take them—Well now, I must ask you whether you really instructed him to do this? In the works there are still several mistakes which are certainly not to be found at all in the manuscript. So be more careful in this respect. Furthermore, I am still convinced that the best arrangement would be for you to send me the first copies, which I promise you to have sung and played through at once. Then I will return to you immediately those passages where there are mistakes. After receiving the corrections you can let me have the other c[opies] at once—I am not well and indeed have not been well for some time, or I should have enclosed in this letter a small list of the mistakes—I will write soon about the idea you put forward for a new work and also about what I am composing—I send you all good wishes for your welfare on German soil!!!!!!!
Kyrie Eleison, wholly your

BEETHOVEN

NB. Thanks for the Musik[alische] Zeitung; and I should like you to continue to send it. About this too I will arrange with you, in due course.—EMILY ANDERSON

The Music

Orchestra

I. BEETHOVEN'S ORCHESTRATION

Before treating of [his] individual style and [his] contribution to the growth of orchestration, an attempt will be made to summarize the gains which accrued to the art of writing for the orchestra from the work of [Beethoven] during the period which extends from a few years before to a few years after, the first quarter of the nineteenth century.

The close of the eighteenth century saw the last of what may be called threadbare or skeleton orchestration. Even the poorest orchestrator in the early nineteenth century provided sufficient harmonic body in the "inside" of his musical structure to ensure sonority and solidarity of effect. The habitual duplication or doubling of parts, which left its traces in the scores of Italian opera composers until even late in the eighteenth century, practically disappeared during the maturity of Haydn and Mozart. Such doubling of parts as appears in nineteenth-century scores is provided more in order to adjust the balance of tone, and to secure the adequate prominence of certain parts, than as the result of habit or indifference.

A very important feature in the growth of orchestration at [the close of the eighteenth century] was due to the increased use of the violoncello as an independent voice. From being at first only a bass instrument, the violoncello had become an occasional tenor instrument toward the close of the eighteenth century, and now early in the nineteenth century it took a new place in the orchestra as a full-blown melodist which, in addition to its former functions, was ready and able to take over the responsibility of presenting entirely melodic matter, either with or without the aid of other instruments. The melody for violas and violoncellos in unison which begins the slow movement of Beethvoen's C minor symphony [is just one] very well-known instance of what became a familiar way of using violoncellos during the first twenty or thirty years of the nine-teenth century, and was a feature of orchestration unknown to eighteenth-century composers.

The upward compass of violin parts began to reach high enough to require the seventh or eighth position for first violins, and the fifth position for second violins.[1] Viola parts were usually kept within the limits of the first position, and only occasionally strayed beyond the upper E which lies within reach of the fourth finger on the A string, while the melodic use of violoncellos, and a tendency to let them sometimes join in the passage-work of the upper strings, freely took the parts for these instruments up to as high as an octave above the sound of their highest string. The brilliancy of higher pitch on violins, and the richness of violon-cello tone on the A string, must be reckoned gains in the treatment of the instruments of the string orchestra which accrued during the period of Beethoven and his contemporaries. The above observations regarding the upward range of the string parts, of course, take no account of special solo parts, which were always more of the *virtuoso* type, and in con-sequence frequently exceeded the usual range of *ripieno* orchestral parts.

Although the richer and more penetrating quality of violoncello-tone on the A string was used to give special prominence to melodic tenor parts, the viola continued to fulfill its function as the normal tenor instrument when the music was merely harmonic or polyphonic in design. Apart from the imitative phrases which occur in the course of ordinary four-part polyphony for string instruments, the violas as a group, and without reinforcement, were as yet hardly recognized as melodists, nor is

[1] The treatment of the second violins as inferior to the first violins both in technical ability and in numbers *was strictly a product of the early nineteenth century.* Thus some passages in Gluck, Haydn, and even Beethoven, where the second violins play melod-ically above the firsts, took on an entirely different balance when they were written from that of today's orchestras.—Editor.

there reason to suppose that the peculiarly attractive and individual *timbre* of viola-tone was really appreciated at this period, in spite of Gluck's suggestive lead, and of Weber's readiness to exploit the dramatic possibilities of this neglected instrument. Both Berlioz[1] and Wagner[2] have testified to the inferior skill and status of orchestral viola players even at a later date, and it is not difficult to see how the prevailing conditions are reflected in the viola parts written earlier in the century. Viola parts, however, tended to lean more and more toward the active and florid nature of violin parts, and to take their patterns from the figures and passages of the upper string voices rather than from the bass parts on which their matter was formerly so largely modeled.

Harmony notes in detached or repeated chords multiplied over and over again by means of double-stopping,[3] the further exploitation of *pizzicato* effects, and the muting of the string instruments, are features which occur constantly in early nineteenth century orchestration, but were not in any case innovations. A general advance in the standard of technique demanded of string players, however, may be added to the list of elements which must certainly be counted as progressive in the string work of the period.

The recent acquisition of clarinets was responsible for some of the most significant developments in the handling of the wood-wind section of the orchestra during the first two or three decades of the nineteenth century. As a solo instrument the clarinet began to assert itself only very gradually in spite of Mozart's example, and not till nearly the end of the first quarter of the century did it stand on an equality with the other wood-wind instruments in this particular capacity. The readiness with which clarinet-tone blends with the tone of bassoons, horns, and with string-tone, had an even more far-reaching influence on orchestration as a whole than the gain of a new solo voice. The smooth-toned combinations of clarinets and bassoons, or clarinets, bassoons and horns, began to replace the wood-wind combinations in which the more incisive-toned oboe had previously always had a place when, early in the nineteenth century, the newcomers had at last secured an assured place in all orchestras. A distinct preference for the warmer and round-toned blends, in which clarinet-tone largely replaced the hitherto predominant oboe-tone, is a feature of orchestration which became very marked during the maturity of Beethoven, and marks the end of the long reign of the oboe as chief and leader of the wood-wind group. Other blends which ex-

---

[1] "Viola players were always taken from among the refuse of violinists." Berlioz, *Instrumentation*, p. 25.

[2] "The viola is commonly played by infirm violinists," etc. Wagner, *Uber das Dirigiren*, English translation, p. 4 (Reeves, London).

[3] The term "double-stopping" is generally understood to embrace either two, three or four-note chords on string instruments.

cluded oboes, and became more common during the same period, were horns and bassoons, and flutes and clarinets.

The occasional use of stopped notes gave early nineteenth century horn parts some more melodic and harmonic flexibility than was possible when only open notes were used. Though retaining the same general style as the Mozartian horn parts, there are more frequent attempts to give the instrument such thematic matter as could be squeezed out of the open and a few stopped notes. The latter also began to be used to supply the minor third of the key in which the horn was crooked, and with the half-stopped leading-note, helped to give a little more fullness to the brass harmony, especially when no trombones were employed. The same object was achieved to a rather more limited extent by making use of four horns crooked in two or more different keys.

Trumpet parts remained much as they were at the end of the eighteenth century, but began to be used, as far as the very limited selection of open notes would allow, for the upper parts in association with the trombone trio. The latter were treated almost entirely as harmonists, except occasionally when suitable matter in the bass part offered opportunity for some thematic interest. The use of trombones at selected moments simply in order to give more volume to particular chords, or to build up and emphasize a climax, shows some advance on the older style which kept these instruments playing more continuously in the movements in which they took part. As a body the brass group still suffered greatly from the want of more flexible upper voices than could be supplied by either natural horns or trumpets; thus, the effect of unmixed brass-tone was one which was largely denied to early nineteenth century composers.

Timpani parts gained in interest and importance by being more freely used for solo passages in soft rhythmical patterns, by the increasing use of soft and *crescendo* rolls, and enjoyed some further expansion of their usefulness by being occasionally tuned at intervals other than the tonic and dominant of the key, also by the use of two drum notes played simultaneously. The early nineteenth century composers seemed to have no idea of using the remaining percussion instruments except to let them hammer away consistently on the accented beats of the bar in loud, and more rarely, in soft *tutti*.

It was the early nineteenth century composers who first began to understand how to build up an extended *crescendo* by adding part after part till all the instruments of the orchestra were engaged. The sense of growing power in these cumulative *crescendi* was a sensation in orchestration hardly understood by Haydn and Mozart, or even by the Mannheimers whose *crescendo* was the admiration of eighteenth century critics. The more careful gradation of tone between *ppp* and *fff* is a noticeable feature in the scores of the period, also more exact indications of phrasing and directions concerning *tempo*, rendering, and effect. More or less novel features were the frequent occurrence of soft *tutti* and a greater sensitiveness for balance of tone shown by the varying marks of expression and dynamics supplied in the parts. The management of loud *tutti* varied very much according to the texture and content of each individual [work]. Balance of tone in the loud *tutti* is often defective when measured by present-day performing standards, and can only partially be accounted for by the fact that rather smaller string orchestras were general at the time, and possibly the prevalence of a less strident manner of tone-production on brass instruments.

The above generalizations, covering the entire first quarter of the nineteenth century, must be modified to some extent when turning to review the work of [Beethoven].

Beethoven's first symphony shows him handling the orchestra with complete confidence, and alive to the resources of orchestration as far as they were developed by the end of the eighteenth century. The handling of the wood-wind shows clearly that the clarinet was hardly yet reckoned the equal of either the flute, oboe, or the bassoon. Beethoven's clarinets at that time were harmony or *tutti* instruments only; all the solo work goes to one or other of the remaining wood-wind. Only the clarinet is excluded from taking a share in the little answering melodic phrases of the second and subsidiary subjects, and oboes take much of the harmonic work which in his later orchestration falls to clarinets. Already in the second symphony (1802) the clarinets are united with bassoons in stating important and essential matter, and in the *Eroica* (No. 3, 1804), a solo clarinet is allowed to take a share in the melodic phrases and essential harmonies of some of the principal themes. After that time clarinets get more extended solo parts, and in smoother-toned blends with bassoons and horns to some extent exclude the hitherto ubiquitous oboe.

Beethoven's earliest horn parts are practically Mozartian in style and scope. The first symphony contains no stopped notes, No. 2 has a solitary B-natural, but several more occur in the *Eroica* and succeeding symphonies, most of them being the half-stopped E-flat and F-sharp. The melodic development of his horn parts is well illustrated by the progress from the style of the earliest symphonies to that of the elaborate parts for three horns in *Fidelio*[1] (1805, rewritten in 1814) and the solo part for fourth horn in the slow movement of the Choral Symphony. The horn parts in the latter work involve a free use of the half-stopped minor third of the key for harmonic purposes in the *tutti*.

Beethoven's trumpet parts show no very marked or progressive characteristics, nor did he advance much on the path of progress in handling trombones. A few dramatic touches in *Fidelio* show more enlightenment

[1] Leonore's Aria, No. 9, Act I.

in using these instruments than the parts in the symphonies. The possibilities of the brass group as a body are very little exploited in Beethoven's orchestration, but to the timpani he gave a prominence and a thematic importance which they had never previously enjoyed.

The earliest symphonies contain much of the three-part writing for the string orchestra, which, as in Haydn's work, gave the viola part a constant tendency to run in octaves with the bass part. Before long, however, the viola seems to transfer its allegiance, and becomes, so to speak, *a large violin rather than a small violoncello.*[1] The emancipation of the violoncello begins in earnest with the *Eroica* symphony. For that work the part soars far beyond the confines of the bass part, and in the fourth, fifth, and later symphonies joins now the first violins, now the violas, in octaves or in unison, in enriching what the uninitiated would call the "tune" of the music.

When for wind instruments alone, Beethoven's orchestration is mostly for wood-wind and horns in combination, or for any of the wood-wind pairs combined with one another, or with the horns. To the second bassoon alone usually falls the duty of sustaining the sole bass part in such combinations, a function which it is often hardly strong enough to undertake quite satisfactorily when horns and all the remaining wood-wind are placed above it.

The accompanying of solo wind parts is generally carried out by strings, without the interference of other wind parts which would clog the clear utterance or distinct coloring of the solo part. Wood-wind, horns and strings are not only often combined, but are also contrasted and opposed to one another in groups antiphonally, answering, echoing, and taking over melodic and harmonic matter, one from the other, sometimes at regular intervals, but at other times quite unexpectedly.

Beethoven's orchestral *tutti* grew from those of the simple Mozartian construction in the early symphonies, to the complex texture of the mighty *tutti* in the first movement of the Choral Symphony. It is in the soft *tutti* of that wonderful movement that Beethoven touched a type of orchestration well ahead of his time, and achieved effects more impressive than any which are brought about by mere noisy brilliance.

The sudden and unexpected *fortes* and *pianos* are characteristic of Beethoven's scores, also the sudden silences, the humorous touches and freakish turns given to the music and orchestration by the master when in his "unbuttoned" mood. Some cases of bad balance occur in several of his symphonies, and are all the result of strings, or strings and brass, overpowering essential matter played by the wood-wind in loud passages. These may possibly be accounted for by the smaller number of string players which were undoubtedly provided in the Vienna orchestras of

[1] Italics by the editor.

his time. Modern conductors usually take upon themselves to "touch up" the orchestration in these places, and by a little readjustment of the parts and the dynamic marks, succeed in letting the hearers hear what the composer undoubtedly meant them to hear.

The above are the hard facts, the tangible features of Beethoven's orchestration which lend themselves to verbal analysis. Others there are, in which orchestration can hardly be separated from musical matter, where nothing ostensibly novel appears on the printed page, yet where the ear finds a something that leaves its trace on the memory, an imprint of instrumental color, simple enough yet indelible, something which is of Beethoven and of no other composer. The thirty or so bars immediately preceding the recapitulation of the first subject in the first movement of the *Eroica*, the alternating wind and string chords just before the recapitulation in the first movement of the fifth symphony, the long passage leading up to the beginning of the *finale*, and the approach to the final *presto* in the same ever-green work; passages such as these, and others there are sprinkled about the scores of Beethoven which linger in the memory of every concert-goer; passages which cannot be considered to be the result of calculation or of skill in the management of orchestral effect; these make the orchestra speak in terms quite unknown to the predecessors or even to the contemporaries of the great master. To some modern ears the scream of undesirably prominent trumpet notes, or the wobble of a horn over an awkward passage in his orchestration, may be distressing. They are but the marks of the time in which Beethoven lived, and have survived with his works the passage of about a hundred years. So let them remain for another hundred.—
ADAM CARSE

II. SYMPHONIES
     a. Symphony No. 3 in E Flat, Opus 55 ("Eroica")
         I. Allegro con brio; II. Marcia funebre, Adagio assai;
         III. Scherzo: Allegro vivace, Trio; IV. Finale: Allegro molto

Those who have listened to the "Eroica" Symphony have been reminded, perhaps too often, that the composer once destroyed in anger a dedication to Napoleon Bonaparte. The music, as one returns to it in the course of succeeding years, seems to look beyond Napoleon, as if it really never had anything to do with the man who once fell short of receiving a dedication. Sir George Grove once wrote: "Though the Eroica was a portrait of Bonaparte, it is as much a portrait of Beethoven himself—but that is the case with everything he wrote." Sir George's second remark was prophetic of the present point of view.

The concept of heroism which plainly shaped this symphony, and which sounds through so much of Beethoven's music, would give no place to a self-styled "Emperor" who was ambitious to bring all Europe into vassalage, and ready to crush out countless lives in order to satisfy his ambition. If the "Eroica" had ever come to Napoleon's attention, which it probably did not, its inward nature would have been quite above his comprehension—not to speak, of course, of musical comprehension. Its suggestion is of selfless heroes, those who give their lives to overthrow tyrants and liberate oppressed peoples. Egmont was such a hero, and so was Leonore. The motive that gave musical birth to these two characters also animated most of Beethoven's music, varying in intensity, but never in kind. It grew from the thoughts and ideals that had nurtured the French Revolution.

Beethoven was never more completely, more eruptively revolutionary than in his "Eroica" Symphony. Its first movement came from all that was defiant in his nature. He now tasted to the full the intoxication of artistic freedom. This hunger for freedom was one of his deepest impulses, and it was piqued by his sense of servitude to titles. Just or not, the resentment was real to him, and it increased his kinship with the commoner, and his ardent republicanism. The "Eroica," of course, is no political document, except in the degree that it was the deep and inclusive expression of the composer's point of view at the time. And there was much on his heart. This was the first outspoken declaration of independence by an artist who had outgrown the mincing restrictions of a salon culture in the century just ended. But, more than that, it was a reassertion of will power. The artist, first confronted with the downright threat of total deafness, answered by an unprecedented outpouring of his creative faculties. There, especially, lie the struggle, the domination, the suffering, and the triumph of the "Eroica" Symphony. The heroism that possesses the first movement is intrepidity where faith and strength become one, a strength which exalts and purifies. The funeral march, filled with hushed mystery, has no odor of mortality; death had no place in Beethoven's thoughts as artist. The spirit which gathers and rises in the middle portion sweeps inaction aside and becomes a life assertion. The shouting triumph of the variation finale has no trap of heavy, crushing feet; it is jubilant exhortation to all mankind, a foreshadowing of the finales of the Fifth and Ninth Symphonies. It is entirely incongruous as applied to the vain and preening Corsican and his bloody exploits. Beethoven may once have had some misty idea of a noble liberator; he was to have an increasingly bitter experience of the misery which spread in Napoleon's wake.

The Third Symphony is set down by Paul Henry Lang in his *Music in Western Civilization*, as "one of the incomprehensible deeds in arts and letters, the greatest single step made by an individual composer in the history of the symphony and the history of music in general." The statement is well considered; it looms in a summation which is broad, scholarly, and musically penetrating.

As his notebooks show, he forged his heroic score with a steady onslaught, expanding the inherited form almost beyond recognition, yet preserving its balance and symmetry. The plans for each movement but the scherzo were laid in the first fever of creation. But Beethoven seems to have been in no great hurry to complete his task. The workmanship in detail is largely attributed to his summer sojourns of 1803 at Baden and at Ober-Döbling. Ries remembered seeing the fair copy in its finished state upon the composer's table in the early spring of 1804.

Musicians have never ceased to wonder at the welded and significant organism of the exposition in the first movement, the outpouring invention and wealth of episodes in the working out, the magnificence and freshness of the coda. The unity of purpose, the clarity amid profusion, which the symphony's early critics failed to perceive, extends no less to the funeral march, the scherzo, the variation finale—forms then all quite apart from symphonic practice. One whose creative forces ran in this wise could well ignore precedent, and extend his score to the unheard-of length of three quarters of an hour.[1]—JOHN N. BURK (2)

It is usual to find that the Eroica symphony marks a definite turning-point in Beethoven's music. We believe this point of view to be entirely justified. Beethoven's music, up to the time that he wrote the Heiligenstadt Testament, is chiefly a music that expresses *qualities*. This is probably what many people mean by "pure" music. Such qualities can only be given the roughest of portmanteau names. We can speak of wit, humor, force, dramatic invention, and so on, but such words are but very pitiful attempts to describe the qualities concerned. Both Voltaire and Tom Hood were witty writers, but the quality of the wit is very different in the two cases. Music of this kind is the very opposite of program music. It need make very little, if any, reference to experience. Elegance, neatness, economy are the sort of terms that can be applied to the productions of an infant prodigy. Music of this kind reveals, as it were, the actual nature of the composer. It reveals the qualities with which he will face life, the qualities that will condition his experience and his presentation of it. In most of Beethoven's early music his

---

[1] Beethoven is said to have retorted to those who vigorously protested the length of the Eroica: "If I write a symphony an hour long, it will be found short enough!" And so he did, with his Ninth. He must have realized, however, the incapacity of contemporary audiences, when he affixed to the published parts (and later to the score) of the "Eroica": "Since this symphony is longer than an ordinary symphony, it should be performed at the beginning rather than at the end of a concert, either after an overture or an aria, or after a concerto. If it be performed too late, there is the danger that it will not produce on the audience, whose attention will be already wearied by preceding pieces, the effect which the composer purposed in his own mind to attain."

experiences of life enter, not as a mastered and synthetic whole, but as moods. He may be somber, melancholy, gay, or anything else, but these alternations in a composition have no organic connection. We are not, when listening to an early Beethoven quartet, for instance, becoming acquainted with the elements of one unified spiritual experience. Movements could be interchanged or very different ones substituted, without harming the composition. The only criteria that would have to be observed are those of aesthetic variety and unity, that a quick movement should follow the slow movement and so on and, perhaps, that certain key relationships should be preserved. In this his early music resembles the vast bulk of the music written by Haydn and Mozart. There are also, of course, technical resemblances, although too much stress can be laid on them. When we say that music expresses qualities we are not, of course, describing the content of the music any more than, in describing *Candide* as witty, we are describing the content of *Candide*. But the music we are speaking of does not possess what we have called a "spiritual content," although it expresses spiritual qualities. We may liken it to a mathematical memoir which exhibits elegance, inventive power, imagination, and even wit, but which has no "external" reference whatever. Particularly unambiguous examples of this purely qualitative music are to be found in some of Beethoven's early scherzos. Besides music of this kind there is to be found some "composed" music in Beethoven's early work. He said himself, for instance, of the Adagio affetuoso ed appassionato of the early F major quartet, that he had in mind the tomb scene in *Romeo and Juliet*. The creative process involved here is not the same as that of a dramatist who records his reactions to an imagined situation that he has himself invented. It is, on the contrary, the same process as is involved in writing opera music, and is subject to the same danger, the danger of losing the note of authenticity that belongs to the expression of a personal experience. The more usual the experience to be depicted, the more likely to be shared by all men, the more likely, of course, that it can secure an adequate musical representation. Most operas deal with stock emotions and experiences, for that is the ground on which the poet and the composer can be most assured of understanding one another. The parting of lovers is certainly a stock situation, and the young Beethoven could treat it adequately. Such stock situations were present, we may suspect, on more than one occasion in his early work. It is not until we come to the Eroica symphony that we find expressed an experience individual, profoundly realized, and in the main line of Beethoven's spiritual development. The early music expresses individual qualities, individual moods, and the young composer's conceptions of a few stock poetic situations. Incomparably the most important part of this music, for our purpose, is the music expressing qualities, for it cannot be denied that Beethoven's "poetic" conceptions are sometimes unconvincing. The onetime "favorite" Largo of the D major sonata Opus 10, for example, is something less than perfectly direct and sincere. It is "made" music, "composed" music, and is altogether inferior to the purely qualitative first movement. What is meant by calling an emotion romantic or sentimental is excessively difficult to define, but unquestionably there is implied the statement that such an emotion is feigned or unearned. An experience is being pretended to that has not, in fact, been experienced. We object to the sorrows of Werther that they are not genuine sorrows. But the sorrows of Werther may be taken seriously either through inexperience or shallowness. The "religious" music of Wagner's last years can only be ascribed to a shallow religious nature, but the overportentous expression of "melancholy" in the young Beethoven is due to the fact that he was young enough to take his comparatively superficial emotion seriously. That it is not due to an incapacity for profounder experience is shown, of course, by what he went on to write.

The first piece of music he composed that has a really profound and important spiritual content is the Eroica symphony. Indeed, the difference from the earlier music is so startling that it points to an almost catastrophic change, or extremely rapid acceleration, in his spiritual development. We have found that such a change is witnessed to by the Heiligenstadt Testament, and we shall see that the Eroica symphony is an amazingly realized and co-ordinated expression of the spiritual experiences that underlay that document. The ostensible occasion of the symphony appears to have been the career of Napoleon Bonaparte, but no amount of brooding over Napoleon's career could have given Beethoven his realization of what we may call the life-history of heroic achievement as exemplified in the Eroica. This is obviously a transcription of personal experience. He may have thought Napoleon a hero, but his conception of the heroic he had earned for himself. It has been objected to the symphony that the Funeral March is in the wrong place and that it should follow the Scherzo. But this objection entirely misses the organic connection of the whole work. The most profound experience that Beethoven had yet passed through was when his courage and defiance of his fate had been followed by despair. He was expressing what he knew when he made the courage and heroism of the first movement succeeded by the black night of the second. And he was again speaking of what he knew when he made this to be succeeded by the indomitable uprising of creative energy in the Scherzo. Beethoven was here speaking of what was perhaps the cardinal experience of his life, that when, with all his strength and courage, he had been reduced to despair, that when the conscious strong man had tasted very death, there came this turbulent, irrepressible, deathless creative energy surging up from depths he had not suspected. The whole work is a miraculously realized expression of a supremely important experience, and is justly regarded as a turning-point in Beethoven's music. The last movement is based on what we know to have been Beethoven's "Prometheus" theme. Having survived death and despair the artist turns to creation. By adopting the variation form Beethoven has been able to indicate the variety of achievement that is now open to his "Promethean" energy. The whole work is a most close-knit psychologic unit. Never before in music has so important, manifold, and completely coherent an experience been communicated.

Although the Eroica symphony is based on a profound personal experience Beethoven was not yet able to express a subjective state in music in a perfectly direct manner. Indeed, it was only toward the end of his life, and principally in the late quartets, that his music became the perfectly direct expression of his inner state. The dramatist may use characters and incidents as symbols, as *carriers* of the state of consciousness he wishes to communicate—as Shakespeare obviously does in *Macbeth*—but the musician, although not so bound to the external world, may also achieve a certain degree of "objectification." There are certain musical forms which are recognized vehicles for certain restricted classes of emotions. Of these forms the funeral march is one. In the Funeral March of the Eroica Beethoven expressed a personal experience, but only to the extent that the form could accommodate it. By using the form he did, to some extent, depersonalize his experience. In this expression it becomes vaguer and also broader, being linked up with the general human experience of death and with the general human foreboding of the darkness beyond. The root content of the movement is Beethoven's personal experience of despair, transformed, by the form adopted, into a representation of a vaguer and more general human experience. Thus it might be supposed to represent the death of Napoleon or Abercrombie or Nelson or of anybody else whose characteristics could be supposed to support comparison with those depicted in the first movement. It is for this reason that the Funeral March, magnificent as it is, seems a little too prominent among the other movements of the symphony. There is a little too much *display* about it, it is a little too suggestive of some great public occasion. The whole symphony is certainly on extremely bold lines, but the other movements are relatively personal and authentic in a way that the Funeral March is not. It is probable that only the Beethoven of the last quartets could have invented a form that should have embodied his experience directly and yet on a sufficiently large scale. To the young Beethoven, who had not yet attained the profound and utter loyalty to his own experience that characterized the music of his later years, there was also the attraction of "great subjects," the triumphant satisfaction of surpassing all other musicians in the treatment of recognized "lofty" themes. The fact, also, that sketches for the Funeral March go back to a period preceding the Heiligenstadt Testament shows that the form chosen was not dictated wholly by the experience that actually inspires it. We need not imagine that the organic unity of the Eroica symphony, or of any other of his greater compositions, was due to considerations that were consciously present in the mind of Beethoven. In an organic work of art the succession of its constituents is not ordered in accordance with any consciously held criterion. The feeling that a certain sequence is "right" is nearly always due to causes the artist could not analyze. In suggesting that the Eroica symphony, in its content and sequence, is the musical expression of the experiences that underlay the Heiligenstadt Testament, we are not suggesting that Beethoven consciously intended this representation. The initial idea of a "Heroic" symphony may indeed have been suggested by the career of Napoleon or Abercrombie or anybody else, but in the process of creation Beethoven had to fall back upon his inner resources, the product of his qualities and his experiences. And the criterion of rightness he employed in the development of his composition was supplied by the order his experience had taken on in the depths of his mind. As a consequence of his own experience the concept of heroism was related, in his mind, within a certain context, largely unconscious, and the conception could only be realized within this context. This explains why the symphony, which makes so great an impression of organic unity, nevertheless defies all attempts to interpret it as representing any particular hero's career. This difficulty has led a recent writer to suppose that the three great movements represent three entirely different heroes, and that the Scherzo is a sort of intermezzo put where it is, either because Beethoven was timid of further outraging popular taste or because he did not fully perceive the connection of the elements of his own work. Such unconvincing shifts are made necessary merely through attaching too great importance to whatever external occasions may be conjectured to have prompted the work. For works of art of the magnitude that we are considering the external occasion is never more than what psychologists call a "tripper" incident, releasing energies and contexts that have been formed in entire independence of it.

Beethoven preferred the Eroica symphony to the symphony in C minor, a judgment that it would be difficult to substantiate on purely musical grounds. The "programs" of the two symphonies are not unrelated, but the Eroica, in spite of the Funeral March, is a more intimate expression of the composer's experience. In Beethoven's outlook on life which, as we have already said, was not philosophic or rational, certain aspects of life had immense importance and became, as it were, personified. Heroism, for him, was not merely a name descriptive of a quality of certain acts, but a sort of principle manifesting itself in life.—J. W. N. SULLIVAN

The designation "heroic" is to be taken in its widest sense, and in nowise to be conceived as relating merely to a military hero. If we broadly connote by "hero" ("*Held*") the whole, the full-fledged *man*, in whom are present all the purely human feelings—of love, of grief, of force—in their highest fill and strength, then we shall rightly grasp the subject which the artist lets appeal to us in the speaking accents of his tone-work. The artistic space of this work is filled with all the varied, intercrossing feelings of a strong, a consummate Individuality, to which nothing human is a stranger, but which includes within itself all truly Human, and utters it in such a fashion that—after frankly manifesting every noble passion—it reaches a final rounding of its nature, wherein the most feeling softness is wedded with the most energetic force. The heroic tendence of this artwork is the progress toward that rounding off.

The *First Movement* embraces, as in a glowing furnace, all the emotions of a richly-gifted nature in the heyday of unresting youth. Weal and woe, lief and lack, sweetness and sadness, living and longing, riot and revel, daring, defiance, and an ungovernable sense of Self,[1] make place for one another so directly, and interlace so closely that, however much we mate each feeling with our own, we can single none of them from out the rest, but our whole interest is given merely to this one, this human being who shows himself brimful of every feeling. Yet all these feelings spring from one main faculty—and that is *Force*. This Force, immeasurably enhanced by each emotional impression and driven to vent its overfill, is the mainspring of the tone-piece: it clinches—toward the middle of the Movement—to the violence of the destroyer, and in its braggart strength we think we see a Wrecker of the World before us, a Titan wrestling with the Gods.

This shattering Force, that filled us half with ecstasy and half with horror, was rushing toward a tragic crisis, whose serious import is set before our Feeling in the *Second Movement*. The tone-poet clothes its proclamation in the musical apparel of a Funeral-march. Emotion tamed by deep grief, moving in solemn sorrow, tells us its tale in stirring tones: an earnest, manly sadness goes from lamentation to trills of softness, to memories, to tears of love, to searchings of the heart, to cries of transport. Out of grief there springs new Force, that fills us with a warmth sublime: instinctively we seek again this force's fountainhead in Grief; we give ourselves to it, till sighing we swoon away; but here we rouse ourselves once more to fullest Force: we will not succumb, but endure. We battle no more against mourning, but bear it now ourselves on the mighty billows of a man's courageous heart.

1 "Wonne und Wehe, Lust und Leid, Anmuth und Wehmuth, Sinnen und Sehnen, Schmachten und Schwelgen, Kühnheit, Trotz und ein unbändiges Selbstgefühl"—I add the German, as the *Stabreims* are so significant of the epoch in Wagner's life (1850-52) at which the above was written.—TR.

To whom were it possible to paint in words the endless play of quite unspeakable emotions, passing from Grief to highest Exaltation, and thence again to softest Melancholy, till they mount at last to endless Recollection? The tone-poet alone could do it in this wondrous piece.

Force robbed of its destructive arrogance—by the chastening of its own deep sorrow—the *Third Movement* shows in all its buoyant gaiety. Its wild unruliness has shaped itself to fresh, to blithe activity; we have before us now the lovable glad man, who paces hale and hearty through the fields of Nature, looks laughingly across the meadows, and winds his merry hunting-horn from woodland heights; and what he feels amid it all, the master tells us in the vigorous, healthy tints of his tone-painting; he gives it lastly to the horns themselves to say—those horns which musically express the radiant, frolicsome, yet tenderhearted exultation of the man. In this Third Movement the tone-poet shows us the man-of-feeling from the side directly opposite to that from which he showed him in its immediate predecessor: there the deeply, stoutly suffering,—here the gladly, blithely doing man.

These two sides the master now combines in the *Fourth Movement*, to show us finally the man entire, harmoniously at one with self, in those emotions where the memory of Sorrow becomes itself the shaping-force of noble Deeds. This closing section is the harvest, the lucid counterpart and commentary, of the First. Just as there we saw all human feelings in infinitely varied utterance, now permeating one an-other, now each in haste repelling each: so here this manifold variety unites to one harmonious close, embracing all these feelings in itself and taking on a grateful plasticness of shape. This shape the master binds at first within one utmost simple theme, which sets itself be-fore us in sure distinctness, and yet is capable of infinite development, from gentlest delicacy to grandest strength. Around this theme, which we may regard as the firm-set Manly individuality, there wind and cling all tenderer and softer feelings, from the very onset of the move-ment, evolving to a proclamation of the purely Womanly element; and to the manlike principal theme—striding sturdily through all the tone-piece—this Womanly at last reveals itself in ever more intense, more many-sided sympathy, as the overwhelming power of *Love*. At the close of the movement this power breaks itself a highway straight into the heart. The restless motion pauses, and in noble, feeling calm this Love speaks out; beginning tenderly and softly, then waxing to the rapture of elation, it takes at last the inmost fortress of the man's whole heart. Once more the heartstrings quiver, and tears of pure Humanity well forth; yet from out the very quick of sadness there bursts the jubilant cry of Force—that Force which lately wed itself to Love, and nerved wherewith *the whole, the total Man* now shouts to us the avowal of his Godhood.

But only in the master's tone-speech was the unspeakable to be proclaimed—the thing that words could here but darkly hint at.—RICHARD WAGNER (3)

No diffuse, moralizing preamble—no high generalization, such as we found in the Introductions to the first two symphonies—but merely two arresting staccato chords serve to focus our attention on the bold mentality that is portrayed in the main theme. The attribute of strength appears in unconscious simplicity, without violence, and even without that righteous indignation which so often imbues Beethoven's sterner utterances. The strange sinking of the theme to C sharp at the fifth bar and the ensuing phrases in the violins seem to suggest a kind of gentleness that does not belie but rather complements the hint of strength.

This hint of gentleness, although of high value, is parenthetical and remains almost unnoticed hereafter. The stronger phrase immediately dominates and gradually reveals what we may (mistakenly) suppose to be its full power. Two episodes follow: the first based on a tender strain whose three-note phrases, passed from instrument to instrument (as with the second theme of the First Symphony), build a continuous melody; the second in the strings, whose animated little figure is soon abandoned in an unmistakable approach to the second subject. Hardly a melody, this subject is rather an elastic succession of harmonies, culminating at its fourth bar in a clinging resolution of subtly introduced discord. Its note of yearning is intensified after the third phrase of its continuation by a momentary dark interjection of the basses. Transition back to the sense of strength is made by a few bars of thirds, moving contrariwise,[1] and that sense is exemplified in perhaps the most emphatic passage thus far heard—an angular melodic line, with the second beat of the measure persistently *sforzato*, that grows to threatening force and with only an instant of release brings the end of the exposition with a hint of the principal theme in B flat.

The development begins in mystery. Out of this the episode of three-note phrases defines itself; then the principal subject, in C minor and in the basses, appears, climbs the ladder of the scale in successive unprepared modulations, and is soon conjoined with the second of the episodes mentioned above. ([During the procedure, the] main theme is presented in "diminution.") The first episode now returns, with a rising staccato scale for enhancement, and the rhythm of this, innervated into a leaping fugue-subject and accompanied by a hint of the second episode as counterpoint, soon eventuates in a tremendous passage of roaring chords, impelled by the rhythm of the fugal figure to a very

[1] This passage "means" nothing, in itself, but it does serve to shift the focus of our attention, which has been sufficiently absorbed with the very actual meaning of the second subject, to the next essential topic.

frenzy of energy—an outburst such as had never before been dreamed of in orchestral music. Articulateness is no longer even attempted; incoherence itself becomes eloquence.

When the music again comes to its senses, it has evolved a wholly new theme, in E minor—essential, no doubt, for the leading of the thought back into familiar channels, but intrinsically as gentle as the restraining hand of God. By this means the main theme is brought back, in C major and quite unharmonized. It almost gets out of control, and the restraining hand has again to be applied; but at last it begins to appear in harmonious imitation, in one after another of the winds, and is supported and vitalized by an irresistible treading, on continually widening intervals, in the basses. Observe that the uproar, earlier, was essentially a descending progression, with a frantic dissonance at the end, while this is a rising progression, with much milder discord and a culmination on the C-flat major triad. The long development ends with that famous passage in which the horns begin the main theme in the tonic while the violins, *tremolando*, still maintain the dominant of the key.[1]

The recapitulation significantly alters the harmony after the C sharp in the theme, subduing the tension and presenting the theme quietly, in F in a solo horn, and in D flat in the flute, before the *forte* reaffirmation. Otherwise, there are no alterations of consequence. The Coda, however, adds an important chapter to the story.

It begins with the main theme, which quietly vaults the modulatory fence into D flat and then, with another leap of that barrier, strikes with full force on the triad of C major. Its first two bars are accompanied by a new rhythmic figure, and begin to rock with a sense of indomitable assurance. The new theme from the development section enriches that sense (which would have become blatant if it had developed at once); but at length, as in the development, the giant strides of the basses again begin their treading. Presently the main theme comes back, joined to the new rhythmic figure, and grows, without ever a tinge of that fatal blatancy, to acknowledged domination of the whole scene. An interlude between the first and second episodes in the exposition is recalled; the dominant chord—first in titanic syncopations and then in the long strides which the violins take over from the basses—makes huge preparation for the tonic; and this, when it arrives, is reinforced by two sharp and forceful strokes, exactly as at the beginning of the movement.

The second movement is entitled Marcia funebre. Few are the poets who have spoken as bravely as here to the shrouded figure. There is neither saintly ecstasy nor meek resignation nor craven terror, but a kind

[1] Ferdinand Ries, Beethoven's pupil, recalls that at the first rehearsal of the symphony he rose at this moment and stopped the orchestra by calling out, "Too soon! too soon! the horn is wrong!" for which display of zeal his only reward was a box on the ears from Beethoven and a furious lecture! (Ries, "*Biographisches Notizen über Ludwig van Beethoven,*" 1838, pp. 79–80).—Editor.

of fortitude, altogether heroic, that seems born of both understanding and faith—truly, a thanatopsis.

The main theme, in the strings, although it is without the customary leaden tramping, is yet instinct with motion. The propulsive energy imparted by the rumbling figure in the basses on "one" in the measure is absorbed by the long G of the theme, so that the ensuing climb from C to E flat seems effortful, and the leap (after silence) to G is of extraordinary tenseness. Even the dissonant A flat (in bar 6) seems less forceful, and its implication of pain is counteracted by the firmness of the ensuing cadence. The oboe, repeating the theme, is a little more decisively propelled by the strings, and its high A flat, longer sustained, descends to a cadence in the major. The hopefulness of the ensuing song comes too soon to be fully realized, but the hint it gives is not lost, however bitter may be the intensifications of these strains that follow.

Now appears a passage in C major whose quiet melody, first in oboe, then in flute, is soon compelled, by mighty reiterations of a sternly marching rhythm, to face that fact of death from whose contemplation it had almost strayed. The melody continues, in spite of this threat, and is tenderly enriched; but at its end there is the threat once more, and a sudden darkening that is one of the most ominous moments in any literature. The main theme starts, as before, but hesitates at its sixth bar; goes on, alarmed, into F minor; achieves its firm cadence there, and enters on a fugue which Weingartner rightly called Aeschylean.

It is really a double fugue. The first subject begins with four rising notes, in the second violins; the second, in the violas, has only long notes, which always accompany the first subject. After announcing the theme, the second violins begin a tremendous countersubject—forceful sixteenths, every one played with a full sweep of the bow—that incessantly adds its elemental energy to the fabric. At the tortured culmination the sixteenths are hastened into triplets, and the four rising notes of the first subject are likewise doubled in speed. Five mighty blows on a single chord end the fugal episode, the last undergoing in a single bar a terrifying diminuendo. There follows a bewildered hint of the principal subject, sotto voce; but a more awful stroke is in store—an insistent and rebellious reiteration of C's in horns and trumpets that goes on for seven bars and then rises to all but intolerable F's to end its outcry.

The tumult of triplet sixteenths in the strings now subsides in force, though it does not cease, and there begins in the basses a figure (similar to that gigantic "treading" we noted in the Allegro) that lends a new solemnity to the main theme of the March, which returns in oboe and clarinet. The triplets halt for a time with the first strain of the theme, so that the second may appear in the full warmth of its simple design. The rest of the theme, with its accompaniment again enriched, appears as before, and there is a little moment of heartbreaking loveliness before the main theme, now torn into little disjointed phrases, fades into the final chord.[1]

How to go on, after such an experience, must have been nearly as much of a puzzle to Beethoven as to us. The very notion of a Scherzo seems for the moment unthinkable. But—a little as if another symphony had begun—a Scherzo does make decorous entrance, maintaining the pianissimo of its beginning until we have been translated back from the contemplation of death to the recognition and even the possible enjoyment of life. Not until the ninety-second bar is there any departure from the quiet hush. Then—and with what singular wisdom!—the full current of vitality bursts forth without transition. But of that impudence which so often characterizes Beethoven's scherzi there is in this one hardly a trace.

With the Trio, whose theme is for three horns (nobody except Haydn, once, in the *Horn Call Symphony*, had ever dreamed of asking for more than two, and Beethoven's extravagance was roundly censured), the full flush of health returns to the cheeks. Even so, the interjections by the rest of the orchestra never become boisterous, unless at the few rhythmically angular passages and the momentary alla breve. For the first time, also, Beethoven composes an epilogue, instead of merely repeating the Scherzo after the Trio; and his keen sense of the meaning that may reside in the sound of the drums is likewise made clear.

The strident D's with which the opening flourish of the Finale begins (Allegro molto, A flat, 2/4 time) are surprising, since they seem to establish G minor as the key; but this is only an approach, like the opening of the First Symphony, which sets the true tonality of E flat more firmly on its base. The theme is not new. Beethoven had first invented it as a contredanse and used it in the *Prometheus* ballet music, and he had later made upon it a set of variations and a fugue for piano, Opus 35. In that work he had built up the whole composite substance of the theme by a gradual addition of its elements, and here he pursues the same plan.

The bass—the fundament of the whole—is [first heard after] the introductory flourish. [It is played] pizzicato in all the strings. It is then repeated with its notes echoed higher in the winds. Next [a gentle countersubject], partly in the cellos and partly in the first violins, is played against the [bass theme, now appearing] in the second violins. Next the most important [lyrical] "tune" in the piece is played together with [the fundamental theme], which has now gone back to the basses.

With this tune ended the movement is now under way, and after a short preparation there comes a fuguing, based on the first four bars

[1] See Ferguson's separate essay on the second movement and its implied meaning from his book *Music as Metaphor*.—Editor.

of [the bass theme] in C minor, in the first violins, with [its original gentle countersubject used] as counterpoint. The texture gets [very] complex, but presently it comes to a ringing end on the dominant-seventh [chord] of C minor. This chord, however, by a lightning change, turns into an augmented sixth chord in B minor. [The "tune,"] in that key, comes floating out of the blue, shifting to D major as it soars. There is not much time for such dainty business as this, and unmistakable preparation is soon made for another new counterpoint to the main bass—a theme [with a characteristic dotted rhythm, somewhat martial, somewhat *Hongroise*]. This, in turn, yields to the [lyrical main "tune,"] and there is soon another fugal variation in which [the bass theme], in the horn, and [the lyrical theme] in the second violins are both turned upside down while [the latter], in the violas, stays right side up, and there is considerable bustling of sixteenths besides. The end is again on the dominant seventh—this time really in E flat; and after its long-held sonority [the lyrical "tune"] comes forth at the summit of the music. But how altered! For it now moves in a stately poco andante and it sings, in a way undreamed of in the *Prometheus* ballet or in the piano variations, of the heart which the Titan put into the breasts of men.

The introductory flourish returns, and there is loud celebration, surely not unjustified, of all that this event implies. It is not strange that this symphony remained for Beethoven, to the end of his days, his favorite among his works.—DONALD N. FERGUSON (1)

The symphony is scored for two flutes, two oboes, two clarinets, two bassoons, three horns, two trumpets, timpani, and strings.

The objection may plausibly be urged against all [examples of music, about which] the original expressive purpose was known, [and, therefore, our emotional reaction to it is predetermined and therefore valueless as an instance of the *direct effect of the music itself*[1]].

We shall now observe what may be called the reverse of this process of analysis. Instead of taking a single musical pattern and exploring its "root meaning" as a factor in a variety of experiences, we shall take [an] example of music which deal[s,] unmistakably, with the experience of death; it is represented under the aspect of that stately ritual—the march—through which men have long found expression for their attitude toward that event. A few bars from the great March in the *Eroica* will suffice.

We shall consider first the element of ideal motion.

As the absence of rhythmic propulsion was important, in [some ex-

1 Italics by the editor.

pressive themes such as the Brünnhilde motive from *Siegfried*[1]], for the suggestion of freedom of movement, so its presence is here significant as conveying the opposite sense. The manner in which that rhythmic energy is applied is notable. The first six bars of this theme begin with notes of identical and impressive length—notes which absorb into themselves the considerable propulsive force supplied by the appoggiatura figure in the basses and by the initial upbeat, so that the weight of these notes is extraordinary. But that force is all but exhausted in the one rhythmic thrust, so that the third and fourth beats (counting the time as 4/8, not 2/4) must themselves gather momentum to reach the next strong beat. Dotted sixteenths here precede thirty-seconds, giving, in the slow tempo, a sense of laboriousness to the ascent; and this sense is augmented by the fall of the long E flat to C.

There is also significant contribution to the laborious motion in the simple relation of height and depth in pitch. The effortful ascent we just noted covers no more than a minor third, from C to E flat (the B natural is too short to create the tension of the diminished fourth); the same rhythmic thrust that propelled the low G is again imparted to the E flat; but so heavy is this note that it absorbs that energy and can do no more than fall back to C. The ensuing moment of silence after the "feminine" phrase-end, seen merely as an aspect of the ideal motion we are considering, is a vivid contribution to that portrayal. For the characteristic rhythmic thrust on the following high G gives to that note, in comparison to all the preceding tones, an almost explosive energy. But again this energy is absorbed into the note, and the descent, now almost precipitous, is made by thirty-seconds *preceding* dotted sixteenths—a vivid inversion of the motion-pattern of ascent in bar 2.

Our somewhat obscure term—ideal motion—for the elemental impression of motion character conveyable by music seems to us here to come quite clear. The whole sense of forward progression in the musical substance (to which the tone-stresses will contribute greatly) is extremely retarded. Its motion is dragged and weighted, heavy-footed and slow; yet the sense of underlying energy is abundant, so that there is no rhythmic sense of weakness or defeat.

Turning now to the values suggested by the tone-stresses, we find the points of activity and rest clearly in accord with, and strongly contributory to, the impressions of motion. We have already had to observe the primary tensions of height and depth to account for some of the values of motion. Observing the melodic notes as active or rest tones, we see that the accented notes in the first phrase (two bars)

---

[1] Ferguson has quoted the beautiful theme in the third act of *Siegfried* in which the very voluptuous turn in thirty-second notes and its inner propulsion to the high note suggest sensuous love.—Editor.

are *all* rest tones. This stability contributes greatly to that sense of weight which we found to be illustrated by the music in its motor aspect. In the second phrase this sense is heightened. The implication of the high G—a rest tone, attacked out of silence—is wonderfully subtle. (Imagine any active note in its place—for example, an A flat—and consider the immediate loss in dignity and character!) It pulls downward with all the force of an active tone; and that downwardness is intensified by the placing of the rhythmic accent on the active thirty-seconds which gains only a precarious foothold on the unaccented (dotted sixteenth) rest tones to which they fall.

The melodic progression E flat—D in the fourth bar forms a kind of rhythmic rhyme to the E flat—C in bar 2. The active note D forms a half-cadence with a feminine ending and, as the first really conspicuous active note thus far, warns the ear of the generally active phrase that is to follow. Indeed, until the final measure, the accented notes are now almost all active tones. The high A flat is the parallel of the earlier explosive G; but this note is not approached by leap, nor is it attacked out of silence. Its intensity is prepared for by stepwise progression on dotted sixteenths (active) followed by thirty-seconds (rest tones), and although it conveys an indubitable sense of pain, its momentary outcry is dominated at once by the extraordinary firmness of the conclusion of the whole theme. This solidity is portrayed by the rythmically even (not dotted) sixteenths of the seventh bar—a fact of ideal motion which we did not observe when dealing with that element of expression, since it was hardly necessary to comment further on that aspect of bars 5–8.

The third aspect of tone-stress—that of harmonic consonance and dissonance—is similarly striking. For the first four bars, except at the half-cadence, there is no other harmony than the minor tonic chord. Although it is unrelieved, it imparts great firmness and dignity. Instead of appearing monotonous, it supports and enhances the directness of the melodic utterance, precluding any suggestion of overweighted misery or nervous abandon. But even here the maintenance of the single harmony produces no impression of stolidity. A singular accumulation of tension is achieved by presenting the one chord in its successive inversions. (The bass, for two bars, is C, the root of the chord; then—approached by two thirty-seconds in a pattern like that of the preceding appoggiatura-figures—it is E flat; then it is G, giving the unstable, almost dissonant 6/4 chord at the half-cadence.) This simplicity in the use of the single harmony for the whole first clause makes effective the use, for the ensuing active melody, of an equally simple active harmony—that of the diminished seventh; but that melodic sturdiness which appears with the even sixteenths is again accompanied by primary triads, so that the cadence, harmonically as well as rhythmically, is on a note of resolute firmness.

This is more than mere marching-music for the dead. Its solemnity is as profound as its sadness. Grief permeates every note and every rhythmic step; but there is no yielding—no indulgence in the alleviating misery of tears. It comprehends heroically and is unafraid.

The title *Marcia funebre* is wholly appropriate to this music—and wholly needless. Where could one find, in poetry or any other art, a truer revelation than Beethoven gives of the heroic mind, confronting unafraid the somber fact of earthly finality?

The Beethoven march [can] be accounted great not because of his superior skill as musician, but because of his ability to reflect, through the medium of music, experience that is in itself neither musical nor in any immediate way aesthetic.—DONALD N. FERGUSON (2)

Announcement of the first public playing of the Eroica:
A grand Sinfonie in D Sharp Minor by Herr Ludwig von Beethoven and dedicated to His Highness Prince von Lobkowitz will be played on Sunday, April 7, 1805, at the Theatre an der Wien. The composer will have the pleasure of conducting it himself.

The Vienna correspondent of the "Allgemeine musikalische Zeitung":
I have heard a new sinfonie by Beethoven in E flat (erroneously announced as being in D sharp major)[1] under the composer's own direction. It was performed by a quite complete orchestra, but even this time I found no reason to change my earlier opinion.[2] Truly this new work of Beethoven's contains some grand and daring ideas, as one might expect from the powerful genius of the composer, and shows great expressive strength as well. But the sinfonie would be all the better—it lasts a whole hour—if Beethoven could reconcile himself to make some cuts in it and to bring into the score more light, clarity, and unity—virtues that were never absent from the Sinfonies in G Minor and C Minor of Mozart, those in C and D of Beethoven, and those in E flat and D of Eberl.[3] Here in place of the andante there is a funeral march in C minor, which is developed fugally, but this fugue is completely lost and confused in the way it is handled. Even after several hearings it eludes the most sustained attention, so that the unprepared connoisseur is really shocked. As a result this sinfonie was anything but enjoyed by the greater part of the audience.

Two and a half years later:
This reviewer remains, in spite of all that has been written on this work, of his original opinion, namely, that this symphony undoubtedly

---

[1] *Sic:* these several discrepancies of key are a telling part of the story. The Eroica is in E flat, the Fifth in C minor.
[2] At a private performance with incomplete instrumental forces, in December 1804.
[3] Anton Eberl (1766–1807), pianist and composer, friend of Mozart's.

contains many beautiful and sublime things, but that these elements are mixed with many harsh things and longueurs, and that it will be able to acquire the purity of form of a work of art only by a thorough revision.

About the same time, a Berlin reviewer:

The symphony is full of originality; it is abundant and even excessive in its harmony, but also full of bizarre ideas. . . . On the whole, this symphony by no means made an impression comparable to that made by Mozart's and Haydn's. The applause of those who know went to the performers, for their skillful overcoming of great difficulties for about three-quarters of an hour.—JACQUES BARZUN

> *b. Symphony No. 4 in B Flat, Opus 60*
> I. Adagio; Allegro vivace; II. Adagio; III. Allegro vivace: Trio;
> Un poco meno allegro; IV. Finale: Allegro ma non troppo

It may have been some inner law of artistic equilibrium which induced Beethoven, after drafting two movements for his C minor Symphony in 1805, to set them aside, and devote himself, in 1806, to the gentler contours of the Symphony in B flat, which, completed in that year, thus became the fourth in number.

Robert Schumann compared this symphony to a "Greek maiden between two Norse giants." The Fourth, overshadowed by the more imposing stature of the "Eroica" and the Fifth, has not lacked champions. "The character of this score," wrote Berlioz, "is generally lively, nimble, joyous, or of a heavenly sweetness." Thayer, who bestowed his adjectives guardedly, singled out the "placid and serene Fourth Symphony—the most perfect in form of them all"; and Sir George Grove, a more demonstrative enthusiast, found in it something "extraordinarily *entrainant*—a more consistent and attractive whole cannot be. . . . The movements fit in their places like the limbs and features of a lovely statue; and, full of fire and invention as they are, all is subordinated to conciseness, grace, and beauty."

The composer has left to posterity little of the evidence usually found in his sketchbooks of the time and course of composition. He has simply (but incontrovertibly) fixed the year, inscribing at the top of his manuscript score: *"Sinfonia 4ta 1806—L. v. Bthvn."* This date has been enough to enkindle the imagination of more than one writer.

It was probably early in May of 1801 that Beethoven took a post chaise from Vienna to visit his friends the Brunswicks at their ancestral estate in Martonvásár, Hungary. There he found Count Franz von Brunswick, and the Count's sisters Therese and Josephine (then a widow of twenty-six), and the younger Karoline. Therese and Josephine ("Tesi" and "Pepi") seem to have had the composer's more interested attention. Romain Rolland, who made more of [Beethoven's] affair with Therese von Brunswick than these subsequent discoveries justify, yet came to the still plausible conclusion that the Fourth Symphony was the direct outcome of Beethoven's stay at Martonvásár, "a pure, fragrant flower which treasures up the perfume of these days, the calmest in all his life."

The felicity of Martonvásár seems to have found its reflection in the Symphony. The gusty lover was in abeyance for the time being. Beethoven dominated the affections of all, but not in a way to ruffle the blessed succession of summer days and nights in the Hungarian manor, secluded in its immense acres where a row of lindens was singled out and one chosen as sacred to each of the little circle, Beethoven included.

The Fourth Symphony, inscribed to *"Monsʳ le Comte d'Oppersdorf,"* bears an example of a convenient and mercenary dedication. In the summer of 1806, the principal works in course of composition were the Fourth and Fifth Symphonies, and to these the "Pastorale" was to be added in 1808. The Fifth and Sixth Symphonies were each dedicated jointly to Prince von Lobkowitz and the Count von Razumowsky, probably in fulfillment of an obligation which honor required. Meanwhile, Beethoven had promised a symphony to a nobleman whom he had met while in Silesia in 1806. Prince Lichnowsky at Castle Grätz had taken him to call upon Count Franz von Oppersdorf, who had a castle of his own in the neighboring town of Grossglogau. The Count favored music and boasted an excellent orchestra of his own; he had Beethoven's Second Symphony performed in the composer's presence. In June of the following year, he ordered a symphony from him and sent an advance of five hundred florins. Beethoven intended to send the Fifth Symphony, but held him off, writing as late as March, 1808, that *"your symphony* has long been ready and I will send it to you by the next post." He mentioned particularly the *Finale* with "3 trombones and flautino," whereby he was to expect "more noise than 6 kettledrums, and, indeed, better noise." But on November 1 he wrote, "You will view me in a false light, but necessity compelled me to sell the symphony which was written for you, and also another to someone else." The Count, who had expected a six months' right of performance, received nothing more than the dedication of the substituted Fourth Symphony, which had been both performed (by Prince Lobkowitz) and sold for publication. There were no further negotiations between Beethoven and Count Oppersdorf.—JOHN N. BURK (2)

The Fourth Symphony is perhaps the work in which Beethoven first fully reveals his mastery of movement. He had already shown his com-

mand of a vastly wider range of musical possibilities than that of Mozart
or Haydn. And he had shown no lack of ease and power in the
handling of his new resources. But now he shows that these resources
can be handled in such a way that Mozart's own freedom of movement
reappears as one of the most striking qualities of the whole. The sky-
dome vastness of the dark introduction is evident at the outset; but it is
first fully understood in the daylight of the opening of the *Allegro*.
The new quick tempo asserts itself with the muscular strength of real
bodily movement. The "spin" of the whole, tremendous as it is, depends
entirely on the variety, the contrasts, and the order of themes and
sequences, varying in length from odd fractions of bars to the 32-bar (and
even longer) processes in the Development. The Second Subject begins
with a conversation between the bassoon, the oboe, and the flute. The
Development keeps up the "spin" by moving on lines far broader than
any yet indicated by the Exposition. The delightful *cantabile* added as a
counterpoint to the entries (in various keys) of the main theme, is
one of the salient features; and nearly half the whole Development is
occupied by the wonderful hovering on the threshold of the remote key of
B-natural major in order to return therefrom to the tonic B-flat by means
resembling, but more subtly and on a higher plane, the return in the
first movement of the Waldstein Sonata (written about a year earlier).
The Recapitulation is quite normal, and the Coda is no longer than one
of Mozart's usual final expansions.

The slow movement is a full-sized Rondo, a form which is extremely
spacious when worked out in a slow tempo. The main theme returns in
a florid variation; and the middle episode, which follows, is one of the
most imaginative passages anywhere in Beethoven. From its mysterious
end arises the return of the main theme in its varied form, this time in
the flute; whereupon follows a regular Recapitulation, including the
transition and the Second-Subject. The Coda consists of a final allusion
to the main theme, dispersing itself mysteriously over the orchestra, till
the drums make an end by recalling the opening stroke of genius.

For the Scherzo no citations are needed: the double repetition of
Scherzo and Trio makes everything as clear as any dance, in spite of
the numerous rhythmic whims. The final repetition of the Scherzo is
abridged (in other cases Beethoven prefers to make full repetition aggressively the point of the joke). Never have five notes contained more
meaning than the Coda in which the two horns blow the whole movement away.

The Finale represents Beethoven's full maturity in that subtlest of ways,
his discovery of the true inwardness of Mozart and Haydn; a discovery
inaccessible to him whenever, as in a few early works (notably the
Septet), he seemed or tried to imitate them, but possible as soon as he
obtained full freedom in handling his own resources. Everything is pres-

ent in this unsurpassably adroit and playful Finale; and it is all pure Beethoven, even when, by drawling out its opening theme into 8th notes with pauses, it borrows an old joke of Haydn's, the excellence of which lies in its badness. Lamb would have understood it—in spite of the Essay on Ears. To do justness to the boldness and power that underlies all the grace and humor of this Finale, it would be necessary to go into details. It is a study for a lifetime; but, once begun, it is in many ways more directly useful to the artist than the study of things the power of which is allowed to appear on the surface. Those who think the Finale of the Fourth Symphony "too slight" will never get nearer than Spohr (if as near) towards a right understanding of the Fifth, however they may admire it.—DONALD FRANCIS TOVEY (2)

The score calls for flute, two oboes, two clarinets, two bassoons, two horns, two trumpets, timpani, and strings.

Here Beethoven entirely abandons ode and elegy; in order to return to the less elevated and less somber, but not less difficult style of the second symphony. The general character of this score is either lively, alert, and gay or of a celestial sweetness. With the exception of the meditative Adagio, which serves as its introduction, the first movement is almost entirely given over to joy. The motive in detached notes, with which the Allegro opens, is only a background upon which the composer is afterwards enabled to display other melodies of more real character; the effect of the latter being to impart a secondary character to what was apparently the principal idea of the commencement.

This artifice, although fertile in curious and interesting results, had already been employed by Mozart and Haydn with equal success. But we find in the second part of the same Allegro a really new idea, the first few bars of which arrest attention, and which also, after interesting the listener by its mysterious developments, strikes him with astonishment by its unexpected conclusion. It is composed as follows:

After a fairly vigorous tutti the first violins parcel out the original theme, by forming a dialogue in pianissimo with their seconds. This terminates with holding notes of the dominant chord of the key of B natural; each instance of such holding notes being followed by two bars of silence interrupted only by a light tremolo of the kettledrum; which, being tuned to B flat, plays enharmonically the part of third to the fundamental F sharp. After two such appearances the kettledrum ceases; in order to allow the string instruments an opportunity of sweetly murmuring other fragments of the theme, and of arriving by a new enharmonic modulation to the chord of six-four; second inversion of that of B flat. The kettledrum now returns upon the same sound; which, instead of being a leading note, as upon the first occasion, is now a veritable tonic; and, as such, continues the tremolo for some twenty bars. The force of tonality possessed by this B flat, only slightly perceptible at first, becomes greater in the same degree as the tremolo proceeds. Afterwards, the other instruments, bestrewing the onward march with slight and unfinished traits, prepare us for a continuous roll of the kettledrum on a general forte, in which the perfect chord of B flat is finally stated by the full orchestra in all its majesty. This remarkable crescendo is one of the best conceived effects which we know of in all music; and its counterpart can scarcely be found elsewhere than in the similar feature by which the celebrated Scherzo of the C minor Symphony is concluded. The latter, however, notwithstanding its immense effect, is conceived upon a scale less vast, starting from piano in order to arrive at the final explosion, without departing from the original key. On the other hand, the episode we are now describing starts from mezzo forte; and is afterwards lost for a moment in a pianissimo, while harmonized in a manner constantly vague and undecided. Then, it reappears with chords of a somewhat more settled tonality, and bursts forth only at the moment when the cloud which enshrouded the modulation has completely disappeared. It might be compared to a river, the peaceful waters of which suddenly disappear and only emerge from their subterranean bed to form a furious and foaming waterfall.

As for the Adagio, it seems to elude analysis. Its form is so pure and the expression of melody so angelic and of such irresistible tenderness that the prodigious art by which this perfection is attained disappears completely. From the very first bars we are overtaken by an emotion which, toward the close, becomes so overpowering in its intensity that only among the giants of poetic art can we find anything to compare with this sublime page of the giant of music. Nothing in fact more resembles the impression produced by this Adagio than that experienced when reading the touching episode of Francesca di Rimini in the "Divina Commedia"; the recital of which Virgil could not hear without sobbing bitterly; and which, at the last line, causes Dante to fall *as a dead body falls*. This movement seems as if it had been sadly murmured by the Archangel Michael on some day when, overcome by a feeling of melancholy, he contemplated the universe from the threshold of the Empyrean.

The Scherzo consists almost exclusively of phrases in duple rhythm, forcibly forming part of combinations in triple time. This means, which Beethoven uses frequently, imparts verve to the style; the melodic outlines become sharper and more surprising, besides which these rhythms, running counter to the ordinary beat, present an independent charm which is very real, although difficult to explain. A pleasure results from this disturbance of the normal accent, which regains its position at the end of each period; the sense of the musical discourse, which had been for a time suspended, then arriving at a satisfactory conclusion and complete solution.

The melody of the trio, confided to the wind instruments, is of a delicious freshness; its movement being slower than that of the rest of the Scherzo, and its elegant simplicity being enhanced by encountering the opposition of short phrases emanating from the violins, which seem cast upon the surface of the harmony like charming traits of innocent mischief. The Finale, which is both gay and sprightly, returns to ordinary rhythmic forms. It is one animated swarm of sparkling notes, presenting a continual babble; interrupted, however, by occasional rough and uncouth chords, in which the angry interspersions, which we have already had occasion to mention as peculiar to this composer, are again manifest.—HECTOR BER-LIOZ

Let us take a lesson from Beethoven in the art of changing a tempo. Only a master who could produce the "Eroica" Symphony could have produced this smaller work at all. As a study in movement, the Fourth Symphony reveals things that we simply have not leisure to notice in larger works. I here refer to the passage in which the Allegro had comfortably settled down to its pace. I am speaking of the momentum, not of the tempo, which is asserted at the outset. The momentum would soon merely send us to sleep if nothing happened from time to time to change it. That is the trouble with so much postclassical music. Few composers seem to realize that, when all your phrases are the same length and all your changes of color and pattern at equal distances, you may cry "Faster, faster," like the Looking-Glass Red Queen when she ran poor Alice to breathlessness and then dumped her at the foot of the same tree that had overshadowed them all the time.

Let us see how Beethoven asserts his allegro vivace. The introduction has been so slow that the young Weber, who was outspoken and honest and died before he had time to understand Beethoven, laughed at it as a display of the knack of spreading the fewest possible notes over a quarter of an hour. So, at all events, he did see something extraordinary in the size of it, which is just what nowadays escapes the intelligence of musicians who can take things in at a glance. This introduction is very quiet, very dark, and tragically mysterious. Tragedies do not often begin in this way. Such darkness arouses expectations, the fulfilment of which may be disappointing. But the contradiction of them may be very refreshing. Weber exaggerates when he talks of a quarter of an hour. Beethoven has kept us in darkness for not much over two minutes; then, with very little warning, the whole orchestra bursts out with two mighty crashes, still in the slow tempo and on the home dominant, now established as that of a major key after the many mysterious and remote modulations of the introduction; and now, here, the crashes are followed up with a drastically clear assertion of the full speed of the allegro vivace. We are, so to speak, hustled into the saddle, and our horse prances off at once. Then comes a playful theme, which consists of four bars closing into four answering bars, the last two of which are unexpectedly prolonged and are followed by two fortissimo bars on the lines of the first crash into the allegro. Then the theme is repeated as a tutti, and its close expanded by further bars. After this, nothing in Rossini could give us so glorious a sense of running comfortably at full speed.

In the exposition of the first movement of the Fourth Symphony, the sense of comfortable settled pace goes with 8-bar phrases, and the tendency is to break these up into shorter elements, until, in one very characteristic passage, we have sequences of which the steps are a bar-and-a-half, with a resulting cross-accent that is very exciting. After the double-bar and repeat (it is a crime to omit the repeat in this move-ment), there comes the development, and, as we shall see in dealing with Beethoven's art-forms, the word "development" is applied to a part of a movement that corresponds more or less with the principal imbroglio of a novel or play. Ingenious contrapuntal combinations may be of use in a development, but they cannot of themselves produce more than an argumentative effect. To develop a theme dramatically, we again need the power to change the size of its phrases and to combine it with other themes rather by building new tunes in partnership with them than by contrapuntal combination. In both the first movement and in the innocent-seeming Finale of Beethoven's Fourth Symphony, the developments are conspicuous examples of the value of wide open spaces. We might recommend the first movement of the Fourth Sym-phony as a breathing exercise to listeners, who may try and hold their breath according to the phrase-lengths. But perhaps the breathing exer-cise will come of itself in a more beneficial form if we listen to the music without thinking of anything else.—DONALD FRANCIS TOVEY (1)

c. *Symphony No. 5 in C minor, Opus 67*
   I. Allegro con brio; II. Andante con moto; III. Allegro; IV. Finale: Allegro

The first movement of the symphony (*Allegro con brio,* C minor, 2/4) opens grandly with three G's followed by a long-held E flat, *for-tissimo* in all the strings and clarinets. What is the key? The ear is in doubt: Is it C minor, or E flat major, or possibly G minor? The next two measures, three F's followed by a long-held D, strike out the possibility of G minor; but it still may be either C minor or E flat major.

The popular legend that Beethoven intended this grand exordium of the symphony to suggest "Fate knocking at the gate" is apocryphal; Beethoven's pupil, Ferdinand Ries, was really the author of this would-be-poetic exegesis, which Beethoven received very sarcastically when Ries imparted it to him. There is a considerable difference of opinion among conductors as to the manner of playing these four opening measures. Some take them in strict *allegro* tempo, like the rest of the movement; others take the liberty of playing them in a much slower and more stately tempo; others again take the three G's and the F's *molto ritardando*, arguing that, although taking the four measures in a stately *Largo* is not permissible—there being no indication in the score to authorize it—the "holds" over the E flat and the D do (at least tacitly) authorize *ritardandos* on the three E flats and three F's, according to the old rule: "You may always make a *ritardando* before a *tenuto*." And, if this retarding of the tempo is cleverly managed, it comes to very much the same thing, in point of effect, as the stately *Largo*, for which there is no authority in the score; it is beating the devil round the bush.

These four grand introductory bars are immediately followed by the exposition of the first theme, of which they furnish the principal figure. The construction of this theme is peculiar: it is really composed of nothing but free contrapuntal imitations on the figure of the introductory bars; but these imitations follow one upon the other with such rhythmic regularity that, to the ear, they form the several successive sections and phrases of a regularly constructed melody, or theme. No single part in the orchestra plays this melody; but take the quaver figures which appear successively on the second violins, violas, and first violins, and write them out in order on a single stave (as one part), and you have the theme. This theme is briefly developed in two sentences, followed by some brilliant passage work for fuller and fuller orchestra, still on the principal figure, ending on the first inversion of the chord of B flat major. Now the second theme enters *fortissimo* on the horns; its opening phrase is but a melodic extension of the principal figure of the first theme, but this is responded to by a more lovely phrase, full of the truest Beethovenian sentiment, which is worked up in a *crescendo* climax, leading to an unspeakably brilliant and dashing antithesis. There is no coda theme, the short concluding sentence being formed by some strong passage work on the principal figure of the first theme. The first part of the movement ends in E flat major, and is repeated.

The development section is not very long, although of sufficient length to be in proportion with the short first part of the movement. It is almost entirely devoted to a contrapuntal working out of the first theme, in which working out, however, new melodic developments keep cropping up. Toward the end, the initial figure of the second theme—which, as will be remembered, is but another version of that of the first—comes in for a brief contrapuntal elaboration, which is followed by the characteristically Beethovenian "moment of exhaustion," the working out gradually dying away in mysterious, unearthly antiphonal harmonies between the strings and woodwind. Then, all of a sudden, the first theme reasserts itself *fortissimo*, and we pass on to the recapitulation.

This part is quite regular in its relation to the first, the second theme now coming in the tonic, C major. It is to be noticed, however, that the development of the first theme is now accompanied by a more sustained, cantabile countertheme—a device of which Mendelssohn was particularly fond (*vide* the recapitulation of the first movement of his "Scotch" symphony)—and one of the long *tenuti* is elaborated into a beautiful little cadenza for the oboe. The change of key for the second theme necessitates a change in the instrumentation also: in the first part of the movement the second theme entered *fortissimo* on the horns, in E flat major; here, in the third part, where it enters in C major, it would have been impossible for the plain E flat horns to play it, so that Beethoven—unwilling to make his horn players change their crooks for only a few bars—found himself forced to transfer the passage to the bassoons. The result is rather unfortunate, for the bassoons sound somewhat veiled and timid, in comparison with the boldly assertive horns in the first part. But composers of Beethoven's day were not infrequently forced to make concessions of this sort. The movement ends with a long and exceedingly brilliant coda.

The second movement (*Andante con moto*, A flat major, 3/8) is in the form of a rondo with variations. It opens with an announcement of its first theme, a stately and expressive melody, sung in unison by the violas and cellos over a simple *pizzicato* bass for double basses, the closing phrase being considerably developed in full harmony by the woodwind, then by the woodwind and strings together.[1] This is immediately followed by the second theme, a heroic, quasi-martial phrase in A flat major, given out in harmony by the clarinets, bassoons, and violins, over a triplet arpeggio accompaniment in the violas, and a *pizzicato* bass. This theme closes with a bold modulation to C major, and is forthwith repeated *fortissimo* in this key by the oboes, horns, trumpets, and kettledrums, while all the violins and violas unite upon the accompanying triplet figure. A short conclusion phrase in mysterious *pianissimo* chromatic harmony, in the strings (without double basses) and bassoons, closes the period with a half cadence to the dominant of A flat major.

The second period corresponds exactly to the first, it being the first

[1] The gradual growth of this theme in Beethoven's mind is to be followed very fully in his sketchbooks; it is a fine and characteristic example of his laborious and carefully self-criticizing method of composition. The first form in which this noble theme appears in the sketchbooks is as trivial and commonplace as possible; every subsequent change it goes through is an improvement, until we at last find it in the form in which it appears in the symphony.

variation thereof. The first theme appears in a figural variation in the violas and cellos (even sixteenth-notes), against a *pizzicato* accompaniment in the other strings and a sustained counterphrase in the clarinet.[1] The variation of the second theme consists simply of substituting arpeggios in thirty-second notes for the triplet arpeggios in sixteenth notes.

In the third variation, which follows, we have the theme figurally varied in running thirty-second notes in the violas and cellos, the counterphrase now coming in the flute, oboe, and bassoon in double octaves, the varied theme soon passing into the first violins, then into the basses, against full harmony in repeated sixteenth-notes in the rest of the orchestra; this extends the first theme to three times its original length. Next follows a little interlude of passage work on the initial figure of the theme in the woodwind. Then the full orchestra precipitates itself *fortissimo* upon the second theme (in C major), in grand plain harmony. Then follows a brief episode in the shape of a staccato melodic variation, based on the initial figure of the first theme, in the flute, clarinet, and bassoon, over plain *pizzicato* chords in the second violins, violas, and basses, and waving arpeggios in the first violins.[2] Some *crescendo* scale passages lead to a *fortissimo* reappearance of the first theme in the tonic in the full orchestra, the theme now appearing in close imitation (not quite strict canon) between the violins and the woodwind. A long coda brings the movement to a close.

The third movement (*Allegro*, C minor, 3/4) is a scherzo with trio, although not so named in the score. It has all the characteristics of the Beethoven scherzo: the rapid tempo, the tricksy effects of modulation and instrumentation, the brilliant humor. It is perhaps the most

[1] One of the progressions in this clarinet obbligato gave rise, according to Berlioz, to one of Fétis's attempted "corrections" in the French edition of the score, which he was editing. The clarinet part begins with a long-sustained E flat, which, in the fourth measure, forms a suspended fourth over the B flat in the bass, and a major ninth over the D flat in the melody. According to the accepted rules of harmony, these dissonances ought to be resolved by the E flat in the clarinet falling to D flat (third of the bass and octave of the melody) on the third beat of the measure. But Beethoven has held this E flat throughout the measure, and made it progress upward to E natural in the fifth measure, forming the third of the chord of the dominant seventh of F major. This upward progress of a suspended dissonant note seemed at first an unpardonable crime to Fétis; but he afterward thought the passage over and found it to be an exemplification of an as yet unformulated law of harmony. This law he then proceeded to formulate as follows in his "Traité d'harmonie": "A dissonant note, instead of falling one degree to a consonant interval, may progress upward by a semitone, whenever, by so doing, it produces a passing modulation to another key." This is just what Beethoven's ascending E flat does: the E natural it moves to produces a passing modulation from A flat major to F major.

[2] Lovers of musical coincidences may be interested to know that both the waving arpeggios and the harmony of this passage (which contains some very characteristic and beautiful modulations) are to be found, in precisely the same rhythm, in the trio of a minuet in one of Boccherini's quintets; only the staccato melody is wanting.

diabolic of Beethoven's scherzos; Berlioz has likened it to a scene from the witches' Sabbath on the Brocken.[1] The first theme is eighteen measures long, the two measures over and above the regulation sixteen-measure cut being added to the third phrase. The thesis is given out *pianissimo* by the basses in octaves, the strings, woodwind, and horns answering with the antithesis in full harmony. This first theme is immediately followed by the second, a bolder phrase, given out *fortissimo* by the two horns in unison over a staccato accompaniment for strings, beginning in C minor, but soon modulating to E flat minor, and carried by the full orchestra through G flat major back to E flat minor again, each phrase ending on the dominant by half cadence. These two themes are worked up, together and in alternation, with some elaborateness in the way of running counterpoint, to the end of the scherzo, in C minor.

The trio (same time and tempo) in C major is a well worked-out fugato on an energetic subject of humorous, almost comic, character, the fugal writing being, however, strictly adapted to the regular scherzo form of two repeated sections. Then comes the repetition of the scherzo. The treatment is somewhat different from that in the first working out, the instrumentation being totally different, now running to *pizzicati* in the strings and staccato phrases in the woodwind, the whole being kept steadily at *pianissimo*. Some little clucking notes in the upper register of the bassoons have a peculiarly weird effect. The elaborate working out of the second theme at last merges into a long dominant pedal for the basses, while the timpani as persistently keep hammering away at the tonic, over which the first violins keep reiterating a figure taken from the first theme at an even, dead, *pianissimo*; then come eight bars of *crescendo*, leading to the finale, with which the scherzo is connected, without any intermediate pause.

The fourth movement (*Allegro*, C major, 4/4) opens with a grand, triumphant, marchlike theme, given out *fortissimo* by the full orchestra. This heroic theme is developed at a considerable length, always *fortissimo* and by the full force of the orchestra, until it is followed by an equally heroic, and somewhat more distinguished, second theme, also in C major. This theme is more briefly developed, still *fortissimo*, until it leads to the entrance of a more vivacious, if not more brilliant, third theme in the dominant, G major. In this third theme, in which *piano* and *forte* phrases keep alternating, the rhythm changes to what is essentially 12/8 time; its development ends with a full orchestral climax in the original 4/4 rhythm

[1] Here is another curious coincidence. The first nine notes (filling four measures) of the principal theme of this scherzo are identical (barring the difference of key) with the first nine notes of the theme of the finale in Mozart's G minor Symphony. But the rhythm is so utterly different that the ear perceives no similarity whatever between the two themes.

of the movement, leading to a fourth, and final theme, also in G major, first announced by the middle strings, clarinets, and bassoons, with brisk little squiblike counterfigures on the first violins, and then briefly developed *fortissimo* by the full orchestra, ending the first part of the movement in the tonic, C major. This first part is repeated.

Then follows a development section, in which the third theme, in triplet rhythm, is most elaborately worked out, the development leading at last to a tremendous climax which closes this section in the dominant key of G major. Now comes a curious and wholly original episode; the theme of the scherzo returns and is worked up briefly in a new way, with new orchestration, ending with a passage of long-sustained *pianissimo* and then *crescendo*, very similar to the one which led over from the scherzo itself to the finale. Indeed, this passage here leads to the triumphant return of the first theme at the beginning of the third part of the movement.

This third part is an almost exact repetition of the first, save that the third and conclusion themes now come in the tonic. The concise development of the conclusion theme leads immediately to the coda, which begins with some brisk passage work on the third theme, worked up to a climax which leads to a strong, and strongly insisted-on, half cadence in the tonic key. This is followed by a *fortissimo* announcement of a figure from the second theme by the bassoons, answered *piano dolce* by the horns. This figure, which is taken from the antithesis of the second theme (as it appeared in the first and third parts of the movement), now appears as the thesis of what might almost be called a new theme, and is worked up in two successive climaxes, the second of which, going *crescendo poco a poco e sempre più allegro*, leads to the final "apotheosis" of the symphony (*Presto*, C major, 2/2), in which the conclusion theme is worked up with the utmost energy, in true Beethoven fashion,—much after the manner of the peroration to the "Egmont" and third "Leonore" Overtures; only that here—as later in the finale to the Eighth Symphony, in F major—Beethoven seems absolutely unable to make up his mind to stop, and keeps hammering away at full chords of the tonic and dominant for forty measures, in sheer mad jubilation.—WILLIAM FOSTER APTHORP

The symphony is scored for two flutes, piccolo, two oboes, two clarinets, two bassoons, double bassoon, two horns, two trumpets, three trombones, timpani, and strings (the piccolo, trombones, and double bassoon, here making their first appearance in a symphony of Beethoven, are used only in the finale).

As a corollary [to Beethoven's conception of heroism] he had a personified idea of Fate. Fate was his name for a personified conception of those characteristics of life that call out the heroic in man. But in this idea of Fate it is something external. The inner state witnessing to its existence is heroism or, it may be, fear. In talking of Fate Beethoven is not talking of an experience, but of something that conditions experience. To that extent his notion of Fate is a construction, not as with his notion of Heroism, an expression of a direct perception. A feeling of the need and importance of the heroic principle persisted in Beethoven up to the end, but his conception of Fate as some kind of personified external menace disappeared. In depicting this menace, as he does in the first movement of the C minor symphony, Beethoven is, as it were, at one remove from reality. Beethoven, with his unequaled capacity for being faithful to his experience, would be obscurely aware of this, and it may be that some such feeling was responsible for his preference for the Eroica. In his later years the experience that he thus interprets in terms of heroism and fate, a contest between what we might call an inner and an outer principle, becomes a contest between two inner principles, assertion and submission. Beethoven had realized that these are the true elements involved, and that a synthesis of them is possible. Fate may still be invoked as some sort of theoretical *rationale* of both attitudes, but the conflicting elements are now both located within the soul itself.

The sketches for the first three movements of the C minor symphony go back to the years 1800 and 1801, when Beethoven was summoning up all his resolution to meet the threatening calamity of deafness. And these three movements, in their final form, still express an earlier stage of the experience that inspires the Eroica symphony. We know from his own words—"Thus Fate knocks at the door"—that Beethoven intended the first movement to convey his sense of the implacable might of that external and maleficent power he called Fate. This is that "Creator" he had "often cursed for exposing his creatures to the merest accident." The conception is simple and straightforward. But out of this conception Beethoven has composed a movement which is not only interesting, but one of the most masterly pieces of music in existence. It has not, perhaps, the wealth of invention that we find in the first movement of the Eroica, for there Beethoven is expressing a more complicated complex of emotions, but it is almost unequaled in the impression it gives of inevitable progression. This is one of the very few compositions of which it can be truthfully said that it does not contain an unnecessary bar. Beethoven often presents to us an organic unity containing within itself dramatic contrasts, but in this movement there is one dominating mood from first to last. Even the little oboe solo serves only to heighten the tension. But a more striking example of the way in which the fundamental impelling urge controls the whole work is shown by the almost imperceptible transformation of the contrasting second subject into a headlong rhythmical figure.[1] Beethoven never wrote anything that sounds more "predestined" from beginning to end, and this is partly due to the lack of complication in the underlying conception. At this time in Beethoven's life the issue was simple and clear-cut. But it is characteristic of him that even so he did not conceive fate as the blind, cold, indifferent, impersonal order of the universe, but as an enemy. We do not suggest that Beethoven ever did anything so ridiculous as to conceive Fate as some powerful and malign being, but his emotional reaction, as the C minor symphony proves, was appropriate to such a conception. In the first movement of the ninth symphony his whole conception has undergone a subtle transformation.

The slow movement of the C minor symphony is one of the less satisfactory of Beethoven's compositions. In the symphony it is a mere resting-place, a temporary escape from the questions aroused by the first movement. In this it plays an altogether different part from the slow movement of the Eroica. It seems as if Beethoven, in working up these early sketches, remained faithful to the experiences of that time. The movement indicates nothing more profound than the "few blessed moments" of the letter to Wegeler. The Scherzo, however, is a very different affair. Dreadful apprehension, defiance, a primitive surging energy, enter into this amazing picture of a tortured mind that has almost abandoned hope. That he should be able to make this material run so swiftly and cleanly is the most striking evidence Beethoven had given up to this time of his immense organizing power. It is too usual, in musical criticism, to call consummate pattern weavers "masters of form," but in making the elements of this Scherzo into a perfectly ordered and economic composition Beethoven has shown a mastery of form that it would be difficult to parallel elsewhere. What might easily have been, in other hands, a desperate chaos of sound and fury, is here a lithe, perfectly controlled, and beautifully shaped movement. At the end of this movement Beethoven carries us, by a crescendo rising out of the brooding expectancy created by the wailing violins and the drum taps, straight into the exultant finale. The whole psychological process of transition depicted in the Eroica is here ignored—probably because it was depicted in the Eroica.—J. W. N. SULLIVAN

There are twenty-four parts participating in the explosion which marks the transition from the Scherzo to the Finale in the C minor Symphony

[1] Cf. Dyson: *The New Music.*

of Beethoven. I speak of the fifty measures of the Scherzo that precede the Allegro. There is a strange melody which, combined with even a stranger harmony of a double pedal point in the bass on G and C, produces a sort of odious meowing, and discords to shatter the least sensitive ear. (A. Oulibicheff, *Nouvelle Biographie de Mozart*, Moscow, 1843)—NICOLAS SLONIMSKY

An appreciation of romantic qualities in art is uncommon; romantic talent is still rarer. Consequently there are few indeed who are able to play on that lyre the tones of which unfold the wonderful region of romanticism.

Haydn conceives romantically that which is distinctly human in the life of man; he is, in so far, more comprehensible to the majority.

Mozart grasps more the superhuman, the miraculous, which dwells in the imagination.

Beethoven's music stirs the mists of fear, of horror, of terror, of grief, and awakens that endless longing which is the very essence of romanticism. He is consequently a purely romantic composer, and is it not possible that for this very reason he is less successful in vocal music which does not surrender itself to the characterization of indefinite emotions but portrays effects specified by the words rather than those indefinite emotions experienced in the realm of the infinite?[1]

Beethoven's mighty genius oppresses the musical rabble; he excites himself in vain before them. But the wiseacres, looking around with serious countenances, assure us, and one can believe them as men of great understanding and deep insight, that the worthy B. does not lack a most abundant and lively imagination; but he does not know how to

[1] *Cf.* Wagner's *Zukunftsmusik:* "The ample heritage and promise of both of these masters (Haydn and Mozart) was taken up by Beethoven; he matured the Symphonic art-work to so engrossing a breadth of form, and filled that form with so manifold and enthralling a melodic content, that we stand today before the Beethovenian Symphony as before the landmark of an entirely new period in the history of universal Art; for through it there came into the world a phenomenon not even remotely approached by anything the art of any age or any people has to show us.

In this Symphony instruments speak a language whereof the world at no previous time had any knowledge; for here with a hitherto unknown persistence, the purely musical Expression enchains the hearer in an inconceivably varied mist of nuances; rouses his inmost being, to a degree unreachable by any other art; and in all its changefulness reveals an ordering principle so free and bold, that we can but deem it more forcible than any logic, yet without the laws of logic entering into it in the slightest—nay rather, the reasoning march of Thought, with its track of causes and effects, here finds no sort of foothold. So that this Symphony must positively appear to us a revelation from another world; and in truth it opens out a scheme (Zusammenhang) of the world's phenomena quite different from the ordinary logical scheme, and whereof one foremost thing is undeniable—that it thrusts home with the most overwhelming conviction, and guides our Feeling with such a sureness that the logic-mongering Reason is completely routed and disarmed thereby."

Translation by W. A. Ellis. *Wagner's Prose Works.* Vol. III. pp. 317-18.

curb it. There can be no discussion of the choice and the formation of his ideas, but he scatters the good old rules in disorder whenever it happens to please him in the momentary excitement of his creative imagination.

But what if the inner, underlying organic structure of these Beethoven compositions has escaped your superficial glance? What if the trouble is with you, that you do not understand the master's speech, intelligible to those to whom it is dedicated? What if the gates to that innermost shrine remain closed to you?—In truth, quite on a level with Haydn and Mozart as a conscious artist, the Master, separating his Ego from the inner realm of sound, takes command of it as an absolute monarch. Aesthetic mechanicians have often lamented the absolute lack of underlying unity and structure in Shakespeare, while the deeper glance could see the beautiful tree with leaves, blossoms, and fruit growing from one germinating seed; so it is that only through a very deep study of Beethoven's instrumental music is that conscious thoughtfulness of composition (Besonnenheit) disclosed which always accompanies true genius and is nourished by a study of art.

What instrumental work of Beethoven testifies to this to a higher degree than the immeasurably noble and profound Symphony in C minor? How this marvelous composition carries the hearer irresistibly with it in its ever-mounting climax into the spirit kingdom of the infinite! What could be simpler than the main motive of the first allegro composed of a mere rhythmic figure which, beginning in unison, does not even indicate the key to the listener. The character of anxious, restless longing which this portion carries with it only brings out more clearly the melodiousness of the second theme!—It appears as if the breast, burdened and oppressed by the premonition of tragedy, of threatening annihilation, in gasping tones was struggling with all its strength for air; but soon a friendly form draws near and lightens the gruesome night. (The lovely theme in G major which is first taken up by the horn in E flat Major.)[1] —How simple—let us repeat once more—is the theme which the master has made the basis of the whole work, but how marvelously all the subordinate themes and bridge passages relate themselves rhythmically to it, so that they continually serve to disclose more and more the character of the Allegro indicated by the leading motive. All the themes are short, nearly all consisting of only two or three measures, and besides that they are allotted with increasing variety first to the wind and then to the stringed instruments. One would think that something disjointed and confused would result from such elements; but, on the contrary, this very organization of the whole work as well as the constant reappearances of the motives and harmonic effects, following closely on one another, intensify to the highest degree that feeling of inex-

[1] G Major entrance of the Second Theme in the development section.—*Tr.*

pressible longing. Aside from the fact that the contrapuntal treatment testifies to a thorough study of the art, the connecting links, the constant allusions to the main theme, demonstrate how the great Master had conceived the whole and planned it with all its emotional forces in mind. Does not the lovely theme of the Andante con moto in A flat sound like a pure spirit voice which fills our souls with hope and comfort?—But here also that terrible phantom which alarmed and possessed our souls in the Allegro instantly steps forth to threaten us from the thunderclouds into which it had disappeared, and the friendly forms which surrounded us flee quickly before the lightning. What shall I say of the Minuet? Notice the originality of the modulations, the cadences on the dominant major chord which the bass takes up as the tonic of the continuing theme in minor—and the extension of the theme itself with the looping on of extra measures. Do you not feel again that restless, nameless longing, that premonition of the wonderful spirit-world in which the Master holds sway? But like dazzling sunlight the splendid theme of the last movement bursts forth in the exulting chorus of the full orchestra.—What wonderful contrapuntal interweavings bind the whole together. It is possible that it may all sound simply like an in-spired rhapsody to many, but surely the heart of every sensitive listener will be moved deeply and spiritually by a feeling which is none other than that nameless premonitory longing; and up to the last chord, yes, even in the moment after it is finished, he will not be able to detach himself from that wonderful imaginary world where he has been held captive by this tonal expression of sorrow and joy. In regard to the structure of the themes, their development and instrumentation, and the way they are related to one another, everything is worked out from a central point-of-view; but it is especially the inner relationship of the themes with one another which produces that unity which alone is able to hold the listener in one mood. This relationship is often quite obvious to the listener when he hears it in the combination of two themes or discovers in different themes a common bass, but a more subtle relation-ship, not demonstrated in this way, shows itself merely in the spiritual connection of one theme with another, and it is exactly this subtle relationship of the themes which dominates both allegros and the Minuet —and proclaims the self-conscious genius of the Master.—E. T. A. HOFF-MANN (1)

d. Symphony No. 6 in F, ("Pastoral"), Opus 68
I. Cheerful impressions awakened by arrival in the country
(Allegro ma non troppo); II. Scene by the brook (Andante
molto moto); III. Merry gathering of country folk (Allegro);
IV. Thunderstorm: tempest (Allegro); V. Shepherd's song;
glad and grateful feelings after the storm (Allegretto)

The hearers should be allowed to discover the situation.—All painting
in instrumental music, if pushed too far, is a failure.—*Sinfonia pastorella.*
Anyone who has an idea of country life can make out for himself
the intentions of the author without many titles.—People will not require
titles to recognize the general intention to be more a matter of feeling
than of painting in sounds.—Pastoral Symphony: No picture, but something in which the emotions are expressed which are aroused in men
by the pleasure of the country (or), in which some feelings of country
life are set forth.—BEETHOVEN.

I. Cheerful impressions awakened by arrival in the country: *Allegro
ma non troppo*, F major, 2/4.

This astonishing landscape seems as if it were the joint work of
Poussin and Michael Angelo. The composer of Fidelio and of the
Eroica wishes in this symphony to depict the tranquillity of the country
and the peaceful life of shepherds. The herdsmen begin to appear in
the fields, moving about with their usual nonchalant gait; their pipes
are heard afar and near. Ravishing phrases caress one's ear deliciously,
like perfumed morning breezes. Flocks of chattering birds fly overhead;
and now and then the atmosphere seems laden with vapors; heavy
clouds flit across the face of the sun, then suddenly disappear, and its
rays flood the fields and woods with torrents of dazzling splendor. These
are the images evoked in my mind by hearing this movement; and I
fancy that, in spite of the vagueness of instrumental expression, many
hearers will receive the same impressions.

The movement opens immediately with the exposition of the first
theme, *piano*, in the strings. The more cantabile phrase in the antithesis
of the theme assumes later an independent thematic importance. The
second theme is in C major, an arpeggio figure, which passes from
first violins to second violins, then to cellos, double basses, and woodwind
instruments. The development of this theme is a gradual *crescendo*.
The free fantasia is very long. A figure taken from the first theme is
repeated again and again over sustained harmonies, which are changed

only every twelve or sixteen measures. The third part is practically a repetition of the first, and the coda is short.

II. Scene by the brook: *Andante molto moto*, B flat major, 12/8.

Next is a movement devoted to contemplation. Beethoven, without doubt, created this admirable *adagio* [*sic*] while reclining on the grass, his eyes uplifted, ears intent, fascinated by the thousand varying hues of light and sound, looking at and listening at the same time to the scintillating ripple of the brook that breaks its waves over the pebbles of its shores. How delicious this music is!

The first theme is given to the first violins over a smoothly flowing accompaniment. The antithesis of the theme, as that of the first theme of the first movement, is more cantabile. The second theme, more sensuous in character, is in B flat major, and is announced by the strings. The remainder of the movement is very long and elaborate, and consists of embroidered developments of the thematic material already exposed. In the short coda "the nightingale (flute), quail (oboe), and cuckoo (clarinet) are heard."

III. Merry gathering of country folk: *Allegro*, F major, 3/4.

In this movement the poet leads us into the midst of a joyous reunion of peasants. We are aware that they dance and laugh, at first with moderation; the oboe plays a gay air, accompanied by the bassoon, which apparently can sound but two notes. Beethoven doubtless intended thus to evoke the picture of some good old German peasant, mounted on a cask, and playing a dilapidated old instrument, from which he can draw only two notes in the key of F, the dominant and the tonic. Every time the oboe strikes up its musettelike tune, fresh and gay as a young girl dressed in her Sunday clothes, the old bassoon comes in puffing his two notes; when the melodic phrase modulates, the bassoon is silent perforce, counting patiently his rests until the return of the original key permits him to came in with his imperturbable F, C, F. This effect, so charmingly grotesque, generally fails to be noticed by the public.

The dance becomes animated, noisy, furious. The rhythm changes; a melody of grosser character, in duple time, announces the arrival of the mountaineers with their heavy *sabots*. The section in triple time returns, still more lively. The dance becomes a medley, a rush; the women's hair begins to fall over their shoulders, for the mountaineers have brought with them a bibulous gaiety. There is clapping of hands, shouting; the peasants run, they rush madly . . . when a muttering of thunder in the distance causes a sudden fright in the midst of the dance. Surprise and consternation seize the dancers, and they seek safety in flight.

The third movement is practically the scherzo. The thesis of the theme begins in F major and ends in D minor; the antithesis is in D major throughout. This theme is developed brilliantly. The second theme, of a quaint character, F major, is played by the oboe over middle parts in waltz rhythm in the violins. "The bass to this is one of Beethoven's jokes. This second theme is supposed to suggest the playing of a small band of village musicians, in which the bassoon player can get only the notes F, C, and octave F out of his ramshackle old instrument; so he keeps silent wherever this series of three notes will not fit into the harmony. After being played through by the oboe, the theme is next taken up by the clarinet, and finally by the horn, the village bassoonist growing seemingly impatient in the matter of counting rests, and now playing his F, C, F, without stopping." The trio of the movement (*in tempo d'allegro*, F major, 2/4) is a strongly accentuated rustic dance tune, which is developed in *fortissimo* by the full orchestra. There is a return to the first theme of the scherzo, which is developed as before up to the point when the second theme should enter, and the tempo is accelerated to *presto*.

But the dance is interrupted by a thunderstorm (*Allegro*, F minor, 4/4) which is a piece of free tone painting:

IV. Thunderstorm: tempest: *Allegro*, F minor, 4/4.

I despair of being able to give an idea of this prodigious movement. It must be heard in order to appreciate the degree of truth and sublimity which descriptive music can attain in the hands of a man like Beethoven. Listen to those gusts of wind, laden with rain; those sepulchral groanings of the basses; those shrill whistles of the piccolo, which announce that a fearful tempest is about to burst. The hurricane approaches, swells; an immense chromatic streak, starting from the highest notes of the orchestra, goes burrowing down into its lowest depths, seizes the basses, carries them along, and ascends again, writhing like a whirlwind, which levels everything in its passage. Then the trombones burst forth; the thunder of the timpani redoubles its fury. It is no longer merely a wind and rainstorm: it is a frightful cataclysm, the universal deluge, the end of the world. Truly, this produces vertigo, and many persons listening to this storm do not know whether the emotion they experience is pleasure or pain.

V. Shepherd's song; glad and grateful feelings after the storm: *Allegretto*, F major, 6/8.

The symphony ends with a hymn of gratitude. Everything smiles. The shepherds reappear; they answer each other on the mountain, recalling their scattered flocks; the sky is serene; the torrents soon cease to flow; calmness returns, and with it the rustic songs, whose gentle melodies bring repose to the soul after the consternation produced by the magnif-icent horror of the previous picture.

There is a clarinet call over a double organ point. The call is answered by the horn over the same double organ point, with the addition of a third organ point. The horn repetition is followed by the first theme, given out by the strings against sustained harmonies in clarinets and bassoons. This theme, based on a figure from the opening clarinet and horn call, is given out three times. This exposition is elaborate. After the climax a subsidiary theme is developed by full orchestra. There is a short transition passage, which leads to an abbreviated repetition of the foregoing development of the first theme. The second theme enters, B flat major, in clarinets and bassoons. The rest of the movement is hardly anything more than a series of repetitions of what has gone before.

It may here be said that most program makers give five movements to this symphony. They make the thunderstorm an independent move-ment. Others divide the work into three movements, beginning the third with the "jolly gathering of countryfolk."

Beethoven did not attempt to reproduce the material, realistic im-pression of country sounds and noises, but only the spirit of the landscape.

Thus in the "Pastoral" Symphony, to suggest the rustic calm and the tranquillity of the soul in contact with Nature, he did not seek curious harmonic conglomerations, but a simple, restrained melody, which embraces only the interval of a sixth (from *fa* to *re*). This is enough to create in us the sentiment of repose—as much by its quasi-immobility as by the duration of this immobility. The exposition of this melody based on the interval of a sixth is repeated with different timbres, but musically the same, for fifty-two measures without interrup-tions. In an analogous manner Wagner portrayed the majestic monotony of the river in the introduction to "Rheingold." Thus far the landscape is uninhabited. The second musical idea introduces two human beings, man and woman, force and tenderness. This second musical thought is the thematic base of the whole work. In the scherzo the effect of sudden immobility produced by the bagpipe tune of the strolling musician (the oboe solo, followed by the horn), imposing itself on the noisy joy of the peasants, is due to the cause named above; here, with the exception of one note, the melody moves within the interval of a fifth.

The storm does not pretend to frighten the hearer. The insufficient kettledrums are enough to suggest the thunder, but in four movements of the five there is not a fragment of development in the minor mode. The key of F minor, reserved for the darkening of the landscape hitherto sunny and gay, produces a sinking of the heart and the distressing restlessness that accompany the approach of the tempest. Calm returns with the ambitus of the sixth, and then the shepherd's song leads to a burst of joyfulness. The two themes are the masculine and feminine elements exposed in the first movement.

According to M. d'Indy the *Andante* is the most admirable expression of true nature in musical literature. Only some passages of "Siegfried" and "Parsifal" are comparable. Conductors usually take this *Andante* at too slow a pace, and thus destroy the alert poetry of the section. The brook furnishes the basic movement, expressive melodies arise, and the feminine theme of the first *Allegro* reappears, alone, disquieted by the absence of its mate. Each section is completed by a pure and prayerlike melody. It is the artist who prays, who loves, who crowns the diverse divisions of his work by a species of Alleluia.

It has been said that several of the themes in this symphony were taken from Styrian and Carinthian folk songs.—PHILIP HALE (2)

The symphony is scored for two flutes, two oboes, two clarinets, two bassoons, two horns, two trumpets, timpani, and strings. Two trombones are added in the fourth and fifth movements and a piccolo in the fourth.

The popularity of the *Pastoral Symphony* is due to the widespread misunderstanding that exists between Man and nature. Consider the scene on the banks of the stream: a stream to which it appears the oxen come to drink, so at least the bassoons would have us suppose; to say nothing of the wooden nightingale and the Swiss cuckoo-clock, more representative of the artistry of M. de Vaucanson[1] than of genuine Nature. It is unnecessarily imitative and the interpretation is entirely arbitrary.

How much more profound an interpretation of the beauty of a landscape do we find in other passages in the great Master, because, instead of an exact imitation, there is an emotional interpretation of what is invisible in Nature. Can the mystery of a forest be expressed by measuring the height of the trees? Is it not rather its fathomless depths that stir the imagination?

In this symphony Beethoven inaugurates an epoch when Nature was seen only through the pages of books. This is proved by the storm, a part of this same symphony, where the terror of man and Nature is draped in the folds of the cloak of romanticism amid the rumblings of rather disarming thunder.

It would be absurd to imagine that I am wanting in respect for Beethoven; yet a musician of his genius may be deceived more completely than another. No man is bound to write nothing but masterpieces; and, if the *Pastoral Symphony* is so regarded, the expression

[1] Jacques de Vaucanson, 1709–1782, a mechanician of Grenoble; his automata *The Duck* and *The Flute Player* are famous.

must be weakened as a description of the other symphonies. That is all I mean.—CLAUDE DEBUSSY

Beethoven was not particularly polyphony-minded. His mind worked in other directions. Yet he, too, knew, or knew without knowing that he knew, the constructive value of the smallest, the most insignificant particle of a theme.

For that matter, what else should such a particle be but insignificant? Suppose you are admiring the exquisitely curved lines of a drawing. If you divide such a line into tiny particles, will not these fragments necessarily lose their prominence and grandeur? By the same token the most wonderful poem is composed of words which, individually, show no trace of uniqueness, but are bound to be used over and over again by the most prosaic mind in the most prosaic connection.

The first theme of Beethoven's Pastoral Symphony consists of four two-four bars.

Short as this theme is, it contains enough material to feed no less than two thirds (to be exact, 337 out of 512 bars) of the movement. This material consists of a number of motifs, each equivalent to a bar, or even a half bar, of the theme. In contrast to [the "motto" in the first movement of Brahms' Second Symphony and the little motifs Brahms created out of it], the diversities of the motifs here are not of rhythmical but of tonal nature, while the rhythm, the more essential motivic element, is retained. The composition shows that *nothing is wasted*; that nothing is too small to form a cell of the structure and to maintain the smooth, undulating flow.

The confinement of the motif material to the leading voice, and the resulting absence of a fine-spun, motivically interwoven texture, make this kind of composition appear simple almost to the point of primitivity, if contrasted to the subtle artistry of Mozart or Brahms.

Does that mean fault or virtue? It certainly means both.—ERNST TOCH

Opinions are much divided concerning the merits of the Pastoral Symphony of Beethoven, though very few venture to deny that it is much too long. The *Andante* alone is upwards of a quarter of an hour in performance, and, being a series of repetitions, might be subjected to abridgment without any violation of justice, either to the composer or his hearers.

(*The Harmonicon*, London, June 1823)—NICOLAS SLONIMSKY

e. Symphony No. 7 in A, Opus 92
I. Poco sostenuto, Vivace; II. Allegretto; III. Presto, Presto meno assai; IV. Finale: Allegro con brio

The first work on a grand scale in which the conflict is taken for granted and ignored, and the fruits of victory enjoyed, is the seventh symphony. In the first movement of this magnificent work we have the impression of a whole world stirring to exultant life. In the year that Beethoven finished the seventh symphony he wrote: "Almighty One, in the woods I am blessed. Happy everyone in the woods. Every tree speaks through thee. O God! What glory in the woodland! On the heights is peace—peace to serve Him." In these stammering words Beethoven expresses something of the joy that is expressed in this symphony. The great introduction to the first movement seems to convey the awakening and murmuring of the multitudinous life of an immense forest. Much more than in the Pastoral symphony do we feel here in the presence of Nature itself.[1] It is life, life in every form, not merely human life, of which the exultation is here expressed. The Allegretto has a similar universal quality. Its dreamy melancholy seems to refer to some universal and far-off sorrow. It passes, like the shadow of a cloud passing across the face of the sun. The exultant note rises higher until, in the last movement, we are in the region of pure ecstasy, a reckless, headlong ecstasy, a more than Bacchic festival of joy. In this symphony Beethoven seems to have emerged into a region where the spiritual struggle that had obsessed him for years is finally done with. Conflict and anguish, to say nothing of despair, are completely absent from this symphony. The hard road to victory, it would appear, has been trodden for the last time. And since this symphony is one of Beethoven's very greatest works we may have confidence that the experience it conveys is fundamental. It is probable that if Beethoven had now been able to marry and to enter fully into the warm human world, the music of his last years would have been very different from what it is. What is called his second-period music is essentially concerned, we believe, with the posing and solution of a problem, and it is very probable that at this time Beethoven felt that his problem was solved. The seventh symphony was finished in the year 1812, although the sketches for [it] precede that date by a few years. And at the very time that Beethoven was engaged in giving final artistic expression to the experience that inspires [this] work he was beginning to realize that the experience was not, for him, a permanent possession.—J. W. N. SULLIVAN

[1] I find in the *Revue Musicale* of April 1, 1927, a similar idea expressed by Romain Rolland: speaking of the sixth and seventh symphonies he says: "Dans l'un et l'autre cas, dans les deux Symphonies, une impression dominante de Nature—champs ou forêts, soleil ou nuit—et l'esprit, qui s'assimile à elle, qui épouse ces forces, qui de l'étoffe de ses vibrations, de ses rythmes, de ses lois, de sa substance, tresse un jeu souverain."

December 8, 1813, is named by Paul Bekker as the date of "a great concert which plays a part in world history," for then Beethoven's Seventh Symphony had its first performance. If the importance of the occasion is to be reckoned as the dazzling emergence of a masterpiece upon the world, then the statement may be questioned. We have plentiful evidence of the inadequacy of the orchestras with which Beethoven had to deal. Beethoven conducting this concert was so deaf that he could not know what the players were doing, and although there was no obvious slip at the concert, there was much trouble at rehearsals. The violinists once laid down their bows and refused to play a passage which they considered impossible. Beethoven persuaded them to take their parts home for study, and the next day all went well. A pitiful picture of Beethoven attempting to conduct is given by Spohr, who sat among the violins. So far as the bulk of the audience is concerned, they responded to the *Allegretto* of the symphony. The performance went very well according to the reports of all who were present, and Beethoven (whatever he may have expected—or been able to hear) was highly pleased with it. The newspaper reports were favorable, one stating that "the applause rose to the point of ecstasy."

A fairly detailed account of the whole proceeding can be pieced together from the surviving accounts of various musical dignitaries who were there, most of them playing in the orchestra. The affair was a "grand charity concert," from which the proceeds were to aid the "Austrians and Bavarians wounded at Hanau" in defense of their country against Napoleon (once revered by Beethoven). Mälzel proposed that Beethoven make for this occasion an orchestral version of the "Wellington's Victory" he had written for his newly invented mechanical player— the "pan-harmonicon," and Beethoven, who then still looked with favor upon Mälzel, consented. The hall of the University was secured and the date set for December 8.

The program was thus announced:

I. "An entirely new Symphony," by Beethoven (the Seventh, in A major).
II. Two Marches played by Mälzel's Mechanical Trumpeter, with full orchestral accompaniment—the one by Dussek, the other by Pleyel.
III. "Wellington's Victory."

All circumstances were favorable to the success of the concert. Beethoven being now accepted in Vienna as a very considerable personage, an "entirely new symphony" by him, and a piece on so topical a subject as "Wellington's Victory" must have had a strong attraction. The nature of the charitable auspices was also favorable.

Both new works were received with great enthusiasm. The performance of the Symphony, according to Spohr, was "quite masterly," and the *Allegretto* was encored. The open letter which the gratified Beethoven wrote to the *Wiener Zeitung* thanked his honored colleagues "for their zeal in contributing to so exalted a result."

The concert was repeated on Sunday, December 12, again with full attendance, the net receipts of the two performances amounting to 4,000 florins, which were duly turned over to the beneficiaries.

The Seventh Symphony had a third performance on the second of January, and on February 27, 1814, it was performed again, together with the Eighth Symphony. Performances elsewhere show a somewhat less hearty reception for the Seventh Symphony, although the *Allegretto* was usually immediately liked and was often encored. Friedrich Wieck, the father of Clara Schumann, was present at the first performance in Leipzig, and recollected that musicians, critics, connoisseurs and people quite ignorant of music, each and all were unanimously of the opinion that the Symphony—especially the first and last movements—could have been composed only in an unfortunate drunken condition (*"trunkenen Zustände"*).—JOHN N. BURK (2)

The main movement is preceded by a long and elaborate intro-duction (*Poco sostenuto*, A major, 4/4). Out of a tutti chord, the oboe prolongs a note and outlines a sort of descending fold of melody which is repeated by clarinets and horns. With an abrupt turn in the harmony, the strings start a series of rising staccato figures which swell to a *fortissimo* and join with the beginning melody. From this emerges a second theme in C major, first heard on woodwinds, against which violin trills stand out in gentle contrast. It is taken up on strings and topped by the piping of a repeated G in oboe and bassoon. Most of what preceded is now repeated, with the second melody in F major. The identical harmonic turn which introduced the rising staccato notes is used to introduce a repeated E, rather grotesquely accented on the first note of each group. Gradually all the interest of the piece becomes concentrated on that E as it is bandied back and forth between violins and woodwind, and from it arises the rhythm which is going to permeate the main movement. This starts (*Vivace*, A major, 6/8) with a *crescendo* on the rhythmic pattern and a sudden drop to *piano* as the flute states the alert first theme. The theme is repeated in a great *fortissimo* passage and developed up to the introduction of the second theme—a sort of fanfare in E major, first given to woodwinds. A fragment of the first theme is given somewhat of a workout which builds up the closing theme, triumphantly loud, but with sudden drops to *pianissimo* in the best Beethoven manner. Bee-thoven marks all of this 6/8 exposition for a repeat which it never receives in performance. It is rather too bad that this is so, because a repeat serves to fix the thematic material in the mind of the hearer, and lack of it alters the proportions of the movement as we may suppose the composer to have imagined them. The development is based principally on the first subject, whose rhythms it treats in a way which is somehow prophetic of the Valkyries' ride of that other composer who was born in the year our symphony received its first performance. The recapitulation brings back the first theme *fortissimo* and then, with a quick modulation, throws it to the oboe in the key of D. What follows is regular but, when the end of the recapitulation is reached, a sudden pause leads to another change of key and the reassertion of the initial rhythm in the bass. The bass keeps dropping lower and finally falls into a grinding and churning mechanism which undergoes a gradual *crescendo* while the upper parts again concentrate on a repeated E. A final recall of the subject brings the movement to a crashing end.

Allegretto, A minor, 2/4. It should be unnecesary to state that this music has no program and could not possibly benefit from one. The solemnity of such a "slow movement" needs no pictorial concomitant; it cannot even be thought of in too solemn terms, if we consider the composer's tempo marking. It is really a series of variations on a harmonic and rhythmic pattern, with episodic material to break up the extreme formalism of the variation technique. At the outset, after a chord of woodwinds and horns, the theme is presented four times, each time in a more complex way. It starts as a series of rhythmic chords in the lower strings. One of the subtlest things about this theme is the way it slips from major to minor, and thus creates an ambiguity of which Beethoven takes full advantage later. In its second statement, the theme picks up a melody in an inner voice. Both ideas are henceforth inseparable in the subsequent variations which rise to a loud statement over triplet figuration. The bleakness of the foregoing is mitigated by the gently flowing theme in A major which now appears, but even here the fundamental rhythm keeps pulsating in the bass. The second phrase of the section verges on sentimental romanticism, but it is finally called back to earth and the minor mode by a severe descending scale which leads in another variation, this time with a bouncing sixteenth-note counterpoint. It is this counterpoint which sets the mood for the following fugato passage. The latter contains some interesting polyphonic writing for strings and gradually involves the other instruments in a *fortissimo* variation. Again the key of A major returns, but only to give the first half of the episodic theme before another shift to minor and the last variation—extremely subtle and tenuous, starting high in flutes and ending in bare *pizzicati*. Finally, as if to frame the whole movement, the chord of the beginning brings it to an end.

Presto, F major, 3/4. This movement is a scherzo, but one expanded to dimensions sufficient to make it compatible with the other movements of the symphony. Usually a scherzo follows the pattern of the old minuet, that is to say, a main part consisting of two sections, both repeated, a trio built on the same plan, also repeated, and a return to the main part, without repeats. Beethoven follows this pattern as far as it goes, but amplifies it by repeating once again both trio and main part. Strictly speaking, it is this last repetition which constitutes the return of the main part, since here, except for the absence of repeats, it is given exactly as at first. In its middle occurrence it wears the same orchestral dress, but without the violent contrasts of *piano* and *forte* which characterize it at the other hearings. The trio is marked *Assai meno presto* and is in D major. The first phrase is given to clarinets, horns, and bassoons, while, until the final climax, the only strings are the violins, which hold an A with only an occasional wavering. When the third occurrence of the main part is over, Beethoven misleads the hearer into the somewhat startling belief that everything is going around for another repeat, but, after the first measures of the trio, the phrase turns to minor, and five sharp chords put an end to it.

Allegro con brio, A major, 2/4. There is something so terrifying about the display of force this movement puts on that it is not surprising that Beethoven's contemporaries believed it to have been composed in a drunken fury. The special rhythmic feature which runs through the movement is a shift of phrasing and accent which brings the stress on the second instead of the first beat. It is especially obvious in the whirlwind of the first subject. The latter extends through a brassily military continuation to end in a passage which elaborates the initial pattern of the theme. The first drop below a *fortissimo* announces a rather flip second theme in C sharp minor. In spite of its key, the theme has a good deal of snap to it, and the cross accents of the movement are very prominent. It works up to a loud and dizzying final theme, at the end of which come the repeat bars, usually disregarded as in the first movement. The idea of the first theme gets a workout in the development, with punctuation supplied by questioning and answering phrases like the bouncing of a huge ball. Soon the orchestra starts a painful upward climb by semitones, but, instead of bursting into the recapitulation, it softens down to present once more the first theme, now in the extremely remote key of B flat, and with the questioning interjections in double time. Only after that does a quick modulation bring in the regular recapitulation. As usual with Beethoven, the coda throws new light on the preceding material. The first subject phrase flashes up and down the various levels of the scale, while the basses steadily descend to arrive at a mechanism recalling that of the first movement, but even more impressive. In a rolling progress as irresistible as that of Juggernaut, it builds up to a climax that leaves one bewildered and torn between panic and exhilaration.—BATEMAN EDWARDS

The symphony is scored for two flutes, two oboes, two clarinets, two bassoons, two horns, two trumpets, timpani, strings.

The merits of Beethoven's Seventh Symphony we have before discussed, and we repeat, that . . . it is a composition in which the author has indulged a great deal of disagreeable eccentricity. Often as we now have heard it performed, we cannot yet discover any design in it, neither can we trace any connection in its parts. Altogether, it seems to have been intended as a kind of enigma—we had almost said a hoax. (*The Harmonicon*, London, July 1825)—NICOLAS SLONIMSKY

In the preceding symphonies, the traces of the third style of Beethoven are limited to a few wrong chords, superimposed intervals of a second, the failure to prepare and to resolve dissonances. In the Seventh Symphony, the phantasm mounts. Look, for instance, at the deplorable ending of the *Andante*. Look, and weep! Can one imagine F sharp and G sharp accompanied by a chord of A minor! Can one imagine a musician who has the sad courage to debase in this way his own masterpiece, to throw the purest part of his genius into the hideous claws of the chimera, as one throws a bone to a dog. It is in the last movement that the figure of the chimera is completed by adding melodic ugliness to harmonic ugliness. When I heard this flayed harmony, I experienced a shudder, and a line of La Fontaine came back to my memory: *On vous sangla le pauvre drille*—and they whipped the poor devil! (A. Oulibicheff, *Beethoven, ses critiques et ses glossateurs*, Paris, 1857) —NICOLAS SLONIMSKY

f. Symphony No. 8 in F, Opus 93
  I. Allegro vivace con brio; II. Allegretto scherzando; III. Tempo di menuetto; IV. Allegro vivace.

This symphony was composed at Linz in the summer of 1812. The autograph manuscript in the Royal Library at Berlin bears this inscription in Beethoven's handwriting: "Sinfonia—Lintz, im Monath October 1812." Glöggl's *Linzer Musikzeitung* made this announcement October 5: "We have had at last the long-wished-for pleasure to have for some days in our capital the Orpheus and the greatest musical poet of our time, Mr. L. van Beethoven; and, if Apollo is gracious to us, we shall also have the opportunity of wondering at his art.[1] The same periodical announced November 10: "The great tone-poet and tone-artist, Louis van Beethoven, has left our city without fulfilling our passionate wish of hearing him publicly in a concert."

Beethoven was in poor physical condition in 1812, and Staudenheim, his physician, advising him to try Bohemian baths, he went to Töplitz by way of Prague; to Carlsbad, where a note of the postilion's horn found its way among the sketches for the Eighth Symphony; to Franzensbrunn and again to Töplitz; and lastly to his brother Johann's home at Linz, where he remained until into November. His sojourn in Linz was not a pleasant one. Johann, a bachelor, lived in a house too large for his needs, and so he rented a part of it to a physician, who had a sister-in-law, Therese Obermeyer, a cheerful and well-proportioned woman, of an agreeable if not handsome face. Johann looked on her kindly, made her his housekeeper, and, according to the gossips of Linz, there was a closer relationship. Beethoven meddled with his brother's affairs, and, finding him obdurate, he visited the bishop and the police authorities and persuaded them to banish her from the town, to send her to Vienna if she should still be in Linz on a fixed day. Naturally, there was a wild scene between the brothers. Johann played the winning card: he married Therese on November 8. Ludwig, furious, went back to Vienna, and took pleasure afterward in referring to his sister-in-law in both his conversation and his letters as the "Queen of Night."

This same Johann said that the Eighth Symphony was completed from sketches made during walks to and from the Pöstlingberge, but Thayer considered him to be an untrustworthy witness.

The [Eighth Symphony was] probably played over for the first time at the Archduke Rudolph's in Vienna, April 20, 1813. Beethoven in the same month endeavored to produce [it] at a concert, but without success.

Beethoven described the Eighth in a letter to Salomon, of London, as "a little symphony in F," to distinguish it from its predecessor, the Seventh, which he called "a great symphony in A, one of my most excellent."

We know from his speeches noted down that Beethoven originally planned an elaborate introduction to this symphony.

It is often said that the second movement, the celebrated Allegretto scherzando, is based on the theme of "a three-voice circular canon, or round, 'Ta, ta, ta, lieber Mälzel,' sung in honor of the inventor of the metronome"[2] and many automata "at a farewell dinner given to Beethoven in July 1812, before his leaving Vienna for his summer trip into

1 See Glöggl's further recollections of this period in connection with the Three Equali for four Trombones, WoO 30.—Editor.
2 Johann Neopomuk Mälzel (1772–1838). See further discussion of him and his "mechanical instruments" in the discussion of the "Battle Symphony," Opus 91. —Editor.

the country." This story was first told by Schindler. Beethoven, who among intimate friends was customarily "gay, witty, satiric, 'unbuttoned,' as he called it," improvised at this parting meal a canon, which was sung immediately by those present. The Allegretto was founded on this canon, suggested by the metronome. Thayer examined this story with incredible patience ("Beethoven's Leben," Berlin, 1879, vol. iii. pp. 219-222), and he drew these conclusions: the machine that we now know as Mälzel's metronome was at first called a musical chronometer, and not till 1817 could the canon include the word "Metronom."

In one of the conversation books (1824) Beethoven says: "I, too, am in the second movement of the Eighth Symphony—ta, ta, ta, ta—the canon on Mälzel. It was a right jolly evening when we sang this canon. Mälzel was the bass. At that time I sang the soprano. I think it was toward the end of December, 1817." Thayer says: "That Mälzel's 'ta, ta, ta' suggested the Allegretto to Beethoven, and that by a parting meal the canon on this theme was sung, are doubtless true; but it is by no means sure that the canon preceded the symphony. . . . If the canon was written before the symphony, it was not improvised at this meal; if it was then improvised, it was only a repetition of the Allegretto theme in canon form." However this may be, the persistent ticking of a wind instrument in sixteenth notes is heard almost throughout the movement, of which Berlioz said: "It is one of those productions for which neither model nor pendant can be found. This sort of thing falls entire from heaven into the composer's brain. He writes it at a single dash, and we are amazed at hearing it."

There has been much discussion concerning the pace at which the third movement, marked Tempo di minuetto, should be taken. Wagner made some interesting remarks on this subject in his "On Conducting" (I use Mr. E. Dannreuther's translation): "I have, myself, only once been present at a rehearsal of one of Beethoven's symphonies, when Mendelssohn conducted. The rehearsal took place at Berlin, and the symphony was No. 8 (in F major). . . . This incomparably bright symphony was rendered in a remarkably smooth and genial manner. Mendelssohn himself once remarked to me, with regard to conducting, that he thought most harm was done by taking a tempo too slow, and that, on the contrary, he always recommended quick tempi, as being less detrimental. Really good execution, he thought, was at all times a rare thing, but shortcomings might be disguised if care was taken that they should not appear very prominent; and the best way to do this was to get over the ground quickly. . . . Beethoven, as is not uncommon with him, meant to write a true minuet in his F major Symphony. He places it between the two main Allegro movements, as a sort of complementary antithesis to an Allegro scherzando which precedes it; and, to remove any doubt as to his intention regarding the tempo, he designates it not as a minuetto,

but as Tempo di minuetto. This novel and unconventional characterization of the two middle movements of a symphony was almost entirely
overlooked. The Allegretto scherzando was taken to represent the usual
Andante, the Tempo di minuetto the familiar Scherzo; and, as the two
movements thus interpreted seemed rather paltry, and none of the usual
effects could be got out of them, our musicians came to regard the
entire symphony as a sort of accidental hors d'oeuvre of Beethoven's muse,
who, after the exertions of the A major Symphony, had chosen to take
things rather easily. Accordingly, after the Allegretto scherzando, the time
of which is invariably dragged somewhat, the Tempo di minuetto is
universally served up as a refreshing Ländler, which passes the ear
without leaving any distinct impression. Now the late Kapellmeister
Reissiger, of Dresden, once conducted this symphony there, and I happened to be present at the performance, together with Mendelssohn.
We talked about the dilemma just described and its proper solution,
concerning which I told Mendelssohn that I believed I had convinced
Reissiger, who had promised that he would take the tempo slower than
usual. Mendelssohn perfectly agreed with me. We listened. The third
movement began, and I was terrified on hearing precisely the old Ländler
tempo; but, before I could give way to my annoyance, Mendelssohn
smiled and pleasantly nodded his head, as if to say: 'Now it's all right!
Bravo!' So my terror changed to astonishment. . . . Mendelssohn's
indifference to this queer, artistic contretemps raised doubts in my mind
whether he saw any distinction and difference in the case at all. I fancied
myself standing before an abyss of superficiality, a veritable void."

At first little attention was paid to the Eighth Symphony. Hanslick
says, in "Aus dem Concertsaal," that the "Pastoral" Symphony was long
characterized as the one in F, as though the Eighth did not exist and
there could be no confusion between Nos. 6 and 8, for the former
alone was worthy of Beethoven. This was true even as late as 1850.
Beethoven himself had spoken of it as the "little" symphony, and so it is
sometimes characterized today.

Leipzig was the second city to know the Eighth Symphony, which
was played in the Gewandhaus, January 11, 1818.

The Philharmonic Society of London did not perform the work until
May 29, 1826, although it had the music as early as 1817.

In Paris the Eighth was the last of Beethoven's to be heard. The
Société des Concerts did not perform it until February 19, 1832. Fétis,
hearing the symphony, wrote that in certain places the symphony was
so unlike other compositions of Beethoven that it gave room for the
belief that it was "written under certain conditions which are unknown
to us, which alone could explain why Beethoven, after having composed
some of his great works, especially the "Eroica," left this broad, large
manner analogous to his mode of thought to put boundaries to the

sweep of his genius." At the same time Fétis found admirable things in the work "in spite of the scantiness of their proportions." But Berlioz saw with a clearer vision. "Naïveté, grace, gentle joy, even if they are the principal charms of childhood, do not exclude grandeur in the form of art which reproduces them. . . . This symphony, then, seems wholly worthy of those that preceded and followed, and it is the more remarkable because it is in nowise like unto them."—PHILIP HALE (2)

Allegro vivace e con brio, F major, 3/4. The terseness of the exultant first theme is balanced by the spacious extent of its continuation, and the unhampered progress of both is brought to an end by the bumpy rhythm and the awkward bassoon solo which introduce the second subject. This starts out gracefully in D major in the violins and, after a retard, modulates to C, in which key it is given by flute, oboe, and bassoon in three octaves over a *pizzicato* bass. As it continues, the second subject alternates a cheerful tutti shout with a softer answer by woodwinds over a graceful string counterpoint, and winds up with a rough and rhythmic teetering on two C's in octaves. This octave figure plays an important role in the following development, while the solo woodwinds count off above it on the opening notes of the movement. The mood changes to minor and there emerges a pattern, unbroken through thirty-six measures, of these opening notes against a heavily accented second beat. The recapitulation begins very loud with the melody in the bass and then takes up with the woodwinds. At the end the bassoon is again heard in the octave figure and the key is turned to D flat, while another persistent figure climbs up the strings. In a loud version of the first theme the cadence is reached. There is a pause, *pizzicato* strings softly bandy the chords about with the rest of the orchestra, and the end comes unexpectedly with an evanescent mention of the theme.

Allegretto scherzando, B flat major, 2/4. In July of 1812, as Beethoven was leaving Vienna to take a trip for his health to the baths of Bohemia, he composed a humorous canon in honor of his friend Maelzel, the inventor of the metronome, and had it sung at a farewell dinner. The canon furnished material for this movement of the symphony, and in the sixteenth-note cluckings of the reeds and horns one can, if one likes, hear the tickings of the inventor's machine. Against them the strings have a comfortable little staccato theme which becomes suddenly and shortly loud once in the course of its presentation and again toward the end as it insists on a cadence. A second, more robust section in F shows humorously impatient *fortissimo* flashes and, after stealthy tiptoeings, ends on a beautifully formal eighteenth-century cadence. A short new version of the first theme leads to the second, now presented as a canon in B flat. The coda gives a questioning phrase to reeds and horns with coy smirks from the violin, whereat the orchestra is moved to violent fury, but the whiplashings receive only the coy reply, and an impetuous final pronouncement ends the movement.—BATEMAN EDWARDS

In the Allegretto of Beethoven's Eighth Symphony, the subdominant appears in a most normal course of events, beginning with a recapitulation of a passage of six bars that has previously returned from the dominant to the home tonic (bars 35–40). To recapitulate these bars *on* the home tonic (not *in* it) is, of course, to assert the subdominant, and Beethoven continues to play humorously with this subdominant for six bars more. He then has three bars of self-repeating final cadence, with a crescendo in burlesque imitation of the already notoriously burlesque style of Rossinian opera. Some musicians feel quite strongly that this has not re-established his tonic, and that nothing short of what I have already called an enhanced dominant could restore the balance. I have not myself noticed that the end of this movement is thus left floating in the air, but those who feel it to be so are entitled to enjoy the sensation as a characteristic example of Beethoven's humor. Even our best modern writers on Beethoven seem not to appreciate the fact that humor is one of Beethoven's most highly developed characteristics. But it would be rash to accuse any writer of failing to describe Beethoven's humor, for what can be more fatal to a joke than to analyze it, especially if the analysis must be musical? I cannot help that. Beethoven without his humor is as inconceivable as a humorless Shakespeare. His tragic power would lose half its cogency if he were not the most drastic of realists and disillusionizers as to the relation between tragedy and comedy. —DONALD FRANCIS TOVEY (1)

Tempo di menuetto, F major, 3/4. Instead of a scherzo, a regular minuet, but not too formal, as the brusque introductory accompaniment figure shows. Not too formal, either, are the repetitions of small figures, the bantering way in which chords are tossed about from strings to winds, and the final horn call with kettledrum bass, where the woodwinds seem to miss their cue and come in wrong. The trio is mostly a duet for horns or for horn and clarinet, with a roving and self-important cello counterpoint.

Allegro vivace, F major, 2/2. This movement is a sonata form with a coda about as long as the rest of the piece. The first subject scurries softly along on the strings to end with an unexpected bump from a *ppp* C to a *fortissimo* C sharp, whereupon the whole orchestra takes over. Having arrived at the dominant of C, a similar rise from G to A flat brings in the graceful second subject in the latter key, but a modulation is effected to get it back to C. It is continued by a carefree and syncopated line which ends in a loud held chord. The development has some trouble getting started but finally settles into a rhythmic pattern which is carried

out for thirty-four consecutive measures. Having repeated the first subject
in A, flutes and strings pump away at an E in octaves which is echoed
by bassoon and kettledrums in a rise to F, and those notes continue
in the bass as the recapitulation starts. Arriving at the held chord, the
coda, like the development, takes a bit of priming to get under way,
but, when it does, a new countertheme accompanies the initial rhythm
and is developed brilliantly in contrary motion. The first subject is again
introduced as at the beginning of the recapitulation. It is here that the
chief use is made of the unexpected C sharp, which now becomes most
insistent and drives the subject into F sharp minor. Everything gets back
into place, however, and the second subject returns, to be repeated by
the basses. Some measures of crisp fooling follow, during one part of
which Beethoven sends a major third up and down a range of four
octaves, and then, lest there be any uncertainty about it, he devotes twenty-
three measures to establishing the final cadence.—BATEMAN EDWARDS

*The symphony was scored by Beethoven for two flutes, two oboes, two
clarinets, two bassoons, two horns, two trumpets, two kettledrums, and
strings.*

Perhaps the most drastic case of [purposeful surprise] is the C sharp
which bursts in so savagely upon the conspiratorial laughter of the first
theme of the Finale of Beethoven's Eighth Symphony (bar 17). This
violent note is a stranger to the audience, but seems no stranger to
the orchestra, who greet it with cheerful uproar. After the Finale has
gone through many adventures and the first theme has returned with the
apparent purpose of making itself comfortable in a quiet coda, this
strange note bursts in again as D flat, and insists upon being taken
seriously as a keynote under the title of D flat (♭VI). When doubt
is cast upon this claim, the note becomes very angry and insists on
being the dominant of an incredibly remote F sharp minor. From this
a return to the tonic is attained only through strong representation, which
perhaps, by a stretch of courtesy, we may call diplomatic.

This illustration of Beethoven's long-distance harmonic effects must
suffice. The refinements of detail in his harmonic style are infinite, and
much harder to describe than those of Bach; especially as they are for
the most part achieved on very familiar material. The searcher for color
effects will miss them, and the old-fashioned grammarians will either miss
them or mistake them for grammatical blunders. They are, for the most
part, the results of great compression of thought. When the simple but
active mind of the Irish peasant combines two unrelated ideas in one
expression, the offspring is known as a "bull." Great poets can overawe
us into taking mixed metaphors seriously. No one laughs at Shakespeare
for making Hamlet talk of "taking up arms against a sea of troubles," nor

at the wrathful Milton for describing the clergy as "blind mouths."—
DONALD FRANCIS TOVEY (1)

The question of the pictorial in music has been much discussed, but the study of its potential for the comic has, on the contrary, been left almost completely in the shade; however, it would seem to us that this study might be of some interest, if it only served to show once more what certain combinations of sounds can accomplish.

The comic intention is manifest but veiled, and therefore remains a little unclear. Thus, in the finale of the *Eighth Symphony*, so sparkling, so animated, so tender, with its middle phrase of a distant farewell, what can that singular A flat signify as it surges abruptly into the middle of the whirlwind and suddenly stops it? The totally strange appearance of this unusual note immediately convinces the listener musical enough to grasp the false relation it presents with that which surrounds it, that here is a humorous passage. But, truthfully speaking, these sallies risk remaining unexplained in instrumental music, and they are hardly detected by the majority of listeners. However, it is certain that there are in Beethoven's music certain deliberate anomalies which remain incomprehensible if one does not attach a humorous connotation to them, the sense of which inevitably goes beyond its purely musical significance. Far be it from us, however, to attribute to these whims more importance than they deserve.—PAUL DUKAS

Beethoven's Eighth Symphony depends wholly on its last movement for what applause it obtains; the rest is eccentric without being amusing, and laborious without effect.

(*The Harmonicon*, London, June 4, 1827)—NICOLAS SLONIMSKY

III. OVERTURES
a. Overtures in General

In the first place, the general compass and specific titles of the separate works[1] recall the "overtures" of previous masters, which had already thrived to a considerable length. What an unhappy name this "Overture" was, especially for tone-works suited for almost any other place than the opening of a dramatic representation, everyone must have already felt who saw himself obliged to keep on giving it to his music-pieces, particularly since Beethoven's great example. But this usage was not the only fetter on his freedom; a far deeper coercion lay within the form itself, the form he was employing. Whoever wishes to rightly

[1] The Liszt symphonic poems.—Editor.

account for the speciality of this form, must study the history of the Overture from its earliest origin; he will be astonished to find that it arose from nothing but a dance, which was played in the orchestra as introduction to a scenic piece; and he will be filled with marvel at what has come of it in course of time and through the inventive genius of great masters.

As you may remember, I once set up Gluck's Overture to Iphigenia in Aulis as a model, because the master, with surest feeling of the nature of the problem now before us, had here so admirably understood to open his drama with a play of moods and their opposites, in keeping with the Overture-form, and not with a development impossible in that form. That the great masters who came after him felt this to be a limitation, however, we may see distinctly by the overtures of Beethoven; the composer knew of what an infinitely richer portraiture his music was capable, he felt equal to carrying out the idea of Development; and nowhere do we find this more plainly evidenced, than in the great Overture to Leonora. But he who has eyes, may see precisely by this overture how detrimental to the master the maintenance of the traditional form was bound to be. For who, at all capable of understanding such a work, will not agree with me when I assert that the repetition of the first part, after the middle section, is a weakness which distorts the idea of the work almost past all understanding; and that the more, as everywhere else, and particularly in the coda, the master is obviously governed by nothing but the dramatic development? But whoso has brains and lack of prejudice enough to see this, will have to admit that the evil could only have been avoided by entirely giving up that repetition; an abandonment, however, which would have done away with the overture-form—i.e. the original, merely suggestive (*nur motivirte*), symphonic dance-form—and have constituted the departure-point for creating a new form.

What, now, would that new form be?—Of necessity a form dictated by the subject of portrayal and its logical development. And what would be this subject?—A poetic motive. So!—prepare to be shocked!—"Program-music."—RICHARD WAGNER (3)

b. Overture to Coriolanus, Opus 62

Coriolanus—a Roman patrician supposed to have been given this name on account of his capture of the Volscian town, Corioli—was by reason of his haughty defiance of the plebeians impeached and banished from the state. Having taken refuge with the Volscians, Coriolanus aided these enemies of the Roman government by leading their armies against his native race. The Romans were panic-stricken at the victorious progress of the exiled patrician; and when Coriolanus appeared with his army at the gates of Rome deputations were sent out to plead with him.

But there burned within the heart of the proud Roman fiercer fires than those fanned by the lust of conquest, or the stirring exultation of victory about to be achieved. Coriolanus had long brooded over the vengeance that he had determined should be his; and now vengeance was at his hand—the hated foes who had condemned him to ignominy and exile were about to be delivered into his keeping to do with as he would. The deputations were sent back, and Coriolanus prepared for his on-slaught on the city. But the Romans now played their last throw for bloodless victory. The noblest matrons of Rome, at their head the vener-able mother of Coriolanus, and his wife, Volumnia, with her two chil-dren, came to the tent of the warrior, and they entreated him for mercy. The humble pleading of the women, their tears, their grievous sorrow went to the heart of Coriolanus. Vengeance which had seemed so goodly a thing before was now a fruit of bitter taste.

The overture commences (*Allegro con brio*, C minor, 4/4) with a *fortissimo* unison on C occurring three times in all the strings, on each occasion being interrupted by an incisive chord in the full orchestra. The principal subject consists of the agitated figure then put forward by the strings, which is worked up to a climax of dramatic power. The second theme sets in, *piano*, in the expressive melody heard (in E flat) in the first violins.

The development is concerned with a working out of a little motive of two notes heard at the end of the second theme. Under this is a restless figuration in the cellos and violas.

The recapitulation of the principal subject is considerably modified, and is in the key of F minor. The second theme now appears in the first and second violins in C major. There is a coda, in which the material of the second subject is brought forward, and following this are to be heard the vigorous unison and the resounding chords which had been used at the opening of the work. The close of the coda has often been held to depict the death of Coriolanus. Note the continuous *diminuendo*, with the fragmentary gasps of the principal theme in the cellos, on each repetition in notes of longer duration.

The overture is scored for two flutes, two oboes, two clarinets, two bassoons, two horns, two trumpets, timpani, and strings.—FELIX BOROW-SKY

Since by an old custom, certainly not to be cast away, every perform-ance in the theater starts with music, every really significant play should have an overture that sets the mood as the character of the piece requires. A number of tragedies have already received overtures, and the genius of Beethoven has now provided Collin's *Coriolan* with a noble work of this kind—even though the reviewer must take note of the fact that it seems to him that Beethoven's purely Romantic genius is not quite on the best of terms with Collin's basically reflective poetry, and that the composer would only begin to grip the soul and fully arouse it for what follows if he should write overtures to the tragedies of Shakespeare and Calderon that express Romanticism in the highest sense. The sober, terrible earnestness of the composition under review, the terrifying chords from an unknown world of spirits, suggest more that is later fulfilled. One really believes that the world of spirits, fearfully announced by subterranean thunder, will be approached in the play, perhaps the armored shadow of Hamlet will cross the stage, or the fateful sisters drag Macbeth down to Orcus. More pathos and brilliance would perhaps have been in order in Collin's poetry. At the same time, apart from the expectations aroused, after all, in only a few hearers thoroughly acquainted with Beethoven's music, the composition is thoroughly well fitted to arouse the determinate ideas: a large tragic event is to be the content of the play about to be presented. Even without reading the program, no one could expect anything else; not a bourgeois tragedy, but explicitly a higher drama, one in which heroes appear and go down in defeat, can be imagined on the basis of this overture.

It consists of only a single movement, Allegro con brio, in 4/4 time, C minor; the first fourteen measures are so written that they sound like an Andante leading into the Allegro. This beginning irresistibly grips and binds the spirit present in the entire idea, but especially in the novel instrumentation. Despite the *ff*, the two first measures of the strings, striking low C, remain muffled and gloomy, shrilly cut into, in the third measure, by the F minor chord for the full orchestra, lasting a quarter note. Then a deathly silence; the strings begin again the same muffled terrible C; once again the shrill chord of the full orchestra; deathly silence once again; for the third time the C of the strings. This time the shrill chord and the ensuing silence are followed by two more chords which lead to the principal theme of the Allegro: everything makes expectancy tense, yes, the breast of the hearer tightens; it is the fearful, threatening murmur of the approaching storm.

The main theme of the Allegro has within it the character of an unease that cannot be stilled, a longing that cannot be satisfied, and for all that it is conceived in Beethoven's own characteristic spirit, it reminded the reviewer vividly of Cherubini; the psychical relationship of the two masters became quite clear to him. Even the further development of the overture is close to several overtures by Cherubini, especially in the instrumentation.

The transposition of this theme down a tone (B flat minor), right after a bar rest, is likewise unexpected and heightens the tension that comes upon one at the first measures. The theme goes to F minor, to C minor in the tutti which follows, and, after the main theme has been touched on in abbreviated form by the second violin and the cello, it goes over into the chord of the sixth on the dominant of the related major key, E flat, closing the first section of the overture.

Now the second main theme enters, accompanied by an undulating figure that recurs frequently in the entire movement, almost always in the cello. F minor, G minor, C minor are the keys most touched in the development of this second theme, down to the closing theme of the recapitulation in G minor, which is characterized by syncopated notes on the first violin, while cellos and violas execute a new agitated figure in eighth notes.

After the conclusion in the dominant, the figure just referred to, with the accompaniment of cello and viola, goes through G minor, F minor, A flat major, D flat major, etc., for thirty-four measures through the movement in F minor, in which the opening music of the overture is repeated. The movement goes into C major, and the second theme enters in C major with the same accompaniment as in the first part, but goes directly over into D minor, E minor and immediately thereafter back to C minor. This is followed by the same figure in syncopated notes with the accompaniment of the cello that first introduced the conclusion in G minor, but now is broken off dramatically after a series of dissonant C's in the oboes, horns, trumpets, and drums, which produces an eerie effect.

Once again before the conclusion, expectation is heightened by the muffled high G's in the horns, followed by the quite unexpected entry of the second main theme in C major. But this bright C major was a fleeting ray of sunshine through the black clouds: for after only four measures the sober minor key returns, and a theme in syncopated notes, resembling the figure mentioned several times, leads back to the beginning of the overture, which now appears differently orchestrated, however. The oboes, clarinets, bassoons, and trumpets hold the muffled C, which at first was only in the strings. Now there are short, interrupted phrases, bar rests, and finally the movement dies out with short references to the agitated main theme, which become broader and broader in their rhythm.

These last measures are scored for only the first violins, the solo bassoon, and the cellos and basses. The rest of the orchestra is silent, and these somber tones, this doleful tone of the bassoon, holding the fifth above the tonic, the diminuendo of the cello, the brief pizzicato of the double bass—everything is profoundly united to form the highest tragic effect, and to produce the tensest expectancy of what the rise of the mysterious curtain will reveal.

The reviewer tried to give a clear idea of the inner structure of the masterpiece, and it will be seen that its artistic structure is put together out of the most simple elements. Without contrapuntal turns and inversions, it is chiefly the artistic and rapid modulation that gives the same themes novelty when they recur and powerfully entrain the hearer. If a number of different themes had been piled up one on the other, then, in view of the unceasing modulation, ever hastening from one key to another, the composition would have become a rhapsody without substance or inner connection, but there are only two main themes; even the connecting middle themes, the powerful tutti, remain the same, and even the form of modulation remains unchanged, and so everything emerges clear and evident for the hearer, on whom the theme impresses itself involuntarily.—E. T. A. HOFFMANN (2) (TR. BY THOMAS K. SCHERMAN)

c. The Three Leonora Overtures and the Fidelio Overture
(a) Overture Leonora No. 1, Opus 138
Andante con moto; Allegro con brio; Adagio ma non troppo; Tempo 1

Leonora No. 1 represents an interesting middle stage in Beethoven's treatment of the Fidelio problem. It also shows amusing signs of the irritation which the whole business of the opera had caused him in 1805 and 1806. When performers were careless in any respect, Beethoven was apt to give them a severe lesson by writing something calculated to betray their weaknesses. The singer of the part of the villain Pizzaro was conceited, so Beethoven asked him if he could sing [a particular] passage at sight. Of course it seemed perfectly easy; but when Pizzaro found that he had to sing it against [another] figure in the whole orchestra[1]— then the worm *did* begin to squirm!

The orchestration of Leonora No. 1 is full of similar disciplinary measures, though none quite so atrocious. For the rest, it is an admirable opera overture, with a broad and quiet introduction containing several distinct ideas: an energetic and terse allegro—with a second group expressive of anxiety and suspense—and with an extensive meditation on Florestan's aria in the dungeon, to replace the development of the overture and to foreshadow the central situation in the opera, [and a recapitulation of the allegro section].—DONALD FRANCIS TOVEY (5)

The score calls for two flutes, two oboes, two clarinets, two bassoons, four horns, two trumpets, timpani, and strings.

(b) Overture Leonora No. 2
Adagio; Allegro; Adagio; Presto

The main movement of the overture is preceded by a lengthy introduction (Adagio, C major, 3/4). After nine measures of this the tenth ushers in the opening phrase of the air "In des Lebens Frühlingstagen"

---

[1] One in which there was a clash of a minor second or major seventh on each strong beat.—Editor.

sung by Florestan in the second act of the opera, here played by clarinets, bassoons, and two horns.

The *Allegro* (C major, 2/2) opens with the principal subject announced *pianissimo* by the cellos, a sustained C being held by the horns, and the same note muttered by the violas. A gradual *crescendo* brings a climax with this same subject *fortissimo* in the full orchestra. The second theme appears in E major in the cellos, an arpeggio figure sounding above it in the first violins. This theme is based on Florestan's air previously heard in the introduction. The development, mainly based on the material of the principal theme, brings in at the close a unison passage in all the strings which leads into a chord of E flat, upon which a trumpet call is heard as from afar. In the opera this call announces the arrival at the prison of the Minister of Justice, Don Fernando, who arrives just in time to prevent the murder of Florestan by his jailer, Don Pizarro. There follows a reminiscence of the principal subject of the movement, and the trumpet call is heard once more. After fourteen measures of modulation Florestan's air appears once again, *Adagio*, in the woodwinds and in C major. Note here the important part for the drum. The violins then bring forward the *Allegro* tempo again in a passage beginning *pianissimo*, but growing in power as the other strings and the woodwind join in, and finally to culminate in a great climax, upon which (*Presto*) the material of the principal subject is heard for the last time in the form of a coda.—FELIX BOROWSKY

The score calls for two flutes, two oboes, two clarinets, two bassoons, four horns, two trumpets, two trombones, timpani, and strings.

(c) Overture *Leonora No. 3*
Adagio; Allegro; Presto

The overture begins with a slow introduction (*Adagio*, C major, 3/4) which opens with a *fortissimo* G in the full orchestra (without trombones, however); this G, struck short by the strings, is sustained and diminished by the woodwind until the strings take it up again and, together with the flute, clarinets, and bassoon, slowly play down the scale of C major in octaves, from G to G, ending on F sharp. This F sharp is thrice swelled and diminished by the strings, while the bassoons come in with soft ascending sighs in thirds, establishing the unrelated tonality of B minor. A measure of full harmony in the strings modulates by deceptive cadence to A flat major, in which key the clarinets and bassoons now sing the opening phrases of Florestan's air, "In des Lebens Frühlingstagen," in the second act of the opera, against an accompaniment in the strings and sustained E flats in the alto and tenor trombones (used there like bass trumpets). Then follow weird, mysterious harmonies in the strings, followed by lighter imitations on a triplet figure between the flute and first violins, while the bassoons and basses come in ever and anon with scraps from the Florestan theme. A short climax leads to a tremendous outburst of the full orchestra on the chord of A flat major; a highly dramatic passage, now tender, now angry chords, now fragments of pathetic melody, interspersed with contrapuntal reminiscences of the triplet figure, leads over to the main body of the overture.

This movement (*Allegro*, C major, 2/2), opens *pianissimo* with the first theme in the first violins and cellos in octaves, against a sustained tremolo in the violas, and nervous rhythmic pulsations in the double basses; a *crescendo* on the initial figure of the theme, by fuller and fuller orchestra, leads to a raging *fortissimo* in which the theme now appears in its entirety, and is developed at some length with the utmost energy. Just before this development comes to an end, there is a sudden change to B minor (like the one in the introduction), and this section of the first part of the movement ends in this key. The beautiful second theme is introduced in the horns, then passes to the first violins and flute, against agitated triplet arpeggios in the second violins and violas; it begins in E major, then passes by a beautiful and sudden modulation to F major, then through G minor, A minor, and B major back to E major again, when a subsidiary passage sets in, in which figures from the first theme are worked up to a climax, ending the first part of the movement.

The free fantasia is shorter and far simpler than the original one (in the No. 2), and consists for the most part of fierce outbursts of the full orchestra, alternating with repetitions of a melodic phrase already heard in the slow introduction; toward the end it becomes, however, more elaborate and contrapuntal, ending with a rushing climax which leads to the key of B flat major. Here comes a dramatic episode: the trumpet call and part of the song of thanksgiving from the prison scene in the Second Act of the opera; some passage work on a figure from the song of thanksgiving leads over to the third part of the movement.

The third part begins *piano* with the first theme in the dominant (G major) as a flute solo; then follows a *crescendo* passage, leading to a return to the tonic, in which key the theme is repeated *fortissimo* by the full orchestra, and developed somewhat more concisely than in the first part, the section now ending in the dominant of the principal key. The second theme now comes in the tonic (C major), and is followed by developments in passage work on figures from the first theme, as in the first part of the movement. But now the second theme returns once more, and one of its figures is made the subject of some rather recitativelike developments, which lead to the coda.

The coda (*Presto*) begins with some rushing scale passages in the first violins, which are soon joined by the second violins, then by the violas, and at last by the basses, leading to a *fortissimo* outburst of the whole orchestra on the first theme, which is now worked up in a tremendous climax to a final apotheosis.—WILLIAM FOSTER APTHORP

This overture is scored for two flutes, two oboes, two clarinets, two bassoons, four horns, two trumpets, three trombones, one pair of kettle-drums, and the usual strings.

(d) Overtures *Leonora No. 2* and *Leonora No. 3*: The Operatic Prelude and the Perfect Tone Poem

Let us compare the two great *Leonora* overtures on this basis, that both are inspired by a theme which Beethoven rightly considered sub-lime, and that they are not related as a sketch and a finished product, but that the earlier is definitely a theatrical prelude, while the later is, though Beethoven did not at first realize the fact, an ideal piece of instrumental music. Otherwise we shall get into a hopeless tangle if we regard the alterations in *Leonora No. 3* as of the nature of criticisms of *No. 2*.

Introduction. The first alteration is in the first bars, which in the earlier version begin with what Grove, in his Irish vein, called a "false start." That is to say, [the falling third (G, F, E)] is given separately in *No. 2* before being embodied in the long descending scale. But the listener who has never heard any of the *Leonora* overtures before must be gifted with a spirit of prophecy if he takes that very emphatic opening of *No. 2* for a "false start." When Beethoven wrote *No. 2*, he must have meant [the falling third] as a definite figure and the long scale as a development of it. And when we inquire into the meaning of [it], we find that it foreshadows Florestan's aria, which, after a mysterious modulation to the distant key of B minor, enters in A flat, the key in which it is to appear in the opera when Florestan sings memories of his wife and his "fight for truth" that brought him to die in chains and darkness.

The two overtures differ in the details of this melody; and they also differ from not less than three other different versions which Beethoven made for Florestan's aria.

The omission of the first three notes of *Leonora No. 2* of course obliterates the reference to [the falling third], and is highly significant as showing how little Beethoven relies on thematic connections as a means of construction.

The continuation of Florestan's theme is a wonderful series of remote modulations on [this falling third]. The first six bars are in *No. 3* com-pressed from the vast but regular eight bars of the earlier version. The next five bars, where [the same falling third] appears in the bassoons and basses, with light triplets in dialogue between violins and flute, are compressed from ten bars of a much more elaborate and exciting passage in No. 2, leading in both cases to a tremendous crash of the full orchestra on the chord of A flat, while the violins rush up and down in gigantic scales. In the earlier version this crash is repeated (with a change of harmony) after a bar's silence, and in this slow time such a silence is surprisingly long. Beethoven then follows the second crash by fortissimo short chords, each at a bar's distance. But in *Leonora No. 3* he does not wish his introduction to be so gigantic or even so impressive. He approves of his earlier material, but prefers to state it in a less startling way. It is enough for him that the new version should cover the same ground as the old in key and phrase, without indulging in effects that leave no room for growth to unexpected climaxes later on. So he has only one great crash in A flat, and fills up the gaps between the short fortissimo chords by [eighth notes] on the woodwind.

Then follows a passage on the dominant of C as a preparation for the allegro. In *No. 3* it is five bars long, and is founded on a phrase, [a series of yearning sighs], that forms the staple of the earlier part of the development in the allegro. The corresponding passage in *Leonora No. 2* was fourteen bars long, and, though closely resembling this in character and outline, was not sufficiently definite to be made the subject of allusions later on. Lastly, Beethoven alters into something much more normal the amazingly impressive notes which in *No. 2* led to the allegro with dark mysterious coloring.

Altogether his revision of his introduction is not pleasing to that habit of mind which studies works of art from one fine point to the next, and neglects to consider them as wholes.

Allegro. The opening of the allegro, up to the end of the second subject, is substantially the same in both versions, except that Beethoven skips four bars wherever he can. In the *crescendo* that continues the theme, Beethoven leaves out four bars at the beginning, in order to put in a fortissimo delay of four bars just where we expect the climax. Then, as the full orchestra takes up the theme, Beethoven takes the opportunity of keeping up the fortissimo more continuously in *No. 3* than in *No. 2.* [The passage in eighth notes starting with the upward leap of the octave C's], which in *No. 2* interrupts the tutti by its appearance *piano* on [the cellos], is in *No. 3* given by the full orchestra. In the passage that follows in *No. 3* he allows *pianos* and *fortes* to alternate rapidly, instead of the fortissimo of *No. 2.* And it is important to note that he uses triplet tremolo [eighth notes] in the first version throughout his tuttis, thereby showing that he was thinking of a slower tempo than that which is obviously right in *Leonora No. 3.* This difference of tempo is of the utmost importance in performance; and throughout *Leonora No. 2* we need to remember that Beethoven knew nothing about *No. 3* until he came to write it.

The passage leading to E major for the second subject is much shortened, and much louder and less mysterious, in the later than in the earlier version; and the second subject itself is rescored beyond recognition by the eye, though to the ear it is much the same in both overtures. It begins with a transformation of Florestan's aria, with wonderful remote modulations, and though the scoring of No. 3 is much easier and simpler than in No. 2, the later version will be seen to divide the melody between instruments on different planes. The sequences and subsidiary themes that follow grow at once to a fortissimo in the earlier version, but in No. 3 they are given intensely, quietly, and mysteriously, only at the last moment coming to a fortissimo as they approach the great syncopated scale-theme, suggested, no doubt, by [the same falling third which sparked the introduction as well as the allusion to Florestan's aria. An examination of the passage in both overtures shows how the wood instruments in No. 3 are following the syncopated theme on the beat, a feature which is not found in No. 2. Moreover, No. 3 disposes of the theme in eight formal bars, whereas No. 2 continues discursively for seventeen. No. 3 ends its exposition with a little cadence theme of two bars in which the horns are answered by the full orchestra, and this is followed by a descending sequence for the violins alone, which leads quietly without a break into the development, the change to the minor mode being one of the well-known romantic moments in No. 3. All this is very different from No. 2, which has substantially the same two-bar cadence theme in quite different scoring, but continues in a triumphant forte, ending in a sustained note followed by a remote modulation, that marks off the development from the exposition by a typical *coup de théâtre*.

At this point *Leonora No. 3* takes leave of *Leonora No. 2*, and has no more in common with it (except the idea of the trumpet-call behind the scene) till we come to the coda. We may still, however, find it profitable to contrast the two versions, as the differences are as unexpected as ever. The mind that lives indolently on fine passages and special effects will find even more to regret here than in the revision of the introduction. The development of *Leonora No. 2* begins, as we have said, by a *coup de théâtre* which plunges us into F major. From this point Florestan's aria is carried on in rising sequences alternating with plaintive dialogues on [the motive derived from the third and fourth measures of the allegro] until the key of D major is reached. Here the whole first theme, as at the opening of the allegro, bursts out in the cellos, leading to G major. (This use of the dominant in the course of the development has a very happy effect; how happy Beethoven himself did not realize until at quite a different point in No. 3 he raised it to a sublime level.) At the present stage (in No. 2) the cellos continue with [the Florestan motive], which is taken up by the woodwind; and now follows a series of mysterious and remote modulations, mostly pianissimo, with an intensely characteristic episodic figure in the bass and woodwind, and a sustained level of lofty inspiration that entitles it to a place among Beethoven's grandest conceptions.

In *Leonora No. 3* Beethoven, with a self-denial almost unparalleled in art, writes as if all this had never existed. He founds all the earlier part of the development on a very large and simple sequence of great orchestral crashes of single chords sustained for four bars, alternating with quiet plaintive eight-bar phrases, founded on [the significant yearning motive] of the introduction, combined with [the first two measures] of the first subject.

Five long steps of this process lead, with a short crescendo, to a stormy tutti in which [the syncopated] figure of the main theme is imitated between violins and basses in rising sequence. In twenty bars this leads, with a rush of ascending scales, to a pause on B flat; and a trumpet-call is heard behind the stage. In *Leonora No. 2* the storm breaks out quite suddenly after a much longer and almost entirely pianissimo development, and it is worked up for forty-four bars before closing with the trumpet-call, which is more florid and in the key of E flat; a not very remote key, and less startling than B flat, which is of all possible keys the most opposed to C major.

We are now about to learn Beethoven's motives for his stern rejection of all the finest features of *Leonora No. 2*. The young author who was advised to strike out all his finest passages would hardly have had that advice given him if they had been as fine as those Beethoven rejected. Beethoven's motives are not those that prompted that advice; he has struck out his finest passages because he needs room to develop something finer. The fact is that *Leonora No. 2* is too gigantic up to the present point to be worked out within the reasonable limits of an orchestral piece in classical style at all. After the trumpet-call Beethoven makes no attempt to treat the rest of it on the same scale, but simply brings in Florestan's aria in C major in its original form (*adagio*, 3/4), and, without attempting any such thing as a recapitulation of the first and second subjects of the allegro, goes straight on to a coda, which we will compare in due course with its vastly larger version in *Leonora No. 3*. Continuing now with *No. 3*, we have, in the surprising key of B flat, the trumpet-call of the watchman on the tower, warning the scoundrel Pizarro that the Minister has arrived to investigate his unlawful detention of his own private enemies in the state prison of which he is governor; and that therefore it is too late for him to put Florestan and his heroic wife out of the way. The flutes and clarinets sing the melody which accompanies Florestan's and Leonora's breathless exclamation: "Ach! du bist gerettet! Grosser Gott!" (There is no trace of this passage in *No. 2,* though the material for it was already present in the opera.)

The trumpet-call is given again (a little louder, according to the direction in the opera); and the song of thanks re-enters in the remote key of G flat, leading very slowly and quietly to G major. We are now beginning to learn a lesson in proportion. Beethoven has, by his compressions and alterations, gained a hundred bars, or nearly a third of the bulk up to the trumpet-call. *Leonora No. 3* reaches that point in 236 bars as against the 335 of *Leonora No. 2.* He has thus left room to grow; and so he continues his development at leisure, with a sunshiny passage in which the flute and bassoon give in G major the substance of the tutti that followed the first subject. This is the sublime and unexpected use of the dominant to which I referred in connection with the development of *Leonora No. 2.* Suddenly all is still, except for the strings climbing upwards with [the syncopated figure based on the opening bars of the main theme of the allegro]. Then there is a perfectly unadorned rising slow chromatic scale in octaves, leading with immense deliberation to the above-mentioned tutti, *fortissimo* in the tonic as at first. This does duty for the recapitulation of the first subject and leads at once to the second, which is given in full, with no alteration except the necessary transposition to the tonic. The syncopated scale theme, [which served as a closing group in the exposition, now] leads straight to the coda, which begins with Florestan's aria once more, as in the second subject. This corresponds roughly with the adagio that followed the trumpet-call in *Leonora No. 2;* but the gain in not changing the tempo is immense, and the passage is much expanded so as to keep us long in suspense.

Again we may note that the alteration obliterates the original connection between the last notes of the Florestan figure and the sequence of scales with which the peroration begins. The idea in *No. 2* is to turn the last notes of the theme into a staccato scale passage, capable of making an effective short crescendo in the original allegro tempo, so as to lead quickly to a brilliant final presto. The idea in *No. 3* is that of a whirlwind of sound, presto from the beginning, twice as long as the earlier passage, and relying upon its intrinsically exciting quality of sound in a way which makes any question of its derivation merely pedantic. The logic of the excitement is rather to be sought in the enormous breadth of the coda to which it leads. In *No. 2* the first theme bursts out presto in a diminution. This is to say, that besides being presto, it is also rhythmically twice as fast, with [eighth notes instead of quarters]. In *No. 3* there is no doubt that this would not do, though after the first two bars the framework is for some time the same in both overtures, the scoring being brighter and less bustling in detail in *No. 3.* Soon we come to the syncopated scale theme. *No. 3* first gives it for eight bars pianissimo. instead of being part of an unvaried fortissimo as in the early version. It gains still greater breadth in *No. 3* from the fact that it is now for the first time prolonged, whereas in *No. 2* it was already as long when it first occurred at the end of the second subject.

The tremendous passage that follows in *No. 3*, leading through another and even more deliberate slow chromatic scale to a really terrific climax on a chord of the *minor* ninth, is entirely new and makes the rejected grandeurs of *No. 2* fade into insignificance. This is the very point at which the coda of *No. 2* ceases to aim higher than an interesting theatrical finish. *No. 3*, the grandest overture ever written, then returns to the joyful reiteration of the figure of its main theme, and ends in the utmost height of triumph.—DONALD FRANCIS TOVEY (5)

(e) Overture to *Fidelio*

Of all the new parts of *Fidelio* none deserves greater reverence than its overture. The mere act of renouncing that mightiest of all overtures, *Leonora No. 3*, is enough to inspire awe. Beethoven was obviously right; *Leonora No. 3*, even in its earlier version (*Leonora No. 2*), referred entirely to the climax of the story in the last act, and was utterly destructive to the effect of the first act. The only chance for the first act of the opera lies in its conveying the impression of a harmless human love-tangle proceeding between certain good-natured young people connected with the jailer of a fortress governed by the villain. Grim forces are thus manifest in the surroundings, together with a growing sense of mystery about one of the persons in the love-tangle—Fidelio, the disguised wife of the unnamed prisoner, who is rescued by her heroism, when she has helped to dig his grave in the dungeon where he has lain in darkness for two years. A music that reveals Leonora's full heroic stature (like the overture *Leonora No. 3*) simply annihilates the first act. In the *Fidelio* overture Beethoven achieves what the first act requires. A formidable power, neither good nor bad except as it is directed, pervades the whole movement, and in the introduction alternates with a quiet pleading utterance—[issued by two horns]—which is soon lost in the darkness of Florestan's dungeon, until, after the drums have entered with slow footsteps, it emerges and leads into the active daylight of the allegro.

This is worked out in sonata form with a terseness and boldness which is more akin to Beethoven's "third period" than is commonly realized. The "second subject" is in the dominant, as usual, and contains several short new themes, of which the first[1] [should be particularly noted] in order that the listener may more readily note a remarkable feature of form in this overture which occurs in the recapitulation.

The development is short and quiet, the drums bringing back the

---

[1] Commencing at measure 82.—Editor.

main theme dramatically. In the recapitulation an unexpected turn of harmony brings the "second subject" into the dark remote key of C major, in which the trumpets, hitherto confined to repeating a single note on the only chords which admitted it, come into their own and dominate mightily. Then at last, with a return to the key of E, the trombones blaze out as the full orchestra breaks into [the opening four-bar assertion of power]. The ensuing adagio passage is adorned with a graceful new triplet figure and soon bursts into a brilliant final presto.

Throughout the overture the scoring is of Beethoven's most subtle and, at the same time, powerful order; and in its form great issues, dramatic and musical, often hang upon a single bar.—DONALD FRANCIS TOVEY (5)

The score calls for two flutes, two oboes, two clarinets, two bassoons, four horns, two trumpets, two trombones, timpani, and strings.

If we attempt to answer a question that hitherto has always been passed over or treated cursorily (i.e., why Beethoven really wrote his fourth overture to *Fidelio*), it will be necessary first of all to visualize the situation that gave rise to this composition.

The first revision of *Fidelio* was due to stress of outward circumstances. The fiasco of the first performance, which was followed by only two more, together with the urgings of trustworthy advisers who saw in the character and disposition of the work itself one reason for its failure, induced Beethoven to subject his score to a thorough revision. That he undertook "this operation" (as Jahn alleges in the preface of his piano reduction of the second version) against "his own conviction and inclinations" is not altogether correct. According to Stephen von Breuning, who made the necessary revisions in the text with Beethoven's concurrence, "Beethoven himself observed a few imperfections in the treatment of the text at the first performances." And the revision of the score, for which Beethoven took his time—Wilhelm Altmann expressly calls attention to this fact in his preface to the Eulenberg *Fidelio*— is something quite different from the concessions wrested from him at the famous December conference at Prince Lichnowsky's in 1805, which ended in his deleting several numbers in their entirety.

The situation was entirely different with the second revision (third version) in 1814. This time it was Beethoven himself who found a new revision necessary for the suggested revival of his work and who, when his permission for the performance was requested, made this expressly contingent on numerous changes being made beforehand.

A comparison of the final *Fidelio* with the first or second version of *Leonora* shows us that this last revision, which was carried out with the highest degree of artistic wisdom, was inspired by the composer's own independent conviction. One follows this revision from number to number with the greatest admiration, noting how, by sacrificing many ideas of value in the earlier versions, it aimed at heightening the theatrical effect and enhancing the musical impressiveness at the same time, and how apparently insignificant retouchings were also designed to intensify the expression, to bring out the important points. From the infinitely loving and infinitely laborious work—"the opera will win me the martyr's crown"—arose the new overture.

A dispassionate appraisal of the actual circumstances of the case in itself refutes an assumption that Beethoven's decision to provide a new overture for the 1814 *Fidelio* was motivated in any way by outward circumstances. What really impelled him to write the E major overture was a purely artistic consideration, which we discover the moment we open the original version of the opera. There we find as the opening number Marzelline's air while the duet between Marzelline and Jacquino holds second place. The position of the two numbers was not reversed until the revised version of 1814, which resulted in the present order. But this rearrangement, a far from incisive measure at the first glance, was for Beethoven a compelling reason for making changes in the overture as well. For the A major duet with the initial motif A-C sharp-E-F sharp would not have been compatible with the C major of the hitherto existing overtures.

If Wilhelm Altmann, in his preface to the Eulenberg *Fidelio* score, asserts that "the new E major overture . . . agrees in tonality with the A major duet, which now opens the opera while the former C major overture was followed by Marzelline's C minor air," we go even further and conclude that the collision of tonalities, which would have arisen between the new opening number of the opera and the original overture, was the primary reason and at the same time the artistic compulsion for composing a new overture. Furthermore, this assumption finds incontestable confirmation in one of Beethoven's sketches of the 1814 version of *Fidelio* cited by Nottebohm. Here, in company with sketches of the new conclusion of Florestan's air (*Ich seh' wie ein Engel*), there is a sketch of a projected E major revision of *Leonora No.* 1 (Opus 138): first of all, the main theme of the *allegro* transposed to E major with transition to the *Seitensatz* and a new progression[1] (also referring to a previous motif of the *Hauptsatz*). Then the theme of the introductory *andante con moto* transposed to E major. Variants and accompanying memoranda show that he intended to rework the material. The project of revising the older composition was abandoned, but the idea of a new key for the overture, which manifested itself in this form for the first time, was retained and led to the conception of the E major overture as we know it.

[1] A few bars are reminiscent of the *Fidelio* overture, another passage of an idea of the great *Leonora* overtures.

In writing to Treitschke of the progress of the work on *Fidelio*, he spoke of the new overture as "the easiest part of it since I can do it new right from the start."

We can be sure that he had already definitely rejected *Leonora No. 2* or *Leonora No. 3* before he drew the logical conclusions from the rearrangement of the first numbers of the opera. For if he had really wished to retain one of the great *Leonora* overtures as introduction for his opera, the problem of the key relationship between the overture and the first number would have been solved, not from the side of the overture, but from the opposite direction—in case the problem had ever actually arisen; that is, should he really have been willing in these circumstances to alter the arrangement of the opening scenes. But the fact that he did so, and perhaps even suggested the new arrangement himself—since it served to heighten the musical effect—is proof conclusive that the question of the overture was already a *cura posterior* and consequently no longer applicable to the two *Leonora* overtures.

This elimination of the grandiose tone poems from the plan of the new *Fidelio* (granting the untenability of any concession on Beethoven's part) is explained solely by his exceptional sense of responsibility towards his art, which, so far as his opera is concerned, amounted to truly heroic self-sacrifice. The German edition of Thayer's biography quotes a remark of the composer in 1823 which occurred in a discussion of the *Fidelio première* of 1814, to the effect that the new overture was not ready in time because of "obstacles which had presented themselves" and had to be replaced by another overture of Beethoven's. "The people applauded [he said] but I stood ashamed. *It did not belong to the rest.*" There indirectly, from Beethoven's own lips, we have the reason for his action in the matter of the overture. In characterizing (a full decade later) the new overture written for the revival as belonging to the "rest," he makes it clear that he composed it expressly because he did not feel that the earlier overtures now met this requirement. The great *Leonora* overtures only belonged to *Fidelio* as a "whole" as regards their origin, but no longer by nature and dimensions. That is probably the thought behind Schindler's assertion that the composer, "to judge by various indications," also recognized himself that *Leonora No. 3* was too long for an opera overture. He was moved by the consideration that either one of the two great C major overtures was prejudicial to the economy of the total structure of the opera. And his remarks on the subject were given only an incorrect and primitive interpretation by the informant who placed his own ideological construction on the "different indications" he observed.

To recapitulate: At the final revision of *Fidelio*, Beethoven for reasons of economy dropped first of all the two great C major overtures. When the necessity of another key for the overture arose, the small *Leonora No. 1*, which was to replace them, still seemed to Beethoven to be worth revising. But the revision in E major was abandoned and led to the composition of a new overture drawing its inspiration from the character of this key.

Marx's opinion, which has been current until quite recently, that the E major overture bore no inner relationship[1] to the opera, was already invalidated by Riemann, so that here we can dispense with the experiment of "interpreting the contents" of the overture to prove its spiritual kinship with the opera. A sentence from [the latter's] discussion of the E major overture is especially significant in the light of our presentation. "Who is not reminded of Leonore's great aria by the tonality and the soft entry of the horns in bar 5?"

If we realize that the C major of the three *Leonora* overtures serves not only to effect an easy, natural connection with Marzelline's C minor-C major aria, that it represents rather the "framework key" of the opera as a whole, common alike to the overture and the final chorus, then at the same time we must view the abandonment of the original tonality of the overture as the loss of a previous factor of unity. This loss, however, is compensated by a solution of the tonality question that is as novel as it is ingeniously simple: through the choice of E major which—solely in view of the duet following the overture—was the obvious but by no means the only possible choice. Instead of the ordinary key agreement between the introduction and final movement, this establishes the relationship between the overture and the spiritual core of the opera: the key reference to the only musical number in which the heroine, revealing her innermost thoughts, stands alone before the spectators of the dramatic action. So, from this point of view as well, the choice of the key is proof that in the new overture Beethoven also had the "whole" in mind.

If, after this, the E major overture can be interpreted—subjective assumptions aside—in the sense of the figure "Leonora," it is perhaps permissible to speak here of a purely musical analogy. Is not perhaps the brooding C major pianissimo that surges up to the great climax in the second adagio (from bar 7) a faint premonition of the passage: "*der* [Florestan] *kaum mehr lebt und wie ein Schatten schwebt*"? *If so*, then in this "unprogrammatic" overture the figure of Florestan would still be introduced indirectly, like an ominous shadow cast by coming events.—LUDWIG MISCH

d. Overture for the Name Day of Kaiser Franz, Opus 115

This work does not deserve to be neglected; and when it is "revived," it should be so played that it can be heard. As far as custom can be imputed

---

[1] "It is one of the most brilliant compositions, sparkling with talent and artistic skill. But it has nothing to do with *Leonore*." The same from Bekker: "Like the *Nameday* overture, the *Fidelio* overture has the general festal character of a concert overture."

to such rare events as its performance, it is customarily played far too fast. Weingartner has remarked that, whereas he takes the finale of Beethoven's Seventh Symphony at an unusually moderate pace, he is constantly told, sometimes in praise and sometimes in blame, that nobody else has ever taken it so terrifically fast. Things will always sound fast when every rhythmic unit bristles with detail. But if we increase the pace until the rhythmic units become a hum, the listener will sleep like a top.

The *Namensfeier* overture is a short and energetic work consisting of a majestic introduction and a bustling *allegro quasi vivace*.[1] (Note the precautionary *quasi*.) The majesty of the introduction and the sledge-hammer power of climax in the allegro bring this work into spiritual alliance with the mighty *Weihe des Hauses*, Opus 124. Eight years passed between the two works; *Namensfeier* being written in 1814, the year of the revival (and revision) of the opera *Fidelio*, and *Weihe des Hauses* being written in 1822. The themes of *Namensfeier* are almost in the nature of short formulas designed to display vivid contrasts of color and phrase-rhythm without attracting attention to themselves. There is nothing perfunctory in the work: like the overture to *Fidelio* (a work of the same date) it is microscopically perfect in detail. Romantic, however, it does not claim to be, except in so far as there is romance in the impulse of a crowd of loyal subjects to greet their sovereign in his progress through the streets of his capital. Beethoven's tremendous sense of movement was still under the impulse of his Seventh Symphony, and his interest in imperial name days was official rather than personal. The crowd interested him more; and after the maestoso introduction has worked its pair of themes (a phrase in loud rhythmic chords and a broad cantabile tune) into a spacious exordium, the rest of the overture suggests an excited and joyful rumor, beginning in whispers and adding information gathered from many different quarters, until the glad news is confirmed and the populace rush together from all sides. No definite "program" can be or need be erected from this basis, but such is the mood of the allegro, which is in very terse sonata form with many abrupt little themes, a short development, and a coda which is by far the largest section of the whole work.

An interesting point in the history of the first theme is that the repeated [eighth-note] figure [of a falling second occurring first in the third and fourth measures of the allegro] was first thought of as a [quarter-note and eighth-note] figure identical [with the rhythm of the first measure]. Nottebohm is probably right in thinking that Beethoven changed it because he did not like to use in this overture a figure so

---

[1] In the Breitkopf & Härtel edition the tempo indication is "allegro assai vivace," thus nullifying Professor Tovey's next sentence.—Editor.

prominent in the scherzo of the Seventh Symphony which he had just produced.

The transition to the second group of themes is effected by the old Italian practical joke of treating the mere home-dominant chord as if it were the dominant key.

But in the recapitulation Beethoven sheds a new light on the old joke by taking it literally. Instead of admitting that those chords were merely *on* the dominant he substitutes tonic chords, with the air of correcting the former mistake.

It is strange, but a fact, that this drastically simple stroke in connection with one of the most hackneyed of structural devices is quite unique.

Less unique but more romantic is [an] impressive detail in the scoring of another short and simple phrase [in the second group of the allegro].[1] The phrase is stated three times, with a sustained inner dominant throughout. The first statement is on violin and violas in octaves, and it closes into a repetition by flute, clarinet, and bassoon in three octaves. An oboe and horn sustain the dominant throughout. Against this, during the second statement, the strings add a seventh, three octaves deep, with a crescendo and an excited uprush.

The overture is full of such typical traits of Beethoven's style. Another great moment is the sudden hush and unexpected move to the subdominant just at the moment of returning to the recapitulation [of the first theme].

The many incidents which thus flee by almost too rapidly for the ear make this overture one of Beethoven's most difficult orchestral works. It does not sound difficult; and if its points are missed either by performers or listeners, no disaster is felt, except by those who have had leisure to study the work. It is an eminently "practical" work, that does not, like the *Fidelio* overture or the Fourth Symphony, court disaster by risky passages. A perfunctory performance can do no worse than make it sound like a perfunctory composition. But if we compare it with a really perfunctory work like the *König Stephan* overture, the difference will soon appear. The harder you work at *König Stephan*, the slighter it becomes; and slight without the engaging frivolity of the *Ruinen von Athen*, but with the insolence of a master who really can't be bothered with such official functions. Beethoven was under no illusions about these patriotic *Festspiele*. The eminent critic Rochlitz devoted one or more articles in his musical journal to rebuking Beethoven for becoming increasingly stagy in these works. Beethoven's legitimate defense might have been that as Kotzebüe's *Ruinen von Athen* and *König Stephan* were the flimsiest of stage spectacles, staginess was the only quality admissible in their music. Instead of this reflection he scrawled upon the margin of his copy of

[1] Occurring first at measure 87.—Editor.

Rochlitz's journal some unprintable remarks as to the relative value of Rochlitz's highest thoughts and his own *pièces d'occasion*. But he implied that his own opinion of these pieces was much severer than Rochlitz's. And the *Namensfeier* overture is not among these pieces, for though its opus number (115) is earlier than that of *König Stephan* (Opus 117), it was written three years later. And the sketches show great care.— DONALD FRANCIS TOVEY (5)

The score calls for two flutes, two oboes, two clarinets, two bassoons, four horns, two trumpets, timpani, and strings.

IV. MISCELLANEOUS WORKS FOR ORCHESTRA
a. "Gratulations-Menuett" for Orchestra, WoO3

Beethoven's friendly feeling for Hensler[1] gave rise to a new orchestral composition which was part of a tribute paid by the members of the company to their director on November 3, the evening before his name day. After a performance of Meisl's drama *1722, 1822, 1922*, the audience having departed, the director was called to the festively decorated and illuminated stage, and surrounded by his company in gala dress. A poetical address was read to him by the stage manager. After he had gone back to his lodgings, the orchestra and chorus serenaded him, the program consisting of an overture to *The Prodigal Son*, by Kapellmeister Drechsel, a concerto for flute, by Kapellmeister Gläser, and what Bäuerle's *Theaterzeitung* called "a glorious new symphony" composed for the occasion by Beethoven, the whole ending with the march and chorus from Mozart's *Titus*. The "new symphony" was the *Gratulations-menuett*. . . . On the next day Hensler gave a dinner in the property room of the theater at 3 P.M. Beethoven, Gläser, Bäuerle, Gleich, Meisl, Hopp, and others were present.[2] Beethoven had a seat directly under the musical clock. Gläser told Reischl,[3] who provided the entertainment to set the clock to the overture to *Fidelio* and then wrote to Beethoven to listen, as he would soon hear it. Beethoven listened and then said, "It plays it better than the orchestra in the Känthnerthor."

The *Gratulations-menuett* was offered to Peters in the letter of De-

[1] Carl Friedrich Hensler (1761–1825), popular dramatist and director of the Josephstadt Theater. He was an old friend and great admirer of Beethoven.—Editor.

[2] Max Unger, "Vom geselligen Beethoven," *Osterreiche Musikzeitschrift*, XII (1957), p. 92, supplies the following identifications: Franz Gläser, son of Beethoven's copyist, Peter Gläser, and theater *Kapellmeister*; Adolph Bäuerle, author and editor of the *Wiener Allgemeine Theaterzeitung*; Joseph Alois Gleich, productive poet for the Josephstadt stage and scholar in the civil service; Carl Meisl, author of the *Weihe des Hauses*; Friedrich Hopp, author as well as actor. This anecdote was told to Thayer on October 28, 1859 by Hopp.

[3] According to O. E. Deutsch, *Osterreiche Musikzeitschrift*, XII (1957), p. 163, Wolfgang Reischl was landlord of the Josephstadt Theater.

cember 20. Beethoven was evidently eager to realize quickly on a work which had cost him but little labor—the product of a period in which his fancy seemed to have regained its old-time fecundity and he his old-time delight in work. He offered it elsewhere and gave a copy (the one that he misdated) to Archduke Rudolph for his collection. Artaria published it in 1832 under the title "Allegretto" with a dedication to Karl Holz. The title on the autograph reads: "Tempo di Minuetto quasi Allegretto" (Allegro non troppo was originally written but then scratched out in favor of): "Gratulations-Menuett."—ALEXANDER WHEELOCK THAYER, EDITED BY ELLIOT FORBES

It is a formal minuet in E flat more akin to his Bonn days than the fast minuets and scherzos he had been writing in the meantime for his symphonies, sonatas, and quartets. Befitting the occasion there is much use made of the brass and timpani.

In form it is a minuet in two parts. The first repeat is written out because it is reorchestrated, the melody given to the clarinet and a humorous staccato accompaniment in the bassoon. The second part is noteworthy for the ingenuous method Beethoven uses to bridge over from the statement of the middle section (much brass and timpani) and the recapitulation of the first phrase.

The trio is in A flat, the melodic material being given mostly to the solo winds. In the second part there is again a humorous accompaniment given to the solo horn, and some delightful imitations among the solo clarinet, bassoon, and flute answered irregularly by the first violins. The second half of the trio is not repeated but modulates to the dominant seventh chord on B flat, which is held, fortissimo. Instead of an immediate da capo of the minuet there are four introductory measures before it reappears. There is no coda.—Editor.

b. 12 Ecossaises for Orchestra, WoO 16
(See 6 Ecossaises for Piano, WoO 83, on page 774.)

V. MUSIC FOR BAND
a. March No. 1 in F for Band, WoO 18; March in C for Band, WoO 20; March No. 2 in F for Band, WoO 19

Beethoven's three *Zapfenstreiche* [military tattoos] have never completely appeared in print. Because there exist several settings of the first and third, the philological problem is not simple and can be solved only by assembling all the relevant source materials and thoroughly examining them.

The first *Zapfenstreich* in F originated in its first setting in the year 1809, without a trio, and under the title "March for the Bohemian Militia." A later autograph bears the inscription *Zapfenstreich No. 1*; in this setting the march contained a small trio section that heretofore had not appeared in print. In 1810 Beethoven reinforced the instrumentation of the main section, dispensed once more with the trio, and combined it in this third form with the similarly worked-out main section of the third *Zapfenstreich* (see below). In this setting both marches were played on the carousel of Empress Maria Ludovica on August 15, 1810, and appeared for the first time in print in 1888 in the supplement to the edition of Beethoven's Collected Works. There exists, however, still another setting! The "March for the Bohemian Militia" appeared shortly after Beethoven's death, in a reworking by an unknown arranger, as No. 37 of a collection of rapid marches published by Schlessinger for the Prussian army. Here it bore the title "March for the Yorkshire Corps."

The words "March" and *Zapfenstreich* differ from each other only in the fact that the latter contains a trio as well as a main section.

Beethoven in the setting with trio exchanges the C clarinet for a B flat clarinet, but says in a footnote to the supplementary B flat clarinet part that it "can also be set for C clarinet." The autograph of the march shows also a notation in Beethoven's handwriting: "One step for each measure." [The march being in 2/4 time,] this indicates that the tempo must be very fast.

The second *Zapfenstreich* in C[1] was composed around 1809/10. It is, by far, the largest [of the three]. There exists only one setting of it that faithfully follows Beethoven's autograph manuscript and is printed in the supplement to the Collected Works. We are spared here all related philological assertions or problems.

This march, in 2/4 time, Vivace assai, is distinguished musically by its extended form, its sudden changes of key, and the delicate accompaniment—unique in band music—of the recapitulation of the main theme. This recapitulation is drawn out, by means of a modulating phrase, by a thematically independent coda, introducing sixteenth notes for the first time. A delicate cantabile trio in F gives the main melody to the piccolo and oboe in octaves. It is connected directly to the repeat of the main section of the march by a subtle reference to the sixteenth notes mentioned above.—Editor.

The third *Zapfenstreich* in F[2] contains the most complex problems. The earliest copy was found by us in an autograph in the archives of the Society of the Friends of Music in Vienna. It bears the title *Zapfenstreich No. 3*. Dr. Luithlen has made the following comment about the endpapers of this autograph: "This autograph is a first copy of the 'fair copy' in the

[1] WoO 20.—Editor.
[2] WoO 19.—Editor.

possession of the Teutonic Order [of Knights]. In this version the piece was originally intended for Archduke Anton.[1] The Society of the Friends of Music possesses a newly prepared copy based on the above-named autograph with a title in the handwriting of Archduke Rudolf." With the revision of the text it is possible to compare this later copy with the first autograph copy and judge its authenticity. The instrumentation is the same as in both the first two *Zapfenstreiche*.[2] Also this third *Zapfenstreich* was rearranged for the carousel of Empress Maria Ludovica and was published in this latter version in the [1888] supplement to the Edition of the Collected Works. The trio to this *Zapfenstreich* version is in Beethoven's handwriting. As to the time of composition of the third *Zapfenstreich*, the year 1810 is considered accurate.

About the chronology of the three marches. That all three marches were composed in the years 1809/10 is now accepted as accurate. However, the question of the trios is not entirely clear. Beethoven offered all three works to the Peters publishing house in Leipzig in the year 1822, a proof of the fact that he considered the original versions worthy of publication. Then he wrote to Peters on September 13: ". . . among the marches there are a few for which I decided to compose new trios." Max Unger judged from this that the trios were first composed in that year. The contrary is obvious due to the fact [we have noted] that the trio to the first march was already in existence in 1809 or 1810 in the same handwriting as the march itself. The question then arises if Beethoven had the intention of substituting new trios for the older ones. This is also contradicted by the correspondence.

The three marches were doubtless conceived as a complete unit. This is indicated by the key relationships: F, C, F. One must observe also that the main theme of the third march already appears in the closing portion of the first march in the trumpet part. Thus a kind of free symmetry exists [among the three marches] and the middle march [in C] can be regarded as an immense trio to the entire structure. The beautiful instrumentation [of this C major march] and notably the accidentals in the waldhorns and the bassoons grant to the wind orchestra a truly Beethovian mildness and warmth. It remains only to hope that these unduly neglected works of the great symphonist will take their rightful place in concert programs. —WILLY HESS (7) (TR. BY THOMAS K. SCHERMAN)

For a humorous presentation of the two F major marches to Archduke Rudolf for an equestrian entertainment given at the Lauenburg Palace on August 24, 1810, see Beethoven's letter 5 (dated August 1810 at Baden) in Part III.—Editor.

1 The older brother of Archduke Rudolf.—Editor.
2 This is: one piccolo in F, two flutes in F, one clarinet in F, two clarinets in C, two F horns, two F trumpets, two bassoons, one contrabassoon, and drums.—Editor.

b. Polonaise in D for Band, WoO 21; Ecossaise in D for Band, WoO 22; Ecossaise in G for Band, WoO 23

Little or nothing is known of the origins of these little works except that they were probably written around the same time as the *Zapfenstreiche*, WoO 18, 19, and 20,[1] that is, in the summer of 1810 at Baden. Of them the polonaise is the most interesting, with its alternating phrases of forte and piano; its offbeat accents in the second half; and the alternation of D minor and D major in the last phrase. Its coda is without interest except for two surprising piano measures in the midst of a fortissimo reiteration of the tonic-dominant formula.

The second ecossaise (in G) exists only in a piano reduction attributed to Czerny.—THOMAS K. SCHERMAN

c. March in D for Band, WoO 24

This march was written in May or June of 1816 for the Civil Artillery Corps, whose commander, Lieutenant Commander Franz Xaver Embel, had written requesting a "March for Turkish music." The letter reads in part: "The Artillery Corps begs for the honor of a March for Turkish Music from the pen of the distinguished Herr Louis van Beethoven." Sketches for it are to be found toward the close of the Sketchbook covering the years 1815-16. It was first published shortly after Beethoven's death in an arrangement for piano two hands and piano four hands by the Viennese Cappi and Czerny. The first published edition of the instrumental score appeared in the Breitkopf & Härtel edition of the Complete Works (1864) in Series 2 (Works for Orchestra). It was one of the four marches (three *Zapfenstreiche*, or Tattoos, and one March) offered by Beethoven to Peters for publication in May of 1823. (See the essay by Willy Hess on the *Zapfenstreiche*.)

In form, harmony, and thematic treatment and development this 1816 march is much more ambitious than the *Zapfenstreiche* dating from 1810. As details in this line there is a four-bar introduction leading to the march proper, which is in two parts, each part repeated; although there is a trio (see below) Beethoven does not simply indicate da capo at the end of the trio indicating a recapitulation of the march proper, but writes out the latter in full, repeats and all, thus ensuring at performances not only the first playing of the march proper but its complete recapitulation after the trio (contrary to the common practice at the time, when the repetitions were eliminated in the recapitulation). Also the instrumenta-

[1] See the essay on these marches by Willy Hess.—Editor.

tion is much fuller than in the *Zapfenstreiche*—the 1816 march calls for
two piccolos, two oboes, three clarinets (one in F, similar to today's E flat
clarinet, which sounds higher than the ordinary clarinet and is much more
piercing in character), two bassoons, one contrabassoon, six horns, eight
trumpets, two trombones, a serpent (the ancestor of the present tuba),
and a larger assortment of percussion instruments.

Harmonically the most interesting section of the march proper is its
second half. The first half having ended in A, the key of the dominant,
Beethoven in very abrupt fashion traverses the keys of D minor, B flat,
C major, and G major before reannouncing the main theme, fortissimo,
in the tonic key. There is also a surprise interrupted cadence when, the
thematic material being completed, the listener expects an assertive D
major triad but hears instead a D-seven chord (the dominant chord of
G major). Also there is a short coda in which there are interesting imitations between the trumpets and the horns while the winds, first the
bassoons in the bass, then the piccolos and high clarinet in the treble,
embellish these alternate imitations with brilliant staccato scales. The
march proper ends as the four-bar introduction began with a typical
trumpet fanfare.

The trio in B flat major is marked "Trio all'Ongarese," which marks its
character. The melody is much more legato, but there are typical Hungarian offbeat accents. Much is made of the triangle. The trio, like the
march proper, is also in two parts, of which, however, only the first is
repeated. The second half, by means of a fall from B flat to A in the
bass and a two-bar molto crescendo, leads directly back into D major and
a complete recapitulation of the march proper.

All in all, this march in D is much more like a symphonic march than
a military tattoo for the exercises of the troops or for use on a carousel,
as were the earlier *Zapfenstreiche*.—THOMAS K. SCHERMAN

d. March in B Flat for 2 Clarinets, 2 Horns, and 2 Bassoons, WoO 29

*The Flötenühr, or musical clock, was a very popular instrument in
Middle Europe in the late eighteenth and early nineteenth centuries.
Well-known composers such as Mozart, Haydn, Gluck, and Beethoven
wrote original works for it, and Viennese manufacturers of the instrument
arranged already composed orchestral and piano compositions by great
composers to be played upon it. One such instrument was manufactured
in 1792 by Teather Primitivius Niemecz, librarian to Prince Esterházy, for
which Haydn, the chief court musician, provided a series of pieces. These
were published by Nagel of Hanover in 1932. Herr Schmid in his article*

discusses the background of the Esterházy Flötenühr *and Haydn's interest in it. He then describes the compositions in the Nagel collection.*

No. 25 [of the thirty-two compositions published by Nagel] brings a small surprise. The work is entitled "*Marsch, von H. Kapellmeister Haydn.*" The same work with insignificant changes transposed to the key of F was published by Kinsky as a *Spielür*[1] composition of Beethoven along with an intermezzo and another march. They all were discovered on a *Flötenühr,* constructed by the Viennese watchmaker Franz Egidus Arzt, that was in the possession of the former Heyer Museum in Köln. The piece appeared under the title "*Granadirs [Grenadiers] Marsch arranchirt [arrangiert] von Herrn Ludwig v. Beethoven.*" Since Arzt died in 1812, the instrument [containing the Beethoven works] was probably created considerably before that date, for it was not delivered posthumously as were [several others manufactured by him]. In the circumstance that the second march coincides with Beethoven's March in B flat for two each clarinets, horns, and bassoons, it can be readily assumed that the first march and the intermezzo also were created by the Master or at least arranged by him. Now, by means of the autograph of the above-mentioned composition attributed to Haydn, it is possible exactly to establish the date of the first march and treat it as also being composed originally for [the same instruments as Beethoven's B flat March]. The expression "*arranchirt*" on the title of the Beethoven work leads us to believe that the Master arranged his own march for *Flötenühr* and combined it with the Haydn march by means of a newly composed intermezzo. The designation "*Granadirs Marsch*" undoubtedly refers to the Prince's Grenadiers in Eisenstadt, for whose *Feldmusik* [military music] (suggested by the instrumentation) Haydn could have composed his march (and probably also Beethoven).[2]—ERNST FRITZ SCHMID (TR. BY THOMAS K. SCHERMAN)

Beethoven's short march in B flat is typical "military music" as attested not only by its instrumentation but also by its predominant dotted rhythm. It is just twenty measures long and is in two parts, both repeated and both of which end with three decisive tonic chords. The voice leading is very sophisticated—for example, the use of the first clarinet and first bassoon in octaves toward the end of the first half, while the horns and second clarinet and second bassoon provide the moving harmonies and the bass underneath their melody; here also a surprise suspension causes a startling discord—quite advanced for "military music" of the time. The most noteworthy spot in the piece thematically is at the last four measures, where Beethoven abandons the rhythm of

---

[1] Same as *Flötenühr.*—Editor.

[2] It is known that Beethoven visited Esterházy in 1807 for the first performance of his Mass in C, Opus 86. It is probable that at that time he composed the *Feldmusik* for the grenadiers, using Haydn's marches as models.—Editor.

dotted eighth and sixteenth notes and has the clarinets and bassoons play impressive half notes in unison over four octaves while the horns provide a syncopated middle voice.—Editor.

VI. CONCERTI

a. Piano Concerto No. 4 in G, Opus 58

I. Allegro moderato; II. Andante con moto; leading to III. Rondo: Vivace.

All three movements of Beethoven's G major Concerto demonstrate the aesthetic principles of concerto form with extraordinary subtlety. In the first movement Beethoven lets the piano state the first phrase—a quiet cantabile phrase [the first two measures of which introduce the rhythmic motive which permeates the entire movement: an upbeat of three repeated eighth notes leading to a downbeat of still another eighth note on the same tone. The piano's complete phrase] is immediately taken up by the orchestra entering softly in a bright, remote key, a wonderful stroke of genius.[1]

Here the orchestra (a small one without trumpets or drums) has the next sixty-eight bars to itself and gives in rapid succession, with beautiful variety of crescendos and fortes and pianos, [six distinct] themes.

[The first is a development of the soloist's opening announcement, stressing the characteristic repeated eighth notes. This leads] through a broad crescendo to another quiet theme, belonging (as we afterwards learn) to the second subject, and modulating through a considerable range of keys. [This theme commences in the surprising key of A minor and is also characterized by a distinct rhythm: a long note (dotted half note) followed by an uneven rhythm of a dotted eighth note and a sixteenth note. After it is repeated in sequence three times and in three different keys, it] is followed by rising sequences [of the first subject's repeated eighth notes on the same tone. The melodic rise is combined with a crescendo] culminating in [still another] important theme [combining in a noble manner the repeated-note upbeat of the first subject with the dotted rhythm of the second subject. This, in turn,] leads to the final figures of the ritornello—[descending scale figures in sixteenth notes, and still another derivative of the opening theme with its four-times-repeated eighth notes. The piano] solo enters with a meditative, long-drawn development of those repeated notes, which broadens and quickens into brilliant running passages.

Fifteen bars (no less) of this broad expanse lead to the restatement of the opening tutti, [this time] with the co-operation of the solo in-

[1] Mozart's interesting early concerto in E flat (K. 271) anticipates Beethoven in allowing the piano to share the first theme with the orchestra, but only in a jocular fashion with results no more than formal and witty.

strument. The restatement begins with [the orchestra] and the piano interpolates a series of brilliant new figures while the orchestra holds the thread with the [constant rhythm of the four repeated eighth notes] and the bassoon and other woodwinds take up the theme in dialogue.

Suddenly the piano becomes contemplative in a dark key [(B flat major) with a lyrical expressive theme of pianissimo eighth notes in the highest register of the piano, accompanied by soft, rolling triplets in the deep bass]. In a few bars of the highest beauty [it] modulates to the dominant, where there is a passage of preparation for the second subject. This soon appears, beginning, to our surprise, with a new melody of which the opening tutti had not uttered a note.

[It starts in the orchestra with a quiet four-bar phrase in the low register of the strings, which modulates, within its gentle frame, to the key of B minor.] This is answered by the piano in a playful variation; and another brilliant solo, in which the orchestra [again] holds the thread with [the repeated-note rhythm], leads to [the minor theme which served as the second subject for the orchestra's ritornello. This begins] in D minor, and [is] soon enriched with an ornate flow of [sixteenth notes] in the piano. This leads through [the rising sequence of the repeated-note motive] (as in the tutti) to [the noble penultimate theme], all with the most brilliant piano accompaniment. These piano figures seem to force their way through the structure till they emerge in a broad expanse, and we hear the long trill which classical composers have generally found the most convenient way of ending the first solo in the exposition of the first movement of a concerto. Beethoven, however, does not [in this case] end with the trill; he makes it lead gently to [still] another repetition of [the penultimate theme], beginning this time piano (so as to reveal the innate tenderness of this [usually] majestic theme). A crescendo brings in the orchestra in triumph with the rest of the ritornello.

Beethoven has now well and truly laid the foundations of his concerto form and is free to raise his edifice to heights undreamed of in earlier music. The composer's main difficulty in the classical concerto is concentrated in the opening tutti [or ritornello] and solo[ist's] exposition of the first movement. Beethoven recognized the errors [which he had made in this troublesome spot] in his first three [piano] concerti. The obvious stroke of genius by which the piano opens the G major Concerto and gives the orchestra occasion to enter in a foreign key is [actually] not more wonderful than the art with which the sequel retains and enhances the processional character of the classical tutti; avoiding alike the dangerous symphonic action which in the C minor Concerto [No. 3] threatens to make the [solo piano] an intruder, and the no less dangerous discursiveness which in the [first two] concerti leaves the [orchestral] tutti at a loose end with matter almost more improvisational than that of the solo.

Contrast those expensive luxuries with the wonderful modulating [second] theme [of the G major Concerto's orchestral exposition], which quietly takes its place in the procession and yet covers a wide range of keys, only to confirm the home tonic more strongly.

[Also], note the complete freedom of the solo exposition in expanding [the orchestral material] in brilliant or ruminating passages, and [even] in introducing [entirely] new thematic matter. Yet every allusion by the soloist to the material of the tutti increases by reflection the cogency of the original orchestral statement.

The development begins with the piano interrupting the quiet close [in D major] of the ritornello [the final derivative of the all-pervading repeated eighth-note motive. It does so] by striking the rhythmic figure on the minor third, F natural. Then follows a series of mysterious modulations, with an entirely new figure [of descending scales in triplets] springing out of the [repeated-note upbeat] as if by accident. Suddenly the piano awakens to an energetic mood, which lasts for a considerable time, while the orchestra quietly works out [the repeated eighth notes] in combination with the new [descending triplet] figure. At length we arrive at an important climax in the extremely distant key of C-sharp minor and another mysterious process begins. [Beethoven reduces the original repeated-note motive to an entirely new syncopated rhythm. This] extraordinary transformation is worked out very quietly as a [fugato] with a running countersubject. [Although this fugato commences in] the home tonic, Beethoven does not expect us to recognize that we have [arrived there], but the fact adds much to the mysterious effect of this very unexpected development. A short crescendo with the [repeated-note] rhythm reasserting itself, first in eighth notes and then diminished [to sixteenth notes], soon brings us in triumph to the recapitulation of the [entire] first subject.

This development section is the most complicated passage in all [of] Beethoven's concerti; yet it is perfectly typical of concerto style. Its breadth of sequence and its copious use of episodic material that has not been heard in the exposition are natural results of the principles we have already seen in operation. The relation between the solo and tutti has made the repetition of the material in the exposition specially impressive and characteristic, and the recapitulation and coda will make it still more so; and therefore the development needs to be more simple and [yet] more contrasted than it would be in a symphony or a sonata.

Beethoven's recapitulation here follows the opening tutti much more closely than did the first solo; but the soloist's repetition of the orchestra's announcement is [suddenly] interrupted by a[n abrupt] modulation to E flat, where [another] lofty contemplative passage, corresponding to [the one introduced at this relative point in the exposition], leads to the second subject recapitulated exactly in the tonic. Where the [orchestra] bursts in, taking up the thread of the penultimate theme in its tender transformation, we have a pause on a 6/4 chord, as in all classical concerti; and the whole responsibility for the greater part of the coda is thrown upon the solo player, who is supposed to extemporize the long cadenza that comes at this point. Here we have the only really conventional element in this much-maligned art form; for obviously a bad cadenza is the very appendicitis of music.[1]

[1] Despite these remarks, or possibly to prove their validity, Tovey himself constructed a most brilliant and appropriately thematic cadenza which I recommend for examination to soloists who are anxious to avoid the one which Beethoven himself published. Tovey's naturally takes fuller advantage of the capacities of the modern piano (as well as the subsequent advance in piano technique since Beethoven's time). There are also published cadenzas by Clara Schumann and Johannes Brahms. Of these three I feel Tovey's is the most appropriate, since it achieves a relative balance between the late-nineteenth-century romantic approach and Beethoven's own modified classical approach to his own themes.

However, since most contemporary performers and most available recorded performances utilize Beethoven's own cadenza, a short description of it follows:

Beethoven's cadenzas written for this concerto in 1809–10 for Archduke Rudolf are much more in keeping with the general mood and style of the work as a whole (written in 1806) than Beethoven's cadenzas written in the same years for his earlier piano concerti. They are formalistically, as well as thematically, unified with the individual movements as a whole. After all, during this particular highly productive period of his life, Beethoven was musically much more thoroughly integrated than he was even three or four years before or ten years after. Sketches for such major works as his violin concerto, Opus 61, his Fourth and Fifth Symphonies, his "Waldstein" and "Appassionata" Piano Sonatas, his entire *Fidelio* (including the first three *Leonora Overtures*), his epoch-making 32 Piano Variations in C Minor, and the three "Rasoumovsky" String Quartets appear side by side in his notebooks during these years. Therefore, it is not surprising that the technical mastery that went into the working-out or development of one inspiration would be reflected in another entirely different creation within the same period. The three *years* in Beethoven's creative output between 1806 and 1809 are much more closely related and identifiable than the three months' output between the production of the arrangements of the Irish folk songs with piano trio accompaniment, in December of 1810, and the "Archduke" Trio, Opus 97, completed in March of 1811!

Beethoven composed and wrote out two cadenzas for the first movement of the concerto. He was evidently giving Archduke Rudolf his choice. The second (entitled, in Beethoven's hand, "*Cadenza, ma senza cadare*") is the more brilliant, more creatively unique, and—to the point—more often played today.

It commences with the repeated notes of the opening theme transformed into the new rhythm of 6/8. Out of this "development" Beethoven extracts first the last three notes, and finally the last two notes of the motive. This leads, after a couple of bravura runs, to a passage in B flat major based on the quiet second subject in its original 4/4. This passage is concluded by a trill on C above the dominant seventh chord of B flat, but the cadence is interrupted and a further extended 6/8 passage (commencing on the dominant-seventh chord of G minor) brilliantly leads through periods of broken chords and descending and rising arpeggios in sixteenth-note triplets to the expected trills on A-B flat (harmonized by chords in G minor) and A-B natural (harmonized by G major chords). A scale passage (non veloce) leads smoothly into the pianissimo coda of the movement, where the closing theme is accompanied by the orchestra for its last time.—Editor.

Fortunately Beethoven has a wonderful way of designing his move-ment so that a long spell of uninterrupted solo, in a style of development [and] extemporization, shall seem necessary and effective, whether it be actually *extempore* or not.

[After the cadenza] Beethoven, knowing that some pages of solo will intervene, repeats [the quiet tender transformation of the penultimate theme], the theme he has just written before [to introduce the cadenza]. Very quietly it floats upward, and is followed by the final cadence theme. As this [too] dies away in upper ether, we are roused by a rapid crescendo with the [repeated-note] rhythm and its diminution (as at the end of the development) surging up till it pervades the entire orchestra, and the movement ends triumphantly.

If I am not mistaken, it was Liszt who compared the slow movement of this concerto to Orpheus taming the wild beasts with his music. This is so apt that it is almost free from the general objection that such comparisons tend at first to substitute their own vividness for that of the music and then to lose their vividness in the necessity for tiresome qualifications of detail. But here the comparison is remarkably spiritual and free from concrete externals. Note, in the first place, that, as in Liszt's own symphonic poem "Orpheus," it refers to the taming of wild Nature, not to the placating of the Furies, though Liszt tells us that he was inspired by the experience of conducting Gluck's "Orfeo." But the spiritual, or, if you prefer popular scientific jargon, psychological depth of the analogy is best shown in the one point of resemblance between this unique movement of Beethoven's and a very different one, Orpheus's first sustained address to the Furies in Gluck's opera. The pleadings of Orpheus are met phrase by phrase with a thunderous No from the Furies in unison, until the last No is a chord which shows that they will at length yield. In this Andante the orchestra does not imitate wild beasts or nature, and the piano does not imitate a lyre or a singer. But the orchestra (consisting of the strings alone) is entirely in octaves, without a vestige of harmony, so long as it remains stubborn and rough in its share of the dialogue with the quiet veiled tones of the solo. After its first soft pizzicato note it melts into harmony. In the supreme moment of darkness at the end, the orchestra and solo join in the same material, whereas they had hitherto been totally contrasted.

The finale breaks in, pianissimo,[1] with an intensely lively theme in that prosaic daylight by which Beethoven loves to test the reality of his sublimest visions. The daylight is the more gray from the emphasis the theme gives to the subdominant chord. [The ten-bar theme is made up of various smaller elements each of which will be exploited later: the

[1] Although Beethoven did not specifically indicate "attacca" at the end of the Andante, he does write "Segue il Rondo." The poetic E minor close of the Andante is greatly enhanced, I feel, by an *immediate* announcement, also pianissimo, of the C major chord which opens the Rondo.—Editor.

rhythmic repetition of the opening note in the first two bars, exploiting one long and two very short notes; the rising arpeggio on the subdominant chord in the third and fourth bars; the succession of melody notes in the next four measures, each ornamented with a neighboring note in another very characteristic rhythm of one eighth note followed by two sixteenth notes; and finally the two final bars consisting of three staccato descending notes ending on the tonic key.]

The first theme, after a variation by the piano, has a countertheme, [commencing with the rhythm of one eighth note followed by two sixteenth notes (drawn from the first theme) and closing with a casual falling figure of two eighth notes and a quarter note. After this casual figure reappears in the two higher octaves in diminution,] the orchestra resumes [the first theme], fortissimo, with trumpets and drums appearing for the first time in the concerto. A transition theme [of gay octave jumps] leads to a very broad passage in [eighth-note triplets] on the dominant of D, taking its own time to bring us at last to the second subject.

This begins with a leisurely and serene melody for the piano in extremely wide three-part harmony, of which the bass is a deep tonic pedal. It intends to repeat itself but the self-repetition impatiently breaks off, as if to say "and all that!" The orchestra then urbanely gives a completed counterstatement, with intricate polyphony.

Then comes the lightest and simplest possible formula, in brilliant arpeggios. We begin to think it unaccountably simple, when suddenly we find ourselves on the dominant of C. The orchestra explains by recalling [the repeated-sixteenth-note rhythm] of the first theme. After keeping us in suspense an enormous time (almost forty bars) on this dominant of C, Beethoven brings us back with a long, rhythmless, [but brilliant] run to our first theme.

This and all its accessories are repeated unaltered, but [the closing subject with the staccato octave jumps] is made to lead to E flat. Here we begin the central episode with a new theme consisting of nothing but energetic arpeggios of tonic and dominant chords. These alternate, however, with rich developments of fragments of the opening theme. [An especially ingenious effect is created by] the drums as a bass to the winds, [constantly reiterating the repeated-sixteenth-note rhythm].

[All of] this leads through various keys to the dominant of our tonic, G, where a brisk chromatic passage for [the] piano brings up to the broad expanse of dominant preparation that culminates in the [leisurely and serene melody of the] second subject. [We have reached this] without having returned to the first subject. [However,] the recapitulation is exact until the end of the humorous arpeggio theme, which this time lands us on a chord of E flat, where, as before, we seem to be dwelling for a long time while the orchestra hints [shyly of the repeated-note rhythm of the first theme]. It gradually dawns on us that [under this florid decoration] we are actually listening to the entire first theme [played legato] in the violas.

The woodwinds become witty [with overlapping appearances of the three final falling notes of the first theme]; and suddenly the full orchestra enters in a rage on a strange chord. [This resolves neatly through a chromatically descending bass] into the dominant of C, our old position of return. The solo piano takes, as before, an unconscionable time in getting back to the first theme in its original key. This time we have it in a new variation, and the orchestra comes blustering in with yet another, leading to the [jumping octaves of the] transition theme.

Now the real business of the enormous coda begins. [The characteristic rhythm and the three staccato falling notes of the first theme] seem to be settling down in a leisurely tonic-and-dominant stride, when the dominant chord overstay[s] its time and slowly changes to the vastly distant key of F sharp major. Here we have the placid second subject, which calmly turns round to C major, and thence back to G, where it is gradually taken up by the whole orchestra with a crescendo, leading [through five short, sharp chords] to a 6/4 chord for a cadenza. Beethoven specifically says that this cadenza must be short.[1]

The cadenza is followed by more witticisms [based] on [the three concluding staccato notes of the main theme] in the horn. Then we settle down comfortably to another variation of the first theme, which is repeated in a remarkably close and persistent canon.

The music dies away in that upper ether which it has never left; but all the time we hear more witticisms on [the falling] figure, which suddenly quickens into presto eighth notes, with a crescendo. On the top of this, the full orchestra storms in with the principal theme, more lively than ever in this quicker tempo. Of course, when it reaches [its closing falling] figure, the irrepressible woodwinds and the piano have a little more to say before ending this audacious masterpiece of gigantic and inexhaustibly varied proportions with that astronomical punctuality which gives solemnity to Beethoven's utmost of high spirits.— DONALD FRANCIS TOVEY (4)

At the beginning [of the first movement] the piano emerges gently from dreams; this is truly Beethoven improvising. Two romantic themes,

---

[1] The one which he wrote out for Archduke Rudolf starts with a repetition in the piano of this five-note motive in octaves in the left hand answered by the similar design in the right hand, and a development of this small melodic idea. The short progress of this is interrupted twice with two cantabile reiterations of the lyric second theme. A series of broken chords, in the pattern with which that second theme was answered by the soloist upon both its appearances within the body of the movement, lead to two fortissimo measures constructed on the chords E flat-G-C sharp and A-G-C sharp, each followed by a measure of silence. The orchestra then re-enters with a pizzicato chord punctuating the beginning of a series of trills by the soloist on the dominant-seventh chord.—Editor.

renunciation and hope, are gradually developed. When, after an orchestral interlude, the piano is heard again solo, it is as if a butterfly rose ecstatically from its cocoon. There are no fortissimos here, and when the call to new adventures sounds, the butterfly sinks back, dreaming. The whole thing is wrapped in dark-red velvet; at times it is as if one were caressing it with one's hands.

EMIL LUDWIG, *Beethoven, Life of a Conqueror* (1943), (tr. by George Stewart McManus)—JACQUES BARZUN

b. Piano Concerto No. 5 in E Flat, Opus 73
I. Allegro; II. Adagio un poco moto; III. Rondo (Allegro)

The Fifth Concerto has a majestic introduction, in which the key of E flat is asserted by the orchestra and pianoforte in a rhapsodic outburst. This introduction reappears once at the beginning of the recapitulation, and plays no further part in the narrative. As in the first movements of all classical concertos, including Brahms's, the main threads of the story are set forth very broadly, but with explicit avoidance of anything like development or combination, in the opening tutti, which is best called by its primitive title of ritornello. In this concerto the ritornello is specially formal and voluminous . . . There are at least five distinct themes, and any number of important derivatives . . . The whole procession of contrasted themes which this great tutti reviews gives an unusually faithful summary of what the pianoforte is going to discuss. The severe monotony of key provides a firm basis for the marvelous richness of the distant keys of B minor and B major (alias C flat), in which the pianoforte is hereafter to present [the second subject] before the orchestra turns it into a rousing march in the orthodox key of B flat. The general plan of the whole movement is as follows:

  I. Introduction.

  II. Opening tutti or ritornello, containing all the themes.

  III. First solo, entering quietly with a chromatic scale, and turning the whole opening ritornello into a vast exposition of a "first" and "second" subject with such devices as the modulations just mentioned.

  IV. Close of the exposition by resumption of the last stages of the ritornello, in the key of the "second subject." By a device first introduced by Beethoven in his Violin Concerto, the end of the ritornello is now diverted into a remote new key. Here in due course the pianoforte again enters with its quiet chromatic scale. (No concerto that boasts a modern or Mendelssohnian "emancipation from the conventional classical ritornello" can achieve such impressive entries of the solo part.)

  V. Development, dealing entirely with [the first theme]. The pianoforte part is, for all its beautiful coloring, at first no more than an accompaniment to the whispered dialogue in which the orchestra discusses [the first theme] . . . By degrees, the rhythmic figure [which occurs at the end of the second measure of that theme] becomes more insistent, till it arouses the full orchestra, and sets the pianoforte off into a furious passage of octaves, descending in dialogue with the strings. What Beethoven wants here [with these "furious octaves"] is the fury of a hailstorm; and you can see daylight through hailstorms, and hear the bassoon through the right sort of octaves in this passage.

The curtain of hail is lifted away into blue sky, and we find ourselves in the very key in which the development started. The calm closing theme of the ritornello reappears; and the bass moves in slow steps up through distant keys to the threshold of home; and the quiet excitement becomes breathless until at last a crescendo leads to—

vi. The introduction, followed by the recapitulation of ii. The modulations at the "second subject" become still more wonderful, the key being now one of those "contradictory keys" (C sharp minor and D flat) of which such subtle dramatic use is made at a similar point in the Eroica Symphony.

vii. The Coda. The saddest chapter in the story of the concerto is the classical custom of leaving all but the orchestral windup of the coda blank, and trusting to a display of the solo-player's powers of improvisation to fill up the bank with a cadenza. Here Beethoven has, for the first time, forbidden extemporization,[1] and written out in full a coda that begins like a cadenza but soon settles down to what turns out to be a final glorified recapitulation of the whole ritornello, from the entry of [the second subject] onward. Gradually the orchestra joins in, beginning with the horns, until the full band is in dialogue with the pianoforte. At last we hear a chromatic scale. It was of this passage that Schumann said that "Beethoven's chromatic scales are not like other people's." No wonder! This quiet scale and the following trills have now borne the Atlas burden of the whole mighty structure for the third time—first, at the outset of the first solo; then at the outset of the development; and now, leading unswervingly to the glorious close.

The slow movement is in B major, the first remote modulation in the first movement, and it has two themes—the serene, devout melody of the muted violins (it is a misprint in the band-parts if the lower strings are muted); and the meditative theme with which the pianoforte enters and moves into a rather remote key on the shaded side (D major) of the harmony. Here the pianoforte seems to be settling down in a cadence with a trill, but the trill rises and rises until it breaks over into

---

[1] In the score at this point Beethoven has specifically written: "*Non si fa una cadenza, ma s'attacca subito il seguente.*" ("Do not play a cadenza [extemporized cadenza, that is], but immediately proceed [from the orchestral fermata on the usual 6/4 chord] to the following." See Ludwig Misch's essay on this unusual feature, directly following this analysis.—Editor.

the tonic key again. Thus the pianoforte comes to deliver its ornamental version of the main theme. As its close fades into a cloud of wavy light, three wind instruments, led by the flute, give out the whole theme again, the pianoforte accompanying with the wavy figure which the admiration of Berlioz has made familiar to all students of orchestration. At last the waves die down, and nothing is left but a cold gray octave. This sinks a semitone, and becomes glowing. As it continues, the pianoforte whispers a strange new theme [which is a rising arpeggio, given out in little spurts in] a mysterious rhythm and, finding itself already in E flat, after a moment's hovering, plunges into the finale, [the] most spacious and triumphant of concerto rondos. Lovers of Schumann's *Carnaval* will easily recognize in the second part of Beethoven's main theme a phrase that enlisted in Schumann's army of Davidites marching against the Philistines. Equally obvious is the great part played by the rhythmic figure [of one dotted eighth note followed by a sixteenth and four more eighth notes] from its first formal appearance as part of the orchestral group of themes to its final mysterious domination in the person of the drum.

What gives this rondo its chief impressiveness is the immense breadth of its middle episode, in which the main theme has three separate escapades, firstly fortissimo in C major (a bright key in this connection), secondly piano in A flat (a sober key), and thirdly pianissimo (breaking into forte) in E major, a remote key. The subsequent exciting return, where the violins remind us of what the pianoforte said at the end of the slow movement, will not escape notice. The drum passage at the end reveals the sublime depths from which all these outbursts of hilarity spring.—DONALD FRANCIS TOVEY (4)

Non si fa una cadenza—Are we really insensitive to this question, or are there weightier reasons for it? An eminent violinist plays the Beethoven concerto and—technical proficiency apart—plays with all the abandon and expression of one who knows and feels what he is playing; in short, one cannot imagine anything more beautiful. Then suddenly—the fatal six-four chord! the inevitable cadenza! And instead of Beethoven we hear the famous virtuoso X. Instead of music bringing us inward joy, we are amazed at a "record" technical exhibition if we do not try to close our ears to it until Beethoven returns again with the liberating trill.

This requires no long aesthetic demonstration. Render unto the virtuoso that which is his. To decry virtuosity as such simply because in certain circumstances it conflicts with higher artistic interests, or to inveigh against it as a principle foreign to art is not only pedantic but also the proof of positive ignorance. The concerto has arisen from the needs and for the needs of virtuosity (certainly not to the detriment of art) as a type of composition "which is intended to display the performer's virtuosity." Beethoven also wrote his concerti (and other works) for "virtuoso" ends, and as far as technique is concerned, took these ends fully into account. But for such purposes and objects (here Beethoven could not help being Beethoven) works arose in which the virtuoso aspect was certainly not neglected, but so applied to higher aims (artistic content, idea, inspiration, or whatever one may choose to call it) that instead of being the goal, it seems to have become the major premise.[1] Beethoven's concerti, along with a number of similar works by other masters, are just as much or just as little "virtuoso pieces" as Chopin's études perhaps —without prejudice to their pedagogic value—are technical exercises. In them we possess art works which we love and listen to for their own sake, and not because of the virtuoso who plays them. On the other hand, we well know that it takes a virtuoso to interpret such art works to perfection. Therefore we are grateful to him and acclaim him for it. And so the virtuoso profits by it. If he is not content with mastering the technical difficulties presented by the work, then he is free to play something else. But he does not tear a homogeneous art work to pieces by interpolations (cadenzas!) intended to display his maximum technical accomplishments, nor does he distort a text, the poetic beauty of which is sacred to us, by parenthetical remarks no matter how clever or amusing they may be.

However, it is quite true that the cadenza is traditional. Did not Beethoven himself write the six-four chord in question at the designated point? And did he not expressly add the direction: "Cadenza"? He would certainly never have hesitated to break with a custom of which he disapproved. Shall we out-Herod Herod?

Let us picture to ourselves the situation when Beethoven brought out his first pianoforte concerti. Composer and virtuoso in one, he whose gift of improvisation was the wonder and admiration of his contemporaries, certainly had no call to oppose a practice which "afforded an opportunity to interpolate a free fantasy in a legitimately artistic form." The cadenzas were *free fantasies* which were intended to show off the player's virtuosity and talent for improvisation in the most brilliant manner. Who would not have heard such cadenzas from a Beethoven!

We learn furthermore that in 1804 he took a cadenza for granted even when his concertos were played by others. The incident recounted by his pupil Ferdinand Ries also dates from this period.[2] Ries was to

---

[1] "It is the composer's secret task [wrote Marx in his still readable Beethoven biography] to overcome the "difficulty" of the concerto form in the form itself through the importance of the content. The difficulty is that the task—to treat one instrument and its performance as the main issue and the incomparably richer and more important orchestra as a mere auxiliary—is really an artistic anomaly."
[2] Wegeler and Ries. "*Biographische Notizen über L. van Beethoven*," quoted from 16, I, p. 93–94.

make his first public appearance with the C minor concerto and asked his Master to write a cadenza for him.

But Beethoven "refused and told me to write one myself and he would correct it." It was characteristic of Beethoven's attitude at that time that he not only permitted foreign matter to be inserted in his works, but actually ordered it. In any case, this time he supervised the procedure and could prevent slips of taste, and so on. We also see Ries's account that Beethoven did not grudge him his triumph as a virtuoso.

"Beethoven was very satisfied with my composition [he continued] and made few changes; but there was one extremely brilliant and very difficult passage in it, which, though he liked it, seemed to him too venturesome; wherefore he told me to write another in its place. A week before the concert he wanted to hear the cadenza again. I played it and floundered in the passage. He again—and this time a little ill-naturedly— told me to change it. I did so, but the new passage did not satisfy me. . . . At the public concert, Beethoven (who conducted) sat down quietly. I could not bring myself to play the easier one. When I now boldly began the more difficult one, Beethoven violently jerked his chair, but the cadenza went through all right and Beethoven was so delighted that he shouted 'Bravo' loudly. This electrified the entire audience and at once gave me a standing among the artists."

Mozart proceeded differently. He wrote cadenzas for his pupils when they played his pianoforte concerti in concert—and he well knew why: they were cut to the measure of each individual's ability. But in the course of time Beethoven, whose creative work in the realm of the concerto (exclusive of the youthful work of 1784), covered a period of a good decade and a half, had evidently changed his original point of view. Otherwise why did he write a series of cadenzas for his own concerti? He no more needed a written cadenza for himself than did Mozart. Did it please him, perhaps, to write down his own improvisations later? Or were these cadenzas new compositions? This would all amount to the same thing: the transitory, the improvised, was replaced by the permanent, the *res facta*. Hence Riemann asserted that "Beethoven also preferred to dictate to the virtuoso what he was to play at this point." In other words, by writing out his own cadenzas to his concerti, he could only have intended to keep others from adding free fantasies to his works.

Beethoven's written cadenzas represent a step forward along the road leading imperceptibly to the abolishment of the cadenza. He took the final step in the E flat major concerto. At the decisive point in the first movement we find the words at the heading of this essay—the terse phrase: *Non si fa una cadenza, ma s'attacca subito il seguente*. There should be no cadenza! An express prohibition. Does this prohibition refer *only* to the E flat major concerto? Is this an isolated case? Or is it not rather the result of a logical development which, once established (and definitely established in this instance), is to be the general rule from now on? In Beethoven's sense the interpretation would perhaps be: in Beethoven concerti no cadenzas but his own.

The art of improvisation is no longer practiced nowadays; therefore the particular soil that gave birth to the cadenza is lacking. Tradition has been unable to maintain the vital element of the cadenza. It has preserved only the dead form as an excuse for indulging in technical tours de force. From this point of view likewise, the existing practice of grafting strange bodies on classical works is artistically untenable.

But there is still another consideration which should not be passed over in silence for the sake of the present point of view. Since the cadenza is prescribed in the classical concerto and has therefore been carefully prepared, its omission might leave the impression of a "cause without effect" so to speak—to reverse a Wagner dictum. This would undoubtedly be a far lesser evil, as compared with the extraneous cadenza. Anyone wishing to avoid [the dilemma] and desiring to have recourse to a cadenza, should at least be governed by Beethoven's other law: *La cadenza sia corta.* In the last analysis, everything rests with the player's sense of responsibility toward the art work.—LUDWIG MISCH

c. Violin Concerto in D, Opus 61, Arranged (by Beethoven) for Piano and Orchestra[1]

From the very beginning, the reception from the vast public was quite different. They accepted the "concerto" with enthusiasm and—because the piano was more popular among them than the violin—it is understandable that they felt the desire to play it on the piano. Muzio Clementi, the celebrated pianist and composer, was among the enthusiasts of the "concerto" and so it was that after his insistent requests Beethoven decided to write the version for piano and orchestra.

The new version was published in 1807, that is, a year before the publication of the "concerto" in genuine form.

In the version for piano and orchestra, Beethoven maintained the orchestral part without alteration; while in that of the soloist he still sought to conserve the maximum of the violin version, he often had to make appropriate changes that had become necessary because of the different mechanism of playing the two instruments and for the desire to exploit the low register of the piano which would otherwise remain inactive.[2] The most notable difference between the two versions is in

---

[1] For a structural analysis see William F. Apthorp's concise essay.—Editor.

[2] Other notable changes between the piano arrangement and the original violin part are:

In the first movement in the third and fourth measures of the solo part the left hand of the piano echoes the orchestra chord (which is on the first beat) on the second beat thereby "filling out" an embarrassing pause.

After the next tutti, where the solo suddenly shifts to F major, the left hand

of the piano fills out the harmonies with a simple Alberti bass in legato eighth-note triplets, thereby contributing to the soft, peaceful other-worldly mood of the passage.

Underneath the long trill on the high E where the winds have two allusions to the main theme (four repeated quarter notes and the *sfp* whole note) the left hand of the piano echoes the winds on the off-measures with ascending arpeggios in eighth-note triplets ending with four repeated high notes similar to the figure with which it answers the orchestra at the very beginning of the solo exposition (after it has announced the first phrase of the theme in the extreme high register).

In the next solo passage after the six measures of ascending sixteenth notes, when it reaches a high F natural held for two bars and resolved into F sharp, the violin held note is unadorned, but Beethoven specifies a crescendo of two measures on the note. As this crescendo would not be possible on the piano, Beethoven in the piano arrangement adorns the whole notes with a trill, thereby allowing for the maximum crescendo.

In the peaceful pianissimo G minor episode the left hand of the piano fills out every other measure with repeated quarter-note chords answering the horns (and later the bassoons) of the orchestra.

At the thirteenth measure after the cadenza where the bassoon twice announces the two-measure closing phrase, answered each time by scale and arpeggio figurations of the soloist, Beethoven in the piano arrangement accompanies the bassoon in those two-measure interstices by similar scale and arpeggio figures in the left hand (and low register) of the piano.

In the second movement the rising arpeggio figures in the first appearance of the soloist are filled out in the third beat by an arpeggio in the left hand under the tenuto high note of the melody.

In the seventh measure of the theme the soloist adorns each quarter note of the theme (as played on the clarinet) with three sixteenth notes. In the piano arrangement Beethoven further adorns it with overlapping three-note figures in the left hand.

The second time the soloist has a fermata on the high F sharp the piano cadenza is infinitely more florid than that of the violin in the similar place.

One of the most difficult passages in the concerto literature for the musicians to *feel* the basic pulse is the passage after the second tutti where the soloist has a quarter note on the third beat of the measure and a free rubato passage on the fourth beat leading up to the next note of the tonic triad on the downbeat of the following bar. In the piano version Beethoven helps this situation (where, as Tovey says, "time seems to stand still") by giving an additional pulse on the *fourth* beat of each bar with a chord in the left hand.

A similar place where Beethoven fills in a musical vacuum with a chord in the left hand is in the very last phrase for the soloist before the sudden fortissimo tutti which bridges the Larghetto over into the sprightly Rondo. Beethoven also wrote out a piano cadenza for this bridge passage. It starts with a fortissimo allusion to the characteristic rhythm of the upbeat to the theme of the slow movement. The repeated notes gather momentum and a brilliant sixteenth-note passage descending and ascending over two octaves remains poised on an eightfold repetition of the falling third A-F sharp (mirrored by F sharp-A in the left hand). This suddenly shifts to B-G and the rhythm shifts to the 6/8 of the Rondo. Tentative allusions to the characteristic falling fourth of the Rondo's main theme leads quite casually into the piano's announcement of the full main theme.

The only major change in the last movement of the piano version is in the second theme (first episode) in A major, where the soloist answers the orchestra's rising phrases of two measures with two-measure descending phrases in thirds. In the piano arrangement Beethoven further elaborates these answers with a sixteenth-note scale in the left hand.

In the coda where the brilliant syncopated eighth-note figures of the orchestra are answered by B flat arpeggios in sixteenth notes of the soloist, Beethoven adds

the question of the cadenzas. For the violin version of the "concerto"
Beethoven did not write any cadenzas (the cadenzas which are played
today were written by David, Joachim, Kreisler, and other celebrated
violinists), while he wrote all the cadenzas for the piano version. The
most important and widespread is that in the first movement (Allegro
ma non troppo). This cadenza has a characteristic part: it is carried out by
the piano with the "timpani obbligati," which accentuates the rhythm and
maintains a type of dialogue with the soloist. This is a novelty probably
without precedent in the history of classical concerti. The cadenza alone
gives a notable interest of artistic and historical nature to the piano version
of the Concerto Opus 61.—WIAROSLAW SANDELEWSKI

d. Concerto for Violin and Orchestra in D, Opus 61
I. Allegro ma non troppo; II. Larghetto; III. Finale: Rondo

1. The first movement (*Allegro ma non troppo*, D major, 4/4) begins
with a long orchestral ritornello. Four soft strokes of the kettledrums
on D usher in the first theme, which is given out by the oboes,
clarinets, and bassoons. After the first phrase of the theme we hear
four more soft kettledrum strokes on A, and the wind instruments
then go on with the second phrase. Now come four soft D sharps in
the first violins; the ear is puzzled; what can come next? Is this D
sharp the leading note of E minor? Or what is it? With the next
measure light comes! The chord of the dominant seventh (on A)
shows the D sharp to have been a semitone appoggiatura below the
second degree of the scale (fifth of the dominant). Upon the whole,
this problematical D sharp, coming no one at first knows whence,
is at once one of the weirdest and most characteristic strokes of genius
in all Beethoven. The exposition of the first theme is followed by
a first subsidiary in the same key; after a modulation by deceptive
cadence to B flat major, it returns to the tonic, in which key the
second theme makes its appearance. This theme (only eight measures
in length) is first given out by the woodwind and horns in D major,
and then repeated in D minor by the violins in octaves against a
running contrapuntal accompaniment in the violas and cellos; it is
developed at some length. It is followed by a short second subsidiary,
which is worked up to a *crescendo* climax, and leads to the triumphant
conclusion theme, which is still in the tonic and brings the first part

---

further intensity the second time by allowing the piano to play along with the tutti
orchestra.

Beethoven evidently did not write out a piano cadenza for the Rondo proper.
The two other cadenzas (plus cadenzas for the first four of his piano concerti)
were composed in 1809 at the request of his august pupil, the Archduke Rudolph.—
Editor.

of the movement to a close with a half-cadence on the dominant chord.

Now the solo violin enters. The first part of the movement is repeated, as is usual in concertos, the solo instrument either playing the themes, or else embroidering them with rich figural tracery. It is, however, worth noting that the irregularity of this part—its second and conclusion themes coming in the tonic—is cured in the repetition, both these themes now coming in the dominant. The conclusion theme is also worked up to a longer climax than before, the solo violin running through a series of bravura scale passages, arpeggios, and ascending trills that lead at last to a resounding tutti in F major. Here the free fantasia begins; the working out is in the orchestra for a while, until the solo violin comes in as it did at first—only now in C major—then modulates to B minor, in which key the first theme makes its reappearance. The remainder of the working out is long, elaborate, and exceedingly brilliant.

The return of the first theme in the tonic at the beginning of the third part of the movement comes as a *fortissimo* orchestral tutti; the solo violin enters on the first subsidiary, and the development proceeds very much as it did in the repetition of the first part. The climax on the conclusion theme leads to a hold of the full orchestra on the dominant, A. Here the cadenza is introduced, after which a brief coda ends the movement.

II. The second movement (*Larghetto*, G major, 4/4) is one of those short, ecstatic slow movements in a perfectly free form, pendants to which may be found in the "Waldstein" Sonata, Opus 53, and the Fourth Pianoforte Concerto in G major, Opus 58. One can almost look upon it as a slow introduction to the finale—with which it is enchained—rather than as an independent movement by itself. The muted strings give out a suave theme, which is forthwith repeated by the clarinet and horns, accompanied by the strings, while the solo violin embroiders it with more and more elaborate figuration. It seems as if the solo instrument were listening in rapture to the theme, and expatiating upon its beauty in its own way. The strings then repeat the theme *forte*, loud calls from the clarinets, bassoons, and horns answering every phrase of it. Then the solo violin enters again and goes through some brief passage work which leads to a more cantabile second theme, given out and developed by the solo instrument and accompanied at first by the strings, then by the woodwind. A free cadenza for the solo violin leads into the next movement.

III. The third movement (Rondo, *Allegro*, D major, 6/8) is built up on one of those rollicking peasant-dance themes, of which we find so many examples in Haydn's final rondos. The second theme, a sort of vivacious hunting call for the horns, is equally bright and cheery.

The movement is in the regular rondo form, and is worked up at considerable length and with immense brilliancy. The composer has made provisions for the insertion of a free cadenza near the end.

The orchestral accompaniment is scored for one flute, two oboes, two clarinets, two bassoons, two horns, two trumpets, timpani, and strings—
WILLIAM FOSTER APTHORP

Beethoven's Violin Concerto [begins] with a mysterious summons to attention by means of a simple rhythmic figure on a drum, a musical note completely detached from all other orchestral experiences. On the top of this, Parratt's[1] pupil suddenly heard a mass of organlike harmony that sounded as if the organ had become as alive and human as Parratt himself.

Beethoven is an untidy artist, though not as untidy as many people seem to think; but he is uncannily accurate in his Violin Concerto, and I had the good luck to begin my orchestral experience with a first-rate performance of it. After the shock of hearing the radiant tones of these wind instruments extended over the mysterious bass of the drums, how could the subtleties of orchestral string tone be more impressively put before me than by the mysterious D sharp with which the violins enter? And what could be more lucky for me than the fact that the D sharp itself had already aroused my curiosity, so that there was no danger of my losing the effect of the strings in a general dazzle of new experiences? Children must be allowed to lose definite impressions in such a dazzle; and nothing could be worse than spoiling their chances of enjoyment, as well as their hopes of constructing their own impressions, by submitting them to the equivalent of a Fairchild-family examination on the contents of Sunday morning's sermon.

My best chance of early appreciating the beauties of string tone was supplied by the fact that the composition is a violin concerto, and that the long-deferred entry of the solo violin gave me the most vivid possible experience of the contrast between the tone of one violin and the tone of an orchestral mass of strings. In his admirable treatise on instrumentation, Cecil Forsyth observed that in a concerto an absurd effect is often produced when the solo violin has given out a phrase which is afterwards taken up by the strings of the orchestra, who seem immediately to demonstrate: "this is how it ought to sound". This is the sort of experience that ought not to happen, and I was lucky in beginning with the experience of a concerto in which nothing of the kind does happen. It is not so easy to learn from the classics as

[1] Sir Walter Parratt, 1841–1924, famous British organist and teacher. He was appointed Master of the Queen's Music in 1893 and was Victoria's private organist for many years. Tovey is identifying himself as Parratt's pupil.—Editor.

you might think, for most of the lessons they teach are negative. A riddle which I always propound to my students is this: Q. What is it which we all wish to learn from the Great Masters, and why can we never learn it? A. How to get out of a hole. Because they never get into a hole.— DONALD FRANCIS TOVEY (12)

In 1828, during the first season of the Société des Concerts du Conservatoire, [the French violinist, Pierre] Baillot played the completely forgotten Violin Concerto of Beethoven, which, since its première in 1806, had received only one performance, in Berlin, in 1812. Another violinist of the French school, Henri Vieuxtemps, played it in Vienna in 1834. But not until the thirteen-year-old Joseph Joachim performed the concerto in London in 1844, with Mendelssohn as conductor, did the work begin to win popularity. As late as 1855, the eminent Louis Spohr—who rejected the late works of Beethoven while enthusiastically approving Richard Wagner—said to Joachim after a performance of the Beethoven Concerto, "This is all very nice, but now I'd like to hear you play a *real* violin piece."[1]

Insensitive as the judgment of Spohr may sound, it was conditioned by the virtuoso practices of the early nineteenth century. In those days few virtuosos were interested in performing concertos other than their own; their display pieces had to be tailored to their "style." Despite its unique beauty, the Violin Concerto of Beethoven suffers from the disparity between a towering musical concept and a comparatively unidiomatic treatment of the solo instrument. Beethoven's knowledge of the violin, though based on actual playing experience, cannot be compared with his creative affinity for the piano. His violin passages are conventional and seem at times to be derived from the keyboard, an impression that may be due to the proximity of the Piano Concerto in G major, composed during the same year. Beethoven was certainly aware of the problem; the original score of the Violin Concerto, as described by Tovey, "assigns four staves to the violin solo, in order to leave room for alterations; and in many places all the four staves have been filled."[2] Beethoven consulted the contemporary concerto repertory of Viotti, Kreutzer, and Rode, who were masters in exploiting the technical resources of their instrument. Broken octaves, which Beethoven favors in the first and last movements of his concerto, were used in similar fashion by Viotti and Kreutzer. A favorite device of Viotti was the elaboration of a melodic line in triplet passages; it reappears prominently in Beethoven's first movement. Kreutzer, too, had a personal manner in writing embellishing passages which seems to have impressed Beethoven. Rode's technique was too intricately violinistic to interest Beethoven. In general,

[1] A. Moser, *Joseph Joachim*, Berlin, 1910, II, 290.
[2] D. F. Tovey, *Essays in Musical Analysis (Concertos)*, London, 1936, p. 87.

Beethoven's technical demands are more modest than those of the Parisian school, for he uses the violin passages not for display but primarily as elaborations of thematic material presented by the orchestra. Double stops are almost entirely avoided, although an effective passage in the finale [the passage in sixteenth notes occurring at measure 68 seq.] seems to point toward a Viotti device [used in the first movement of his Fifth Concerto]. Nor does Beethoven care to exploit the rich register of the G string, except for the juxtaposition of the Rondo theme—an effective contrast previously tried by Viotti.[1] In general, however, Beethoven shows a predilection for the silvery high register of the E string. Whether the violinist Franz Clement, for whom Beethoven wrote the concerto, was consulted in matters of technique is difficult to ascertain. His playing was graceful rather than vigorous, his tone small but expressive, and he possessed unfailing assurance and purity in high positions and exposed entrances. Perhaps in keeping with the temperament and technical idiosyncrasies of his interpreter, Beethoven stressed the lyrical aspects of the violin while shifting the dramatic accents into the orchestra.

Despite its implied march pulse, the first movement of Beethoven's Violin Concerto is far removed from the contemporary concept. It is conceived along symphonic lines; the orchestra carries most of the thematic material while the solo violin appears at times almost incidental. The idea of embedding, as it were, the solo part into the orchestral texture was novel and alien to the virtuoso concept of the nineteenth century; it found no imitators except Brahms. Another departure from convention was the withholding of the *cantabile* theme from the soloist until the coda of the movement. The formidable and unusual length of the first movement is caused by two full expositions; by a development section expanded through the addition of a new episode; and by a rather full recapitulation with cadenza and coda. The lack of contrast between the two principal themes is mitigated somewhat by the opening four-four motif, which provides a measure of dramatic contrast.

The Larghetto, perhaps the most perfectly realized movement of the three, has in its closing section an affinity with Viotti's most famous work, the Concerto No. 22.[2] It is noticeable not only in the melodic line and supporting harmonies but in the whole manner in which the phrase is placed within the context of the movement. The *forte* preparation of the cadenza at the end also seems to have a certain relationship.

[1] In the finale of his Sixth Concerto (also interestingly enough a rondo in 6/8 time) Viotti states the gay main theme first on the E string and later on the G string. Beethoven reverses this.—Editor.

[2] Brahms was particularly fond of Viotti's Concerto No. 22, to which he seems to allude in his own Violin Concerto; he appears to have been more enthusiastic about it than about even the Beethoven Concerto. See A. Moser, *Geschichte des Violinspiels*, Berlin, 1923, p. 391 f.

Beethoven's Rondo finale approximates perhaps most closely to the contemporary taste. The theme is not of startling originality, and it is used somewhat repetitiously. From the point of view of violin technique, the last movement is definitely more idiomatic and inventive than the first.

When the concerto is considered as a whole, one must admit that while Beethoven may not have matched his French colleagues in the efficient handling of the solo part, in the end his genius was bound to relegate the violinistic shortcomings into the background. Indeed, one is not aware of them unless deliberately scanning the work from that point of view.—BORIS SCHWARZ

e. Triple Concerto For Piano, Violin, and Violoncello, Opus 56
I. Allegro; II. Largo, leading to III. Rondo: alla Polacca.

Once or twice in the middle of Beethoven's career we meet with what is usually described as a reversion to an earlier style. This description generally means that certain works make a less powerful and less definite impression on us than others. A close study and a sympathetic hearing of such works is a valuable experience not obtainable from greater things. Without the Triple Concerto Beethoven could not have achieved the Piano Concertos in G and E flat, nor the Violin Concerto. It is in some sense a study for these works; and if it were not by Beethoven, but by some mysterious composer who had written nothing else and who had the romantic good fortune to die before it came to performance, the very people who most blame Beethoven for writing below his full powers would be the first to acclaim it as the work of a still greater composer. Let us take it on its own terms, and see what it can tell us.

None of Beethoven's three previous concertos[1] had satisfied him as to the treatment of the opening orchestral ritornello. In the first two he had allowed the orchestra to develop themes and sequences in a rather discursive way; in the third (in C minor) he had frankly begun like the exposition of a symphony, and had allowed the orchestra to change its mind abruptly just after that impression had been irrevocably conveyed. He is now going to solve the real problem of stating the vast procession of themes on the orchestra in such a way as to prevent any group from seeming to mark a separate development of dramatic action. If the procession can thus be kept, so to speak, on one plane, then the solo instrument or instruments can produce the grandest dramatic effects by spacing all this material out and adding their own material so as to build up a gigantic sonata form, with a second group in a suitable foreign key.

[1] The first three piano concertos, Opus 15 (1795), Opus 9 (1794), and Opus 37 (1800).—Editor.

But the opening tutti, in maintaining its processional movement, must also have its own dramatic character, and must arouse in more than a negative way some expectation that the orchestral crowd is going to be addressed and dominated by an individual.

The true solution of an art problem is often first achieved on the largest possible scale. Beethoven thoroughly enjoyed spacing out this first solution of his mature form of concerto on the huge scale required by three solo instruments, of which the piano will generally demand its separate statement of each theme, and the violin and cello (as a pair) their own statement. The dimensions of nearly everything except the opening tutti in this work are thus at least twice those of any normal concerto, even on Beethoven's scale. Moreover, he is so profoundly interested in the elements of trio writing against an orchestral background, that his piano part is very light, and his cello has, in virtue of its opportunities and position, quite the lion's share of the ensemble. Lastly, the material both of ornaments and themes is severely simple. It demands from performers and listeners the fullest recognition of the grand manner in every detail.

The statement of the opening theme pianissimo in the basses is one of those mysterious simplicities peculiar to great works. If the composer were Cherubini, every history of music would refer to it as epoch-making; and indeed the continuation is in its severe formality not unlike what Cherubini might have made it. The ensuing crescendo is in Beethoven's grand style, but not beyond lesser powers of invention. I [call attention to] its climax [appearing from measure 21 to 33] for reasons which will appear later. Suddenly the unapproachable Beethoven shows himself very quietly in the calm entry of what is afterwards to become the second subject [measure 31, seq.] Formal as this theme appears, it gives us that Greek combination of simplicity and subtlety which is the highest quality in art. It appears here in G major, but under circumstances which make it impossible for the ear to take that key seriously. We simply accept it as the dominant of C, and are not surprised when the theme continues in that key. A beautiful, purple patch—[from measure 44 on, where Beethoven dips mysteriously into foreign keys—] asserts for a moment a note of romantic solemnity, but leads to another tonic-and-dominant tributary theme in the same nonchalant marching rhythm as [the second subject]. Then there is a formal and emphatic process of "presenting arms" in G major, which again cannot possibly be taken as an established key. There is something mysterious in the way in which this passage lets fall an unharmonized cadence figure; but it seems quite natural that, this being so, the cadence figure should go a step farther and end emphatically in C. Evidently we are waiting for something or somebody.

The cello enters quietly with [its own statement of] the main theme;

the violin answers it in the dominant; and the two move back to the tonic with great breadth, gracefully ushering in the piano, which, with its third statement, rounds off the theme in trio dialogue with proportionate brilliance and climax. The orchestra then surprises us by bursting in with a new military march.

The solo trio takes this up calmly, and proceeds to shed an unexpected light upon the whole past and future of the movement by modulating toward a key of which no hint has been given, the key of A, the submediant. The preparations for this are laid out on a huge scale; and we have the full power of Beethoven revealed in the radiant effect of the entry of [the] second subject in A major [—that theme which appeared so calmly in the orchestral introduction.] The cello and the violin have divided its two phrases between them; and the orchestra begins vigorously with a counterstatement, which, however, the solo trio instantly catches up as a variation, carrying it through the purple patch. The variation now develops on a large scale, and comes to a deliberate close in A minor. Or rather, just as it is going to do so, the violin and the cello rush in with an energetic new theme. The first four bars of this they turn into an expanded variation, and then they join the piano in a vigorous counterstatement, presenting it in yet another variation, and expanding and delaying the close in the grandest style. Indeed, the close is interrupted by a sudden *piano*, and the approach and building up of the characteristic trill is an intense pianissimo unsurpassed even by the closely similar passages in the Violin Concerto. The orchestra bursts in with the new transition theme [—the orchestral military march which originally appeared in a blazing comment after the three soloists' first entry with their commentaries on the main theme. The march theme now appears] in the unexpected key of F major. From this it passes back to A minor, in which key it concludes matters with the passage of "presenting arms" at the end of the opening tutti. And now is revealed the mystery of the unharmonized cadence which this otherwise formal passage let fall [on its first appearance from measure 241 on]. That cadence is made once more to swing round to A major, while the cello embroiders a beautiful cantabile upon it and passes straight on to an immense restatement of the opening theme in A major. The solo trio works this out at complete leisure as at the outset, as if there were no such things as modulating developments to trouble about. But when at last the trio chooses, it has no difficulty in starting the development with a sudden plunge into B flat. Indeed the trio seems rather to have been storing energy for this very purpose, and pursues a simple and direct course of dialogue in staccato triplets, while the woodwind accompany with the [eighth-note] figure of [the opening theme.] Soon the dominant of C is reached; the cello and the violin, joined in due course by the piano, call for the recapitulation in an expressive cantabile, followed by provocative references to [the opening theme] in a diminuendo that reaches an exciting pianissimo, until suddenly the anticipatory scales gather up strength and bring back the orchestra with the first theme in full harmony and full scoring.

In the recapitulation Beethoven shows an appreciation of a point established by Mozart, in that he follows this time the course of the original tutti, breaking the fortissimo so that the solo trio can participate in [the climax of the long crescendo. The material] is now so developed as to lead to the solo transition material on the dominant of C. This brings the second subject with all its solo accessories into C major; and fresh light is shed upon the vigorous new solo theme, [the vigorous theme in a dotted rhythm which was announced in the exposition by the two solo stringed instruments. The new light is shed] by the fact that after the first four bars it is continued throughout in the major. In due course the orchestra bursts out again with [a transition theme] in the key of A flat. This is so worked as to lead easily back to C; and we are now surprised by a huge symphonic coda in which the solo trio calmly takes up a phrase which has not been heard since the opening tutti, and follows it up by making something very brilliant and full of color out of the passage of "presenting arms." This broadens out and makes, for the last time, one of Beethoven's characteristic pianissimo climaxes, which settles down to a beautiful cantabile for the solo trio, while the orchestra has fragments of the main theme in the bass. Then the orchestra wakes up (più allegro) pulling the figure of that theme into a livelier form; and so the huge movement comes to a brilliant end.

The slow movement foreshadows that of the E flat Concerto in the dark and solemn tone color of its opening melody with the muted violins.

The melody is severely reserved; though here, as elsewhere in the byways of Beethoven's art, it would have become famous for its warmth and breadth if it had been ascribed to Cherubini. After the fourth bar the cello lifts the whole continuation to a higher octave. As the melody comes to its close the piano enters with a florid accompaniment, and the whole is restated, the first four bars being given by the woodwind, and the rest continued by the violin and cello in the heights. The resulting impression is that of a very large opening indeed; and this impression is strengthened by the broadly dramatic sequel which swings slowly round to the dominant of C, whereupon the solo trio proceeds to make preparations in an intense pianissimo. What it is preparing for turns out to be not a central episode but the finale.

The style of the polonaise was not uncommon for rondos and finales in Beethoven's time (an example may be found in the slow movement of one of Mozart's piano sonatas); but Beethoven has left us only three polonaises, one in the middle of the Serenade Trio, Opus 8, one a solitary piano piece, Opus 89, dedicated to the Tsarina, and the finale of this concerto.[1] None of these shows any of the formidable temper of Chopin's polonaises; nor is it overdressed or in any other way similar to the polonaises of Spohr and Weber, who, when they write a *polacca brillante*—which is the only kind they ever do write—are inclined to make a very smart-society person of it indeed. Otherwise all three of Beethoven's polonaises are eminently aristocratic and charmingly feminine. The genius and romance of the main theme lie in its exquisite modulation to E major and back again.

There is a crowd of orchestral and transitional accessories which will turn up at the end of the movement in the coda. The listener should look out for the characteristic way in which the second subject lands on its subdominant and thereon seems to evaporate, until the chord flutters down among the three solo players as a tonic chord and so leads back to the first theme. The second episode fills the middle of the movement with two contrasted themes which no one but Beethoven could have written. Against the athletic energy of the first, [given out by the solo violin,] we have a note of reproachful pathos in the second, [played espressivo by the solo cello.] This leads to a very dramatic passage of preparation on the dominant of C; and when the placid main theme returns it is accompanied by one of the most Beethovenish of thunderous trills in the piano. A full recapitulation of the first episode ensues, which in due course evaporates on the subdominant chord. This chord the solo trio now turns into something rather more mysterious, which instead of leading to the first theme, delights us by drifting into [the second espressivo part of the theme of the second episode.] This leads melodiously back to the dominant of C, but instead of a thunderous trill we have a more matter-of-fact pause of anticipation. Then the first theme astonishes us by trotting away at a brisk pace in duple time—a version which, after due statement and following up, the orchestra transforms into [a smoother variant]. The orchestra stops abruptly on a 6/4 chord; whereupon the solo trio executes a written-out cadenza accompanied with occasional chords on the orchestra, and suddenly dropping into a pianissimo at its climax. The final trill swells out and fades away; and then the full beauty of Beethoven's design is revealed in the fact that instead of ending brilliantly in this double-quick tempo, the polonaise theme returns in its original rhythm, broken up into dialogue for the solo trio, punctuated by acclaiming chords from the orchestra, and finally settling down in calm triumph to the unquoted accessory themes before the transition. These rise to an end the brilliance of which lies in its formal and ceremonial fitness.—DONALD FRANCIS TOVEY (4)

Besides the three solo instruments, the concerto is scored for one flute, two oboes, two clarinets, two bassoons, two horns, two trumpets, timpani, and strings.

[1] As well as one for military band in D major, WoO 21 (1810).—Editor.

f. Choral Fantasia for Piano Solo, Chorus, and Orchestra, Opus 80

I. Adagio. (Pianoforte Solo.) C minor.

II. Finale: Allegro (Introductory dialogue with orchestra).

III. Meno allegro. C major (Statement of theme, with group of variations and coda).

IV. Molto allegro. C minor (Variation followed by development).

V. Adagio. A major (Slow variation with coda), leading to

VI. Alla Marcia: assai vivace. F major (Variation followed by development).

VII. Allegro. C minor (the first introductory dialogue resumed).

VIII. Allegretto moderato quasi Andante con moto. C major Vocal statement of the theme to a poem by Kuffner).

IX. Presto (Coda).

The Choral Fantasia is neither a concerto for the pianoforte nor just a setting of a poem to music for a chorus. It is an improvisation and a vision. In the Golden Age all music was improvisation; creation and performance were one and the same thing. In Beethoven's days, and throughout the whole eighteenth century, public extemporization was quite a common thing; indeed it was expected as a matter of course from any musician who aspired to be something more than a mere player.

A composer of Beethoven's reputation would be expected to exhibit his creative powers on a more extended scale. Arpeggios and sham recitative were hardly enough. The two obvious forms for an extemporization are fugue and variations; they may also be combined.

The first duty of a prelude is to arrest attention and concentrate it. So we begin with a few full chords, or a long held bass note; the choice of our chords will depend on whether we wish to settle our audience quietly or to startle them. We must make acquaintance with the touch of our instrument, indeed get our own fingers into practice; for we have only consented to extemporize after much pressure and it is part of our pose that we have not touched a keyboard for weeks. So we run about a little in sixteenth notes; if we are in the mood for it we may even turn our prelude into a toccata or an étude. If we are really none too fluent we may try a little recitative, or hint at a fugato if we cannot manage a fugue. The fact is that we have to gain time, and try to think out some sort of real idea while we are supposed to be waiting for the divine afflatus. We can keep our audience in a state of interested suspense for a space with effects of pleasant or unpleasant sound and vague reminiscences of some musical convention with which they are familiar. The works of J. S. Bach will illustrate all these methods.

The Choral Fantasia has the characteristic form of an extemporization on the grand scale. It has its plan; one could not expect the chorus and orchestra to extemporize as well as the pianist. But it is planned to suggest an extemporization, and we know that at the first performance Beethoven did himself actually extemporize the whole of the introductory movement. The score as printed still bears the trace of that extemporization in the direction which heads the first entry of the orchestra: *Qui si da un segno all'orchestra o al direttore di musica.* And it is curious to note that this entry, which one might have thought to be the real beginning of the work, is also headed in large letters "Finale." The main scheme of the work is a theme and variations. The variations fall into two groups, the first instrumental, the second vocal. They are preceded by a long quasi-extemporary introduction for the pianoforte, after which comes a rhapsodical dialogue between pianoforte and orchestra. Between certain variations there are developments on the lines of a concerto; before the voices enter there is a short reference to the rhapsodical dialogue, and the work concludes with a long coda.

Let us consider the Choral Fantasia from a more romantic point of view. Our first clue to its meaning should naturally come from the words which are sung. The author of them was one Christoph Kuffner, author of numerous plays, poems and novels popular in their own day but now utterly forgotten. The words of the Choral Fantasia have no great literary merit, but they have nonetheless a certain significance. Kuffner was a devoted lover of music and had in his youth been the friend of Haydn and Mozart. His poem sings the praise of music and its power. And it is clear that this friend of Haydn and Mozart was trying to express in his verses something which lay very near the hearts of those two musicians—the ideas which inspired "The Magic Flute," the mystical spirit of eighteenth-century Freemasonry, the new religion of liberty, equality, and fraternity. Here is a translation, or rather, a free version of Kuffner's poem, which can be sung to Beethoven's music if slight modifications are made to fit certain bars.

> Strains of secret music hover
>   Round the wisely listening ear;
> Eyes that Beauty once has opened
>   Find her flowers everywhere.
>
> Happy souls, by her enlightened!
>   Sweet content is theirs and joy;
> Toss'd no more on passion's tempest,
>   Wafted toward the life on high.

When the singer's notes are wedded
    To the poet's word of might,
Forth from formless void and darkness
    Breaks the new created light.

Blest are those to whom 'tis granted
    To behold that wondrous ray,
Why by Truth and Beauty guided
    Find the realm of endless day.

Every seed of noble nature
    That within their hearts was sown
Wakes to nobler life and fragrance
    In that glorious light alone.

There the seer of inward visions,
    Borne aloft on Music's wing,
Hears a thousand echoing voices
    To his own in answer ring.

Haste, O soul, that voice to follow,
    Haste, O soul, that joy to share,
Led by Love, by Strength and Beauty
    On to Music's final sphere.

The pianist in the Choral Fantasia represents the poet. The introductory pages set us in the atmosphere of rhapsody and inspiration; he strikes magnificent attitudes, hints at visions, breaks off suddenly with a gesture of mystery. A new theme enters, given out by the basses of the orchestra—quiet, but resolute and threatening. The poet protests in pathetic phrases of recitative. It is interesting to note that on the occasion when Beethoven first played the Choral Fantasia, in 1808, it was preceded by the Pianoforte Concerto in G major, the slow movement of which presents us with a very similar situation. And it was followed by the C minor Symphony. Beethoven knew what he was about when he arranged that program. Gradually the voices of the orchestra assemble, soft, mysterious, secretive and troubled, like the citizens in "Egmont." There is a pause. Two horns call, and are echoed by two [oboes] softly, as if asking a question. They answer it themselves; then after two clear assertions of agreement, the poet propounds his theme. It is one of those utterly naïve and childlike tunes such as Beethoven alone could write—infinitely trivial or infinitely sublime, according as it strikes the hearer. It is a tune which one must receive in a childlike spirit, and the first few variations seem to show it to us in a state of happy infancy, surrounded by the little fluttering noises of wind instruments—cooing horns, a butterfly flute and twittering [oboes]. A new emotion comes into it with the altered line which the clarinets present; the period covered by Beethoven's lifetime is an interesting field in which to study the gradual evolution of the personality of the clarinet, and the change which the personality of the [oboe] underwent as the result of the clarinet's ascendancy. I refer the reader to "Così fan Tutte." The bassoon part which accompanies these two clarinets still belongs to the eighteenth century; the romantics would never have allowed the bassoon to be so publicly industrious.

With the entry of the [strings] the theme becomes more vigorous until the full orchestra presents it grown to man's estate. The pianoforte has been silent for some time. Prometheus the poet has been watching the development of his creatures; now, when they have reached their first maturity he can speak to them, urge them on, show them yet further ideals to which they may press forward. He leads them on to a new key; it is only the dominant, but at this stage even the dominant is an adventure. There are reminiscences of the Waldstein Sonata, hints at the theme of the "Ode to Joy," an unexpected stab of pain, and then the crash of battle. At this point the variations are interrupted by a long development section which foreshadows the Pianoforte Concerto in E flat, composed in the following year although published under an earlier opus-number. After wandering through a wide range of new experiences we come to another variation. It is an adagio, and in a strange key, A major. It brings us a new type of sentiment. The theme is remembered by the clarinets, and we recall Berlioz's association of them with the voices of "noble heroic women." The poet at the pianoforte decorates their version of the theme with delicate phrases of caressing tenderness, while, underneath, violas and violoncellos seem to murmur a recollection of

Mir ist so wunderbar—

That subsidiary theme on the arpeggio of the subdominant chord, with which the poet first waved on his followers to adventure, here reappears, but more like a lingering farewell. Horns call again in the distance, the key changes to F and the hero rides off to a jingling march. But his thoughts are elsewhere. He is "the eternal dreamer" of Germany, and as he dreams an anxious pizzicato phrase becomes more and more insistent until once more that threatening motive with which the orchestra first set in after the poet's introduction returns. But the poet has no more fear or hesitation. One great startling chord interrupts the murmur and he has the crowd under his control. The poet is certain of his power; he knows the spell of Orpheus whose song draws all living things after him. We have for some time been becoming conscious that the emotional scheme of the Choral Fantasia is much the same as that of Richard Strauss's "Ein Heldenleben." Like Strauss, Beethoven ends his story with the hero as poet.

It is at this point that the voices of the singers are first heard. Beethoven has always had the reputation of writing music which no singers can ever sing. If he does so it is not for want of sympathy with the singers or for want of understanding of the expressive powers of the human voice; it is because he regards the human voice as the only medium for his most sublime and exalted inspirations. In this respect the Choral Fantasia is the conscious forerunner of the Choral Symphony and the "Missa Solemnis." Like Haydn in his "Creation," Beethoven demands a chorus not of men and women but of angels. Later generations have always regretted that there was not a closer personal contact and collaboration between Beethoven and Goethe; but had personal contact been possible, there was another poet living in those days whose visions ought to have been interpreted by Beethoven—William Blake.

Once more the horns and [oboes] call; this time they have no hesitating pauses, for the rushing arpeggios of the poet at the pianoforte carry them on to their affirmative C major chord, and the basses of the orchestra enforce their affirmation by the proud logic of their descent from the dominant chord of G through the relentless (as so often in Beethoven) four-two on F to the six on E which buttresses the arch to the E above. The upper voices gently introduce the familiar theme; it should have had words by the author of the *Songs of Innocence*. Tenors and basses take it up, while the pianoforte elaborates it with yet more sparkling embroidery until the full chorus and orchestra burst in with the words

> Grosses, das in's Herz gedrungen,
>   Blüht dann neu und schön empor,
> Hat ein Geist sich aufgeschwungen,
>   Hall't ihm stets ein Geisterchor.

This stanza gives the clue to the meaning of the Fantasia and to most of Beethoven's choral music—it is the chorus of the "sons of God shouting for joy" whom the poet's word and song have transubstantiated for us.

We see now the technical value to the musician of a melody so simple and direct. It is suitable to any instrument and to any voice. It will take any words and will take on the emotion of any words. Beethoven requires words which have color and individuality, even more awkward consonants that shall force the singers to realize the sense of struggle which must of necessity precede the joy and glory of achievement. And just as this simple tune can be made to take on a new emotion by some minute change of harmony, so it can take on another kind of new emotion by the slight changes of phrasing and accent which are imposed upon it by the shape and sense of the words which are sung to it. It is a dreary work for a choral society to practice, if they have no idea of the work as a whole. Like so many of Beethoven's compositions, it requires an understanding of its moral intention as well as a mere performance of the notes. Choral societies love such a work as Bach's Mass in B minor because the actual notes are so difficult to learn that even good sight-readers can find something to worry them right up to the end of the whole season's rehearsals. Most village choruses could get the notes of the Choral Fantasia right at the first reading. What has to be studied and carefully rehearsed is something which very few choral conductors— Stanford, I need hardly say, was the most penetrating and inspiring of exceptions—ever seem to understand: the subtle values of vocal color and phrasing which depend partly on pure vocalization and partly on a fine sense of literary values. And in any choral work of Beethoven we must always be intensely conscious of moral values too. That may be difficult for us, because we have to make some considerable effort to put ourselves back into the frame of mind of a hundred years ago.

The hero of the Choral Fantasia, the poet, the seer, the man of genius, is Beethoven himself. It is Beethoven whom we must imagine seated at the pianoforte, evoking for us his vision of the poet's life, swaying us as the orator sways the crowd, catching us up into the glorious company of the elect who shall follow him to the fashioning of a newer and happier world.—EDWARD J. DENT

The fantasia is scored for solo piano, four-part chorus, two flutes, two oboes, two clarinets, two bassoons, two horns, two trumpets, timpani, and strings.

Operas and Incidental Music

I. FIDELIO, OPUS 72

Opera in two acts by Ludwig van Beethoven. Text by Joseph Sonn-leithner and Georg Friedrich Sonnleithner after the drama by Jean Nicolas Bouilly. First produced at the Theater an der Wien, Vienna, November 20, 1805 (in three acts), with Anna Milder, Louise Müller, Demmer, Meier, Rothe, Weinkopf, and Cache, conducted by Beethoven; given in two acts on March 29, 1806. First given in its final form at the Kärnthner-thor Theatre, Vienna, 1814. First performed in London at the Haymarket (in German), 1832, at Covent Garden (in English), 1835, with Malibran; New York (in English) 1839, (in German) 1856; at the Metropolitan, New York, 1884, with Marianne Brandt, Auguste Kraus, Anton Schott, Adolf Robinson, Josef Miller, Josef Staudigl, and Otto Kemlitz, conductor Leopold Damrosch.

CHARACTERS

Florestan, *a Spanish Nobleman* . . . . .Tenor
Leonora, *his wife, in male attire as Fidelio* . . . . .Soprano
Don Fernando, *the King's Minister* . . . . Bass
Don Pizarro, *Governor of the prison* . . . . Bass
Rocco, *chief jailer* . . . . .Bass
Marcellina, *daughter of Rocco* . . . . .Soprano
Jacquino, *assistant to Rocco* . . . . .Tenor
Soldiers, Prisoners, People
Time: Eighteenth century.   *Place:* A fortress near Seville,
Spain, used as a prison for political offenders

The libretto, which appealed to the composer by reason of its pure
and idealistic motive, was not written for Beethoven. It was a French
book by Bouilly and had been used by three composers: Pierre Gaveaux
(1798); Simon Mayr, Donizetti's teacher and the composer of more than
seventy operas (1805); and Paër (1804).

It was Schikaneder, the librettist and producer of Mozart's *Magic Flute,*
who commissioned Beethoven to compose an opera. But it was finally
executed for Baron von Braun, who had succeeded to the management of
the Theater an der Wien.

Beethoven's heart was bound up in the work. Conscientious to the last
detail in everything he did, there are no less than sixteen sketches for the
opening of Florestan's first air and 346 pages of sketches for the opera. Nor
did his labor in it cease when the opera was completed and performed.

Bouilly's libretto was translated and made over for Beethoven by Schubert's friend Joseph Sonnleithner. The opera was brought out November
20 and repeated November 21 and 22, 1805. It was a failure. The
French were in occupation of Vienna, which the Emperor of Austria
and the court had abandoned, and conditions generally were upset. But
even Beethoven's friends did not blame the nonsuccess of the opera
upon these untoward circumstances. It had inherent defects, as was apparent even a century later, when at the *Fidelio* centennial celebration in
Berlin the original version was restored and performed.

To remedy these, Beethoven's friend, Stephen von Breuning, condensed
the three acts to two and the composer made changes in the score. This
second version was brought forward April 29, 1806, with better success,
but a quarrel with von Braun led Beethoven to withdraw it. It seems to
have required seven years for the *entente cordiale* between composer and
manager to become re-established. Then Baron von Braun had the book
taken in hand by a practical librettist, Georg Friedrich Treitschke. Upon
receiving the revision, which greatly pleased him, Beethoven in his turn
rerevised the score. In this form *Fidelio* was brought out May 23, 1814,
in the Theater am Kärnthnerthor. There was no question of failure this
time. The opera took its place in the repertoire and when, eight years

later, Mme. Schröder-Devrient sang the title role, her success in it was sensational.

There are four overtures to the work, three entitled *Leonore* (Nos. 1, 2, and 3) and one *Fidelio*.[1] The *Leonore* overtures are incorrectly numbered. The No. 2 was given at the original performance and is, therefore, No. 1. The greatest and justly the most famous, the No. 3, is really No. 2. The so-called No. 1 was composed for a projected performance at Prague, which never came off. The score and parts, in a copyist's hand, but with corrections by Beethoven, were discovered after the composer's death. When it was recognized as an overture to the opera, the conclusion that it was the earliest one, which he probably had laid aside, was not unnaturally arrived at. The *Fidelio* overture was intended for the second revision, but was not ready in time. The overture to *The Ruins of Athens* was substituted. The overture to *Fidelio* usually is played before the opera and the *Leonore*, No. 3, is frequently inserted between the two scenes of Act II.[2]

In the story of the opera, Florestan, a noble Spaniard, has aroused the enmity of Pizarro, governor of a gloomy medieval fortress, used as a place of confinement for political prisoners. Pizarro has been enabled secretly to seize Florestan and cast him into the darkest dungeon of the fortress, at the same time spreading a report of his death.

One person, however, suspects the truth—Leonora, the wife of Florestan. Her faithfulness, the danger she runs in order to save her husband, and the final triumph of conjugal love over the sinister machinations of Pizarro, form the motive of the story of *Fidelio*, a title derived from the name assumed by Leonora, when, disguised as a man, she obtains employment as assistant to Rocco, the chief jailer of the prison. Fidelio has been at work and has become a great favorite with Rocco, as well as with Marcellina, the jailer's daughter. The latter, in fact, much prefers the gentle, comely youth, Fidelio, to Jacquino, the turnkey, who, before Fidelio's appearance upon the scene, believed himself to be her accepted lover. Leonora cannot make her sex known to the girl. It would ruin her plans to save her husband. Such is the situation when the curtain rises on the first act, which is laid in the courtyard of the prison.

Act I. The opera opens with a brisk duet between Jacquino and Marcellina, in which he urges her definitely to accept him and she

[1] See the excellent essays on the comparison among these four overtures by Tovey and Misch.—Editor.

[2] But this practice is by no means universally approved (except, maybe, among conductors, since it gives them a solo opportunity). *Leonore* No. 3 repeats much of the material of the scene it follows; sacrifices the effect of sunshine and of solution which the C major of the final scene can produce when *not* preceded by music in the same key; and entirely destroys the dramatic balance of the whole act. Professor Dent has pointed out in addition that the careful balance of the instrumentation of the opera is upset (compare the dynamic ranges of the *Fidelio* overture and *Leonore* No. 3) and has suggested that the piece be played at the end of the whole opera for the benefit of those who must have it and of the prima donna conductors who must play it!

cleverly puts him off. Left alone, she expresses her compassion for Jacquino but wishes she were united with Fidelio. ("O *wär ich schon mit dir vereint*"—O were I but with you united.)

Later she is joined by her father. Then Leonora (as Fidelio) enters the courtyard. Marcellina, seeing how weary Leonora is, hastens to relieve the supposed youth of his burden. Rocco hints not only tolerantly but even encouragingly at what he believes to be the fancy Fidelio and Marcellina have taken to each other. This leads up to the quartet in canon form, one of the notable vocal numbers of the opera, "*Mir ist so wunderbar*" (How wonderous the emotion). Being a canon, the theme enunciated by each of the four characters is the same, but if the difference in the sentiments of each character is indicated by subtle nuance of expression on the part of the singers, and the intonation be correct, the beauty of this quartet points the tragic implications of much of the rest of the opera. The participants are Leonora, Marcellina, Rocco, and Jacquino, who appears toward the close. "After this canon," say the stage directions, so clearly is the form of the quartet recognized, "Jacquino goes back to his lodge." Rocco sings a song in praise of money and the need of it for young people about to marry. ("*Hat man nicht auch Gold beneben*": Life is nothing without money.) Its jocular, vulgar character is curiously at variance with the style of the quartet it follows.

The situation is awkward for Leonora, but the rescue of her husband demands that she continue to masquerade as a man. Moreover there is an excuse in the palpable fact that before she entered Rocco's service Jacquino was in high favor with Marcellina and probably will have no difficulty in re-establishing himself therein when the comely youth Fidelio turns out to be Leonora, the faithful wife of Florestan.

Through a description which Rocco gives of the prisoners, Leonora, now suspects what she had not been sure of before: her husband is confined in this fortress and in its deepest dungeon. The scene ends with a trio dominated by Leonora's "*Ich habe Muth*."

A short march, with a pronounced and characteristic rhythm, covers the change of scenes and announces the approach of Pizarro. He looks over his dispatches. One of them warns him that Fernando, the Minister of State, is about to inspect the fortress, representations having been made to him that Pizarro has used his power as governor to wreak vengeance upon his private enemies. A man of quick decision, Pizarro determines to do away with Florestan at once. His aria, "*Ha! welch' ein Augenblick!*" (Ah! the great moment!), is one of the heaviest and most difficult solos for bass voice in the dramatic repertory, but its effectiveness is undeniable.

Pizarro posts a trumpeter on the ramparts with a sentry to watch the road from Seville. As soon as a state equipage with outriders is sighted, the trumpeter is to blow a signal. Having thus made sure of being warned of the approach of the Minister, he tosses a well-filled purse to Rocco, and bids him "for the safety of the State," to make away with the most dangerous of the prisoners—meaning Florestan. Rocco declines to commit murder, but when Pizarro takes it upon himself to do the deed, Rocco consents to dig a grave in an old cistern in the vaults, so that all traces of the crime will be hidden from the expected visitor. The music of this duet, effective enough to begin with, is later subjected to repetition in a way which brings it perilously out of line with the dramatic situation— it provides evidence for those who doubt the existence in Beethoven of a sense of the stage.

Leonora, who has overheard the plot, now gives vent to her feelings in the highly dramatic: "Abscheulicher! wo eilst du hin!" (Accursed one! Where hasten'st thou!); a deeply moving expression of confidence that her love and faith will enable her, with the aid of Providence, to save her husband's life. The recitative, andante air, and quick final section is on the pattern made familiar by Mozart's "Dove sono," and, later, in the operas of Weber. "Abscheulicher" is one of the most famous examples of such a scena. Soon afterwards she learns that, as Rocco's assistant, she is to help him in digging the grave. She will be near her husband and either able to aid him or at least die with him.

The prisoners from the upper tiers are now, on Leonora's intercession and because it is the King's birthday, permitted a brief opportunity to breathe the open air. The cells are unlocked and they are allowed to stroll in the garden of the fortress, until Pizarro, hearing of this, angrily puts an end to it. The chorus of the prisoners, subdued like the half-suppressed joy of fearsome beings, is one of the significant passages of the score.

Act II. The scene is in the dark dungeon where Florestan is in heavy chains. The act opens with Florestan's recitative and air, a fit companion piece to Leonora's "Komm Hoffnung" in Act I.

The whispered duet between Leonora and Rocco as they dig the grave and the orchestral accompaniment impress one with the gruesome significance of the scene, and with Beethoven's delicate juxtaposition of melodrama and accompanied song.

Leonora thinks she recognizes her husband and obtains Rocco's permission to give him some food and drink. His heartfelt thanks for the unexpected kindness, her anguished recognition, and Rocco's premonition that the prisoner is beyond human aid combine in a trio of wonderful beauty.

Pizarro enters the vault, makes himself known to his enemy, and draws his dagger for the fatal thrust. Leonora throws herself in his way. Pushed aside, she again interposes herself between the would-be murderer and his victim, and, pointing at him a loaded pistol, which she has had concealed about her person, cries out: "First slay his wife!"

At this moment, in itself so tense, a trumpet call rings out from the direction of the fortress wall. Jacquino appears at the head of the stone stairway leading down into the dungeon and announces (in spoken dialogue) that the Minister of State is at the gate. Florestan is saved and the quartet ends with Pizarro's discomfiture. There is a rapturous duet, "*O namenlose Freude*" (Joy inexpressible) for him and the devoted wife to whom he owes his life.

In Florestan the Minister of State recognizes his friend, whom he believed to have died, according to reports set afloat by Pizarro, who himself is now apprehended. To Leonora is assigned the joyful task of unlocking and loosening her husband's fetters and freeing him from his chains. A chorus of rejoicing, "*Wer ein solches Weib errungen*" (He whom such a wife has cherished), brings the opera to a close.—GUSTAV KOBBE

As far as character goes, the *Fidelio* libretto, which as we know was founded on fact, does not represent an isolated case. On the contrary, it belongs to a type of material which was popular at the turn of the eighteenth century and figures in the history of music under the heading of "horror" or "rescue" opera.[1] The original French text on which the opera was based had already been set to music by Paer in an Italian translation just previous to, or during, the time that Beethoven was working on *Fidelio*. After the Dresden première of Paer's opera *Leonora ossia l'amore conjugale* (Leonore, or Wedded Love), Beethoven to his great annoyance naturally had to select another title for his work, which came out later and was to have been called *Leonore*.

Unexpected rescue from death is unquestionably an effective theme for a drama. And at the proper point (the quartet of the second act, *Er sterbe, doch erst soll er wissen*), Beethoven developed it to a scene which for sheer dramatic impact and breathtaking suspense has no peer in the entire literature of music drama. But this scene alone, which it is true represents the climax and turning point of the action, could not have been the deciding factor in the choice of the text. What really attracted him to the libretto and made him overlook the much-discussed dramatic weakness of the first version, which as we know underwent two revisions, was the inner content of the drama, which corresponded to his own deepest nature. He saw in it the reflection of an idea that he had nurtured in his heart all his life long and to which—after *Fidelio* —he as symphonist was to give artistic expression in [one] of his most grandiose creations, the Ninth Symphony; an idea that we usually formulate as "through darkness to light," or which might also be expressed in his own words: "through suffering to joy."

In a letter in 1815 [Beethoven wrote:] "We mortals with the immortal

---

[1] That is, melodramatic material characterized by sensational incident and violent appeal to the emotions, but with a happy ending.

spirit are only born to joy and suffering, and one might almost say that the Elect receive joy through suffering." In this sense the dramatic action of *Fidelio* took on for Beethoven a personal-programmatic and, at the same time, universal significance. And viewed in this light, we can understand why the second finale had to undergo such a tremendous development after the real action was already over. The broad treatment of the *Hymn of Joy* is also conditioned by artistic-economic considerations through the necessity of balancing off the heavily charged atmosphere, and anyone who is tempted to condemn it as a lapse into the cantata-like has failed to grasp what Beethoven had at stake here. The second *Fidelio* finale, which plays the same role with respect to the whole as the final movement of the Ninth Symphony, does not represent the end of an opera according to the stereotyped pattern, but it is the actual goal of the drama's development.

Writers on musical aesthetics have likened the Minister's entry to the introduction of the famous *deus ex machina*, which in antique drama and in opera up to the time of Gluck was called upon to untie man's inextricable knots. It is true that the Minister appears by chance just at the right moment (and even a *deus ex machina* disguised as Providence would also be no real dramatic factor), but the Heaven-sent savior merely completes the work which was begun by Leonore through her own strength alone and which she would also have brought to culmination even without this miraculous intervention. After the foregoing development, we never for a moment doubt that she would be capable of carrying out her threat and killing the mortal enemy in order to save her husband. Leonore—with all her confidence in help from on high—embodies Beethoven's own heroic ethics: "I will seize Fate by the throat." But this womanly figure must also have appealed to him in other ways than as a heroine. The opera was first produced under the title *Fidelio, or Wedded Love* and is still known today as the "Song of Songs of wedded love." "Love only—yes—this alone can give thee a happy life!" he wrote on another occasion. "O God, let me find her at last, she who will strengthen me in virtue, who is destined to be mine!" To him on whom Fate (the daemon of his genius and the misfortune of his deafness) had imposed the life of a solitary, Leonore became the symbol of an ideal wife, of the ethical principle of marriage. "Let him who has attained such a wife join in our joyful song." Beethoven glorifies the happiness of wedded love in almost the same words as he did many years later[1] in the finale of the Ninth symphony. And even before she recognized her husband in the suffering figure in the dungeon, Leonore by her oath: "Whoever thou art, I will save thee!" had transmuted wedded love into the all-embracing love of mankind—into humanity.

[1] We even find the identical text in the original version: "*Wer ein holdes Weib errungen.*" *Leonore*, piano arrangement by Erich Prieger.

He who inspired Leonore's heroic love must also have awakened Beethoven's humanity and deep compassion over and above the appeal to his creative imagination. For Florestan, the victim of cruel despotism, whose lament, *In des Lebens Frühlingstagen ist das Glück von mir geflohn* (Happiness fled from me in the springtime of life), might well have touched the chord of Beethoven's own sorrow, is not only an object of "tragic interest," he is the very personification of violated human rights. Furthermore, "the noble person who contended for truth" and now lies in fetters for his pains is the martyred champion of an ethical ideal. One can, without hesitation, substitute "right" for "truth" in the given connection and in so doing actually have "human rights" in mind.[1] We know what human rights signified for Beethoven by his outburst at the news of Napoleon's coronation as emperor: "He's nothing but an ordinary mortal! Now he'll trample all human rights in the dust . . . become a tyrant!"

Thus the saving of Florestan's life, the undertide of the dramatic action, became at the same time an artistic confession of faith in the ultimate victory of justice and the triumph of human love. For the figure of the Minister, whose intervention finally crowns Leonore's work, simply embodies the idea of humanity. At this fateful turn of events brought about "by justice linked with mercy," the question is no longer one of Florestan and Leonore. Their individual destinies merge into the collective and are raised to a symbol of the fate of mankind. "O God, Thou lookest into my inmost soul [we read in the *Heiligenstädter Testament*], Thou knowest it and understandest that love of humanity and a desire to do good dwell therein." Beethoven, who in the finale of the first act expresses the suffering and hope of the nameless prisoners with the same sympathetic fervor as he does the soul turmoil of the heroes of his opera, expands in the finale of the second act the "Song of Songs of wedded love" to the "Song of Songs of the love of mankind." This is brought out even more clearly in the quietly moving episode, which a phrase in the Minister's speech ("Brother seeks brother, and when he can help, he does so gladly") raises to tremendous significance, than in the exultant opening chorus of the folk and the prisoners. These wonderful bars overflowing with purest good will deserve the name "*Humanitätsmelodie*" no less than the inspired sostenuto assai ("O God what a moment!") which was taken from the cantata on the death

[1] There can be no doubt that Florestan, whom the Minister addressed as friend and the champion of truth, is a political fighter. When in Pizarro's case "he ventured to uncover a crime," no paltry rascality was meant such as a "corruption scandal" and the like, for otherwise the words, "I made bold to speak the truth," would smack too much of pathos. Pizarro must have been finally convicted for an analogous or the same crime —the misuse of executive power to put the troublesome out of the way. From the action taken against a transgressor of Pizarro's stamp (an individual case unknown to the Minister), we can easily see the nature of the whole struggle waged by Florestan for the cause of truth.

of Joseph II and, in the words of Riezler, "has been fittingly called the melody of humanity."

But the besmirched human dignity of the oppressed is restored by the glorified message of the brotherhood of man: the same spirit that imbued Beethoven's words to the "Immortal Beloved" when he wrote, "Man's humility before men pains me." The Minister turns to the prisoners: "Kneel no longer slavishly before me. The severity of the tyrant is foreign to me!" Given the actual theme of the opera, it is unnecessary to point out that the entire action is permeated by the ideal of freedom, which is invoked by the prisoners in hopeful yearning and by Florestan in transports of ecstasy. It is the same idea that Beethoven refound and glorified in *Egmont*.

The heroism of love and the heroism of moral conviction—optimism in deed and faith in divine and human justice and goodness—these were the ideas that Beethoven deduced from his libretto and through the might of his genius and the ethos of his personality formed and fashioned to an art work and profession of faith. His ethical creed also comes out distinctly, conclusively, and upliftingly in his instrumental works. But there it is less easy to define and demonstrate than in the opera where it has the assistance of the text. Therefore his ethics and philosophy of life come out more comprehensibly in *Fidelio* than in any of his works. And it is in this sense that Walter Riezler's words are to be taken: "Never did Beethoven reveal his soul as here."—LUDWIG MISCH

In the Prisoners' Chorus in *Fidelio*, the prisoners have, contrary to the orders of the governor, been let out of their cells and allowed to walk in the garden. Beethoven did not know how to bully his librettist, and after several revisions the libretto of *Fidelio* remained a hindrance to him, even in its final form; but he was a master of stage-timing where the libretto permitted, and the entry of the prisoners is of an overpowering pathos, achieved by the simplest means. The key of B flat is straightforwardly established, in a few slow chords arising from a deep bass; and when all the prisoners are assembled, they sing, at first in hushed voices, a pathetic strain of joy at seeing daylight and breathing fresh air; but the highest pathos is reached when one of them, with a sudden hope of real release, begins a new melody in G major. To have modulated from B flat to G would have been as infuriating as to preach to the prisoners a sermon on the blessings of liberty. The proper occasion for modulations is very different. The prisoners see that they are watched by a sentry, and they whisper to each other to speak softly and keep carefully within bounds. For this counsel, modulations are appropriate, and the more obscure the better. Beethoven deliberately avoids establishing any sense of key until, having landed on what happens to be a chord of D major,

evidently in the sense of a dominant, he drops from it, not to G major, but back to B flat, and there resumes the first strain of the chorus fortissimo; after which, with further apprehensive whispers that "we are watched and must keep within bounds," the prisoners disperse into the garden.—
DONALD FRANCIS TOVEY (1)

The dungeon scene is, in its now extant version, from first to last, "one of the greatest thrillers to be seen on any stage." That expression is as out of date as Pizarro's thirst for "crimson blood and the hour of my revenge":—but 1814 is pretty near to the actual date of that expression. Thus, even the humble literary values of the libretto are those of an original and not of an imitation. And they are faithfully translated into the music of Beethoven. The elements of operatic convention in [this scene] are clear enough to justify themselves, and they actually bulk much smaller in reality than in common report. Moreover, as we are dealing with first-rate melodramatic thrills, it is only fair to compare them with parallel phenomena in the cinema during the few years in which that modern art shall still give us opportunity to observe such phenomena.

For instance, it has been remarked, and justified as a good operatic convention, that Pizarro would in real life have a dozen chances of still killing Florestan while the music of the great quartet is pursuing its torrential course. I rather doubt this; few dramatic critics, and even fewer modern composers, know how short the apparently formal processes of classical music really are. However, supposing that Beethoven's quartet does stretch the action beyond realistic limits in order to achieve a musical purpose, that musical purpose fully occupies the listener's mind here and now, and only increases the dramatic tension; whereas in the cinema the only reason why the hero is tied to a barrel of gunpowder and left there to await the burning down of a six-inch candle is because common sense on the part of the assassins would make it impossible to announce that another episode of this hair-raising drama will be given next week.

An orchestral introduction gives an impression of darkness and of echoing vaults. At first there are no themes, but time is slowly measured out with sounds that build up rhythm, while the harmony firmly asserts its dark key from the outset. An articulate theme is heard on the dominant. Mysterious drum notes deepen the darkness. A gleam of consolation appears in a new key [D flat, with a tender, syncopated figure], but the darkness returns like the black waves that drown the afterimages in tired eyes.

The curtain rises. Florestan, chained to a stone block, is dimly seen by the light of a small lamp that shines high up on the wall of a vaulted dungeon.

FLORESTAN. Dark! and always dark![1]
How horrible the silence.[2]
Here in my lonely cell ne'er a living thing I see.
  O cruel fortune!
Yet the will of God is righteous.[3]
I'll not complain, for all my suffering comes from Him.

Florestan's great aria now begins. Its melody [appears] in two different versions [in] the *Leonora* Overtures [No. 2 and No. 3]. The version of *Fidelio* differs slightly from both.

> Ere my life is half completed
> All that gave me joy is flown.
> Words of truth too boldly spoken.
> Brought me here to die alone.
> All my pain I gladly suffer;
> End my life without a groan.
> This alone consoles my sorrow,
> That my duty I have done.

Suddenly the aria closes into a bright foreign key; and soon from a state of "half dreaming" the starved prisoner passes into feverish exaltation, Allegro, 4/4:

> Yet sometimes, half dreaming, I think I can see
> A vision that rises before me;
> An angel appearing in garments of light,
> With soft words of comfort and love to restore me.
> Or is it Leonora?
> Leonora, my angel, my wife?[4]
> Yes? Whom God sends to lead me to heavenly life.
> I see her; she comes to me now,
> To lead me to freedom and heavenly life.

He falls back exhausted. Footsteps are heard. Enter Rocco the jailer, and Fidelio, the youth who has come from nowhere, has entered his service, and has earned his wholehearted approval as his prospective son-in-law. Their task is to dig up a part of the dungeon floor that conceals an old well, so that the murderous commander of the fortress, Pizarro, may get rid of the body of his enemy Florestan before the arrival of the [King's Minister], whom Pizarro has been secretly warned to expect as a surprise visitor.

Accompanied spoken dialogue.
FIDELIO. How cold it is in this underground vault!

---

[1] This is followed in the orchestra by the first articulate theme which appeared in the introduction.—Editor.
[2] The drumbeats of the introduction are repeated here.—Editor.
[3] The accompaniment to this line is built on the tender syncopated figure which momentarily relieved the gloom of the introduction.—Editor.
[4] This line is set to a brilliant rising and falling motive in eighth notes.—Editor.

Rocco. Of course it is; it's a long way down.

Fidelio (*trying to see her surroundings*). I thought we should never find the entrance.

Rocco. There's the man.

Fidelio. He seems not to move at all.

Rocco. Perhaps he is dead.

Fidelio. You think so?

(*She tries to throw the light of her lamp on his face.*)[1]

Rocco. No, no, he is only asleep. We must get to work at once; we have no time to lose.

Fidelio (*aside*). It is so dark, I cannot distinguish his features. Oh, God help me if it is my husband.

(Quotations from a passage in Act I relevant to Rocco's next words.)

Rocco. Somewhere here under this rubbish is the old well that I told you about. We shall not have to dig far to clear the opening. Give me the pickax: you stand there and clear the stuff away. You're shivering. Are you frightened?

Fidelio. No, no; I'm only so cold.

Rocco. Well, then, set to work; that will soon make you warm.

Duet

This movement is a study in atmosphere, instrumentation, and declamation from the first shadowy, vibrating chords to the stark unison phrase with which it, and the gravediggers' task, ends. Rocco urges his fellow worker in tones that have little more than the rise and fall of speech. Fidelio replies in melody while at work, and the melody becomes heroic during the aside in which the determination is formed to save the prisoner, whoever he may be.

Rocco. Come, set to work, for time is pressing;
   There's not a moment to be lost.

Fidelio. You ne'er shall say that I was idle,
   Or left the task I had to do.

Rocco (*lifting a great stone*). Here, come and help me lift this stone up. Take care! and hold it fast.

Fidelio. I'm holding it! Push below!
   I'll do the best I can to move it.

Rocco. 'Tis nearly out. It moves! Come, lift again!

Fidelio. Take care! 'Tis nearly out. We have it now.
   (*The stone rolls away.*)

Rocco. Come, set to work: Pizarro's coming!
   We must have done before he's here.

Fidelio. A moment's rest and I am ready;
   Not much remains for us to do.
   (*aside*) That man, whoe'er he be, I'll save him,
   I swear I will not let him die.

[1] Here the orchestra plays the eighth-note rising and falling motive which accompanied Florestan's outburst: "Leonora, my angel, my wife." But they gain pathos by appearing not Poco allegro as he sang them at first, but Poco adagio and cantabile.—Editor.

Rocco. Come, come, I'll have no idling here.

Fidelio. Indeed, sir, not one single moment will I waste.

Rocco. Come, set to work, etc.

Fidelo. You ne'er shall say, etc.

The mouth of the well is cleared. The prisoner awakens. Fidelio (Leonora) recognizes him. Her quest is over: he is her husband. But she must not reveal herself. She must remain in her role of Fidelio until she can surprise Pizarro in the moment of his murderous intention. Meanwhile the goodhearted Rocco, considering that Florestan's sufferings will soon be over, ventures to answer the prisoner's questions at last. Florestan learns that he is in the power of Pizarro, whose crimes he had two years ago discovered and tried to reveal. Rocco gives Florestan a draught of wine.

Terzet.[1]

Florestan. Be this good deed in Heaven rewarded,
 For surely 'twas Heaven sent you here,
 My last remaining hours to cheer,
 Although by me with thanks alone rewarded.

Rocco (*aside to Fidelio*). Poor soul, the wine I gladly give;
 Few moments more he has to live.

Fidelio. My heart beats loud within my breast;
 With joy is, yet with pain, opprest.

Florestan (*aside*). How strangely moved the lad appears;
 And even the man seems half in tears.
 Together—

Fidelio. One only hope to me remains,
 To die with him or break his chains.

Florestan. And hope again returns to me
 That I may yet see liberty.

Rocco. I have my duty here to do,
 But hate the deed no less than you.

Fidelio (*aside to Rocco*). This piece of bread, may I not give him?
 He makes my heart with pity bleed.

Rocco. A kindly thought that was indeed,
 But yet I know I must forbid it.

Fidelio. Ah! yet you yourself this wine did give.

Rocco. I have my orders to fulfil,
 I must obey my master's will.

Fidelio. Few moments more he has to live.

Rocco. Then give him what you will, I'll not refuse you.

Fidelio. Then take, oh take this bread, oh hapless man!

Florestan. Oh take my grateful thanks.
 Together—

---

[1] A tender melody in A major (Moderato, 4/4).—Editor.

FIDELIO. Oh place your trust in Heaven above.
You know not yet how near its help may be.
FLORESTAN. 'Twas surely Heaven that sent you here
My dying hours to cheer.
ROCCO. Your sufferings filled my heart with pain,
Although to help I was not free.
Together—
FLORESTAN. 'Tis more than I can e'er repay.
FIDELIO and ROCCO. 'Tis more than I can bear to see.

All is now ready. Rocco gives a signal which brings down the waiting
Pizarro. He confronts Florestan and reveals himself.

Quartet.[1]

PIZARRO. So die then! Yet before you perish,
I'd have you learn who strikes the blow.
No more I'll hide my secret vengeance.
My name you, ere you die, shall know.
Pizarro. Did you seek my ruin?
Pizarro. 'Twas your own undoing.
He stands before you, and wreaks his vengeance now.
FLORESTAN. So murder, not justice, is your end!
PIZARRO. 'Twas you alone who sought my overthrow,
One moment more is all you have to live.
(*Fidelio rushes forward between Pizarro and Florestan.*)
Together—
FIDELIO. No, no!
FLORESTAN. O God!
ROCCO. How now?
FIDELIO. You shall not, while I stand by his side.
You shall not wreak your vengeance
Till I for him have died.
Together—
FLORESTAN. O God, help me now.
PIZARRO. What, would you dare? Yes, you shall die for this.
ROCCO. Stand back! Would you dare?
FIDELIO. I am his wife.
FLORESTAN. My wife!
PIZARRO and ROCCO. His wife?
(We may now call Fidelio by her real name.)
LEONORA. Yes, I am Leonora.
I am his wife, and I will not let him die.
For all your power.
Together—

[1] Allegro, 4/4, D major, starting with an agitated four-measure introduction played in
unison by the strings.—Editor.

LEONORA. His wrath I can defy, and all his power.
FLORESTAN. My heart stands still for joy!
PIZARRO. Does she my power defy?
ROCCO. My heart stands still for fear!
   Together—
PIZARRO. Shall I before a woman tremble?
LEONORA. You shall not wreak your vengeance
   While I stand by his side.
LEONORA (*presenting a pistol*). Say but a word, I shoot you dead.
(*A trumpet is heard from the tower,* as in the Overture *Leonora No. 3*)
   Together—
LEONORA. Ah! You are delivered! Thanks to God!
FLORESTAN. Ah! I am delivered! Thanks to God!
PIZARRO. Ah! That was the signal! All is lost!
ROCCO. Oh! What is that sound? Thanks be to God!
(*The trumpet sounds again.*)
   A voice speaks from the top of the stairway.
   Rocco! Rocco! The [King's Minister] is here! His outriders are at the gates!
   Together—
LEONORA and FLORESTAN. Now strikes the hour of vengeance!

$$\left. \begin{array}{l} \text{My} \\ \text{Your} \end{array} \right\} \text{dangers are all past.}$$

$$\left. \begin{array}{l} \text{Through} \\ \text{Your} \end{array} \right\} \text{courage and devotion}$$

$$\left. \begin{array}{l} \text{I'll} \\ \text{Will} \end{array} \right\} \text{set you free at last.}$$

PIZARRO. Accurst who thwarts my vengeance!
   Not yet my hour is past.
   Despairing frenzy fills me;
   I'll have revenge at last!
ROCCO. Now strikes the hour of vengeance.
   Are all his dangers past?
   Her courage and devotion
   May set him free at last.

                     (*Exeunt* PIZARRO and ROCCO.)

Duet.[1]

LEONORA and FLORESTAN. Oh joy beyond expressing,
   When heart finds heart again,
   Our anguish all forgotten
   In love's exultant strain.
LEONORA. Once more within my arms I fold you!

---

[1] An impassioned Allegro vivace 4/4 in G major in which the singers echo one another with a brilliant florid phrase expressive of the almost total abandon of their joy.— Editor.

FLORESTAN. By God's great mercy I behold you!
[Here the entry of the double-basses two octaves below the cellos
is a *locus classicus* for an orchestral risk taken with sublime results.]
LEONORA and FLORESTAN. O thank we Him whose tender care
Has given us now this joy to share.
My love! My life! Oh joy beyond expressing.
FLORESTAN. Leonora!
LEONORA. Florestan!

Recapitulation.—One cannot help wishing that Beethoven could
have retained a glorious modulation into B flat, which gave to the
original recapitulation and coda of this duet a glow which the excessive length and vocal strain of the sequel could not weaken; but
he is certainly right in now pressing on straight to the end, though
the composer of *Fidelio* in 1814 is undoubtedly sometimes very
severe in his treatment of the composer of *Leonora* in 1805.

The finale of *Fidelio* is a delightful festive scene in the open air,
with exactly the right lightness of touch to bring us into the mood
for winding up matters less sublime, though not less human, than
Leonora's heroism. But in the concert-room we may at this point
most fitly rise to the height of what Beethoven had in 1814 discovered to be altogether too sublime for any conceivable stage-music,
and we may measure the happiness of Leonora and Florestan by the
musical values of the Overture *Leonora No. 3.*—DONALD FRANCIS
TOVEY (6)

II. MUSIC FOR EGMONT, OPUS 84

When a commission came to Ludwig van Beethoven to provide music
for a performance of Goethe's *Egmont*, the composer took it up with
eagerness and excitement. For one reason, there was no one in German
life whom Beethoven admired more than Johann Wolfgang von Goethe,
poet, dramatist, philosopher, and twenty-one years the composer's senior.
Another reason was the theme of the drama itself which, set in the
Netherlands in 1567–68, dealt with the struggle for freedom from Spanish rule. The thought of "liberty against tyranny" always kindled a fire in
Beethoven, as his opera *Fidelio* had shown. And a possible third reason
might have been Beethoven's awareness of his own Flemish ancestry.

And so Beethoven produced the most remarkable example of "incidental music" in history, one in which drama and music of genius
were so well matched that the music seemed to take up without break
where the words left off. The performance of the play with the music
took place at the Burgtheater on June 15, 1810. In April 1811, Beethoven
wrote to Goethe about "this glorious *Egmont* which I read so ardently,
thought over and experienced again and gave out in music—I would
greatly like to have your judgment on it and your blame, too." Goethe,

who as Counselor at the Court of Weimar was a step higher in the social ladder than Beethoven, and who also did not love music as much as Beethoven loved poetry, answered courteously that he had heard the *Egmont* music "spoken of with praise by several," and that he planned to use it for a projected performance at the Weimar theater. In July 1812, at Teplitz, the two great men met for the first time.

The *Egmont* Overture was performed several times in Beethoven's later years as an independent work and today deservedly ranks in the concert hall as an outstanding masterpiece of its kind, a concentrated example of the musical dramaturgy that had made the *"Eroica"* and *Fifth Symphony* turning points in music history. But the loving care with which Beethoven shaped the rest of the score as an integral part of Goethe's drama caused it to suffer in terms of an independent concert life, despite its glowing inspiration. Beethoven felt this keenly. In 1814 he wrote to the poet and theatrical producer Georg Friedrich Treitschke, urging that the drama be staged and offering to write additional music if necessary. "Thus the music to *Egmont* would not be quite lost." Attempts have been made by Mosengeil, Grillparzer, and Bernays to write a declamatory text that could knit all the numbers together as a concert presentation. But it has remained for modern recording to make the beauties of the full score available to music lovers. And it is not amiss to suggest that modern listeners will find themselves much closer to Beethoven's mind if they hear the music in the context of a knowledge of Goethe's drama, either in German or in English translation.

Goethe's play, which had been written between 1775 and 1788, opens with a picture of the Netherlands seething with religious and political unrest. As an arm of the tightening Spanish grip upon the land, the Inquisition is persecuting Protestants, heretics, and dissenters. The city burghers and artisans are beginning to agitate for an uprising. Count Egmont is a dashing Netherlands nobleman, a hero to the people for the victories he led over the French, a Catholic, loyal to the Spanish king, and governor of the land. He counsels that Spanish rule be moderate, tolerant, and respectful of the ancient rights of the people. But King Philip sends the ambitious, harsh, and cruel Duke of Alva at the head of Spanish troops to establish "order" with terror and an iron hand. Shrewd political minds like William of Orange advise Egmont to guard himself and move to a place of safety. But Egmont is confident that his princely status will protect him, and that his suggestions for less despotic rule will be given some attention. Treacherously, Alva arrests Egmont and arbitrarily condemns him to death as a traitor.

The one major protagonist who is not a historical figure is Clara (or Klärchen), a burgher's daughter with whom Egmont is in love. (The actual Count Egmont was married and had eleven children.) She tries to instigate an effort to rescue Egmont and when she fails poisons herself.

Egmont meets his death bravely, knowing that it will kindle an insurrection that will bring about what Alva and Philip fear most, an independent Netherlands.—s. w. BENNETT (2)

The overture to *Egmont* begins with a concise slow introduction, (*Sostenuto ma non troppo,* F minor, 3/2); a long-held F for full orchestra, diminished from *forte* to *piano,* is followed by a stern theme in sarabande rhythm, given out strongly in full harmony by all the strings. Soft sighing responses come in imitation from oboe, clarinet, bassoon and strings, leading to another *fortissimo* F for full orchestra, which is followed in turn by a resounding repetition of the sarabande theme. Then come some more imitations on the sighing figure, followed by a new motive, repeated over and over again by the first violins, doubled by various woodwind, over a close *tremolo* for second violins and violas, soft chords on the bassoons and brass instruments, and a bass which still adheres to the sarabande rhythm.

The main body of the overture (*Allegro,* F minor, 3/4) opens with four introductory bars of *crescendo,* in which the first violins and cellos repeat a more rapid version of the last violin figure from the introduction; then the strings pounce upon the passionate first theme, each phrase of which consists of a descending arpeggio on the cellos, ending with an ascending sigh on the first violins. The antithesis of the theme begins with another strenuous sigh from the woodwind, which is forthwith answered by the strings, and developed in passage work in a livelier and livelier rhythm; this continues *crescendo* until the theme returns *fortissimo* on the full orchestra, with a new and more fiery antithesis. Some subsidiary passage work, which wavers between the tonalities of A flat and E flat major, leads into the second theme. The thesis of this is a modified version of the stern sarabande theme of the introduction, now given out in *fortissimo* chords in A flat major by the strings; the antithesis is a lighter, waving triplet figure for woodwind. The entire change of character noticeable in the thesis—from the sternness of the original sarabande to triumphant energy—is due to a slight melodic transformation, and especially to the change of mode from minor to major. A second subsidiary idea begins with a melodious phrase in ascending thirds on the woodwind, and then develops in more and more brilliant passage work; it leads to a third theme in A flat major, which consists of a series of closer and closer imitations on the initial figure of the first theme by the woodwind, interrupted at every eighth bar by crashing chords for full orchestra. A short transitional passage, beginning with reminiscences in C minor of the first theme in the basses, and developing into some more repetitions of the introductory figure of the violins, leads directly over to the third part of the movement.

The relations between this third part and the first are tolerably regular for a while. The second theme now comes in D flat major. But, at the point where the third theme entered in the first part, the original plan is abandoned: the clarinets, bassoons, and horns sound *fortissimo* chords in the sarabande rhythm of the thesis of the second theme, to which the strings softly respond with the sighing figure of the second subsidiary. Soft, sustained, mysterious harmonies in the oboes, clarinets, and bassoons lead over to the coda.

The coda (*Allegro con brio*, F major, 4/4) is based upon entirely new thematic material; it is the dramatic "apotheosis" of the overture. It begins *pianissimo* with a constantly repeated rising turn in the first violins, against tremolos in the second violins and violas, and sustained harmonies in the woodwind and horns, over a dominant organ point in the basses and kettledrums. This goes on in *crescendo* climax until the thoroughly Beethovenish explosion comes: the full orchestra precipitates itself in *fortissimo* upon a triumphant fanfare figure; then comes a strongly accented theme in the violas, cellos, and bassoons (the accents being reinforced by the horns), against which the violins pit a brilliant contrapuntal counterfigure; one could swear that one of Beethoven's well-nigh frantic fugatos was coming. But no, the development goes on purely homophonically, and rises to one of the most tremendous final climaxes in all orchestral music. Particularly famous are the little whistling shrieks of the piccolo flute in its highest register, against the fanfare of the brass and bassoons, between the resounding crashes of the rest of the orchestra in the last five measures.

This overture is scored for two flutes (the second being interchangeable with piccolo), two oboes, two clarinets, two bassoons, four horns, two trumpets, one pair of kettledrums, and the usual strings.—WILLIAM FOSTER APTHORP

The song *Die Trommel gerühret* (Vivace) is sung by Clara in the closing scene of Act One. She is at home in a gay mood, and this lighthearted soldier's song with rousing orchestral interjections expresses her thought of her lover, the brave and handsome Egmont.

Die Trommel gerühret!	The drum is resounding,
Das Pfeifchen gespielt!	And shrill the fife plays;
Mein Liebster gewaffnet	My love for the battle,
Dem Haufen befielt,	His brave troop arrays;
Die Lanze hoch führet,	He lifts his lance high,
Die Leute regieret.	And the people he sways.
Wie klopft mir das Herze!	My blood it is boiling!
Wie wallt mir das Blut!	My heart throbs with fire!
O hatt' ich ein Wämslein	Oh if I had a hat
Und Hosen und Hut!	And a soldier's attire!

Ich folgt' ihm zum Tor 'naus	How boldly I'd follow
Mit mutigem Schritt,	And march through the gate;
Ging' durch die Provinzen,	Through all the wide province
Ging' überall mit.	I'd follow him straight.
Die Feinde schon weichen	The foe we would shoot at
Wir schiessen darein—	And beat till they ran—
Welch Glück sondergleichen,	What joy it would be
Ein Mannsbild zu sein!	To be changed to a man!

Entr'acte No. 1 is in two parts, carrying on the tender feelings of the preceding scene (Andante) and then picturing the agitation of the people in the city streets (Allegro con brio) which makes up the opening scene of Act Two. *Entr'acte No.* 2 (Larghetto) is a touching slow movement doubly effective in context. It follows the end of Act Two, when William of Orange has warned Egmont to beware of Alva, and its reflectively tender music is troubled by the muffled "tyrant" theme of the overture and the undercurrent of drumbeats. *Freudvoll und leidvoll* is Clara's beautiful love song, in the closing scene of Act Three.

Freudvoll und leidvoll	Blissful and tearful
Gedankenvoll sein;	With thought-teeming brain;
Langen und bangen	Hoping and fearing
In schwebender Pein;	In wavering pain;
Himmelhoch jauchzend,	Praising heaven with joy,
Zum Tode betrübt:	Then with death-thoughts riven;
Glücklich allein	Happy the soul
Ist die Seele, die liebt.	To which love has been given.

S. W. BENNETT (2)

Freudvoll und Leidvoll.—This is the second of the two songs which *Clärchen* sings in Goethe's tragedy, "Egmont." Concerning the songs, Mr. Thayer prints the following statement in his biography of Beethoven from a letter written to him in 1867 by the first representative of *Clärchen* who sang the music. This was Antoine Adamburger, afterward the wife of the archaeologist von Arneth.

"I was then a childish, happy, merry little thing, quite unable to appreciate the worth of the man, who did not seem at all imposing to me; while now, seventy-six years old, I deeply feel the joy of having known him. It was because of this that I advanced toward him without the slightest embarrassment when my blessed aunt, my benefactress, had me called to her room and introduced me to him. His question, 'Can you sing?' I answered unhesitatingly and frankly with a 'No.' Beethoven looked at me in surprise and said with a smile, 'No? Why, I am asked to compose the songs in "Egmont" for you.' I replied simply that I had sung only four months and, becoming hoarse, had quit lest my voice should suffer from the strain of excessive use, since I was practicing declamation diligently. Then in a jovial tone, playfully assuming the

Vienna dialect, he said: 'Humph! that will be a pretty mess!' (*Nun das wird was sauberes werden*); but so far as he was concerned it turned out to be something glorious. We went to the pianoforte, and turning over the music piled on it—old pieces inherited from my father, whose singing I imitated like a parrot (I can sing the things by heart, at this moment)—he found on top the familiar rondo with recitatives from Zingarelli's 'Romeo and Juliet.' 'Sing that,' he cried, with a laugh that shook him as he sat down doubtfully to play the accompaniment. I rolled off the air as ingenuously as I had chatted with him. Then an amiable look came into his eye, he brushed my forehead with his hand and said: 'Good, now I understand.' (*Ah so, jetzt weiss ich es.*) Three days afterwards he came and sang the songs for me several times. A few days later, after I had learned the songs, he left me with the words: 'Now, that's right; that's the right way, sing that way, don't permit anybody to persuade you to something else, and don't put in a single mordent.' He went, and I never saw him in my room again. Only at the rehearsal while he was conducting he often nodded to me pleasantly and benevolently."—H. E. KREHBIEL (1)

Entr'acte No. 3 (Allegro) develops orchestrally the love-song motif, and then changes abruptly (Marcia-Vivace) to marching music, raising the curtain on the agitated and rebellious city people whose scene opens Act Four. This act brings the drama to its climax, the curtain falling on Alva's arrest of Egmont. *Entr'acte No. 4* (Larghetto) begins with a cry of outrage and pain, and then moves into a sad, troubled, yet consoling melody, ending quietly. In the third scene of Act Five, Clara has been with Brackenburg, the young suitor whom she had rejected but who is still in love with her. She, unobserved by him, drinks poison, the two walk off, and at this point, with the curtain still up on an empty stage lit by a flickering lamp, the music for *Clara's Death* (Larghetto) is heard. Its tenderly lamenting song over soft throbbing ostinatos, speaks as only music can for what is in everybody's heart.

The *Melodrama* is music written for the last scene of the play. It begins with soft melodies accompanying Egmont's falling asleep.

Süsser Schlaf! Du kommst wie ein reines Glück ungebeten, unerfleht am willigsten. Du lösest die Knoten der strengen Gedanken, vermischest alle Bilder de Freude und des Schmerzes; ungehindert fliesst der Kreis innerer Harmonien, und eingehüllt in gefälligen Wahnsinn, versinken wir und hören auf, zu sein.

Sweet sleep! Like the purest happiness, thou comest most willingly, uninvited, unsought. Thou dost loosen the knots of earnest thoughts, dost mingle all images of joy and of sorrow; unimpeded the circle of inner harmony flows on, and, wrapped in fond delusion, we sink away and cease to be.

The music swells, as a vision appears to Egmont of Clara in the garb of a Goddess of Liberty, bringing him the laurel crown of a victor, and signifying that the Netherlands will win their freedom.

Verschwunden ist der Kranz! Du schönes Bild, das Licht des Tages hat dich verscheuchet! Ja, sie waren's, sie waren vereint, die beiden süssesten Freuden meines Herzens. Die göttliche Freiheit, von meiner Geliebten borgte sie die Gestalt. Mit blutbefleckten Sohlen trat sie vor mir auf. Es war mein Blut und vieler Edeln Blut. Nein, es ward nicht umsonst vergossen. Und wie das Meer durch eure Dämme bricht, so brecht, so reisst den Wall der Tyrannei zusammen und schwemmt ersäufend sie von ihrem Grunde, den sie sich anmasst, weg!

The crown is vanished. Beautiful vision, the light of day has frightened you away! Yes, they appeared before me, they appeared, the two sweetest joys of my heart. Divine Liberty disclosed herself, taking the face and form of my beloved one. With bloodstained feet she approached me. It was my blood and the blood of many brave people. No, it will not be shed in vain. And just as the ocean breaks through the dikes, so you will smash through the bulwark of tyranny and sweep it out of your land, which it tries to possess.

(Drums, continuing through the following passages)

Horch! Wie oft rief mich dieser Schall zum freien Schritt nach dem Felde des Streits und des Siegs! Auch ich schreite einem ehrenvollen Tode aus diesem Kerker entgegen; ich sterbe für die Freiheit.

Listen! How often has this sound summoned my joyous steps to the field of battle and of victory! And now I go forth from this dungeon to meet a glorious death; I die for freedom.

(The background is filled with Spanish soldiers carrying halberds)

Schliesst eure Reihen, ihr schreckt mich nicht! Ich bin gewohnt, vor Speeren gegen Speere zu stehn und, rings umgeben von dem drohenden Tod, das mutige Leben nur doppelt rasch zu fühlen.

Freunde, höhern Mut! Im Rücken habt ihr Eltern, Weiber, Kinder!

Close your ranks, you do not frighten me! I am accustomed to standing where spears clash with spears, and, menaced by death on every side, I feel even redoubled life and courage welling up within me.

Friends, have courage! Behind you are your parents, wives and children!

(He points to the guard)

Und diese treibt ein hohles Wort des Herrschers, nicht ihr Gemüt. Schützt eure Güter! Und eure Liebsten zu erretten, fallt freudig, wie ich euch ein Beispiel gebe!

And these are men driven slavishly by their Lords' commands, they have no spirit of their own. Defend your land! And to liberate your loved ones, give yourselves joyfully, as I have given you an example!

As Egmont walks past the guards to the door, the curtain falls, and the last movement of the score is heard, the *Siegessymphonie*, which is the paean to victory that had ended the overture.—S. W. BENNETT (2)

III. INCIDENTAL MUSIC TO *The Ruins of Athens*, OPUS 113
   (a) Overture
   (b) Chorus: Daughter of high-throned Zeus
   (c) Chorus of Dervishes: Thou who didst draw the moon
   (d) Turkish March
   (e) Chorus: Where freedom hath triumphed
   (f) March and Chorus: Twine ye garlands

"The Ruins of Athens" forms the second part of a festival play by August von Kotzebue, written to celebrate the opening of a new German theater in Pest; the first part was called "King Stephen, Hungary's first Benefactor." Beethoven was commissioned to supply music for the whole evening, and obliged in a great hurry, though the premiere had to be postponed four months to February 1812. "The Ruins" was an extremely tactful piece describing how Minerva awakes from two thousand years of sleep. Her first thought is to return to Athens, her old cultural stamping ground, but she is appalled to see the Parthenon in ruins, and the home of Socrates under the dominion of the Ottomans. The last straw is the order given by the chief Janizary:

> Here is the very thing we want; this trough
> Of stone will make a famous manger for
> Our Pasha's horse.

Minerva shudders at this desecration of a sarcophagus and calls to be taken to Rome; but here too it seems she is forgotten. Only in Pest, Mercury tells her, are culture and reason honored and cultivated, under the enlightened patronage of the Emperor Franz, to whom choruses of thanksgiving are duly sung.

Beethoven's score consisted of an overture and eight numbers. The well-known overture begins with a slow, mysterious introduction based on the duet "*Ohne Verschulden Knechtschaft dulden,*" which is sung later by Hector and Helen, two Greeks who bemoan their fate under the Turks. A fragment of march in G major, which is later extended in the last chorus, leads to the main Allegro of the overture, based on three themes, only one of which is at all developed; the material here is all unconnected with the music of the masque.

The curtain rises on an Olympian cavern where Minerva is chained to a rock. The invisible chorus wakens her in "Daughter of high-throned Zeus," which is solemn and andante in E flat, much of it unaccompanied. Transported to Athens, Minerva hears the Greek couple in their duet, but is interrupted in her conversation with them by the noisy approach of dervishes, who enter singing and dancing grotesquely to the comic chorus that Beethoven wrote for them in the popular Turkish style (Mozart was a dab hand at this style too). The Kaaba, which they mention repeatedly, is the holy stone of Mecca by which Mohammedan folk swear. Alborak was Mohammed's magic steed.

The dervishes cross the stage and enter a temple. Then come the stern oppressors the Janizaries, to the famous Turkish march in B flat. The gentle, almost Mendelssohnian chorus in G major, which follows (Beethoven had already used this style in the second movement of his Opus 90 piano sonata), allows the chorus of Pestians to declare their peace of mind and fondness for art and beauty in all manifestations. Actually [in the original this chorus] follows "Twine ye Garlands," but [the latter] makes a more effective end to [a concert performance of the complete music], being the most extended number, a noble march in E flat which gradually grows in power and impressiveness while the chorus fills the stage and then bursts into its grand hymn of praise.—WILLIAM S. MANN (1)

From: Letter to Camille Bellaigue, Las Palmas, January 23, 1897— First, concerning the famous "Chorus of Dervishes": Since you, just as I, have witnessed those mystical "spinning tops" whirling in Cairo, how is it that you have never noticed the identity of the triplets played by the flutes which accompany them with those in the chorus of *The Ruins of Athens?* In my opinion, it is impossible that Beethoven, through the simple intuition of genius, could have thought it up; he must have had an authentic document at his disposal. Obviously, the effect is much more beautiful in his work than in its "natural" state, but that is not the important point.— CAMILLE SAINT-SAËNS

IV. MARCH AND CHORUS FROM *The Ruins of Athens,* OPUS 114; CHORUS: "Wo sich die Pulse," WoO 98

[In 1822] Beethoven began the work which was to call him back into public notice. This was the music for the opening of the Josephstadt Theater, which the director of the theater, Carl Friedrich Hensler, director also of the combined theaters of Pressburg and Baden, asked of him immediately after his arrival at the watering place.[1] Hensler (1761–1825) was a popular dramatist as well as manager and an old acquaintance of Beethoven's, by whom he was greatly respected. He had bought the privilege of the Josephstadt Theater in Vienna. Carl Meisl, who was a commissioner of the Royal Imperial Navy, had written two festival pieces for the opening, which had been set down for October 3, 1822, the name day of the emperor. The first piece was a paraphrase of Kotzebue's *Ruinen von Athen,* written for the opening of the theater in Pesth in 1812, for

[1] Baden.—Editor.

which Beethoven had composed the music. Meisl took Kotzebue's text and made such alterations in it as were necessary to change *Die Ruinen von Athen* into *Die Weihe des Hauses*. Nottebohm's reprint in *Zweite Beethoveniana* (p. 385 *et seq.*) enables a comparison to be made with the piece as it left the hands of Meisl and the original. The new words did not always fit the music and caused Beethoven considerable concern. A choral dance:

> *Wo sich die Pulse*
> *jugendlich jagen,*
> *Schwebet im Tanze*
> *das Leben dahin*, etc.

was introduced and to this Beethoven had to write new music, which he did in September. He also revised, altered, and extended the march with chorus[1] Beethoven wrote a new overture also, that known as *Die Weihe des Hauses*, putting aside the overture to the *Ruinen von Athen* because that play had served as a second piece, or epilogue, at Pesth. On a revised copy of the chorus "*Wo sich die Pulse*" Beethoven wrote: "Written toward the end of September 1823, performed on October 3 at the Josephstadt Theater." The 1823 should be 1822, of course, but singularly enough the same blunder was made on a copy of the overture and another composition, the *Gratulationsmenuett*, which was written about the same time. The explanation is probably that offered by Nottebohm, viz.: that Beethoven dated the copies when he sent them to the archduke. Beethoven's remark in a letter to Johann that he had finished the chorus with dances and would write the overture if his health allowed also fixes the date of the composition of the overture in September.—ALEXANDER WHEELOCK THAYER, EDITED BY ELLIOT FORBES

V. INCIDENTAL MUSIC TO *King Stephen*, OPUS 117

In October 1811 a new German theater was due to be opened in Pest (now part of Budapest), and Beethoven was commissioned to write incidental music for the double bill by Kotzebue which was to open it. *King Stephen* or *Hungary's First Benefactor* was the curtain raiser to this entertainment; the subsequent play was *The Ruins of Athens*. Both were occasional pieces, and Beethoven had only a month to compose music for the two of them. The opening of the theater was postponed, in the end, until February 1812, so that the composer had time to polish what he had written, which was quite extensive. *King Stephen* consists of this overture and nine musical numbers. Beethoven was fond of his Kotzebue music,

[1] Published as Opus 114 and designated as "new" by Beethoven, though not a measure had been added, but only a few lines of text, and the choral music simplified. Steiner published pianoforte arrangements for two and four hands in 1822, and the score in 1826.

and referred to *King Stephen* and *The Ruins* as "my little operas." Later, in financial straits, he resold both overtures to the Philharmonic Society in London—and claimed, I regret to say, that both were brand new.

The *King Stephen* Overture begins with a slow introduction: a chain in powerful descending fourths (anticipating Bartók), and then a slow, decidedly Hungarian tune, as if it were the *Lassu* of a Hungarian rhapsody (it appears later, in a female chorus from the play). The fourths interrupt once, and soon the *Friss*, or quick dance breaks in (at one moment it reminds us of the "Ode to Joy" in the Ninth Symphony). In due course the fourths interrupt again, this time ascending; and the two sections are recapitulated, with a brief reference to the *Lassu* before the coda.—WILLIAM S. MANN (2)

The score calls for two flutes, two oboes, two clarinets, two bassoons, contrabassoon, four horns, two trumpets, timpani, and strings.

Besides the overture the music for King Stephen *consists of the following:*

No. 1. Chorus of Elders (C major, Andante maestoso e con moto). Its main interest is in the four-measure introduction, which gradually unfolds the C major chord from the low C of the bassoon upward through the horns and woodwinds to the C above middle C, accompanied by a smooth undulating figure of eighth notes in the cellos.

No. 2 Chorus of Elders (C minor, Allegro con brio). This describes the crowd wandering in the dark woods by a breathless theme of short quarter notes treated in canon among the voices. Suddenly the high winds of the orchestra play a group of repeated dominant triads in eighth-note triplets (similar in sound and effect to the Prelude to Act III of Lohengrin). Light enters the woods as the music breaks out into a fortissimo C major chord and the chorus sings a jubilant strophe of praise to their savior (King Stephen).

No. 3. War March (G major, Feurig und stolz). This accompanies the entrance of armored Hungarian warriors who place their weapons at the feet of their king. The march starts piano, with the horns and timpani alone, but a sudden crescendo within the space of one measure brings in the entire orchestra.

No. 4. Chorus of Handmaidens (A major, Andante con moto all'Ongarese). The music of this delightful Hungarian dance appears in the overture. It cleverly alternates between A major and minor in much the same way as Schubert later did in many of his songs.

No. 5. A melodrama (dialogue accompanied by music) leads without pause to

No. 6. A jubilant chorus (F major, Vivace) praising the beauty of Gisela, their new queen, Stephen's bride.

No. 7. A melodrama, accompanies King Stephen's speech to the elders and also describes musically the lift of the fog in the background revealing the city of Pesth in all its brilliance.

No. 8. "Geistlicher Marsch" (B flat, Moderato). This accompanies a procession of Roman elders who enter carrying a crown which they present to Stephen. This is followed by a dramatic musical background to Stephen's speech of thanks and his promise to the folk to protect them and keep them forever free.

No. 9. Final Chorus (D major, Presto). A paean of praise, based musically on the Friss that appeared in the overture. There is a loud B flat chord toward the end followed by silence, then a mysterious soft passage before the final peroration. This is, in embryo, the musical substance of the close of the finale of the Ninth Symphony.—Editor.

VI. INCIDENTAL MUSIC TO Leonore Prohaska, WoO 96

Of some minor compositions belonging to this spring, this is the story: The Prussian king's secretary, Friedrich Duncker, brought to Vienna, in the hope of producing it there, a tragedy, Leonore Prohaska, "which tells the story of a maiden who, disguised as a soldier, fought through the war of liberation." For this Beethoven composed a Soldiers' Chorus for men's voices unaccompanied: "Wir bauen und sterben"; a Romance with harp, 6/8 time, "Es blüht ein Blume"; and a Melodrama with harmonica. Also he orchestrated the March in the Sonata, Opus 26,[1] Duncker preferring this to a new marcia funebre.—ALEXANDER WHEELOCK THAYER, EDITED BY ELLIOT FORBES

Chamber Music With Piano

I. TRIOS
a. 2 Trios for Piano, Violin, and Violoncello, Opus 70

How deeply, O! exalted Master! have your noble piano compositions penetrated into my soul; how hollow and meaningless in comparison all music seems which does not emanate from you, or from the contemplative Mozart, or that powerful genius, Sebastian Bach. With what joy I received your Opus 70, the two noble trios, for I knew so well that after a little

[1] The autograph of this version is in the Library of the Paris Conservatory of Music. It is published in the Complete Works Edition, Ser. 25, No. 272. Kinsky-Halm (p. 553) dates the music to Leonore Prohaska, the fall of 1815—an advance over Thayer's date of the spring of 1814.

practice I could play them to myself so beautifully. And it has been such a pleasure to me this evening that now, like one who wanders through the sinuous mazes of a fantastic park, among all kinds of rare trees, plants, and wonderful flowers, always tempted to wander further, I am unable to tear myself away from the marvelous variety and interweaving figures of your trios. The pure siren voices of your gaily varied and beautiful themes always tempt me on further and further. The talented lady who today played the first trio so beautifully just to please me, the Kapellmeister Kreisler, and before whose piano I am now sitting and writing, brought it home to me most clearly that we should honor only that which is inspired and that everything else comes from evil.

Just now I have been playing over from memory some of the striking modulatory passages from the two trios. It is true that the piano (Flügel-Pianoforte)[1] as an instrument is more adaptable to harmonic than to melodic uses. The most delicate expression of which the instrument is capable cannot give to the melody that mobile life in thousands and thousands of shadings which the bow of the violinist or the breath of the wind-instrument player is capable of giving. On the other hand there is no instrument (with the exception of the much more limited harp) which has control to such a degree as the piano, with its completely grasped chords, of the kingdom of harmony, the treasures of which it discloses to the connoisseur in the most wonderful forms and images.

How wonderfully the Master understood the characteristic spirit of the instrument and consequently handled it in its most appropriate manner!

At the bottom of each movement there lies an effective singable theme, simple but fruitful of all the various contrapuntal developments, such as diminution, etc. All the other secondary themes and figures are organically related to this principal idea so that all the material divided among the different instruments is combined and ordered in the most complete unity. Such is the structure of the whole; but in this artistic structure the most wonderful pictures, in which joy and sorrow, melancholy and ecstasy, appear side by side, change in restless succession. Strange shapes begin a merry dance, now dissolving in a blur of light, now sparkling and flashing as they separate, chasing and following one another in kaleidoscopic groups; and in the midst of this unlocked spirit-world the ravished soul listens to the unknown language and understands all those mysterious premonitions by which it is possessed.

Only that composer penetrates truly into the secrets of harmony who is able to stir the soul of man through harmony; to him, the mathematical proportions which to the grammarian without genius are only dry arithmetical problems, are magic combinations from which he can build a world of visions.

In spite of the geniality which predominates in the first trio, not ex-

[1] The newly invented "Hammerklavier."—*Tr.*

cepting the emotional Largo, Beethoven's genius, as a whole, remains serious and religious in spirit. It seems as if the Master thought that one could not speak of deeply-hidden things in common words but only in sublime and noble language, even when the spirit, closely penetrating into these things, feels itself exalted with joy and happiness; the dance of the priests of Isis must take the form of an exultant hymn.—E. T. A. HOFFMANN (1)

(a) Trio No. 5 in D, Opus 70, No. 1
I. Allegro vivace e con brio; II. Largo assai ed espressivo; III. Presto

The opening *Allegro vivace e con brio*, a sprightly and spirited piece, recalls somewhat the first movement of the Eighth Symphony, both by its straightforward, strongly rhythmical first subject, and by its immediate confrontation with a graceful melodic theme marked *dolce*. The most important subject-matter of the whole movement has thus been presented in a mere dozen bars, for all that follows in the course of the comparatively short exposition—which is to be repeated—is but an elaboration of the foregoing material. The two contrasting elements, which up to then have alternated in a rather playful way, come to a real conflict of Beethovenian stature in the course of the development, but still without any hint of tragedy whatsoever. This is music of healthy high spirits, showing the composer's most genial, sunny side. The movement finds an energetic conclusion with a final affirmation of the opening motive, the culmination of a coda that began *pianissimo* with the "melodic" element.

Now follows the famous *Largo assai ed espressivo*, a highly original, prophetic "night-piece", sometimes forecasting Schubert's most fantastic moods, or even the later Impressionists. Its dark and mysterious beauty again takes its thematic support from two small contrasting elements played during the very first bars. But here there is nothing as clearly definable as the evident Sonata-form scheme of the preceding movement. In fact, this is one of the first atmospheric "mood-pieces" in music history, where elements of tone-color tend to blur the formal outline. The dark gloom of this *Largo*, which stands in such striking contrast to the brightness of the outer movements, is further enhanced by the frequent low rumblings on the piano, which account for the piece's nickname. It is interesting to know that at the time he wrote it, Beethoven was sketching an opera about Macbeth! At the ninth bar—very slow bars indeed—a slightly more extended melody appears (on the piano) as an outgrowth of the original cells, much in the way of Sibelian "thematic growth." This leads to the first climax, landing on a shrill augmented chord. A second "wave" dwells in the wierd *pianissimo*, with dark, "ghostly" keyboard *tremoli*, leading to a deceptive dying-out. After two further elaborations of the main melody, the movement ends with a faintly glimmering coda, dissolving the subject-matter to the point of immateriality, and dying with a hush.[1]

A swiftly moving *Presto* in Sonata-form closes the work in a gay and relaxed atmosphere. Both themes are straightforward and easy to grasp, the formal outline unfolds itself without surprises, but many a felicitous harmonic stroke helps lift an otherwise deliberately lightweight piece— an almost necessary contrast to the preceding "ghost" *Largo*—to a poetic level of its own.—HARRY HALBREICH (2)

Very grand slow movements can be constructed in a sonata form that omits the development. The omission of the development reduces the bigness of the total impression far less than any perfunctoriness in the transition or shortness in the recapitulation.

It is of some importance to be able to recognize where a slow movement is in full sonata form, because this is one of the things that can be done by ear, and must not be entrusted to the eye. The commonest mistake which the merely optical analyst makes is that of counting the bars and supposing that seven or eight of them cannot be enough to constitute a development. The listener need make no such mistake. The single dominant chord that marks off a bar in the middle of the slow movement of Opus 10, No. 1, obviously does not amount to a development. The eight bars in the same position in the middle of the slow movement of the D major Trio, Opus 70, No. 1, are scarcely longer by the ticking of the seconds hand, but there are three modulations in the first three bars, a complete change of topic in the next four, and the last bar is equivalent to a full-sized preparation for the home tonic. More has happened here than in the quite orthodox, though short, development of the finale, which occupies about a couple of pages.— DONALD FRANCIS TOVEY (1)

(b) Trio No. 6 in E Flat, Opus 70, No. 2
I. Poco sostenuto; Allegro ma non troppo; II. Allegretto; III. Allegretto ma non troppo; IV. Finale (Allegro)

Less striking at first hearing, and consequently less well-known than its neighbor, the Trio in E-flat Major, Opus 70, No. 2, a most beautiful equipoised piece of music, shows us Beethoven at his felicitous lyrical best. This is true chamber music, intimate and serene, and while boasting nothing so startling as the "ghost" largo, the E-flat Trio probably

---

[1] See Tovey's appraisal of the scope of this Largo.—Editor.

achieves a more satisfying balance between its four movements which offer comparatively little contrast.

The first movement begins with a slow peaceful introduction, marked *Poco sostenuto*, first unfolding some gentle canonic writing, and then leading more freely into the lyrical *Allegro ma non troppo*, whose lilting six-eight time suggests Haydn. Indeed it avoids any dramatic conflict in the course of its spacious, but transparent development. A short reminiscence of the canonic introduction precedes the graceful and merry coda.—HARRY HALBREICH (2)

One of Beethoven's profoundest works is the Trio in E flat, Opus 70, No. 2, and one of the duller futilities of criticism is that which accuses its style of a relapse into Mozartean phraseology. One of its most Mozartean phrases [is the passage in the first movement where the development section links with the recapitulation (measures 110–12 of the *Allegro ma non troppo*). The cello, which has carried the bass line for the latter part of this section through a multitude of keys, has duly descended to the tone B flat, the dominant of the home key. Beethoven (as are we) is prepared for the recapitulation to commence when this bass descends one tone further to A flat, with which the cello bursts out forte with the main theme, and is promptly corrected by the right hand of the pianoforte in the home key. From here on the recapitulation proceeds with an air of noticing nothing unusual. This is perhaps the most unexpected return in all music.

The left hand of the piano, having taken over the bass line from the cello, rises chromatically from the A flat (dominant of the key of D flat) to B flat (the "correct" dominant for the recapitulation in the home tonic of E flat). But note the rhythmic subtlety.]

If any survivor of the method of teaching harmony by describing the roots of chords thinks he can treat these progressions as chords in themselves, he is welcome to make the attempt. In *Madam How and Lady Why*, Charles Kingsley pointed out that chemical analysis might work forever at the contents of a plum-pudding without any chance of arriving at the essential fact that the cook had boiled it in a cloth. What has happened in this suavely Mozartean utterance of Beethoven's is that he has compressed into two bars what could not have been said in less than four *if the bass had not taken upon itself to move faster than the treble and so give a more than double meaning to the melody!*[1]

The real influence of Mozart and Haydn was slow to show itself in Beethoven's style, and what did eventually appear was the integration of Mozart's and Haydn's resources, with results that transcend all possibility of resemblance to the style of their origins, and are nowhere

[1] The italics and the exclamation point are mine.—Editor.

more transcendent than in a work like the E flat Trio, Opus 70, No. 2, where Beethoven discovers new meanings for Mozart's phrases and Haydn's formulas.—DONALD FRANCIS TOVEY (1)

This [Trio], in its intended avoidance of strong contrasts, dispenses with a genuine slow movement. Instead, we have an *Allegretto*—as in the Seventh and Eighth Symphonies!—, of a slightly *scherzando* character, which again, and more markedly, recalls Haydn by its casting in "double variation" form (one of Haydn's favorite devices, but very rarely found in Beethoven's work, and not at all in Mozart's). The two contrasting themes are in C Major and C Minor respectively, but the movement's closing in the latter key, far from implying any feeling of tragedy, rather suggests some harmless teasing.

Next comes an *Allegretto ma non troppo*, halfway between a *Minuet* and a *Laendler*, a songful movement in A-flat Major, whose strikingly beautiful Trio, twice alternating with the main part, uses piano and strings antiphonally.

The final *Allegro* brings a wealth of colorful material, sometimes of near folksong-like quality, into a spacious Sonata-form. This is the most extrovert and vigorous of the four movements, a typical expression of the jocular, "unbuttoned" Beethoven, ending this delectable work with the most infectious and tonic of high spirits.—HARRY HALBREICH (2)

With Beethoven, there is never any difficulty in seeing where his recapitulation begins, though we may be surprised when we find ourselves already in the swing of it; but, where we are thus surprised, we may find it worth while to remark that the recapitulation is continuing a process begun by the development, especially when the development has been very short in itself. The stupendous example is in the finale of the E flat Trio, Opus 70, No. 2. In the exposition, three short themes, all on the tonic, are thrown at us with no further explanation at the moment than antiphonal repetition as between the pianoforte and the strings. The transition offers no apology for this abruptness, and, though it broadens out effectively, the broadening is surprising rather than explanatory. [The second group, however, is not in the expected key of the dominant, but in the key of A.]

Now, if there is any device that could make an opening sound sequential and formal, it would be the device of answering the first clauses in the supertonic, as at the beginning of Beethoven's First Symphony. When we come to the recapitulation, this is what happens. The first pair of themes, having returned in conspiratorial whispers, begins to repeat itself, and modulates deliberately to the supertonic, there to begin a counterstatement which also includes the third theme. This is one of the grandest architectural effects Beethoven ever produced, and it leads to a unique feature of form. The second group had been in one of Beethoven's remoter key-relations, the major mediant (III). Beethoven's usual practice when he uses this remote key is to let the recapitulation of the second group represent it by its twin brother, the major submediant (VI); but only for a few bars. With or without the expense of an extra repetition of the first phrase, the group shifts to the home tonic, and so the normal key balance is preserved, though the recapitulation has gained a touch of brilliant color. [However], in the finale of the E flat Trio, nothing could be more natural than that this supertonic, which has so greatly enlarged the design of the first group, should lead to the major submediant (VI); but what is unusual and unexpected is that the whole second group is given in that key, and that afterwards there is another complete recapitulation in the home tonic.—DONALD FRANCIS TOVEY (1)

b. Trio No. 7 in B Flat, Opus 97 (the "Archduke")
I. Allegro moderato; II. Scherzo (Allegro); III. Andante cantabile; IV. Allegro moderato

Written in 1811 (but not published till 1816) and dedicated to Archduke Rudolph, younger brother of the Emperor of Austria, and a keen amateur musician. The Archduke was a portly, unattractive young man who took lessons from Beethoven from 1803 to 1806, composed a little, and played the piano well enough to tackle some of Beethoven's concertos. Nearly all the Hapsburgs were musical, a fact which did much to establish Vienna's position as the chief music center of Europe. The Archduke was fully capable of distinguishing between Beethoven's greater and lesser works, and was observed to show displeasure on those occasions when a masterpiece was dedicated to someone else. He should be remembered with gratitude for having organized an annuity for Beethoven in 1809 which kept him from want.

The Trio opens with a theme of sufficient breadth and spaciousness to establish the mood of the whole work. Beethoven's alchemy is such that he scarcely needs any more material than this. However, as a brief interlude, he gives us a gently descending second subject in the unexpected key of G; this too comes first as a piano solo, to be immediately repeated by strings. After a solid, rather pompous climax the composer turns to what must have been for him the most pleasurable of tasks: the development of his opening theme. He draws a broad sustained paragraph from each phrase of it. The cello introduces bar 1, and this is taken up as a suitable subject for conversation by all three instruments. Eventually the cello switches the conversation to the phrase starting at the end of bar 2, trying it out first *arco* and later *pizzicato* against curious trills on the piano. Soon the rising scale of bar 3 is speeded up into [eighth notes], and discussion of this leads to a climax, after which Beethoven returns to his opening music, restating his themes and adding a short coda of suitable grandeur.—ROGER FISKE (2)

Shakespeare chooses to begin *Twelfth Night* with a piece of music. He does not write the music, but something must be played or sung and brought to a definite end, in order to explain the first spoken words: "If music be the food of love, play on. . . . That strain again; it had a dying fall." In this case, therefore, a lyric opening becomes the dramatic means of revealing the character of the sentimental Orsino. But it is not often that a drama can afford to begin with a lyric, and for the same reason it is not often that a movement full of active development can afford to begin with a square tune. Listeners whose fondness for melody has not risen far superior to my own sinful fondness for square tunes will find that their insight into Beethoven's larger designs will grow rapidly if they select those cases where Beethoven has begun a highly developed movement with a dangerously broad and symmetrical melody. Nothing can be more quiet than the way in which such a melody will disengage itself from symmetry and broaden into something evidently part of a larger whole; and the process is as dramatic as it is quiet. [One] clear instance [is] the opening of the B flat Trio, Opus 97.

[This] takes the risk of rounding off its melody with some symmetry. One reason for this is that the pianoforte naturally forms one mass of harmony, while the violin and the violoncello form another, and this gives occasion for antiphonal correspondences; but the melody having reached a dominant close at the eighth bar, the violin and cello intervene quite dramatically with six bars of sustained declamatory dialogue, which removes all premature effect of symmetry from the counterstatement that now follows. A counterstatement is a restatement of an idea with a change of direction, and thus is eminently a device suitable for exposition—though it may hamper dramatic movement if it is too symmetrical. Here, however, apart from the intervention of those six bars of dialogue, the counterstatement broadens and deepens till no doubt of the dramatic scope of the music remains.—DONALD FRANCIS TOVEY (1)

The *Scherzo* is innocently impish. The piano is silent until the strings have picked out the main tune. The Trio or middle section has two tunes, the first a mysterious *fugato*, the second by way of contrast a *bravura* affair with all the dash of a Weber waltz. Beethoven asks for more repetition than usual; *scherzo—trio—scherzo—trio—scherzo—*coda (based on the mysterious *fugato*).

The slow movement, which is very long, has one of those broad sustained tunes only Beethoven could write. Then follows a set of variations in which the harmonic structure of the theme is more carefully preserved than the melodic outline.

Var. I. The piano decorates the theme in triplets.

Var. II. For a few bars the piano picks out the theme against a new [sixteenth-note] figure on the strings, but soon the [sixteenth-note] figure takes command and the theme appears only intermittently.

Var. III. The violin has a version of the theme as a background to decorative music in [thirty-second notes] on the piano.

Var. IV. So far each variation has had more movement than its predecessor. Beethoven now returns to the simple [quarter notes] and [eighth notes] of his opening; in fact, the theme is scarcely varied at all, except for some fascinating short-lived modulations. The music leads into a warm romantic coda with something of the feeling of a nocturne. Violin and cello alternate with rhapsodic snatches of the original melody.

—ROGER FISKE (2)

In the B flat Trio, Opus 97, Beethoven uses variation form in order to express a sublime inaction in his slow movement. On paper, the very gorgeous ornamentation of the variations in the Trio, Opus 97, may present the same appearance of blackness as a set of brilliant variations on "Home Sweet Home" by a Victorian salon writer, but its quality is really quite different. If anyone is under the delusion that such ornamentation as that of the third variation in the Trio, Opus 97, is easy to compose, or much easier to play than to compose, I do not know how the delusion is to be dispelled, for those who suffer from it will be quite satisfied with their own attempts to parody such work.

In the B flat Trio, we encounter drastic examples of Beethoven's disposition to shock his listeners after he has deeply moved them. He used, we are told, to extemporize with such effect that his listeners were in tears, whereupon he would burst into a loud guffaw and call them fools. Now this may be impish, but it is not Mephistophelean. It is an outward sign of one of the highest qualities of Beethoven's spiritual grace. In a more conciliatory form, it is represented by William James's profound observation that it is not good for us to be content to enjoy art passively, and that, if we cannot ourselves be artists, we must at all events not receive without giving.

The blazing effect of a major supertonic which cannot be explained away as an enhanced dominant is shown very dramatically on a melodic scale in the last variation of the Andante of the Trio in B flat, Opus 97. Here, again, nothing can be learned by taking the passage out of its context. We must have heard the sublime melody with its repeats and its penultimate climax on the subdominant, and we must have heard the four complete variations on the plan of *doubles*—that is to say, of increasing subdivisions of rhythm—until in the fourth variation the tempo has to become slower to make room for the notes, and, when the theme returns at its original pace without any ornamentation, we must be enjoying as a novelty its pathetic new harmonies, which construe part of it as in keys related to its tonic minor. Only then shall we see the dramatic force of the query to which these harmonies lead, as if by accident, in its twelfth bar. The query is twice repeated, and its incredible answer is an outburst of the supreme climax in E major (II). As this is indeed incredible, the final cadence halts and is repeated with differences, eventually passing through a deep shadow, which happens to be the dominant chord of C major. As the whole procedure is, after all, only on a melodic scale, it is enough for this chord to explain itself away enharmonically, and so to pass by easy harmonies into the home tonic.—DONALD FRANCIS TOVEY (1)

There is no break between the third and fourth movements. The finale, which is in rondo form, is something of an oddity, different in mood from any other music. The main tune trips along with a gaiety that is somehow not quite real, while the principal episode is definitely uncouth: perhaps it is one of Beethoven's jokes. The music has an indefinable quality that is continuously fascinating. The fourth and last appearance of the rondo theme is in a new rhythm, six-eight, and marked *presto*; and here the music is more obviously lighthearted. Throughout this movement the piano writing is noticeably more difficult than that for the strings. The violin part is kept unusually low, the player scarcely using the top string at all. On the other hand, much of the cello writing is extremely high.

This trio is Beethoven's supreme achievement for piano and strings.—ROGER FISKE (2)

When the finale of the B flat Trio shocks us with unseemly conviviality before the slow movement has finished dying away, Beethoven has no apologies to offer. The outrageous jocularity continues unabashed, until not only the proportions, but the actual mysterious quality, of the finale develop a sublimity of their own. [It] is a marvelous study in

Bacchanalian indolence. The theme begins in the subdominant (that is to say, its tonic is dominant to the subdominant), and it makes very little effort to maintain its proper balance against this bias. Even its second group hardly succeeds in establishing more than the home dominant, without any enhanced dominant to give the orthodox effect of the dominant key, and whenever the main theme returns, the warning necessarily takes the form of preparation for the subdominant. It is true that a diminished seventh interposes a faint cloud-veil over the procedure, but who minds what a diminished seventh says? With still further effrontery, the middle episode chooses to begin in the subdominant, and modulates only to nearly-related keys. Again, there is the warning of return to our main theme; but now comes a final effrontery, namely that our little second group, which only succeeded in maintaining itself on, and not in, the dominant, is now recapitulated, not only in the subdominant, but with particular emphasis upon the subdominant's own subdominant chord. A belated apology is made for this by repeating the main second-group theme in the home tonic, but then we have for the last time the warning of a return to the main theme. The cloudy diminished seventh is present, and this time we are compelled to listen to it, for it changes its meaning and takes us into a remoter key than those mapped out in the gorgeous key-system of the other three movements.—DONALD FRANCIS TOVEY (1)

c. Trio No. 8 in B Flat, WoO 39
Allegretto (B flat, 6/8)

As a pendant to the customary seven trios well known to music lovers, this work has its interest, though little history, esoteric or otherwise. The best opinion is that it was produced in the same year (1812) as the famous "Archduke" (Opus 97) in the same key, but it was obviously written for a special purpose, perhaps even a special person. To judge from its lack of complexity, that person might have been one of Beethoven's piano pupils with an interest in chamber music performance.

The cheerful, lighthearted movement begins with a sparkling little theme in the piano against chordal strings. The progress to F for the second subject is according to customary practice, with a double ending. The second ending moves rather pertly into D major, which is emphasized to the extent of a signature change to two sharps, for sixteen measures. An engaging feature of the recapitulation is the comparatively elaborate coda, with much use of the opening matter in the contrary motion to which its character predisposes it.—IRVING KOLODIN

II. SONATAS

a. Sonata No. 10 in G for Violin and Piano, Opus 96

I. Allegro moderato; II. Adagio espressivo; III. Scherzo (Allegro); IV. Poco allegretto

[In] the last Sonata (Opus 96) [there exists an] intimacy of dialogue we have not yet encountered, an understatement in conveying the message, a certain indecision in formulating answers—these are new aspects of the violin-piano Sonata that seem to be the goal of the master who always started afresh.

The last Sonata (Opus 96) is the only one of the ten that states its theme unaccompanied, unharmonized, giving the bare essence only of the germinal idea. It is also (along with the Sixth—the only one that is in ternary meter. (The main body of the first movement of the Kreutzer is in duple meter.)

We can also say that it is the only one whose theme has no rhythmical gesture or "gesticulation" to it, [such as the opening bars] of the "C minor" or the [varied rhythm and texture of the opening theme of] Opus 30, No. 1.

But all these stock-takings and descriptions of its structure do not explain the hold it has on our imagination and the special niche it occupies in our affections. Perhaps the similar statement of the opening movement of the last Quartet (F major, Opus 135), [slightly tentative], or the [equally incomplete] opening of the Piano Sonata Opus 54 (published in 1806), can serve as a clue and lead us to an explanation of sorts.

We can only ask: "Isn't it precisely this "stillness," this lack of gesture and of emphasis (in this soft-spoken exchange of the two voices) that casts the spell? Or is it the sparseness, the understatement of the first movement that creates the right receptivity for the sublimities of the Adagio and the continuity of pastoral good humor in the remaining two movements? (The similarity in "climate" in these last two movements is a very unusual feature of this work.)

The goal of a greater integration of four movements into a whole must have hovered before him when after a gap of some eight years he set himself the task of writing a sequel [to the nine earlier sonatas]. Doesn't the attacca link to the following bucolic, pastoral Scherzo show us that this goal was guiding his pen? Isn't the serene lilt of the Trio a link to the "gemütlich" climate of the theme of the last movement? It is when we hear the first statement of the noble theme of the

Adagio expressivo and the meditative commentary of the violin which postpones the restatement of this theme, until quite late in the movement (in fact, not until thirty bars before the end do we hear it), it is only then that we realize in retrospect the wisdom and inevitability of just this type of first movement. Brahms in the Adagio of his Violin Concerto follows exactly this plan of withholding the theme proper from the Solo Violin. And from now on everything falls into place, and the unity of purpose of the whole is revealed to us.

What contrast between the staccato sforzando plan of the Scherzo in the minor key and its Ländler-like "horizontal" Trio and how inevitably does the Coda in the major key lead into the Poco allegretto variation movement, the theme of which calls up reminiscences of that Alla danza tedesca of the Quartet Opus 130, [a movement also in G major,] written thirteen years later.

One can only repeat: Coming events cast their shadow years before in the case of a Beethoven!

Beethoven in a letter to his pupil Archduke Rudolph says in mock-seriousness that the last movement of the Opus 96 Sonata written for Pierre Rode and dedicated to the Archduke, does not have a Finale of the "roaring (rauschend) kind that we like to have," and explains that it is consideration of Rode's playing style that guided his pen. The remark of Beethoven's may have been made in a tongue-in-cheek manner, for the last variation of this supposedly esoteric work certainly has an unbridled élan and is a fitting climax to the mature gaiety of this earthy set of variations on a theme borrowed to a certain extent from a contemporary "Singspiel," with its unprecedented centerpiece of a cantabile, contemplative, dialogue between the two instruments. The two final flourishes, the one for piano following the risky violin run up to the high "D," belie Beethoven's professed intention of avoiding uno stilo molto concertante this time!—JOSEPH SZIGETI (2)

b. Sonata No. 3 in A for Violoncello and Piano, Opus 69
I. Allegro ma non troppo; II. Scherzo—Allegro molto; III. Adagio Cantabile; IV. Allegro vivace

After Opus 5 we must go to Opus 69 before we find another sonata for piano and cello.[1] An interval of twelve years! We have no idea of what occasion led Beethoven to write this composition, and no performance of it is known prior to 1812, when it was played at the Schuppanzigh

---

[1] Beethoven's variations for cello and piano on Handel's *Judas Maccabeus* were written in 1796. Those on Mozart's *Ein Mädchen oder Weibchen* date from 1799, and the others, also on [an air from *The Magic Flute* ("*Bei Männern, welche Liebe Fülen*")] from 1801.

concerts,[1] with Czerny[2] at the piano and Linke[3] at the cello. Since Beethoven honored these two brilliant executants with his friendship and held them in high esteem, it might be supposed that it was for them that he composed the sonata; this hypothesis of mine would also be supported by the fact that it was the same cellist, Linke, that later provided him with the occasion to write Opus 102.[4]

The Sonata, Opus 69, is dedicated to Baron Gleichenstein, but the dedication was purely a matter of occasion. This work, with Boccherini's Sixth Sonata in A major (the identical tonality is a strange coincidence), a piece of quite a different genre but likewise a masterpiece, is the ideal of every cellist, the touchstone of artists, the dream of amateurs.

The first movement, Allegro ma non tanto, characterizes the entire sonata. It begins with a calm, solemn song given to the solo cello, with its deep sounds on the third and fourth strings. It is the main theme [of the movement], which although full of sweetness and feeling never becomes sentimental. Triplets on the piano accompany a new and interesting motif in A minor which becomes a bridge to the second theme, which unfolds in episodes of varying character. [In the development section, a passage which is] truly Beethovenish in its strength and vigor, twelve measures of sixteenth notes are played on the cello while the theme appears in the low register of the piano, beginning fortissimo and ending piano. A sublime outburst of feeling follows, arriving by way of an unexpected diminuendo to pianissimo, in which the cello, with its deep sounds faintly whispered, leads us into mysterious regions. This new section, likewise twelve bars in length, recalls the initial theme and keeps the mind in suspense until before we realize it we are embarked on the recapitulation. Contrary to what usually takes place in Beethoven when he arrives at the recapitulation, here he does not apply any variants of notes. [However, as if to drive home his point, Beethoven allows the main theme] to assert its dominance over the secondary theme [by appearing] toward the end in the form of a coda with the two instruments in unison, first pianissimo then fortissimo, departing gradually and tenderly in bright trills and vibrant chords.

In the Scherzo the phrases follow one another in the most natural of manners, with the syncopated rhythm giving us the impression of a timid, anxious joy. [The movement] begins with two similar eight-

[1] These concerts were named after the first violin of the famous quartet supported first by Prince Lichnowsky and then by Count Rasumovsky. The members were: Schuppanzigh, first violin; Sina, second violin; Weiss, viola; Linke, violoncello.
[2] Czerny was a pupil of Beethoven's and gave the first performances of many of the compositions of the Master.
[3] Schindler asserts that Kraft and Linke taught Beethoven the mechanism of the cello, Punto that of the horn, Friedlowsky that of the clarinet.
[4] The last two cello and piano sonatas, written in 1815, in the full flush of his mature "third period" style.—Editor.

measure phrases, each one announced first by the piano[1] and repeated by the cello. These lead directly to a second theme in E minor [where, briefly, the syncopation ceases]. After a suggestion of the main theme in another key, there follows a very lively syncopated passage in A minor. This strong and agitated section ends with a diminuendo, dying away in the low notes of the piano and leading to the magnificent Trio. Bekker points out the striking resemblance between this Trio and the one in the Seventh Symphony, "in which, as here, a melody in the form of a *lied* appears in colors, now light, now darker, through changes in the dynamic effects." The repeat of the Trio, which occurs twice, interrupted by the scherzo, is [also similar to the form of the corresponding movement] in the symphony.

The close [of the Scherzo] is marvelous, with its mysterious pianissimo as the movement fades, timidly and anxiously, as it had started. Next comes the Adagio cantabile. There are eighteen measures in all, but so full of ideas and so full of feeling that one regrets it when, at the end of the cello cadenza, there is a sudden transition to the Finale, after the two instruments have sounded only once that divine song in E major.

But Beethoven's vein is inexhaustible in this sonata! The Adagio is but a majestic prelude to the Allegro vivace [, the Finale], which repays us with interest for the interruption of our pleasure. In it the melody knows no limits; as Wagner says, "Everything becomes melody: the very accompaniment, every rhythmic note, even the pauses."

The first theme is extremely brilliant and the second one somewhat pensive, but each imparts its own character to this movement; and yet in the development they are so perfectly merged that the movement expresses just the joy that the composer stated so magnificently in the previous movements. The Allegro vivace seems to double the interest of the hearer, who, already imbued with the beauty of this great masterpiece, feels more and more moved as the movement goes forward, with its immortal, light-filled, warm gaiety, to close magically in the most dazzling of sonorities.

It is often said, and I think fairly, that this sonata is the best concerted work written for two instruments. It might be thought that Beethoven had conceived it in one of his rare moments of felicity. Instead, we read these words in the manuscript: *Inter lacrimas et luctum* (In the midst of tears and sorrow).—EUGENIO ALBINI (TR. BY THOMAS K. SCHERMAN)

---

[1] Beethoven took great pains to play up the syncopation of these two phrases by prescribing a change of finger on each tied note. Whenever Beethoven took pains to write his own fingering for passages in his piano sonatas, chamber music, or concertos, it was for a very special effect!—Editor.

Chamber Music Without Piano

I. STRING QUARTETS
   a. 3 String Quartets, Opus 59

The true Beethoven of any period is more accurately reflected in the string quartets than in the symphonies. Beethoven wrote string quartets only with great circumspection and with a very keen sense of responsibility. In these he is more rigorously faithful to his experience, less "dramatic," less "objective," than anywhere else in his music. The string quartet is probably the most sincere form of musical expression. The greater intimacy, the great *faithfulness*, as it were, of his string quartets is admirably illustrated by the three Rasoumovskys, composed in 1806. At this time, Beethoven's fundamental attitude toward life was based on his realization of the victory that may be achieved by heroism in spite of suffering.[1] He was to exult, for a few years, in the confidence this realization brought him. He thought he had found the key to life. The life history of this realization is depicted in both the "Eroica" and the C minor symphonies, although it is only in the last movement of the C minor that the full joy and confidence of the victor are revealed. In both these works the whole process is objectified. It is "dramatized" and presented on the biggest possible scale. The hero marches forth, indubitably heroic, but performing his feats before the whole of an applauding world. What is he like in his loneliness? We find the answer in the Rasoumovsky quartets.

The opening theme of the first Rasoumovsky quartet has not the dramatic, arresting quality of the "Eroica" theme, but it is nevertheless "heroic." Its sober resolution is appropriate to a more mundane world than that of the grandiose visions of the "Eroica." It conveys a truer impression, we may be sure, of Beethoven's daily spiritual food. Its assurance is less conscious, less willful. But, except that they have a more intimate and less obviously dramatic quality, the Rasoumovsky quartets are essentially concerned with the psychological process with which we are familiar. This is [especially] true of the first.—J. W. N. SULLIVAN

[1] See Sullivan's comments on the Third and the Fifth Symphonies.—Editor.

(a) String Quartet No. 7 in F, Opus 59, No. 1
I. Allegro; II. Allegretto vivace e sempre scherzando; III. Adagio
molto e mesto; IV. Thème Russe—Allegro

In Beethoven's case, the revolutions marking the major style changes
can be seen to have been precipitated by circumstances in his ill-managed
emotional life. It seems beyond coincidence that the shattering move into
the second period should come at exactly the same time as the shattering
Heiligenstadt Testament of October 1802. Drafted as a letter to his
brothers, this famous document reads less as a letter or a will than as a
great unburdening cry of grief at his deafness and solitude—mingled with
apology, self-justification, self-pity, pathos, pride, hints of suicide, and
presentiments of death. The date is what seems so significant, given the
facts of Beethoven's artistic activity. To this date, possibly, can be related a new awareness of himself as artist—if not as man—in a repeated
side-reference: "It seemed to me impossible to leave the world until I
had brought forth all that I felt was within me . . . With joy I hasten
to meet death—if it comes before I have had the chance to develop all
my artistic capacities, it will still be coming too soon. . . ." He had
never spoken in quite this way before. The neurotic details are not much
to the point. Other artists have suffered neurosis, breakdown, chronic
depression, extreme illness, and destructive love affairs without experiencing the amazing artistic after-effects that such things seem to have produced in Beethoven.

The situation around 1802 in Beethoven's music can be reconstructed
from the sketchbooks, if not quite fully, certainly much more so than
the private details bearing on the Heiligenstadt Testament. As he wound
up work on the early set of quartets, in 1800, Beethoven turned back to
the sonata, with the *Grande Sonate* in Bb, Opus 22. He devoted the next
two years to this genre, by and large, along with work on the ballet
Prometheus, the Second Symphony, and some other compositions. In
half a dozen piano sonatas (Opus 26; Opus 27, Nos. 1 and 2; Opus 28;
Opus 31, Nos. 1, 2, and 3) and in another half dozen for violin and
piano (Opus 23; Opus 24; Opus 30, Nos. 1, 2, and 3), he rapidly pressed
experiment and solution, bending the classicism of the 1790's into astonishing tensile spirals. But a marked change occurs soon after the Heiligenstadt Testament—or, for all we know, directly afterwards; that closely
the sketches are not dated. His thoughts turned from sonatas to compositions of an ambition never before imagined: in particular the Third
Symphony, the *Eroica*, during 1803, and the opera *Leonore* (renamed
Fidelio) during 1804 and 1805. Again, it can be no coincidence that
these two works are so strongly, so unusually shot through with extramusical ideas, and that the ideas should be ideas of heroism. Other works

of 1803 and 1804 fall under the sway of these two, in mood and scope. Even the few sonatas are now heroic—the "Waldstein" and the *Appassionata*. With this set of works Beethoven made his revolution: not a sharp cut with the past, but an abrupt phase of evolution forced by psychological factors which necessarily remain obscure.

The key work is the symphony—a real "watershed" work, not only in terms of his own *oeuvre*, but also in terms of our whole musical tradition considered as broadly as we please. There will be occasion to say something about this great work in the following pages. With his (to some people) embarrassingly simple but unerring sense of symbolism, Beethoven inscribed the piece to Napoleon, as is very well known, and then tore up the title page when he saw revolution betrayed. But he did not tear up the symphony, and now there was no more chance of turning back to the aesthetic of Viennese classicism than there was of returning to the *ancien régime*. Though efforts were made, even by this composer. After the *Eroica*, Beethoven's quartets like everything else he wrote breathe in a different world from that of the 1790's. Hearing the second-period quartets today, one breathes and listens differently than one does to Haydn, Mozart, and the Quartets of Opus 18.

In response to the difference, criticism has to bring in new techniques and methods of articulation, learn a new metabolism, and at the very least commit itself to a new intensity of attention. What has to emerge first of all is a fitting stance for this music in general. The F-major "Razumovsky" Quartet—greatest of the three in Opus 59, I should say, in spite of something unsettled in the sequence of the movements; certainly greatest in its superb opening *Allegro*—can serve, almost as well as the symphony, to introduce Beethoven's second period and whatever critical equipment may be brought to bear upon it.

Beethoven's theme simulates a long lyric utterance, surging up four octaves, filling the entire quartet space. One is reminded—but only very dimly!—of the slender theme of the Quartet in B♭, Opus 18, No. 6. Rhythmically very square, the theme serves almost ostentatiously as an arsenal of well-defined motivic material: a fundamental rising-scale motif covering a fourth, an eighth-note motif, and a cadence motif on a firm anapaest rhythm. Everything sounds direct and crudely powerful, yet the real basis for power rests in a rather celebrated point of harmonic subtlety.

If Beethoven's idea was to bring his theme up from the depths, he was more or less bound to begin it in the cello, with no bass below. This was a plain invitation to fruitful ambiguities. Not only does the first phrase begin low, it also lays low, turning suspiciously around C, the dominant degree. The recurring C vaguely implies a harmonic root, biasing these first bars already in the dominant direction—a bias helped by the throbbing C on the top of the accompaniment, and tacitly allowed by the hollow accompaniment chord (there is only one) itself. Of course, the little phrase speaks so firmly that one can scarcely credit the harmonic indefiniteness with which it offers to tell its story—and in any case, two F's unofficially confirm the tonic stability. The total impression, if we have time to think, is less delicate than willful, less equivocal than forthright but askew.

The cello melody rises from C to F and then to a half-cadence on G, supporting a no-longer-ambiguous dominant 4/3 chord. This G in bar 8 develops as a key detail. The next phrases (in the violin) deploy themselves like a balancing lyric continuation of the original two; but the inflexible way in which they parrot the original motivic material jars just as much as the fact that a single harmony (the same V4/3 on top of the same G) is sounding all through the eight-bar section. In spite of first appearances, then, Beethoven is dealing less with tunes here than with a great *crescendo* of preparation. The novelty comes in combining such a passage with thematic exposition, and in bringing it so explosively early in the piece.

The opening statement of the "Archduke" Trio, Opus 97—a later work —bears a certain superficial similarity to this one, in its rhythmic profile and in its general impetus toward melodic climax. But the comparison (which can be extended past the themes to the pieces as wholes, and even, indeed, to the periods during which the pieces were written) simply points up the radical nature of the quartet and the normality of the trio. The trio is what the quartet only pretends to be—genuinely lyric. Less dynamic and disruptive than the quartet, it was just the work to impress such composers as Schubert and Brahms.

In the quartet, clouded harmony in the first phrase has clarified into a dominant chord at the cadence of the second. The dominant chord holds fast for a full eight bars, its cadential quality turning into a very strong sense of anticipation. Then bars 17–18 add more sinew—a solid root for the dominant, and a strong ninth resolving up through D–E–F to the first stable tonic sonority in the composition. This makes for an arrival of the greatest force. Throughout these eighteen bars, the feeling of preparation has grown in urgency as the melody thrusts up and up. And one sore spot stands out: the note G, which marked the first change of harmony. This G, the second degree of the scale, rears itself out of F, then seems to get stuck and to beat away very determinedly before marching back.

As usual in the largest sonata movements, the main theme will return at the main hinges of the form. But in this piece the theme is transformed more deeply than ever before. After a broad close to the exposition, the theme seems to return verbatim, and in the tonic key too; the listener supposes that the formal repetition of the exposition is under way. However, the sixth bar of the theme moves up not to F but on the spur of the moment to G♭, a degree higher and infinitely more intense. We have been thrust into the development section, and the intensity of the shock, as much as the intensity of the chromatic note G♭ itself, suffices to stir a long series of developmental modulations pointing, as will appear, to D♭.

Later the sense of this G♭ is expounded, as well as its connection with D♭. During the first 12 bars of the recapitulation—during three out of the original four phrases—the theme follows its original path; the V4/3 chord on G has started its pulsing. By bar 13, however, the rising sequences in the violin turn to the minor mode, whereupon the cello G♮ sinks to G♭—which holds even more persistently for another *ten* bars, the violin threshing around the same G♭ in various other registers. In other words, G♭ is now heard as a warp of the original "sore" G♮. The tension grows quite intolerable. At last G♭ resolves to F, treated not yet as the tonic but as the third degree of D♭ major. It takes another sixteen-bar period before these flat regions can be forgotten, and the parallel step D♭–C♮ can bring D♭ back again around toward the tonic F major.

So Protean a theme must in the coda be somehow contained. Beethoven takes one obvious course: he gives out the theme not as a slow *crescendo* but as a triumphant *fortissimo* from the start, not with a harmonic question mark but (at last) with full and frank harmonization underneath. The passage sharply contrasts F and G by juxtaposing their major triads. This stabilizing version of the theme pares it down to two phrases, the sequel evaporating harmlessly up to the heights and down again. A few cadential periods later, the theme is suggested once more in a sort of inspired sublimation. Only three elements endure—elements which we now see to be of the very essence: the first motif (the other two are lost); the idea of a great sweeping ascent from the depths; and the "sore" note G, with its pulsation, desiring the tonic. The great ascent is revealed as the outcome of the modest rising-scale motif, and the G is "explained" downwards from A. While G beats violently again in the bass, the violin climbs a scale up to the highest note in the piece, three octaves above middle C. There it rests for five whole bars, seeming to dispose the G fathoms below to resolve, resume, and resolve again to an F that is finally a serene, unclouded tonic.

Those other motifs are not entirely lost, either. The violin in its descent recalls the eighth-note motif, and the concluding modal cadence contains a hint of the cadence motif.

These are extraordinary transformations of a theme that was already extraordinary enough in its plain statement. In their grandiose way, the transformations are perfectly in scale: the theme itself invites the catastrophe of the recapitulation, which in turn requires the huge double affirmation of the coda. Of course the full scope of Beethoven's conception reveals itself only in the light of all the rest of the movement. We should look back over it in some detail, starting [with the end of the first statement of the theme], the point at which the main theme arrives so forcefully at the first true tonic sonority.

The interesting fact about this arrival is that it is an artificial one. Or, more correctly, Beethoven seems to have wanted only the fact of arrival; he had no intention of doing anything with the F that is arrived at (the basic exposition, after all, was accomplished by this time). The next six bars prevaricate: a low C deliberately undercuts the harmony, and inconclusive diminished-seventh chords build up to a cadence which in effect restates that of [the end of the rising theme]. Here a solid tonic passage commences—only to take on the air of a bridge starting up. So although a great deal seems to be happening, there is no really definitive statement, only a brilliant show of motivic energy. The prevaricating bars suggest the anapaest rhythm of the cadence motif. The bridge makes a bucolic extension of the eighth-note motif, running into canons on the first motif. These in turn sprout new, useful triplet figures.

The actual modulation to the second group is done just a little roughly —but significantly—by juxtaposing F- and G-major triads. Suddenly there is a very forceful new arrival, at G. The high melodic line E–F♯–G and the dominant ninth chord echo the prior arrival, D–E–F, which can now be heard as a stage toward the present one. F and G, the notes around which the long opening revolved, stand out as the cadential goals in the first large section of the movement.

But by this time serious action is to take place. A solo cello theme in G erupts out of the triplet figuration [which accompanied the foregoing high melodic line E–F♯–G], relaxing rather majestically into C major and a lyric second theme (in whose cadence notes A–B–C we may hear a resonance of the two prior arrivals). The subsequent cadence figures bear a very individual stamp, and seem bent on exploring the total pitch firmament once again. The first of them uses entwining triplet *arpeggios* in all the instruments. The second uses a series of cryptic half-note chords, irregular harmonically and very widely spaced; one thinks, oddly, of Webern. In sonata form, the section after the second theme was a traditional place for small harmonic clouds, but Beethoven is extremely bold (and, with his new touch in the recapitulation, even capricious). A third and final cadence idea picks up the light canons of the bridge, devising a new motif—a variation of the rising-scale motif in the rhythm of the eighth-note motif. This admirable combination does important service in the development, and reappears in the last passage of the coda.

One of Beethoven's most tremendous development sections is to follow; but as Tovey remarked, there is at first no sign of unusual scope or even of unusual imagination. The development starts with the main theme in the tonic (or is it *on* the dominant? a nice paradox at this point), its second phrase forced up to a dramatic new note, G♭. This sets up a modulating dialogue on the theme, whose accents, harmonies, and accompaniment figuration all prove to be grist for Beethoven's developmental mill. The eighth-note motif forms itself into a neat sequence; the harmonies proceed in standard fashion from I to IV to ii to vi; the Webernish half-note chords turn up, and also a strong dominant which the listener takes (correctly enough) as that preparing the home key. All this holds to a predictable scheme, but gradually unpredicted greater rhythms begin to assert themselves. The first violin extends the eight-note motif into a leisurely rhapsody, while the harmonies move away with sublime unconcern. After about sixteen bars Beethoven settles in the key of D♭, a much more remote region than those touched earlier in the development (even though it was foreshadowed by the rupturing G♮ at the start). He is loath to leave; for another sixteen bars he makes up warm, nostalgic versions of the last cadence theme in D♭, expanding it and rounding it lyrically. There is a sudden lurch, and an even grander landscape is revealed.

Contrapuntal episodes had haunted the development sections of the Opus 18 Quartets, but Beethoven had never before worked on a scale that allowed or demanded the massive formality achieved by counterpoint here. A giant double fugue unfolds, with a secondary subject grown out of the combination motif of the cadence theme, and with a principal subject that is to all intents and purposes new, in spite of the familiar anapaest rhythm. The entries of these subjects, at five-bar intervals, sound stately, rather scholastic, and enormously deliberate for a sonata-form episode. There is enough time for three regular entries, plus two different *stretto* ones, before the second *stretto* turns extremely loud and dissonant, and grinds its way harshly up to a stop. This abrupt climax—it is on an inchoate diminished-seventh chord—smashes the fugue, only to collapse numbly to a new strong dominant. After yet another lengthy diversion, the true dominant is sounded while the violin soars quietly up to the highest part of its range, to high B♭–B♮–C in solo whole-notes. The two arrivals in the opening period of the exposition flash back to the ear.

An arrival—but not yet at the main theme: at its prevaricating, chromatic, anapaestic sequel. And not yet at a firm tonic sound; the material is given initially over a I6 chord, which is undercut as before by a loud C. Beethoven must have felt reluctant to dispel the harmonic ambiguities of his first theme any earlier than the coda. But of course he wanted a *forte* recapitulation; if the decision was to hold the lucid *forte* version of the main theme in reserve, it was a brain wave to use the prevaricating passage in its place at this juncture. The passage starts *forte*, continuing a little differently in view of a different and clearer goal: pre-establishment, in fact, of the hollow accompaniment harmony (A and C) of the coming theme. When [this] main theme arrives, it arrives *piano* again, so that it can make a *crescendo* again—the catastrophic *crescendo* with the G♭ that has already been discussed. The ambiguous note C is stressed further by means of repeated scales. If one still hears A trumpeting away on the cello, it will seem to sink to the G, thence to G♭, and finally—after the shattering new build-up—to an equivocal F.

Equivocal in that F is treated not as the tonic, but as the third degree of a temporary D♭ tonality—resuming the key of the main center of the development, and with it a great sense of range and exploration. Only after sixty-five bars of this recapitulation is a real tonic sonority heard, at the majestic entry of the lyric second theme. In honor of its new role, perhaps, Beethoven reorchestrated the second theme richly. Thereafter things move directly to the gigantic double affirmation which makes up the coda. Preoccupation with tonic stability here, to the exclusion of even so much as a gesture in any other direction, helps balance the extended digression to D♭ in the recapitulation. Rarely, in any case, did Beethoven end a composition with such serene breadth, such a perfect inertia.

Our account of the movement has been mainly descriptive, perhaps to the point of drabness. But there is so much to describe. A study of the quartets alone does not trace Beethoven's development step by step; coming upon the first "Razumovsky" Quartet after the six of Opus 18 is like coming into a new artistic universe. It is like a first reading of Chapman's Homer, a first visit to Athens or Venice, a first kiss. The richness of detail, the originality and fertility of musical idea, the commanding coherence, the sheer smooth density and complexity of it all, are fairly breathtaking. Little wonder that in the 1800's quartet players who like Opus 18 found Opus 59 a closed book. There had never been such a quartet before; and the piece remains breathtaking in any context.

Yet perhaps the primary impression is not so much of fecundity as of span, purposeful span. Already indicated by the opening theme itself, a sense of horizon grows on the listener with every large gesture of the piece. Contractions—for there are a few in the second portion of the exposition—only contribute to this sense as a foil to the pulse of the essential progress. The modulations which mark the stages of this progress are few and monolithic, and manage to give the piece such slow-swinging power, that by the time D♭ forces its way into the recapitulation we are not at all amazed (as well we might be) that it maintains itself so long and so successfully. Unusually large digressions have been placed within our experience—the unexpected warm detour to D♭ in the development, and the protracted cool explorations of the double fugue. In the coda, detail is stripped away to reveal the sure framework. Multiplicity without confusion, extension without vacuity, prolongation without delay, scope without either flaccidity or tedium: all this falls within the new range of Beethoven's second period.

Of all the compositions between Opus 18 and Opus 59, one in particular springs to mind in connection with the F-major Quartet: the *Eroica* Symphony itself. So much is remarkable about the symphony, in purely technical terms as well as in terms of "program" or extramusical impetus. But the most remarkable single fact about it is its span. It dwarfs every previous effort of the classic composers, and opens the door to *The Damnation of Faust,* the *Ring,* and the Mahler symphonies, to say nothing of Beethoven's Ninth. Something of this scope is attempted in the F-major Quartet—though the quartet medium might seem to be the last place to try for it—and stands out as the commanding feature of the work. Only Beethoven would have forced open this door, and only Beethoven cared to pass through to conceptions such as that of the Quartet in B♭ of 1825 with the Great Fugue.

In quality, the *Eroica* Symphony is entirely different from the quartet; as different as the key of E♭ major, in Beethoven's ear, from the key of F. But technical parallels between the two works are quite close. At the heart of the conception of each opening movement lies the idea of a theme destined for earth-shaking reinterpretations—not so much in the development section, as in the recapitulation and coda. In both movements, the change in the recapitulation hinges on one "sour" note. In the quartet, an ostensibly bland G gets stuck and has to be bent violently to G♭. In the symphony, a far from bland—in fact, a distinctly mysterious —C♯ becomes D♭ at the recapitulation, causing luminous digressions in distant keys. The quartet theme and the symphony theme both lie in the bass region, accompanied above by a pulsation which refuses to budge (this is true in the symphony at least for the duration of the C♯). Then climactically in the coda, each theme is simplified, and coarsened, into a triumphant statement, up in the treble register. This is done differently in the symphony than in the quartet, by means of a fourfold fanfare. But the principle is much the same.

Great contortions in the recapitulation and coda go hand in hand with the singular aspect of the development sections in these works. Writing the *Eroica,* Beethoven experienced his vision of a gargantuan development, less a digression than a journey of exploration, proliferating into many distant episodes which bespeak personal energies over and beyond the prescriptions of the exposition proper. Not only do the developments of the *Eroica* and the Quartet in F run longer than the respective expositions—in itself an unusual circumstance—but the proportional lengths are almost identical, about 3:2 in each case. The development of the *Eroica* includes a fragmentary but very impressive double *fugato;* the double *fugato* in the quartet is larger, more formal and more central. In each case Beethoven mops up the *fugato* in the same curious way, by swirling it up into a passage of inchoate, angry noise. Here, certainly, the palm goes to the treatment in the symphony—the matchless stripping away of melody, harmony, and rhythm until only dissonant noise remains, a descent into the dark night of the heroic soul. By comparison, the diminished seventh chord in the quartet seems more than a little perfunctory.

For Beethoven, massive developments like these needed to incorporate some decidedly new material. In the quartet, as we saw, this is the main fugue subject. The fugue is central here. The new element in the symphony is the famous E-minor theme introduced after the inchoate crisis following the *fugato*. The symphony includes a number of effects of slow tonal diversion recalling the rhapsodic violin deflection from F major to D♭ early in the quartet development. Both works, finally, plan some special excruciation at the point of recapitulation—they had to, after the immensity of developmental action. The "wrong-beat" horn entry of the *Eroica* finds a parallel in the brilliant reversal of first-group material in the quartet recapitulation.

The analogy between the two first movements comes in scope and technique, not at all in mood. Lacking in the quartet is the sense of inner conflict that first drove Beethoven, it would seem, to his heroic vision. He was not doing a *quartetto eroico*; the piece rather resists programmatic imaginings. For all its powerful drives and sharp explosions and new revelations, the quartet breathes an abstract quality that sets it in a different emotional sphere from the symphony. Its drives and explosions and revelations do not seem to emerge in response to conflict; rather, they are working out certainties, investigating tonal properties. Massive control, even a certain commanding serenity marks this movement—symbolized, perhaps, by the double fugue in the development, with its new theme, its energetic level gestures, and its crowning position within the movement as a whole.

As for the quality of tonal investigation in the quartet movement, this hinges on a crux of two notes, F and G, the tonic and second degree of the F-major scale. One may hear, or construe, the step from F up to G as a kernel not only of the rising-scale motif, but also of the whole idea of ascent. This basic idea is expressed at the beginning, as the theme screens tonal space; at the end, as F and G extinguish themselves below the violin high C; and at many striking points between. F and G mark the first forceful arrivals in the exposition, capping the dramatic tension of the theme itself. G supports the quite long, majestic preparation for the second theme (the G-major triad, dominant of C). Indeed, the juncture of F-major and G-major triads becomes a familiar sound in this composition. (The triads arise, of course, as a deepening of the crux of the notes themselves—another instance of the harmonic extension of a melodic detail such as occurs prominently already in the earliest of the Opus 18 Quartets.) F- and F-major sonorities make the abrupt modulation in the original bridge, and they sharply salt the triumphant harmonized version of the theme in the coda. [In it] the G-major triad alters the fourth degree of the F-major scale, B♭, to B♮, canceling the subdominant (IV). In fact, the coda and the recapitulation avoid subdominant sounds like the plague. Harmonies of the sixth degree are used instead: that long D♭ (♭VI) in the recapitulation, and the ultimate progression in the coda, using D minor (vi). The latter progression makes a curiously effective modal cadence; does not the piece as a whole tend toward a loose modality, Lydian in fact? It is a later F-major composition, the *Heiliger Dankgesang* of the Quartet in A minor, Opus 132, that will strike a self-conscious Lydian pose. But already this movement —by its avoidance of the subdominant, by its insistence on G with B♮ above it, by its concluding modal touch—cultivates the slightly ethereal, very distinctive harmonic flavor of the Lydian mode.

This fact may help explain why the next movement of the quartet, the *Allegretto vivace e sempre scherzando*, was set by the composer in the unprecedented key of B♭, the subdominant. And this *Scherzando* is an even more extraordinary movement than the opening *Allegro*. Unprecedented indeed.

At the start, thematic material is presented in what Tovey would call "a vision of dry bones." The monotone rhythm that inspires the whole piece appears first as an antecedent phrase, answered—with a sharp, characteristic dissociation of register—by a consequent phrase which modulates. To compare this with the unaccompanied opening of the *Scherzo* (also in B♭) of the "Archduke" Trio is to see, once again, the extremity of Beethoven's intention in the present work, and to clarify the "normality" of the trio.

Later in the piece, the consequent phrase proves susceptible to radical melodic transformations. [The first of these transformations occurs directly after the rhythmic "dry bones" are repeated *fortissimo* in the tonic harmony. It is in the key of D minor and consists of prolonging the little phrase and varying it with dotted rhythms. A second transformation takes place shortly thereafter, when the monotone reappears as it did at the beginning, *pianissimo* and on the tonic, B♭. At this point the consequent phrase is altered to start *on* instead of before the beat as it did originally. This shifting of accent completely changes its character by making it into a perky mazurka-like phrase.

This mazurka-like aspect] can be bodied forth in many different ways, [as] in a very important *fortissimo* combination with canonic overtones [at the close of the exposition.

At the] recapitulation (in G♭ major) [it reappears in its original form] with wispy new countersubjects. Later on the mazurka-like transformation reappears with one of those countersubjects in free inversion, and a free canon thrown in. Contrapuntal work is ostentatious, once again, just as in the first movement of the quartet and in every one of the Opus 18 series.

What seems to be central to this *Allegretto vivace e sempre scherzando* is not counterpoint in the ordinary sense, but the very process of bodying out. That sounds Beethovenian enough in spirit, though as a matter of fact he never elsewhere worked in just this way. A parallel may be thought to exist with the dynamic principle of the first movement of the quartet, which relies on the expansion of a theme in its repetitions and on the reinterpretation of one note within it. The *Eroica* first movement does something similar. But instead of the more typical sense of deepening or revelation in the thematic transformations, here on the contrary the effect is one of wonder and whimsy—Beethoven starts from something impossibly slight and carries it to implausible lengths, in bewildering diversity. There, a sense of cumulative growth, here of discontinuous transformation. The quality, in a word, is exactly appropriate to the sentiment named: *sempre scherzando.*

And if the fact of paradoxical bodying-out was central to Beethoven's conception, one can see why traditional sonata form—no less than the simple A B A "minuet and trio" scheme—proved inadequate to the intrinsic urge of his material. Sonata form is antithetical to the idea of paradoxical variation. At least in Beethoven's hands, sonata form worked out the given potential of themes, rather than displaying them in fascinating, novel, essentially additive guises. That was the sphere of the theme and variations, a much less dynamic musical form which a less sophisticated aesthetic had been able to encompass perfectly well. One thinks of the chaconnes and passacaglias of the Baroque era. Significantly enough, the closest parallel to the inner process of the present movement comes in Beethoven's so-called *Eroica* Variations, Opus 35, and in the work developed from them, the Finale of the *Eroica* Symphony.

So in the present instance Beethoven was driven to a thoroughly novel formal synthesis. Though the piece contains such obvious sonata-form elements as an exciting development section, it cannot without absurdity be pressed into a standard sonata mold—Vincent d'Indy and most other commentators to the contrary. The form—which is to say, the expressive shape—of this movement is *sui generis*, an imaginative combination of elements familiar in themselves from the dance forms and from the more highly organized sonata forms, but never associated in just this way. Sonata principles are in play, but the customary framework for these principles, "sonata form," is simply not present.

What is present—as a first level—is a ground-plan that was now interesting Beethoven in the Fourth Symphony and in the E-minor "Razumovsky" Quartet, a double Scherzo | Trio | Sherzo | Trio | Scherzo alternation. But the plan is raised to quite another level by tonal activity and by the corresponding inserted development section:

Scherzando I	Trio I→Development	Scherzando II	Trio II→Scherzando III
B♭	F minor modulates	B♭—but re-written with broad tonal digressions	Same as Trio I, transposed to B♭ minor	B♭, much abbreviated

What I wish to hear (with Riemann) [is that] the "trio" behaves on the whole conventionally, beginning after a stop and ending after a formal cadence prior to the transition into the development section. It introduces a fairly sharp contrast of mode, tone, and material; it shapes itself as an elementary little ternary structure, with the second member repeated, and with only one odd bar to disturb the dancelike regularity of four-bar phrases. At its second appearance, in B♭ minor, the "trio" barely changes.

The *scherzando* sections, on the other hand, are unique in construction and in rhetoric; they fall into nothing resembling a conventional dance form. Furthermore, they differ radically from one another, not so much in material as in harmonic action:

```
                                        A
                            D——D        D
Scherzando I:     Bb            Bb         Bb       Bb
                        Cb
                    Ab                      .

                                        E
                                          A
                            G——G
                              F
Scherzando II:                  Bb                  Bb
                          Ab
                      Db
              Gb
```

These diagrams are meant to chart the sequence of keys, from left to right, with boldface type reserved for the clear tonic sections, which are the centrally important ones. Modulations happen so abruptly, even in *Scherzando* I, that in spite of really revolving around B♭, this section sounds unstable enough to encourage (indeed, to require) a development section later. It is the first and third boldface B♭ areas that accommodate the mysteriously quiet "dry bones" versions of the thematic material; in each place, the paradox of texture is compounded by paradoxical harmonic movement (B♭–A♭–C♭, then B♭–A–D). Both kinds of paradox are soon dispelled by the loud, triumphant, fully harmonized version of the theme, in the second and fourth B♭ areas. (The second B♭ area, near the beginning of the piece, does double service: as resolution of the paradox and as transition to the long contrasting D-minor section following.) The third and fourth B♭ areas act together as a loose *da capo*. The fourth one does not cadence, however, running instead to an expectant dominant and the stop which demarcates the "trio."

Scherzando II makes a wonderful free expansion of this tonal dynamic. Here the "dry bones" versions are always fleshed out with kaleidoscopic counterpoints, and the harmonic digressions are more serious than before —much more serious: G♭–D♭–A♭ in the first instance, and F–E–A in the second. These doubly paradoxical statements resolve to the same loud, fully harmonized tonic versions. But now the tonic has been reached in the first instance by a deeply subdominant route (I am reminded of the Finale of Schubert's C-major Symphony) and in the second, as though to balance, by way of the dominant.

Tonic centrality is kept in all three *scherzando* sections, then, though in *Scherzando* II Beethoven certainly seems to have stretched things as far as he dared. Much depends on recollection of the first time around and on the brute fact of *fortissimo* in the resolving B♭ places. Throughout, the tonal pattern is more dissociated (on the diagrams, more spread out vertically) than that of *Scherzando* I. All this runs contrary to sonata-form orthodoxy, of course, which would have the last statement of a large section harmonically *more* stable than the first, not less so, as here. A strong new dominant (the F) in a "recapitulation" would be particularly shocking. But once again, this is no sonata-form movement. Because after *Scherzando* II Beethoven intends to return at length to the tonic with "Trio" II, he can dare and profit from unorthodox tonal fragmentation.

Scherzando III, a concluding summary statement, brings the original theme in its original tonal position (but not in its original bare-bones texture). There is a reminiscence of the distant modulations of the development, dispelled once again by the theme fully harmonized (but no longer *fortissimo*):

Scherzando III:	**B♭**		reminiscence of	**B♭**
		C♭	development	
	A♭		modulations	

At this reminiscence, what serves to jog the memory is the progression F–F♯, for a hard juxtaposition of F and F♯ (G♭) had served both to begin the development and to end it. The first-movement development comes to mind, too. The present development, it should be said, works excitedly up the circle of fifths—and introduces its own radical thematic transformations and bodyings-out.

One other technical feature should be mentioned, one that associates the movement with the opening *Allegro*: the conspicuous play of registers. There is even a parallel to the odd Webern-like place in the first movement, [where the violent shift of registers is accompanied by equally violent shifts of harmony. These occur twice: at the end of the first theme in the exposition (measures 35–38), and at the similar place in the recapitulation (measures 271–74)].

As can be seen in part (but only in part) from the various music examples [described] above, the main theme itself tends to reappear with its octave registers freshly dissociated. The tension established by the first bars—the melodic consequent phrase octaves above the monotone antecedent—develops dizzily up to the amusing "sprung" gestures at the very end of the movement.

But these descriptions, once again, can give only a bloodless impression of this extraordinary piece of music. A. B. Marx dutifully counted (so Helm dutifully reports) ten shifting moods within it; that was his way of articulating something about its imaginative juxtapositions and its intense inflections of detail. By these qualities, he might have added, the movement forecasts Beethoven's third period in technique, if not in mood. Since fertility is at the heart of the conception, all the explosions, contortions, dartings, contrasts, and paradoxes are in a certain sense functional. This posed Beethoven an interesting formal problem, which he solved a great deal better than most analysts have been able to trace. Brilliant flexibility was needed in the form, too—and achieved, certainly; but on the other hand, the form had to hold all the manifold unpredictabilities in shape. So it is that the Scherzo | Trio | Scherzo | Trio | Scherzo alternation provides a certain humdrum stability offsetting all the adventure; and the adventure itself moves, after all, almost always to the same goal, the triumphant embodiment of the vision of dry bones in the home tonic B♭, *fortissimo*. Through it all, even somehow through the contrasting "trio," the original monotone rhythm broods or mutters or clangs: now subsidiary, now bodied out, now only a vestige, now—and ultimately—the bare loud resolving substance of the whole machine.

It is tempting to speak of this movement as an experimental one, if only because Beethoven never wrote anything else remotely like it. But that cannot be because of any lack of success in the "experiment"; the piece was never conceived as a study in some kind of *cul de sac*; the analogy of experimental method simply does not hold in art. Everything works—and "everything" includes incredible things. As an individual musical structure, this *Allegretto vivace e sempre scherzando* is one of the signal masterpieces of the second period, as much so as the opening *Allegro*.

The *Scherzando* had defected to the subdominant, B♭; the main key of the quartet is restored by the third movement, *Adagio molto e mesto* in F minor. A full-scale slow movement in the minor mode is a rarity in Beethoven, especially past the first period. Besides the present quartet and the C-major "Razumovsky," the important examples occur in the *Eroica* and Seventh Symphonies, the "Ghost" Trio and the D-major Cello Sonata, the Fourth Piano Concerto—a rather special case—and the Piano Sonatas in Bb and Ab, Opus 106 and 110. Of all these, the present *Adagio molto e mesto* is doubtless the most profoundly tragic in intention,[1] an essay in misery scarcely relieved by any response of sobriety or solace. The contrast with the ebullience of the first two movements is likely to catch the listener up very sharply.

In this respect the piece looks back to the *Adagio* of another F-major Quartet, Opus 18, No. 1, and it looks back in other respects too. For both movements, programmatic notes of pathetic import have been found scribbled against the sketches—a curious coincidence: with the early quartet, *Les derniers soupirs* of Romeo and Juliet, with the present one, *Einen Trauerweiden oder Akazien-Baum aufs Grab meines Bruders*, "A Weeping Willow or Acacia Tree over my Brother's Grave." The inspiration was as fictional in the one case as in the other, by the way: neither of Beethoven's brothers was dead when the quartet was written. In each case, one strongly suspects that an extramusical impetus must have stayed too close to the surface to permit the work of art to succeed as a free emotional artifact. Sentimentality was clouding Beethoven's vision; the technique is very impressive indeed, once again, but there is something overblown in the expression, something in the feeling that the technique does not properly support.

The actual sentiment naturally differs from that of Opus 18, No. 1. The rage, energy, and high tragedy of the *Adagio affettuoso ed appassionato* have turned into anguish, dejection, *mestizia* here. The mood is much richer, it must be said, and closer to the ceremonial grief writ large of the *Marcia funebre* in the *Eroica* Symphony, some of whose accents seem echoed here. Yet a certain objectivity and decorum makes the symphony seem both more genuinely touching and more sincere. The main theme of the *Adagio e mesto* is admirably calculated, with its hollow 5ths, its *appoggiaturas*, and its extreme compounded series of melodic dissonances. (The emphasis on the bVII degree, Eb, recalls the "trio" of the *Scherzando*, which had also figured in F minor; perhaps something Russian already informs these melodies, with their slight modal shading.) Calculation apart, however, the theme strives too greedily for gloom by means of insistent *appoggiaturas*, and it risks more than it prudently should through the weeping descant of its repetition. The

[1] I would place the slow movement of the Piano Sonata Opus 106 on a par with the *Adagio* of Opus 59, No. 1, in its feeling of "profound tragedy." Its only "release" from tragic tension is the second theme in the subdominant major, which in itself is short-lived and unresolved.—Editor.

gesture toward the relative major [which begins the second phrase] sounds a little glib; Beethoven makes it sound more so by repeating it at once with a decoration; and by adding a florid touch [of staccato thirty-second notes together with an operatic neighbor note] at the recapitulation, he will make it sound positively tawdry.

Even the second subject of this movement must come in the minor mode, the dominant minor. The rich, very beautiful sequence emerging from it takes care to flush out many minor-mode sonorities; more of the traditional rhetoric of the minor mode is manipulated in the long series of cadences that follows. But these cadences harp on a note of despair ill sustained by the structure of the exposition as a whole. Once it occurs to the listener that one of them may be supererogatory, the entire emotional façade falls under suspicion. And the tempo, according to Beethoven's metronome mark, is set extremely slow.

A development section starts with a rather inexplicable turn to the major mode—which denatures the second subject when it now appears in this mode. After some modulations, a superb section ensues in which *pizzicato* cello *arpeggios* hold together fragmented, and agonized, canons on sections of the first theme. By the largest reckoning, the subsequent dominant preparation prior to the recapitulation lasts seventeen bars—this in a movement whose entire exposition lasts only forty-five. The reckoning includes a striking digression to a new hymnlike tune perched in Db major, over and away from the dominant C. This frank *maggiore* balances the Ab major which opened the development; perhaps both of them were needed to relieve the continual *minore* sonorities elsewhere in the piece. The note of consolation is unmistakable, yet once again excessive, fulsome, and essentially unearned.

Instead of an independent coda, this *Adagio* has another return of the desolate main theme (complete with its unpleasant florid touch, in octaves). For a last point of intensity, the violin brings the melody slowly down two octaves as the cello moves up and up to meet it; the converging lines almost meet, in a fine ultimate excruciation of D and Db. At this point an emotional resolution is maneuvered which rings truer than the prayerful Db episode in the development. Gradually the violin shakes itself free of the texture and of the tragic obsession, and curls its way upward in a sort of fluttering cadenza. (One remembers the leisurely rhapsody of the violin in the development of the opening *Allegro*.) This transition—to the Finale—is perfectly gauged in psychological justness and in its larger rhythm. With a sense of almost physical release, the violin ascends to the very high C, three octaves above middle C, while the other instruments ground it airily by means of scales down to the low cello C. Then the violin too cascades down to a trill, still on C, waiting for the Finale.

"*Allegro. Thème russe,*" Beethoven writes at the head of the new

movement, with some satisfaction, it would seem, and with evident satisfaction the little Russian folk song turns up at once in the cello. According
to rather imprecise tradition, the incorporation of Russian material in
these quartets was the idea of Count Razumovsky, who was not only a
Russian but the Russian Ambassador. The violin extends its trill unchecked; there is no further accompaniment. Perhaps the first thing we
sense—besides relief after the mourning *Adagio*—is a curious external
similarity to the theme of the first movement. A pulsing C on top of
a hollow harmony, and a deep cello melody rising from the fifth degree
to the tonic: Beethoven is making a subtle parallel with, or comment on,
or parody of his opening *Allegro*.

The distinctions are egregious, of course, and they arise from the
nature of the *thème russe*. The indefatigable Nottebohm found both this
theme and the one used in the E-minor "Razumovsky" Quartet in a
certainly contemporary folk song collection, one particular copy of which
bears annotations in Beethoven's hand. The present song really belongs
in D minor; originally dubbed *Molto andante* by its collector, it gains
gusto from its emphasis on the "modal" ♭VII degree, C. The parallel
with the two F-minor themes of the "trio" and the *Adagio*, with their
E♭'s, is interesting, all the more so because Beethoven now refuses to
take the song in its proper mode. Without having to change any notes,
he wrests it into a cheery paradoxical F-major context by further emphasis of that very C. The initial D becomes an *appoggiatura* on to
the dominant C, instead of a tonic, and later outlines of D minor
in the tune are swept under the rug. Clear results of this odd procedure
enliven the further progress of the movement.

An air of good-natured parody is present: for example, in the canons,
which instantly start chiming away at the folk song, and, a little later,
at the otherwise rather slight second subject. At the end of the piece,
Beethoven plays various tricks on the *thème russe*, combining two of its
phrases to make a comic double counterpoint, and then slowing it
down to a pretentious *adagio*. This last transformation is not all for fun.
Mock-expressive chromatic harmonies light up a not-so-secret A-major
harmony (dominant of D minor) which is implicit in the tune but
which had been avoided in the F-major interpretation previously.

The beginning of the song combines with bridge material, amusingly,
in the development section, which modulates far before settling. It settles
to a suspiciously long and vigorous D-minor plateau; this key would
seem to make amends for the D minor that was short-changed within
the *thème russe* itself. The way out is ingenious. Quietly things slip
down from D minor to C minor, then to B♭—and in this key, the
subdominant, the recapitulated folk song returns unexpectedly, its initial
D now treated as a full-fledged subdominant. Altering one of the notes,
Beethoven now wants us to hear the modal melody—which is really in

D minor, which he has previously always pressed into F—as beginning in a third tonality, Bb. This reinterpretation bears a certain fantastic, lightly touched analogy to the reinterpretations of thematic material that are at the basis of the conception of the opening movement of the quartet.

Recapitulation by way of the subdominant certainly counts as an original effect, which Beethoven was to employ less wittily, and more expressively, in the first movement of the Sixth Symphony. (The symphony is in F, too.) Is the subdominant episode here an inverted reflection of the *avoidance* of the subdominant in the opening *Allegro?* or of the aberrant placement of the *Scherzando* in the subdominant key? The present recapitulation, in any case, makes no reference to the opening texture of the exposition, which so strikingly recalled the first movement —the solo cello with the violin C pulsing above it. That texture, one must therefore conclude, does not serve as an important functional thing in this movement, as it does in the other. Its role can only be understood as one of reminiscence or linkage.

There is another similar situation. The end of the exposition in the Finale employs the same cascade down from high C to the trill as was used to graft the Finale on to the *Adagio* (the notes in the violin correspond exactly, even though the notation differs and the speed is half as fast again, according to Beethoven's metronome marks). Since this detail too is omitted at the balancing place at the end of the recapitulation, presumably it too has to be understood principally as a link with the earlier movement.

In all this, we may come to feel some of the same exhilaration in the abstract investigation of tonal properties as informs the great opening *Allegro*. The last movement of the Quartet in F, besides being the only Beethoven movement to engage seriously with a Russian tune, ranks as one of the most elegant, spirited, and forthright of his finales—and the finale was always the touchy movement. That it strikes a tone wrongly scaled to the quartet as a whole, however, has been generally felt and expressed by the commentators in one way or another. The problem is a subtle one, because the Finale fits excellently with the *Adagio;* its slightly strained high spirits make a fine intellectual foil to those exaggerated tears, and the psychological transition is very wonderfully managed. But whereas the *Adagio*, sentimental or not, will pass as sheer relaxation after the two exhaustive early statements, the Finale leaves one wanting something more or at least something different— something heavier, I am afraid. There are some intrinsically less interesting movements that succeed better at the end of Beethoven pieces. The Finale of the Sixth Symphony is one. In the quartet, Beethoven was writing at the very top of his form, but his instinct for the larger coherence faltered.

In the light of this, the links mentioned above are especially interesting.

The need for binding up the whole did not escape the composer. Already with the quartets of Opus 18, he was concerning himself with unification of the four-movement form; interrelationships of one kind or another are to be observed in all the early quartets. But in a way, the revolution of the *Eroica* Symphony seems to have marked a temporary setback to this development, or rather, a radical deepening of the terms of the problem, which was bound to delay its solution. The individual movements now grow so terrific that even Beethoven cannot always face them appropriately one to the next.

With the F-major Quartet, the *hubris* that conceived and executed the opening movement must have destined the difficulties to come. By a fantastic effort of energy Beethoven matched the opening movement by the *Scherzando*; then he seems to have felt driven to a lament as excessively mournful as the *Scherzando* is excessively brilliant. The suspicion of flatulence about this formidable *Adagio molto e mesto* suddenly suggests something unwieldy, and therefore inexpressive, about the sequence of the composition as a whole. The Finale can convincingly dispel the lament—in itself an emotional accomplishment of great power—but Beethoven really gave up the ambition to produce another statement on the scale dictated by the earlier three. Or did the very medium of the string quartet begin to appear insufficient to accommodate his grandiose vision, in spite of the *tour de force* of the opening *Allegro?*

Again the *Eroica* Symphony comes to haunt this discussion of the Quartet in F; for these are exactly the two main masterpieces of Beethoven, I think, that wrestle most seriously with the problem of the individuation of single movements. One feels after the first movement of the *Eroica* much as one feels after the first or second movement of the quartet—that so exhaustive an experience has been conveyed, and in so many facets, as to make any further communication superfluous. The *Marcia funebre* in the symphony carries off the impossible, but in both works the later movements are set awkwardly for the total impression. Mention has been made of the obvious technical parallels between the opening movements in the two compositions, and of a certain emotional kinship between their tragic *Adagios*. There are other parallels: for sheer overflowing variety of material and treatment, no compositions at this period can approach the first movement of the symphony and the *Allegretto vivace e sempre scherzando* of the quartet, though the two movements may have nothing else in common beyond their astonishing exuberance. Even the two finales are alike in setting themselves a delicate and uncommon task, the treatment of pre-existing material.

To say that the quartet occupies the same place within the genre as does the symphony within its genre is to say little, for after the Opus 18 Quartets anything written in 1805 would have had much the same effect. More than that: in various ways, the quartet seems to refer back to

the *Eroica* Symphony itself, not merely in a general way to its revolutionary new sense of scope and freedom. Even though clear evidence from
the sketchbooks is lacking, one would wish to think of the Quartet
in F maturing in Beethoven's mind not long after the *Eroica*—the first
towering peak, perhaps, this side of the watershed. It was inevitable that
the Fourth Symphony and the next quartets should represent in some
sense a retrenchment.

The image of what we take as our musical tradition is marked indelibly by the strengths and weaknesses of Beethoven's second period—
or better, by its perfections and its excesses. The F-major "Razumovsky"
Quartet stands with the *Eroica* at dead center of that image, magnificent
embodiment of both.—JOSEPH KERMAN

(b) String Quartet No. 8 in E Minor, Opus 59, No. 2
I. Allegro; II. Molto adagio; III. Allegretto; IV. Presto

Placed side by side, the first movements of the F major and E
minor *Rasoumowsky* quartets afford a vivid study in contrasts. In the
first, there is an Olympian deliberateness and expansiveness of design; in
the second there is terseness of form and epigrammatic forcefulness of
syntax. The firm lyrical contours of the first are offset by the ejaculatory
motifs ("*tantôt plaquée, tantôt brisée*," as d'Indy puts it) of the second.
The wide part distributions of the first are sharply contrasted with the
compact sonorities of the second. The first has the reasoned eloquence
of the "Eroica," the second has the curt and pithy style of the "Coriolanus" Overture.

What could be more revealing than the sketches for the principal
theme of this first movement? The progressive stages through which the
composer eventually achieves the "eloquent silences" go far to underline the dramatic purport. [The first sketch in E minor and 6/8 time has
the outline of the melody intact; however, the subtlety of the final
form is missing because the high note (B) is reached on the second
beat and immediately the descending passage of sixteenths brings us back
to the tonic, which appears on the main beat of the second measure.
The rest of the second measure is silent before the same phrase is repeated a half note higher. This makes for two silences of five eighth
notes' duration, unlike the much more dramatic silences of eight eighth
notes' duration which occur in the completed form. This longer silence
is achieved by the simple expedient of holding the high note for a half
bar's duration before going into the descending figure. Another sketch
experiments with the same melodic outline but in 3/8 time. This sketch
does suggest the holding onto the high note but only in the second
phrase. The third sketch is practically identical in rhythm and melodic
outline to the final form, but it leaves out the most significant feature

of the theme—in fact of the whole first movement: the two peremptory tonic and dominant chords followed by a measure of silence which usher in the first theme and which in varying harmonies usher in the "consequent" portion of the principal theme, the development section, the recapitulation, and the coda.]

The "consequent" portion of the principal theme injects a plaintive note which is intensified by the expressive underlying phrase of the viola.

To the tempo indication of the second movement, *Molto Adagio*, the composer added the characteristic direction "*Si tratta questo pezzo con molto di sentimento*." We have the authority of no less a person than Carl Czerny that this movement owes its origin to Beethoven's contemplation of the starry sky. The story was corroborated by Holz, the violinist, an intimate friend of Beethoven and member of the famous Schuppanzigh Quartet. Holz tells how the composer conceived the idea one night at Baden, near Vienna, as he gazed up at the stars. Whether this be fact or fancy, the mood is both serene and contemplative. By actual playing time this *Adagio* is the longest of all Beethoven's slow quartet movements.

The third movement, *Allegretto*, falls but loosely into the category of Scherzo. This Allegretto reveals, nevertheless, the typical round and round alternation of Scherzo and Trio (a-b-a-b-a) which was later to be expanded into what d'Indy designates the "Grand Scherzo" or *Scherzo developpé* with new material for the second Trio: a-b-a-c-a.

The Trio section of this E minor Scherzo makes use of a Russian theme which appears also in Rimsky-Korsakoff's opera, *The Tsar's Bride*, where it symbolizes the majesty of the Tsar. It bobbed up also in Moussorgsky's *Boris Godounov* as a descriptive theme for the great Kremlin scene.

The substance of the finale is anything but weighty; the principal theme itself is about as inconsequential and carefree as many another finale theme of Haydn, and yet there is a wide discrepancy between the crude sketch of this rollicking tune and its final form. [In the sketch the uneven dotted rhythm is present, but significantly absent is the smoothing out of the melody into even eighth notes in the latter part of the phrase. Also absent in the first sketch is the arrival on the tonic note (E) of the scale at the end of the phrase when the tonic harmony (E minor) appears for the first time: the sketch ends the phrase on the note G, which could just as easily be harmonized as the fifth of a C major triad as the third of an E minor triad.]

Despite the nonchalance of the thematic material, there are a good many points of unique interest. A certain pungency is achieved through the insistency of the rhythm and the five-measure consequent of the initial period. The form is that of the Sonata-Rondo, the second digression expanding into a development section. But there is one feature that seems to have been a considerable shock to Vincent d'Indy's orthodoxy as regards the ordering of tonalities. There is an arrogant contradiction between the key-signature (E minor) and the actual tonality—that of C major—in which the principal theme sets out. Within the consequent phrase, there is, to be sure, a two-measure digression into E minor, and in the final *presto*, there is a hasty conclusion in the nominal key of the quartet; but these are not, in d'Indy's estimation, enough to establish a true tonal equilibrium. "It is difficult to say," he remarks, "to what one may attribute this singular prank on the part of a composer who was such a scrupulous observer of the laws of tonality. Despite the implication of the key-signature, this Rondo is not, and never was in E minor. The eight repetitions of the theme in the key of C are in formal opposition to E minor. Without doubt the preoccupation of the composer was elsewhere. . . ." To one less deeply orthodox, it might appear that Beethoven had had an ample sufficiency of the E tonality (minor and major) in the three preceding movements, and felt the necessity of establishing a contrast at the outset of his Finale. This is achieved by means of reversing the usual order of the minor key and its submediant major, i.e., C-e instead of e-C. It appears from this that Beethoven gave precedence to the *law* of Contrast which momentarily overrode the *rules* of key corroboration.—ARTHUR SHEPHERD

The second [Rasoumovsky] quartet, in E minor, stands somewhat apart from the others. It suggests that the "Fate" that is to be overcome is not some external menace, some threatening and maleficent power, but Beethoven's own loneliness. The first movement, with its suggestion of an enforced and bitter loneliness, its yearnings, and its outbursts of something very like rage, is one of the greatest and most dramatic movements in this group of quartets. The slow movement of this quartet [is one of] the greatest slow movements that Beethoven wrote at this period. [It is a] magnificent example of that function that music performs with unequaled subtlety, the function of presenting us with a synthesis of emotions or, as Gurney called them, "fused emotions." The complexity of [its] effect can be realized if we compare [it] with such a composition as the slow movement of the C minor symphony, for example. Such fusions are not obtained by contrast. Contrast gives the effect of a psychological transition. The different elements of the music we are discussing are not contrasted, but unified. A more elementary example of such a synthesis is to be found in the broken-winged gaiety of the Allegretto of the E minor quartet.—J. W. N. SULLIVAN

(c) String Quartet No. 9 in C, Opus 59, No. 3
I. Andante con moto; Allegro vivace; II. Andante con moto quasi Allegretto; III. Menuetto (grazioso); IV. Allegro molto

The opening of this quartet, not only in the mysterious introduction through which clouds cloak as it were a landscape revealed only in glimpses, but in the first or tentative element of its twofold main theme, Allegro, exemplifies Beethoven's now completely matured skill in spreading suspense over wide spaces. His power to seize and dominate our imagination so that a passage like this introduction, once heard, can never be forgotten, depends directly on this structural control, since in music it is structure that makes drama, and not vice versa. Thus the suspense we feel here is almost painful in its uncertainty as we peer like aviators through rifts in clouds at the distant earth, seeming now to glimpse A minor, now E flat major, a little later F minor and G major, yet never anchoring in any of them until, after nearly thirty measures, we alight at last, with the first two chords of the Allegro, firmly on C major earth.

Yet all this intentionally vague progression is controlled by a master hand. The bass, through all these many measures, from the opening F sharp to the final B, descends step by step (albeit the cello lacks the low B and has to substitute a higher one) with the inexorable logic of fate. "The introduction," writes Rebecca Clarke from the point of view of the player, "is one of those things in which the tension is so great both technically and musically that one hardly dares breathe, and can almost see the internal counting of one's companions floating like an astral shape above them. It is such a trying thing to play—wonderful as it is—that the entry into the *Allegro vivace* feels exactly like a sigh of relief at gaining solid ground again."

Even in the main theme, however, at least in its first, tentative member, the mood is still suspense, though created by different means. Conclusiveness is to come only in the second, positive member, measures 43–59, firmly stabilized on the C major tonic. The tentative air of the opening member is ensured by single suspensive chords, each spread wide: the dominant seventh through the opening violin recitative of four and a half measures, the parenthesis dominant seventh of the II (D minor chord), through the following still longer recitative. The question naturally follows: if these sections do not have, as the introduction did, a systematically moving bass to unify them, to what do they owe their no less satisfying unity? The answer seems to be that the little germinal motive of the first two notes of the *Allegro*, E—F, embodying a scalewise rise of a single step, suffices to generate, in the hands of the great master of thematic development, not only this theme, but the greater part of the whole movement. As we go on we find its fertility ever more amazing.

During the bridge, for instance, it steals at measure 65 into one instrument after another, becoming now a half step instead of a whole one, and sometimes falling instead of rising. In the second theme, [starting at measure 77], it reappears at crucial rhythmic points in falling inflection, and by expansion creates a lovely lyric movement in *pianissimo* E minor. Even the droll short phrases of the conclusion theme (99 seq.) are shot forth, each from its sixteenth note trigger, along the scale-line. In last analysis, as we realize especially in retrospect, it is the little two-note scale-step that dominates the whole exposition.

More than that, it dominates the development too. For although this starts off with the violin recitative, it soon devotes itself to new interlocutory play between the instruments on the two scale-steps, eventually falling to the cello and so leading to a new key, F, and a return to the bridge theme. Yet hardly has that started before its attention is diverted by the scale-steps again, in the original rhythm of their first appearance (a short followed by a long). This time the melodic aspect is pushed aside by the rhythmic, and at the *fortissimo* begins a queer sort of hobbling march of the instruments by pairs, viola and cello leading off, violins following as if pulled along against their will by *force majeure*—a crab-like progress later to become a mannerism with Brahms. The strenuous jumps insensibly expend their power, restrict their range, and abate their vehemence, reviving only briefly when the dominant of the original key is reached and a violin trill on G ushers in the recapitulation.

It is here that we find what is perhaps the most remarkable bit of prestidigitation of all. The entire passage, in essence, is but the restatement of the tentative member of Theme 1 that began the *Allegro*. But its details have been so rethought, so fresh-created, that the little two-note scale-rises now shared out among the instruments are like the oranges of a conjurer—they flash through the air to our bewildered admiration, never falling, never colliding, but carrying us over this tightrope moment until with a sigh of pleasure we land safely on the *forte* tonic triad that starts the positive member. In the course of this as well, ingenious transformations of the minute cell may be found, including at measure 218 rhythmic diminutions and, two measures later, even double diminutions.

As for the reduction of his idea to its "lowest terms," its ultimate simplicity, Beethoven reserves that, as we have seen him doing before, for his final shot. In the last fourteen measures he almost suppresses, by quick answer, each two-note question. But when the cello insists a little, it forces up the other three voices from their *pianissimo* hesitations, through an insistently loudening and accelerating chromatic scale, to a jubilant trilled cadence, verified by two victorious *fortissimo* chords.

The haunting *Andante* begins to move away from the dramatic contrasts of the two other great slow movements of Opus 59, toward the more contemplative vein of the later quartets. The subjectivity of Beethoven's last years is even thus early beginning to displace drama. This movement of over two hundred deliberate measures, in the overwhelming majority of which six eighth notes hypnotically pulsate, lacks the trenchant contrasts of earlier ones; by no means devoid of contrasts less obvious, especially in its subtly opposed tonalities, it verges almost dangerously on rhythmic monotony. Yet this rhythmic monotony is indispensable to its mood of unrelieved melancholy. . . .

It is interesting to note how many differing means the composer bends to his purpose of maintaining this air of sad monotony: melody, harmony, mode, register-color, tonality-color, and most striking of all, form. The themes, especially the first, but also even the more cheerful second starting at measure 42, move along the scale-line, without any bolder jumps. The harmony subordinates action to repose, notably in the long-drawn-out cadences. The opening phrase prolongs the A minor tonic it reaches at the first ending by two whole measures (that is, by half its own length) wearily punctuated by the plucked notes of the cello; and the second half of the theme ends in the wonderful codetta insisting on the same A minor chord for no less than six measures (20-25), as the heart dwells on a cherished grief. The unforgettable poignancy with which the movement ends (to look forward a moment) is due to two repetitions of this codetta. The first devotes to the chord of conclusion the same six measures (176-81) as before. The second maintains it for no less than fourteen measures, counted off by the solemn plucked notes of the cello, rising a moment as if summoning new energy, only to descend at last to the destined A in stoic acquiescence.

From measure 25 on, the phrases that follow the theme subserve the same expressive purpose, with increasing emphasis, by color both of register and of tonality. The viola, descending to its darkest register, accompanied only by the thudding plucked notes on the cello open C string, explores the dark tonality of F, in minor mode, darker even than A minor, and made still more menacing by its lowered second step, G flat. The sadness of the mood is now raised to tragic intensity by the interjected cries of the violins. The relief of the more cheerful C major second theme is but temporary, and the whole middle section is somberly colored by E flat minor and other keys far from the A minor center—harmonies furthermore rhythmically weighted by lasting a whole measure each.

Finally, even the sonata form, supposed by the unobservant to be a rigid mold, is here elastically responsive to the needs of the intangible atmosphere Beethoven wishes to preserve. The movement in its haunting ebb and flow makes us feel as if he were improvising it, and we with him, and neither of us quite knowing where we were coming out. Both its deep melancholy and its fascination somehow inhere in this sense of groping. Those plucked notes of the cello seem to be feeling their way: if they come out on E the theme repeats; if on C, lower and heavier on the lowest open string, they launch us into F major and new experiences. After the descent of the viola to its darkest register following the codetta, and its hoarse trills there, it seems, as it turns upward once more, to feel its way like a snail—"teasing," as a poet has said, "with its jellied prong"—until it finds the G from which the second theme takes off.

This theme, too, in its later appearance in the tonic, A major, Beethoven bodily transfers from the recapitulation to the earlier development section, in order that its cheer may not break in upon the passive grief he is reserving for his final impression.[1] When at last he reaches the codetta that so epitomizes his whole mood, he not only gives it twice, the second time extended, but deepens its despair by interjecting the tragic F minor cries, now concentrated to their essence. Yet they too die away, to leave only the long chord of A minor; and as that at last fades out in the two plucked A's, we sigh as if awaking from a dream.

Between the deep sadness of the Andante and the boisterous, almost brutal energy of the fugue (*Allegro molto*), we need a moment of respite; and we get it in the minuet, appropriately bearing the single direction *grazioso*, and achieving its grace by means as simple as they are sensuously delicious. Minuet and Trio, taken together, delight the ear with one of the most primitive of contrasts—that of smooth legato with crisp staccato, while each by itself, thanks to thematic imagination, delights also the mind by the much it makes from little. Thus the minuet, never pausing in the ease of its proliferation, grows entirely out of its naïve opening six-note motive. This generates a four-measure phrase four times repeated; and anyone unversed in quartet sonorities, simply reading the score and noticing that its third and fourth appearances are transpositions down an octave of its first and second, might expect this lowering to result in anticlimax. Especially liable to such error would be one judging by the piano, where low register is usually duller than high. In the quartet, on the contrary, the low G and C strings are so much richer than the middle strings that the danger of the low phrases is the opposite of dullness; they are likely to be pulled out from the G strings of vain players hunching their shoulders in the mus-

---

[1] It is my conviction that the recapitulation actually starts here, at measure 102, but with a reversal of the order of the three themes: first, this second naïve, simple theme; then, the bittersweet first theme at measure 137; and finally the codetta, long delayed, at measure 177.—Editor.

cular *molto appassionato*. It takes a genuinely musical group to achieve the lovely rich yet clear *piano* that can make them smooth and soft as velvet.

After the double bar the six-note motive continues to be the subject of discourse, first in a solo violin passage where its entrances are ingeniously crowded nearer and nearer together, then in a sort of roll-call of all the players. On the other hand the final cadence is made of the same obliging fragment, now no longer compressed, but encouraged by the composer's contrapuntal facility to expand until it fills no less than six measures—and seeming in the process, far from being diluted, to increase its potency.

More than half of the trio, again, is spun out of cadences, during which busy inner voices keep up a stir-about while the violin emits syncopated cries of joy. D'Indy's comment that "this minuet is a return to the style of 1769" is apparently meant in a deprecating sense; but it is a part of great art to know when to be simple and let the tensions relax.[1]—DANIEL GREGORY MASON (2)

If we now turn to the finale of the C major quartet, our aim is merely to clarify the form and not to furnish an exhaustive description or aesthetic evaluation of the composition. We can hereby dispense with musical notations under the assumption that the reader has the score before him.

The movement begins like a fugue. In the interchange of dux and comes, three parts enter one after the other (viola, second violin, cello). Since the theme modulates to the dominant, the return modulation falls to the comes, which is effected by the usual device of deviating from the

---

[1] The coda of this movement is especially interesting. What, we ask, is its harmonic or thematic significance? It makes use of the six-note opening motive (the rising scale), passing with it through several remote keys. The scale figure is extended further upward by the cello and then by all the instruments, ending in an unanswered question B, C, D, E, F, over a dominant harmony followed by a pause, pungent with meaning. It takes the opening theme of the last movement with its falling scale figures A, G, F, E, D and G, F, E, D, C musically to answer this question. The coda of the minuet has served, we realize, as an effective bridge between the two movements, connecting them not only physically but thematically.

In Beethoven's sketchbook, over the first outlines of this triumphant final movement, the composer scrawled the following words: "Never need you again feel ashamed of your deafness! Can anything . . . prevent you from expressing your soul in music?" Later on in the same group of sketches is another equally positive, self-confident exclamation: "It is now possible, despite social hindrances, to continue your work! Let your deafness no longer be a secret—not even in art." Marliave, in his exhaustive study of the quartets of Beethoven, is, I feel, entirely justified in calling this movement "Beethoven's first great song of victory."

I am taking the liberty of substituting for Professor Mason's highly instructive but musically complex analysis of this great final movement of Opus 59, No. 3, the fascinating study of it by Ludwig Misch—one of today's outstanding musicologists. Dr. Misch's comments are particularly valuable because they put into very clear perspective the important differences between a fugue and a sonata-allegro movement with a fuguelike principal theme.—Editor.

fifth to the fourth. But the entry of the third part already manifests a divergence from the norm of the fugue exposition; that is, the original version of the dux is not strictly maintained, but undergoes a change in the penultimate (ninth) bar, which leads to a tonic, instead of a dominant, close. And at the entry of the fourth part (first violin) which follows immediately, we find the dux again, contrary to the rules. The further development of the movement will show the reason for this ostensible anomaly.

First of all another feature strikes us about this independent "fugue exposition" and that is the lack of any consistent contrapuntal treatment, which from the very outset is contrary to the assumption that Beethoven ever intended to write a real fugue. The "contrast" that answers the theme each time[1] and at first continues the theme's eighth-note motion and then changes to quarter notes naturally has a very marked rhythm. But even at the first counterpoint, the quarter-note motif group (limited to chordal notes) leads to two bars of mere harmonic transcription (dominant-seventh chord). At the next entry of the theme, two voices with the same rhythmic motion are counterpointed, the eighth-note figures of which (doubled sixths and thirds)[2] converge in quarter-note chords. And after the entry of the fourth voice of the quartet (first violin) the potentially four-part movement becomes two-part, doubled in octaves, in which the theme is allocated to the upper voices, the counterpoint to the lower.

The polyphonic texture ends temporarily with the compression to two parts. The last dux carried out verbatim for only seven bars progresses freely by means of a motif derived from the beginning of the theme—and destined for independent development later—which over a later equally important bass rhythm in half notes leads to the cadence in the tonic key. The pure homophonic section that this introduces modulates to the dominant of the dominant through a motif group of its own derived from the foregoing. And now a new idea appears in the key of the dominant[3] prepared by a connecting solo passage of the first violin—a short motif which is again destined for polyphonic treatment carried out by means of repetition, limitation, and exchange of parts in double counterpoint (the eleventh) in periodic symmetry and expanded through elaboration of the motifs to a sort of binary song form with a cadential and again homophonic close.

In surveying the development of the movement up to this point, we recognize the ground plan of a sonata exposition. The presumable fugue

[1] Not strict counterpoint, to be exact; only the rhythmical configuration has been retained but not the melodic outline.
[2] Doubled thirds and sixths in a contrapuntal part as a Beethoven intensification device. See the trio of the E minor quartet and the trio of the Ninth Symphony.
[3] In order to prevent any misunderstanding, the theme in G major begins on the dominant, that is, it is only apparently in D.

exposition forms the *Hauptsatz*, the second contrapuntal section, the *Seitensatz*, while in between lies the usual modulatory part in homophonic texture. Now we understand why the *Hauptsatz*, contrary to all the rules of fugue exposition, states the theme twice in succession in the form of the dux. Here the object is to strengthen the principal key and to save the key of the dominant for the *Seitensatz*.[1] And the entry of the homophonic element into the fugue texture proves to be a special stylistic finesse, or more correctly speaking, the effect of a wonderful sense of homogeneous form, so that even the parts are imbued with the underlying idea of the work as a whole: The fusion of two different form types.

What the structure of the movement up to this point has revealed to us regarding the form is—to state the matter straightway—confirmed by a recapitulation which, *mutatis mutandis*, exactly corresponds to the exposition and in the fugal *Hauptsatz* even repeats the order of entry of the voices and the variants of the theme.[2] Beethoven's usual method of intensification in a recapitulation is achieved here "by means of a new contrast," which is associated with the fugue theme from its very first entry and with its sharply profiled outline in half notes (only varying in unimportant details) plays the role of an independent and striking countersubject. Thus the quasi fugue of the beginning is now completed and even surpassed by a quasi double fugue!

We have skipped about 120 bars lying between the exposition[3] and the recapitulation: the development section, which proceeds directly from the exposition without any noticeable separation, in fact with not even so much as a double bar as a visible dividing line. It lies beyond the scope of our task to go into this part more closely, interesting as it is. The sole purpose of this study is to show that it is really a "development section" in the sonata-form sense, in which the fugue-form main theme is never once stated in its entirety,[4] much less undergoing a fugue-form "development." The contrapuntal technique, as an important device in Beethoven's art of development, naturally requires due space even here— and here especially—without interfering in any way with the brilliant unfoldment of other thematic elaboration.

[1] If we remember that Beethoven likes to introduce the modulatory part of his sonata movements with a (curtailed) repetition of the principal theme, the last (only seven bars) entry of the theme can also be interpreted in this sense.
[2] The only slight divergence is that the last dux retains eight instead of seven bars of its primordial form.
[3] It cannot be definitely decided where the development section begins, since the motivic chain work and the metrical motion extend beyond the usual tonal limits of the exposition and only reach a connecting point of repose in the realm of a new key (dominant of E flat major). The same is true of the transition from the recapitulation to the coda.
[4] The material of the modulatory section is taken into consideration, but not the *Seitensatz*.

A word still remains to be said on the coda, which corresponds with the development section not only in length (there are even more bars) but through the parallel form of the beginning (wherever one may assume the beginning to be). Yet so far from unusual as such proportions are with Beethoven, just so little is this "parallelism" an isolated case (see, for example, the first movement of the Waldstein sonata). And furthermore, the last 105 bars (out of a total of 135 or 124) bear so unmistakably the character of a coda, even that of a *stretto*, that there can be no doubt about the form.

From all this it is difficult to understand how musicologists in general, and Beethoven specialists in particular, can consider this a fugue. It is far more justifiable to speak of a "sonata movement with fugal treatment." But this does not characterize the essential element of this form, namely, the fusion of the sonatalike and the fuguelike to a new structural form, which is identical with neither the one nor the other. For here the fugue parts do not represent inlays in the sonata texture, nor (as so often in Beethoven development sections) are they a result and product of thematic elaboration. They appear rather as structural carriers of the sonata idea, subject to the law of the sonata (as shown above) and in turn affecting the organism of the sonata (contrapuntal *Seitensatz!*).—LUDWIG MISCH

[Beethoven's primary concern in] the Rasoumovsky quartets with the psychological process [rather than with bold dramatic canvases] is true, more particularly, of the third. The slow movement of the third Rasoumovsky quartet is not [as] complex [as those of the other two], but the emotion it conveys, although simpler, is much more strange. This movement, indeed, stands alone among Beethoven's compositions, and throws an unexpected light upon his imaginative resources. Beethoven's imagination and emotional nature, although so intense, are, on the whole, of a normal kind. Most of the very great artists may be regarded as huge extensions of the normal man, which is the chief reason why they are so valuable. Beethoven, in his last years, was speaking of experiences which are not normal, but which are nevertheless in the line of human development. But this strange slow movement, as more than one writer has remarked, makes on us the impression of something strictly abnormal. It is as if some racial memory had stirred in him, referring to some forgotten and alien despair. There is here a remote and frozen anguish, wailing over some implacable destiny. This is hardly human suffering; it is more like a memory from some ancient and starless night of the soul. What it is doing in this quartet we cannot imagine. If Beethoven wanted a contrast to the victorious note of the first movement he has certainly got it. But even the magnificent fugue at the end, the most triumphant movement in all Beethoven's quartets, is no resolution of the cold despair of this movement. It does not belong to the same world. Nowhere else has Beethoven's imagination been exercised in so strange a region.

Each of the three Rasoumovsky quartets has a victorious conclusion, They are essentially poems of conflict, and although the experiences they communicate are very varied they may be regarded as springing from the root experience that also inspires the C minor symphony. Such a root experience, as we have said before, can assume many different embodiments. A parallel example is probably furnished by Shakespeare's great group of tragedies which, different as they are from one another, surely sprang from some root experience which conditioned his whole attitude toward life.—J. W. N. SULLIVAN

> b. *String Quartet No. 10 in E Flat, Opus 74 (the "Harp")*
>   I. Poco adagio—Allegro; II. Adagio ma non troppo; III. Presto
>   —Più presto quasi prestissimo—Tempo I—Più presto quasi pres-
>   tissimo—Tempo I; IV. Allegretto con variazioni

1809 was an important year in terms of exterior event. The annuity from the princes was a major victory[1]; Beethoven was elated. His immediate response was to plan marriage, however, and the subsequent rejection of his proposal to (presumably) Therese Malfatti appears to have hit him extremely hard. During this crisis, Zmeskall may have proved an especially true friend. In May 1809, Vienna suffered its second invasion by the French (the first invasion had helped to spoil the premiere of *Fidelio*); this time the occupation lasted five months, and was enlivened by a two-day siege of shelling. Thayer repeats the well-known story about Beethoven sheltering his ears with pillows in his brother Carl's cellar, and remarks on the general disruption of life and harassment under foreign rule, inflation, and the rest. Beethoven could not take his habitual long summer holiday; what was perhaps worse, most of his friends and patrons had left the city—and one could not repeatedly divert oneself by writing *Les Adieux* sonatas. More to the point, Nottebohm claimed to read in a sketchbook of 1809 evidence of Beethoven's inability to settle down to work on major projects:

> The appearance of the following pages bears witness to the fact that Beethoven lacked the composure and inner peace for the continuation of his usual activity and the execution of larger compositions. Except for work on a sonata movement, which, to judge from the number and character of the sketches, came rapidly to its final form, these pages reveal no continuous larger sketches. Rather they are filled in part with drafts left undeveloped, in part with theoretical examples and exercises, and in part with notations of various kinds.

[1] Princes Lobkowitz and Kinsky, together with Archduke Rudolph, banded together as patrons to provide Beethoven with a steady annual income of four thousand florins. —Editor.

The period in which this blocking of compositional activity can be remarked may be ascribed to the middle two or three months of the year.

Give or take a few months, this sounds very much like the Quartet in E♭: a rather marvelous piece written at a time when the composer could not fully concentrate.

The slow introduction that opens the Quartet in E♭ grows mainly from a single motif, a sort of *"Muss es sein?"* or (better) *"Möchte es sein?"* which is presently to be answered—*forte* and *allegro*—in the affirmative. The motif always concludes tentatively, and it leans strongly toward the subdominant, but for seventeen bars of *poco adagio* the piece seems to take pains not to modulate properly to the subdominant key or to any other. Modulation, it will appear, is no prominent feature in any of the movements of this quartet. The final phrase of the introduction, though starting with a dramatic minor-subdominant chord, does not modulate either, but slides upward to the dominant through a series of deep harmonic obfuscations. Mystery-making after an initial clear tonic was traditional in slow introductions, and Beethoven was following tradition here—more closely at least than in the introduction of the C-major *"Razumovsky"* Quartet. He made material for his obfuscation by picking out the two middle notes of the main motif and multiplying them into a rising chromatic sequence; the phrase as a whole sounds like an astonishing protraction of the motif. The chromatic step returns modestly at one point in the ensuing *Allegro*, within the bridge.

The *Allegro* is touched off by an *arpeggio* motif which resembles the introduction motif just closely enough in melodic and rhythmic profile to suggest its affirmation or resolution. After this bright antecedent, a peaceful consequent phrase touches the subdominant over a tonic pedal (bars 28–31). This harmonic arrangement calls to mind a Mozartian habit heeded by Beethoven in his very first quartet, Opus 18, No. 3, in D; at present it recalls to the ear the subdominant inclinations of the *Poco adagio* which has just been heard. Unlike any of the quartets of Opus 59, this Quartet in E♭ is ostentatiously at peace with itself. The sense of supreme and easy technical control strikes the listener forcibly.

Calm extends to the formal plotting of the first movement too, very noticeably so. The recapitulation involves no serious functional changes from the exposition, and the few modifications that do occur seem to proceed out of a kind of relaxed improvisation, imaginative froth thrown up almost without calculation by the superb technical machine. A passage such as [the] burgeoning of the cadence of the original theme lacks the momentousness of the reinterpretations of prior material in the F-major "Razumovsky" Quartet, or for that matter in any of the first three numbers of Opus 18. One cannot feel that the change was "necessary" for the total formal coherence; it feels more like a rich spontaneous gesture, of a kind that is rather new, I believe, in Beethoven's music of this period. Certainly the preceding quartets were too high-strung to allow much of it. The quality looks forward to another Quartet in E♭, the Opus 127, whose first movement features an almost continuous process of dreamlike variation.

A further instance of calm or simplicity of structure comes with the development section. Concise and facile, the second group of the exposition has concluded with a sharply rhythmicized figure in the new key of B♭ (V), stressing D, the third degree of B♭. On this D the harmony pivots, the development opening abruptly with the main theme in G major (III), so that the brisk *arpeggio* goes up from G to B to D (the same D). During ten bars of the development, only a single modulation takes place, as for once Beethoven allows the subdominant urge of his material to ease the tonality around from G to C. But no further. When the consequent phrase appears a second time, it stays in C for a full eight bars; whereupon this key is celebrated for fourteen additional bars, with very strenuous orchestral sounds and with repeated cadential phrases slicing the melody away into smaller and smaller fragments. Then things quiet down of themselves and the harmony moves directly back to E♭, over a long, highly colored sixteen-bar period. Fourteen bars of the simplest dominant preparation, still impressively scored, lead to the recapitulation.

Now the interesting fact about all these figures is the great length of the development, and at the same time its relative vacuity. It lasts sixty-two bars, by the clock 20 per cent longer than the exposition, yet it encompasses less real action than any opening sonata-allegro that Beethoven had written up to that point. Not altogether unfairly, this development could be described as a single great C-major statement led into by two routine modulations and led out of by a single monolithic swing back to the tonic E♭. Such a section differs in principle from the development of the *Eroica* Symphony or the F-major "Razumovsky" Quartet. In a sense, it operates by a diametrically opposed principle. In those movements the middle section consists of unstable, uncertain explorations, the instability achieved chiefly by means of modulation. In this movement the middle section amounts to an impressive nonmodulating plateau. To stretch a point, there is here a rather startling suggestion of static *da capo* construction.

What is obviously the most striking special feature of this movement, its unusual emphasis on instrumental devices of several kinds, should probably be thought of as compensation for the modulatory reticence and the studied simplicity of form. The *pizzicato* passages, the brilliant first-violin passage work, and the rich coloristic mood effects make their formidable contribution to the over-all temper. And the way Beethoven blends them into the quartet texture—where they do not really belong— bears witness again to technical control, to a compositional virtuosity matching the purely instrumental virtuosity. *Pizzicato* comes up right away in the bridge of the exposition; one by one, the four instruments pluck away busily at the *arpeggio* in the main theme. (This passage and its more sensational derivatives earned the quartet its nickname "The Harp"—for no very commanding reason, we may think today, with the Bartók quartets twanging in our ears. But at that time probably no quartet had ever employed *pizzicato* so brashly.) The impressive fourteen-bar dominant preparation for the recapitulation has the *pizzicato arpeggios* swept up through three octaves and accelerated from quarter-notes to triplets, from triplets to eighth-notes, and from eighth-notes, to *arco* triplet-eighths. Doubtless this made a thrilling sound in 1809. Some instrumental effects dim with habitude, though; the passage does not seem so strong today.

More successful, at least in my opinion, are the extended fireworks at the start of the coda, which provides a surprisingly broad, slow-moving, and strong peroration for the piece as a whole. Although the first-violin part looks like a concerto, with its cross-the-string figuration in sixteenth-notes, there is no disparity of effect. And most successful of all is the very last idea, resuming the *pizzicato arpeggios* in contrary motion. The musical stream is distilled down to its simplest basis in the E♭ triad; there is a flash of whimsy here, and a sense of intellectual show-off, and above all an unintellectual feeling of inspired spontaneous play. Something a little similar ends the first and last movements of the Eighth Symphony, which Thayer (but only Thayer) believed to have been sketched at the same time as the quartet. This instance of thematic "liquidation" is the most genial touch in a genial movement—an unusually brilliant yet unostentatious piece, taut yet in essence serene, intellectual yet unproblematic in its musical thought, raising no major new issues.

The slow movement falls for once into the subdominant key, A♭, the traditional place for it, but also a place that accords well with the inclinations of the first movement. This *Adagio ma non troppo* is a lovely piece of music, relaxed, almost slack by comparison with the serious slow movements of earlier quartets. It banks almost entirely on its opening melody, and this melody makes no effort to generate anything like a sonata dynamic, as usually happened before. It simply appears three times in increasingly rich versions (which can be classed as light variations), with episodes between. By keeping the two episodes tentative in organization, and by leaning them both in the subdominant direction, Beethoven minimizes contrast with the main tune. Even the motivic work tends to minimize contrast: the first period of the melody, scored rather poignantly high, revolves around the third degree (C) and the step that stresses it, D♭–C; then this descending step recurs insidiously—often intensified by two or more quick notes—as a motif or motivic element in both episodes.

The step D♭–C (IV–III) also forecasts the tendency of the episodes to modulate to the subdominant.

That Beethoven in his earliest years revealed little gift for melody pure and simple is an old criticism. The superb lyric achievements of the last period came only after years of experience: after continual external tinkerings with melodic lines, which can be discerned in sketches for slow movements, and after continual internal testings of feeling, which can only be hypostatized, but which must have been as rigorous as the technical apprenticeship. The melody of this *Adagio* occupies an important place; it is certainly one of Beethoven's best lyric ideas to date. Tender, and yet at the same time slightly remote in emotional quality, it manages to avoid anything weighty or pretentious, slow as it may go.

Once the main melody has come to a slightly drawn-out, peaceful full close, the first episode begins directly with what promises to be a contrasting tune in the tonic minor—as though in apposition to the main melody; one thinks of those Haydn slow movements built on the naïve alternation of major and minor sections. But the pathetic accents of the new tune are not given a chance to take hold. After a normal four-bar phrase, the lyricism cedes to solemn, rather abstract dramatic gestures pulling the music along to a tentative close (in C♭) and then to a second stab at the episode tune in the minor subdominant, D♭ minor. A single four-bar phrase is still all that will crystallize; the new four-bar consequent that emerges serves as a transition rather than as a genuine lyric member. It settles into lengthy—indeed diffuse—dominant preparations for the return of the decorated main melody.

As for the second episode, it starts with a cursory turn to the major subdominant and forms an innocently soulful eight-bar period modulating to its own dominant (i.e., from D♭ to A♭). The period is duly repeated, with touching new comments from the first violin (fascinating, as well as touching: they make a sort of free canon). Instead of rounding out this lyric beginning, Beethoven appears to lose interest; having reached A♭, he takes the opportunity to commence his main melody again, in the minor mode. (Probably more than one listener has thought of Schubert's *Das Wirtshaus* here.) This potential minor-mode variation has the effect of a very curiously placed false start, for after only one phrase, new dramatic gestures interrupt and hurry into the entrance of the entire melody, in the major mode, for its third and last appearance. So there is not much to get one's teeth into except for the main melody, which grows more gorgeous in each successive manifestation. Both the delicate ornamentation of the melodic line and the involved figuration below it are progressively elaborated. Some of the opulent sonorities resemble points in the slow variation movements of the late quartets.

The gigantically calm coda is perhaps the most admirable part of this whole calm movement. Instead of resolving, the main melody halts for a moment on its last dominant chord—which is run directly into the minor tune of the first episode. This sounds less like a statement in apposition, then, and more like a recollection or something insubstantial. The familiar four-bar *minore* phrase gets no further than before, and thematic fragments in light counterpoint attenuate themselves pensively. The important step D♭–C echoes in a repeated series of slow dying closes. Things are becoming very ethereal; but the low cadential chords, eight bars before the end, restore a sense of involvement. In a movement that has self-consciously eschewed strong dominant harmonies, these chords sound wonderfully warm.

After so quiescent a slow movment, an intense scherzo is definitely in order. The piece (which Beethoven does not mark *Scherzo*, only *Presto*) is evidently a benign twin of the famous third movement of the Fifth Symphony; but what counts as benign in relation to the symphony still sounds violent enough within the framework of this quartet. Among features that show kinship with the symphony are (of course) the notorious driving rhythm; the key of C minor—which Beethoven never took lightly; the jocose, noisy contrapuntal trio; the *da capo* of the *Presto* in a deepening *pianissimo*; and the grandiose deceptive cadence at the end, running into A♭ (♭VI) and a long passage of transition to the Finale. Since this piece of mystification is leading not to triumphant C major— as in the symphony—but to cheerful E♭, things will proceed differently, and Beethoven actually contrived a repetition of the deceptive cadence one step higher, on the Neapolitan degree, D♭. The "availability" of this passage to Schubert is manifest in his first impressive quartet, the unfinished *Quartettsatz* in C minor of 1821, as well as in his last quartet, Opus 161, in G major.

The *Presto* goes fast and furious, in a well-behaved sort of way; nothing here will raise Prince Lobkowitz's eyebrows. It manages a bold sequence through the Neapolitan degree (D♭) without losing its grip on formal checks and balances in the correct classic spirit. The trio, which behaves less well, Beethoven originally marked *Più presto quasi prestissimo*, as well as *fortissimo* throughout, but it is interesting to see him in effect change his mind about the former direction when he comes to supply metronome marks for the quartet a few years later. He sets identical marks for both *Presto* and trio, $\downarrow$.=100 and $\circ$.=100. [This indicates he was thinking of two measures of the *Più presto*, 3/4, to be equal to one measure of the former *Presto*. Also it makes it easy for the listener to feel *two* measures of the faster 3/4 as equal to *one* full measure of 6/4. This interpretation] takes one cue from Beethoven's own dotted-wholenote indication, and another from his rubric "*Si ha s'immaginar la battuta di 6/8*" (in later years he might have written simply "*temo di due battute*").

The initial odd-footed phrase [is] in gauche double counterpoint. [One of the themes is the fast staccato quarter-notes going up and down the scale with every third note gruffly accented. This is played against staccato dotted quarters outlining a theme which might well be choral-like if it were not played at such a fast tempo.] When, immediately, this phrase is to be repeated, it gathers extra voices and becomes a parody textbook exercise in third- and fourth-species counterpoint, nine bars long. There follows a pair of derivative phrases, modulating. Then the initial phrase sounds out the form by roaring through its material in contrapuntal inversion—a belly-laugh at all pedants, and a belly-laugh at the composer himself.

For during the difficult months of the French occupation, he was occupying himself with the compilation of counterpoint exercises for his patron-pupil the Archduke Rudolph. Copybook models for this trio would have been running around in his head—doubtless to Beethoven's own disgust. But in any case, formal counterpoint in a quartet was practically a tradition with him by this time, a point of honor, an automatic response. In this piece, as in the E-minor "Razumovsky" Quartet, the obligatory contrapuntal display comes as a raucous major-mode trio. Beethoven repeats the *Presto* literally and the trio literally a second time and then the *Presto* once again, as though to be sure nobody misses the schoolboy naughtiness of it all (but the effect, as in the Fifth Symphony, is a good deal better than that). Only after the third time round for the *Presto*, when it is progressively hushed, does the long transition which so impressed Schubert usher in what must surely be some particularly formidable concluding statement.

But not at all. What ensues is a particularly refined and economical variation movement on a slight, elegant *allegretto* theme. This is as conspicuously light a finale as could have been conceived.

The tune has two main points of interest: the quaint syncopated harmonic rhythm and the piquant modulation scheme, the first half closing on a G-major triad (III) and the second half pausing on a D-major triad (VII) before returning to the tonic key E♭. The six variations, all in tempo and in time, hew closely to the theme and range themselves in an almost childlike order. Odd variations (Nos. 1, 3, and 5) are each marked *sempre forte* and concentrate on figuration, whereas even variations (Nos. 2, 4, and 6) are each marked *sempre dolce e piano* and concentrate on lyric expansion and small harmonic subtleties. Each of the variations, like the theme (but more so), harps on a single kind of rhythmic motion. Taking an idea from the cadences of the original theme, Variation No. 1 joins various canonic eighth-note patterns to simulate continuous eighth-note motion. Variation No. 2, a warm, smooth viola solo, moves in continuous triplet-eighths. No. 3 speeds up to continuous sixteenth-notes. No. 4 slows down to continuous quarters. No. 5 uses a synocopated motif involving sixteenths. No. 6 combines continuous eighth-notes and triplet-eighths simultaneously. It is all lucid in the extreme.

In the three quiet, lyric-harmonic variations, the central cadence can be deliciously altered. The note G, it is demonstrated, may seem at first to act as V of [the relative minor key of C minor], but it may also act as [a genuine G major harmony] in Variation No. 4, or simply as the third degree of the Eb triad, in Variation No. 6. Here Beethoven boils the whole tune down harmonically to the scheme Tonic | Nontonic | Tonic; and with a quiet show of mastery, he chose for the "nontonic" sonority a completely unexpected one, a rich Brahmsian bVII (Db) in place of VII (D) as before. This simplifying or liquidating variation recalls in a way the coda of the opening movement of the quartet, which reduces everything to a buoyant, spiritual play of Eb *arpeggios*.

A coda commences with fragments of the melody of Variation No. 6, in which I seem to hear the elegant folk-accents of *An die ferne Geliebte* echoing or fore-echoing across the years. An amusing repeated cadence pattern resumes that Db, again in the bass, with small regard for grammatical orthodoxy, after which a series of accelerating half-variations leads to a rather sudden quiet ending. But the suddenness points out the sly disposition of the final tonic chord with G on top!

In his *Cobbett's Cyclopaedia* article, Vincent d'Indy brushed aside this movement as one that "adds no element of novelty." In point of fact, suave, half-humorous, nicely balanced variation movements that build from *allegretto* tunes and feature slightly remote modulations *are* new in Beethoven's works at this time. These characteristics are missing in earlier sets of variations, such as that of the Quartet in A, Opus 18, No. 5, and in later ones, such as those of the last quartets. Other examples at the present period occur in the Violin Sonata in G, Opus 96, the Piano Fantasy, Opus 77, and the Piano Variations, Opus 76 (on the tune that later became the Turkish March in *The Ruins of Athens*).

D'Indy was just not interested in this sort of novelty, that is all. He sensed what is obvious enough: that the radical fresh areas of experience which Beethoven has led the listener to anticipate, in one composition after another, are left aside here. This holds for the quartet as a whole, a work of consolidation rather than of exploration, a work which though by no means content to repeat something that has been done before, is content to move within an expressive framework laid down by its predecessors. I have suggested that some retrenchment may have been called for after the disruptive tendencies in the "Razumovsky" Quartets, and also that the stance may have been partly "political" on the part of the composer, and that it may have been partly forced on him by the difficult conditions of 1809. To put it another way, in J. W. N. Sullivan's famous formulation, the Quartet in Eb cannot be said to contribute seriously to Beethoven's "spiritual development." For Sullivan,

The transition from the fourth to the fifth symphony is not the transition from one "mood" to another, both equally valid and representative; it is the transition from one level of experience and realization to another; one might say that the transition is vertical, not horizontal. And the third and fifth symphonies are more important than the fourth in the history of Beethoven because it was the deepest things in him that conditioned his development. The greater importance the world has always attributed to the third, fifth, seventh and ninth symphonies compared with the fourth, sixth and eighth, is not because of any purely musical superiority they possess, but because everyone is more or less clearly aware that greater issues are involved, that something more important for mankind is being expressed.

The Quartet in E♭ is not one to raise deep questions and great issues—that is what D'Indy saw. Liberation from the necessity to raise and meet them, indeed, helps give the piece its special *élan*, as does also a sense of quiet exhilaration in artistic processes circumscribed and carried through with elegance and tact and perfect accuracy. These qualities, which are hardly to be dissociated from the fact of technical control, do rather definitely represent an element of novelty in Beethoven's bank of expressive resource.[1]—JOSEPH KERMAN

c. String Quartet No. 11 in F Minor, Opus 95

I. Allegro con brio; II. Allegretto ma non troppo; III. Allegro assai vivace ma serioso; IV. Larghetto espressivo—Allegretto agitato—Allegro

The F-minor Quartet is not a pretty piece, but it is terribly strong —and perhaps rather terrible. One does not hear it with the joy and the *Mitgefühl* that the E♭ Quartet should evoke; the piece stands aloof, preoccupied with its radical private war on every fiber of rhetoric and feeling that Beethoven knew or could invent. Everything unessential falls victim, leaving a residue of extreme concentration, in dangerously high tension. But strength, not strain, is the commanding impression; the listener is confronted with expressive authority as secure as that of the E♭ Quartet. Once again, this authority is not to be dissociated from consummate technical control, a quality that comes out clearly, I believe, if the composition is considered together with the E-minor "Razumovsky" Quartet. That Beethoven was dissatisfied with the E-minor Quartet I should not dare to say, but certainly in the first movement of the F-minor he addressed himself all over again to expressive and technical problems broached there: to pain and violence and the raging alternation of

[1] For a comparison between the techniques of Opus 74 and Opus 95, written a year later, and the way those techniques foreshadow the mastery of the late quartets, written fifteen years later, see the closing paragraphs of Kerman's essay on Opus 95, which follows.—Editor.

feelings, to the minor mode and the Neapolitan step and the rationalization of rhythmic discontinuities. What was often merely brusque and
hypersensitive in the earlier composition has become entirely forceful
here. The F-minor Quartet is a nugget statement of the world of the E-
minor.

If the opening period of the earlier work was original, complex, and
even eccentric in construction and expression, these qualities are pushed
to some kind of limit here. As in the E-minor Quartet, the initial outburst
[, a unison passage revolving up and down the F minor scale,] is cut off
by a rest and then answered by a sharply contrasted new idea [a dotted
rhythmic one revolving around the harmony of the dominant]. Also as in
the E-minor Quartet, the first theme theatrically offers to repeat itself up
a step on the Neapolitan degree, Gb. But we have experienced that sort of
thing before; the violins suppress the cello with a twelve-bar lyric passage
contradicting the explosions of the start in a quite remarkable way. Turning pathetically back toward the tonic key, this passage dwells upon the
semitone C–Db, upper reflection of the original Neapolitan step F–Gb.
Repeatedly Db sinks down to C. What is this leisure doing in the drastic,
shotgun atmosphere of the opening five-bar statement?

In the F-minor Quartet, individual notes and individual note-rela-
tionships are forced into the consciousness more strongly, perhaps, than in
any previous composition by Beethoven. This is partly a consequence of
the extreme sense of compression. We have seen Beethoven working to
convince us of the significance of certain notes—with G and Gb in the
first movement of the F-major "Razumovsky" Quartet, for instance—and
we have admired the massive draftsmanship by which such points were
made. Here the same sort of thing is accomplished in a single stroke, with
a violence unknown to the earlier music. There is an urgency to every
"sore" note that sticks out of the fabric, and with this new responsibility,
a new opportunity for expressive manipulation. The Neapolitan step is of
course unshakably planted, and the tritone C–Gb between [the end of
the dotted rhythmic passage and the beginning of the repetition of the
original outburst a semitone higher than it first appeared] haunts the
ear for the rest of the work. So does the step Db–C which has emerged
as the principal substance of the lyric interruption. Then, as the opening
figure is resumed, compressed, erupted, and evaporated into the second
group, the progression F–Gb–G♮ stabs a wound that will somehow have to
be healed in the sequel.

In the E-minor Quartet, the modulation to the second group was done
abruptly enough, with scarcely any buffer. Here the switch almost alarms;
three or four bars suffice. The shuddering inflection in [the final cadential
bar, a mere six measures later,] seems to legitimize the move to Db, the
second key, which in any case had been anticipated by the harping Db–C
of that lyric passage. The second group itself is just as curt: a rocking figure

several times repeated (10 bars) running into an extraordinary cadence (nine bars) settling into a little tonic *ostinato* (four bars); then the cadence, even more intense, and the *ostinato* are both repeated.

All through the Quartet in F minor one senses Beethoven's impatience (or fury) with conventional bridge and cadential passages of every kind—the more or less neutral padding material of the classic style. In the "Razumovsky" Quartets he labored to individuate such passages. In the Eb Quartet he enjoyed stylizing them. Now he will simply do without them. The particular radical ellipsis of the F-minor Quartet may never be needed again, but through it Beethoven gained a new resource of expressive immediacy which is drawn on in all the later music.

As for that extraordinary cadence, its contributions include sheer ferocity; extreme dissonance as preface to extreme relief and swift resolutions; and a recollection of the first group. The opening gesture of the movement is recalled by the *fortissimo* unison scale followed by the long rest, and the lyric passage that interrupted those gestures is recalled by the poignant answer here with its semitones. Even more important, the progression again involves an upward semitone step to the Neapolitan degree, I–bII (Db–Db, or strictly speaking Db–Ebb; this is in the new key of Db major). Eight bars earlier, the cadence had come on the upper reflection of this step, Ab–Ab (Ab–Bbb). Since the passage counts as the most memorable in the whole exposition, its handling in the recapitulation faced Beethoven with a problem and a rare opportunity. The solution is analyzed by Tovey:

> The development is a short process of Mozartean straightforwardness and Beethovenish violence, and it leads punctually to a recapitulation in which the first group is represented merely by the moment at which it executed the transition [that is, from the measure where the opening outburst returns in unison a second time after the lyrical interlude and traverses from F through G [flat to G]; and here it has the audacity to execute the original transition to the original complementary key (bVI). After four bars in this key, the second group quietly swings round to the tonic major; but now comes the evidence of Beethoven's imagination at its highest power. Only two other masters could have been trusted to see the right thing here—viz. Schubert and Brahms. Anybody else would have exactly transcribed the fierce outbreaks upon bII; but the colour value of bII has gone. It is hardly distinguishable from bVI. Beethoven substitutes the ordinary supertonic [ii, G minor], and does not even sophisticate it by making it major. The glare of common daylight is the one thing that can inspire terror at this juncture.[1]

This brilliant stroke occurred to Beethoven at the last moment. Nottebohm gives a very late sketch of the recapitulation which simply moves to

[1] *Beethoven*, p. 107.

♭II, like the exposition. The ordinary supertonic, it should be added, serves as an iron resolution to the Neapolitan sounds earlier, a resolution upward: F–G♭–G♮, from to ♭II to ♮ii. Such upward resolution is carried further yet in the Finale of the quartet.

What Tovey calls a "short process of Mozartean straightforwardness and Beethovenish violence" is indeed a single "process," a single arc of twenty-two bars without preface, postface, or any real interior seams. That in itself is remarkable—though how characteristic and how right for this particular piece!—but not as remarkable as the harmonic situation. For the entire passage hovers around the tonic key, which is ambushed at the beginning and glimmers through all the admirable fracas of diminished sevenths, ninths, and enhanced dominants. The dotted-rhythm motif of [the opening], though introduced nowhere else in the movement, does find a role here, perhaps on account of its naturally stormy quality; the whole twenty-two-bar section wants to sound like the storm in the Sixth Symphony (which is also in F minor), with its echoes of operatic *temporali* back and forth from Gluck to Rossini and on. Lightning strokes, rainy hushes, soughing branches, roars of thunder—all are maneuvered with much verve and with instrumental virtuosity worthy of the "Harp" Quartet. Characteristic intervals batter the ear: F–G♭–G♮, D♭–C, and finally a splendid crux of D♭ and E♮ [in the cello, under an insistently repeated C in the inner voice,] before the composer plunges into a harshly truncated recapitulation of the first group.

The whole formal scheme is as ingenious as it is original. For the sake of over-all compression, an abrupt modulation was wanted in the exposition; so the new key—not even a very close one, by the way—was suggested ahead of time by an unusual lyric passage right in the first group. Meanwhile the very placement of this lyric passage adds to the general mood of discontinuity. Then in the recapitulation, for greater brusqueness, amputate that lyric passage entirely; there is no new key to prepare. When Beethoven anyhow "has the audacity to execute the original transition to the original complementary key," this will have a novel feeling of instability about it. Which in turn can be very beautifully dispelled by the subsequent inevitable swing back to the tonic (within the second theme, at the third repetition of its rocking figure). Since the exposition and the recapitulation include such vivid harmonic contortions as those of the opening bars and of the repeated second-group cadence, the middle section—one rather hesitates to call it a "development"—can forgo modulation and achieve its violence simply by means of dynamic and orchestral storm-effects. Here perhaps lies the fundamental difference in conception between the treatment of the Neapolitan step in the F-minor Quartet and in the E-minor. The earlier piece works out the tensions of the step in a large, complex development section. The later piece handles them tersely, almost aphoristically, within the exposition and the recapitulation. The difference reflects a swing in Beethoven's practice that will become more and more pronounced in his later music, a swing away from traditional development procedures toward more flexible and more gnomic expression.

In reparation for the truncated recapitulation, a coda is required lasting almost exactly as long as the "development," after starting with a very similar ambush. D♭ is recalled, and also the opening motif, more brazenly than ever before. In the final liquidation, the cello flings out the same crux of D♭ and E♮ that had emerged at the end of the "development." This now sounds like a skeleton of the opening bars: F–E♭–D♭–C–D♮–E♮–F reduced to D♭–C and E♮–F. The cello D♭–C, in particular, on the bottom of the C string, seems to crystallize all the semitone obsession of the piece—the Neapolitan steps, the harping lyric passage of the exposition, and the poignant conclusion of the second-group cadence.

It also provides a fantastic promontory from which the second movement can be experienced. For it seems to me that the famous unaccompanied cello scale which introduces the *Allegretto ma non troppo* takes at least half of its tension from its relation to this liquidating D♭–C in the cello. D♭ at the end of the first movement is answered by D♮ at the beginning of the second; only after several halting *portamento* notes does D–C♯ explain itself as a simple scale in the new (and far from simple) key of D major. This makes for an excruciating discontinuity, of course, and arguing from a discontinuity may seem like arguing from a vacuum. However the excruciation is far from unprepared. The opening movement bristled with semitone relations, the step D♭–D♮ occurring at its most memorable juncture, the second-group cadence in the exposition. And does not the cello now gingerly line out the very sonority that Tovey describes as climatic in the first movement, the supertonic G triad—sophisticated, now, into the major mode?

In any case, the confrontation between D major and F minor stands as the most extreme between movements in any Beethoven work, bar none. The second key of the first movement already represented an enhanced dominant, D♭ (♭VI) in place of C (v). D♮ in the second movement represents an enhancement of the enhancement.

A lyric slow movement poised—one might even say, racked—in this way is obviously not designed to register any sort of consolatory relaxation. When Beethoven wants that, he may as well leave the slow movement in the key of the first movement, as he does with the Quartet in E minor. But at this point the F-minor Quartet parts company for good with the E-minor: in place of a grandiose, mystic, somewhat sentimental turn away from the preoccupations of the start, here the prior disturbance is continued and actually enhanced. It is not often that an extended lyric statement in the classic style attains a level of psychological intensity as high as that of the opening movement. The most obvious

technical index of this is the continuing chromaticism—in itself an unusual feature for a slow movement, particularly for one ostensibly in
the major mode. This *Allegretto ma non troppo* has a subtlety and a
deep sense of involvement that are even rarer. It does not represent a
resting place or a point of reflection but a newly intense stage on
the journey that was initiated by the outburst at the very beginning
of the quartet.

After the introductory cello scale, an emotional, fluid melody emerges.
It comes to a formal full close; a fugue is developed; the melody returns
with a greatly spun-out coda. This would amount to the familiar A B A
dynamic if not for the fact that the fugue ruptures hugely in the middle, so that the piece is experienced as a sort of retrograde A B / B A arc,
hinging on a crisis of expressive intensity. Indeed the hinge acts as a
climax for the quartet as a whole.

In orthodox fashion, the fugue begins with one instrument following
another at fairly regular four- and five-bar intervals. A marvelously melancholy subject winds downward through ambiguous chromatic steps, with a
countersubject mirroring and thus intensifying the chromaticism. A chromatic subject in D brings to mind Book II of *The Well-tempered
Clavier*, and this may also have occurred to Beethoven; but for Beethoven
a chromatic fugue subject was pretty well committed to modulatory
vicissitudes well beyond Bach's expressive range. Only a fugue so committed, of course, could serve his purpose at the present juncture.

Already at the fourth (first-violin) entry, the charged chromatic lines
are causing problems in terms of the harmonic underpinning. The Neapolitan harmony suggested by the end of the subject (i.e., the B♭ [in the
last bar]) works its way back into the prior bar; then a dark piercing
tritone figure (second violin) obtrudes enough to repeat itself in triple
counterpoint, the figure thrown up to the top of the churning harmonies.
Strettos begin to crack the fugue apart. Things happen very fast, until
the outer instruments strike a catastrophic new tritone (G–D♭) in place
of the original fourth-leap of the subject. The tritone *incipit* cannot continue. Instead the violin singles out the lamenting chromatic essence of
the subject, the descending semitone motif of its first full bar.

This makes for a climax of passion rarely matched by Beethoven himself. The effect is helped by a sudden stoppage of the involuted harmonic
rhythm, on a strong low E♭. The E♭ harmony resolves pathetically to a
very distant tonic, A♭. This is a tritone away from the point at which
the fugue began, D.

The rupture has to be healed from the outside—by the opening cello
scale, moving enharmonically through incredible, unfathomable tonal
spaces. The cello is treading on razor blades, and the upper instruments
are whispering through their teeth memories of the semitone lament,
which, indeed, seems to be frozen into the cello line itself. The semitone

step B♭–A, finally, hollowed almost to nothing, marks the tenuous return of D major. The fugue tries again.

At this point the fugue subject seems to want to get along; witness the new hasty countersubject. Perhaps it no longer dares explore the chromaticism of its fourth bar, which had proved so disruptive. Entries now stumble in at three-bar intervals, a compression which masks the well-calculated lowering of intensity on other grounds. The harmony will not attempt to digress any further: it comes simply to the dominant, and the subject takes on fresh blunt energy by submitting to inversion (a standard fugal resource used in a rather unusual way). Imitations press more closely; the new countersubject coalesces; rich tritone figures emerge again, only to be fobbed off around a circle of fifths in preparation for a very strong, leisurely return. The passion of the previous climax is recalled, but it is passion resolved and encompassed.

This return involves the entire opening melody, complete with the cello scale, reduced from its original *mezza voce* to *sotto voce*. But after the melody there is yet another breath-taking reminiscence of the crisis that halted the fugue. The final cadences of the melody are interrupted by the fugue subject (or rather, gently combined with it, for the first violin continues very elegantly with its cadence line). Free *strettos* starting G–D, A–D, and D–D are topped by a high tritone A–E♭, and as before this tritone *incipit* collapses into a lamenting semitone step, B♭–A. Supported by another unanticipated low bass note, an open-string C, this step has just the flavor of the prior D♭–C over the bass E♭. But [there] when E♭ moved to F♭, that was a feint. Here, when C moves to C♯, the harmonic aberration is guided directly back.

All this may seem to imply that the original *allegretto* melody, the A of the A B | B A structure, is overshadowed by the fugue (B). That cannot be, of course; the movement lives on the mysterious balance of the two. Beethoven thought enough of the melody to build an exceptionally long, serene coda out of repetitions of its cadential figures. Yet there can be no doubt that the lyric flow was restrained with the brooding fugue in mind, and the coda bolstered by way of compensation. The melody itself, after a heavy surge toward the minor subdominant in the first phrase, hangs largely around the dominant. Sensitive—indeed hypersensitive—inflections around B♭, A, and B♮ take the place of modulation or even of other incidental harmonies. (Perhaps that is the price for venturing so frankly on an early strong subdominant. Perhaps the cello scale, twisting the other way, was needed to keep us on an even keel.) In short, this [is] not quite a "melody" in the self-contained sense that melodies figure in slow movements of the E♭ Quartet or the C-major "Razumovsky." The *Empfindsamkeit* (almost debilitation) and unrest (almost uncertainty) and curious muted pathos that mark this melody apart from any other in Beethoven are as much a matter of over-all construction as of the highly refined sense of scoring and nuance.

Next to this, even the glum fugue subject sounds almost craggy and predictable. That it bears distinct analogies with the start of the melody was observed (and exaggerated) by Hugo Riemann. The point surely lies in the way Beethoven coaxes from the fugue the same lamenting semitone (Bb–A) that is of primary importance in the melody too. The recollection of the fugue after the return of the melody, before the coda, aggregates and reconciles the two. They cleave together, we now under-stand, as an inseparable dyad. The many repeated Bb's within the superb long coda cement this impression, as well as preparing for the new link forward to the next movement.

The third movement of the Quartet in F minor is as surprising as its predecessors, though for an opposite reason: not for its complexities but for its simplicities. Essentially it ranks in the familiar category of Bee-thoven's driving scherzos, which generally set out to strike a gross con-trast with their slow movements. Here the contrast sounds like a real denial, in view of the link between the movements through the dimin-ished-seventh chord on B [the last chord of the slow movement, which sounds so mysterious after the quiet repeated chords of D major]. The rhythmic idea itself, especially as aerated by rests at its first appearance, is likely to recall the [second phrase in dotted rhythm] of the first movement.

The main section of the piece is ostentatiously dry and square—dry on account of the gritty writing in thirds, which can slip into real double counterpoint at the tenth or as easily into hollow unisons; square be-cause its brief, single span of forty bars is made up of five eight-bar phrases of two four-bar phrases each, balancing rigidly left and right. The whole effect is rather constipated. We must not call the movement a scherzo, because Beethoven specifically marks it *Allegro assai vivace ma serioso*, so perhaps we may call it a march—a serious, three-legged, tough little quick-march.

The contrasting trio is neither dry nor square nor even fully organized. A sort of *schwärmerisch* chorale in block chords never gets past its initial phrase; between repetitions of the same phrase, the simple violin figuration keeps going in a curious clubfooted fashion. The whole interest here is in the harmonic treatment. The march, after the diminished-seventh link from the previous movement, fell directly back from the dominant key to the central tonic F minor, which it hammered loudly and stiffly for its remaining twenty-four bars. It did not have the time (or the inclination) to modulate. The trio does not have the wit to modulate; it simply finds itself in certain extremely distant keys: first in Gb, the Neapolitan degree which started all the fury in the first place, and then in D major, the excruciating plateau of the slow movement.

This amounts to a kind of irresponsible summary—*ma serioso!*—of harmonic regions achieved with great expressive labor earlier in the piece. After a strange passage in B minor, F minor returns by way of the same diminished-seventh chord on B.

Crotchety, succinct, asthmatic—the march runs through its motions again, and then the trio and march are brought around another time, but in contracted versions. The second trio starts the chorale first directly in D (a very pointed reference to the crux of F minor and D) and then safely at last in C. For the third march, the twenty-four *forte* bars suffice, played *più allegro*. The compression begins to border on the grotesque.

As though to dispel any such suspicion, Beethoven introduces the Finale with a moment of decided relaxation: eight bars of *Larghetto espressivo* before the advent of the *Allegretto agitato*. Technically, these bars may be considered to liquidate the obsessive dotted rhythms of the march, and certainly they contribute to the general coloring by piling up D♭ on top of C, with B♮ thrown in for good measure. However, their main role would seem to be to modulate the feeling into something more familiar and available, after the fine eccentricity of the march and trio. They reproduce the standard heavy accents on high lament which Beethoven had sounded in (for example) the F-minor *Adagio molto e mesto* of the first "Razumovsky" Quartet. This tone would have been too obvious for the slow movement of the present work, and even now it maintains itself for no longer than two short phrases. In emotional terms, this suffices to prepare a movement designed to bring the quartet a modicum of normality in shape and sentiment.

Not that the construction of the *Allegretto agitato* fits any textbook prescription; it makes its own combination of sonata and rondo features. But though the transitions may still be as brusque and passionate as ever, and though the recapitulation may happen before one quite notices, the dynamic is always immediately comprehensible. One is not always being confronted by those searing harmonic intrusions and rhythmic juxtapositions which give the earlier movements their sense of the problematic. Details of counterpoint and figuration, particularly at the recurrences of the taunt main theme, are marvelously varied, resulting in an almost Wagnerian overload of rich inflection; yet these details sound like no more than decorations of the always more or less predictable swing of the rondo repetitions. In consequence, this movement avoids the harshness that had shadowed earlier parts of the quartet. In particular, its pathos is simpler and more direct than that of the opening *Allegro*.

Some distinctly stormlike effects are heard, as in the first movement, but the first movement includes nothing so innocent as the second subject here. A somewhat halfhearted development runs into a false recapitulation in the subdominant. Everything is exceptionally laconic, and the *agitato* humor (in one sketch Beethoven glossed it with the non-existent word *languente*) is excellently projected. Less garrulous than the Finale of the E-minor "Razumovsky" Quartet, the Finale of the F-minor also blusters less. This movement, this quartet as a whole, is not going to end in the oblivion of sheer raging exhaustion.

Beethoven's concluding touch reopens unexplored expressive vistas. Grandiose Db's have slowed down the coda to a strange halt on a *tierce de Picardie*, that is to say, a major-mode tonic, scored low in the strings and marked *ppp*. For the first time in its life the piece seems positively to mark time. Then, as though something silently snapped, a very fast *alla breve* section emerges in the major mode, a fantastic evoca-tion of an *opera buffa* finale in which all the agitation and pathos and tautness and violence of the quartet seem to fly up and be lost like dust in the sunlight. Through the speedy repeating cadential figures, a single chromatic motif isolates itself: F♯–G–G♯–A, a reflection of the F–Gb–G♮ of the opening movement, and at the same time a way of resolving it into the clear major 3rd, F and A. There are evanescent con-trapuntal touches—as evanescent as *"Questo è il fin di chi fa mal"* in the final scene of *Don Giovanni*. Everything is effortless and amusing and trite; the texture glistens; it is all over in a second or two (like everything else in this compressed quartet). A perfectly astonishing con-clusion.

Also thoroughly problematic, like so much else about the Quartet in F minor. Was Beethoven "serious" in calling a piece with such an ending *"Quartetto serioso?"* The seriousness seems kicked in the rear—delicately kicked, but kicked all the same. Vincent d'Indy, who congenitally grew tight-lipped as Beethoven grew playful, was prepared to dismiss the whole passage as one "without interest or utility of any sort." It is hard to argue with a joke except by saying that you don't want to hear one. Yet there is a genuine idea about how to end a piece of music here, in spite of something uncertain reflected in the joke and in the lack—or at best tenuousness—of relation between the ending passage and the rest of the composition.

Perhaps Beethoven did not exactly see how to end the Quartet in F minor, or to put it better, did not exactly "feel" how to end it. He had perhaps never engaged so directly with the darker emotional forces. He was perhaps himself overwhelmed. But in 1810 he had reached a stage of compositional virtuosity—the point has been made in connection with both the Eb and F-minor Quartets—that allowed him to gloss over doubts with great ease and with a certain impressive show of *sang-froid*. The suspicion is strengthened by what seems clearly to be a much deeper success with a similar problem later, in the Quartet in A minor, of 1825. Beethoven had a habit of returning to half-solved problems.

One more Beethoven piece belongs in this discussion: the Overture to *Egmont*, which was written at just the same time as the F-minor Quartet, and which also resolves its basic tonality of F minor by means of a new concluding section in the major mode. The process is rare enough with Beethoven to make it certain that the parallel with the quartet was interesting him. One has the distinct impression of an inversion of means, as though the composer had seized upon a single technical idea to see how opposite emotional effects could be wrung out of it. For in place of the evanescent play of the quartet, the F-major "Symphony of Victory" at the end of the Overture strikes a loud and violent (and indeed rather blatant) note of triumph. This much was directly inspired by Goethe. Yet by comparison with the late quartet, both earlier compositions may be seen together as thrusting aside their prior action a little too hastily—in the one case humorously, vehemently in the other. Only in the A-minor Quartet did Beethoven achieve a really integral sense of dissolution.

In the opinion of the present writer, and not his alone, certainly, the Quartet in F minor stands at the highest summit of Beethoven's artistic achievement up to the end of the second period. I trust the judgment is not unduly influenced by the seemingly proleptic tendencies of this composition, tendencies which have struck all the commentators with varying degrees of force. The matter of the finales is only one of many ways in which the quartet seems to look forward over the relatively lean years of the next decade, and to store techniques, attitudes, and actual ideas for the composition of the late quartets in 1825–6.

In more general terms, the Quartet in F minor seems to foreshadow aspects of the technique of the late quartets in its dominant qualities of conciseness, directness, and instant confrontation of contrast. But in the later works, even when contrast is forced very hard, the effect may not be so abrupt—as is true of the Finale of the A-minor Quartet by comparison with the F-minor.

Both the E♭ and the F-minor Quartets handle sonata form much more coolly than the earlier pieces. They pay little attention to sonata procedures in any of their movements save the first, and even there the development sections have become surprisingly simple—in the E♭, little more than a lengthy tonal plateau, and in the F-minor, a single stormy process hovering around the tonic key. Beethoven was moving away from the "heroic" type of development section, the development on the *Eroica* model. Here too the quartets of 1809–10 anticipate the later ones, which develop all kinds of astonishing new alternatives to the traditional exposition, development, recapitulation scheme, without at all abandoning the underlying principles of sonata form.

Another matter is the tendency to interrelate and link movements of the cyclic work. With Beethoven, as has been seen in one composition after another, this was accomplished largely by harmonic means. And the quartets of 1809–10 carry this tendency forward more subtly and more securely than the "Razumovsky" series. That the Quartet in E♭ employs as many as three different keys for its four movements (E♭, A♭, C minor, E♭) is already indicative; previously Beethoven had used three keys in only one sonatalike work—the recently composed Piano Trio in E♭, Opus 70, No. 2, using exactly the same three!—but in such later works as the Quartets in B♭ and C♯ minor, he will find a need for four keys and six, respectively. With the E♭ Quartet, he must have attached importance to the fact that the plateau-key of the first movement development, C, is the very one that recurs so surprisingly in the *Scherzo*. Relationships among the movements extend further. To cote one: C–D♭ is a prominent step in the *Adagio* and D♭ is its main subsidiary key; the *Scherzo* moves dramatically through D♭ too; and the Finale makes its most arresting harmonic point by the insertion of D♭ into the otherwise bland E♭ tonality.

Things work even more interestingly, or in any case more intensely, with the Quartet in F minor. The first movement throws D♭ and D♮ against F minor; the second movement can therefore maintain itself in the extraordinary key (for this context) of D major. The solo cello scale at the beginning of this movement accepts the situation, in some awe, and so stresses it. Then the parallel degrees B♭ and B♮ color the D major of this second movement, and it is by way of a diminished-seventh chord on B♮ that the end of it links back to F minor. In F minor again, the march takes care to strike one resounding G♭ Neapolitan chord, sufficiently reminiscent of the opening movement, with its arresting Neapolitan steps. The trio reiterates not only G♭ but also the D major of the second movement. Semitone articulation continues to be important in the Finale, from the brief *Larghetto espressivo* introduction through the *Allegretto agitato* up to and including the major-mode conclusion, *Allegro, molto leggieramente*. The new motif F♯–G–G♯–A dismisses and dissolves all the convoluted B♭'s and D♭'s, as everything resolves up into lucid major thirds.

The significance of these technical details, it should be said, is not uncontroversial; even so, one is reminded of how much more confidently technicalities can be talked about than their aesthetic results, which are what finally matter. That the two are connected feels very sure; greater intimacy among the movements makes the total experience more continuously self-aware, and seems to raise the level of insight to a special plane. A certain kind of discipline implied in the concept of an ordered totality reflects back on the individual movements, too. Even considered separately, their new flexibility makes for a new sensitivity of response, and their remarkable directness of expression seems to preclude sentimentality, bombast, or any sort of overextension of feeling. Thus in the first movement, although the pain and the spleen will cow the listener sooner than charm him, he will as likely submit to the integrity of the experience contained there as to the sheer ferocity of the action. The emotional current is altogether too intense to be turned off with the next movement, the superb *Allegretto ma non troppo*, which deepens the sense of disturbance and tempers it with a very equivocal sweetness. Toward the end of the work, as often happens with cyclic compositions in the minor mode, the complex experience of the beginning is resumed and simplified. If here less seems to be lost than usual, that is partly because the last two movements seem almost to set about analyzing aspects of the first: the march filtering out its quirkiness and anger, the Finale concentrating all its agitation and pathos. And then the delightful, astonishing, problematic major-mode conclusion, with its curious glance ahead to Opus 127 and Opus 132.

Forward-looking stylistic tendencies, too, can be talked about much more confidently than the qualities of individual works of art—and to do so is a considerable temptation at this particular point in a book on the Beethoven quartets, when attention is about to turn to the last period. Reviewing the last works of the second period, the Quartets in Eb and F minor of 1809–10, we can formulate the contrast between them in terms of one of them looking backward, the other forward. But to consider one looking outward, the other inward, is closer to the aesthetic point. The Quartet in Eb seems public and available, an open book by contrast with the surrounding quartets, an essay in sophisticated—if temporary—retrenchment. Perhaps it occupies the true turning point among the Beethoven quartets. At the turning point of a pendulum, the momentum is temporarily zero. The Quartet in F minor, written only a year later, is Beethoven's most self-absorbed and uncompromising and fraught with energy, the energy turned squarely in on itself.

A quartet is not a spiritual diary, but some quartets much more than others appear to take substance from a deep inner process of introspection and emotional synthesis. It is the penetration and (I believe) the hitherto unmatched directness of the inward look that establishes the particular greatness of the Quartet in F minor. It would be pleasant to think that in entitling it *Quartetto serioso* Beethoven was referring to its unmatched seriousness in insight. That quality too points to the future. It is, in fact, ultimately the chief signpost to the third period.—JOSEPH KERMAN

II. Three Equali for 4 Trombones, WoO 30
I. Andante; II. Poco adagio; III. Poco sostenuto

An *equale* (plural: *equali*) is a composition for equal voices, i.e., all male or all female, or for a group of similar instruments. Specifically, it became known in the seventeenth and eighteenth centuries as a composition written for four trombones, for a solemn occasion.

In response to a request by Thayer (Beethoven's famous biographer), Franz Gläggl wrote the following reminiscences of Beethoven's stay in Linz (1812) with his brother, Johann:

"Beethoven was on intimate terms with my father, *Kapellmeister* in the Linz cathedral. He was at our house every day and several times took meals with us. My father asked him for an equale for trombones. Beethoven asked to hear an equale such as were played at funerals in Linz. One afternoon when he was expected to dine with us, my father had three trombonists from the cathedral play an equale as desired, after which Beethoven sat down and composed one which my father had his trombonists play."

These three *equali*, all slow and solemn, are written mostly in block chords, like four-voice hymns; however, there are a few polyphonic passages such as might be found in a Renaissance motet. There are two very exciting interrupted cadences in the first *equale* in D minor, the first one seeming to prepare for a close in F major, the second one completing a cadence in D minor, where the opening phrase is repeated. The piece ends with a plagal cadence in major—very reminiscent of Renaissance harmonies.

The second *equale*, in D major, is softer and gentler. A late Beethoven touch is a surprise cadence in the remote key of C, in which the opening theme is repeated. Its second phrase is adjusted with chromatic harmonics to close, as expected, in the tonic key of D.

The third *equale*, in B flat major, is in triple time (3/2). It is the most solemn and moving of the three. The harmonies are all in the Renaissance vein, albeit taking the short piece (it is only sixteen measures long) as far afield as D flat and A flat.

In 1827, Ignaz von Seyfried, Beethoven's confidant and later biographer, who prepared the music for Beethoven's funeral, wrote Latin words to the first (*"Miserere"*) and third (*"Amplius lave me"*) and had them alternatingly sung by the choir and played by the trombones.—THOMAS K. SCHERMAN

Piano Sonatas

I. PIANO SONATA NO. 21 IN C, OPUS 53 ("WALDSTEIN")
  I. Allegro con brio; II. Introduzione (Adagio molto); III. Rondo (Allegretto moderato)

This, the so-called "Waldstein" Sonata (it is dedicated to Beethoven's patron, Count Waldstein), is one of the most famous and favorite, as well as one of the most brilliantly effective of the series. It is the perfect example of the composer's "middle period," by reason of its self-confidently vigorous, triumphant attitude, the bold grandeur of its design, and its well-balanced mastery.

The first movement, Allegro con brio, has, with all its marvelous depth and miraculous power of expression, that clarity, plasticity, and simplicity which are associated with the classic style of Goethe. A magnificent play of lines, rhythms, accents; rather than opalescent colors or expressive melodies. From the very beginning there pulsates an uncommonly stirring energy, even in the quickly reiterated pianissimo chords of the opening theme. The elemental character of the natural key of C major is strongly felt. There are contrasts—light and dark, high and low, strong and weak, etc.—yet not in the sense of changing emotions; only as shadings of that fundamental mood, the energy and gladness of creative activity. If mountains, cliffs and forests could sing, they would praise their Creator in such tones as these.

The place of a slow movement[1] is taken by an Adagio introduction to the finale. This short but important piece is of preludelike character. In it, toward the middle, there rises—for the first time in the sonata— a warm melody, as though it were sung by a cello delighting in the beauty of its tone. But after only six measures it is interrupted by the preludizing phrase of the opening, which now raises its question even more intensely and impressively.

The answer to this question is given by the Rondo. It begins with a happy, quasi-pastoral tune, which, gradually increasing, rises to a jubilant key. Four times the tune appears, and the third and fourth times it grows into a full-throated hymn of joy. Episodes separate or connect these repetitions of the chief theme. These episodes provide contrasting moods, symphonic combinations, grandiose climaxes; and finally they whip the music into a delirium of joyful ecstasy. But always the joy is that of humanity at large. Even in its finale this sonata preserves its unlyrical character, never voicing the sentiment of an isolated individual. It is the music of universality.—HUGO LEICHTENTRITT

Passages that prepare for the advent of a new key are essentially like well-worked-out preparations for the first entry of an important character in a drama. Much more exciting, though not different in harmonic structure, are the passages that prepare for the return to the home tonic. Let us begin for convenience with one of the most exciting—that in the first movement of the "Waldstein" Sonata, Opus 53, bars 136-155. You will not appreciate the full force of this until you hear it in its

[1] See Rolland's essay on the "Andante Favori" in F major, WoO 57, which was originally intended as the slow movement for this sonata.—Editor.

place in the whole movement, and the "Waldstein" Sonata is enormously more difficult to play than most people think. (Beethoven suffers cruelly from teachers and players who have not outgrown the delusion that the difficulty of a piece is to be gauged by the presence or absence of types of passage which come sooner or later in one's technical studies.)

In later works, Beethoven discovered that there are more exciting ways of returning to the home tonic. We shall do well to mistrust the common explanation that he grew tired of the dominant or was anxious to get away from it, or even the explanation, more flattering to ourselves, that the listener grows more intelligent and less in need of such explanatory devices. We shall never understand a work of art unless we take it as a whole. And it is only small and incomplete artists whose way of broadening from precedent to precedent is to narrow from boredom to boredom. Dominant preparation becomes crowded out of Beethoven's works because his wider harmonic range has made it inadequate. The history of the "Waldstein" Sonata itself exquisitely demonstrates the process, for the new harmonic wealth of its first movement and Finale crowded out the very beautiful Andante in F which Beethoven afterwards published separately, substituting for it the single page called *Introduzione* which now stands in the Sonata and is harmonically its richest feature. . . .

Beethoven soon discovered that there was no excuse for [the reactionary though intensely beautiful Andante] and that what the sonata really wanted in that place was no reaction but, on the contrary, a deeply emotional assertion of its new harmonic principles in their highest concentration. You have only to see how he modulates from F to D flat in bars 245–249 in the first movement, to say nothing of the miracle of bars 167–168 compared with bars 12–13, and you will see that when, in the Andante in F, Beethoven's chief purple patch is the modulation from F to D flat spaced out in the emphatic way [of proceeding directly, without any intervening chord, from an F major harmony (leaving the high F hanging precipitously) to a D flat chord (in which the same F becomes the third step in the scale of D flat)]—he is in the position of a writer who says, "Then a strange thing happened," by way of introducing an event which is obviously less strange than many things which he has already told with full power and restraint of style.—DONALD FRANCIS TOVEY (1)

II. PIANO SONATA NO. 22 IN F, OPUS 54

I. In tempo d'un menuetto; II. Allegretto

In tempo d'un menuetto.—There is no musical form and no classical precedent to which this first movement can be made to conform. It has been called a minuet with a modulating trio, part of which recurs between the varied repetitions of the minuet strain; but as trios never behave like that and minuet themes do not recur with variations in any normal dance movement of this sort, it is not more fantastic to think of this piece as representing a very special treatment of sonata form, which is after all much more elastic than a dance form that remained conventional even after it had produced the new offshoot of the scherzo. And as Beethoven, when all is said, did call this work a sonata, why not think of it thus?

We will call [the first four measures] the first subject. It continues rather than develops (for it is always stopping on full closes) for a while and has two more extended cadences slightly sophisticated by chromatic harmony. Then comes what we may take as the second subject [—a canon between the left and right hands played in vigorous eighth-note triplets. We will seemingly exaggerate its importance by calling it a full-fledged subject because,] although as such it shows its lack of classical breeding by not being definitely in the key of the dominant, it at least never holds for long to any other center of tonality. It is developed at much greater length than [the opening theme] until at last it begins to spin around a figure of three semitones, rather tentatively, all over the keyboard. This eventually becomes fixed in the bass and after two bars alters its note sequence as though making a humorous compromise with the first subject, for which it seems anxious to pave the way in the original key. Thus re-established, [the main minuetlike theme] dresses up in its first variation, after which [the triplet canon] makes a much briefer reappearance, ending on the dominant seventh of F major, broken into two triplet groups followed by a pause on the chord, the first time fortissimo, the second piano.

[The main theme] comes back again, treated still more elaborately this time and ending with a cadenza in which all metrical distinctions are blotted out. A coda follows with the first theme planted firmly on a low pedal F and still varied, though no further developed. On the contrary, it is simplified and gradually dissolved into a merely harmonic, nonmelodic close. But the harmony is extremely interesting and, for its time, daring. [There are dramatic] dissonant clusters in the [final] cadence. The tonic pedal (F), [however], is retained throughout.

Allegretto.—Here we have another moto perpetuo of continuous [sixteenth notes] a fascinating movement made of the kind of music one would hum to oneself in a train going at a steady pace—but a train that would have to take one into some land of fantastic beauty to awaken such music. What is even more remarkable than the unbroken flow of even notes is the fact that practically throughout the music is written strictly in two single parts, with the result that such harmony as is produced is transparent and constantly shifting in the most alluring way.

There are two main thematic features: [a] rising figure [of broken chords in sixteenth notes] with a kind of Scotch snap at the end, and [a] falling one [played by both hands, the one acting as the mirror of the other].

When both have been exposed and repeated, their development begins in a key as far removed as A major; but the falling figure, which has an incorrigible tendency to modulate, almost at once takes the music into other tonal regions. After chromatically descending half notes, heard strongly accentuated in the bass, a new rhythmic figure comes to complicate the music with its syncopations.

Shortly afterwards a melodic idea makes itself heard in the left hand, but tentatively, for it introduces its initial figure repeatedly and brokenly, as though somebody with a stammer endeavored to contribute to the discourse. Over a phrase derived from this theme the music modulates through the whole "cycle of fifths," an occurrence that is unique in the whole of Beethoven's work, as Sir Donald Tovey points out, except for the two preludes in all the major keys, published as Opus 39.

At last the music lands back in F major, and there is a kind of recapitulation, though the texture is differently laid out, [the ascending figure] appearing over a pedal F. A new allusion to the left-hand melodic feature gives rise to chords that make their appearance for the space of ten bars and almost for the only time in the whole movement.

A long repeat turns back to the beginning of the development, where [the figures] appear for a moment in A major. When we have once more arrived at the chord passage of ten bars—during which, by the way, the [sixteenth-note] motion does not stop—there is a regular full close into F major instead of an interrupted cadence tumbling into A major. A short coda, stirred into più allegro and containing references to the chief thematic features, brings this remarkable, fantastically humorous and curiously shaped but formally quite satisfactory movement to an end.—ERIC BLOM (1)

The neglect of this subtle and deeply humorous work comes not so much from its being overshadowed between its gigantic neighbors, as from the fact that it is almost, if not quite, as difficult as either of them. Moreover, it is utterly unlike any other work of Beethoven, just as *Meistersinger* is utterly unlike any other work of Wagner. The enormous size of *Meistersinger* compels the enthusiast to recognize that without a knowledge of it a whole aspect of Wagner's mind, and that perhaps the wisest remains unknown and hardly suspected. Beethoven's Opus 54 represents only what can be comprised in ten minutes of his most Socratic humor; but that is too important to deserve neglect. The humor is not bitter: Socratic irony approaches it nearly. But its purport is not philosophic. The two movements speak naïvely in their own characters, and Beethoven does not intrude with any indication that he could write a different kind of music with his fuller knowledge. The first movement seems quite happy with a main theme that cannot get through 4 bars without a full close, and prefers to sit down after 2. The finale, on the other hand, cannot stop at all, though its initial range of sentence is only 2 bars, with a hiccup at the 3rd. It does not seem to have heard of any other texture than 2-part writing, with occasional nodules of double notes, nor of much internal rhythm beyond perpetual motion; nor, strangest of all, does it seem to have heard of counterpoint beyond note against note, or rather arpeggio against arpeggio, with an occasional syncopated figure in monotone. Hence we can hardly explain it as a reversion to Bach, though nobody but Bach and Beethoven can have had anything to do with it. So much, then, for what it is not. It resembles all Beethoven's other works, great and small, late, middle, and early, in this,—that it can be properly understood only on its own terms. If Beethoven uses an old convention, we must find out how it fits the use he makes of it, instead of imagining that its origin elsewhere explains its presence here. If Beethoven writes in a form and style which cannot be found elsewhere, we must, as Hans Sachs says, find its own rules without worrying because it does not fit ours.

Beethoven's contemporaries knew their Haydn better than we do; and they probably saw nothing unorthodox in the outward aspect of a sonata consisting merely of a minuet and the sort of *perpetuum mobile* which by some obscure process had, since the time of Paradies, acquired the name of toccata. The contemporaries of Beethoven and Clementi would probably have said that Beethoven's Opus 54 was a small work consisting of a minuet and a toccata; and they would see nothing calling for further explanation in the title sonata for a group of two movements in the same key, in manifestly good contrast of form, and by no means lyric in style.— DONALD FRANCIS TOVEY (9)

III. PIANO SONATA No. 23 IN F MINOR, OPUS 57 ("APPASSIONATA")[1]
I. Allegro assai; II. Andante con moto; III. Allegro ma non troppo

This is one of the *chefs d'oeuvre* of Beethoven's art. This sonata, called "Appassionata," is a great hymn of passion, of that passion which is born of the never-fulfilled longing for full and perfect bliss. Not blind fury, not the raging of sensual fevers, but the violent eruption of the afflicted soul, thirsting for happiness, is the master's conception of

[1] Highly recommended further reading is the famous essay entitled "The Appassionata," by Romain Rolland.—Editor.

passion. To Beethoven the difference between ideal happiness and what mundane life offers as a substitute to true happiness is so violent as to rouse his sensitive nature to almost brutal outbursts. But in all of Beethoven's passionate outbursts there is a moral element, a conquest of self, an ethical victory. And this is true, of course, of Opus 57, this deeply personal avowal and one of the most moving documents of a great and fiery soul that humanity possesses.

The first movement begins with a sinister, brooding motive, issuing convulsively from the depths, and ending, after two measures, in a surprisingly imploring gesture. Thus already at the outset we have that precipitous change of moods which continues throughout the mighty proportions of this piece. Hesitant knocking at the door, terrifyingly furious response; touchingly simple appeal, and haughty, imperious bursts of passion; glimmering hope and staggering despair; fear-inspired stillness and heart-rending cries of distress; dark depth and sun-bathed height—these are some of the contrasts which tear at the heartstrings of the listener in this work. Never before this had music spoken in such glowing accents of passion.

The development of the first movement of the *Sonata Appassionata* contains the most famous of the climaxes he achieves by this means. Being an incident in the course of development, it is not restrained by the conditions of an exposition. The passage in question is that which leads to the recapitulation (bars 109–35). The essential points are as follows.

The calm theme with which it begins had first appeared in the exposition in A flat (bars 35/36–39) as a four-bar melody on a bass which happens to rise simply because an orderly rising bass is here in good style, whereas a bass of root notes would be clumsy. In the exposition, the entry of the theme has been prepared by a very long passage of dominant preparation. Its appearance in the development in D flat is still more impressive, because Beethoven has taken the extraordinary risk of arresting his action by not only reproducing his whole passage of dominant preparation on the threshold of this D flat, but by actually adding four more bars to it, bars for which he is obliged to invent entirely new matter, since the original preparation had purposely contained very little matter at all, being of the nature of long-drawn sighs and gasps ending in exhaustion.

The calm theme, having thus entered with enhanced impressiveness in D flat, should after four bars begin to repeat itself in the upper octave. Instead of this, the bass continues rising. This forces the theme in a crescendo through a series of keys which it is not worth while specifying. The point is: first, that the bass rises for two octaves, and that at the top of its climb articulate music ceases. So far, we may hope that the driest of grammarians, once he has been convinced that harmonies on a gradually rising bass are not aesthetically replaceable by harmonies in

root positions, will have seen the point of this tremendous climax. Beethoven, like many Germans of his and of later days, knew his Shakespeare remarkably well, at all events in very good translations. His rising bass is the *hysterica passio* to which Lear, already dreading the approach of madness, cries "Down!" Its climax is inarticulate. Melody disappears and harmony becomes ambiguous, for the diminished seventh, though it implies a dominant, happens to omit the dominant from its notes, and is notoriously ready to shift its intonation and imply any of three other widely remote dominants. Rhythm itself would disappear but for the fact that, so long as we remain conscious, we cannot get rid of time. In the present passage, the first sign of the return to articulate speech is in an ominous rhythmic figure (bar 120), and the diminished seventh resolves into the home dominant, and so leads us to the recapitulation.
—DONALD FRANCIS TOVEY (1)

The second movement (Andante con moto) is a return to peace and self-control. The tempest is silent for a while. Solemn, prayerful thoughts inspire the theme. From the depths of sorrow the spiritual eye looks upward to the serene, forgiving countenance of the Supreme Being. Accents of hope and confidence are heard. There are four variations. Proceeding from the hesitant rhythms of the first, the motion becomes freer and more fluid in those which follow. Beginning in the bass, the music rises upward by degrees, so that the last variation seems as if suspended in heavenly regions.—HUGO LEICHTENTRITT

The variations in the *Sonata Appassionata* are *doubles* (that is to say, progressive subdivisions of the rhythmic units) on the boldest of all themes of this kind. All its cadences are tonic at every two bars, both in the first part and in the second, and the melody itself is, in its first part, as near monotony as possible. If the listener can see anything in the *Sonata Appassionata* at all, he cannot fail to understand that the point here is the contrast between the Nirvana-like inaction of the slow movement and the terrible tragedies that surround it. It is, in fact, a vision of a world away from action, and the most dramatic moment in the sonata is that in which the last variation substitutes an unexpected chord at the end. With this the vision is shattered, and all is overwhelmed in the torrential passion of the finale.—DONALD FRANCIS TOVEY (1)

The finale's atmosphere is one of terror. A shrill cry of pain bursts forth suddenly. A howling flood of tones is released, and flows wildly, irresistibly through the entire piece, now whispering softly, now roaring loudly. Only once, in the middle section, this demoniacal onrush is interrupted; yet what is revealed in these pauses is not comforting calm, but a desperate glimpse into Nirvana. Still more madly than before the whole first part of the movement once again rushes past, its savagery emphasized by a sort of march of triumph in the coda, followed at the end by a despairing crash to the depths. It is music reminiscent of the Inferno visions of Dante's fancy.—HUGO LEICHTENTRITT

IV. PIANO SONATA No. 24 IN F SHARP, OPUS 78
I. Adagio cantabile, Allegro ma non troppo; II. Allegro vivace

Beethoven had a special affection for this sonata and quite decidedly expressed his preference of it to the so-called "Moonlight" Sonata, in C sharp minor. Each of the two works is dedicated to a beloved woman, the earlier one to the Countess Giulietta Guicciardi, the later to the Countess Therese von Brunswick. It is tempting to see some correspondence at least between a favorite work and its inscription to a favored woman. It is certain that the Sonata Opus 78 is emotionally as well as musically riper than the "Moonlight," which is an affair of moods, of setting three states of mind against each other by way of contrast, whereas the F sharp major Sonata is concentrated throughout upon the expression of one dominating emotion.

Content and form are at once unusual and strictly logical, for Beethoven was the man to persuade himself that the unprecedented could be made reasonable. The musician in love with a countess, and by no means without a chance of requital, was a new thing hardly thinkable before the French Revolution; to the fierce humanitarianism of Beethoven there was nothing unsuitable in it, apart from merely practical considerations. Much less did he hesitate to treat the sonata form, previously approached with a great deference for its conventions, with a proud superiority that put the frank expression of feeling before ceremony. It is noteworthy that the earlier work, dedicated to Giulietta, was called a *Sonata quasi una fantasia*, and the later, devoted to Therese, simply a sonata. But the qualification *quasi una fantasia*, now done away with as an apology for formal irregularity, has not become inappropriate to the later sonatas merely because of what is, from the point of view of each separate work, perfect cohesion, since they do not conform to a general pattern any more than the earlier works in question.

Adagio cantabile—Allegro ma non troppo.—The *adagio* begins as though it would develop into one of Beethoven's great slow melodies. Indeed, how such a development was to be resisted passes comprehension. At the same time, it is the very fact of its being interrupted in the middle of the fourth bar that imparts to this brief introductory remark its effect of tense expectancy. The music remains suspended on a pause for an instant, then merges quietly into the very moderately paced *allegro*. The first subject, or rather the first strain of a group of short motifs that constitute the first subject, is now stated at once. [It starts with a dotted-rhythm upbeat passing scalewise from the third to the fifth step (A sharp to C sharp) of the F sharp major scale. Then starts a broad lyric melody in quarters and dotted half notes which gently outlines the F sharp major tonality.] There is no need to enlarge upon the placid beauty of this melody, and its functional significance will appear presently; but it is worth while drawing attention at this point to Beethoven's subtilization of a time-honored device—the Alberti bass. Mozart and Haydn, who still applied it almost mechanically at times, or even Beethoven himself in his early days, would probably have written the bass of such a passage in the manner of an accompaniment pure and simple. Here it acquires a melodic significance of its own, almost as though a viola and a cello were contributing independent parts of their own to a quartet. It is very characteristic of Beethoven's piano writing that it should often convey the impression of a consort of instruments. A hint of anything from a string trio to a full orchestra may surprise the ear at this or that moment. Thus, if his piano texture is not ideally adapted to the keyboard instruments, it is at any rate something more rather than something less than sheer pianism.

The first-subject group continues [with tentative sixteenth-note groups in the right hand and answered in the left, followed by a descending scale in eighth-note triplets outlining the I-IV-V portion of a cadence in F sharp major in the bass, which is thereupon concluded in quarter notes].

The next five bars are a superb example of Beethoven's use of thematic fragments in a manner that is at once purposeful and economical. The three-chord figure [with which the previous phrase ended] is at first restated in a hesitant way a degree of the scale higher. One of the [sixteenth-note] groups is then followed by the [dotted rhythmic upbeat to the first strain], which leads directly into a transitional episode of [sixteenth-notes] in the right hand and chords in the left. The important point about [this] passage is the perfect naturalness with which three thematic scraps are made into an incident that would be beautiful and significant even if its derivation remained unnoticed.

The [sixteenth-note motion] that follows is again so interesting as a specimen of that concerted instrumental texture implied by Beethoven's keyboard writing that one cannot resist [pointing out that the seemingly ornamental sixteenth-note figures actually outline a very potent melody in quarters and eighths and finally half notes].

The transition culminates in an emphatic cadence of C sharp major, in which key the second-subject group opens half a bar later. It will be

noticed that Beethoven makes the new departure in the orthodox key—
that of the dominant—very deliberately in this instance; as much so,
in fact, as the eighteenth-century composers, who often advertised their
arrival at this turning-point by a flourish on the dominant that had in
itself no musical significance. He compromises characteristically by retaining the emphasis but insisting on significance to the last.

The opening of the second subject is [in triplet rhythm]. In its very
brief course a new [sixteenth-note] figure surges up twice, then descends
into the bass to form a bridge passage that leads to the repeat of the
exposition from the beginning of the *allegro*.

The concluding bridge passage now takes a turn into F sharp minor,
in which key reappears the opening strain of the first subject. A bold
modulation through A major brings [the same strain] back in G sharp
minor, after a first hint at it in the bass. Then the small [upbeat figure]
alone lends its rhythm, with a different melodic formation, to a stretch
of development that leads, through a variety of keys, to the dominant of
F sharp major, and so to the recapitulation. The working-out, therefore,
has been extremely brief, but then, so is the whole movement, and
since Beethoven achieves a remarkable feat of thematic concentration
within less than twenty bars of closely reasoned discourse on his first-
subject material, he has said all that needed saying at this juncture. His
terseness, in fact, combined with unswerving relevance to the main
topic, is one of the secrets of his greatness.

The recapitulation is of great interest as conforming to tradition or
departing from it just as it suits the inspiration of the moment. The
return of the second-subject group is managed in the orthodox manner:
the [sixteenth-note] transition is reintroduced in such a way as to reach
its final cadence, not on the dominant this time, but on the tonic, in
which key (F sharp major) the second subject duly reappears with
[its pervading triplet rhythm]. But before this, the transition itself is
approached by a startlingly new disposition of the first-subject group. It
opens as before, but the [tentative sixteenth-note groups which followed
it] are so extended that the triplet scale is now displaced into the key
of E major. The [quarter-note chords which ended the second strain]
also are differently managed, for they now appear five times in succession
instead of only twice. After the normal unfolding of the second subject,
a very brief coda is built up from the bass previously used as a bridge,
first to the repeat of the exposition and then to the working-out. Its
importance is now emphasized by a passing reference to [the opening
strain of the first subject]. The whole of the second part, like the first,
is repeated, *an unusual procedure at this stage of the evolution of the
Beethoven sonata, but justified by the great concision of the whole
piece.*[1]

---

[1] Italics by the editor.

Allegro vivace.—The second movement being also the final one, Beethoven is constrained to use the same key as he did for the first. With great subtlety, therefore, he avoids insisting on it as long as possible, and whether this was done consciously or not, the fact remains that it is a master stroke. It does not vastly matter in art whether greatness be achieved by or thrust upon genius, and it will not always do to inquire how its most astonishing feats come about. Whether intentionally or by intuition, Beethoven here exhibits one of the most convincing proofs of his technical cunning.

The movement opens [with a kaleidoscopic pattern of harmonies and only tentative two-bar melodic groups]. The chord of the augmented sixth at the beginning at once aims at ambiguity of key, and until the [twelfth bar of the piece] the composer sedulously avoids stating the tonic chord in root position. He makes, in fact, a perfect cadence to B major before he asserts F sharp major. It is with the fluttering [sixteenth-notes] heard a moment later that the tonic key definitely establishes itself. After a few bars the figuration is changed to rapid, broken pairs of notes in rising steps, distributed between the two hands. Then the main theme returns, the impression made being that of restating a rondo subject after the first episode. However, it is not followed by a new incident, as it should be in a regular rondo, but by the same as before, except that the broken two-note figures [are] now [descending] instead of ascending.

A new notion now comes to the fore, which a glance at the movement as a whole reveals as a definite second subject. Not that this would mean that the piece could not be a rondo; but it does not contain a sufficient variety of episodes to be definitely classed as such, so that it must be regarded as partaking as much of the sonata as of the rondo form, though the feature of a working-out section is lacking. It is characteristic of the concision of this sonata that Beethoven should have chosen this curious hybrid form for the finale, almost as though he had wished to condense three movements into two.

The second subject, which is in a mixture of D sharp major and minor, begins [with pairs of sixteenth-notes rising boldly in D sharp major, answered by a soft cadence figure in D sharp minor. After a short working-out, this pattern ends in a *fortissimo* augmented sixth chord spaced very widely across the keyboard. This] leads back to the broken figures, which both rise and fall this time, and so to the main theme again, with its phrases now distributed between treble and bass. For some time no new material is used, and the second subject reappears in F sharp major and minor. A last return to the chief theme marks the introduction of a short but highly significant coda that admirably sums up the musical argument. The rhythm of the [second short tentative melodic group of the main theme] is used a dozen times in a new

melodic formation and followed by three unexpected chords that hold up
the rhythm, the last broken into arpeggios. The movement is then
rounded off by a brief sentence based on the fluttering [sixteenth-notes]
heard before. Like the first movement it ends abruptly: Beethoven has
said all he set out to say as economically as possible and disdains to
announce the fact by any merely rhetorical conclusion.—ERIC BLOM (1)

V. PIANO SONATA No. 25 IN G, OPUS 79
I. Presto alla tedesca; II. Andante; III. Vivace

This slender work was composed in 1809 and published in December
1810 by Breitkopf & Härtel of Leipzig. In February 1810 Beethoven
offered it to the publishers together with the Sonatas Opus 78 and
Opus 81a. The present sonata was, of course, much the least important
of the three, and the composer himself entitled it *Sonate facile ou
sonatine*. But although the second and third movements are very slight
indeed, the first is neither as easy to play as Beethoven claims nor in
the least sketchy or even unusually condensed in form.

Presto alla tedesca.—The tempo indication is curious and requires
some care in its interpretation. Beethoven's "presto" simply qualifies
the "alla tedesca," which is the tempo of the ländler or early waltz;
in fact this "in the German manner" is the exact equivalent of the
Deutsche of Mozart and Schubert, whose dances of that type, however,
are in a very moderate tempo which Beethoven's "presto" is intended
to speed up.[1]

The first subject [opens abruptly with the characteristic melodic turn
G-B-G-D outlining the G major triad and follows it with a smooth
eighth-note ornamental line descending over an octave to the slower
outlining of [the chord of] the dominant seventh. The bass is a series
of broken chords in eighth notes outlining the harmonies of G, C, and
D7 all with a pedal note of the tonic G].

At its first appearance Beethoven's harmony in the fifth bar [shifts
from C to D7 on the third quarter]; but he seems later to have decided
not to repeat this dissonant anticipation of the dominant (together
with the tonic bass), feeling perhaps that its effect would be attenuated if
it occurred more than once. [Some] editors put down this irregularity to
forgetfulness [and attempt to "correct" it]. They deserve Sir Donald
Tovey's snub, which I cannot forbear to quote. He says that these
different versions:

[1] See Ludwig Misch's comparison of the main theme with the Alla tedesca of the
Quartet, Opus 130, written sixteen years later (in his book "Beethoven Studies," pp.
14–18).—Editor.

. . . are characteristic in themselves and in their discrepancy. We, who take Beethoven's style seriously, can only say: "Why throw away upon music talents intended by nature so plainly and so exclusively for the more perfectible art of book-keeping by double entry?"

The [opening characteristic melodic turn] is of special structural importance and will occur later in three different forms [:G-B-G-D; then merely G-B-G; and finally merely B-G preceded by silence]. The [first theme ends with a descending scale which] also assumes a certain constructive significance in the future developments, but it must decidedly not be regarded as having influenced the accompanying scales of the second subject. The exposition closes with four isolated statements of [the two-note version of the opening motif], which lead to the repeat of the whole section.

The same figure serves as a bridge to the working-out, but with the addition of two more statements which bring the music into the distant region of E major. In this key the first seven bars [of the opening theme] are heard, and then comes a development of [the three-note version of the opening motif] in E major and C major, which covers sixteen bars. [It] is so altered as to make its first [quarter note] into a bass note and the other two into falling thirds played by the left hand over the right [in the treble register]. Bars 8-11 of [the opening theme] then reappear in C major, and [its concluding descending scale] is detached to provide a modulation into C minor. The process just heard is now repeated in C minor and E flat major, and [the descending scale] again forms a connection with yet another appearance of [the truncated version of the opening motif] in its modified form. This seems to be in D major, but the intrusion of a C natural soon shows that it stands for the dominant of G major. In that key the recapitulation begins—and remains. It is so brief that Beethoven adopts the (for him) unusual device of repeating the whole working-out and recapitulation, which the second time, by a new use of [the two-note version of the opening motif], merges into a coda.

Andante.—The slow movement, in G minor with a middle section in E flat major, is short, simple and easy to play. In character it resembles those songs without words by Mendelssohn which bear the title of *Venezianisches Gondellied*: in other words, it is of the barcarolle type affected by many composers of the nineteenth century, for whom it may be said to have been what the *siciliano* was to those of the eighteenth. This sonata, in fact, does not look back, but rather forward, in spite of its brevity and simplicity. The main G minor section is repeated note for note after the E flat major episode, but amplified by a three-bar echo of its principal strain and three concluding pairs of chords.

Vivace.—The chief theme of the finale, which is a very condensed rondo, [is a regular phrase made up of figures of alternating eighth-notes and two sixteenth-notes harmonized in the left hand by harmonies descending scalewise in the key of G].

The second strain of the main theme [in which an eighth note and two sixteenth-notes veer off into an angular melody of straight eighth notes and quarters] is more important than the episodes.

The first episode in E minor and the second in C major are well contrasted and both very brief. A characteristic procedure of this rondo is the linking up of the episodes with the returning main themes by means of passages derived from the latter. Apart from the changed accompaniment [(the bass harmonics now appear in triplets)] the first return leaves the theme unaltered. At the second and last return its shape is still retained, but the melody soon becomes disintegrated into broken triplets. A short but conclusively phrased coda is then constructed from alternate appearances of [the second and the first strains of the chief theme] in various modified forms.—ERIC BLOM (1)

VI. PIANO SONATA No. 26 IN E FLAT, OPUS 81a ("LES ADIEUX")
I. Les adieux (Adagio, Allegro); II. L'absence (Andante espressivo); III. Le retour (Vivacissamente)

The emotions represented by this sonata are not those of a love-story. The music is a monument to the friendship of two men, deep as any friendship formed in schooldays or in the full stress of life, and manly as Beethoven's ripest art. The Archduke Rudolf was a musician who might have made a reputation as such if he had been cast adrift upon the world. At the age of sixteen he became a pupil of Beethoven; and it is impossible not to recognize a special quality in the numerous important works that Beethoven dedicated to him—the present sonata, the E flat Concerto, the last Violin Sonata, Opus 96, the last Trio, Opus 97, the Seventh Symphony, and the Missa Solemnis in D. These do not exhaust the list of works dedicated to the Archduke Rudolf; and they have in common a magnificence of scale, a gorgeous wealth of invention, and, almost more conspicuously than any other quality, a beauty at once majestic and energetic that may indeed be found wherever Beethoven has much to say, but here more obviously than in other works. One might almost assign dedications to this particular patron on internal evidence, though not without risk of mistake—*e.g.*, there is something very Rudolfian in the first Rasumovsky quartet.

We need harbor no doubts as to the sincerity of Beethoven's emotion in the present sonata. Court etiquette was no more to Beethoven than the mace to Cromwell. The published dedication to the Archduke was formal; but in Beethoven's sketches, which he showed to nobody, the sonata is described as "written from the heart and dedicated to H.R.H." In the lower orders of sentimental journalism persons may be found to whom the true circumstances of this sonata are not romantic enough. But sane and manly friendships formed in schooldays and in the full stress of life are very fine subjects for Beethoven's music.

It is with the emotions of parting, absence, and reunion of such friends, and with no external circumstances, that this sonata deals. Nothing in it would lead us to guess that while Beethoven's friend was absent (with the rest of the royal family) Vienna was being attacked by Napoleon's forces, and that Beethoven's chief anxiety during the bombardment was to spare the last remains of his rapidly failing hearing. For this reason alone he spent long hours in the cellar, taking refuge from the noise, though otherwise he expressed great contempt for the inefficient gunnery on both sides. All that he chose to tell of these terrible days in his music was that he had said farewell to a dear friend and that he was longing for the friend's return. For that return he waited, and wrote not a note of the music for it until the happy time had really come.

There is any amount of minute psychological accuracy in the form and style of each movement of the sonata; and its external story, in revealing Beethoven's capacity for friendship, helps us to understand the depth and subtlety of the music. To look for more pictorial details is to miss all that matters. "Not painting, but the expression of feeling" is an excellent description of all Beethoven's music, whether absolute or associated with things that can be explained in words.—DONALD FRANCIS TOVEY (9)

[The sonata starts with an Adagio introduction constructed on a harmonized falling third G-F-E flat over which Beethoven writes, in the score, the three syllables "Le-be-wohl." Harmonized simply as they are, the three notes sound like a posthorn. As in the Sonata, Opus 78], everything is so interrelated that it even is doubtful where the second subject begins: if it is in bar 35 (bar 19 of the Allegro) then neither of the themes begins in the tonic and the treble is an inversion of the main subject; but perhaps it is the *espressivo* passage of bar 50 (bar 34 of the Allegro) which repeats the main subject note for note: we meet the three notes of the introduction everywhere. The clear B flat major in bar 50 is more of a quiet contrast to the main theme than bar 35; most likely, this is the second subject proper. That Beethoven used the notes G-F-E flat with conscious intent in the Allegro subject is shown by the tenuto mark in bar 18 [the second measure of the Allegro].

The coda is particularly tender and poetic. We hear the posthorn vanishing in the distance and the beloved friend disappearing in a cloud of dust, yet the realm of absolute music is never abandoned.—EDWIN FISCHER

If, the introduction to the first movement of Beethoven's Piano Sonata, Opus 81a, is regarded as an extended prolongation of the opening E-flat major harmony, the main point of the introduction is, it seems to me, missed. For the passage is heard just the other way around: the opening progression leads us to expect a cadence in E-flat, and the whole introduction consists, in a sense, in delaying the arrival of such a cadence until after the allegro has already begun. The meaning of the passage and its affective power derives from this inhibited tendency toward a perfect cadence in E-flat. All this is missed if the introduction is considered as a prolongation of E-flat major. At best, we understand the introduction as a prolongation only after it is finished.[1]—LEONARD B. MEYER

One of his most subtle harmonic devices, is Beethoven's characteristic way of putting two keys together by cutting away part of a chord and replacing it by notes which transform the remainder into a new key. Beethoven sometimes presents us with a single note, or a fragment of unsupported melody, which he gives out just slowly enough to make us wonder what its key is to be. The most wonderful of all passages on this principle is to be found in the development of *Les Adieux* (Allegro, bars 57–74), where the fragments of the "farewell" figure descend without accompaniment and find themselves in an incalculably remote new key at each step, the crowning surprise being that the eventual drift is toward the home tonic.—DONALD FRANCIS TOVEY (1)

The interwoven style also predominates in the second movement, entitled *L'Absence*, which recalls the introduction to the first movement. It has two themes of contrasting mood: a sigh of forsakenness at the beginning, and then a consoling cantabile—with the left hand entering somewhat rudely in staccato [thirty-second notes].

The movement falls into two halves: from bar 21 onwards the first half is repeated note for note in another key. In this lament, the fingers must become spiritual feelers conveying the finest tremors of emotion to the listener's mind and heart.—EDWIN FISCHER

[1] Actually the resolution of the E flat chord doe snot occur until the fifth bar of the Allegro.—Editor.

This *Intermezzo*, deals with a series of short themes in rotation, recapitulating them in another group of keys, and making as if to recapitulate again, but it is interrupted by a change leading to finale.

This form, musically very simple, admirably solves the problem of expressing the sorrow of absence without inflicting its tedium on the listener. The cycle of thoughts, at first wistful, then yielding to a mood of affectionate reminiscence, which is interrupted by a passionate protest against the present solitude—this cycle must recur forever unless miracles happen. Beethoven allows us to witness one recurrence, which suffices to show that there is no prospect of escape. But [at measure 37] the wistful first theme rises for a third time with a new, if forlorn, hope, and the miracle happens—for Beethoven's enharmonic modulations do succeed in being miracles instead of bad puns or duodecuple theorems. [Actually, what happens musically is that] the diminished seventh resolves onto the dominant of E flat (B natural-C flat), [and leads down to B flat. On this dominant harmony] two more bars arise from [the wistful figure] and lead to the finale.—DONALD FRANCIS TOVEY (9)

After the introduction to the finale, which stands for the first embrace of the reunited friends, there is the difficulty of giving adequate expression to the simple triads of the main theme. The movement is in sonata form. Its technical difficulties, especially those of the left hand, can best be overcome by using a loose hand and loose arm. The joy of reunion should not be stifled by too much panting and puffing but expressed in a free and happy style of playing.—EDWIN FISCHER

VII. PIANO SONATA NO. 27 IN E MINOR, OPUS 90
    I. Mit Lebhaftigkeit und durchaus mit Empfindung und Ausdruck;
    II. Nicht zu geschwind und sehr singbar vorgetregan

The publication of Opus 90 in 1815 was announced with the statement, "All connoisseurs and friends of music will surely welcome the appearance of this sonata, since nothing by L. van Beethoven has appeared now for several years." To be exact, not quite four years separated the publication dates of Opuses 81a and 90. The review of Opus 90 early in 1816 [in the *Allgemeine Musikalische Zeitung*] was cordial, beginning, "With much pleasure the reviewer calls attention to this new sonata. It is one of the most simple, melodious, expressive, intelligible, and *mild* among all [the sonatas] for which we are indebted to Beethoven." Perhaps part of this changed attitude may be credited to the musical public, which was beginning to catch up a little more with Beethoven.

For Opus 90, with its motivic concentration on the main idea in the first movement and its lyrical finale that extends to a "heavenly length" in Schubertian fashion, is quite as subtle and original in its way as Opus 78 or 81a. It is an exceptionally introspective work, which followed several patriotic works appropriate to the restored freedom in Vienna, and which developed alongside the revision of *Fidelio*. The German inscriptions over each movement are indicative in themselves: i) "Lively, but with sentiment and expression throughout"; ii) "Not too fast and very songful."—WILLIAM S. NEWMAN

The interwoven style again predominates in this work. Rhythms and motifs undergo metamorphoses producing patterns which differ externally but are inwardly related. Like the nymph who is turned into a laurel tree or a reed, the divine soul lives on within the new form. Thus, the driving force in the first movement of Opus 90 is the rhythm [of the first two measures,] which occurs all over the place, even in the transition to the second subject and in the second subject itself [measures 47–50] though there it loses its anacrustic character, going, as it does, from a strong to a weak beat. The melodic element G-F sharp of the opening subject undergoes similar changes, in the second subject (measure 55 on], in the codetta [measures 69–70, 73–74, etc.] and at the end of the development. Bar 25 results from a combination of the rhythmic element of the main subject with the beginning of its melodic consequent.

The form is simple. Whether, as Riemann thinks, the second subject begins at bar 45 is open to doubt. Surely, the character of the movement does not change until bar 55, and Beethoven's ritard before bar 55 and the subsequent a tempo show that the composer felt that something new was starting at this point. Before the recapitulation there is a transition skillfully worked by augmentation and diminution, which it is quite difficult to bring off.—EDWIN FISCHER

[At the close of the development section there occurs one of those magic moments which look forward to Beethoven's late style. From measure 110 to 117 the tender cantabile phrase (which made up the second part of the main theme)] in two-part harmony in C major [appears] for four bars, answered in F major by two lower parts, while [sixteenth-note] arpeggios arise above. [From measures] 118 to 132 a bass voice enters with [the cantabile phrase] in D minor, ousting the other voices, while the arpeggios continue above. [The second half of the cantabile phrase], starting on G sharp as dominant of A minor, rises for ten one-bar steps in the bass, soon passing into the home tonic, and culminating in the home 6/4 [chord] at bars 130 and 131. [In bars] 132 to

143, over the 6/4 [harmony] the arpeggios have coalesced into a new conjunct [scale figure: G F sharp E D sharp E]. This is suddenly left unsupported except for an echo in a lower octave. As if in bewilderment, this figure is then developed in imitative two-part dialogue, transformed by augmentations in a kind of geometrical progression, in the course of which it is reduced to the three notes G, F sharp, E. The meaning of these seems to attract attention. The three notes speed up their rhythm again in various ways: the two voices, shifting among three octaves, collide and rebound, until the figure, now in eighth notes, proves to be a version of [the first measure of the main theme], into which it finally closes. And so the development is finished, and the home 6/4 chord has never resolved onto the dominant at all. And this is the most important point in the whole process. If the main point lay in the ingenious thematic transformation, those critics would be justified who find it farfetched. Nothing is easier than to derive anything whatever from anything else whatever on such lines. Again, if Beethoven had not carried out the whole process in our actual hearing, it would have been mere lunacy to impute any connection between the main theme and the casual [scale figure] in bar 132. Nor would it be less foolish if that figure had been clearly related to some other theme. Indeed, an essential point of the passage is that the [scale figure] is the most casual of accidents. The main theme is made to emerge dramatically from something as nearly nothing as can be embodied in sounds at all. The 6/4 chord is evaporating while awaiting its resolution; the anxious voices ask, Where? Where? When? and How?—and all the time the answer is "Here and now"; and the answer is at last given without troubling to remind us that the 6/4 chord has not been resolved. This *locus classicus* thus introduces us to what becomes a prominent feature of Beethoven's third manner—viz., the avoidance of the dominant chord in cadential positions. All such avoidances are expressive of the dramatic discovery that the questions "When and where" are to be answered by "Already here and now."—DONALD FRANCIS TOVEY (9)

In the wonderful Rondo of Beethoven's E minor Sonata, Opus 90, you may, if you like, consider that the main theme consists of AA BB AA. Even here, the term "ternary" misses the point. In the first place, the A is not a repeated strain of four bars, but a self-repeating 8-bar strain. Though the cadence into bar 4 is tonic, it is melodically obviously not final, as is its answer in bar 8. In the second place, B is twice as slow, or, as we had better call it, twice as large, as A, in as much as it consists of 8 bars that are not self-repeating; but this whole 8-bar strain is repeated. The proper way to regard the whole 32-bar section is not to classify it at all, but to treat it as unique.

The characteristic of a rondo has been well described by Parry as "the frequent and desirable return of a melody of great beauty." People have been known to complain that the Rondo of Opus 90 repeats itself too much. They should join company with the sea-captain who took up a copy of *Gulliver's Travels* and, after reading several chapters, flung it down, exclaiming: "I don't believe a word of it." Tastes may differ about the desirability of hearing the beautiful melody of the Rondo of Opus 90 three times unvaried in full, with its own self-repetitions, and a fourth time as a duet between treble and bass, plus a compressed final version in the coda, making ten times in all for the first clause. But when this rondo is cited as an unusually long movement, taste has nothing to do with the matter. It so happens that the whole thing is compressed into six and a half minutes. Beethoven has written some of the longest movements that have ever been held together in perfect form. But no other composer is a match for him in power of compression; nor, until Wagner changed the whole time-scale of music, has anybody approached Beethoven in power of expansion.—DONALD FRANCIS TOVEY (1)

Piano Variations

I. 6 VARIATIONS IN D, OPUS 76

These variations, composed at the latest in 1809, and published in December 1810, are written on the Turkish March which Beethoven afterwards introduced into his music to the Ruinen von Athen, Opus 113, composed in 1811. In this fact lies the chief interest of the variations for us. Apart from the historical interest, we may perhaps take some musical interest in the second and fourth variations; but they are too Turkish (or whatever else it may be) to make a pleasing impression upon us, and grotesque rather than characteristic.

Some of the sets of variations—especially those on "God Save the King" and "Rule Britannia"—have shown us how low a man of genius may fall.—FREDERICH NIECKS (2)

II. 7 VARIATIONS ON "GOD SAVE THE KING," WoO 78; 5 VARIATIONS ON "RULE BRITANNIA," WoO 79

These two series, whose destination is unknown, date from 1803. They are thus contemporaries of the "Kreutzer" Sonata and, paradoxically, of the "Eroica" Symphony. For in 1813, having got over his enthusiasm for Napoleon and celebrating instead Wellington's victory, it was to be precisely the two themes that Beethoven would develop in *"La bataille de Vittoria,"* by contrasting them with *"Malborough s'en va-t-en guerre!"* Both are less ambitious than several of the other sets of variations and look toward the past. Nevertheless the first series is a success, with its supple minor variations and its march.—JACKET NOTES FOR TURNABOUT TV 34162

III. 32 VARIATIONS IN C MINOR ON AN ORIGINAL THEME, WoO 80

The 32 Variations in C minor, composed in 1806, is based on an energetic original theme only eight bars long, very pregnant harmonically. In each of its bars there is a definite change of harmony, and after the second and fourth bars a modulation: the bass presents, from the first to the sixth bar, the chromatic scale descending from the tonic to the dominant, then returning to the tonic by way of the IV and V degrees. From this it could be expected that in the main the variations would have to take this harmonic process, the primary characteristic of the theme, as the "pole at rest in the flight of appearances," as the fixed line of support backing up all of its transformations, however diversified. But it is not only the harmonic design of the theme that is maintained unchanged, apart from a few imperceptible modifications; the same key (except for a few changes from minor to major), the same time signature and the same basic tempo continue throughout the entire work. This leaves only the melody and rhythm as the elements to which the master's art of variation are applied here. Now, although these elements occur in almost inexhaustible diversification, and give rise to such sharply marked designs, despite the limitation imposed on them, still in and of themselves they would not suffice to give the work the character of a modern set of variations unless there were a train of logical connection running through them, such as we do not find with equal clarity and thoroughness of plan in any other of Beethoven's works in this form. The design principle of building groups, of having several variations grow out of a rhythmic or melodic or figurative motif, which previously had occurred only sporadically, runs through the entire work as a basic formal idea. We clearly distinguish the following groups of variations: Nos. 1, 2, 3; 7, 8; 10, 11; 13, 14; 15, 16; 20, 21; 26, 27; 31, 32. Within each group there is a slight heightening of tension, either because the previously more rapid rhythm in one hand is extended to both hands (Groups I and II) or because the movement spreads from the lower parts to the more accessible upper registers (Groups III and VI) or because the number of parts involved is doubled (Group IV) or because a livelier rhythm sets in although the design is otherwise the same. Further, in some cases several groups come together with other variations outside them to produce a continuing heightening on a larger scale (Variations IV to XI), while other variations owe their creation only to the need of effects of contrast (XII, XXIII, XXX). All this gives rise to a totality that is so rich in relations and so meaningfully interconnected in its various parts that despite the absence of changes in modulation, key, and time signature, the hearer's interest is captured undiminished, even increased, down to the very end. We see from this work how Beethoven always kept approaching the problem of the variation form from a new side and how his primary aim, in contrast to the stereotyped ideas of an earlier period, was to give his sets of variations individuality and raise them to the level of his other works.—OTTO KLAUWELL (TR. BY THOMAS K. SCHERMAN)

Miscellaneous Piano Works

I. FANTASIA IN G MINOR, OPUS 77

This illustration of the quest of joy is sometimes described as the Fantasia in G minor; but a couple of dominant scales and a single Adagio cadence-phrase constitute the only assertion of that key in the whole scheme. It must begin in some key (as Beethoven wrote it early in the 19th century and not in the 20th); and an essential point in its design is that whatever key it starts in must never be heard again. The opening scales are a note of interrogation; the Adagio cadence-phrase is an expression of resigned hopelessness. The question and the hopeless resignation are repeated in F minor, a key contradictory to G minor. If Beethoven wished to build a design on the harmonic basis thereby implied he could easily explain the contradiction (the openings of the Waldstein Sonata and the Sonata in G, Opus 31, No. 1, are on much the same principle); but his intention is to drift entirely away. A new theme in a new rhythm begins tenderly in the remote key of D flat; the note of interrogation interrupts drastically. The new theme pleads its cause again, with an anxious turn of harmony; the note of interrogation becomes menacing. A childlike Allegretto enters, with confiding zest; it becomes shy and anxious, with good reason, for the chords which now thrust it aside are angry and persistent, ending indignantly with the old note of interrogation. A fiery Allegro in D minor builds itself up in formal phrases, but shows no better capacity to develop than its predecessors. It quickly exhausts itself, and a solemn change of harmony to another immensely distant key (A flat) leads to a deep impulse toward thoughts that are neither childish nor angry. The new idea is a slow rhythm, not yet ready for melody.

The interrogatory scale becomes subdued and wistful. The solemn harmonies move steadily toward a certain key (the dominant of B). This key arouses a wild and tragic excitement, and the ensuing Presto has what none of the previous movements have shown, a clearly introductory character; that is to say, it is not an idea that enters as a beginning and fails to continue; its whole outlook is forward, and it presses on until the solemn rhythm re-enters and leads, with a glow of welcome, to a Theme and Variations in B major, the object of all these questions and efforts.

The seventh variation broadens out into a Coda, in which the note of interrogation reappears only in order to give itself the pleasure of a happy affirmative; and so when the theme also pretends to suggest doubts as to its key the scale-figure, no longer a note of interrogation, dismisses this impromptu with a laugh.—DONALD FRANCIS TOVEY (13)

II. POLONAISE IN C, OPUS 89

The polonaise is a ceremonial marchlike composition and is usually associated with a certain amount of pomp and grandeur.[1]

In the present instance Beethoven commences with an ornamental cadenza passage, and the polonaise itself is in a graceful, poetical and partly playful mood. The middle section beginning in C minor has some charming modulations ending with a flowery succession of [trills] and chromatic passages which lead again to the playful first subject. A pleasing contrapuntal episode and final entry of theme with coda complete the work.—HERBERT WESTERBY

III. BAGATELLE IN C, WoO 56

This remarkable little Allegretto was originally conceived, according to Nottebohm, as an intermezzo for the C minor Sonata, Opus 10, No. 1. Actually in the context of a second or third movement of that sonata it would have been slightly *de trop*, not because of the added length to an otherwise taut composition but because of its mood in relationship to the already existing movements. If it were to be one of four instead of

[1] The piece was written for, and presented to, the Empress of Russia, for which Beethoven received a present of fifty ducats and a long-overdue present of one hundred ducats from her husband, Alexander I, to whom he had dedicated the three violin sonatas, Opus 30, a dozen years earlier.—Editor.

the now three movements, it would have to come either *after* the fiery, passionate opening Allegro con brio, where its slight frame would have been swallowed up in advance and the beauty and repose of the elegiac A flat Adagio would be diminished by a foretaste of the major mode; or *before* the breathless Prestissimo, in which position its intricate polyphonic writing and its delicate pianissimo close would take away from the impetuous nervousness of the equally soft opening of the last movement. Were it to stand alone as a middle movement, replacing the present Adagio, it lacks sufficient contrast to the two outside movements. When we listen to the sonata as it stands, we can admire Beethoven's flawless taste in rejecting the idea of the C major intermezzo, even if it meant discarding this delightful piece of music.

Standing by itself, it is a little gem. It is full of surprises. In construction it resembles a short sixteen-measure scherzo with a trio and a coda. The first four measures for left hand alone, written in impeccable two-part polyphony and fraught with tension by syncopation and suspensions, are answered in the right hand over a pedal point in the left. How subtle Beethoven is to start a crescendo when the right hand enters, which would lead our ears to expect its climax at the cadence in the last bar, then to deny that satisfaction by prescribing a sudden piano at that exact point. The second eight measures reverse the procedure and also heighten the interest with double counterpoint. Here, however, Beethoven allows the crescendo to reach its climax in the final bar but somewhat dims its effect by having a feminine cadence, that is, resolving the chord not on the first beat but on the second. Incidentally, these feminine cadences are almost a trademark of Beethoven's last style, suggesting as they do complete repose. The Diabelli variations, the Sonata, Opus 109, the String Quartet, Opus 127, and the second movement of the Ninth Symphony are but a few examples that come to mind.

This particular feminine ending is "corrected" in a witty manner in the coda. Here Beethoven, after repeating it twice more forte in two different registers, answers it by two soft chords in a still lower octave suggesting a quiet cadence in that register. But he again denies even this satisfaction by flippantly repeating it in that register. Then by a rhythmic trick of speeding up still another repetition, he shifts the emphasis of the dominant chord so the tonic chord comes on the downbeat. It is a musical subtlety forecasting his mature third style.

The trio too is quite sophisticated by seeming to be in A minor because of its running bass, but proving to be in C major. Or, rather, Beethoven begs the issue of key by leaving the trio suspended in mid-air on a dominant-seventh chord, which, after a pregnant silence, is followed by the recapitulation of the Scherzo proper.—THOMAS K. SCHERMAN

IV. ANDANTE GRAZIOSO IN F, WoO 57

The lovely Andante grazioso con moto in F major was published without an opus number, May 1806. It will be found in Breitkopf's collection of *Kleinere Stücke für das Pianoforte.*

This work has a delicacy of touch that ought to ensure its being better known. It is an exquisite piece of painting, slightly lost in too large a frame; its dreamy languor shows how young Beethoven's heart was even at that date. But the second motive, repeated three times, has in its outline and the variations of its accompaniment, the values of which vary from the [eighth note to sixteenth and thirty-second notes], a hint of the heroic fanfare of the andante of the C minor symphony. And in the coda there is an abrupt modulation from F major to G flat minor the lovely melancholy shadow of which evokes the *Wehmut* of one of the songs to *The Distant Beloved.* I have no doubt that Beethoven put into this andante many of his more intimate emotions at this period of his life. Dare I say that this is perhaps why he sacrificed it? Too little notice has been taken of an extraordinary fact—the extended slow movements into which Beethoven poured the deepest depths of his heart, those adagios and largos that were the jewels of his first twenty sonatas and were the special delight of the public of the time, afterwards disappear from his piano sonatas. Either he dispenses with them altogether or he drastically cuts the proportions of them down, reducing them to the role of an introductory link to the finale. It is not until we come to the monumental adagio of Opus 106, fourteen years later, that we meet again, in the piano music, with those soliloquies the gates of which are closed to the external world. It is as if in the maturity of his classical age Beethoven stood on guard against his natural propensity toward sentimental expression. From the *Waldstein* onwards to Opus 106 he reduces the confidences of his adagios to the minimum.—ROMAIN ROLLAND (2)

V. "FÜR ELISE," WoO 59

This small occasional piece, sometimes called *"Albumblatt für Elise,"* has also been described (in the list of Beethoven's works in Grove's Dictionary, for instance) as another bagatelle. The former name meets the case more adequately, the composition being written "for remembrance," as Beethoven wrote at the head, but the latter does well enough, since he also called his bagatelles *"Kleinigkeiten"* (trifles), and this is very much of the same size and in the same vein.

Who "Elise" was has never been definitely settled. Emerich Kastner, the editor of a selection of Beethoven letters, suggested the singer Elise Keyser; but as Theodor Frimmel, in his *"Beethoven-Handbuch,"* points out, a song rather than a piano piece would surely have been inscribed to a vocalist. Frimmel inclines more toward the view of Max Unger, who thinks that the dedicatee was Therese Malfatti, with whom Beethoven was in love at the time this piece was written (April 27, 1810). "Elise," according to Unger, may be a misreading for Therese, to which Frimmel tentatively agrees by giving instances of similar mistakes, though he points out that Unger disregards the fact that former owners of the manuscript explicity stated that the piece was not addressed to Therese Malfatti. The fact remains, however, that the autograph was found among the papers of Therese von Drossdick, nee Malfatti, after her death. Another ms. of it, which is no more than a sketch, is in the Beethoven house at Bonn.

The piece is a miniature rondo with two episodes.—ERIC BLOM (2)

VI. *"Ziemlich Lebhaft"* (*Klavierstück*) IN B FLAT, WoO 60

Like the more familiar, *"Für Elise,"* this short piece is an *Albumblatt,* written on August 14, 1818, for a young lady named Marie Szymanowski. It was first published in 1824 by Schlesinger in Berlin; whether Beethoven authorized its publication or not is not known. A second edition the following year bore the title "Impromptu Composed at the Dinner Table," and an edition published in 1840 bore the inaccurate legend "Beethoven's last musical thought." The ethics of music publishers have improved somewhat since then.—JACKET NOTES FOR TURNABOUT TV 34162

VII. MINUET IN E FLAT, WoO 82

This piece was published at Vienna in 1805, but is tentatively dated 1783 by Grove and others. The early date is credible, for, although it is a composition remarkably serious in tone for a boy of thirteen, it shows nothing that cannot be confidently placed in the eighteenth century.

Here again there is no need to quote the opening strain. [But] the beginning of the second part is worth [noting] for its interesting suspensions and its attempts at strict four-part writing—[it is almost as adroit as the remarkable Mozart minuet in D, K. 594,[1] composed seven years later (in 1790)].

The main section of the minuet, both parts of which are of course repeated, is written in regular four-bar periods, except for two bars interpolated before the return of the chief theme in the second part. But

[1] The minuet used by Tschaikowsky in his fourth orchestra suite (Mozartiana), Opus 61.—Editor.

in the trio Beethoven is metrically as free as Haydn, from whom indeed we may take it that he learned the value of irregular periods, particularly as applied to minuets, of which there are hundreds in Haydn's symphonies, quartets and sonatas, and where it was thus essential to avoid rhythmic sameness. The first part of Beethoven's trio proceeds by two six-bar periods; in the second there is first a thematic period of five bars, then a group of three transitional bars, followed by a conclusion in seven bars.

The key of the trio is A flat major—subdominant. This is in itself original, and the music as such is very characteristic. The theme slips into the left hand at the seventh bar, while the right hand instantly adjusts its matter from the previous left-hand accompaniment, in a way that shows the born composer unmistakably. In character the trio is rather closer to the country-dance type than the more courtly and formal minuet; and here one thinks not so much of Haydn as of Mozart, whose minuet trios have a marked tendency to approximate to the German dances and country dances of which he wrote a large number during the later stages of his career, and which on the one hand derived from the Austrian folk dance, the *Ländler*, and on the other pointed forward to the waltzes of Schubert, Lanner and the Strauss family.—ERIC BLOM (2)

VIII. 6 ECOSSAISES FOR PIANO (ALL IN E FLAT), WoO 83

Time of Composition: 1806? There is a probability, even a likelihood, that these écossaises were not originally composed for piano but were transcriptions of orchestra dances and are portions of the twelve écossaises that were published by Johann Traeg for two violins, two flutes, two horns (ad lib.), and bass, according to an advertisement in the *Wiener Zeitung* of March 21, 1807, and were quoted in a piano arrangement. The piano transcription ("12 Ecossaises for Pianoforte") also appears in Artaria's Catalogue of Beethoven's Work as Opus 106 [sic!]. *Autograph:* unknown.
GEORG KINSKY, EDITED BY HANS HALM (TR. BY THOMAS K. SCHERMAN)

The reason all six of the short écossaises are in E flat is that collectively they make one continuous composition. The second sixteen measures of the first écossaise act as a refrain. At the end of all of the succeeding dances (all of sixteenth-measure duration) there is the indication "Da capo al segno," the sign being at the beginning of the refrain. Thus the entire series becomes a primitive form of rondo. The refrain itself, with its rising line and its Scottish snap, has a delightful, impish quality. —Editor.

Music for Voice

I. MASSES AND ORATORIOS
a. "Christus am Ölberge," Opus 85

On April 5, 1803, the thirty-two-year-old Beethoven gave a concert of his own music at Vienna's Theater an der Wien. The program contained four large works: the *Symphony No. 1*, the *Symphony No. 2*, the *Piano Concerto No. 3*, and the oratorio *Christus am Olberge*—of which all but the *First Symphony* were receiving their first public performance. Although Beethoven himself played the piano in the *C minor Concerto*, the undoubted hit of the occasion was the oratorio, which was to be repeated in Vienna three times within one year. By 1814 oratorio-demented England had heard a performance of *Christus am Olberge* which had netted the clever impresario, Sir George Smart, something like one thousand pounds. The text, however, offended English taste, largely because one of the singers represented Jesus, and it was not long before the music became epidemic at choral festivals throughout England as sung to an English text entitled *Engedi, or David in the Wilderness*, which had less than nothing to do with the words Beethoven had set or with the character and profile of his music. Sometime after the middle of the century, the popularity of *Christ on the Mount of Olives* began to recede, and by our time the only part of it which remains familiar is its concluding chorus, often referred to as "Beethoven's 'Hallelujah Chorus.'"

Beethoven's only oratorio was composed in something of a hurry, though it seems likely that he had been preparing himself for it over a period of several years. The text was written, with much help and prodding from the impatient composer, by Franz Xaver Huber, a popular opera-librettist of the time, who closely followed the narratives of the Evangelists in the German Bible. The two men spent fourteen days at this thankless task, and then Beethoven swept through the labor of composition at high speed, completing the oratorio during 1800. Although it was successful in 1803, and was repeated many times thereafter, it was not published until 1811, by which time Beethoven had rather come to dislike it (he did not even bother to dedicate it to anyone).

There can be no doubt that *Christus am Olberge* is in some respects a curious work. For example, the idea of having Jesus sing a duet with a seraph remains somewhat strange. But neglect of the oratorio by our choral and orchestral societies cannot be justified. For it contains much truly Beethovian music of the period of the *"Eroica"* *Symphony* and *Fidelio*. If the whole piece were listened to often enough, more of it than the concluding chorus would certainly achieve familiar popularity.

The entire text of *Christus am Olberge* is given below, [in] a literal English translation.

1. *Orchestral introduction; recitative and aria* (JESUS)

JESUS: God, Thou my Father! O send me comfort and force and strength. The hour of my suffering draws near, already chosen by me even before the world burst forth from chaos at your command. I hear the thunder-voice of Thy Seraph. She demands one to place himself in man's stead before Thy judgment. O Father, I appear at Thy call. I wish to be the reconciler, I, I alone to atone for man's guilt. How can this race, made out of dust, bear a judgment that presses me, Thy son, to the ground? Oh see, how dread, how fear of death, strongly grips my heart. I suffer greatly, O my Father; oh see, I suffer greatly; have mercy upon me. *Aria:* My soul is shattered from the torments, from the torments that threaten me; fear takes me, and my being shudders horribly. Like an ague, anxiety grips me, anxiety over the nearby grave, and from my face, instead of sweat, blood drips, instead of sweat, blood, blood. Father! deeply bowed and weeping, Thy son prays to Thee, to Thee; all is possible to Thy power; take, take the cup of sorrow from me, take the cup of sorrow from me.

2. *Recitative; aria* (SERAPH), *with* CHORUS OF ANGELS

SERAPH: Tremble, earth. God's son lies here, His face pressed deep into the dust, completely forsaken by His Father, and suffers unending torment. The Good One! He is ready to die the martyr's utter death so that man, man whom He loves, may be resurrected from death and live eternally, eternally. *Aria:* Praise, praise the goodness of the Liberator, man, praise His grace. He dies for you out of love, for you out of love. His blood, His blood wipes out your guilt; praise, man, praise his grace. O hail to thee, you who are released, to you peace beckons if you are loyal in love, in belief, and in hope. But woe to those who dishonor the blood that flowed for them; the curse of the Judge will strike them; damnation is their lot.

3. *Recitative; duet* (JESUS, SERAPH)

JESUS: O Seraph, does your mouth announce to me the mercy of my eternal Father? Does he remove the fear of death from me? SERAPH: Thus saith the Lord: Before the holy secret of absolution is fulfilled, so long does the race of man remain condemned and deprived of eternal life. *Duet.* JESUS: So, then, O my Father, let Thy judgment rest upon me with complete severity, with all its severity, O my Father. Pour over me the stream of suffering, only do not be angered with Adam's children, do not be angered. SERAPH: Shaken, I see the Exalted One enveloped in death's suffering. I tremble, and the terror of the grave which He feels encircles me. JESUS, SERAPH: Great are the torments, the anxiety, the fears, which God's hand pours upon Him, but greater, greater yet, is His love, with which His heart encloses the world.

4. *Recitative* (JESUS); CHORUS OF SOLDIERS

JESUS: Welcome, death, which for the healing of mankind I undergo, bloody on the cross! O be blessed in your cool cave, ye whom an eternal sleep holds in his arms, ye will joyfully awaken to happiness. CHORUS OF SOLDIERS: We have seen him walking along this mountain; he cannot escape; the judgment waits for him.

5. *Recitative* (JESUS); CHORUS OF SOLDIERS; CHORUS OF DISCIPLES

JESUS: Those who have come out to capture me come near. My Father! O let the hours of suffering go by me in a quick flight, let them fly quickly to Thy heaven as the clouds that a storm-wind drives. Yet may not my will, no, but Thy will only, be done. CHORUS OF SOLDIERS: Here he is, here he is, the condemned one, who to the people boldly names himself King of the Jews. . . . Seize and bind him. . . . CHORUS OF DISCIPLES: What is the meaning of this uproar? It has happened because of us! Surrounded by rough soldiers, what will befall us? Mercy, mercy. . . . CHORUS OF SOLDIERS: (repetition).

6. *Recitative* (PETER, JESUS); *trio* (PETER, JESUS, SERAPH); CHORUS OF SOLDIERS; CHORUS OF DISCIPLES; CHORUS OF ANGELS

PETER: Not unpunished does the insolent mob with impudent hands seize Thee, Thee the Exalted One, my Friend and Master. JESUS: O let your sword rest in its scabbard. If it were the will of my Father to rescue me from the power of mine enemies, then legions of angels would be prepared to save me. PETER: In my veins righteous anger and wrath churn. Let my vengeance grow cool in the determined blood. JESUS: You shall not practice vengeance! I taught you only to love all people, to forgive your enemies willingly. SERAPH: Mark, O man, and hear: Only a mouth of God will speak holy teaching of the love of neighbor, only a mouth of God speaks such holy teaching. SERAPH, JESUS: O child of man, understand this holy command: love him who hates you; only so, only so, will you please God. PETER: (repetition). JESUS: (repetition). SERAPH, JESUS, PETER: (repetition). CHORUS OF SOLDIERS: Up, up, seize the betrayer; stay here no longer; away now with the evil-doer; drag him quickly to judgment. CHORUS OF DISCIPLES: O, because of him we shall also be betrayed hatefully. They will bind us, make martyrs of us, and sacrifice us to death. CHORUS OF SOLDIERS: (repetition). CHORUS OF DISCIPLES: (repetition). CHORUS OF SOLDIERS: (repetition). JESUS: My torment is quickly vanished; the work of release is accomplished; the power of Hell is soon conquered and put down. CHORUS OF SOLDIERS: (repetition). CHORUS OF DISCIPLES: (repetition). CHORUS OF ANGELS: Sing, worlds; sing, worlds—thanks and honor to the exalted Son of God. Praise him loudly, you angel choruses, in holy tones of joy. . . .—HERBERT WEINSTOCK

The oratorio is scored for soprano, tenor, and bass soloists, four-part chorus, and an orchestra consisting of two flutes, two oboes, two clarinets, two bassoons, two horns, two trumpets, three trombones, timpani, organ, and strings.

b. Mass for Four Solo Voices, Chorus, and Orchestra, Opus 86
I. *Kyrie* (Andante con moto assai vivace quasi allegretto ma non troppo); II. *Gloria* (Allegro con brio); III. *Credo* (Allegro con brio); IV. *Sanctus* (Adagio); V. *Benedictus* (Allegretto ma non troppo); Vi. *Agnus Dei* (Poco andante)

The Mass in C major, composed in 1807 at the request of Prince Esterházy and designed for normal liturgical use, bears the imprint of Catholic custom but is nevertheless a direct approach by Beethoven to the words set.

It shows how far he had traveled as man and musician since 1800. His creative powers had matured—he was at work on the C minor Symphony—and his spiritual understanding had quickened. Where his honesty has once betrayed him into the religious crudities of the *Mount of Olives*, that same honesty now led him to study the text of the Mass free from any dogmatic or ecclesiastical intermediation between himself and his Maker. Given such a mind as Beethoven's, the results were bound to be remarkable. "I do not like to say anything about my Mass or myself," he wrote to Breitkopf, "but I believe I have treated the text as it has seldom been treated." He was perfectly right. Looking at his Mass today, we can see that the familiar words had become translucent for him to the truths behind. His setting followed the words and painted their ideas with extraordinary fidelity. At the same time he strove for a musical design that should evolve logically, without depending on the verbal clauses to make it intelligible. The Mass, in fact, was to be as self-sufficing as a symphony or sonata. It was planned on a noble scale for a quartet of solo singers, chorus and full orchestra —a decision justified by the ample resources of the Esterházy musical establishment. Unfortunately there is reason to believe the rehearsals were grossly inadequate, so when the Mass was performed on 13th September 1807 it was a fiasco. "But my dear Beethoven, what is this you have done now?" quizzed Prince Esterházy. Hummel, standing by, smiled. The Esterházy family taste in masses was distinctly "tuney." But Beethoven believed the smile had been directed at himself. It hurt atrociously.

The Esterházy entourage was not altogether wrong in detecting the experimental element in the Mass in C. But our business now is to revalue the Mass both for its own sake and for the light it brings to Beethoven's *Missa Solennis* and his still later works.

On the constructional side the Mass in C is divided into the customary movements, the Osanna being repeated after the Benedictus. During the first three numbers, the Kyrie, Gloria and Credo, Beethoven employs the key of C major, as the point of departure and arrival, but the modulations within those movements follow a different circle in each case. Then, as if to show the change to some condition above the earth, he sets the Sanctus and Osanna in A major, while between them comes the Benedictus in F major—a favorite key with him to express tranquillity and blessedness. For the Angus Dei he uses C minor, and comes back to C major for the "Dona nobis." But to confirm the scheme he does a thing which is an aesthetic and psychological master-stroke: he repeats the pleading music with which the mass had opened on the words "Kyrie eleison" as a coda to the whole work on the supplication "Dona nobis pacem." Thus he unified the work and linked its emotional sequence into a perfect circle. Here was the principle of his *Liederkreis*, applied nine years ahead of the time when he is said to have invented it.

This rounding of the work was all the more valuable that the relative proportions of the movements were not quite perfect. But the choral writing in the Mass in C is more feasible for singers than that of the *Missa Solennis*, and the orchestration is beautiful. The instruments take their part beside the chorus almost like living creatures. It is possible that the loveliness and depth of Beethoven's intentions were a little greater than the thematic material in which he expressed them, but every movement of the mass has wonderful beauties. Note the Kyrie, in which the first long-phrased melodies are followed by short points of imitation and brief ever-shifting modulations, as if Beethoven looked out and saw imploring hands lifted everywhere over the world beseeching help. The broad diatonic harmonies and the stability of the choral writing in the following Gloria give a wonderful impression of the unchanging eternal strength of God. Beethoven's close illustration of the text is seen at his setting of the words "Laudamaus te, benedicimus te, adoramus te, glorificamus te," where at "adoramus" he bows himself down clean out of C major into the chord of B flat major. (The Victorians called it a Gothic progression!)

For the "Qui tollis" Beethoven goes into F minor—a key which he seemed to associate with suffering and punishment borne by the innocent, since he used it in *Fidelio* for Florestan and in the overture to *Egmont*. At the words "Qui sedes ad dexteram Patris" he reduces the voices from four-part harmony to octaves for the first time, as if to show the oneness of Christ with God, and thereafter throughout the work, octaves or unison are often employed in connection with the idea of God as the One, for example, at the words "Quoniam tu solus sanctus" and later in the Credo at "Deum verum de Deo vero."

Up to the "Quoniam" the style has been mainly melodic and harmonic, with some canonic imitation, but at the words "Cum Sancto Spiritu," Beethoven introduces a movement in fugal style which is developed with brilliant effect. The Credo, musically very fine, is psychologically profoundly interesting. If the descending phrases at "descendit" might have been done by any composer, no one except Beethoven would have set the "Et incarnatus" thus, with so much meaning in such subtle simplicity. As if to make his progressions clearer, he allots this section to solo voices. The poignancy of the harmony in the orchestra at the words "et homo factus est" gives an indescribable impression of Beethoven's view of manhood—just as if he said: " 'Tis glorious misery to be born a man"—and the extraordinary slither of semitones at "sub Pontio Pilato" (like water falling away) expresses Beethoven's contempt for Pilate's despicable weakness. The fugal element reappears briefly at "Et resurrexit" and at the "Et vitam venturi saeculi, Amen," a great choral fugue rolls forward on glorious waves of melody.

This association in Beethoven's mind between the idea of Life Everlasting and fugue as its musical symbol is not a mere chance, nor even a secondhand acceptance of the practice of other composers who had introduced fugal writing at this point. I am convinced he adopted it deliberately. Beethoven never accepted anything for his great works to which he could not subscribe with his whole being. Fugue and invertible counterpoint offered him material almost as sure as the progesssions of pure mathematics. For example, the interval of the perfect fifth when inverted can only produce the perfect fourth and vice versa; the major third can only become a minor sixth, and so on. Musically, therefore, fugue would be right as the symbol for Beethoven's conception of the life of the world to come, and metaphysically he was right in identifying that life with God "in knowledge of whom standeth our eternal life," as the collect says.

The Sanctus is a short movement like a sojourn in heavenly peace. It contains beautiful harmonic textures, and an enharmonic modulation so characteristic of Beethoven [where an F sharp chord changes its meaning from the V of B minor to the VI flat of B flat major].

The Benedictus is a long flowing movement, beautifully orchestrated;

the Agnus Dei is heartfelt; the "Dona nobis" contains an almost too graphic passage in which the voices mutter antiphonally "miserere, miserere," and the mass ends—as I have already said—with a return of the lovely melody with which it had opened.—MARION M. SCOTT

The mass is scored for soprano, alto, tenor, and bass soli, four-part chorus, two flutes, two oboes, two clarinets, two bassoons, two horns, two trumpets, timpani, strings, and organ.

c. "Der glorreiche Augenblick," *Cantata for Four Solo Voices, Chorus, and Orchestra, Opus 136*
I. Chorus ("*Europa steht*"), Allegro ma non troppo; II. Recitative ("*O seht sie nah*"), Andante, and Chorus ("*Vienna!*"), Allegro; III. Recitative ("*O Himmel, welch Entzücken!*"), Allegro, and Aria ("*Alle die Herrscher darf ich grüssen*"), Allegro ma non troppo; IV. Recitative and Cavatina with Chorus ("*Dem die erste Zähre*"), Sostenuto; V. Recitative (*Der den Bund im Sturme festgehalten*"), Allegro, and Quartet ("*In meinem Mavern baven*"), Allegretto; VI. Chorus ("*Es treten hervor die Scharen der Braven*"), Poco allegro

Beethoven did not get to the country for any lengthy sojourn [in the] summer [of 1814]; he had only a brief stay at Baden. The Congress of Vienna was originally scheduled to meet on August 1 but was postponed until the early fall. That Beethoven was bearing this congress and its visiting dignitaries in mind is shown by the next series of "occasional compositions."

Next to Opus 90 in the "Fidelio" sketchbook are a few hints for "*Ihr weisen Gründer*," which, though called a "cantata" in the sketchbook, is but a chorus with orchestra—a piece of flattery intended for the royal personages at the coming congress. It was not finished until September 3. This was the only work which Beethoven now had on hand suitable for a grand concert, but he was working on others. Over the title of the manuscript of "*Ihr weisen Gründer*" is written in pencil by him: "About this time the Overture in C." This work, what was to be called the "*Namensfeier*" Overture, he now had in hand.

At the same time he was working on a vocal composition of some length. The eventual result would be *Der glorreiche Augenblick*, with text by Alois Weissenbach, but at this point he was attempting to set a text whose author, whoever he was, must have profoundly studied and heartily adopted the principles of composition as set forth by Martinus Scriblerus in his "Treatise of Bathos, or the Art of Sinking in Poetry": for anything more stilted in style, yet more absurdly prosaic, with nowhere a spark of poetic fire to illuminate its dreary pages, is hardly conceivable.

A short excerpt from the body of the text will suffice:[1]

ALLE STIMMEN
Hört ihr klirren der Knechtschaft Ketten?
Hört ihr seufzen des Ebro Fluth?
Seht die Donau Ihr roth von Bluth?
Wer soll helfen? ach, wer soll retten?

ALL VOICES
Hear ye the clang of captives' chains?
Hear ye the sighs of the Ebro's flood?
See ye the Danube red with blood?
Who shall succour? who wipe up the stains?

ERSTE STIMME
Und Karl, aus Habsburg altem Haus
Zog, Gott vertrauend, gen ihn aus.
Wo Habsburg schlug am Donaustrand

Da schlug er ihn—und Oestreich stand.

FIRST VOICE
And Karl of Habsburg, ancient line,
Battled with trust in God divine.
Where Habsburg struck on the Danube's strands
There struck he him and Austria stands.

ZWEITE STIMME
Und Wellington, der Spanier Hort,
Zog, Gott vertrauend, get ihn fort,
Und bey Vittoria schlug er ihn,
Dass schmachvoll heim er musste fleih'n.

SECOND VOICE
And Wellington, the Spanish hoard,
Battled against with trust in the Lord,
And at Vittoria struck them he
Till home with shame they had to flee.

DRITTE STIMME
Die heil'ge Moskwa flammet auf,
Der Frevler stürzt in Siegeslauf;
Porussia sieht, die Völker sehn der Freyheit Gluth,
Und Moskwa gleich flammt Aller Muth.

THIRD VOICE
Holy Moscow burst in flame,
The villain plunged ere victory came;
Prussia sees, the people see Freedom's glow,
And Moscow's flames to all courage show.

(and so forth, *ad nauseam*)

Beethoven announced a grand concert for November 20 in the large Redoutensaal, but advertisements in the *Wiener Zeitung* of the eighteenth postponed it till November 22, then till the twenty-seventh, and finally till the twenty-ninth. On November 30, the newspaper reports: "At noon yesterday, Hr. Ludwig v. Beethoven gave all music lovers an ecstatic pleasure. In the R. I. Redoutensaal he gave performances of his beautiful musical representation of Wellington's Battle at Vittoria, preceded by the symphony which had been composed as a companion piece. Between the two works an entirely new . . . cantata, *Der glorreiche Augenblick.*" One would like to know what Beethoven said when he read this; for the symphony supposed by the writer to be composed as a companion piece (*Begleitung*) to the "Wellington's Victory" was the magnificent Seventh!

[1] Text given by Wilhelm Virneisel, "Kleine Beethoveniana," in *Festschrift Joseph Schmidt-Görg zum 60 Geburtstag*, ed. Dagmar Weise (Bonn, 1957), pp. 363–64.

The solo singers in the cantata were Mme. Milder, Dem. Bondra, Hr. Wild, and Hr. Forti, all of whom sang well, and Mme. Milder wonderfully. "The two Empresses, the King of Prussia" and other royalties were present and "the great hall was crowded. Seated in the orchestra were to be seen the foremost virtuosi, who were in the habit of showing their respect for him and art by taking part in Beethoven's Akademies." All the contemporary notices agree as to the enthusiastic reception of the symphony and the battle, and that the cantata, notwithstanding the poverty of the text, was, on the whole, worthy of the composer's reputation and contained some very fine numbers. The concert, with precisely the same program, was repeated in the same hall on Friday, December 2, for Beethoven's benefit—nearly half the seats being empty! And again in the evening of the twenty-fifth for the benefit of the St. Mark's Hospital, when, of course, a large audience was present. Thus the cantata was given three times in four weeks, and probably Spohr, who was still in Vienna, played in the orchestra; yet he gravely asserts in his autobiography that "the work was not performed at that time."—ALEXANDER WHEELOCK THAYER, EDITED BY ELLIOT FORBES

The finest of the new things was Beethoven's "Glorreicher Augenblick," a long cantata (three-quarters of an hour, choruses, solos, etc.) in honor of the three monarchs who met at the Vienna Congress. There are splendid things in it, among others a cavatina, a prayer, quite in Beethoven's grand style but with wretchedly stupid words, where "heller Glanz" is made to rhyme with "Kaiser Franz," followed by a great flourish of trumpets. And now Haslinger has actually put other words to it, and calls it the "Praise of Music," and these are even more wretched, for "poesy" is made to rhyme with "noble harmony," and the flourish of the trumpets comes in—still more stupidly. And so we spend our days in Germany . . .—FELIX MENDELSSOHN-BARTHOLDY

d. Duet for Soprano and Tenor with Orchestral Accompaniment: "Nei giorni tuoi felici," WoO 93

Those who believed that of the so far unprinted works of Beethoven the most worthy of note to be discovered would be among the "occasional" compositions and the smaller works such as canons and album remembrances and the like, would be thoroughly impressed that one of the more significant of his vocal compositions has been announced in the press on February 10, 1939, in Winterthur. Only a few Beethoven specialists knew of the very existence of that work—"Nei giorni tuoi felici," a duet for soprano and tenor with full orchestra accompaniment.

[Actually research discloses that] it was composed between the end of the year 1802 and the beginning of 1803, [which] signifies the conclusion of his studies in Italian vocal composition with Antonio Salieri. Many compositions of those years give evidence of the assiduity and zeal with which Beethoven pursued these studies: close on two dozen two- to four-part Italian *a cappella* songs,[1] the song with piano accompaniment "O *care selve antiche*,[2] the Scena ed Aria "No, *non turbati*" for soprano and string orchestra[3]—these represent only the most important items. Beethoven never made any attempt to have these compositions published, for he regarded them as mere student's exercises.[4]

The position regarding this duet is entirely different. In this work we meet Beethoven as a mature master who knows how to utilize his acquired knowledge and how to handle his material with complete independence of his teacher. This is attested to by the care with which he handled the orchestral accompaniment—it is scored for two flutes, two oboes, two bassoons, and two horns besides the usual strings. In it, one finds no trace of Salieri's "corrections." Beethoven's own high estimation of the work is best proved by the fact that as late as 1822 he offered it to the Viennese publisher S. A. Steiner.

[Hess here traces the copy of the orchestral and vocal score and the orchestral parts from that date up to the Second World War, when they were lost, although the autograph manuscript found its way to the Prussian State Library.]

In the winter of 1929/30 I discovered the autograph by Beethoven in the Prussian State Library. When the score was handed to me, I was astounded by the great bulk of a so-far-unprinted and thoroughly unknown work of Beethoven—it contained twenty-eight twelve-stave pages of which the last five were empty. I immediately realized the importance of making a clear copy for publication or performance.[5] It appeared to me that it was one of the more beautiful concert arias. The text by Metastasio is from his *Olimpiade* (Act I, Scene 10) [and consists of a dialogue between two star-crossed lovers]. The work opens with an Adagio in E major of wonderful charm and of chamber-musiclike polish. This closes [and leads without interruption] into a highly dramatic Allegro in E minor. Although in the first section there are perhaps reminiscences of Mozart (possibly the "*Porgi amor*" from Act II of *Figaro*), the second section with its [wide] breadth and its great exciting surges undoubtedly heralds the master of *Leonora-Fidelio*. "It is not saying too much,"

---

[1] Grouped by Kinsky-Halm collectively under the listing of WoO 99.—Editor.
[2] Song with unison chorus, with text by Metastasio from his *Olimpiade*, WoO 119.—Editor.
[3] See Hess's essay.—Editor.
[4] Many of them contain "corrections" in Salieri's hand.
[5] Actually this copy by Hess was used for a belated first performance in February 1939 in Winterthur, and later for a publication of the score and parts by the publisher E. Eulenburg.—Editor.

wrote Max Unger of the first performance in Winterthur, "that apart from his choral music and the aria 'Ah, perfidio,' it is the most important work for voice and orchestra from Beethoven's pen!"—WILLY HESS (8) (TR. BY THOMAS K. SCHERMAN)

It is interesting to note that, for publication, Beethoven crossed out the seven last bars of his manuscript (the orchestral coda, which bore little or no thematic relationship to the body of the allegro) and substituted a highly dramatic and musically much more relevant coda of six measures.—Editor.

e. "Ihr weisen Gründer," for Chorus and Orrchestra, WoO 95

This is one of several works (such as the Cantata "Der glorreiche Augenblick," Opus 136; the "Namensfeier" Overture, Opus 115; and the "Wellington's Victory" Symphony, Opus 91), which Beethoven composed for the congress of Vienna.[1]

The flowery text is by Josef Karl Bernard (1775–1850), an author and journalist who in 1815 became the editor of the Wiener Zeitung." (He was incidentally extremely helpful to Beethoven with advice during the court proceedings concerning Beethoven's nephew, Karl.)

The words are merely one after another praise of the deeds and decisions of the allied rulers "which will be felt by sons and grandsons for generations."

It is set for four-part chorus with orchestral accompaniment. The introduction and the accompaniment of most of the words feature the dotted rhythm, so associated with pomp and circumstance. There is a literal setting of the words "Aonen lang" ("aeons long")—the first time they appear at the close of a regular eight-bar phrase, but when they are repeated Beethoven has the unison chorus hold the single note for several measures while the orchestra stresses the ceremonious dotted accompaniment. The climax is a fortissimo fermata on the subdominant chord (shades of the "Ihr Millionen" section of the finale of the Ninth Symphony). In its present context the impressive chord graces the words "beglücklende Fürsten" ("blessed princes").—THOMAS K. SCHERMAN

II. SONGS WITH PIANO ACCOMPANIMENT
a. General Survey of Beethoven's Lieder

Lesser contemporaries of the great classical masters took up what Haydn had not had time to do, and it was first in the compositions of Anton Eberl, J. E. Fuss, Nikolaus von Krufft, as well as in the works, extending

---

[1] Among these works must also be included the Polonaise for Piano, Opus 89, dedicated to the Empress of Russia.—Editor.

well into the Beethoven period, of Hofmusikgraf Moritz Dietrichstein, that the songs of Vienna linked up fully with major German poetry, to which Beethoven then lent the most powerful musical effect.

The unlucky saying of E. T. A. Hoffmann, the poet and composer, that Beethoven, the born instrumental composer, was less successful in vocal music, ran through the last century like an *ignis fatuus*. It was only logical that this mistaken judgment, born of a romanticization of Beethoven, should only have disappeared in our times, along with the last residue of the romantic image of Beethoven. Today we see Beethoven's song style as the only thing it could be, conformably to the over-all attitude of the composer, as the perfection of the classical song.

Beethoven carries out what Mozart and Haydn could do only very incompletely for the classical song, and he could do so because he was the creative spirit standing at the summit of the total culture of his time. He, who was never oppressed by the narrowness of what was only musical, is fully responsible for the song as an artistic total organism and he left no doubt that he was ready to take the responsibility in full.

From his final classical peak he surveyed the entire domain of the song, from its new beginnings around the turn of the century. This holds true for the text as well as for the musical aspect. Beethoven wrote songs in all the forms of the time, both German and foreign; but, much more, he gave his song forms such a personal imprint that the generally typical aspect of form underlying it became all but insignificant.

In his choice of texts Beethoven often, quite consciously, took to poets of the second rank, for reasons that he did not conceal with reference to his favorites, Klopstock and Schiller, whom he seldom set to music. These poets started "from too high up," and left him, as a musician, too little freedom of movement.

In the motivation of his song writing, in his experiential urge and drive to making songs, there was in Beethoven a significant change from what had been normal for previous songs of the century. Love is not at all the basic motive of Beethoven's lieder. It was at least equally important for Beethoven to express fundamental ethical views in and through his songs. If his lieder are grouped according to the most important pillars of their content, those pillars would be ethics—fellow feeling—love. What is beyond that is of little weight.

For almost four decades, from the beginnings in Bonn down to the middle of his last period, the song was Beethoven's companion, having its full share in his general working and creative characteristics, as is shown by the sketchbooks. For him, the song is not a product of the moment, quickly thrown together, but it fights its way out of him with the same difficulty as the major works.

Among the evidences of his first major victory in song, the "Sechs Lieder von Gellert," Opus 48, have an important place. Anything Viennese-Southern is alien to these songs, which tower in almost North German-Prussian rigor and whose spare single-stanza form (except for the "*Busslied*," which has a large plan in several parts) give the lead entirely to the text. The element of declamation prevails in these songs, without the slightest borrowing from recitative; their inner greatness, which speaks most nobly in "*Die Himmel rühmen des Ewigen Ehre*," makes them worthy of being contemporaries of the "Eroica."

The path to the composition of the Goethe songs can be found in the accounts given by Bettina Brentano, where she speaks of Beethoven's relationship to Goethe's poems.

This Beethoven of Bettina's, spinning imaginings in words and sounds on Goethe's poetry, has this much in common with the real Beethoven: that he felt himself, as compared with the poet, only in the position of an equal creative spirit. Unassuming as he otherwise always is with respect to his knowledge, the name of Goethe, the idea of Goethe (who seemed to him the greatest jewel of the nation), called forth all the powers of his being, in readiness for highest art. When he sets poems by Goethe, he is not merely a song composer, he is Beethoven the musician—in the panoply of all his knowledge as a composer. Thus, from the height of musical greatness he had reached, he rushed in 1800 at the Lili song "*Neue Liebe, neues Leben*," on which he forced the laws of his great form, the sonata. Here are, in their main outlines, the forms on either side:

Beethoven	Goethe
Herz, mein Herz, was soll das geben?	Sonata form
Was bedränget dich so sehr?	Stanza 1: First theme and transition group.
Welch ein fremdes neues Leben!	
Ich erkenne dich nicht mehr.	
Weg ist alles was du liebtest,	
Weg warum du dich betrübtest,	
Weg dein Fleiß und deine Ruh —	
Ach, wie kamst du nur dazu?	
Fesselt dich die Jugendblüte,	Stanza 2: Verses 1 to 4: second theme.
Diese liebliche Gestalt,	
Dieser Blick voll Treu' und Güte	
Mit unendlicher Gewalt!	
Will ich rasch mich ihr entziehen,	Verses 5 to 8: third theme.
Mich ermannen, ihr entfliehen,	
Führet mich im Augenblick	
Ach mein Weg zu ihr zurück!	

— — — — — — — — — —
— — — — — — — — — —
— — — — — — — — — —
— — — — — — — — — —
— — — — — — — — — —
— — — — — — — — — —

Development:
(Short concentrated development on
the words *"Herz, mein Herz, was soll
das geben?"*)

Recapitulation:
Stanzas 1 and 2.

Und an diesem Zauberfädchen,
Das sich nicht zerreißen läßt,
Hält das liebe lose Mädchen
Mich so wider Willen fest;
Muß in ihrem Zauberkreise
Leben nun auf ihre Weise.
Die Veränderung, ach wie groß!
Liebe! Liebe! Laß mich los!

Stanza 3: Coda.

Despite Beethoven's masterful repetitions, no violence is done the poem
in this superimposition of an alien form, rather an artistic domination,
which transposes the poetical work of art from one peak of genius to another. Beethoven tried once more, in the song *"Mit einem gemalten
Band,"* to adapt Goethe's four-stanza form to the sonata (sonatina) form,
although less convincingly.

These songs in themselves are enough to show that the saying of Beethoven handed down by Friedrich Rochlitz, the writer on music, to the
effect that no poet can be "so well composed" as Goethe, can be merely
a momentary flash; and the settings from *Wilhelm Meister* prove this
even more. Although the statement may apply more or less for the music
to *"Kennst du das Land,"* whose varied stanza form is much less complicated than the poet assumed, it definitely does not hold true for
"Nur wer die Sehnsucht kennt." Beethoven struggled with this text in
four settings, with three different beats, in the obvious intention to
work out the utmost degree of a sculptural melody shape, in which every
word would have the correctness of tonality that hovered before him.
This effort already points to the songs that Beethoven too could have
called his "declamations," in which at the outset he used the familiar
means of recitative and aria. But finally, what in Bürger's *Seufzer eines
Ungeliebten und Gegenliebe*[1] had been no problem at all became a problem of creativity, which gave rise to songs of the highest order in
Goethe's *Wonne der Wehmut*, [Opus 83, No. 1, written in 1810], the
second setting of Tiedge's *An die Hoffnung* [Opus 94, written in 1813],
or the *Wachtelschlag* [WoO 129, written in 1803]. It is precisely the

[1] WoO 118, written in 1794.—Editor.

Wachtelschlag, which Hans Böttcher, in his special study of Beethoven as a song composer, calls a dramatic solo cantata that shows the overcoming of the old cantatalike characteristics by the genuinely Beethovenish means of the fusion of motifs into a total form. As he did soon thereafter in the first four measures of the Allegro con brio of the Fifth Symphony, Beethoven, in that song, states the basic material in the instrumental introduction, and out of it the entire song grows. It is no cantata, but a free-form Beethoven variation song! [It also] however is as a song of nature, a marvelous image and repetition in artistic creation of that creative basic process of nature brought to light by Goethe.—HUGO MOSER

b. Mignon: "Kennst du das Land?," Opus 75, No. 1

This is the first of six songs, the words by Goethe, for solo voice and pianoforte, published as Opus 75 and dedicated to the Princess von Kinsky. A pretty story connected with its early history is told by Bettina Brentano, afterward Bettina von Arnim, in a letter to Goethe. One day in May 1810, a young woman stole into Beethoven's room as he sat at his pianoforte, and placed her hands on his shoulders. The great composer, who had just finished writing a song, looked up with a scowl, but the cloud left his face when he saw the handsome Bettina, who put her lips to his ear and said: "My name is Brentano." She needed no further introduction. Beethoven reached out his hand to her without rising from his chair, smiled, and said: "I have just made a pretty song for you; do you want to hear it?" Then he sang "Kennst du das Land," in a harsh, penetrating voice, but with a passionate intensity that moved his listener deeply. "Well, how do you like it?" he asked. She nodded her appreciation. "Nicht wahr, it is beautiful, very beautiful—I'll sing it for you once more." And he sang it again, looked at his lovely visitor with a triumphant light in his eyes, and when he saw his own delight reflected in her features he rejoiced in her cheery approval. "Ah, ha!" he said, "most people are touched by a thing of beauty; but they are not artistic natures. Artists are fiery; they do not weep." And then he sang another song by Goethe: "Trocknet nicht Thränen der ewigen Liebe." In August of the same year Beethoven sent the young woman a copy of the song, with the words: "I send you 'Kennst du das Land' written with my own hand, as a souvenir of the hour when I made your acquaintance."

Very many composers have made musical settings of Goethe's exquisite romance (and that of the Frenchman, Ambroise Thomas, which becomes the motif of his opera Mignon, is by far not the least praiseworthy), but I know of none to be placed beside Beethoven's—certainly not Schubert's or Liszt's. Not only is the music beautiful in itself and the declamation natural and correct (while that of Liszt's setting is strained and perverted), but Beethoven seems to have based his treatment on Goethe's description of the manner in which the strange child sang the song before *Wilhelm Meister's* door—with breadth and solemnity in the beginning, mystery and reflection in the *"Kennst du es wohl?"*; irresistible longing in the *"Dahin, dahin!"* and petition and urgency alternating in the *"lass uns ziehn."* Read the description in the first chapter of the third book of *Wilhelm Meister's Lehrjahre*: *"Sie fing jeden Vers feierlich und prächtig an, als ob sie auf etwas Sonderbares aufmerksam machen, als ob sie Wichtiges vortragen wollte. Bei der dritten Zeile ward der Gesang dumpfer und düsterer; das 'Kennst du es wohl?' drückte sie geheimnisvoll und bedächtig aus; in dem 'Dahin, dahin,' lag eine unwiderstehliche Sehnsucht und ihr 'lass uns ziehn' wusste sie bei jeder Wiederholung dergestalt zu modifizieren, das es bald bittend und dringend, bald treibend und vielversprechend war."*

In the "Goethe Jahrbuch," vol. 22, page 262, Franz Kahn called attention to an error in the text of the romance (as proved by the only existing autographs) which seems to have been propagated since the first publication unless, indeed, it had the sanction of the poet himself. In the first stanza the line *"O mein Geliebter"* was originally written *"O mein Gebieter."*—H. E. KREHBIEL (1)

c. *"Neue Liebe, Neues Leben," Opus 75, No. 2*

No. 2 of the six songs to which *Mignon* belongs. The songs seem to have been composed about the same time. Beethoven sent *"Neue Liebe, neues Leben"* to Bettina Brentano, together with *Mignon* on August 11, 1810. In the letter accompanying the two songs he wrote: "I send you also the overture which I composed after I bade you farewell, dear, dear heart!

> Herz, mein Herz, was soll das geben,
> Was bedränget dich so sehr?
> Welch ein neues, fremdes Leben—
> Ich erkenne dich nicht mehr.

Now answer me, my dearest friend, and say what is to become of me since my heart has turned such a rebel."—H. E. KREHBIEL (1)

d. Goethe Songs, Opus 83

Opus 83, composed around 1810, contains three songs, the poems by Goethe. Nineteen—almost a quarter of Beethoven's songs—have texts by Goethe. Beethoven was the first musician to sense deeply the worth of these poems. The romantic stress of the highly personal finds illustration in a poem, *Wonne der Wehmuth*, born out of the sorrow of separation from Lili.[1] Goethe has expressed in these few lines what Beethoven had often experienced, tears of unhappy love. After exaltation, the sting of bitterness, and yet the pleasure of remembrance, is so great that the cry is for the tears to remain. Beethoven's great loneliness and his search for the "Immortal Beloved" well up through these lines in music that is filled with poignant beauty. The repeated phrase *"trocknet nicht"* takes but half a measure, the accompaniment continuing with a solo line of descending scale. In this song, so short of length, so great in value, the accompaniment in thirteen of the twenty-three measures rises to solo position. The voice and piano are true complements, in an interplay suggestive of Schumann. Yet within its short space we are led back to the first phrase in the home key (measure 16); so rich, however, is the inspiration that only one measure is an exact repetition. There is a quiet tenderness in the few measures of the coda; in its final measure, the descending scale motive of measure 1 sinks resignedly through to the tonic.—JAMES HUSST HALL

e. "In questa tomba oscura," WoO 133

This music of this song, sublimely solemn and beautiful in its expression of the sentiment of the underlying text, is one of the few examples of Beethoven's co-operation in a set task with other composers, its instrumental parallel being the famous variations for pianoforte on a waltz theme by Diabelli. It was composed in 1808, and formed the last of sixty-three settings of the poem written by Giuseppe Carpani, an Italian poet and writer on music, undertaken at the request of a lady of quality of Vienna. The compositions were published in 1808 in a volume bearing the title:

IN QUESTA TOMBA OSCURA. Arietta con Accomp. di Pianoforte composta in diverse maniere da molti Autori e dedicata a S. A. N. Sig. Principe Giuseppe di Lobkowitz, etc. Vienna, Pressa T. Mollo.

Amateurs as well as professional musicians contributed to this singular *olla podrida*, some of the latter with a number of settings. Beethoven was content with a single and simple treatment, but his is the only one that has lived, though Salieri, Sterkel, Cherubini, Asioli, Righini, Zingarelli, Weigl, Paër, and Czerny were among his pseudo competitors. Carpani was long a resident of Vienna and spent his last years in the Austrian capital as a pensioner of the emperor. He translated Haydn's *Creation* into Italian and wrote a charming book on the composer entitled *Le Haydine*, which was audaciously plagiarized by Henri Beyle, who

[1] Lili Schönemann (1758–1817), Goethe's first true love.—Editor.

published a French translation under the name of L. A. C. Bombet without credit to the author. I have attempted a new translation of the words of Carpani's song:

> Here, in the grave's dark portals,
>   Disturb not my repose.
> While I was 'mongst the living
>   You thought not of my woes.
> Within these gloomy shadows
>   Let my heart peace regain.
> Nor, ingrate, grieve my ashes,
>   By feigning sorrow's pain!

H. E. KREHBIEL (1)

In marked contrast [to the religious songs, Opus 48 (texts by Gellert)] is Beethoven's treatment of Carpani's text, "*In questa tomba oscura*," which appeared as the sixty-third and last in a volume of settings of the same text by different composers. Among others commissioned by a Viennese patroness to make their contribution to this strange volume were Cherubini, Salieri, and Zingarelli. "*In questa tomba oscura*" is the embittered cry of a spirit who seeks the peace of death and commands her who was faithless during his life to disturb not his ashes with her poisoned tears. The solemn tread of the first division recurs, but with a repeated "*in questa*" at the beginning and with a coda of a twofold "*ingrata*." After the repressed grimness of the opening, the middle section rises naturally to dramatic fervor, the rich dissonant chords of the accompaniment tremolando adding to the intensity of the emotion. The march of the bass starting in measure 7 on the tonic (original key A flat), reaching the dominant below two measures later, offers a bit of scoring that must have been due to the limited range of the piano of that day. Although the six octave piano (C_1–c'''') had appeared, more common were the five-and-one-half-octave instruments with F_1 the lowest note. Since, at the time, Beethoven could not in the original key go lower than the bottom F in the beginning of measure 8, he perforce breaks the tread of the bass octaves and has to be content with the single upper F flat. It seems legitimate here for accompanists to continue the octaves to the dominant.—JAMES HUSST HALL

III. FOLK SONG ARRANGEMENTS WITH ACCOMPAINMENT OF PIANO, VIOLIN, AND VIOLONCELLO

a. Beethoven and George Thomson

Among the less known works of Beethoven are a series of Scottish, Welsh and Irish tunes to which he set accompaniments and "symphonies," as the word was used a century and a quarter ago, to the order of

George Thomson, a zealous and enterprising musical amateur of Edinburgh. There are no fewer than 127 of these songs, plus three English and two Italian songs, that found their way into the collection, now published in the complete edition of Beethoven's works. They form a rather bulky part of Beethoven's output. To them he devoted a good deal of valuable time, extending over five years of his creative period. Thomson was not a publisher or a businessman; he was a clerk of the Board of Trustees for the Encouragement of Literature and Manufactures in Scotland. He was forced into the publishing business by the development of his plans to rescue the Scottish folk song. In one of his letters to Beethoven he burst out emphatically in answer to a letter of the composer in which he had spoken of Thomson as a "music seller": "Don't call me a music seller: I sell nothing but my national airs, and those wholesale." He formed ambitious schemes for the collection, arrangement and publication of Scottish, Welsh and Irish tunes—apparently in those days there was little thought of English folk tunes, and what there was, was to the effect that they were not worth publication. Thomson himself did some collecting, in Wales; but he displayed considerably more zeal than knowledge, from a modern point of view, in his treatment of the material.

His scheme was at first concerned with Scottish airs; he wished to "furnish a collection of all the fine airs, both of the plaintive and lively kind, unmixed with trifling and inferior ones: to obtain the most suitable and finished accompaniments, with the addition of characteristic symphonies to introduce and conclude each air, and to substitute congenial and interesting songs [i.e., words] every way worthy of the music, in the room of insipid or exceptionable verses." He had the right intention "to procure the airs in their best form," but realized a difficulty here, and thought that the "original" forms could not now be obtained. But he devoted a much larger amount of his energy and funds to getting his accompaniments and "symphonies" than would now be thought necessary or, indeed, at all desirable. Thomson, as also, no doubt, all the music lovers of his day, considered that the value of his tunes would be immensely enhanced by their "treatment" by some noted contemporary composer, no matter whether or not he had any special knowledge of the kind of folk song he was commissioned to deal with, or any special sympathy with it. He first engaged Ignaz Pleyel, one of the best known and popular composers of the day, whose music stood as high then as it stands low now in the estimation of music lovers, and then Leopold Anton Kozeluch, whose reputation has proved to be even more unstable.

With these collaborators Thomson began his activities about 1790. One of his first ideas for popularizing the Scottish tunes and extending a knowledge of them was to order from his distinguished composers sonatas in part based on such tunes as thematic material. He advertised in his first volumes of songs "Grand sonatas for pianoforte, the middle and last movements of which are founded upon Scottish subjects"—six each by Pleyel and Kozeluch. In these "the first movement of each sonata (the subject of the composer's fancy) forms a delightful variety contrasted with the familiar subjects of the middle and last movements. And the publisher flatters himself they will be found the most interesting works for the pianoforte which these composers have ever produced." Unfortunately, it will be difficult for the critic of the present day to come upon copies of these interesting works to enable him to judge and compare. In fact, the name of Kozeluch is not much more than a name to any at present; and that of Pleyel has come down to us as of one who turned to the manufacture of pianos after spending half his active life in the rather futile manufacture of music.

Pleyel soon gave out as a contributor to Thomson's undertaking; after a while the enterprising editor got Haydn, who had been doing the same thing for another publisher to take his place. With no little justified pride he announces that he was so fortunate as to engage "Dr. Haydn" to proceed with the work, "who, to the inexpressible satisfaction of the Editor, has all along wrought *con amore*." He quotes an optimistic expression conveyed to him by Haydn, in Italian: "I boast of this work and by it I flatter myself my name will live in Scotland many years after my death." Haydn's name lives still in Scotland; but there may be reasonable doubt as to how much his accompaniments to the Scottish songs have contributed thereto.

To help toward an understanding of the taste of the day, another quotation from Thomson's preface might be made. Haydn had been engaged to do only part of the songs. Should any ask, "why Haydn was not employed to do the *whole* work, the Editor would say that, though he himself idolizes Haydn, yet the public have long admired the other two composers also, whose style unquestionably possesses great sweetness, elegance, and taste; and that a greater variety is obtained from all than could have been expected from one of the composers."

It might also be added that in Thomson's estimation "the symphonies form an introduction and conclusion to each air, so characteristic, so elegant and so delightful, and comprise such a rich collection of new and original pieces, that they must be regarded by every musical amateur as an invaluable appendage to the airs." Nor should it be overlooked, as a final statement of Thomson's theory of folk song treatment, that "the accompaniments are admirably calculated to support the voice and to beautify the airs, without any tendency to overpower the singer. Instead of a thoroughbass denoted by figures, which very few can play with any propriety, the harmony is plainly expressed in musical notes, which every young lady may execute correctly. Here, therefore, the pianoforte will alone be found a most satisfactory accompaniment in chamber singing. At the same time, when the violin and violoncello are joined to the pianoforte, they certainly enrich the effect highly." In these first volumes the airs are printed with accompaniments and "symphonies" for the pianoforte alone. Those who desired the highly enriching effect of violin and violoncello could buy parts for those instruments separately and simply join the pianist.

Into this happy family Beethoven was finally invited to enter. It took Thomson a good while to get him; but when he finally did enter, it was something after the fashion of a bull in a china shop. By the beginning of the nineteenth century Beethoven's fame had reached Edinburgh; so that in the year 1803 Thomson wrote to order of him six of the same kind of sonatas that Pleyel and Kozeluch had so happily provided. But Beethoven's prices were higher than Thomson thought he could pay: "three hundred ducats [about £150] for six sonatas will not be too much," answered Beethoven, "seeing that in Germany they give me as much for the same number of sonatas even without accompaniment," *i.e.*, without violin and violoncello. He loved Scottish airs particularly, he said, and would take a special pleasure in the composition of such sonatas. The negotiations went no further then; and neither then nor later did Beethoven write any Scottish sonatas. It would be interesting to speculate what such sonatas from Beethoven's hands would have been like, had not Thomson's business prudence forestalled their composition. The two Rasoumoffsky quartets with movements derived from the Russian themes (Opus 59, Nos. 1 and 2) give the only clue for such speculation. There was apparently no question at that time of accompaniments and "symphonies" to songs to be written by Beethoven. The correspondence was dropped.

Haydn had been laboring valiantly with the songs, but he was getting old and was also beginning to suspect that Thomson was screwing him down a good deal in the matter of terms. He was ready to give up the commission. In 1806 Thomson again approached Beethoven, proposing the composition of six "easy and pleasant" string trios and six string quintets. Beethoven accepted for three of each; and in place of the other three proposed three quartets and two sonatas for "pianoforte with accompaniment"—that is, with violin—and a quintet with two violins and flute. For flute alone, or with pianoforte, he roundly declined to write, as Thomson seems to have asked him to do, because the flute was "too limited and imperfect." For all this Beethoven demanded £100. Thomson also asked him, at the same time, to do some Scottish songs, but Beethoven relegates this matter to a short postscript, in which he says he awaits "a more exact proposal"; meaning, evidently, a higher offer, for he adds that he knows well that Haydn was getting one pound per song.

But again nothing came of it; and not till three years later was there further parleying. Thomson this time sent Beethoven forty-three Welsh and Irish melodies with a request for a very speedy setting of them for pianoforte or pedal harp, violin, and violoncello, accompanying the voice. Beethoven was ready himself this time with his "exact proposal": asking £10 more than Thomson had offered—£60 instead of his £50. Thomson again wanted also quintets and sonatas, but again did not offer enough to tempt the composer. Beethoven was willing to do the songs, though the task was "no great pleasure for an artist," but realizing that there was in them "something useful for business." They finally came to an agreement about the terms for the songs and Thomson published the first Beethoven volume of his collection in 1814. He naturally expatiated with pride in his preface upon securing Beethoven's co-operation. He speaks of Haydn's death, and goes on:

> Of all composers that are now living, it is acknowledged by every intelligent and unprejudiced musician, that the only one who occupies the same distinguished rank with the late Haydn, is *Beethoven*. Possessing the most original genius and inventive fancy, united to profound science, refined taste and an enthusiastic love of his art—his compositions, like those of his illustrious predecessor, will bear endless repetition and afford ever new delight. To this composer, therefore, the Editor eagerly applied for symphonies and accompaniments to the Irish melodies; and to his inexpressible satisfaction, Beethoven undertook the composition. After years of anxious suspense, and teasing disappointment, by the miscarriage of letters and manuscripts, owing to the unprecedented difficulty of communication between England and Vienna, the long-expected symphonies and accompaniments at last reached the Editor, three other copies having previously been lost upon the road.

The correspondence went on for a number of years, during which Beethoven worked on a large number of songs. Delivery was always slow and uncertain, because of the wars and rumors of wars that distracted Europe in those years. There was incessant chaffering about terms, Thomson always pleading poverty and the impossibility of getting his money back from his publications, Beethoven always demanding more, generally double what Thomson thought right, or what he could afford. Talk about the instrumental pieces kept up; but, as we know, Beethoven never wrote, or apparently never seriously considered writing, anthing of the kind for Thomson.

One of Thomson's theories as to how the folk songs could be popularized involved getting many distinguished poets to write new words for them—a plan which mades the modern "scientific" collector writhe with anguish. Among his poets were Burns, Scott, Joanna Baillie, Mrs. Opie, Samuel Rogers, and several others whose names loomed larger a century ago than they do now. He had what seem now strange ideas about what the poets needed to guide them in fitting their verses to the airs, as well as what the musicians needed to fit their accompaniments and symphonies to them. Sometimes the poets knew nothing of the tunes and sometimes the musicians knew nothing of the texts. Sometimes Thomson sent the poet a line or a stanza of the original words that were to be superseded, as a model for rhythm and meter. In other cases the poet, as well as the musician, got only the tune and some indication of the tempo and character of the music, such as might be suggested by the words "allegro," or "moderato," or "affetuoso," or "scherzoso." Beethoven, in one of his letters, complains of the ambiguity of the word "andantino," which, he says, may mean either faster or slower than "andante." He is often quite dissatisfied with the sparing indications of the character of the songs he is to work on, and more than once asks for the complete words. In one letter, he says:

> I urgently beg you always to add the texts to the Scottish songs. I do not understand how you, who are a connoisseur, cannot understand that I should produce quite different compositions if I had the texts at hand; and that the songs never can become perfect products unless you send me the texts. Unless you do you will force me, in the end, to decline your commissions.

Thomson's ideas about "improving" the words of the songs strike the modern lover of folk song as peculiar. In a letter to Burns, proposing the task, he says he wants "the poetry improved for some charming melodies"; and declares himself in favor of verses in English instead of the Scottish vernacular, because "English becomes more and more the language of Scotland." Burns promptly accepted the invitation; but says he will accept no "wages, fee or hire," and would alter no songs unless he could "amend them"; and if his own were not approved, they could be rejected without offense: "I have long ago made up my mind as to my reputation of authorship," he writes to Thomson, "and have nothing to be pleased or offended at in your adoption or rejection of my verses." Thomson seems to have had the best of the arrangements with Burns, at any rate. He altered his verses when it suited him to do so, added stanzas, changed rhythms by inserting or removing words, and adapted verses to unauthorized tunes. Burns advised him to "let our native airs preserve their native features," but Thomson had the notion of the day that "improvement" was necessary.

Thomson's proceedings with Burns's poem "Scots wha hae wi' Wallace bled" were among those least to the modern taste. Burns contributed the poem to this collection; the tune is not one of those assigned to Beethoven for setting, as it was disposed of before he began to work for the Scottish editor. Burns wrote the verses to the old tune of "Hey tutti tattie" and in a letter to Thomson called them "a kind of Scots' ode, fitted to the air that one might suppose to be the gallant royal Scot's address to his heroic followers on that eventful morning"—that is, Bruce's to his followers before the battle of Bannockburn. But Thomson did not like the tune and considered it "utterly devoid of interest or grandeur"; so he adopted another one in his publication. As this was in a different meter, a foot had to be added to every fourth line of Burns's song! Burns seems to have had no remedy, and Thomson printed it in his own improved version three years after the poet's death. Then Thomson saw the light, after there had been an acrimonious public discussion, admitted his error, and in his next volume reprinted "Scots wha hae" with a note to the effect that the tune Burns had selected "gave more energy to the words" than his own choice. And so, thenceforth, the words have been married in the hearts and mouths of all Scotsmen to that tune.

The matter of prices was never dropped in the correspondence between Thomson and Beethoven, Beethoven always demanding more, Thomson always protesting that he could not pay so much. Beethoven refers to Haydn and what he was paid, or said he was paid—and, at that, "he wrote only for the pianoforte and one violin alone, without ritornellos and without cello." A charming touch is given in his reference to "Monsieur Kozeluch," who worked for lower prices; he ironically congratulates his correspondent thereon and also the English and Scottish publishers, if they liked that sort of thing. He values himself twice as much in this line as Monsieur Kozeluch (with the thoroughly Beethovenish parenthesis, "Miserabilis") and he hoped that Thomson could discriminate between them, which would enable him to do him, Beethoven, justice.

Thomson in his letters to Beethoven is also constantly urging him to greater simplicity in his writing. He realizes that there is not one of his accompaniments "but is marked with the stamp of genius, learning and taste. Certain of the accompaniments, however, will fail to please, because the taste of the public is not sufficiently refined to appreciate their excellence." Will Beethoven, therefore, oblige by altering here and there? Thomson is willing to grant extra pay for such changes. "Your great predecessor, Haydn, invited me to point out frankly everything which was likely not to please the national taste, and very readily altered all those to which I took exception." Thomson then specifies nine airs in which he thought alteration was necessary. Here is an instance: "In this song there is not one pianoforte player in a hundred who could make both hands go properly together in the first ritornello; I mean, play four notes with one hand and three with the other at the same time." In another case the "style" is complained of: "the accompaniment is brilliant and the runs totally unsuited to a tender and plaintive air." He apologizes for such candid criticism, "which is not from personal prejudice, but is only for the success of the work." In his next letter he still complains of the difficulties of Beethoven's writing: "there is not one young lady in a hundred who will do so much as look at the accompaniment, if it is ever so little difficult."

But Beethoven, alas! was not a Haydn. He was emphatically not willing to oblige; and having written a thing in his way, he intended that it should stay so. His answer ran: "I regret that I am unable to oblige you. I am not accustomed to tinker with my compositions!" But he did get so far as to rewrite the accompaniments and ritornellos of all the nine songs complained of—and sent in a bill for doing it, much to Thomson's disgust. "I am surprised at your re-writing nine ritornellos and accompaniments," was the answer he got, "and making me pay 27 ducats [about £13 10s.] when there were only three that needed re-writing. I never imagined you would have any objection to making the very slight alterations I desired in the other six airs."

Notwithstanding all these woes and misunderstandings, and though he found Beethoven a very different character from the docile Haydn, and still more different from the tame cats with whom he had begun his enterprise, Thomson persevered. He proposed to Beethoven an additional six English songs which he described as "ditties for young females." Beethoven never worked upon the ditties for young females. Whether in order to escape, or because his name and fame had by this time risen to greater financial values, he answered Thomson that he considered the honorarium he offered totally inadequate. Thomson thereupon burst out in indignation at what he considered Beethoven's "extortionate demands"—"nearly three times what you asked two years ago." Nothing daunted, Thomson in 1811 asked Beethoven to write not only more song accompaniments, but also a cantata based on James Thomson's "Battle of the Baltic," and an oratorio. Beethoven was ready to undertake the cantata for 60 ducats, and the oratorio for 600; but he made the condition that in the cantata there should be no unfriendly words about the Danes—as, in fact, there are not—and that the text of the oratorio should be "singulièrement bien fait." Nothing, of course, ever came of either.

Among the songs arranged by Beethoven are some of the best known of Scottish and Irish tunes, as: "Faithfu' Johnnie," "Bonnie Laddie," "Garyone" (twice), "Let Brainspinning Swains," "O Erin, to thy Harp Divine," "St. Patrick's Day," "The Banner of Buccleuch," "Auld Lang Syne," "God Save the King," "The Soldier" (better known to the words "The Minstrel to the Wars has Gone"), "O Sanctissima" (called "Sicilian Folk-Song," sung nowadays as a hymn-tune) and "Robin Adair." "Sally in our Alley" also appears, with the true English folk-tune to which Carey's words were adapted (and to which they are now sung) after his own air was abandoned about the middle of the eighteenth century. There are also several sets of simple variations for pianoforte alone, or with flute or violin, devised by Beethoven on airs of various nationalities, for Thomson's collections.

At this late day it is hard to see how the public of that time could have been so enamored of the accompaniments and "symphonies" of Pleyel and Kozeluch as Thomson says it was; or could have hesitated a moment between them and Haydn's. Both presented only the baldest possible outline of accompaniment, reduplicating the tune with "tum tum" chords in the bass. Even in many of Haydn's the right hand duplicates the air, but usually with some harmonic enrichment. The obstreperous Beethoven went to greater lengths in devising independent figures and in making his work of an independent artistic value, even to the extent of perplexing the young females of the day. But his accompaniments and ritornellos seem now, for the most part, pretty simple, little differentiated in accordance with the character of the song. There is often, or generally, an independent part, and by no means always a literal duplication of the tune. There is an effort to obtain a variety of figuration—no doubt the cause of some of Thomson's moans about the difficulty of the work. In the accompaniments for a trio, of pianoforte, violin, and cello, the strings do not as a rule double the pianoforte part, and there is something lost in presenting them for pianoforte alone, as Thomson did in his later quarto editions. All this should be said in justice to Beethoven, as well as to put in their places Pleyel and Kozeluch, who were so well matched to the musical stature of Thomson's young ladies. But it need not be supposed that Beethoven, after all, contributed much to Thomson's publications that he had great reason to be proud of. What Beethoven really thought of the business may be gathered from a remark he made in a letter to an Austrian friend, Hauschka, that he "had to do a lot scribbling for bread and for money"—the "scribbling" being, as Thayer interprets it, nothing other than his folk song arrangements for Thomson. It may be remarked that Beethoven prudently refrained from calling it "scribbling" in his letters to his Scottish correspondent. It seems today mostly hack work, though it may be the hack work of a genius; such work as almost any well-schooled conservatory pupil could do about as well. There is not much that seems to reflect or to intensify the spirit of the folk songs. It seems all too plainly to be work done with the composer's eye firmly fixed on the English pound sterling, which had so stable a value in days when values such as the "Wiener Währung" were crumbling; something "useful for business." In other words, to quote one of his own most withering remarks about an unfortunate contemporary, who was thereby swept out of consideration, he "wrote for money." There may be, of course, degrees in "writing for money," a difference in the degree to which money is the controlling factor. If Beethoven's own expressions, frequently recurring in his letters to Thomson, may be believed, he had a real interest in the Scottish folk songs. On the other hand, they seem to have made

little impression upon him as musical material; and he never referred
to them as anything to touch upon in his own compositions. This
Scottish episode in his life seems to have made only a transitory effect
upon anything except his bank account.—RICHARD ALDRICH

b. The Irish Songs

Irish national music, which we rather loosely designate as folk music,
has several sources, only a few of which are truly representative of the
people. The most ancient, patrician, and valuable of these is the work
of the bards. In their songs we find not only a major part of all Irish
melody, but also most of the bilingual heritage of Gaelic-into-English
poetry. Another source is also bardic in origin. It consists of nonvocal
harp tunes. These were jigs and reels for dancing, planxties for convivial
uses, and dirges for funerals. The most accessible source is represented
by the ballads, usually in English, which were so widely sung and heard
at fairs, in taverns, theaters, and on the streets, that they may truthfully
be called folk songs. In this group we find the familiar Cockles and
Mussels, Garryone, and The Wearing of the Green. The ballads are far
more modern than the songs or harp tunes of the bards, and, in general,
less distinguished musically and poetically. They are of significance chiefly
for the sometimes humorous, sometimes pathetic, and sometimes savagely
satirical comment they provide upon the fortunes or misfortunes of the
Irish peasantry.

Beethoven's Irische Lieder are derived from all three of these sources.

Curiously enough, one of the very few early bardic songs that can be
reliably accounted for as regards poem, tune, and composer, is the
familiar Eileen Aroon, which Handel was to admire. It is the work
of a 14th-century bard, Carroll O'Daly, who came of a family of bards
and who was "chief composer of Ireland and musical doctor of the
County of Corcomroe"—the County Clare of today. The second edition
of Grove's Dictionary contains an article by W. H. Grattan Flood on this
song in which it is related how, by a set of amusing circumstances,
Eileen Aroon "wandered" to Scotland and there became Robin Adair.

Eileen Aroon appears among Beethoven's Irische Lieder as do two
other medieval tunes. These are Summer is Coming and Paddy Whack.
Summer is Coming has caused a good deal of musicological controversy,
having been claimed by Irish scholars as the original version of Sumer
is icumen in, with British scholars, among them Burney, dissenting. In
Beethoven's arrangements Summer is Coming appears as Sweet Power
of Song, while Paddy Whack is transformed into English Bulls or The
Irishman in London.

The patrician Gaelic society to which the bard had chiefly addressed
his songs was virtually annihilated, as such, by the successive campaigns
of the Elizabethans and Cromwell and by the stand in Ireland of

James against William of Orange. To quote again from *The Irish* of Sean O'Faolain: "Irish literature in Gaelic, like the Irish aristocracy, had received in the 17th century, blows from which it never recovered. Being the literature of a caste, it must die with the caste."

As the great ruling families such as the O'Donnells and O'Neills of the north, and the O'Briens and O'Conors of the west, were scattered by exile, death, and bankruptcy, or dwindled into the frustrated existence of disenfranchised aristocrats, the status of the bard as court musician came also to an end. No longer a private performer, he became step by step a public institution.

The two most important figures of this period of transition are Rory Dall Cahan of the early 17th century and Turlough O'Carolan, who was born in the 1670s. Both, as was frequently the case with bards, were blind, because according to a later account, "At that period all harpers were blind, this profession having been humanely reserved for the sons of reduced gentlemen who happened to be blind, a calamity then much more common than at present, owing to improvements in the treatment of small pox."

Cahan, or O'Cahan, prudently left Ireland for Scotland, early in the 17th century, and there performed for the future James I of England. He was essentially a musician rather than a poet. His compositions include many lessons or "Ports" for the harp which he usually names, in characteristic Irish fashion, in honor of the patron for whom they had been written. At least one of these "Ports" has (also characteristically) strayed from its intended instrument into the vocal repertory. As *Lough Sheeling*, it inspired Robert Burns's *Ae Fond Kiss* and it is to be found in the *Irische Lieder* as a duet for tenor and bass called *Fare Well Bliss and Farewell Nancy*.

In Turlough O'Carolan we find the greatest, though not "the last," of the bards. He was a contemporary of Bach and Handel and, as such, can be said to belong both to the old Gaelic world and to the Anglo-Irish ascendancy of the 18th century. His career was a modification of the traditional role of the bard to a patrician household. As a gifted blind boy, he was patronized by the families of the west, and moved as an honored guest among the O'Conors and McDermotts of Roscommon— a life he pursued to a ripe and apparently bibulous old age. In fact, his planxties, dance tunes, and convivial songs were considered his forte. As a bard, he excelled in melody rather than poetry, with the result that we have over 200 of his tunes and only 30 poems.

To O'Carolan, Beethoven owes *The Elfin Fairies* (one of its composer's finest planxties), *I'll Praise the Saints*, and *Return to Ulster*.

So many tunes were composed, collected, and revived during the 18th century that it is impossible to comment on them in detail. There is, however, one tune or family of tunes that is especially interesting.

It is the song *Ned of the Hill,* which with its numerous variants is the tune from which *The Last Rose of Summer* was devised.

Ned of the Hill, whose composer is unknown, was sung in honor of Edmund Ryan, himself a bard who turned in the years after the defeat of the Boyne to the life of a Rapparee. The original tune soon gave rise to many variants such as *The Young Man's Dream* and *The Green Woods of Truagh.* Toward the middle of the century an absurd effusion in praise of a country estate called Castlehyde was "dubbed" into one of the variants. The poets Millikin of Cork and Francis Sylvester Mahony collaborated in writing a parody of this nonsense; they appropriately called it *The Groves of Blarney.* It is the melody associated with this facetious member of the *Ned of the Hill* tune group that Moore made famous as *The Last Rose of Summer.* Beethoven uses another version of the same tune for his *Sad and Luckless.*

It was to be, however, the bard in his capacity as harper, rather than the bard as composer or the bard as poet, who was to play the stellar role in the restoration of Irish song to the civilized world.

In July 1792 certain "gentlemen of Belfast," motivated by nationalistic, not to say revolutionary zeal, organized a Congress of Harpers. It was intended as a patriotic salute to Irish music. To this meeting came ten virtuosos of the ancient instrument. By all accounts they were a colorful crew; six were blind, several were of advanced years (the great Denis Hampson was ninety-seven), and one, William Smith, was a lad of fifteen.

A young musician, Edward Bunting, was engaged to take down the music played by the harpers and to record whatever they could tell him of their instrument, their technique, and their careers. In selecting the nineteen-year-old organist for so congenial a task, the "gentlemen of Belfast" builded better than they knew. Bunting was fired with enthusiasm not only for the melodies he heard but for the harpers themselves, as gallant exponents of a declining art. The days he spent with them determined his future as the first of Irish musicologists. It also gave rise to his three collections of Irish tunes, which were to be extensively ransacked in the subsequent promotion of the Irish folk song.

In 1796 Bunting issued his first collection.[1] Among the tunes it contains are songs, jigs, planxties, a lullaby, and several solos for the harp, including Carolan's "Concerto." There is, in addition, an interesting preface in which Bunting gives many particulars of the Congress of 1792 which had stimulated him to make further study of his country's music. The preface makes it quite clear that Bunting preferred the harp as the medium for the performance of all Irish melodies, even where a song with known text is concerned. He goes so far as to regret that some vocal music is not better adapted to his favorite instrument.

Bunting's collection came promptly to the attention of a group of nationalistically-minded undergraduates at Trinity College in Dublin.

[1] *A General Collection of the Ancient Music of Ireland,* Dublin, 1796.

Among them were the martyr-to-be, Robert Emmet, and seventeen-year-old Thomas Moore. Moore had, at a very early age, achieved something of a reputation in middle-class Dublin society for spontaneous musicality and graceful versification. A self-taught pianist, young Moore was noted for singing verses of his own composition to his own accompaniment. A collection of singable tunes, which were to all intents and purposes wordless, provided Moore with an irresistible incentive for the composing of what was to become in Moore's *Irish Melodies* a whole literature of patriotic, convivial, and amorous verse.

Although Moore's participation in the revolt of 1798 was slight, it made London, ironically, a safer city than Dublin for a performing poet of his political convictions. By the opening of the new century, suddenly stylish Tom Moore could be found almost nightly in one or another of the great Regency houses moving his hearers to tears, to laughter, to wine, and to indignation over Ireland's wrongs.

Scottish music was esteemed many years before Irish music fought its way back to the drawing room. During the years when Moore was re-enacting the bard to fashionable London, an Edinburgh business man, George Thomson, was engaged in promoting Scotch song. Since the early 1790s he had been collecting tunes which he published at his own expense. He retained various poets, chief among them Burns, to "improve" the texts where they existed, or to write new verses where they did not, or were unsuitable. In selecting Burns for so appropriate a task, Thomson established himself as a major benefactor of English poetry. Burns wrote lyric poetry of the greatest beauty to already-existing melodies, of which to name only two—*My Love is Like a Red, Red Rose* and *Mary Morrison* are familiar examples. For the musical research and arrangements, Scotland lacked a Bunting. There was no musician at hand of Burns's stature. Thomson, therefore, conceived the grandiose idea of securing the services of the most famous Continental composers, among whom the most distinguished was Haydn. Haydn entered in on this task with enthusiasm and over a period of several years supplied Thomson's tunes with accompaniments and "symphonies." In 1797 Burns died and in 1806 Haydn discontinued his work for Thomson because of ill health.

Haydn's gift for pastoral utterance and his familiarity with the British musical scene proved encouraging to Thomson's faith in the congeniality of Vienna and Edinburgh. He communicated in 1803 with Beethoven, proposing a set of six sonatas in which the composer would utilize Scotch songs. This plan came to no more than Beethoven's consent, but it was eventually to lead, after much correspondence in which money plays a larger part than music, to Beethoven's not only completing Thomson's Scottish collection, but to his arrangements of Welsh airs and to the 62 *Irische Lieder* that are our present concern.

Since Thomson had not the firsthand experience of Irish song that he had of Scottish melodies, he entrusted the selection of tunes to be forwarded to Vienna to a Dr. Latham of Cork. He drew, as was to be expected, on Bunting, and also on any other source being utilized by Moore and Stevenson. The result is that of Beethoven's 62 *Irische Lieder*, about thirty of the same tunes exist in Moore's *Irish Melodies.*—ALICE ANDERSON HUFSTADER

c. 25 *Scottish Songs, Opus 108*[1]

1. Music, love, and wine (Allegretto più tosto vivace, G major, 4/4)
2. Sunset (Andante con molto espressione, A minor, 2/4)
3. Oh, sweet were the hours (Andante con moto e semplice, F major, 3/4)
4. The Maid of Isla (Allegretto ma con espressione, D major, 2/4)
5. The sweetest lad was Jamie (Andantino un poco allegretto, G minor, 4/4)
6. Dim, dim is my eye (Andante amoroso con molta espressione, D major, 3/4)
7. Bonny laddie, highland laddie (Allegretto quasi vivace, F major, 2/4)
8. The lovely lass of Inverness (Affetuoso assai ed espressivo, D minor, 3/4)
9. Behold, my love, how green the groves (Grazioso, E flat major, 6/8)
10. Sympathy (Andantino più tosto allegretto, D major, 4/4)
11. Oh! thou art the lad of my heart (Allegretto più tosto vivace, E flat major, 6/8)
12. Oh, had my fate been join'd with thine (Andante teneramente con molto espressione, D major, 4/4)
13. Come fill, fill my good fellow (Spirituoso ma non troppo presto, G minor, 9/8)
14. O, how can I be blithe and glad (Andante poco allegretto, D major, 4/4)
15. O cruel was my father (Andante con molto espressione, F major, 2/4)
16. Could this ill world have been contriv'd (Allegretto grazioso e un poco scherzoso, D major, 6/8)
17. O Mary, at the window be (Andantino quasi allegretto, D major, 4/4)
18. Enchantress, fare well (Andantino grazioso con espressione, A major, 6/8)
19. O swiftly glides the bonny boat (Andante poco allegretto, D Major, 4/4)
20. Faithfu' Johnie [sic] (Andantino simplice amoroso teneramente, E flat major, 2/4)

21. Jeanie's distress (Andantino quasi allegretto, D major, 6/8)
22. The Highland watch (Spirituoso e marziale, G minor, 2/4)
23. The shepherd's song (Allegretto, A major, 4/4)
24. Again, my lyre (Andante affetuoso assai, F major, 4/4)
25. Sally in our alley (Andante con molto grazioso e semplice assai, D major, 3/4)

Titles. After the "Index to the Poetry" in [George] Thomson's original edition (see below) the English texts (which are printed under the melodies) are by the following poets: Joanna Baillie (Nos. 19 and 23), Alexander Ballantyne (No. 15), Robert Burns (Nos. 8, 9, 14, 17), Lord Byron (No. 12), Mrs. Grant (No. 20), James Hogg (Nos. 7, 16, 22), Walter Scott (Nos. 2, 4, 18) and William Smythe (Nos. 1, 3, 5, 6, 10, 11, 13, 24); No. 25 is entitled: "The old English Ballad of Sally in our Alley." (In the original German edition the names of the [translators] are not mentioned.) After the main title to A. M. Schlessinger's second edition the author of the German translations [is mentioned as] S. H. Spiker, that is, the Berlin librarian Samuel Heinrich Spiker (1786–1858; see Frimmel's *Beethoven Handbook*, Vol. II, pp. 227 ff.).

Composition. 1815–16 (commissioned by [George] Thomson). That Scottish [publisher and] friend of music, who was born in 1757 in Limekilns, Dunferline, and died in his ninety-fifth year (1851) in Leith, held for fifty years—until 1839—the distinguished position of Secretary of the Board of Trustees for the Encouragement of Arts and Crafts. From 1792 on, he had started a collection of the songs of his homeland. On the advice of the poet Robert Burns, he later enlarged his plan to include Irish and also Welsh folk songs. With untiring zeal and the help of considerable financial means he made this his life's work. He was a "dilettante" in both senses of the word, for at his own expense he published the musical arrangements between 1793 and 1841, only as musical "curiosities," while the folklorist value of the collections seemed to elude him entirely. For the musical arrangements of the melodies and the fitting together of these with accompaniments for piano trio with introductions and codas, he commissioned well-known foreign composers (Pleyel, Koseluch, Haydn), and, to this end, he also turned later to the "famous" follower of the elderly Haydn, Beethoven. A steady correspondence with Beethoven about the project from 1803 to 1806 resulted, in the autumn of 1809, in a firm commitment, and the carrying out of this well-paid drudgery (the total honorarium amounted to 550 British pounds!) occupied the Master with interruptions until the year 1823. In a covering letter to the first consignment of fifty-three songs, Beethoven wrote to Thomson, on July 17, 1810: "*Voilà, Monsieur, les airs écossais dont j'ai composé la plus grande partie con amore [sic] voulant donner une marque d'estime à la nation écossaise et anglaise en cultivant leurs chants nationaux . . .*" ["Here, Sir, are the Scottish songs which I have composed for the most part with great joy and satisfaction, wishing to give a mark of esteem to Scotland and England by cultivating their national songs . . ."] When Beethoven in his letters and manuscripts refers to *"schottische,"* he obviously uses the adjective as all-inclusive of songs of the British Isles, for it is used to describe Irish and Welsh songs as well as truly Scottish. In all there are 126 of his arrangements that appeared in various of Thomson's collections—41 Scottish, 59 Irish, and 26 Welsh songs.

Original English Edition (June 1818):

"A Select Collection of/ORIGINAL SCOTTISH AIRS/With Introductory and Concluding Symphonies [sic] and Accompaniments for the/PIANOFORTE, VIOLIN AND VIOLONCELLO/By/Haydn and Beethoven./With Select Verses adapted to the Airs, including upwards of/One hundred new Songs by/BURNS,/Together with his celebrated Poem of/The Jolly Beggars/Set to Music by/HENRY R. BISHOP./Price of each Volume, the Voice and Pianoforte One Guinea.—The Violin and Viol^{co} parts separate 6 shillings./[Vignette]/Vol. 5 Ent^d at Stationers hall/London. Printed and Sold by Preston, 97 Strand. And by G. Thomson the Editor and Proprietor Edinburgh."

That volume includes, besides 5 songs by Haydn (see below) all of the complete Opus 108 of Beethoven. Haydn's arrangements are under the [original Thomson] numbers 218 ("O Marion is a bonny lass"), 220 ("Oh was I to blame to love him?"), 224 ("A soldier am I"), 225 ("Poor flutt'ring heart"), and 227 ("Now bank and brae are cloth'd in green").

Original German Edition (July 1822):

"SCHOTTISCHE LIEDER/*mit englischem und deutschem Texte./ Für eine Singstimme und kleines Chor* [sic]/*mit Begleitung/des Pianoforte, Violine und Violoncelle obligat* [sic]/*componiert von* LUDWIG Van BEETHOVEN./Sr *Durchlaucht/dem Fürsten und Herrn,* Anton Heinrich Radzivil [sic]/*Statthalter im Grossherzogthum Posen, Ritter des schwarzen Adler-Ordens,/unterthänigst zugeeignet/vom Verleger./Opus 108/. . . In der A. M. Schlesingerschen Buch- und Musik-handlung./NB. Diese Lieder können auch für eine Singstimme mit Pianoforte allein executirt* [sic] *werden/ . . .*"[1]

About the dedication. In a letter of March 7, 1821, Beethoven wrote to

---

[1] "Scottish songs, with English and German texts, for one voice and small chorus with accompaniment of pianoforte, violin, and cello obbligato, composed by LUDWIG Van BEETHOVEN. Humbly dedicated to the Prince and Gentleman Anton Heinrich Radziwill, Ruler of the Archduchy of Posen, Knight of the Order of the Black Eagle, by the composer. Opus 108. N.B. These songs can also be performed by one voice and pianoforte alone . . ."

Schlessinger: "The dedication to the Crown Prince of Prussia [who later became King Friedrich Wilhelm IV] is free for His Highness; since I have considered no one else, I will gladly consider this." On the title page of the printed edition, the dedication—as well as that of the Choral Fantasia, Opus 80, as early as 1811 by [the publishers] Breitkopf & Härtel—was, however, already committed to Anton Heinrich, Prince Radziwill (1755–1833). Prince Radziwill, from 1796 brother-in-law of Prince Louis Ferdinand of Prussia, from 1815 ruler of the Archduchy of Posen, was also known as a composer through his stage music for Goethe's *Faust*, which was published in 1835. A personal friendship between him and Beethoven, whom he honored as a composer, was never established, however, although the Master—probably as thanks for a subscription toward the publication and performance of the *Missa Solemnis*—dedicated the "Namensfeier" Overture, Opus 115, which appeared in 1825, to him.

Literature: Felix Lederer, "*Beethovens Bearbeitung schottischer Volks-lieder*," Bonn, 1934. Willy Hess, "*Neues zu Beethovens Volkslieder-Bear-beitung*" in *Zeitung für Musikgewissenschaft*, Vol. XIII, pages 317–24. Literature on G. Thomson, see the monograph on Thomson (". . . the friend of Burns, his life and correspondence with Haydn and Beethoven") by J. Cuthbert Haddon, London and New York, 1898; the entry in Grove's Dictionary, Fifth Edition, Vol. III, pages 322–24; and, above all, "Thomson's Collection of National Songs, with Special Reference to the Contributions of Haydn and Beethoven," by Cecil Hopkinson and C. B. Oldman in "The Transactions of the Edinburgh Bibliographical Society," Vol. II, Part I, 1940.—GEORG KINSKY, EDITED BY HANS HALM (TR. BY THOMAS K. SCHERMAN)

d. Various Folk Song Arrangements, WoO 152–58

About the groupings and order: The grouping of the following numbers [WoO 152–58] follows Nottebohm's thematic index, since this has been followed without deviation in the complete edition of the songs by Breitkopf & Härtel. The original English edition of Thomson, in which the songs appear in a highly different order, has been largely ignored. The justification for this procedure is that the *Gesammtausgabe* [Breitkopf & Härtel's publication of the complete works of Beethoven] completely defies that of Thomson and is essentially an easier method of grouping. For instance, a disagreement between Thomson's numbering and that of the *Gesammtausgabe* occurs already in Opus 108 (see above[1]) in the exhaustive study of Hopkinson and Oldman ["Thomson's Collection of National Songs, with Special Reference to the Contributions of

---

[1] See the essay on Opus 108 arrangements that appears in the Kinsky-Halm *Verzeichnis.*—Editor.

Haydn and Beethoven," Edinburgh, 1940], in which the reprinting of single songs in Thomson's later collections is well catalogued.

About the composition (as witnessed in the collected letters): As already mentioned in the discussion of Beethoven's Opus 108, the composer's association with the Scottish music publisher George Thomson (1757–1851) in Edinburgh was inaugurated in the years 1803 and 1806, and the firm commitment on both sides that was reached in the autumn of 1809 remained intact, although with many interruptions, until the year 1820 [Thayer says 1823]. Beethoven was very pleased with this well-paid *"Brotarbeit,"* as he called it [compositions to keep him, literally, alive]. Already in the postscript to his letter of November 1, 1806, Beethoven declared his willingness *"d'harmoniser de petites airs écossais,"* whereupon Thomson, in the beginning of 1807, promptly sent him twenty-one songs to arrange. It is not known whether Beethoven received this first group, as Thomson wrote him on September 25, 1809: *"Les 21 premiers de ces airs ont été envoyés, il y a près de trois ans, mais j'ignore si vous les avez reçu."* ["The first 21 songs were sent you almost three years ago, but I am not sure whether you have received them."] With this letter was forwarded forty-three more *"petites airs"* [to which Thomson begged that Beethoven compose "as soon as possible" the *Ritornelles* and accompaniments for the pianoforte "or the pedal harp" [sic] as well as for the violin and violoncello]. Beethoven took the project in hand and promised the delivery already for the beginning of December (letter of November 23, 1809). It was not delivered, however, until the following July (letter of July 17, 1810). This delivery contained seventeen Irish songs (From WoO 152 and 153) and almost all the collected twenty-six Welsh songs, WoO 155. The dispatch of the manuscripts to Edinburgh and the payment of the honorarium was handled in all cases by the Viennese banking firm Fries and Company.

In Beethoven's own hand the titles of two of the songs are altered, and also in Beethoven's letter of July 17, 1810, fifty-three songs are mentioned and reckoned at a price of 150 ducats. Evidently, this was intended to include the remaining ten Irish songs.

The next letter is written a year later on July 20, 1811. In it Beethoven states that since the fifty-three songs which over the space of a year had been sent to Scotland had gone astray, [he was forced to recompose many of them a second time]. This letter included the manuscript of the last [No. 15] of the twenty-six Welsh songs.

On February 29, 1812, Beethoven mentions the delivery of nine further songs. [These were] likewise Irish songs: eight from the twenty-five of WoO 152, and a new arrangement of No. 9 ["Oh! would I were but that sweet linnet"—a duet] of the twelve songs, WoO 154. Again he repeats his request that the texts of the melodies be sent him, as they "are indispensable to me for proper composition!"

A year later, on February 19, 1813, Beethoven insisted that Thomson finally had in his possession all sixty-two songs. He resisted [Thomson's] request to alter nine of the song arrangements: "I am not accustomed to retouch my compositions," he wrote in French, "for I feel that any change whatsoever alters the character of the composition." However, these nine altered songs were dutifully delivered.

The next letter, of September 15, 1814, was written after the receipt of the first volume of Thomson's A Select Collection of Original Irish Airs, which appeared the previous March. Of the thirty songs in the collection, with the exception of the last (by Haydn), all were composed by Beethoven (the complete twenty-five Irish songs of WoO 152 and Nos. 1-4 of WoO 153). Beethoven also acknowledges the honorarium of four ducats offered for the "altre arie scozzesi" which Thomson wished. By these "altre arie scozzesi" he meant the true Scottish songs[1] (Opus 108 and WoO 156), work on which was now begun in earnest. On February 7, 1815, he wrote [Thomson] through his friend Johann Häring: "All your songs with the exception of a few are ready to be forwarded."

The letters of January 18, 1817, brought the news that all of the songs ordered on July 8, 1816, would be ready by the end of September, the delivery having been delayed by sickness. Also Beethoven broaches the subject of a collection of "chansons de divers [es] nations," a plan which had engaged him since 1815 (see WoO 158).

The importance of this is manifested by the publishing on November 18, 1818 (together with an honorarium of over 140 ducats) of his varied themes for piano and flute (Opuses 105 and 107) and eight new Scottish songs. Beethoven and two witnesses signed [upon this occasion] the following declaration: ". . . all the Ritornellos or Symphonies and Accompaniments which I have before at different times composed for Scottish, Irish and Welsh Melodies, that is for one hundred and eighteen[2] of those melodies sent to me by . . . George Thomson . . . are also the sole and absolute property of the said George Thomson . . . without any reservation." This declaration included the Twenty-five Melodies of Continental Nations, that is, the arrangements of several songs of various nations, that Thomson had already received but had not yet published (see WoO 158).—GEORG KINSKY, EDITED BY HANS HALM (TR. BY THOMAS K. SCHERMAN)

WoO 152 is a set of twenty-five Irish songs—some duets—which includes among other familiar melodies "The massacre of Glencoe" (No. 5), "The deserter" (No. 10), "Dermot and Shelah" (No. 14), "The wand'ring

---

[1] As mentioned in the discussion of Opus 108, Beethoven used the adjective "écossais" not only for songs of Scotland, but also those of Ireland, Wales, and even England.—Editor.

[2] Italics by the editor.

gypsy" (No. 23), and "Oh harp of Erin" (No. 25). They were originally published by Thomson in March 1814.

WoO 153 is a set of twenty more Irish songs including "The British light dragoons" (No. 3), "I dreamed I lay where flow'rs were springing," with a text by Robert Burns and set as a duet (No. 5), "The kiss, dear maid, thy lip has left," with a text by Lord Bryon (No. 9), "Paddy O'Rafferty, merry and vigorous" (No. 14), and "Judy, lovely matchless creature" (No. 19). They appeared in May 1816 in the second volume of Thomson's "A Select Collection of Original Irish Airs."

WoO 154, twelve Irish songs, contains a second setting of "From Garyone, my happy home," the melody of which also appeared as No. 22 of WoO 152. There is also a beautiful arrangement of "Oh! would I were but that sweet linnet" the introduction of which was changed several times by Beethoven and which ultimately appeared as a duet rather than for solo voice. These songs also appeared originally in a separate volume of Thomson's "A Select Collection of Original Irish Airs," published in May 1816.

WoO 155 consists of twenty-six Welsh songs, all of which were composed by the end of 1810 with the exception of No. 15, "When mortals all to rest retire," which was worked on around the end of February 1812, and No. 25, "The parting kiss," which was not composed until the summer of 1814. Familiar melodies in the collection include: "A golden robe my love shall wear" (No. 5), "To the Aeolian harp" (No. 9), "The vale of Clwyd" (No. 19), and "The old strain" (No. 23). The entire collection was published by Thomson in May 1817 in "A/ Select Collection of/Original/WELSH AIRS/Adapted for the Voice/ UNITED TO CHARACTERISTIC/English Poetry/never before Published,/With Introductory and Concluding Symphonies/and Accompaniments for the PIANOFORTE, VIOLIN, AND VIOLONCELLO/Composed Partly by/Haydn but chiefly by Beethoven."

WoO 156, twelve Scottish Songs, includes among other familiar melodies "Glencoe" (No. 10) to the same text by Sir Walter Scott that was used for No. 5 of the Irish songs (WoO 152) and with the same melody, this time, however, appearing in C major, 2/4, Andante espressivo, in contrast to its first setting in A Minor, 4/4, Andante lamentabile; also a setting with a gay, flippant character (Allegretto, 2/4) of "Auld Lang Syne" composed as a vocal trio! In Beethoven's lifetime six of the songs were published by Thomson, with accompaniment for piano alone without violin and violoncello, in the second volume of "Select Melodies of Scotland interspersed with those of Ireland and Wales, united to the songs of Robert Burns, Sir Walter Scott, and other distinguished poets: with Symphonies and Accompaniments for the Pianoforte by Pleyel, Koseluch, Haydn, and Beethoven . . . in five volumes" published in London in 1822. Others appeared in the sixth volume of "Thomson's

Collection of the songs of Burns, Sir Walter Scott, and other eminent lyric poets ancient and modern, united to the select melodies of Scotland, Ireland and Wales" published in Edinburgh, 1824-25.

WoO 157 is a collection of arrangements of folk songs of various countries. It includes two British songs, including "God Save the King," five Irish, including "Robin Adair" and "The wandering minstrel," two Scottish, including "Charlie is my darling," one old Jacobite song, "Sir Johnie Cope," one Sicilian song, "O sanctissima, o piissima," and the famous Venetian "La gondoletta" which Mendelssohn also used later. They all were composed during the years 1814 and 1815. Four of the Irish songs appear in original proofs with corrections in Beethoven's own hand and dated May 1815. The Sicilian and Venetian songs were intended for the projected collection of songs of different nations, which Thomson however did not publish (see below).

WoO 158 is a group of arrangements of songs of different nations. They are grouped by Kinsky-Halm into three broad headings, the first of which contains twenty-three Continental songs—one Danish, two German, five Tyrolean (including the familiar "Teppichkrämerlied"), two Polish (including the melody "Poszla baba po popia!" which Chopin used as the theme for his variations on a Polish air), two Portuguese, four Russian (including the famous "Darling Minka, I must leave thee"), a Swedish lullaby, a Swiss song (with words in Schweizerdeutsche), two Spanish boleros (one "a solo" and one "a duet"), another Spanish song "Tiranilla española" (the melody of which is similar to the Mexican hat dance), a Hungarian drinking song, and the Italian "Canzonetta veneziana." The melodies and texts of the Russian songs appeared in a volume, published by Ivan Pratch in 1790, which Beethoven had studied in connection with his three "Russian" quartets, Opus 59. Two of the Tyrolean songs were used by Beethoven as themes for his folk song Variations for Flute and Piano, Opus 107. As we have seen, these were all intended for a collection to be published by Thomson which never materialized. The first actual edition of the works was in 1941 by Breitkopf & Härtel.

The second grouping is of seven British songs (three Irish and four Scottish) which appear without texts but with the accompaniment arranged for piano, violin, and violoncello as with all of the folk song settings Beethoven composed for Thomson.

The third grouping is of six songs (also without text) whose melodies are unidentified as to the country of origin.—Editor.

His Life

AFTER the sustained creative energy of the years 1800 to 1812, Beethoven's genius slept, or at least dozed, so far as published works are concerned, for a number of years. A pair of piano sonatas, another pair for cello, an overture (not one of the best), and a song cycle are the pick of his works in these lean years. But in 1817 the flame bursts out again and he sets to work simultaneously on three of his mightiest undertakings, the Piano Sonata in B flat, Opus 106, the Mass in D, and the Ninth Symphony, which occupy him between them till 1824, the three last piano sonatas being thrown off during intervals of work on the two gigantic choral masterpieces. Then he turns to quartets, producing his last five compositions in this genre between 1824 and the onset of his illness in 1826. The quartets were by no means intended as his final word. There are sketches for a new symphony and a string quintet in C, and he often spoke of another Mass, a second opera, possibly a *Faust* to crown his life's achievement. But these things were not to be.

For most serious musicians these last works are the greatest of all. It is not merely their size that gives us this impression though in fact they are his biggest; nor is it their novelty, though in them Beethoven innovates more boldly than ever before. It is not even their wealth of ideas, though the last quartets are perhaps more closely packed with thought than any other music in the world. It has been said that there is a spiritual, mystical quality about them, but the same is true of many compositions by Palestrina, Bach and others. What is unique about this music is not its spirituality, but its particular *kind* of spirituality, the note of authentic experience, the peace that is only won through strife, the wisdom that only suffering can teach.[1] There is no sudden crisis to account for this final development of Beethoven's style; it was the result of a gradual process that included the whole man and proceeded unin-

[1] On this subject see J. W. N. Sullivan's "Beethoven: His Spiritual Development."

terrupted to the end. The last quartets take us a step further than the ninth symphony. Had Beethoven lived to write yet other works, it is safe to surmise that they would have taken us further still.

The sketchbooks in which Beethoven worked out his ideas afford interesting evidence of his creative processes at this time. Many are still extant and have been made the subjects of most careful study. Nottebohm is our chief authority here, and one of the things that strikes him most is the profuseness of invention. No one, he says, who has not seen the sketchbooks can appreciate the full measure of Beethoven's fertility. The published works, rich though they be, contain but a tithe of what the composer might have produced.

Even during the barren years 1813–17 his inspiration was still flowing and the scarcity of works must be attributed in part to sheer lack of resolution. His character always lacked decision and his infirmity of will grew on him as he got older. It was this that kept him from going to England. He had always admired the English, he wanted to visit London, and during his later years he received more than one invitation. He was assured that such an expedition would be highly remunerative, and once, at any rate, he almost made up his mind to go. Almost!—and then that fatal irresolution came over him and he jettisoned his plans. It was the same with composition on the large scale: his projects had become so vast that he simply could not bring himself to embark upon them. It must be admitted that he had cause for hesitation, for when, in 1817, he took the plunge and started work on the Mass and the Ninth Symphony he thereby committed himself to some six years of arduous labor. His artistic conscience was more sensitive than ever, his critical faculty keener. What might have been good enough ten years earlier was not nearly good enough now. He wrote and rewrote with astonishing assiduity and patience; the contrapuntal sections in the Mass were only hammered out by sheer tenacity and indomitable perseverance; he would wrestle with them for hours and then come from his study exhausted as if by actual physical conflict. Even when the score was finished he was loath to part with it, keeping it by him day after day, week after week, in the hope that some improvement might suggest itself.

Unhappily this extreme scrupulousness, so conspicuous in matters connected with his art, was by no means so evident at this time in his dealings with his fellow men. One records with regret that the Ninth Symphony, after being definitely commissioned by the London Philharmonic Society, received its first performance in Vienna[1] and was dedicated to the King of Prussia; and that the Mass, after being promised to three rival publishers simultaneously, was ultimately given to a fourth. Throughout these dubious negotiations Beethoven was loud in his protestations of his own uprightness, and it may be that, with his curious

---

[1] On May 7, 1824.

incapacity to adjust himself to the external world, he was blind to the discreditable nature of his transactions. But while we may seek to understand his attitude we cannot condone his conduct. If Beethoven really regarded as honorable his proceedings in the matter of the Mass, then one can only lament the flaw in his moral sense. One might even suspect him of avarice, were it not that in his later years he was badly in need of money. This was due in part to his own improvidence, in part to the unfruitful years that preceded 1818; but there were more serious causes, and these we must now investigate.

In 1812 his financial position seemed secure. He was drawing a considerable income from his compositions and in addition he was in receipt of an annuity of four thousand florins that had been settled on him in 1809 by three rich patrons, the Archduke Rudolph (youngest son of the Emperor Leopold II), Prince Kinsky, and Prince Lobkowitz. Through no fault of its generous guarantors this annuity became a source of endless worry to Beethoven. First there was a fall in the Austrian currency, then Prince Kinsky was killed in an accident and Prince Lobkowitz went bankrupt. Beethoven found himself involved with a swarm of lawyers, executors, and creditors. In the end he got his annuity—or most of it. But the business dragged on till 1815, making serious inroads on his time and energy.

Meanwhile he had undertaken another lawsuit on his own account. Mälzel, the inventor of the metronome, had also invented a strange mechanical instrument which he called the panharmonicon, and in 1813 he prevailed upon Beethoven to write a work for it. This composition, perhaps the worst but in its day the most popular that ever came from Beethoven's pen, was the Battle Symphony: Wellington's Victory at Vittoria. At Mälzel's suggestion he orchestrated it, and it was performed at a concert on December 8, 1813, amid scenes of great enthusiasm. Afterwards, however, Mälzel and Beethoven fell out over their respective rights in the work, and Beethoven went to law. Mälzel fought the case and there were years of fruitless conflict before the litigants made peace. Beethoven gained nothing, and this time he had wasted money as well as energy.

Far more serious was the family lawsuit that raged round his nephew Karl. Both Beethoven's brothers had married, Caspar Karl in 1806, Johann in 1812. Johann had prospered and become, in his own eyes at any rate, a person of some consequence. Caspar Karl had been less successful and in 1815 he died, leaving a young son, Karl, who was placed under the joint guardianship of his mother and his uncle Ludwig.

His sisters-in-law Beethoven hated with a deep and bitter hatred. Since both ladies were shameless in their infidelities his feelings are comprehensible enough; but they did not help him in his position as guardian. His first action was to remove Karl entirely from his mother's influence, in direct opposition to the terms of the will, on the plea that she was not a fit person to have charge of him. The mother's resentment was natural, for whatever her faults she loved her son; and it is not in the least surprising that she sought redress at law.

She had more to complain of than the usurpation of her rights as a mother. In everything except his motives Beethoven was the most unsuitable of guardians. His habits were irregular, his lodgings untidy, uncomfortable, even dirty; and his frequent preoccupation prevented him from giving proper attention to the boy's material needs. Evidence was brought to show that Karl's feet and hands were frostbitten, that he had no seasonable clothes, that his linen and his baths were neglected. On the moral side Beethoven was equally unwise, kind and harsh by turns. Never knowing what treatment to expect, Karl grew deceitful, lying freely to his uncle when there was danger of an outburst. He was not naturally a vicious boy and he became eventually a decent member of society, but it was inevitable that he should react unfavorably to the unhappy influences of such a childhood. He told the court that he "would like to live with his uncle if he had but a companion, as his uncle was hard of hearing and he could not talk to him."

As for Beethoven, he was entirely convinced of the justice of his own cause, and, as usual, he was completely unable to look at things from the point of view of other people. In Karl he had found at last an abiding object for his love, and this time he did not love by halves. The boy was all in all to him, and on him he lavished all the passionate affection of his lonely spirit. "God help me," he writes in one place, "Thou seest me deserted by all men, for I do not wish to do wrong, hear my supplication, only for the future to be with my Karl." For all his wrongheadedness the desperate sincerity of the man compels our sympathy. Toward him, as toward Karl and his mother, there is no room for any feeling but a profound pity. Providence granted his prayer: at last, in 1820, the court gave final judgment and Beethoven was confirmed in his guardianship of Karl. But his nephew's heart he could not win. Karl merely accepted the situation. His feelings for his deaf old uncle with the queer temper and bearish ways included both fear and impatience, but no love.[1]

The lawsuit had been a heavy drain on Beethoven's resources, and Karl's education involved a considerable further expense. He was poor now, for the first time since his early days in Vienna, and he was very much alone. It was about 1812 that he began to withdraw from society. His law cases occupied much of his time, there was his composition, and

[1] See W. J. Turner's essay on Karl. Also of extreme interest is the book *Beethoven and His Nephew*, by Editha and Richard Sterba, M.D. (New York, 1954), which implies a homosexual relationship adduced from a Freudian analysis of the known facts. The extremely high morality which Beethoven professed must be equated with the "easygoing" sexual mores of the early nineteenth century. Both points of view should be considered in context.—Editor.

soon his nephew provided an all-absorbing interest at home. Besides, he was now too deaf to mingle easily with a crowd of people. In 1814 he took part in chamber music for the last time and in the next year he made his final public appearance at the piano, playing accompaniments for the singer Wild.[1] By 1819 it was no longer possible to converse with him even by shouting. *Fidelio* was revived in November 1822, and it was at a rehearsal for this performance that he had to abandon conducting. In spite of the utmost good will on the part of all concerned it soon became impossible to go on. Beethoven looked around, hesitating, anxious. Then realization came to him. "He leaped from his place in the orchestra, hastened from the theatre to his lodgings, threw himself on the sofa, covered his face with his hands."[2] It was the end. At the first performance of the Ninth Symphony in 1824 he stood in the orchestra near the singers and was quite unaware of the storm of applause till Fräulein Unger drew his attention to the clapping hands he could see but not hear.

He gradually became something of a recluse, and people who had come to Vienna on purpose to see him were sometimes unable to discover whether he was in the city or not. His poverty never amounted to destitution, but he was hard pressed, and his pathetic inability to govern his household with order and economy added greatly to his difficulties. There was indeed a nest egg (amounting to over seven thousand florins) on which he might have drawn, but this had been put aside as his legacy to Karl, and, whatever his need, he refused to touch it. We hear of threadbare coats and soiled linen. Once, out walking in the country he was arrested as a tramp, and his protests that he was the composer Beethoven were met with amused incredulity. Not so, in the opinion of the police, would the great Beethoven appear. Ill-health was added to his other woes: he had trouble with his eyes, he suffered from various ailments that kept him for a while in bed, and in 1821 he was laid up with a serious attack of jaundice.

Neither poverty, loneliness nor suffering could teach him to understand the world and its unaccountable human inhabitants. Yet few men have been purged like Beethoven, and the white flame of the chastened spirit was often visible through the mask of misery that was his face. Sir Julius Benedict describes him in 1823, his "white hair flowing over his mighty shoulders [and] with that wonderful look." Rellstab, in 1825, is more explicit: "Suffering, melancholy and goodness showed in his face, but not a sign of harshness." Beethoven had learned something more than resignation, an ultimate wisdom the clue to which we must seek in the

[1] The audience at this concert was full of notabilities (including crowned heads) assembled for the Congress of Vienna.
[2] The story is Schindler's, who was present.

last quartets. Even then we may perhaps seek in vain, for there are high mysteries here.

In 1826 his relations with his nephew reached a crisis. Karl, now a young man of university age, was lazy and neglectful of his uncle. Beethoven was suspicious and reproachful, always carping at him and accusing him of visiting his mother—the unforgivable sin! At last, exasperated and desperate, Karl tried to shoot himself; but the wound was not mortal and after a sojourn in hospital he recovered. The tragedy occurred at the end of July and the shock aged Beethoven visibly. It was now clear even to his vacillating mind that a decisive step was necessary, and on the advice of his family he resolved to gratify Karl's own wishes and send him into the army.

A vacancy was found, but there was an inevitable interval after Karl's discharge from hospital on September 25 before he could take up his cadetship. Johann van Beethoven stepped into the breach and invited uncle and nephew to stay with him on his estate at Gneixendorf. The visit was planned to last a fortnight. But the fortnight passed and Ludwig, his usual indecision reinforced by his dread of losing Karl, made no move to leave. Johann's wife returned to Vienna; Johann himself stayed on, behaving all the time with exemplary patience. When toward the end of November he pointed out to Ludwig that Karl's prospects in the army might be jeopardized if there was further delay, he was doing no more than his duty, and it is Ludwig's hasty temper that we must blame for what ensued. He took deep offense at his brother's well-meant intervention and insisted on leaving at once. Johann, after vainly urging him to postpone his departure till adequate arrangements could be made, did his best to secure a suitable vehicle at short notice and speed the travelers on their way. But the journey in the raw winter weather was inevitably uncomfortable, Beethoven had to spend the night in a drafty room at an inn, and when he arrived in Vienna on December 2 he was already in a fever.

At first he made light of it, and it was only on the third day that Dr. Wawruch was called in. He found his patient suffering from pneumonia, prescribed the proper treatment and in a week had him on his legs again. But the next day he relapsed with alarming symptoms and it was soon clear that all sorts of complications had developed, including jaundice and dropsy. The real root of the trouble was cirrhosis of the liver. He had probably been suffering from this complaint for a long time; it may well have been the cause of his jaundice in 1821, and now it killed him.

Karl had to join his regiment at the beginning of the new year (1827). He departed and never saw his uncle again. But Beethoven's friends, Schindler, Breuning, his brother Johann and several others were assiduous at his bedside. His illness did nothing to sweeten his temper, but at first he was in good heart in spite of the wretchedly insanitary conditions in which he lay. He read Scott and Ovid and was immensely pleased with an edition of Handel's works sent him by an English admirer. News of his illness spread and he received many gratifying evidences of the veneration in which he was held. But as time went on and, in spite of a change of doctors and several changes of treatment, he got no better, hope gradually sank. On March 16 the doctors declared him lost. He knew it already.

Yet he lingered on. They brought him news that one of his last quartets had been performed but had failed to please. "It will please them someday," he answered tranquilly. The London Philharmonic Society, hearing of his illness and his need, sent him a loan of a hundred pounds; and one of his last actions was to dictate a letter of thanks to "the generous Englishmen." On March 23 it was apparent that the end was near. He signed his will, and his friends, in some trepidation (for they doubted his orthodoxy), asked if they might send for a priest. He raised no objection, received the Last Sacraments and offered a courteous word of thanks. All was now accomplished, and turning to those present he exclaimed with a flicker of his old spirit, "*Plaudite, amici, comaedia finita est.*" Next day, the twenty-fourth, a present of good Rhine wine arrived from Schott's, his publishers. "Pity, pity," he murmured, "too late!" They were his last words. That evening he relapsed into unconsciousness, but for hour after hour his iron constitution fought a last great fight with Death. He lived through the night, through the next day, and on the afternoon of the twenty-sixth he still breathed. That evening there was snow in Vienna, and an unexpected thunderstorm. A particularly violent thunderclap seemed to rouse Beethoven. He raised his clenched right hand with a "very earnest" expression in his eyes. When it fell back he was dead.

They buried him with what honor they might. A huge crowd that included the elite of the Viennese aristocracy followed the coffin to the Währing cemetery, and there they laid him, putting above him a stone inscribed with the one word "Beethoven." Among the torchbearers was Franz Schubert, whom Beethoven never knew but whose songs he had admired on his deathbed. Late in the following year Schubert was to travel that road again, to be laid near him. But neither Beethoven nor Schubert was left undisturbed. In 1888 the remains were exhumed, to be reinterred, let us hope finally, in the central cemetery of Vienna. Not far off lies Hugo Wolf.—PETER LATHAM

The Places

———◆———

Mödling

The rather complete catalogue of Beethoven's workshops must trace his Odyssey through houses in the heart of the old city as well as country villas in more distant suburbs such as Mödling, where the *Missa Solemnis* was composed. Again we owe a vividly drawn picture of Beethoven's last apartment, where death reached him in March 1827, to von Breuning and we freely quote from the account:

One reached the apartment by way of an attractive staircase. Entering the second floor on the left side through a somewhat low door, one arrived in a spacious foreroom with one window facing the court. From this hall one went straight to the kitchen . . . to the left was a very spacious room with one window facing the street.

The two rooms right off the foyer were Beethoven's real living quarters: the first one was chosen as his bed- and piano room, the other, the "cabinet," was his study for composition.

In the middle of the first room (containing two windows) stood two pianos with their keyboards on opposite sides, arranged in this way so that the players could face each other. Beethoven preferred this arrangement for the purpose of teaching and also for performances on two instruments. With its keyboard facing the entrance stood the English piano which the Philharmonic Society in London had presented to him; toward the other side, with the keyboard facing the study, stood the grand piano which the Austrian manufacturer Graf had put at his disposal.

A chest with drawers was placed against a pillar between the two windows. On top of it was a bookcase, painted black and containing four shelves full of books and writings. Upon this chest lay several hearing aids and two violins. Everything was in pitiful disorder and usually covered with dust. Papers and music were thrown everywhere— over the bookcase, under the table, on the floor, on the piano. The rest of the furniture consisted of Beethoven's bed, his night table, a small extra table and a clothes hanger.

The cabinet room with one window was Beethoven's study. Here,

on his desk, framed under glass and always in front of him, he had the
following sayings written in his own handwriting:

> I am what is;
> I am everything that is, what has been, what will be; .
> No mortal being has lifted my veil.
>
> He is unique in His kind and to this unique One
> All things owe their existence.

These sentences are parts of inscriptions from the ancient temple of
the Goddess Neith in Saïs, found by the French Egyptologist, Cham-
pollion-Figeac. Obviously, Beethoven was captivated by their mystic connotation.

His desk was rather large and also served as a table for knickknacks.
Among other things, he kept on it letter weights, silver bells, several
candleholders of various forms, a figure of a Cossack and of a Hungarian
Hussar and a few statuettes of old Greeks and Romans, one of them
being Brutus, for whom Beethoven had deep admiration. There was
more in these gadgets than meets the eye. They were tokens of Bee-
thoven's spirit. The Brutus statuette symbolized freedom, liberation from
Caesar's tyranny. The Beethoven whom we know from the Eroica, the
Egmont music and *Fidelio* responded to the democratic hero—to Brutus
who freed Rome from its dictator. These farewell living quarters of
Beethoven do not show the sordidness of the surroundings in which
Mozart and Schubert struggled in neighboring times and places. Here, at
last, we feel that Beethoven had a certain comfort and ample space.—
FREDERICK DORIAN

Gneixendorf

After Karl's attempted suicide, Beethoven decided that he should take
Karl away from Vienna for a time so as to remove him from easy access
by the police. It would be just as well if he were to be asked no further
questions. Before he could join the army, time was needed to let his
hair grow over the wound so that when he did become a soldier there
would be no visible marks to shame him. Where could uncle and nephew
find a retreat, a place where Beethoven would be left alone and Karl
could quietly recuperate?

Johann has acquired an estate in Gneixendorf, in the Danube Valley, a
few miles from Krems. The estate comprised nearly four-hundred acres,
most of which were leased to tenants. Johann and Therese lived in a

large and handsome house surrounded by a garden and isolated by a sheltering wall. Johann had invited Beethoven several times to visit him, and Beethoven, no doubt because he knew he would have to endure the company of his sister-in-law, had consistently refused. Beethoven wrote to Johann:

July 13, 1825

As for your desire that I should visit you, I already expressed my opinion long ago. I beg you never to mention the subject again, for in this you will find me, as always, adamant.

After Karl's "accident," Johann must have repeated the invitation. On August 28, 1826, Beethoven replied:

I am not coming—
                    Your brother??????!!!!
                    Ludwig

A few weeks after that, Johann was in Vienna and again offered his place as a haven to Beethoven and Karl. This time Beethoven, who had declared himself "adamant," *accepted* the invitation. He wanted to get away from the scandal, the inquisitive looks, the whispered comments— he would go anywhere, away from Vienna.

Three days after Karl was discharged from the hospital, Beethoven and he started off and, passing the night at an inn on the road, reached Gneixendorf on September 29 in the afternoon.

They were a curious pair of guests, the older man ailing and sick at heart, the young man with his wound still raw, afraid of his uncle and yet secretly rejoicing that at last there seemed to be a prospect of obtaining what he wanted most, to free himself from Beethoven's Argus-eyed fretting and to live a life of his own. Late in the afternoon of their arrival, Johann showed Beethoven around his property. The walk through the fields and woods cheered him up. The next day he and Karl took a very long stroll.

At first everything went well. Beethoven had been given a pleasant room with a view of the Danube Valley. Being in the country let him breathe more easily. He took an interest in the activities of the estate. One day Johann went to a nearby village to visit a doctor named Karrer, who was a friend of his. The doctor had been called away to a patient, but there were other guests at the home, and the doctor's wife, very pleased by the visit of the estate owner, whom she could show off to her friends, entertained Johann lavishly. She noticed a man, sitting by himself on a bench behind the stove, who took no part in the general conversation. Thinking that he was somebody's servant, she filled a little jug with wine and handed it to him, saying, "He too shall have a drink." When the doctor came home that night and heard an account of the incident, he exclaimed, "My dear wife, what have you done? The greatest composer of the century was in our house today and you treated him with such disrespect!"

Therese assigned one of her servants, a young man named Michael Krenn, to look after Beethoven. The cook, a woman, was supposed to make up his room. One day, while she did so, she saw Beethoven sitting at a table waving his arms violently, beating time with his feet, muttering and singing. This struck the woman as funny, and she burst into a loud guffaw. Beethoven saw her laughing and chased her out of the room. Michael followed, but Beethoven drew him back, gave him a tip, told him not to be afraid, and said that from now on *he* was to make the bed and clean the room by himself. He was told to come to the room early in the morning, but usually he had to knock for a long time before Beethoven opened the door.

Beethoven got up at half-past five, immediately sat down to work, and went through the business of singing, stamping, and shouting. But Michael got used to it. At half-past seven Beethoven would go down for breakfast, after which he went into the fields and roamed for miles, shouting and waving his arms, stopping at times to write in a notebook. At half-past twelve he would return home for dinner, after which he would rest until about three. Then he resumed his walks until shortly before sunset. Supper was at half-past seven, and after eating he worked until about ten and then went to bed. Nobody was allowed to enter his room except Michael. On one or two occasions Michael found money lying on the floor, and when he carried this to its owner, Beethoven made him show him the exact spot where he had found the money. Then he gave him the coins. Sometimes Beethoven asked Michael what had been said about him at dinner or at supper, and Michael would obligingly write down the answers to his questions.

While Beethoven was walking, the peasants working in the fields used to observe his wild gestures. At first they thought he was mad and carefully kept out of his way. When they found out that he was the brother of the estate owner, they used to greet him politely. Lost in thought, he seldom noticed their greeting. One day a peasant who was driving a pair of young oxen scarcely broken to the yoke saw Beethoven's gesticulations; the peasant, being afraid for his oxen, called out, "Hold on a little." But Beethoven paid no attention. What the peasant feared would happen did happen: the oxen took fright, ran down the steep hill, and were calmed only with the utmost difficulty.

One day Therese sent Michael shopping and gave him a five-florin note. Michael lost the money. He went back to the house in consternation and told Therese. She promptly discharged him. That night, when Beethoven came to dinner, he asked where Michael was, and Therese told him what had happened. Beethoven grew terribly angry, gave her five florins—whether Therese accepted them we do not know—and demanded that Michael be recalled to his job. It was done. After that, Beethoven never had dinner or supper with the family but had the meals brought to his room, and Michael prepared breakfast for him.

Karl enjoyed himself doing nothing. He visited people in nearby villages, played billiards, sat in the wine cellars, and talked to the peasants. He did continue to practice the piano. "Karl plays very well," Therese notes in the Conversation Book.

Experience had taught Beethoven nothing; even now he often reproached Karl. There were scenes between uncle and nephew. Karl writes: "Yours is the right to command, and I must endure it all." The reproaches continued, Karl replying, "I beg you once and for all to leave me alone.". . . .

Beethoven, looking at Karl with the gun wound showing, must have been under continual nervous apprehension. Once, when Karl stayed away for a few hours, Beethoven's fears mounted. Where was Karl? Was he contemplating some new irresponsible deed? Therese tried to calm him:

Do not be concerned. He will certainly come home by 1 o'clock. It seems that he has some of your rash blood. I have not found him angry. It is you that he loves, to the point of veneration.

The visit was supposed to have been a short one. But the two stayed on. Beethoven avoided Therese and spoke little to Johann; he was totally immersed in the completion of the Quartet in F. Karl was anxious to stay until he could appear "without any visible sign left of what happened to me." I believe he may have wanted to stay also because he did not have enough strength to face life. Much as he hated the fetters with which his uncle bound him, he may yet have been afraid to break them and to walk alone. Being taken care of in Gneixendorf suited his weak nature. Schindler says that Karl slept with Therese. That may be another of Schindler's inventions,[1] but if it was true, it would furnish an additional reason for Karl's wanting to stay.

[1] Schindler indulges in particularly wild fabrications when he comes to relate the last days of Beethoven. He writes that Karl was playing billiards in a coffeehouse when Beethoven needed a doctor and Karl told the marker in the billiard room to fetch one. The marker, being himself unwell, could execute this commission only after a few days. Schindler implies that Karl did nothing about caring for his uncle. This story (told also by Gerhard Breuning) has been exposed as false. Schindler also says that during Beethoven's stay at Gneixendorf "there was an unbelievable lack of consideration for the master's physical needs as to both lodging and food." Donald W. MacArdle, the editor of the present edition of Schindler's book, *Beethoven as I Knew Him*, comments: "The painstaking inquiries conducted by Thayer in Gneixendorf in 1860, corroborated by the evidence that he educed from the Conversation Books, give so completely different a picture of the composer's life with his brother during these two months that no effort can succeed in reconciling the two accounts. Thayer's integrity and the care with which he conducted his researches and formed his judgments are beyond challenge. One can assume only that Schindler allowed his malice toward brother Johann to get the better of his obligations as a biographer."

The weather turned colder, and still they stayed. Beethoven quarreled with Johann; he wanted Johann to make a will in favor of Karl, bypassing his wife. By that time Johann must have been more than anxious to get rid of brother and nephew both. Near the end of November, when they had been there two months, Johann wrote his brother a letter (Thayer suggests that he wrote a letter to avoid a face-to-face argument) which reads in part:

> I cannot possibly remain silent concerning the future fate of Karl. He is abandoning all activity and, grown accustomed to this life, the *longer* he lives as at present, the more difficult it will be to bring him back to work. At his departure *Breuning* gave him a fortnight in which to recuperate, and now it is two months.— You see from Breuning's letter that it is his decided wish that Karl *shall hasten* to his calling; the longer he is here the more unfortunate will it be *for him,* for the harder it will be for him to get to work, and it may be that we shall suffer harm.
>
> It is an infinite pity that this talented young man so wastes his time; and on whom if not *us both* will the blame be laid? For he is still too young to direct his own course; by which reason it is your duty, if you do not wish to be reproached by yourself and others hereafter, to put him to work at his profession as soon as possible. Once he is occupied it will be easy to do much for him now and in the future; but under present conditions nothing can be done.
>
> I see from his actions that he would like to remain with us, but if he did so it would be all over with his future, and therefore *this is impossible.* The longer we hesitate the more difficult will it be for him to go away; I therefore adjure you—make up your mind, do not permit yourself to be dissuaded by Karl. I think it ought to be *by next Monday.*

A reasonable and forthright statement. Instead of acting upon it immediately, Beethoven let several more days elapse before he decided that he wished to return to Vienna with Karl. Having so decided, and probably having taken offense at Johann's letter, he could do nothing but leave *at once.* Johann seems to have told Beethoven that if he wanted to leave on Monday (the Monday mentioned in Johann's letter), the carriage must be got ready on Sunday. Whether Beethoven did not let Johann know that he needed the carriage, or whether the carriage was broken, or whether Therese had driven in it to Vienna is unclear.

No public conveyance was available, because none went from the tiny village to Vienna. So Karl and Beethoven set out in an open wagon—"a vehicle of the devil, a milk wagon," Beethoven described it— early in the morning of a cold December day.

Before following the two on this journey, we must ask—is it possible that Johann would let his brother depart in so perilous a conveyance, exposed to the winter winds? Even if the departure had been preceded by a quarrel, could Johann have been so heartless as to endanger Beethoven's health, which was already precarious? What were Johann's feelings toward his brother? Here we are treading on uncertain ground. Johann's motives are irreconcilable with one another. At one moment he seems genuinely eager to help his brother, is fond of him, concerned for him. Just the contrary in his next action. He did want Beethoven to live with him; that is proved by his repeated invitations, extended in spite of Beethoven's refusals.—GEORGE R. MAREK

His Friends

Did not all who were privileged to live in the sphere of Beethoven's influence batten on his magnanimity? In a certain sense they all did; everyone enriched himself at his expense either directly through his mind or indirectly through his music. But there were many who in spite of their presumably sincere devotion sought rather their own advantage, or at least the satisfaction of their self-importance or vanity, from the Master who deigned to let them come into contact with him because in return they showed themselves grateful by services of all kinds.

In addition to his real friends from whom in any case he exacted a great deal, but on whose shoulders he could not cast anything, he needed such men who could relieve him of mechanical duties, run errands, or write letters for him. Chief of these was the good-natured, unselfish and obliging bookkeeper Oliva, who, as happened to many others, was suddenly forgotten. For a time, too, his brother Carl, who could be of help in copying music, even in the making of piano arrangements, was his amanuensis.

Oliva's successor was the young Anton Schindler, who in the evening played the violin in the Josefstädter Theater, and in the day worked for the Advocate, Dr. Bach, to whom the Master often entrusted business when he required legal advice, and who one day had occasion to send Schindler to Beethoven with a letter. Once there were difficulties about a passport at Brünn, which nearly led to the young man's arrest, and this so incensed Beethoven—as indeed did all interference with personal liberty during this period of police dominance—that he insisted on obtaining further information from Schindler about the proceedings of the Moravian authorities. This was the beginning of a personal connection which soon became a daily one and lasted from the year 1814 to the day of Beethoven's death. There were naturally not a few interruptions which (it is always the same story) were due to the Master's irritable suspicions and outbursts of hot rage, but also often to Schindler's meddling and unreliability. Anton Schindler was the typical clerk, the real "famulus Wagner" of this magical Dr. Faustus. He was a prematurely aged, jejune, unimaginative and humorless person, with shortsighted eyes peering from a prematurely wizened [face], a long, thin, parchmentlike man with a nasal voice and a dominie's movements of his bony hands, a busybody, pedantic, pompous, born old. With his owl-like solemnity and his self-important angular gestures, he was rather comic withal, but his inclination to scandalmongering and mischief-making made him a little dangerous, and his servility and his tendency to magnify his office and to boast of the confidence that Beethoven reposed in him often led to unpleasantness. All in all perhaps a grotesque and somewhat unpleasant, fundamentally unstable, type of national schoolmaster. He was not dishonorable and in no way stupid. On the contrary, he had plenty of mother wit, but he never made the right use of it, for his fidgety love of detail alternated with a curious slovenliness. He was a self-taught, half-cultivated man, and his musicianship was real but limited, and was directed mainly to practical ends. The magniloquent boasts with which he gave himself out as Beethoven's *alter ego* made him a doubtful and dangerous companion for the Master, who with all his suspicions was often amazingly trustful and easily disconcerted by any strange or evil experience. Beethoven gave him many things to do, but certainly never revealed to him as much of his outward experiences or his inner life as Schindler later tried to gull the world into believing.

There are possibilities which are truer in the highest sense than any mere facts can be. Thus I should like to interpret as a real happening, and not only as an illuminating possibility, the fact that, if we are to believe Heine's playful and half-spiteful statement, he had had engraved on his visiting cards after his name the words "*Ami de Beethoven*" as if they sufficiently described his profession in life. Or did he perhaps regard it as a distinction just as others put on their cards "Knight of the Order of the Red Eagle"? In a certain sense either would have been possible.

His intercourse with Beethoven certainly reflected credit on him. It cannot, however, be denied that after the Master's death Schindler turned this intercourse and his reminiscences and experiences into hard cash, and later made them his chief means of livelihood.

We need not be astonished that this dry, conceited gentleman's chief ambition was to have been selected by his "Great Friend" as the official Beethoven biographer. We may well imagine how it galled him that he was twice passed over, and how it must have hurt him that the Master nominated to this honorable office—and what was worse by a written declaration—the hated Carl Holz and later Friedrich von Rochlitz. His ability and real claim to such an ambitious task may be recognized only in so far as he had more material at his disposal than the others. But he clearly had not the faintest notion that Beethoven could never have dreamed of choosing him for such a mission, for he lacked two indispensable qualities, in addition to those of the mind and the heart: truthfulness and reliability. Never would the Master, who always demanded of his biographer the most rigid sincerity and right understanding, have entrusted the task to Anton Schindler of all men. He often called him Papageno on account of his lack of discretion, and was often obliged to request him not to take the lock from his mouth. He even had to allow Beethoven to say of him: "With all your commonness, how would it be possible for you not to misunderstand all that is uncommon?" Moreover, his reckless way of acting on his own responsibility and using the name of Beethoven often caused both of them many a bad quarter of an hour.

More than once he was simply thrown out of the house, and the most humiliating abuse was hurled at him, and over and over again he was scolded for his unreliability: "To invite yourself and then not to come is just part and parcel of what you are and what you never should be. *Dixi*."

It is true indeed that immediately after such an outburst and as soon as his anger had evaporated, Beethoven would be friendly, even touchingly anxious about Schindler's well-being. Even during his last illness, when he was told of an accident which had caused his *adlatus* financial embarrassment, he placed all his possessions at his disposal as he always did: "None of my friends must starve as long as I myself have a penny," he said in his downright way, and: "At least, take your food from me—it is most gladly given."

Once before, things had come to such a pass that Beethoven angrily refused to accept even any gratuitous services from that "contemptible object" and "miserable rogue." He was obliged to teach him his place and emphatically ask him kindly not to appear until he was asked. But he was always befooled by his good-natured heart, while at the back of his mind he knew perfectly well who were his true friends and who the riffraff.

Of all those who threatened to put a spoke in Schindler's wheel and whom he therefore pursued with his venomous hate, no one was as unwelcome to him as Carl Holz, the young cellist of the Schuppanzigh Quartet. Many people called him the Master's Mephisto, and the world suspected him of having led Beethoven into crooked ways, although as far as I know not a single fact of this kind has actually been established. It cannot be denied, however, that he often dragged the Master, who withdrew himself more and more from his fellow-men, and sank deeper and deeper into black despondency, out of himself into cheerful company with a bottle of respectful wine.

It was a good work to do.

It is just as unreasonable to draw the inference that these escapades were only an excuse for alcoholic excess, as to reproach Holz with having set Beethoven a bad example and put temptations in his way, which led to the early fatal issue of his illness.

The fact that the treatment ordered by the doctor, which was based on these false premises, was mistaken, was proof how unfounded these accusations were. They were indeed refuted by the small fact that just at this time Beethoven even handed on a present of valuable Tokay which had come to him, to the "Samothracian good-for-nothing" Schindler, as Beethoven loved to call him when he was in a good temper, bidding the thirsty theater musician to refresh his throat with it. A real toper, such as some people have not hesitated to call Beethoven, would certainly have drunk it all himself.

Holz knew very well what he was doing when he dragged the Master from his solitude. His actions certainly smacked of opportunism, and he imagined he would make himself very pleasant to the Master when he tried to cheer him by releasing him from the unpleasant company of his worthless brother, or the tedious Schindler. He was versatile, clever, always ready for high-spirited fun, and never took offense. Compared with Schindler the Moderato, he was the Presto. He was perhaps not exactly a valuable and sincere companion of Beethoven's lighter hours, but he certainly was not the evil spirit that the fancy of some people has created, and his must have been a really shrewd and sympathetic brain, if Beethoven could even think him capable of writing a description of his life and his work.

Nevertheless, it was not because Schindler tried to make him suspicious of Holz by spreading all kinds of rumors that the Master never trusted him fully, even when he sent him on important and delicate missions. Any machinations of Schindler would rather have roused him to opposition, yet there was in his mind an uneasy feeling against Holz which was never set at rest. It is significant in this connection how a chance remark of an innocent child was enough to turn the scales against him. The little Gerhard von Breuning confessed that he could not stand Holz, and urged Beethoven not to trust him too much, for most people were saying that he was a false friend. Now there was no positive evidence to prove this, and it is doubtful whether it was a good thing that Schindler should have succeeded in driving Holz from the Master's bedside, for he was always cheerful and ready to do a service, and knew better than anyone else how to dispel the patient's morbid fancies. Had he been allowed to stay the patient would not have been so grossly neglected.

Beethoven was in any case difficult to handle when ill, but remarkably ready to submit to any measures which he felt to be sensible. Had Gerhard been at hand, he would never have been tended with so little care and such neglect of even the most elementary cleanliness. On this point we have once more the evidence of the little Gerhard who one day wrote in positive alarm in the Conversation Book: "I heard today that you are so disturbed by insects that you are awakened every moment from your sleep, but as sleep is so good for you now, I will send you something to drive them away."

We cannot help admiring the touching anxiety of that vivacious, sympathetic boy who better than the adults could appreciate the mental and physical needs of the Master.

But there was no power that could bring him any means of driving away the human vermin who disturbed his waking hours.—RICHARD SPECHT

His Nephew, Karl

Beethoven's nephew Karl was born on September 4, 1806. He was the only child of Beethoven's brother, Karl Kaspar. This brother died of consumption on November 20, 1815, aged forty-one. He was a cashier in the R. I. Bank and Chief Treasury. He had married Theresia Reiss, a daughter of a rich upholsterer. In Karl Kaspar's will there was the following clause:

> I appoint my brother Ludwig guardian, since my deeply beloved brother has often helped me with true brotherly love in the most conscientious and noble manner I ask in full confidence and trust in his noble heart, that he shall bestow the love and friendship he has often shown to me upon my son Karl, and do all that is possible to advance the intellectual training and future welfare of my son. I know that he will not deny me this request.

But Karl Kaspar added a codicil, dated November 14, 1815, which reads as follows:

> Having learned that my brother Herr Ludwig van Beethoven desires after my death to take wholly to himself my son Karl, and wholly withdraw him from the supervision and training of his mother, and since my brother and my wife are not on good terms, I have

found it necessary to add to my will that I by no means wish
my son to be taken from his mother; but that he shall always and
for so long as his future career permits remain with his mother,
to which end the guardianship of him is to be exercised by her
as well as my brother. The object which I have in view in appointing my brother guardian of my son can only be obtained by unity.
Therefore, for the well being of my child, I recommend submission
to my wife and more moderation to my brother. God permit them
to be harmonious for the sake of my son's welfare. This is the
last wish of the dying husband and brother.

KARL VAN BEETHOVEN.

Beethoven disliked his brother's wife, partly because she had been
unfaithful to him, having had an intrigue with a medical student. He described her as the "Queen of the Night." Since years of Beethoven's life
were wasted in the quarrel with this woman over the guardianship of
Karl, her son and his nephew, it is advisable to give a short account of it
here. In 1816 Beethoven appealed to the Upper Austrian Landrecht to
have the guardianship of his nephew transferred solely to him, on the
ground that the boy's mother was an unfit person. A decision was given
in his favor, and an order was made on the nineteenth of January 1816
empowering Beethoven to take possession of Karl, who was still with
his mother. Beethoven sent his nephew to a private school directed by
Giannatasio del Rio. He petitioned the Landrecht to prohibit Karl's
mother from communicating with her son; but this was granted with
the reservation that the mother should be allowed to visit her son
in his leisure hours without disturbing his education. In January 1818
Beethoven removed Karl, who was now twelve years old, from Giannatasio and engaged a tutor for him. Although Beethoven, in a letter to
Streicher, dated January 1818, admitted that a mother, "even a bad one,
remains a mother," yet he was very headstrong and jealous, and endeavored constantly to prejudice Karl against his mother. Consequently,
in September 1818, Madame van Beethoven petitioned the Landrecht
to remove the guardianship from [Ludwig van] Beethoven. The petition
was rejected; but at the end of the year 1818 Karl ran away from Beethoven, and the mother made a fresh petition. In the course of Beethoven's
examination before the Landrecht he stated that he got his nephew back
from his mother with the aid of the police, and that the boy's means
of subsistence were half of his mother's pension and the interest on
two thousand florins. Up to that time Beethoven himself had paid the
difference between this sum and the expense of Karl's education and
upbringing. In the cross-examination of Karl, aged twelve years, he was
asked why he had left his uncle, and he replied that it was because
his mother had told him that she would send him to a public school, and
he did not think he would progress under private instruction. He said

his uncle treated him well, and that he would rather live at his uncle's if he had a companion; his uncle was hard of hearing and he could not talk with him. The boy was asked whether his uncle admonished him to pray, and he replied yes, that he prayed with him every night and morning. During this process the question was raised whether Beethoven was of noble birth or not, and as it was decided that he was not, the matter was transferred to a lower court. This lower court took the side of Madame van Beethoven. In 1819, Beethoven retained the right to look after the education of his nephew; but in March 1819 he was persuaded to resign his guardianship, and at the suggestion of Beethoven the court appointed Counselor Matthias von Tuscher guardian of the boy on March 26. In May of that year Beethoven appealed to the Archduke Rudolf to use his influence to aid him in getting his nephew sent far away from his mother's influence; but his plan to send his nephew out of the country was frustrated. Later in 1819 Tuscher resigned his guardianship, and Beethoven gave notice to the court that he himself would resume the guardianship, and made application to be recognized as sole guardian. This was not granted, and an appeal to a higher court was made in the year 1820. Beethoven's case was prepared by Dr. Bach, and after a great deal of litigation, the Court of Appeal ultimately gave its decree in Beethoven's favor. Karl's mother now appealed to the emperor, who upheld the decision of the Court of Appeal, and on July 24, 1820, Beethoven finally won his case. All his friends were delighted when this litigation was at last over. It cost Beethoven a great amount of energy, and his relations with his nephew, who had become the sole object of Beethoven's emotions, were a source of constant worry and distress. It is possible that this business was partly responsible for Beethoven's nonproductiveness during the years 1816–1820.

We now [skip] to an incident which caused Beethoven great distress. His nephew Karl was a young man of twenty years of age, clever but unreliable. He had matriculated at the University of Vienna sometime in 1823 and studied philology. In 1824 he expressed a wish to enter the army, but in 1825, he entered the Polytechnic Institute, where he idled a good deal, was extravagant, and got into debt. Beethoven, who, since finally gaining his lawsuit in 1820, has been entirely responsible for Karl's upbringing and treated him as his adopted son, was constantly worried and tormented by his overwhelming feeling for Karl. Karl for many years had been the sole human object of Beethoven's affections, and in his passionate ambition for Karl's future he expected from this quite ordinary and not unintelligent young man what only a boy of extraordinary gifts and exceptional character could have achieved. Many of Beethoven's biographers denounce Karl as worthless because he caused Beethoven such suffering. This is pure bathos. The fact is that the extraordinary genius and powerful personality of Beethoven weighed like a range of Alps upon this quite decent young man. And Beethoven in spite of his inward struggle to be fair to the boy's mother—a fairness which he occasionally practiced, as we have already seen from letters quoted—occasionally gave way to the most violent jealousy. The following extract from a letter to his nephew in the year 1825 give[s] a good picture of Beethoven's feelings.

BADEN, *May* 22

Although I have been informed by somebody that again there have been secret meetings between you and your mother, up till now I have only suspected it—have I once more to suffer the most abominable ingratitude? No, if the tie between us is to be broken, let it be so, but you will be hated by all impartial people who hear about it. The statements of my Herr Bruder and those of Dr. Reissig, as he says, and yours yesterday concerning Dr. Sonleitner who necessarily must feel offended with me, as the law court decided exactly the opposite of what he demanded, do you think that I would risk once more to be mixed up in these vulgarities?—No, never more—if the *Pactum* is irksome to you, then, let it be so, I leave you to Divine Providence; I have done my part, and can appear fearless before the highest of all judges. Do not be afraid to come to me tomorrow, I still only suspect. God grant that nothing of it is true, for in truth there would be no limit to your unhappiness, likely as this scamp of a brother of mine and perhaps your mother, may think of your gossiping with the old woman. I shall expect you with certainty.

One day, about the middle of 1826, Holz rushed into Beethoven's room and told him that Karl was going to shoot himself. Holz and Beethoven immediately set out for the house of Schlemmer, were Karl had been living. The following conversation began:

Schlemmer. I heard that your nephew intended to shoot himself. . . . I gather it was on account of debts. I made a search and found in his drawers a loaded pistol. I sent you notice that you might act as his father. The pistol is in my charge. Be gentle with him or he will be driven to despair.

Holz. What is to be done? He said "what is the use of preventing me: if I do not succeed today it will be done another time."

Beethoven. He will drown himself.

Holz. If he had already made up his mind to destroy himself he would certainly have told no one.

Holz and Beethoven then went to the police station. From there they went on to his mother's, where they discovered a note in a pocketbook written by Karl: "Now it is done, torment me no more with reproaches and complaints."

Beethoven. When did it happen?

Karl's mother. He has just come. The coachman carried him down off a rock at Baden. He has a ball in the left side of his head.

Beethoven visited Karl in hospital and said, "If you have a secret trouble, reveal it to me through your mother." Holz told Beethoven that Karl had said to him that it was not hatred, but "quite another feeling which irritates him against you. He gives no other reason but imprisonment at your house, the existence under your surveillance," and Breuning told Beethoven that his nephew stated at the police station that "it was your constant worrying him which had driven him to the deed." Karl said to the magistrate who conducted the inquiry after his recovery: "I have become worse because my uncle insisted upon making me better." The result of this escapade was to steady Beethoven's nephew somewhat. Schindler relates that Karl's attempted suicide was a terrible blow to Beethoven, and that after this affair "he looked like a man of seventy." Beethoven's friends tried to persuade him now to resign his guardianship; but he writes in his conversation book:

I wanted only to accomplish his good. If he is abandoned now something might happen.

At last Beethoven consented to his nephew becoming a soldier. In January 1827 Karl went to his regiment at Iglau, and Beethoven was greatly relieved. Karl never saw his uncle again; but Beethoven left him all his property. A very interesting incident occurred when Beethoven made a codicil just before his death appointing Karl as his sole heir. The codicil reads

My nephew Karl shall be my sole heir. The capital of my estate shall, however, descend to his natural heirs or to those appointed by him through a Will.

Signed,

LUDWIG VAN BEETHOVEN

VIENNA, *March* 23, 1827

This codicil was signed by Beethoven three days before his death in the presence of Stephan von Breuning. To Breuning's great surprise Beethoven changed the word "legitimate" before "heirs" into "natural" and refused to restore the word "legitimate," which was originally written.

—W. J. TURNER

Karl and His Descendants

In his article, "The Famliy van Beethoven," published in the Musical Quarterly,[1] Donald W. MacArdle has presented an admirably complete history of the composer's family and a thorough bibliography on the subject.

At the time of his uncle's death, Karl van Beethoven was enrolled in Archduke Ludwig's 8th Infantry Regiment under Baron von Stutterheim at Iglau in Moravia. He hurried to Vienna upon hearing the news but arrived too late for the funeral.

In 1832 he resigned from the army and in August of that year married Caroline Naske. After two years as an administrator of a farm in Niklowitz, he received an appointment as frontier commissioner, which he held for two more years. In 1848 his uncle Johann died. Since Johann's wife, Therese, had already died twenty years before, Karl received the entire estate of his uncle, which amounted to 42,123 florins. He was now the beneficiary of the estates of both his uncles and was able to live the last ten years of his life in comfortable circumstances. He died on April 13, 1858.

Karl's widow was left with five children, one son and four daughters. From the marriages of these daughters there were twelve children. The name of Beethoven was continued through Karl's son, Ludwig, who was born on March 8, 1839. In a codicil to his will dated March 23, 1827, Beethoven had indicated that the capital to his estate was to be used by Karl's "natural or testamentary heirs." Thus, from 1858, the year of Karl's death until 1874, the date of her last withdrawal, Caroline received financial support from this source. According to her daughters, she also received help from a pension provided by music-lovers in Vienna as well as from royalties from foreign theaters. She died in 1891.

Karl's son, Ludwig, married Marie Nitche in 1865. He had a varied career which became less and less distinguished as it developed: noncommissioned officer in the army, employee in the Chancellery of the German Order, traveling correspondent or salesman in various cities where, increasingly, he came afoul of the law, and finally, ordinary swindler. According to Sandberger,[2] Richard Wagner gave him introductions in Munich in 1868 and 1869 which led to his wheedling over a thousand

[1] MQ, xxv, No. 4 (1949), pp. 528-50.
[2] Adolph Sandberger, "Beiträge zur Beethoven-Forschung" in Archiv für Musikwissenschaft, Vol. 2 (1920), p. 398.

florins from King Ludwig. His activities during the next three years, which included his trading in a variety of fictitious Beethoven memorabilia, led to his imprisonment in 1872 for a term of four years. Nothing definite is known about his life hereafter, but MacArdle has found clues that indicate that he may have come to the United States and been employed as a foreman-inspector on the Pacific Railroad.

Ludwig had a son, Karl Julius Maria, who was born in 1870. He spent most of his childhood in Belgium, where he became a journalist. At the beginning of World War I he was living in England with his mother and an adopted brother. Then the family returned to their native Munich, and Karl enrolled in the army. In 1917, he died in an army hospital in Vienna, the last in the composer's branch of the family to bear the name Beethoven.—ALEXANDER WHEELOCK THAYER, EDITED BY ELLIOT FORBES

Beethoven and His Copyists

Geniuses, as a rule, are not even-tempered, and Beethoven was certainly no exception. Misunderstandings and quarrels with relations and friends were of common occurrence, though for the most part of short duration. Many were doubtless due to his state of health and to his great infirmity, deafness. His blunt, outspoken manner and his strong conviction for the moment that he was right did not tend to smooth matters. Only the surface of the sea is agitated during a storm, and in like manner Beethoven, despite passing passions, was at heart true and well-meaning.

Of his relations with his copyists there are few details, yet enough to show that at times his temper was tried, and, as will be seen, in one instance lost:

Schlemmer

Beethoven was very fortunate in his copyist Schlemmer. Dr. Gerhard von Breuning, who wrote "Aus dem Schwarzspanierhause," giving an account of the composer's last days, heard from his mother that Schlemmer had worked for Beethoven for thirty years. In that case he must have begun in 1793, soon after Beethoven's arrival in Vienna, to study under Haydn. Schlemmer may have done occasional work for him, but he was not regularly engaged until about 1811. In that year Beethoven wrote to his great friend Zmeskall, who helped him in all kinds of ways—servant-hunting, buying hats and looking-glasses, cutting quill pens, etc.—informing him "that I am thinking of taking into my service a man who copies music, and who has offered to come." The unpractical composer, however, would first like to talk over the matter with his friend.

That man was, we presume, Schlemmer; for in a letter written in March, 1812, Beethoven says: "The illness of my copyist—since I cannot trust my works to any other—is the greatest hindrance." On a paper attached to this letter was the following: "I confess that up to now I was unable to copy the two Overtures—but I promise to deliver the copies by Thursday about 12 o'clock." And this was written and signed by Schlemmer.

In Dr. Frimmel's "Beethoven-Jahrbuch," vol. ii., a letter to Ries, Beethoven's former pupil, dated March 8, 1819, was published for the first time. Beethoven, who had sent him a manuscript, ascribes the many faults in it to the fact that "my *copyist* Schlemmer, poor fellow! is getting old—as, indeed, we all are." And in a letter written the following month (April 19), also to Ries, he speaks about not being able to afford to have his own copyist. But that breat was only temporary, since four years later we find Beethoven apologizing to another publisher on account of many corrections in a manuscript he had sent, and saying: "My old copyist can no longer see, and the younger man must first be trained."

Thus poor Schlemmer is not only getting older, but soon he will be unable to do any more work. Beethoven evidently meant "can no longer see clearly," for four months later (July 1, 1823) Schindler is told to give Schlemmer some fine paper, "as it will be easier for him to write the trombone parts on it."

On June 1, just a month before this letter, Beethoven wrote to the Archduke Rudolf:

"The Variations [in the last sonata, Opus 111] were copied at least five or six weeks ago; meanwhile my eyes prevented me from revising them; in vain I hoped for a thorough restoration. I therefore got Schlemmer himself to do so; and if they do not look very elegant, still they are, very probably, correct."

The words "Schlemmer himself" seem to say, "as a last resort, for I did not like troubling him." Beethoven, suffering at the time with his own eyes, was no doubt in a sympathetic mood.

In that same month Beethoven hears that Schlemmer is dying.

It is a common saying that health is not valued until it is lost. And

Beethoven felt his loss deeply when Schlemmer died, and all the more when he had to engage new men. In a letter to the publisher Schott, he refers to a manuscript score which he promises in a week, and says:

"As the score must be printed correctly, I must still go through it several times, for I have no skillful copyist. He whom I had was buried a year and a half ago. I had full confidence in him, but a new man, to become anything like him, must first be trained."

And to Ries in 1825, respecting a manuscript of the "Opferlied" in which he had made corrections, he says:

"Here you have an example of the wretched copyists[1] whom I have had since Schlemmer's death. There was scarcely a note I could trust."

Of the copyists with whom he had dealings three are known by name—Rampel, Gläser, and Wolanek; and a few lines shall be added concerning them.

Rampel

This copyist began to work for Beethoven, as we have seen, while Schlemmer was still alive. He seems to have got on fairly well. Yet at times he was incorrect. In a letter to Holz, his secretary, the composer writes: "Do for heaven's sake impress on Rampel to write everything as it stands," and he gives certain cases in which this was not done. The work in question was the Quartet in A minor (Opus 132). One letter from Beethoven to Rampel has been preserved:

BEST RAMPEL,

Come early tomorrow morning, but go to the devil with your calling me gracious. God alone can be called gracious. The housemaid I have already engaged; only impress on her to be honest and attached to me, and punctual in her small services.—Your devoted

BEETHOVEN

[1] Those who have seen Beethoven's handwriting will at once understand the difficulty the new copyists must have had in reading his scores. Schlemmer at first may have made mistakes, but Beethoven, accustomed for many years to the clever deciphering of his hieroglyphics, may have forgotten them.

Peter Gläser

Franz Gläser, the composer, was conductor at the Josephstadt Theater, Vienna. In 1822 he sent for his father, Peter Gläser, who was in poor circumstances, hoping to procure work for him as copyist. Beethoven's Overture, "Die Weihe des Hauses," was produced at a concert in the Josephstadt Theater in 1822 (October 3). At the final rehearsal Beethoven sat at the piano with Gläser close to him as assistant, though really, on account of the composer's deafness, chief conductor. At a concert in November in the same theater, Beethoven conducted his "Gratulations-Menuett," and Gläser an overture of his own. These facts are mentioned to show that the two men were well acquainted with each other, so that Gläser no doubt spoke to Beethoven about his father.

Peter Gläser, however, did not seem very experienced. While he was copying the Choral Symphony, Beethoven wrote him a long letter, begging him to write the words under the notes exactly as in the manuscript score which he was copying.

Ferdinand Wolanek

In a letter to Ries, Beethoven points out certain grave faults in copies of the Choral Symphony and Mass in D, and says: "You will see what kind of a copyist I have now"; and he describes Wolanek as "an out-and-out Bohemian."

This man sent back his work unfinished, and with it an insolent letter. The composer returned it scratched through, and wrote underneath some caustic remarks. Here is one: "Scribbler! Stupid fool! Correct your own faults, caused through ignorance, arrogance, self-conceit, and stupidity."

Had the composer been able to control his feelings, he would not have condescended to answer the letter. Wolanek, apparently, was the last and worst of Beethoven's copyists, for when the composer wrote the

Second Finale to the Quartet in B flat (Opus 130), in place of the Fugue, which at the earnest request of his friends he discarded, he himself wrote out the parts. This was only a few months before his death, and that Finale was his last composition.—J. S. SHEDLOCK (2)

Contemporary Reminiscences

Gioacchino Rossini

[It must not] be imagined that all the German musicians were against Rossini, though they might deplore the stupid excesses of his admirers. Beethoven said that Rossini would have been a great composer had his teacher only given him a good licking, and surprised a certain organist and composer called Freudenberg by declaring that Rossini, though his music was the embodiment of the frivolous spirit of the times, was a man of talent and an excellent melodist, whose facility was such that he could write an opera in as many weeks as a German would take years. His own ardent supporter, the composer Kanne, wrote a detailed and laudatory analysis of *Zelmira*, while Carpani, another of Beethoven's friends, produced a paean of praise on the subject so fulsome that one understands only too easily the irritation of Weber and those who thought like him.

If Rossini gave much to Vienna he received from it much in return. Previously, he can have known little of Beethoven's music except a few early quartets and piano sonatas. During his stay there he was introduced for the first time to several new quartets and, above all, to the *Eroica* Symphony. This seems to have made such a deep impression on him that he ardently desired to pay the composer a visit, an ambition by no means easy of accomplishment, for Beethoven remained notoriously unapproachable. The publisher Artaria was first tried as an intermediary without success; next Salieri. It was Carpani, whom Beethoven much liked, who eventually procured for Rossini the desired interview.

A strange meeting! On the one hand, the thirty-year-old Rossini, elegant, popular, successful, bubbling over with the joy of living; on the other hand, the prematurely aged, Titan-like Beethoven, disheveled and dirty, racked with care and disease. In any case, the interview must have been difficult, for Beethoven was totally deaf, and Carpani had to write down everything Rossini said. Rossini later gave Wagner an extremely vivid account of the visit, describing with much feeling how deeply he had been affected by the squalor of Beethoven's lodgings, so filthy and untidy, with large holes in the ceiling. The story is best related in his own words:

"The familiar portraits of Beethoven give a good general idea of what he looked like but no picture could express the indefinable sadness apparent in his every feature. Under the thick eyebrows his eyes shone as if from the back of a cavern; they were small but they seemed to pierce. His voice was soft and rather veiled.

"When we entered he at first paid no attention but continued to correct some proofs. Then suddenly, raising his head, he said in fairly good Italian: 'Ah, Rossini, so you're the composer of *The Barber of Seville*. I congratulate you; it is an excellent *opera buffa* which I have read with great pleasure. It will be played as long as Italian opera exists. Never try to write anything else but *opera buffa*; any attempt to succeed in another style would be to do violence to your nature.'

"'But,' interrupted Carpani, 'Rossini has already composed a large number of *opere serie—Tancredi, Otello, Mosè*. I sent you the scores a little while back to look at.'

"'Yes, and I looked at them,' answered Beethoven, 'but, believe me, *opera seria* is ill suited to the Italians. You do not possess sufficient musical knowledge to deal with real drama, and how, in Italy, should you acquire it? Nobody can touch you Italians in *opera buffa*, a style ideally fitted to your language and your temperament. Look at Cimarosa; how much better is the comic part of his operas than all the rest! And the same is true of Pergolesi. You Italians have a high opinion of his religious music and I grant that there is much feeling in the *Stabat*; but as regards form it is deficient in variety, and the effect is monotonous. Now *La Serva Padrona . . . !*

"I then expressed my profound admiration for his genius and my great gratitude for having been allowed to voice it in person. He answered with a deep sigh: 'O un infelice!' "[1]

After a pause Beethoven asked for certain details about theaters and singers in Italy, whether Mozart's operas were frequently performed, and so on. Finally, with an expression of good wishes for the success of *Zelmira*, he led Rossini and Carpani to the door, his last words being: "Remember, give us plenty of *Barbers*."

Rossini told Wagner how, going down the dilapidated stairs and thinking of Beethoven's isolation and destitution, he could not restrain his tears. Carpani remarked that it was Beethoven's own fault; he was a morose old misanthrope incapable of keeping any friends. Rossini, how-

[1] The necessary paraphrase, "O, unhappy I!" gives perhaps some idea of the dramatic misery of Beethoven's original Italian.

ever, could not drive the impression of sadness out of his mind; the sigh of "infelice" haunted his ears. That evening there was a dinner party at Prince Metternich's house. Conscious of a feeling almost of resentment against the consideration shown to himself by the brilliant society of Vienna, he tried to persuade several of the people he met to subscribe toward a permanent income for Beethoven. Nobody, however, would have anything to do with the scheme, assuring him that, even if Beethoven were provided with a house, he would very soon sell it, for it was his habit to change his abode every six months and his servant every six weeks.

After dinner there was a reception at which the whole of Viennese society was present. Among the music performed was one of Beethoven's trios, rapturously applauded. The contrast between the squalor in which the composer lived and the elegance of the surroundings in which his work was given, again struck Rossini with a sense of tragic incongruity. Later, he tried once more to do something for Beethoven, himself heading a subscription list. To no purpose, however. The answer was always the same: "Beethoven is impossible."—FRANCIS TOYE

Maurice Schlesinger (1819)

Born as Moritz, son of the Berlin music-publisher Adolf Martin Schlesinger, he went into business for himself at Paris in 1821 or 1822 and, as a farsighted, shrewd and progressive music-publisher, soon helped to make musical history. Of Beethoven's works he acquired principally the Pianoforte Sonatas, Opus 109, 110, 111 and the Quartets, Opus 132 and 135. How he won the good will of Beethoven, he amusingly told A. B. Marx in a letter of February 27, 1859, printed in the latter's Beethoven biography.

I cannot refrain from telling how, in the year 1819, I made Beethoven's acquaintance, and owing to what chance I was lucky enough to have him become fond of me. I was in Steiner & Company's vault when Haslinger, their partner, said: "There comes Beethoven. Do you care to make his acquaintance?" When I said that I did he added: "He is deaf. If you have something to say to him write it down at once. He does not like to reveal his affliction to people." He then introduced me and Beethoven invited me to visit him in Baden. This I did a few days later. Stepping from my carriage I entered the tavern, and there found Beethoven stalking out of the door, which he slammed to after him, in a rage. After I had removed some of my travel stains, I went to the house pointed out as his dwelling. His housekeeper told me that I probably would be unable to speak to him, since he had returned home in a rage. I gave her my visiting-card, which she took to him and, to my great surprise, returned a few minutes later and told me to enter. There I found the great man sitting at his writing-desk. I at once wrote down how happy I was to make his acquaintance. This (what I had written) made a favorable impression. He at once gave free rein to his feelings and told me he was the most wretched man in the world; he had but just returned from the tavern, where he had asked for some veal which he felt like eating—and none had been available! All this he said in a very serious, gloomy way. I consoled him, we talked (I myself writing) about other things, and thus he kept me for nearly two hours; and though, afraid of boring or molesting him, I several times rose to go, on each occasion he prevented me from taking my departure. Leaving him, I hurried back to Vienna in my carriage; and at once asked my innkeeper's son whether he had some roast veal ready. When he said he had, I made him put it in a dish, carefully cover it and, without a word of explanation, sent it back to Baden by the man, in the carriage I had kept, to be presented to Beethoven with my compliments. I was still lying in bed the following morning when Beethoven came to me, kissed and embraced me, and told me I was the most kindhearted person he had ever met; never had anything given him such pleasure as the roast veal, coming at the very moment when he so greatly longed for it.—O. G. SONNECK (1)

Sir John Russell (1821)

The following is taken from Sir John's book "A tour in Germany, and some of the southern provinces of the Austrian Empire, in 1820, 1821, 1822." (Edinburgh, 1828.)

Beethoven is the most celebrated of the living composers in Vienna and, in certain departments, the foremost of his day.[1] Though not an old man, he is lost to society in consequence of his extreme deafness, which has rendered him almost unsocial. The neglect of his person which he exhibits gives him a somewhat wild appearance. His features are strong and prominent; his eye is full of rude energy; his hair, which neither comb nor scissors seem to have visited for years, overshadows his broad brow in a quantity and confusion to which only the snakes

---

[1] [Footnote of Sir John.] Beethoven has died since this was written. He died, moreover, in want, amid a people who pretend to be the most devoted worshipers of music and musicians.

round a Gorgon's head offer a parallel. His general behavior does not ill accord with the unpromising exterior. Except when he is among his chosen friends, kindliness or affability are not his characteristics. The total loss of hearing has deprived him of all the pleasure which society can give, and perhaps soured his temper. He used to frequent a particular cellar, where he spent the evening in a corner, beyond the reach of all the chattering and disputation of a public room, drinking wine and beer, eating cheese and red herrings, and studying the newspapers. One evening a person took a seat near him whose countenance did not please him. He looked hard at the stranger, and spat on the floor as if he had seen a toad; then glanced at the newspaper, then again at the intruder, and spat again, his hair bristling gradually into more shaggy ferocity, till he closed the alternation of spitting and staring, by fairly exclaiming "What a scoundrelly phiz!" and rushing out of the room. Even among his oldest friends he must be humored like a way- ward child. He has always a small paper book with him, and what conversation takes place is carried on in writing. In this, too, although it is not lined, he instantly jots down any musical idea which strikes him. These notes would be utterly unintelligible even to another musician, for they have thus no comparative value; he alone has in his own mind the thread by which he brings out of this labyrinth of dots and circles the richest and most astounding harmonies. The moment he is seated at the piano, he is evidently unconscious that there is anything in exist- ence but himself and his instrument; and, considering how very deaf he is, it seems impossible that he should hear all he plays. Accordingly, when playing very *piano*, he often does not bring out a single note. He hears it himself in the "mind's ear." While his eye, and the almost imperceptible motion of his fingers, show that he is following out the strain in his own soul through all its dying gradations, the instrument is actually as dumb as the musician is deaf.

I have heard him play; but to bring him so far required some manage- ment, so great is his horror of being anything like exhibited. Had he been plainly asked to do the company that favor, he would have flatly refused; he had to be cheated into it. Every person left the room, except Beethoven and the master of the house, one of his most intimate acquaintances. These two carried on a conversation in the paper book about bank stock. The gentleman, as if by chance, struck the keys of the open piano, beside which they were sitting, gradually began to run over one of Beethoven's compositions, made a thousand errors, and speedily blundered one passage so thoroughly, that the composer con- descended to stretch out his hand and put him right. It was enough; the hand was on the piano; his companion immediately left him, on some pretext, and joined the rest of the company, who in the next room, from which they could see and hear everything, were patiently waiting the issue of this tiresome conjuration. Beethoven, left alone, seated himself at the piano. At first he only struck now and then a few hurried and interrupted notes, as if afraid of being detected in a crime; but gradually he forgot everything else, and ran on during half an hour in a fantasy, in a style extremely varied, and marked, above all, by the most abrupt transitions. The amateurs were enraptured; to the uninitiated it was more interesting to observe how the music of the man's soul passed over his countenance. He seems to feel the bold, the commanding, and the impetuous, more than what is soothing or gentle. The muscles of the face swell, and its veins start out; the wild eye rolls doubly wild, the mouth quivers, and Beethoven looks like a wizard, overpowered by the demons whom he himself has called up.—O. G. SONNECK (1)

Wilhelmine Schröder-Devrient (1822)

This great dramatic artist (1804–1860) made her operatic *début* in 1821 as "Pamina" in Mozart's "Magic Flute." The very next year she established herself as one of the consummate artists of her time as "Leonore" in Beethoven's opera "Fidelio." Indeed, this until then ill-fated work owed much of its rise to permanent popularity to her. Richard Wagner's admiration for her is well attested by his treatise "About Actors and Singers" (1872). Two years before her death she received an offer to tour America, but could not accept it. The following reminiscences of Beethoven she contributed in 1846 to Schilling's "Beethoven Album."

It was in the year 1823 [actually November 3, 1822] when for the birthday of the defunct Emperor Francis I, Beethoven's "Fidelio," which had been lying dormant for several years, was put in rehearsal again at the Vienna *Kärnthnertor* theater. My children's shoes no more than discarded, I already had made my first timid attempts as a budding singer and probably owing more to the lack of some other, more fitting impersonatrix, than because of any conviction that I already was capable of singing the role of Leonore, that difficult part was entrusted to me.

With youthful unconcern, and far removed from realizing the magnitude of my task, I undertook the study of the role to which, at a later period, I was principally indebted for the fact that my name was mentioned abroad among the names of other German artists with especial recognition. Under the guidance of my intelligent mother many a trait of Leonore's character became clear to me; at the same time I was still too young, too little developed inwardly completely to conceive what was taking place in Leonore's soul; those emotions for which Beethoven had found his immortal harmonies. At the rehearsals, directed by the then conductor Umlauf, the inadequacies of my undeveloped child voice were soon recognized, and many alterations were made in my part so that it would not suffer too greatly in effect. The last rehearsals already had been announced when, before the dress rehearsal, I learned that Beethoven had requested the honor of conducting his work himself on the ceremonial day. At this news I was seized with a nameless dread, and I still recall my illimitable awkwardness at the last rehearsal, which had driven my poor mother and the assisting artists who surrounded me to despair.

But Beethoven sat in the orchestra and waved his baton above the heads of us all, and I never had seen the man before!

At that time the Master's physical ear already was deaf to all tone. With confusion written on his face, with a more than earthly enthusiasm in his eye, swinging his baton to and fro with violent motions, he stood in the midst of the playing musicians and did not hear a single note! When he thought they should play *piano*, he almost crept under the conductor's desk, and when he wanted a *forte*, he leaped high into the air with the strangest gestures, uttering the weirdest sounds. With each succeeding number we grew more intimidated, and I felt as though I were gazing at one of Hoffmann's fantastic figures which had popped up before me. It was unavoidable that the deaf Master should throw singers and orchestra into the greatest confusion and put them entirely off beat until none knew where they were at. Of all this, however, Beethoven was entirely unconscious, and thus with the utmost difficulty we concluded a rehearsal with which he seemed altogether content, for he laid down his baton with a happy smile.

Yet it was impossible to entrust the performance itself to him, and Conductor Umlauf had to charge himself with the heart-rending business of calling his attention to the fact that the opera could not be given under his direction. He is said to have resigned himself with a sorrowful heavenward glance; and I found him sitting behind Umlauf in the orchestra the following evening, lost in profound meditation. You probably know with what enthusiasm the Vienna public greeted "Fidelio" on that occasion, and also that since that performance this immortal work has found a permanent place in the repertoire of the German operatic stage. Every artist taking part in the performance accomplished his task that evening with enthusiastic devotion; for who would not gladly have given his last breath for the wretched Master who heard nothing of all the beauty and glory he had created! Beethoven followed the entire performance with strained attention, and it seemed as though he were trying to gather from each of our movements whether we had at least half understood his meaning.

In those days they already insisted on calling me a little genius; and that evening it really seemed as though a more matured spirit possessed me, for several genial original traits flashed up in my portrayal which could not have escaped Beethoven's notice, since he himself, the exalted Master, came the following day to express to me his thanks and recognition. I moistened the hand he offered me with hot tears, and in my joy would have exchanged all the earth's worldly possessions for this praise from Beethoven's lips. He promised me at the time to write an opera for me, but unfortunately that was as far as it went. Soon afterward I left Vienna and a few years later Beethoven's lofty spirit winged its way back to that primal bourne from whence it had come. He did not live to see his "Fidelio" become domiciled in the capitals of France and Albion, nor to realize that his childishly timid Leonore of 1823, who later herself had developed a greater comprehension of his genius, was able to do her part in securing due and full recognition for so tremendous a work in its German fatherland as well. The consciousness of having laid down even one more wreath in Beethoven's spreading hall of fame—whom would it not fill with joy? And so may these lines also testify to the gratitude, the veneration I have vowed and shall continue to vow his lofty spirit as long as I live.—O. G. SONNECK (1)

Franz Liszt (1823)

It is a curious fact that occasionally those who began their career as prodigies in later years develop an aversion against "Wunderkinder." This was true of Beethoven and it required considerable urging on the part of Schindler, as we know from a conversation of his with Beethoven on April 13, 1823, to persuade the master to attend a concert of Franz Liszt, then eleven years old, on the following day. Apparently there is a chronological conflict between this authentic conversation and Liszt's reminiscences of his only visit to Beethoven, which he communicated in 1875 to his pupil, Ilka Horowitz-Barnay. If Czerny took Liszt to Beethoven on the morning of his concert, the discrepancy would disappear.

I was about eleven years of age when my venerated teacher Czerny took me to Beethoven. He had told the latter about me a long time before, and had begged him to listen to me play sometime. Yet Beethoven had such a repugnance to infant prodigies that he always had violently objected to receiving me. Finally, however, he allowed himself to be persuaded by the indefatigable Czerny, and in the end cried impatiently: "In God's name, then, bring me the young Turk!" It was ten o'clock in the morning when we entered the two small rooms in the *Schwarzs-panier* house which Beethoven occupied; I somewhat shyly, Czerny amiably encouraging me. Beethoven was working at a long, narrow table by the window. He looked gloomily at us for a time, said a few brief words to Czerny and remained silent when my kind teacher beckoned me to the piano. I first played a short piece by Ries. When I had finished Beethoven asked me whether I could play a Bach fugue. I chose the C-minor Fugue from the Well-Tempered Clavichord. "And could you also transpose the Fugue at once into another key?" Beethoven asked me. Fortunately I was able to do so. After my closing chord I glanced up. The great Master's darkly glowing gaze lay piercingly upon me. Yet suddenly a gentle smile passed over his gloomy features, and Beethoven came quite close to me, stooped down, put his hand on my head, and stroked my hair several times. "A devil of a fellow," he whispered, "a regular young Turk!" Suddenly I felt quite brave. "May I play something of yours now?" I boldly asked. Beethoven smiled and nodded. I played the first movement of the C-major Concerto. When I had concluded Beethoven caught hold of me with both hands, kissed me on the forehead and said gently: "Go! You are one of the fortunate ones! For you will give joy and happiness to many other people! There is nothing better or finer!" Liszt told the preceding in a tone of deepest emotion, with tears in his eyes and a warm note of happiness sounded in the simple tale. For a brief space he was silent and then he said: "This event in my life has remained my greatest pride— the palladium of my whole career as an artist. I tell it but very seldom and—only to good friends!"—O. G. SONNECK (1)

Franz Grillparzer (1823)

Possibly the great Austrian poet's reminiscences of Beethoven would never have been recorded had he not in 1840 felt compelled to take issue with statements by Ludwig Rellstab affecting the miscarriage of the project to write in collaboration with Beethoven an opera on "Melusine." With all his growing respect and admiration for Beethoven, Franz Grillparzer (1791– 1872) never quite seems to have shared Beethoven's aesthetic views. His aphorism "Beethoven: Chaos," however, quoted by Mr. Philip Gordon in his able article in *The Musical Quarterly* on "Franz Grillparzer: Critic of Music" ought not to be taken too literally. Mr. Gordon also quotes Grill-parzer's touching words on how he came to write his famous funeral oration for Beethoven: "Schindler had come to me with the news that Beethoven was dying and that his friends wanted me to write a funeral address to be spoken by the actor Anschütz at his grave. . . . I had come to the second part of the oration, when Schindler came again and told me that Beethoven had just died. Then something snapped inside me; the tears rushed from my eyes, and I could not finish the speech as elegantly as I had begun. However, the address was made . . . I had really loved Beethoven. . . ."

I first saw Beethoven in my boyhood years—which may have been in 1804 or 1805—at a musical evening in the home of my uncle, Joseph Sonnleithner, at that time an associate partner in an art and music business in Vienna. Besides Beethoven, Cherubini and the Abbé Vogler were among those present. Beethoven in those days was still lean, dark, and contrary to his habit in later years, very elegantly dressed. He wore glasses, which I noticed in particular, because at a later period he ceased to avail himself of this aid to his shortsightedness. I no longer recall whether he himself or Cherubini played, and only remember that when the servant already had announced that supper was served, Abbé Vogler sat down at the piano and commenced to play endless variations on an African theme which he had brought in person from its natal land. During his musical exploitation of it the company gradually drifted into the dining-room. Only Beethoven and Cherubini remained. At last Cherubini also disappeared, and Beethoven alone remained standing beside the industriously working pianist. Finally he, too, lost patience, though Abbé Vogler, now entirely deserted, never ceased caressing his theme in every way, shape and manner. I myself had stayed in the room in my dazed astonishment at the monstrous nature of the entire proceedings. As to what transpired from that moment on, my memory, as often is the case where the recollections of childhood are concerned, is entirely at fault. Who sat beside Beethoven at the table, whether he conversed with Cherubini, and whether Abbé Vogler joined them later—I feel as though a dark curtain had been dropped over all of it in my mind.

One or two years later I was living with my parents during the summer in the village of Heiligenstadt, near Vienna. Our dwelling fronted on the garden and Beethoven had rented the rooms facing the street. Both sets of apartments were connected by a hall in common which led to the stairs. My brothers and I took little heed of the odd man who in the meanwhile had grown more robust, and went about dressed in a most negligent, indeed even slovenly way, when he shot past us with a growl. My mother, however, a passionate lover of music, allowed herself to be carried away, now and again, when she heard him playing the piano, and entering the connecting hall would stand, not beside his door, but immediately beside our own in order to listen with devout attention. This she may have done a couple of times when suddenly Beethoven's door flew open, he himself stepped out, saw my mother, hurried back and at once rushed down the stairs into the open, hat on head. From that moment he never again touched his piano. In vain my mother, since every other opportunity was lacking, had a servant assure him that not alone would she no longer eavesdrop on his playing, but that our door leading to the hall should remain locked, and her household, in place of the stairs in common, would make a broad detour and use only the garden entrance. Beethoven remained inflexible and his piano stood untouched until finally the late autumn brought us back to town again.

During one of the summers which followed I made frequent visits to my grandmother, who had a country house in the adjacent village of Döbling. Beethoven, too, was living in Döbling at the time. Opposite my grandmother's windows stood the dilapidated house of a peasant named Flohberger, notorious for his profligate life. Besides his nasty house, Flohberger also possessed a pretty daughter, Lise, who had none too good a reputation. Beethoven seemed to take a great interest in this girl. I can still see him, striding up the *Hirschgasse*, his white handkerchief dragging along the ground in his right hand, stopping at Flohberger's courtyard gate, within which the giddy fair, standing on a hay- or manure-cart, would lustily wield her fork amid incessant laughter. I never noticed that Beethoven spoke to her. He would merely stand there in silence, looking in, until at last the girl, whose taste ran more to peasant lads, roused his wrath either with some scornful word or by obstinately ignoring him. Then he would whip off with a swift turn yet would not neglect, however, to stop again at the gate of the court the next time. Indeed, his interest was so great that when the girl's father was put in the village lockup (known as the *Kotter*) for assault and battery while drinking, Beethoven personally interceded for his release before the village elders assembled. But as was his habit, he handled the worthy counselors in so tempestuous a manner that he came near keeping his captive protégé company against his will.

Later I saw him mostly on the street, and once or twice in a coffee-house, where he spent much time with a poet of the Novalis-Schlegel guild, now long since dead and gone, Ludwig Stoll. It was said that they were projecting an opera together. It is inconceivable how Beethoven could have expected to secure something serviceable from this unstable dangler; in fact, anything but—well versified, it is true—mere fantastic fantasies.

Meanwhile I myself had set my feet in the road of publicity. The *Ahnfrau, Sappho, Medea, Ottokar* already had been published, when suddenly Count Moritz Dietrichstein, then intendant of both the Court theaters, sent me word that Beethoven had applied to him to ask whether he could induce me to write an opera libretto for the composer.

The inquiry, I may as well confess, placed me in a decided quandary. First of all, the idea of writing an opera libretto in itself was far from my thoughts; and then I doubted whether Beethoven—who had become totally deaf in the interim, and whose last compositions, despite their lofty value, had assumed a harshness which to me seemed in contradiction with the treatment of the voice-parts—I doubted, I repeat, whether Beethoven still was able to compose an opera. The thought, however, of supplying a great man with a possible opportunity of writing a work which, in any event, would be highly interesting overweighed all other considerations, and I gave my consent.

Among the dramatic subjects I had noted down for future development were two which, at any rate, seemed to admit of treatment in operatic style. The one moved in the domain of the most exalted passion. Yet aside from the fact that I knew of no singer who could have undertaken the leading role, I did not wish to give Beethoven an opportunity, by spurring him on with a half diabolic subject, of drawing still nearer those extremest boundaries of music which already yawned before his feet like threatening abysses. Hence I chose the legend of Melusine, separated and put aside, so far as was possible, its reflective portions and attempted, by the dominance of the choruses and tremendous finales, and by giving the third act a well-nigh melodramatic shape, to adapt myself as well as might be to the peculiarities of Beethoven's last trends.

In the course of the summer of 1823, I visited Beethoven in Hetzendorf, on his invitation, together with Mr. Schindler. I do not know whether Schindler told me while we were underway, or whether someone else had remarked before that Beethoven hitherto had been prevented by urgent work he had been commissioned to do from undertaking the composition of the opera. Hence I avoided touching on the subject in conversation.

We took a walk and conversed together as well as was possible, half-talking, half-writing, while walking. I still recall with emotion that Beethoven, when we sat down to the table, went into the adjoining room and himself brought in five bottles. One he set down by Schindler's plate, one before his own and the remaining three he stood up in a row before me, probably to tell me, in his naïvely savage, good-natured way that I was at liberty to drink as much as ever I wished. When I drove back to town without Schindler, who remained in Hetzendorf, Beethoven insisted upon accompanying me. He sat down with me in the open carriage, but instead of merely going to the outskirts of the village he drove back all the way to town with me, and getting out at the gates started off on his long hour and a half journey home alone, after heartily pressing my hand. As he got out of the carriage I saw a paper lying on the spot where he had been sitting. I thought he had forgotten it and beckoned him to return. But he shook his head and laughing loudly, like one who thought he had been successful in playing a trick, ran off all the faster in the opposite direction. I unwrapped the paper, and it contained the exact amount of carriage-hire I had agreed to pay my driver. So thoroughly had Beethoven's manner of life estranged him from all the habits and customs of the world that it never occurred to him how insulting such a procedure would have been under any other circumstances. I took the thing, however, as it was meant, and laughingly paid the coachman with the gift money.

Later I saw him, I no longer remember where, only once more. At that time he said to me: "Your opera is finished." Whether by this he meant completed in his head, or whether the countless notebooks in which he was accustomed to jot down individual thoughts and figures for future development, comprehensible only to him, also may have contained the elements of this opera in fragmentary form, I cannot say.

It is certain that after his death not a single note was discovered which with positivity might have had reference to our work of collaboration. I myself, incidentally, remained faithful to my resolve not to recall it to him even in the most indirect manner and, since I found our written conversation very inconvenient, did not come near him again until, clad in black and with a burning torch in my hand, I walked behind his coffin.—O. G. SONNECK (1)

Sir George Smart (1825)

In his two volumes of Beethoven-reminiscences of contemporaries, Kerst begins his note on Sir George Smart (1776–1867) with the words "George Smart, an English music-publisher, visited Vienna in 1825." The date is correct, but this could have been a visit in spirit only, since George Smart, the father of Sir George (knighted in 1811) had died long ago. However, in a sense Sir George was a "publisher" of music, too, for he conducted with eminent skill many concerts of the Philharmonic Society of London and numerous music-festivals. Among many other noteworthy events he had to his credit the first performance of the Ninth Symphony at London on March 21, 1825. Indeed, it was because of his ardent championship of Beethoven's symphonies that he visited Vienna and called on Beethoven with whom he thus far had formed an acquaintance by correspondence only. He went to Germany in company with Charles Kemble whose object it was to engage Weber to compose an opera for Covent Garden and it was at Sir George's house that the composer of "Oberon" lived as a guest and died on June 5, 1826.

Sir George kept a diary of his experiences. They were published as "Leaves from the Journal of Sir George Smart" by Longmans, Green & Co., in 1907, and the following narrative is quoted from that delightful book.

Friday, September 9th. . . . We then went to Mecchetti's music shop, they too are publishers, and bought three pieces for Birchall. . . . Mr. Holz, an amateur in some public office and a good violin player, came in and said Beethoven had come from Baden this morning and would be at his nephew's—Carl Beethoven, a young man aged twenty—No. 72 Alleegasse. . . . At twelve I took Ries to the Hotel Wildemann, the lodgings of Mr. Schlesinger, the music-seller of Paris, as I understood from Mr. Holz that Beethoven would be there and there I found him. He received me in the most flattering manner. There was a numerous assembly of professors to hear Beethoven's second new manuscript quartet, bought by Mr. Schlesinger. This quartet is three-quarters of an hour long. They played it twice. The four performers were Schuppanzigh, Holz, Weiss, and Lincke. It is most chromatic and there is a slow movement entitled "Praise for the recovery of an invalid." Beethoven intended to allude to himself, I suppose, for he was very ill during the early part of this year. He directed the performers, and took off his coat, the room being warm and crowded. A staccato passage not being expressed to the satisfaction of his eye, for alas, he could not hear, he seized Holz's violin and played the passage a quarter of a tone too flat. I looked over the score during the performance. All paid him the greatest attention. About fourteen were present, those I knew were Boehm (violin), Marx (cello), Carl Czerny, also Beethoven's nephew, who is like Count St. Antonio, so is Boehm, the violin player. The partner of Steiner, the music-seller, was also there. I fixed to go to Beethoven at Baden on Sunday and left at twenty-five minutes past two. . . .

Saturday, September 10th. . . . Previous to this sightseeing I called for the music at Artaria's for Birchall, for which I paid, and on our return found a visiting-card from Earl Stanhope and also from Schlesinger of Paris with a message that Beethoven would be at his hotel tomorrow at twelve, therefore, of course, I gave up going to Baden to visit Beethoven, which he had arranged for me to do. . . .

Sunday, September 11th. . . . From hence I went alone to Schlesinger's at the "Wildemann," where was a larger party than the previous one. Among them was L'Abbé Stadler, a fine old man and a good composer of the old school, to whom I was introduced. There was also present a pupil of Moscheles, a Mademoiselle Eskeles and a Mademoiselle Cimia, whom I understood to be a professional player. When I entered Messrs. C. Czerny, Schuppanzigh and Lincke had just begun the trio, Opus 70 of Beethoven, after this the same performers played Beethoven's trio, Opus 79—both printed singly by Steiner. Then followed Beethoven's quartet, the same that I heard on September the 9th, and it was played by the same performers. Beethoven was seated near the pianoforte, beating time during the performance of these pieces. This ended, most of the company departed, but Schlesinger invited me to stop and dine with the following party of ten. Beethoven, his nephew, Holz, Weiss,

C. Czerny, who sat at the bottom of the table, Lincke, Jean Sedlatzek
—a flute player who is coming to England next year and has letters
to the Duke of Devonshire, Count St. Antonio, etc.—he has been to
Italy—Schlesinger, Schuppanzigh, who sat at the top, and myself. Beethoven calls Schuppanzigh Sir John Falstaff, not a bad name considering
the figure of this excellent violin player.

We had a most pleasant dinner, healths were given in the English
style. Beethoven was delightfully gay but hurt that, in the letter Moscheles
gave me, his name should be mixed up with the other professors. However, he soon got over it. He was much pleased and rather surprised
at seeing in the oratorio bill I gave him that the "Mount of Olives"
and his "Battle Symphony" were both performed the same evening. He
believes—I do not—that the high notes Handel wrote for trumpets
were played formerly by one particular man. I gave him the oratorio
book and bill. He invited me, by his nephew, to Baden next Friday.
After dinner he was coaxed to play extempore, observing in French
to me, "Upon what subject shall I play?" Meanwhile he was touching
the instrument thus,[1] to which I answered, "Upon that." On which
theme he played for about twenty minutes in a most extraordinary
manner, sometimes very fortissimo, but full of genius. When he rose at
the conclusion of his playing he appeared greatly agitated. No one could
be more agreeable than he was—plenty of jokes. He was in the highest of
spirits. We all wrote to him by turns, but he can hear a little if you
halloo quite close to his left ear. He was very severe in his observations
about the Prince Regent never having noticed his present of the score
of his "Battle Symphony." His nephew regretted that his uncle had
no one to explain to him the profitable engagement offered by the
Philharmonic Society last year. I have had a most delightful day.
Schlesinger is very agreeable, he knows Weber and Franz Cramer's
family. About seven I took a little walk with Carl Czerny—whom Neate
taught, he says, to speak English. I then went to his house and played
four or five duets with him, they are clever compositions but not easy.
He taught young Liszt. About nine I went home by myself, having
promised to go to C. Czerny's on Wednesday evening.

On Friday, September 16th, at half-past eight in the morning young
Ries came and we went in a hired carriage from Mödling to Baden. The
distance is about six miles south of Mödling and sixteen miles south-
west of Vienna. The journey cost five florins in paper money and took
us about an hour. After walking in the little park and looking at the
baths we went to Beethoven's lodgings according to his invitation. These
are curiously situated, a wooden circus for horsemanship has been
erected in a large court before his house. He has four large-sized
rooms opening into each other, furnished *à la genius*, in one is the grand
pianoforte, much out of tune, given him by Broadwood, in which

---

[1] Smart writes out a two-measure scherzando phrase.—Editor.

is written, besides the Latin line, the names of J. Cramer, Ferrari, and C. Knyvett. Beethoven gave me the time, by playing the subjects on the pianoforte, of many movements of his symphonies, including the Choral Symphony, which according to his account took three-quarters of an hour only in performance. The party present, namely Holz, the amateur violin; Carl Beethoven, the nephew; besides young Ries, agreed that the performance at Vienna only took that time; this I deem to be totally impossible. It seems at Vienna the Recit. was played only with four celli and two contra bassi which certainly is better than having the tutti bassi. Beethoven and we deservedly abused Reicha's printed specimen of fugueing. He told me of a Mass, not yet published, which he had composed. We had a long conversation on musical subjects conducted on my part in writing. He is very desirous to come to England. After ordering his dinner with his funny old cook and telling his nephew to see to the wine, we all five took a walk. Beethoven was generally in advance humming some passage. . . . On our return we had dinner at two o'clock. It was a most curious one and so plentiful that dishes came in as we came out, for, unfortunately, we were rather in a hurry to get to the stagecoach by four, it being the only one going to Vienna that evening. I overheard Beethoven say, "We will see how much the Englishman can drink." *He* had the worst of the trial. I gave him my diamind pin as a remembrance of the high gratification I received by the honor of his invitation and kind reception and he wrote me the following droll canon[1] as fast as his pen would write in about two minutes of time as I stood at the door ready to depart.

He was very gay but I need not write down more, for memory will ever retain the events of this pleasurable day with Beethoven.—O. G. SONNECK (1)

Gerhard von Breuning (1825–27)

Moritz *Gerhard* von Breuning (1813–1892) was the son of Court-Councilor of War Stephan von Breuning, the friend of Beethoven since youth and whom by a strange coincidence of Fate he survived by only two months: he died at Vienna on June 4, 1827. Late in life, in 1874, Gerhard von Breuning gave to the musical world his delightfully reminiscent book "Aus dem Schwarzspanierhause" which was to be the great composer's last lodging.

[1] The canon Sir George mentions [is on the words "*Ars longa, vita brevis*,"] and the dedication translated into English reads as follows:

Written on the 16th of September, 1825, in Baden, when my dear talented musical artist and friend Smart (from England) visited me here.

LUDWIG VAN BEETHOVEN

Beethoven took a fancy to the bright boy, calling him his "Trousers-button" and his "Ariel." He also interested himself in his musical education. On one occasion, for instance, he had Gerhard play for him, listened critically and recommended Clementi's method instead of Czerny's. The lad's droll remarks often cheered Beethoven but his great friend's misery also weighed heavily at times on the kindhearted boy. Of this we possess a pathetic proof in one of the *Conversations Hefte* shortly before Beethoven's death: having heard that the sick master's nights were made sleepless by vermin, the solicitious Gerhard brought with him a disinfectant to relieve the dying Beethoven from such torture.

In August, 1825, while taking an afternoon walk with my parents, I was fortunate enough to make Beethoven's acquaintance. We were walking along the promenade which runs around the city of Vienna and cuts its Escarpment (*glacis*) and at the moment we were between the *Kärnthnerthor* and the *Karolinentor*, into which latter gate my father meant to turn to take his way to his office, when we saw a man walking alone making directly for us. Our meeting, no sooner had we sighted one another, was followed on both sides by an unusually friendly exchange of greetings. He was powerful looking, of medium height; his walk as well as his very lively movements were energetic; his dress was not elegant but rather that of a plain townsman; and yet there was something about his appearance as a whole which escaped all classifications of caste.

He spoke almost uninterruptedly, asking how we were, questioning us about our present mode of life, our relatives on the Rhine and many other things and—hardly waiting for an answer to his query why my father had not visited him for so long a time, etc.—told us that some time ago he had been living in the *Kothgasse* and of late in *Krugerstrasse*, but that he was spending the summer in Baden. It was with quite special and joyous haste, however, that he informed us that soon—toward the end of September—he would move into our immediate vicinity, into the *Schwarz-spanierhaus* (we were living in the so-called "Red" house belonging to Prince Esterházy, lying opposite to it at right angles) and this information called forth increased interest on our part. He added that he expected to see us much and often; and at once begged my mother at last to put his poorly managed housekeeping arrangements into order, to keep eye on them, etc.

My father, though he said less when he did speak, spoke in a manner noticeably loud and distinct and with lively gesticulations; and amid hearty and repeated assurances of both the wish and the will to see much of him in the near future we parted from him for that day.

The wish I often had expressed to my parents: that I might meet Beethoven, had at last been granted, and with youthful impatience I counted the days which would bring me into that long-yearned for closer touch with the friend of my father's youth, whose name had so often been mentioned to me. . . .

On various occasions the flames of love leaped high in Beethoven's heart, yet ever at bottom with the honest fundamental thought: "Not until I have the right to call you mine!"

Once my father told my mother, when she had incidentally said to him that she could not quite understand how Beethoven, since he was neither handsome nor elegant, but looked positively unkept and unkempt, could have been such a favorite with the ladies: "And yet he always has been fortunate with women." Beethoven always, where women were concerned, showed himself possessed of noble, elevated sentiments, whether in his friendships or in his love affairs.

On one occasion I visited Beethoven in his house in the *Ungargasse*, near the Escarpment. He happened to be standing at the piano with his hands on the keyboard. When he saw me he brought down both hands on the keys with a crash, laughed and walked away from the piano. With this he probably meant to say to me: "You thought I was going to play something for you, but that is just what I am not going to do!" Nor did I ask him.

Though all his household affairs were now in such good order [Frau von Breuning had put Beethoven's housekeeping arrangements into shape], the way in which he kept his room continued to be just as disorderly. His papers and possessions were dusty and lay about higgledy-piggledy; and in spite of the dazzling whiteness and cleanliness of his linen and his repeated bodily ablutions, his clothes remained unbrushed. This inordinate bathing may, perhaps, in some past time have been the primary incidental cause and origin of his deafness—perhaps owing to a rheumatic inflammation—rather than his "predisposition for intestinal complaints," as so often has been taken for granted. He always had been in the habit, after he had sat for a long time at the table composing and this had heated his head, of rushing to the washstand, pouring pitcherfuls of water over his overheated head and, after having thus cooled himself off and only slightly dried himself, of returning to his work or, even, in the meanwhile, hastening out into the open for a brief walk. All this was done in the greatest hurry, so that he might not be snatched out of his imaginative flight. How little he thought at the time of the need of drying his thick hair, sopping wet, is proven by the fact that, without his noticing it, the water he had poured over his head would flood the floor in quantities, leak through it, and appear on the room-ceiling of the lodgers living beneath him. This, on occasion, led to annoyances on the part of his fellow lodgers, the janitor and, finally, the owner of the house and even was responsible for his being given notice.

He liked to have us invite him to dinner, and would often send us a portion of fish, if he had ordered some bought for himself in the market; for fish was one of his favorite dishes and when he himself liked something he liked to share it with his friends.

Beethoven's outward appearance, owing to that indifference to dress peculiar to him, made him uncommonly noticeable on the street. Usually lost in thought and grumbling to himself, he not infrequently gesticulated with his arms as well when walking alone. When he was in company, he spoke very loudly and with great animation and, since whoever accompanied him was obliged to write down his answers in the conversation notebook, the promenade was interrupted by frequent stops, something which in itself attracted attention and was made more conspicuous by the replies he made in pantomime.

Hence the majority of those whom he met turned around to look when he had passed, and the street boys even poked fun at him and called after him. For this reason nephew Karl disdained to go out with Beethoven and once told him plainly that he was ashamed to accompany him in the street because he looked such a fool, a remark anent which Beethoven expressed himself to us in a deeply hurt and wounded manner. For my own part, I was proud to be allowed to show myself in the company of this great man.

The felt hat then worn, upon Beethoven's homecoming, though it might be dripping wet with rain, after merely giving it a slight shake (a habit he always observed in our house, without concern for what was in the room) he would clap on the very top of the hatrack. In consequence it had lost its even top and was vaulted in an upward bulge. Brushed infrequently or not at all, before and after it had rained, and then again allowed to grow dusty, the hat acquired a permanently matted appearance. In addition he wore it, so far as possible, back from his face in order to leave his forehead free; while on either side his gray, disordered hair, as Rellstab so characteristically says, "neither curly nor stiff, but a mixture of all," stood out. Owing to his putting on and wearing his hat away from his face and back on his head, which he held high, the hat's hinder brim came into collison with his coat-collar, which at that time shot up high against the back of the head; and gave the brim in question a cocked-up shape; while the coat-collar itself, from its continual contact with the hat brim, seemed to have been worn away. The two unbuttoned coat-fronts, especially those of the blue frock coat with brass buttons, turned outward and flapped about his arms, especially when he was walking against the wind. In the same manner the two long ends of the white neckerchief knotted about his broad, turned-down shirt-collar streamed out. The double lorgnette which he wore because of his nearsightedness hung loosely down. His coattails, however, were rather heavily burdened; for in addition to his watch, which often hung out on the one side, in the pocket of the other he had a folded quarto notebook, anything but thin, besides a conversation notebook in octavo format and a thick carpenter's pencil, for communication with friends and acquaintances whom he might meet; and also, in earlier days, while it still aided him, his ear-trumpet. The weight of the notebooks considerably extended the length of the coattail containing them and, in addition, the pocket itself because of its own frequent pulling out and that of the notebooks, hung down visibly on the same side, turned outward.

The well-known pen and ink drawing [Böhm's drawing, since Lyser's apparently first came into being after Beethoven's death] gives a fair idea of Beethoven's figure, even though he never wore his hat pressed sideways, as the drawing—with its usual exaggeration—presents it. The above sketch of Beethoven's outward appearance had been inextinguishably impressed upon my memory. It was thus that I so often saw him from our windows, toward two o'clock—his dinner-hour—coming from the direction of the *Schottentor* across the Escarpment where the Votive Church now stands, his body and head, as usual, projecting (not stooping) forward, and bearing down alone upon his own house; or I myself might be walking with him.

In the street, where there was not always sufficient time to write, conversation with him was most difficult, and, that he was absolutely deaf was attested to me by the following striking proof, had proof been needed. Once we expected him for dinner, and it already was almost two o'clock, our dinner-hour. My parents, always suspecting that, lost in composition, he might not remember the appointed time, sent me out to fetch him over. I found him at his work-table, his face turned toward the open door of the room in which stood the piano, working at one of the last (Galitzin) quartets. With a brief upward glance, he bade me wait awhile, until he had set down on paper the thought which preoccupied him at the moment. For a short time I remained quiet, then I moved over to the piano standing nearest at hand, the one by Graff (with the attached resonance-gatherer) and, not convinced of Beethoven's tone-deafness, began to strum softly on the keys. Meanwhile I looked over at him again and again, to see whether this disturbed him. But when I saw that he was quite unconscious of it I played more loudly; then, purposely, very loudly—and my doubts were resolved. He did not hear me at all, and kept on writing with entire unconcern until, having at last finished, he summoned me to go. In the street he asked me something: I screamed the answer directly into his ear; but he understood my gestures rather than my words. Only once, when we were sitting at table, one of my sisters uttered a high, piercing shriek; and to know that he still had been able to hear it made Beethoven so happy that he laughed clearly and gleefully, his dazzlingly white and unbroken rows of teeth fully visible.

Characteristic, too, was the liveliness with which he discussed circumstances that interested him, and at such times it might even chance that walking up and down the room with my father, he would spit into the mirror instead of out of the window, without knowing it.

On September 24, 1826—it was my birthday—Beethoven was again our dinner guest in honor of the occasion. While we were eating, he told us that the Vienna city council had made him a Vienna citizen, and in this connection had informed him that he had become, not an ordinary but an honorary citizen, whereupon he had replied: "I did not know that there were also scandalary citizens in Vienna." [A pun on "Ehrenbürger" and "Schandbürger".]

In the afternoon we all went out to Schönbrunn together, on foot. My mother had a visit to make in Meidling (bordering on Schönbrunn) and I accompanied her. My father, Beethoven and my teacher waited for us on one of the benches in the parterre of the Schönbrunn Garden. When we then went walking in the garden, Beethoven, pointing to the leafy alleys trimmed in wall-pattern according to the French style, said: "Nothing but artifice, shaped up like the old hoop-petticoats! I feel benefited only when I am out where nature is free!" An infantryman passed us. At once he was ready with a sarcastic remark: "A slave, who has sold his independence for five *Kreuzer* a day!"

When we were going home, several boys in the middle of the right-hand park alley in front of the Schönbrunn bridge were playing bowls with a small ball, and the latter accidentally struck Beethoven's foot. Thinking it had been done with malicious intent, to plague him, he at once turned violently on them, calling out: "Who gave you permission to play here? Why do you have to pick out this particular spot for your carrying on?" And he was on the point of rushing on them to drive them away. My father, who feared the brutality of the street arabs, however, soon calmed him, and, besides, the ball which had grazed him had caused him no more than a passing pain.

It was already dark when, returning over the "Schmelz," we lost our way and were compelled to walk straight across the plowed fields. Beethoven growled melodies to himself, as he swayed rather helplessly from one hummock to the next, and, in view of his nearsightedness, was glad to have a guide for the time being.

When his nephew Karl was about to take his examination in technics and, in addition, loaded with debts, felt himself as unprepared in purse as he was in knowledge; besides, furthermore, dreading his uncle's reproaches, of which "he had already long since tired and which he found silly"—he resolved to kill himself. He bought two pistols, drove out to Baden, climbed the tower of the ruinous Castle Rauenstein, and high up in the air, putting both pistols to his temples pressed the triggers—and merely superficially injured the periosteum, yet so that he had to be taken to the General Hospital in Vienna.

The news was a terrible blow to Beethoven. The sorrow which the occurrence caused him was indescribable; he was as downcast as a father who has lost his well-beloved son. My mother met him, seemingly quite deranged, on the Escarpment. "Do you know what has happened to me? My Karl has shot himself!" "And—is he dead?" "No, he only grazed himself; he is still alive and they hope to be able to save him. But how he has disgraced me, and I love him so very dearly!"

I must preface what comes next by telling how now that my ardent desire to enter into close daily communion with Beethoven had been most fully gratified, I nourished the further wish to be able, like my father, to call him "du" [in German the "you" of intimate friendship and affection]. Had I not long since attached myself to him with all my soul, and taken no little pride in knowing he loved me and that I, too, was one among the few chosen ones in this connection? I asked my father how I might introduce the subject and whether he would act for me in the matter. My father replied offhand: "If it will give you pleasure all these circumlocutions are unnecessary; simply address him as 'du,' and he will in nowise be offended, but more apt to be pleased. In any event it will not even seem strange to him." Relying on this encouragement, since I was well aware of how entirely at home my father was where Beethoven's mental processes were concerned, I at once made the venture on the occasion of my next visit, when I was alone with Beethoven (this was during the first earlier period of his illness). With a beating heart, it is true, and yet with venturesome boldness I made my attempt and in the first sentence I wrote down of our conversation, I used this form of address. I watched his features with tension when I held up the slate to him. And—it was as my father had foretold—Beethoven never even noticed it, and thus I henceforth continued to address him.

During his illness (toward the end of February, 1827) one forenoon, Handel's complete works—in a handsome bound quarto volume edition —arrived as a present, sent by the harp virtuoso Stumpff. Beethoven had long cherished the wish to own them, and it was in accordance with this very wish, which he had once expressed, that the gift had been made. When at noon I entered his room, as was my daily custom when the clock struck twelve, he at once pointed to the volumes heaped up on the piano, his eyes radiant with pleasure: "See, this is what I have received as a present today; they have made me very happy with these works! I have wished to own them for a long time because Handel is the greatest, the most solid of composers; from him I still can learn something. Fetch the books over to me!" These and other things he said in connection with them, speaking with joyous excitement. And then I began to hand one after another volume to him in his bed. He turned the pages of one volume after the other, as I gave them to him, at times dwelling a while on certain passages, and then at once laying down one after another book to the right, on his bed, against the wall; until at last all were piled up there, where they remained for several hours, for I found them still there that afternoon. Then once more he began to deliver the liveliest eulogies on Handel's greatness, calling him the most classic and thorough of the tone poets.

Once, as often was the case when I arrived, I found him asleep. I sat down beside his bed, keeping quiet—for I hoped the rest might be strengthening—in order not to awaken him. Meanwhile I turned the pages and read one of the conversation notebooks which was still lying ready for use on the little table next the bed, to find out who had lately visited him, and what had been said. And there, among other things, I found in one place: "Your quartet which Schuppanzigh performed yesterday did not appeal to me." When he awoke a short time after I held the sentence up to him and asked him what he had to say to it: "Someday it will suit them," was his laconic reply. He at once added with legitimate self-confidence some brief remarks to the effect that he wrote as seemed well to him, and did not allow himself to be led astray by contemporary opinion: "I know that I am an artist!"

I improved an opportunity to ask him why he had written no second opera. He answered: "I wished to write another opera but I found no suitable textbook for it. I must have a text which stimulates me; it must be something moral, elevating. Texts which Mozart could compose I would never have been able to set to music. I never have been able to get into the mood for setting lewd texts. I have received many textbooks, but as I have said, none which I would wish to have." And furthermore he said to me: "It was my wish to write many another thing. I wanted to compose the Tenth Symphony, and then a Requiem as well, and the music to 'Faust,' and even a piano method. This last I would have done in a way different from that in which others have written them. Well, I shall no longer get around to that, and, anyhow, so long as I am sick, I will do no work, no matter how much Diabelli and Haslinger may urge me; for I have to be in the mood for it. Often I have been unable to compose for a long time and then all at once the desire returned to me."

Another time I found a sketchbook lying on a piece of furniture in the room. I held it up to him, asking whether he really found it necessary to note down his inspirations. He replied: "I always carry a notebook of the kind about me, and when an idea occurs to me, at once note it down. I even rise at night when something happens to occur to me, since otherwise I might forget the idea."—O. G. SONNECK (1)

His Letters

———◆———

To the Archduke Rudolph

[*Autograph in the Gesellschaft der Musikfreunde, Vienna*]
YOUR IMPERIAL HIGHNESS!

[VIENNA, 1813]

Neither presumption nor a belief that I could intercede for some-body nor a desire to boast of some special favor bestowed upon me by Your Imperial Highness impels me to put forward a request as simply as in itself it is simple—Old *Kraft*[1] came to see me yesterday—He wonders whether it would not be possible for him to be given a lodging in your palace. He said that in return for this privilege he would be at Your Imperial Highness's disposal whenever *you required it*. He told me that he had now spent twenty years in Prince L[obkowitz]'s[2] household, that for a long time he had received no pay and that now he had also to leave his lodging without receiving any compensation—The plight of this poor, old and deserving man is hard and I would certainly have been guilty of callousness had I not made bold to put his case before you—Count Troyer[3] will ask Your Imperial Highness for a reply—Since it is a question of relieving the difficult situation of a human being, I know that you will forgive Your Imperial High-ness's loyal and obedient servant

LUDWIG VAN BEETHOVEN

[1] Anton Kraft (1752–1820), the famous cellist.
[2] Kraft had joined the orchestra of Prince Lobkowitz in 1795. He had not spent twenty years in the Prince's household, for owing to his financial difficulties Lobkowitz had had to leave Vienna in July, 1813.
[3] Count Ferdinand von Troyer, born in 1780, and his brother Franz were cham-berlains to the Archduke Rudolph. The former was a competent clarinettist.

To the Countess Anna Marie Erdödy

[Autograph in the Beethovenhaus, Bonn, H. C. Bodmer collection]

VIENNA, *February* 29, 1815[1]

I have read your letter with great pleasure, my beloved Countess, and also what you say about the renewal of your friendship for me. It has long been my wish to see you and your beloved children once again. For although I have suffered a great deal, yet I have not lost my former love for children, the beauties of nature and friendship— The trio and everything else that has not been published are most certainly at your service, my dear Countess— As soon as the trio has been copied you shall have it.[2] It was not without sympathy and interest that I frequently enquired after your state of health. But now I will call on you sometime in person and I shall have the pleasure of being able to participate in everything that concerns you— My brother has written to you. I beg you to make allowances for him, because he is really an unhappy, suffering man[3]—

The prospect of the coming spring will, I trust, have an excellent influence on your health as well, and perhaps surround you with the happiest of life's realities— May all that is good be your portion, dear and beloved Countess. I send my greetings to your dear children whom I embrace in spirit— I hope to see you soon— Your true friend

LUDWIG VAN BEETHOVEN

[1] The autograph is dated thus. No doubt the letter was written on March 1st.
[2] Probably Opus 97. This trio for pianoforte, violin and cello was first performed by Beethoven, Schuppanzigh and Linke at a charity concert held on April 11, 1814 in the Hotel zum Römischen Kaiser.
[3] Caspar Carl, who died in November, 1815.

To the Archduke Rudolph

[*Autograph in the Gesellschaft der Musikfreunde, Vienna*]
YOUR IMPERIAL HIGHNESS!   VIENNA, *July* 23, 1815
When you were in town a few days ago, this chorus again occurred to me.[1] I hurried home to write it down. But I delayed over it longer than I first thought that I should, and thus to my very great grief I missed Y.I.H.— The bad habit I formed in childhood of feeling obliged to write down my first ideas immediately, apart from the fact that they certainly have often come to nothing, let me down on this occasion also— So I am sending Y.I.H. my own indictment and my apology and hope to receive your gracious pardon— I shall probably to able to betake myself soon to Y.I.H. in order to inquire about your health which is so precious to all of us— Your Imperial Highness's faithful and most obedient
LUDWIG VAN BEETHOVEN

To the Archduke Rudolph, Baden

[*Autograph in the Gesellschaft der Musikfreunde, Vienna*]
YOUR IMPERIAL HIGHNESS!   VIENNA, *July* 11, 1816
In view of your gracious favors to me I am surely justified in hoping that you will not attach *any ulterior motive* to the dedication I am enclosing, a dedication which I have rather mischievously ventured to make (but only so as to give you a surprise). The work was composed for Y.I.H. or, rather, owes its existence to you; and is the world (the world of music, I mean) not to know about it?[2]— I shall soon have the pleasure of being able to wait upon Y.I.H. at Baden. Until now the condition of my chest has not allowed me to do so, notwithstanding all the efforts of my doctor,

[1] According to Kinsky this was Beethoven's setting of Goethe's poems "Meeresstille" and "Glückliche Fahrt" for four voices with orchestral accompaniment. The work was first performed on December 25, 1815, at a charity concert in the Grosser Redoutensaal. It was dedicated to Goethe and published in score by Steiner in February, 1822 as Opus 112.
[2] The sonata for violin and pianoforte, Opus 96, was published by Steiner in July, 1816.

who on that account did not want me to leave Vienna. All the
same, I am better. I hope to hear only good and heartening news
about the condition of your health which is causing us anxiety—
Your Imperial Highness's loyal and most obedient

LUDWIG VAN BEETHOVEN

To the Archduke Rudolph, Baden

[Autograph in the Gesellschaft der Musikfreunde, Vienna]

YOUR IMPERIAL HIGHNESS!   NUSSDORF, *September* 1, 1817

I have been hoping all this time that I should be able to betake
myself to you at Baden. But my ailing condition still persists;
and although in some respects there is an improvement, yet my
complaint is still not absolutely cured. What I have taken and am
still taking to cure it are medicines of all kinds and in all forms.
Well, at last I must abandon the hope I so often cherished of
making a complete recovery—I hear that Y.I.H. is looking wonderfully
well; and though it is quite possible to draw therefrom wrong
conclusions about excellent health, yet I hear people talking about
the improvement in Y.I.H.'s condition, and in this I certainly do
take the most lively interest. I hope too that when Y.I.H. returns
to town I shall be able to assist you in the sacrifices you make
to the Muses—Surely God will hear my prayer and will once more
liberate me from so many calamities, seeing that since my childhood I have served Him trustfully and have performed good
actions wherever I could. Hence on Him alone I place my reliance
and hope that in all my manifold miseries the All-Highest will
not let me utterly perish—

I wish Y.I.H. all the good and beautiful things that can be
conceived; and as soon as Y.I.H. has returned to town, I will
immediately betake myself to you.

Your Imperial Highness's faithful and most obedient servant

L. V. BEETHOVEN

To the Archduke Rudolph, Baden

[*Autograph in the Gesellschaft der Musikfreunde, Vienna*]

YOUR IMPERIAL HIGHNESS!   MÖDLING, *July* 15, 1819

Ever since I was proposing to wait upon Y.I.H. the last time I was in town I have been very unwell. But I hope to be in a better state of health by next week when I shall immediately betake myself to Baden to visit Y.I.H.— Meanwhile I have been in town a few times to consult my doctor— The persistent worries connected with my nephew who has been morally almost completely ruined are largely the cause of my indisposition. At the beginning of this week I myself had again to assume the guardianship, for the other guardian had resigned after perpetrating a good many misdemeanors for which he has asked me to pardon him.[1] The Referent too has resigned his office because, although he was really interested in our good cause, he was being publicly described as prejudiced.[2] So this confusion persists, the end is not in sight, and I am without help or comfort. Everything I built up has been blown down by a hurricane, as it were. Moreover the present proprietor of a boarding school where I have placed my nephew (he was a pupil of Pestalozzi)[3] thinks that it will be difficult for him and for my poor nephew to achieve his desired objective. And he is now of the opinion that by far the best solution would be to send my nephew abroad!— I hope that the health of Y.I.H., which is the health of one of those persons dearest to me, leaves nothing to be desired; and I am already looking forward to being able soon to be with Y.I.H. again and to prove to you my zeal to serve you—

Your Imperial Highness's most obedient and most faithful servant

BEETHOVEN

[1] Matthias von Tuscher resigned early in July.
[2] A "Referent" was an official who reported on the findings of a committee or acted as its secretary.
[3] Joseph Blöchlinger, at whose boarding school Karl was placed on June 22, 1819.

To the Archduke Rudolph, Baden

[Autograph in the Gesellschaft der Musikfreunde, Vienna]

YOUR IMPERIAL HIGHNESS!   MÖDLING, *July* 29, 1819

I was indeed distressed at receiving the report of Y.I.H.'s fresh indisposition; and, as I have had no further definite news, I am extremely anxious— I was in Vienna in order to collect in Y.I.H.'s library what was most useful for me. The chief purpose is *rapid execution* united to a *better understanding of art,* wherein *practical considerations,* however, may of necessity admit certain exceptions[1]; in which connexion the older composers render us double service, since there is generally real artistic value in their works (among them, of course, only the *German Händel* and *Sebastian Bach* possessed genius). But in the world of art, as in the whole of our great creation, *freedom and progress* are the main objectives. And although we moderns are not quite as far advanced in *solidity* as our *ancestors,* yet the refinement of our customs has enlarged many of our conceptions as well. My eminent music pupil, who himself is now competing for the laurels of fame, must not bear the reproach of being one-sided—et iterum venturus judicare *vivos* —et *mortuos*[2]— Here are three poems. Perhaps Y.I.H. might choose one of them to set to music. The Austrians are now aware that the *spirit of Apollo* has come to life again in the Imperial dynasty. From all sides I am receiving requests to obtain something composed by you. *The editor of the Modenzeitung*[3] will send Y.I.H. a *written* request. I trust that *I shall not be* accused in any quarter of *taking bribes— At court and no courtier, why, the possibilities are infinite??!!! His Excellency the Obersthofmeister raised a few objections* when I wanted *to select the music* in Vienna.[4] It is not worth while to trouble Y.I.H. with this in writing. But let me just say this, that by such behavior many a talented, good and noble person would let himself be put off from associating with Y.I.H., unless he had the

---

[1] The words from "united" to "exceptions" are added at the foot of the page.
[2] Quoted from the Nicene Creed, but with the omission of "est cum gloria" after "venturus," i.e. "and will come again in glory to judge the living and the dead."
[3] Johann Schickh (1770–1835), a Viennese draper, founded in 1816 the *Wiener Zeitschrift für Kunst, Literatur, Theater und Mode,* called the *Modenzeitung,* a periodical which he edited until his death. As supplements it had fashion plates, chiefly from French models, and sheet music, mostly songs.
[4] This was Count Ferdinand von Laurencin d'Armont, who was Obersthofmeister (i.e. Chief Steward) of the Archduke Rudolph.

good fortune to have intimate knowledge of your excellent qualities of mind and heart— I wish Y.I.H. a very, very quick recovery and for *myself* some news *to set my mind at rest.*

Your Imperial Highness's most obedient and *most faithful servant*

L. v. BEETHOVEN

To the Archduke Rudolph, Vienna

[*Autograph not traced*][1]

YOUR IMPERIAL HIGHNESS!   MÖDLING, *October* 15, 1819

On account of the vintage not a single carriage was to be had at Mödling; and only today have I been promised one for tomorrow. Hence Y.I.H. will understand why I shall not have the honor (*and the pleasure*) of waiting upon you until tomorrow. I shall be with Y.I.H. punctually at half past three in the afternoon, for I now know that this is the most suitable hour and the one which Y.I.H. prefers— Y.I.H. will remember the written statement about the removal of my nephew from Vienna which you were so kind as to deliver to His Imperial H[ighness] the Archduke Ludwig. I most earnestly beg Y.I.H. to ensure that this document is returned to you, because I urgently need it *on account of the enclosures.* Indeed I should find myself in an exceedingly awkward position if these enclosures were not available. A fresh attack has been launched upon me by the venal Magistrat of Vienna acting in collaboration with my nephew's mother, so that, although I am almost too exhausted to take any further steps in the interest of my nephew under such unworthy auspices, yet for the sake of my honor I must address myself to the Court of Appeal. The impudence, the vulgarity, the ignorance and the wickedness of this Magistrat have now reached the point that even Y.I.H., is, so to speak, almost an object of their attack as well. You will be amazed to hear this. On the other hand, the entire cabal is so brainless that one doesn't know whether to feel distressed or almost to die of laughing. I fancy that the result of this whole disgraceful story will be that Y.I.H. will most graciously have a testimonial written for me about two points in the statement. Y.I.H. will forgive me for again entreating you to be so kind as to have the written statement I sent you returned to me as promptly as possible— Steiner has now received Y.I.H.'s var[iations] and will himself express his thanks to you. By the way, it has just occurred to me that the Emperor Joseph traveled under the name of Count von Falken-

[1] Taken from Frimmel, *Beethovenforschung*, February, 1913, no. 4, pp. 114–115. The autograph was then in private ownership.

stein.[1] This remark refers to the title.— Baumeister, as I have seen in the Gazette, has built his house in eternity[2]— Without laying the slightest claim to being a good *adviser*, I know someone who would fill this post in Y.I.H.'s household to your complete satisfaction — I am greatly looking forward to being with Y.I.H. tomorrow. I dreamt about Y.I.H. last night. Although no music was performed, yet it was a musical dream. But in my waking hours too I think of Y.I.H. The Mass will soon be finished—May Heaven empty the cornucopia of its blessings every day, nay, every hour, upon your illustrious head. As for me I am and shall remain until the last moments of my life

Your Imperial Highness's most faithful and most obedient servant

L. v. BEETHOVEN

To the Archduke Rudolph

[*Autograph in the Gesellschaft der Musikfreunde, Vienna*]

YOUR IMPERIAL HIGHNESS!   [VIENNA, 1819]

I have the honor to send you herewith by the copyist Schlemmer Y.I.H.'s masterly variations, I myself will call on Y.I.H. tomorrow and I already look forward to being able to serve my eminent pupil as his companion in a glorious undertaking—Your Imperial Highness's most humble and most faithful

L. v. BEETHOVEN

To the Archduke Rudolph, Olmütz

[*Autograph in the Gesellschaft der Musikfreunde, Vienna*]

YOUR IMPERIAL HIGHNESS!   VIENNA, *April* 3, 1820

So far as I remember, when I wanted to wait upon you I was informed that Your Highness was indisposed. But I went on Sunday

---

[1] Evidently the Archduke Rudolph was proposing to adopt the *nom de plume* of Count Falkenstein, which Joseph II had used on his travels in 1780. No doubt Beethoven had suggested some similar disguise for his royal pupil. In the end, however, the variations were published under the composer's name.

[2] Baumeister, the private secretary and librarian of the Archduke, had died on October 6th. As usual Beethoven took the opportunity of making a pun, this time on "bauen," to build.

evening to inquire, because I had been assured that Y.I.H. would not leave on Monday. In accordance with my habit of not waiting about for long in the antechamber, I hurried off quickly after receiving this information, although I noticed that the footman wanted to say something more. I was distressed to hear on Monday afternoon that Y.I.H. had really gone off to Olmütz.[1] I admit that this news produced in me an extremely painful emotion. But my conviction that I had not done anything wrong soon persuaded me that just as such incidents frequently occur in similar moments of our mortal life, here was another instance of the same phenomenon. I fully understood that Y.I.H., who was excessively overwhelmed by ceremonies and by your many new experiences, would not have much time at O[lmütz] for anything else. Otherwise I would certainly have hastened to anticipate Y.I.H. in the matter of writing —But now I should like Y.I.H. kindly to inform me how long you have arranged to stay at O[lmütz]. I was told here that Y.I.H would return to Vienna about the end of May. A few days ago, however, I heard that Your Highness would remain at O[lmütz] *for a year and a half*. On that account perhaps I have already taken the wrong steps, *not in respect of Y.I.H.*, however, but in respect of myself. But as soon as I receive some information on this point, I shall explain everything more fully. By the way, I do beg Y.I.H. to pay no attention to some reports about me. I have already heard in Vienna several remarks, which one might describe as gossip, with which people fancy that they can be of service even to Y.I.H. Since Y.I.H. calls me one of your precious possessions, then I can say with confidence that Y.I.H. is to me one of the most precious objects in the whole world. Even though I am no *courtier*, yet I think that Y.I.H. has got to know *this much about me*, that it is no mere frigid interest that attaches me to you, but a true and deep affection which has always bound me to Your Highness and has ever inspired me; and I might say in truth that Blondel has been found long ago and that if there is no Richard for me in this world, then God will be my Richard—It seems that my idea of forming a quartet will certainly be the very thing. Even if similar arrangements are generally made at O[lmütz] on a large scale, yet by means of your quartet wonderful things might be achieved for music in Moravia— If, as the above reports declare, Y.I.H. is to return to Vienna in May, I advise you to save up your spiritual children until then, because it would be better if I were first to hear them performed by yourself. But should your stay at Olmütz be really so prolonged, I shall be extremely delighted to receive them and I shall endeavor to guide Y.I.H. to the highest peak of Parnassus.

God keep Y.I.H. in perfect health for the benefit of humanity and, especially, of those who admire you; and I beg you to be so

[1] In 1820 April 3rd fell on a Monday.

kind as to delight me soon again with a letter. At any rate Your Highness is convinced of my readiness to comply at all times with your wishes.

Your Imperial Highness's faithful and most obedient servant

L. v. BEETHOVEN

To Adolf Martin Schlesinger, Berlin

[Autograph in the Koch collection]

SIR!   VIENNA, March 7, 1821

You have probably formed an unfavorable opinion of me. But you will soon think better of me when I tell you that for six weeks I have been laid up with a violent attack of rheumatism. However, I am better now. But you will understand that many plans had to be set aside for the time being. I shall soon make up for lost time— Well now, let me just give you a brief outline of what is most necessary. Opus 107 is to be written on the songs.[1] If I remember rightly, the names of the *English authors*, which include those of Lord Byron, Scott and so forth, were not added. You will soon receive them— You are at liberty to make the dedication to the Crown Prince of Prussia.[2] Although I had intended the work for someone else, yet in this case I will defer to your wishes— But as to the sonata which you must have received a long time ago, I request you to add the following title together with the dedication, namely,

Sonata for the Hammerklavier
composed and dedicated to
Fräulein Maximiliana Brentano by Ludwig van Beethoven
Opus 109[3]

Would you agree to add the year as well? I have often wanted this, but no publisher would do it.[4]

The other two sonatas will soon follow[5]—and I shall inform you

---

[1] This is a slip of Beethoven's, for Simrock had published Opus 107 during the summer of 1820. In the end the twenty-five Scottish songs published by A. M. Schlesinger in July, 1822, were given the Opus No. 108.

[2] The Crown Prince (1795–1861) became in 1840 Friedrich Wilhelm IV. But Schlesinger dedicated Opus 108 to Prince Anton Heinrich Radziwill (1755–1833), who was also a composer of merit and to whom Beethoven later dedicated his Opus 115.

[3] Schlesinger published this sonata in November, 1821.

[4] Beethoven's wish was carried out in the case of only one of his compositions, his "Missa Solemnis," published by Schott in 1827 as Opus 123.

[5] The pianoforte sonatas, Opuses 110 and 111, were first published by A. M. Schlesinger's eldest son Moritz (Maurice) Schlesinger in Paris in 1822.

of the fee in good time— I have not got your letters beside me. But if I remember rightly, you wanted to have some other works as well. If you send me particulars about these soon, I can then make my arrangements and create what is desirable for my art also to suit my convenience— I wish you all that is to your advantage. You will probably be able to read my manuscript. If you find that proofreading is necessary, please send me proofs both of the songs and of the sonatas. But the manuscript of the songs must be sent with them. This manuscript, I admit, is only a very hastily written copy of my own manuscript, which, however, I do not possess.—

All good wishes, most honored Sir, from your most devoted
                                                            BEETHOVEN

To the Archduke Rudolph, Vienna

[*Autograph in the Gesellschaft der Musikfreunde, Vienna*]

YOUR IMPERIAL HIGHNESS!   UNTERDÖBLING, *July* 18, 1821

I heard yesterday of Your Highness's arrival here which, however gratifying this might have been to me, has now proved to be a sad event for me, for it may be a rather long time before I can enjoy the happiness of waiting upon Y.I.H. I had been very poorly for a long time when finally *jaundice definitely* set in; and in my case it seems to be an extremely objectionable disease. I trust, however, that I shall have recovered sufficiently to be able to see Y.I.H. here before your departure— Last winter too I had the most violent attacks of rheumatism—a great deal of this is to be ascribed to my distressing situation, and particularly to my economic circumstances. Until now I have hoped to overcome the latter eventually by the most strenuous exertions. God who sees into my innermost heart and knows that as a man I perform most conscientiously and on all occasions the duties which humanity, God and Nature enjoin upon me, will doubtless rescue me in the end from my afflictions— The Mass will be delivered to Y.I.H. while you are still in Vienna. Y.I.H. will kindly spare me an enumeration of the reasons for the delay, in as much as such details could not but be, to say the least, unpleasant for Y.I.H. to hear—I would very gladly have written to Y.I.H. from here occasionally. But Y.I.H. had told me here that I should wait until Your Highness should write to me. Well, what was I to do? Perhaps it would have displeased Y.I.H. if I had not paid attention to what you had said. Besides I know that there are people who like to slander me to Y.I.H.; and this hurts me very deeply. So I often think that all I can do is to

keep quiet until Y.I.H. desires to see or hear something of me.—
I have heard that Y.I.H. is indisposed. I trust that your indisposition
is not serious. May Heaven shower blessings in richest measure on
Y.I.H. I hope that it will not be too long before I shall have
the happiness of being able to tell Y.I.H. how much I am

　　　　Your Imperial Highness's most obedient and faithful servant
　　　　　　　　　　　　　　　　　　　　　　　　　　BEETHOVEN[1]

To Anton Felix Schindler

[*Autograph in the Deutsche Staatsbibliothek, Berlin*]

[VIENNA, *January*, 1823]

MOST EXCELLENT OPTIMUS OPTIME!

　　I am sending you herewith the calendar. The paper markings
indicate all the legations in Vienna. If you could just extract from
it quickly a list of the courts, we could then expedite the task in
hand.[2] By the way, as soon as my brother butts in, please—*co-operate
with him*. For, if you don't, we may well experience *sorrow* instead
of *joy*—

　　Do try to get hold of some philanthropist who will lend me
money on the security of a bank share, so that, in the first place,
I may not put the generosity of my exceptional friends, the
B[rentanos], too severely to the test, and so that I myself may not be
financially embarrassed owing to the holding up of this money, for
which I have to thank the splendid arrangements and precautionary
measures of my *dear* and worthy brother—It would be pleasant if
you were to turn up at Mariahilf[3] at about half past three this
afternoon or perhaps in the morning—

　　Other people must not notice that we should like to have the
money[4]—

[1] Beethoven added his address, Unterdöbling, No. 11, at the end of the letter.
[2] I.e. of making a list of possible subscribers to the "Missa Solemnis" and sending
them a circular letter.
[3] Mariahilf was, and still is, a suburb of Vienna. Beethoven is evidently referring
to some coffeehouse where he and Schindler frequently met.
[4] Schindler adds the remark "because we sorely need it."

To King George IV of England, London

[*Autograph in the Deutsche Staatsbibliothek, Berlin*][1]

VIENNA, *February* 24, 1823

I now venture most submissively to put forward to Your Majesty my most humble petition. At the same time I make bold to add another one.

As long ago as 1813 the undersigned, complying with many requests put forward by several Englishmen residing in Vienna, took the liberty of sending to Your Majesty his work entitled "Wellingtons Schlacht und Seig bei Vittoria," because nobody in England yet possessed a copy. Prince von Razumovsky,[2] who was then Russian Ambassador to the Imperial Court and happened to be in Vienna, undertook to forward this work to Your Majesty by a courier.

For many years the undersigned cherished the agreeable hope that Your Majesty would most graciously have him informed of the safe arrival of his work. But as yet he has not been able to boast of this happiness and has had to content himself merely with the brief announcement of Herr Ries, his worthy pupil, who duly informed him that Your Majesty had most graciously condescended to give the above-mentioned work to Herr Salomon, then Director of Music, and to Herr Smart, who were to have it performed in public at the Drury Lane Theatre.[3] The English papers announced this too and even added, as Herr Ries did also, that this work had been received with extraordinary applause both in London and everywhere else.

Your Majesty will forgive, no doubt, the sensitivity of the undersigned for whom it has been very mortifying to have to hear all this through indirect channels. And Your Majesty will most graciously allow him to mention that he spared neither time nor expense when presenting this work to Your Most Excellent Majesty in the most proper manner in order therewith to afford you the greatest pleasure.

From all these circumstances the undersigned draws the conclusion that the work may have been presented to Your Majesty in

[1] This is the draft of a letter which was presumably sent to the King of England. In the Royal Archives at Windsor, however, there are no letters from Beethoven.
[2] Count Razumovsky was created a Prince in 1815.
[3] The work was first performed in London at the Drury Lane Theatre in February, 1814.

some unsuitable way; and as his most humble petition, which he again puts forward, affords him the opportunity of approaching Your Majesty, he now ventures most submissively to send to Your Majesty an engraved copy of the score of the Schlacht bei Vittoria. This copy has been lying ready for this purpose ever since the year 1815 and has been kept back so long only on account of the uncertain position in which the undersigned was placed about the whole affair.

As he is convinced of the great wisdom and favor with which Your Majesty has always known how to value and to bring happiness to art and to the artist, the undersigned flatters himself that Your Majesty will most kindly consider, and most graciously comply with, his most humble petition.[1]

To Johann Baptist Bach
[Autograph not traced][2]

DEAR AND HONORED FRIEND!   VIENNA, *March* 6, 1823

Death can come without any previous warning; and at the moment there is no time to make a legal will. I inform you, therefore, in this letter written in my own hand that I nominate my beloved nephew Karl van Beethoven heir to my entire property and that I declare that after my death everything, without exception, *which can be described as being in my possession shall belong to him as the sole owner*—I appoint you his curator; and, should this will not be superseded by another one, you are entitled and requested to find for my beloved nephew K[arl] v. Beethoven a guardian, who must not be, however, my brother Johann van Beethoven,[3] and to entrust my nephew to this guardian in accordance with the traditional laws.

I declare this written document to be valid for all time, just as if it were my last will and testament before my death—I embrace you with all my heart—Your sincere admirer and friend,

LUDWIG VAN BEETHOVEN

NB.[4] The capital amounts to seven bank shares; and whatever additional cash may be available will, like the bank shares, become my nephew's property.

1 Beethoven's draft has this addition written in another hand: "Convaincu de la haute Sagesse dont Votre Majesté a toujours su apprecier l'art ainsi que de la haute faveur qu'elle accorde à l'artiste le soussigné se flatte que Votre Majesté prendra l'un et l'autre en consideration et vaudra en grace condescendre a sa tres humble demande."
à Vienne le 24 fevrier.
2 From a photostat in the Beethovenarchiv, Bonn.
3 The words from "who" to "Beethoven" are added at the foot of the third page.
4 The NB. is added on the first page.

To Ferdinand Ries, London

[*First portion of the autograph not traced,*[1]
second portion of the autograph in the Universitätsbibliothek, Bonn]

DEAR RIES! VIENNA, *April* 25, 1823

The Cardinal's stay in Vienna for about four weeks, during which period I had to give him every day a lesson lasting two and a half, and sometimes three, hours, has robbed me of a great deal of time. For after such lessons one is hardly able on the following day to think and, still less, to compose.

Yet my persistently distressing situation demands that for the time being I should compose whatever can bring me in money to spend for my immediate needs. What a sad discovery you are making!! And now owing to the many worries I have been enduring I am not well and even my eyes are troubling me! At the same time you must not be anxious about me. You will soon receive the symphony.[2] Only this miserable state of affairs is really the reason why you have not received it sooner— In a few weeks too you will receive a new set of 33 variations on a theme, a work which I have dedicated to your wife.[3]

Bauer has the score of the Schlacht von Vittoria, dedicated to the then Prince Regent,[4] for which I have yet to receive the cost of having it copied— All I ask is that you should interest yourself in this matter, dear friend! I[5] shall be satisfied with whatever you can get for it. But do see that the C minor sonata is engraved immediately.[6] I promise the publisher that it will not appear anywhere else first. And, if necessary, I will also send him the copyright for England. But it must be engraved at once— As the other one in Ab, even though it may already have arrived in London, has been engraved inaccurately, well then, the English publisher if he engraves it too, can announce his edition as the correct one.[7] I am inclined to think that a matter of that kind merits the grateful recognition of an English publisher (in clinking coins, I mean)— After all we both know what sort of people those worthy publishers are. They are the most barefaced black-

---

[1] The first portion of this letter has been taken from Franz Wegeler and Ferdinand Ries: *Biographische Notizen*, pp. 185–186.
[2] Opus 125.
[3] Opus 120, the 33 pianoforte variations on a waltz theme by Diabelli, was published in June, 1823, by Cappi & Diabelli with a dedication to Antonia Brentano.
[4] Since 1820 George IV of England.
[5] From this point the remainder of the autograph is in the Universitätsbibliothek, Bonn.
[6] Opus 111 was engraved by Clementi & Co. (1823?) with a dedication to Antonia Brentano.
[7] Opus 110 was engraved by Clementi & Co. (1823?).

guards. Well now, all good wishes, my dear R[ies]. May Heaven bless you. With all my heart I embrace you. Give my greetings to all those who would like to have them— As for the tender subject of your marriage, *you yourself* will always find a sort of *opposition* from me, I mean, an opposition to *you* and a proposition *for your wife*.—Ever your friend

BEETHOVEN

To Antonio Diabelli, Vienna

[Autograph not traced][1]

[HETZENDORF, *June*, 1823]

I absentmindedly sent you my manuscript yesterday instead of the French edition of the C minor sonata.[2] Please return it. If you would like to have the French edition returned to you, I will send it to you immediately, although I should be glad to be allowed to keep it. The text of the corrected proofs of the variations will surely be finished; and please be so kind as to send it to me for my further approval.[3] As for the promised eight copies, I have come to the conclusion that your first offer to let me have the eight copies on fine paper would be, after all, very welcome, since I could put a few of my friends under an obligation to me by presents of that kind.

The metronome will be attended to, though this will have to be postponed for a little, because I am now too hard pressed for time. Your friend

BEETHOVEN

[1] The autograph of this letter was stuck into the cover of a Beethoven sketchbook of 1825, which belonged to Cecilio de Roda, who published it in *Un quaderno di autografi di Beethoven del 1825* (Torino, 1907).
[2] Opus 111.
[3] Opus 120.

To the Archduke Rudolph, Vienna

[Autograph in the Gesellschaft der Musikfreunde, Vienna]

YOUR IMPERIAL HIGHNESS!   HETZENDORF, *July* 1, 1823[1]

Since Y.I.H.'s departure I have been ailing almost the whole time; and latterly I have been having bad pain in my eyes. This has subsided, however, but only to the extent that during the last week I have been able to use my eyes again, though sparingly. From the accompanying receipt dated June 27th Y.I.H. will see that I have sent you some music. As Y.I.H. seemed to enjoy hearing the C minor sonata, I thought that I should not be too presumptuous if I gave you the surprise of dedicating it to Your Highness.[2] The variations were copied certainly five or even six weeks ago. But in the meantime the condition of my eyes did not allow me to check them all; and I hoped in vain for a complete recovery. So in the end I let Schlemmer check them; and although they may not look very tidy, yet they should be correct.[3] The C minor sonata was engraved in Paris, and very inaccurately; and as it was engraved again here, I made certain so far as possible that it would be correct—

I shall soon send you a finely engraved copy of the variations.[4] With regard to the Mass which Y.I.H. would like to see more generally available, the condition of my health, which had then been rather poor for several years, demanded that I should think out a way of improving my situation to some extent, the more so as on its account I had incurred heavy debts and had to refuse, for the same reason also, invitations to go to England. The Mass seemed to be the very thing. I was advised to offer this work to several courts. However difficult I found it to do this, yet I was convinced that if I failed to take this step I should only have myself to blame. I sent therefore to several courts an invitation to subscribe to this Mass. I fixed the fee at 50 ducats, because the general opinion was that this was not an excessive sum and that if there were several subscribers some profit would be made. So far the list of subscribers has brought me honor, it is true, for their Royal Majesties of France and Prussia have subscribed. Moreover I received a few days ago from Petersburg a letter from my friend Prince Nikolaus Galitzin in which that

[1] The autograph is dated June 1st in Beethoven's hand. But on internal evidence this must be a mistake for July 1st.
[2] Opus 111.
[3] Evidently a manuscript copy of Opus 120 made specially for the Archduke Rudolph.
[4] Opus 120 was published in Vienna by Cappi & Diabelli.

truly amiable Prince informs me that His Imperial Russian Majesty has also become a subscriber and that I shall soon have more details about this from the Imperial Russian Embassy in Vienna.[1] At the same time, although a few others have subscribed, I have not yet received as much as the amount of a publisher's fee for this Mass. On the other hand there is for me the advantage that the work is still *mine*. The expense of having the work copied is also very great and will be even greater, because I am adding three new movements, which when I have finished composing them, I shall immediately send to Y.I.H.— Perhaps Y.I.H. would not find it troublesome to use your influence on behalf of the Mass with the Grand Duke of Tuscany so that His Highness too might order a copy. An invitation to the Grand Duke of Tuscany was already sent off, it is true, a long time ago by von Odelgha, his agent in Vienna[2]; and Odelgha solemnly assures me that the invitation will certainly be accepted. But I am rather doubtful, for several months have now elapsed and I have heard nothing more.[3] Since this business has now been set going, it is only natural that I should do my utmost to achieve the purpose I have in view.— I have found this undertaking most difficult; and I have found it even more difficult to tell Y.I.H. about it or to express my feelings about it, but "*Necessity knows no law*"— I am only too grateful to Him who rules the stars in the firmament, that I can now begin to use my eyes again. At the moment I am composing a new symphony for England, i.e. for the Philharmonic Society, and I hope to finish it in less than a fortnight.[4] As yet I cannot put any strain on my eyes for long. So I beg Y.I.H. to be patient a little longer about Your Highness's variations.[5] I think them charming; but all the same they require a more thorough examination than I have been able to give them. Y.I.H. must now continue, in particular, your exercises in composition and when sitting at the pianoforte you should jot down your ideas in the form of sketches. For this purpose you should have a small table beside the pianoforte. In this way not only is one's imagination stimulated but one learns also to pin down immediately the most remote ideas. You should also compose without a pianoforte; and you should sometimes work out a simple melody, for instance, a chorale with simple and again with different harmonies according to the laws of counterpoint and even neglecting the latter. This will certainly not give Y.I.H. a headache; nay, rather, it will afford you real enjoyment when you thus find yourself in the very swim of artistic production.— Gradually there comes to us

---

[1] Prince Galitzin's letter, dated June 2nd, is quoted in full in *TDR* IV, 554.
[2] Carlo di Odelgha was the envoy of the Grand Duke of Tuscany.
[3] The Grand Duke of Tuscany did become a subscriber.
[4] According to Schindler II, 56, the score of the ninth symphony (Opus 125) was finished in February, 1824.
[5] Evidently Beethoven had given the Archduke Rudolph another theme on which to compose variations. This second theme has not been identified. See Kinsky-Halm, pp. 592–593.

the power to express just what we desire and feel; and to the nobler type of human beings this is such an essential need— My eyes bid me stop writing.— I wish Y.I.H. all that is beautiful and good; and in sending you my compliments I describe myself with the deepest reverence as Your Imperial Highness's most faithful servant

L. V. BEETHOVEN

To Anton Felix Schindler, Vienna

[*Autograph in the Deutsche Staatsbibliothek, Berlin*]

HETZENDORF, *July* 2, 1823

MOST EXCELLENT HERR VON SCHINDLER!

The landlord's brutality which has persisted from the very beginning of my stay in that house until now, demands the help of the Imperial and Royal Police.[1] Just apply to them. As for the winter windows, the housekeeper had been ordered to see to them, especially after the very heavy rain, and to find out whether it was necessary to fit them owing to the possibility of rain pouring into the rooms. But she did not find that rain had poured in nor was then pouring in at all. So acting on this conviction I had the bolt padlocked in order that that particularly brutal fellow should not open my rooms during my absence, as he had threatened to do— Tell the police how he behaved later on when you were there and how he displayed the card without my having given him notice, which in any case I need not do until July 25th—

He is acting quite as unfairly in refusing to let me have the receipt for the quarter from April 24th to July 25th, as this notice shows, seeing that I am to pay for lighting, a thing I had never heard of; and those horrible rooms without *stove* heating and with the most wretched *general heating* cost me at least 250 gulden V.C. as an extra expense apart from the rent,[2] merely in order to keep body and soul together during the winter I spent there—

It was deliberate swindling on his part, seeing that I was never allowed to see the rooms on the first floor but only those on the second, so that I should know nothing of the many drawbacks of the former. I really cannot understand how it is possible *for the Government to tolerate such a disgraceful method of heating which is so injurious to human health.* You remember what the walls in your room looked like with the smoke and how much it cost even

---

[1] Beethoven is referring to his rooms at Kothgasse 60.
[2] The words from "as an" to "rent" are added at the foot of the page.

to lessen, let alone entirely to remove, that nuisance. Meanwhile the main thing is that he should be ordered to take down the notice card and let me have my receipt for the rent which I have paid. In no circumstances will I pay for that wretched lighting, seeing that, in any case, I was faced with excessive expenses merely in order to keep alive in those rooms.— The condition of my eyes does not yet allow me to stand town air; otherwise I would go to the Imperial Police myself— Your most devoted

L. V. BEETHOVEN

To Anton Felix Schindler, Vienna

[Autograph in the Deutsche Staatsbibliothek, Berlin]

[HETZENDORF, Summer, 1823][1]

S[COUN]D[RE]L OF S[AMOTHRACI]A!

Why, you were sent word yesterday that you were to betake yourself to the South Pole, while we were to go off to the North Pole, although indeed Capt[ain] Parry has already smoothed out the slight difference.[2] But there was no potato pureé there— I request Bach, to whom I send my best regards and very many thanks for his efforts on my behalf, to inform me to what price the rooms at Baden may possibly soar. And moreover we should have to see how we could manage to bring Karl out there every fortnight (and cheaply, Heaven help us over poverty and cheapness!). You could make that your business, for you have admirers and friends among the bosses and country coachmen[3]—

If this letter reaches you in time, it would be well for you to go to Bach today, so that I may have the reply tomorrow morning. For if you don't, it will be almost too late—

Tomorrow too you could pounce on that rascal of a copyist from whom I do not expect anything good. He has had those variations now for a whole week.[4]— Your amicus

BEETHOVEN

[1] Noted by Schindler on the autograph. The letter was probably written in July, for Beethoven moved to Baden on August 13th.
[2] Sir William Edward Parry (1790–1855), a naval officer and explorer, rendered good service in preparing the way for the eventual discovery of the North Pole.
[3] Schindler had noted on the autograph that Beethoven is alluding to patrons.
[4] Rampel was probably making a copy of the Diabelli variations to be sent to London. This work, Opus 120, had been published by Cappi & Diabelli in June, 1823.

To Johann van Beethoven, Gneixendorf

[Autograph in the Beethovenhaus, Bonn, H. C. Bodmer collection]

BADEN, *August* 19, [1823][1]

DEAR BROTHER!

I am delighted to hear that you are in better health. As for me, my eyes are not yet quite cured; and I came here with a ruined stomach and a horrible cold, the former thanks to that arch-swine, my housekeeper, the latter handed on to me by a beast of a kitchen-maid whom I had already chucked out once and then taken on again— You should not have taken up the matter with *Steiner*. I will see what can be done. It may be difficult to arrange for the songs *in puris*, as the text is in German. It would probably be easier to do this with the overture.—

I received your letter of August 10th through that miserable rascal *Schindler*. Remember that you need only send your letters straight to the post where I shall certainly receive them all. For I avoid as far as possible that low-minded, contemptible fellow— Karl can't join me until the 29th when he will write to you.[2] But you will not be entirely neglected,[3] and you will receive letters from Karl and from me through him. For, however little you may deserve it so far as I am concerned, yet I shall never forget that you are my brother; and in due course a good spirit will imbue your heart and soul.[4] Now for something else. You have my own manuscript of some numbers of the "Ruinen von Athen." I really need it because the copies were made from the Josephstadt score from which a good many passages were omitted which are only to be found in my manuscript scores. As I happen to be composing something else of this kind I badly need my manuscripts. So let me know in writing where I can get hold of them. I earnestly beg you to do this. I will let you know some other time about coming to stay with you. Am I

---

[1] On the verso of the autograph another hand has noted "written in the late summer of 1824." But on internal evidence the year must be 1823.

[2] At the end of August, 1823, Karl left Blöchlinger's boarding school for good. He was then just 17.

[3] The following passage, deleted by another hand, is still legible: "whatever those two *canailles*, that loutish fat woman and her bastard, may do to you."

[4] The following passage, deleted by another hand, is still legible: "a good spirit which will separate you from those two *canailles*, that former and still active whore, with whom her fellow miscreant slept no less than three times during your illness and who, moreover, has full control of your money, oh, abominable shame, is there no spark of manhood in you?!!!"

to become so degraded as to mix in such low[1] company? But perhaps this could be avoided and we might still spend a few days with you?! I will write some other time about the remaining points in your letter. All good wishes. I hover over you unseen and influence you through others so that the scum of the earth[2] may not strangle you— Ever your faithful

brother.

You should address your letters direct to me in Vienna[3]—

To Ferdinand Ries, London

[Autograph in the Beethovenhaus, Bonn][4]

MY DEAR FRIEND!

BADEN, September 5, [1823]

You say that I ought to look around for someone to attend to my affairs. Well, that is the very thing I did in respect of the variat[ions], I mean, my friends and Schindler looked after them for me, but alas! how badly! The variations were to appear first of all in Vienna after they had been published in London.[5] But everything went wrong. The dedication to Brentano[6] was only to apply to Germany. I was under a great obligation to her and could publish no other work at the time. In any case only the Viennese publisher Diabelli got those variations from me. But everything went through the hands of Schindler. I have never yet met a more wretched fellow on God's earth, an arch-scoundrel whom I have sent packing— I can dedicate some other work to your wife instead. You must have received by now my last letter about the Allegri di Bravura. Well, I think that I might get 30 ducats apiece for them. But I should like to be able to publish them immediately in Vienna as well, a connection which could be easily established. Why should one let those Viennese scoundrels make such a profit? The work would not be given to a publisher here until I had heard that it had arrived in London. By the way, you

---

[1] This adjective has been deleted by another hand.
[2] The previous four words have been deleted by another hand.
[3] This reminder is added at the top of the first page to the left of the date.
[4] The autograph, which bears no address consists of one leaf written on both sides.
[5] Opus 120.
[6] Antonia Brentano. The first edition published by Cappi & Diabelli has this dedication. A manuscript copy made by Rampel and corrected by Beethoven, now in the Beethovenhaus, Bonn, H. C. Bodmer collection, was dedicated to Ries's wife. It is dated April 30, 1823, and was intended to serve for a London edition. See Kinsky-Halm, p. 349.

yourself must fix the fee, for you know best what London conditions are— The copyist finished the score of the symphony a few
days ago.[1] So Kirchhoffer and I are only waiting for a good opportunity to send it off— I am here, where I arrived in a very sick
condition. For my health, when all is said and done, is very shaky
and, Good Heavens, instead of enjoying as others do the pleasures
of bathing, my financial straits demand that I should compose
every day. And as well as taking the baths I have to drink mineral
waters— The Mass will be sent off in a day or two. I am waiting to
hear from Kirchhoffer how it is to be dispatched, for it is too bulky
to be given to a courier— In my last letter you will have read
all my remarks about the Mass— I will send you choruses. Let me
know soon about commissions for oratorios so that I may fix the
time immediately— I am sorry for both of us—and particularly about
the variations, seeing that I composed them more for London than
for Vienna. It is not my fault— Reply soon, very soon, both about
the conditions and about the time. My best greetings to your family
from [your] true [friend]

BEE[THOVEN][2]

To Louis Spohr, Cassel

[MS in the possession of the Spohrgesellschaft, Cassel][3]

MY VERY DEAR FRIEND!   BADEN, *September* 17, 1823
    It has afforded me much pleasure that you have honored me
with an immediate reply to my letter. In regard to the point referred to about the Mass I remember that somebody told me not
to have an invitation sent to Hesse-Cassel because he was convinced
that it would not be accepted. So far as I know, no invitation was
sent off. In this connection Hauser made me think differently. Having ascertained from him that my works were not quite unknown at
Cassel I gathered fresh hope that perhaps after all His Excellency
the Elector too might accept my invitation, seeing that even the
Emperor of Russia, the King of France, and the King of Prussia are
among the number of my illustrious subscribers.[4] I have already
made inquiries several times at the Hessian Legation, but each time
there was nobody there and I was told that everyone was in the

---

[1] Opus 125.
[2] At the end of the autograph the ink has faded so badly that the bracketed
words and the remainder of Beethoven's signature have been supplied by the present
editor.
[3] Written by Schindler and signed by Beethoven.
[4] The Elector of Hesse-Cassel did not subscribe to the Mass.

country. But as I am now at Baden for the sake of my health, it is very inconvenient to forward this invitation through the Legation. Hence I have thought it best to send it to you direct; and I venture to request Geheimrat[1] Rivalier to deliver it to His Excellency the Elector. I myself will thank the Geheimrat later on in writing for this kind action—

My health was not yet fully restored when Hauser came to see me. I was very poorly when I came here, but I now feel better than I did. My *eye complaint* too is rapidly clearing up.

As to your enquiry about *my opera* it is true that *Grillparzer* has written a libretto for me and that I too have already made a start.[2] But on account of my poor health several other works were set aside which I must now take up again. When these are finished I will set to work again at the opera and will let you know with what success.

Hauser told me that you had composed double quartets.[3] I was delighted to hear this. They will certainly be welcomed by the musical public. I am equally delighted to see from your letter that you are leading a peaceful country life with your family, to whom I send my best regards. My most ardent desire is to be able to lead that kind of life. But unfortunately my circumstances have not yet permitted it.

I send you my wishes for all that is good and to your advantage, and I trust that you will keep me in your friendly remembrance.

I remain, as always, your friend and fellow-artist

BEETHOVEN

PS. Please ensure that I shall soon have a reply. Let me add that admittedly the undertaking appears on the surface to be very successful; but there are also certain difficulties connected with it. The copying expenses have greatly exceeded the amount I expected to have to disburse. Once more I urgently beg you for an early reply. And so that no distrust may be harbored, the copy will be delivered to the Electoral Hessian Legation on receipt of the fee. Although the number of subscribers is not large, yet it is sufficient to enable me to dispatch a copy at once. The fee is 50 ducats.

[1] The full title is "Geheimer Cabinetsrat." This official has not been identified. But Professor O. E. Deutsch has suggested Count Karl de la Rivalière.
[2] On Grillparzer's libretto "Melusine."
[3] Among many other chamber music works for unusual combinations of instruments Spohr composed four double string quartets.

To Frau Johanna van Beethoven

[*Autograph in the Beethovenhaus, Bonn, H. C. Bodmer collection*]

[VIENNA], *January* 8, 1824

Our many occupations made it quite impossible for Karl and me to send you our best wishes on New Year's Day. But I know that even without this explanation you are fully assured of both my and Karl's sincerest wishes for your welfare—

As for your need of money, I would gladly have helped you out with a sum. But unfortunately I have too many expenses and debts and am still waiting for certain payments, so that I cannot prove to you at once and on the spot my readiness to help you.[1]— Meanwhile I assure you now in writing that henceforth and for good you may draw Karl's half of your pension. We shall send you the receipt every month and then you yourself can draw it. For it is no disgrace whatever to draw it in person every month (I know that several acquaintances of mine draw their pensions every month). Should I be comfortably off later on and in a position to provide you from my income with a sum large enough to improve your circumstances, I will certainly do so— Further, I undertook long ago to pay the 280 gulden, 25 kreuzer which you owe Steiner.[2] No doubt you have been informed of this. Moreover for a considerable time you have not had to pay any interest on that loan—

You have received from me through Schindler pension payments for two months— On the 26th of this month or a few days later you will receive the amount of the pension for this month— As for your lawsuit, I will soon discuss that matter with Dr. Bach[3]—

Both Karl and I wish you all possible happiness— Your L. v. BEETHOVEN who is most willing to help you.

[1] A short fragment, the end of a letter from Beethoven to an unknown recipient, of which there is a photograph in the Beethovenarchiv, Bonn, mentions the same private difficulty: ". . . to be remitted soon, for just now, as usual, I must disburse, and I should be receiving, a good deal of money—"

[2] According to a note dated March 28, 1818, the autograph of which is in the Beethovenhaus, Bonn, Beethoven's sister-in-law Johanna undertook to pay Steiner by August 1, 1818 this amount of five per cent interest on capital formerly borrowed from him and already repaid.

[3] It has not been possible to discover any particulars of this lawsuit.

To Johann Andreas Stumpff, Vienna

[*Autograph not traced*]

MY ESTEEMED FRIEND!   BADEN, *October* 3, 1824[1]

It would be very charming of you if you would call on the gentleman who lives in the Landstrasse[2] and kindly tell him exactly what ought to be done to my Broadwood instrument.

I send you my heartfelt greetings and I request you not to forget me in England and, moreover, to remember that tortoise of £600 from the King of England for my Schlachtsymphonie.

Your willing friend and so forth

LUD[WIG] VAN BEETHOVEN

To Ignaz Schuppanzigh[3]

[*Autograph in the Beethovenhaus, Bonn, H. C. Bodmer collection*]

MOST EXCELLENT MYLORD!   [VIENNA, *February*, 1825]

You may perform the quartet from today until the second Sunday.[4] It was impossible to let you have it before, because I have been far too busy with other work which *only one copyist* can manage; and altogether my not very prosperous circumstances, which compel me to undertake only what is most necessary, are partly to blame— Meanwhile the quartet will not be published for a long time, and thus remains *your sole property here in loco.* You have not sent me word about the concerts, *so we shall not hear anything*— All good wishes. I shall let you know as soon as that machine of mine is ready which will enable you to be lifted up quite comfortably to me on the fourth floor.[5]—Yours

BEETHOVEN

1 Thayer states that Stumpff seems to have added on this letter "or September."
2 Matthäus Andreas Stein, the younger brother of Nanette Streicher. Stumpff added Stein's name on this letter.
3 The address on the verso of the autograph runs as follows:—Al Signore Milord stimatissimo nominato Sciuppanzig grand' uomo della Città di Vienna.
4 Opus 127 was first performed by Schuppanzigh's quartet on Sunday, March 6, 1825.
5 Possibly Beethoven is referring to Falstaff's appeal in Shakespeare's *Henry IV*, Part I., Act II., sc. 2, where he says; "Have you any levers to lift me up again, being down?"

To [Anton Felix Schindler, Vienna?][1]

[*Autograph not traced*]

BADEN, *May* 6, 1825[2]

In no circumstances are you to leave the bell and the bell-ropes and so forth in my former rooms. No suggestion was made to those people that they should *take over anything* from me. The locksmith never came to remove the bell when I was there, and my ill health has prevented me from sending somebody from here into town. Surely those people could have had the bell taken down, seeing that they have *no right* to keep it—Well, whatever happens, I absolutely refuse to leave the bell there. I need one here and can make use of this one. For a bell would cost me twice as much here as in Vienna, since *bell-ropes are the most expensive articles* to buy from locksmiths—If necessary, go at once to the Imperial and Royal Police—The window in my room was exactly like that when I moved in. But you may pay for it and also for the one in the kitchen; the two will cost 2 gulden, 12 kreuzer—The key must not be paid for, since we found no key there. Instead of being locked, the door was nailed up or bunged up when we moved in; and it remained in that condition until I left. There never was a key there, since none was used either by us or by the person who occupied the rooms before us—Perhaps a collection will be arranged for. If so, I will put my hand in my pocket.

LUDWIG VAN BEETHOVEN

To Karl van Beethoven, Vienna

[*Autograph in the Deutsche Staatsbibliothek, Berlin*][3]

DEAR SON! BADEN, *June* 28, [1825]

Since you perhaps like to bathe in this heat, I am sending you another two gulden. But I insist that everything be put down in writing both conto as well as by those who have received some-

---

[1] According to Thayer, this letter was addressed to Karl. Nohl maintains that it was addressed to Beethoven's brother. On internal evidence it was probably intended for Schindler, with whom Beethoven seems to have lived for a short period.

[2] As Beethoven did not move to Baden until May 7th, there must be some mistake in the first transcription from the autograph, which was published in *Signale für die musikalische Welt*, 1857.

[3] Autograph not available. Text taken from Thayer.

thing from you.[1] For proof of the mistakes you made are the blue cloth and the three gulden for the mirror. You are already a Viennese although I hope that you will not become a sport of Viennese currency. Nevertheless it does you no harm at your age to have to give a full account of the money you receive, since you do not reach your majority until you are 24 and since you yourself, if you had money of your own, would at your age have to give a full account of it to your guardians—Do not make me recall incidents of long ago, which would be easy to do but only painful for me; and in the end you would just say as usual "after all you are a very good guardian" or something similar. If only you had some depth of character, you would always act quite differently —Well, to turn to this contemptible tribe of domestics. The kitchen-maid disappeared yesterday but returned later. What it is all about is very difficult to fathom in the case of such an old witch, who is now all smiles again and refuses to admit that *she was the loser when the accounts were made up*. What do you say to that?[2]

To Karl Holz, Vienna

[*Autograph in the Koch collection*]

BADEN, *August* 24, [1825]

MOST EXCELLENT PIECE OF MAHOGANY!

We have no quills available, so you will have to put up with this[3]— Your letter made me laugh. Yes indeed, *Tobias* will always be a T[obias], but we will make him even more of a Tobias— Castelli must lend a hand, and our story will be printed and engraved for the benefit of all poor Tobiases— I am writing this moment to Karl telling him to postpone sending the letters to Peters and Schlesinger, which means that I am awaiting a reply from Herr A[rtaria] at Mannheim.

On the other hand it is all the same to me what hellhound licks or gnaws away my brain, since admittedly it must be so; but let us hope the answer will not be delayed for too long. That hellhound at L[eipzig][4] can wait and in the meantime enjoy in Auerbach's cellar the company of Mephistopheles (the editor of the

[1] Beethoven evidently means that Karl himself should keep an account of the sums he disburses as well as the recipients of the sums.
[2] The remaining portion of this letter was written on two pages of a sheet, half of which has been torn off. Hence what is left is quite unintelligible.
[3] Beethoven is apologizing for his rather illegible scrawl.
[4] Obviously a reference to C. F. Peters.

L[eipziger] Musikal[ische] Zeitung)[1] Beelzebub, chief of the devils, will shortly seize the latter by the ears—

My dear fellow, the last quartet too is to have six movements; and I hope to complete them by the end of the month.[2]— If only somebody could give me something for my sick stomach— My worthy brother has again been to the P.N.G.[3] Heigho! But, my dear fellow, we must see to it that all these newly invented words and expressions will survive into the third and fourth generations of our posterity[4]— Come on Friday or Sunday— Come on Friday when Satan's performances in the kitchen are most tolerable— My best wishes— A thousand thanks for your devotion to me and for your affection. I trust you will not be punished for it.

In love and friendship, your

BEETHOVEN

Yes, yes! The little Paternostergasse and our *Director* are implicated quite nicely. It is a good thing to know all this even if one doesn't gain anything by it.[5]

Do write to me again, but it would be even better if you would come!![6]

N'oubliès pas de rendre visite à mon cher Benjamin.[7]

To Bernhard Schotts Söhne, Mainz

[MS *in the Stadtbibliothek, Mainz*][8]

GENTLEMEN! VIENNA, *January* 28, 1826

In reply to your latest communication I inform you that you will soon receive the metronome markings for all the works. Please do not forget that the first quartet is dedicated to Prince Galitzin.[9] —So far as I know, Matth[ias] Artaria has already received from you

---

[1] Breitkopf & Härtel, Leipzig, had founded in 1798 the *Allgemeine Musikalische Zeitung*, which they continued to publish until 1848. From 1798 until 1818 it was edited by J. F. Rochlitz, who continued to supervise its publication until 1835.

[2] Beethoven had begun to compose the B♭ quartet, the third of the Galitzin quartets, Opus 130. He had finished the second one, Opus 132, in July.

[3] Paternostergasse, i.e. Steiner's firm.

[4] A reference to Castelli's endeavors to restore the purity of the German language and to invent new expressions.

[5] This postscript is written at the top of the first page.

[6] This sentence is written at the left side of the second page.

[7] I.e. Karl. The remark, written in French so that the bearer of the letter should not understand it, is added on the fourth page below the address to Karl Holz, who was then living "im Bergenstammischen Hause, Mölkerbastei 96."

[8] Written by Karl and signed by Beethoven, who also added the musical phrase at the end of the letter.

[9] Opus 124, published by Schott in December, 1825.

two copies of the overture.[1] I too should very much like to receive several copies of this work and also of the quartet. If I have not yet thanked you for the previous copies, well, that was really due to my forgetfulness. By the way, you may rest assured that I never sell nor act as agent for the sale of a single copy. Only a few artists whom I really esteem are to receive copies; and that will not injure you, seeing that in any case they could not afford to buy these works.

Well, there is something else I should like to hear and that is whether Prince Galitzin when he sent you particulars of the title for the dedication asked you at the same time for the number of copies of the quartet and the overture which he required. For, if not, I must send them to him from here.

By the way, I request you to arrange for your deliveries to me to be made in future through Matth[ias] Artaria and no longer through Steiner, because I hope to receive everything more quickly through the former.

In the Mass the list of subscribers should be printed first and then followed by the dedication to the Archduke worded exactly as I have sent it to you.

I will soon let you have particulars about the dedication of the symphony. It was to have been dedicated to the Emperor Alexander.[2] The delay has been caused by the events which have taken place.

You would again like to have some works of mine?
Excellent fellows!!
You have grossly insulted me!
You have played several wrong notes!
Therefore you must first purge yourselves before my judgment seat here in Vienna. As soon as the ice has thawed Mainz must betake itself hither. The reviewing Councillor of the Supreme Court of Appeal must turn up here in order to answer for his actions. And now I send you all good wishes!

We are far from being particularly attached to you!

Handed in on the heights of Schwarzspanien without handing anything.

BEETHOVEN

BEETHOVEN

il
Posaun
16 fussig

trillo

minacciando

---

1 Opus 127.
2 Alexander I of Russia had died on December 1, 1825.

To Stephan von Breuning

[*Autograph in the Beethovenhaus, Bonn, H. C. Bodmer collection*]
[VIENNA, *Spring*, 1826]

You, my esteemed friend, are up to the eyes in work and so am I. And, what is more, I am not yet quite well— I would have invited you to dinner before, but even now I still need the assistance of several people, of whom the gifted leading spirit is the cook. Their intellectual works are *not indeed* to be found *in their own cellar*, for they pry into kitchens and cellars and their company would serve you ill. But things will soon be changed— Don't use Czerny's Klavierschule.[1] During the next few days I shall receive fuller particulars about another one—

Here is the fashion journal[2] which I promised your wife, and here is something for your children. If you like, I can continue to provide you with the fashion journal. And indeed you have only to order from me anything else that I possess and that you would like to have—

I hope that *we* shall soon meet again.

BEETHOVEN

With love and deep regard, your friend

To Karl Holz, Baden[3]

[*Autograph in the Stadtbibliothek, Vienna*]
MY VERY DEAR FELLOW!   [VIENNA], *September* 9, 1826

One can see how much good can be done by better and purer air and also by the good influence of women. For in less than three days your icy surface has wholly melted. I notice this is your letter written yesterday, whereas your letter of September 17th is *like a dried fish*—I received it only last night because I had gone off to Nussdorf yesterday to enjoy cooler and more pleasant air. I would join you at Baden too; and indeed *perhaps* I shall go tomorrow. That reminds me, I would like to look around for an apartment. But I

---

[1] This work was published by Haslinger in 1826.
[2] Probably the *Wiener Zeitschrift für Kunst, Literatur, Theater und Mode*, familiarly called the *Wiener Modenzeitung*, which was edited by Johann Schickh and published by Anton Strauss.
[3] Karl Holz's address at Baden, written on the verso of the autograph, was "Im Sauerhof, Tür 75."

must really hurry to finish the corrections for His Majesty[1]— K[arl] insists on joining the army. He has written about this; and I have discussed it with him too. Surely it would be better for him to go first to some military college, such as the one at Neustadt. If you and your friends happen to go to Neustadt, you might just inquire from *Colonel Faber*[2] there whether *the years* in Vienna would be counted *for that purpose*. I don't think so, for *one has to pay there*; and K[arl] could very likely *leave the college as an officer*. For I do not think that it would be a good thing for him to be a *cadet* for long; and if we want him to become an officer *in that way*, we must ensure, first of all, that he receives his officer's pay and, in addition, provide a little extra to enable him to live. For he must certainly not be treated as a *convict*. On the whole I am *not at all* in favor of the army as a profession. Now that you are *there*, everything will surely go very quickly. I am worn out; and happiness will not be my portion again for a very long time. The terrible expenses which I now have to meet and shall have to meet in future are bound to worry me; all my hopes have vanished, all my hopes of having near me someone who would resemble me at least in my better qualities!— Enjoy yourself to the full out there, empty the cornucopias of all-enchanting Nature; and on Monday[3] I hope to see you again for certain and to embrace you.

Grateful as always I remain your

BEETHOVEN

To Franz Gerhard Wegeler, Coblenz

[*MS in the possession of Julius Wegeler*][4]

MY BELOVED OLD FRIEND!   VIENNA, *December 7*, 1826[5]

Words fail me to express the pleasure which your letter and Lorchen's have afforded me.[6] And indeed an answer should have been sent off to you as swiftly as an arrow. But on the whole I am rather slack about writing letters, for I believe that the best people know me well in any case. Often I think out a reply in my

---

[1] I.e. corrections to the ninth symphony, dedicated to the King of Prussia.

[2] Philipp von Faber, then in charge of the military academy at Wiener-Neustadt, held the rank of Lieutenant-Field-Marshal. The Director-General was the Archduke Johann (1782–1859), an elder brother of the Archduke Rudolph.

[3] Beethoven was writing on Saturday.

[4] Written by Karl and signed by Beethoven.

[5] In all the German editions of Beethoven's letters the month is given as October. But it is undoubtedly December. The autograph has 10br and on internal evidence it must be that month.

[6] Wegeler and his wife Eleonore had written to Beethoven on December 29, 1825.

head; but when it comes to writing it down, I usually throw away my pen, simply because I am unable to write as I feel. I remember all the love which you have always shown me, for instance, how you had my room whitewashed and thus gave me such a pleasant surprise,—and likewise all the kindnesses I have received from the Breuning family. Our drifting apart was due to the changes in our circumstances. Each of us had to pursue the purpose for which he was intended and endeavor to attain it. Yet the eternally unshakeable and firm foundations of good principles continued to bind us strongly together.— Unfortunately I cannot write to you today as much as I should like to, for I have stayed in bed. So I shall confine myself to answering a few points in your letter. You say that I have been mentioned somewhere as being the natural son of the late King of Prussia. Well, the same thing was said to me a long time ago. But I have adopted the principle of neither writing anything about myself nor replying to anything that has been written about me. Hence I gladly leave it to you to make known to the world the integrity of my parents, and especially of my mother.— You mention your son. Why, of course, if he comes to Vienna, I will be a friend and a father to him; and if I can be of any use to him or help him in any way, I shall be delighted to do so.

I still possess Lorchen's silhouette. So you see how precious to me even now are all the dear, beloved memories of my youth.

As for my diplomas I merely mention that I am an Honorary member of the Royal Scientific Society of Sweden and likewise of Amsterdam, and also an Honorary Citizen of Vienna. A short time ago a certain Dr. Spiker took with him to Berlin my latest grand symphony with choruses; it is dedicated to the King, and I had to write the dedication with my own hand. I had previously applied to the Legation for permission to dedicate this work to the King, which His Majesty had granted. At Dr. Spiker's instigation I myself had to give him the corrected manuscript with the alterations in my own handwriting to be delivered to the King, because the work is to be kept in the Royal Library. On that occasion something was said to me about the Order of the Red Eagle, Second Class. Whether anything will come of this, I don't know, for I have never striven after honors of that kind. Yet at the present time for many other reasons such an award would be rather welcome.— In any case my motto is always: Nulla dies sine linea; and if I let my Muse go to sleep, it is only that she may be all the more active when she awakes. I still hope to create a few great works and then like an old child to finish my earthly course somewhere among kind people.— You will soon receive some music from the Gebrüder Schott at Mainz.— The portrait I am sending with this letter is certainly an artistic masterpiece, but it is not the latest one which has been done for me.— Speaking about my honors which I know you are pleased to hear of, I must add that the late King of France sent me a medal with the inscription:

Donné par le Roi à Monsieur Beethoven. It was accompanied by a very courteous letter from the Duc de Chartres, Premier Gentilhomme du Roi.

My beloved friend! You must be content with this letter for today. I need hardly tell you that I have been overcome by the remembrance of things past and that many tears have been shed while the letter was being written. Still we have now begun to correspond and you will soon have another letter from me. And the more often you write to me, the greater will be the pleasure you afford me. Our friendship is too intimate to need inquiries from either of us. And now I send you all good wishes. Please embrace and kiss your dear Lorchen and your children for me and when doing so think of me. God be with you all!

Ever your true and faithful friend who honors you,

BEETHOVEN

To Johann Andreas Stumpff, London

[MS not traced][1]

MY VERY DEAR FRIEND! VIENNA, February 8, 1827

My pen is quite unable to describe the great pleasure afforded me by the volumes of Handel's works which you have sent me as a gift—to me a royal gift![2]—This present has even been mentioned in the Viennese papers, and I am sending you the notice.[3] Unfortunately since December 3rd I have been confined to bed with dropsy. You can imagine the situation to which this illness has reduced me. Usually I live entirely for the support of my intellectual work and manage to earn everything for the support of myself and my Karl. But unfortunately for the last two and a half months I have not been able to write a single note.

My income only suffices to pay my half-yearly rent, leaving me a few hundred gulden V.C. Bear in mind too that the end of my illness is not by any means in sight. Nor do I know when it will be possible for me again to soar through the air on Pegasus in full flight! Physician, surgeon, everything has to be paid for—

I well remember that several years ago the Philharmonic Society wanted to give a concert for my benefit. It would be fortunate for me if they would now decide to do so. Perhaps I might still be rescued from the poverty with which I am now faced. I am writing

---

[1] Taken from Thayer. The letter was doubtless dictated to Schindler.
[2] Samuel Arnold's edition of Handel's works, published 1787–1797.
[3] According to Thayer, this notice appeared in the Vienna *Modenzeitung* and a copy of it was among Stumpff's papers.

to Mr. S[mart] about this. And if you, dear friend, can contribute something to this object, do please come to an agreement with Mr. S[mart]. A letter about this is being written to Moscheles as well. And if all my friends combine I do believe that it will be possible to do something for me in this matter.

In regard to supplying Handel's works to His Imperial Highness the Archduke Rudolph I cannot say anything definite yet. But I will write to him in a few days and draw his attention to this suggestion.

I thank you again for your splendid gift. Please make use of me and if I can serve you in any way in Vienna I shall be delighted to do so— Once more I appeal to your philanthropic feelings in regard to my situation which I have described to you in this letter. I send you my best and most cordial wishes and my warmest compliments.

With kindest regards, your

BEETHOVEN

To Ignaz Moscheles, London

[MS in the possession of Julius Wegeler][1]

MY DEAR KIND MOSCHELES!   VIENNA, March 14, 1827

During the last few days I have heard through Herr Lewinger[2] that in a letter to him dated February 10th you inquired whether I was recovering from the illness about which people have been spreading such varying reports. Although I have not the slightest doubt that you have by now received my first letter of February 22nd which will inform you about everything you want to know, yet I cannot but thank you warmly for your sympathy with me in my sad misfortune and ask you once more to take a keen interest in my request which you will have read about in my first letter—Moreover, I feel almost assured in advance that by collaborating with Sir Smart, Mr. Stumpff, Mr. Neate and other friends of mine you will certainly succeed in obtaining a favorable result for me from the Philharmonic Society— Since my first letter I have written again to Sir Smart, as I happened to find his address, and once more urged him to deal with my request.

On February 27th I underwent a fourth operation; and already there are again visible signs that I must soon undergo a fifth. What is to be the end of it all? And what is to become of me, if my illness persists for some time?—Truly my lot is a very hard one! However,

1 Written by Schindler and signed by Beethoven.
2 A bank clerk in Vienna.

I am resigned to accept whatever Fate may bring; and I only continue to pray that God in His divine wisdom may so order events that as long as I have to endure this living death I may be protected from want. This would give me sufficient strength to bear my lot, however hard and terrible it may prove to be, with a feeling of submission to the will of the Almighty.

So, my dear Moscheles, I again ask you to deal with this matter which concerns me; and I remain with my most cordial regards ever
                                                                            your friend[1]
Hummel is here and has already visited me a few times.[2]

To Ignaz Moscheles, London

                                        [MS *in the possession of Julius Wegeler*][3]
MY DEAR, KIND MOSCHELES!   VIENNA, *March* 18, 1827
I cannot put into words the emotion with which I read your letter of March 1st. The Philharmonic Society's generosity in almost anticipating my appeal has touched my innermost soul[4]— I request you, therefore, dear Moscheles, to be the spokesman through whom I send to the Philharmonic Society my warmest and most heartfelt thanks for their particular sympathy and support.

I found myself obliged to draw immediately the whole sum of 1000 gulden A.C., for I just happened to be in the unpleasant position of having to borrow money; and this would have caused me fresh embarrassment.

In regard to the concert which the Philharmonic Society has decided to give for my benefit, I do beg the Society not to give up this noble plan but to deduct from the proceeds of this concert the 1000 gulden A.C. which they have already advanced to me. And if the Society will be so kind as to let me have the remainder, I will undertake to return to the Society my warmest thanks by engaging to compose for it either a new symphony, sketches for which are ready in my desk, or a new overture, or something else which the Society might like to have.

May Heaven but restore my health very soon and I shall prove to those magnanimous Englishmen how greatly I appreciate their sympathy for me in my sad fate.

[1] Moscheles gave away Beethoven's signature.
[2] On hearing of Beethoven's serious illness Hummel and his wife immediately repaired to Vienna where they remained until after the composer's death. The last quill used by Beethoven is still in the possession of Frau Margarete Hummel.
[3] Written by Schindler and signed by Beethoven.
[4] Beethoven had just received a gift of £100 from the Philharmonic Society in London.

But *your* noble behavior I shall never forget; and I will shortly proceed to express my thanks particularly to Sir Smart and Herr Stumpff.

I wish you all happiness! With the most friendly sentiments I remain your friend who highly esteems you

LUDWIG VAN BEETHOVEN

My heartfelt greetings to your wife.

I am indebted to the Philharmonic Society and yourself for a a new friend, namely, Herr Rau.[1] Please let the Philharmonic Society have the metronome tempi for the symphony. I send you the markings herewith.

Metronome markings of the tempi of Beethoven's last symphony, Opus 125,

Allegro ma non troppo	88 =	♪
Molto vivace	116 =	♪.
Presto	116 =	♪.
Adagio tempo I	60 =	♪
Andante moderato	63 =	♪
Finale presto	96 =	♪.

Allegro ma non troppo	88 =	♪
Allegro assai	80 =	♪
Alla Marcia	84 =	♪.
Andante maestoso	72 =	♪
Adagio divoto	60 =	♪
Allegro energico	84 =	♪.
Allegro ma non tanto	120 =	♪
Prestissimo	132 =	♪
Maestoso	60 =	♪

[1] Race was the steward of the house and property of the banker Baron Eskeles.

To Baron Johann Pasqualati

[Autograph in the Nationalbibliothek, Vienna]

ESTEEMED FRIEND!   [VIENNA, *March*, 1827]

Please send me some more stewed cherries today, but cooked quite simply, without any lemon. Further, a light pudding, almost like gruel, would give me great pleasure. My good cook is not yet competent to provide me with invalid diet. I am allowed to drink *champagne*; but please send me a champagne glass as well with your first delivery.— Now about wine. At first Malfatti said that it should be only Moselle. But he declared that there was no pure Moselle to be had in Vienna. So he himself gave me several bottles of Krumpholz Kirchner,[1] and declared that this was the best wine for my health, as it was impossible to obtain any genuine Moselle— Forgive me for giving you so much trouble; you must ascribe this in part to my helpless condition.

With kindest regards, your friend

BEETHOVEN

To Baron Johann Pasqualati

[Autograph not traced][2]

ESTEEMED FRIEND!   [VIENNA, *March*, 1827]

How can I thank you sufficiently for that excellent champagne which has so greatly refreshed me and will continue to do so! I need nothing more for today and I thank you for everything— Please note down what further result you achieve in respect of the wines, for I would gladly compensate you as much as my strength allows.— I cannot write any more today. May Heaven bless you in every way and reward you for your affectionate sympathy with your respectful and suffering

BEETHOVEN

—EMILY ANDERSON

[1] Gumpoldskirchner.
[2] Taken from Ludwig Nohl's *Neue Briefe Beethovens*, no. 320. Nohl transcribed the letter which was then in private ownership.

The Music
_____◆_____
The Last Style

What a great man has to say at the end of his life, whether this has been long or short, has in most cases certain special characteristics. Moreover the late works of all creative artists—whatever the art and whatever the epoch—have something in common: they resemble each other like old trees of different species, in which characteristics of the particular species are obliterated or at least hidden by the common quality of old age. The second *Oedipus* of Sophocles and Goethe's *Faust*, Part II, entirely different as they are in externals, have kindred sounds that meet across the millennia. And that it is not merely the octogenarian mind that thus expresses itself is shown by a last work such as Shakespeare's *Tempest*, Michelangelo's *Descent from the Cross*, his *Pietà* in the Palazzo Rondanini, and the Capella Paolina frescoes; Titian's *Crown of Thorns* in Munich; and Rembrandt's last paintings—the *Prodigal Son* and the Brunswick group: all seem to have had their origin in the same world. Nor will those capable of recognizing the existence of a general law governing all the means of expression of the various arts fail to see that even Bach's late works—the *Art of Fugue*, the *Musical Offering*, and the last Choral Prelude—belong to this same world. It is not only that the "style" of every great artist ceases gradually to develop: as he approaches the end of his life, so the individuality—the uniqueness—of his genius becomes less clearly defined, and so all that points to "eternity" in his works shines out the brighter. Only to the greatest, whose gaze has always been fixed on the eternal, is it granted to draw nearer and nearer to this distant aim. The ultimate depths have from the very beginning been closed to all that lack the power, even in old age, and though the spring then flows less freely, to say something new—unless perhaps, as in the case of Schumann, exhaustion is the outcome of disease.

In the case of Beethoven as in that of all other composers, no hard and fast line can be drawn between the last period and the preceding one. Nevertheless a broad division is plain enough: it occurs during the "barren" years, when it was thought that his creative power was exhausted; the years, that is to say, following the completion of the Seventh and Eighth Symphonies and the Opus 97 Trio. The great works that he subsequently wrote—the Ninth Symphony, the D major Mass, and the last Sonatas and Quartets—show us Beethoven on "new paths." Not that he broke with the past or denied his old aims: it was merely that his means and methods of expression were gradually changing. And when, with his last Quartets, he had run his earthly course, his "last style" had achieved its perfect development. Looking back from this stage we can clearly perceive in some of his earlier works the first indications of that style.

Unlike Goethe, Michelangelo, and Titian, Beethoven, it is true, did not live to over eighty; he did not even glimpse from afar the threshold of the age when the passions relax their hold: in certain of his later works, indeed, there are movements, such as the first of the Opus 111 Piano Sonata and the Finale of the C sharp minor Quartet, in which there is deep and genuine passion. And the most impassioned of all Adagio tunes, the second F sharp minor theme of Opus 106, is to be found in one of his last Sonatas. Nor had he lost his humor: it happens, even, that the last movement he wrote, shortly before his death, is one of the most humorous—the second Finale that he composed for the Opus 130 Quartet. The last Quartet, Opus 135, which he had written shortly before this, is full of light-winged humor. It can by no means be said that in general these last works lack the passionate outbursts to be found in his earlier ones, any more than it can be said that they no longer contain the contrasts that are so typical of him—on the contrary these contrasts are bolder and more imposing than ever. Nor, generally speaking, did his thematic material become more complicated or less easily comprehensible, for even in his last Quartets we still find any number of themes and melodies of the greatest and most truly "popular" simplicity. Examples of this are the *Danza tedesca* of the B flat Quartet, and the two themes of the Scherzo of the C sharp minor, in which moreover the formality and (apparent) artlessness of his periods are very striking.

Wherein then consist the peculiar features of his late works, which cannot escape the notice of any Beethoven student, or indeed of any musically sensitive person? If we look for the answer in the big works we shall find that the earlier ones lack the weight and fullness, the spaciousness of form, and the synthetic power of the later ones. Beethoven's control over the greatest forms of all was, in his last period, no less than stupendous, and the fertility of his invention never waned, as is proved by the Ninth Symphony, the great Mass, and the last Sonatas and Quartets. If we examine these latter for indications of his new style we shall discover a refinement and sensitiveness in the part-writing, and a feeling for the depth and significance of the smallest detail, such as is to be found in none of his earlier works. His anxiety to attain the highest perfection in part-writing became immeasurably greater. In a sketchbook he wrote out the last four bars of the variations of the C sharp minor Quartet twelve times in all, leaving the first violin part unaltered and making hardly any changes in the bass, merely because he was not entirely satisfied with the writing of the middle parts. And this was at a time when, owing to his deafness, he was popularly supposed to be indifferent to the sound of his music! There are innumerable passages in his last Sonatas and Quartets in which in a few bars of music he opens up a whole world of feeling. Among his earlier works there are indeed short movements, pieces in the smaller forms; but never before did he take them as seriously as he did in the composition of the Bagatelles, Opus 126. These were composed at the same time as the Ninth Symphony, and on them he expended the utmost care. Nor is it often that we find among his earlier works short movements such as occur in the last Quartets— movements that say so much in so few bars, and that of such moment. On the strength of these, we might well imagine that Beethoven had become a master of the small form, which he filled with music of the deepest significance.

And if we examine his late works for the individuality of their musical language—of their melodic and thematic material—the result is no more definite and the extent of the possibilities is as great. Nowhere are the firmness and significance of his musical structures greater or more immediately comprehensible than, say, in the principal theme of the first movement of the Ninth Symphony, the theme of the last movement, or the subject of the Fugue in the *Gloria* of the D major Mass. These and many other themes of a similar kind show that his power not only of invention but also of shaping and moulding his material, had become still greater with age. The same applies to the melodies of his Adagio movements, such as that of the Ninth Symphony or the last movement of Opus 109: the spiritual depth that permeates them is combined with a perfection of form and a structural firmness that assigns to every note its foreordained place in the harmonic scheme. But when we find an Adagio melody like that of the Ninth Symphony, firm and solid in its construction, avoiding the broadly prepared perfect cadence, and exactly the same thing happening immediately afterwards in the episode that follows, we see something that is characteristic of Beethoven's "last style." The same is to be seen still more clearly in melodies such as that of the *Benedictus* of the Mass. The beginning of this, indeed, has a well defined harmonic foundation; as it proceeds, however, it becomes more and more irresolute, until, at the point where we expect the perfect cadence, the melody comes to an end with the far less decisive plagal cadence. (During the whole of the very long movement, in fact, the hearer is again and again intentionally put off in his expectation of the perfect cadence, until the entry of the *Osanna*, which again ends with

the indecisive plagal cadence.) We find similar cases in many of Beethoven's later tunes, such as the principal theme of the slow movement
of Opus 106, the theme of the variations of Opus 127, and the
Cavatina of Opus 130. It is this last that Beethoven considered the
finest tune he had ever written; as he once said: "even the memory
of it brings a tear to the eye." The harmonic construction is always
either looser, or else disguised by the bass of the middle voices; or, as
in the Arietta of Opus 111, the elementary harmonization precludes any
possibility of expression—only in the variations does this emerge.

In 1818 Beethoven made notes for a "Symphony in the ancient
Modes," which it was his intention to compose simultaneously with
the one that was to become the Ninth. This fact is of the greatest
importance to our understanding of Beethoven's last style. Since 1810
he had had experience in writing music in another system than that
of the present-day major and minor. He had undertaken the arrangement
of some English, Welsh, and Scottish folk songs for an English publisher,
and had seriously devoted himself to this work. His efforts were not
directed to modernizing the harmonies of these ancient songs, most
of which were in one or other of the old modes, but, on the contrary,
to harmonizing them so as to emphasize as strongly as possible their
exotic flavor. He wrote to his publisher: "There are any number of
harmonies to choose from, but only one that suits the particular character
of the tune." Bach's method of treatment, when he copied a mass of
Palestrina, was the direct opposite, for he altered much of the harmony in
order to make the music more "tonal." Beethoven, on the contrary,
not only allowed these unfamiliar harmonies to stand as the accompaniment to melodies not of his composition, but in his later years even
introduced them into his own works. This it is that gives special
significance to the famous "Thanksgiving of a Convalescent to the
Divinity, in the Lydian Mode," from the A minor Quartet, Opus 132.
This mode corresponds to the modern key of F, but with B natural
instead of B flat, so that the whole sphere of the subdominant, and
thus one of the "dimensions" of the music, is lacking. The result is
that the key perpetually fluctuates between C major and F major; and this
is most strongly felt toward the end of the movement, where the apparent
C major asserts itself more and more, only to give way at the end to F
major. Never since Palestrina has such incorporeal, freely floating music
been written. True, it is only an episode in the whole work, and
Beethoven immediately ensures the return to tonality by means of the
D major episode that follows: "Feeling new Strength." The effect of
this return is very striking, giving as it does the impression of a descent
to solid ground; though at the same time the florid figuration veils the
robust clarity, so to speak, of the tonal harmonies. In the Credo of
the Mass the same effect is created by the Et homo factus est, coming

after the modal *Et incarnatus*. Similar effects are also to be found elsewhere in the Mass—vacillating tonality, or the juxtaposition of triads whose relation to any definite tonality is uncertain, e.g. the *In gloria dei* in the *Gloria*, the last sixteen bars of the movement, and the *Et resurrexit* in the *Credo*. In the Ninth Symphony, at the passage in the Finale *"Brüder überm Sternenzelt . . ."* the F major-C major harmony is obscured by the unaccompanied, freely floating melodic line, so that no tonal basis is apparent. Similarly at the words *"Ahnest du den Schöpfer . . . wohnen,"* though we may perhaps hear the series of triads as if they were in the key of G minor; yet the real effect of the passage is created by these unattached triads, which more than anywhere in Beethoven remind us of Palestrina, the man he held in such high esteem.

Beethoven, to be sure, never wrote his modal Symphony; "tonality" was to the last his true domain. But it must not be overlooked that in his later years he often felt the need of departing from this domain, not indeed for the sake of contrast or new color effects, as was later the case with Brahms and others, but in the effort to free himself even now from the remains of those "rational" bonds with which the tonal system fettered him. Almost infinite as are the possibilities of expression that this system brought to music, its resources do not extend to the realization of the full "transcendence" of modal Church music. Thus it was always the precincts of religion that Beethoven approached in the passages concerned, just as his modal Symphony was to be religious in character. But he had already written Church music without making use of these means. It was not until his last period that he felt the need of this ultimate degree of "spiritualization"; and this is by no means confined to his modal passages. It is the principle that governs all his late compositions, and all the new means of expression that we can discover in these works serve the cause of this spiritualization. Only by a detailed analysis would it be possible to show this convincingly, and in particular to show that even at the moments of its greatest power and weight of expression this music is leavened with spiritualizing elements. One of the commonest and most important cases in which this happens is that of the perfect cadences, whose function as the pillars supporting the edifice was always specially emphasized in his earlier, monumental style, but which are now very often disguised. One example, from the first movement of the Ninth Symphony, will serve for many: at the first statement of the principal theme, although its close is prepared in a broad and resolute cadential phrase, when the decisive moment comes the 6/4 chord on A is followed, not by the expected dominant, but by the tonic of D minor, which is still further disguised by the downward-rushing figure for violins. Thus even this powerful musical phrase is left, so to speak, hanging in the air. We see much the same thing in Michelangelo's Capella Paolina frescoes, in which we should expect the figures, overflowing as they are with strength and vigor, to be standing with their feet firmly planted on the ground. Yet so far from any such firm stance being emphasized, it is altogether absent, with the result that the figures seem to be floating in mid-air. The same applies to those in Rembrandt's *Prodigal Son,* and to the "cliffs" in the last scene of Goethe's *Faust,* Part II, which "lean upon the billowing forest."—WALTER RIEZLER

Orchestra

I. THE "BATTLE" SYMPHONY, OPUS 91

Should not everyone, the dearer Beethoven and his art are to him, the more fervently wish that oblivion might very soon draw an expiatory veil on such an aberration of his muse, through which he has desecrated the glorified object, Art, and himself.

(Gottfried Weber on Beethoven's *Wellington's Victory,* in *Caecilia,* Berlin, No. 10, 1825)

(Beethoven showed his anger at this, in a marginal note scrawled in his copy of *Caecilia:* "O *du elender Schuft! Was ich* scheisse, *ist besser als du je gedacht!*"[1])—NICOLAS SLONIMSKY

a. The Background

Johann Nepomuk Mälzel, the famous maker of automata, exhibited in Vienna during the winter of 1812–13 his automatic trumpeter and panharmonicon. The former played a French cavalry march with calls and tunes; the latter was composed of the instruments used in the ordinary military band of the period,—trumpets, drums, flutes, clarinets, oboes, cymbals, triangle, etc. The keys were moved by a cylinder. Overtures by Handel and Cherubini and Haydn's Military Symphony were played with ease and precision. Beethoven planned his "Wellington's Sieg," or "Battle of Vittoria," for this machine. Mälzel made arrangements for a concert,—a concert "for the benefit of Austrian and Bavarian soldiers disabled at the battle of Hanau."

This Johann Nepomuk Mälzel (Mälzl) was born at Regensburg, August 15, 1772. He was the son of an organ builder. In 1792 he

[1] Freely translated: "O you miserable scoundrel! What I shit is better than anything you ever thought!"—Editor.

settled at Vienna as a teacher of music, but he soon made a name for himself by inventing mechanical music works. In 1808, he was appointed court mechanician. In 1816 he constructed a metronome,[1] though Winkel, of Amsterdam, claimed the idea as his. Mälzel also made ear trumpets, and Beethoven tried them, as he did others. His life was a singular one, and the accounts of it are contradictory. Two leading French biographical dictionaries insist that Mälzel's "brother Leonhard" invented the mechanical toys attributed to Johann, but they are wholly wrong. Fétis and one or two others state that he took the panharmonicon with him to the United States in 1826 and sold it at Boston to a society for four hundred thousand dollars, an incredible statement. No wonder that the Count de Pontécoulant, in his "*Organographie*," repeating the statement, adds, "I think there is an extra cipher." But Mälzel did visit America, and he spent several years here. He landed at New York, February 3, 1826, and the *Ship News* announced the arrival of "Mr. Maelzel, Professor of Music and Mechanics, inventor of the Panharmonicon and the Musical Time Keeper." He brought with him the famous automata—the Chess Player, the Austrian Trumpeter, and the Rope Dancers—and opened an exhibition of them at the National Hotel, 112 Broadway, April 13, 1826. The Chess Player was invented by Wolfgang von Kempelen.[2] Mälzel bought it at the sale of von Kempelen's effects after the death of the latter, at Vienna, and made unimportant improvements. The Chess Player had strange adventures. It was owned for a time by Eugène Beauharnais, when he was viceroy of the kingdom of Italy, and Mälzel had much trouble in getting it away from him. Mälzel gave an exhibition in Boston at Julien Hall, on a corner of Milk and Congress Streets. The exhibition opened September 13, 1826, and closed October 28 of that year. He visited Boston again in 1828 and in 1833. On his second visit he added "The Conflagration of Moscow,"[3] a panorama, which he sold to three Bostonians for six thousand dollars. Hence, probably, the origin of the panharmonicon legend. He also

[1] There were two kinds of this metronome radically different in construction. "This accounts for the different metronome figures given by Beethoven himself, as for instance for the A major symphony." Beethoven thought highly of the metronome; he thought of "giving up the senseless terms, Allegro, Andante, Adagio, Presto."

[2] Señor Torre y Quevedo, who claims to have invented a chess-playing machine, had a forerunner in Baron von Kempelen, who, at the beginning of the last century, traveled through Europe with what he described as an unbeatable chess automaton in the likeness of a Turk. Kempelen used to conceal a man in the chest on which the Turk was seated, but so ingenious was the contrivance that for a long time everybody was deceived. Napoleon played chess with the pseudo-automaton when stopping at Schönbrunn, after the battle of Wagram. He lost the first game, and in the second deliberately made two false moves. The pieces were replaced each time, but on the Emperor making a third false move the Turk swept all the pieces off the board. (*Daily Chronicle*, London, Summer of 1914.)

[3] See in *The Life and Writings of Major Downing*, by Seba Smith (Boston, 2d ed., 1834), Letter LXIX. (page 231), dated Portland, October 22, 1833, "in which Cousin Nabby describes her visit to Mr. Maelzel's Congregation of Moscow."

exhibited an automatic violoncellist. Mälzel died on the brig *Otis* on his way from Havana to Philadelphia on July 21, 1838, and was buried at sea, off Charleston. The *United States Gazette* published his eulogy and said, with due caution: "He has gone, we hope, where the music of his Harmonicons will be exceeded." The Chess Player was destroyed by fire in the burning of the Chinese Museum at Philadelphia, July 5, 1854. An interesting and minute account of Mälzel's life in America, written by George Allen, is published in the *Book of the First American Chess Congress*, pp. 420–84 (New York, 1859). In Poe's fantastical "Von Kempelen and his Discovery" the description of his Kempelen, of Utica, N.Y., is said by some to fit Mälzel.

The arrangements for the charity concert at which the "Battle of Vittoria" was to be played were made in haste, for several musicians of reputation were then, as birds of passage, in Vienna, and they wished to take parts. Among the distinguished players were Salieri and Hummel, who looked after the "cannon" in "Wellington's Sieg"; the young Meyer-beer, who beat a bass drum and of whom Beethoven said to Tomaschek: "Ha! ha! ha! I was not at all satisfied with him; he never struck on the beat; he was always too late, and I was obliged to speak to him rudely. Ha! ha! ha! I could do nothing with him; he did not have the courage to strike on the beat!" Spohr and Mayseder were seated at the second and third violin desks, and Schuppanzigh was the concert-master; the celebrated Dragonetti was one of the double basses. Beethoven conducted.

The program was as follows: "A brand-new symphony," the Seventh, in A major, by Beethoven; two marches, one by Dussek, the other by Pleyel, played by Mälzel's automatic trumpeter with full orchestral ac-companiment; "Wellington's Sieg, oder die Schlacht bei Vittoria." "Wel-lington's Sieg" was completed in October, 1813, to celebrate the victory of Wellington over the French troops in Spain on June 21 of that year. Mälzel had persuaded Beethoven to compose the piece for his pan-harmonicon. He furnished material for it and gave him the idea of using "God Save the King" as the subject of a lively fugue. He purposed to produce the work at concerts, so as to raise money enough for him and Beethoven to visit London. A shrewd fellow, he said that if the "Battle Symphony" were scored for orchestra and played in Vienna with success, an arrangement for his panharmonicon would then be of more value to him. Beethoven dedicated the work to the Prince Regent, afterwards George IV, and forwarded a copy to him, but the "First Gentleman in Europe" never acknowledged the compliment. "Welling-ton's Sieg" was not performed in London until February 10, 1815, when it had a great run. The news of this success pleased Beethoven very much. He made a memorandum of it in the notebook which he carried with him to taverns.

This benefit concert was brilliantly successful. There was a repetition of it December 12 with the same prices of admission, ten and five florins. The net profit of the two performances was four thousand six gulden.

Beethoven was delighted with his success, so much so that he wrote a public letter of thanks to all that took part in the two performances. "It is Mälzel especially who merits all our thanks. He was the first to conceive the idea of the concert, and it was he that busied himself actively with the organization and the ensemble in all the details. I owe him special thanks for having given me the opportunity of offering my compositions to the public use and thus fulfilling the ardent vow made by me long ago of putting the fruits of my labor on the altar of the country."

The symphony was repeated in Vienna on February 27, 1814. On November 29 of that year it was performed with a new cantata, "*Der Glorreiche Augenblick*," a pretentious work written to celebrate the gathering of most of the crowned heads in Europe on the occasion of the peace treaty.—PHILIP HALE (1)

b. Beethoven's Lawsuit Against Maelzel

As we embark upon the narration of the torments suffered by our master, it is necessary to think back to the glorious days of 8 and 12 December 1813, when the A major symphony and the *Battle of Vittoria* were performed for the first time. Furthermore we must remember the letter of thanks that Beethoven prepared on this occasion, and how at the end of the letter he said explicitly that the court mechanic, Maelzel, had given these concerts, that Beethoven had written the *Battle* symphony solely for this purpose, and that he had presented it free of charge to the mechanic. The letter also mentions this man's intention of traveling to England.

In order to clarify what happened between these two friends, it is necessary to explain a previous incident. In 1812 Maelzel had promised the composer that he would make him devices that would enable him to hear better. Hoping to spur him on, Beethoven composed a piece called *Battle* symphony for the panharmonicon that Maelzel had just invented. The effect of this piece was so unexpected that the mechanic urged Beethoven to orchestrate it. The composer, who had long entertained the idea of writing a long "battle symphony," took his friend's advice and went to work immediately. Eventually four hearing devices were produced, but only one of them, the smallest and simplest, was found to be useful.[1]

---

[1] These are probably the ear trumpets shown by Ley in *Beethovens Leben in Bildern*, p. 77.

The first clash between the two friends came about in 1813 when Maelzel, who made all the arrangements for the 8 December concert by himself, took the liberty of printing on the notice posters that the *Battle* symphony was his own property, a gift to him from Beethoven. The latter lost no time in protesting against such an act of usurpation. Maelzel countered by stating publicly that he claimed the work in question in exchange for the hearing devices together with a considerable sum of money. This disagreeable argument formed the prelude to the forthcoming artistic celebration. The court mechanic's conduct toward his friend was certainly beneath the dignity of a cultivated man, and remained for a long time the object of general disapprobation.

Immediately after the first performance on 8 December, Beethoven was warned that Maelzel was trying to get possession of the score. When this attempt failed, he managed to procure some of the instrumental parts, which had been carelessly guarded. He put them together to reconstruct the score; the missing voices were filled in by some hireling. In April of 1814 Beethoven received word from Munich that the *Battle* symphony had been performed there by Maelzel, who had proclaimed that with this work he must clear 400 ducats to meet Beethoven's demand for payment.

It was now time to seek the protection of the law in guarding his own property. In the deposition drawn up for his attorney (this document is still in existence and is reproduced word for word [following this essay]). Beethoven explains:

We agreed to give this work and several others I had written in a concert for the benefit of the veterans. At this time I was beset by severe financial embarrassments. I was alone here in Vienna, abandoned by the whole world, awaiting a change for the better, and Maelzel offered me fifty gold ducats. I took them and told him that I would repay him here or, if I did not go with him to London, I would give him the work to take along and would direct an English publisher to pay him the fifty ducats.

Two other documents must be noted, one an explanation drawn up by Baron Pasqualati and the court lawyer, Dr. von Adelsburg, and the other an announcement addressed by Beethoven to the musicians in London. The first document still exists in the original; dated 20 October 1814, it states that Beethoven had in no way relinquished his claims to the work in question. In his letter to the London musicians, Beethoven tells what happened in Munich and declares: "The performance of these works (the *Victory* symphony and *The Battle of Vittoria*) by Herr Maelzel is a deception on the public and an injury to me, for he procured them in an unlawful way"; he concludes by warning the musicians against these "mutilated" works.[1]

As a result of the letter, Maelzel did not dare to attempt a performance

[1] This document is given in the supplementary material.

of these works in London. The lawsuit in Vienna was inconclusive, for the defendant was far away and his representative managed to postpone the trial for an indefinite time, causing the plaintiff considerable expense and perpetual vexation. Our master decided not to prosecute further, for in the meantime the affair had become well enough known to deter the bad friend from making any new attempts. The legal expenses were equally divided. Maelzel never returned to Vienna[1] but later resumed his correspondence with his former friend in the hope of gaining Beethoven's endorsement of the metronome. We have here his letter written from Paris on 19 April 1818. In it he claims to be working on a hearing device that Beethoven could use when conducting (!), and even suggests that they go to England together. The master informed the mechanic of his satisfaction with the metronome, but he heard nothing more about the hearing device.[2]

Papers With Reference to the Legal Controversy With the Mechanic Maelzel

1. *Deposition*

Of my own volition I composed for Maelzel, without honorarium, a composition for his panharmonicon, the *Battle* symphony. After he had had this for a while he brought me the score, the engraving[3] of which had already been started, and asked that it be arranged for full orchestra. I had already conceived the idea of a battle piece that would not be adaptable for his panharmonicon. We agreed to give this work and several others I had written in a concert for the benefit of the veterans.[4]

At this time I was beset by severe financial embarrassments. I was alone here in Vienna, abandoned by the whole world, awaiting a change for the better, and Maelzel offered me fifty gold ducats. I took them and told him that I would repay him here or, if I did not go with him to London, I would give him the work to take along and would direct an English publisher to pay him the fifty ducats.

The concerts took place, and meanwhile Herr Maelzel's plan and character first showed themselves. Without my permission, he caused to be placed on the posters the statement that the work was his property. Though indignant, he was forced to have these posters taken down. Then he placed upon them, "Out of friendship, for his journey to London." I

---

[1] Schindler's memory again plays him false: his own words in a Conversation Book state that he and Maelzel took part together in an impromptu performance of the *Ta, ta* canon at a Viennese tavern in 1817 when the friendship between Beethoven and Maelzel was restored.

[2] The quarrel with Maelzel is discussed impartially and at length in Thayer's *Life of Beethoven*, revised and edited by Elliot Forbes, Princeton, 1964, pp. 1097 ff.—Editor.

[3] Thayer makes the very logical suggestion that the "engraving" referred to was the preparation of the cylinder for the panharmonicon.

[4] The reference to the concerts of 8 and 12 December 1813, at which the Seventh Symphony and *Wellington's Victory* received their first performances.

consented to this, since I believed that I still retained the freedom to stipulate the conditions under which I would let him have the work. I remember having quarreled violently with him during the printing of the posters, but the time was too short— I was still writing the work. In the heat of inspiration, wholly absorbed in my work, I gave little thought to Maelzel.

Immediately after the first concert at the University Hall, I was told from all sides by trustworthy men that Maelzel was broadcasting the word that he had lent me 400 ducats in gold. I forthwith had the following statement inserted in the newspapers, but the writers for the papers did not insert it, since Maelzel stood well with all of them. Immediately after the first concert I gave Maelzel back his fifty ducats and told him that since I had come to know his character here, I would not travel with him—righteously angered at the fact that without asking me he had placed on the placards the statement that all arrangements for the concert had been badly handled, and also that his own unpatriotic character had shown itself in the following statement: "I [obscenity] upon L[ondon?] if only they say in London that people here paid ten gulden; I did this not for the wounded but for—"; also, that I would give him the work for London only upon conditions that I would communicate to him.

Then he asserted that it was a gift of friendship, and had this statement published in the newspapers after the second concert, without in any way asking me about it. Since Maelzel is a crude fellow, entirely without education or culture, one can imagine how he comported himself toward me during this time and thus constantly increased my wrath. And who would force a gift of friendship upon such a person?

I was now offered the opportunity of sending the work to the Prince Regent. It was thus wholly impossible to give Maelzel the work unconditionally. He then came to you and made proposals. He was told on what day he should appear to receive the answer, but he did not come, left the city, and had the work performed in Munich. How did he obtain it? Theft was impossible. Thus, Herr Maelzel had some of the parts at his house for a few days, and from these he had the whole work reconstructed by a vulgar musical craftsman, and is now hawking about the world with it.

Herr Maelzel promised me some ear-trumpets. To encourage him, I arranged the Victory symphony for his panharmonicon. His ear-trumpets were finally ready, but they were of no use to me. For this slight service Herr Maelzel would have one believe that after I had arranged the Victory symphony for full orchestra and composed the Battle for it, I should make him sole owner of this work. If we assume that I was in some small degree obliged to him for the ear-trumpets, this obligation is canceled by the fact that with the Battle compiled from parts stolen from me or made up in a mangled condition, he has made for himself at least 500 gulden CM. Thus he has paid himself off.

He had the audacity to say here that he had the *Battle*; indeed, he showed it in writing to a number of people, but I did not believe it, and was correct to the extent that the whole work was not by me but had been assembled by someone else. Moreover, the honor that he claims for himself alone might be reward enough. The War Council did not refer to me in any way, yet everything that was presented at the two concerts was by me.[1] If, as Herr Maelzel says, he delayed his journey to London because of the *Battle*, this was said only in jest: Herr Maelzel stayed here until he had completed his job of patchwork [?], since the first attempts were unsuccessful.

Beethoven m. p.

2. Explanation and Appeal to the Musicians of London by Ludwig van Beethoven

Herr Maelzel, who is at present in London, on his journey thither performed my *Victory* symphony and Wellington's *Battle at Vittoria* in Munich, and according to reports will also give it in London, just as he planned to do in Frankfurt. This induces me to declare publicly that I never and in no way made over or surrendered the above-mentioned works to Herr Maelzel, that no one possesses a copy of them, and that the only one that I gave out I sent to His Royal Highness the Prince Regent of England.

The performance of these works is accordingly either a fraud upon the public, since according to the explanation given herein he does not possess them, or if he does possess them it is an encroachment upon my rights since he acquired them in an illegal manner.

But even in the latter case the public will be deceived, since what Herr Maelzel offers it under the title "Wellington's Victory at Vittoria and Victory symphony" must obviously be a spurious or mutilated work, since he never received anything of these works from me except a single part for a few days.

This suspicion becomes a certainty when I add the assurance of musicians of this city, whose names I have been authorized to give if necessary, that at the time of his departure from Vienna he told them that he possessed this work and that he showed them parts for it, which however, as I have already proved, could only be mutilated and spurious.

Whether Herr Maelzel is capable of doing me such an injury is ascertained by the fact that he announced himself in the public papers as the sole entrepreneur for my concerts that took place here in Vienna for

---

[1] According to Thayer, the second number at each of the concerts was "Two Marches played by Maelzel's Mechanical Trumpeter, the one by Dussek, the other by Pleyel."

the benefit of the soldiers wounded in the war, at which only my works were performed, without mention of my name.

I therefore call upon the musicians of London not to allow such an injustice to me, their colleague in art, by a performance of the "Battle of Vittoria and the Victory symphony" arranged by Herr Maelzel, and to keep the London public from being deceived in the aforementioned manner.

Vienna, 25 July 1814

3. Certificate

We, the undersigned, certify in the interests of truth (and can if necessary testify under oath) that there were several conferences between Herr Louis van Beethoven and the Court Mechanic Herr Maelzel, both of this city, at the home of the undersigned Dr. Carl v. Adlersburg, at which the first of the musical compositions, the *Battle of Vittoria*, and the journey to England were discussed. At these conferences, Herr Maelzel made various proposals to Herr van Beethoven to secure for himself the above-named work or at least the rights for its first performance. Since, however, Herr Maelzel did not appear at the last appointed meeting, nothing came of the matter, the proposals that he made to the former not having been accepted. In witness thereof, our signatures.

Vienna, 20 October 1814

> Joh. Freiherr v. Pasqualati,
> k. k. patented wholesaler
> Carl Edler von Adlersburg
> Court and trial attorney and
> k. k. patented notary

—ANTON FELIX SCHINDLER, EDITED BY DONALD W. MACARDLE

c. The Music

One would think that by this time Beethoven's entire creative work would be the intellectual property of the world of music. But this is not the case. There are a considerable number of compositions that are never played, or as good as never. It is a widespread belief among musicians and music lovers that, when one knows the works that appear regularly on our concert program, one knows the whole Beethoven. So it is generally assumed that the less familiar things, or those which have been entirely shoved into the discard, are of no importance, or even weak. Of course, there are a number of compositions, those dating from his very early youth or *pièces d'occasion*, written hastily and without interest, which from the purely artistic point of view no longer mean anything to us.[1] But these apart, there is still a sufficient amount of musically rewarding material among the unused stock to fill several chamber music, orchestral, and choral concerts as well as song recitals.[2]

How can we explain that? With the exception of works that are inappropriate in style for the concert hall, such as the canons for example, it is a question in part of works unsuited for ordinary concert performance owing to their scoring (chamber music for curious combinations, wind instrument ensembles, etc.) or of those which no longer have any message for us owing to a purely topical text. In addition, there are certain compositions which are outweighed by others of a similar category, and finally, those against which there is simply a traditional prejudice.

One work of this last group, which played a decisive role in Beethoven's life but has been simply jettisoned by later generations without considering it further, is the subject of this essay, the famous and discredited so-called Battle Symphony, Opus 91, or as the complete title reads, *Wellington's Victory or the Battle of Victoria.*

[After its first performance], voices gradually began to be heard that condemned the work as mediocre, some even going so far as to call it "unworthy of a Beethoven." And this verdict has become so firmly implanted in the consciousness of later generations that the work can be characterized as a forgotten or, more exactly, suppressed work.

It takes tremendous impertinence on the part of small-minded persons to defend Beethoven's artistic dignity from Beethoven himself. The motives back of the Master's acceptance of Maelzel's suggestion (the real reason was the pecuniary difficulties in which he found himself) required neither justification nor extenuation. The question remains: how did Beethoven carry out the assumed task from an artistic point of view?

Naturally the Battle Symphony cannot sustain comparison with Beethoven's symphonies. But such a comparison would be totally erroneous. Here his sole aim and purpose was to write one of those battle pieces played at the outdoor band concerts at the beginning of the twentieth century, which in Beethoven's time and even long before were equally popular with broad masses of the public. That a genius who had created the *Eroica* should find no inner compulsion to depict a realistic battle in music is as reasonable an assumption as that Beethoven (quite apart from his having to write it hastily) did not feel called upon to expend any great amount of brain work on such a primitive artistic project.

---

[1] Personally I feel that nothing of Beethoven's is lacking in interest, even if only as a contribution to our knowledge of his personality and development as an artist. It is also difficult to understand that only a part of the conversation books have been published as yet and that a large number are still awaiting examination and publication.

[2] And also an evening in the theater if—apart from the original *Leonore*—one thinks of the beautiful music to the *Ruins of Athens* and the final chorus *Zur Weihe des Hauses,* which was written later, to say nothing of a reconstruction of the choreography to the *Prometheus* ballet and a halfway practical text for the music to *King Stephan.*

It is significant enough that he took over from Maelzel not only the idea but also the entire compositional plan of the battle music. He let Maelzel conceive and sketch in detail the drum marches and trumpet flourishes of the enemy armies and adopted his suggestions regarding the use of the English and French national anthems.[1]

And still Beethoven did not renounce his principles even in this occasional work, planned deliberately for its sensational and popular appeal. There is no doubt that he wanted to satisfy the demands of the average public for once; and he ventured into an ambit far removed from the sphere of Beethoven spirituality. But just because he correctly gauged the genre with which he had to do, he was able to turn out a work that was a brilliant example of its kind. The themes are not suited to a symphony. But his ideas invariably strike the bull's-eye. Furthermore, he not only dedicated all his technical skill to it, but warmed up to the task and the sparks from the flint of his genius took fire. So without any violation of style he wrote in the Beethoven hand an unprecedented, and in its way unsurpassable, composition in the given genre. The *Battle of Victoria* is not a work "unworthy of a Beethoven," but a curiosity, and a curiosity at that which only a Beethoven could produce and which, if taken as it was intended to be taken, would cause a furor even today. Some of the orchestral players are said to have looked on it as a "terrific" joke, and they were not entirely in the wrong. Here Beethoven undertook something that from the point of view of art was alien to his style. But he carried it off in his own distinct way—with his tongue in his cheek.

How highly he himself thought of it is shown by the detailed instructions and explanations for concert performance that he indicated in the score. These designate the number of instruments, the position of the different choirs, and the direction of the unusual apparatus. He specifies in detail the instruments for the percussion "battery" and how the "approach of the armies" is to be simulated realistically. Thus he demanded two complete and entirely independent wind choirs for the English and French armies, which combine during the further course of the work but must be maintained "by all means" right up to the end— duly considering the dynamical requirements. "The rest of the orchestra must naturally be as strong as possible in proportion," and the "larger the hall, the more instruments there should be." He considered it very important not to substitute the normal Turkish drums ("the real Turkish drum does not belong in the orchestra") for the two large drums "which were to imitate the cannon." Here he expressly wished the large instruments used in theaters for "making thunder" ("five Viennese feet square"). These heavy guns, along with the rattles for imitating gunfire,

[1] Some years before, in fact, Beethoven had written pianoforte variations on the themes of *God Save the King* and *Rule Britannia*.

and the fanfares and drum rolls (approaching from the distance) were to be located outside the orchestra at the farther end of the hall, out of sight of the audience. But with all his delight in this din and hubbub, he did not want the racket of the salvos to "darken" the orchestral music. Therefore the gunfire (except the final *presto* of the battle) should never begin at the opening of a new section. He wanted "the theme of each section" to be heard. Moreover, he himself marked the gunfire in the score, particularly the cannonades, using special indications for it. It is strange—one might almost say fantastic—to see large black and white circles above the staves of an ordinary orchestral score, to indicate the English and French cannonades!

Let us now try to describe the unusual score, as far as this is possible in mere words. First of all we hear a drum march which begins softly in the distance, and then increases to a *fortissimo* to symbolize the approach of the English army. An English military fanfare enters, followed by the English anthem, *Rule Britannia*, which, beginning softly, also gradually grows louder. This is scored in the manner of the military bands of that day and augmented later by the string choir. The same is repeated on the French side.[1] After a new drum march and fanfare, we hear the then popular French marching song, *Marlborough s'en va-t-en guerre*. The French open the attack. A new trumpet call resounds as "challenge" from their positions which is returned by the enemy forces. And then the battle begins.

The movement is in three sections. First a motif flares up which illustrates the discharge and whirring of a shell. Intensification (stepwise harmonic progressions and explosive rhythms, recalling the thunderstorm of the *Pastorale* symphony) is effected at first by simple transposition, then after a few bars by thrilling diminution of the groups. A Beethoven storm bursts forth. This first section, which is naturally accompanied by the necessary cannonades, clatter of musketry, and trumpet calls, passes quickly into a *meno allegro*. Harking back to a French trumpet fanfare carried by *fortissimo* chords, the orchestra prepares the entry of a new motif, [of rising and falling arpeggios in a distinctive 3/8 rhythm. This motif,] by means of inversion, syncopated counterpoint, etc., is developed to an effective battle picture, stalling finally in an organ point. And now the climax. Under the designation *Sturmmarsch* (assault) the seemingly simple theme of the *allegro assai*, which begins at this point, progresses by the very primitive compositional device of a stepwise ascent (cobbler's work!).

One must only imagine this theme in a unison of the deepest notes of the strings, accompanied by a thrilling drum rhythm and supported by more and more wind instruments; then one can readily picture the really

[1] Strange to say, both times the same except that the English is in E flat while the French is in C with the penultimate bar omitted.

stirring effect of this assault. Here in the deafening discharge of elementary rhythmical-dynamical forces we have a foretaste of twentieth-century orchestral effects (Stravinsky, the Potemkin film). In addition, a continuously increasing pace leads to a *presto*. A trumpet call of the English merges into the familiar theme of *Rule Britannia*, which now amid the swirling arabesques of the strings proceeds in *strettos* to a mighty climax. A fragment of the Marlborough theme vainly tries to maintain itself (symbol and status of the battle), but it breaks up more and more, pulls itself together again, and finally succumbs in the sighing wind instruments. The Marlborough theme, in minor mode and in funeral-march rhythm, fades away in a quivering tremolo of the strings, which characterizes the end of the battle. As a strategist also, Beethoven "goes the whole works," even to the knockout. The English guns thunder up to the last moment, after the French have long been silenced.

The Victory Symphony then follows as part two. After a short *intrada*, thundered out by four trumpets over a drum bass, a stirring festal march begins which, rhythmically related to the second *Fidelio* finale, has something of the triumphant character of the final theme of the C minor symphony. Even though the movement may seem lighter in weight and more loosely put together than the corresponding thematic structures of Beethoven's greater works, there is no mistaking the claws of the lion. The superhuman shout of exaltation of the dominant-seventh chord as it swings from the dominant of the dominant of the parallel key back to the main key[1]—the ecstatic gasps of the syncopated close—this could only have been written by a Beethoven! The English national anthem (*piano*, carried by woodwinds) interrupts the march with a sudden change of harmony. The march resounds again and the national anthem is repeated, now more richly ornamented—interrupted by acclamations and a flourish of trumpets as it were—then, in a stirring development, to lead to the great final apotheosis after a highly original transition to a short but extremely artistic and ingenious fugato. Beethoven (as he expressed it) "wanted to show the English in a way what a blessing *God save the King* is!"

It goes without saying that the *Battle of Victoria*, in view of its genre and unusual scoring, can claim no permanent place in the repertory. But it is equally certain that it deserves to be known and for this reason should be played from time to time. This deliberate and intentional potboiler and thriller in its day (as its history shows) has been raised through Beethoven's fantasy far above all topical considerations and represents a curiosity which, taken as such, would "bring down the house" even today.—LUDWIG MISCH

[1] Somewhat related to the wild outbreak in the *fortissimo* of the diminished-seventh chord on the simultaneous words, "*befrei'n*," "*Rache*," and "*Wütrich*" in the quartet of the second act of *Fidelio*.

II. SYMPHONY NO. 9 IN D MINOR, OPUS 125, ("CHORAL")
Lifelong Pursuit: Brotherhood of Man

The choral finale of Beethoven's Ninth Symphony is the coronation of a lifelong artistic pursuit springing from a tonal vision which already the young composer had tried to realize. Since his youthful years in his native Bonn, Beethoven had been impressed with the poetry of his great contemporary, Friedrich Schiller. It was more than the beauty of his verses and the rhythm of a truly musical language that early attracted the composer: he felt a deep affinity with the idealism of Schiller's poetic world, and artistically responded to the classical balance of form and content.

On January 26, 1793, Schiller's sister, Charlotte, received a letter from a friend in Bonn, Fischenich, who inquired about her reaction to the musical setting of Schiller's "Feuerfarb," "by a young man of this place whose musical talent is becoming known and whom the elector has just sent to Haydn at Vienna. He intends to compose Schiller's 'Freude,' verse by verse."

It is through this letter that we learn for the first time of young Beethoven's intention to compose Schiller's "Hymn to Joy." The theme of joy was already the driving force behind Beethoven's cantata, *On the Ascension of Leopold II* (September 30, 1790). It is jubilant music; choruses sing joyfully for the happy occasion. Moreover, the evolution from darkness to light, which is the psychological curve of the Ninth, underlies also the structure of the cantata: the music first mourns the death of Emperor Joseph, and then turns to the jubilant greeting of his successor. Here, too, the fugato technique is integrated in the enthusiastic chorale. The exuberance of the "Heil" chorus sounds in D Major just as the finale of the Ninth. When the basses intone "Stürzet nieder Millionen" in the cantata, this passage anticipates, in mood and text, the phrase "Ihr stürzt nieder Millionen" of the Ninth. In the cantata, the people are urged to "look up to the Master of all thrones" and the analogous invocation of God occurs also in the symphony.

Beethoven was twenty years old when the coronation of the Emperor inspired him to a score forecasting artistic events of paramount importance. But it needed a deeper message and a stronger experience than the enthronement of a monarch to stimulate the imagination of Beethoven—the greatest republican of all the artists—to a work of immortal significance.

Yet the cantata proves that the young Beethoven already envisioned masses joyously marching along and singing together: a tone-poetic conception, which decades later culminated in the choral scene of the Ninth Symphony. While the actual composition of the symphony is biographically related to the years 1817–1823, more than two decades after the quoted letter to Charlotte Schiller, we have, however, tangible evidence of Beethoven's occupation with the problem (known to us as that of the Ninth) in sporadic notes dating throughout all the intervening years.

What lies between such creative beginnings and such ends is a fascinating interplay of sketches, studies and enterprises—of subconscious and conscious work. Already in a sketchbook from 1798, we find a reference to the great unison passage, "Brüder über'm Sternenzelt muss ein lieber Vater wohnen." The sketch, however, hardly permits a clue to the final shape of tones to come. Only the words point to their later tie-up. This early flash occurs most unexpectedly between drafts for two piano compositions, namely the Rondo in G, Opus 51, No. 2, and the Sonata in C Minor, Opus 10, No. 1. Such a process of interrupting one work and suddenly shifting to another occurs frequently with Beethoven.

From about the year 1803, Beethoven was engrossed in the composition of his only opera, *Fidelio*, first performed in Vienna, Theater an der Wien, November 20, 1805. Here, too, the way to its final conquest is one of long search and struggle. The finale of the opera (originally laid in the prison, later on the outside) is again a tone picture of joy, of an hour of gladness; an outburst of suffering people into jubilant singing. The minister, Don Fernando, liberates the oppressed: "I seek my brethren as a brother." We face here again pillars upon which the choral scene of the Ninth was built: a score for soli, chorus and orchestra in jubilant expression, a text based on the theme of brotherly love—a culmination of all preceding music into a finale of overpowering joy.

In 1808 Beethoven wrote his Fantasia for Piano, Orchestra, and Chorus, Opus 80. This work appears, in retrospect, as the chief study for the form of the choral scene in the Ninth. Beethoven himself interprets the close relationship between these two scores, Opus 80 and Opus 125, in a letter on March 10, 1824, to his publisher, Probst: "The Ninth Symphony is in the style of my Choral Fantasia but very much more extended." While the fantasia is less complex in character than the Ninth, it clearly anticipates the musical contours of the Ode to Joy. Both scores introduce their vocal sections with recitatives which are followed by variations on a theme of a simple diatonic character. And even the themes resemble each other in their construction upon neighboring tones. There are numerous other analogies, which the stylistic comparison of Opus 80 and Opus 125 readily yields.

In the years 1811 and 1812, Beethoven planned the composition of three new symphonies. He finished the manuscripts of those in A Major and F Major (the Seventh and Eighth) in May and October 1811, respectively. As to the third in this series of symphonies, little progress was made at this time. Yet its key was settled—D Minor, which indeed remained the key of the Ninth. Between sketches for the Seventh and Eighth appears the following comment:

"Finale, Freude schöner Götter Funken Tochter aus Elysium. The symphony in four movements; but the second movement in 2/4 time like the first. The fourth may be in 6/8 time—major; and the fourth movement well fugued."

But the integration of Schiller's hymn into the planned symphony could not have been definitely established in Beethoven's mind because his sketches for an Overture in C, called Namensfeier (published later as Opus 115) and finished in October 1814, surprisingly refer to the Schiller verse, "Freude schöner Götter Funken" with the remark "vielleicht so anfangen" (perhaps begin thus).

When Beethoven in 1817 contemplated plans for a new symphonic composition of great dimensions, he entertained various and, as we shall see, conflicting ideas. The sketches show, under a headline "Zur Sinfonie in D," rather extensive work pertaining to the scherzo. Yet the plan at this date did not call for the characteristic feature which distinguishes the finished Ninth from all symphonic works written before, namely, the use of a choral finale. Like Beethoven's preceding eight symphonies and the preceding movements of this new one, the finale of the planned score was to be a purely orchestral movement based on a fugal theme which is preserved as the theme of the scherzo. In 1818 the drafts for the symphony again occupy Beethoven's mind. Yet they are soon repressed by extensive work on the Hammerklavier Sonata. In spite of the intense effort expended on this great polyphonic score, Beethoven shows, at this time, enough strength to plan his pair of symphonies:

Adagio Cantique:—
Religious song in a symphony in the old modes (Herr Gott dich loben wir—Alleluja), either independently or as introductory to a fugue. Possibly the whole second symphony to be thus characterized: the voices entering either in the Finale or as early as the Adagio. The orchestral violins, etc., to be increased tenfold for the last movements, the voices to enter one by one. Or the Adagio to be in some way repeated in the last movements. In the Adagio the text to be a Greek mythos (or) Cantique Ecclesiastique. In the Allegro a Bacchus festival.

In these words, Beethoven sets the stylistic attitude of his never completed Tenth Symphony. It was to be a thanksgiving in archaic colors, an alleluia, a polyphonic adoration of Deity. The idea of blending the symphonic with vocal expression is now in the foreground. The point at which the human voice was to enter the symphonic cycle might have been the adagio or the allegro finale. The planned festival of Bacchus points to orgiastic expression and jubilation, the ecclesiastic song to the mood of thanksgiving.

In 1822, Beethoven again refers to his pair of symphonies. Rochlitz relates in his *Für Freunde der Tonkunst* Beethoven's confession that he had "two grand symphonies round his neck, different from each other and different from any of the preceding ones." The first of the symphonies is referred to as "Sinfonie Allemande." And in the preliminary work, the irrefutable evidence of the diatonic D Major theme, "Freude schöner Götter Funken," appears and variations are mentioned as the underlying form scheme. Schindler reports how Beethoven walking up and down his room suddenly exclaimed: "I have it, I have it." What Beethoven "had" was the solution as it appears in two pages of his sketchbook. The first page contains the exclamation: "Lasst uns das Lied des unsterblichen Schiller singen." (Let us sing the song of the immortal Schiller.) "Freude, Freude, Freude" (Joy, Joy, Joy). And on the next page, Beethoven notes the beginning of the bass recitative: "Bass: nicht diese Töne, Voce[1] fröhlichere Freude!" (Bass: not these tones; let us sing something more pleasant and full of joy!)

In spite of all these powerful proclamations, the plan for a choral finale was still not firmly entrenched in the master's mind. Facing one of the conflicts so characteristic of Beethoven's creative life, we find in the sketchbook as late as the summer of 1823, in the middle of drafts for the Ode to Joy, a plan for a "finale instrumentale." Yet the basic thought of this sketch eventually found its place in the finale of the String Quartet, Opus 132. Such a shifting of material was a typical procedure with Beethoven: the tonal substance of important inventions is preserved. If not used for a current enterprise, the material is stored for future work. Often it was not until after extended experimentation that Beethoven found the proper environment for his ideas.

The draft of the second movement of the new symphony was finished in August 1823—the notebook from May to July contains sketches for the first, second, and third movements. Two fugal themes written in 1815 and 1817 are transplanted into this new environment and their prolongation eventually becomes the theme of the scherzo. But the second of the planned pair of symphonies did not materialize in spite of a new and intense period of planning. He gave the project up although he had already sketched extensive parts of the symphonic score. The scherzo, in particular, had taken on form. But the following note expresses his decision: "instead of a new symphony, a new overture on B-A-C-H,[2] intensely fugal with three."[3] The negative decision to postpone or definitely

[1] The word *voce* is not clearly legible and seems to be a reminder for Beethoven to use the human "voice" at this place.

[2] German-speaking musicians refer to the note which we know as "B flat" simply as "B"; our "B natural" is their "H." Thus B-A-C-H becomes a very identifiable musical motive, used extensively by J. S. Bach himself. See his *Kunst der Fugue.*—Editor.

[3] The "three" might refer to the employment of three fugal subjects. Grove, however, believes that Beethoven meant three trombones. The planned contrapuntal work was to be a triple fugue honoring the spirit of Bach by an extended piece of polyphony.

reject a tenth symphony turns into a creative opportunity: from the moment the Tenth is given up, the idea of the choral finale is available for the Ninth. And this plan seizes Beethoven's mind, excluding all other possibilities, at a time when he is intensely occupied with the idea of choral variations on the Ode to Joy. Gradually the vision emerges with a sufficient degree of clarity and gains final impetus. It is the plan which triumphs in the Ninth as we know it today.

This then is the life story of the choral symphony: the budding of a tonal vision in the mind of the youth, its slow ripening in the early venture of the Cantata for Emperor Leopold and in the later one of the Choral Fantasia. Passing through stages of trial, the youthful vision finally reaches a new form in the jubilant singing of the opera, *Fidelio*. But it is not until the human voice is transplanted into the symphonic realm that the lifelong tonal vision of the Ninth is truly fulfilled. Beethoven, the creator, who had set his art free, crowns classicism in its greatest human message: the Ode to Joy lights the way to the brotherhood of man as a still unfulfilled promise of a better tomorrow.—FREDERICK DORIAN

SYMPHONY IN D MINOR, No. 9, WITH FINAL CHORUS ON SCHILLER'S "ODE TO JOY," OPUS 125
I. Allegro ma non troppo, un poco maestoso; II. Molto vivace, Presto; III. Adagio molto e cantabile, Andante moderato; IV. Allegro assai, Quartet and Chorus

1. *Allegro ma non troppo, un poco maestoso*, D minor, 2/4. Themes which are gradually unfolded from mysterious murmurings in the orchestra—no uncommon experience nowadays—all date back to the opening measures of the Ninth Symphony, where Beethoven conceived the idea of building a music of indeterminate open fifths on the dominant, and accumulating a great *crescendo* of suspense until the theme itself is revealed in the pregnant key of D minor, proclaimed *fortissimo* by the whole orchestra in unison. It might be added that no one since has quite equaled the mighty effect of Beethoven's own precedent—not even Wagner, who held this particular page in mystic awe, and no doubt remembered it when he depicted the elementary serenity of the Rhine in a very similar manner at the opening of the "Ring." The development in this, the longest of Beethoven's first movements, moves with unflagging power and majesty through many an episode, many a sudden illumination from some fragment of his themes. At the restatement of the main theme the orchestra is flooded with the triumph of the D major long withheld. The long coda, coming at the point where it would seem that nothing more could be said on a much developed subject, calls forth new vistas from the inexhaustible imagination of the tone magician who needed little

more than the common chord upon which to erect his vast schemes. Tovey writes of this movement (in "Essays in Musical Analysis") that it "dwarfs every other first movement, long or short, that has been written before or since," attaining its stature, in his opinion, by a perfect balance in the organization of its parts. And Grove goes further still ("Beethoven and His Nine Symphonies"): "Great as are the beauties of the second and third movements—and it is impossible to exaggerate them—and original, vigorous and impressive as are many portions of the finale, it is still the opening *Allegro* that one thinks of when the Ninth Symphony is mentioned. In many respects it differs from other first movements of Beethoven; everything seems to combine to make it the greatest of them all."—JOHN N. BURK (2)

The opening measures of Beethoven's Ninth Symphony furnish a striking example in which a progressive weakening of texture, together with both harmonic and motivic incompleteness and ambiguity, creates powerful expectations whose inhibition and ultimate resolution into a clearly defined theme produce a powerful affective experience. In the sixteen measures of introduction the structural gaps are not only melodic, they are harmonic as well. For within the cultural context in which this work is heard, the complete triad is the norm, and the open fifths presented throughout the introduction are felt to involve incompleteness. Indeed, this incompleteness is signified by the very fact that such fifths are commonly referred to as "empty." Moreover, the harmonic incompleteness creates ambiguity as to mode; the listener is in doubt as to what the completion will be. Thus, the powerful effect of the first theme is, at least in part, due to the fact that it presents a completed triad and in this way removes the previous ambiguity and completes what was clearly incomplete.

But the forceful impression of the first theme is even more the product of the fact that it is a distinct, substantial shape. The whole introduction is built upon a motive which is obviously psychologically unsatisfactory. It is not merely incomplete, it lacks direction and coherence. The listener senses that it must have meaning, but he has no idea of what that meaning is since he can envisage its consequents only in the vaguest terms. Because motive establishes no progressive motion, either melodically or harmonically, the listener has little feeling for where this passage is leading; he is merely aware that it seems to presage some momentous, fateful event.

In a sense, the only really satisfactory, unambiguous aspect of measures 1–12 is the relationship between the figure and the ground. All the factors making for a clearly articulated relationship are present: not only is the ground much more uniform than the figure, but it begins before the figure is introduced, thus surrounding it in a temporal sense. But this clarity also gives way to ambiguity. For as the point of culmination approaches, the figure becomes progressively weaker—more like the ground. First, the rhythmic articulation of the motive is lost in the rising crescendo of volume and the psychological accelerando (measures 13–14). Then its intervallic definition becomes obscured in the general octave motion; and, in the end, when the distinction between figure and ground is obliterated altogether, the texture becomes completely ambiguous and the listener is uncertain as to what the textural organization is.

The feeling that a momentous event is impending is heightened by the crescendo which begins in measure 11 and by the increased psychological tempo at that point. For the figure instead of being repeated every two beats is now repeated on every beat. And in measure 13 it occurs at a still shorter time interval. It should also be noted that when the motive is stated in sixteenth notes (beginning in measure 13), the metric opposition of twos against threes, implicit in the opening measures, becomes actualized and tends to increase the general ambiguity of the whole texture.

Although the entrance of the low D in the horns and bassoon in measure 15 is not strongly emphasized, not marked for consciousness, it plays an important part in intensifying expectation at the very end of the passage. Since it creates the first harmonic motion in the whole introduction, the listener senses that "this is it," that at last he will know and understand what heretofore had been only a powerful premonition.

The sense of the relentless power of inexorable fate which characterizes the main theme of this first movement is a result not only of the elemental force of the theme itself and of the ambiguities and expectations excited by the introduction but also of the particular manner in which the introduction leads into the theme. Unlike most introductions this one does not conclude with a dominant preparation, a waiting period, in which the listener is given an opportunity to orient himself to what has passed and prepare for what is to come. Instead the music moves on without pause, without pity, to its stark and awful declaration:

> As flies to wanton boys are we to the gods.
> They kill us for their sport.

These compelling lines call attention to those inexplicable and inescapable events of our existence which the Greeks attributed to "fate," the Renaissance to "fortune," and we ascribe to "chance."—LEONARD B. MEYER

II. *Molto vivace*, D minor 3/4. For the only time in his symphonies, Beethoven in this case put his scherzo second in order and before the slow movement. A scherzo it is in everything but name, with the usual repeats, trio, and *da capo* (with bridge passages added). There is the dancelike character of earlier scherzos, and an echo of rusticity in the trio, recalling the Sixth and Seventh. Yet all is lifted to the prevailing mood of rarified purity as this movement, like the others, adds a new voice to an old form. This scherzo has been called "a miracle of repetition in monotony," by virtue of the incessant impact of its rhythm (associated with the kettledrums, tuned in octaves) which keeps its constant impact through the most astonishing variety in modulation, color, counterpoint. The movement begins as a five-voice fugue, recalling the fact that Beethoven first conceived the theme as the subject for a fugue—the earliest of his sketches which eventually found its way into the symphony. The trio continues the contrapuntal interest by the combination of two themes. The famous passage for the oboe against wind chords reminded Berlioz of "the effect produced by the fresh morning air, and the first rays of the rising sun in May."

III. *Adagio molto e cantabile*, B flat major, 4/4. The slow movement is built upon two themes whose structural relation lies principally in contrast: the first, *Adagio* in B flat, 4/4 time, the second, *Andante moderato* in D major, triple time. After the almost static *Adagio*, the second theme attains flowing motion in its melody, which Beethoven has marked *espressivo*. This theme recurs in alternation with the other, but unlike the other is hardly varied, except in the instrumentation. The *Adagio* theme undergoes variations of increasingly intricate melodic ornament like those by which Beethoven also lifted his last sonatas and quartets to such indescribable beauty.

IV. *Allegro assai*, D major, 4/4. The finale opens with a frank discord, followed by a stormy and clamorous *presto* of seven bars. It is as if the composer, having wrested from his first three movements the very utmost drop that was in them, is still restless and unsatisfied. He must still advance upon his divine adventure, cast off his tragic or poignant moods, find some new expression, spacious and radiant. A few measures of each movement are reviewed, and after each a recitative in the cellos and basses gives an answer of plain rejection; in the first two cases brusquely, in the case of the *Adagio* softened by a tender memory. Beethoven's instruments seem on the very verge of speech. A hint of the coming choral theme is breathed in gentle accents by the woodwinds, to which the recitative, now no longer confined to the strings, gives a convincing affirmative. Thereupon the theme in full is unfolded in its rightful D major. It is first heard in the utter simplicity[1] of the low

[1] The choral theme has come in for some slighting remarks, probably on account of its A B C simplicity. It need scarcely be pointed out that a basic simplicity, treated with infinite subtlety and variety, is the very essence of the score from the first measure to the last. It is not without significance that Beethoven refined and polished his theme through two hundred sketches, to attain its ultimate beauty and perfection. There are

strings in unison, *piano*. Gradually harmonies and instruments are added, until the exposition has been completely made, but not even yet has the composer left the instrumental field.

Once more there is the noisy *presto* passage, and the composer introduces words for the first time into a symphony. The baritone has this recitative:

"*O Freunde, nicht diese Töne,*	"O brothers, these sad tones no longer!
sondern lasst uns angenehmere	Rather raise we now together our voices,
anstimmen, und freudenvollere."	And joyful be our song!"

There immediately follow the first three verses of Schiller's ode,[1] by the solo quartet and chorus:

Freude, schöner Götterfunken,	Joy, thou spark from flame immortal
Tochter aus Elysium,	Daughter of Elysium!
Wir betreten feuertrunken,	Drunk with fire, O heav'n born Goddess,
Himmlische, dein Heiligthum.	We invade thy halidom!
Deine Zauber binden wieder,	Let they magic bring together
Was die Mode streng getheilt;	All whom earth-born laws divide;
All Menschen werden Brüder,	All mankind shall be as brothers
Wo dein sanfter Flügel weilt.	'Neath thy tender wings and wide.
Wem der grosse Wurf gelungen,	He that's had that best good fortune,
Eines Freundes Freund zu sein,	To his friend a friend to be,
Wer ein holdes Weib errungen,	He that's won a noble woman,
Mische seinen Jubel ein!	Let him join our Jubilee!
Ja—wer auch nur eine Seele	Ay, and who a single other
Sein nennt auf dem Erdenrund!	Soul on earth can call his own;
Und wer's nie gekonnt, der stehle	But let him who ne'er achieved it
Weinend sich aus diesem Bund.	Steal away in tears alone.

---

no lack of distinguished advocates for the theme. Grove wrote: "The result of years and years of search, it is worthy of all the pains which have been lavished on it, for a nobler and more enduring tune surely does not exist." Wagner: "Beethoven has emancipated this melody from all influences of fashion and variations of taste, and has raised it into a type of pure and lasting humanity." Tovey (to use a recent authority) says as much, in his way, in three words, calling it simply "a great theme."

[1] It may be noted here that of the eight verses of Schiller's poem, Beethoven chose the first three verses, at first without their four-line choruses, and then added three choruses in succession, one of them, "Froh, wie seine Sonnen fliegen," belonging to the fourth verse, which he did not use, and obviously chosen for its militant possibilities. Beethoven could scarcely have set more of the text; to set three stanzas required from him the longest symphonic movement which had ever been composed. Yet Grove thought that Beethoven was deterred by the "bad taste" of some of Schiller's verses. A line which the Englishman fastens upon in horrified italics as "one of the more flagrant escapades" is this: "Dieses Glas dem guten Geist!" ("This glass to the good Spirit!")

Freude trinken alle Wesen	Joy doth every living creature
An den Brüsten der Natur;	Draw from Nature's ample breast;
All Guten, alle Bösen	All the good and all the evil
Folgen ihrer Rosenspur.	Follow on her roseate quest.
Küsse gab sie uns und Reben,	Kisses doth she give, and vintage,
Einen Freund, geprüft im Tod;	Friends who firm in death have stood;
Wollust ward dem Wurm gegeben,	Joy of life the worm receiveth,
Und der Cherub steht vor Gott.	And the Angels dwell with God!

The four line chorus (to the unused fourth verse) summons in Beethoven's imagination a marching host, and he gives it to proud and striding measures *alla marcia*, adding piccolo, double bassoon, triangle, cymbals, and bass drum to his orchestra (again for the first time in a symphony). This is the verse, given to the tenor solo and chorus:

Froh, wie seine Sonnen fliegen	Glad as burning suns that glorious
Durch des Himmels prächt'ten Plan,	Through the heavenly spaces sway,
Wandelt, Brüder, eure Bahn,	Haste ye brothers, on your way,
Freudig, wie ein Held zum Siegen.	Joyous as a knight victorious.

After the excitement of this variation, Beethoven allows himself to be alone with his instruments once more, and for the last time, in a double fugue. The chorus next sings (*Andante maestoso*) the following short verse of far-flung import, calling upon three trombones to add to the impressiveness of the sonority:

Seid umschlungen, Millionen!	O embrace now all you millions,
Diesen Kuss der ganzen Welt!	With one kiss for all the world.
Brüder—überm Sternenzelt	Brothers, high beyond all stars
Muss ein lieber Vater wohnen!	Surely dwells a loving Father.

A religious *Adagio* in a mood of mystic devotion is the setting of the following verse:

Ihr stürzt nieder, Millionen?	Kneel before him, all you millions
Ahnest du den Schöpfer, Welt?	Know your true Creator, man!
Such' ihn überm Sternenzelt!	Seek him high beyond all stars,
Ueber Sternen muss er wohnen.	High beyond all stars adore Him.

But the key verse of the movement is the first: "Freude, schöner Götterfunken," and this, with its chorus: "Seid umschlungen, Millionen," is resumed by the quartet and chorus, and finally exalted to its sweeping climax in the coda, *prestissimo*.

The symphony is scored for two flutes, piccolo, two oboes, two clarinets, two bassoons, contra-bassoons, four horns, two trumpets, three trombones, timpani, bass drum, triangle, cymbals, and strings.—JOHN N. BURK (2)

[After the seraphic close of the *Adagio*, all] hell breaks loose! Wagner thought it an inadequate hell and wanted to improve it: his emendations are chiefly concerned with the trumpet parts.

The opening chord of the finale is [a] grinding discord. But the trumpets and horns in Beethoven's day were incapable of playing both the chord of D minor and discordant B flat, which, therefore, had to be left to the woodwind, who, it must be confessed, perform the task rather feebly. Also Beethoven had a disconcerting habit, here and elsewhere in his tuttis, of putting notes for the trumpets where their "natural" scale fitted into the harmony, and leaving them out where they did not, which gives a scrappy sound to the music. Wagner wished to use the possibilities of the modern trumpet to fill in these gaps, but with doubtful success. It seems that the only thing to do is to take Beethoven for better for worse, as we find him. At all events, the "harsh din" is hellish enough to arouse a cry of remonstrance from the orchestral basses. Again the din, and once more the protest from the basses. They seem to be looking for some great tune which should solve all the doubt and dismay of what has gone before. How about the first movement? says the orchestra —again rejection and despair by the basses. The scherzo is next suggested; angry dismissal by the basses. Surely, then, the slow movement was good? "Ah! that was lovely," the basses seem softly to sigh, "but it won't do now. Quick! let us find the solution of our troubles before it is too late —before joy is lost for ever!"

Then the woodwind answers: "There used in the Golden Age to be a tune which went somehow like this." "That's it," say the basses, "we are saved; joy will once more be ours," and with that they start softly, serenely, and seriously to hum to themselves their "immortal chant of old"—the "Joy" tune as it shall hereafter be called.

Then the violas take up the tune—still softly, but with full voice, while the cellos join them in a loving unison: the first bassoon improvises a heavenly descant, while the double basses far below murmur a deep foundation.

It has been proved by musicologists that Beethoven intended the second bassoon to play with the double basses here, as all good bassoons should when the double basses are left alone, and that in printing the score it was accidentally omitted. The omission is one of those lucky accidents on which masterpieces often depend; the unobtrusive murmur of the double basses would be quite spoiled by a snorting bassoon.

Then the violins sing the tune, the bassoon helping from time to time, and the lower strings play sonorous countermelodies, and lastly the trumpets take up the theme and make it into a solemn march.

After this last repetition Beethoven adds [a] refrain which is, of course, suggested by the last phrase of the tune. This is extended, modulating in a perfectly orthodox fashion to the dominant A major, and we are led to expect a "second subject" in regular symphonic form. But suddenly the composer appears to change his mind, a little wraith of a subject appears in an uncertain manner, both as to tonality and tempo, there is an angry outburst, and suddenly hell breaks loose again with renewed force. This time it is rebuked, not by the orchestral basses, but by the human voice crying out to them to cease this din and to sing of joy.

What are we to make of all these hesitations, these apparent changes of purpose, which are characteristic of the symphony as a whole?

If we knew only the printed page and knew nothing of the historical facts, we might well guess that Beethoven originally designed a purely instrumental finale on "sonata" lines, that he changed his mind and decided instead on a choral conclusion, but that he forgot when he sent the work to the printers to cut out the discarded version: if this were indeed so, we should have to count it as another lucky accident, for we should have lost some of the most beautiful pages in the whole of music.

The choral Finale may be described technically as a set of variations with episodes, like the slow movement.

After an initial shout of "Freude, Freude," the bass soloist sings the "joy" tune to the words of Schiller's *Ode to Joy*. The melody is in the bass, while the oboe[1] plays a joyful little countermelody. The chorus joins in when the second half of the melody is played. Between each variation the refrain is repeated.

The first variation is not much more than a repetition of the theme with different texture, sung by the solo voices while the chorus joins in as before, but this time in four-part harmony. The second variation[2] is an ornamentation of the theme in [eighth notes]. Like the first variation it is sung by the solo voices and taken up by the chorus. Again the refrain follows, this time covered by heavy [half-note] chords for the voices, and the variation finishes with a shattering modulation to F major on the words "vor Gott" ("before God"). I once played this passage to a pupil well versed in "modern" harmony. I shall never forget her cry of surprise and delight at this modulation.

There is a pause: then what are we to expect? Well, Beethoven was a truly religious man, and was therefore not ashamed to place earthly jollity cheek by jowl with deep adoration.

Softly we hear the grunt of the contrabassoon and the thump of the big drum, gradually there emerges a jolly marching tune, a variant of the "Joy" tune. This is, I believe, the music which deeply shocked the Victorian Beethovenites.

---

[1] And the clarinet plays a second countermelody alternating with the oboe.—Editor.
[2] Vaughan Williams in another place objects to this and certain other Beethoven variations as being "overlaid with trite mechanical formulas."—Editor.

It is played chiefly by the wind band, very softly. The army of joy (freedom?) is advancing in the distance. Beethoven, great artist that he was, had no false shame in introducing this "Turkish Patrol" effect. Then, against the march tune, a man's voice is heard singing—probably a drunken soldier. He is without doubt a Welshman, for he is obviously singing a "Penillion" to the principal melody, though he probably has not obeyed all the rules of "Penillion"[1] singing. Gradually his companions join in, and the song culminates in a lusty shout.

Incidentally, it should be noted that Schiller's text here refers to the March of the Stars across the heavens. Beethoven evidently considered that the stars were jolly good fellows, fond of a rousing chorus, fond of a glass of beer and a kiss from the barmaid.

As the chorus finishes, the orchestra takes up the tale with a double fugue of demoniac energy. [There are] two subjects. One is made up on the march tune; the other is a rhythmical variant of the "Joy" tune. Wagner, I believe, says that this figure "means" the hero rushing into the fight. This unfortunate explanation has been the cause of much bad music by later composers.

The fugue continues with unabated exuberance for about a hundred bars. The [eighth-note] subject is unceasing, altering and extending itself as the occasion requires. [It] lands us on an F sharp, the dominant of B, when the rhythm only is repeated; then comes a diminuendo on the horns.

The "Joy" tune puts in a claim, sadly: "Have you forgotten me?" "No," shouts the chorus, and plunges hurly-burly into the "Joy" tune while the strings scamper around in excited [eighth notes].

I know no parallel to this moment except perhaps the great "Battle Piece," No. 5 of Bach's Cantata *Ein' Feste Burg.*

The music ends abruptly: there is a silence. Then the trombones sound (for the first time since the scherzo) and the men's voices declare the brotherhood of man [in solemn hymnlike tones].

The full choir repeats the strain, then the orchestra, joined later by the chorus, with hushed voices gives the reason that it is because man, lowly as he is, is made in God's image.

Never has the mystery of the universe been so portrayed. Note the strange color of the strings, without violins or double basses, enriched by the soft tones of low flutes, clarinets, and bassoons. Note also the strange quasi-modal melodic and harmonic scheme.

Then, at the words "He lives beyond the stars," first a great shout and then an awe-struck whisper, we seem to see the whole star-studded universe and for a moment to penetrate into the mystery which lies beyond.

The great shout is on the chord of E flat. The whisper is on [a

[1] Penillion: an ancient form of Welsh song in which a harp plays a well-known tune and the singer extemporizes words *and* music to it.—Editor.

mysterious discord made up of a diminished ninth on the bass note A].
On this chord the strings shimmer, the winds throb, the trombones and
lower voices hold soft chords, while the women's voices murmur in their
highest register. It may be worth notice that Brahms thought this passage
worth cribbing for his *Requiem*.[1]

Then joy breaks out again, joined with the assurance of the brotherhood of man in another wildly exciting double fugue, or rather, it would
be wildly exciting when sung by a choir of supermen and women; of the
two subjects, the upper is a rhythmical variant of the "Joy" tune and
the lower a version of the "brotherhood of man" theme.

There is also a third subject or rather an ejaculation, [two repeated
notes on the word "Freude"].

The fugue rises to its highest point at the famous passage where the
sopranos hold the high A for twelve bars, a terror to the average choralist.
Then, at the very height of the excitement, a sudden hush; again we
ponder in awe and wonderment on the deity and man's likeness to him.

This soft unison, these augmented intervals, the repeated notes: are
they not well-worn devices for expressing mystery in eighteenth-century
music? So is the diminished seventh of Bach's "Barabbas" a well-worn
device; so are the chromatic scales in Beethoven's pastoral thunderstorm.
But when a master hand guides these devices, they remain ever new and
startling, and excite us more each time we hear them; while the farfetched
tricks of lesser composers seem stale even the first time.

This section ends with a great shout, "brothers," and then the music
softly and beautifully dies away as we once more contemplate the stars
and the mysteries that lie behind them. Quite naturally, there succeeds
to this a mood of childlike happiness. *Beethoven did not put on his
top hat when he went to church*,[2] indeed, if he had lived in modern
times he would probably have joined the Salvation Army. At all events
he could pass without any feeling of impropriety from awe-full wonderment to simple merriment, then back to the emotion of deeply-felt joy;
and without a break to riotous junketing.

> I am of old and young,
>   of the foolish as much as the wise,
> Regardless of others, ever regardful of others,
> Maternal as well as paternal,
>   a child as well as a man,
> Stuffed with the stuff that is coarse
>   and stuffed with the stuff that is fine . . .

The strings trip lightly onto the scene in terms of the "Joy" tune.
The chorus now takes its share, adding a great shout "All men shall

[1] In the third movement on the words: "*Nun Herr, wess soll ich mich trösten?*" just
before the cadenzalike passage leading into the final "joyful" fugue: "*Der Gerechten
Seelen sind in Gottes Hand.*"—Editor.
[2] Italics by editor.

be brothers"—but suddenly the voices are hushed when they sing of the "soft wings of Joy." Then the music repeats itself in shortened form; again we have the great shout of brotherhood, and again the hush, but this time it takes the form of that famous vocal cadenza which Brahms was, again, not ashamed to crib in his *Requiem*.[1] Especially magical is the final cadence. The voices reach the chord of B major, with the soprano holding the high B, then gently drop to F sharp while the alto sounds D natural, making the chord of B minor. Then the bass voice softly slides down to A and we are back in the home key: this progression has been foreshadowed earlier in the movement.[2]

The orchestra takes up the idea with gusto: B, A, B, A, it repeats, over and over again, with ever-increasing speed, until at last we burst into the final unrestrained jubilation. No Sunday school about this, no angel choirs but real rowdy human beings:

> Pour out the wine without restraint or stay,
> Pour not by cups but by the belly full,
> Pour out to all that will.

The drums thump, the cymbals crash, the trumpets blare, the chorus sings [what seems to me an] atrociously vulgar tune, which nevertheless, or perhaps, therefore, is one of the great inspirations of the symphony. But Beethoven has one more act of daring up his sleeve. The climax to all this rowdyism is a sudden choralelike paean in praise of Joy, "the daughter of Elysium." Then once more the drums beat, the cymbals clash, the trumpets blare and in twenty quick bars the symphony is over.—RALPH VAUGHAN WILLIAMS

First Movement.—The first movement appears to be founded on a titanic struggle of the soul, athirst for joy, against the veto of that hostile power which rears itself 'twixt us and earthly happiness. The great chief theme, which steps before us at one stride as if disrobing from a spectral shroud, might perhaps be translated, without violence to the spirit of the whole tone-poem, by Goethe's words:

Entbehren sollst du! Sollst entbehren! Go wanting, shalt thou! Shalt go
wanting!

Against this mighty foe we find a noble forwardness, a manly energy of defiance, advancing in the middle of the piece to an open fight with its

---

[1] Also in the third movement on the words: "*Ich hoffe auf dich!*"—Editor.
[2] The author is obviously referring to the passage at the end of the first double fugue (the combination of the "march" tune and the "joy" tune). It is the point at which the horns repeat the naked F sharps; the winds tentatively start the joy tune first in B major, then B minor; then the strings, which have been supplying the bass of the chords, slip quietly down from B to A, and the chorus, realizing this is the home key, shouts out with joy. Measures 525-43.—Editor.

opponent, a fight in which we think we see two giant wrestlers; each of whom desists once more, invincible. In passing gleams of light we recognize the sad-sweet smile of a happiness that seems to seek for us, for whose possession we strive, but whose attainment that archfiend withholds, overshadowing us with its pitch-black wings; so even our distant glimpse of bliss is troubled, and back we sink to gloomy brooding that can only lift itself again to stern resistance, new war against the joy-devouring demon. Thus force, revolt, defiance, yearning, hope, midway-attainment, fresh loss, new quest, repeated struggle, make out the elements of ceaseless motion in this wondrous piece; which yet falls ever and anon to that abiding state of utter joylessness which Goethe pictures in the words:

Nur mit Entsetzen'wach'ich Morgen- *sauf,*	Grim terror greets me as I wake at morn,
Ich möchte bittre Thränen weinen,	With bitter tears the light I shun
Den Tag zu sehn, der mir in seinem *Lauf*	Of yet another day whose course for- lorn
Nicht Einen Wunsch erfüllen wird, *nicht Einen.*	Shall not fulfil one wish, not one.

At the movement's close this gloomy, joyless mood, expanding to colossal form, appears to span the All, in awful majesty to take possession of a world that God had made for—*Joy*.

Second Movement.—With the very first rhythms of this second movement a wild excitement seizes us; a new world we enter, wherein we are swept on to frenzied orgy. 'Tis as if, in our flight from despair, we rushed in breathless haste to snatch a new and unknown happiness; for the older, that erewhile lit us with its distant smiles, now seems to have vanished clean away.

With the abrupt entry of the middle section there suddenly opens out to us a scene of earthly jollity: a certain boisterous bluntness seems expressed in the simple oft-repeated theme, a naïve, self-contented mirth.

But we are not disposed to view this banal gaiety as the goal of our restless quest of happiness and noble joy; our gaze clouds over, and we turn from the scene to trust ourselves anew to that untiring force which spurs us on without a pause to light upon that bliss which, ah! we never *thus* shall light on; for once again, at the movement's close, we are driven to that earlier scene of jollity, and now we thrust it with impatience from us so soon as recognized.

Third Movement.—How differently these tones address our heart! How pure, how heavenly the strain wherewith they calm our wrath, allay the soul's despairing anguish, and turn its turbulence to gentle melancholy! It is as if a memory were awakened, the memory of purest happiness from early days.

With this memory we reach again that tender yearning so beautifully expressed in this movement's second theme, to which we might appropriately apply these other lines of Goethe's:

Ein unbegreiflich holdes Sehnen	A fathomless enraptured yearning
Trieb mich durch Wald und Wiesen	Drove me through woods afar from
hinzugeh'n,	mortal eyes,
Und unter tausend heissen Thränen	And midst a flood of teardrops burning
Fühlt' ich mir eine Welt ensteh'n.	I felt a world around me rise.

It appears as the yearning of love, and in turn is answered by that hope-inspiring, soothing first theme—this time in a somewhat livelier dress; so that with the second theme's return it seems to us that Love and Hope came arm-in-arm to wield their whole persuasive force upon our troubled spirit.

Thus the still-quivering heart appears to waive aside their solace: but their gentle might is stronger than our already-yielding pride; conquered, we throw ourselves into the arms of these sweet messengers of purest happiness. This exaltation is not yet free from all reaction of the out-lived storm; but each recurrence of our former grief is met at once by fresh exertion of that gracious spell, till finally the lightning ceases, the routed tempest rolls away.

Fourth Movement.—The transition from the third to the fourth movement begins with a shriek of horror.

With this opening of the last movement Beethoven's music takes on a more definitely *speaking* character: it quits the mold of purely instrumental music, observed in all the three preceding movements, the mode of infinite, indefinite expression,[1] the musical poem is urging toward a crisis, a crisis only to be voiced in human speech. It is wonderful how the master makes the arrival of Man's voice and tongue a positive necessity, by this awe-inspiring recitative of the bass-strings; almost breaking the bounds of absolute music already, it stems the tumult of the other instruments with its virile eloquence, insisting on decision, and passes at last into a songlike theme whose simple stately flow bears with it, one by one, the other instruments, until it swells into a mighty flood.

---

[1] Tieck [see below], regarding this character of instrumental music from his own standpoint, was moved to the following dictum: "At deepest bottom of these symphonies we hear insatiate Desire forever hieing forth and turning back into itself, that unspeakable longing which nowhere finds fulfilment and throws itself in wasting passion on the stream of madness, battles with every tone, now overwhelmed, now conquering shouts from out the waves, and seeking rescue sinks still deeper." It almost seems as if Beethoven had been prompted by a similar consciousness of the nature of instrumental music, in the conception of this symphony.—R. Wagner.

Johann Ludwig Tieck (1773–1853), a German poet who provided the libretto for Robert Schumann's opera *Genoveva*, and whose long epic poem *Liebesgeschichte der schönen Magelone* provided words for Brahms's song cycle "The Fair Magelone," Opus 33. He wrote a long essay "*Phantasien über die Kunst, für Freunde der Kunst*," published in 1799, from which Wagner quoted the passage about instrumental music, above.—Editor.

This seems to be the ultimate attempt to phrase by instrumental means alone a stable, sure, unruffled joy: but the rebel rout appears incapable of that restriction; like a raging sea it heaps its waves, sinks back, and once again, yet louder than before, the wild chaotic yell of unslaked passion storms our ear. Then a human voice, with the clear, sure utterance of articulate words, confronts the din of instruments; and we know not at which to wonder most, the boldness of the inspiration, or the naïveté of the master who lets that voice address the instruments as follows:

Ihr Freunde, nicht diese Töne! Sondern lasst uns angenehmere anstimmen und freudenvollere!

No, friends, not tones like these! But let us sing a strain more cheerful and agreeable!

With these words Light breaks on Chaos; a sure and definite mode of utterance is won, in which, supported by the conquered element of instrumental music, we now may hear expressed with clearness what boon it is the agonizing quest of joy shall find as highest, lasting happiness.

Warlike sounds draw nigh; we believe we see a troop of striplings marching past, their blithe heroic mood expressed in words. This leads to a brilliant contest, expressed by instruments alone: we see the youths rush valiantly into the fight, whose victor's spoil is *joy*. The battle, whose issue we never had doubted, is now fought out; the labors of the day are crowned with the smile of joy, of joy that shouts in consciousness of happiness *achieved* anew.

In the transport of joy a vow of *Universal Brotherhood* leaps from the overflowing breast; uplifted in spirit, we turn from embracing the whole human race to the great Creator of Nature, whose beatific Being we consciously attest,—ay, in a moment of sublimest ecstasy, we dream we see between the cloven skies.

And now it is as if a revelation had confirmed us in the blest belief that *every human soul is made for joy*. With all the force of strong conviction we cry to one another:

Seid umschlungen, Millionen!
  Diesen Kuss der ganzen Welt!

Hand to hand, earth's happy millions! This fond kiss to all the world!

and:

Freude, schöner Götterfunken,
  Tochter aus Elysium,
Wir betreten feurtrunken,
  Himmlische, dein Heiligthum.

Joy, thou fairest of immortals, Daughter of Elysium, Fired by thee we pass the portals Leading to thy halidom.[1]

With God to consecrate our *universal love*, we now dare taste the

[1] We find this one paragraph to be the most enlightening interpretation of the musical "meaning" of the great double fugue we have encountered up to the present. If it is possible to plow through the romantic bathos of Wagner's verbiage, gems such as this are the rewards of tortuous labor.—Editor.

purest joy. Not merely in the throes of awe, but gladdened by a blissful truth revealed to us, we now may answer the question:

Ihr stürzt nieder, Millionen?   To your knees, ye favor'd millions?
  Ahnest du den Schöpfer, Welt?   Knowest thy Creator, world?

with:

Such' ihn über'm Sternenzelt!   Seek him where the stars are strewn!
  Brüder, über'm Sternenzelt   Brothers, o'er the starry dome
Muss ein lieber Vater wohnen!   Surely dwells a loving Father!

In intimate possession of our granted happiness, of childhood's buoyancy regained, we give ourselves henceforth to its enjoyment.

To the gentle happiness of joy succeeds its jubilation:—we clasp the whole world to our breast; shouts and laughter fill the air, like thunder from the clouds, the roaring of the sea; whose everlasting tides and healing shocks lend life to earth, and keep life sweet, for the *joy* of Man to whom God gave the earth as home of *happiness*.—RICHARD WAGNER (7)

A fog of verbiage and criticism surrounds the *Choral Symphony*. It is amazing that it has not been finally buried under the mass of prose which it has provoked. Wagner intended to complete the orchestration. Others fancied that they could explain and illustrate the theme by means of pictures. If we admit to a mystery in this symphony we might clear it up; but is it worth while? There was not an ounce of literature in Beethoven, not at any rate in the accepted sense of the word. He had a great love of music, representing to him, as it did, the joy and passion piteously absent from his private life. Perhaps we ought in the *Choral Symphony* to look for nothing more than a magnificent gesture of musical pride. A little notebook with over two hundred different renderings of the dominant theme in the *Finale* of this Symphony shows how persistently Beethoven pursued his search and how entirely musical his guiding motive was; Schiller's lines can have only been used for their appeal to the ear. Beethoven determined that his leading idea should be essentially self-developing and, while it is of extraordinary beauty in itself, it becomes sublime because of its perfect response to his purpose. It is the most triumphant example of the molding of an idea to the preconceived form; at each leap forward there is a new delight, without either effort or appearance of repetition; the magical blossoming, so to speak, of a tree whose leaves burst forth simultaneously. Nothing is superfluous in this stupendous work, not even the *Andante*, declared by modern aestheticism to be overlong; is it not a subtly conceived pause between the persistent rhythm of the *Scherzo* and the instrumental flood that rolls the voices irresistibly onward to the glory of the *Finale?*

Beethoven had already written eight symphonies and the figure nine seems to have had for him an almost mystic significance. He determined to surpass himself. I can scarcely see how his success can be questioned. The flood of human feeling which overflows the ordinary bounds of the symphony sprang from a soul drunk with liberty, which, by an ironical decree of fate, beat itself against the gilded bars within which the misdirected charity of the great had confined him. Beethoven must have suffered cruelly in his ardent longing that humanity should find utterance through him; hence the call of his thousand-voiced genius to the humblest and poorest of his brethren. Did they hear it? That is the question.

The Ninth Symphony was a demonstration of genius, a sublime desire to augment and to liberate the usual forms by giving them the harmonious proportions of a fresco.

Beethoven's real teaching then was not to preserve the old forms, still less to follow in his early steps. We must throw wide the windows to the open sky; they seem to me to have only just escaped being closed forever. The fact that here and there a genius succeeds in this form is but a poor excuse for the laborious and stilted compositions which we are accustomed to call symphonies.—CLAUDE DEBUSSY

We find Beethoven's Ninth Symphony to be precisely one hour and five minutes long; a fearful period indeed, which puts the muscles and lungs of the band, and the patience of the audience to a severe trial. . . . The last movement, a chorus, is heterogeneous. What relation it bears to the symphony we could not make out; and here, as well as in other parts, the want of intelligible design is too apparent. (*The Harmonicon,* London, April 1825)—NICOLAS SLONIMSKY

Beethoven always sounds to me like the upsetting of bags of nails, with here and there an also dropped hammer.

(From John Ruskin's letter to John Brown, dated February 6, 1881)— NICOLAS SLONIMSKY

The whole orchestral part of Beethoven's Ninth Symphony I found very wearying indeed. Several times I had great difficulty in keeping awake . . . It was a great relief when the choral part was arrived at, of which I had great expectations. It opened with eight bars of a commonplace theme, very much like Yankee Doodle . . . As for this part of the famous Symphony, I regret to say that it appeared to be made up of the strange, the ludicrous, the abrupt, the ferocious, and the screechy, with the slightest possible admixture, here and there, of an intelligible melody. As for following the words printed in the program, it was quite out of the question, and what all the noise was about, it was hard to form any idea. The general impression it left on me is that of a concert made up of Indian warwhoops and angry wildcats.

(Quoted from a Providence, R.I., newspaper in *The Orchestra*, London, June 20, 1868)—NICOLAS SLONIMSKY

III. OVERTURE: *"Zur Weihe des Hauses,"* OPUS 124

An instinct, which the event proves to be well grounded, has prevented me from attempting an extended analysis on the numerous occasions on which I have performed this work; for a more indescribable piece of music I have never yet encountered. Even précis-writing gives but little help, for none of the incidents can be summed up in technical terms. Beethoven's fugues have always been considered such debatable ground that for many amateurs and critics the mere statement that the allegro of this overture is a fugue suffices to bar all further inquiry. But this prejudice is now a little old-fashioned. Fugues are coming into their own; and in this overture it is probably the introduction which most takes listeners, conductors, and critics by surprise. Beethoven has never written anything that is quite so unlike everything else. This would cause no difficulty if the unusual features were obviously strokes of genius. But they are mostly formulas; only we have never met them elsewhere.

The first four bars consist of introductory chords. If we compare these with the introductory chords of two of Beethoven's most cautious early works, his first symphony, and his first overture, that of *Prometheus*, we find that those early works begin with a stroke of genius, which did in fact shock the contemporary critics. It is the same stroke of genius in both cases, [that of beginning on the dominant seventh of the subdominant instead of with the expected tonic] and is far more powerful in the relatively unimportant *Prometheus* Overture than in the symphony. The *Prometheus* Overture anticipates the *Weihe des Hauses* in the tone and scoring of the solemn tune which follows the introductory chords. But the first four bars of the *Weihe des Hauses* Overture are plain tonics, dominants, and subdominants, with no systematic interest in the bass. Their purpose is, of course, to define the key, but they also have the more important purpose of measuring out the rhythm, from the broad end foremost. They stimulate the listener to do what he should always do with music, to listen from point to point and allow each musical fact to enter the mind without letting gratified anticipation degenerate into information received. Thus, it is not until the third bar that we can know that the long intervals of silence are not unmeasured pauses. During the third bar the intervals are halved, and in the fourth bar the quarter beats and the rhythm of the trumpets have set us in step with a slow march. Elementary as all this may seem, it has surprisingly few parallels in other music. Mozart separated the opening chords of the *Zauberflöte* Overture by unmeasured pauses; but Beethoven is here contriving his chords so that in the course of the third bar we discover not only what the rhythm is but that it has been in swing from the beginning. For this purpose it is essential that the opening chords should not be monotonous. If they were mere reiterations we should in the retrospect feel as if the rhythm had begun before the music. On the other hand, it is equally important that they should not contain a stroke of genius, nor, as in the *Prometheus* Overture, a systematic feature such as a bass descending by steps. Lastly, there must be no air of mystery about them. I have not seen any sketches of this overture; but Beethoven's sketches often show elsewhere (as in those for the "Eroica" Symphony) that these architectural formalities give him endless trouble. Beethoven follows his chords by a big tune, given out first by soft winds and then by the whole orchestra. It is full of harmonic subtleties, such as the sudden bare octaves at the end of its first clause. The trombones, though intimately associated with the trumpets, have a symbolical meaning of their own, for they are confined to the introductory chords and to the echoing of each cadence in this great tune in both its soft and its loud statements. When the loud statement is finished the echo cadence of the trombones marks their final exit from the overture. Then (un poco più vivace) the trumpets erect a series of typical flourishes into a symmetrical theme of two four-bar sections, each repeated, the rest of the orchestra marking the time in big tonic and dominant chords. At the repetition of the first section, it is the bassoons which supply what I have above described as the sound of hurrying feet. This gives occasion to remark that there is no doubt that the overture was calculated for performance with at least double wind. Beethoven probably quite understood that even a Handelian proportion of bassoons would not make these runs more than a background effect. The suspicion that there is any miscalculation here seems to be quite out of the question, although I must admit that in the previous loud scoring of the big tune the bassoons have been given some independent [eighth-note] movement which I see no prospect of ever making more audible than the independent low flutes of Haydn's tuttis.

The opening chords I have shown to be unusual in spite of their commonplace appearance. The big tune is obviously impressive, and its restatement with full orchestra deepens its impressiveness. But this fanfare-theme, with its square repeats and its eccentric scoring, throws the orthodox Beethoven-lover completely out of his step. Nevertheless, I find myself enjoying it as a convincing item in one of Beethoven's greatest inspirations, and it certainly throws into high relief the more dramatic passage that follows. The close of the fanfare-theme has been echoed; and the horns, relapsing into slower time, fix the echo on to the dominant.

Now throughout this overture the dominant is kept, so to speak, out of office. The main modulation of the big opening tune was to the mediant, E minor; and this re-echo of the last fanfare is the first moment in which the dominant is emphasized. It is now promptly treated as a key, G major, but that key will never be established until we hear its own dominant, and this Beethoven does not allow.

Musical philologists may enjoy the suggestion that in what follows Beethoven has a mild attack of the Rossini fever which about this time was devastating Vienna. Rossini himself, if not the Rossinians, may have intended some dramatic thrill in the tramp-tramp-tramp of his favorite accompaniment of monotonous staccato chords, though I find the earlier and Mozartean Cimarosa already using it with the vulgarest inanity in the overture to a tragic opera. To Beethoven it is evidently, when taken in the right tempo, an intensely dramatic thing, whether he got it from Rossini or invented it himself. Here it accompanies a fugato at the octave on a staccato theme, which for all its fugal treatment is almost as Rossinian as the accompaniment. A bassoon and the violoncellos bring the fugato into the home tonic, and soon afterwards all the strings take it up, massed four octaves deep on the dominant, which is now maintained as a long pedal-point. The strings rise in cross-rhythmed sequences to a climax where the Beethoven lover may find himself on more familiar ground. Yet both the climax and the decline from it are as unique as everything else in this work, and are typical of its drastic severity. The sure way to misunderstand the whole work is to regard its features as deviations from Beethoven's style. The most Beethovenish thing about it is the composer's grasp of the fact that a deviation *into* Beethoven's normal style would be a fatal lapse. Nobody but Beethoven could have written a line of it, for nobody but Beethoven could have maintained its style consistently. If I were less afraid of the musical philologists I should say that it realizes what Beethoven saw in his beloved Cherubini; the sublimity which that unresponsive master always intended but missed because he lacked that which could cast out his fear.

A sudden diminuendo leads to a passage of the most halcyon calm, of which the first faint stirrings give rise to a lyric turn of melody which moves into the key of the dominant and almost comes to a close therein. The first faint stirrings might be by Cherubini, but are much more sublime in a music that does not consist wholly of inhibitions; the lyric turn is pure Beethoven.

But the cadence is interrupted. Harmonically the interruption is a drastic example of the subtleties with which this overture is full; for the quite unaccented first note of the following short upward runs disclaims any intention to bear the strain of resolving the previous leading note. The sweet concession to lyric melody has simply been disavowed by a moment of silence, followed by the first stirrings of the pentecostal wind.

Notice again the extreme simplicity and originality of the crescendo and stringendo that lead from the introduction to the fugue. The stringendo is no exception to the rule that Beethoven does not accelerate his pace except in approaching the last section of a finale, for, as my short summary has indicated, the essence of this whole composition is finality.

With all its audacious simplicity, this uprush is ingeniously calculated to avoid accent on the previously emphasized dominant; and just before the tempo has reached allegro con brio the lower octaves have deviated and ended on the tonic, leaving the violins alone [on the dominant] to find their way into the first note of the double fugue. I have some reason to believe that the thrice three [eighth-note] chords that accompany [the fourth and fifth measures of both themes] are a Masonic symbol, like the *Dreimaliger Akkord* in Mozart's *Zauberflöte*. The structure of the subjects would in any case enable Beethoven to preserve these chords as thrice three more often than to repeat them indefinitely or to cut them short; so they may be an accidental feature. But I doubt whether anything is accidental in this very solemn *Weihe*; and there are several places where the thrice three is preserved without being associated with the subjects.

The first subject of the double fugue starts with the violins poised on G as a sort of a springboard to a busy theme which descends in a startlingly Handelian manner. The second theme, played simultaneously, is a more solemn descent of syncopated [half notes] ending, at the bottom, in a rush of [sixteenth notes].

The two subjects are duly answered in the dominant; and the third entry, giving the first subject to the bass and the second to the treble, returns to the tonic. Another entry follows in the dominant, with the first subject in the violins and the second in the basses. All this has been delivered apparently with full strength, but Beethoven is able to make still more powerful fifth and sixth entries by giving one subject to the united winds and the other to the strings.

The sixth entry shows that the fugue has passed beyond the stage of exposition, for the first subject is now definitely in G major by its own right, instead of entering as a tonal answer to C. By this time it ought to be clear why the dominant has not hitherto been more definitely asserted as a key. The swing from tonic to dominant is so essential a part of the exposition of a fugue that, if the subject is long enough to make it a matter of alternating keys instead of noncommittal chords, there is no sense in treating the dominant as an important center of contrast.

The counterpoint of this overture gives neither Beethoven nor the listener the slightest difficulty, its whole material being contained in its classically simple and formal combination of fugue subjects. When Beethoven's polyphony deals with themes that are less comfortable to old fugue types, the harshness of his counterpoint becomes open to criticism, though not to disrespect.

To return to the study of Beethoven's irregular fugues. So far we have had six entries of the pair of subjects, and the sixth entry, by being definitely *in* the dominant instead of *on* it, has begun to make us feel that the fugue has passed beyond the stage of exposition. Accordingly, events now begin to move more rapidly, and this is where the difficulties of fugue-writing begin. The difficulties are not matters of counterpoint, but of composition. The first question is: does the composer intend the whole piece to be a fugue? Or (as in Mozart's *Zauberflöte* Overture and the finale of Beethoven's C major Quartet, Opus 59, No. 3)[1] has he merely stated his first theme in the form of a fugue exposition? The only difference between a fugue exposition and other ways of stating a theme is that the fugue exposition takes up more room than most ways of stating a theme, and has a decidedly argumentative effect. In the sonata forms there is neither more nor less difficulty in passing from such argument to action than there is in drama. The difficulty begins when you determine *not* to abandon the argumentative fugue style. This is partly inherent in the nature of the orchestra. When Bach and Handel begin an orchestral movement with a fugue exposition, they soon take to alternating the fugue with matter in the style of a concerto. Really the problem of an overture so consistently fugal as the *Weihe des Hauses* is essentially new. The orchestral aspect of it Beethoven has mastered in his stride. Here, as in all his fugues, the themes are at once contrapuntal, rhetorical, and magnificently instrumental. Their distribution in the orchestra is entirely unhampered by irrelevant notions of choral style with a definite number of voices. Beethoven knows very well how far anything is to be gained by applying such notions to keyboard music, and in the fugue of the Sonata, Opus 106, he is justifiably proud of the fact that the *alcune licenze* consist in so few departures from three-part writing. But such questions of license are mere grammatical trivialities compared to the difficulties and dangers that arise at the point when Beethoven's instrumental fugues have irrevocably committed themselves to continue beyond the stage of exposition. Quite apart from "real" part-writing, the scoring, whether it be for pianoforte alone, for string quartet, or full orchestra, is inseparably associated with a dramatic style. This in itself is not incompatible with maintaining the fugal argument style. It merely enhances the elements of drama proper to all rhetoric. The trouble is that it is also inveterately associated with sonatalike methods of phrasing, of modulation, and of establishing keys. And here we have Beethoven at the

---

[1] See essay by Misch which points out the difference regarding the beginning of the last movement of Opus 59, No. 3, as a fugue and regarding it as an essential part of the laying out of a highly sophisticated movement in sonata-allegro form.—Editor.

height of his powers taking up the problems of fugue, when he has already summed up and transcended the whole experience of Haydn and Mozart in the totally opposite system and habits of the sonata style.

Consider the matter for a moment in the light of the things which Beethoven must not do. The most obvious Don't is that which every student has to learn: he must not make sectional full-closes. Like most Don'ts, this rule is much more accurate and helpful when it is turned into a Do. Anybody can avoid full-closes by simply not having enough meaning to distinguish a grammatical subject from a predicate: your music and your philosophy will sound learned enough if nobody can make head or tail of them. The true advice is to think as clearly as you can from one full-close to the next, and to undermine your full-closes after you have drafted and arranged your propositions. Much the most serious difficulty for fugue-writing in Beethoven's style is that you must not prepare and establish your keys in the sonata fashion. Your home tonic must be like the horses of the Red and White Knights in *Alice Through the Looking-Glass:* however wide the range of modulation, the tonic must allow the fugue to get off it and on again as if it were a table. There is thus no scope for a dramatic return to the tonic, and the necessary architectural preponderance of the home tonic at the end must be, as with Bach and Handel, unaided by any such interest. Similarly, anything like the process of firmly establishing other keys will tend to be associated with a dropping-away from fugue-writing. In plenty of classical fugues some such license has proved a welcome diversion; but the strictest fugue-writing in the world could not digest such a process as harping on the dominant of a new key by way of establishing that key.

Let us see how Beethoven modulates now that his fugue is in full swing. His sixth entry having been definitely in the dominant, he annuls the effect of that key by passing quickly through the tonic into the subdominant; and at the same time he indicates a nuance which is one of the most impressive characteristics of his fugues, and significantly related to their whole esthetic system. The all-pervading fortissimo quickly subsides into a whispering piano. Just as the tonic is not allowed to assert the "here and now" aspect of the music with undue pride, so the dynamics of the sound have a way of receding abruptly into illimitable space, and of bursting upon us in full strength, not as dramatic surprises, but as thunders and lightnings too unconcerned with our little temporalities to warn us to get out of their way. Beethoven, having now retired into the subdominant, takes occasion to show us that this fugue is not concerned with contrapuntal paraphernalia in themselves. Stretto, the overlapping of subject and answer, is a device usually explained to students as an effective and ingenious means of producing climaxes in the later stages of a fugue. The orthodox teaching on this point goes so far as to assume that it is the main means of climax and a positive necessity, so that a rule is laid down that "every fugue subject must be capable of at least one harmonious and effective stretto." Of this doctrine it is enough to say that it wipes out thirty of the fugues in Bach's Forty-Eight, besides at least seven in the *Kunst der Fuge*. Where Bach does use stretti his habit is to bring them on at an early stage of his fugue, and only in a minority of cases does he rely upon them as a means of climax. Beethoven knew his Bach well enough to give little weight to the already orthodox doctrine that the stretto is necessarily a method of climax; and he takes early opportunity deliberately to minimize its effect by making this first soft passage begin with a perfunctory indication of a stretto in the subdominant before the full-sized subject enters. The first subject is then allowed to complete itself in F major, the second having lost emphasis by being disguised in tremolo. Then [the motives move] easily through related keys back through the tonic to the unexpectedly bright region of A major, where in another adumbration of stretto Beethoven perfunctorily inverts the first figure of the main theme. The momentary gleam of A major is the first excursion beyond the key-relationships of Bach and Handel. It is a mere natural addition to the harmonic vocabulary, but its effect is as accurately calculated as every other subtlety in this extraordinary composition.

The impression of stretto now becomes more serious, though the device remains rigorously debarred from dealing with complete themes. [The music] shows a strong drift toward E minor, and on the dominant of this key there is enough pause with a short crescendo to produce a moment's feeling of sonatalike preparation, as if the key had some dramatic meaning. It has, and the meaning exactly shows how far such plotting and preparation are admissible as a means of reconciling the fugue style with that of the symphonic orchestra.

The pair of subjects now bursts out in the full orchestra in E minor and leads to a magnificent dispute between E minor and the home tonic. I do not know a finer stroke of genius in musical architecture and accurate delimitation of style. The key (E minor, the mediant) is that of the only modulation in the big tune of the introduction. That is its precise dramatic meaning; it has a just perceptible association with a memorable melody. Not with any event that could have interrupted the flow of that melody or made its tonic vanish below the horizon. Had the dominant, or any major key, such as the bright A major which we have already heard, been chosen either in that tune or in this place, the magnificent effrontery of [this passage] would have been impossible, with its obstinate attempt of the home tonic chord to overbalance the key of E minor and its contemptuous yielding to the E minor cadence at the last [quarter note]. Moreover, any major key, related or remote, would have had the wrong kind of dramatic importance. Thus emphasized, it would have definitely looked forward to actions and excursions in sonata style. And such things have already long ceased to be possible to this music. Beethoven is still as free to abandon polyphony as Bach is to let his orchestral fugues drop into concerto passages; and he does at this point need to mark that the fugue has reached its middle stage and closed an epoch in its course. Accordingly, Beethoven allows himself a drop into sonata style in its most inactive phase, that of a tonic and dominant winding-up process, which [culminates in] the more drastic effrontery of ordinary tonic and dominant chords ending with unisons on the tonic.

Upon this mundane conclusion fugal wisdom suddenly descends as from the heavens, and the chord of E minor changes in Beethoven's most characteristic way into that of the home tonic [by the mysterious descent in the winds and horns E-B-G-E, ending with C in the bass, while the upper voices retain the G-E of the original E minor chord].

The fugue is resumed pianissimo, the second subject being still more disguised with [sixteenth-note] ornament. The entries are crowded closer together with a more serious effect of stretto. Suddenly [at measure 181 seq.] the sequences begin to rise instead of falling, and in four bars of crescendo the full orchestra is ablaze over a dominant pedal, the [first] theme swinging to and fro in the middle part, while the rhythmic figure which I believe to be Masonic assists as accompaniment. The Beethoven-lover is now on more familiar ground. For, while the sonatalike dramatic treatment of keys, themes, returns, and recapitulations is inadmissible to an orchestral fugue, sonatalike methods in emphasizing the home tonic in the coda will, however unknown to Bach and Handel, always be welcome as soon as the fugue has reached its final stages. And now, with no physical conditions to fatigue us, we can enjoy climbing the last stages of a mountain with a series of surprises at discovering again and again that there is yet another stretch before the summit. With all its symphonic resources, this coda never lapses into a merely symphonic style. It never implies that the return to the home tonic has been a return from a long journey. The first deceptive cadence, without dropping into a Handelian idiom, uses Handel's device of being an ordinary full-close played very slowly. As will be seen, this close is interrupted by Bach's characteristic flattened seventh on the tonic, which brings us into the subdominant regions associated with plagal cadences. Beethoven [then] drifts mysteriously into dark modulations, climbing up through the flat supertonic. These dark modulations are the accurately timed counterpoise to the momentary flash of A major which occurred early in the fugue. The home tonic is again reached in a two-bar crescendo, and we again have an ordinary tonic and dominant swing with the Masonic rhythm. We have heard it descend in sequences, but it is a new thing to have it brought to a cadence on the last beat of the bar [as it does in measure 224]. By means of this behavior, it leads to a quite new four-bar phrase as unexpected as the little notch in the last ridge of the Matterhorn which

Edward Whymper feared might block his way at the last moment, but which turned out to be an easy change of slope when he came to it. And so [the busy] figure begins climbing again, this time on a tonic pedal. Suddenly, on the fourth beat of the bar, the subdominant appears in its grandest solemnity, and the main theme is given a new epigrammatic turn as a two-bar phrase repeated and leading once more to the tonic. Then the whole first theme is given in the tonic, and its close is insisted upon in a new way, on the tonic without the dominant, until a passage of scales with strings and wind in antiphony seems to be leading us toward the summit. But again there is an obstacle. At first the sudden dark intervening A flat [in measure 257] seems to be merely alternating with the tonic, but on repetion it becomes a serious dark modulation. When this has yielded, nothing interferes with the final tonic and dominant cadential climaxes, which Beethoven keeps spinning with all his astronomical momentum. He knows a good deal about the music of the spheres and is not afraid in his Ninth Symphony to make the stars march to the Turkish music of big drum, cymbals, and triangle, and the singing of a tenor whose rollicking and broken rhythms suggest that, at all events for humanity, the sublime spectacle is almost too intoxicating. Whatever the difficulties of the *Weihe des Hauses* Overture, it does not shock decorum; but, though it does not use the big drum, it agrees with the Ninth Symphony that the stars in their courses do not thump on tubs.— DONALD FRANCIS TOVEY (3)

The score calls for two flutes, two oboes, two clarinets, two bassoons, four horns, two trumpets, three trombones, timpani, and strings.

IV. 11 *Mödlinger Tänze* (1819), WoO 17

If the 12 Country Dances bring us to the shadow of the "Eroica" Symphony,[1] the 11 Vienna Dances, also known as the Mödling Dances, bring us to the shadow of another great masterpiece, the Ninth Symphony. They are believed to have been written in 1819 at Mödling, a forest suburb of Vienna much frequented by Beethoven. At this time Beethoven had just completed his tremendous *"Hammerklavier"* Sonata, Opus 106, with its most tragic of all slow movements and most complicated of all fugal finales, and was beginning work on the Ninth. If these lovely dances seem to strike a strange note in such company, the fact is that Beethoven in these late years wrote a good deal of light music, such as witty songs and vocal canons, and the piano bagatelles. While at Mödling he also tossed off a set of waltzes for some local musicians, which have unfortunately been lost.

[1] See Finkelstein's comments on those 12 Country Dances written in 1801–02.—Editor.

The period was one of great difficulties for Beethoven. These dances may have been written to make some needed money. Beethoven said, in a letter of 1819, "The sonata (Opus 106) was written under painful circumstances, for it is hard to write for bread, and to that I have now come."

Yet writing "for bread" does not necessarily diminish the greatness of a composer, and it is worth noting that in this late period a number of Beethoven's serious compositions directly use popular material. Apparently Beethoven then was taking a very deep interest in what could be done with popular music. There are for example the variations on a waltz by Diabelli. Furthermore the lofty chorale finale of the Ninth Symphony makes many bows to "popular" style, in its main swinging melody and its march passages.

The eleven Vienna Dances comprise a little anthology of Austrian popular dance, including four waltzes, five minuets, and two ländler. In the trio of the sixth dance we have another link to a Beethoven symphony. It is the main theme of the slow movement of the Second Symphony, written seventeen years before, which reappears here, much changed in rhythm and tempo and yet unmistakable.[1]

While it would be arrant hindsight to find Beethoven's late style in these jovial works, it is true that they show an artistry far above that of the earlier delightful country dances. The touch of the great master is seen in the right, antiphonal structure of these dances, with their sparkling statements and answers, in the constantly varied inner rhythmic patterns, and in the fresh, unhackneyed harmonies and cadences, which nevertheless never depart from the simplicity of feeling of music for dancing. Each of these dances is a little gem, and so much do they all grow on repeated hearings that they deserve the title of great art in miniature.— SIDNEY FINKELSTEIN

The score calls for two flutes, two clarinets, two horns, bassoon solo, and strings (without violas).

V. 6 ÉCOSSAISES, WoO 83

These short dances, all in E flat major, are of uncertain date. Some musicologists feel that they may be half of the set of écossaises published in orchestral form in 1807 but since lost; others assign them to 1822–23. In any event, their first modern appearance was in the supplementary volume to the *Gesamtausgabe* in 1888. The first and fourth dances are twenty-four measures long, the others thirty-two measures; they all have the characteristic Scottish snap.—JACKET NOTES FOR TURNABOUT TV 34162

[1] There are also turns of phrase in Dance No. 5 and Dance No. 10 that show up in the Bagatelles, Opus 119, Nos. 7 and 3 respectively.—Editor.

VI. INCIDENTAL MUSIC TO *Tarpeja*, WoO 2

Christopher Kuffner (born June 28, 1780, in Worzach; died 1846 in Vienna) was, like Kotzebue and Treitschke, a thoroughly copious Austrian playwright and very well admired at his time, and his name, like theirs, is hardly known today. As a music pupil of Wranitsky and a friend of Haydn, he was very close to music, but quite early he went into public service and in later years as court secretary he practiced his art only as a dilettante. His most important literary work is his adaptation of the works of the Roman comic poet Titus Plautus, which appeared in the year 1805. Kuffner was acquainted with Beethoven only in the master's later years, at which time Beethoven eagerly was searching for opera and oratorio texts.

If Czerny's report[1] holds, it was Kuffner who gave practical form to the text of Beethoven's *Choralphantasie* [Opus 80], doing so in all haste, as the music had already been sketched. However, this is questioned by Nottebohm, as the text does not appear in the twenty-volume collected works of Kuffner which appeared in 1845.

So there remains but one work of Kuffner for which Beethoven definitely wrote music—the tragedy *Tarpeja*,[2] which appeared for the first time on the stage of the Vienna Hofburgtheater on March 26, 1813, and was repeated. It surprisingly reminds one definitely of Collin's tragedy *Coriolan*, for both plays take place in legendary Rome, and both are concerned with the same problem—a noble, high-minded man shattered in conflict between personal feelings and public duty. For both heroes death is the only solution. We know how closely Beethoven felt about such a situation, and in his overture to Collin's *Coriolan* he brought a truly immortal expression to the poet's words.

But what about the music to *Tarpeja*? We know with some certainty that Beethoven, for the benefit of Mozart's brother-in-law Joseph Lange (1751–1831), a pensioned actor, wrote a short *Triumphmarsch* in C major for the performance of the play on March 26, 1813. (The march, however, does not appear in the edition of Beethoven's complete works.) The theater playbill of the time states: "The march is newly composed by Herr van Beethoven." A short marchlike movement in D major entitled "*Introduzione de* [!] *II do atto*" might also have been intended for *Tarpeja*, but it is surprising that the playbill does not mention it, and that the orchestral parts and score have not been discovered up till now. Beethoven's autograph, full of corrections and cuts, could hardly

[1] In Otto Jahn's *Die Errinerungen an Beethoven*, Vol. 1, Stuttgart, 1913.
[2] Tarpeja is the daughter of Tarpejus, general and friend of King Romulus. She is in love with Tatius, the noble king of the Sabines, those same Sabines who seek secret revenge for the Roman desecration of their women.—Editor.

have been used at the performance. And that Beethoven in truth wrote the *Introduzione* for *Tarpeja,* but that it was not used at the performance, also seems hardly likely. In short, the question is still not solved.

However, Georg Schünemann did not hesitate to make a naked conjecture of the truth when he asserts, in his edition of the "Music to the tragedy Tarpeja" (B. Schotts Sohne, Mainz, 1938) that these two pieces (the introduction to the second act and the *Triumphmarsch*) are the only two numbers necessary for a complete performance with incidental music of Kuffner's tragedy. What basis he has for this thesis is not divulged.[1]—WILLY HESS (5) (TR. BY THOMAS K. SCHERMAN)

The introduction opens with the full orchestra playing a unison D (the tonic key) and held under a fermata—similar, in fact, to the opening of the *Coriolanus* Overture. The short movement is in a moderate march tempo, and Beethoven makes use of the horns and trumpets in the same formal way in which they are used (for similar effect) in the opening of the "*Weihe des Hauses*" overture. One odd feature is that the phrases are of three-bar length instead of the usual four. The middle section features light staccato triplets in the strings accompanied by repeated chords (also in triplets in the winds). The orchestration here is similar to that of the second movements of the Eighth Symphony. After the march theme returns there is a short coda also featuring the light triplets.

The short C major march has more of musical interest although it is only fifty-nine measures long. The main theme is merely an ascending and descending arpeggio on the tonic chord in a characteristic march rhythm of a dotted quarter note followed by an eighth note and two more quarters. But the handling of this primitive theme, which at first seems nothing but a fanfare, is noteworthy. It is initially announced by the brass alone, but softly instead of the expected forte. Then as the brass continue with their second phrase the strings play the theme in unison pizzicato as a background. One of Beethoven's highly charged crescendos commences as the strings redecorate the basic rhythm with dotted eighths and sixteenths. As the crescendo approaches its climax the strings change to arco to reinforce the sound. A flourishing scale figure in the violins and violas leads to a third announcement of the theme, very grandiose, by the full orchestra, fortissimo. The middle section, which follows, is lighter and makes use, as in the introduction to the second act, of light triplets and repeated triplet chords in the winds. A typical Beethoven surprise occurs in this section. While the brass instruments are

[1] Hess in his article points out several spots in the text which call for music of one kind or another, and concludes that Beethoven might have given his permission to use the march but did not feel called upon to supply the other material. The complete text of the tragedy is also published following the article.—Editor.

playing repeated C's in eighth-note triplets, the rest of the orchestra plays the first two notes of the C major triad—C, E—in half notes. Our ears expect this to be followed by the G on the down-beat of the next bar (probably by unconscious association with the last movement of the Fifth Symphony); but although the brass continue their repeated C's, Beethoven shocks us with a G sharp. He quickly rectifies the situation by using the G sharp as a leading tone to A, and a triplet scale in thirds in the winds establishes the subdominant harmony. The main theme returns, this time fortissimo, with the brass and winds playing it harmonized and the unison strings embroidering it with sixteenth-note scales. The coda is based on the thematic and rhythmic elements of the middle section.—THOMAS K. SCHERMAN

Masses and Cantatas

I. *Missa Solemnis*, FOR FOUR SOLO VOICES, CHORUS, ORCHESTRA, AND ORGAN, OPUS 123
I. Kyrie (Assai sostenuto. Mit Andacht); II. Gloria (Allegro vivace); III. Credo (Allegro ma non troppo); IV. Sanctus (Adagio. Mit andacht); V. Praeludium (Sostenuto ma non troppo); VI. Benedictus (Andante molto cantabile, e non troppo mosso); VII. Agnus Dei (Adagio)

During the work on this grand mass [*the* Missa Solemnis] *my main purpose was to evoke in both the singers and the auditors religious sentiments and to instill them permanently.* (To Andreas Streicher, September 16, 1824)—MUSICAL QUARTERLY, APRIL 1927 (BEETHOVEN'S OWN WORDS)

We stand in the presence of one of the greatest masterworks in the realm of music. Only works like Bach's Mass in B minor and Wagner's *Parsifal* can be compared with it. During four consecutive years Beethoven constructed this prodigious monument; "he seems as though transfigured by it," say those who approached him. He dwells above terrestrial contingencies, and he knows that he is writing on a divine text. He has had the sense and the accentuation of the Latin words of the Holy Sacrifice minutely explained to him. He is armed to compose the sublime hymn of prayer, of glory, of love and of peace, to which he adds the epigraph: "Coming from the heart, may it go to the heart."
Should the *Missa Solemnis* be regarded as liturgical music? Let us

answer boldly, No! This admirable art would surely not be in place in church. Quite out of proportion to the ceremonies of the divine office, the Mass requires the employment of a considerable orchestra, hardly suited for the music appropriate to a place of worship.

Not liturgical music;—but sacred music of the loftiest rank, and, further-more, essentially Catholic music. We are very far from regarding with suspicion the good faith of those among Beethoven's historiographers who have sought to attach to this unique monument of religious art a purely philosophical significance—to set this Mass down as a work out-side of Christian belief, as a manifestation of free thought (they have gone as far as that!); but not to recognize the very spirit of Catholicism in the tenderness wherewith the divine personages are enveloped, in the emotion accompanying the announcement of the mysteries, is in itself proof of blindness—or ignorance.

How can one venture—even had the author not taken pains to tell us clearly—to assert that this entire Mass is not an ardent "act of faith," that this Credo does not proclaim on every page "I believe, not merely in a vague divinity, but in the God of the gospel and in the mysteries of the incarnation, the redemption, and the life eternal"? How gainsay the penetrating emotion—so new in music—which attends these affirma-tions, and which springs solely from a Catholic comprehension of these dogmas and mysteries? How, finally, can one misconstrue the piously meticulous care with which the sacred words are treated and translated into music, and the marvelous meaning of the expressive accents which unveil their signification to those who can and will understand? For the rest, it suffices to know and to feel, in order to be convinced. We shall endeavor to bring this knowledge home to the reader, hoping to inspire within him that sentiment for beauty and truth to which Beethoven himself laid claim when he wrote to Streicher: "My chief design when writing the Mass was to arouse *religious emotion* in singers and auditors alike, and to render this emotion lasting."

From the beginning of the Kyrie one receives an impression of grandeur which finds an equal only in that given by the similar entry in Bach's great B-minor Mass. It is the whole human race that implores divine clemency. The tonality is speedily inflected to the relative minor; a sort of distressful march shows us the Son of God come down to earth; but the word *Christe*, grounded on the same music as *Kyrie*, symbolizes the identity of the two Persons in one God; whereas the third *Kyrie*, rep-resenting the Holy Ghost, the third Person participating in the same divinity as the two others, is based upon the third harmonic function, the subdominant, as a bond of union for the three representations of the single God.

The Gloria enters with impressive brilliancy in a trumpet-fanfare confided to the contraltos of the chorus. It is important to bring out this

typical motive with due effect amid the din of the orchestra; the conductor should see to this. After the shout of glory, all suddenly grows
calm on the words *pax hominibus*, etc.; and one can already trace the
sketch, in its essential features, of the grand theme of Peace with which
the work ends. We cannot dwell on each phrase of the Gloria; but we
shall mention, in passing, in the *Gratias agimus tibi*, the emergence of a
melodic design later to be cherished by Richard Wagner, principally in the
Meistersinger and the *Walküre*. The trumpet-signal which serves as a
pivot for the whole piece is almost constantly in evidence; every time,
at least, that the words imply an appeal to force or a symbol of power. We
may regret that the final fugue on *in gloria Dei Patris* is not more unlike
its congeners, and develops with no more of interest than the fugues
written by the *Kapellmeister* of the period on the same words. It is the
weak point of the word.

With the Credo, we re-enter the cathedral, not to leave it again. And
what is this Credo, even plastically considered, but a real cathedral; this
sublime monument of Catholic faith, so strikingly divided into three
naves, the central nave ending with the sacrificial altar "*Et homo factus
est*"? The architectural arrangement is a marvel of construction, a miracle
of harmonious, nay, mystical equilibrium. Judge for yourselves.

The Credo is planned in three grand divisions, following the *trini-
tarian* system customary in a great number of liturgical works.

The first division, an exposition of faith in one God, in itself comprises
two affirmations: "I believe in one God, the Father Almighty," and "in
one Lord Jesus Christ." Both are established in the principal key of B-flat
major, with a transition to the subdominant; after which the two Persons
are reunited, on *consubstantialem Patri*, in the tonic.

The second division presents the Evangelical drama of Jesus descended
to earth. It consists of three acts: The Incarnation, going over to the
tonality of D major (which is that of the synthesis of the Mass) on the
words *Et homo factus est*; the scene of the Passion ("*Crucifixus*"),
beginning in D major and progressing in depression on the words of the
burial; and the Ressurection, which of a sudden soars upward to the
luminous dominant, F major.

The third division is consecrated to the Holy Ghost. Like the first, it
contains two subdivisions: The affirmation of belief with regard to the
Holy Ghost and the dogmas of the Church; and the celebration of the
mystery of eternal life. All this last part does not leave the tonality of the
piece.

And there may be found critics so superficial as to assert that the
theological sense of the sacred text was a matter of indifference to
Beethoven!

We cannot enter into a detailed analysis, for everything would have to
be quoted. Let us study only the central portion—the drama. Succeeding

the *Incarnatus*, written in the first Gregorian mode, there begins the awful ascent of Calvary. We can follow the Savior's faltering steps, so rudely underscored by the orchestra. And now there arises, under the bows of the first violins, the moan of the most moving plaint, the sublimest expression of suffering, that ever issued from musician's heart; a plaint yet more intense than the sorrowful melody in Opus 110, in that here it expresses, not human suffering, but the anguish of a God made man. The final fugue is altogether of admirable luminosity. It requires a *very slow* movement; for it should be remembered that when Beethoven writes in 3/2 time, or even in 6/4 (as, for instance, in the overture to *Egmont*, the twentieth variation in Opus 120, the religious theme in the Finale of the Ninth Symphony, etc.), he attributes to this notation a signification of majestic slowness; no exception to this rule can be found in his works. This fugue—as regular, with its *stretti*, its *contrary motion* and *diminutions*, as the finest fugues of Bach—is a model of masterful poesy. It might be called a representation of the joys of heaven, as they were imagined by Lippi or Giovanni da Fiesole. It is, in fact, like a fresco from the golden age translated into music; the fancy depicts a mystic dance, a roundel of the blessed pressing with naked feet the flowerets of the celestial meadows. It sounds afar off, this majestic round, scarce to be heard. It approaches, it is close at hand, we are entwined in its hallowed circles—it departs, wellnigh vanishes, but only to return as with an augmented host, yet more enthusiastic, to bear us away in its whirl and to subside, in adoration, before the throne of the Almighty!

In the Sanctus, Beethoven, respecting the Catholic liturgy and knowing that, during the mystery of the consecretion, no voice should make itself heard, Beethoven, by the might of his genius, has raised silence into sublimity. This Praeludium, which allows the celebrant time to consecrate the elements, is to our mind an inspiration infinitely loftier in conception than the charming concerto for violin and voice which follows. This Praeludium is admirable in every aspect! What grandeur of *religious* art! —and obtained by means so simple as to be astonishing, did not enthusiasm in this case overwhelm astonishment.

We have now reached the Agnus Dei, that division of the work which we should consider the finest, and the most eloquent of genius, had not the Credo preceded it.

It is here, and in the prelude for the consecration, that Beethoven's religious feeling is most clearly in evidence. The whole long entrance-section, wherein mankind implores the pity of the divine Lamb, is of a beauty still unequaled in musical history. Careful examination will show how greatly this supplication in *Latin*, that is to say, endowed with a peculiarly Catholic expression, differs from the Greek prayer of the Kyrie; —a prayer more carefully ordered, it is true, after the manner of antique art, but less affecting and less urgent. And that the accents of this appeal rise so brokenly toward the throne of the Lamb, the victim of Hate, is because it beseeches Him for peace, "peace *within* and *without*," wrote Beethoven. No more hateful thoughts, no more soul-conflicts or profound dejection; the theme of Peace has emerged, calm and luminous, out of the irresolute key of B minor, and has at last given us back the tonality of D major, that of Faith and of Love, that wherein the Love of all Mankind is enwreathed in the Ninth Symphony. This theme takes on a pastoral character which gives the impression of a walk in the fields; for Peace is not in the city—it is by the brooks of the valley, among the trees of the forest, that the restless town dweller must seek her; for Peace is not of the world, therefore it is beyond the world that the artist's heart goes forth on her quest: *Sursum corda!*

A simple, quite regular fugue-exposition prepares the blossoming of the peaceful Flower, this affirmative theme which, descending straight from heaven, bears witness that the soul has finally won the enjoyment of that so longed-for peace. This *four*-measure theme appears only four times in the Agnus, but is of such penetrating charm that the spirit of the hearer is left, as it were, impregnated with its perfume, and still feels its spell long after the tones have died away.[1]

Suddenly—in homage to the traditional *in tempore belli* of Haydn's Masses—distant drums and trumpets twice announce the army of Hate. And the soul is anew seized with dread; again it implores; it begs for the promised peace as yet but transiently felt: "We must pray, pray, pray."[2] But it cannot gain peace without conquering itself. This is the musical apology of Christian renunciation. The theme of peace is transformed; a conflict in the human heart is introduced in the course of the extraordinary orchestral presto in which the peace-motive turns upon itself in a self-annihilating struggle brought to a close by a victorious fanfare. "Above all, the power of the peace within—Victory!" And here we find the one point whence are derived all the arguments going to show that the *Missa Solemnis* is an exclusively human work, bare of religious spirit—a *layman's* Mass. "What!" we are told. "A military signal, and twice repeated, at that! It is an opera; it has nothing to do with religion." And without further ceremony the label *irreligious* is plastered on the Mass! This reasoning is as just as that which would adduce the bird songs in the Pastoral Symphony to prove a lack of internal feeling for nature in that symphony—"*Empfindung*," as Beethoven says—and make it a purely descriptive work. Ancient sophism always consisted in taking *the part for the whole*. And wherein—to speak plainly—does this episode of an appeal to arms, giving way, after a short though bitter struggle, to an ardent prayer, conflict with the religious spirit of the Mass?

---

[1] The penetrative power of this melody is due, technically speaking, to the fact, that, of the nine notes of which it is formed, not one stands on a degree previously heard; thus the melodic design is new in all its elements.

[2] Written in Beethoven's hand on his sketches.

On the contrary, this fight against the spirit of Hate within us, so destructive of peace, a fight already[1] depicted in the Ninth Symphony in almost the same musical forms, realizes one of the most familiar traditional conditions of Christian life. And Beethoven, writing to Count Dietrichstein, the Intendant of the imperial music, "It is not necessary to follow habitual usage when the purpose is sincere adoration of God," does he not himself declare that, if the Mass in D is not liturgical, it was at least dictated by a religious spirit beyond question? The episode in whose behalf we have just made this digression is therefore simply and solely a vital commentary on the words; the distressful "Have mercy upon us!—upon us, whom the demons of Hate assail from every side," gives way to the confident appeal, "Give peace unto our souls!"

And, in truth, it is Peace that anew intervenes. Tender, radiant Peace waxes like a miraculous plant, and while faraway drums are beating the retreat of the spirits of Evil, there spreads for the last time from the height of its upraised stem the brilliant bloom of the four incomparable measures, as if to exhale heavenward the perfume of the grateful soul's act of faith. Is there anything more beautiful in the realm of music?—And, for the expression of peace won by God's aid, can one imagine a more sublime offering from a human being to his divine Creator?

[Beethoven's] masterworks, brought forth in sorrow according to Biblical law, conducted him through sadness and suffering, as he himself said, to the possession here below of the joy within the heart, to the peace of those blessed souls who have joined with so great love in the song of his sublime Credo.

May his example be of profit to us, and may devotion to his art hasten the reign among us of sweet peace and the bountiful love of all mankind.—VINCENT D'INDY (1)

The score calls for four solists, chorus, two flutes, two oboes, two clarinets, two bassoons, contrabassoon, four horns, two trumpets, three trombones, timpani, strings, and organ (ad lib).

Many of my works were immediately effective; others, not equally fathomable and compelling, required many years to achieve recognition. In the meantime, these years, too, have passed, and second and third generations have doubly and triply made good to me what I had to endure from my earlier contemporaries.

These words of Goethe, from the introduction to *West-Ostlicher Divan*, were found underlined in Beethoven's copy and written out in his own hand in his diary. Beethoven was convinced that he would not live to see his later, more difficult works understood by his contemporaries,

---

[1] The adverb is wrong. Actually the Ninth Symphony was completed in February 1824, whereas the *Missa Solemnis* was completed early in 1823.—Editor.

and he was resigned to his fate. The hope for which he sought sustenance in Goethe's words did not deceive him. Of this we had an opportunity to convince ourselves recently when a performance of his *Missa Solemnis* in the Redoutensaal was so mobbed that the adjoining Small Redouten-saal had to be opened to accommodate the overflow.[1]

The impression was powerful. Of that there can be no doubt, however difficult and oppressive much of it may have seemed to the audience. There is no other work of Beethoven's which crushes the unprepared listener with such gigantic strength, at the same time raising him up again, deafened, delighted, confused. The Mass in D, and its companion piece, the Ninth Symphony, are creations which recall Zelter's dictum: "I admire Beethoven with awe."[2] Only devoted and extensive study can dispel this awe. A work by Beethoven conceived in the full power of his imagination and fully characteristic of his utter lack of compromise is not to be enjoyed as easily, as freely, as a symphony by Haydn. In the Mass in D, Beethoven set down everything he possessed in the way of sublime ideas and religious feelings; he gave to this music three years of his life, then in its sunset and brilliantly aglow with its double majesty of genius and adversity.

There is no doubt that the Mass, in its whole and in its parts, stands at the outermost boundary of sacred music. And yet one must be careful about accepting the often repeated objection that it is "unchurchly." Whether a church composition is appropriate to the requirements of a particular service, or whether it is imbued with a religious spirit, presents two entirely different questions. Although both are perfectly justified, they are not of equal validity when reviewed from a more elevated standpoint. Beethoven's relationship to the Catholic Church was casual, probably limited largely to the friendly echo of childhood impressions. After the oratorio *The Mount of Olives*, which he himself later disparaged, and his first Mass, which already overstepped the boundaries of the churchly in many aspects, he let years pass without further thought of sacred music. Then the installation of his noble pupil and friend, Archduke Rudolph, as Archbishop of Olmütz, provided an occasion for the composition of a great religious office. He obviously began the work, intending, for all its immensity of concept, that it should meet the requirements of the church.

I have remarked before that Beethoven was never especially attached to the articles of the Catholic faith, that his belief had rather the

[1] By the Society of Friends of Music on 17 March, Herbeck conducting. This performance represented the climax of a musical renaissance which began in the forties with Nicolai's performance of the Ninth Symphony with the newly founded Philharmonic Orchestra and in which Beethoven's late works were finally accorded general popular recognition.

[2] Karl Friedrich Zelter (1758-1832). German composer and longtime friend of Goethe. Mendelssohn was one of his pupils.

character of a liberal theosophy, responsive only to ethical dictates. His faith—tested in adversity—in an unalterable moral order, in a just and supreme being, never left him. The consecration of a lofty and liberal religiousness and the earnestness of an unbending morality are discernible as a principle in all of his life and works. Would he have deserted these principles in the very work in which he devoted his best efforts to a religious subject? On the contrary, he offers us in the Mass the ultimate intensification of that devotion which we find in all his greater works.

All his music was to him religious; in art he always felt himself to be in a church, and that is why, in this particular case, it did not occur to him to don specifically churchly raiment. "With devotion," he wrote at the beginning of the "Kyrie" and the "Sanctus"; and, indeed, what music has the character of devotion if not this? The imposing and austere spirituality of this holy office strikes me as significantly more religious than the brighter spirit of the Haydn Masses, although the latter may be incomparably more valuable and useful to the church.

Heinse[1] once said of an effective piece of sacred music, and with reason, that "it filled the spirit of the listener without making itself felt." In this sense we have the ideal of true church music in the Masses of Palestrina; they are the community sublimated in music. The harmonious stream, crystal clear, moves with calm repose; there is no melodic excitement, no rhythmic stimulation, no disconcerting instrumental color. Palestrina represents that point in the history of music where music had advanced sufficiently far to command respect as an art, but not so far that its resources had outgrown the purposes of the church. Palestrina's music is what the church likes music to be, namely, a means of intensifying religious devotion. It belongs completely to the church, just as do the sacred pictures, the painted windows, the costly vestments, and other art products which the church employs, not to awaken the artistic senses but to stimulate devotion. The ultimate advancement of art is not profitable to the church. People think that they, too, are devout when they listen to a Mozart or Beethoven Mass in church, but therein they confuse aesthetic devotion and religious dedication.

Beethoven himself, after completing his Mass in D, wrote to Zelter that he "regarded the *a cappella* style as the one true church style." Thus, despite the forceful, symphonic treatment of his Mass, he had at heart the correct feeling that the interests of the church require simpler music. In the conflict as to whether the church or music itself should dominate in his own sacred music (in the concept of any sacred music there is an inner conflict), he decided in favor of art, courageously, and fully conscious of the import of his decision. And it is on this basis that one must follow the grandeur of his genius, wholeheartedly, without

[1] Johann Jakob Wilhelm Heinse (1749–1803), German novelist and critic who was influential in the romantic movement.

concern as to whether this passage or that seems too dramatic or too symphonic. Even as the composer of a Mass, Beethoven neither could nor would deny his own great artistic personality; he was inspired by the idea of faith, and in his music he gives us religion as he saw it. After the impression which I experienced myself and which I observed in others, I cannot doubt that for the Mass in D, as for the Ninth Symphony, the time is approaching when shock and surprise will give way to understanding, admiration, and love.[1]—EDUARD HANSLICK

The *Missa Solemnis* was generally regarded as an incomprehensible production, the depths of which (if they really were depths) it was impossible to fathom. This opinion I confess I adopted. After poring for hours over the ponderous pages, the only result was an absolute bewilderment among its mazes.

(London *Morning Chronicle*, quoted in the *Musical Times*, London, October 1845)—NICOLAS SLONIMSKY

[1] The identical public and critical outcry against theatricalism in a Religious Work (the capitals are used advisedly) was witnessed when Hanslick first heard the Verdi *Requiem* performed under the direction of the composer in Vienna in 1879. Fortunately musicology has progressed twentyfold since Hanslick's time. Erudite knowledge, which had hitherto been the jealous possession of an elect and devoted few scholars—knowledge of the great musical heritage before the seventeenth century—has, through the advent of long-playing records and the wide advances in communication media, become common knowledge to the average concertgoer and record listener.

Now that the enormity of the brass bands, the double-, triple-, or quadruple-string orchestras, and the mammoth choirs that participated in the festival Masses of the French and Italian Renaissance and in the baroque Masses, are well known by most aware music lovers, there is little reason for surprise at the grandeur, the spectacle, the drama of Beethoven's and Verdi's masterpieces, *which were also conceived as "oeuvres d'occasions."* These two very practical composers had very precise knowledge of the vocal and instrumental forces they might expect for the performances of these two gigantic works. The size, the opulence, the use of certain melodramatic and theatrical devices in these works, have no bearing on whether they are "churchly" or "unchurchly," as both were conceived with specific cathedral performances in mind. What *is* important is that the eighteenth-century-oriented Beethoven and the nineteenth-century Verdi *do* reveal to us, through these works, their innermost convictions. (Sometimes, it may be felt, their revelations of personal faith become so sincere as to border on the embarrassing.) However, the two composers do express themselves in the approved words of the Missal. Those familiar words are, at times, interpreted in meanings—poignant, terrifying, or awe-inspiring—which we may not heretofore have realized were inherent in them. This only proves that these two great geniuses felt deeper about those sacred syllables than do many of us, who, through constant repetition, roll them almost mechanically off our tongues. It does *not* and should *never* mean that those same words should be said and sung in anyplace but a sanctuary!—Editor.

II. *"Meeresstille und Glückliche Fahrt,"* CANTATA FOR CHORUS AND ORCHESTRA, OPUS 112

When Beethoven composed his Cantata, Opus 112, on Goethe's two poems *Meeresstille* and *Glückliche Fahrt,* [he] dedicated the work to Goethe and sent him the score (which was published in 1822). Goethe merely noted in his diary: "Received a score from Beethoven," but never replied.

Almost nine months later Beethoven, who had a healthy sense of his own worth and could be arrogant to dukes and princes, wrote humbly to his adored Goethe:

VIENNA, *February* 8, 1823

YOUR EXCELLENCY!
Still ever living, as I have lived since my youth, in your immortal and ever youthful works, and never forgetting the happy hours spent in your company, I am now faced with the fact that I too must remind you of my existence—I trust that you received the dedication to Your Excellency of *Meeresstille und Glückliche Fahrt* which I have set to music. By reason of their contrasting moods these two poems seemed to me very suitable for the expression of this contrast in music. It would afford me much pleasure to know whether I had united my harmony with yours in appropriate fashion. Indeed your criticism, which might almost be regarded as the very essence of truth, would be extremely welcome to me. For I love truth more than anything; and in my case it will never be: *veritas odium parit* . . . How highly would I value a general comment from you on the composing of music or on setting your poems to music!

Still no answer from Goethe!
Beethoven's cantata, *Meeresstille und Glückliche Fahrt,* was composed in 1814 and 1815, during the Congress of Vienna. The full score was written out during the month following the Battle of Waterloo. The first performance took place on Christmas Day of that year in the grand Redoutensaal in Vienna at a benefit for the *Bürgerspitalfonds* (Citizens' Hospital Fund).

The first half, the description of the calm sea, is held to a very simple chordal, hymnlike style, beginning almost in a whisper and expanding suddenly in both volume and pitch range on the "infinite expanse" of the penultimate line.

For the second poem, the music takes on a lively tempo, as whispering scales, first in the string choir, then in woodwinds suggest the mists that are rent. As the heavens are cleared, the orchestral texture grows bright.

And as Aeolus loosens the "restraining ties," Beethoven indulges in an innocent pun, by tying five dotted half notes in all four choral parts simultaneously. Orchestral woodwinds suggest the winds of the poem, the excitement grows as the ship leaps forward and cries of *"das Land, das Land, das Land"* echo from section to section of the chorus, like a shout of triumph.

The orchestra for Beethoven's cantata uses two flutes, two oboes, two clarinets, two bassoons, four horns, two trumpets, kettledrums, and the traditional string choir.

Meeresstille	Calm Sea
Tiefe Stille herrscht im Wasser	Calm and silence rule the water,
Ohne Regung ruht das Meer,	Motionless the ocean lies,
und bekümmert sieht der Schiffer	And the sailor's anxious gaze
glatte Fläche rings umher.	Finds glassy flatness far and wide.
Keine Luft von keiner Seite!	Not a breath of air is stirring!
Todesstille fürchterlich!	Fearful, deathly stillness reigns!
In der ungeheuern Weite	On the infinite expanse
reget keine Welle sich.	Not a single wavelet moves.

Glückliche Fahrt	Prosperous Voyage
Die Nebel zerreissen,	The mists are rent,
der Himmel ist helle.	The heavens shine,
und Aeolus löset	And Aeolus loosens
das ängstliche Band.	Restraining ties.
Es säuseln die Winde,	The winds now are whistling,
es rührt sich der Schiffer.	The sailor bestirs himself.
Geschwinde! Geschwinde!	How swiftly; how swiftly
Es teilt sich die Welle,	The waves part before us,
es naht sich die Ferne;	The distance draws near;
schon seh' ich das Land!	And now I see land!

EDWARD DOWNES

Chamber Music with Piano

I. Variations for Piano, Violin, and Violoncello on Müller's Song *"Ich bin der Schneider Kakadu,"* Opus 121a

The series of Beethoven's piano trios closes with a [thoroughly] significant though [little known] composition. The variations on *"Ich bin der Schneider Kakadu"* ("I am the tailor Kakadu"), Opus 121a, were written, perhaps as a relaxation, in 1823, the year of completion of the *Missa solemnis*, when Beethoven began his final struggle with the Ninth

Symphony. The theme "The Sisters from Prague" is borrowed from a then fashionable Singspiel by Wenzel Müller. That Beethoven could draw most magnificent and deeply felt music from futile or even trivial material had been magnificently shown three years earlier with the composition of the stupendous "Diabelli" Variations. The use of such insignificant material even acted as a stimulating challenge to his mind, and it must be said that the present "Kakadu" Variations are a genuine if minor masterpiece. The trifling little tune in G major is preceded by a lengthy and pathetic Adagio introduction in the tonic minor, where snatches of it are forecast, as in a dream. There are eleven variations in all, the first being committed to the piano alone, whereas the cello keeps silent during the second, and the violin during the third. From now on, the music alternates between delightful and brilliant instrumental display—not at all easy in performance!—and more tightly wrought contrapuntal sections, such as the graceful invention for violin and cello (without piano!) of No. 7. The ninth variation brings more deeply felt music, changing the up-to-now prevailing Allegretto into an Adagio espressivo while reverting to the G minor key of the introduction. The two last variations are of the "amplificatory" type, No. 10 being a six-eight Presto lightly dashing through G major to G minor, with some interesting fugal working-out of the theme, and No. 11 a genuine Finale, where the theme tries to assert itself in its original form but soon gives way to Beethoven's unleashed fantasy, culminating in an impetuous and effective virtuoso ending.—HARRY HALBREICH (2)

II. 2 Sonatas for Violoncello and Piano, Opus 102

After so much political music[1] and military fanfare,[2] it is a joy to find the beloved poet again in the wonderful 2 Sonatas for Cello and Piano (Opus 102), composed in July and August 1815 and dedicated to Countess Marie von Erdödy. We find our great Beethoven again in [these sonatas]. The Master of the last quartets had himself already well in hand in these compositions, in which the lyric improvisation rejects all restraint. The adagio of the D major Sonata (Opus 102, No. 2) expresses a feeling of sadness with almost a spiritual solemnity that seems to set it quite apart. Let us not even speak of skill, so much has the concern for form disappeared. One thinks of Lamartine's Méditations, which appeared shortly after, and which were poured forth with the same abundance and the same natural ingenuousness. The voice that speaks to us in the D major Sonata has no need of words; the melodic texture unfolds itself; the phrase is inflected, interrupted by pauses, it murmurs or declaims, becomes animated with a reflection of gaiety, or is darkened by a passing

---

[1] "Glorreiche Augenblick," Opus 136.—Editor.
[2] "Wellington's Sieg" Symphony, Opus 91.—Editor.

shadow, is stated precisely in a fixed design, or evaporates like incense. Technical skill is manifested in the fugato of the finale. Throughout the andante, will seems to be abandoned; it is life that is expressed while avoiding, even in its fury, all excessive violence.

With the two sonatas of Opus 102, Beethoven leads us back to the heights from which his military extravaganzas had driven us; there is the same insight, the same pure melody as in the *Archduke Trio*; but already gleaming are the lights that flash through the last quartets.—EDOUARD HERRIOT

a. Sonata No. 4 in C, Opus 102, No. 1
I. Andante, Allegro vivace; II. Adagio, Allegro vivace

The Sonata in C (Opus 102, No. 1) has no printed dedication; but it is said that the composer, on being visited by the English pianist Charles Neate, inscribed the work to him in his own hand. The slow introduction presents the cello in cantilena mood, the theme being simple in shape, moving first down, then up. The opposite happens with the theme of the *Allegro vivace*, thus heightening the contrast between C major and A minor. There is a coquettish corollary to this theme, and the second group is dominated by an insistent triplet-figure. The jerky rhythm of the opening bars plays a large part in the development, and when the return proper comes there is a hint of canon. An *Adagio* follows, with filigree figuration linking the two instruments. Then the melody of the first *Andante* returns, decorated and enhanced by its own recollections. But the tranquil mood soon passes, the end of a trill turning itself into the germ of the final *Allegro*. Here, a number of bright and bustling themes are heard, the rhythm of the first being well to the fore. The great moments, however, are in the dramatic pauses, ended each time by a low note on the cello: the fifth is added, and the piano comments pointedly. The coda brings with it a reluctant farewell to the staid beauty of a C major close.—DENIS STEVENS

b. Sonata No. 5 in D, Opus 102, No. 2
I. Allegro con brio, II. Adagio con molto sentimento d'affetto; III. Allegro fugato

The second sonata of Opus 102 begins, as the sonata in A major does, with an Allegro, one full of energy. But the form of this movement, with sudden leaps of octaves and tenths from the very first measures and with frequent modulations, makes us realize that we are face to face with something new, something never encountered in the previous sonatas.

Even after we have passed to the lyric-sentimental part, the first theme returns, first peeping through and then becoming aggressive and imperious, dominating the entire movement. In the development of the sonata the "duet" is perfectly carried out and the dynamic effects are stunning, with frequent and surprising contrasts. After a repeat in D major of the second theme, we come to the coda, with a marvelous crescendo up to a fortissimo of three measures in unison. To these fortissimi, and sforzati in the fortissimi, the "sempre pianissimo" of the coda makes a sudden contrast, until the initial power is resumed in the last four bars, with which the imposing first movement comes to a close.

Without any preparation whatever, we pass to the Adagio con molto sentimento d'affetto, one of Beethoven's most beautiful creations, the heart and soul of the entire work. The first notes, grave and deep, whispered "a mezza voce," at once impose rapt attention; then gradually this religious song becomes so convincing and moving that the listener is swept away, abandoning himself softly to the indefinable spiritual enjoyment it provides. Passing from the minor to the major, the voices rise to higher regions while a new episode enters in the chorale, an episode all the more welcome in its profound genius because it attains the most delightful effects of expression and takes us for a moment from the dream into which we are to lapse again when the return is made to the minor key. This return is marked by a section in staccato notes. The bel canto comes out in splendor, first on the piano and then on the cello, passing to piano and pianissimo in the form of a duet until it fades mysteriously and delightfully into [a fermata on a dominant-seventh chord]. But instead of the resolution, there is an attack by the cello, echoed by the piano; then, more strongly than ever, the cello begins the fugato with a lovely original theme. The piano comes in, in turn, and the development is made with admirable mastery, presenting richness of rhythms and accents in a form that is absolutely modern. Moreover, the voices, although involved in a great variety of ideas and harmonic accompaniments, are able to maintain a melody that is always pleasing and natural.

It is worth dwelling a little on this fugato,[1] if only because of the criticisms it arouses, and aroused even in Beethoven's time.

It has been accused of muddiness; in point of fact, this criticism could be confined, as Schindler notes, to the few measures before the fermata on the hard F sharp chord. If the modulations had been less accentuated, the clarity would have gained to some extent, as also some

---

[1] Beethoven's adversaries, and especially the music critics (his worst enemies), who had already decreed that he was unable to write a fugue, picked up the ball on the rebound once more and attacked him with such violence as to endanger the artistic and financial success of this work. They even spread the story that the publisher had asked Beethoven for compensation for his losses and that he had given him Opus 107 without remuneration. When the sonatas were published by Artaria in a new edition in 1818, they used this fact as if to prove the truth of their slander. In this they were helped by various Vienna publishers to whom Beethoven had always refused his works.

hardnesses would have been attenuated, but all this and the difficulties of execution are no reasons for undervaluing the powerful work. It is true that the fugato is carried out very freely, "tantôt libre, tantôt recherché," as is written before the fugue for the Quartet, Opus 133, but are we to say that Beethoven is to be censured for that? On the contrary, it should lead us to admire his genius even more, once again in advance of his time. Toward the end, there is a splendidly successful point on the tonic, which gives Beethoven the occasion to arrange the harmony in the most varied combinations, using the theme and secondary ideas; the coda is very effective, reaching its culmination in the fortissimo, in which the parts, no longer pursuing one another, finally unite and proceed in an in-dissoluble knot to the last chord. This finale recalls the austerity of the first movement and, even without succeeding in absorbing the senti-mental episodes of the Adagio, gives form to the entire sonata.—EUGENIO ALBINI (TR. BY THOMAS K. SCHERMAN)

The vigorous finale is really a fugue. In that stands the innovation, and one of the earliest signs of Beethoven's new orientation toward counterpoint. Hitherto in instrumental music he had treated the fugue as ancillary to variation form or sonata form; now he employed it in its own right. He told Holz later: "To make a fugue requires no particular skill. In my student days I made dozens of them. But the fancy wishes also to assert its privileges, and today a new and really poetical element must be introduced into the traditional form."—MARION M. SCOTT

III. 6 THEMES AND VARIATIONS FOR FLUTE AND PIANO, OPUS 105

[Beethoven's arrangements for voice with trio accompaniment for the Scottish editor, George] Thomson were ultimately to pave the way later on for his Opus 105 (6 Themes and Variations for Flute and Piano). More precisely, Opus 105 [is] conceived "for piano or for piano and flute or violin." These works, some autographs of which are kept at the British Museum, were published by Thomson in July 1819, and by Artaria in Vienna in September of the same year. It is interesting to note that Beethoven referred to indiscriminately as "Scottish" everything which originated in the British Isles—that is to say also airs which were in fact Welsh and Irish.

Opus 105, No. 1, in G Major (Irish Air entitled "The Cottage Maid").— This is an Andantino quasi allegretto in 2/4 time followed by three variations. The first variation is for piano alone. The second is entrusted to the flute. The third, marked Allegro, after a few measures of Adagio, has a central episode in minor.

Opus 105, No. 2, in C Minor (Scottish Air).—This is an Allegretto scherzoso in 4/4 time followed by three variations. The theme is more elaborate than the preceding one. The first variation for the most part is ornamental, the second complicated rhythmically. The third, an Allegretto, opens in 6/8 time in the major key and ends with the marking Allegro in the minor on a seventeen-measure trill.

Opus 105, No. 3, in C Major (*Austrian Air entitled* "A Schussel und a Reindel ist all mein Kuchelq'schirr").—This is an Andantino in 2/4 time followed by six variations, and one of the most successful pieces in the series. The main theme is fairly simple, and the variations are in their turn melodic, comic, singing, martial (piano solo), serious (Adagio sostenuto ma non troppo in C major), and symphonic (Andante con moto in the major key).

Opus 105, No. 4, in E Flat Major (*Irish Air entitled* "The Last Rose").— Andante expressivo in 3/4 time followed by three variations. Beethoven also set this tune and the next two with piano, violin, and cello accompaniment. The theme is characteristic; with its accent syncopated. The first variation is in legato triplets (piano only). Through the next two, the theme is given to the flute while the piano accompanies.

Opus 105, No. 5, in E Flat Major (*Irish Air*).—This is an Allegretto spiritoso in 6/8 time followed by three variations. The theme has the air of a country dance, and the first variation, with displaced accent, is handled with great skill. The second is for piano solo. The third (Allegro assai in 2/4) brings the piece to its conclusion in a gay mood.

Opus 105, No. 6, in D Major (*Irish Air*).—Allegretto piu tosto vivace in 6/8 time followed by four variations. The theme is similar to the preceding one, but here the first variation is for piano alone. In the second, the theme is enforced by incisive strokes in [eighth-note triplets] on the piano accompanied by the flute. The third, Dolce and sempre legato, is curiously in G sharp. The fourth returns to D major, and to the Allegretto feeling of the beginning—it is a kind of study in rhythms.—JACKET NOTES FOR TURNABOUT TV 4059

IV. Variations for Flute and Piano, Opus 107

The ten sets of variations for flute and piano have an interesting history. This history concerns only their begetting, since of their later existence there is almost no record at all. Although they are unquestionably first-rate late Beethoven, written in the years 1818–20, and although they were published at once and have since been republished in several editions, the writer of these notes has not, in the twenty years he has known them, heard of a single performance, either contemporary or in the past. Not one of the score of flutists he has queried about the pieces has shown any knowledge of the music.

In view of the exhaustive literature on every other work of Beethoven's last years, and in view of the fact that almost all other late Beethoven is well known in recital and concert hall, this neglect is astonishing. These pieces are in no way trifles, but a series of vignettes manifesting all the characteristics of the famous works of the master from the A major sonata, Opus 101, to the end of his life. In an attempt to appeal to a wider public, the original publishers issued Opus 107 as for "piano alone or with accompaniment of a flute or of a violin, *ad libitum.*" The result may have been that the pieces were considered a curious bastard novelty of Beethoven, not to be taken seriously. But the truth is that the music can no more be considered a piano solo than Beethoven's violin or cello sonatas could successfully be played without the stringed instrument.

George Thomson, born in 1757, the Edinburgh publisher of Robert Burns and secretary to the Board of Trustees for the Encouragement of Arts and Manufactures in Scotland, was a musical dilettante and a devotee of the cultural improvement of the peoples of the British Isles. Over a period of years he commissioned and published several hundred British songs harmonized and arranged by leading European musicians. Among those who wrote for him were Haydn, Beethoven, Kozeluch, and Pleyel. He paid well, and the tremendous number of settings he published may be some indication of the willingness of even the greatest and best-established composers to work for him.

As early as 1806, it seems, Thomson endeavored to interest Beethoven in writing popular pieces of various kinds. Beethoven at first was occupied with other things, but about 1815 he began setting the poems that Thomson sent him for solo voice or small chorus, or a combination of the two, with the invariable accompaniment of piano, violin, and cello. In all he wrote 140, to Scottish, English, Welsh, and Irish poems by, among others, Burns, Byron, Walter Scott, and Campbell.

Between 1818 and 1820, that is, at the time of the height of his creative powers, he selected ten of the tunes and wrote sets of variations on them for piano and flute. These variations were published by Thomson (and also in Germany) as Opus 107.

Opus 107, No. 1. This is the most original piece of all the sixteen sets of variations—a musical parody comparable only to Mozart's *"Ein Musicalischer Spass,"* K. 522. Extended musical jokes are rare, being confined almost exclusively to operatic or other vocal music in which the text abets the fun.

With a popular Alpine yodeling theme as framework, Beethoven maliciously sets out to make fun of the poor flute player. For four measures the flutist seems to be able to make sound only the bare skeleton of a tonic-dominant accompaniment. Then he breaks into octaves with the piano, losing his place after a fermata. After a pause to catch his breath, he finishes the theme in triumph.

The first variation is a fast piece in running eighth notes. The flutist is completely at sea. He manages very little but repeated E flats and B flats, except for a moment when he finds himself playing bass to the piano, and introduces a wicked G flat.

The second variation, in which the left hand of the pianist becomes a bassoon, and the right a complete village band, finds the flute eager to assert himself. He comes in a measure late with the tune, so omits the second bar to be properly in place for the third. Thereafter he lives a hectic existence to the end of the variation.

After the second variation ends in E flat major, the third opens in E natural minor, certainly the most awkwardly abrupt key change in all classical variations. The theme is played lugubriously in octaves by the piano, with the upbeat of each phrase tacked onto the end of the preceding one. After a single terrified high E, the flute is lost for measures, until it recovers itself with its inevitable octaves. Then it asserts its passionate character with a series of minor ninths in various rhythmic disguises.

Empty fifths on E flat land the music back in E flat major for the last variation, in which Beethoven relents and gives the flute a new tune it can handle against syncopated triplets in the piano.

Opus 107, No. 2. This set is notable for a beautiful siciliana as the fourth variation.

Opus 107, No. 3. A wild Russian dance. The pace is broken only by the adagio sostenuto in which the Arietta of Opus 111 is clearly foreshadowed. The base of the theme is used as the subject of a fughetta in the finale.

Opus 107, No. 4. Variations on the well-known Irish tune "The Pulse of an Irishman." A profound Beethoven adagio is broken into by a two-four scherzando with strong offbeats that make it oddly jazzy. The set ends with an unforgettable flowing melody in which a curious feature is the collision of seven consecutive notes of the flute with sevenths and ninths in the piano.

Opus 107, No. 5. The biggest and most bravura of all the ten sets. The third variation is an endless melody in the piano under and over long trills, with incredible sustained pedals in the flute.

Opus 107, No. 6. A bucolic air with a first variation reminiscent of Brahms's piano writing, and a second that returns to the Scene by the Brook of the Pastoral Symphony.

Opus 107, No. 7. The theme is a popular Russian tune not unknown to Tin Pan Alley. It was used some years ago in the Broadway hit *Le Chauve Souris*.

Opus 107, No. 8. These five adroit and sensitive commentaries on the theme are music seldom surpassed by Beethoven.

Opus 107, No. 9. The familiar "Scottish snap" of the allegretto theme appears again in the slow variation—a movement not unworthy of the "Hammerklavier" Sonata, which Beethoven was working on at the time.

Opus 107, No. 10. A march in a minor key. The adagio with its incandescent melody in thirty-second notes is in a style the composer returned to in the thirty-first "Diabelli" variation.—DAY THORPE

Chamber Music Without Piano

I. STRING QUINTET IN C MINOR, OPUS 104

At the time of the Viennese Classics house-music was in full flourish, but although original string quartets and quintets were plentiful, piano sonatas, -duos, -trios, etc., were frequently arranged for string instruments, or "translated," as one termed it at that time. In the case of several of Beethoven's works this was also done; he himself created from his piano sonata in E major, Opus 14, No. 1, a string quartet half a tone higher. In a declaration published in the *Wiener Zeitung* of October 20th, 1802, he protested that clever publishers had published his First Symphony and his Septet as string quintets without making it clear on the titles that these were "translations," and that they were not by him.

In 1817 a composer of unknown name submitted to Beethoven for his criticism a string quintet arrangement of the very popular piano trio Opus 1, No. 3 in C minor. It was so unfortunate that Beethoven felt induced to carry out such an arrangement himself. In his humoristic manner he gave this work, the original manuscript of which is unknown, but a copy of which carefully corrected by himself is the property of the Prussian State Library in Berlin, the following title written in his own hand[1]:

"*Bearbeitetes Terzett zu einem 3 stimmigen Quintett von Herrn Gutwillen und aus dem Scheine von 5 Stimmen zu wirklichen 5 Stimmen ans Tageslicht gebracht, wie auch aus größter Miserabilität zu einigem Ansehen erhoben von Herrn Wohlwollen 1817 am 14. August. NB. Die ursprüngliche 3 stimmige Quintett-Partitur[2] ist den Untergöttern als ein feierliches Brandopfer dargebrachtworden.*"

The quintet was published in February, 1819, as Opus 104, only in parts as was the custom, with the title: "*Quintett für 2 Violinen, 2 Brat-*

---

[1] "Arranged terzetto for a three-part quintet by Mr. Goodnature, drawn to the light of day from 5 mock parts to 5 real parts, and raised from great miserableness to some repute by Mr. Goodwill, 1817, the 14th August. N.B. The original three-part quintet score has been sacrificed to the Undergods as a solemn burnt offering."
[2] The bad arrangement of the unknown composer.

schen und Violoncell von Ludwig van Beethoven nach einem seiner schönsten Trios für's Piano-Forte von ihm selbst, frey bearbeitet und neu eingerichtet[1] *Eigenthum der Verleger. Wien bei Artaria und Comp."* It was evidently Beethoven's intention to recompense the publishers with this work for the fact that he had not yet supplied a string quintet promised on June 1st, 1805.

The difficulties which must be overcome when piano compositions are transcribed for string instruments were dealt with by Beethoven in his letter to Breitkopf & Härtel dated 13th July, 1802, in which he says *inter alia:* "Since not alone whole passages must be entirely omitted and rearranged, additions are necessary, and it is here that the awkward stumbling block lies, and to overcome it one must either be the master himself, or at least have the same skillfulness and invention." Unquestionably he has succeeded in transcribing his early opus for string instruments without leaving out a bar and without adding one, frequently retaining the violin part of the trio for the second violin of the quintet; occasionally, e.g. in the Trio of the Scherzo, he could not veil completely the original character of the piano passages. In some instances he based the middle parts on new motifs invented by imitation. The transcription of the variation movement seems the most successful. In any case there is no reason why this quintet, whose first public performance took place in the *Gesellschaft der Wiener Musikfreunde* on the 13th December, 1818, should be treated grudgingly, i.e. not be brought into the concert hall. Above all, amateurs should play it. Unfortunately string quartet is little played in the family home these days, string quintet even less. Let us hope that the near future brings a revival of house-music as it flourished in the times of Haydn, Mozart and Beethoven.—WILHELM ALTMANN (3)

II. FUGUE IN D FOR STRING QUINTET, OPUS 137

[In the year 1817] there was the composition of a Fugue in D major for five stringed instruments, which was completed on November 28, 1817. This piece was written especially for a manuscript collection of Beethoven's works projected by Haslinger, to be discussed below, and was published by him in the fall of 1827 as Opus 137. Beethoven was particularly interested in fugues at the time. "To *make* a fugue requires no particular skill," he said later to Holz, "in my study days I made dozens of them. But the fancy wishes also to assert its privileges, and today a new and really poetical element must be introduced into the old traditional form." The sketches for the conclusion of the quintet fugue

[1] ". . . being his own free and new arrangement of one of his most beautiful Trios for Piano-Forte."

are mixed with notes from Bach and others showing how zealous were his studies in the form at that time.

A fugue theme, identical, so far as the first three measures go, with that of the Scherzo of the Ninth Symphony, presented itself to him and was imprisoned in his notebook in 1815, being recorded among the sketches for the Sonata for Pianoforte and Violoncello in D, Opus 102.[1] The fugue theme appeared again in 1817 in an altered form but with the same rhythmic outline.[2] According to Nottebohm, this was to be the main theme for the fugue for five stringed instruments. The Fugue, Opus 137, was worked out, however, in D major.—ALEXANDER WHEELOCK THAYER, EDITED BY ELLIOT FORBES

III. THE LAST STRING QUARTETS

Late in 1824, the project of the trip to England again came up. The London Philharmonic Society made Beethoven another generous offer. But after haggling with them for a hundred pounds more, which they refused, he raised so many difficulties as to wreck this project. This was bad for Beethoven's purse. But we are probably the gainers. If he had gone to London the last five quartets might never have been written.

A century ago wealthy Russian amateurs of music were doing as much for their art as M. Koussevitzky is doing today. When, in 1806, Beethoven had begun longing to write again in this form, Count Rasoumowsky had earned the enduring gratitude of all quartet lovers by ordering Opus 59. Toward the end of 1822 Prince Galitzin, another Russian enthusiast, chose an equally happy moment. He ordered "two or three string quartets." This commission was heartily welcomed. Beethoven was weary of his long struggle with the text of the *Missa* and desirous of returning to his own field of absolute music—that art which escapes the profanation of concrete programs.

For the experience of hearing the last five quartets the listener should be prepared at least as carefully and seriously as a schoolboy for the university, or a freemason for initiation into the higher degrees, or a child for confirmation. Indeed, more carefully and seriously. For these quartets give a glimpse of an evolutionary stage not yet attained by many human spirits. They reveal the Alpine blossom of experience growing farther above the workaday levels of normal Twentieth Century humanity than most visions of the average scholar or freemason or churchman.

[1] The sketch differs from the ultimate theme of the Scherzo in the fourth measure, where instead of the three quarter-notes F, E, D, Beethoven embellishes the first two notes with eighth notes: F, G, F, E.—Editor.
[2] The theme is in 3/8 instead of 3/4. It is similar to the theme of the Quintet fugue, Opus 137, in that there is a tied note at the end of the third measure, thus delaying the conclusion of the cadence until *after the entrance of the second voice.*—Editor.

"Behold, I show unto you a mystery!" says the Master. He does not proceed to enunciate an enigmatic intellectual proposition such as "We shall not all die." Rather he sets beating within us the heart of the mystery itself. He actually exhibits to us the incorruptibility of this corruption. He shows forth the mortal in the very act of putting on immortality, and the will of the superman, by a supreme rite of renunciation and resignation, drawing the very sting of death itself.

It is of Beethoven in this last rarefied phase that the writer always thinks in reading a superb page of Marcel Proust[1]:

> There is a unique accent to which those great singers who are the original musicians elevate themselves, to which they return despite themselves, and which is a proof of the irreducibly individual existence of the soul. . . . Every artist seems thus the citizen of an unknown fatherland, forgotten by himself, different from that land whence comes, equipped for earth, another great artist. . . . This lost fatherland the musicians do not recall. But each of them remains forever unconsciously tuned in a certain unison with it; he is delirious with joy when he sings in accordance with his fatherland.

Proust goes on to say that this song is composed of all that

> residue of reality which we are obliged to keep to ourselves, which words may not even transmit from friend to friend, from master to disciple, from lover to mistress, this ineffable something which qualitatively differentiates that which each has felt and which he is obliged to leave on the threshold of phrases in which he may not communicate with another, except in limiting himself to exterior points common to all and without interest.

Then the great artist appears,

> exteriorizing in the colors of the spectrum the intimate composition of these worlds which we call individuals and which, without the aid of art, we never would come to know. Wings, another respiratory apparatus which would allow us to traverse immensity, would be of no service to us. For if we went to Mars and to Venus still keeping the same senses, they would invest themselves for us with the same aspect as all this which we are able to perceive of Earth. The only veritable voyage, the sole true fountain of youth, would be not to seek new landscapes, but to have other eyes, to look upon the universe with the eyes of another, of an hundred others, to see the hundred universes which each of them sees, which each of them is; and this we may do with [great artists]; with beings like them we truly fly from star to star.

Some such experience of extraterrestial grandeur awaits the music lover who can acquire ears and brains attuned to appreciate the last quartets of

[1] *La Prisonnière*, Vol. II, p. 73, in that great modern epic, *A la Recherche du temps perdu*.

Beethoven. In them the Master attained such other-worldly altitudes that, in connection with this *finale* of his career, one might appropriately reverse the title of Strauss's famous tone-poem, and speak of Beethoven's "*Verklärung und Tod*"—his transfiguration and death. No pinprick thoughts of his irritability, his avarice, his dishonesty can count for a moment in the atmosphere of the *adagios* of the E flat, the A minor, and the B flat quartets and the fugue which opens the C sharp minor.

We are eternal debtors to his deafness. It is doubtful if such lofty music could have been created except as self-compensation for some such affliction, and in the utter isolation which that affliction brought about. Perhaps that very deafness acted as a sort of protection against the too dazzling intensities of the mystic revelation. It may be that his shrouded hearing was like the veiled vision of him who was warned that he might not "see God and live." At times these quartets seem to have the celestial quality of

> The light that never was, on sea or land.

Only three years before they were begun, another great artist, in a distant land, sickening like Beethoven for his deathbed, wrote some lines[1] strangely applicable to this last and supreme work of his loftiest contemporary:

> Heard melodies are sweet, but those unheard
> Are sweeter; therefore, ye soft pipes, play on:
> Not to the sensual ear, but, more endear'd
> Pipe to the spirit ditties of no tone.

When one has entered into intimacy with them, these last "ditties"—the quartets that were of "no tone" to the Master's poor outer ear, gradually become "more endear'd" than any other mortal music.

Nothing could have been a fitter vehicle for Beethoven's swan song than the string quartet—the most perfect means for conveying absolute music yet discovered. It is made up of instruments strongly individual yet capable of merging their personalities into one. These instruments are almost uniquely equipped for pure intonation. They interpose less mechanism between hand and ear than the piano. They form an organism far more intimate and pliable than the orchestra—a perfect medium for the high subjectivity and the rich and independent polyphony of these last utterances.

The old quartet form did not suffice for the intense personalism of this music. So Beethoven invented new forms. In these the tempo changed more often and more capriciously than ever.[2] The usual four movements

---

[1] John Keats, *Ode on a Grecian Urn.*—Editor.
[2] Not counting *ritardandos*, the quartets of the first and second periods usually change tempo about four times, reaching ten times in the Sixth Lobkowitz and the "*Harp*." But of the three greatest quartets of the last period the A minor (Opus 132) changes tempo twenty times; the B flat (Opus 130) twenty-one times; and the C sharp minor (Opus 131) no less than thirty-one times.

grew to five—six—and even seven, as if in memory of the rococo *divertimento* and Suite. There was less strictness in the sonata-form movements. Their modeling was not so formally pronounced. The second subject sometimes burst in unprepared. The development grew shorter and more polyphonically intensive (e. g., in the first movement of the B flat quartet). The most astonishing contrasts of naïve folk tunes with the music of philosophical reverie were forged into a whole by sheer sorcery. The voice-leading became wonderfully free and daring. In these quartets there are no neutral passages where the hearer may nod and recover. Every moment he must give all he has; for each note is packed with significance.

The only way to make these quartets one's own is by repeated hearings and much detailed study with score in hand. The excellent phonograph records of them now available are godsends. They are powerful aids in speeding up the processes of comprehension.[1]

But a still more powerful aid is a knowledge of how to draw near them. They should be approached in the humble spirit which Mr. Havelock Ellis advocates as necessary for the comprehension of graphic art.

> Schopenhauer long ago pointed out that a picture should be looked at as a royal person is approached, in silence, until the moment it pleases to speak to you. For if you speak first (and how many critics one knows who "speak first"!) you expose yourself to hear nothing but the sound of your own voice. In other words, it is a spontaneous and mystical experience.[2]—ROBERT HAVEN SCHAUFFLER

a. String Quartet No. 12 in E Flat, Opus 127
    I. Maestoso, Allegro; II. Adagio ma non troppo e molto cantabile; III. Scherzando vivace; IV. Finale

Beethoven had composed a quartet in the key of E♭ once before, the "Harp" Quartet, Opus 74, in 1809, and one ostensible similarity between the two first movements is worth mentioning. The composite theme of Opus 127 can be thought of as a more "extreme" version of the theme-type employed in Opus 74, namely, an antecedent-consequent idea passing from force to gentleness. There a brisk tonic-to-dominant *arpeggio*, isolated by an evocative pause, was answered by a lyric "doublet phrase" biased to the subdominant. Here a resonant fanfare, marked *Maestoso*, slowly builds up the E♭ tonic triad to the dominant B♭ and beyond to a rhetorical pause on C. This melts into a lyric doublet (*Allegro*) circling

---

[1] Readers will find much of help and interest in certain books of detailed analysis: Theodor Helm, *Beethoven's Streichquartette*, 3d ed., 1921 (Leipzig: Siegel); Hugo Riemann, *Beethoven's Streichquartette*, Meisterführer No. 12 (Berlin: Schlesinger); Joseph de Marliave, *Les Quatuors de Beethoven*, 1925 (Paris: Felix Alcan) (English translation, 1928).

[2] *The Dance of Life*, 1923, p. 329.

down four times from C harmonized as the subdominant or as the closely related chord ii$_6$.

Subsequently, in Opus 74, the brisk antecedent *arpeggio* serves to open the development, drifting from G around to C, which turns out to be the one important key of the section. Likewise in Opus 127, the antecedent *Maestoso* returns to start the development in G, drifting round to C, which is again—and more organically—the strong development key. The *Maestoso* even returns once more within the development in such a way as to stress this key.

At this point any parallel ceases, abruptly, for the *Maestoso* never appears again, neither to introduce its consequent in the recapitulation, nor anywhere in the coda. It falls victim to the single-minded lyric ambition of the movement as a whole. In Opus 74 the consequent phrase seems to complement the antecedent, according to the best classic principles of checks and balances; together they form a neat symmetrical pair whose intrinsic contrast fructifies the movement up to its final gesture. In Opus 127 the consequent seems rather to escape out of, articulate, and supersede the antecedent, which therefore can and does wither away. The rhetoric is after all quite different. This movement lives not on contrast but on the inherent beauty of the consequent doublet phrase.

No quartet fast movement in Beethoven moves so lyrically as this one. Among the quartets its gentle utterance occupies a special place analogous to that occupied by the opening of the Sonata in A, Opus 101, among the sonatas. "*Mit innigster Empfindung,*" he writes on the earlier composition, "*teneramente,*" "*sempre piano e dolce*" on the present one. The phrase structure of the exposition seems unbelievably simple, hardly conducive to dramatic tensions:

FIRST GROUP:	antecedent (Maestoso)	6 bars	
	consequent (Allegro)	|:8:|	(|:2×4 bars:|—"doublet")
	forte	10	
BRIDGE:		8	(4+4 in sequence)
SECOND GROUP (iii):	second theme	|:8:|	
	1st cadential phrase	8	(3×2+2)
	2nd cadential phrase	8	(2×4)

Only the *forte* passage following the first theme involves any rhythmic sophistication on the level of the phrase; everything else tends to fall into repeating 4- or 8-bar patterns. We might almost be listening to a garland of folksongs.

Yet in spite of its almost voluptuous tenderness, the basic doublet phrase of the first theme is inherently contrapuntal, more so than any earlier quartet theme. It combines three important elements: the melody itself, a *cantus firmus* in unobtrusive parallel motion (cello), and a murmuring syncopated voice (viola).

This skeletal species counterpoint will clarify itself as the work proceeds. At first the phrase is repeated in a loosely knit variation (bar 15 ff.) involving an aborted gesture at imitation, a fresh *appoggiatura*, and a sequential melisma in the cello. Action of this kind becomes very characteristic of the piece and contributes greatly to its particular loveliness, its unique sense of efflorescence. New details, often of a light contrapuntal nature, decorate the first theme at every one of its repetitions, and the same is true for the second theme.

Indeed, a process of continuous free variation seems to supplant traditional developmental energy in this movement, in interest at least, even perhaps in function. Certainly the development section proper is undercut. It begins forcefully, with a return of the *Maestoso* spread out over four octaves of G, melting as before into the lyric consequent phrase. But instead of modulating or fragmenting, the latter molds itself into long lyric periods, more ample than before on account of an inversion stretching upward (bars 85–9, etc.), and much more emotional on account of a cadential detail reminiscent of the second theme (bars 96, 112). The new lyric periods are absolutely plain in harmony: sixteen bars in G major followed with the least possible fuss by sixteen or more in C. Here a thoroughly novel quality of flatness is achieved by the use of canons, and essentially strict ones, at the unison or octave. Work of this sort probes the contrapuntal potential of the theme in a timeless aspect without touching on possibilities for dramatic movement. This very impressive passage—but it does not appear to have impressed many commentators— is one of Beethoven's most extraordinary conceptions for a development section, comparable only to the first-movement development in the Quartet in B♭, Opus 130.

And dramatic modulations do not really interest the composer in the 50 bars remaining for his development section, any more than in the first 42. C minor feints at the key of A♭ and shakes with some conventional modulatory bluster, but the *Maestoso* fanfare that emerges remains on C (in which direction it had pointed at its very first appearance, at the start of the movement). C is already heard as a dominant of F, forecasting a second lax swing around the circle of 5ths (G-C, C-F). Thereafter new blusters and a new nod to A♭ return simply enough to dominant-9th chords built on the same C.

What all this is preparing is not the anticipated tonic key E♭, but the first note of the doublet, C, and its first harmony, the F-minor triad, ii$_6$ of E♭. The intention is to recapitulate the consequent phrase alone, without its antecedent; and almost absent-mindedly the *Maestoso* drops out of the quartet once and for all, never to be heard of again (though possibly it will be heard echoing behind certain phrases of later movements). The paradoxical idea of preparing not the actual key of a theme but the off-tonic sonority on which the theme happens to begin, Beethoven had learned from Haydn and employed in several earlier quartets: in the first movement of Opus 18, No. 3, and most spectacularly in the Finale of Opus 59, No. 2. The direct precedent for the present situation, however, comes not in quartets but in piano sonatas. There are two Sonatas in E♭, Opus 31, No. 3, and Opus 81a, *Les Adieux*, which have first-movement themes starting on ii$_6$ of its close relatives ii$_6$ of IV$_6$ and which re-capitulate them by means of secondary dominants.

Whatever Beethoven had in mind with the sonatas, with the present composition he seems certainly to have meant to soften the recapitulation. The feeling is altogether different from the emphatic, forceful, or tri-umphant recapitulations in most of the previous quartet first movements. The doublet slips in obscurely, with an effect neither of enhanced strength nor of Haydnesque wit, but simply of a paradoxical new lease on life and staying-power. As its phrases repeat themselves in gorgeous variation, the sense of the return is perhaps left in doubt; some sort of developmental action could still be going on. However the recapitulation unfolds quite symmetrically—which is to say lyrically. There is a new modification to the last of the cadential phrases. The expressive semitone inflection in [the cello in the measures of the dominant seventh chord], absent from the exposition, seems to trace back to a poignant detail of the second theme. In turn, the semitone allows Beethoven to move very beautifully toward the subdominant, again, in order to start the coda.

This coda consists of a sweetly obsessive series of repetitions of a newly touching and newly repetitive version of the doublet (bars 249–56) together with recollections of the inverted version of the development and of the original form. Seven times the song circles its way down from II or IV or ii$_6$ to the tonic, while the *cantus firmus* isolates itself and migrates now above, now below the melody. The whole effect approaches that of an inexact, ruminative, and inexpressibly tender round.

This movement is a burgeoning, not a dramatic statement. It soon shakes free of the strong, benign, inchoate *Maestoso* that launched it ini-tially and concentrates on the intimate *aveu* of its contrapuntal doublet. Of this Beethoven never tires. He caresses it endlessly, melting and shuf-fling the melody itself, urging the syncopations back and forth, exploring fresh regions and registers with touches that are always familiar and never quite the same. The composite theme itself provides the single impressive element of contrast, but contrast is abandoned with the *Maestoso* halfway through the piece. The second theme, far from con-trasting with the first, adopts its gait and mien and also a suspicious number of its melodic details. Even its key, G minor (iii)—a minor key!—seems chosen to contrast as little as possible. No less lyric than the first theme, the second sits over a static pedal G which scarcely budges all through the transparent cadential phrases; when the second theme recapitulates in the tonic major, certain original minor-mode inflections are preserved, so that the change of mode makes surprisingly little difference. Strong contrasting articulation is avoided at the point of recapitulation also, as has been mentioned. From the development, what remains in the memory is the section of canons, with its timeless, almost mystic quality.

Sensibility, not structure, is the heart of this piece. Obviously form as such is not the major expressive element. Yet the art required to mold unobtrusive form that will support the repetitive leisure of such a piece is very considerable, as many nineteenth-century composers (or their listeners) learned to their sorrow. The expressive climax of the development comes with the lyric phrases at the beginning and the canonic mediation, for the blustering passages go nowhere and develop nothing significantly. Beethoven must have thought them necessary to set off the recapitulating theme in an unexpected fresh softness. As the fragile little recapitulation might hardly have sufficed to discharge all that curiously dissociated violence, the repetitions of the coda are required or justified. There is about the structure of the movement an ease and instinctive mastery that hides itself, yet frees the lyricism that the composer wished most to develop.

The melody that generates the second movement of the Quartet in E♭, *Adagio ma non troppo e molto cantabile,* is a famous miracle of beauty. "Were some malignant power to permit us to retain but a single page of Beethoven," wrote Daniel Gregory Mason, as usual a little stiff-necked, a little moving, "this page, which gave him such endless trouble in the writing, might well be the one we should cherish for our solace and delight." Mason was referring to the extensive sketches for the melody, which so struck Nottebohm that for once he printed a whole set rather than just a sample. (The suspicion is that Beethoven's best music was the most laboriously sketched, and the most laboriously sketched the most spontaneous-sounding.) In addition to sketches, a sort of early draft for the melody may perhaps be recognized in Leonore's aria *Komm, Hoffnung* in *Fidelio.* However this may be, its natural vocal quality has never been in doubt. Three months after Beethoven's death, it was sliced off the front of the *Adagio* and published as a song upon that occasion: *Beethoven's Heimgang,* with words beginning *"Es wand sein Geist sich von des Staubes Randen los."*

What one cherishes is its calm directness, its sense of freedom, its simplicity and its economy. The form is spare, the harmony plain. Everything devolves upon the melodic line ranging through the great span of an octave and a half—the opening upbeat 4th capped by an entire 6th; the soaring octave leaps in the first strain; the new 6th in the second strain, flowing all the way up from the subdominant D♭ to a high B♭; and the beautiful gapped octave—like catching one's breath—down to the delicate cadence.

The quite unusual luxuriance of the movement as a whole is already forecast within the melody, simple as it is in outline. Half-improvisatory contrapuntal graces are accumulated by almost every segment of it, especially when the cello repeats the two strains originally played by the violin. The free variation technique of the opening movement of the quartet is recalled in such details as the disembodied descant of [the violin over the main theme the second time played on the high strings of the cello]; the opulent fattening of the melody by the second violin [upon the repetition of the second phrase also played on the cello]; and a whole series of imitations or half-imitations of the opening upbeat 4th. Even the harmony changes a little in the repetitions of the strains. [During the repeat of the second strain] the important subdominant climax shines because it was shadowed [on its initial appearance].

After the repetition of the last strain, there are yet two and a half bars of highly articulated concluding material to come—this melody is in no hurry to proceed. [The antepenultimate bar] provides an echo for the gapped-octave fall of the violin. [The next bar] (after first suggesting a further echo) makes a rich chromatic close. [The last bar] adds a halting three-note cadence-figure. Each of these three ideas—the echo, the chromatic close, the three-note cadence—plays its role later in the movement.

Listening to the melody, we have scarcely been worrying our heads about the likely continuations. When a very ornate but essentially regular variation of it ensues, however, it may occasion some surprise, for the melody had certainly not advertised itself as a peg to support a variation chain. The repeated structure of the melody is normal, but variation themes do not normally indulge themselves in leisurely threefold cadences, nor do they at once start gathering to themselves pregnant yet (it would seem) carefully unorganized decorations, as this melody has done so beautifully. Even the opening ground for the peg has been softened, by two bars of preliminary dominant. Not surprisingly, then, with such a beginning, the present variation movement turns out to be a much more organic conception than that of the traditional classic variation model.

All Beethoven's late variation movements, with one exception, move so far from the classic model as to leave it almost unrecognizable (and sometimes unrecognized).

In Opus 127 the six variations and coda are formed, not like a chain with seven links and a plummet, but like a symmetrical A B A design with a very significant cap in the coda. The theme and Variations 1 and 2 together constitute the first element. Variation 3 constitutes the second.

Variations 4, 5, and 6 as a unit complete the design. The essential articulation is harmonic, but Variation 4 emphasizes the three-part arc by means of thematic recapitulation to go along with the tonal return.

As for that essential harmonic articulation, Beethoven recaptures it in an extraordinary fashion, in a few bars of terse revelation within the coda. These harmonic digressions *are* functional; by relating the tonic key of A♭ to E major by way of C♯ (D♭) minor, they pull together the three key-areas of the movement as a whole. The theme and the first two variations stay in A♭. Variation 3, the B section, moves with a spasm to E major (F♭, ♭VI), a key which creates the highly charged sense of an enhanced dominant, as is usually the case with the minor sixth degree. Variation 4 returns just as abruptly to A♭, with Variation 5 balancing the digression to E by stressing the deep minor subdominant (iv, C♯ or D♭ minor), and Variation 6 resuming the tonic.

(One can hark back to the original melody for a scent of these harmonies. Possibly its most striking melodic progression, in bars 3–4, links the tonic to the sixth degree of the scale—albeit the major scale, not the minor. The climactic harmony [in the last measure of the second strain] is the subdominant, albeit the major subdominant—but the minor subdominant gleams in the chromatic close [two bars later] which counts as the most colorful harmonic progression.)

The first variation in Opus 127, as has been said, is thoroughly complex in detail—the most complex Beethoven ever wrote—although it follows the phrase structure of the theme strictly enough. All the variations in this movement seem to cleave a little to their predecessors; here the opening texture resumes the opulent parallel sixths which ornamented strain 2 of the original melody in its repetition. The sixths melt into dense, flexible imitations on motifs derived a little energetically from each fragment of the melody in turn, and destined to expand each harmonic detail into a tiny moment of intensity. The invention is too spontaneous to allow close parallelism between the strains and their repetitions; everything burgeons as freely as the variations to the doublet phrase in the first movement of the quartet. The lush, vibrant texture dries up only at the very last bar, as the three-note cadence-figure follows the echo and the chromatic close. This serves to prepare the more highly strung variation to follow.

Still in A♭, Variation 2 changes to duple time and slightly accelerates the tempo: *Neue Kraft fühlend,* as Beethoven expresses a not dissimilar transition on another occasion. Here he tries out a distinctive light *obbligato* style used a number of times in the late quartets—in the contrasting section of the *Heiliger Dankgesang* of Opus 132, in the *Andante con moto* of Opus 130, and in certain variations of Opus 131. What is typically involved is some kind of fast-dancing dialogue, with crisp syncopations and trills, lucid harmonies, a deceptively popular swing in the bass, and much air—small rests separating fugitive motifs making much play with *staccato*. Beethoven likes to write these passages very "black," that is, in sixteenth, thirty-second, and sixty-fourth notes. There exists a letter (analyzed by Heinrich Schenker[1] and Oswald Jonas[2]) in which the composer discusses a refined point of technique in this variation.

The climactic subdominant harmony from [the last bar of the second strain] of the theme now obtrudes angrily as a minor subdominant, preparing another touch of minor subdominant (C♯ minor) at the very end—which can twist abruptly to E major for the crucial Variation 3. The echo, the cadential close, and the 3-note cadence-figure are all smoothed together by the florid figuration.

That the central contrasting key-area should be led into not by a proper modulation but by a spasm, and that it should be left in just the same way, is entirely typical of Beethoven's methods in the last period. Similar dissociated strokes isolate the B sections of the slow movements of the Ninth Symphony and the Quartet in A minor. There are cases close to home; each of them "nonmodulates" to a form of the sixth degree, as here, and each of them creates its own variety of that insistent religious experience which also inspires the *Cavatina* of the B♭ Quartet and the climactic *Adagio* variation of the C♯ minor. Indeed, Variation 3 is a hymn-variation of the melody, slowed to *Adagio molto espressivo* and simplified into *alla breve* time. Sustained by quiescent chords, the elemental melody picks out only certain chief notes of the original theme, a procedure quite opposite to the busy ornamenting of the early variations. The decided tone of prayer makes a spiritual crown for the movement, and for that matter, for the quartet as a whole.

E major makes one think back to the slow variation-finale of the Sonata in E, Opus 109, whose half-cadence resonates so curiously in a harshly scored augmented-6th chord here. This chord clarifies itself into plain ♭VI of E (as though to remind us that E major arose in the first place as ♭VI of A♭) and marks a displaced variation of the cadential echo before falling into an alarmingly Brahmsian version of the chromatic close. In this variation the three-note cadence-figure is passed over.

Almost with a sense of relief, Variation 4 drifts back to the original mood—back to Tempo I and A♭ major, with figuration first resembling that of Variation 1, but sprouting into new riches of trills and slow-sweeping *arpeggios*. Presently the melody is restored almost verbatim, in the same pair of dialoguing instruments that had it originally; this accentuates the strong sense of return in the *A B A* structure. By

---

[1] "*Beethoven zu seinem Opus 127*" in *Der Tonwille*, IV, 1924.—Editor.
[2] "A Lesson with Beethoven by Correspondence" in *Musical Quarterly*, Vol. 38. This is a précis in English of Schenker's article. Both articles unfortunately are so dependent on musical examples that they are impractical for the present volume. The editor recommends them highly to students of composition technique.—Editor.

eliminating subdominant harmonies from the second strain, Beethoven makes the melody sound all the more emphatic in its return, and circumspectly keeps the sequel fresh. After the chromatic close, a brief extension of the three-note cadence-figure leads innocently to the subdominant and to Variation 5.

Perhaps this wonderful passage does not altogether earn the name of variation; if you wish, call it an episode in the subdominant with strong thematic connections. Of its 13 bars, the theme is followed only by the first 4, a bare gentle canon tracing the characteristic melodic sixth and ending on the characteristic half-cadence. Thereafter Beethoven falls, abstracted, into a meditation upon the subdominant note Db (C♯) and upon its minor triad—the note itself spread out as a sonorous four-octave pedal, the triad wound around in sequential double counterpoint (derived from the chromatic close that had first glowed with C♯ minor, many variations ago). Beethoven is celebrating the subdominant climax of the original melody, in bar 17. This becomes clear as almost tentatively things slip back on the track with a recollection of the end of the melody. From Db (C♯) the line moves not up the major scale to high Bb, but up the minor scale to Bbb (A). The cadential echo is heard one extra time, in the cello, as though to confirm the return to the major mode as the rich trills break in once again; but the chromatic close and the three-note cadence-figure are saved for Variation 6.

The last and simplest and shortest variation glides over the melody in continuous flowing sixteenth-notes. It sounds similar to the second variation in the *Adagio* of the Ninth Symphony, and just as serene. Again the subdominant is avoided, to save its darkening color for the terse coda which retells the whole harmonic story of the movement. The main material of this coda is that which is due after the chromatic close: the three-note cadence-figure. This was bypassed in Variations 3 and 5, but now comes into its cadential own.

The treatment of the three cadential ideas is only one aspect of the superb shaping of this piece. Besides being the most sensuously beautiful movement Beethoven ever wrote, it is one of his masterpieces of expressive form and without much doubt his most sophisticated structure in a slow movement. The rudimentary A B A arc is articulated as subtly as a great cathedral articulates its basic cruciform plan (the simile is Tovey's): the first member freely embroidering the theme, the central member reducing it to a mystic vision in a remote tonality, and the final member restoring the theme to its original aspect—more or less, in spite of the placid decoration of the last variation. In spite of the subdominant meditation of the penultimate one, Variation 5, Variations 4–6 sound together as a unit, moving as they do in the same tempo and with figuration that is not identical but not very variable either. Speaking purely (if one can) of architectural eloquence, this movement goes deeper and further than other slow movements of the last period. In terms of structure, the Ninth Symphony seems bulging by comparison, Opus 130 merely happy and correct, Opus 132 austere, Opus 131 permissive. Only the *Lento assai* of the last quartet, the Quartet in F, Opus 135, inscrutably the simplest of all is built so perfectly and so eloquently.

In essence—to resume the burden of the present chapter—the vocal impulse represents a grandiose impulse toward directness of communication. Elemental song in the form of the country dance, the folk song, and the nursery song, and sophisticated song in the form of the aria, lied, recitative, and hymn, all converge in the major effort for immediacy of contact. The gradual development of Beethoven's lyric sensibility, from the gauche beginnings of Opus 18 to the superb flights of the last period, is too large a matter for treatment here; say only that the process proved as laborious and as valuable to him (and can prove as inspiring to us) as his development of harmony, motivic work, fugue, and so on. Yet I think one misses the point if one views this progress purely or even mainly in technical terms. All the developments were forging language; the development of song was forging language straight for the "common listener." This was, after all, Beethoven's most significant response to the Romantic stirrings of the 1820's, a response that did not fail to impress the nineteenth century. If perhaps the impression has dimmed for later, revisionist generations, something has been dimmed of Beethoven's essential voice.

In Opus 127 one can trace in certain movements exactly the opposite or complementary tendency: a tendency to maximize contrast. This may provide a key to the understanding of a sometimes misunderstood piece, the *Scherzando vivace* of the Quartet in E♭.

Song, not drama, grounds the tender first movement of this quartet, and song, however superbly and strongly molded, inspires the theme and variations of the *Adagio*. Somewhere the later movements had to find a place for another quality—for something tougher, more intellectual, and more disruptive. As Beethoven planned the total sequence of feeling, the Finale was to return to the relaxed simplicity of the opening, leaving only the *Scherzo* to introduce the essential note of contrast. Indeed the *Scherzando vivace* is one of Beethoven's most explosive pieces, bursting with energy and malice, crackling with dry intelligence. To make the dance movement the center of tension in a cyclic work was in any case unusual, though something of the sort had been accomplished in the earlier E♭ Quartet, Opus 74.

Internal high contrast, I think one can say without forcing the case, is the clue to the quality of this movement in itself, as well as to its admirably calculated role within the quartet as a whole. Having recently conceived the second movement of the Ninth Symphony, Beethoven was in the right frame of mind for an unusually involved *Scherzo*; from the Ninth Symphony, too, he carried over the idea of fugue for a start. After a prefatory *pizzicato* fanfare—there are no timpani in a string quartet!—a fugal exposition stamps out a shaky path: subject in the dominant (cello), answer by inversion (viola), a humorous six-bar echo episode, subject in the tonic (first violin), answer by inversion (second violin). And thereafter, fugality and counterpoint cease abruptly, and begin, and cease, and begin again. Much more pointedly than in the Ninth Symphony, the issue here seems to be not the fact of fugue, but the tension between contrapuntal material and the noncontrapuntal surroundings in which it is placed. This provides an ideal matrix for the play of contrasts.

The basic material smells of the schoolroom: a stiff, musty piece of ostentatious two-part counterpoint recalling, at first glance, something out of the Great Fugue or the third movement (*Allegro assai e vivace, ma serioso*) of the Quartet in F minor, Opus 95. In Opus 127, some of the rigidity results from the fact that everything about the first fifteen bars works to stress the third beat of the bar; so that when in bar 16 the second beat is struck chromatically in preparation for the tonic entries, there is a particularly dirty bump. Accompanying these entries, a loose new countersubject continues to strike away at the second beat, a sharp contrasting detail carrying through into the homophonic section marked—in the language of the Ninth Symphony—*ritmo di tre battute*: which is not musty at all. The A section of the *Scherzo* closes promptly and in good order on the dominant. In the repeat, the *pizzicato* fanfare of bars 1–2 is skipped; nor is it ever heard of again.

The B section piles contrast upon contrast, pressing dangerously and deliberately toward the breaking point. A gesture of unprecedented strength begins it: a *fortissimo* unison sweeping up almost four octaves, a compression of the total rhythm of the subject. What the unison leads to is an idea of unprecedented weakness: a a miniature dancelike phrase for the first violin which cheapens the subject (or rather the inversion) into a two-bar sequence. This is made even more grotesque by fussy accompaniment *arpeggios* in the cello and by continuing little squawks on the second beat. But contrapuntal habits die hard. The dance-phrase instantly inverts itself and starts deploying its elements through the various instruments; and by the time it also doubles itself in thirds and accompanies itself by its own inversion, the counterpoint is assuming a kind of nightmare seriousness. A fleeting but quite distinct suggestion of more majestic movement is knocked down by a second loud upward-sweeping unison. (This happens to be a precise compression of the main subject in the minor mode, with some of its most unexpected notes accentuated.)

In this whole series of madly contrasted ideas, none lasts more than a few bars. It is perhaps hardly surprising that the piece cracks up at this point. A fragmentary, hushed, grinning 2/4 *Allegro* free-associates its way in, and by the time we get over the shock we have perhaps been made to see how rigid the rhythm had been becoming. The interruption has a heavy gestural quality, something like recitative. Though it sounds shocking, it does not sound quite wild because the whole atmosphere has been getting surreal, because tenuous melodic connections obtain with the previous unison [the first three measures of the 2/4 consist of a rhythmical variant of the two preceding measures of the 3/4]. Tonally speaking everything is reined in hard. The prior dissociated action had been taking place in a tonal field more restless than anything else in the entire quartet: the original unison deviated to C minor, and then the harmony jerked its way up from C–F to Db–Gb to D–G. But now a circle-of-fifths sequence rolls back from the second unison, starting on D, to G minor (the 2/4 interruption) to C minor (the same interruption a second time) to C₇ to F minor to Bb₇ (very briefly) and thence to a return of the initial fugal exposition in the tonic Eb.

As compared with the one at the beginning, this second fugal exposition is much less shaky, admitting no deviation from the tonic and no episode. In compensation, its four regular entries accumulate new accompaniment or countersubject material of increasing density and brilliance. A drawling coda seems designed to set up a concluding witticism which plays on the second beat once again.

The rhythmic figure of the witticism accelerates neatly into the trio. Two main ideas, one in the minor mode and the other alternating in the major, rush through a series of keys that seem to make no particular expressive point:

|: i–VII :|: VII–v–III–i–V :|

One is reminded of the rambling trio of the Quartet in F minor or of the dance-tune "medleys" in the quartets to come; but the present *minore* has less intrinsic character—very little, in fact, except as a gross foil to the overstimulated *Scherzando* itself. This is duly repeated, and the trio begins whirling away for a second time until suddenly checked by a rest, after eight bars, as though someone had misread the directions. Much the same thing happens in the Ninth Symphony. Beethoven compounds the joke about the second beat in the sardonic close.

And then the Finale: one of Beethoven's sweetest and simplest-sounding, as well as one of the most perfectly conceived and executed. The folklike tone is so magical and true, so lively and calm, that one feels solemn to talk about subtleties of construction, long-term harmonic relationships, goals and contrast—all that. But folk accents can sound banal just as easily as enchanting. What sets and assures the tone is the way the musical elements are put together.

Beethoven was getting less and less inclined to start a movement directly with its main thematic material. The opening four-bar phrase here, beginning squarely off key, serves as a preface to the theme, *not as a theme per se*.[1] [An] analogy [is] the opening of the Finale of the *Eroica* Symphony, though the present preface seems to look forward to the rest of the movement in a far more integral way.

Thus the prefatory lunge toward G proves to be the main spur of harmonic contrast in a movement which otherwise can afford to stay very quiet in this respect. Twice at important junctures a strong G breaks in on the E♭ harmony—though the preface as such recurs only once; it drops out unobtrusively before the piece is half over, like the *Maestoso* antecedent in the first movement of the quartet, like the *pizzicato* fanfare in the third. Rhythmically, the half-note A♭ on the second beat (bar 1) establishes a pattern for the main theme itself (which also as A♭'s on the second beat) as well as for one element of the second group, later. After rearing up to the step G–A♭ (in bar 1), the preface collapses by degrees, making little scrambling echoes of G–A♭ by means of several other upward steps. The same step G–A♭ grounds the first bars of the main theme; G–A♮ seems all the more piquant thereafter, in bar 7. The same step G–A♭ is perhaps heard supervising the climactic step B♭–C in bar 8.

Oddly prepared, the main theme itself is decidedly odd, in spite of its homely swing. A♮ in [the second bar] grates because it contradicts the stolid A♭'s [which appear earlier], because it blunders into a tritone with E♭ at the beginning of [the measure], and because its modulatory ploy is so thoroughly cold-shouldered. There is something odd about the large rhythm, too. Though the phrase falls into a regular eight-bar module, inside it feels lopsided, with its fourth bar somehow out of place. Are we quite sure how many A♭ bars and how many A♮'s are required? The third movement of the "Pastoral" Symphony comes to mind, with its village bassoonist who has trouble counting his cadences. The second half of the tune ambles just a little loosely. Later, indeed, Beethoven actually does remove one of the A♭ bars; at present, terse propulsion is certainly not wanted. The ambiguity of phrase construction rubs quietly against the folklike innocence of the tone. And some subtlety of construction is welcome to offset great plainness everywhere else.

No ambiguity clouds the immediate sequel, for example, a guileless "doublet" tune which becomes a faithful pendant of the main tune. This doublet [is an] example [of] how heavily Beethoven relied on the note of popular lyricism in the last quartets. In the Finale of Opus 127, one soon gets the feeling of a "medley" of folklike phrases, a feeling that is experienced even more clearly with certain dance movements and trios in slightly later quartets. After the first theme, the tunes are square

[1] Italics by the editor.

and ingenuous, jogging along in all-but-continuous quarter-notes. These tunes follow one another amiably with next to no transitional material.

In the course of [the] discussion of the first movement, a diagram showed the extreme regularity and simplicity of phrasing in its exposition. A parallel diagram will show a parallel situation in the exposition of the Finale (italics being used for phrases which in the recapitulation are simply excised). Transitional material scarcely exists; one can hardly speak of a "bridge," for Beethoven merely breaks the first four bars off the main theme—a paradoxical break—and runs them successively through the four instruments: a pair of statements in the tonic, and then, without any modulatory interlude, a pair in the dominant. (This will work, on account of the modulatory itch of the original A♮.) A two-bar extension, and we are quite ready for a new folklike doublet in the new key.

For sheer effervescence it would be hard to match this garland of themes in Beethoven's earlier music, though their quality is captured

FIRST GROUP:	Preface	4 bars
	main theme	|:8:|
	secondary theme	|:8:| (|:2×4 bars:|—"doublet")
	main theme	4 cello
		+4 viola
	in V:	+4 second violin
		+4 first violin
		$_2$
SECOND GROUP:	third theme	8 (2×4 bars—"doublet")
		+4 (variation of second half of doublet)
	fourth theme	6+|:4:|
	cadential phrases	4
	to 1:	6
		6

again and even heightened in the Finale of the Quartet in F, Opus 135. *Bonhommie rustique*, Romain Rolland called it. What is so striking is the combination of an evocation of cloddishness, on the one hand, and the most utterly refined treatment of melodic and harmonic detail, on the other. Perhaps the combination, so stated, seems classical enough. But it does not seem Haydnesque any more—the detail is altogether too elegant. Nor Mozartian—the connotation is too earthy and plain.

At the close of the exposition, after the fourth of the tunes has made an extra-heavy cadence in the dominant, light cadential phrases turn back to the tonic and begin to concentrate on the backward step A♭–G. Thus prepared, the preface booms in again on G. A tonic return seems to be just around the corner. However, we are denied the full sense of security that a rondo would provide, in favor of a very playful development section heading toward C minor (which is of course the direction implied by the G of the preface). Beethoven amuses himself by making frivolous combinations of the first theme and the third, by running away with the eighth-note figure of the first theme, and by somersaulting around a warm and thoroughly contrapuntal circle-of-fifths sequence. This leads smilingly but rather swiftly to the key of A♭. Here, in the subdominant, the main theme returns very high in the viola, and following it the secondary doublet theme complete with all its repetitions.

Commentators have tended to brush off the formal plan of this movement as lucid and obvious. Certainly nothing about it is likely to strike any listener as abstruse. All the same, the enormous subdominant return —thirty-two bars, encompassing the main theme and the subsidiary theme —must be the most obstinate "false reprise" in the whole classic repertory. Doubtless the lengthy emphasis on A♭ can be heard as outcome of the G of the preface when it returned to open the development—the large relationship G–A♭ expanding the step G–A♭ within the preface. After thirty-two bars, at all events, a brilliant transition (almost the only one in the piece) climbs up very ethereally to E♭; the modulation is grounded by G–A♭–G high in the cello.

In the tonic key, E♭, the full recapitulation takes place, beginning with the same thirty-two bars, which are (wisely) now handled with some variation. Rhythmic compression would still be out of the question. The first theme merely concentrates on canonic decorations and new harmonies, and takes more time to solidify its harmonic underpinnings.

At the close of the recapitulation, cadential phrases settle around the note G, just as they did at the close of the exposition. This time the preface does not ensue. The tonality lightens miraculously, and yet securely for the moment, into C major, as the tempo softens into 6/8 time. Rustling, dizzying scale figures in triplet sixteenths begin to blur all the edges. Beethoven evaporates the first phrase of the main theme into a three-bar phrase, by following bars 5, 7, and 8 of the original but dropping the redundant second A♭ bar. Velvet-gloved, this phrase swings powerfully from instrument to instrument, from the key of C major (where G moves once again to A♭) to A♭ to E to E♭, again without any real modulations between. At last, after seeming not to notice, the composer accepts the awkward modulatory energy of the original A♮ and whirls the tune through incredible, forbidden regions. Home in E♭—there is a ten-bar tonic pedal—the phrase begins to reiterate the upward step B♭–C of [the fourth bar of the main theme], which appears in the repeating cadential phrases. The scoring grows very exquisite, the sonority very full. [The second four measures] of the original tune are swept into the stream, their bluntness like everything else melted into the eddying 6/8 flow. A flash of major and minor sonorities around B♭ and C, a further crystallization of the theme, and the piece is suddenly silent. It is the clownish A♮ that emerges as the final irreducible essence.

—JOSEPH KERMAN

b. String Quartet No. 13 in B Flat, Opus 130
I. Adagio ma non troppo—Allegro; II. Presto; III. Andante con moto ma non troppo; IV. Alla danza tedesca—Allegro assai; V. Cavatina—Adagio molto espressivo; VI. Finale—Allegro

The Quartet in B flat major was the second of the three commissioned by and dedicated to Prince Nicholas Galitzin. Its opus number is chronologically confused with the A minor and C sharp minor quartets of the same set. The actual order in which these works were written is Opus 132, Opus 131. The B flat quartet was written toward the end of 1825, and was given its first performance by Schuppanzigh's Quartet on March 21, 1826. The reception varied with the different movements; the Cavatina was not understood. The Scherzo-*Presto* and the Danza alla Tedesca were enthusiastically encored, but the formidable fugal finale was positively disliked. Though Beethoven rarely paid any attention at this period to the sort of reception his compositions met with, his friend Breuning reported that on his deathbed Beethoven replied to a report that the new quartet did not please: "It will please them someday."

At the instigation of the publisher Artaria, Beethoven suppressed the fugal finale, and wrote a new last movement which was destined to be his last completed composition. The private performance of this movement by Schuppanzigh and his fellow-players was warmly applauded.

Artaria had succeeded in securing the publishing rights to the quartet in spite of the sly bargaining of the Parisian publisher Schlesinger. Beethoven, who was indifferent to the competition as long as he received proper remuneration wrote to his friend Holz: "It is immaterial which hellhound licks and gnaws my brains since it must needs be so; only see that the answer is not delayed too long. The hellhound in Leipzig can wait and meanwhile entertain himself with Mephistopheles [editor of the *Leipziger Musikalisches Zeitung*] in Auerbach's Keller; he will soon be plucked by the ears by Beelzebub, the chief of devils."

Beethoven had a great fondness for this quartet. In one of his conversation books he refers to it as his "Lieb Quartet." When Holz suggested to the composer that perhaps this was his greatest work in quartet form, Beethoven replied: "Each in its own way. Art demands of us all that we shall not stand still. You will find a new manner of voice treatment (part-writing) and, thank God! there is less lack of fancy than ever before." On another occasion Beethoven referred to the C sharp minor as his greatest quartet.

The much discussed "three periods" of Beethoven's creative output are not to be accounted for solely on the basis of chronology and the normal evolution of style from youth to maturity. "The tone forms," to adopt a felicitous term of Raul Bekker, "afford the real ideas which stirred in the composer. . . . they display the poetic idea underlying each phase of his life under the tone-symbolism of three separate styles: that of the sonata-improvisation, that of the monumental symphony, and that of the abstract quartet."

It is more than likely that an artist's impulse to abstraction is the normal result of a constantly deepened perception of, and sensitiveness to, the essential nature of his chosen medium. It is hardly credible that Beethoven's reawakened interest in quartet writing, after a lapse of fifteen years, is to be fully accounted for on the circumstance of Prince Galitzin's commission. Is it not more plausible, that the composer deliberately turned to the homogeneous timbre of the four strings as the medium best adapted to his maturest thought? At any rate, it so transpired that his creative labors between the Spring of 1824 and Winter of 1826 were entirely devoted to quartet writing.

Taking due account of the imposing attributes of the E flat quartet (Opus 127) and its clear tokens of a new style, it must still be accounted as only the outer portal of the sanctuary.

Many will be content to remain within its radiance, and it is not without reason that the remaining four quartets represent, collectively, a tonal arcanum that is difficult to penetrate.

The great "Triptych" represented in the B flat, C sharp minor, and A minor Quartets, should, indeed, be studied consecutively and with regard for their significant interrelation; nor should the "Grosse Fuge" (originally placed in the final movement of the B flat quartet, Opus 130, and afterwards published separately as Opus 133) be looked upon as a separate work in any way extraneous to the others of its mighty neighbors. But let us summarize at this point the salient features of the "last manner" to which the B flat quartet is the "open sesame":

I. Departure from Sonata (first movement) form.
II. Divergence toward the group of contrasted pieces analagous to the Suite.
III. Incorporation of the Fugue.
IV. Inclusion of the Choral Variation (A minor Quartet).
V. Reversion to modal melody and its resultant modal harmony.

These, in addition to the "grand" variation, represent the Beethoven of the last period, wherein it will be seen that any significant departure or innovation moves invariably in the direction of *form* and *structure,* and not toward the reconstitution of tone-relations, *per se,* in the harmonic sense. Melodic ideas, too, are made subservient to structural considerations. From first to last, structure and organic development were the fundamental determinants and the *foci* of Beethoven's art.

Yet another feature pertaining to the processes of *development* gains steadily in significance in the last period: the interpenetration of thematic ideas based upon contrapuntal principles tends to displace the harmonically conditioned processes of the earlier *developments*. The train of thought, as manifested in the thematic interplay; in a sort of grand cross-reference system, becomes a great tonal complex that is unparalleled since the polyphonic art of J. S. Bach. It is, moreover, in the hands of Beethoven, more convincing, more subtle and more inevitable as regards the inner expressive processes of composition than the "thematic transformations" of the Berlioz-Liszt-Wagner school or the deliberate "cyclic" procedures of César Franck and the French symphonists so ardently championed by M. d'Indy. With Beethoven, the interrelation of ideas is more genuinely the result of spiritual compulsion than the more externalized thematic involutions of the later Romanticists.

Taking into account this particular phase of the composer's "last manner" it becomes intensely illuminating, and well-nigh indispensable to follow the invaluable studies and deductions of such devoted scholars as Nottebohm, Bekker and d'Indy as they bear upon the last quartets.

Let us then follow these scholar-musicians for a better apprehension of the Master's train of thought. Thus Bekker observes:

> The most remarkable testimony to the organic connection between these three quartets—a witness hitherto seldom recognized or fully appreciated—is the thematic bond which undoubtedly exists between them. It must be remembered that for any critical aesthetic valuation of the B flat major quartet the original version with the fugue as closing movement, not the later version with its final *Allegro*, should be reviewed. Nottebohm has shown that the fugue theme of Opus 130 and the opening theme of the A minor quartet are contemporaneous and closely associated, and he believes that "there can scarcely be a doubt that Beethoven drew from studies of the fugue theme the motive of four long notes with which he opens the first movement of the A minor quartet and which he uses again later in that work. The fugue studies thus served a double purpose.
>
> But Bekker—in hot pursuit—discovers that "the purpose served was, as a matter of fact, not double but threefold. This theme formed not only the main subject of the first movement of Opus 132 and the fugue subject of Opus 130 (now Opus 133), but by a change from ascending sixths to descending thirds it became the principal theme of the first and, reversed, of the last movement of Opus 131. It is the leading idea of the whole group of Beethoven's three greatest quartets, and recognition of the fact throws new light on the composer's train of thought. . . . The fact that the center of gravity is thus placed in the fugue finale affects the relationship of the other movements to each other. . . . . This idea once grasped, the fantasia-like sequence of movements and kaleidoscopic changes of mood are easy to understand."

Our next step will be to make, as nearly as possible, a [melodic] verification of these deductions, beginning in retrograde order, with the first subject of the *Grosse Fuge*:

[a) The theme in its outline is B flat, B natural, high A flat, G, low B natural, C, high A natural; for convenience let us designate these notes by the numbers of their respective order in the scale: one, one-sharp, seven-flat, six, one-sharp, two, seven, eight.

b) The slow opening of the A minor quartet, Opus 132, consists of four even half-notes in the cello—one-flat, one, six, five (corresponding to the first four notes of the *Grosse Fuge* theme)—answered five bars later in the violin with the following steps in the key of the dominant: seven-flat, six, one-sharp, two (corresponding to the third, fourth, fifth, and sixth notes of the theme).

c) The first four notes of the opening fugue of Opus 131 are again even half-notes—B sharp, C sharp, A, G sharp—which are again identical to the outline of the first four notes of the Opus 133 theme, although the rise of the interval of a sixth between the second and third notes of the latter receives a poignant sadness in the former by changing the register of the last two notes and falling the interval of a third instead.

d) The skeleton of the vigorous unison theme of the last movement of Opus 131 is almost identical to the Opus 133 theme, though its melodic outline is filled out by notes of the implied harmonies.

e) The same filling out of the bare outlines of the Opus 133 theme is noticeable in the first lyrical four measures of the main first movement theme of Opus 130, although here they are filled out by neighbor notes instead of harmonic ones.]

Had Herr Bekker looked for still more definite corroboration of the "threefold" thematic bond he would have found it (in the last movement of the C sharp minor) [at the recapitulation of the main theme where the second phrase of the second theme has as a surprise counterpoint three *sforzando* notes in the cello which are characterized by the rise of a sixth and the fall of a minor second].

This pointed entrance of the "basic motif" in the cello is followed by successive entrances, equally emphatic, in the viola, second violin, and first violin.

And now, viewing the B flat quartet individually, apart from its fellows, the feature that attracts immediate attention is its division into six movements, thus bringing it into general alliance with the older design of the *Suite* or *Divertimento*. As regards the structural design applied to the several movements the distribution is as follows: I—*Sonata allegro*; II—*Scherzo*, form (a-b-a); III—*Lied-Sonata*, i.e., Sonata without central development (designated by some analysts as "*Sonatina*"); IV—*Scherzo* form; V—*Lied* (designated by some as "first rondo" form); VI—*Sonata allegro*.

The first movement presents a capricious aspect by reason of the persistent alternation of slow and fast tempi: *Adagio ma non troppo—Allegro*. Note the further interplay between the initial basic motif and the second subject:

The following Scherzo is exceedingly deft in style and concise in form.

The third movement, *Andante con moto*, in D flat major, is not "easy going" on first hearing; it is, in fact a very elusive movement, by reason of its closely woven texture and the variation-like unfolding of the melodic lines and their accompanying arabesques. It brings to mind the observation of von Lenz,[1] that it is "not so much a quartet as a discourse between four string instruments." Robert Schumann characterized this movement as an *"intermezzo."* In addition to the tempo mark, Beethoven added the direction *poco scherzando*.

History records that the fourth movement *Alla danza Tedesca*[2] was encored on its first performance, as was also the B flat minor scherzo movement (No. 2). Freely interpreted, the term *"Alla Tedesca"* means— in the German style. *"Tedesca"* and *"Deutsch"* are both derived from an ancient term which appears in medieval Latin as *Theotisca*. (Grove's Dic.)

The *Cavatina, Adagio molto espressivo*, which comes next, is the movement regarding which Beethoven said to his faithful friend Holz: "Never did music of mine make so deep an impression upon me; even the remembrance of the emotions it aroused always costs me a tear." Most deeply affecting is the passage in C flat major, with its ensuing modulations, bringing a return to the principal song theme. The composer's pent up emotion is herein indicated by the expression mark *"Beklemmt"* (afflicted).

Poignant interest attaches to the sixth movement of this quartet in as much as it is the last composition that came from Beethoven's pen. This is the movement which finally displaced the great fugue (subsequently published as Opus 133), which was found to be incomprehensible to its first audience.

This gay and exuberant finale was written under the most distressing circumstances. The composer was staying at his brother John's house at Gneixendorff, near Krems; the same brother who had darkened the last years of his life by cruelty and avarice. Beethoven had recently recovered from a serious illness, and was already feeling the early symptoms of the disease to which he was soon to succumb. And so in this characteristic fashion the Master defiantly tossed a final challenge into the face of the grim "Intruder."—ARTHUR SHEPHERD

---

[1] Wilhelm von Lenz, 1808–1883, Russian Councillor at St. Petersburg and author of *Beethoven et ses trois styles*, in which the idea, originally suggested by Fétis, that Beethoven's works may be divided into three separate epochs, has been carried out to its utmost limits.

[2] See the remarks by Professor Misch about this movement and its relationship to the Piano Sonata, Opus 79, in his book: *Beethoven Studies*, pp. 14–18.—Editor.

c. String Quartet No. 14 in C Sharp Minor, Opus 131
I. Adagio ma non troppo e molto espressivo; II. Allegro molto vivace; III. Allegro moderato; IV. Andante ma non troppo e molto cantabile; V. Presto; VI. Adagio quasi un poco andante; VII. Finale (Allegro)

The idea that Beethoven, in such works as this, "broke the mold" of the classical forms is fatally well expressed in that metaphor. There was no mold to break. The art forms of Haydn, Mozart and Beethoven were not molds into which music could be cast, but inner principles by which the music grew. The great family likeness between hundreds of Mozart's movements does not prove that they are not alive. Their differences are as vital as those which distinguish one Chinaman from another; and with study the differences soon become vital to us. But with Beethoven's later works the differences are more conspicuous than the resemblances. If form means conformity to a mold, then indeed Beethoven's last works require a separate mold for each. Does this, then, mean that there is more form in these works, or less form than in works that will all fit one mold? Evidently the mold metaphor is unprofitable: when we come down to anything more detailed than the most childish generalization, Mozart is no more comfortable in a mold than Richard Strauss. Let us take the C sharp minor quartet from point to point and see what it tells us when we are unencumbered by *a priori* notions.

It begins with a fugue. The method of a fugue is argumentative; and while its argument is proceeding dramatic action is in abeyance. This fugue is clearly bent on its own business and shows no sign of being an introduction to anything else. Space forbids a detailed analysis, and only a detailed analysis can throw any light on a fugue. Three points, however, can be made here. First a fugue in as much as it is not a dramatic form, has no tendency to emphasize its changes of key, or even to single out a return to its tonic as an important event. Hence there is something unusually formal in the eight bars of clearly cadential tonic and dominant at the return to C sharp minor (marked by a double bar and four sharps in this score, bars 83–90); and the preceding ethereal passage in A for the two violins, answered by D for the viola and violoncello, is also considerably more like a distinct event than one would expect in a mere fugue. In short, this fugue has subtle signs that it is part of a work in sonata style, though the hard dramatic facts of that style are not allowed to disturb its quiet flow. Secondly, the range of key is very small, being practically confined to "directly related" keys; that is to say, keys in which the chord of our tonic (C sharp minor) can be found. Thirdly, both the beginning and the end of this fugue throw strong emphasis on the flat supertonic (D natural). In the subject

the minor sixth (A) with its sforzando is reflected by D natural in the
answer, which has been put into the subdominant (instead of the orthodox dominant) for this very purpose. The counterpoint of this answer
even emphasizes G natural, the flat supertonic of this subdominant. At
the end of the movement the flat supertonic is so strong that the major
tonic chord is almost in danger of sounding like a dominant. As the
final chord dies away, the violoncello rises an octave; the harmony
vanishes into unison as the other instruments echo the rising octave. . . .

The rising octave, a semitone higher, begins a lively self-repeating
eight-bar tune pianissimo in a quick six-eight (allegro molto vivace).
So the key is D major, flat supertonic to C sharp minor, and, in spite of
all the emphasis that prepared it, utterly unexpected. The viola repeats
the tune, which the violin resumes at the fifth bar and continues with
another eight bars which overlap into a new theme, evidently destined
to be a transition theme. We are unquestionably moving in sonata style
and have left the fugue behind us. Now what will become of the
sonata form in these extraordinary circumstances? From the fact that
the movement is in this strange key, we may expect that it will not
modulate very widely, for fear of losing its bearings or damaging its
special key-color by reminding us of the C sharp minor which is so
firmly established by that great and solemn fugue as the key of the
whole work. Again, the development of a sonata form movement is bound
to be argumentative: and here again the fugue has forestalled us. Accordingly this D major movement, which has started with a rondolike
tune, sets out at bar 24 with a highly organized transition theme which
expands until at bar 44, having overshot A major, the dominant, it
finds itself poised on a chord of C sharp major, dangerously near the
key of the fugue. After a pause the situation is saved by the bold
stroke of playing the first theme again actually in E, the dominant of
the dominant. This is "dominant preparation" with a vengeance; and
four more bars lead safely into A major, where (at bar 60) a lively
second subject begins. But it behaves like the second subjects of Beethoven's rondos and allied types of finale, and soon shows a hankering
for the tonic and for a return to the first theme. At bar 84 the theme
does return. At bar 100 it moves to the subdominant, and thence
takes a new course leading to a passage on the chord of F sharp
major, corresponding to that which ended on the chord of C sharp.
From here, however, six bars lead easily back to D, where (at bar 133)
the second subject is recapitulated. This, of course, leads to the subdominant just as happened in the rondo of Opus 22; and here, as
there, the main theme enters in the subdominant before swinging round
to the tonic. A spacious coda, greatly developing the transition theme,
now ensues and brings this delicate movement to quite a brilliant
climax which, however, dies away abruptly.

Eleven bars of declamatory interlude lead,[1] in a few firm steps of harmony, to A major. A theme in two repeated strains (andante ma non troppo e molto cantabile) initiates a great slow movement in the form of a set of six absolutely strict variations, with a coda which, as is typical of Beethoven's procedure, begins as if to make another variation but drifts away, after the first phrase, into foreign keys. Most of the variations reflect only the harmony of the theme, and in the second variation (più mosso, common time) an extra bar at the beginning displaces the rhythm, while in the second part of the mysterious syncopated fifth variation (allegretto 2/4 there is an extra bar in a more unexpected place. Otherwise the fact that each variation is in a different tempo and style cannot in any way weaken the strength with which the theme is grasped. It is not the naïve listener who finds this movement "chopped up" by these changes of tempo. After the sixth variation (in 9/4 time with a most original rhythm and more resemblance to the melody of the theme than has hitherto been shown) the florid triplet passages which the four instruments give out in dialogue are unmistakably beginning a seventh variation, but at its eighth bar a long trill leads slowly to C major, the first change of key in the whole movement, which of course has hitherto been confined to the harmonies of its theme. In C major a fragment of the original melody is given in a quicker tempo (allegretto) and it moves excitedly back to A major, where the first eight bars of the theme appear in their original tempo, surrounded by a glory of trills. Again at the eighth bar a trill rises slowly, this time to F major. The fragment of the theme in an increasingly excited allegretto leads back to A, again in the original tempo (Beethoven's intention is certain though his directions are confused); and in a coda of fourteen bars, the details of which cost Beethoven immense pains, this slow movement dies away with broken accents from the cadence of its theme.

Now follows the most childlike of all Beethoven's scherzos. Beyond being in alla breve instead of triple time it does not differ from the form laid down by him in the Fourth and Seventh Symphonies. The key is E major. The trio begins with a tune in E and contains four distinct ideas, the last two of which are in A. The first da capo of the scherzo has its repeats written out in full in order that (as in the Seventh Symphony) a large portion may be at first kept mysteriously subdued. The whole trio is made to come around again, and so there is a third appearance of the main body of the scherzo. The tunes of the trio then try to prove themselves irrepressible. But repressed they are, and the scherzo dies away in a mischievous whispering passage which suddenly swells out to a fortissimo end. So far this description might apply to half-a-dozen of Beethoven's other scherzos. What is peculiar

[1] Actually marked by Beethoven as the third movement.—Editor.

to the scherzo of the C sharp minor quartet (apart from its childlike spirit) is the joints of the form; the humorous treatment of its first four notes, a humor which is heightened at each recurrence when the trio leads back to the main theme; and the strange diminuendo leading to poco adagio in the middle of the second part of that theme. Such things are always typical and yet always unique.

Catastrophe overwhelms the end of the scherzo. Its last three notes are savagely repeated on a G sharp, and then a solemn slow tune (adagio quasi un poco andante) is given out by the viola in G sharp minor.[1] Its first strain is repeated by the violin, and a second strain, finishing the tune in eight bars, is divided among the instruments and repeated. After this, three more bars move to C sharp minor, and so lead to the finale.

At this point we must survey the keys which have been heard in the course of the work. The fugue may be taken to have established C sharp minor with a firmness beyond the power of any mere introduction. The allegro molto vivace was then able to maintain itself in D major, the flat supertonic, but could not venture far afield, and so had a finalelike second subject that speedily returned to its tonic. The slow movement, in A major, was confined to the key of its theme throughout six-and-a-half variations. It then made the only modulatory purple patch in the whole quartet, by going outside the circle of directly related keys into C major and F major (the pair of keys that are so important in the introduction of the Seventh Symphony). The scherzo was confined to E major and A major.

Now, at last, in the introduction to the finale we have heard the dominant of C sharp minor. And now, at last, it will be, at all events theoretically, possible to cover a wide range of key and have some expansive and argumentative development. Let us see what happens. The finale begins with four bars of a savage tonic and dominant theme in [eighth notes] and [quarter notes]. (We will call this the anapaest theme.) Thereupon follows a wild yet square-cut tune in dotted rhythm and tragically sardonic mood. It occupies sixteen bars, of which the last four are a sad echo, emphasizing D natural (our flat supertonic) in an ominous way. Then follows (over an undercurrent in the sardonic dotted rhythm) a new theme.

We will call it the mournful theme. With its rondolike symmetrical eight-bar shape and its immediate full repetition in the bass, this theme strengthens the conviction that the finale is in no hurry to take action as yet. The anapaest theme reappears below the dotted rhythm and

[1] François Joseph Fétis, the nineteenth-century French musicologist, claims this theme is taken from an old French folk song, a theory which is backed up by the somewhat archaic harmonic texture (such as the F major chord appearing at the end of its second measure, and the flatted second step of the scale in its fourth measure).— Editor.

then pretends that it was part of the sardonic tune which is resumed from its fifth bar. Suddenly, after its twelfth bar, action is taken. In four bars we reach E major (the usual "relative major") and a theme of extraordinary pathos, in dialogue between the instruments, occupies twelve bars of tonic and dominant before it reluctantly moves up first one step, then another, and then tries hesitatingly to come to a close, which is frustrated by the drift of the harmony into F sharp minor. Thus the second subject has occupied only twenty-one bars and has been thoroughly typical of Beethoven's ways in a finale of this kind. The first themes, anapaests and sardonic tune, burst out in F sharp minor, the subdominant. Now if this finale were going to be a rondo, these themes would have entered here in the tonic; and the fact that they are in another key, however closely related, at once convinces us that this is no rondo, but a movement of highly organized development. And after the twelfth bar of the sardonic tune we find the development in full swing. The austere simplicity of its first process may be realized if we [observe] the new counterpoint of rising [whole notes] which accompanies the figure of the sardonic tune.

If this line does not stretch to the crack of doom,[1] it at all events lands us in a key which, though not remote from C sharp minor, is quite incompatible with it. In this key of B minor a new development of the anapaest theme arises. Modulating in seven bars to D it now proceeds in a couple of six-bar periods (thrice two) to land itself on the dominant of C sharp minor. Here, relapsing into four-bar periods (trust your ear, not your eye) it continues for eight bars. Suddenly all trace of any theme vanishes. Beethoven writes *Ritmo di tre battute*, and in this three-bar rhythm the music vibrates grimly on the dominant for twelve bars. Then the recapitulation begins. The vibration still continues above while the anapaest theme is tossed to and fro in the bass. Its four bars are expanded to eight. The sardonic tune, on the other hand, is expanded in another way. It is not allowed to take its original shape, but its first four bars are treated in a tonic and dominant dialogue, with a new counterpoint of semibreves. This occupies sixteen bars which seem much more spacious than those of the original tune. The mournful theme now enters in the subdominant, and we are surprised to find that after its repetition in the bass it drifts into a quiet passage on the last figure of the sardonic theme with a running accompaniment like that of the later stages of the development. And this passage lasts some time: thirteen bars. What does it mean?

It means that the second subject is going to be recapitulated in the flat supertonic! The wheel has come full circle. The whole quartet is a

---

[1] Alternating among the four instruments and changing register, this scale of whole notes actually rises almost three complete octaves from E sharp (harmonized as the leading tone in F sharp minor) to D natural (harmonized as the third of B minor). —Editor.

perfect unity, governed by the results of the initial event of that modified first movement which maintained itself in the flat supertonic after the opening fugue had firmly established the key of C sharp minor. Hence the restraint in the matter of modulation, even in the finale where Beethoven was free to expand in argumentative development. His power of modulation is really unsurpassed even by Wagner, but this fact is generally ignored or disbelieved, because the occasions on which Beethoven exercises the power in any obvious ways are very rare.

We have now reached this wonderful recapitulation in D major. But a more wonderful stroke is pending. The pathetic way in which that second subject wandered into a key a tone higher (originally F sharp minor) leads it here to the dominant of E, and a further similar step leads it to a chord of C sharp major. This, instead of behaving as a dominant, is taken as the tonic major; and the whole subject is recapitulated again. The pathos is enhanced by the fact that the tonic major has never before been heard in the whole work since the end of the first movement. This beautiful gleam of hope and consolation is a typical example of tragic irony; for the ensuing coda is unsurpassed anywhere in Beethoven for tragic power. A detailed analysis would take up too much space and would raise no issues that have not been dealt with to the best of my ability already. Two points must be mentioned. First, the "answer" to the mournful theme is taken up and turned into an emphatic and unmistakable allusion to the first four notes of the fugue. I am generally skeptical about such long-distance resemblances, where the composer has no means of enforcing his point. But here in the C sharp minor quartet he goes out of his way to accentuate his point; the point refers to the very beginning of the work, and not to some transitional passage heard only twice in its course; and not only is the point thus explicable but it has no other explanation. The other matter is the reappearance of the flat supertonic in a shuddering cadential passage that breaks in upon the height of the passion; having no connection of theme with its surroundings, and requiring no such connection.

The forms of Beethoven's last works show, the more we study them, a growing approximation to that Bach-like condition in which the place of every note can be deduced from the scheme. The more the forms differ from each other the more strictly do they carry out their own principles. As to the "strictness" of poor Spohr's projected set of quartets with [trills] at the end of the passages, it compares with the strictness of Beethoven's C sharp minor quartet as railway trains in a fog compare with the stars in their courses.—DONALD FRANCIS TOVEY (11)

The quartet in C sharp minor is the greatest of Beethoven's quartets, as he himself thought. It is also the most mystical of the quartets, and the one where the mystical vision is most perfectly sustained. It counts seven movements, but, regarded as an organic unity, it is the most complete of Beethoven's works. For the purposes of description, however, it is convenient to divide it into three parts. The opening fugue is the most superhuman piece of music that Beethoven has ever written. It is the completely unfaltering rendering into music of what we can only call the mystic vision. It has that serenity which, as Wagner said, speaking of these quartets, passes beyond beauty. Nowhere else in music are we made so aware, as here, of a state of consciousness surpassing our own, where our problems do not exist, and to which even our highest aspirations, those that we can formulate, provide no key. Those faint and troubling intimations we sometimes have of a vision different from and yet including our own, of a way of apprehending life, passionless, perfect, and complete, that resolves all our discords, are here presented with the reality they had glimpsed. This impression of a superhuman knowledge, of a superhuman life being slowly frozen into shape, as it were, before our eyes, can be ambiguous. That passionless, remote calm can seem, as it did to Wagner, like a melancholy too profound for any tears. To Berlioz it was terrifying. To Beethoven himself it was the justification of, and the key to, life. In the light of this vision he surveys the world. That this vision was permanent with Beethoven is inconceivable. No men ever lived who could maintain such a state of illumination. This, we may be sure, is the last and greatest of Beethoven's spiritual discoveries, only to be grasped in the moments of his profoundest abstraction from the world. But it was sufficiently permanent to enable him to write the C sharp minor quartet in the light of it, a feat of concentration, of abstraction, of utter truthfulness, that is without equal. In the light of this experience we arrive, in the next movement, as a new-born creature in a new-born world. The virginal purity of this movement, its ethereal and crystalline quality, suggests to us a spirit not yet made flesh. After a brief introduction, which seems to usher in the act of incarnation, we find ourselves fully present in the warm, familiar human world. And yet how different it has become! The various aspects of experience that make up this human life, surveyed in the variations that follow, all have this different quality. They have the delicacy of shadows, but without their suggestion of impermanence. It is a transfigured world, where both our happiness and our prayers have become more pure and more simple. There is an indescribable lightness in this air; our bonds have become gossamer threads. And after floating through this outspread world we do, at that rapturous outbreak of trills in the last variation, rise up on wings and fly. And it is not only we, but all creation, that seems to be taking part in this exultant stirring. If ever a mystical vision of life has been presented in art it is here, in the sequence beginning with the fugue and ending with the last variation. It is this sequence, more than anything else in Beethoven's music, that

convinces us that he had finally effected a synthesis of his whole experience. In these moments of illumination Beethoven had reached that state
of consciousness that only the great mystics have ever reached, where
there is no more discord. And in reaching it he retained the whole of his
experience of life; he denied nothing. There follows an outbreak of the
most exultant gaiety. There is no trace in the scherzo of anything but
the purest joy. Its most human quality is its humor, but humor so carefree and radiant is scarcely human. The adagio introduction to the finale
has all the quality of a sorrowful awakening. It is as if the whole of the
quartet preceding this movement had been a dream. But that, we are
passionately convinced, cannot be true. The note of complete authenticity in that opening fugue cannot be mistaken. But it is certain that
there is a withdrawal of the vision. It signifies, perhaps, a return from
those heights on which no man may permanently live to this less real
but more insistent world in which we are plunged in the last movement,
a world where a heroism which is also pathetic marches to its end attended by yearning and pain. It may or it may not be of symbolic
significance that Beethoven makes some use of the fugue theme in this
last movement. But the character of the theme, as it occurs here, is entirely changed, and any symbolic significance it may have is not obvious.—
J. W. N. SULLIVAN

d. String Quartet No. 15 in A Minor, Opus 132
I. Assai sostenuto, Allegro; II. Allegro ma non tanto; III. Can-
zona di ringraziamento (Molto adagio); IV. Alla marcia (Assai
vivace); V. Allegro appassionato

Like the piano sonata in A flat major, Opus 110, the whole of this
quartet is a representation in music of the issue of a crisis, in this case
probably a bodily one, since the date of the composition coincides with
Beethoven's illness, lasting from April to August 1825, and serious enough
to necessitate a month in bed.

But, unlike the sonata, this is not a description of a crisis at its height,
ending in a song of triumph; it is, on the contrary, a remembrance of
those terrible hours of pain, and a hymn of thanksgiving to Him in
whose hands is the life of man.

The whole work, in fact, breathes a spirit of deep religious feeling and
filial gratitude.

The introduction, a short phrase of four notes, given out at the start
by the violoncello, provides the master key without which none can
enter the superb edifice which forms the first movement.

This movement, in fact, is cast in a very remarkable form. It consists
of three successive expositions, interrupted by developments of the introductory theme. It is this theme which throws open each chamber of the

palace and gives rise to the appearance of the two constituent ideas, the first of which reflects the memory of the hours of suffering, while the second, in F major, bearing the impress of hopeful charm, combines in its third phrase the rhythm of the initial idea with the rather peculiar harmony of the key phrase of the introduction.

The second entry of this key phrase, blending with the development of the first idea, leads shortly to a second exposition of the two constituent themes, in the dominant; a third, and last, intervention of the key phrase, blended with the development, opens a last door, through which rushes the hopeful theme (second subject) in A major, soon borne along by the theme of suffering, now transformed into a hymn of joy.

Indeed, one need only read through this first movement, so entirely new in form, to be perfectly convinced that Beethoven *knew how to compose!*

A scherzo, in A major, with a pastoral trio—a last echo of some wandering musician's bagpipe—suggests to us once more the still uncertain steps of the convalescent in his first outings.

Then we come to the "Song of Thanksgiving, in the Lydian mode, offered to the Divinity by a convalescent"—a note written in French, in Beethoven's hand, on the autograph manuscript, and translated later, into Italian, at the instigation of some publisher.

At that time, as an aid to the composition of the great *Missa Solemnis,* Opus 123, Beethoven was closely studying the liturgical melodies of the Catholic faith which were to be found in the voluminous library of the Archduke Rudolph, paying special attention to the works of Palestrina.

There is no doubt that to his knowledge of the masters of vocal counterpoint is due that newly found understanding of polyphonic writing which enhances all his later works. We shall not, then, be astonished that the *Chant de reconnaissance* is written in the scale of the *sixth Gregorian mode,* whence the indication: *"en style lydique,"* in *modo lidico* in the Italian translation.

The movement is an example of an aria (lied) in five sections. The hymn is set out at first in four phrases each prepared by a short instrumental prelude; then comes an episode (second section, in D major), treated at some length, wherein the sick man feels his strength returning. Second exposition of the hymn, line by line this time, and, around this line, the orchestral theme, which at first served as a formal prelude, now adds movement and emotion. After a fresh episode (fourth section) indicative of the renewed strength, very closely similar to that of the second section, there is a third strophe of the hymn, but this time it appears only in fragmentary form and leaves all the expressive interest to the instrumental theme, which the composer notes as to be played "con intimissimo sentimento." This theme then becomes the true song of gratitude of the human soul, while the melody of the hymn takes wing to celestial regions. And this indeed is pure Beauty!

A short march, almost military—a sharp contrast—brings us abruptly back to earth, after which a recitative, which lacks only words, comes to give wings to the finale—allegro appassionato, filled with radiant joy and constructed in the old rondo form, which Beethoven consents to revive for this one occasion.—VINCENT D'INDY (2)

Of the three great last quartets, the one in C sharp minor is the most unearthly and serene. The first of them, in A minor, is the least mystical and the one most full of human pain. It is, as a matter of historical fact, connected with a serious illness of Beethoven's and he himself wrote over the slow movement "Heiliger Dankgesang an die Gottheit eines Genesenen, in der lidischen Tonart." Acting on this hint the commentator A.-B. Marx sees in this quartet the description of a physical illness. This idea, as with so many apparently ridiculous "programs" suggested by musical compositions, does, although inadequately, testify to certain genuine perceptions on the part of the commentator. The whole quartet may be taken as illustrating the normal aspect that life presented to the late Beethoven. Witness after witness testifies to the expression of profound sorrow that was habitual with him in the last years of his life, so that in mere contemplation of that dumb countenance the more emotional of them felt moved to tears. As we have said, we believe that in his most profound moments of insight and abstraction Beethoven was granted the solace of a more complete understanding. But such moments must have been comparatively rare, and could have occurred only in the midst of the artist's most profound isolation. We can well believe that no man ever saw the face of the transfigured Beethoven. But we believe that this man had suffered so greatly that the Beethoven men saw was the normal Beethoven of those days, poor, ill, stone-deaf, wretchedly housed, utterly alone, betrayed and abandoned by the one human being whose love he so desperately and pitifully craved. And from the depths of this man rose that solemn, pure and profound song of thanksgiving to the Godhead. The yearning and the pain of the first movement (which ends, as only Beethoven would end, with what sounds like a startling and celestial trumpet call) is but little lightened in the second movement, where there reigns a spiritual weariness which is quite unmistakable. But again there comes that intimation of something celestial in an *alternativo* (that some writers find "curious" and others "humorous"!) where the first violin soars high over a pedal, and then comes the first moment of joy, real joy without any *arrière-pensé*, in the whole quartet. The first part is then repeated; the dominant mood is re-established. From this matrix rises the slow movement, the most heartfelt prayer from the most manly soul that has expressed itself in music. From this pure and sincere communion with his God there comes a quickened life, a rush of celestial joy, in the passage marked "Neue Kraft fühlend." The psychological resemblance between this transition and that in the second movement is obvious. Relief from pain, in this most pessimistic of Beethoven's quartets, comes only from above. Two main experiences form the texture of this quartet, exhaustion and defeat, and the new life bestowed as an act of grace from on high. With this "new strength" the next movement steps forth, but there is a wistfulness in its bravery. This is one of those movements that occur only in the late Beethoven, where the very quality of the heroism reveals the heartache it is intended to conceal. This forlorn and lonely little march is marching to no victory. It is a gesture, brave but pathetic. With the più allegro section our forebodings are realized. Here is a shudder of realization, a resigned and hopeless cry, and we are again in the darkness of the struggle. Great waves of anguish seem to sweep over the struggling soul and at moments it seems that no resolution and faith can prevail against them. But a permanent strength, we may suppose, has come from those earlier celestial visions, from that pure and profound prayer, and the theme which before seemed to strive with difficulty against despair accelerates, until, in the final Presto, it rings out victoriously, but victor in a victory so hard-won that we are left with none of that feeling of exultant triumph with which we have watched so many of Beethoven's victories, but rather with a feeling of slightly incredulous relief, of thankfulness still tinged with doubt.—J. W. N. SULLIVAN

e. String Quartet No. 16 in F, Opus 135
I. Allegretto; II. Vivace; III. Lento assai e cantante tranquillo; IV. "Der schwergefasste Entschluss" (Grave: "Muss es sein?," Allegro: "Es muss sein!")

Beethoven's last quartet, following as it does such masterpieces as the A minor, the B flat, and above all the C sharp minor, is likely at first hearing to make upon us the impression of a lamentable falling off in quality, or at any rate in depth of expression. . . . The predominantly high-spirited finale has been forced to bear on its shoulders three literary tags: the famous *Muss es sein* ("Must it be?"), *Es muss sein* ("It must be"), and heading both the still more enigmatic epigraph, *Der schwergefasste Entschluss* ("The difficult decision"). Here is an invitation to read into the work a mystic significance, a philosophic "message" its innocent and gay music is far from suggesting—an invitation irresistible to devotees of mystery at all costs. . . .

It appears that a certain Dembscher, a rich amateur at whose house the E flat Quartet had been played, wished to give there also the B flat.

As he had failed to subscribe fifty florins, however, for its ill-fated March performance, he was refused the loan of the parts by the composer. He then asked Holz how he could reinstate himself in the master's good graces, and to the suggestion that he begin by paying the fifty florins, replied ruefully: "Must it be?" On learning this through the *Conversation Books*, Beethoven, delighted, at once improvised the words and music of a canon: "It must be! It must be! Yes, yes, yes, yes. Across with the wallet! Across! Across! It must be!¹ The *Es muss sein* theme thus struck out in a moment of amusement, as high-spirited and quite as saucily vulgar as the words, no doubt recurred to Beethoven's mind as often as the joke itself, a stock favorite in the *Conversation Books*. The trivial little motive evidently ran on in his head through the summer, picking up at some undiscoverable time and by some unconscious process its more serious companion. Such is the meager external evidence available.

The internal evidence builds up the picture of a work using already familiar techniques with the accumulated skill of a lifetime, but so far as structural types are concerned, breaking few new paths. From his recent experiments in fugue, in variations, in recitative, in chorale-prelude style, and in the general multiplication of movements, Beethoven returns to the customary four movements in traditional forms. . . .

But if the structures suggest labor-saving conformity to familiar types, there is novelty and powerful originality in the textures. It is in these that the technique of the last quartet makes unprecedented advances. Here Beethoven carries much further than in the B flat that "new manner of voice treatment" he had announced to Holz, vindicating afresh his claim that as artist he "does not stand still," and that each of his latest quartets is great "in its own way." The way now is one of economy hushed to its limits—a Spartan spareness. Utmost brevity is secured by relentless concentration; "big sonorities" disappear; not a note is conceded to luxury; rests are frequent, climaxes infrequent and brief. The essential ideas, reduced to lowest terms, are stated as if in shorthand or a series of graphs.

Already in the terse exposition [of the Allegretto first movement], only sixty-two measures in all, we feel the charm of this economy, both in the simultaneities (chords) and in the successions (themes). Yet in each theme is found room for more than one characteristic motive—in the opening theme for no less than three. This first theme, propounded softly by the viola with sole support of the cello, presents already the interval of a falling fourth that in the *Es muss sein* is to dominate the finale. In this initial form it owes its brooding character not only to the somber tone of the viola, but even more to harmonic progression from

¹ Schauffler's spirited translation, fitted to the music. Schindler gives a different story of the origin of *Es muss sein*, equally trivial; but as he appears to have forged support for it in the *Conversation Books*, its truth may be doubted.

minor subdominant to dominant, with pause there—in suspense. This gives it, as d'Indy remarks, the character of a "question," despite its downward inflection.[1] The little running start of grace notes both emphasizes the initial B flat and supplies, however inconspicuously, the G completing the *Es muss sein* reference. The menacing, almost sinister air of the motive is enhanced by the bareness of the two low voices; had the harmony been "enriched" by the addition of violins, the effect would have been proportionately impoverished. The violins are used instead, as Mies points out, "to bridge polyphonically the halts and rest in the theme."

In the "answers" to this viola question that follow in the three upper instruments, whether they distribute the melody as they first do or combine on it in unison later, there is the same rigor; the harmonies, never fully realized, are outlined or sketched, for the most part in but two voices. Still barer—and in their bareness still more provocative—are the over-all unisons of the third member of the theme, that curious pattern of even quarter notes sounding in a single composite voice the scale steps 5–6–3–2: 6–7–4–3, seeming to breathe some cryptic message. Marked *piano* and heard but once, they leave volumes unsaid, address the mental rather than the physical ear, and by their reticence for the moment promise all the more interest to come.

It may even be questioned whether some of this withheld interest is not realized sooner than we expect. The eight measures of playful badinage with the "answer-rhythm" taken from measure 6, which complete the first theme and lead over to the bridge, seem at first to have no significance beyond their own playfulness. But as we grow more familiar with them, an uneasy sense of some hidden tendency gains upon us—something behind seems to be guiding them. . . .

The second theme, following the brief thirteen-measure bridge, is only sixteen measures over all, yet manages to find room for two contrasting ideas: first, a naïve, almost childish tune in arpeggios; second, two phrases (from measure 46) that for all their brevity sing themselves indelibly into our memories. We cannot but wonder how such unpretentious bits can so intrigue our interest. Partly, no doubt, it is here by the thematic significance of the falling fourth in the melody, recalling in so changed a color the somber fourth of the viola at the start. Partly it is by the use of the suggestive type of texture again: the shorthand that realizes with four instruments only two effective voices implies so much more than it makes explicit that we find our imaginations delightfully provoked. . . .

Here, moreover, the harmony stimulates not only by remaining in-

[1] One may feel with Marion Scott that this phrase is "fatalistically made from the falling fourth of *Es muss sein*" without necessarily following her interpretation of the program to the point of agreeing that "With the very first notes of the first movement . . . the shadow of death lies upon the threshold."

complete but by becoming slightly enigmatic. In his profounder moods, as we have seen, Beethoven clings close to the commonest chords. The coming Lento will demonstrate once again the same instinctive choice. But lighter, more fanciful moods may prompt harmonic adventures further afield. So in this measure 46 he seems to be playing with augmented triads that by their indeterminateness of resolution amuse a composer as puns or plays on words amuse a writer. He may here be experimenting with a procedure that was to become systematic only with Debussy and other users of the even more equivocal whole-tone scale. It need not surprise us to find in so seminal a mind many seeds he could scatter but not wait to see germinate.

After the exposition has ended with a conclusion theme as concise as all its surroundings—only two phrases—supplemented by a few scattering recalls of the "answer-rhythm," development begins in a cryptic passage highly characteristic of the new manner. One pair of instruments after another lays out, as methodically as if they were problems in mathematics, combinations of the curious quarter-note pattern with brief returns of the viola's opening question, clinching the cadences. The pattern is always on the same steps 5–6–3–2: 6–7–4–3, but always from a new pair of players and in a new key: first G, then C, then (by a modulation more lovely than anything less coherent than a theme could effect) C minor to A flat, and finally A flat. These four permutations of two elements arrive by relentless logic at ever fresh and novel charm. For the rest, whenever there is danger at the cadences of stagnation or a sense of thinness, a flash of arpeggio sketches in a harmony as a skilled draftsman will indicate by a single well-placed line a ship, a nose, or a mountain.

The "answer-motive" next reappears, twice brusquely asserted and after pauses coyly completed. Its last three notes, which as early as measure 6 were briefly echoed, are now repeated with more emphasis and even a slight retardation, obstructing momentarily the melodic current, but quickly breaking the dam, so to speak, and foaming into rapids of triplets. These plunge powerfully forward into recapitulation of the viola's opening question, now reinforced canonically by both violins. Similarly the answers return in fuller instrumentation than at first, but still kept within two-voice texture. When the curious unison pattern in turn reappears it becomes, as Alice in Wonderland would say, "curiouser and curiouser," its quarters broken into eighths, so that each of the essential intervals, 5–6–3–2: 6–7–4–3, is attended by a "side note" that masks and disguises it. Thus bent like a stick seen through water, it combines with the "question" to produce stranger effects than ever.

Its final state is reserved for the coda. Here the combinations begin more closely to dot the page, while interjected among them are many of the little running starts of grace notes and flashing harmony-outlining arpeggios—until at the *forte* the grace notes foam downward in a cascade. This too dies away; the questions are asked for the last time on a high, almost hysterical note; and to the answer motive fall the last phrases, precise, deftly dovetailed, starting in the subdominant to give themselves extra elbow-room and enhanced finality, and for emphasis twice enunciating their cadence, like one proudly proclaiming the result of an irrefutable syllogism.

The scherzo, equally playful, seems less spontaneous. Its thematic material pushes frugality to the borderline of poverty. The meager *mi-re-do* violin theme, melodically jejune, saved from dullness only by persistent syncopation, gains little from its cello countersubject wandering up and down the scale. When after the contrast of the unison E flats both subjects return, *forte* and reversed by double counterpoint, cello and viola pounding out the *mi-re-do*'s while violins shriek the countersubject, these bare bones of the design hardly give our minds satisfaction enough to compensate our suffering ears. What saves the situation is the rhythm. Bearing in mind that in so fast a tempo measures become as beats, alternately heavy and light, we see that the theme begins just after a rest on a heavy (an 'empty first') and ends on a light, that is, with a feminine cadence. These delays in both beginnings and endings produce, as phrase follows phrase, elusive dovetailings to which the little piece owes much of its charm. Rhythm and harmony frolic together. The sudden fillip we so relish, for example, at the eighth measure from the end [measure 59], results from the witty repetition of the dominant harmony of the preceding measure, with the rhythmic change that this harmony, formerly suspensive in a light measure, now falls in a heavy, and initiates the final series of feminine cadences. It is the unexpectedness of this shift, almost eluding us as it slips by, that is so fascinating.

The musette trio recalls, with its tunes, the masquerade balls of Beethoven's youth. [It uses] as background a bagpipelike drone and affords the violin gay figures to play across the strings. There [is a] half-crazy humor [in] this headlong Vivace. Here, as if throwing on the rubbish heap all conventions and most traditions, Beethoven seems bent on finding out just how irresponsibly he can improvise on paper.

The new theme releases from the coiled spring of a five-note turn a long, elastic, up-soaring scale, its one wide curve in welcome contrast to the syncopations of the scherzo. Through six measures of tonic chord its staccato notes dance up, like bubbles through still water, from viola and cello depths to violin. Here, tossed across the strings through two measures of dominant, they complete the phrase by overlap into a second one almost its exact fellow. These twin phrases remain entirely in F major as if that were to be the key of the trio as well as of the scherzo. But now some freakish badinage, tossing the five-note turn back and forth between low and high instruments, arrives almost accidentally, as it seems, at the key of G, one melodic step above F, but foreign to it harmonically. Here the bubbling process more or less repeats itself, arriving with equal inconsequentiality at A, another step above the G—and to it foreign! Yet this seems to be what we were aiming at all along; for the business of the bustling phrases now begins in earnest, with frequent interpolations of the five-note turn. And at the *fortissimo* the madcap violin, alone in its glory, begins a wild dance across the strings, backed by its three companions in a unison ostinato that seems as if it would never stop—forty-seven consecutive repetitions of the five-note turn. Sometimes the solo performer seems about to sink in the melee; always his harmonic whereabouts is problematical, as the long tonic seems unarticulated by any cadences; and the sound of the whole conglomeration is not unlike that of a poorly greased wheel. When the long spin begins to lose momentum, gradually runs down, and at last comes to a standstill in triple *piano*, we are more relieved than sorry.

Yet here too works the unquenchable experimentalism of Beethoven's mind. May not the choice of keys in the trio, strange in one to whom tonality was so fundamental an instinct, be simply an experiment suggested by the scherzo theme itself—a reversal of its *mi-re-do* to *do-re-mi*? One might so construe it, especially in view of the counterreversal of the triple piano passage wherein A, G, F steal slyly back.

The Lento, briefest slow movement in the later Quartets, is also unequaled by any of the others in the rigor of its simplicity. All on one tonic, devoid of modulation, varied only by a change of mode quickly canceled, it clings so closely to its sober diatonic theme that Tovey is able to hear and describe it as a set of variations. Its medial *più lento*, however, departs just far enough from the opening to make more plausible d'Indy's division into the statement, contrast, and restatement of a highly concise song form. In any case, its melody and syntax are severe almost to bareness. After a two-measure curtain, a solemn period of ten measures moves soberly along the scale, to reach in its last three measures cadence echoes in Beethoven's last manner. The same period is then repeated in higher register and with intensifications of the harmony—and that is all.

The middle part, still briefer and even more severe, consists of a two-measure echo of the major theme, now minor, an echo of this echo in the theme. This time the opening period is almost literally repeated, but in relative E major, and six measures to get back to the original mode and the bass, with canonic echoes from the violin. The second period, represented only by its underlying harmonies, is commented on by a touching violin obbligato, and consummated by two measures of plagal cadence derived from it. In early hearings so extreme a simplicity may strike us as empty. We may try to account for this fancied "emptiness" by attributing it to its composer's old age, illness, and lassitude—possibly even quoting in testimony his own phrase placed against one of the sketches: *Süsser Ruhegesang oder Friedensgesang:* "Sweet song of rest or peace."

As we hear the music oftener, becoming more at home in it, and above all as phrases from it begin to sing themselves in our minds unexpectedly at odd times, its simpleness may come to seem full rather than empty, strong rather than weak, rich rather than poor. It may grow to reflect for us not the physical exhaustion of old age, but its spiritual breadth of vision, balance, magnanimity. The plainness of its technical procedures may then come to seem necessitated by the impression it is to produce: its parenthetic dominants giving warmth without overemphasis; the diminished sevenths to which they are intensified in the second period (chords notoriously prone to melodrama) all the more eloquent here for their freedom from any taint of excitement; the pauses of the *più lento* made arresting and dramatic without loss of dignity; the violin, as it accompanies the cello's resumption of the main theme, quiet for all its tenderness; its sighing obbligato, full of sentiment, never becoming sentimental; and at the end the gentle cadence, sounding on its third step and light beat as happy as it is timid, remembering the whole journey in resignation and final acquiescence. Viewed from this standpoint Beethoven's notation "Sweet song of rest or peace" takes on a new and deeper significance, and we realize that this slow movement, less dramatic than the greatest of them, is inferior to none of them in essential nobility.—DANIEL GREGORY MASON(2)

Beethoven's last set of variations is the slow movement of the last String Quartet, Opus 135. Here the theme consists of a single strain with echoes. The second variation is in the tonic minor, and takes advantage of the very clear and self-repeating structure of the theme by answering the first two bars in a foreign key, with the result that the following shorter sequences modulate more widely. It is to be hoped that the present comment leaves or restores to the listener enough naïveté to enable him to hear this movement as the perfectly straightforward set of variations which it happens to be. The last variation, like the minor variation, quits the melody of the theme, and can afford to do so, as there is no mistaking the very simple phrasing and harmonies. A slight expansion of the echoing cadences produces enough climax to end the movement almost in the ordinary course of the theme.—DONALD FRANCIS TOVEY(1)

The finale is the hardest of the four movements to understand, even when we abstract, so far as possible, its purely musical elements from the elaborate verbal labels with which Beethoven has encumbered them. It consists of two Allegros built up from the *Es muss sein* motive, introduced by two Graves on the *Muss es sein*; and these Allegros and Graves seem to inhabit musically disparate worlds, with no point of contact save a possible relation between the melodic intervals of their motives, pretty well disguised by contrasting rhythms. In style and expression they stand off sharply from each other. The Allegros, winningly light, gay, even jaunty, with an undertone of irony, maintain the bare textures of the first two movements. The sketch method there developed is pushed toward a limit in the charming little A major second theme beginning at measure 53, called by Dickinson "one of Beethoven's best short tunes," and likened by Marliave to a popular march. . . . Pure quartet style reaches in these Allegros a high point of development at which it is able to suggest through the smallest body the greatest soul.

How disappointing, in comparison, is the opening Grave! After four measures congruous enough in style with the Lento but suggesting in their questions something new and disturbing, we are abruptly plunged into the alien world of opera, a world of frenzied diminished seventh chords punctuated by portentous pauses, in which the questions first grow hysterical, then die away into shuddering silence. The appeal is baldly to nerves rather than to mind or heart. This dichotomy of styles, though it cannot but seem a blemish, may be regarded as the inevitable result of the program. The *Es muss sein*, as we have seen, came to Beethoven spontaneously, in the improvised canon. He had to have a *Muss es sein* to explain and complete it; this he got as an afterthought; and mercifully he made it short in both its appearances, keeping it strictly introductory.

We delight in leaving it behind us, to return in the Allegro to the laconic lightness, the epigrammatic wit, the deft workmanship of the opening movements. Everything goes quickly here. Two statements of the elastic subject suffice to lead to a more flowing countersubject, destined to reveal its full function only in the development section, but serving now as a bridge to A major and the little popular march of Theme II. This in turn is followed, still in A major, by an equally concise conclusion theme in which the *Es muss sein*, to complete the exposition, beats a tattoo as slick as an impudent repartee.

Announced by a fourfold unison on the *Es muss sein* subject, development now begins by combining it, for the first time, with the flowing countersubject already awaiting it. Far more seizing than the *forte* unison, though kept *piano* and later even *pianissimo*, this colloquy holds our interest by its ingenious permutations of the two fragments. As quietude descends on the scene there now steals in the little popular march in a new guise, deprived of even its rudimentary accompaniment, and thus all the more piquantly precise. With the magic of his recreative imagination Beethoven makes from these unpromising ingredients, countersubject and march, a page of indescribable charm. As the momentum of the earlier busy rhythms abates, leaving hardly more than a murmur punctuated by slow pulsations, lower and lower registers accompany darker and darker keys. Starting in D major, we gravitate through G minor and C minor, to settle in F minor where, static in its somber atmosphere and scarcely leaving its tonic chord, violins on their dark G strings, viola and cello on their C's, silhouette the mere ghost of the little march formerly so childishly gay. The eerie magic of this reminiscence is unforgettable in its suggestion of some inarticulate menace, though it hold us but a moment in limbo before a short *crescendo* leads to the second Grave, and so to the recapitulation.

Beethoven has still in store for us a last surprise: one that is highly characteristic of a lifelong devotee of practical joking. As the coda commences and we feel the end approaching, the *Es muss sein* for a moment takes on a serious, even a tender and pondering air. Three times, over provocative harmonies, it is whispered by the violin, and echoed from lower instruments. The third time its harmony becomes almost cryptic, its tempo *poco adagio*. What is about to befall? Some undreamed solemnity, we may fancy, some final mystic revelation. We are wrong. Suddenly, in the original key (hardly expected from what precedes) the little march, stripped for final action, pops up once more, no longer played with the bow, but plucked. So sounded, its notes are hardly longer than its pauses; all have the brevity that is the "soul of wit." Who would have dreamed it could take on so novel a personality? Above the plucking begins a quicker dance, bowed by the first violin; the second, debonair, cries many times on end "It must be"; and all the other voices finally fall in with it as if asserting in grim chorus: "I *told* you! I *told* you! I *told* you so!" All mystical explanations of the motive that reaches thus its gay apotheosis, all vague abstractions, seem merely irrelevant in face of so epigrammatic a deftness as this, a spontaneity so unpredictable and winning. Nearer the mark is Dickinson's conclusion that this final section at least "has no transcendental axe to grind." Rather it seems to be thumbing its nose at us before it slams the door.—DANIEL GREGORY MASON(2)

It so happens that Beethoven's last complete work, the quartet in F major, Opus 135, makes a fitting end to his great series of explorations. It is the work of a man who is fundamentally at peace. It is the peace of a man who has known conflict, but whose conflicts are now reminiscent. This quality is most apparent in the last movement, with its motto "Muss es sein? Es muss sein!" According to Schindler this motto had its origin in a joke but, as used here, it is a summary of the great Beethovenian problem of destiny and submission. But Beethoven had found his solution of that problem, and he treats the old question here with the lightness, even the humor, of one to whom the issue is settled and familiar. There is no real conflict depicted in this last movement; the portentous question meets with a jovial, almost exultant answer, and the ending is one of perfect confidence. The question raised here is, indeed, seen in the light of the profound peace which dominates the slow movement of this quartet. If we may judge from this quartet, it would appear that at the end of his life the inner Beethoven, the Beethoven who expressed himself in music, was content.—J. W. N. SULLIVAN

f. Grosse Fuge in B Flat for String Quartet, Opus 133

It rests with the trained musician with a thorough knowledge of compositional technique to fathom the extraordinarily artistic structure of [Opus 133] in all its details. But the music lover who wishes to carry away a musical impression will also do well to familiarize himself as far as possible with its plan.

The fugue, which is preceded by a special introduction (*overtura*), consists of three main sections along with a coda. Outwardly these three sections,

a. *Allegro*—4/4—B flat major.
b. *Meno mosso e moderato*—2/4—G flat major,
c. *Allegro molto e con brio*—6/8—B flat major,

conform to the movement plan of a sonata. But only outwardly so, as will be seen on closer inspection. The first section presents the homogeneous theme of the entire fugue linked with a "countersubject" (second theme) and represents a normal and complete double fugue. In the *meno mosso e moderato*, a rhythmically altered version of the (principal) theme is treated fugally, wherein we find a new "counterpoint" which dominates the entire section. The third section, which is framed by a short, marchlike passage and its expanded repetition, brings new developments.[1] However, not only a new rhythmical variant of the theme is worked out here, but the theme itself, broken up into smaller fragments as in a sonata, is also treated fugally. Next comes a section employing the "countersubject" of the double fugue, and finally one that recapitulates the *meno mosso*. The decisive point in arriving at a complete understanding of the form is to recognize that, in the *third* section, the tech-

[1] The term "development," unless otherwise indicated, is used with reference to the fugue, i.e., "progression of the theme through the individual voices."

nique of the fugue is merged with sonatalike thematic elaboration. We now grasp in retrospect the secret of the form of the Grand Fugue.

a. Each section consists of a group of "developments" which unite in Section I to form a complete fugue.

b. Sections I and II are in contrast. Section III not only presents new elements but draws from the preceding sections. Above all, it combines sonata-form "development" with fugue-form "developments." *The relationship between the first two sections is that of a first and second "thematic group" (Hauptsatz and Seitensatz).*[1] *The third section bears the same relationship to them as the development section of a sonata.*

This interpretation is further confirmed by the fact that between the close of Section II and the coda, we find quotations from Sections I and II—the sketched suggestion of a recapitulation.

OVERTURA

The *Overtura* forms not only the organic fundament of the entire work, but at the same time an interesting general heading by stating the most important versions of the theme. First [the theme appears] with tremendous emphasis, in heavy *fortissimo* dotted half notes (one to a bar) sounding in three different octaves at once. A second version, which follows an exciting *fermata*, requires only a simple *forte*, in keeping with its [giguelike] rhythmical movement. The repetition of this theme effects the modulation to F major (the dominant key of B flat) where we now find the third version of the theme with harmonic accompaniment [in quarter notes and legato]. In the repetition, it is counterpointed with the [sixteenth-note] motif that appertains to it later in the working out. If here the theme is heard in a yearning *piano*, in the fourth version it is stated in a timid *pianissimo*, [on the weak beats of the measure]. But it is this version that will soon undergo a hard battle in the double fugue, which now begins.

FUGUE
Allegro

(Section I, double fugue). At this point the theme can hardly hold its own against the first stormy countersubject, especially since the other

---

[1] The *Hauptsatz* is the first section of the exposition which establishes the tonic key. It opens with the principal theme (1. *Thema*), but in movements of larger dimension contains more than just the principal theme (the working out of motifs of the principal theme, new ideas, cadences, etc.). It extends to the beginning of the "modulatory part." The *Seitensatz* is the section in the contrasting tonality. It contains (with Mozart and Beethoven but rarely with Haydn) the contrasting second theme *Seitenthema*), but can likewise contain more than the second theme itself. It extends to the beginning of the closing group (Epilogue or *Schlussgruppe*); that is, in cases in which a closing group is distinguishable as a special section. With Beethoven the closing group usually reverts to the motifs of the principal theme but can also employ new material (as frequently occurs with Mozart). The closing group should not be confused with the coda, which with Beethoven and at times with Haydn and Mozart also, is the section immediately following the recapitulation.

voices powerfully support the [dotted] rhythm of the countersubject. The conjoined pair of themes runs through the four voices (first development); then a fifth entry of the theme closes the "exposition." A change to E flat major introduces the "modulatory part," which comprises two developmental sections.

Owing to the continued *fortissimo* of the conflict between the two themes, an increase in effect (*Steigerung*) can be achieved only by quickening the pace. At the beginning of the second development section, the counterpointed voices oppose the themes with a triplet rhythm. In the third development, the rhythm [of continuous alternation of one eighth note and two sixteenth notes] is even more lively (simultaneously with a rhythmical variant of the theme). In the battle of the episodes the first theme seems to go under completely. Only its rhythm maintains itself stoutly against the superior force (bass leaps over three octaves!) but it gains renewed strength and also holds its own against the hostile theme in the fourth development, which brings us to the closing section. In a last rush of excitement, the themes scurry by at redoubled speed, now compressed into two bars as compared with the previous four. Furthermore, the "countersubject" is in triplet rhythm. In the coda the "countersubject" triumphs in the end. But now the picture changes. A modulation to G flat major leads to the:

Meno mosso e moderato

(Section II, likewise a double fugue). A [sixteenth-note] motif [in G flat] derived from the (principal) theme prepares the entry of one of those wonderful melodies that only the Beethoven of the last period could write. Accompanied harmonically at the beginning, the melody is revealed as "counterpoint" to the fugue theme [which appears in the ninth measure]. But this "counterpoint" dictates the character of the entire section, although the fugue theme, in keeping with all the rules of the art, is worked out here. In a unison of all four voices, the "counterpoint" then has the last word in this lyrical section of the work.

Allegro molto e con brio

(Section III). The treatment of the fugue theme (in the [giguelike rhythmical version, 6/8]) would lead one to believe that a fugue were in the making (entry as *dux* and *comes*). But nothing comes of it. A contrapuntal motif is developed freely to a stirring, triumphant marching air around which in turn the theme now eddies contrapuntally. We know what marching airs mean with Beethoven. A battle is in the offing. There is an energetic shift from B flat major to A flat major and then the fugue theme in its mightiest form (as it first appeared in the introduction) enters threateningly in the bass. Desperate cries [in the 6/8 rhythm] answer it. After the first development, the fugue theme breaks to pieces in the battle. Its members continue to fight on independently, the first half during the second development and the second half during the third development with its galloping inrush of triplets. The first violin, which tries to carry the theme above a fearful organ point, trills over a *stretto* of the lower voices, and the triplets, which assume more and more the form of the fugue theme, rush by. The [original] "countersubject" (now changed to 6/8 rhythm) of the double fugue is announced with a soft signal call. The "countersubject," which tests its mettle victoriously in this contest, now crosses swords with the remaining portions of the great fugue theme, which arm themselves for the last battle with a *stretto* of all four voices.

Meno mosso moderato [2/4]

"Feeling new strength," as it were, the fugue theme now raises its head in a movement corresponding to the first *meno mosso*, though differing from it greatly in character. The soft, delicate G flat major has given place to the lusty energy of A flat major.

Allegro molto e con brio

The return of the march signals the end of the battle. The movement is spun out longer this time. It pauses a moment in mystical reflection and then fades away softly, in a mood of deep spiritual inwardness.

Allegro, meno mosso e moderato

Here we find the aforesaid quotations of the two first sections, but as already pointed out they have another sense than the outwardly similar "reminiscence motif" of the Ninth Symphony (aphoristic recapitulation).

Allegro molto e con brio

(The coda.) Here the theme is stated in the first version, which is now revealed as the primordial and principal form, but in an expanded, triumphant configuration in the bright key of E flat major answered by the quiet 6/8 version of the theme. A mystical mood, over an organ point (*stretto* in the upper voices)—a breath-taking transition. Triumphant and yearning, joyous and pleading at the same time, the "countersubject" now surges up in the octave doubled bass, carried by the first theme and accompanied harmonically by an inner voice. A conclusion of overpowering majesty and exhalting ethos.

A great deal more might be said about the Grand Fugue, but only to one who has the wonderful score before him.—LUDWIG MISCH

IV. "BEETHOVEN's *letzter Gedanke*," WoO 62 (FROM AN UNFINISHED STRING QUINTET)

In September 1824, Beethoven wrote two different letters to Diabelli concerning the completion of a quintet. In the one he promised the quintet in a little over six weeks for one hundred gold ducats; in the other he promised a flute quintet. Nothing more is known of a quintet at the time. But in November 1826, according to Nottebohm, there were sketches for the first movement of a string quintet in C major on a page originally to be used for the new finale of Opus 130. There were also sketches for other movements. Holz told Jahn that the first movement of a quintet in C for strings, which Diabelli had bought for one hundred ducats, was finished in the composer's head and the first page written out. In the catalogue of Beethoven's posthumous effects No. 173 was "Fragment of a new Violin Quintet of November 1826, last work of the composer." Diabelli's firm bought the twenty-four-measure fragment and published it in pianoforte arrangement, two and four hands, with the title "Ludwig van Beethoven's last Musical Thought, after the original manuscript of November 1826," and the remark "Sketch of the Quintet which the publishers, A. Diabelli and Co., commissioned Beethoven to write and purchased from his relics with proprietary rights. . . . The published work is a short movement in two divisions, having a broad theme of a festal character, andante maestoso and a polonaise rhythm.[1]—ALEXANDER WHEELOCK THAYER, EDITED BY ELLIOT FORBES

V. *Kleines Stück* IN A FOR 2 VIOLINS, WoO 34

At Breslau, [Alexandre] Boucher[2] changed his itinerary[3] and went to Austria. He did not wish to give up the opportunity of visiting the renowned Beethoven, to whom he had [several] letters of introduction. On his arrival at Vienna, he knocked on the door of the modest dwelling where the great musician lived. A servant told him that Beethoven was not at home.

"At what time might I see him?"

"It is impossible to say."

Boucher left one of his letters of introduction with the servant and left.

---

[1] It appears to be part of a consciously old-fashioned (baroque) overture. There are, however, glimpses of the late Beethoven such as a "nonmodulation" from E minor to a fortissimo C major chord, and a false harmonization of the repeat of the second theme.—Editor.

[2] French violinist (1778-1861); friend of Spohr; somewhat of a charlatan, but an international star. His wife, too, was an accomplished musician.—Editor.

[3] Concert tour during the winter of 1821-22.—Editor.

Next day, he was not satisfied and left a second letter. He returned that evening without success, and left a third letter, and each of the following days he did the same. Beethoven, [evidently,] conscientiously threw into the wastebasket all the letters which his servant delivered to him from M. Boucher, despite the fact that they were signed by dukes, princes, music publishers, or financiers, all of whom had the same value to him [Beethoven]. But hardly had he scanned the sixth letter when he seized his hat and left like a madman in search of Boucher. That letter was written and signed in the handwriting of his good friend Goethe.[1] A protégé of Goethe's could not, in his eyes, be a mere opportunist. He must be a great artist. Wishing to see him immediately, he rushed to [Boucher's] hotel and met on the way the dramatic composer Salieri.

"Find me," he said [to Salieri], "the violinist Boucher, the protégé of my friend Goethe, and bring him to my lodgings. I won't budge from home until I have seen him!"

Salieri had no trouble finding him and took pleasure in accompanying him as far as Beethoven's house; on the way, he took from his pocket a canon, which, he said, he had composed the previous night and which he would be delighted to try out with him, and in the middle of the street the two of them proceeded to sing the canon.

[After several other distractions] Boucher finally arrived at Beethoven's residence, where he was received with open arms and invited to listen to his latest compositions. To this end, the Maestro asked the violinist to enter with him into a large acoustical box which he had constructed because of his deafness, and which completely enclosed the auditors. It was there, tête-à-tête with the great genius, that Boucher had the privilege of hearing played the overture to *Prometheus*, a passage from *Fidelio*, and several symphonies [sic!] extraordinarily pretty. The violinist, in his admiration, asked Beethoven permission to give him a lock of his [Beethoven's] hair, and begged him to write for him several lines of music. Beethoven complied with both requests and immediately jotted down his momentary inspiration [a short seven-measure piece for two violins in A major, 4/4], which he followed with these simple words: "*Ecrit le 29 avril 1822, lorsque M. Boucher, grand violon, me faisait l'honneur de me faire une visite,*" and signed it "Louis van Beethoven." However, he must have realized that, although he was thoroughly conversant with the French language, he had written these few words very hastily and he had confused the words *faisait* and *de faire*, for he erased *faisait*, replacing it by another word; and in turn erased that and finally superimposed the passage so thoroughly with his jerky handwriting that it became illegible.—GEORGE VALLAT (TR. BY THOMAS K. SCHERMAN)

[1] See essay on Beethoven's relationship to Goethe. Theirs was hardly a close friendship!—Editor.

VI. *Kleines Stück* IN A FOR 2 VIOLINS (AN INSTRUMENTAL CANON), WoO 35

Otto de Boer was a member of the Academy of Fine Arts in Amsterdam. To gain an audience with Beethoven, he probably had used his predicate as a member of this academy, which had already elected Beethoven as one of its honorary members. This man from Holland must have diverted the composer with his broken German, which looks no more comical in the Conversation Book than it must have sounded; but a canon without words which he carried away with him on August 3 may be said to bear witness to the fact that he made a good impression on Beethoven, to whom he gave information concerning the state of music in Holland.— ALEXANDER WHEELOCK THAYER, EDITED BY ELLIOT FORBES

Piano Sonatas

I. PIANO SONATA No. 28 IN A, OPUS 101

Etwas lebhaft, und mit der innigsten Empfindung
Lebhaft, marschmässig
Langsam und sehnsuchtvoll; Geschwind, doch nicht zu sehr und mit Ent-schlossenheit
(Composed probably in 1815 and 1816; published February, 1817, as "Sonate für das Hammer-Klavier"; dedicated to the Baroness Dorothea Ertmann.)

The space of only a year between Opus 101 and its predecessor, Opus 90, seems surprising as the two are compared. Each is as subtly handled as its ripe year would suggest, but the earlier one, with its easy sentiment, and leisurely amplitude, is backward-looking, while the A major Sonata shows the composer on his mettle. Fantasy, while lightly lyrical, can reach boldly toward a new expressive mold. Perhaps the dedications are a sign of what Beethoven thought of each—the first as suitable for a Count in love, the second for the far more expert and discriminating Dorothea von Ertmann.[1] The Sonata in F sharp major (Opus 78), though written in

---

[1] Beethoven's "Dorothea-Cäcilia," as he called her, was accounted a pianist of great distinction, a bond which helped to cement a long friendship. Mendelssohn, meeting the Baroness and her military husband years later as an elderly couple, had this anecdote from her which he related in a letter: "When she lost her last child, Beethoven at first did not want to come into the house; at length he invited her to visit him, and

1809, six years before, is decidedly more akin to Opus 101, and this little Sonata, be it remembered, was dedicated to the sensitive intellectual, Therese von Brunswick. Like this one, and unlike the sonata which complimented the affianced Count Moritz Lichnowsky with commodious periods of romantic melodiousness, Opus 101 draws carefully aside from all ruts of comfortable custom and takes a distinctive course, cultivating conciseness. The first movement occupies two pages. The second, "march-like," but by no means heavily shod, is soon over by its tempo. The *Adagio* consists of nineteen measures. The *finale*, with its fugal development, is a movement of normal length—and more than normal moment. As in Opus 27, 53, 57, or 81a, the finale is the substance and climax toward which the earlier movements lead. Beethoven makes his points with delicacy and constant variation, never lingering over them; it is a sonata, in a word, which asks for alert listening. The usual segments of sonata form can be discovered in the first movement, but they are not rhetorically ushered in; the articulation is so close that the joints are scarcely perceived. The movement is a fluent whole, its melodic idea continuously changing, maintaining its character by a constant rhythm.[1] There is no contrasting theme. The dominant serves to bring in a syncopation of the rhythm. The second movement replaces the usual scherzo with the first of the "march" episodes to which Beethoven would twice again turn in his last years.

The rhythm has a resemblance to the key rhythm of the first movement, but its swiftness changes graceful pulsation to a springing activity. Only the trio, with its canonic imitations, relieves the rhythmic persistence. The *Adagio* is introductory, but instead of mere chordal harmonies proposes a melodic phrase of great beauty in A minor, with a *gruppeto* which, with the economy and directness characteristic of the whole Sonata, develops in a few measures a momentary intensification of the until now even mood. A cadenza suggests a new disclosure, but first makes a parenthetical, dreamy allusion to the opening of the Sonata, with a hold after each phrase.[2]

But the poetic reflections are swept aside. The finale proper puts its proposition with hard clarity and vigorous assertion. This was not a fugue finale, with its problem of style contradiction still to be solved, but a regular sonata-form movement with a fugue planted in the development.

when she came he sat himself down at the pianoforte and said simply: 'We will now talk to each other in tones,' and for over an hour played without stopping. She remarked: 'He told me everything, and at last brought me comfort.' "

[1] It was surely in such movements as this that Wagner found his delightful expedient of using a rhythmic *ostinato* as a loom for unbroken melodic strands and a constant variegation of color.

[2] The direct reference to an earlier movement was an innovation. A similar incident is to be found in the C major Cello Sonata, Opus 102, written at the same time.—Editor.

The hybrid justifies itself with exciting results. The exposition, in double counterpoint, predicts weighty doings, which presently come to pass. Tovey once aptly remarked that the fugue style and the sonata style are as different as a court trial and a stage scene. The one is a closely worded, narrowly conditioned procedure; the other free and open for the interplay of contrast, stress and subsidence, every device of which drama is made. But a highly charged trial scene placed within a play, and cunningly set off, becomes its crux. So, too, a fugue within a sonata movement. This fugue in four voices, having excitingly clinched its contrapuntal argument, gives way to a free recapitulation and coda, where chordal clarity returns with heightened effect.—JOHN N. BURK (1)

II. PIANO SONATA NO. 29 IN B FLAT, OPUS 106 (*"Hammerklavier"*)

Apropos of this work, composed in 1818–19, one may quote a declaration Beethoven was fond of making: "What I have now written bears no resemblance to what I wrote in the past: it is *a little better!*" Again, in 1817, speaking of the Septuor Opus 20, he declared, "At that time I knew nothing about composition. Now I am a composer." At the age of 47 he felt himself completely master of his craft. His natural musical talent had been trained and developed to such an extent that he felt he had at his disposal a technique adequate for the thoughts and feelings which clamored for expression.

The so-called Hammerklavier[1] sonata, which Beethoven himself considered the finest pianoforte work he had yet produced, is so rich in characteristics of the third period that it is worthy of a somewhat closer analysis than we have given the others.

1st Movement: *Allegro: Bb major: Sonata Form.*

The opening theme occupies the first sixteen bars, to the beginning of bar 17. Comparing it with the first subjects of the earlier sonatas, we are at once struck by its terrific concentration. The generator of the whole is the first two bars, [with a propulsive upbeat in the bass, a sweeping leap of over two octaves, and the first bold announcement of the characteristic rhythms which will dominate the entire movement]. These [two bars] are repeated with the melody a third higher. The continuation is developed from the [rhythm and falling figure of the second half of that opening motive]. Its more melodic style contrasts well with the first thought, while unity is preserved by its derivation. We have thus an example of Beethoven's favorite principle of opposing ideas (masculine and feminine, as we might call them) making its presence felt in one and the same theme.

---

[1] It is not impossible that Beethoven was prompted to compose this sonata by a pianoforte which he received about this time from John Broadwood.

[When that lyric continuation reaches its logical conclusion with a cadence in the tonic key,] a "transition" of huge proportions commences. It continues [for forty-six bars], and is thus nearly three times as long as the first subject. At first sight this would seem ill-judged, but we shall find it so logically developed from the first subject that it is not so. It is in three sections. The first, [with proud chords carrying the melody in the right hand accompanied by a vigorous repeated chord accompaniment,] is related to [the opening measure of the movement] and, after some rapid modulations, reaches the dominant F. The second part starts by restating [the characteristic opening motive, but] repeating it in an altered form [with the insistent rhythm being hammered out] in the chord of D major, dominant of G. The continuation is clearly suggested by [the upward leap of the main subject] and the rhythm leading to the next section, [an upbeat of two eighths, is clearly derived from its characteristic rhythm] and reappears in the third section and also in the second subject.

The third section is a long [flowing] passage in dominant harmony in the key of G.

The second subject overlaps the end of the transition, beginning in the bass [in the key of G major]. The second section of the second subject emphasizes dominant harmony up to [a graceful falling arpeggio figure in the right hand], after which it modulates toward the subdominant (C). At [its climax] the rhythm [of the main subject] appears, [fortissimo,] in C major treated imitatively, after which a return is made to G major, a full close in that key overlapping the entry of the third part of the second subject (coda). The latter for the most part emphasizes tonic harmony in G. The first part is a cantabile passage which is of the nature of a plagal cadence (with the *minor* subdominant chord, however) followed by a perfect cadence.

The conclusion is a more animated passage ending in repetitions of tonic and dominant harmonies in G.

A link based on [the upward leap and the characteristic rhythm of the main subject] leads to the repetition of the exposition. It will be noticed that Beethoven's treatment of the exposition of a movement in sonata form is here quite different from that to be found in the sonatas of the second period. Instead of waiting till after the exposition to develop his themes, he starts to develop them right away. It is as if they have an inherent vitality of their own, and set forth adventuring as soon as they are born. Though we have used the conventional labels, 1st Subject, Transition, 2nd Subject, and so on, the whole of the music is so closely knit, so much an efflorescence from the germinal ideas, that the usual labels seem an impertinence.

After the repetition of the exposition further development takes place. First the link with the exposition G, A, B is repeated a third higher, then a curtailed version of [the concluding phrase] leads to the key of E♭ major (through C minor), in which key the three-note link is repeated twice. Then follows canonic treatment of a subject based on [the movement's opening two measures], in two, then three, then four parts, in E♭ and related keys. This form of development continues till [a climax] is reached [on the chord of G major]. At this point two rhythms derived from [the opening motive] are introduced [alternating fortissimo statement of one with a piano statement of the other]. These seem to enter into conflict throughout this passage, the [first] rhythm ultimately proving victorious, being left emphasizing dominant harmony of G.

We are suddenly plunged into B major, [the cantabile portion of the second subject] appearing in that key. [It is followed by] an embellishment [of itself] in eighth notes against the constant triplets in the left hand, leading to dominant harmony. An allusion to the opening theme appears in F♯ major, and is imitated in stretto. This figure is gradually condensed, its last notes dropping off till we are left with the rhythm alone, which leads naturally to the recapitulation, a modulation to the dominant of B♭ having been carried out during the process of condensation.

If the harmonies of the development section be studied closely, it will be found that an underlying principle appears, viz. the alternation of passages remaining more or less in one tonality with passages of more or less rapid modulation through several keys.

The recapitulation introduces still further developments. Right at the beginning the principal subject is accompanied by a figure [in the left hand which is closely linked rhythmically to the theme itself]. This gives additional verve and makes the continuation the most natural thing in the world. The modulation to G♭ is new, and consequently the transition takes on a new color. Starting in G♭ major, it leads to B (C♭) minor for its second section and the dominant of B♭ for its third. These darker harmonies throw the second subject into strong relief when it enters in B♭ major. Its three sections occur without much modification, and lead to a coda which consists of a further development of (1) [the concluding theme] characterized by rapid modulation, (2) the third section of the second subject, and (3) [the opening motive,] which is treated fragmentarily, first modulating out of the tonic key, then returning and remaining in dominant and tonic harmonies.

This whole movement is a colossal example of economy of means and variety of resource. None but Beethoven could have written it: it bears the stamp of his personality in every bar.

2nd Movement: *Scherzo: Assai vivace: B♭ major: Ternary Form.*

The first part of this movement is developed from the opening sentence of seven bars [characterized by a rising figure in dotted rhythm as an upbeat, and a falling figure of two even quarters].

The contour of the melody shows that this consists of two three-bar phrases, followed by two cadence chords. The affinity between this theme and the opening of the first movement is evident. [The opening sentence is repeated an octave higher and is followed by a second sentence (also repeated an octave higher) ending with] two repeated B♭'s.

The middle section in B♭ minor is more melodic in character, its long rhythmic sweep contrasting well with [the opening section] while its rising and falling thirds provide a unifying feature. [Eight bars later it] is treated in canon at the octave, the melody being implicit in the triplets of the right-hand part.

After a repetition in the relative major an episodical presto in duple time begins in B minor; it modulates to F minor and back again. A repetition of this (ff, in chords) ends in dominant harmony and leads to a short cadenza, after which [the opening section] returns with a texture rhythmically richer.—A. FORBES MILNE

The coda [of the scherzo] opens with the following process of eight bars. [The two repeated octaves] on the final tonic [are] softly answered by the impertinent suggestion, "I think you mean B♮." The B♭ indignantly reasserts itself. The B♭ says, "Oh, very well; but I suppose you are really A♯ so [the opening rising and falling motive of the main theme] will kindly turn itself into B minor, and I shall remain where I am." A ritardando during these last four bars indicates some hesitation; and in another four bars of presto in [duple] time the B♮ breaks out in panic, losing its rhythm and rising in octaves, and finally collapsing on B♭ after all. So it was not the B♭ that was really A♯, but the B♮ which was really C♭; in other words, the perfectly respectable [flattened supertonic.] But [the allusion to the opening motive] had certainly gone into minor, not major.

B♭ and triple time being restored, [the rising and falling opening] figure concludes the whole matter, rising three octaves and accompanied by [a] rhythmic click in the inner voice. This inner voice descends below the bass, making the final tonic [of the movement] a 6/4 chord; but the progression of the true bass leaves the ear perfectly satisfied.— DONALD FRANCIS TOVEY (9)

3rd Movement: *Adagio sostenuto: F♯ minor: Sonata Form.*

In *The Rhythm of Modern Music* Mr. Abdy Williams refers to this movement as "a long contemplative Adagio of a character so noble, so elevated, so dignified, that it could only have been written by a composer who was completely out of touch with the everyday world, whose thoughts were entirely occupied with the highest expression that music is capable of. . . . It is the expression of a lofty soul communing with itself, wandering in a region of sound that existed in his brain, and made accessible to ordinary mortals by a genius so transcendent, so grand, as occurs only once in many centuries."

M. d'Indy also bears testimony to the wonderful elevation of this movement. "One might affirm with perfect justice," he says, "that he who did not feel himself moved to the depths of his soul by such a manifestation of sublime beauty, was not worthy of the name of musician."

It is impossible to convey by mere words the effect of this amazing music. There are moments when Beethoven soars to heights of sublimity which are so far removed from the emotional plane of ordinary men that it is only on rare occasions, when one is for the moment "in the spirit," that one can savor their ineffable beauty.

The first theme of the Adagio occupies twenty-seven bars (the first two notes, added later, form a "preliminary" bar).[1] A noteworthy feature is the transitory modulation to G major [in the second phrase], so unexpected, original, and strangely beautiful. A return to the key of F♯ is made through the first inversion of the chord of G major (Neapolitan 6th in F♯). Just as in melody, chromatic notes are used decoratively between diatonic notes, so here this modulation is used between diatonic harmonies. It is an extension of the use of the Neapolitan 6th as a point of color between two diatonic chords.

At [its conclusion] an expressive melody enters which fulfills the function of a transition, gradually leading to the key of D. It grows out of what precedes it quite naturally.

The second subject enters in the key of D major (submediant), quiet and consolatory. [It consists of the quiet falling outline of the triad, first in the depths of the keyboard and then in the brighter upper register.] This is continued by another [rising] theme accompanied by rich polyphony of a kind favored by Beethoven in his latest works. The harmony in this section is in a state of flux, but ultimately D major tonality is reached and the final section appears.

A short development of the opening theme with the "preliminary" bar in the bass leads, through C♯, E♭ (D♯), G♯ minor, and D♯ minor, to the dominant of F♯ minor, in which key the first subject reappears in full, highly decorated in [thirty-second notes] (cf. Adagio of the Ninth Symphony).

The transitional melody starts in D major, but leads to F♯ major, in which key [the falling outline of the major triad, first in the bass and then in the treble,] reappears followed by the rest of the second subject in due course.

[1] See Ernest Newman's discussion of this added bar.—Editor.

At [the close of the recapitulation] the "preliminary bar," [coupled with the first true bar of the opening theme], occurs in B minor and starts a coda in which further development of [the second subject] occurs in G major, modulating to dominant harmony of F♯, in which key [the main theme] appears and forms the basis of the rest of the coda, which ends with the tonic major chord (tierce de picardie).— A. FORBES MILNE

The strangest case of [Beethoven's] unconscious urge toward an up-beat commencement in certain circumstances is that of the adagio of the *Hammerklavier* sonata. Beethoven's pupil Ries tells us of his astonishment at a letter he received one day in 1819 from Beethoven. The huge sonata was already engraved, and Ries was daily expecting the announcement of its publication, when Beethoven wrote to him that a bar containing the two notes A and C sharp was to be prefixed to the bar with which the adagio had commenced. "Two notes to be added to so great and so carefully wrought a work, six months after it was completed!" says Ries in amazement. He could not know, as we do, how subject Beethoven was to the unconscious in him. The original impulse to add a "curtain," as Hugo Riemann aptly calls a preliminary bar of this kind, had probably been suppressed during the composition of the adagio. But though suppressed it could not be killed; and when at last it rose into Beethoven's upper consciousness he *had* to add the upbeat bar, even though the sonata was then on the point of being published.—ERNEST NEWMAN

4th Movement: *Largo: Modulating Introduction*

The purpose of this Largo is simply to find its way down a series of descending thirds until the right key for the finale has been reached. (For purposes of analysis, Beethoven's groups of four sixteenth notes may be treated as a bar.)

The process starts with a five-octave F. After the key of the slow movement (G flat) this is a leading note, which will presumably turn into a dominant. From it mysteriously syncopated triads descend in thirds. Halts are called at four significant places, and the situation debated at each.[1]

At "bar" 5 the descending thirds have reached G flat. This was the key of the slow movement. Three voices, with a hesitating little subject for imitation, explore the key for four "bars," but see no way out.

The steps are resumed. Two of them arrive at C flat. Whether this is C flat or B natural (as written), it is a semitone above the required mark, and two voices discuss it canonically in running figures with some anima-

[1] The editor has taken the liberty to divide Tovey's short essay into paragraphs for easier assimilation.

tion. In their seventh "bar" they move to its dominant chord and pause there. It closes onto B again, and another step is taken.

Bother! This lands us in G sharp minor (A flat minor) which is absolutely contrary to our purpose. The debating voices brace themselves up into strict common time, and explore the key with a new theme.[1] After three bars of two-part discussion, two more voices crowd in, to bring the question to a head, the key having been thoroughly explored with its subdominant and even its [flattened supertonic].

A pause cuts the debate short on the dominant. The steps are resumed from G sharp. In three steps we reach A. This is promising. It is a semitone below the mark; but that means a leading tone. The A fills five octaves (like the F at the beginning), and a leisurely recitative descends over a dominant chord, filling two bars of irregular slow common time, with sustained pause.

Now let us continue. The steps continue without interruption in pairs at the end of every second four-sixteenth-note "bar." After eight steps why are we not in sight of our goal? We must have taken a wrong turning! Hurry up! Here is D; let us break the circle and jump down a fourth instead of a third to A again.

(Prestissimo.) Ah! there was our mistake; from A we must drop a *major* third, not a minor. Here we are on F, knowing at last that it is the required dominant!—DONALD FRANCIS TOVEY (9)

Fugue a tre voci, con alcune licenze

The subject of the fugue starts with a leap recalling the opening of the first movement, [followed by descending scales in sixteenth notes and a modulating passage also in sixteenths. It is eleven bars long and overlaps with the first *answer*.] The three "voices" enter in turn, the *answer* having a definite countersubject against it, which reproduces the characteristic leap, [followed by a gentle motive in eighth notes. After the third voice has stated the theme,] an episode occurs based on the [sixteenth notes] of the subject and [the rhythm] of the countersubject. This leads from the key of B flat to D flat [eleven bars, later] in which key [the fugue theme] enters in the bass.

The next episode is based on the [eighth notes] of the countersubject and the [sixteenth notes] of the main subject, and modulates to G flat. Examples of double counterpoint occur during this episode. A new [flowing] figure is heard in G flat major and developed by imitation. This carries out a modulation to its relative minor (E flat). At [this point] the subject enters in augmentation in E minor in the bass, the upper part being derived from [the countersubject].

After a cadence in D flat the previous material is developed till a new

[1] In the manner of a Bach toccata.—Editor.

[cantabile] theme [in quarter notes and half notes] occurs in B minor against [the main subject] "cancrizans" (backwards). This is inverted freely and joined by the [countersubject]. After further development of fragments of [the main subject], the latter enters in D major (shortened), and is answered by inversion in G major, [first] in the treble and [then] in the inner part.

An episode follows based mostly on the subject and ending in A major.

A [totally] new idea is presented fugally in D major, [a dolce theme which alternately falls and rises on the steps of the scale]. This forms the basis of the next twenty-eight bars, leading to B flat, when it is combined with part of [the main subject]. A free inversion of this follows and leads to a stretto in which [the main subject] inverted (in the bass) is combined with [the same subject] direct (in the treble) in the key of F. This is then repeated in B flat with the inverted version *above* the other. Then follows further development in which almost every conceivable device of imitation and inversion is displayed. [At the climax of this passage] several partial entries of [the main subject] occur [fortissimo], but it is not till [thirteen bars later] that a fairly complete entry appears, leading to a double (tonic and dominant) pedal point.

The conclusion, after a poco adagio, consists of the [sixteenth-note] figure from the subject followed by emphatic repetitions of the shake figure, and a final cadence.

Certainly this is a fugue con alcune licenze: it bears little resemblance to the academic type! It is a gigantic example of the form rich, indeed overrich, in technical devices. As Sir Henry Hadow says, it "would be a vigorous and forcible piece of eloquence if it would ever allow us to forget that it is a fugue: we can hardly catch its meaning for the strettos and inversions and other laborious devices of the counterpoint school." The fact is that Beethoven at this time was very much occupied with the older contrapuntal forms. He felt that therein lay a possibility of enriching the sonata. He sought in some way to effect a fusion of the sonata and the fugue. In the last movement of Opus 101 the development section is completely monopolized by a fugue based on the main subject of the movement. The result is unsatisfactory, the fugue sounding merely a gratuitous addition to a sonata movement. Here he goes to the other extreme, the fugue is everything, there being little to suggest sonata principles (though there is a resemblance to rondo form in the use of two episodes on new material). The problem of fusion is satisfactorily solved.—
A. FORBES MILNE

Beethoven's nonproductivity during the years 1810–17 was only partly due to "external storms." His nonproductivity was not absolute, but none of his greatest works were originated and matured during this period.

Such works, in the case of Beethoven, always sprang from some profound and mastered experience. The same root experience could serve as the spiritual content of many different works, for any such experience is rich in aspects and may be explored from many points of view. Thus both the Eroica and C minor symphonies are inspired by the same root experience, but they are entirely distinct works of art. Such an experience is really composed of many elements which can be formed by the artist into different organic wholes. So far as the inner history of Beethoven's non-productive years are concerned we may regard them as occupied by the as-similation of another root experience, an experience which, by the nature of the case, could only gradually be realized. This experience was his growing consciousness that what is called the "human" life, the life that includes love, marriage, children, friends, was withheld from him. This emotional and passionate man was condemned to a fundamental isolation from the warm human community. How much this isolation meant to Beethoven we see most clearly in his behavior in connection with his nephew Carl. Into this one narrow channel was poured Beethoven's wealth of emotion; from this one being he demanded the love and sympathy that had been denied him; and the young man very nearly died under the strain. But Beethoven's idolatrous love for his nephew was merely a blind, irrational, pitiful attempt to make at least one point of contact with that warm human world from which he was shut out. Deep within himself the artist in him knew that his isolation was irretrievable. Personal relations that should give him a sense of completeness and satisfy his hunger were impossible. Henceforth his only escape from an isolation become intolerable was to reach out to an Eternal Father, to God the Companion, or to merge his private aspirations into the aspirations of mankind at large.

At the time that he wrote the Hammerclavier sonata, finished in 1818, Beethoven's realization of his essential loneliness was terrible and com-plete. But we may suppose that even then he was becoming aware that his separation from the world was the entry into a different and more exalted region. But the Hammerclavier sonata is the expression of a man of infinite suffering, of infinite courage and will, but without God and without hope. At the time that he depicted this experience it is possible that Beethoven had already passed beyond it. The sonata is the complete expression of an important stage in Beethoven's spiritual development, but it was only after passing through this stage that the wonderful new world lay open before him, and that all his greatest work was achieved. From the Hammer-clavier sonata itself nothing more could come. Its spiritual content is at the end of a process, an end that contains within itself no new beginning. The completely naked Beethoven, relying upon nothing whatever but his inner resources, has said his last word in the Hammerclavier sonata. Without some new life added to him, without some new organization of his experience, the undying energy of the Hammerclavier fugue can be used only to say over again what it has already said. The Hammerclavier sonata does not, in its spiritual content, belong to what is called Beethoven's third period. Neither does it belong to his second. It stands alone, a great and grim memorial to the long and painful journey between the two worlds.

The courage and resolution we find in the first movement are curiously austere. The old experience is once again to be lived through, but the spirit in which it is approached is very different. Those cold harmonies, so characteristic of Beethoven's later work, no longer convey the warm human confidence of a man who knows that victory lies at the end. There is expressed a stark, bare resolution, courageous enough, but uncolored by any joy in conflict. And the other elements that go to make up the wealth of a Beethoven first movement have all become colder. The man who wrote this music is already a great solitary. He has abated nothing of his courage, but it has become more grim. Suffering, it would appear, has hardened him; never again, one would think, can this man melt. And there is no good-humor in the Scherzo. A curiously laconic savagery, with hints of the formidable passion that is expressing itself so abruptly, entirely separate this movement from the frank energy of the earlier Scherzos. The slow movement is the deliberate expression, by a man who knows no reserves, of the cold and immeasurable woe in whose depths, it would seem, nothing that we could call life could endure. It seems as inimical to human existence as the icy heart of some remote mountain lake. Whether it be faithfulness to psychological experience, or whether it be the instinct of an unmatched artist, the Largo that follows the slow movement is a miracle of art. To end with the slow movement would be unendurable, and any sudden shattering of the hypnotic state it produces would be equally unendurable. The gradual awakening effected by the Largo from our state of dumb suspension fulfills a craving of the spirit that surely only this one artist could ever have formulated. And we awake to what? To the blind and desperate energy left in this man when there was no longer any reason to live. We are presented here with a will to live which is inexpressibly furious and inexpressibly bare. It is the expression of the final refusal of annihilation, even if no hope and no object be left in life. The sheer blind energy, this insistence on mere existence, does not contain within itself dramatic contrasts. To be expressed at all it must be expressed in a form within which its swiftness and violence can rage unchecked. No form permits so unidirectional and unhampered a flow as the fugue, and Beethoven chose the fugue. And having chosen it, he exhausts its resources to keep his mass moving with the requisite momentum. At one point the mass rises to a climax and there is an interruption. We are given a glimpse, a few bars, dolce and cantabile, of that serene, inhuman eternity that surrounds this blind, furious striving. But it is only a glimpse, a meaningless stare, and we are once more involved in this headlong rush, this most primitive, fundamental, and unconquerable of the impulses that manifest themselves in creatures that have life. The spiritual content of this fugue is the fitting complement to the Adagio, in the sense that nothing else could have survived. And the greatness of Beethoven is shown in the fact that, having passed through an experience that left him so little to express, he yet expressed so much.—J. W. N. SULLIVAN

Beethoven was not a man of the fugue, and he was never less so than in this nightmare—*a raw and undigested mass!*

(W. de Lenz on the Finale of the Sonata, Opus 106, in *Beethoven et ses trois styles*, Paris, 1855)—NICOLAS SLONIMSKY

III. PIANO SONATA NO. 30 IN E, OPUS 109

1st movement: *Vivace ma non troppo*, alternating with *Adagio espressivo*.

Two ideas in contrasted tempi, worked out in terse but free sonata form.

Fantastic as this first movement is, its form is not unprecedented. But the precedents have no such rhapsodic or mysterious character, and they are all on the opposite basis, beginning in the slow tempo, with their second group in the quick tempo.

Domenico Scarlatti produced several movements of this kind; and Mozart's violin sonata in C major (Köchel No. 303) begins with a delightful example.

In three points Beethoven's form in the present movement is unprecedented. First, there is this reversal of the order of the two tempi. Already this fact implies that the purport of the movement is much graver than in the earlier cases. It is a lighthearted thing to break from a slow tempo to a lively one—unless, of course, the quicker music is loaded with tragic passion. But nothing short of a serious dramatic event can suddenly check the course of a quick movement and then proceed in a slow tempo, nor can the slow music be less than solemn in such a position.

But, in the second place, Beethoven has given the quick tempo only the minimum of time to assert itself at all. In it we hear just two four-bar phrases of short bars. Only the first of these asserts the tonic; the second modulates straight into the dominant. As to the rhythm, the word "bar" is not so meaningless here as we often find it in classical rhythms; the 2/4 bars are here a genuine accentual frame for a uniform series of iambic feet; and we have eight such feet without disturbance. This is certainly enough to establish a sense of tempo, if the player is not careless. In the same way, the tonality is clear; the tonic is unmistakable at the outset, and so is the deliberate modulation to the dominant.

But this uniform rhythm and this clear tonality are destined to receive a shock. The *Adagio cantabile* interrupts with a chord that casts a deep shadow on the dominant key that had been so quickly established. One bar of this *Adagio* takes considerably more time than four of the *Vivace*; and until we have heard at least two *adagio* bars we shall not know what the new pattern of rhythm is to be. Meanwhile this cloudy harmony takes the greater part of the huge new bar to show that it is impinging on the supertonic of our dominant key. The second bar brings things into shape by imitating the 1st sequentially a step lower; and the third bar rounds off the period by a cadence which closes into what is evidently going to be a repetition of the whole. This repetition begins quite clearly with the cloudy diminished seventh. But the cloud does not evaporate in time, and the supertonic drift does not show itself in that bar at all. On the contrary, a chromatic appoggiatura that adorned the melody in the second bar now attracts attention and claims harmonic rights of its own; misleading the bass into supplying it with the root of the quite remote chord of which it is the major third. This strange chord fills almost the whole second bar; but at the end of the bar the major third flattens and becomes, as if nothing had happened, part of the tonic chord; so that the cadential third bar follows in due course and is greatly expanded, closing into a fourth bar on the tonic (*i.e.*, of the present key). Thus, although the supertonic has entirely disappeared, giving place to an utterly remote modulation, bars 12, 13, and 14 have preserved the form of the three which they purport to repeat— viz., two bars in falling sequence and a third cadence-bar.

With the return of the *Vivace* the third unique feature of this movement becomes evident—viz., that the *Vivace* is entirely uniform both as to its iambic rhythm and its arpeggio texture. In the finale of Opus 54 Beethoven had already written such a movement; but it was not exposed to shocks, though it already showed that in Beethoven's view the texture of Bach's arpeggio preludes could be steadily maintained in a fully mature sonata style. The ordinary notion of sonata-development does not quite meet such a contingency: a figure cannot be said to develop when it has been present unchanged all the time. Keys, however, may cover fresh (if not more extensive) ground; and the omnipresent figure may group itself into larger or differently proportioned phrases. In the present case Beethoven expects that the player and listener will have taken the opening seriously enough to appreciate the fact that, whereas bars 1–2 were in falling sequence, bars 16–17 are in rising sequence. This is typically a case of normal development; but after this point a new melodic process begins. To connect this with the descending scale of the bass of bars 1–8 would be to put inaudible resemblances that may well be accidental on a level with things that must be understood if the music is to make sense at all. The organizing of harmonies and modulations on a rising or falling bass is important; but such a bass is not in itself a theme and is not to be emphasized as if it were. But here we have a theme; necessarily a new one, because there is no other way in which the uniform figure of this *Vivace* can develop except by building new melodic sequences. These lead, by no means hurriedly, to a quite emphatic insistence on the home dominant; which makes the eventual return to the opening bars (49 foll.) give the unmistakable effect of a recapitulation. And nothing could, in retrospect, more thoroughly confirm the importance of the opening than the way in which bars 5–6, after moving to the dominant as at first, are repeated in the tonic. And so the *Adagio* is recapitulated in due course; it is expected and can no longer startle us. But the harmonic surprise of bar 13 would also no longer be a surprise, and Beethoven will not reproduce it as it was then. It is an accessory, not a fundamental idea. The duly placed repetition of a fundamental idea is welcome: the repetition of an accessory, that loses thereby the power to surprise, is weak. And so Beethoven has, at bar 61, a new harmonic surprise, of a dark instead of a bright color. Its results are just as faithful to the scheme as was the former device; and, besides the new color, there is the gain that certain rhythmic matters have needed slight compression in order to resolve the new chords in time.

After the *Adagio* has been recapitulated the *Vivace* returns, forming a Coda which alludes to points in the development and ventures to drop the [sixteenth-note] rhythm for eleven bars, resuming it with twelve bars of a final tonic pedal.—DONALD FRANCIS TOVEY (9)

2nd Movement: *Prestissimo in E minor: Sonata Form.*

This delightful movement is a good example of the closely-knit organic style of Beethoven's later period. There is little contrast between the main themes, the whole being largely developed from the rhythms contained in the first four bars. Its key-system, however, conforms to that of the "First-Movement" or "Sonata-Form" type. The polyphonic nature of the music will be obvious to all.

The first subject starts [with a vigorous rising theme. It is made up of two four-bar phrases, the first ending on the dominant, the second passing through the subdominant chord and closing in the tonic]. At bar 9, over a long dominant pedal, it is contained in [a more polyphonic] fashion, till bar 24 is reached, where there is a full close in the tonic.

A transitional passage, based on the rhythm of bars 3 and 4 [of the first subject], first in bare octaves and then harmonized, leads to the "second subject" in B minor (on a dominant pedal). This preserves much the same rhythm as [the first subject and the same polyphonic texture of its continuation]. It overlaps the end of the transition. Note the freedom of modulation within the second subject. (B minor, F sharp minor, E minor, D minor, C major, B minor; the keys of F sharp minor, E minor, and D minor never being really established, however.)

The development section starts [after the abrupt close of the second subject with two unison octaves spelling out the V-I in the key of B minor. It starts] with a reference to the [first] theme. [Four bars later,] over a pedal B, the bass of [that theme] is treated in canon in two parts. Note how the figure of three [quarter notes] is developed and how the bass of [the theme] is transferred to the top part and harmonized.

The recapitulation starts [vigorously, after three tentative chords followed by silences]. There are some differences in treatment in this section: e.g., the theme is transferred to the bass [upon the repetition of the first eight measures,] while the original bass is inverted and transformed in rhythm. The syncopated version of its first two notes was foreshadowed in [the development section]. The rest of the movement proceeds normally, a short coda founded on the bass of [the last phrase of the second subject] bringing it to an abrupt end.

In its economy of material and its concentration, this movement recalls the methods of the "sonatas" and suites of the early eighteenth century.—
A. FORBES MILNE

3rd Movement: *Andante molto cantabile ed espressivo*. Binary melody with six variations.

Already in the playful little slow movement of Opus 14, No. 2, Beethoven had devised a theme which deliberately closed on the dominant five times in ways as little different as it was possible to keep distinct at all. The point of this subtle and dangerous game lies, of course, in the fact that the theme is meant for variations, and that these, if they are genuine variations, will make its subtleties clear by emphasis and repetition. Therefore the subtleties must not be weaknesses. This particular game of the delicately graded cadences fascinated Beethoven to the end of his life; and each time he played it his theme became more subtle and less of a joke. The theme of the variations in the A major Quartet, Opus 18, No. 5, is as witty as that in Opus 14, No. 2, but it aims primarily and successfully at being beautiful. The theme of the variations in the well-named Sonata Appassionata achieves the extreme *tour de force* of consisting entirely of tonic cadences; but that very fact is an element in its profound solemnity. There are heights and depths beyond that solemnity; and these are attained in melodies externally more normal and with greater liberty to move, in spite of their being built upon subtle cadences. Such are the present theme, The Arietta in Opus 111, the themes of the slow movements of the Quartets Opus 127, 132 (the Lydian chorale), Opus 135 (the last quartet) and the Ninth Symphony. One direct result of the subtlety of these themes is that many people have no idea how strict the variations are. The slow movement of the last quartet has been seriously discussed as a curious bundle of detached episodes, though it sticks to its theme more closely than would have suited Mozart's convenience. The student and listener must not take a mistaken view of what a set of variations is supposed to convey to the ear. If the variations are mere embroidery, then we may be expected to trace the melody in them. But if the principle of the variation lies deeper, we are intended to appreciate the depths in the same way as we appreciate other depths: we attend to what reaches our senses, and we allow the sum of our experience to tell us more in its own good time. A painter shows his knowledge of anatomy by the skin-deep merits of his work. His surface is so true that he must have produced it from a knowledge that penetrates beneath the surface. Accordingly, in the analysis, as in the performance of variations, we have no authority to prefer those points in which the variation resembles the theme to those points in which it differs from them. The naturalist knows that the bird of paradise is a crow, but he does not mistake either for the other.

Theme: Binary melody.

Variation 1: Melody mostly new; and bass simplified, moving at first only once a bar. The later part of the second strain approaches more nearly to the melody of the theme.

Variation 2: A double variation on two contrasted ideas; in fact, two different variations dovetailed by means of the repeats.

Variation 3: Allegro vivace. A double variation by development, the repeats being variations of the variation.

Variation 4: (A little slower than the theme.) Single variation (with repeats) developing a pair of figures in free imitative polyphony. The distinction between the dominant chord of bar two and the dominant key of bar four is lost, but the augmented sixth of bar 8 is clear.

Variation 5: Allegro ma non troppo. Double variation by development.

Variation 6: Double variation by continuous development.

Yet another kind of double variation, first found here and afterwards carried out on a larger scale in the slow movement of the C sharp minor Quartet. There is neither the alternation of two ideas nor the varied repetition of one; but the variation steadily increases its resources as it pursues its course, until the end of it has no resemblance to the beginning.

There was already a suggestion of this possibility in the second idea of Variation 2. There we found that the second idea itself produced a new idea after four bars. What happens here is that the radioactive breakup appears after every two bars. [At the end of the repetition of the second strain, the] suspension in the eighth bar does not resolve at once, but the syncopated [eighth notes] descend the dominant-over-tonic chord for three extra bars, which bring them into position to close into the opening theme. (Therein lies the beauty of the well-attested reading according to which [the last] bar is *not* completed by the expected F sharp, D sharp, but the isolated A shares with the trill the honor of closing into the melody.)

[The] da capo of the original theme concludes the sonata. Thus the three bars [which preceded it] and the extra repetition of the second strain in Variation 5 are the only points in this movement which are not comprised within eight exact lengths of a symmetrical binary melody with repeats.—DONALD FRANCIS TOVEY (9)

IV. PIANO SONATA No. 31 IN A FLAT, OPUS 110
   I. Moderato cantabile, molto espressivo; II. Allegro molto; III. Adagio ma non troppo; Fuga (Allegro ma non troppo)

Almost all Beethoven's works (at least, the important ones) bear, as we know, significant dedications, Opus 110 alone has none. Should we feel surprise at this? Could Beethoven dedicate to anyone but himself this expression in music of an internal convulsion in his life? Triumphing for the moment over the first attacks of the malady to which he was to succumb six years later; triumphing also, through his recent winning of a lawsuit, over grievous family cares—worse sufferings for him than the sickness itself; exulting in the serene joy of work on the Mass, he sought to transcribe in music the moral drama in which he had been the chief actor. Four years thereafter he will put forth a complement of like nature to this sonata: the fifteenth quartet. But, whereas the quartet, almost in its entirety, is a religious burst of gratitude to God, the vanquisher of evil, the sonata carries us into the very midst of a crisis; it resembles a cruel and desperate conflict with this Evil, the principle of annihilation, followed by a return to Life celebrated by a hymn of triumphant jubilation. This work might be likened to Opus 57, constructed on nearly the same plan; but in our present sonata in A♭ the reascension toward the light is treated in a far more moving and dramatic fashion.

At the outset of the first movement Beethoven presents, as the second element in the initial idea, that theme from Haydn[1] which he treated

---

[1] Haydn's Symphony in G (Breitkopf & Härtel No. 88)—the main theme of the slow movement.—Editor.

so often. And here this theme, the last tribute of the aging Master to the teacher who guided his first steps in composition, seems like a symbol of moral and physical health; likewise the direction *con amabilità* instructs us concerning the manner of its interpretation. After a Scherzo whose restlessness already intrudes on the *amiable* calm of the first movement, a Recitative intervenes, alternating with ritornelli in orchestral style. We have previously encountered this form of declamation without words (sonata Opus 31, No. 2), and shall meet with it again in the last quartets and the Ninth Symphony. Now there arises, in the key of A♭ minor, one of the most poignant expressions of grief conceivable to man. Too soon the phrase dies away. It makes way for the fugue in A♭ (major), whose subject is derived from the *amiable* theme of the first movement. It might be termed an effort of will to shake off suffering. But the latter is the stronger. And the grief-stricken phrase is repeated, this time in G minor. This reappearance in a tonality so distant and strange, transporting us into a *place* so different from that wherein the rest of the sonata takes its way, has the effect of bringing us face to face with the final throes of an implacable moral agony. But now Will asserts itself against the forces of annihilation, and a dynamic succession of tonic chords ushers in the key of G major, in which the fugue resumes its progress, though presented in *contrary motion:* It is the resurrection!

And here it is impossible to misunderstand the author's intentions when he writes, at the head of this new appearance of the health-motive reversed, the direction "Poi a poi di nuovo vivente"; whereas the second arioso is marked "Perdendo le forze." Yes, strength revives according as we approach the *place* where health was transmuted into music, that is to say, the initial key. Finally, as a conclusion, a song of thanksgiving enters in victorious amplification of the melodic phrase, triumphantly closing this work, which will remain a type of eternal beauty. Opus 110 was dated "on Christmas Day of the year 1821."— VINCENT D'INDY (1)

In the first movement of Beethoven's A flat major sonata (Opus 110) the transition from the *Hauptsatz* to the *Seitensatz* takes the form of a running passage in [thirty-second] notes, which represents a series of chord figurations employing an independent motif which is neither evolved from the *Hauptsatz* nor introduced in the *Seitensatz* and which only approximates to the motif of the new theme (octave leaps) just before the entry of the *Seitensatz*.

Although this finely-etched and musically-melodious figure work, which represents the ornamental accompaniment of the first section of the recurrent principal theme at the beginning of the recapitulation, forms

such a characteristic component of the exposition that it can lay claim
to a place not only in the parallel passage of the recapitulation but
also in the coda, it still seems that as far as substance is concerned we
must consider it a purely figurative interpolation between the actual
"thematic" parts. And this gives rise to the question how an apparently
unrelated running passage in a late Beethoven work achieves structural
independence as the carrying idea of the transition and how the figurative element comes to operate as an organic component of the composition and to give the effect of being artistically homogeneous—as an
expressive medium—with the rest of the material.

So long as there was no clear understanding of the formal disposition
of the movement, it was difficult to view the [thirty-second-] note section
other than as episodic passage work, which one had to accept—with
or without any attempt at motivation—as an anomaly in style and form.
Nagel[1] still holds this point of view.

Through an erroneous designation of the second theme, he has so
distorted the form that he is now unable to find a place for the
[thirty-second-] note section in the regular structural scheme of the
sonata. And since he can adduce no organic reason for it, his explanation
can be nothing more than a makeshift.

Once we admit that bars 12–19 form the transition, from the *Hauptsatz*
to the *Seitensatz*, we arrive at the following.[2] In a number of his sonata
movements, Beethoven lets the transition grow directly out of an already
initiated and more or less intensified repetition of the principal theme
by fusing the repeated portion of the principal theme and the following
modulation into one uninterrupted section.[3] If we visualize this structural
process, then in seeking some relationship between the transition and
the principal theme in the first movement of the A flat major sonata,
we will not overlook the fact that the first four bars of the transition
correspond to the harmonic progression after the first four bars of the
movement—the "head motif," as Riemann calls this essential idea, or
core, of the main theme[4]—i.e., the chord series of bars 12–15 is com-

---

[1] Willibald Nagel, *Beethoven und seine Klaviersonaten*, Langensalza, 1924.—Editor.
[2] What stood so long in the way of a proper understanding of the structure is obviously
the harmony. [Walter] Riezler [in his book, *Beethoven*, Berlin, 1936] analyzes the
harmonic progression through which "the entry of the second theme is curiously disguised, for it opens, immediately after the sixteenth-note arpeggios, in what sounds like
A flat major but is really the subdominant of E flat. Only by degrees, after the series
of trills in the bass, is the E flat clearly asserted."
[3] Examples: first movements of the pianoforte sonatas Opus 31, No. 1; Opus 53; Opus
57; Fourth and Seventh symphonies; *Egmont* overture (borderline and transition cases
apart). Mozart employs the same procedure in the first movement of the great G minor
symphony.
[4] The whole *cantilena* up to the beginning of bar 12 is to be understood of course as
the "main theme." The relationship of the "head motif" (which is really a motif complex, forephrase of a virtual period) to the following thematic section will be clear when
one recognizes, first of all, that the rhythm of the melody from bar 5 on is a variant

posed of the principal harmonies (chords at the beginning of the bars)
of bars 1-4:

> Bars 1 and 12, tonic;
> Bars 2 and 13, dominant, passing four-three chord;
> Bars 3 and 14 tonic, sixth chord;
> Bars 4 and 15, dominant.

The fact that the dominant in bar 4 (expanded to the dominant-
seventh chord on the second quarter note) does not return to the root
position in bar 15, but to the six-five chord, does not affect the agreement, but is premised by the different architectonic mission of the two
analogous bars. The object of bar 4 with the fermata is a strong caesura,
wherein the "head motif" is contrasted with the following; bar 15,
on the other hand, a further development without caesura. At first there
still seems to be no tangible basis for this statement; for in spite of
the striking similarity of the bass progression, the analogy after all consists only in a symmetrical interchange of tonic and dominant.

But from the beginning of the recapitulation, a clear, new light
falls on the relationship of the two passages. Here where the figures
of the transition play round the "head motif" in the manner of "ornamental variations," it is revealed that bars 12-15 (the rest is a logical
continuation of the content of these bars) represent the ornamental
form allotted to it (and actually added in the recapitulation).[1]

The beginning of the recapitulation, which at first glance seems to
confirm the purely figurative character of the transition, shows in point
of fact that the tendrils of these running passages have sprung from
thematic soil. This explains the logical and organic effect inherent in
the seemingly free play of the sixteenth-note arabesques. The transition
really goes back to the beginning of the principal theme, but it merely
indicates the thematic idea (to which it has reference) between the
lines, so to speak. It presents the harmonic ground plan of the primordial
theme by means of a new motif (variation motif). Instead of the
actual corporeality, it brings merely the fragrance, as it were, of the
theme in question.

Here we have an example of the "veiled texture" which Riezler cites

---

of bars 1-2, and further when one notes that the bass line of bars 5-8 is a variant of
the bass fundament of bar 1 up to the first beat of bar 3 (extension of the dominant
bass from bar 2 over two bars), and last of all when one takes into consideration the
analogy of the melodic factors bars 3-4 and 10-11 which correspond to a half and full
close.

[1] The connection will come out more clearly if the three passages are envisaged in a
different order: (a) the "head motif" as it appears at the beginning of the movement;
(b) the "head motif" with its ornamental sheath as it appears in the recapitulation; and
(c) the ornamental sheath without the thematic core, as presented in bars 12-15 (beginning of the transition).

as a criterion of Beethoven's last style.[1] But—leaving aside the irrational in the creative process—it was an artistic-economic motive that impelled Beethoven to let the "head motif" in the transition appear only "latent" behind the veil of a newly introduced figuration: he did not wish to weaken the effect of the wonderful *cantilena* through prolonging repetition, but to enhance it by contrast. And so the running passage, which was added with the unaffected ease of "unpremeditated music-making" and developed to an "important constituent" of this inward tone poem was inspired by the same "great wisdom" which, according to Riezler, induced "Beethoven to refrain from allowing the song theme to appear again in the recapitulation."—LUDWIG MISCH

V. PIANO SONATA No. 32 IN C MINOR, OPUS 111
I. Maestoso; Allegro con brio ed appassionato; II. Arietta (Adagio molto semplice cantabile)

Great works form in the vast organism of man's creative thought like crystals in a saturated solution. History cannot explain them; but they seem to explain history. Beethoven's Opus 111 is a work of this kind.

This Sonata, wrought in the fires of profound experience, can command a lifetime of devotion, can be entered into so thoroughly that every note becomes engraved on the deepest tissue of the mind, can call forth the utmost in imaginative insight—and yet lie forever beyond the realm of the familiar and the known. Its essential mystery is not unlike the remoteness of a noble character, the strange and unconscious serenity of a beautiful woman. It is full of significance; but instead of understanding it we only idealize it. It demands that we die a thousand deaths before we can enter its own sphere of being. Even then we never possess it. It possesses us. In some indefinable way our minds are suspended in and through the spiritual power with which it is so abundantly charged. It has a plenitude of being; our own mode of consciousness, which makes the experience of it possible, is yet "lower" than the experience it gives us. We are the dewdrops in the ocean of its being, the motes in its atmosphere.

New generations of musical experience bring new critical insights, and there is something like a progressive unfolding in our musical understanding. In the case of Beethoven's late-period works this critical lore has taken on a distinct metaphysical tinge. "Where I find Beauty and Goodness," he wrote once, "there I make my home." He is also known to have believed, in common with later philosophers, that music is the closest link between the spiritual and the sensuous.

Another reason why Beethoven criticism has tended toward the meta-

---

[1] "It is just the transparent, almost immaterial texture, and the delicacy of contour and tenderness of expression that is most truly representative of his last style."

physical may be the fact that Beethoven was creating his profoundest music when Hegel and others were soaring into the abstractions of a romantic and mystical metaphysics. The temptations to associate Beethoven and the philosophers doubtless proved irresistible to many a nineteenth-century critic. Whatever we deduce from this, it would be wrong to forget that the later Viennese masters were composing music during the most fruitful period of German philosophy and literature. Lastly, there is music itself. If the romantic philosophers felt, like Socrates, that philosophy is the highest music, it seems equally true that Beethoven, and others who followed after, believed no less fervently that music is the highest philosophy.

All this has probably helped to confirm the feeling that in Beethoven's greatest works appreciation is much more than listening. The listener is involved in something supremely greater than himself. Because Hegel had believed that the very act of philosophizing was a mode of experience in which reality unfolded itself "to itself," and through which the individual mind flowered into the absolute experience, "great experiences" in art and music, consciously invested by composer or critic with the dignity of philosophic communication, seemed like a poetic and intuitionist pathway to the heights of pure being. And many people who, in fact, believe that they are are probably more influenced by romantic ideas than they might be prepared to admit. An English philosopher, Bosanquet, who would not, I think, have described himself as a romantic, once said that the man who commits *il gran rifuto*—the man who turns away from the great experiences—will never tread the path which leads to the vision of truth.

[One] trend in nineteenth-century thought may have helped to perpetuate the metaphysical approach to Beethoven. This was the train of ideas set in motion by Max Müller's oriental studies, the influence of which upon Schopenhauer is well known. Buddhism especially gave romantic idealism a further push in the direction of ethereal absolutism. Buddhism lends itself very much to romantic misinterpretation. The concept of Nirvana, for instance, which is now taken to refer to a plenitude of being, was often held in its more negative aspects. Hence the idea of annihilation in a sort of blue remoteness took root in certain minds as the final truth about the nature of things. Overshadowing the last movement of Mahler's "Das Lied von der Erde" is the deep ocean of the unconscious conceived as a solvent for world-sick souls.

It is probable that true perception and misunderstanding have both colored the way in which Beethoven's music has been regarded. The late works, and especially Opus 111, are like jewels in the tissue of history. Before Beethoven are trends in sonata composition which certainly reach a culmination early in the nineteenth century. After Beethoven both music and criticism reflect the impact of sublime compositions upon minds attuned to speculation. It is natural that whatever true perception there is should express itself in the forms of thought which are in the air. One task of the modern critic is to see how far old-fashioned ideas are still adequate to modern insight and interpretation.

I think it is axiomatic that Opus 111 enshrines profoundly significant experience so unmistakably that analysis from purely abstract formal points of view seems to leave the central fire untouched. The most unmetaphysical musician feels compelled to say "Yes!" to something far more than a pattern of beautiful sounds. It demands even more than the fullest resources of musical intellect and refined emotional sensitivity, because the "wealth" of surprisingly "commonplace" material it contains makes it very open to misunderstanding and caricature. This is true for both performer and listener. There must be "conditions corresponding to the conditions of the thing to be expressed." There can be nothing surprising in Beethoven's own attitude. He said his last music was "better" than his earlier works. This shrewd understatement, no doubt prompted by an absurd attitude on the part of those of his contemporaries who could not see wood for trees, could almost be regarded as a clue to the way his music ought really to be approached. In other words, granting developed intellect and emotional refinement, the listener (and performer) have still to exercise the higher faculty of intuition. To grasp the more-than-music in Opus 111 the listener has to take one step beyond the normal categories of musical understanding. Beethoven himself had taken this step because his experience demanded it, and he confidently forecast that others would take it eventually.

There are many moments in the last works which pull the mind into the sphere of intuitive perceptions—sometimes suddenly, sometimes after meditative preparation, as in the variations of Opus 111. Other examples are the hollow octaves at the end of the exposition in the first movement of Opus 110, the ending of the fugue in the C sharp minor Quartet, and the opening of the fugue in Opus 110. All these moments have one element in common, and this is apprehended rather than comprehended. The common element is a significant emptiness, a kind of tonal void which has a profound effect upon the formal movement of the music. Purely formal analysis and ordinary emotional response break down at such points, as we shall see later, and it was Beethoven's intention to break them down. I am confident that such technical devices can be grasped only in the actual tonal moment of performance, unlike most musical devices which can be comprehended very well on paper (given, of course, a fair share of imagination) and that this is because the faculty of apprehension—intuition—which they bring into play always works only in the concrete immediacy of the present moment. In music, the present moment can only be a moment of actual sound.

It was intuition which inspired these "empty sounds," and it is intuition only which will help us to grasp them. Intuition of what, then? In so far as there is an answer to this question, we can only say that the very exercise of the faculty in these higher levels of musical appreciation involves a state of consciousness which is self-sufficient and self-explanatory. The way in which the listener interprets his own experience after the event will depend upon his poetic insight and his background of philosophical ideas and religious beliefs.

The classical example of sublime misunderstanding is, of course, enshrined in Schindler's puzzled inquiry. Why did not Beethoven write a triumphant finale to Opus 111 and wind up the work in the grand symbolic manner? Beethoven said he had no time. He was too much engrossed with other things, the Ninth Symphony for instance. Another answer to this question has been supplied by Wendell Kretschmar, a character in Thomas Mann's "Dr. Faustus." This answer is, in essence, a formulation of another romantic idea with which we may all have toyed at one time or another. The *Adagio molto semplice e cantabile* is, of all musical compositions, the finale to end finales. It is the end not only of Opus 111, in C minor, it is the end of sonatas. "A return after this parting?" asks Kretschmar. "Impossible!" The sonata had come to an end, an end without any return. The sonata as a species, as a traditional art form, had finished.[1]

When we survey the subsequent history of the sonata, it is difficult not to feel that *something* intrinsic to the sonata style had been worked out in Beethoven's work, that an essential formative force had reached a high peak from which there could be no descent to a re-expression. To the classical sonata the *Adagio* seems, in truth, a farewell. Kretschmar symbolizes the dominant motive (C–G–G . . D–G–G) with a few phrases: "Fare thee well," "Heaven's blue," and the final embroidery on the last page (C–C♯–D–G) with "Great was God in us," " 'Twas all but a dream." There is sentimentality in all this; but the idea of eternal ending, departure to a blue remoteness, is not easy to shake off once the seed has been sown in the imagination. In much the same way the psychological content of the final pages of "Das Lied von der Erde" where, again, the idea of departure is associated romantically with a blue infinity of emptiness, persuades the entranced listener that here, indeed, is the end of the romantic symphony. A healthy corrective to overmuch dwelling on this kind of thing is the possibility that there might have been more sonatas had Beethoven lived longer. And yet . . . the *Adagio* seems like a last word.

Be this as it may, a similar idea has been even more clearly formulated. There is an analysis of Opus 111 in Lenz's "A Critical Catalogue of Beethoven's Works." In the discussion of the relationship between the two movements, the first is characterized as "Resistance" and the last

[1] Quoted from the English translation published by Secker & Warburg.

as "Resignation," or as "Samsara" and "Nirvana" respectively. In Buddhism the term "Samsara" denotes the world of striving, becoming, effort, toil and, in a certain sense, illusion. Nirvana means "a state of something-ness to the nth degree," as opposed to a state of nothingness.[1] Here we wander in strange seas of thought; but we are by no means alone. This problem of insight into the psychological basis of the work faces any pianist who strives to understand the relationship between the *Allegro* and the *Adagio*. But we have to beware of confusion. I cannot interpret Lenz's mind, but his use of "Resignation" and "Nirvana" as alternative characterizations of the *Adagio* suggests that he is thinking in somewhat Mahlerian terms; and there is a universe of difference between Mahler's farewell and Beethoven's. Mahler's leavetaking is retrospective, and the emphasis is all upon the world that is being left behind. Pure negation seems to be the essence of the hopeless "Ewig" with which the work ends. Mahler's resignation is the resignation to loss.

This is in no sense true of Beethoven. If it were, I doubt very much whether the listener would have that experience of being "sustained" by the music, as if by something greater than himself. I doubt, too, whether Beethoven would have been idealized to the extent he has been had it been possible to characterize the psychological basis of the last great works so precisely. The very point about Beethoven's profound-est utterances is that they defy adequate formulation. There is no puzzle about Mahler. We feel with him perhaps, but his utterances in the "Abschied" do not require any special intuitive effort. Very little is left to the imagination—a typical Wagnerian trait. If Beethoven is resigned, then his resignation has a supremely positive quality. The *Adagio* is certainly not negative. It communicates "a state of something-ness to the nth degree," and its prevailing mood is rather one of percep-tion, contemplation and acceptance. Taking for granted that this wonder-ful movement has its place purely in the world of spiritual experience, then perception, contemplation and acceptance seem to characterize three well-marked stages through which the variations ascend.

It may be, then, that the Nirvana analogy is not entirely out of place, provided that it is taken in its positive sense. For it is the supremely positive character which marks Opus 111 as one of the greatest achieve-ments of the *classical* era. The last sonata is, before all else, a classical masterpiece, and is best approached in terms of its classical background and, so far as possible, its structural features regarded not as abstract formal properties but as concrete moments of experience. This does not mean that the romantic approach is false as a whole, but only that romantic categories of explanation do not originate in the art of music itself. They may therefore obstruct a more essentially musical approach,

[1] Francis Younghusband.

and thus a more penetrating musical understanding. This can be arrived at only after a thorough study of the musical experience.

The most powerful dynamic in Beethoven's sonata-form movements is the sublimation of direct emotional expression in objective form. In fact, this is probably the most fruitful element in the compositions of the entire Viennese school. During the course of Beethoven's evolution as a sonata composer, expression and form are each brought to a limit, and both are transformed in serving each other. The storm and stress element, which, at bottom, is little more in music than emotional conflict, develops gradually into a dialectical struggle in which conscious expression and communication take second place to intense and sustained tonal thinking. The sonata-form idea on the other hand, transformed by the dialectical tension into a much more plastic principle of structure, becomes itself a transforming element in that it directs the dialectical movement toward coherence and wholeness determined by the basic tonal material. Hence a movement like the *Allegro* of Opus 111 is much more impressive than mere emotional expression. It does not, regarded as a vehicle, communicate anything at all. It consists solely of a vigorous and relentless *attacca* involving extreme resources of harmony and counterpoint. This very intellectual rigor establishes a mode of experience in the listener which, in and of itself, is far more satisfying than that state in which we receive "messages." The message idea demands that we regard music as the vehicle of nonmusical contents, and this in turn makes the contents one stage removed from the immediacy of what we hear. Perhaps we sometimes forget that the greatest power of sound is known in performance. The immediacy of the musical thought establishes a condition of immediacy. In other words, the vitality of pure musical thinking establishes a form of consciousness which is itself a significant way of experiencing. The *Allegro* is not a message about reality. It is nothing less than reality itself because all we know of reality is the present moment, and, in music, the present moment is formed by musical thinking and tonal experience which are one in essence. The conviction of sigificance which arises in the experience of Opus 111 would not be so assured if the formal thought were any less self-contained than it is.

All art implies idealization; but idealization can be of two kinds. On the one hand there is romantic idealization, which is always tending toward falsification of life in accordance with the private fantasy of the artist. A work grounded in an aesthetic of romantic idealization will convey more about the artist's psychological state than it will about life as a whole. Not that it is the purpose of music to reveal the theme of our life; but it just happens that some romantic composers, consciously striving toward a quasi-philosophical ideal—Mahler in his symphonies, for example—achieved only a revelation of their personal inwardness. Thus Mahler may be said to idealize the world without conveying any essential truth about it. His fourth Symphony is a case in point. On the other hand, works which were "just music" as far as the composers were concerned, may unconsciously project something universally valid in our experience which commands immediate assent. Such compositions, whenever they were composed, embody classical idealization. Hence, romantic idealization may involve an element of withdrawal from life regarded as something universal to be involved in, and hence a rejection of reality. Classical idealization is always a formal enhancement of "lived-through" experience, and seems to imply an acceptance of reality. I say "lived-through" because romantic idealization may project experience at second-hand, which the artist would like to have but fails to grasp. This may very well turn the composer into a false prophet. The pseudo-mysticism of César Franck is possibly a case in point.

There can be no doubt that classical idealization is the essence of Opus 111. The relentless counterpoint which plows roughly through hollow-sounding harmonic vastnesses, the restless changes of tempo and the emphatic threefold statement of germinal ideas which is a special feature of the *Allegro*—all these amount to an idealization of something universal and unceasing in experience which Beethoven himself knew with a special intensity. This is why the listener is immediately involved in something he feels to be greater than himself. Consciousness, in any mode other than the religious, is concerned with the world of forms. We dwell in the realm of fluctuation, struggle, tension and movement, and these are universal. These are all properties of the world of form, and it follows that any idealization of form must be in terms of struggle, tension and movement. It also follows that the experience of the successful idealization of these properties of form must expand, sustain, define and "bring to a head" the consciousness of the individual involved in it. Any artistic expression of an extreme state of form-consciousness must necessarily demand tremendous intellectual virility, and must necessarily appear an idealization of form. The *Allegro* of Opus 111 is, then, the idealization of form itself. There is no "message." Its "truth" is simply what it is.

All this may help to explain why so many listeners find a tragic element in the first movement of Opus 111. Consciousness, in its world of forms, is shot through with tragedy and suffering, and such a powerful crystallization of the essence of form must inevitably concentrate and bring to a focus the tragic element in life which seems so inextricably mixed with the whole field of human experience.

How was Beethoven able to progress to the point where he could use formal methods traditionally associated with emotional expression to idealize form itself? Because, I suggest, he was always in earnest with the formal properties of the expressive emotional fragments with which he worked, and thus with their universal properties. So much at least is revealed by the notebooks. Had Beethoven put most emphasis upon the content of the fragments he used, he would have lapsed into romanticism, and the grammar of the third-period works would have been very different. But the pursuit of form, the continual wrestling with the formal properties and implications of germinal ideas—in this case of themes and harmonic intuitions crystallized out of the stuff of life as he knew it—led to an intense concentration upon the tissue of musical thinking as itself a mode of lived-through reality. Hence the seriousness and swamping immediacy of the *Allegro* are fundamental to the realm of becoming in which our consciousness unfolds.

There is another answer, of course: the *Adagio* itself. How could Beethoven concentrate such intensity of experience into an "abstract" movement in sonata form? How could he idealize the realm of form with such telling objectivity? Because he had penetrated to a realm of experience which is beyond form? This may well be the truth of the matter, and the reason why metaphysics and mysticism link hands with music in the minds of so many who try to fathom the secret of the last works. Penetration to the realm of experience without form would imply a high state of religious awareness, an insight into the being of things transcending their becoming.

Now variation form is fundamentally static, of all musical forms the one least associated with tension. It lends itself to analogous interpretation in terms of musing, speculation, lingering contemplation of a central nucleus, absorption and the like. In this respect it is something like fugue, and it is significant that both variation and fugue are prominent in Beethoven's third period. Fugue, however, contains a ratiocinative element. A composer idealizing his highest intuitions of being would turn to the dynamic immobility of variation form, which seems to hold its point of origination in suspension.

Another factor is supremely important. A state of being (as distinct from a state of becoming) could not be idealized in classical musical terminology by anything other than simple, rudimentary ideas fundamental to the idiom of thought the composer has used all his life. These are the being of the composer's style—the essential wholeness within which his works have flowered into conscious life. This may explain the innocence of the theme in the C sharp minor Quartet which affected Wagner so deeply, and especially the essential fourths and fifths of the Arietta in the last sonata. Consider, too, the basic simplicities of Diabelli's theme from which Beethoven distilled so many sublime moments. According to traditional records, one of the most characteristic features of mystical experience is the transfiguration of the commonplace. If the Arietta is religious music of the kind many believe it to be, this fact cannot be anything but intimately connected with the inclusion of so much rudimentary C major material. Indeed, looked at from one point of view, the whole movement is like an idealization of the ultimate substance of the classical style.

But there is more to it than this. Like the preceding one, this movement has to be approached in purely musical terms. Only then is it possible to develop analogies which, after all, are subjective and personal to all of us.

The material of the Arietta, like all the affecting themes which Beethoven uses in his third period, seemed to him to invite elaboration not only in terms of its emotional content, but also in terms of its intrinsic formal properties. Now in music a property of form is not simply a property of thematic structure. If it were, formal elaboration would only be thematic elaboration, and the variations of the Arietta in Opus 111 would unfold only as melodic embroidery. It requires but one performance of the Arietta to realize that the caressing fourths and fifths of the theme are presented against a wide harmonic spacing, and that this harmonic "depth" is possibly the dominating formal feature of the entire movement. Almost everything that happens floats in a tonal void. Therefore the variations are not only accounted for in terms of thematic elaboration, but more significantly in terms of harmonic space. The variations unfold in terraces, and each terrace opens up a broader aspect of the relation of the melody to its harmonic background. At certain points the insistence upon this is overwhelming.

The theme and its first three variations constitute the first section of the movement, the first terrace of tonal exploration based primarily upon thematic treatment against the given harmonic spacing. A new phase is initiated by Variation IV, which, by contrasting treatment of the repetitions, very explictly enlarges the tonal depth. This seems tremendously significant when we compare the vibrating bass in fifths (echoed in the last Opus 126 Bagatelle) with the shimmering cascade high in the treble which immediately follows. The two taken together epitomize the higher and the lower of tonal experience. Neither seems to *move* in any "forward" sense. Both the weighted and darkling chords of the former and the glistening ripple of the latter exert a hypnotic influence upon the hearer, and this simple formal device of contrasting registers goes a considerable way toward negating the impression of formal motion. The motion of music is, of course, movement in time toward a conclusion formally implicit in the basic material. In this set of variations we have, I suggest, a unique example of sustained "lateral" movement in time being waned out by the effect of deep vertical spacing. In this connection it is important to remember that the effect of notes is always dependent upon the relationship established between them. This relationship can be temporal—*i.e.* the notes can follow one another in time, or it can be "spatial" or "immediate." In the latter case relationship determines *the quality of a moment*. In temporal relationship, the intervals between the notes determine *the quality of moments*. Hence it follows that a prolonged movement characterized by a sameness or identity of "spatial" or "immediate" relationship will all seem to be taking place in the immediacy of a single moment. A short but powerful example of this is the bare octave space on the note D♭ which links the exposition with the development in the first movement of Opus 110. At this instant the music "stops"; the temporal movement is momentarily arrested as the consciousness of the hearer is jolted into a new mode of musical apprehension. The startling quality of this moment is such that it seems to contain in itself the why and the wherefore of the whole movement.

In the case of the *Adagio* and its variations, it is still true that the spacing is essential to the structural and thus formal being of the music. Music, however sublime, and however it is understood, is a formal art and must be understood as form before any other mode of appreciation can legitimately supervene. If, then, this music seems to guide the listener toward the sphere of no-form, through the exploitation of a device which seems to cancel out formal movement, Beethoven is using form to negate form. If this seems like a paradox it may help to call the plight of the mystic to mind. The mystic can only use the formal means of language to convey the essence of his vision. If Beethoven is striving to express (though there seems to be no conscious striving in the variations) a high state of consciousness, then in trying to make his means of expression correspond to "the conditions of the thing to be expressed" he is compelled to embrace a paradox. It is not irrelevant to remark here that some kinds of mysticism explicitly underline the paradox of "form—no-form" as central to reality. In other words, the sphere of form is given its meaning and final justification by the sphere of formlessness. If this really is so, then the contradiction implied in using formal means to express that which is beyond form —in this case an exalted consciousness—only appears a contradiction to those who cannot themselves enter a phase of awareness which is beyond the everyday and the familiar world.

This is where intuitive perception supervenes upon intellectual comprehension. It was suggested above that intellect and emotional sensitivity are not the "open sesame" to the last period, that the listener has to go that one step farther. If we go the first mile in Opus 111, Beethoven demands that we go another. In Variation IV the appeal of the music is no longer to the intellect, and no more to emotional sensitivity. There is a challenge now to direct perception. We are asked to experience music the essence of which is neither intellection nor emotion and which, if we can rise to it, will lift the plane of consciousness to a level untouched by any of his earlier work. The crisis is reached in the long chain of trills which immediately follows the fourth variation. The initial trill, mounting in semitones, reaches a dizzy height, hovers a moment, and eventually resolves five octaves above the solitary notes in the bass. There follows the profoundest moment in all music, a still emptiness transcending thought and emotion, which finally brings home the significance of the deep spacing which is apparent throughout the entire movement. If the relation of the Arietta and its transformations to the *Allegro* is not grasped at this point, the work must forever remain a puzzle.

If the romantic "farewell" interpretation has any real application, this is surely in the hushed and wistful episode which introduces the next variation. This is the real farewell, and it is a loosening, a letting go of more familiar things. Kretschmar interprets it as a "start of fear that such a thing could happen." That trill surely climbed too high, that emptiness was too vast, too deep . . . ? Whatever meaning we give to it, this C minor episode has a pathetic air. But its pathos has a note of reverence, and its languishing cadences lead inevitably to the acceptance and ecstasy of the fifth variation.

The theme floats serenely like a planet in the void, a star born in the emptiness of that motionless moment which gives the clue to the whole tremendous work. The intensity mounts again, and this time there is no looking back, no hesitation—only a trembling nerve of exquisite perception, a final sealing of the bond between the spiritual and the sensuous.

The final bars are very nearly like those which have conventionally ended a hundred sonatas in C major. But in this movement the conventional and the commonplace have been transfigured. The downward-rippling scale and the last tonic-dominant cadences are all one with the last transformation of the theme—Kretschmar's "Lebewohl, Lebewohl, Great was God in us. . . ."

Samsara-Nirvana? A great experience leading to the heights of pure being? The vision of a mystic? A revelation of God? Is there, then, some truth in the romantic interpretations after all? We never really denied it. . . . But the only truth this music contains which we can *know* is the state of consciousness which exists as we listen. And who can find the words to express it?—PHILIP T. BARFORD

Beethoven is not only still numbered among the living, but is at a period of life when the mind, if in *corpore sano*, is in its fullest vigor, for he has not yet completed his fifty-second year. Unfortunately, however, he is suffering under a privation that to a musician is intolerable —he is almost totally bereft of the sense of hearing; in so much that it is said he cannot render the tones of his pianoforte audible to himself. . . . The Sonata, Opus 111 consists of two movements. The first betrays a violent effort to produce something in the shape of novelty. In it are visible some of those dissonances the harshness of which may have escaped the observation of the composer. The second movement is an *Arietta*, and extends to the extraordinary length of thirteen pages. The greater portion of it is written in 9/16, but a part is in 6/16, and about a page in 12/32. All this really is laborious trifling, and ought to be by every means discouraged by the sensible part of the musical profession. . . . We have devoted a full hour to this enigma, and cannot solve it. But no sphinx ever imagined such a riddle as the 12/32 time presents. Here we find twelve [thirty-second-notes], and eight [sixty-fourth-notes] in one bar; twelve [thirty-second-notes] and twelve [sixty-fourth-notes] in another, etc., and all without any appearance of a misprint! The general practice of writing notes apparently very short, then doubling their length by the word *Adagio*, is one of the abuses in music that loudly cries for reform; but the system of notation pursued in this *Arietta* is confusion worse confounded, and goes on, as we have before stated, to the extent of thirteen pages; and yet the publishers have, in their title, deemed it necessary to warn off all pirates by announcing the Sonata as copyright. We do not think they are in much danger of having their property invaded.

(*The Harmonicon*, London, August 1823)—NICOLAS SLONIMSKY

Wendell Kretschmar, at that time still young, at most in the second half of his twenties, was born in the state of Pennsylvania of German-American parentage. He had got his musical education in his country of origin; but he was early drawn back to the old world whence his grandparents had once migrated, and where his own roots lay and those of his art. In the course of his wanderings he had become our organist in Kaiseraschern. He had even appeared as composer and produced an opera which was well received and played on many stages. He honored the principle, which we repeatedly heard from his lips, first formed by the English tongue, that to arouse interest was not a question of the interest of others, but of our own; it could only be done, but then infallibly was, if one was fundamentally interested in a thing oneself, so that when one talked about it one could hardly help drawing others in, infecting them with it, and so creating an interest up to then not present or dreamed of. And that was worth a great deal more than catering to one already existent.

What did he talk about? Well, the man was capable of spending a whole hour on the question: Why did Beethoven not write a third movement to the Piano Sonata Opus 111? It is without doubt a matter worth discussing. We who were present at the explanation had indeed an uncommonly enriching evening, and this although the sonata under discussion was to that date entirely unknown to us. Still it was precisely through these lectures that we got to know it, and as a matter of fact very much in detail; for Kretschmar played it to us on the inferior cottage piano that was all he could command, a grand piano not being granted him. He played it capitally despite the rumbling noise the instrument made; analyzing its intellectual content with great impressiveness as he went, describing the circumstances under which it—and two others —were written and expatiating with caustic wit upon the master's own explanation of the reason why he had not done a third movement corresponding to the first. Beethoven, it seems, had calmly answered this question, put by his famulus,[1] by saying that he had not had time and therefore had somewhat extended the second movement. No time! And he had said it "calmly," to boot. The contempt for the questioner which lay in such an answer had obviously not been noticed, but it was justified contempt. And now the speaker described Beethoven's condition in the year 1820, when his hearing, attacked by a resistless ailment, was in progressive decay, and it had already become clear that he could no longer conduct his own works. And then Kretschmar talked about the Sonata in C minor, which indeed it was not easy to see as a well-rounded and intellectually digested work, and which had given his contemporary critics, and his friends as well, a hard aesthetic nut to crack. These friends and admirers, Kretschmar said, simply could not follow the man they revered beyond the height to which at the time of his maturity he had brought the symphony, the piano sonata, and the classical string quartet. In the works of the last period they stood with heavy hearts before a process of dissolution or alienation, of a mounting into an air no longer familiar or safe to meddle with; even before a *plus ultra*, wherein they had been able to see nothing else than a degeneration of tendencies previously present, an excess of introspection and speculation, an extravagance of minutiae and scientific musicality—applied sometimes to such simple material as the arietta theme of the monstrous movement of variations which forms the second part of this sonata. The theme of this movement goes through a hundred vicissitudes, a hundred worlds of rhythmic contrasts, at length outgrows itself, and is finally lost in giddy heights that one might call other-worldly or abstract. And in just that very way Beethoven's art had overgrown itself, risen out of the habitable regions of tradition, even before the startled gaze of human eyes, into spheres of the entirely and utterly and nothing-but personal—an ego painfully isolated in the absolute, isolated too from sense by the loss of his hearing; lonely prince of a realm of spirits, from whom now only a

[1] Schindler.—Editor.

chilling breath issued to terrify his most willing contemporaries, standing as they did aghast at these communications of which only at moments, only by exception, they could understand anything at all.

So far, so good, said Kretschmar. And yet again, good or right only conditionally and incompletely. For one would usually connect with the conception of the merely personal, ideas of limitless subjectivity and of radical harmonic will to expression, in contrast to polyphonic objectivity (Kretschmar was concerned to have us impress upon our minds this distinction between harmonic subjectivity and polyphonic objectivity), and this equation, this contrast, here as altogether in the masterly late works, would simply not apply. As a matter of fact, Beethoven had been far more "subjective," not to say far more "personal," in his middle period than in his last, had been far more bent on taking all the flourishes, formulas, and conventions, of which music is certainly full, and consuming them in the personal expression, melting them into the subjective dynamic. The relation of the later Beethoven to the conventional, say in the last five piano sonatas, is, despite all the uniqueness and even uncanniness of the formal language, quite different, much more complaisant and easygoing. Untouched, untransformed by the subjective, convention often appeared in the late works, in a baldness, one might say exhaustiveness, an abandonment of self, with an effect more majestic and awful than any reckless plunge into the personal. In these forms, said the speaker, the subjective and the conventional assumed a new relationship, conditioned by death.

At this word Kretschmar stuttered violently; sticking fast at the first sound and executing a sort of machine-gun fire with his tongue on the roof of his mouth, with jaw and chin both quivering, before they settled on the vowel which told us what he meant. But when we had guessed it, it seemed hardly proper to take it out of his mouth and shout at him, as we sometimes did, in jovial helpfulness. He had to say it himself and he did. Where greatness and death come together, he declared, there arises an objectivity tending to the conventional, which in its majesty leaves the most domineering subjectivity far behind, because therein the merely personal—which had after all been the surmounting of a tradition already brought to its peak—once more outgrew itself, in that it entered into the mythical, the collectively great and supernatural.

He did not ask if we understood that, nor did we ask ourselves. When he gave it as his view that the main point was to hear it, we fully agreed. It was in the light of what he had said, he went on, that the work he was speaking of in particular, Sonata Opus 111, was to be regarded. And then he sat down at the cottage piano and played us the whole composition out of his head, the first and the incredible second movement, shouting his comments into the midst of his playing and in order to make us conscious of the treatment demonstrating here and there in his enthusiasm by singing as well; altogether it made a spectacle partly entrancing, partly funny; and repeatedly greeted with merriment by his little audience. For as he had a very powerful attack and exaggerated the *forte*, he had to shriek extra loud to make what he said halfway intelligible and to sing with all the strength of his lungs to emphasize vocally what he played. With his lips he imitated what the hands played. "Tum-tum, tum-tum, tum-tr-r!" he went, as he played the grim and startling first notes of the first movement; he sang in a high falsetto the passages of melodic loveliness by which the ravaged and tempestuous skies of the composition are at intervals brightened as though by faint glimpses of light. At last he laid his hands in his lap, was quiet a moment, and then said: "Here it comes!" and began the variations movement, the "*adagio molto semplice e cantabile.*"

The arietta theme, destined to vicissitudes for which in its idyllic innocence it would seem not to be born, is presented at once, and announced in sixteen bars, reducible to a motif which appears at the end of its first half, like a brief soul-cry—only three notes, an eighth note, a sixteenth note, and a dotted quarter note to be scanned as, say: "heav-en's blue, lov-ers' pain, fare-thee well, on a-time, mead-ow-land"— and that is all. What now happens to this mild utterance, rhythmically, harmonically, contrapuntally, to this pensive, subdued formulation, with what its master blesses and to what condemns it, into what black nights and dazzling flashes, crystal spheres wherein coldness and heat, repose and ecstasy are one and the same, he flings it down and lifts it up, all that one may well call vast, strange, extravagantly magnificent, without thereby giving it a name, because it is quite truly nameless; and with laboring hands Kretschmar played us all those enormous transformations, singing at the same time with the greatest violence: "Dim-dada!" and mingling his singing with shouts. "These chains of trills!" he yelled. "These flourishes and cadenzas! Do you hear the conventions that are left in? Here —the language—is no longer—purified of the flourishes—but the flourishes —of the appearance—of their subjective—domination—the appearance— of art is thrown off—at last—art always throws off the appearance of art. Dim-dada! Do listen, how here—the melody is dragged down by the centrifugal weight of chords! It becomes static, monotonous—twice D, three times D, one after the other—the chords do it—dim-dada! Now notice what happens here—"

It was extraordinarily difficult to listen to his shouts and to the highly complicated music both at once. We all tried. We strained, leaning forward, hands between knees, looking by turn at his hands and his mouth. The characteristic of the movement of course is the wide gap between bass and treble, between the right and the left hand, and a moment comes, an utterly extreme situation, when the poor little motif seems to hover alone and forsaken above a giddy yawning abyss—a procedure of awe-inspiring unearthliness, to which then succeeds a distressful making-of-itself-small, a start of fear as it were, that such a thing could happen. Much else happens before the end. But when it ends and while it ends, something comes, after so much rage, persistence, obstinacy, extravagance: something entirely unexpected and touching in its mildness and goodness. With the motif passed through many vicissitudes, which takes leave and so doing becomes itself entirely leave-taking, a parting wave and call, with this D G G occurs a slight change, it experiences a small melodic expansion. After an introductory C, it puts a C sharp before the D, so that it no longer scans "heav-en's blue," "mead-ow-land," but "O-thou heaven's blue," "Green-est mead-ow-land," "Fare-thee well for aye," and this added C sharp is the most moving, consolatory, pathetically reconciling thing in the world. It is like having one's hair or cheek stroked, lovingly, understandingly, like a deep and silent farewell look. It blesses the object, the frightfully harried formulation, with overpowering humanity, lies in parting so gently on the hearer's heart in eternal farewell that the eyes run over. "Now for-get the pain," it says. "Great was—God in us." " 'Twas all—but a dream," "Friendly—be to me." Then it breaks off. Quick, hard triplets hasten to a conclusion with which any other piece might have ended.

Kretschmar did not return from the piano to his desk. He sat on his revolving stool with his face turned toward us, in the same position as ours, bent over, hands between his knees, and in a few words brought to an end his lecture on why Beethoven had not written a third movement to Opus 111. We had only needed, he said, to hear the piece to answer the question ourselves. A third movement? A new approach? A return after this parting—impossible! It had happened that the sonata had come, in the second, enormous movement, to an end, an end without any return. And when he said "the sonata," he meant not only this one in C minor, but the sonata in general, as a species, as traditional art-form; it itself was here at an end, brought to its end, it had fulfilled its destiny, reached its goal, beyond which there was no going, it canceled and resolved itself, it took leave—the gesture of farewell of the D G G motif. consoled by the C sharp, was a leave-taking in this sense too, great as the whole piece itself, the farewell of the sonata form.

With this Kretschmar went away, accompanied by thin but prolonged applause, and we went too, not a little reflective, weighed down by all these novelties. Most of us, as usual, as we put on our coats and hats and walked out, hummed bemusedly to ourselves the impression of the evening, the theme-generating motif of the second movement, in its original and its leave-taking form and for a long time we heard it like an echo from the remoted streets into which the audience dispersed, the quiet night streets of the little town: "Fare-thee well," "Fare thee well for aye," "Great was God in us."—THOMAS MANN

Miscellaneous Piano Works

I. 33 Variations in C on a Waltz by A. Diabelli, Opus 120

Diabelli's theme has often been cited as a proof that Beethoven could make the most enormous works out of nothing. This is not true. He could not have made an enormous set of variations out of the sublime themes which he treats in variation form in his sonata works. Diabelli's theme is as prosaic as the hard-shell businessman who wrote it, but it does mean business, and a stronger structure has never been realized in reinforced concrete. It is a theme which sets the composer free to build recognizable variations in every conceivable way. It was sent by Diabelli to fifty-one eminent musicians living in Austria, and Diabelli's purpose was to collect from each musician a variation and to publish the whole fifty-one for the benefit of the widows and orphans in the late wars. Beethoven was about to begin on the Ninth Symphony, and his first impulse was doubtless to advise Diabelli with Beethovenish precision to go elsewhere. Instead of which, after keeping Diabelli on tenterhooks for a considerable time, he sent a contribution which had to be published in a separate volume. I have seen the volume containing the other fifty contributions. The glance I have taken is quite enough to show that most of the composers, from the excellent Assmayer to the gentleman with a name like a sneeze, found Diabelli's theme a surprisingly plastic object. It will be seen that the short sequential lines are placed between a couple of long lines and what might be called a prize last line in a scheme closely resembling that of a limerick. Now it is obviously legitimate to substitute one tonic and dominant form for another as long as they both fill up the same space. For instance, the formal TTTD, DDDT is a legitimate alteration for Diabelli's four tonics and four dominants. Then again, Diabelli's melody (and why not call it melody when railway companies classify typewriters as musical instruments?) begins with a twiddle around the tonic, and repeats the twiddle a step higher over the dominant. Accordingly it is quite natural, and productive of great variety, to translate the first eight bars from a tonic and dominant antithesis to a tonic and supertonic sequence (Variation 8); and, if supertonic, why not flat supertonic (Variation 30)? Again, the bass is as recognizable a melody as the treble. In fact, poor Leporello sang it at the beginning of *Don Giovanni*, when the curtain rose upon his unwilling sentry-go during his master's most wicked escapade

(Variation 22, *Alla "Notte e giorno faticar" di Mozart*). Very rarely does Beethoven take liberties with the actual size of the theme. In two variations, he omits a bar, almost certainly by inadvertence, which is not unlikely, considering the desperate hurry in which this most wonderful of variation-works was written. In the Mozart parody, he adds two bars to the end, which does no harm. In the fughetta, Variation 24, the four entires of subject and answer do duty for Diabelli's tonic and dominant, and the rest of the pair of limericks evaporates into fugal ether. Variation 29, though in a slow tempo, compresses each part of the theme into six bars, of which the first four represent Diabelli's eight. Variation 30 is quite strict, but for the fact that, in representing Diabelli's upward step by the flat supertonic, Beethoven sends all the subsequent modulations to remoter regions. Instead of repeating either part, he elects to repeat the last four bars in the style of the French *petite reprise*, or refrain. Variation 31, being in enormously slow tempo, begins by quite adequately repeating each of Diabelli's four bars by one bar of 9/8, and then becomes rhapsodic on a much larger scale at the hint of Diabelli's rising sequence. The fugue merely takes a few notes from Diabelli's thrumming right hand as one fugue subject, and a vague hint of the rising sequences turned into falling sequences as the countersubject, or second subject. Perhaps, again, as in the fughetta, we may say that the scheme of a fugue exposition may do duty for Diabelli tonic and dominant; but otherwise the point of this fugue is that it has definitely flown off at a tangent.—DONALD FRANCIS TOVEY (1)

Beethoven's "Diabelli" Variations, Opus 120, present many puzzling features to the scholar, performer and listener, who—apart from occasional programme notes and Tovey's exposition in "Chamber Music"—can get little more than brief mentions in books on the composer. The prime question is: why did Beethoven make use of what is apparently a trivial theme for such a gigantic work and when only asked to supply a fragment toward a publisher's novelty? The notion that such a theme was too good for a pasticcio and that he, Beethoven, would show its possibilities to the composer, will not bear sustained consideration. Although a complete answer may never be known with certainty, one or two points are worthy of consideration.

Diabelli's theme has features akin to Beethoven's own method of construction. Binary in form, the theme has in its first section an opening of four bars tonic, followed by four bars dominant, and a rosalia repeat with sequence leading to a dominant cadence. The second section, opening with dominant harmony, proceeds in the pattern of the first section and concludes on the tonic. This pattern is mechanical enough both on paper and aurally but given the Beethoven emphasis, much that is trivial tends to disappear, the balance of section partially acquiring one of Beethoven's characteristic opening methods of thematic construction. A few examples of this tonic-dominant dominant-tonic opening will suggest themselves: theme of "Eroica" Variations (Opus 35); Sonata in C minor (Opus 111), second movement; and String Quartet in C sharp minor (Opus 131) variation theme. That Beethoven had observed this feature in earlier masters (i.e. Mozart's Rondo in D) can hardly be doubted, but it is of interest that it is only in his late works that this simple harmonic pattern takes on unexampled grandeur. To return for a moment to an early work, the Piano Trio in E flat (without opus number, published posthumously in 1830) has an opening to its scherzo which bears a striking resemblance to the Diabelli theme and tempts the thought that Diabelli's theme recalled to Beethoven his own former work.

The very squareness of Diabelli's theme seems to have presented a firm basis for Beethoven since very few variations adhere to both its harmonic and its melodic patterns. Much is brought about by suggestion which should leave no doubt to the listener concerning the relationship to the theme. Perhaps it might be said that the wider the variation, the squarer the foundation needs to be in order to create a rational organic unity.

A second puzzling point is the length of the whole work: approximately 55 minutes. It had a precedent in Bach's "Goldberg" Variations but as far as number of variations go both are easily outstripped by Handel's 62 Variations on a chaconne theme. The "Goldberg" variations, unlike Handel's, show an organic pattern which for performance may be split into two halves or some repeats missed out, but any attempt to do this with the "Diabelli" is unthinkable. It has been privately suggested that perhaps the "Diabelli" variations are not in a fixed order and that a more satisfactory grouping of certain variations could be achieved. This is very unlikely since if what may be termed a graph of the work is made, in terms of performing times, dynamics, expression marks and pitch levels, it shows a pattern beginning with steady rise to a medium climax in Variation 10 with sudden drop of speed, dynamic and tension leading through a series of checkered motions until the slow minor variations—29, 30, 31,—give way to an energetic fugue as the great climax, followed by a gentle variation with a quiet coda relieving the mind and ear of all previous storms. Seen in perspective, the work shows a vast single form which may only be arbitrarily divided in four sections for the purpose of study, not as a basis for playing or listening as suggested by some programme notes. The end of the supposed first section does not suggest finality if properly interpreted. A pause between Variations 10 and 11 is needed aurally and emotionally rather than formally, since an impetus built up by four forceful variations in two pairs separated by a deliberate contrast, requires a pause in order to prepare and properly hear the first bars of the quiet eleventh variation. The same may be said of a slight pause between 28 and 29, and also in a lesser degree between 23 and 24. Bearing this in mind a thoughtful yet inspired interpreter could remove one of the listener's problems when injudicious pauses tend to split a unified work into four movements. Any calculation of these pauses depends on many factors such as speed, dynamics, type of piano, size of hall, and to some degree on the audience's concentration. Since listening speeds differ from performing speeds, the "Diabelli" needs much playing to audiences before performing balance and correct spacing between variations are achieved. It is possible in Variation 20 to slow down the audience's listening speed in order to put over to them this variation's strange sounds and at the same time disarm them for the avalanche of Variation 21 which, possessing two speeds, checks its own impetus and prevents 22 from being misheard. For the performer, 32 (fugue) also presents a problem. After an immense [quarter-note] hammering has reached its climax, Beethoven, as in his usual fugue patterns presents a variation or a new subject that can be woven into the fugue material and at the same time can be perhaps thought of as a coda. In 32 there is a temptation to wait overlong at the climax before beginning this second section. In editing his fine edition, Schnabel surprisingly adopted this procedure, alloting a 13-beat pause and at the same time reducing the second section to less than half-speed with an acceleration to half Tempo 1 just before the ending. This bifurcating of a form is unlikely to help the listener recall the original binary theme and although perhaps a limited spaciousness is added to this variation, the torrential effect of the original is obscured and the following variation, 33, becomes just another variation instead of a revelation in part of a vast scheme. Variation 32 in some ways becomes a vast stretto, summing up not only the preceding emotional patterns but also containing a variant or fragment in motive, key or dynamic form of early every variation, distributed within the fugue.

Without entering the controversy of e'''' and e''' flat in Opus 106 and 111, it is noteworthy that the "Diabelli," a later work, is contained within six octaves, from $C_{,,}$ to c'''' when some pianos were being made up to f'''. Although fully exploiting a six-octave range, some of the variations are somewhat unpianistic and seem to have been composed for an ideal piano. Pianos of Beethoven's day may have produced a certain amount that approximated to his notion of how the work should sound, yet it must be allowed that by the time the finer developments in the pianoforte were coming into being, Beethoven was deaf and nearing his end. Many pianos of his day contained octave couplers (octaves in the "Waldstein" Sonata?), "pizzicato" pedals, drums, and occasionally lute or harp relics of harpsichord days. We may discount his pianoforte arrangement of the "Battle" Symphony, yet in an occasional sonata there is a reminder of contemporary instruments; but the "Diabelli" rejects every mechanical device except *una corda* as if to reveal the very substance of piano tone.

In the pianos of 1825, metal frames were unknown (with the exception of an occasional Broadwood), hammer covering was not stablized, nor were strings uniform, pianos were bichord, trichord and on occasions were made with four unison strings to a note—as with Beethoven's Graf instrument. Even the striking place was not known to piano-makers in Beethoven's early days. Numerous devices were patented and manufactured to produce sustained tone and rapid repetition, yet despite the lack of a suitable instrument Beethoven made great use of these features and probably felt that these problems would be solved without mechanical means. A reminder of early pianoforte voicing and bass stringing is found in the wide spacing of treble and bass parts in many cadences concluding either section of the variations. It is recorded that Beethoven preferred his Broadwood to Viennese instruments on account of the greater depth of tone. For contemporary performances it would seem that a Viennese action with straight stringing on an iron frame would perhaps be nearer to his ideals in the "Diabelli" than the modern roller-action, cross-strung grand which is inclined to jangle slightly during the many passages containing reiterated loud low-placed chords.

Very few octaves are to be found in the entire work, but counterpoint of varying kinds is evident in at least twelve variations and many have a bass running counter to the treble melody. Broken chord and pure arpeggio passages are rare, yet one borrowed figuration which appears in gentle terms in Clementi's "Gradus ad Parnassum" becomes impressed with energy in "Diabelli" Variation 23 (bars 1–4 and 9–12). Harmonic vocabulary is conservative; in the entire work there is only one somewhat remote appoggiatura chord: yet there is nothing that can be described as datable.[1]

This puzzling feature may result from the extreme conciseness of style; the composition may be said to consist of mortised stone rather than bricks and mortar.

In such a work the performer's problem is insurmountable. Should an attempt at interpretation be made to help both the performer and audience or should the performance be, as it were, dehumanized and the stark colorlessness of the notes be presented as a framework for contemplation? There is a parallel in "King Lear"; in both the performer can never hope to offer much more than an aspect or introduction.

[1] Variation 30, measure 8.—Editor.

Also, in spite of its pianistic qualities, it may be fairly asked of the "Diabelli" whether it is akin to the "Art of Fugue" which, although playable on a keyboard, hardly reaches its fullness in any medium. One further problem is to foresee the length of the "Diabelli" when beginning a performance, since each succeeding variation contains some aspect or motive from the preceding one; from this grows the difficulty of spacing, some variations needing longer time than others. One curious contrast is found between Variation 14 (*Grave e maestoso*), taking approximately four minutes, and 15 (*Presto*) lasting three-quarters of a minute, followed by 16 and 17 (*Allegro*). Owing to the extreme slowness of 14, Variation 15 seems much shorter than it really is, its very lightness being soon swallowed up by two furious adjoined *Allegros*. Variation 24 is often admired by Bach enthusiasts but its placing after the explosive 23 helps toward appreciating the nobleness of its character.

Another puzzle is, why in the presence of the composer's manuscripts and an original edition revised by Beethoven, there should be so many variants in editions. There are more than thirty differences. Of these about twenty between the manuscript and the original edition are mostly of minor importance. Some editors, thinking that Beethoven's ability was waning, have added an unauthorized bar to Variation 4, between bars 5 and 6, making the variation up to sixteen bars to correspond with the theme. Variation 12 has also suffered; Beethoven's revised version of forty-eight bars has been published in at least one edition with only forty-six bars owing to a slight difference between manuscript and first edition.

A percussive element, derived from the theme permeates most of the work. In Variations 9 and 29 the same motive and key are used with opposite effect, while 9 begins with the same motive and notes as the theme. Only three variations do not match the theme having a dominant cadence to conclude the first section. The very archaisms of pattern used by Beethoven seem to be covered completely and simultaneously by the quality of the music and by each variation in many cases being a variation on its own, often dispensing with its initial motives without involving a sense of loss.

In keyboard literature, the "Diabelli" Variations belong to a category of works that sum up the possibilities of the instrument of its day yet point forward to the future. Just as Bull's "Walsingham" Variations show the highest point of virginal technique, and the Bach "Goldberg" that of the harpsichord, the "Diabelli" set sounds the uttermost reaches of true pianoforte technique in the first quarter of the nineteenth century. Yet its starkness, its choice of somber or sharp-edged pianoforte tones, and its rigid pattern relieved only by a miraculous coda make it unapproachable to many listeners.—WILLIAM YEOMANS

II. 11 New Bagatelles for Piano, Opus 119

Of the miscellaneous pieces, the Bagatelles, Opus 119 and 126 (1823), I take to have originally been sketches for various sonata or other movements, or, as it were, experiments in various styles, rounded off and made available for educational or recreative purposes. In the Opus 119, the Allegretto, No. 1, in G minor, is a graceful and sprightly minuet. No. 2, the Andante con moto, in C, is a neat and melodious songlike movement with crossing of hands. No. 3, à l'Allemande, in D, is in the style of a German waltz. No. 4, Andante cantabile, in A, might have been intended as an andante movement for a sonatina. No. 5, Resoluto, in C minor, reminds one of a movement in the violin sonatas, while No. 6 is a playful and effective Scherzo, preceded by an introductory Andante. The others are of a more miscellaneous nature.[1]—HERBERT WESTERBY

III. 6 Bagatelles for Piano, Opus 126

These small pieces were written at various times around 1823, and completed that year, when Beethoven was finishing the Ninth

[1] I would like to point out some musical gems in the next five pieces.

No. 7, in C major, is a study in trills where in strict four-voice writing a trill passes from the soprano voice to the alto and ends up as a pedal point on the tonic in the bass. An ingenious harmonic feature is that there is no final cadence as such: when the tonic in the bass finally arrives, it does so as the dominant of the subdominant key, F, and after this trill the two top voices start an exciting sequence of rising harmonies, first in eighth notes, then in sixteenths, sixteenth-note triplets, and finally thirty-second notes, ending with a brilliant arpeggio.

No. 8 is a gentle minuet in two parts also in C. Very typical of late Beethoven is the sudden "unexplained" change of harmony at the double bar. The first part ends smoothly enough in the dominant, G. The second part begins abruptly in B flat, whose significance is not realized until four bars later. It is first the tonic of B flat major, then the third step in the key of G minor, and only in passing does it reveal itself as the seventh in the chord of C7 which leads to the key of the subdominant, F, which leads the music gracefully back to the tonic.

No. 9 is an agitated waltz in A minor with an opening broken-chord motive as fiery and intent as the opening of the C minor piano sonata, Opus 10, No. 1.

No. 10, in A major, is a gay little wisp which is over before we know it. Starting on the dominant of the dominant, it does not reach the tonic until the end of the eight-measure first part, which is repeated. We expect a second part of at least equal length if not longer. All we actually get is a hurried four-bar coda which never strays from the tonic key!

No. 11, in B flat, is a peaceful andante with a simplicity of melody and harmony which bring the listener into the spiritual realms of the later quartets. Its only ruffling moment is a sudden diminished-seventh chord in the second half which resolves smoothly (by a chromatic shift in the bass) to a dominant-seventh chord, and after a short florid run we are back on a smooth even keel harmonically.—Editor.

Symphony and the *Missa solemnis*, so that we may regard them as relaxations from the two most exacting tasks he had ever undertaken. They are also contemporary with the "Diabelli" Variations. But although Beethoven did call them "bagatelles," we need not suppose that he regarded them as mere frivolities. Small as they are, [they] at once strike one as having absorbed his whole creative faculty. They are in their own way as original and representative as anything he wrote in the last three or four years of his life, and doubly precious because they are not quite like anything else.

We know that Beethoven was subject to moods and that these moods varied greatly and were apt to change suddenly and violently. Now all this is reflected with extraordinary vividness in the bagatelles, and it is therefore permissible to imagine that each of these pieces is a faithful reflection of Beethoven's frame of mind on this day or that. Indeed one may plausibly argue that in this respect they reveal his character more intimately than anything else he ever wrote. They are, if anything in music can be, self-portraits, whereas his larger compositions express not so much personal moods as ideal conceptions requiring sustained thought and an unchanging emotional disposition for many days or weeks —indeed in Beethoven's case sometimes years. But these short pieces could be dashed off by the composer, whatever he felt like at the moment, while the fit was on him. No doubt there is an element of exaggeration in this theory of the difference between composition on a large and a small scale; but the fact remains that in the bagatelles we have some perfect and almost graphically vivid sketches of Beethoven in his changeable daily moods, tender or gently humorous one morning and full of fury, rude buffoonery or ill-temper the next. Not even his letters, in which we may find all these turns of mind too, reveal him more clearly than that.

No. 1—*Andante con moto.*—G major.—The additional Italian directions Beethoven gives the performer of this first piece (cantabile e compiacevole) seems to contradict what has been said above, for whatever he may have been Beethoven was never complacent! We may perhaps better interpret his indication of the nature of the music as "songful and agreeable." It is perfectly urbane and has no trace of tenderness or lyricism about it, qualities which are kept out by a kind of gruff undertone in the accompanying lower parts.

A curious feature occurs in the second part of the piece which is much longer than the first and still further extended by a repeat.[1] This is a change from triple time to duple time. The effect on the ear is not as startling as that suggested to the eye [for the motive of this short 2/4

[1] The sixteen measures of the first part are not repeated but the second eight measures are merely ornamented variations of the first eight, thereby implying, to the listener, a repeat.—Editor.

section is a mere contraction of the measure before, in 3/4]. At the resumption of the 3/4 there is first of all a short cadenza, which for a moment destroys all sense of meter. [However,] after this the music [continues] in the first tempo and in the same mood, but takes a quite different turn [for] the opening melodic phrase appears not in the treble but in the bass.

No. 2—*Allegro.*—*G minor.*—Here Beethoven is impish and capricious. An impetuous rush of [sixteenth notes] alternates with a more caressing episode in [eighths]. The first part of the piece continues with these contrasts, [the little opening motive of sixteenth notes] being made use of separately for a moment. After the repetition of that part the second opens with a new melodic theme [which is marked "cantabile." The lovely melody] is immediately repeated with more piquant harmony as well as with a suspicion of counterpoint. Then the [little sixteenth-note motive] bursts in all alone, as in angry remonstrance and with pauses between, as though words failed it to express its indignation. But the pauses grow shorter and its expostulations more fluent. The tirade that follows seems to subdue its anger by its own eloquence, so that the music grows almost tender and playful in the end, though it still has its peevish movements. For all these changes of mood this second part is so beautiful and fantastically original throughout that one cannot fail to welcome its repetition.

No. 3—*Andante.*—*E flat major.*—Another complete change of feeling. This piece is in the nature of some of Beethoven's slow sonata movements, but on a very small scale, and in its form it may be said to constitute a tiny set of variations with a coda. The single theme opens [in a graceful 3/8 rhythm and in the sensuous "tenor" register of the piano]. It covers eight bars, which are repeated and followed by a short extension and by two chords broken into arpeggios. Then comes the first variant, which occupies no more than the eight bars. [Under a trill in the right hand, the left hand breaks up the eighth notes of the original theme into sixteenth notes.] The second [variant] is equally brief, [consisting of flowing, melodic thirty-second notes]. The coda is built on the final phrase of the third and last variant and concludes with a magically beautiful pianissimo passage in which tonic and dominant harmony is blended in an impressionistic manner by means of the sustaining pedal.

No. 4—*Presto.*—*B minor and major.*—Here we have a perfect picture of Beethoven in a furiously bad temper, and also of the extraordinary quickness of that temper to appear and to calm down again. There are two alternating sections, in B minor and major respectively. The former has these two irascible phrases for its outstanding features:—[the first consisting of a legato melody over a rude staccato accompaniment in the bass; the second of an angular climbing figure interrupted by imperious sforzandi]. Both occur in the very short first section, which is repeated. Then [the first phrase] appears in E minor in the bass and is followed by a lighter, fluttering theme played by the right hand. After a loud double knock of F sharp in bass octaves [it] incongruously appears in C major, only to be rudely interrupted by the F sharp again, which has an effect of comic roughness not unlike that of the famous C sharp in the finale of the Eighth Symphony. Beginning in F sharp minor again, [the same phrase] makes a pretense of embarking upon a fugato passage, which it almost immediately abandons, however, to make room for a more suave and sweet-toned transformation into E minor. But the original loud B minor version very soon returns and the hammering figure of [the second phrase] is extended into a concluding passage of eight bars.

The key now changes to B major, and with it the mood. Over a drone-bass of an open fifth there is a soft syncopated chiming of three-note groups which suggests a kind of constrained amiability, but a brief, muttered interruption ominously hints that all is not well and that we may expect another outbreak of rage. Sure enough, [the first phrase] returns, and with it the whole first section, which is played over again exactly as before. So, for that matter, is the second: the piece ends quietly but abruptly in B major.

No. 5—*Quasi allegretto.—G major.*—The fifth piece is the simplest and least original in the set, but it has its own character nevertheless, a kind of urban, sunny peacefulness that somehow makes one think of Sunday afternoon in the Vienna of Beethoven's time—perhaps a scene of a family's walk in the Prater, the middle episode in C major, with its suggestion of drums and fifes, hinting that soldiers on parade are not far off. The placid G major section returns, played an octave higher and with a different ending—a full close instead of the original half-close.

No. 6—*Presto, Andante amabile e con moto.—E flat major.*—The last piece begins with a frantic rush, but calms down at once to the andante amabile, than which nothing could have made a greater contrast. Here is a stillness and peace that pauses even from great emotion. There is not a vestige of fervor, and once again one is made to think of a kind of placid Austrian *Gemütlichkeit*, an impression which is perhaps enhanced by the gentle yodeling triplet figures that appear at the end of the first part. The first part is repeated. The triplet figures continue in the second part and modulate in a sharp curve through B flat major and C minor to A flat major, in which key the principle theme returns over a soft drum-roll base of alternating tonic and dominant in [sixteenth-note] triplets. These triplets are carried on under the lovely continuation of the theme, but now formed into melodically moving basses.

When the second part, which again closes with [the yodeling figure] but this time in the principal key, has been repeated, a coda begins with an exquisite expansion of [those triplets] by means of sequential passages, not mechanically contrived as so often in the case of minor composers, but with the Beethovenian imagination at the height of its power. Yet even here no passion intrudes—and only a supreme master can produce music, or indeed any art, showing the greatest pressure of the imagination unaccompanied by emotional heat. A drooping cadence based on [the peaceful first theme] tries to bring the piece to a conclusion in complete tranquillity, but suddenly the opening presto rushes in once more with the effect of a door that is being violently slammed on a peaceful scene.—ERIC BLOM (2)

IV. Klavierstück IN B MINOR (für Ferdinand Piringer), WoO 61

On February 18, 1821, appeared a noteworthy Albumblatt, [a short Allegretto in B minor, 2/2]. The style suggests Beethoven's later manner and the whole composition breathes a certain transitoriness which suggests that it was an "occasional" composition. Ferdinand Piringer [1780–1829] had approached Beethoven for an entry in his Autograph Album. This was the instigation.

[Piringer was a Viennese music lover who acted as assistant conductor of the Concerts Spirituel. The conversation books of 1821 and 1822 indicate that he became a very close friend of Beethoven's. The Allegretto is only twenty-seven measures long, but it is noteworthy for its clean three-part polyphonic writing, which does not detract from but rather adds to its warm lyricism.]—THEODOR FRIMMEL (1)

V. Klavierstück IN G MINOR (für Sarah Burney Payne), WoO 61a

Time of Composition: September 27, 1825.
Autograph: Louis Krasner, Syracuse, N.Y.—one page of four staves. Over the beginning of the manuscript in Beethoven's own hand [appear the words]: "Allegretto quasi Andante." At the foot of the page also in his hand [appears] the dedication: "Comme un souvenir a Sarah Burney Payne [one word blotted out]/par Louis van Beethoven/le 27 septemb., 1825." Previous owner: Thomas Massa Alsager, patron of contemporary music in England in the 1830's and 1840's. See O. E. Albrechts: "A Census of Autograph Music Manuscripts of European Composers in America," Philadelphia, 1953, No. 210 (p. 30).
About the dedication: Sarah Burney Payne, the daughter of Charles Burney [the English music historian], was on friendly terms with the owners of the magazine Harmonicon. It is therefore highly likely that it

was she who was the author of an article in that magazine in the volume 1825 entitled "A visit to Beethoven," and not, as Albert Leitzmann in his "Ludwig van Beethoven" (Volume 1, p. 331) states, a certain Lady Clifford.—GEORG KINSKY, EDITED BY HANS HALM (TR. BY THOMAS K. SCHERMAN)

The piece is in 2/4 time in two voices and starts out as a very smooth canon at the octave. It is only thirteen measures in length.

VI. *Klavierstück* IN C, *"Letzter musikalischer Gedanke"* (FROM THE UNFINISHED STRING QUINTET OF NOVEMBER 1826), WoO 62

Three different compositions of Beethoven have been identified as his last. The first to mention is a short piece for pianoforte in B flat which was published in Berlin by Schlesinger in the year 1840, with the title *"Dernière pensée musicale."* Beethoven wrote it for an album book [of Marie Szymanowska] in August 1818, at the same time as the last movement of the [Piano] Sonata, Opus 106. Obviously it cannot be considered, therefore, as Beethoven's "last thought." Another matter, however, presents itself in the case of the last movement of the String Quartet in B flat, Opus 130. This movement, according to authentic statements, was completed in November 1826, thus approximately four months before Beethoven's death. This movement appears to be Beethoven's last *completed* work.

The third composition to be mentioned is a piece in C major for pianoforte, two hands as well as four hands, which was published in 1838 by A. Diabelli and Company in Vienna with the title and description "Beethoven's last musical thought, from the original manuscript of November 1826; sketch of a quintet which A. Diabelli, music dealers, commissioned of Beethoven and the proprietary rights to which were purchased posthumously."[1] The manuscript is described in the auction catalogue of Beethoven's effects as "No. 173—fragment of a new Violin Quintet of November 1826, the last work of the composer." Page 28 of the Leipzig Universal Musical Press of January 1828 describes the purchase as follows: "The firm of Diabelli bought Beethoven's last work, a quintet begun in November 1826, of which regretfully however barely 20 or 30 measures in sketch were transcribed to paper." This statement contradicts itself in one respect. In one place it refers to the piece as a fragment, thus presumably finished up to a certain point whereas in another place it is described as merely a sketch. We cannot now determine which interpretation is correct, as the autograph is not at present in

[1] See the two letters to Diabelli quoted below.—Editor.

existence.[1] In any case the piece is not known to us in its original form as part of a movement of a quintet but only in two arrangements [:for piano, two hands, and piano, four hands].

All statements about it however agree that it was composed in November 1826. Now the finale of Opus 130 was also composed in November of 1826. Therefore one can ask: which of those two pieces was the last to be composed? An answer is supplied by one sheet of the sketchbook which begins with a passage written out in score of the finale of the B flat Quartet but which evidently Beethoven felt needed further work. These passages referring to the finale were written in ink, then after several empty staves there appear sketches for the quintet movement in C,[2] which were written in pencil.

Therefore the quintet movement was written later than the finale of Opus 130. On the same page of the sketchbook there appear, later on, sketches for another movement [also in C], which apparently were intended for the quintet.[3] It is not known whether Beethoven did further work on this passage. Probably only his death prevented him from completing it.—GUSTAV NOTTEBOHM (TR. BY THOMAS K. SCHERMAN)

VII. WALTZ IN E FLAT, WoO 84; WALTZ IN D, WoO 85; ÉCOSSAISE IN E FLAT, WoO 86

During the years 1824–25 and 1825–26 the well-known publisher C. F. Müller in Vienna issued a collection of dances for pianoforte "especially composed for this occasion" by famous composers. About the personality of the editor another entire essay should be written. Let us say here only that, unlike what has been believed up to now, a *non*composer of dance music (by the same name) would not have presumed to put out a collection of Viennese dance music even if he were from Berlin. The fact that Beethoven approached him (even for his so-called "bread-and-butter work") is enough testimony. Beethoven delivered to him three small works—two waltzes in E flat and D major, and an écossaise in E flat. The original manuscripts (now in the so-called "*Zürcher Beethovensammlung*) are noted in the Master's own handwriting, "*Walzer [Eb-dur] von L. v. Beethoven—Wien, am 12*ten *Novemb., 1824*"; "*Walzer [D-dur] Geschrieben am 14*ten *Novemb., 1825 von L. v. Beethoven*"; and "*Ecossais, Geschrieb am 14*ten *Novemb., 1825 von L. v. Beethoven.*"

[1] Kinsky in his description of WoO 62 states that it has not been traced. Nottebohm was writing in 1871 and Kinsky in 1955.—Editor.

[2] Nottebohm quotes five measures of the beginning which differ only slightly from the piece in its ultimate form as anonymously arranged for the Diabelli publication. —Editor.

[3] Nottebohm quotes twelve measures marked moderato 2/4, which are distinctly dancelike in character—not unlike the spirit which pervades the finale of Opus 130.—Editor.

Both waltzes and the écossaise for C. F. Müller were Beethoven's last dance compositions. As they were composed during his work on the last quartets, they are too easily dismissed. Certainly the thought of the great tone-poet has little in connection with them. But is it not proper that we ourselves should know what came from the great mind of a genius who at the same moment was creating [Opus 131 and Opus 135]?—MAX UNGER (2) (TR. BY THOMAS K. SCHERMAN)

In studying the three morsels I was at a loss to try to discover some subtlety of harmony, some one measure of surprise, some melodic turn, that I would be able to quote to refute Herr Unger's argument that these light compositions are difficult to consider as from the same pen and the same mind that at the same moment was molding the great Opus 131 and Opus 135. I did find one or two samplings that renewed my faith that a creative genius of that magnitude would not—no, could not—turn out any work that smacked of bad taste.

The first part of the E-flat Waltz (eight measures) ends on the tonic. The second part consists of sixteen measures, the first eight of which glide through neighboring keys landing, poised, in its eighth measure, on the dominant-seventh chord, after which the first eight measures are repeated to round out the waltz. There is a crescendo indicated at the beginning of the second part, which one would expect to continue up until the crucial dominant-seventh chord. But Beethoven, very slyly, indicates a diminuendo from the seventh measure on—thus negating the entire importance of the journey into slightly foreign parts and giving the listener a feeling that he had been listening to the same key and same refrain for the entire time.

To balance this, the trio of the waltz is constructed entirely on a pedal point of A flat, the key of the subdominant. The manner in which he establishes this pedal point, with its fifth step also included, suggests the bagpipe or drone bass which was so common in the village dance bands. At the same time the immense spread between the bass and the treble (a spread of five octaves) is definitely the product of the same creative mind that was hearing, in his inner ear, the scherzos of the last quartets.

The voice leading of the D-major Waltz suggests the smooth writing of the composer in his middle period. However, I too must admit I can find no subtlety, sophistication, geniality, or tenderness that can recommend the sixteen-measure écossaise. Be that as it may, its composer, at the time, had more important things to consider.—THOMAS K. SCHERMAN

Arrangement for Piano Four Hands
of the Great Fugue, Opus 134

A letter to Karl Holz found its way to America many years ago. It is now owned by Mr. Harold Randolph of Baltimore and possesses particular significance because apparently it has remained *unpublished*. As generally in such cases, the contents of the letter help to clarify a special episode in Beethoven's life. The letter taxes the gift of divination of the transcriber, but fortunately the obscure words (obscure to me) do not complicate the sense for the translation.

> Best Wood of Christ!
> Here the piano score for 4 hands—for the H. Mathias. God give [?]
> —he will understand that I could not possibly lose so much time for
> nothing. Also, it has now become a special work of mine. Nevertheless
> I do not ask more than 12 ducats in gold. Suppose the case that
> I had agreed from the beginning to make the piano-score myself,
> one could not have offered me a fee of less than 25 to 30 ducats.
> In consideration, however, that A[rtaria] has also lost the 100 florins,
> Viennese Currency I content myself with the amount indicated
> above. You know that I hereby *do not profit but on the contrary lose.*
> The already agreed Poenale could also still be paid off rightly, be-
> cause our best H. Mathias has really given me a raw deal in view of
> his wanting to take [?] the quartet then not taken—However,
> Hr. M. knows anyhow that we gladly and often are at his service
> without payment and shall be—but the present service which I
> rendered him is too slavish not to have to insist on compensation—
> Appointing you now Executor in this matter, I beg of you, honorable
> Sir, to receive everything.

> (No Address)

> YOUR
> BEETHOVEN

The mere fact that the letter was written to Holz assigns it to either 1825 or 1826, but the context definitely places the letter in 1826. For the reason that this epistle of instructions to Karl Holz as Executor refers plainly to Beethoven's Opus 133, the "Grande Fügüe tantôt libre, tantôt recherchée" for string quartet published by Mathias Artaria of Vienna on May 10, 1827.

The active interest of the firm of Artaria in Beethoven's works will appear from this array of his works published by it: Opus 2, 4, 5, 7, 8, 9, 12,

46, 48, 51, 63, 64, 66, 72 (Fidelio, third version), 87, 102, 103, 104, 105, 106, 113, 114, 130, 133, 134, not to mention sundry works without opus numbers. That Beethoven occasionally felt irritated by this publisher as he did, when the temper seized him, by practically every other of his various publishers, goes without saying, just as he must have irritated all of them time and again. Perhaps the allusion to a quartet which Beethoven expected Artaria to take, relates to some such incident. At any rate, we know that Artaria was among the unsuccessful competitors for the E flat major Quartet, Opus 127. This, the first of the three quartets commissioned by Prince Galitzin, was acquired by Schott; the second (in order of composition), Opus 132 in A minor, Schlesinger took and only the third, the one in B flat major, Opus 130 went to Artaria. That quartet was composed in 1825 with a fugue as the last movement and that fugue particularly taxed the executive powers of the Schuppanzigh Quartet and the receptive powers of the audience at the first performance on March 21, 1826.

Among those who questioned the wisdom of retaining the fugue and persuaded the composer to substitute as last movement the one composed in the Fall of 1826, with which the work was then published, was precisely Mathias Artaria, with whom Beethoven had become quite intimate. Artaria proposed that, if the master followed his advice, he would issue the fugue separately and would pay him for the new movement. Thus it came about that the original last movement of Opus 130 saw the light of day, with a dedication to Archduke Rudolph, as Opus 133 under the title quoted, though on Artaria's autograph score called "Overture." Shortly after Beethoven's acceptance of the advice of his critical friends, Artaria, in a Conversations-Heft belonging to about April 11, 1826, remarked: "There have been already many requests for a four-hand arrangement of the Fugue. Do you permit that I publish it in that form?—Score, the parts, the Fugue à 4 Mains arranged by you, to be published simultaneously." Beethoven evidently approved of this practical idea but, instead of making the arrangement himself, requested the pianist Anton Halm who had played the B flat major Trio at Schuppanzigh's concert of March twenty-first, to do so. Halm submitted his arrangement on April 24th with a very respectful letter to Beethoven who disliked the pianistic distribution of the parts as Halm many years later told Thayer: "Therefore, Beethoven arranged the Fugue himself and so it was published." As Opus 134, which explains Beethoven's remark about "a special work." No less a pianistic celebrity than Franz Liszt made it his business to edit the work for the "first complete" edition of Beethoven's pianoforte compositions published by L. Holle (Wolfenbüttel) long ago forgotten, but preserved in the New York Public Library. A copy of the still scarcer original edition is at the Library of Congress. Harold Bauer, whose attention I drew to the whole episode,

examined both editions and favored me with the following note on Beethoven's own arrangement:

> Beethoven seems to have kept Halm's arrangement while making
> his own, which in my opinion, he wrote impatiently and hastily,
> reversing, for the sake of visual effect of separate voices, and totally
> regardless of difficulty in performance, all that Halm had done in
> order to make it pianistically playable.
>
> Because of certain unnecessary, and in most cases, quite ineffec-
> tive modifications in the passage work, it appears doubtful that
> Beethoven referred to the original score in making his arrangement,
> the main value of which lies in his implicit recognition of the fact
> that the composition exceeds the technical limitations of a string-
> quartet, for, commencing with the first notes of the introduction,
> the basses are frequently doubled, and throughout the entire work
> there is an obvious intention to suggest a greater continuity to effect
> in the use of the thematic material than the four stringed instruments
> with their unavoidable changes of register could possibly obtain.

The piece does not appear in the "Gesamtausgabe" of Beethoven's
works. Perhaps because the editors thereof accepted Schindler's statement that the arrangement published by Artaria was actually that of
Halm and not of Beethoven. Halm's own narrative refutes Schindler
definitely and, furthermore, Artaria would hardly have dared mislead the
public by giving to Opus 134 the same main title as to Opus 133, merely
adding "et arrangée pour le Pianoforte par l'auteur même. Oeuvre 134."

One can hardly blame Beethoven for demanding payment for his
service of slavery—ordinarily he detested making arrangements of his
works—but, on the other hand, Artaria at first could not quite see the
matter through Beethoven's eyes. He had paid on May 12, 1826, Halm
40 ducats in good faith, not expecting that Beethoven, beyond perhaps
suggesting this or that improvement, would reject Halm's arrangement.
How Beethoven felt about the matter we know from the quoted unpublished letter not only, but from a published (rather courteous) letter to
Artaria's confidential agent. In this he said:

> I do not at all wish to compel him [Artaria] to take my arrange-
> ment for piano. I therefore send you the piano score of Halm so
> that, upon receipt of my piano score, you may deliver Halm promptly
> to M. A. [Mathias Artaria]. If, however, Herr A. wants to retain
> my piano-score for the fee of 12 ducats in gold, I demand only that
> he put that in writing or pay you the fee in hand—for which purpose
> I inclose a receipt. The piano-score cannot be debited to me in any
> way.

To this ultimatum he added "you know my situation,"—one of his
numerous allusions to straitened circumstances. From a question of Holz

in July we know that the dispute had not yet been settled, but Artaria then finally decided to drop Halm's arrangement and to accept and publish Beethoven's own and on Beethoven's terms, the only decision compatible with normal business acumen. His expense-books show that he paid Beethoven the stipulated 12 ducats in gold on September 12, 1826.

From the above sequence of events it follows that Mr. Randolph's letter best be dated May or June, 1826.—O. G. SONNECK (2)

Music for Voice with
Piano Accompaniment

I. SONG CYCLE: "An die ferne Geliebte," OPUS 98

The art song had not developed a cult in Beethoven's day and was not a fruitful source of revenue, and Beethoven was [not] able to ignore the commercial side of his profession. Nevertheless, [he] gave attention to the song form at the beginning and the climax of his career: he was scarcely eleven years old when his song "Schilderung eines Mädchens"[1] was published, and he [composed] a setting to "Ich war bei Chloen" [words by Weisse][2] less than five years before his death when he was absorbed with the completion of the Ninth Symphony.

The six songs of the cycle "An die ferne Geliebte" have never been entirely in or wholly out of vogue, yet I shall never quarrel with a singer who shall say that their sanctity is such that he would not wear them on his sleeve "for daws[3] to peck at." Their sentiment is at once so simple, yet profound, [and] their emotional content so personal and precious. Aside from their beauty, moreover, they have a historic significance which ought to be brought forth. [Opus 98] is not only the first song cycle; it is still the most perfect of all song cycles in respect of unity. There is both a spiritual and a material bond which knits the six poems into a whole, as the various parts of a Beethoven symphony are molded into a oneness.

[Opus 98] was composed in 1816. Alois Jeitteles,[4] the [poet], was a young man of twenty-one, studying medicine in Vienna at the time. It has been thought that he handed the poem[s] to Beethoven in person.

---

[1] WoO 107. See Prod'homme's essay on the early songs.—Editor.
[2] "Der Kuss," Opus 128.—Editor.
[3] Krehbiel is alluding to music patrons and music critics.—Editor.
[4] 1794-1858. Schindler states that Beethoven thanked him for the happy inspiration. —Editor.

Sketches for the songs appear in a sketchbook [of the spring of 1816].
They disclose Beethoven's habitual care in the study of declamation and
descriptive effect.

The first phrase of the first song is repeated several times with its
characteristic fall [of a major sixth], so suggestive of the poet's longing
glance in the direction of his love. [This was an afterthought according
to the many sketches, as also were] the detached tones of the melody of
No. 3, designed to give the effect of lightness and airiness to the description of the floating clouds.

The tenderness and warmth of feeling led Thayer to suspect there was
a bit of autobiography in the composition: [he] quotes, as corroboration,
a letter of Beethoven to Ferdinand Ries in 1816: "My kind regards to
your wife. I, alas, have no wife. I have met only one and her I shall
probably never get." [The loved one referred to is Amilie von Sebald.]—
H. E. KREHBIEL (2)

In the late songs too the songs of nature play an important part,
headed by the song cycle "*An die ferne Geliebte.*" Thayer, and surely
correctly, already linked the highly personal nature of this special creation
with a surging love experience of the master, which is referred to in a
statement by Beethoven at that period concerning the one woman that
he would never possess. It is not an arbitrary act to link the gripping
sorrow that runs through the song cycle with what the man Beethoven
felt at that time in the bitter renunciation of what he "had regarded as
the highest happiness of his life." But this sorrow does not twitter in
some sort of formless romantic subterranean emotion; in the true Beethoven manner it is summed up in a basic motif—the "Farewell" already
known from Opus 81a and distributed in variation transformations among
the individual songs. And the composer takes still further measures to
keep the exploration of "the blue cloud land" within bounds, as his
larger form shows in two ways, in the symmetrical arrangement of the
key grouping and in the song forms chosen in each case:

No. 1	No. 2	No. 3	No. 4
var. stanza song	three-part	var. stanza song	var. stanza song
		(single form of accompaniment)	
E flat major	G major	A flat major	

No. 5	No. 6
three-part	var. stanza song
C major	E flat major

HUGO MOSER

II. *"Der Kuss,"* ARIETTE WITH PIANO ACCOMPANIMENT, OPUS 128

In his chapter of three sketchbooks from the years 1819 to 1822, Nottebohm has the following remarks about the sketchbook containing copious work on the *"Weihe des Hauses"* overture:

"In between and later appears a multitude of various notes. Among them are the following: exercises in figured bass based in the second volume of Phillip Emanuel Bach's 'Versuch [*uber die wahre Art des Clavier zu spielen*' (1762)] and without doubt apropos of the later undertaken addition of figured bass in the Missa Solemnis; also a small sketch for the song 'Der Kuss,' Opus 128." [Nottebohm quotes the sketch: the first four measures of the melody, with only the first three words of the text written underneath.]

In discussing a sketchbook of 1798 containing work on the Quartet in D, Opus 18, No. 3, the author writes the following paragraph:

"Soon [after the sketches of the quartet] appeared a draft of a melody to Chr. F. Weisse's text 'Der Kuss.' [Only the first twelve measures appear, with the full text underneath.] This draft proves that the song which appeared under the opus number 128 already existed as an earlier composition, which was somewhat worked over in the year 1822. A substantial difference between the [1798] sketch and the [1822] publication appears in the voice part in the first two measures."

Despite the early sketches the 1822 song has many earmarks of the late Beethoven. Firstly there is the detailed tempo indication in German instead of Italian, which Beethoven adopted only after 1814. Secondly, there is a delightful nine-bar introduction for the piano, in which the first phrase of the song melody is highly developed, using material that does not occur again throughout the song in either the vocal line or the piano accompaniment. Thirdly, there are many humorous pauses and sudden accents which greatly enhance the charming text. On the whole, although harmonically there are no novelties, the highly declamatory style is certainly a product of the Master's late years. One titillating detail is the way Beethoven treats the word *"lange"* in the closing line: *"Ja wohl sie schrei doch lange hinter her"* ("Yes, certainly she cried but much later"). The full line is repeated three times in full, but the last time the word *"lange"* is repeated by itself all of nine times, ending with a ritard and a fermata.—THOMAS K. SCHERMAN

III. *"Un lieto brindisi,"* A SMALL CANTATA FOR SOPRANO, TWO TENORS, AND BASS, WITH PIANO ACCOMPANIMENT, WoO 103

Meanwhile[1] one of Beethoven's minor productions was now composed for his friend Bertolini.[2] The occasion was an evening festival arranged by the doctor at his own expense on the name day (St. John's day, June 24) and in honor of Malfatti. It was a little piece for four voices with pianoforte accompaniment to a text written by Abbate Bondi[3]:

> Un lieto brindisi
> Tutti a Giovanni,
> Cantiam così, così,
> Viva longhi anni, etc.[4]

Invitations were extended not only to Malfatti's relatives and personal friends but to a large number of artists of the various professions, resident or temporarily in Vienna—Dragonetti among the musicians. The scene was Malfatti's villa in Weinhaus. There they feasted; the wine flowed; the cantata was sung; Beethoven, "thoroughly unbuttoned," improvised; fun and frolic ruled the hour. "The sport cost me a few hundred florins," laughingly said the good doctor fifty years afterwards.—
ALEXANDER WHEELOCK THAYER, EDITED BY ELLIOT FORBES

IV. *"Resignation,"* WoO 149; *"Abendlied unterm gestirnten Himmel,"* WoO 150

If we seek to observe the final goal of Beethoven's development in song, we may look to "Resignation" (1817) and the *"Abendlied unterm gestirnten Himmel"* (1820), his last song.

The first one is in three parts, for the most part limited to what could be called a Handel-like three-voicedness which, by adding an octave to a section with only two voices, presents the sound of misery that corresponds to the sadness of the text, reinforced by dissonant retards and passing notes for the voice; this harsh coloration and spare motifs show a sort of Pfitzner tonality (e.g., *"Zum Abschied meiner Tochter"*). The primitive quality of the chord repetitions is accentuated even more in the

---

[1] During the preparations for the production of the revised version of *Fidelio* in 1814.—Editor.

[2] Andreas Bertolini, the close friend and personal physician of Beethoven from 1806 to 1816.—Editor.

[3] Clemente Bondi (1741–1821), a poet and Jesuit priest.—Editor.

[4] The autograph of the work was lost. The work itself was reconstructed by Willy Hess in 1945 from a transcript by Otto Jahn. The words, however, are in German. It was published in this form for the first time in the *"Jahrbuch der Literarischen Vereinigung,"* Winterthur, 1945, as part of an essay by Hess describing the circumstances of the creation of the work.—Editor.

"*Abendlied*," which is made up of four eight-line variation stanzas. Despite the brilliance of the full accompaniment, the melody in notes of uniform length in the fifth and sixth lines can hardly be surpassed for angularity.

The first four lines have more feeling; the two last lean toward the social song. This might almost seem like negative criticism, and yet, out of the song, illuminated by the poem's idea of imminent death, there shines forth a transfiguration that makes the contemporaneity of the Ninth Symphony not at all an anachronism. Here we see one of the end points of Beethoven's classicism attained, and it is understandable that this sparing absence of sensuous quality could be followed only by a break: Schubert's songs and Loewe's ballads derive from quite other ancestors than the harshly sublime style of Beethoven's late songs. From this point of view Beethoven's lyricism as a whole appears as a noble special case, as a proudly detached ceremonial region that was never a road open to traffic but ended as a blind alley; or rather a consecrated still square, on which allegorical statues of gods stand in rows to receive offerings of pious memory.

We are taken still further into the world of the late Beethoven by the song "Resignation," whose indication "With feeling, but decisively, well accented and eloquently delivered" already shows the sphere it belongs to. This is Beethoven's last word in the declamatory song style, which he carried to the extreme of its possibilities, beyond which every step had to lead back to recitative.

It is with deep reverence that the German spirit must accept the gift of a final completion of the song style, in which the greatest musician of the age proves himself to be, to the point of self-denial, the protector and defender of the rights of words and verbal expression in the combination of words and sounds.—HUGO MOSER

V. WEDDING SONG FOR ANNA GIANNATASIO DEL RIO, WoO 105

On February 6, 1819, Nanni Giannatasio, the daughter of Giannatasio del Rio, the proprietor of the boarding school where Beethoven's nephew Karl was enrolled, married Councilor Leopold von Schmerling. For the occasion Beethoven composed a short song for a male voice, with a refrain for a small male chorus in unison, and piano accompaniment. On the wedding morning the participants, one of them being Beethoven himself, lay in wait in a corner of a room and greeted the young couple as they entered with the new song. Later Beethoven presented the manuscript, the text for which had been written by Dr. Stein, professor of philosophy at the University of Vienna. The subsequent fate of this manuscript was eventful. In some way, as yet unexplained, it disappeared from Mrs. Schmerling's possession and got to England, where it was owned by Ewer & Company, publishers, and disappeared completely after 1858. These publishers put out the song on the occasion of the marriage of the subsequent Emperor Friedrich III to Princess Victoria of England, with a new English text for the occasion and with certain changes in the notes of the original. After that the manuscript vanished, until by good fortune it reappeared in November 1924 in the archives of the house of Breitkopf & Härtel.

The song has the unmistakable imprint of Beethoven, unpretentious though it may be in other respects; as Thayer says, it is "a well-contrived piece, which would be effective on any similar occasion." The remark is justified; if the little opus had a suitable text that applied generally, it could be a source of joy today too on festive occasions. It is significant of the master's sense of responsibility that he felt it necessary to make a goodly number of sketches even for so light and temporary a bit; his mind and artistic conscience always tested the artist's ideas, even when God-given, and forced them in the correct form that suited them in each case. And it is this kind of work that distinguishes him from the so-called "original geniuses," the only-musicians and dilettantes, who do not have enough power to match their often correct and great ideas and bring them, like jewels, into the right form, without which they have no brilliance and no value.—WILHELM HITZIG

The short wedding cantata is a solemn, festive strophe song for solo voice and chorus accompanied by piano—a genuine example of a fervor-inspired Beethoven composition. There is a grandiose fortissimo intro-duction whose tremolo bass and brilliant octave scale suggest a piano reduction of an orchestral work. The flourish ends in a fermata on a dominant-seventh chord elaborated by a sweeping arpeggio from the lowest to the highest register of the paino. This is followed by a simple melodic figure twice repeated (again in naked harmonics and different registers suggesting the orchestral winds). This turns out to be the first measure of the soloist's melody. The soloist sings each verse, which is made up of three short phrases with the accompanying piano filling out the pauses in between each phrase. The last phrase is the most interesting to students of Beethoven, as it is an exact note-for-note reproduction of the second phrase of the "Ode to Joy" of the Ninth Symphony. As if to reinforce the similarity, the chorus repeats this phrase (as it does in the symphony) in unison with an increasingly full accompani-ment. There is a five-measure postlude by the piano, a repetition of the melodic fragment, and the next verse begins. There are three verses. —Editor.

VI. *"Lobkowitz-Cantata,"* WoO 106

"The late prince esteemed you highly, and you are held in the like esteem by his children"; so writes Court-Councillor Peters, in the year 1819, in the so-called conversation-book of Beethoven, which the then completely deaf master always had to carry in his pocket. Historical dates prove that this entry could only have reference to Prince Lobkowitz, in Vienna, who died in 1816, leaving two sons. It must have been highly interesting to the author to peruse these about one hundred and thirty conversation-books in the Berlin library, and to find the following notice, which was, no doubt, published by the authority of O. Jahn, the author of Mozart's biography, and who collected facts for a Beethoven biography, which notice appeared in 1865 in A. W. Thayer's Chronological list of Beethoven's works. There we read (page 208):—"Cantata for a special occasion, composed in 1816." This cantata, which is supposed to be at the present time in Prague, was written by Beethoven, both words and music, for his friend Peters. It was the intention that this little piece should be sung by the young princes, the pupils of Peters, to their father on the anniversary of his birthday. The death of the prince, however, which took place on the 7th of December, 1816, frustrated their plan. The 7th of December was not only the day of the prince's death, but also that of his birth. The fact is, so far, without doubt, the cantata has not only never been sung, but up to the present time[1] it has been thought to be lost. Among the documents belonging to the late wife of the elder of the two princes, I succeeded in discovering the manuscript. Here it is just as it was performed in the year 1823, on the birthday of the same prince (then 27 years of age), and as I have found it in the musical archive of the Castle of Eisenberg in Bohemia. The autograph is in the possession of Herr Ottokar Zeithhamer, in Prague, and on comparing my copy with the autograph, I find it perfectly correct.

Although the little work is not of great importance, yet, being a composition of Beethoven, associated with the memory of one of his most excellent friends, it possesses a double interest. The dedication to the prince by Beethoven of seven of his most important works testified to the mutual esteem which existed between them. It has been related to me by the daughter-in-law of the prince, who died 15th of December, as mentioned in my little book, "New Pictures from the Life of Music and its Masters" (Munich, 1870), that Beethoven wrote a letter, dated 8th January of the following year, 1817, to the young noble heir, revealing the intense regard with which he had enjoyed the friendship of the

[1] February 1, 1882.—Editor.

prince. He writes:—"I take the liberty of sending you this dedication, which was intended for your lamented father, but by untoward circumstance did not reach him. I hope you will accept this little offering of thankfulness I had intended for your good father. Pray, believe me to be one of those who know you will fulfill all his expectations, and perform those great deeds men will expect from you in your exalted position of life." Court-Councillor Peters certifies, as we have before indicated, that the son faithfully followed in the footsteps of his father, at least in regard to Beethoven. C. F. Pohl's "History of the Vienna Conservatoire" shows for the years 1833 to 1848 not less a sum than 16,000 florins subsidized by the prince. That "Dedication" was Beethoven's "Liederkreis" to his greatly beloved Amelie Sebald in Berlin, and then just published. The prince had a strong and fine baritone voice, and frequently sang.[1]—F. NOHL

Music for Voice with
Orchestral Accompaniment

I. *"Germania"* FOR BASS SOLO, WITH CHORUS AND ORCHESTRA (FINAL SONG FOR FRIEDRICH TREITSCHKE's *Singspiel "Gute Nachricht"*), WoO 94

The French armies had so often taken possession of the capitals of the various Continental states that the motives are inconceivable, which induced Schwarzenberg to restrain the approach of the allied armies on Paris, until Blücher's persistence, enforced by his victories, at last com-

---

[1] The work is based on the following slightly pompous but appropriate words (written by Beethoven himself):

"Es lebe, es lebe, unser theurer Fürst!	(Long live our dear Prince!
Er lebe, er lebe!	He lives, he lives!")
Edel, edel handeln sei sein schönster	Let noble deeds be his handsome
Beruf!	profession.
Dann, dann wird ihm nicht entgeben der	Then he will receive the noblest of
schönste Lohn.	rewards!
Es lebe, es lebe, unser theurer Fürst!	Long live our dear Prince!
Er lebe, er lebe!"	He lives, he lives!")

It starts with a martial theme first announced by the accompanying piano and repeated immediately by the soprano soloist and punctuated by the chorus on the words *"Er lebe."* A short piano interlude of scales and fanfares slows down to an Adagio assai which ushers in the middle section, much more lyric in character for the soloist, ending with a florid cadenza. The original tempo and original theme re-enter on the repetition of the words *"Es lebe, unser theurer Fürst"* but this time the chorus sings the entire phrase. The whole short work ends with a brilliant postlude for the piano.—Editor.

pelled the commander-in-chief to yield the point. When this became known in Vienna, it was determined to celebrate the event, so soon as news of it should arrive, by an appropriate performance in the Court Opera. To this end, Treitschke wrote a *Singspiel* in one act entitled *Gute Nachricht* (Good News). Of the nine pieces of music in it, the overture was given to Hummel and the concluding chorus, "*Germania, wie stehts du jetzt im Glanze da,*" to Beethoven.—ALEXANDER WHEELOCK THAYER, EDITED BY ELLIOT FORBES

It is a strophe song of five verses in which the chorus answers the bass soloist after each line. The accompaniment is typical of a Festspiel work with many brass fanfares and timpani rolls. The only touch of originality is the interruption of the second line of the last verse with a ritard and a fermata followed by a very operatic outburst of the soloist to the words "Franz, Kaiser Franz Victoria!"—Editor.

II. "*Es ist vollbracht,*" FOR BASS VOICE WITH CHORUS AND ORCHESTRA, WoO 97

[In 1815] while [Beethoven] was employed [on the composition of the two Sonatas for Cello and Piano, Opus 102], Treitschke[1] called upon him for a closing chorus, "*Es ist vollbracht*" to a little dramatic piece, similar to the *Gute Nachricht*, entitled *Die Ehrenpforten*, and prepared to celebrate the second capitulation of Paris. It was performed July 15, 16, and 23; and, on the occasion of the emperor's name day, was revived "with appropriate changes" October 3 and 4; but (according to the theater bills) with the chorus "*Germania*"[2] substituted for "*Es ist vollbracht.*"—ALEXANDER WHEELOCK THAYER, EDITED BY ELLIOT FORBES

It is a strophe song each verse of which begins and ends with the words "Es ist vollbracht." The musical interest is kept alive by the changing instrumental accompaniment to each verse. The odd length of Treitschke's lines gives Beethoven an opportunity for subtle phrase lengths tied together by the orchestra introducing the second line which overlaps the entrance of the voice part.

The chorus echoes the soloist's last phrase in each verse. At the end of the fourth verse the orchestral interlude is suspended on the chord of the dominant seventh, at which point the tempo changes to poco adagio and, to the words "Gott sei dank, und unser'm Kaiser, es ist vollbracht," Beethoven quotes the Austrian national anthem.—Editor.

[1] Georg Friedrich Treitschke, author of the revised *Fidelio* libretto.—Editor.
[2] Beethoven had written this for Treitschke's earlier *Singspiel* "*Die Gute Nachricht.*" —Editor.

III. *"Elegischer Gesang,"* FOR FOUR VOICES AND STRING QUARTET, OPUS 118

In the year 1804, Beethoven found lodgings in a house on the ramparts of Vienna on the Mölkerbastei, three or four houses away from that of Prince Lichnowsky. It was owned by Baron Johann Baptist von Pasqualati, a musical amateur and physician to the Empress Maria Theresa. According to Ries: "Beethoven's room was on the fourth story from which there was a lovely view over the broad Glacis, the northwestern suburbs of the city and the mountains in the distance. Although he moved out several times he always returned to it." The baron was evidently good-natured enough to remark, "The lodging will never be rented; Beethoven will come back."

Obviously Beethoven was on good terms with both the baron and his wife, Eleonore. The latter died in childbirth on August 5, 1811, and upon the third anniversary of her death Beethoven presented to his friend a short song for four solo voices with string quartet accompaniment, with the inscription: "To the memory of the transfigured (*"verklärte"*) wife of my honored friend, Pasqualati, from his friend Ludwig van Beethoven." The poet is unknown but the words beautifully express Beethoven's sympathy:

> *Sanft wie du lebtest*
> *Hast du vollendet*
> *Zu heilig fur Schmerz!*
> *Kein' Auge wein*
> *Ob die himmlischen Geistes Heimkehr.*
>
> Tender as thou lived
> So thou died
> Too holy for sorrow!
> No eye can weep
> At the homecoming of a heavenly soul.

Its musical setting is filled with the other-worldly tranquillity that so often appeared in the slow movements of Beethoven's works at this time. His sensitivity to the declamation of the text and its inner meaning is amazing. The first forte in the piece is on the work *"Schmerz,"* on which there appears also the first discord to mar the calm harmonies. But the dynamics recede immediately to pianissimo. That first forte is mirrored by another loud chord on the words *"himmlischen Geistes Heimkehr,"* but this time in a clear harmony of the subdominant, which to Beethoven always signified the approaching close of a composition. The ending is particularly haunting. Twice the voices without accompaniment enter one after another to complete a feminine cadence which is echoed each time by the strings, the last time in voice leading worthy of the slow movement of the Opus 95 quartet.—THOMAS K. SCHERMAN

IV. *"Opferlied,"* FOR SOPRANO WITH CHORUS AND ORCHESTRAL ACCOMPANIMENT, OPUS 121b

A treatise on Beethoven would not be complete today without a sufficient discussion of the date of composition of various works of the master. It is not enough to say that a composition was created "between such and such a date," as is now the case with many of Beethoven's works. With this in mind we shall try to sort out the confusion which now exists about the various settings by Beethoven of Matthison's poem *Opferlied,* and in doing to use as our guide the stylistic differences among them.

We call to mind the "three" arrangements of Matthison's text that appear in the collected works:

Setting No. II—in Series 23 of the collected works, Number 233
Setting No. III—in Series 25, Number 268
Setting No. IV—in Series 22, Number 212

With this arrangement it is evident that a hitherto unknown Setting No. I must exist. Further we must note that the above-mentioned "three" settings seem to appear in the following order: Setting II, Setting IV, Setting III. As evidence:

Setting II appeared in the collection "3 German Songs," first published by Simrock in 1808. The year of composition is placed by Boettcher[1] as 1795, Nottebohm-Frimmel [in the thematic catalogue of Beethoven's compositions] place it "at the latest" 1795, while Thayer [in his biography, Vol. II] gives the indication 1796-97. As evidence of these dates the various authors quote the sketchbooks and the opinions about the publication of Matthison's text. We will discuss the sketches later and bring to them a well-authenticated clarification of the various authors' interpretations. Also the argument about the appearance of the text needs one supplementation: Matthison wrote the poem *Opferlied* in 1788 and it was published around 1790 in the *"Musen-Almanach"* of Voss. Later the poet came to the attention of Bonn (and specifically the Bonn of Beethoven's days) by means of his journey there on September 6, 1786, as evidenced by his diary. Therefore, the time of the appearance of the text would not stand in the way of an interpretation that the musical setting of the *Opferlied* was worked on as early as the Bonn days of the composer.

Setting IV is placed by Boettcher as being composed in 1822; for evidence he cites a handwritten score in the archives of the Society of the

---

[1] Hans Boettcher: *"Beethoven as Liederkomponisten."*—Editor.

Friends of Music in Vienna. The designation of Setting IV as Opus 121b—also erroneously as Opus 121a—resulted from the piano arrangement published by Schött and Sons in Mainz. This designation was repeated in the above-mentioned appearance in the collected works. In search of a more accurate date of composition, the author obtained the following information from the publishing house of Schött:

"At the request of Beethoven, the edition was placed under the supervision of Gottfried Weber, who also assembled the corrections and managed the correspondence. This must be the reason also for the fact that nothing further is found concerning the work in our files."

Setting III is generally not mentioned in the catalogues of Beethoven's works by Thayer and Nottebohm-Frimmel. [It] was for a long time unquestioned as an independent composition until we discovered an allusion to it in the [*Encyclopedia of German Concert Literature*] of Müller-Reuter, which was quoted by Hans Boettcher in his comprehensive essay on Beethoven's vocal compositions. The latter gives the year 1823 as the date of composition.

[Herbst here goes into great detail as to the identification of the various scores and parts of the composition and quotes a letter from the publisher Peters to Beethoven dated March 4, 1823, in answer to a letter of Beethoven's dated February 15, that he was returning the manuscripts of three songs, one of which was the "*Opferlied.*" He also points out that the "*Opferlied*" (Version 3 for three solo voices—soprano, alto, and tenor—and four-part chorus with accompaniment of two clarinets, two horns, violas, and violoncello) was written in 1822 for the tenor Wilhelm Ehlers and performed at a concert in Pressburg for the latter's benefit. He also quotes the program of a concert which took place at the Society of the Friends of Music in Vienna on April 4, 1824, of which the fourth piece performed appeared as "Opferlied von Matthison, Musik von L. van Beethoven for Solo voices and Chorus with accompaniment of a few instruments."]

The similarity of the titles with respect to Settings III and IV (the former for solo voices, the latter for solo voice, both with chorus and instrumental accompaniment) gave rise to the decade-long confusion between the two works. A short examination of the works themselves discloses the difference between the two: The title "Solo voices and Chorus" in Setting III signifies merely the distribution of the chorus in solo and tutti sections for dynamic reasons, whereas Setting IV discloses a fully worked-out concert-aria form.

Beethoven [himself] gave the manuscript of Setting IV [which was evidently intended for the Pressburg concert of Ehler and the Vienna concert of April 4, 1824] to his brother Johann. The latter offered it to the publisher Schött on November 14, 1824, and wrote of it as follows: "3 songs of which 2 are with chorus with accompaniment of piano alone or with wind instruments alone, the other with accompaniment of full orchestra."

Here we perceive for the first time the words "accompaniment of full orchestra," the characteristic of Setting IV, which Schött also published as Opus 121b. In this connection, we can now make sense of Beethoven's own words upon presenting the song to Ehlers, that he has finally "rediscovered the true [musical] concept [of the text]." Then where does this place Setting IV, which Beethoven by his own words had already composed? Doubtless Beethoven wished to pay off his brother completely and could not do so by offering him only Setting III, which had already been refused publication.

The composer also sent the "*Opferlied*" to Ries for the Music Festival of the Lower Rhine. In the covering correspondence Beethoven wrote on April 9, 1825: "You will by now have received a second copy of the Opferlied. Mark it at once *as corrected by me* so that it may not be confused with the copy you have already."

A last reference [to the "*Opferlied*"] occurs in a letter of Ehlers on August 1, 1826, thanking him for the trouble he [Ehlers] had taken to restore the music for "The Ruins of Athens": "I shall also write to Schött to let you have the *Opferlied* should you write for it. For the original and true draft was only found later."

We have now examined all the available literature on the "*Opferlied*" and will briefly summarize our findings:

1. The placing of the date of composition of Setting II as 1795–97 is not entirely proved by the existing material. However, Boettcher's supposition of the year 1822 for Setting IV and 1823 for Setting III has considerably more justification. It is, however, false to regard Setting III as a preliminary study for Setting IV.

2. It is quite false, in the case of the "*Opferlied*," to correlate the year of composition with the year of publication.

3. The supposition that the [Vienna] concert of April 4, 1824, was the first performance of Setting IV is proved false.

We will now examine the various settings from a stylistic standpoint as well as from their appearance in the sketches. Setting I for voice and piano exists as an unpublished autograph in Berlin. On the back of this single page are unidentified sketches which must have been added later when the song was of no further use. Stylistically they bear a thematic and harmonic resemblance to the first piano sonatas and the C minor Trio [Opus 1, No. 3].

Setting I differs from Setting II in the following way: The melody of the first four measures of each is characterized by the unfolding of the tonic chord in a downward fall of an octave. However, Setting I starts on the fifth, while Setting II starts on the octave. Also in measure 23 of

Setting I, as opposed to Setting II, there occurs a pause on the last quarter, which is transformed in Settings III and IV into a distinct fermata, thereby developing the declamatory nature of the musical setting of the text. The melody and piano accompaniment of Setting I are further distinguished from Setting II. For example, in measures 4 and 13 of Setting I these quarter notes result in a suspension on the accented beat, while in Setting II the constant half-note rhythm eliminates any such suspension.

[The evidence of the sketches for both Settings I and II pinpoints the dates of composition as 1796 and 1799 respectively.]

Why did Beethoven in 1808 give up the octave opening [of Setting II] in favor of the melodic opening on the fifth [as in Setting I]? From the so-called "Kessler Sketchbook" (Autograph No. 34A of the Society of the Friends of Music of Vienna) we can infer with certainty that around 1802 the composer developed the intention of an instrumental version [of the song]. The sketches of this period universally utilize the melodic opening on the fifth. The inference is that Beethoven had chosen the octave opening for the piano edition and the fifth opening for the orchestra version; thus through the difference of the melodic line the two versions would become independent.

A definitive view about both instrumental versions can be based upon the very pertinent definition of E Bükkens [in his article entitled "*Die Lieder Beethovens*" in Volume II of the *Neues Beethoven-Jahrbuch* (1925)], in which he points out that "the structure of the vocal melodies of the late Beethoven represent the most pungent working-out of declamation within the scope of classical melodic structure." This thesis proves wholly correct as regards Setting IV of the "*Opferlied*" when it is compared with Setting III. Setting III stands stylistically in close relationship with Settings I and II. If we follow this factor of the declamatory construction of a vocal melody and apply it to the late Beethoven style, we come to the conclusion that the order of development [of the various settings of the "*Opferlied*"] is actually: Settings I, II, III, and IV.

This order of composition is also confirmed by the formalistic viewpoint. If we examine the place where the words "*und Weihrauchdüfte wallen*" ["and waves of incense float about"] appear, we are struck, in Settings I and II, by the less than convincing five-bar phrase—a distinguishing stylistic mark of the young Beethoven, whose early songs often contain such uneven phrases. Setting III, at this point, approaches the classical ideal with its eight-bar melody, but is scarcely an improvement from the declamatory point of view. In Setting IV we hit upon the earlier five-bar phrase; however, the actual phrase is already concluded in the fourth measure and is merely prolonged by the musical extension of the last two syllables of the word "*Weihrauchdüfte*." This extension does not contradict the classical melodic structure, yet it infinitely enhances the sense of the text and reveals the declamatory character of the song. Another such critical point of comparison among the four settings is the various melodic structure at the words *"und lass des Jünglings Opfer Dir, Du Höchster, wolhlfallen!"* ["and may the offering of the youth please Thee, Thou Almighty One!"].

[Herbst concludes his essay with a comparison of the instrumental accompaniments of Settings III and IV, pointing out the much more highly developed orchestral voicing in the latter.]—KURT HERBST (TR. BY THOMAS K. SCHERMAN)

V. *"Bundeslied"* (POEM BY GOETHE), FOR TWO SOLO VOICES AND THREE-PART CHORUS WITH ACCOMPANIMENT OF SIX WIND INSTRUMENTS, OPUS 122

Time of Composition: Judging from a sketch page entitled "trifling song" in the possession of the Society of the Friends of Music in Vienna, [the work dates from] around 1797 but [was] reworked in 1822; for the sketches see [Gustav] Nottebohm['s *"Zweite Beethoveniana"*] page 207 ff. and page 542 ff. The work was offered to C. F. Peters in Leipzig on February 15, 1823, for publication, [but it was turned down], and in the next year it was probably worked over again (see Thayer's biography [page 141 of Vol. III of the Krehbiel edition]), before [the publishers] Schött [and Sons] in Mainz obtained it at the beginning of February, 1825.[1] According to a remark in a conversation [between] Carl Holz [and Thayer] it received its first performance in Vienna in 1826.

Report of the Composition in [the magazine] *Caecelia,* August 1825 (Vol. XI): "How spiritually Beethoven is integrated with Goethe is pointed out by the present work. Only so would Goethe, were he as great a composer as he is a poet, have set [the wedding song] to music."— GEORG KINSKY, EDITED BY HANS HALM, (TR. BY THOMAS K. SCHERMAN)

The song is in four verses. As befits a wedding ceremonial song it is set for female voices—two soprano soli and a three-part female chorus. It is accompanied only by two clarinets, two horns and two bassoons. Beethoven treats it as a regular strophic song until the last verse. There is an eight-measure staccato introduction by the winds, gay as the words themselves suggest. The first three verses commence with the two soprano soli taking up the melody and continuing it, in two-part harmony, in a

---

[1] Thayer goes on to say that it was one of three songs offered to Peters and turned down and ultimately published by Schött. The two others are the third version of *"Opferlied,"* Opus 121b, which contains the same instrumental setting for accompaniment, and *"Der Kuss,"* Opus 128.—Editor.

*foursquare manner, but touched with Beethovian subtleties in the ac-
companiment and in certain surprising chord progressions. The last two
lines of each verse are repeated by the chorus. The fourth verse commences the same way, but on the last line there is a surprise ritard and
a brilliant technical display by the first clarinet under a held note by the
singers.—Editor.*

Music for Voice *a Cappella*

I. *"Abschiedsgesang,"* FOR THREE MEN'S VOICES A CAPPELLA, WoO 102

This choral trio was written in 1814 at the request of Magistrate
Mathias von Tuscher, whom Beethoven had favored for the unrewarding
task of guardian of his nephew, Karl. The *raison d'être* of the composition was the farewell party for their mutual friend, Dr. Leopold
Weiss, who was leaving Vienna for good to take up residence in Steyer.

The capricious nature of the work is attested by Beethoven's inscription: *"Um nicht weiter tuschiert zu werden."* This pun on the magistrate's
name is lost in translation. Literally the inscription reads: "In order
not to be touched up (corrected)."

There are many musically humorous touches in the piece. It starts
off in a stately fashion in B flat, like many drinking songs. There are
several adroit examples of imitation among the three voices. When the
words *"Stadt Steyer"* appear, repeated sixteenth notes interrupt the stately
flow, but the first part ends with dignity with a threefold cadence in
the tonic key. Then without interruption and without modulation the
scherzo-like second section begins in G major in a fast 6/8. It starts as
a three-part canon and is a veritable patter song. It is a faster, jollier drinking song with an allusion in the text to Ganymede (the wine pourer to
the Greek gods). Whenever his name appears, there is a long held note
in one of the voices while the two others comment in the patter rhythm.
This section ends also in G major; the stately movement returns starting
in G minor. Then (without changing bass) we are in E flat, the subdominant of the original key of B flat, and within two measures we are back in
that key but thematically in the middle of the phrase. The piece ends
in this dignified tempo with the three voices singing in turn: *"Lebwohl!"*
—THOMAS K. SCHERMAN

II. *Gesang der Mönche,"* FROM SCHILLER'S *William Tell,* FOR THREE
MEN'S VOICES A CAPPELLA, WoO 104

Beethoven's correspondence of the winter is full of references to his
continued ill-health. In several letters he described the "feverish cold"
with which he had been afflicted in October 1816, the effects of which
hung on during the winter and spring, limited his activities in the summer, and made his domestic difficulties seem the more intolerable. The
picture of his domestic affairs will gain in vividness by imagining the
following extracts from the so-called *"Tagebuch"* of the Fischoff manuscript to be scattered through these preceding pages. Dates are nowhere
given, but memoranda of letters to Brentano in April follow which prove
these notes to belong to the previous months:

> Never again live alone with a servant; there is always danger,
> suppose, for instance, the master falls ill and the servant, perhaps,
> also.
> He who wishes to reap tears should sow love.
> The Compassionate Brothers the monks in Tell, form a semicircle
> around the dead man and sing in deep tones:

Rasch tritt der Tod den Menschen an	Quick comes the death of man;
Es ist ihm keine Frist gegeben	For him is granted no delay,
Er stürzt ihn mitten in der Bahn	Down he is thrust amid his span,
Es reisst ihn fort vom vollem Leben	From a full life he is torn away
Bereitet oder nicht zu geh'n!	To go, prepared or not!
Er muss vor seinen Richter stehen!	Before his judge he must learn his lot![1]

On May 2 Beethoven's old friend the violinist Wenzel Krumpholz[2]
died very suddenly of apoplexy while walking on the Glacis. Beethoven
commemorated the event by writing his *"Gesang der Mönche"* (from
Schiller's *Tell*) for three male voices with the superscription: "In memory
of the sudden and unexpected death of our Krumpholz on May 3, 1817."
The twelve-measure composition with its superscription was written out
for the musical scholar Franz Sales Kandler (1792–1831), who, with a
letter of introduction from Beethoven, was leaving Vienna for Italy.—
ALEXANDER WHEELOCK THAYER, EDITED BY ELLIOT FORBES

[1] The scene is at the end of Act IV. Hermann Gessler, the cruel viceroy and
tyrant, has just been shot by an arrow from a cliff overlooking the Hohle Gasse,
by William Tell. Gessler realizes who his murderer is, but Tell escapes. A wedding
procession which is passing through stands around the dying man in horror. As
the viceroy's soldiers start to leave, a procession of monks enters. They form a
semicircle around the body. Just before they sing their song, Stüssi, one of the
Swiss freedom fighters, says sarcastically: "The victim's dead, and so the ravens
come!" At the last line of the monks' song, the curtain falls.—Editor.
[2] Wenzel Krumpholz (1750–1817), violinist and revered friend of Beethoven.—Editor.

It is in C minor, just twelve measures long, in a slow 4/4 measure. It is written entirely in block chords as befits a song of death sung by a group of monks. There is a suspension at the end of each line followed by an unmeasured silence which adds to the dignity of the work. The poignancy of the words "To go, prepared or not!" is enhanced by a crescendo and then a sudden piano on the words "su geh'n" ("to go"). Equally well portrayed musically is the mystery of the last line, "Before his judge he must learn his lot!" by means of an unexpected Neapolitan cadence.—Editor.

PART FIVE

Beethoven's Death,
Contemporary Reports

The Last Days

Schindler to Moscheles.

February 22, 1827.

WHEN you last were here, I already had described to you Beethoven's financial circumstances without suspecting that the time was so near at hand when we would see this estimable man approach the end of all in so wretched a manner. Yes, one may well say "the end of all," for with regard to his present illness his recovery is out of the question, though this is something he is not allowed to know, for all he himself suspects it.

Not until December 3d did he arrive here with his worthless nephew. While on his journey hither, bad weather compelled him to stay overnight at a wretched inn, where he contracted such a cold that an immediate inflammation of the lungs resulted and it was in this condition that he arrived. No sooner had this been removed, than he developed all the symptoms of a dropsy which made such rapid headway that he already had to be tapped for the first time on December 18th, since otherwise he would have burst. On January 8th the second operation followed, and on January 20th the third. After the second and third tappings the water was allowed to flow from the wound for eleven days; but no sooner did the wound heal than the rush of water was so tremendously swift that I often feared he would choke before we could get to the operation. Only now do I observe that the rush of water is not so swift as before, since now, if matters continue as at present, some eight or ten days may easily pass before the fourth puncture is made.

Well, my friend, think of Beethoven with such a terrible disease, given his impatience and, above all, with his temperament. Think of his having been brought to this pass owing to that despicable creature, his nephew, and also in part by his brother; for both physicians, Messrs. Malfatti and Professor Wawruch, declare his illness due to the terrible mental disturbances to which this good man was for so long a time subjected by his nephew, as well as to his long stay in the country during the rainy season of the year, something which could not easily be altered because the young gentleman could not remain in Vienna owing to a police order and an opening in a regiment could not at once be found for him. Now he is a cadet with the Archduke Ludwig and treats his uncle just as he did before, though now as then, he depends on him absolutely. The letter to Sir Smart already had been sent him by Beethoven fourteen days ago, for translation into English, yet up to this day no answer has been returned, though he is but a few steps from this place, in Iglau.

Should you, my dear, splendid Moscheles, in connection with Sir Smart, be able so to arrange that the Philharmonic Society accedes to his wish you doubtlessly will be doing him the greatest of benefits; the expenses of this tedious illness are extraordinary, and hence the supposition that as a consequence he will have to suffer privations, torments him day and night; for to be obliged to accept anything from his horrible brother would certainly kill him.

As it is now evident his dropsy is turning into a wasting away, for now he is no more than skin and bones; yet his constitution bids fair to withstand this terrible end for a very long period of time.

What hurts him greatly is the fact that no one here takes any notice of him; and in truth this lack of interest is most striking. Formerly people drove up in their carriages if he were no more than indisposed; now he is totally forgotten, as though he had never lived in Vienna. I myself suffer the greatest annoyance, and earnestly wish that matters may soon take a turn with him, in one or another way, for I am losing all my time since I devote it altogether to him, because he will suffer none other about him, and to abandon him in his absolutely helpless condition would be inhuman.

He now often speaks of a journey to London when he is well again, and already is calculating how both of us may live most cheaply during the trip. But, good God in heaven! Let us hope the journey will take him further than England. He distracts himself, when alone, reading the ancient Greeks, and he also has read with pleasure several of the Walter Scott novels.

Ferdinand Hiller, the composer, in Landau's Beethoven
Album, 1877.

Though at that time one heard less about the greatest men than we now
do every week about the least noteworthy, the news of Beethoven's illness, nevertheless, had reached Weimar. He was suffering from dropsy. In
Vienna, the artists who had visited Hummel reported the worst with
regard to his condition. On the one hand it was hopeless; on the other
unspeakably sad. Absolute deafness, a continually increasing distrust of
everyone on earth, and now, added to this, bodily sufferings—unsuccessful
operations—discontent and loneliness—and an appearance which almost
excited horror. Thus forewarned we drove out to the suburb. Through
a commodious anteroom in which tall closets held thick, corded masses
of music, we came (how my heart beat!) into Beethoven's living-room,
and were not a little surprised to see the Master to all appearances quite
comfortably seated at the window. He wore a long, gray dressing-gown,
completely open at the moment, and high boots which reached to his
knees. Emaciated by his evil malady he seemed to me, as he rose, to be
tall in stature. He was unshaven, his heavy, partly gray hair hung in disorder over his temples, the expression of his features grew very mild and
gentle when he caught sight of Hummel, and he seemed to be extraordinarily glad to see him. The two men embraced with the utmost heartiness; Hummel presented me; Beethoven was entirely gracious and I was
allowed to sit down opposite him at the window.

As is known, verbal conversation with Beethoven was in part carried
on in writing. He spoke, but those with whom he spoke were obliged to
write out their questions and answers. For this purpose thick notebooks
of ordinary writing-paper in quarto format and lead-pencils always lay
near him. How annoying must it not have been to this lively man, who so
easily became impatient, to have to wait for every reply, to have to endure
a pause at every moment of conversation, during which his own mental
activity, so to say, was condemned to inaction. Then, too, he followed the
writer's hand with greedy eye and seized what had been written with a
glance rather than read it.

The continuous manual labor of writing on the part of his visitors
naturally greatly hampered liveliness of conversation. I can hardly blame
myself, no matter how greatly I regret it, that I did not write out in
greater detail all that Beethoven said at the time; in fact, I must even
rejoice that the fifteen-year-old boy, who had come to a great city for the
first time in his life, had enough self-control to note down any details at all.
I can vouch for the absolute exactness of all that I am able to reproduce, however, with a clear conscience. The conversation at first,
as was customary, turned on house and Court, our journey and visit,

my relations to Hummel and other matters of the sort. Beethoven asked after Goethe with quite special sympathy, and we were able to give him the best of news. Had not the great poet, only a few days before, written some verses alluding to our trip in my album. Poor Beethoven complained greatly about his condition. "Here I have been lying all of four months," he cried, "one loses patience in the end." And much else in Vienna did not seem to suit him and he expressed himself in the most cutting manner with regard to "the present taste in art," and anent "the amateurishness which ruins everything here." Nor was the government, up to its highest heads, spared. "Write a book of penitential psalms and dedicate it to the Empress!" he said laughing morosely, to Hummel who, however, did not follow this well-meant advice.

Hummel, who was a practical person, took advantage of Beethoven's momentarily favorable condition to communicate to him something which cost considerable time to tell. Reprinting was then in fullest blossom. In publishing one of the Master's concertos (I think it was the one in E-flat major) it had chanced that the composition, of which a copy had been purloined from the office of the rightful publisher, had not only been *re*printed, but *pre*printed as well, for the thief, in fact, issued it before the date on which the owner was permitted to print it.

And now Hummel wished to address himself to the illustrious Diet with petition so that this might be done away with, for which purpose he laid great weight on Beethoven's signature. He sat down in order to explain the matter on paper and in the meantime I had the honor of carrying on the conversation with Beethoven. I did my best and the Master continued to give rein to his part melancholy, part passionate outpourings in the most confidential way. The greater part of them had reference to his nephew, whom he greatly loved, and who—as is known—caused him much unhappiness, and at the time owing to some trifles (for thus Beethoven seemed to regard them) had gotten into difficulties with the authorities. "They hang the little thieves and let the big ones escape!" he cried out peevishly. Asking about my studies and encouraging me he said: "One must always transmit art"; and when I spoke about the exclusive interest which Italian opera then commanded in Vienna he burst out into the remarkable words: "They say, *vox populi, vox Dei*—I never have believed it."

On March 13th Hummel took me to Beethoven the second time. We found that his condition had changed decidedly for the worse. He lay in bed, seemed to be suffering violent pain and occasionally gave a deep groan, although he talked a good deal and with animation. He now appeared to take it to heart that he never had married. Already, on our first visit, he had joked about the matter with Hummel, whose wife he had known as a young, beautiful girl. "You," he said to him on this occasion, with a smile. "you are a lucky man. You have a wife who

takes care of you, who is in love with you, while I, poor unfortunate!—"
and he sighed heavily. He also begged Hummel to fetch his wife to visit
him, though the latter had not been able to bring herself to see in his
present state the man whom she had known when he was at the height
of his powers. A short time before Beethoven had been presented with a
picture of the house in which Haydn had been born: he had it near
his bed and showed it to us: "I was as pleased as any child," said
he—"the cradle of a great man!"

Not long after our second visit the news spread through Vienna that
the London Philharmonic Society had sent Beethoven one hundred pounds
sterling, in order to ameliorate his sufferings. It was added that the surprise
had made so deep an impression on the poor great man that he even
felt himself bodily much relieved. When we once more stood by his bedside on the 20th, his remarks, it is true, showed how much the attention
had rejoiced him, but he was very weak and spoke only in a low voice
and in broken sentences. "I shall probably soon make my way up above,"
he whispered after we had greeted him.

Similar exclamations he uttered frequently, yet together with them he
voiced hopes and projects which, unfortunately, were not to be realized.
Speaking of the noble action of the Philharmonic Society and praising
the English, he opined that as soon as his condition had improved he
would undertake the journey to London. "I shall compose a great overture and a great symphony for them." And then he also wished to visit
Madame Hummel (she had come with us) and stop, I no longer recall
just where, at all sorts of places. It did not even occur to us to write down
anything for him. His eyes, which when last we had seen them, still had
shown considerable life, had collapsed, and he found it hard, from time
to time, to sit up. It was impossible longer to deceive one's self—the worst
was to be anticipated.

Altogether hopeless was the appearance of this extraordinary man when
we once more visited him on March 23d, for the last time. He lay there
faint and wretched, at times sighing gently. No further word passed his
lips; the perspiration stood out on his brow. Seeing that by some chance
he did not have his handkerchief at hand, Hummel's wife took her dainty
wisp of batiste and at different times dried his face. Never shall I forget
the grateful glance which his broken eyes sent up to her when she did
this. While we were spending March 26th in the home of the art-loving
Mr. von Liebenberg (who formerly had been Hummel's pupil) in merry
company, we were surprised between five and six o'clock by a heavy
thunderstorm. A dense fall of snow was accompanied by violent thunder
and lightnings which illuminated the whole chamber.

A few hours later guests arrived with the news that Ludwig van Beethoven was no more; that he had died at quarter to five.

Beethoven's physician, Dr. Wawruch, in retrospect.

May 20, 1827.

Ludwig van Beethoven declared that from earliest youth he had possessed a rugged, permanently good constitution, hardened by many privations, which even the most strenuous toil at his favorite occupation and
continual profound study had been unable in the slightest degree to im-
pair. The lonely nocturnal quiet always had shown itself most friendly to
his glowing imagination. Hence he usually wrote after midnight until
about three o'clock. A short sleep of from four to five hours was all he
needed to refresh him. His breakfast eaten, he sat down at his writing-desk
again until two o'clock in the afternoon.

When he entered his thirtieth year, however, he began to suffer
from hemorrhoidal complaints and an annoying roaring and buzzing in
both ears. Soon his hearing began to fail and, for all he often would
enjoy untroubled intervals lasting for months at a time, his disability
finally ended in complete deafness. All the resources of the physician's art
were useless. At about the same time Beethoven noticed that his digestion
began to suffer; loss of appetite was followed by indigestion, and annoying
belching, and alternate obstinate constipation and frequent diarrhea.

At no time accustomed to taking medical advice seriously, he began to
develop a liking for spirituous beverages,[1] in order to stimulate his decreas-
ing loss of appetite and to aid his stomachic weakness by excessive use
of strong punch and iced drinks and long, tiring excursions on foot. It was
this very alteration of his mode of life which, some seven years earlier,
had led him to the brink of the grave. He contracted a severe inflammation of the intestines which, though it yielded to treatment, later on
often gave rise to intestinal pains and aching colics and which, in part,
must have favored the eventual development of his mortal illness.

In the late fall of the year just passed (1826) Beethoven felt an
irresistible urge, in view of the uncertain state of his health, to go to the
country to recuperate. Since owing to his incurable deafness he sedulously
avoided all society, he was thrown entirely upon his own resources under
the most unfavorable circumstances for days and even weeks at a time.
Often, with rare endurance, he worked at his compositions on a wooded
hillside and his work done, still aglow with reflection, he would not
infrequently run about for hours in the most inhospitable surroundings,
defying every change of temperature, and often daring the heaviest snow-
falls. His feet, always from time to time edematous, would begin to
swell and since (as he insisted) he had to do without every comfort of
life, every solacing refreshment, his illness soon got the upper hand of
him.

[1] This medical statement, of course, in no way implies that Beethoven was a
heavy drinker. On the contrary, he was temperate in his habits.

Intimidated by the sad prospect, in the gloomy future, of finding himself helpless in the country should he fall sick, he longed to be back in Vienna, and, as he himself jovially said, used the devil's own most wretched conveyance, a milk-wagon, to carry him home.

December was raw, wet, cold and frosty. Beethoven's clothing was anything but suited to the unkind season of the year, and yet he was driven on and away by an inner restlessness, a sinister presentiment of misfortune. He was obliged to stop overnight in a village inn, where in addition to the shelter afforded by its wretched roof he found only an unheated room without winter windows. Toward midnight he was seized with his first convulsive chills and fever, accompanied by violent thirst and pains in the side. When the fever heat began to break, he drank a couple of quarts of ice-cold water, and, in his helpless state, yearned for the first ray of dawn. Weak and ill, he had himself loaded on the open van and, finally, arrived in Vienna enervated and exhausted.

I was not sent for until the third day. I found Beethoven with grave symptoms of inflammation of the lungs; his face glowed, he spat blood, when he breathed he threatened to choke, and the shooting pain in his side only allowed him to lie in a tormenting posture flat on his back. A strict anti-inflammatory mode of treatment soon brought the desired amelioration; nature conquered and a happy crisis freed him of the seemingly imminent danger of death, so that on the fifth day he was able to sit up and relate to me with deep emotion the story of the adversities he had suffered. On the seventh day he felt so passably well that he could rise, move about, read and write.

Yet on the eighth day I was not a little alarmed. On my morning visit I found him quite upset; his entire body jaundiced; while a terrible fit of vomiting and diarrhea during the preceding night had threatened to kill him. Violent anger, profound suffering because of ingratitude and an underserved insult had motivated the tremendous explosion. Shaking and trembling, he writhed with the pain which raged in his liver and intestines; and his feet, hitherto only moderately puffed up, were now greatly swollen.

From this time on his dropsy developed; his secretions decreased in quantity, his liver gave convincing evidence of the presence of hard knots, his jaundice grew worse. The affectionate remonstrances of his friends soon appeased the threatening excitement and Beethoven, easily conciliated, soon forgot every insult offered him. His illness, however, progressed with giant strides. Already, during the third week, nocturnal choking attacks set in; the tremendous volume of the water accumulated called for immediate relief; and I found myself compelled to advocate the abdominal puncture in order to preclude the danger of sudden bursting. After a few moments of serious reflection Beethoven agreed to submit to the operation, the more so since the Ritter von Staudenheim, who had been called in as consulting physician, urgently recommended it as being imperatively necessary. The premier chirurgeon of the General Hospital, the Mag. Chir. Hr. Seibert, made the puncture with his habitual skill, so that Beethoven when he saw the stream of water cried out happily that the operation made him think of Moses, who struck the rock with his staff and made the water gush forth. The relief was almost immediate. The liquid amounted to 25 pounds in weight, yet the afterflow must have been five times that.

Carelessness in undoing the bandage of the wound at night, probably in order quickly to remove all the water which had gathered, well-nigh put an end to all rejoicing anent the improvement in Beethoven's condition. A violent erysipelatous inflammation set in and showed incipient signs of gangrene, but the greatest care exercised in keeping the inflamed surfaces dry soon checked the evil. Fortunately the three succeeding operations were carried out without the slightest difficulty.

Beethoven knew but too well that the tappings were only palliatives and hence resigned himself to a further accumulation of water, the more so since the cold, rainy winter season favored the return of his dropsy, and could not help but strengthen the original cause of his ill, which had its existence in his chronic liver trouble as well as in organic deficiencies of the abdominal intestines.

It is a curious fact that Beethoven, even after operations successfully performed, could not stand taking any medicine, if we except gentle laxatives. His appetite diminished from day to day, and his strength could not help but decrease noticeably in consequence of the repeated large loss of vital juices. Dr. Malfatti, who henceforth aided me with his advice, a friend of Beethoven's for many years and aware of the latter's inclination for spirituous beverages, therefore hit upon the idea of recommending iced punch. I must admit that this recipe worked admirably, for a few days at any rate. Beethoven felt so greatly refreshed by the iced spirits of wine that he slept through the whole of the first night, and began to sweat tremendously. He grew lively; often all sorts of witty ideas occurred to him; and he even dreamed of being able to complete the oratorio "Saul and David" which he had commenced.

Yet, as was to have been foreseen, his joy was of short duration. He began to abuse his prescription, and partook freely of the punch. Soon the alcoholic beverage called forth a powerful rush of blood to the head; he grew soporose and there was a rattle when he breathed like that of a person deeply intoxicated; he wandered in his talk and to this, at various times, was added an inflammatory pain in the neck with consequent hoarseness and even total speechlessness. He grew more violent and now, since colic and diarrhea had resulted from the chilling of the intestines, it was high time to deprive him of this valuable stimulant.

It was under such conditions, together with a rapidly increasing loss of flesh and a noticeable falling off of his vital powers that January, February and March went by. Beethoven in gloomy hours of presentiment, foretold his approaching dissolution after his fourth tapping, nor was he mistaken. No consolation was able longer to revive him; and when I promised him that with the approaching spring weather his sufferings would decrease, he answered with a smile: "My day's work is done; if a physician still can be of use in my case (and then he lapsed into English) his name shall be called wonderful." This saddening reference to Handel's "Messiah" so profoundly moved me that in my inmost soul and with the deepest emotion I was obliged to confirm the truth of what he had said.

And now the ill-fated day drew ever nearer. My noble and often burdensome professional duty as a physician bade me call my suffering friend's attention to the momentuous day, so that he might comply with his civic and religious duties. With the most delicate consideration I set down the admonitory lines on a sheet of paper (for it was thus that we always had made ourselves mutually understood). Beethoven, slowly, meditatively and with incomparable self-control read what I had written, his face like that of one transfigured. Next he gave me his hand in a hearty, serious manner and said: "Have them send for his reverence the pastor." Then he grew quiet and reflective, and nodded me his: "I shall soon see you again," in friendly wise. Soon after Beethoven attended to his devotions with the pious resignation which looks forward with confidence to eternity.

When a few hours had passed, he lost consciousness, began to grow comatose, and breathed with a rattle. The following morning all symptoms pointed to the approaching end. The 26th of March was stormy, and clouded. Toward six in the afternoon came a flurry of snow, with thunder and lightning.— Beethoven died.— Would not a Roman augur, in view of the accidental commotion of the elements, have taken his apotheosis for granted?—O. G. SONNECK (1)

The Autopsy

Beethoven having expressed a wish that the cause of his deafness might be investigated, it may not be out of place to give a detailed account of the post-mortem examination which was undertaken by Dr.

Joseph Wagner[1] at the house of the deceased, in presence of Professor Wawruch, M.D.[2] The principle results were as follows:

The external ear was large and regularly formed, the scaphoid fossa, but more especially the concha, was very spacious and half as large again as usual; the various angles and sinuosities were strongly marked. The external auditory canal was covered with shining scales, particularly in the vicinity of the tympanum, which was concealed by them. The Eustachian tube was much thickened, its mucous lining swollen and somewhat contracted about the osseous portion of the tube. In front of its orifice and toward the tonsils some dimpled scars were observable. The principal cells of the mastoid process, which was large and not marked by any notch, were lined with a vascular mucous membrane. The whole substance of the os petrosum showed a similar degree of vascularity, being traversed by vessels of considerable size, more particularly in the region of the cochlea, the membranous part of its spinal lamina appearing slightly reddened.

The facial nerves were of unusual thickness, the auditory nerves, on the contrary, were shriveled and destitute of neurina; the accompanying arteries were dilated more than the size of a crow quill, and cartilaginous. The left auditory nerve, much the thinnest, arose by three very thin grayish striae, the right by one strong clear-white stria from the substance of the fourth ventricle, which was at this point much more consistent and vascular than in the other parts. The convolutions of the brain were full of water, and remarkably white; they appeared very much deeper, wider, and more numerous than ordinary.

The calvarium exhibited throughout great density and a thickness amounting to about half an inch.

The cavity of the chest, together with the organs within it, was in normal condition.

In the cavity of the abdomen four quarts of grayish-brown turbid fluid were effused.

The liver appeared shrunk up to half its proper volume, of a leathery consistency and greenish-blue color, and was beset with knots, the size of a bean, on its tuberculated surface, as well as in its substance; all its vessels were very much narrowed, and bloodless.

The gall bladder contained a dark brown fluid, besides an abundance of gravelly sediment.

The spleen was found to be more than double its proper size, dark-colored and firm.

---

[1] Thayer refers to him as Dr. *Johann* Wagner.—Editor.

[2] Dr. Andreas Wawruch, 1771–1842, professor of general pathology and pharmacology at the General Hospital in Vienna. He was an amateur cellist and an ardent admirer of Beethoven's music. He was Beethoven's attending physician in the illness which ended in his death.—Editor.

The pancreas was equally hard and firm, its excretory duct being as wide as a goose quill.

The stomach, together with the bowels, was greatly distended with air. Both kidneys were invested by a cellular membrane of an inch thick, and infiltrated with a brown turbid fluid; their tissue was pale red and opened out. Every one of their calices was occupied by a calcareous concretion of a wart-like shape and as large as a split pea. The body was much emaciated.

(Signed) Dr. Joseph Wagner, Assistant in the Pathological Museum

IGNATIUS SEYFRIED, EDITED BY HENRY HUGH PIERSON

The Funeral

I. Description

Vienna, March 29, 1827[1]

No sooner had his friends, with bleeding hearts, done him love's last services than they came together to determine the solemn details of his funeral, which, owing to the preparations necessary, was set for the afternoon of March 29. Cards of invitation were at once printed and distributed in lavish quantity. The mild, beautiful spring day lured a countless number of the curious into the open, to the Escarpment of the Alser suburb before the Schottentor, at the so-called Schwarzspanierhaus in which Beethoven had lived. The crowding incident to a gathering of some twenty thousand persons of every class finally became so great that the gates of the house of mourning had to be locked, since its spacious court, in which Beethoven's corpse had been biered, no longer could accommodate the densely packed multitude. At four-thirty the clerical dignitaries appeared, and the procession set out and, for all the distance to the church, in a straight line, amounts to no more than five hundred feet, yet it took more than an hour and a half to traverse because of its extremely slow progress made through the swaying crowds, which could not have been kept in order without using violence. Eight singers of the Royal and Imperial Court Opera carried the coffin. Before they raised it to their shoulders, however, they intoned the chorale from B. A. Weber's opera, *Wilhelm Tell*.[2] Then all the mourners—

[1] Contemporary report, reprinted from Landau's *Beethoven-Album*, 1877.
[2] Bernard Anselm Weber, 1766–1821, German piano virtuoso, conductor, and composer. He composed incidental music for a production in Berlin in 1804 of Schiller's *Wilhelm Tell*, of which the chorale of the monks: *"Rasch tritt der Tod den*

artistic colleagues of the deceased, friends and admirers of his exalted genius, poets, actors, tone poets, etc., all in deepest mourning, with black gloves, fluttering crape, bouquets of white lilies fastened to their left arms and torches with crape ribands—formed in order. After the crucifer who led the procession came four trombone players and sixteen of the best singers in Vienna, who alternately blew and sang the *Miserere mei Deus*, whose melody had been composed by the deceased Master himself.

It was, in fact, in the late autumn of the year 1812, when he was staying with his brother in Linz, that choirmaster Glöggl of the local cathedral had asked him for some short trombone pieces for his *"Turners"* (city musicians) to be used on All Saints' Day. Beethoven wrote a so-called *Equale a quatro tromboni*, true to the venerable ancient style, but stamped with the originality of his own bold harmonic structure. Out of this four-part composition for the brasses, choirmaster von Seyfried, quite in the spirit of the creator of these serious devotional mortuary hymns, then shaped a four-part vocal chorus to the words of the psalms mentioned which, thus admirably sung and alternating with the hollowly reverberating chords of the trombones, made a tremendously moving impression. After the band of priests, including all those in the funeral procession, followed the splendidly ornamented bier, surrounded by the conductors and choirmasters Eybler, Hummel, Seyfried, and Kreutzer, on the right, and Weigl, Gyrowetz, Gänsbacher, and Würfel on the left, holding the long white ribbon-ends which hung down from above. They were accompanied on each side by the torchbearers, among them Castelli, Grillparzer, Bernard, Anschütz, Böhm, Czerny, Lablache, David, Pacini, Rodichi, Meric, Mayseder, Merk, Lannoy, Linke, Riotto, Schubert, Weidmann, Weiss, Schuppanzigh, etc.

The pupils of the Vienna Konservatorium and Saint Anna Music School, as well as the most distinguished notabilities, such as Count Moritz von Dietrichstein, Court Counselors von Mosel and Breuning (the latter the friend of Beethoven's youth and executor of his testament) brought up the rear of the ceremonially inclusive processional.

Upon reaching the church the corpse received the blessing before the high altar, during which ceremony the sixteen-voice male chorus sang the hymn *Libera me, Domine, de morte aeterna*, which Seyfried had set in the "lofty style." When the splendid hearse, drawn by four horses, drove off with the lifeless clay past the aligned crowd, it was escorted by more than two hundred equipages. At the cemetery gates Master Anschütz with the most solemn pathos and emotion spoke the incomparably beautiful funeral oration written by Grillparzer, whose profound

---

Menschen an," is the same passage set by Beethoven in 1817 as the *"Gesang des Monches,"* WoO 104, in memory of his friend, the violinist Krumpholz.—Editor.

feeling and masterly presentation moved every heart, so that many a burning tear flowed from generous eyes in memory of the departed prince of tone. Many hundreds of copies of the two poems by Castelli and Schlechta, respectively, were distributed among those present who, after the coffin together with its three laurel wreaths had been lowered into the grave, departed the sacred resting place, profoundly touched, as the twilight shadows began to fall.—O. G. SONNECK (1)

II. The Oration by Franz Grillparzer

Standing by the grave of him who has passed away, we are in a manner the representatives of an entire nation, of the whole German people, mourning the loss of the one highly acclaimed half of that which was left us of the departed splendor of our native art, of the fatherland's full spiritual bloom. There yet lives—and may his life be long!—the hero of verse in German speech and tongue; but the last master of tuneful song, the organ of soulful concord, the heir and amplifier of Händel's and Bach's, of Haydn's and Mozart's immortal fame is now no more, and we stand weeping over the riven strings of the harp that is hushed.

The harp that is hushed! Let me call him so! For he was an artist, and all that was his, was his through art alone. The thorns of life had wounded him deeply, and as the castaway clings to the shore, so did he seek refuge in thine arms, O thou glorious sister and peer of the Good and the True, thou balm of wounded hearts, heaven-born Art! To thee he clung fast, and even when the portal was closed wherethrough thou hadst entered in and spoken to him, when his deaf ear had blinded his vision for thy features, still did he ever carry thine image within his heart, and when he died it still reposed on his breast.

He was an artist—and who shall arise to stand beside him?

As the rushing behemoth spurns the waves, so did he rove to the uttermost bounds of his art. From the cooing of doves to the rolling of thunder, from the craftiest interweaving of well-weighed expedients of art up to that awful pitch where planful design disappears in the lawless whirl of contending natural forces, he had traversed and grasped it all. He who comes after him will not continue him; he must begin anew, for he who went before left off only where art leaves off. Adelaïde —and Leonora! Triumph of the heroes of Vittoria—and the humble sacrificial song of the Mass!—Ye children of the twice and thrice divided voices! heaven-soaring harmony: *"Freude, schöner Götterfunken,"* thou swan song! Muse of song and the seven-stringed lyre! Approach his grave and bestrew it with laurel!

He was an artist, but a man as well. A man in every sense—in the highest. Because he withdrew from the world, they called him a man hater, and because he held aloof from sentimentality, unfeeling. Ah, one who knows himself hard of heart, does not shrink! The finest points are those most easily blunted and bent or broken! An excess of sensitiveness avoids a show of feeling! He fled the world because, in the whole range of his loving nature, he found no weapon to oppose it. He withdrew from mankind after he had given them his all and received nothing in return. He dwelt alone, because he found no second Self. But to the end his heart beat warm for all men, in fatherly affection for his kindred, for the world his all and his heart's blood.

Thus he was, thus he died, thus he will live to the end of time.

You, however, who have followed after us hitherward, let not your hearts be troubled! You have not lost him, you have won him. No living man enters the halls of the immortals. Not until the body has perished, do their portals unclose. He whom you mourn stands from now onward among the great of all ages, inviolate forever. Return homeward therefore, in sorrow, yet resigned! And should you ever in times to come feel the overpowering might of his creations like an onrushing storm, when your mounting ecstasy overflows in the midst of a generation yet unborn, then remember this hour, and think. We were there, when they buried him, and when he died, we wept.—
O. G. SONNECK (1)

The Estate and the Auction

Legal Inventory and Assessment
dated August 16, 1827
of the legacy of music and books of the tone master Ludwig van Beethoven, who died in Vienna on March 26, 1827, at the Schwarzpanier House No. 200.

Those present:
Brandstätter (Ferdinand), secretary to the magistrate
von Ortowitz (Franz), commissar of closures
Ohmeyer, representative of Dr. Bach as curator
Hotschever (Jacob), royal guardian of the nephew

In addition to those especially summoned here:
Czerny (Carl), composer and sworn witness
Piringer (Ferdinand), royal registrar of dwellings

Haslinger (Tobias), privileged music dealer
and the two treasurers:
Artaria (Dominik), privileged music dealer
Saver (Ignaz), former music dealer

Works already spoken for
for Count Lichnowsky
1 volume of the Inventions and Preludes of Bach
6 volumes of Handel's works, boxed

for H. Schindler
Mass in D sharp [sic] written in three hymns by Beethoven

Herr von Zmeskall
Gluck's *Iphigenia in Tauris*
Orpheus and Eurydice is missing

Herr von Kuffner
Text of a Cantata, 1st Part. "Saul turns to lustrous battles, etc.

for the Royal Theater
Textbook of *Fidelio*
Textbook of *The Noblest of Men*

Herr von Piringer
"Gradus ad Parnassum" by Fux

Steiner and Company
Complete original score of the Seventh Symphony in A sharp [sic]
Battle symphony of the Battle of Vittoria. Original score.
Finale of the Eighth Symphony. F major *"Der heiligen Augenblick."*
Score of cantata.
Written-out parts and score of a cantata for
the choral director in 2 packages

Artaria and Company
(their property, because Beethoven had borrowed them)
6 volumes of Metastasio's works
Score of the *Prometheus* ballet
Rondo: *"Primo amore"* for voice
Trio for 2 oboes and English horn
Overture to *Fidelio*
Andante vivace with voice
Sonata for pianoforte

F. Starke, conductor
No. 175. Miscellaneous pieces for pianoforte for
Starke's school for piano.

No. 204. Reutter. Count Lichnowsky

AUCTION CATALOGUE[1]

I

Notes and Notebooks in Beethoven's Own Hand
[There follow fifty-one entries, all of which are appraised at 1 florin (except No. 51: "The Prompter's cue-book from 'Fidelio,' two acts, with notations in Beethoven's own hand," which is appraised at two florins) and of which the highest bid was three florins, one krone.]

II

Sketches and Fragments of Unpublished or Unfinished Works in Beethoven's Own Hand

NO.	APPRAISED		SOLD	
	Fl.	Kr.	Fl.	Kr.
52. Sketches for a quartet	2	–	2	36
53. Sketches	2	–	2	30
54. Sketches for a quartet	2	–	2	30
55. Completed sketches and pieces	3	–	3	30
56. Completed sketches	3	–	3	01
57. Sketches for a quartet	2	–	3	–
58. Italian ariettas	2	–⎫		
59. Sketch for a quintet, as yet unknown	2	–⎬	6	30
60. Sketches already used	2	–		
61. Copy of the Piano Trio, Opus 1, anonymously arranged for quintet	1	–	1	–
62. Copy of Trio No. 2	2	–	3	–
63. Sketches for a mass	2	–	3	–
64. Sketches for a quartet and bagatelles for pianoforte	2	–	2	30
65. Sketches for a concerto for pianoforte	2	–⎫		
66. Bagatelles	2	–⎬	3	–
67. Vocal work with orchestra, completed but not entirely orchestrated	3	–	9	30
68. Song	1	–	1	16
69. Sextet	2	–	2	30
70. Original Songs	3	–	3	30

[1] See Thayer's "Verzeichniss," pages 175 through 182 for complete numbered description of the various items.—Editor.

III

Autographs of Printed Works
[Nos. 71–143, the most valuable being No. 103, score of "Christ on the Mount of Olives," appraised at 6 florins and sold at 7 florins; and No. 126, score of the Last Mass, appraised at 6 florins and sold at 7 florins. Also Nos. 144–148, which are copies in another hand of some of Beethoven's works, of which the copy of the score of the "Eroica" Symphony (No. 144) contains notations in Beethoven's own hand (appraised at 3 florins and sold at 3 florins, 10 kronen).]

IV

Remaining Original Beethoven Manuscripts, Incomplete but Not Yet Published
[Nos. 149–89, of which the most valuable are No. 149, five packages of contrapuntal studies by other composers with notations in Beethoven's own hand (appraised at 10 florins and sold at 74 florins); No. 164, an incomplete score of "The Ruins of Athens" (appraised at 10 florins and sold at 8 florins); No. 173, "Fragment of a new violin quintet dated November 1826, the last work of the composer" (appraised at 10 florins and sold at 30 florins, 30 kronen); and No. 177, Rondo for Pianoforte with Orchestra, "unknown," (appraised at 10 florins and sold at 20 florins). No. 189 is a score of a Symphony in B flat by Haydn which "appears to be in Haydn's manuscript."]

V

Copied Parts to Beethoven's Works
[Nos. 190–99
Copies of music by various composers including some by Beethoven, himself, Nos. 200–16, the most valuable being No. 212, score of *Fidelio* together with the libretto (appraised at 8 florins and sold at 15 florins).]

VI

Published Music
[Nos. 217–46. The most valuable item is No. 239, the London edition of Handel's works in forty leather-bound volumes (appraised at 50 florins and sold at 102 florins). Also of interest is No. 226, piano score of *Fidelio* and the "Select Collection of Irish Melodies by Beethoven in 2 volumes published in Edinburgh," (both of which items were sold together at 15 florins, 49 kronen).]

Books on Music
[Nos. 247–51, including fourteen volumes of works of Haydn in score.]

Clavier, bought by Spinna	181 Fl.
Medals	
Two Violins	33 Fl.

ALEXANDER WHEELOCK THAYER, TR. BY THOMAS SCHERMAN

Sale of Beethoven's MSS. and Musical Library.[1]

Vienna, March 16, 1828.

The sale of the lamented Beethoven's MSS. and musical library, which lately took place here, excited uncommon interest among the lovers of music, amateurs as well as professional men. The following are the heads under which the articles were arranged in the catalogue:—

1. Fragments from Beethoven's musical portfolio, consisting of noted paper, scraps of various themes, &c. 2. Fragments and sketches in a more complete form. 3. Autographs of scores already published. 4. Autographs of unpublished music. 5. Copies of various Symphonies, Choruses, Overtures, Masses, &c., corrected by the composer's own hand. 6. Printed music and theoretical works. 7. A small collection of works of general literature. 8. A small collection of musical instruments. The contest for several of the articles was warm and spirited, particularly between the well-known music-sellers Artaria, Haslinger, and Steiner. More than forty works, unknown to the public, were brought to the hammer, the greater part of which are productions of Beethoven's earlier years. No doubt the present possessors will, ere long, afford the world an opportunity of enjoying these works of the lamented master. We observed that the greater proportion of them became the property of Artaria, after a severe contest with his brother publishers; several fetched extraordinarily high prices. Besides a great many other articles, Beethoven's last work, an unfinished Quintet, begun in November, 1826, fell to the lot of Diabelli, who triumphantly bore it away, at a very high price, from a host of competitors. The same gentleman also became possessor of a Solo-Capriccio, of a Rondo for pianoforte and orchestra, and of the English pianoforte which Beethoven had received as a present from the Messrs. Broadwood. The gold medal which the composer had the honor to receive from Louis XVIII. on receiving the copy of one of his grand masses was bought by some anonymous collector. But by

[1] From the Harmonicon, April, 1828.

far the most interesting article of the whole sale fell to the lot of
M. Haslinger—the collection of contrapuntic exercises, essays, and finished
pieces, which Beethoven wrote while under the tuition of his master,
the celebrated Albrechtsberger, all in his own handwriting, with the
interlineal corrections of that master, and his remarks on the margin.
It is in five thick volumes, which were evidently preserved with great
care. The struggle for the possession of this invaluable relic—the fruit
of Beethoven's first studies—was long and spirited; but the stamina of
M. Haslinger brought him through: after many a fiercely-contested round,
he was at length declared the victor, none of his antagonists coming
to time. We are happy to be able to state that this collection of studies,[1]
so interesting to the whole musical world, is immediately to be placed
in the hands of Kapellmeister Seyfried, who is to prepare it for the
press. M. Haslinger also became the fortunate possessor of a pianoforte
Trio, consisting of an Allegro, Adagio, Finale, and Variations, composed
while Beethoven filled the place of organist in Cologne; of a short
Sonata for four hands; of several songs and other vocal pieces; of a
small collection, entitled *Zapfenstreiche für Türkische Musik*; of two
violins, with the possessor's seal on each; and lastly, of Beethoven's copy
of the works of Handel, Dr. Arnold's edition, in forty volumes folio.
The latter, as is well known, was presented to the lamented composer
by his friend M. Stumpff, of London, the possession of which tended
so much to soothe Beethoven during his last protracted illness. The
mind and talents of Handel were kindred to his own, and he was
seen for hours hanging over these volumes in rapture and forgetting his
sufferings. Two other competitors contended warmly for this prize—M.
Gläser of Gotha, and Mr. Schenk, the well-known composer of *Der
Dorfbarbier*; but M. Haslingler still retained his honors as champion
of the field.[2] We must, however, observe, that, warm as the opposition
was between these different opponents, the contest was still conducted
with becoming respect—not to say with a certain solemnity due to the
relics of the mighty dead. Some of the prices given astonished even
the most enthusiastic admirers of the composer, and are the most satisfactory proofs of the deep zeal and love for the art predominant among
US.—ANTON FELIX SCHINDLER

[1] This work has indeed been published.—Ed.
[2] M. Schindler has informed us that this valuable collection was bought by Haslinger for 100 florins, about £10 sterling—a price which would not seem to
bespeak much spirit in the rival bidders; and the writer of the above account of
the sale adds, in a note, that the purchaser almost immediately advertised it for
sale in the Leipzig Musical Gazette, price 450 florins, or £45.—TRANSLATOR.

The Projected Works

Operas

I. *Vestas Feuer*

"Beethoven is working on an opera by Schikaneder," the *Zeitung für die elegante Welt* of Vienna was able to report on August 2, 1803. The text on which Beethoven was working was *Vesta's Fire*, Schikaneder's last opera libretto. The enterprising and business-wise man of the theater had convinced Beethoven to undertake the composition, after the success of an "Academy" directed by Beethoven in the Theater an der Wien in April of that year had made him feel that Beethoven was the man he needed to make sure of a big success for his text. But on this occasion the speculation of the keen businessman turned out to be mistaken. Beethoven's interest in the text faded after he became acquainted with the text to *Fidelio* that Sonnleithner had worked up from the French, and *Vesta's Fire* remained unfinished.

The original score of this, the largest and also the musically most valuable of all the as yet unprinted works of Beethoven, is in the possession of the Gesellschaft der Musikfreunde in Vienna. A. W. Thayer, as early as 1865, entered the work in his chronological list of Beethoven's works (Berlin, Fr. Schneider) as No. 266, without being able to define it more exactly. Gustav Nottebohm gave the first thoroughgoing discussion of it in his *Beethoveniana* (Leipzig and Winterthur, 1872); he recognized the piece as a scene from an unfinished opera on which Beethoven was working in 1803, that is, just before embarking on *Fidelio*. He assumed, because of the rousing final trio, that it was a finale. In *Ein Skizzenbuch Beethovens aus dem Jahre 1803* (A Sketchbook of Beethoven's of the Year 1803) he presented long sketches for this unknown opera, including the beginning of an aria of revenge, which was to come *after* the Vienna score. The latter, therefore, could not be a finale.

It was not until 1930 that a Vienna man, Raoul Biberhofer, established the existence of the libretto in the Austrian National Library; he reports on it in the March issue of *Musik* for 1930. This collected all the material in one place.

The main characters of this story, which Schikaneder described as a "Grand Heroic Opera in Two Acts," are the following:

> Romenius, a decemvir
> Ponteus, a tribune
> Sericia, a noble Sabine woman
> Porus, a noble Roman[1]
> Volivia, his daughter
> Sartagones, her beloved
> Malo, a slave of Porus

and servants, Vestal virgins, augurs, bodyguards of Romenius, common people, etc.

Schikaneder gives the following stage directions for the *first scene*, for which Beethoven composed the music: "The theater is an enchanting garden of cypresses; a waterfall gushes forth in the center and runs into a brook at the right. Left is a tomb, with several steps leading down. The dawn is shining through the trees." Malo, the slave, tries to incite Porus against Sartagones, the beloved of Volivia. The two, in hiding, spy on the lovers, who plight their eternal troth and then are surprised by Porus (Malo stays in the background from this point on). In view of Sartagones' noble character, the father, after some hesitation, consents to their union, and a trio of the three happy people closes this first scene.

The rest of the text gives us, in eight more scenes, a rank tangle of intrigues and conflicts. Malo, enflamed by passion for the fair Volivia, alleges he is her brother and publicly accuses the absent Porus of having kidnaped him and his sister Volivia when they were small children. But Romenius too is in love with the beautiful Roman girl and for her sake throws over his fiancée Sericia. In order to get obstacles to his plans out of the way, he plots to send Ponteus, Porus, and Sartagones out of Rome with the army. Ponteus, for his part, hopes to win Sericia, the Sabine woman, for himself. Volivia, deprived of the protection of her father and her betrothed, seeks refuge in the temple of the vestal virgins, but Romenius does not respect even this holy place, but destroys it with his hordes. The sacred fire of Vesta goes out. Malo, who is a rival standing in the way of Romenius, is drowned in the Tiber, but Romenius survives his victim for only a few moments, since his fiancée Sericia stabs him. And now that the two villains are dead, a miracle occurs. The sacred fire of Vesta blazes up spontaneously, the vestals and the people flood in, Sartagones, Porus, and Volivia are rejoined, and a final chorus announces the marriage of the lovers, overcoming all the powers of evil:

[1] In the MS copy of the libretto before me the name is written as "Poros," which must be an error, since it concerns a Roman. Beethoven always writes "Porus."

>Cast yourselves down to earth,
>Vesta's fire flares again,
>Praise eternal to ye gods there,
>Ever hallowed be the spot.
>Gods, your blessing on this pair
>At the bridal altar there.

With such a banal and stereotyped opera intrigue, it is not hard to see why Beethoven put the text aside after composing the music for its best part, the first scene.

All the same, we must be grateful to Schikaneder for this work. Not only was it the source of the splendid music of the duet of rejoicing in *Fidelio*, which is present in embryo in the trio *"Nie war ich so froh wie heute, niemals fühlt' ich diese Freude"* (Never have I been so happy as today, never have I felt this joy), but the four numbers Beethoven composed are genuine masterpieces. The threatening undertone of the first scene is as impressive as the ardor and warmth of the love duet (in E flat major); in the recitative that follows, the music gives sculptural form to the actions of the singers, and the musical expression of the internal feelings and events is fascinating in impressiveness and intensity. Marvelous too is the ascending line of the change of heart in Porus (*"Warum soll Vaters Schuld er büssen?"* (Why should he suffer for his father's guilt?), leading to the joyful trio, which gives the entire scene a magnificent climax and close.

As a matter of fact, this quartet of pieces left by Beethoven forms a totality that is complete in itself, in both poetry and music, and could very well stand on its own feet in the concert hall. It could also be given student performances on the stage. Since the two tenors (Malo and Sartagones) never have to sing at the same time in any number, they could readily be taken by a single singer in concert versions.—WILLY HESS (4)

II. *Macbeth*

In December [1807], Rust,[1] writing to his brother Carl, was obliged to correct what he had said about Beethoven's new opera: "All new products which have appeared here are more or less mediocre except those of Beethoven. I think I have written you that he has not yet begun his new opera. I have not yet heard his first opera; it has not been performed since I have been here." These last sentences of Rust remind us of the once current notion that disgust and disappointment at the (assumed) failure of *Fidelio* prevented Beethoven from ever undertaking the composition of another opera. The error was long since exploded and indeed amply refuted by his proposition to the "princely theater rabble"

[1] Wilhelm Rust (1787–1855), a once famous *Wunderkind* from Dessau.—Editor.

for a permanent engagement. It is now universally known how earnestly Beethoven all his life long sought a satisfactory text for an opera or an oratorio; his friends always knew it; and his essays in vocal composition had, in spite of the critics, so favorably impressed them and the dramatic writers of the day that all were eager to serve him.

Thus Schneller[1] writes to Gleichenstein[2] from Graz, on March 19, 1807: "Speak at once to your friend Beethoven and particularly with the worthy Breuning, and learn if Beethoven has a mind to set a comic opera to music. I have read it, and found it varied in situation, beautiful in diction. Talk to him over a good dinner and a good glass of wine." Nothing came of this, nor is it known what the libretto was.

The new directors of the theaters began their operatic performances at the Kärnthnerthor January 1 and 2, and at the Burg January 4, 1807, with Gluck's *Iphigenia in Tauris*. It was new to Collin[3] and awakened in his mind new ideas of the ancient tragedy, which he determined to embody in a text for a musical drama in oratorio form. According to his biographer, Laban, he projected one on the liberation of Jerusalem, to offer to Beethoven for setting; but it was never finished. Another essay in the field of musical drama was a *Macbeth* after Shakespeare, also left unfinished in the middle of the second act, "because it threatened to become too gloomy." Nottebohm (*II Beeth.*, pp. 225 f.) says that the first act of Collin's *Macbeth* was printed in 1809 and must have been written in 1808 at the latest. He also prints a sketch showing that Beethoven had begun its composition. Collin's opera begins, like Shakespeare, with the witches' scene, and the sketch referred to is preceded by the directions: "Overture Macbeth falls immediately into the chorus of witches." In a letter to Thayer, Röckel[4] wrote: "That Beethoven did not abandon the idea of composing another opera was shown by the impatience with which he could scarcely wait for his friend Collin to make an opera book for him of Shakespeare's 'Macbeth.' At Beethoven's request, I read the first act and found that it followed the great original closely; unfortunately Collin's death prevented the completion of the work."

However, Collin did complete a grand opera libretto, *Bradamante*, for which he had an unusual predilection. It also was offered to Beethoven,

---

[1] Julius Franz Schneller, professor of history at Graz, and responsible for raising support for charitable institutions there. He arranged a charitable concert which included Beethoven's Sixth Symphony in its first performance in that city.—Editor.
[2] Ignaz Gleichenstein (1778–1828), born of a noble family from Breisgau. He was one of Beethoven's closest friends and was the husband of Anna Malfatti, the sister of Therese (one of the possible candidates for the "Immortal Beloved").—Editor.
[3] Heinrich Joseph von Collin (1771–1811), famous Viennese poet and dramatist. He was the author of the tragedy *Coriolan*, for which Beethoven wrote the famous overture.—Editor.
[4] Joseph August Röckel (1783–1870), tenor, who was the Florestan in the revised version of *Fidelio* and was active in persuading Beethoven to make certain changes.—Editor.

but seemed too venturesome to him in respect of its use of the super-natural; there were probably other reasons why it did not appeal to him. "And so it happened," says Laban, "that although at a later period Beethoven wanted to undertake its composition, Collin gave the book to Reichardt, who set it to music during his sojourn in Vienna in the winter of 1808–09."

The consequence of Beethoven's fastidiousness and indecision was that he had no text for a vocal composition when he moved to the country for the summer.—ALEXANDER WHEELOCK THAYER, EDITED BY ELLIOT FORBES

III. *Faust*

This article contains many facts and several quotations from letters, books, and contemporary reminiscences which appear elsewhere within this volume. The reason the editors are presuming to subject the reader to what at first might appear to be unnecessary repetition is that here, in a discussion of unfinished or proposed works by Beethoven, those facts and historical viewpoints have been so arranged and interpreted by Professor Unger as to form a fascinating picture of two creative giants and of their converging temperaments which played such a part in molding their own generation and those up to the present.—Editor.

"It is certainly a gratifying phenomenon to see two great masters united in one magnificent work and thus to witness a happy fulfillment of every expectation of the shrewd connoisseur of the works of each." So, almost 150 years ago, wrote E. Th. A. Hoffmann, the most famous contemporaneous critic of Beethoven's music, in his review of the Egmont Overture, the most significant work in which the master of tone combined his name with the master of the German word. Their relationship, how-ever, did not remain confined to the stimulus supplied by the poet to the composer: three years after the production of the Egmont music—in July 1812—they were combined in another and even more personal project.

Numerous qualified authors, mostly musical, have discussed this artistic relationship. In all the great biographies of both masters one finds it thoroughly covered. A whole list of authors have even written separate essays upon it, from Theodor Frimmel through Romain Rolland, Walter Nohl, Otto Erich Deutsch, and Walter Englesmann up to Richard Benz. It is understandable that the authors of books and essays, like Ferdi-nand Hiller, Wilhelm Bode, Max Friedländer, Hermann Abert, Joseph Müller-Blattau, Ferdinand Küchler, Friedrich Blume, Hans Joachim Moser, etc., have discussed in thorough depth Goethe's relationship to music and musicians, of whom the Viennese tone poet holds a particularly impressive position. However, hardly any monograph has placed the correspondence between Goethe and Bettina Brentano in its proper perspective and none has given full enough value to the conversation books in which the deaf Beethoven was forced to record his questions and answers. Hitherto also one highly important conversation which took place between the two great men during their meeting in Teplitz has been generally overlooked—although its subject matter has already been known since the end of the last century.

This long-overlooked but far-reaching discussion of the relationship between two artists cannot be covered in a few pages or in a short essay, but could well afford a complete volume. In the following treatise, therefore, we will confine ourselves essentially to an outline of Beethoven's endeavors relative to the Faust poem and a review of the plan, which the composer and the poet agreed upon during the few days together in Teplitz in 1812, of converting that dramatic masterpiece into an opera.

That Beethoven had been engrossed in Goethe's creative works since his early youth is confirmed in the two letters which the poet received from him. "Since my childhood I knew you," he declares in a letter of April 12, 1811. And the longer note of February 8, 1823, begins with the assurance: "Still, ever living, as I have since my youthful years in your immortal and eternally young works, etc." These words are also confirmed by several early works of the composer. As the manuscript of a musical sketch to the "Song of the Flea" proves, Beethoven had already absorbed himself with the so-called "Faust, a Fragment"—which appeared in 1790— in his last years in Bonn; also two arias on texts from a Goethe *Singspiel* probably exist from even earlier years. "The Sorrows of the Young Werther"—that novel of sentimental old age—held a deep fascination over him, which in later years he finally understood and admitted himself; also equally penetrating was the effect of *"Göte von Berlichingen"* in those early, impressionable years. This interest in and sympathy for contemporaneous literature was hardly nurtured in Beethoven's own home, but his maturer understanding came about through his association from his earliest days with personalities on a higher and more penetrating intellectual level. Above all it came about in the home of the young widow Countess Helene von Breuning, as well as through the influence of his first music teacher of note, the *"Musikdirektor"* Christian Gottlieb Neefe, a born catalytic agent.

When the name of Ludwig van Beethoven came to Goethe's attention is unfortunately unknown to us. It is questionable if the poet saw the first press notice about the young pianist and composer in Cramer's *Magazin der Musik* in 1783; probably he became aware of the name ten years later when Beethoven was described by Neefe, in Spazier's *Berliner Musikalischen Zeitungung*, as "one of the foremost pianists" which imprinted itself on Goethe's memory. Around the end of the century he must have associated Beethoven's name among the foremost contemporary musicians, from the contents of the *Jenaischen Allgemeiner Literaturzeitung*, [the foremost literary magazine of Jena] which often commented on Beethoven's newest published works; and the Leipzig *Allgemeinen Musikalischen Zeitung* in which Goethe was accustomed to acquaint himself with the latest performing musicians. But an answer to the question as to the poet's first actual acquaintance with Beethoven's music is not absolutely clear. We know only that the orchestra of the Weimar Royal Theater often performed Beethoven's orchestral compositions at the turn of the century, but it is probable that the poet might have come in contact even earlier with the frequently performed piano and chamber music of the young artist.

It is known that Beethoven traveled by the post from Bonn to Vienna on November 2, 1792, for the purpose of concluding his studies with Joseph Haydn in the musical capital. The route was by way of Koblenz, Ehrenbreitstein, Frankfurt am Main, and Munich. A noteworthy occurrence that has not been pointed out in any comparison of the lives of the two great artists is: if Goethe's [biographical] work *Vacation in France* is examined, it will be seen that, barring an accident en route, the paths must have crossed; for at the time that Beethoven was traveling through Koblenz, Goethe was already in that city or in the nearby Ehrenbreitstein. Who would not believe that, if the ambitious young Beethoven had knowledge that he was in such close vicinity of the poet whom he admired so much, he would at the very least have sought to develop a personal acquaintanceship with his idol by exchanging a few words.

But the personal meeting of the two great men was not to take place for another twenty years. It did not happen accidentally, but was worked out with true devotion by a mediator: the young, attractive Bettina Brentano, Goethe's "child" and intimate friend.[1] Besides being a very imaginative and prolific writer, she was also musically talented. Around the middle of May 1810 she stayed for a few weeks with the family of her brother Franz in Vienna, and through this circumstance journeyed in Beethoven's musical circle. She discusses her intimacy with the composer in a letter to Goethe on July 28, 1810, from which only the following overrefined and exuberant introduction is preserved. It has just been made available within the last decade through the last will and testament of Reinhold Steig:

"When I see anyone who loves you[2] as deeply as the One about Whom

---

[1] "Duzfreundin," one who is addressed by the familiar "*Du*" rather than the formal "*Sie*."—Editor.

[2] Throughout this letter Bettina used the familiar "*Du*," "*Dich*," and "*Dir*."—Editor.

I am about to tell you, I forget the entire world; the earth withers away for me, when that memory grips me; forsooth it vanishes and my horizon begins at my feet, arches around me, and I find myself in the washes of that Heaven which emanates from you. You know not what you give to others; or are you aware that all thoughts remain in the background and a peace, that envelops me like a flood, takes possession of my heart? . . . And the same is true of this Beethoven about whom I would now speak with you. People may say that he is offensive and ugly; but the love that he bears for you has invested him with an armor which disguises all his outer weaknesses from me. Now pay attention! In him the entire world comes to life and no one but . . ."

Here, unfortunately, the letter breaks off, all too suddenly. Its last sentence can be approximately reconstructed from "Goethe's correspondence with a child," which Bettina published in a rather fabricated form in the year 1835. There it appears in the following form: "The striving of mankind reverberates like clockwork within him back and forth, he alone is able to produce the unproducible, catalogue the thoroughly diversified . . ." Probably the young dreamer in the painting of this picture allowed her fantasy too much freedom. Nevertheless, she retains the merit of having brought about the meeting between the poet and the composer through her heartfelt co-operation.

The letter, so full of respect, in which the composer through Bettina's mediation informed the Weimar poet of his imminent arrival, is reprinted here unabridged in order to recall it to the reader's memory[1]:

Vienna, April 12, 1811

YOUR EXCELLENCY!

The pressing opportunity afforded by a friend of mine and a great admirer of yours, who is leaving Vienna very soon, allows me only a moment in which to thank you for the long time I have known you (for that I have done since my childhood)— That is so little for so much— Bettina Brentano has assured me that you would receive me kindly, or, I should say, as a friend. But how could I think of such a welcome, seeing that I can approach you only with the greatest reverence and with an inexpressively profound feeling of admiration for your glorious creations!— You will shortly receive from Leipzig through Breitkopf & Härtel my music for Egmont, that glorious Egmont on which I have again reflected through you, and which I have felt and reproduced in music as intensely as I felt when I read it[2]— I should very much like to have your opinion on my music to Egmont. Even your censure will be useful to me and my art and will be welcomed as gladly as the greatest praise.

Your Excellency's profound admirer,

LUDWIG VAN BEETHOVEN

[1] As translated by Emily Anderson (*The Letters of Beethoven*, Vol. 1, p. 318). —Editor.
[2] Goethe's diary states that he received the music in January 1812.—Editor.

Goethe's polite but cool answer (as attested by the fact that it was not written until June 25) begins by praising the young lady with the following words: "The good Bettina has well gained the sympathy which you expressed. She spoke with delight and the happiest disposition of you and recalled the hours which she spent with you among the happiest in her life. . . ."

Around the middle of April 1811, a certain Franz Oliva, on a commission of the firm of Ofenheimer Brothers in Vienna, by whom he was employed, made a journey to middle Germany. He was at that time Beethoven's right hand in everyday affairs and occasionally helped the composer in business matters. He must have come from a highly musical family. He was certainly himself a musician, for along with his other work he also gave piano lessons, and was acutely aware, as Beethoven's conversation books from the years 1819–20 testify, of many musical subjects and events which he discussed with erudition.

On that journey Oliva made his first visit to Goethe on May 3, 1811, as his own diary testifies, and must have delivered Beethoven's letter to the poet, although no mention of this appears in Goethe's reminiscences. Sulpiz Boisserée (who by means of his collection of [old Dutch and German] paintings and his own drawings of the cathedral in Köln was attempting to secure for himself a place in artistic society) describes in great detail the events of that afternoon. In writing to his brother Melchior, he recounts that when Goethe listened to Beethoven's music which Oliva delivered: "Goethe remarked that I should look at the sort of stuff it is: 'enough to drive one crazy, beautiful and mad at the same time.' I answered, 'Yes, it is certainly an echo of our times.' 'Exactly,' he said, 'it tries to encompass everything and in so doing always loses itself in the elemental!'"

In the spring of 1812 Napoleon invaded Russia with half a million soldiers. Two months later Teplitz was the gathering place of Emperor Franz and a number of German and Austrian rulers or their representatives; seemingly by merest coincidence, but in truth in order to conspire against the conqueror. On July 7, Duke August von Sachsen-Weimar traveled there, two days before Beethoven arrived, presumably to take the baths.[1]

At the summons of Duke August, Goethe came there from Karlsbad on July 14. On the seventeenth Beethoven mentioned in a letter to Breitkopf & Härtel in Leipzig, "Goethe is here." He had evidently not seen the poet, but was undoubtedly aware of his presence from the registration book at the Kurhaus.

---

[1] See Unger's mention of that journey and its significance in shedding certain light on the mystery of the "Immortal Beloved" in his essay on the letter.—Editor.

July 19, 1812, must be recorded in golden letters in every history of art as one of the immortal days in German culture. It was the day that the most transcendent German poet and the most honored German composer first saw each other and shook hands.

On that day Goethe recorded Beethoven's name first in his list of social calls he made. Also on the same day he wrote to his wife Christiane, who had remained in Karlsbad: ". . . I have never seen an artist more concentrated, more energetic and more sincere. I can well understand how singular he must stand in his relations with the world." As Goethe's diary later states, the two men took a walk to the nearby Bilin on July 20, and on the evenings of the twenty-first and twenty-third Goethe was again at Beethoven's lodgings. In his entry of July 21, Goethe recorded: "He plays exquisitely."[1]

[About the subject of the conversations] between the two great men, not only one but two documents have come down to us, one discovered over fifty years ago, the other less than twenty-five. They are both as reliable as a biography should hope to be; for the one is extracted from one of Beethoven's own letters, and the other in a note of a man high up in Goethe's circle of friends.

The composer himself, delighted with his intercourse with the poet, wrote to his Leipzig publishers another letter,[2] dated July 24, a day after their last conversation, according to Goethe's diary. In it he describes a plan of artistic collaboration with the poet which the two had evidently discussed:

> We send you our most friendly greetings and expect the same from you even without any tangible proofs.— That Goethe is here I have already told you. I spend some time with him every day. He has promised to write something for me. If only I do not have the same experience with him as others have with me!!!— Send me by "letter post" [these words are heavily underscored] my six songs [Opus 75], one of which is Goethe's "Kennst du das Land."— Have an offprint made on the thinnest and finest paper as quickly and speedily, with the greatest expedition that one cannot express

[1] Bettina Brentano wrote several letters about those meetings and in her own fantasy world spread the spurious anecdote of the two great men meeting the Emperor Franz on the promenade—Goethe, moving to one side, according to Bettina, bowed deeply, while Beethoven strode defiantly by and afterwards rebuked the poet for his subservience. A far more realistic picture of that incident, if it did in fact occur, is seen in the following remarks in a letter by Beethoven to Breitkopf & Härtel on August 9: "Goethe delights far too much in the court atmosphere, far more than is becoming to a poet. How can one really say anything about virtuosi in this respect, when poets, who should be regarded as the leading teachers of the nation, can forget everything else when confronted with that pomp and circumstance."—Editor.

[2] Besides the one previously mentioned, dated July 17, in which he told them that Goethe was also in Teplitz.—Editor.

it in words, and send it to me here on the wings of thought for I am an Austrian bungler—*povero musico!*[1]

About Goethe's conversation with him, Beethoven could only be referring to an opera text; for he had since 1806 been in search of a [suitable] opera libretto. Not only had he approached various Austrian poets, but foreign ones as well. But always without success.

Beethoven's foregoing announcements have been made even more precise through a few lines of Count Otto Heinrich von Loeben. According to the book *Justinus Kerner's Correspondence With His Friends* (which Theobald Kerner edited in 1897), Loeben wrote to the South German doctor, mystic, and poet on August 29, 1814: "Do you know that our Master [Goethe] has written a drama for October 18? I dream of it! And that Beethoven has instigated a project to set his "Faust" to music? When two such crowning personalities strive toward such a work . . . we may well consider ourselves on the return to the time of Olympus!" Stimulated by the nobility of thought that Goethe and Beethoven would participate together in a major work of modern German poetry, Loeben (who, under the pseudonym Isidarus Orientalis, published some insignificant verse and prose) sounds surprisingly like E. Th. A. Hoffmann in the latter's comments on the "Egmont" Overture with which this essay began.

Loeben had undoubtedly received his knowledge of the plan for an opera by Beethoven based on *Faust* from the poet himself. He had spent the winter of 1813–14 in Weimar and had visited Goethe many times.

How high Beethoven stood in his reputation is shown, outside of Loeben's letters to Kerner, in the form of two poems in which he glorifies the composer. In the public library of Berlin, there is a volume of posthumous literary works in Loeben's hand which contains a few such works. It is in three octavo pages. On the first two pages there appear the following two sonnets: *To Beethoven,* and *To Beethoven after Hearing One of His Symphonies":*

I

An Beethoven
Das alte Feuer will sich neu entzünden,
Ins Meer der Nacht soll sich der Seher wagen,
Die Felsen, die gemacht das Wellenschlagen,
Sie werdon im kristallnen Arm verschwinden.

Das Fernrohr lehrt die Götterstrasse uns finden,
Die Sterne im Chore singen nahes Tagen,
Auch nach Vergangnen muss der Blick nun fragen,
Im einstigen Chaos, was da ward, empfinden.

[1] Translation by Emily Anderson in her *Letters of Beethoven,* London, Macmillan and Co., Ltd., 1961, pp. 382–83.—Editor.

Da werden Töne, wird Musik uns Denken,
Du heissest mich zum Chaos niedersteigen,
Die Kampfposaune schlägt durch alle Tiefen.

Es will ihr Blitz mit Licht den Abgrund tränken;
Sell sich aus Nacht das Feuer göttlich zeigen,
Man muss mit dir ins Werden sich vertiefen.

II

An Beethoven, über eine seiner Symphonien
Wie alle die tiefen Wunder uns umringen,
Die Elemente blitzen in der Waffen,
Recht Gottes Lust sich zeiget in den Schaffen,
Erzengel der Musik! Hebst du die Schwingen.

Da kommt das Licht, das Chaos zu bezwingen,
Die Tiefen eilen sich emporzuraffen,
Dein Flügelschlag hat grosse Ruhe geschaffen,
Man hört die Engel in der Höhe lobsingen.

Doch irdisch Sträuben kommt, sich zu erzeugen,
Aus Kampf zum Frieden treibt nun die Posaune,
Sehnsucht gebiert sich in den flüchtigen Schmerzen,

Da gibst du den Takt dem Sternenreigen,
In einzeln Tönen, dass die Erde erstaune,
Dir strömen sie von Gottes Sonnenherzen.

I[1]

The ancient fire will be once more rekindled,
In night's vast ocean shall the Seer awake,
The rocks on which its raging waves are breaking
Within His mighty arms shall crumble to dust.

In that distant hour we'll learn God's way,
The stars in chorus sing forth that bright new day,
Yet from the past we all in terror ask,
What shall befall us in that future Chaos.

Where once was noise there now is melodious music,
That showest me how to rise from out those depths;
The horns of war resound throughout the Vast.

Thy lightning shall illuminate the abyss;
At night celestial fires will reappear;
With thee, we all shall greet our metamorphosis.

[1] There has been no attempt on the part of the translator to reconstruct the rhyme scheme, which is in classical sonnet form. The flowery language is in itself a key to the poet's intention.

II

As all these mystic wonders thus engulf us—
The elements lit up as if in war—
True godly joy appears on the horizon,
Archangel of music, when thou spreads't out thy wings!

Through thou there comes the light that conquers Chaos,
The lowest depths all hasten to respond,
The beating of thy wings creates rare quiet,
One hears the heavenly angels singing praise.

Though worldly strife seems ever to recurr,
On battlefields thy trumpets sing us joy,
As longing is fulfilled in floods of tears.

Thou beatest out the rhythmic march of stars
In tones unique, which hold the world in awe,
Thou pourest out the melodies of God.

Already in his last years in Bonn, Beethoven, as mentioned above, became familiar with the first part of Goethe's *Faust*. The drama occupied
him pressingly throughout his entire life, as is shown by numerous musical works as well as by many diversified sketches. The thought of transforming it into an opera had already occurred to him before he wrote
the incidental music to "Egmont." Scarcely two years before the composition of the latter, a Viennese correspondent to the Stuttgart *Mor-
genblatt für gebildete Stände* wrote: "The ingenious Beethoven has
the concept of composing Goethe's 'Faust,' but so far he has found no-
one who can adapt it, to his satisfaction, for the stage. That he has other
musical projects before him cannot be doubted, but we may be certain
that a deep and truly sensitive product will result from his spirit [in the
event the opera comes to life]."

In a letter to Breitkopf & Härtel, dated January 28, 1812, Beethoven
mentions that he has written to Goethe a second time, in which he has
promised to send the poet a complete score of "Egmont." Unfortunately
the letter no longer exists. On the same day he also wrote to August von
Kotzebue[1] in Riga with the request that he supply him with an opera
text. Is it not possible, in fact probable, that in the letter to Goethe
he also mentioned the wish that the poet transform *Faust* into an opera
libretto for him?

A half year later [as we have seen] Beethoven had the opportunity to
put his request to the poet directly face to face, and one must suppose that
this is exactly what happened in their first meeting. Both of them had
only a few days together in Teplitz. According to Goethe's diary they

---

[1] The poet and dramatist and manager of the Burgtheater in Vienna from 1798
to 1799.—Editor.

were from the nineteenth to the twenty-third of July. On orders of his doctor, Beethoven traveled on the twenty-seventh to Karlsbad and around August 8 proceeded to Franzenbrunn, returning to Teplitz on September 8. On the return trip he stopped off in Karlsbad once again, manifestly to give a farewell handshake to Goethe, who in the meantime was staying there. After that the master of music and the master of words never again saw each other.

"When I am with him [Goethe], nothing else matters!!! Much has been said about this [project] but one can speak with the best intentions and nothing comes of it!" Unfortunately it happened in that manner: the Faust opera of Goethe and Beethoven remained unwritten. Both had sought it out and hit upon it but found that they could not achieve a true artistic meeting of minds.

In a letter of September 2 to his musical counselor, Carl Friedrich Zelter, Goethe shows that he is essentially taken aback by Beethoven the man: "His talent amazed me; however, unfortunately, he is an utterly untamed personality, which, indeed, is by no means wrong if he finds the world detestable, but it certainly does not make the world more enjoyable for himself or for others." But how did he feel about Beethoven the artist? He admired him greatly but was neither equipped through his musical education nor through the musical advice he received from Zelter fully to understand his compositions. He used the expression *"Teufelzeug"* [stuff of the devil] in a conversation with Boisserée in which he was comparing Beethoven's style [to that of Haydn]. Another significant scene occurred when the young Felix Mendelssohn-Bartholdy played on the piano the first movement of the Fifth Symphony for the poet in 1830, three years after Beethoven's death. The listener felt it very strange and remarked: "That moves one not at all—it merely astonishes one; it is merely grandiose!" After a long period of silence he began again: "It is tremendous, quite mad; one could fear the whole house might collapse—imagine the whole lot of them [the entire orchestra] playing it together!"

No, Goethe grew up in the classical musical world of Haydn and Mozart, and [was influenced also] by the somewhat Philistine opinions of Zelter and could not comprehend the "massive style" of the young master; the elemental power of the "new music" disturbed him, brought about within him an unstable equilibrium; it even frightened him. Goethe was well aware of the force and greatness of Beethoven's music, but it was a world which was not in tune with the classical symmetry of his own. No wonder that toward the end of his life, in a conversation with Eckermann[1] about a musical setting of *Faust*, Goethe hardly mentions

[1] Johann Peter Eckermann (1792–1856), who compiled from his notes the book *Conversations with Goethe During the Last Years of His Life.*—Editor.

Beethoven, but especially expresses the viewpoint that Mozart would have been the ideal musical interpreter of the tragedy. Eckermann reports:

"The conversation turned to Zelter. 'I have a letter from him,' said Goethe; 'he says among other things that the performance of the 'Messiah' was spoiled by a pupil of his, who sang a particular aria too gently, too weakly, too sentimentally. This weakness is a characteristic of our century. I have a hypothesis that it is a consequence of an effort to get rid of the French. Painters, scientists, sculptors, musicians, poets, are all (with few exceptions) weak, and the masses are hardly any better.'[1]

"'But,' I said, 'is there no hope for me that I will see a satisfactory musical interpretation of "Faust"?'

"'It is entirely impossible,' he replied. 'The repulsive, the annoying, the frightening, which it must contain here and there, is antipathetic to the present outlook. The music must be in the character of Don Juan: Mozart would have been a perfect composer for it!'"

Rather than the "repulsive" and "frightening" that Goethe had imagined for a truly artistic musical interpretation, Beethoven's mighty style seemed to him too brutal and barbaric.

Thus the poet found the composer neither personally nor artistically congenial to his work.[2]

Beethoven, on the contrary, retained till the end the highest honor and enthusiasm for the poet despite the ambivalent impression Goethe the man (and only the man) made upon him. No other poet or philosopher is so frequently mentioned in Beethoven's letters and conversation books as Goethe, and not a single unkind or disgruntled word about him as a human being appears. Once it appears that he even stood up for Goethe in a conversation with one of his (Beethoven's) best friends, Privy Councilor Peters[3]—Peters wrote (in the conversation book): "Goethe should not write any more, the muse seems to have left him for good," which obviously drew forth a quick response on the part of Beethoven, for the following placating words follow: "Yet he remains the first poet of Germany." This is a verdict that Beethoven is known to have agreed with.

Yet in spite of their mutual agreement on arranging Faust as an opera, neither of the two masters was stirred to put pen to paper in a letter about

---

[1] See Paul Henry Lang's discussion of the Biedermeier tradition in German culture, in his *Music in Western Civilization*, pages 805–8, which echos this evaluation of Goethe's.—Editor.

[2] It is interesting and unfortunate that Goethe has, in his existing writings, never made mention of Spohr's opera *Faust*, which appeared in 1816, and the music to which would undoubtedly be more to the poet's taste than any by Beethoven! —Editor.

[3] Karl Peters, the tutor to the children of Prince Lobkowitz and appointed in April 1820 as co-guardian of Karl, Beethoven's nephew.—Editor.

it during the first year after their meeting. Beethoven, to be sure, was well known not to correspond except under some pressure. Did his silence signify that he was quits with the project because the poet never heard from him? The latter is not entirely out of the question.

So far as we are informed, in the course of the all too sparse correspondence between the two great personalities of the beginning of the nineteenth century, it was Goethe who first wrote to Beethoven—ten years after their meeting at the Bohemian bathing resort. It probably amounted to a mere short introduction of a musician: the French violinist Alexandre Boucher[1] had made a visit to Weimar early in 1822 on one of his concert tours, and came soon thereafter to Vienna, where he appeared in concert several times that spring with his wife. Unfortunately Goethe's letter of introduction to Beethoven is lost.

Soon thereafter around the middle of May of the same year, the composer sent a copy of the newly published first edition of the choral work *Meerestille und glückliche Fahrt*[2] to Weimar. The composition, which appeared in 1914-15, is dedicated "with highest esteem to the author of the poem, the immortal Goethe." The poet noted the receipt in his diary; however, as was the case ten years earlier with the receipt of the Egmont music, Beethoven was never thanked for it. (It had, to be sure, arrived without a covering letter.) At least the composer was not restrained by that oversight from turning again to Goethe at the beginning of the next year with a request that lay especially close to his heart.

It came about at the time he was attempting to make the publication and performance of his recently completed great work, the *Missa Solemnis*,[3] economically practical. Seeking friendly advice, he had sent Goethe the orchestral score of the work, for the proper publication of which he was seeking the subscription of as many royal personages and music societies as possible. In this connection Beethoven had approached the Duke of Sachsen-Weimar and used this as an excuse to write on February 8, 1823, to Goethe containing a request that the poet put in a friendly word for him to the duke. As twelve years before, in respect to his music for Egmont, he again this time asked for Goethe's opinion of this latest composition. About the Faust project there was no word. The Master closed the letter with a superabundant yet sincere avowal to the poet, confident that he would intercede with the duke for him[4]:

> The admiration, the love and the esteem which already in my youth I cherished for the one and only immortal Goethe, have

[1] An exceptional violinist who lived from 1778 to 1861, but a slight charlatan who excited European audiences more by his tricks than by his musicianship. His wife was an equally gifted harpist.—Editor.
[2] Opus 112.—Editor.
[3] Opus 123.—Editor.
[4] The translation of the letter is by Emily Anderson, from her already cited book, pages 998-99.

persisted. Feelings like this are not easily expressed by an uncouth fellow such as myself, for my *one* aim has been to master the art of music. However a strange feeling is constantly prompting me to say these things to you, seeing that I live in your writings—I know that you will not fail to use your influence on this particular occasion on behalf of an artist who feels only too keenly to what an extent *mere gain* detaches him from *his art*. Yet *need* compels him to act and to work *on behalf of others and for others*. We can always see clearly what is good; and thus I know that Your Excellency will not reject my petition—A few words from you to me would fill me with happiness—

I remain, Your Excellency, with my most profound and infinite regard,

BEETHOVEN[1]

Many Beethoven biographers have thrown much suspicion upon Goethe because he left this letter, a touching appeal, unanswered. Especially Rolland has particularly harsh words about it, but softens them by the following passage in defense of the poet: "If an ego is without proportion to the extent that it comprehends the universe, that it becomes the basis for the enlightening and beautifying of the entire world, who would dare to criticize it? Do we accuse the sun for indiscriminately sending out its rays?"

Unfortunately, however, this interpretation is not adjudged within the context of Goethe's above-mentioned letter of introduction of Boucher. Beethoven's pressing appeal was left unanswered by the poet, yet scarcely a year earlier the poet had presumed to write an equally practical, worldly, and self-seeking letter to the composer in behalf of the violinist!

It remains to us hardly any other possibility than to return to the explanation given by most earlier interpreters of the artistic relationship between Goethe and Beethoven. Most of them cite the fact that Goethe's livelihood was already impaired in the year 1823: A few days after the arrival of Beethoven's letter the poet was stricken by a highly dangerous illness. He recovered from it only after a lingering battle. After a short time—not even age, it seems, had protected the wisest of Germans from folly—the heart of the seventy-four-year-old was burning in its last flame of love, for the nineteen-year-old Ulrike von Levetzow, and he even thought in terms of a new marriage. (Only the understanding of the Levetzow family thwarted the plan.) This event toward the end of the year had resulted for the poet in a new serious illness and a feeling of unutterable loneliness, and only slowly did he recover from them.

[1] This quotation is merely the end of the letter, as Professor Unger explains. However, it is interesting to note that the letter also contains mention of the composer's setting of the poet's *Meerstille und Gluckliche Fahrt*, but with assurance that the dedication of it to Goethe was in no way connected with the present favor being asked.—Editor.

During these occurrences, upsetting alike to his soul and body, he must have found little sympathy for Beethoven's letter. The composer was probably almost completely forgotten to him but was suddenly forcefully returned to his mind. Naturally Goethe's silence vis-à-vis the Master, whose reputation and honor were secure in the entire cultural world toward the end of his life, must remain a sin of omission. Has anyone criticized Goethe in these terms for considering unworthy of answer the receipt from the yet unknown Schubert of his setting of the poet's *Erlkönig?*

After Beethoven's encounter with Goethe at the Bohemian watering place, the choral work *Meerestille und glückliche Fahrt* remains his only large-sized composition based on words of the poet. However, already around the time of his last letter to Goethe, Beethoven appears to be absorbed in the former's lyrics. In a sketchbook of the second half of 1822 there appear several attempts at *Heidenröslein* which were evidently left unfinished. It was probably in the following year that his setting of *Bundeslied* ("In allen guten Stunden . . .")[1] originated; it is set for two solo voices and three choral voices with accompaniment of a few wind instruments. Above all the composer in these years repeatedly took in hand the opening words of Goethe's poem *Das Göttliche:* "Edel sei der Mensch, hülfreich und gut." A six-voice canon based on them is altogether the most ambitious vocal work of this type by the composer.[2] Yet he had also experimented with a three-voice canon on the slightly rearranged words, "Edel, hülfreich sei der Mensch." Just a few weeks before his letter to Goethe he had given as an album leaf to a Countess Wimpffen,[3] a short vocal piece with piano accompaniment on the likewise rearranged words: "Der edel Mensch sei hülfreich und gut!" [It is] a simple and heartfelt work. It appeared first in 1843 in the *Allgemeinen Wiener Musikzeitung.* The editor, August Schmidt, makes the clever observation: "Just as the composer had through his choice of text done honor to [the poet], he had also made the latter's name tangible in the first five notes of the accompaniment: namely, g, e, d, h,[4] e." (That is the way of spelling Goethe's name in Saxon dialect.) Doubtless an homage was intended. He was known to have made plays on words in many of his conversations and letters, as well as in his riddle canons, and he undoubtedly had fun with this musical pun. Be that as it may, it is seen that the magnanimous friend of man, Beethoven, linked his name with the poet's no less than three times in this humanistic verse: ["The noble man is helpful and good!"]

---

1 Opus 122.—Editor.

2 Kinsky-Halm identifies it as WoO 185 and it appears in the Breitkopf & Härtel edition of the collected works.—Editor.

3 Countess Marie von Wimpffen, daughter of the Baron von Eskeles, Beethoven's banker.—Editor.

4 "H" is the German way of spelling the note B natural.—Editor.

In the summer of 1822, through Friedrich Rochlitz, the Leipzig editor, the firm of Breitkopf & Härtel delivered to Beethoven the commission to compose music for *Faust* in the same manner as he had previously for "Egmont." Speaking of Goethe's lyrics [to Rochlitz], the composer remarked: "There is no one who lends himself to musical setting as well as he." "When I mentioned the Faust project," Rochlitz writes, "'Ha!' [Beethoven] cried, and flung up his hand. 'That would be a man-sized job! That might yield something!' He went on in this fashion for sometime, picturing the thought to himself in a manner anything but inept, while, with his head thrown back he stared at the ceiling. 'But,' he continued, 'for some time now I have been carrying about in my head the idea of three other great works. I have done a good deal of work upon them [in my head].' Though I doubt the success of the 'Faust' project, let us live in hopes, since the suggestion caught his fancy, and he assured me again and again that he would not forget it."[1]

And in the beginning of April 1823, Dr. [Johann] Bihler wrote in the conversation book concerning an oratorio commissioned by the Handel and Haydn Society of Boston. Beethoven answered in the following words: "I cannot write now what I should best like to write, but that which I am obliged to through the pressing need for money. Yet when this period is past I hope to compose what for me and for art is above all: Faust!"

Even a few months before his death Beethoven continued to play around with the idea of a musical setting of *Faust*. From information given us by Beethoven's young friend Anton Schindler, the composer's last conversation about the *Faust* plan closed with these words: "Something definitely will come of it!"—MAX UNGER (3) (TR. BY THOMAS K. SCHERMAN)

IV. *The Ruins of Babylon*

[By 1811] Hartl[2] had retired from the direction of the Court Theaters, and Lobkowitz and Palffy[3] were again at the helms respectively of the theater next to the Kärnthnerthor and that An-der-Wien. Beethoven was

[1] From Rochlitz's *"Für Freunde der Tonkünste"* (1830–32), as reprinted in *Beethoven—Impressions of His Contemporaries*, edited by O. G. Sonneck, New York, 1926, G. Schirmer, Inc.—Editor.
[1] Joseph Hartl, court councillor and director of the Court Theaters from 1808 to early in 1811. It was he who secured Beethoven's services, in April and November, to conduct two benefit concerts of his own compositions.—Editor.
[3] Count Ferdinand Palffy de Erdödy (1774–1840), Viennese nobleman and patron of the arts and sciences. In 1806 he joined a group of distinguished aristocrats, including the Princes Lobkowitz, Scharzenberg, and Esterházy, to take over the running of the Court Theaters.—Editor.

busy with dramatic compositions[1] and so, very naturally, the project of another operatic work was revived. He had also obtained a subject that pleased him—a French melodrama *Les Ruines de Babylon*—probably from the Prussian Baron Friedr. Joh. Drieberg. This composer, much more favorably known for his researches into ancient Greek music than for his operas, had been five years in Paris, "where he studied composition under Spontini and probably for a short time also under Cherubini," and now for two years in Vienna.

A series of notes from Beethoven to . . . Count Palffy, written in June and July 1811, show how the operatic project was shaping itself in his mind. On June 6, he was anxious to know if Treitschke had read the book, and wished to reread it himself before Treitschke began work on it. He expressed dismay to Palffy on June 11, because he had heard that a performance of the melodrama *Les Ruines de Babilone* was projected for the benefit of an actor, Scholz. He set forth how much more desirable it would be to have this work given as an opera, a "work of lasting value." "It is so difficult to find a good libretto for an opera; I have rejected no less than twelve or more in the last several weeks." Beethoven said that he had told the archduke about the subject and had even written to foreign newspapers of his intention to set it to music. He hoped the count would forbid the intended performance. Palffy evidently co-operated, for on July 3 the composer again wrote to Treitschke that he had received a translation "along with Palffy's instructions to arrange everything that is necessary with you. There is nothing now to prevent your keeping your promise to me. But I am again asking you if you really are going to keep it, so that I may know where I stand in the matter—" There the matter seems to have rested. . . .—ALEXANDER WHEELOCK THAYER, EDITED BY ELLIOT FORBES

V. *The Return of Ulysses*

Theodor Körner[2] informs us that [in 1812] Beethoven's desire again to try his fortune on the operatic stage was in no wise abated. On June 6 the youthful poet writes: "If Weinlig does not intend soon to compose my *Alfred*, let him send it back to me; I would then, having bettered my knowledge of the theater and especially of opera texts, strike out several things, in as much as it is too long, and give it to the Kärthner Theater, as I am everlastingly plagued for opera texts by Beethoven, Weigl, Gyro-

1 Primarily work on *The Ruins of Athens*, a play by Kotzebue, for which he was invited to compose the incidental music.—Editor.
2 1791–1813, poet and hero, he was also an ardent music lover. In 1811 he became engaged to Toni Adamberger, the famous actress, who in 1810 created the role of Clärchen in Beethoven's musical version of Goethe's tragedy *Egmont*. —Editor.

witz, etc." On February 10, 1813, he writes: "Beethoven has asked me
for 'The Return of Ulysses.' If Gluck were alive, that would be a
subject for his Muse."—ALEXANDER WHEELOCK THAYER, EDITED BY ELLIOTT
FORBES

VI. *Romulus and Remus*

In a letter of early December [1814] to the archduke, who was then in
Prague attempting to hasten a settlement of the Kinsky payments, Beethoven writes: "—then there is the *matter of a new opera*—the *subject* of
which I must decide in the next few days—" The *Sammler* of December
13 explains the allusion to an opera: "It is with great pleasure that we inform the music-loving public that Herr van Beethoven has contracted to
compose an opera. The poem is by Herr Treitschke and bears the title:
Romulus und Remus." The notice was based upon this note to Treitschke:
"I will compose Romulus and shall begin in a few days, I will come to
you in person! first *once*—then *several times* so that we may discuss the
whole matter with each other."

Now here was a promising operatic project, but before six weeks had
passed came the *Allgemeine Musikalische Zeitung*, bringing Johann
Fuss's musical "Review of the month of December," wherein among the
items of Vienna news was a notice that "Hr. Fuss had composed an opera
in three acts entitled *Romulus und Remus* for the Theater-an-der-Wien!"
And this was so; portions of it were afterwards sung by a musical society
of which Dr. L. Sonnleithner was a member, and in Pressburg it was
put upon the stage in 1818, but it never came to performance in
the theaters of Vienna. . . .—ALEXANDER WHEELOCK THAYER, EDITED
BY ELLIOT FORBES

VII. *Bacchus*

The opera book . . . was entitled *Bacchus*, a "Grand Lyric Opera in
Three Acts." The libretto was preserved among Schindler's papers in the
Berlin Library. It seems likely that Beethoven gave some thought to the
opera and experimented with some themes. There are interesting notes
on a work with a classical subject, the words apparently the beginning of
an invocation to Pan, in a sketchbook of 1815, which Nottebohm[1]
describes without deciding whether they belong to Treitschke's *Romulus
und Remus* or von Berge's *Bacchus*:

[There is a curious syncopated measure which is probably the motive
of Pan, because Beethoven has written the words "*gütiger Pan*" underneath
the notes. This is followed without interruption by a bucolic dance

[1] *II Beeth.*, pp. 329–30.

motive in 3/8. Beethoven then writes:] "not quite so characteristic, it must be evolved out of the B.M." [probably standing for the Bacchus Motif, according to Reimann. That motive is also a dance motive in 3/8 indicated by Beethoven to be played by horns. Beethoven continues:] "Throughout the opera probably dissonances, unresolved or [resolved] very unusually as our refined music cannot be thought of in connection with those barbarous times.—Throughout the subject must be treated in a pastoral vein."—ALEXANDER WHEELOCK THAYER, EDITED BY ELLIOT FORBES

VIII. *Melusine*

[While] Grillparzer has left on record his [boyhood] recollections of Beethoven, which date back to the year 1804 or 1805, [he] did not really make Beethoven's acquaintance until some time after the perform-ance of "König Ottokars Glück und Ende,"[1] when he was informed by Count Dietrichstein, the nominal head of the two imperial theaters, that Beethoven had expressed a desire to have a libretto from his pen. Grillparzer, after some hesitation—due to a doubt whether the composer, at that time already completely deaf, was still able to write an opera—consented to furnish a libretto, and chose for it the subject of Melusine. When the book was ready, he sent it to Beethoven, leaving it to his judgment whether to use it or not.

"A few days afterward," he writes, "Schindler, then Beethoven's busi-ness manager—the same who afterward wrote his biography—called on me and told me that his master, who was indisposed, requested me to visit him. I dressed, and we started immediately for Beethoven's house. He lived at the time in the Landstrasse, and I found him lying, in untidy night attire, on a disarranged bed, a book in his hand. At the head of the bed there was a small door, leading, as I subsequently perceived, to a little cabinet containing some eatables, on which he kept an eye. When a servant finally appeared, with butter and eggs, Beethoven, although en-gaged in animated conversation, could not refrain from casting a search-ing glance at the quantity of food carried out of the cabinet, which gave me a sad insight into the troubles of his domestic life.

"When we entered, Beethoven rose from his bed, gave me his hand, overwhelmed me with expressions of esteem, and immediately began talking about his opera. 'Your work is right here,' he said, pointing to his heart; 'in a few days I shall go to the country and then I shall at once begin to set it to music. But the hunters' chorus, with which the libretto opens, troubles me. Weber used four bugle-horns in his chorus, you will

[1] Written in 1823; produced for the first time in 1825. It was severely cen-sored by the royal authorities and cost its author a remunerative job in the civil service.—Editor.

therefore see that I shall have to have eight, and what then?' Although I could not see the logic of his argument, I told him that the hunters' chorus might easily be spared altogether, without injury to the whole—a concession with which he seemed to be very much pleased."

Grillparzer was entirely indifferent to the commercial aspects of their partnership, on which Beethoven laid great stress. In spite, however, of his eagerness to draw up a contract at once, and his apparent entire satisfaction with the libretto as it stood, Beethoven for some reason delayed the execution of the work; and when, in the course of the summer, Grillparzer visited him in the country, there was no further talk about the opera between them. Their conversation was carried on by Grillparzer's writing down what he had to say on loose sheets of paper, which have been preserved.

"I remember vividly," continues the autobiography, "that Beethoven, when we sat down at the table, went into the adjoining room and brought out five bottles of wine. One of these he put before Schindler's plate, one before his own, and three he placed in a row before me, probably in order to indicate, in his naïvely ignorant, good-natured way, that I was at liberty to drink as much as I pleased. When I started to drive back to the city, without Schindler, who remained in Hetzendorf, Beethoven insisted on accompanying me. He sat down next to me in the open wagon, but instead of going merely to the limits of his district, he drove with me back to the city, at the gates of which he alighted; and after a hearty handshake, he started alone upon his return tramp of an hour and a half. As he left the carriage, I saw a paper lying in the place where he had sat. Thinking he had forgotten it, I motioned to him to return, but he shook his head, and laughing loudly, as if delighted with the success of his ruse, he ran off with increased speed in the opposite direction. I opened the paper, and found that it contained the exact amount of the fare which I had agreed upon with the driver. So estranged had he become, through his manner of living, from all worldly customs, that it never entered his mind what an insulting proceeding this might be considered by anyone else. I took the matter as he intended it, and laughingly paid the driver with the money presented to me.

"I saw him—I do not know where—but once more after that. He then told me: 'Your opera is ready.' Whether he meant, 'all thought out,' or whether the countless notebooks in which he jotted down, for future elaboration, detached thoughts and notes, intelligible to him only, contained fragments of that opera, I cannot say. Certain it is that after his death not a single note was found which could have been identified as relating to our common work. For my part, I remained true to my resolution not to remind him, in any way, of my libretto, and as I found it burdensome to converse with him by means of a writing tablet, I never more approached him until, dressed in black, and a burning taper in my hand, I walked behind his coffin.[1]

"I may say that I truly loved Beethoven. If I can relate but little concerning my talks with him, the principal reason is that I am not interested in what an artist has to say, but in what he does. If talking were a criterion of artistic capacity, Germany would be as full of artists as, in reality, she is devoid of them. Among the things Beethoven told me, I remember his high praise of Schiller, and his remark that he considered the lots of poets a far happier one than that of musicians, inasmuch as their field was so much wider. I recollect that his estimate of Weber's 'Euryanthe' was no higher than my own. On the whole, it was probably the successes of Weber that suggested to him the thought of writing another opera himself. But his imagination had become so unbridled that no libretto in the world would have been able to confine his creations within given limits. He looked far and wide for one, but could not find it."

Grillparzer's recollections of Beethoven are supplemented by the preserved records, on loose sheets, of his remarks written down by him while conversing with the deaf composer. On one of these sheets we find Grillparzer suggesting to him an expedient which, as Ehrhard remarks, is nothing less than the employment of a *Leitmotiv* in the manner of Richard Wagner. "I have asked myself," he wrote, "whether it would not be advisable to mark each appearance or action of 'Melusine' by some catching and regularly recurring melody. Why could not the overture begin with this melody?"

The leaves commemorating the last conversation that took place between the two men, early in 1826, reflect the melancholy to which Grillparzer was then a prey, shortly after he broke off his engagement to Katharina Fröhlich. The sentences, brief and detached, are full of meaning. "The censorship has killed me.—One has to emigrate to North America if he wants to give free expression to his thoughts.—I have become stupid.—The musician is not subject to censorship.—The literary men of other countries are opposed to everything that comes from Austria.—In spite of everything I love Austria.—At bottom my works are finding less and less favor.—I have the misfortune to be a hypochondriac.—My works give me no pleasure.—Ah, if I had the thousandth part of your energy and firmness!"

During his last interview with Beethoven, Grillparzer expressed himself disparagingly about Weber, whose "Euryanthe," he said, contained more poetry than music. The North Germans, he added, reason too much, and Weber is merely a critic turned composer. He considered the critical habit characteristic of the present age. "The world has lost its innocence, and without it one cannot create or enjoy a work of art."

---

[1] See text of Grillparzer's funeral oration.—Editor.

Ehrhard surmises that in answer to all these despondent reflections Beethoven must have exhorted Grillparzer to take courage, for on the same day the violinist Holz spoke to Beethoven about Grillparzer's lack of firmness and remarked: "The lecture you have given him must have made a great impression on him." Holz mentioned "Melusine" to Beethoven in terms of praise, but the composer emphatically condemned the hunters' chorus. Grillparzer's libretto subsequently passed into the hands of the composer, Konradin Kreutzer, who set it to music, without, however, achieving the success scored by his "Nachtlager von Granada."— GUSTAV POLLAK

Choral Works

I. Requiem

[Besides an opera and an oratorio] his friends also urged him to compose a requiem mass, and such a composition belongs in the category with the oratorio as a work which he had been paid to undertake. Among the ardent admirers of Beethoven and most zealous patrons of the Schuppanzigh Quartets was Johann Nepomuk Wolfmayer, a much-respected cloth merchant. One of the methods chosen by Wolfmayer to show his appreciation of the composer was occasionally to have a new coat made for him which he would bring to Beethoven's lodgings, place upon a chair and then see to it that an old one disappeared from his wardrobe. We have already heard a similar story from Mayseder.[1] It is said that Wolfmayer sometimes had difficulty in getting the composer's consent to the exchange, but always managed to do it. Early in the second decade of the century Wolfmayer commissioned Beethoven to write a requiem for him and offered him one-hundred ducats as honorarium. Beethoven promised but never set to work, though Holz says he was firmly resolved to do so and, in talking about it, said that he was better satisfied with Cherubini's setting of the mass for the dead than with Mozart's. A requiem, he said, should be a memorial of the dead and have nothing in it of the noises of the last trumpet and the day of judgment. ALEXANDER WHEELOCK THAYER, EDITED BY ELLIOTT FORBES

[1] Josef Mayseder (1789–1863), excellent Viennese violinist.—Editor.

II. ORATORIO: *The Victory of the Cross*

Mödling, June 15, 1819

Your Well-born!

I lie in bed and, therefore, cannot immediately discuss at length the subject of the oratorio.—However, I shall write you about it in a few days or speak with you in person. The receipt of the 400 florins Vienna Currency I herewith acknowledge to you over my own written signature

With esteem Your most devoted

BEETHOVEN

(Address) [illegible. Oliva?]

I believe myself on [very firm] ground[s] that [Franz] Oliva [was] the recipient of the above letter, preserved at the Isabella Stewart Gardner Museum of Boston. Not only does the barely legible name on the address-side resemble that name, but Franz Oliva still functioned as the composer's *factotum*, especially in matters financial. Moreover, in a Conversation-Book which belongs to that year and contains entries partly written in Vienna and partly in Mödling after Beethoven had gone there in May for the summer, Oliva asks in an entry apparently of the month of April, 1819: "is the oratorio finished? I can't understand with what he keeps himself busy—his professional activity amounts to nothing and otherwise he does nothing and yet he continually talks of his many tasks and affairs."

The *he*, referred to in so uncomplimentary a fashion by Oliva, was Josef Karl Bernard who, five years younger than Beethoven, by a queer freak of circumstances died in 1850 in the very same house where the composer breathed his last on March 26, 1827—the Schwarzspanierhaus. Bernard, since 1817, editor of the Wiener Zeitung, added to his journalistic endeavors an ambition for literature and that ambition seems to have brought him into contact with Beethoven. At any rate, he undertook to revise or improve Weissenbach's miserable text for Beethoven's cantata "Der glorreiche Augenblick," composed in 1814 in honor of the Vienna Congress with its galaxy of crowned heads, precisely the reason why Haslinger found it necessary to take refuge in an *Ersatz*-text by Rochlitz, "Preis der Tonkunst" when he published this unimportant cantata as Opus 136 in 1836.

"Bernardus non Sanctus" or "Dominus Bernardus non Sanctus" as Beethoven's banter would designate him, soon entered the inner circle of the master's friends and advisers and comparatively many are the letters addressed to him by Beethoven in the years of their intimacy. Curiously enough, however, all these letters, with one exception, occupy themselves with the tragic troubles of Beethoven as guardian of nephew Karl and only casually with a collaboration between Beethoven and Bernhard which had practically miscarried when the one exception (of 1824) was written. This collaboration concerned precisely the oratorio to which Beethoven alludes in his Mödling letter of June 15, 1819. Though that letter throws no new light on the history of that abortive collaboration, the episode will be sketched here somewhat fully because my views of Beethoven's actions in the matter noticeably diverge from those of Thayer and others.

"His Excellency, the Chairman (Count Apponyi) reported that Herr L. v. Beethoven has expressed himself through Herr v. Zmeskall as willing to *deliver* for the Society a large work and that the Executive Committee looks forward to his conditions." Thus the minutes of the meeting on December 22, 1815, of the Gesellschaft der Musikfreunde, founded in Vienna the year before, and it has been said that the Friends of Music—to whom Beethoven jokingly would refer as The Enemies of Music—desired an oratorio from Beethoven with which to rival the success of Abbé Stadler's "Die Befreiung Jerusalems" in 1813. However that may be, Beethoven neglected to put his verbal acceptance in writing for Zmeskall until January, 1816, "with dismay" at his discourtesy for which he could only offer as an excuse his state of mind after the death of his brother Karl two months previously. Apparently Zmeskall had been instructed to ask Beethoven what fee he would consider and also to convey to the composer suggestions about the nature of the work and its technical and artistic demands. Otherwise Beethoven in his delayed answer, when proposing a fee of 400 ducats in gold (one ducat equivalent to about $2.30), hardly would have expressed himself willing in principle to take the "artistic means for performance" under advisement, while reserving for himself the privilege to depart "from those already established." If he also wrote that "in the meantime the poem of H. von Seyfried is already begun and I shall also soon set it to music," this may refer to a tentative text for this oratorio or to some other work, commissioned by the society—a point I leave to others to determine.

There the matter seems to have rested until May 17, 1818, when Vincenz Hauschka, a member of the society and an intimate friend of Beethoven, was instructed to negotiate with him for the composition "of an oratorio of the heroic type for the exclusive use of the Society for one year from the day of the first performance, the fee to be 200, at the most 300 pieces in gold." Beethoven countered from Mödling, apparently in 1818, with a letter to Hauschka, such as only a composer in good humor, and among composers only he could or would write. In that letter he observed silence about his own remuneration, humorously trusting to the good will of "friends of music," but remarked "Herr von Bernard would be quite agreeable to me; only pay him," and on the subject of the oratorio "no subject other than a sacred one have I, but you want something heroic. Very well, only I believe that to mix in something sacred would be quite in order for such a mass" of performers. This would seem to be the first reference to Bernard as the final choice of "the enemies of music" as Beethoven's collaborator. Rumors of this reached the public press, for on December 1, 1818, the "Wiener Zeitschrift für Kunst" whetted the appetite of its music-loving readers for "a work from the pen of our genius Beethoven with text by Bernard next year." The public was to be disappointed in these expectations, just as Beethoven was to be—and until the end of his life—in his expectation to visit England which he so admired for her institutions, her interest in him and, last not least, as *Eldorado* for the remainder of his career. One of his frequent references to these British plans happen to contain an allusion to the oratorio. It occurs in his letter of March 30, 1819, to Ferdinand Ries:

> At present it is impossible to go to London, enmeshed as I am by so many circumstances; but God will assist me certainly to go to London next winter, when I shall bring along the new symphonies. I expect very soon the text for a new oratorio which I am composing for the Musikverein and which is likely to be of service in London.

The next item to round out the scanty material for the history of that oratorio is the autograph of the Mödling letter of June 15, 1819. It rounds it out for the reason that the editors of Thayer assume that the letter to Hauschka was merely an informal communication and that after further negotiations, it was followed, as the minutes of the Gesellschaft der Musikfreunde show, by a formal communication on June 15, 1819. Evidently they never saw the autograph of that letter which seems to have reached the Society through Oliva; otherwise they could hardly have considered it a formal document except for Beethoven's acknowledgment of receipt of an advance of 400 florins in Vienna Currency (practically $64, figuring the paper florin in Vienna Currency at about 40 per cent of the florin in "Convention" currency which was worth about 40 cents). Nor does Pohl, the historian of the Gesellschaft, appear to have had firsthand knowledge of that letter and he, by the way, adds a puzzling flavor to the record by his reference to the books of the Society that Beethoven actually did not receive the advance until August 18, 1819. If true, then Beethoven receipted for an advance payment considerably in advance of payment—not exactly a normal procedure in matters of business!

The subject chosen by Bernard for the oratorio was "Der Sieg des Kreuzes" (The Victory of the Cross), that is, the victory of Constantine

the Great over Maxentius, and an indigestible confection he made of it![1]
But this is anticipating the final result, for his progress on the libretto
was woefully slow. Apparently too slow for those who commissioned
the work. That one may read between the lines of an entry in the
minutes of the meeting of the Gesellschaft on November 22, 1819,
according to which Beethoven had answered a communication from
Prince Odescalchi "that he, too, was anxious to deliver a work which
would do honor to the Society and that he would push this work to the
best of his ability." In a Conversation-Book of April, 1820, Bernard then
remarked: "this month I must finish the oratorio so that you may begin
work on it at Mödling," but in August we *hear* from a different hand
that Hauschka is still pressing for completion of the text and that
"sanctus Bernardus" appeared "embarrassed," as if he desired to "conceal his poetical impotence" but that he expected to "complete his
work in 5 days," etc. Again months passed and Bernard, according to the
minutes of the Gesellschaft on December 17, 1820, could merely report
"that he would deliver the text of the oratorio destined for Beethoven
by January 15, 1821, and that he would then express himself about
his remuneration."

Now, Beethoven's remark to Rochlitz in 1822, that before essaying
"Faust" he would have to "rid his chest of two symphonies and an
oratorio," is sufficient proof that he had no intention of abandoning
his promises to the Gesellschaft der Musikfreunde, but one cannot
very well compose an oratorio, even after receiving an advance of 400
florins Vienna Currency, without a libretto. *Bernard did not deliver it
unto his collaborator until October 23, 1823*, though there is no reason
for doubting his word (anyhow confirmed by Beethoven) that he entrusted to the composer the first part with a sketch of the rest two
years earlier. Bernard also delivered the complete text to the Gesellschaft
at the end of October, 1823, and it voted at its meeting of January 9, 1824,
to pay Bernard his fee only "when Beethoven will have declared the
Oratorio suitable."

The same meeting voted that "Beethoven in this connection was
energetically to be asked *peremptorily* to indicate the time required for
completing the composition." In other words, the Gesellschaft had lost
patience and in January, 1824, did remind energetically both Beethoven
and Bernard at length and in detail of their contractual obligations.
For this energetic reminder the Gesellschaft cannot very well be criticized,

---

[1] The book was based on the ancient legend of the apparition to Constantine
of the Cross and the words "*In hoc signo vinces*" upon it. The plot is heavily
complicated by the side plot about Constantine's daughter, Julia, who was the
wife of his foe, Maxentius, and who was converted to the true faith by hearing
angelic voices accompanying the apparition, later becoming a martyr in its cause.
The crucial battle scene is weakened by allegorical figures of Hate and Discord
on the one hand, and Faith, Hope, and Charity on the other.—Editor.

but the action, in retrospect, nevertheless does not give us the true color of the situation! It is just a bit unfair to Beethoven to quote that vote in biographical literature without calling attention to what preceded it. According to Pohl, L. v. Sonnleithner, a prominent member of the Gesellschaft proposed to perform the Ninth Symphony and the "Missa Solemnis" because, so he said, "Beethoven had declared that he would leave the second receipts [i.e., receipts from a second performance] to the Society, in case this would assume the expenses for copying and all other such incidentals." That the Executive Committee viewed, at least in principle, this proposition with favor is proved by the fact that estimates of cost were prepared. The estimate ran to 1842 florins, whereupon the matter was dropped. Now, the point I wish to make in Beethoven's defense is that his proposition, Sonnleithner's report (though secondhand, as it turned out to be) and the estimates of cost *all preceded* the Society's vote for energetic reminder in the oratorio matter on January 9, 1824. In other words, Beethoven, embarrassed by his predicament with Bernard's long delayed and unsatisfactory text, proposed a means for squaring his financial account with his creditors which they seriously considered! That they, because of prohibitive cost to themselves, rejected it, certainly does not detract from the debtor's good and honest intentions!

The reminder brought forth from the composer on January 23, 1824, one of the longest letters he ever took the time or trouble to write. It was not a letter of apologies nor even of excuses but of explanations and he refused to see the matter in the light presented by the Gesellschaft. He flatly contradicted their assertion that he had *asked* for an advance-payment and averred that 400 florins had been paid him without any solicitation on his part. Could he have foreseen that the project of the oratorio would encounter such delays, he would have returned the money long ago. It became so painful for him to have to keep silent in the matter that he conceived the idea of protecting the Society at least against a loss of the interest on the amount advanced by proposing a joint concert. If Schindler and his brother Johann let the cat out of the bag, they certainly did not have his authorization to make a proposition to Sonnleithner *just in that manner* which was very far from his mind. Thanking the Society for their proffered help for the forthcoming performance of his "Ninth Symphony" and "Missa Solemnis," he assured it that he would with pleasure put at its disposal those two works after his own concert. Plainly, Beethoven was not in a mood to let reflections on his good faith in the matter go unchallenged, but his main point was the unfitness of Bernard's text for composition and the necessity for essential changes. Because of Bernard's editorial duties, he found it difficult to confer with him in person, an inevitable source of delay. Secondly, Bernard had never written anything in the nature of a libretto except that for the opera "Libussa" and from the defects of that Beethoven foresaw trouble for himself in setting the oratorio text. He then continued:

All the more reason why I had to insist on receiving the whole. True, I at last received the first part, but Bernard said that it would have to be changed and, if memory fails me not, I had to return that part to him. Then at last, at the same time that the Gesellschaft received the whole libretto, my copy reached me. Other obligations which I had not been able to fulfill on account of past illnesses, then pressed on me for the keeping of my promises, the more so, as you surely know, because unfortunately I am able to make a living only from the works I have to write. Now, sundry and much must be changed in Bernard's oratorio. I have already indicated some of these changes and shall soon be through with them, when I shall acquaint Bernard with them. As it is, though the subject is well invented and the poem has a value, it simply cannot remain. "Christus am Oelberg" was written by me and the poet in 14 days, but that poet was musical and had written several things for music and I could consult with him any moment. Do not let us discuss the value of such poetry. We all know the allowances one must make—the merit lies in the middle. As for myself, I would rather set even Homer, Klopstock, Schiller to music. At least, if one has to conquer difficulties, these immortal poets deserve it. As soon as I have finished the changes of the oratorio with Bernard, I shall have the honor to inform you and at the same time to let the Society know when it may with certainty count on it. That is in the meantime all I can say about it.

Stung by the Society's letter of reminder he apparently followed up his letter to the Society by one to Bernard himself from which I quote the following lines:

My dear, worthy friend! As for your oratorio several things in it and even its plan would have to be changed for me. To indicate all that immediately now, is impossible because of urgent tasks which I cannot retard. Furthermore, these changes would take time. If you find someone who is of a different opinion, and that is easily possible, I cannot and must not take it amiss, if you entrust to him your worthy work. Do not believe because of this remark that I do not appreciate your talent and your merits, but it has always been a principle with me not to be a cause of injury for others. As for the Society which, confident of seeing the oratorio materialize sooner, expressed itself to me as I had neither asked nor expected, I shall certainly see to it that it is in no way injured.

These long quotations from letters have been inserted here because of my disagreement with those who desire to see in Beethoven's protestations and arguments an element of insincerity and an attempt at evasion of the issue—of composing Bernard's text. Beethoven, in my opinion, had no intention of shirking his responsibilities toward the Gesellschaft, but as a composer he desired to forestall failure of his share in the oratorio by insisting on whatever improvements were possible. That the task of composing Bernard's text occupied his mind in 1822 we already know from his remark to Rochlitz and that remark may be supplemented, I think, rather significantly by further sentences from that conversation: "Much I have already hatched [the Ninth Symphony, a tenth symphony never composed and the oratorio]; that is, in my head . . . that will take a long time. You see, for some time past I do not easily get myself to write. I sit and meditate and meditate. I have had it for a long time [that is, the music in his mind]; but it will not go down on paper. It horrifies me to begin such big works. Once in it, then things move. . . ." And an oratorio was a big work! Is it any wonder that Beethoven preferred to keep the Gesellschaft waiting until the Bernard text answered his requirements, rather than fulfill promises in a hurry with indifference to the artistic result? Those who answer this question in the affirmative, simply do not comprehend the workings of an artist's mind and his higher sense of duty towards his employers and the world.

The tragi-comedy dragged on for two more years. In April, 1824, Schindler informed Beethoven that Archduke Rudolph had accepted the dedication of Bernard's text and had expressed his desire to see it composed by Beethoven. Apparently other intimates thought likewise, but Schikh, a journalistic colleague of Bernard, voiced the sentiments of the opposition party with his scathing remark: "if I were Beethoven, I should never compose this extremely dull oratorio text." As for Beethoven himself, the changes Bernard is actually known to have made in the text—his manuscript libretto has been preserved—could not possibly remedy its fundamental defects for composition sufficiently to cast a magnetic spell over the composer. According to Holz, he sighed "how can I enthuse over it" and yet as late as September 23, 1824, his letter to Hauschka shows his determination to fulfill his obligations towards the enemies of music. "That there may be no mistake about it, we report that we shall certainly set to music Bernard's oratorio, according to our signature and seal," he writes and asks Hauschka to obtain for Bernard his fee. We know that, indeed, Hauschka was instructed to pay Bernard the balance of his fee, but it is also a matter of biography that Beethoven never composed "The Victory of the Cross."

Not even sketches for the oratorio have been discovered, but that neither proves that Beethoven carried no music for the work in his mind, nor that he abandoned the project. As a matter of fact, he did not, though naturally his last String Quartets had the right of way. Whether the ultimate miscarriage of collaboration peeved Bernard so as henceforth to cause or not a degree of frigidity in his relations with Beethoven, certain it is that in 1825 Beethoven, instead of giving up Bernard's text as hopeless, believed in it sufficiently to entrust F. A. Kanne, a stout champion of his art as editor (1821–24) of the Allgemeine Musikzeitung of Vienna, author and composer, with a revision of it which obtained the approval of Hauschka. Rumors that Beethoven had actually begun to compose this revision appear reflected, at the end of 1825, in a remark of Karl Holz in one of the Conversation-Books. If Holz later on stated that Beethoven "never seriously worked on 'The Victory of the Cross,'" that may be true but the statement implies that the composer *did* work to some extent on that ill-fated oratorio. The matter simply had become a futile conflict between his artistic scruples and his sense of obligation towards those whose commission he had accepted ten years previously. His experiences with Bernard's text, however, had nourished his ambition to write oratorios and, as a matter of record, Beethoven before his untimely death gave not a little thought to at least two oratorios, one on "The Elements," the other on the subject of "Saul." In that connection his deep veneration for Handel asserted itself, as we incidentally know from a remark of his recorded by Holz: "In the future I shall write after the manner of my grand-master Händel annually only an oratorio or a concerto for some string- or wind-instrument, provided I have completed my tenth Symphony (C minor) and my *Requiem.*"— O. G. SONNECK (2)

III. ORATORIO: *Saul and David*

In April Kuffner[1] told Beethoven that he had read Bernard's oratorio book[2] but could not find in it even a semblance of an oratorio, much less half-good execution. These protests could only strengthen Beethoven's distaste for the text. At any rate the plan was definitely laid aside. . . .

Perhaps there was something of personal equation in Kuffner's judgment of the Bernard text, for he was ready to write not only one but even two oratorio texts if Beethoven would but undertake their composition. He presented the plan of a work to be called *The Four Elements*, in which Man was to be brought into relationship with the imposing phenomena of Nature. Meanwhile, there was discussion of the subject of Saul. Holz relates that "Beethoven had given much study to Handel's *Saul* and read a lot about the music of the ancient Hebrews; he wanted to write choruses in the old modes." In April the conversation was lively on the subject. Kuffner was to revise the text for Beethoven; he was already thinking of a place for the performance. Kuffner intended in his treatment of the story of Saul to make it a representation of the triumph of the nobler impulses of Man over untamed desire.

[1] Christoph Kuffner (1780–1846), Viennese playwright; Beethoven wrote incidental music to his tragedy *Tarpeja* in 1813.—Editor.
[2] For *The Victory of the Cross.*—Editor.

Kuffner set to work and Holz brought a few sections of the text to the composer. In a Conversation Book he says:

> I must take back this one in Kuffner's handwriting by the day after tomorrow. I will take care of your copy.

> I copied this quickly from Kuffner.

> Here there might be a chorus in the Lydian mode as you wanted to bring one in.

Holz urged that it would be a shame if this mode were heard only in a quartet. In May he brought greetings from Kuffner, who was now at work on it body and soul. He also explained that Kuffner intended to treat the chorus as an effective agent in the action, for which purpose it was to be divided into two sections, like the dramatic chorus of the Greek tragedians. Kuffner was sufficiently encouraged to write the book, and Holz says that Beethoven finished the music for the first part "in his head." If so, it stayed there, as far as the sketchbooks bear testimony.[1]— ALEXANDER WHEELOCK THAYER, EDITED BY ELLIOT FORBES

Instrumental Works

I. OVERTURE ON B-A-C-H

A project which cropped out intermittently during 1823 was the writing of an overture on the musical motive suggested by the letters composing the name of Bach. The thought seems to have become fixed in his mind in 1822, though the device of using

as a motive in composition was at least as old as the Leipsic master's "Art of Fugue," and no doubt familiar to Beethoven. However, he was deeply engrossed in fugal writing at this period and it is very likely, as Nottebohm suggests, that he conceived an overture on the motive as a tribute to Bach's genius. Several sketches showing different forms of the theme appear in the books of 1823; and a collateral memorandum, "This overture with the new symphony, and we shall have a concert (*Akademie*)

[1] Beethoven mentioned the project as late as January 1827, during his final illness. —Editor.

in the Kärnthnerthor Theater," among sketches for the last quartets in 1825, shows that he clung to the idea almost to the end. Had Beethoven carried out all the plans for utilizing the theme which presented themselves to him between 1822 and 1825, there would have been several Bach overtures; unfortunately, he carried out none.

The last relevant sketch in the [sketch-] book of 1822 is a sort of thematic index to the [D minor] symphony as it now lay planned in Beethoven's purpose.[1] The second movement [Beethoven indicates] was to be a fugued Scherzo with the theme of 1815, the fourth the Presto in 2/4 time which first appeared in this year, the fifth the "Ode to Joy." In the midst of these sketches appears the significant remark: "Or perhaps instead of a new symphony, a new overture on *Bach*, well fugued with 3—."[2]

The conclusions to be drawn from the sketches thus far are that, as was the case in 1812 when the Seventh and Eighth Symphonies were brought forth as a pair, Beethoven was again contemplating the almost simultaneous production of two symphonies. He did not adhere to the project long, so far as we can know from the written records, and the remark about the substitution of an overture on B-a-c-h probably marks the time when he began seriously to consider the advisability of abandoning what would then have been the Tenth Symphony. With the exception of a portion of the first movement, the Ninth Symphony was still in a chaotic state. Taken in connection with negotiations which had been concluded with the Philharmonic Society of London, it may be assumed, however, that the present Symphony in D minor was associated in Beethoven's mind with the English commission, and that the second, which he had thoughts of abandoning in favor of the overture, was to have been a "Sinfonie allemand." For a time, at least, Beethoven is not likely to have contemplated a choral movement with German words in connection with the symphony for the London Philharmonic Society: this was to have an instrumental finale. The linguistic objection would be invalid in the case of the German symphony, however, and to this was now assigned the contemplated setting of Schiller's poem.—ALEXANDER WHEELOCK THAYER, EDITED BY ELLIOT FORBES

II. TENTH SYMPHONY

The first intimation of the existence of a Tenth Symphony by Beethoven was given by Schindler, his well-tried companion. It was about the

---

[1] It contains two measures which are marked "Comincia" and are practically identical as to the main theme of the first movement as it now stands; over the words "2tes Stück" are the first four measures of the present scherzo; there is a blank under the inscription "3. Adagio"; there are 3 measures marked "2/4 Presto" which represent his thoughts for the fourth movement; the fifth movement is represented by the first four measures of the present "Ode to Joy" theme.—Editor.

[2] Nottebohm fills the hiatus with "Trombones? Subjects?"

time when, reduced to a condition of absolute material want by his last wearisome illness, the master, upon repeated application, had received the sum of a hundred pounds sterling from the London Philharmonic Society "on account of the forthcoming concert." In a letter dated March 24th, 1827, and addressed to Moscheles, the chief promoter of the concert in question, undertaken in aid of the composer, Schindler writes; "During three days after the receipt of your letter he was greatly excited, and wanted again to see the sketches of the Tenth Symphony, about the design of which he spoke to me a good deal. He has now quite made up his mind to give it to the Philharmonic Society." This letter I discovered in 1864, at Mannheim, among Schindler's valuable Beethoven papers (now in Bohemia). It was published by me in the following year, and I have subsequently given it a place in my "Musikalisches Skizzenbuch" (Munich: 1866; p. 282). In the same volume may also be found a passage from Beethoven's letter to Moscheles, intended to accompany that of Schindler, and which runs thus: "Tell these worthy men that when God shall once more have restored me to health, I will endeavor to realize my feeling of gratitude also in works, and that therefore I leave to the Society the choice of that which I am to write for them. An *entirely sketched-out Symphony* lies now in my desk" (Eine ganze skizzirte Symphonie liegt in meinem Pulte). These words, although forming part of the original manuscript as dictated by Beethoven, have afterwards been crossed out by Schindler, and are consequently not to be found in the letter actually sent. Nevertheless, their substantial accuracy is confirmed by the above-quoted remark on the part of Schindler even though the words "entirely sketched out" should not, perhaps, be applied in too literal a sense. And here I insert the statement made by Karl Holz, who was for some years the confidential friend and companion at table of the composer, and who expressly declares that he is citing "Beethoven's own words" viz: "I shall in future, after the manner of my grand-master Handel, content myself with writing one oratorio and one concerto only every year—provided I have completed my *Tenth Symphony* and my 'Requiem.'" This conversation dates from the year 1826, and we shall hear anon that Holz had moreover obtained some actual knowledge of the work itself. Here, also, I will quote a conversation, carried on in the well-known manner with the deaf composer on his sickbed by the friend of his youth, Gerhard von Breuning, in January or February, 1827, and published subsequently in the *Berliner Conversations Hefte*: "I am better pleased with you today than ever before. Are there, then, vocal parts in the Symphony?—An entirely new idea!" It is, in fact, a work conceived and matured many years previously according to his distinct plan, with which we are here dealing, and which, indeed, embodied an "entirely new idea."

Thus the fact of an intended Tenth Symphony after the gigantic Ninth, which appears to us today as the keystone of Beethoven's monumental creations, being regarded by some, indeed, as the last of all symphonies, after which further development can only be hoped for in new forms— may be considered as historically established. It will be my endeavor now to show this idea of yet another symphonic work to have been the natural outcome of the composer's strivings, forming part, in fact, of his entire artistic development. . . . Of the Tenth Symphony itself we have the following traces, which imperfect though they be, will nevertheless indicate clearly enough the leading idea and character of the projected work.

Consulting Schindler again (in his report to Moscheles already alluded to) we meet with the following passage: "But, my dear friend, if Beethoven should really be able to write this Tenth Symphony, I fear the generation has yet to be born which would be capable of understanding it." It is, however, scarcely surprising that in the words of "Faust," all hope should "forsake this simpleton," in as much as to the very end of his life the *famulus* here referred to has been incapable of truly appreciating the genius of his master. Nevertheless, he has succeeded in retaining for us the impression made upon his mind by the vision of the tone-picture which on this occasion Beethoven unfolded before him, and which will enable us to arrive at a conclusion as to the importance and grandeur of its intended design. "In the confusion of his domestic arrangements," continues Schindler, "it was impossible to commit to writing all that he said, and the more so since he continually referred to the gigantic projects he meant to carry out, but which he would never once pause to explain." The music to "Faust" is then again mentioned, touching upon which Beethoven is said to have exclaimed: "That shall be something!" (Das soll was geben.) Our informant concludes his observations with the appropriate remark: "It is a thousand pities that during this overflow of his imageries, when his conversation would assume a poetic fluency such as I had but rarely noticed with him when in his normal state of health, some intelligent listeners, or better still, shorthand writers, have not been present! The benefit conferred by such instruction upon art would have been immense!"

Turning now to this remarkable plan of the Tenth Symphony itself, we rely upon the following note from the year 1818, which, after the above manifold references and allusions, we are justified in associating with that projected work. The memorandum says: "*Adagio cantique*, hymnlike song, in a symphony, written in the old modes (Lord God we praise Thee, Hallelujah!) either separate or as introduction to a fugue. Perhaps in this manner the entire second symphony to be characterized, in which case the voices would appear in the last movement, or already in the *Adagio*. The orchestral violins, etc., will in the last movement be increased tenfold. Or else the *Adagio* will in the last movement be repeated when the voices will only gradually enter. The text to be Greek *mythos; cantique ecclésiastique;* in the *Allegro,* 'Feast of Bacchus.'" Not the introduction of the human voice, even though in this instance it might have been already intended in the *Adagio,* was the "entirely new idea" to which we have heard Breuning make allusion; for already the Ninth Symphony had included it, nay even the Choral Fantasia. Nor was it the direct interconnection of the different movements, however significant that may be as regards the further development of the poetic capabilities inherent in the sonata-form. But important in the highest degree is the ethical significance of the work which might, likewise and most appropriately be called "The Victory of the Cross," because the most profound Greek *mythos*—the Mysteries of Dionysos (containing in itself already the germs of religious regeneration)—was by this *cantique ecclésiastique,* by the religion of divine grace and love, to be superseded or rather fulfilled and sanctified.

And this reconciliation and union of old and new world ideas—a theme which occupies the minds of all modern poets and thinkers—was to have been artistically illustrated in symphonic language; beyond doubt "An entirely new idea"; an idea which in the directness and correctness of the poetic intention foreshadowed an enormous augmentation of the dramatic power within the organism of the Symphony! The religious disposition of the composer's mind had long since been prepared alike by bitterest sufferings and purest spiritual elevations. His soul was irresistibly drawn toward "the Eternal, the All-powerful, the Infinite," and far more profoundly than in the "Missa Solemnis," this fact is proclaimed by the Ninth Symphony in the words "Ihr stürzt nieder Millionen, Ahnest Du den Schöpfer, Welt?" and in the joy of an all-embracing Love, which is the result of a similarly exalted state of mind. And were not the English known to be particularly orthodox in matters concerning the Christian faith and doctrine? What then, could be more natural than that he should select a subject which would appeal directly to the sympathies of the people for whom this tone-picture was intended, and which would at the same time afford him an opportunity of solving after "his fashion" a problem of the highest ethical import. . . .

Concerning the question of key, Beethoven's friend Holz (who during these last years of the composer's life had been on specially intimate terms with him) gives the following account. "The Tenth Symphony commences with an *Andante* in E flat, 3/4 time, assigned to wind instruments, and changes suddenly into a stormy *Allegro,* representing the Feast of Baccuhus." The latter, of which the sketches are extant, has 6/8 time and the key of C major, while Holz mentions C minor as being the key of the entire conception; a supposition which is also borne out by the subsequent sketches. When in the year 1824, after the brilliant performance of the Ninth Symphony, the old project of the composer's visit to England had again revived, the Tenth was at once thought of. Neate had again written, assuring him that his talents were more appreciated in England than in any other country, adding that the master would indeed become a happy man if he could make up his mind to visit a country where he would meet with none but friends, and where the fame of the "great Beethoven" surpassed that of any other composer. The Philharmonic Society, the writer continues, were anxious to renew their former offer, while expecting a second symphony; the first of the two (namely the Ninth) having already been received. Thus the old scheme was again discussed, and the sketches for the composition in question (now in the possession of the Royal Library of Berlin) again looked over. When, on his deathbed, the master once more asked to see these sketches, they were handed to him by Schindler, and it was on this occasion that the latter was made acquainted with the general design of the work. Subsequently Schindler communicated what he knew about the subject to "Hirschbach's Musikalisch—Kritisches Repertorium" (Leipzig 1842) and it was then, for the first time, that the world obtained some positive information concerning the Tenth Symphony. The *motive* of the *scherzo*, C minor, 3/4, is the first of the sketches. Then follows a *motive* B, A, C, H, (the latter being the B of the German scale) originally appertaining to a long-projected overture in honor of the "arch-father of Harmony," Sebastian Bach. This is followed by the jubilant theme in 6/8 time, the Feast of Bacchus, which is superscribed "Finale of the first movement." Next comes a notation, "2/4, A flat major," referring, according to Schindler, to the adagio; but neither an "old mode," nor a Te Deum laudamus, nor a Hallelujah can be discovered. Finally to the word "Fugue," the sketches contain a *motive* in C minor, 2/4, resembling the second portion of the theme of the Fugue in E major from the second part of Bach's "Wohl-temperirtes Clavier," evidently the *finale* of the work, since, as we have heard, the adagio was to have culminated in a Fugue.

Thus everything is found together which constitutes a "great" symphony, and the idea thus shadowed forth is indeed as worthy of the genius of Beethoven as it is of the "magnanimity of the generous men" who had bespoken the work, and who had been instrumental in conveying to the dying master the last ray of hope and comfort. Here too, then, the twin-character of Beethoven's symphonies has been *de facto* maintained, although, unfortunately for our art, we do not possess the full measure of this final conception since it has never been actually realized. Nevertheless, it will be admitted that the "poetic idea" or rather the spiritual design of the Tenth Symphony, renders it to the fullest extent the equal of its companion, the Ninth, while we recognize therein at the same time the first step toward a mighty development of the Symphony itself, and toward the participation of musical art in the solution of the highest problems of modern life and culture.—LUDWIG NOHL

PART SIX

Evaluations by Composers

Carl Maria von Weber

From: Letter to Hans Georg Nägeli, May 21, 1810 [Repudiating Nägeli's remark that one of Weber's works reminded him of Beethoven]

In the first place, I hate everything that bears the stamp of imitation; secondly, my views differ far too much from those of Beethoven ever to come into contact with him. The fiery, almost incredible inventive faculty which inspires him is attended by so many complications in the arrangement of his ideas that it is only his earlier compositions that interest me; the later ones, appear to me a confused chaos, an unintelligible struggle after novelty from which occasionally heavenly flashes of genius dart forth, showing how great he might be if he chose to control his luxuriant fancy.

—Ludwig Nohl, *Letters of Distinguished Musicians*, tr. Lady Wallace, London, Longmans, Green, 1867, p. 209.—SAM MORGENSTERN

Richard Wagner

It was *Beethoven* who opened up the boundless faculty of Instrumental Music for expressing elemental storm and stress. His power it was that took the basic essence of the Christian's Harmony, that bottomless sea of unhedged fullness and unceasing motion, and clove in twain the fetters of its freedom. *Harmonic Melody*—for so must we designate this melody divorced from speech, in distinction from the Rhythmic Melody of dance—was capable, though merely borne by instruments, of the most limitless expression together with the most unfettered treatment. In long, connected tracts of sound, as in larger, smaller, or even smallest fragments, it turned beneath the Master's poet hand to vowels, syllables, and words and phrases of a speech in which a message hitherto unheard, and never spoken yet, could promulgate itself. Each letter of this speech was an infinitely soul-full element; and the measure of the joinery of these elements was utmost free commensuration, such as could be exercised by none but a tone-poet who longed for the unmeasured utterance of this unfathomed yearning.

Glad in this unspeakably expressive language, but suffering beneath the weight of longing of his artist soul—a longing which, in its infinity, could only be an "object" to itself, not satisfy itself outside—the happy-wretched, sea-glad and sea-weary mariner sought for a surer haven wherein to anchor from the blissful storms of passionate tumult. Was his faculty of speech unending—so also was the yearning which inspired that speech with its eternal breath. How then proclaim the end, the satisfaction, of this yearning, in the selfsame tongue that was naught but its expression? If the utterance of immeasurable heart-yearning be vented in this elemental speech of absolute tone, then the *endlessness* of such utterance, like that of the yearning itself, is its only true Necessity; the yearning cannot find contentment in any finite *shutting-off* of sound,—for that could only be Caprice. Now by the definite expression which it borrows from the rhythmic dance-melody, Instrumental Music may well portray and bring to close a placid and self-bounded mood; for reason that it takes its measure from an originally outward-lying object, namely the motion of the body. If a tone-piece yield itself *ab initio* to this expression, which must always be conceived as that of mirth, in greater or in less degree,— then, even mid the richest, most luxuriant unfolding of the faculty of tonal speech, it holds within itself the necessary grounds of every phase of "satisfaction"; while equally inevitably must this "satisfaction" be a matter of caprice, and therefore in truth unsatisfying, when that sure and sharp-cut mode of utterance endeavors merely *thus* to terminate the storms of endless yearning. The transition from the endless agitation of desire to a mood of joyous satisfaction can necessarily take place no otherwise than by the ascension of desire into an *object*. But, in keeping with the character of infinite yearning, this "object" can be none other than such an one as shows itself with finite, physical and ethical exactitude. Absolute Music, however, finds well-marked bounds dividing her from such an object; without indulging in the most arbitrary of assumptions, she can now and never, of her own unaided powers, bring the physical and ethical Man to distinct and plainly recognizable presentment. Even in her most

infinite enhancement, she still is but *emotion*; she enters *in the train* of
the ethical deed, but not as that *Deed itself*; she can set moods and feelings side by side, but not evolve one mood from out another by any dictate of her own Necessity;—she lacks the *Moral Will*.

What inimitable art did Beethoven employ in his "C-minor Symphony,"
in order to steer his ship from the ocean of infinite yearning to the
haven of fulfillment! He was able to raise the utterance of his music
almost to a moral resolve, but not to speak aloud that final word; and
after every onset of the Will, without a moral handhold, we feel tormented
by the equal possibility of falling back again to suffering, as of being
led to lasting victory. Nay, this falling-back must almost seem to us more
"necessary" than the morally ungrounded triumph, which therefore—
not being a necessary consummation, but a mere arbitrary gift of grace—
has not the power to lift us up and yield to us that *ethical* satisfaction
which we demand as outcome of the yearning of the heart.

Who felt more uncontented with this victory than Beethoven himself? Was he lief to win a second of the sort? 'Twas well enough for the
brainless herd of imitators, who from glorious "major"-jubilation, after
vanquished "minor"-tribulation, prepared themselves unceasing triumphs,
—but not for the Master, who was called to write upon his work the
world-history of Music.

With reverent awe, he shunned to cast himself afresh into that sea of
boundless and insatiate yearning. He turned his steps toward the blithe-
some, life-glad Men he spied encamped on breezy meads, along the
outskirt of some fragrant wood beneath the sunny heaven; kissing, dancing, frolicking. There in shadow of the trees, amid the rustling of the
leaves, beside the tender gossip of the brook, he made a happy pact with
Nature; there he felt that he was Man, felt all his yearning thrust back
deep into his breast before the sovereignty of sweet and blissful *manifestment*. So thankful was he toward this manifestment that, faithfully
and in frank humility, he superscribed the separate portions of the tone-
work, which he built from this idyllic mood, with the names of those life-
pictures whose contemplation had aroused it in him:—"Reminiscences
of Country Life" he called the whole.

But in very deed they were only "Reminiscences"—pictures, and not the
direct and physical actuality. Toward this actuality he was impelled with
all the force of the artist's inexpugnable ("*nothwendig*") yearning. To
give his tone-shapes that same compactness, that directly cognizable and
physically sure stability, which he had witnessed with such blessed solace
in Nature's own phenomena,—this was the soul of the joyous impulse
which created for us that glorious work the "Symphony in A major."
All tumult, all yearning and storming of the heart become here the
blissful insolence of joy, which snatches us away with bacchanalian might
and bears us through the roomy space of Nature, through all the streams

and seas of Life, shouting in glad self-consciousness as we tread throughout the Universe the daring measures of this human sphere-dance. This symphony is the *Apotheosis of Dance* herself: it is Dance in her highest aspect, as it were the loftiest Deed of bodily motion incorporated in an ideal mold of tone. Melody and Harmony unite around the sturdy bones of Rhythm to firm and fleshy human shapes, which now with giant limbs' agility, and now with soft, elastic pliance, *almost before our very eyes*, close up the supple, teeming ranks; the while now gently, now with daring, now serious,[1] now wanton, now pensive, and again exulting, the deathless strain sounds forth and forth; until, in the last whirl of delight, a kiss of triumph seals the last embrace.

And yet these happy dancers were merely shadowed forth in tones, mere sounds that imitated men! Like a second Prometheus who fashioned men of clay ("*Thon*") Beethoven had sought to fashion them of *tone*. Yet not from "*Thon*" of Tone, but from both substances together, must Man, the image of life-giving Zeus, be made. Were Prometheus' moldings only offered to the *eye*, so were those of Beethoven only offered to the *ear*. But only *where eye and ear confirm each other's sentience of him, is the whole artistic Man at hand.*

But where could Beethoven find *those* men, to whom to stretch out hands across the element of his music? Those men with hearts so broad that he could pour into them the mighty torrent of his harmonic tones? With frames so stoutly fair that his melodic rhythms should *bear* them and not *crush* them?—Alas, from nowhere came to him the brotherly Prometheus who could show to him these men! He needs must gird his loins about and start *to find out for himself the country of the Manhood of the Future.*

From the shore of Dance he cast himself once more upon that endless sea, from which he had erstwhile found a refuge on this shore; the sea of unallayable heart-yearning. But 'twas in a stoutly-built and giant-bolted ship that he embarked upon the stormy voyage; with firm-clenched fist he grasped the mighty helm: he *knew* the journey's goal, and was determined to attain it. No imaginary triumphs would he prepare himself, not after boldly overcome privations tack back once more to the lazy haven of his home; for he desired to measure out the ocean's bounds, and find the land which needs must lie beyond the waste of waters.

Thus did the Master urge his course through unheard-of possibilities of

---

[1] Amid the solemn-striding rhythm of the second section, a secondary theme uplifts its wailing, yearning song; to that rhythm, which shows its firm-set tread throughout the entire piece, without a pause, this longing melody clings like the ivy to the oak, which without its clasping of the mighty bole would trail its crumpled, straggling wreaths upon the soil, in forlorn rankness; but now, while weaving a rich trapping for the rough oak-rind, it gains for itself a sure and undisheveled outline from the stalwart figure of the tree. How brainlessly has this deeply significant device of Beethoven been exploited by our modern instrumental-composers, with their eternal "subsidiary themes!"

absolute tone-speech—not by fleetly slipping past them, but by speaking out their utmost syllable from the deepest chambers of his heart—forward to where the mariner begins to sound the sea-depth with his plumb; where, above the broadly stretched-forth shingles of the new continent, he touches on the heightening crests of solid ground; where he has now to decide him whether he shall face about toward the bottomless ocean, or cast his anchor on the new-found shore. But it was no madcap love of sea-adventure, that had spurred the Master to so far a journey; with might and main he willed to land on this new world, for toward *it* alone had he set sail. Staunchly he threw his anchor out; and this anchor was *the Word*. Yet this Word was not that arbitrary and senseless cud which the modish singer chews from side to side, as the gristle of his vocal tone; but the necessary, all-powerful, and all-uniting word into which the full torrent of the heart's emotions may pour its stream; the steadfast haven for the restless wanderer; the light that lightens up the night of endless yearning: the word that the redeemed world-man cries out aloud from the fullness of the world-heart. This was the word which Beethoven set as crown upon the forehead of his tone-creation; and this word was:—"*Freude!*" ("Rejoice!") With this word he cries to men: "*Breast to breast, ye mortal millions! This one kiss to all the world!*"— And *this Word* will be the language of the *Art-work of the Future*.—

The Last Symphony of Beethoven is the redemption of Music from out her own peculiar element into the realm of *universal Art*. It is the human Evangel of the art of the Future. Beyond it no forward step is possible; for upon it the perfect Art-work of the Future alone can follow, the *universal Drama* to which Beethoven has forged for us the key.— RICHARD WAGNER (1)

Felix Mendelssohn-Bartholdy

It is of the utmost significance that Mendelssohn's coming of age coincided with the last years of Beethoven. The heaven-storming Titan, in his sonatas, chamber works and symphonies, had developed the Classic form to its seemingly furthest limits. Little more was to be done in this direction, and his younger contemporaries, looking for fresh blood to pour into their work, took their cue from the *Pastoral Symphony* which contained the first intimations of a new poesy and emotional accent. The field was large and unworked and the newcomers seized upon it avidly. This was the origin of Romanticism.

Mendelssohn, whose veneration for Beethoven was only second to that of Bach, advanced to the edge of the alluring new field. But being weighted down by his severely Classical training, he only sniffed at it delicately through well-bred, intellectual nostrils. Like his grandfather, who stood between the old and new Judaism, and like his father, "a dash uniting Moses and Felix Mendelssohn," Felix Mendelssohn was a dash uniting Classicism and Romanticism—the old and new styles in music. He was thus not only a product of his training but a victim of his heredity as well.

Returned to home, Felix ordered every composition of Beethoven's as fast as it was published. The great Titan's last years significantly coincided with his own period of growing maturity, and he longed to go to Vienna, to stand in the hallowed presence and humbly offer his quantum of silent respect. Perhaps the Master would deign to look at his sheaf of modest pieces and say a few kindly words of encouragement. He could not believe the stories of gruffness and frenetic irritability that swept into Berlin. Berlin table-talk had to be taken with a grain of salt. Beethoven would welcome him as a brother, as a son, for between kindred spirits there was a mystic bond indissoluble by time and distance. He avidly memorized every sonata and symphony that bore the sanctified name. Timdly he approached his father on the feasibility of the pilgrimage to Vienna.

It was ill-timed. "Nonsense," Herr Mendelssohn roared in a passion. "Your taste is execrable. The man is a lunatic who writes meaningless stuff."

"Is this 'meaningless stuff'?" Felix sat down to the piano and commenced the heaven-storming Sonata in B flat.

"Hallucinations," the father responded with growing rancor. "Stop it."

Felix became defiant, switched stubbornly to the Allegretto of the Seventh Symphony. While he played the somberly marching introduction, he spoke as if in a bitter incantation: "They condemn him for the hectic manner of setting down his music, a piece here, a piece in the middle, a piece at the end. Why should he not? The thing is complete in his mind, unified and flowing. Yet the final result of blossoming, personal, living beauty is ignored because the mechanics are not those prescribed by Professor Paidogogus. See," here he came to the glowing C major theme, "see how it grows from a bud to a flower? They say he knows little of melody, less of counterpoint. Listen to this fugato in the strings. No counterpoint? . . . Meaningless stuff? . . ." But his father was not listening. On the subject of Beethoven he could be an unloosed demon. He walked to the door in a towering rage, and ordered Felix out of the room.

The defender of the embattled Beethoven went to his little study, pale, shaken and bemused. It was not the first tussle they had had on the matter. All had ended the same way. Nor was it to be the last. He was unconscious of his father's powerful domination of him, and yielded placidly enough to every direction. But when Genius was attacked, Truth was attacked, and that he could not bear. Each time he had innocently returned to a discussion of Beethoven's music, hoping to finally win his father over, a scene was sure to follow. That, however, did not mean that Beethoven was no genius. Beethoven was undervalued, had many enemies. The brilliantly cantankerous Weber had turned from scornful contempt for the Master's music to worshipful adoration. Weber himself had enemies without number, and that, despite his overwhelming popularity and the passionate Weber *cultus* that had sprung up around him. Every composer had enemies. Perhaps he too would some day have them: jealous, vaunting dyspeptics who minimized one's efforts before they were made, and refused to listen to them afterward. Reverently, he took a newly arrived score from his neatly kept cupboard, and lost himself in musing.

At the next Sunday musicale, Spohr turned up. Felix anxiously inquired his opinion of Beethoven. The famous Kappelmeister had come to Berlin to supervise the production of his opera *Jessonda,* and was consequently solely immersed in himself. Some folk had set him up as the superior of the composer of *Fidelio,* and the humorless man took them seriously. He had not much to hand Beethoven, nor any other composer, save Spohr. "Beethoven," he pontificated, "has no aesthetic culture, no sense of beauty."

Felix was shocked. "There can be no arrogance among priests!" he gasped. But he soon learned that there could be arrogance among peacocks and composers.

A far different man was the pianist, Ignaz Moscheles. He had just come from Vienna on his way to Paris and London. He eulogized Beethoven's talent and played his music superbly. Nor was he sparing of praise in other quarters. Felix and he became enthusiastic friends, and "the prince of pianists," as Frau Mendelssohn called him, came to the house almost daily.

Of late, huge financial transactions that strained every fiber of his intense person had left Abraham Mendelssohn worn and irritable. He made a great effort to subdue the violent inner clamor and awkwardly patted his son's hand. Felix was the source of most of his happiness and pride. He could not be long angry with him.

"Obedience," the distracted banker held his forefinger up playfully.

"But still I cannot understand," Felix immediately forgot his promise, "why you hate Beethoven so, and rate Cherubini above him. Surely the Viennese is the greater master. Why, his symphonies alone . . ."

Herr Mendelssohn passed a displeased look to his son. "Your endless

Beethoven," he exploded, "is nothing but a bore and an impostor, and his compositions rank gibberish. Although it would have been much less trouble to take you to Vienna, I choose to bring you here to be adjudged by a great contrapuntist, a man who knows his business and writes music an intelligent person can listen to. And mind, what Cherubini says of you, shall be finally so!"—SCHIMA KAUFMAN

Nicolò Paganini

Codignola questions the truth of these assertions[1] and attributes them to Paganini's romantic urge to create a dramatic effect. It is, of course, not at all implausible that here, with his innate mimicry, he was playing the sedulous ape to Beethoven and deliberately fabricating a picture of his childhood that in the eyes of later generations would place him in the company of his idol. For he was extraordinarily receptive to suggestions, even his most quoted mots being all derivative and easily traceable to their original sources. We know from his own words and contemporary testimony that, like Berlioz, he too "put Beethoven at the summit of his musical Olympus."[2] Hardly a day passed, we are told, that he "did not play some work of Beethoven's," while the programs of all his important concerts—particularly his first appearances abroad, on which so much depended—almost invariably opened with a Beethoven work, as though he were invoking the spirit of his great colleague. In Vienna a year after Beethoven's death, he must have had many opportunities of discussing him with former associates and of hearing that his "father had been a pitiless tyrant, the boy a victim and a slave . . . compelled to unremitted application through fear, or the actual infliction, of punishment for neglect on the part of his harsh and unjust parent, his father keeping him at his studies with inflexible severity."[3]—G. I. C. DE COURCY

[1] Miss De Courcy is referring to Paganini's assertions that his father was terribly strict and made him practice the violin inordinately long hours as a boy. This is quoted (in 1830) by one of Paganini's early biographers, Julian Schottky.—Editor.

[2] Jacques Barzun, Berlioz and the Romantic Century, I, 152.

[3] Compare Beethoven's "music became my first youthful pursuit in my fourth year" and Paganini's "I was enthusiastic about my instrument and studied it unceasingly." Thayer wrote: "Johann van Beethoven's main object was the earliest and greatest development of his son's musical genius so as to make it a marketable commodity. . . . Urged forward by his father's severity, by his tender love for his mother, and by the awakening of his own tastes, the development of his skill and talents was rapid." A. W. Thayer, Life of Beethoven, I, 58–59.

Georges Bizet

"Like you, I place Beethoven above the greatest, the most renowned. The symphony with chorus is for me the culmination of our art. Dante, Michelangelo, Shakespeare, Homer, Beethoven, Moses!—Neither Mozart, with his divine form, nor Weber, with his powerful, colossal originality, not Meyerbeer, with his overwhelming dramatic genius, can, in my opinion, contend for the crown of the *Titan*, the *Prometheus* of music. You see, we still understand each other. . . .

"I suspect anything that smells of improvisation.—Look at Beethoven. Take the vaguest, the most ethereal works; they are always deliberate, always sustained. He dreams, yet his idea has body. You can grasp it.— Only one man has been able to do quasi-improvised music, or what seems like it, and that is Chopin.[1]—MINA CURTISS

Louis Gottschalk

[NORFOLK, VIRGINIA, *April* 4, 1862]

Beethoven, taken as a symphonist, is the most inspired among composers, and the one who composes best for the orchestra. The instrumental effects he combines on paper are always realized in the orchestra as he has conceived them. As a composer for the piano he falls below mediocrity—the least pianist of any intelligence, in our days, writes infinitely better than Beethoven ever did. "Hue and cry on the robber!" are you all about to exclaim? You brawlers will never attain that height of admiration which I have for Beethoven when he is great, and it is through this admiration that I am forced to see his feebleness. I will explain: The piano is an instrument that Beethoven knew but imperfectly, and that at the period he wrote was but the embryo of the piano made by modern manufacturers. The instrumentation of the piano is a special matter. The point in question is not only to have ideas, but to know how to adapt them to the piano, and this is what Beethoven only imperfectly knew. The ideas so beautifully and so marvelously clothed in

[1] From a letter to Paul Lacombe.—Editor.

all the splendor or all the tenderness that the orchestra affords him in his profoundest originality are clumsy and often tame when he adapts them to the piano. The number of formulae he prepared for the piano was extraordinarily limited, and in many passages we feel what he has wished by perceiving that he has not attained it. Many of the effects he combined from his knowledge of the orchestra have failed on the piano, from not knowing how to translate them into the peculiar language of this instrument.

Imagine Raphael engraving his pictures himself after having painted them. The lines, the contours, the design of them would always be pure, the first conception always inspired, but the execution, the details, the tints, the shadows, the lights, the life, finally—do you think he would have obtained them? The poorest engraver would have succeeded better.
—LOUIS MOREAU GOTTSCHALK

Peter Ilich Tschaikowsky

To the Grand Duke Constantinovich.

"FROLOVSKOE, *September 21st (October 3rd),* 1888.

". . . Fet[1] is quite right in asserting, as you say he does, that 'all which has no connection with the leading idea should be cast aside, even though it is beautiful and melodious.' But we must not deduce from this that only what is terse can be highly artistic; therefore, to my mind, Fet's rule that an exemplary lyric must not exceed a certain limit is entirely wrong. All depends upon the nature of the leading idea and the poet who expresses it. All that is good, but superfluous, we call 'padding.' Can we say we find this padding in Beethoven's works? I think most decidedly we do not. On the contrary, it is astonishing how equal, how significant and forceful this giant among musicians always remains, and how well he understands the art of curbing his vast inspiration, and never loses sight of balanced and traditional form. In his last quartets, which were long regarded as the productions of an insane and deaf man, there seems to be some padding, until we have studied them thoroughly. But ask someone who is well acquainted with these works, a member of a quartet who plays them frequently, if there is anything superfluous in the C♯ minor Quartet. Unless he is an old-fashioned musician, brought up upon Haydn, he would be horrified at the idea of abbreviating or cutting any portion of it. In speaking of Beethoven I was not merely thinking of his latest period. Could anyone show me a bar in the *Eroica*, which is very lengthy, that could be called superfluous,

[1] A well-known Russian poet.

or any portion that could really be omitted as padding? So everything that is long is not *too long*; many words do not necessarily mean empty verbiage, and terseness is not, as Fet asserts, the essential condition of beautiful form. Beethoven, who in the first movement of the *Eroica* has built up a superb edifice out of an endless series of varied and ever new architectural beauties upon so simple and seemingly poor a subject, knows on occasion how to surprise us by the terseness and exiguity of his forms. Do you remember the Andante of the Pianoforte Concerto in B flat? I know nothing more inspired than this short movement; I go cold and pale every time I hear it.

"Of course, the classical beauty of Beethoven's predecessors, and their art of keeping within bounds, is of the greatest value. It must be owned, however, that Haydn had no occasion to limit himself, for he had not an inexhaustible wealth of material at command.

"That inspired musician who expresses himself with such breadth, majesty, force, and even brusqueness, has much in common with Michael Angelo. Just as the Abbé Bernini has flooded Rome with his statues, in which he strives to imitate the style of Michael Angelo, without possessing his genius, and makes a caricature of what is really powerful in his model, so Beethoven's musical style has been copied over and over again. Is not Brahms in reality a caricature of Beethoven? Is not this pretension to profundity and power detestable, because the content which is poured into the Beethoven mold is not really of any value? Even in the case of Wagner (who certainly has genius), wherever he oversteps the limits it is the spirit of Beethoven which prompts him. Beethoven never repeats an entire movement without a special reason, and, in doing so, rarely fails to introduce something new; but he has recourse to this characteristic method in his instrumental music, knowing that his idea will only be understood after many statements. I cannot understand why your Highness should object to the constant repetition of the subject in the Scherzo of the Ninth Symphony. I always want to hear it over and over again. It is so divinely beautiful, strong, original, and significant! It is quite another matter with the prolixity and repetitions of Schubert, who, with all his genius, constantly harps upon his central idea—as in the Andante of the C major symphony. Beethoven develops his first idea fully, in its entirety, before repeating it; Schubert seems too indolent to elaborate his first idea, and—perhaps from his unusual wealth of thematic material—hurries on the beginning to arrive at something else. It seems as though the stress of his inexhaustible inspiration hindered him from the careful elaboraton of the theme, in all its depth and delicacy of workmanship."—ROSA NEWMARCH

"Probably after my death it will not be uninteresting to know what were my musical predilections and prejudices, especially since I seldom gave opinions in verbal conversation.

"Shall start gradually and shall speak to the point, touching upon musicians living at the same time with me and about their personalities.

"Shall start with Beethoven, whom it is usual to praise unconditionally and whom it is commanded to worship as though he were a god. And so what is Beethoven to me?

"I bow before the greatness of some of his works—but I do not *love* Beethoven. My attitude toward him reminds me of what I experienced in childhood toward the God Jehovah. I had toward Him (and even now my feelings have not changed) a feeling of wonder, but at the same time also of fear. He created Heaven and earth, He too created me— and still even though I bow before Him, there is no *love*. Christ, on the contrary, inspires truly and exclusively the feeling of *love*. Though He was *God*, He was at the same time man. He suffered like us. We *pity* Him, we love in Him His ideal *human* side. And if Beethoven occupies a place in my heart analogous to the God Jehovah, then Mozart I love as the musical Christ. Incidentally, he lived almost as long as Christ. I think that there is nothing sacrilegious in this compassion. Mozart was a being so angelic, so childlike, so pure; his music is so full of unapproachable, dvine beauty, that if anyone could be named with Christ, then it is he.

"Speaking of Beethoven, I come to Mozart. According to my deep conviction, Mozart is the highest, the culminating point that *beauty* has attained in the sphere of music. No one has made me weep, has made me tremble with rapture, from the consciousness of my nearness to *that something* which we call the *ideal*, as he has done.

"Beethoven has also made me tremble. But rather from something like fear and the pangs of suffering.

"I cannot *discourse* on music and shall not go into details. However, I shall mention [that] in Beethoven I love the middle period, at times the first, but I fundamentally *detest* the last, especially the last quartets. Here there are *glimmers*—and nothing more. The rest is *chaos*, over which, surrounded by an impenetrable fog, hovers the spirit of this musical Jehovah."[1]—JACQUES BARZUN

Nicolas Rimsky-Korsakov

When the student works alone, the best plan is to study full scores and listen to an orchestra, score in hand. But it is difficult to decide what music should be studied and heard. Music of all ages, certainly, but

[1] From Tschaikowsky's diaries of the year 1886.—Editor.

principally the fairly modern. This music will teach the student how to score; classical music will prove of negative value to him. Weber, Mendelssohn, Meyerbeer (*The Prophet*), Berlioz, Glinka, Wagner, Liszt, and modern French and Russian composers—these will prove his best guides.

The gigantic figure of Beethoven stands apart. His music abounds in countless leonine leaps of orchestral imagination, but his technique, viewed in detail, remains much inferior to his titanic conception. The use of the trumpets, standing out above the rest of the orchestra, the difficult and unhappy intervals he gives to the horns, the distinctive features of the string parts and his often highly-colored manner of employing the wood-winds are features that will cause the student of Beethoven to stumble upon a thousand and one points of contradiction.

—Nicolas Rimsky-Korsakov, *Principles of Orchestration*, tr. Edward Agate, London, Russian Music Agency, 1922, p. 2.—SAM MORGENSTERN

Modeste Moussorgsky

(From Letter to V. V. Stasov, St. Petersburg, October 18, 1872)

In poetry there are two giants: coarse Homer and refined Shakespeare. In music there are two giants: the thinker Beethoven, and the super-thinker Berlioz. When around these four we gather all their generals and aides-de-camp, we have a pleasant company; but what has this company of subalterns achieved? Skipping and dancing along in the paths marked out by the giants—but to dare to "go very far ahead," this is terrifying!

—Jay Leyda and Sergei Bertensson, *The Musorgsky Reader*, New York, W. W. Norton, 1947, p. 199.—SAM MORGENSTERN

Ferruccio Busoni

Only psychological tragedy suits Beethoven; his handling of a tragic situation is quite dull. A tragic situation requires a conflict between *at least* two people, while a psychological one takes place in a single person. Beethoven would have been the man for a higher kind of comic opera. Aphoristically: Humor is the blossom from the tree of seriousness. One sees it in Shakespeare and in Ibsen.

Los Angeles, 15 *March* 1911.
Melody belongs to the Future

It can be said—contradict it who may—that Wagner was the first to recognize melody as the supreme law, not only theoretically. On the whole, the older art of composition suffers from a neglect of melody. Unconsciously we feel another standard in the classical works and we do not measure them so strictly.

With Beethoven, this strikes one most forcibly in his *Second period*, which is the weakest, and is exemplified in its principal compositions, the Fifth Symphony, the "Waldstein" Sonata, the "Appassionata," and the three Quartets, Opus 59.

I should like to repeat—and let them contradict me again—that in Beethoven's first period feeling conquers helplessness; in the third feeling stands above the mastery which he has gained. But in the second period feeling is overshadowed by symphonic breadth and symphonic brilliance. Beethoven, in his second period, exploits the forceful ideas contained in the first.

The heroically passionate defiance of the "Pathétique" continues to be the basis for all pieces similar in feeling (only more extended) in the following period, headed by the Fifth Symphony. But the melodic element does not keep step with this extension and gets lost in—what shall I call it?—a kind of table-land of modulatory and figurative eloquence. I am thinking, for example, of the working out in the first movement of the "Appassionata" where the persistent rush and intensity of temperament fill the place where the content should be.

The deepest feeling needs the fewest words and gestures. It is a historical commonplace, repeated like a continuous cinematograph performance, that as each new composition appears it is accused of a lack of melody. I have read this kind of accusation in criticisms after the first performance of Mozart's Don Giovanni, Beethoven's Violin Concerto, and Wagner's operas. And it is always taken for granted that the increase in technical complications is the reason for the decrease in melodic invention.

It almost seems as if technical mastery makes its effect by being unusual, whereas melody is only perceived as such when it appears in commonplace and familiar ways.

But as a matter of fact Mozart, as a maker of melodies, was richer than his predecessors; Beethoven broader, more ingenious than Mozart, and Wagner more voluptuous than Beethoven (if perhaps less noble and original).

Beethoven himself in his *third* period—at times in the string quartets —dissolves the rigid symphonic mechanism into melody and—psychology.
—FERRUCCIO BENVENUTO BUSONI

Claude Debussy

Beethoven furnishes material for several articles. His works, particularly the symphonies, somewhat overburdened programs, so Debussy considered. We have already quoted his dogmatic statements regarding the symphonic form adopted by the German master. His paradoxical criticism of the "Pastoral Symphony" has often been quoted and keenly discussed. It was written after a performance at the Concerts Lamoureux. Weingartner had conducted the symphony "with the care of the meticulous gardener. It was so neatly cleared of caterpillars that it gave the impression of a landscape varnished with a brush, the gentle undulations of the hills being represented by plush at ten francs a meter, and the trees crimped with curling tongs." The excessive detail of this interpretation helped, perhaps, to provoke the critic's ill humor.

His mockery and censure have their origin in an intense love of nature: "In short, the popularity of the 'Pastoral Symphony' is due to the misunderstanding which not commonly exists between nature and man. Notice the scene by the stream! . . . a stream where the oxen apparently come to drink (or so the bassoons lead me to suppose), not to mention the wooden nightingale and the Swiss cuckoo which belong rather to the art of M. de Vaucanson[1] than to nature. . . . All this is useless imitation or a purely arbitrary interpretation. How much more deeply is the beauty of a landscape expressed in some pages of this old master, and this simply because there is no direct imitation, but merely a transposition of his feeling for all that is *invisible* in nature. Can one render the mystery of a forest by measuring the height of the trees? Is it not rather its unfathomable depths that appeal to the imagination? Besides, in the symphony Beethoven is dependent upon a period when nature was observed only through books. . . . This is apparent in the storm which forms part of this same symphony, where the terror of beings and things is cloaked in romance though the thunder that growls is not very alarming."

Ten years later there appeared another ironic criticism of this imitation of nature. The "Pastoral Symphony" "certainly remains one of the best examples of mechanical expression. . . . To hear an orchestra imitate the cries of animals is a real joy to young and old. To assist at a storm from an armchair is sheer sybaritism." Thanks to Gabriel Pierné's charming interpretation, "we were really in the country. The trees did not wear white

[1] A famous maker of mechanical toys (1709–82) [translator's note].

ties; the stream, beside which the most German of idylls takes place, was delightfully fresh. A little more and we should have smelled the cowshed!"

Debussy, fearing that his mockery might be misinterpreted, is careful, before concluding his article of 1903, to introduce a note of admiration: "It would be absurd to think that I am wanting in respect to Beethoven, but a musician of his genius could err more blindly than another. . . . No man is expected to write only masterpieces; and if the 'Pastoral Symphony' is classed as such, the term loses force when applied to his other works. That is all I mean to say."

The title of masterpiece is, in Debussy's opinion, wholly deserved by the "Ninth Symphony." He writes of it with reasoned enthusiasm. He even rejects the charge of lengthiness which authorities on music have brought against certain parts of the symphony. In the first place he deplores the mass of literature which the great work has called forth: "The Choral Symphony has been enveloped in a fog of words and high-sounding epithets. This work and the famous Mona Lisa smile (which has been forever labeled 'mysterious') are the two masterpieces about which the greatest amount of nonsense has been written. The wonder is that it has not been buried under the heap of prose it called forth. Wagner proposed to complete its orchestration; others planned to explain its story by means of descriptive tableaux. In short, this clear, powerful work was turned into a bogy for the public. Presuming that there is a mystery in this symphony, it might perhaps be elucidated,—but to what purpose?"

Here is the actual critique, full of musicianship and feeling: "Beethoven was not in the least literary. (At least, not in the sense now attached to this word.) He loved music with pride. Music was to him the passion, the joy, so painfully lacking in his private life. The Choral Symphony should perhaps be regarded as merely a more unbounded gesture of musical pride—nothing more. A little notebook, in which are noted down more than two hundred different aspects of the main theme of the finale of this symphony, bears witness to the persistent research, the purely musical speculation which directed it. (Schiller's verses have really only a sonorous value.) He wished this idea to contain its own inevitable development; and apart from its marvelous intrinsic beauty, it is magnificent in its fulfillment of his expectations. There exists no more triumphant example of the adaptability of an idea to the mold that is designed for it. At every advance there is new joy, achieved without weariness, without apparent repetition, suggesting the budding of a fabulous tree whose leaves all burst forth at once. In spite of its huge proportions, there is nothing superfluous in this work—not even the Andante which, according to recent critics, is long drawn out. Does it not constitute a rest, arranged with delicate forethought between the rhythmic persistence of the scherzo and the rushing instrumental torrent leading the voices triumphantly to the glory of the finale? Besides, Beethoven had written eight symphonies; the figure 9 must therefore have impressed itself upon his mind with an almost fatalistic significance, and Beethoven labored to surpass himself. I do not see how anyone could doubt that he succeeded. The human feeling which bursts through the customary bounds of the symphony springs from a soul panting for freedom, a soul which, by the irony of fate, dashes itself against the gilded bars fashioned by the unkind friendship of the great. Beethoven must have suffered intensely and burned with the desire for communion with humanity. Hence the cry addressed by the thousand voices of his genius to the humblest and poorest of his brethren. Was he heard by them? . . . A disturbing question, this."

Beethoven's orchestration is excellent in the opinion of Debussy, or rather, of Monsieur Croche, who contrasts it with that of Wagner: "Beethoven's orchestra, which appears to him a formula in black and white, resulting in the whole exquisite gamut of grays; that of Wagner which is a species of polychromatic putty, spread almost uniformly, in which he assured me he could no longer distinguish the sound of a violin from that of a trombone."

On the other hand, Monsieur Croche does not approve of the way the sonatas are written for the piano, for they exceed the scope of the instrument: "Beethoven's piano sonatas are very badly written for the piano. The later ones in particular are rather transcriptions from orchestral scores. A third hand is often required, and this Beethoven must have realized—at least, I hope he did."

Apart from the greater works, Debussy wrote only of the song "Adelaïde," which an artist had sung "with an elegant tremolo." This page he considers unworthy of its author: "I think the old master must have forgotten to burn this melody, and the overcupidity of his heirs is probably to blame for the mistake of its exhumation." This lack of reverence need not astonish us. Debussy admired Beethoven as he admired Wagner, but as he stated one day: "I refuse to admire them *en bloc* because I have been told that they are Masters! That, never! In my opinion, the attitude that people adopt toward Masters nowadays is unpleasantly servile. If a dull page annoys me, I insist on my right to say so, whoever its author may be. . . ."

Beethoven [and] Mozart are [two] sovereign masters, differing one from the other by reason of development in taste: "Genius can, of course, dispense with taste: of this Beethoven is an example. Mozart on the other hand, his equal in genius, has, in addition, the most delicate taste."—
LEON VALLAS

Charles Ives

Thoreau was a great musician, not because he played the flute but because he did not have to go to Boston to hear "the Symphony." The rhythm of his prose, were there nothing else, would determine his value as a composer. He was divinely conscious of the enthusiasm of Nature, the emotion of her rhythms and the harmony of her solitude. In this consciousness he sang of the submission to Nature, the religion of contemplation, and the freedom of simplicity—a philosophy distinguishing between the complexity of Nature which teaches freedom, and the complexity of materialism which teaches slavery. In music, in poetry, in all art, the truth as one sees it must be given in terms which bear some proportion to the inspiration. In their greatest moments the inspiration of both Beethoven and Thoreau expresses profound truths and deep sentiment, but the intimate passion of it, the storm and stress of it, affected Beethoven in such a way that he could not but be ever showing it and Thoreau that he could not easily expose it. They were equally imbued with it, but with different results. A difference in temperament had something to do with this, together with a difference in the quality of expression between the two arts. "Who that has heard a strain of music feared lest he would speak extravagantly forever," says Thoreau.—CHARLES IVES

Igor Stravinsky

In our early youth we were surfeited by his works, his famous *Weltschmerz* being forced upon us at the same time, together with the "tragedy" and all the commonplaces voiced for more than a century about this composer who must be recognized as one of the world's greatest musical geniuses.

Like many other musicians, I was disgusted by this intellectual and sentimental attitude, which has little to do with serious musical appreciation. This deplorable pedagogy did not fail in its result. It alienated me from Beethoven for many years.

Cured and matured by age, I could now approach him objectively so that he wore a different aspect for me. Above all I recognized in him the indisputable monarch of the instrument. It is the instrument that inspires his thought and determines its substance. The relations of a composer to his sound medium may be of two kinds. Some, for example, compose music *for* the piano; others compose *piano music*. Beethoven is clearly in the second category. In all his immense pianistic work, it is the "instrumental" side which is characteristic of him and makes him infinitely precious to me. It is the giant instrumentalist that predominates in him, and it is thanks to that quality that he cannot fail to reach any ear that is open to music.

But is it in truth Beethoven's music which has inspired the innumerable works devoted to this prodigious musician by thinkers, moralists, and even sociologists who have suddenly become musicographers? In this connection, I should like to quote the following passage taken from an article in the great Soviet daily, *Izvestia:*

"Beethoven is the friend and contemporary of the French Revolution, and he remained faithful to it even when, during the Jacobin dictatorship, humanitarians with weak nerves of the Schiller type turned from it, preferring to destroy tyrants on the theatrical stage with the help of cardboard swords. Beethoven, that plebeian genius, who proudly turned his back on emperors, princes and magnates—that is the Beethoven we love for his unassailable optimism, his virile sadness, for the inspired pathos of his struggle, and for his iron will which enabled him to seize destiny by the throat."

This chef-d'oeuvre of penetration comes from the pen of one of the most famous music critics in the U.S.S.R. I should like to know in what this mentality differs from the platitudes and commonplaces uttered by the publicity-mongers of liberalism in all the bourgeois democracies long before the social revolution in Russia.

I do not mean to say that everything that has been written on Beethoven in this sense is of the same quality. But, in the majority of these works, do the panegyrists not base their adulation far more on the sources of his inspiration than on the music itself? Could they have filled their fat volumes if they had not been able to embroider to their hearts' content all the extramusical elements available in the Beethoven life and legend, drawing their conclusions and judgments on the artist from them?

What does it matter whether the Third Symphony was inspired by the figure of Bonaparte the republican or Napoleon the emperor? It is only the music that matters. But to talk music is risky, and entails responsibility. Therefore some find it preferable to seize on side issues. It is easy, and enables you to pass as a deep thinker. . . .

It is in the quality of his musical method and not in the nature of his ideas that his true greatness lies.

It is time that this was recognized, and Beethoven was rescued from the unjustifiable monopoly of the "intellectuals" and left to those who seek nothing in music but music. It is, however, also time—and this is perhaps even more urgent—to protect him from the stupid drivel of fools who think it up-to-date to giggle as they amuse themselves by running him down. Let them beware; dates pass quickly.

Just as in his pianistic work Beethoven lives on the piano, so in his symphonies, overtures and chamber music, he draws his sustenance from his instrumental ensemble. With him the instrumentation is never apparel, and that is why it never strikes one. The profound wisdom with which he distributes parts to separate instruments or to whole groups, the carefulness of his instrumental writing, and the precision with which he indicates his wishes—all these testify to the fact that we are in the presence of a tremendous constructive force.

I do not think I am mistaken in asserting that it was precisely his manner of molding his musical material that led logically to the erection of those monumental structures which are his supreme glory.

There are those who contend that Beethoven's instrumentation was bad and his tone color poor. Others altogether ignore that side of his art, holding that instrumentation is a secondary matter and that only "ideas" are worthy of consideration.

The former demonstrate their lack of taste, their complete incompetence in this respect, and their narrow and mischievous mentality. In contrast with the florid orchestration of a Wagner, with its lavish coloring, Beethoven's instrumentation will appear to lack luster. It might produce a similar impression if compared with the vivacious radiance of Mozart. But Beethoven's music is intimately linked with his instrumental language, and finds its most exact and perfect expression in the sobriety of that language. To regard it as poverty-stricken would merely show lack of perception. True sobriety is a great rarity, and most difficult of attainment.

As for those who attach no importance to Beethoven's instrumentation, but ascribe the whole of his greatness to his "ideas"—they obviously regard all instrumentation as a mere matter of apparel, coloring, flavoring, and so fall, though following a different path, into the same heresy as the others.

Both make the same fundamental error of regarding instrumentation as something extrinsic from the music for which it exists.

This dangerous point of view concerning instrumentation, coupled with today's unhealthy greed for orchestral opulence, has corrupted the judgment of the public, and, being impressed by the immediate effect of tone color, people can no longer solve the problem of whether it is intrinsic in the music or simply "padding." Orchestration has become a source of enjoyment independent of the music, and the time has surely come to set things to rights. We have had enough of this orchestral dappling and these thick sonorities; we are tired of being saturated with timbres, and want no more of all this overfeeding, which deforms the entity of the instrumental element by swelling it out of all proportion and giving it an existence of its own. There is a great deal of re-education to be accomplished in this field.

From Igor Stravinsky, *Chronicle of my Life*, London, Victor Gollancz, 1936, p. 189.—SAM MORGENSTERN

Beethoven, the greatest orchestral master of all in our sense, is seldom praised for his instrumentation; his symphonies are too good music in every way, and the orchestra is too integral a part of them. How silly it sounds to say of the trio of the Scherzo of the Eighth Symphony, "What splendid instrumentation"—yet, what incomparable instrumental thought it is.—IGOR STRAVINSKY AND ROBERT CRAFT

Evaluations by Performers
Wilhelm Furtwängler

Where, for example—to put it paradoxically—would the whole of our concert life be today, if Beethoven had not written his symphonies? It was Beethoven's predecessors and followers, and, above all, he himself, who *created* the concept of a "concert audience" by their works. To be sure, then, this audience is something other than just a formless mass without a will of its own. Suddenly, through the formative influence of these composers, it is possessed of standards. It makes demands. The composer must resist these demands. There is, after all, a difference between a mass of people welded into a whole by watching a horse race or a boxing match and a crowd made one by listening to a Beethoven symphony. It is the manner of unification which matters.

These differences also exist within the sphere of music. Effects made upon the audience from without are described by Wagner as "sensationalism" which can turn it perhaps into a momentarily intoxicated mass, but cannot make it a true "community." Such sensationalism he laconically defines as "effects without causes." It was precisely in Wagner's time, the dawn of the age of the great virtuosos, that musicians began to strive after these "effects without causes," and to make use of them. Thus, the audience-composer relationship became for the first time the problem it has remained to this day. The craving for effect at any price, which started in the age of Wagner and Liszt, was symptomatic of this estrangement.

This much is certain: those works alone succeed in turning an audience if only for seconds into a *genuine* community, that take hold of the individual in such a way that he is no longer a separate entity, but a part of his people, a part of humanity, a part of the Divine Nature operating through him. It is those works alone that men need and desire. This does not alter the fact that in daily musical life it is to just such works that the audience, as we know from experience, shows the strongest opposition and yields least willingly. In this it is like a woman who wants her happiness forced on her.

To reject Beethoven's works on the grounds that they are effective with the audience would indeed be emptying the baby out with the bath. It is just such a phenomenon as Beethoven that offers the best examples of genuine, of "legitimate," effect. His works make their impression precisely and exclusively because of what they *are*, and not because of what they seem; by their character, and not by their façade. But that Beethoven's effects are what they are is thanks to the clarity with which he says what he has to say. The greatest possible clarity of expression is thus the way—the only way—in which the composer can take into account the existence of the audience. It was Goethe who said: "If a man would tell me anything, he must say it clearly and simply. I have enough within me that is problematic." There is of course a precedent condition: namely, that one should *have* something to say, that is, that one can dare to show oneself naked, without any covering, just as one is. To do so is not for everybody, and those who express themselves in a complicated way—especially if they are artists—may generally have their reasons.

With Beethoven, music became for the first time capable of expressing what in Nature is the catastrophic element. The catastrophe is no less natural than is the slow organic development of evolution: it is another form of Nature's expression. So far the character of music had been epic, now it gradually became dramatic. In ancient Greece, too, Homer preceded the tragic poets. Such things do not happen by chance. The great epic corresponds to a more primitive stage of development than the drama, which presupposes the possibility of isolating the fates and characters of individuals, of allowing them to develop according to inherent laws. Epic precedes drama because description is the first sort of encounter with reality. Not until reality has been mastered by description does the creative artist acquire the degree of detachment necessary for his characters to develop according to the law inherent in each: not until then can he treat his creatures as though they no longer depended upon him but lived their own lives, fulfilling private destinies.

Bach, of course, achieves certain "tragic" effects—one has only to think of the Passions. But Bach, in spite of this, remains essentially epic; with him, a subject represents an unalterable entity, which, although it is developed, never has a life of its own. The decisive factor which was introduced into the history of music by Haydn and which became a complete reality in Beethoven's work was that the subject should develop organically within the work, like a Shakespearian character. With Bach, the entire potential development of a work is implicit in the subject as such, in reality he never does anything which is not in accord with his main theme, even when he introduces countersubjects (e.g., in a fugue). He is monothematic in the real sense of the term. The forms he employs—the fugue, the aria etc.—are all presented to us in the same broad flow. Each piece runs its predestined course with iron consistency. With Beethoven, the course of a piece of music is not prescribed to the same extent, although it would be entirely wrong to say that the degree of cogency in the development of the piece is less than it is with Bach. But with Beethoven this development is not predetermined solely by the first subject; Beethoven uses several subjects from the opposition and permutation of which the piece develops. These different subjects live and develop in interaction. They have to bear a destiny of their own. The work is molded—to no one else in the whole history of music does this apply to the same extent—into a whole from parts which in themselves often represent the greatest contrasts imaginable.

For some time it was publicly argued that Beethoven's ideas as such had no special virtue: it was what he made of his ideas that mattered. There was one school of thought which rightly held that intuition must always be the essential factor, even in works such as Beethoven's, which show evidence of much "hard work." The other school of thought— tending for the most part, though without saying so, to make the part played by intuition appear as small as possible because they themselves were intellectuals—represented Beethoven as the typical example of an artist with an infinite capacity for taking pains. It is true that certain of Beethoven's subjects (e.g., the first subject of the *Eroica* or of the fifth symphony) cannot be considered as particularly brilliant. But Beethoven's genius consists in surrounding every subject with an appropriate aura, an appropriate "climate"; and secondly—and this is the most important point—in managing to find for every subject the very companions which enable its possibilities to be developed to the fullest extent. Beethoven's supreme genius, which is unsurpassed in this respect in the history of music, consisted in his ability to invent seemingly within the scope of one and the same over-all "mood" several subjects of entirely different individual characteristics which only attain their full development by establishing a living contact with each other, thus forming a new and all-embracing unity which exceeds by far the limitations of the individual themes. It is not, therefore, a genius for the invention of themes that is Beethoven's only characteristic—though in this respect, too, he has something to show (so that those who favor the "hard work" theory are not entirely wrong). His intuition goes far beyond this; at his best he succeeds in finding a whole series of subjects which appear to cling together by fate, one might almost say by a law of nature, and which, in supplementing one another, endow the work with all the fullness and strength of life that their creator has to impart.

This is a method which I call "dramatic" in the real sense of the word. Beethoven's subjects develop in mutual interaction like the characters in a play. In every single subject of every Beethoven work, a destiny is unfolded.

In the *Klassischer Walpurgisnacht* in *Faust*, Part II, Goethe represents the clash of . . . two diametrically opposed concepts, obvious archetypes of a possible interpretation of nature. And there really are different kinds of organic development. There is the more feminine, or evolutionary principle, and the catastrophic, which may be called the masculine principle. The latter, too, is part of organic nature—in contrast to everything purely intellectual or mechanical, which operates on an entirely different level of existence.

Wagner is a poet who pursues his poetic dreams with the aid of music. But he is in a category by himself. As far as Beethoven is concerned, we can say that he succeeds in attaining within the most restricted frame, within the scope of a sonata, the kind of effect which Aristotle ascribes to tragedy. And it is this point which shows in what respect the two arts of music and poetry are related and where they differ. In a tragedy, the catastrophe—the wreck of clashing forces—tears apart and refashions those who participate in it, establishing thereby a harmony on a higher plane, that "tragic catharsis" of which Aristotle speaks. If we apply this to the realm of music we find, curiously enough, that music itself is incapable of achieving tragic effects of this kind, and that a real musical tragedy has therefore never been written. A work with a tragic ending can be a music-drama like *Tristan* or *The Twilight of the Gods*, it is the subject, the drama, which is tragic, not the music as such. Attempts have of course been made in this direction from time to time, even in the field of pure music—the most recent of these was made by Tchaikovsky in the *Pathétique*, which has great powers of suggestion, and is deeply rooted in the Slav national character—but their effect is nevertheless very different from that of the great spoken tragedy. Not "tragic catharsis" but gloom, despair, and resignation have the last word. One cannot help feeling that a climax of sorrow and struggle and conflict can only be transitory, because in music the tragic element does not possess the same liberating power as in poetic tragedy: it does not exalt man above his normal condition, but confines him within himself as within a prison. It is by no means accidental that the funeral march is only the second movement of the *Eroica*. The *ultimate* effect of tragedy (a subject on which Goethe and Schiller conducted an extensive correspondence), its liberating effect, its power to save, is released by music—and this shows the profound difference between the two arts—by the opposite of the "tragic element," that is, by *joy*. It is at this point that the essentially dionysiac character of music stands revealed. And no one has shown this more clearly than Beethoven. No matter what the prevailing mood of individual movements may be, every sonata, every string quartet is in its way a drama, not infrequently a real tragedy, whose concentrated ecstasy is altogether beyond the reach of poetry. Richard Wagner realized this. At the point where poetry acquires wings and soars into the grandeur of the superhuman, music will somehow always appear tongue-tied, imprisoned, as it were, within itself. At the point of ecstasy which marks the limit of poetical expression, music only begins to reveal what it is capable of. This abandonment to the dionysiac side of life, to joy, is as alien to Goethe, whose approach is essentially bounded by poetry, as it was to the epic sense and feeling for form of the Greeks—though they, of course, possessed the other as well. This is fundamentally the explanation of Beethoven's great finales in a major key, a monumental example being the finale of the ninth symphony.

The character of Beethoven's works is as rich and diversified as Nature herself. But, in calling them dramatic, I was referring not to the "world" or to the "mood" which they express, but to the mode of expression on which they are based; what I said just now about the manner in which the subjects are formulated—the bringing together and integration of entirely disparate elements—in the creative principle by which he works. It informs and permeates all his compositions in the smallest detail as in the whole, in the individual theme as well as in the division of the whole into movements, comparable to the acts of a play. For the profoundly necessary relationship between these movements in their sequence is undeniable. And the sense of the "fruitful contrast," as I should like to call it, which dominated Beethoven, the contrast from which is born a *new* entity, is shown clearly in all his work. There is such tremendous variety in Beethoven's works precisely because it is this synthesis which is aimed at, because every piece consequently has a world of its own to express. This even affects details of form, style, the growth of a composition. No two works by Beethoven are similar in form, whereas, for example, Bruckner's few are as alike as peas in a pod as far as the various elements of form (the codas, for instance) are concerned.

It seems as if Beethoven has been deliberately searching for apparently irreconcilable antitheses. Thus a dramatic and hard movement full of action (first major example, the Kreutzer sonata, last example, sonata

Opus III) is followed by a set of variations written in the most relaxed and serene musical style imaginable. But it is only the two together that constitute for Beethoven a *whole*.

These sets of variations on a slow theme, especially the ones written during the last years of his life, are, of course, by no means accidental. They are not variations in the usual sense. They presuppose the existence of that type of Beethoven theme which is so balanced in itself, which has its being so completely within itself that the whole great set of variations which follows is as it were no more than an exhalation, an unfolding, an expansion of the theme, with nothing added that does not spring from its own nature. And such a movement—representing the highest degree of relaxation ever dared in music—is then inserted between movements in which tension seems to have been heightened to breaking-point. Think for a moment of the ninth symphony. Consider the theme of the adagio, steeped in an other-worldliness which properly belongs to the sphere of religion: how it expands in the variations which follow, how it is lost in innumerable arabesques—as if a stylistic urge were at work which, in terms of art history, would probably have found expression in the Gothic style: in Beethoven's case not, however, for its own sake, as with the Gothic builders, but rather as a necessary part of an ordained whole. It seems as if the full purpose of the adagio—which in spite of its profoundly contemplative character must remain an episode, part of one uniform creative process—were only revealed in retrospect, when the finale is announced in frightening tones. Nothing is merely strung together, everything is developed organically from what has gone before. Thus was Beethoven enabled not only to write this first movement of the ninth symphony—a world in itself, whose contents and style have formed and overshadowed whole generations of composers—but also to follow it up, as its necessary supplement and contrast, with a scherzo which is the archetype of all large-scale symphonic scherzi; then to represent, in the adagio, the obverse side of the world, here too, as in the preceding movements, going to the limits of human ability; to feel and finally to put all these movements into his very own type of perspective—perspective by means of the last movement, thus revealing in their entirety the tragic and dionysiac possibilities of music. That is creative power indeed!

But I should like to go back for a moment to what [was] said about the undramatic character of certain works by Beethoven, especially the "even number" symphonies. Of course there are such works; they even outnumber those which are of a more tragic and dramatic nature. Beethoven enjoys an extraordinary wealth of moods. But each of these moods—and this is the point—is expressed with the absence of ambiguity peculiar to him. Each expression is always pursued and exploited to its utmost limitations. Those half-moods of Mozart or the early Romantics, in which

the soul itself seems not to know what it wants, are as foreign to
Beethoven as are the bourgeois-inspired hesitancy, the inability to "go
the whole hog," which are to be found constantly in Schumann and
Brahms, or the incapacity to transcend the limitations of the given
means that we so often see in more recent music. Especially in his latter
period Beethoven frequently expresses spiritual extremes.

But this makes him more difficult for the mass of the public to
understand, so that the effect of his music loses in breadth what it
gains in depth. A work like the seventh symphony, with its unearthly
serenity and its wild gigantic high spirits is, I think, intelligible in its
entirety only to the few. This also applies to the sweet idyllic strains of
the "pastoral," which Wagner has apostrophized so aptly with the words
of Christ: "This day shalt thou be with me in paradise." Long passages
of this symphony are imbued with a kind of natural piety, a quality of absorption which is related to the religious sphere and nowadays does not
appeal universally either to audiences or performers.

The remarks and prejudices voiced again and again by performers as
well as audiences show very clearly to what extent these works, which are
after all accessible to the public, are misunderstood: that the eighth
symphony is "harmless," that the "pastoral" is "weak," that it has "no
end," that the last movement of the ninth is "banal," etc. Beethoven,
the great unknown, is a subject which reflects mainly on the inadequacy
of our performers.

Beethoven more than anyone else had an urge to express everything
in a purely musical form. This is demonstrated particularly clearly by
his attitude toward a given text. No matter how hard he may try, e.g.,
in parts of *Fidelio*, or in the *Missa solemnis*, to express the meaning of
every word in music, he never entirely succeeds in getting away from
his purely musical conceptions of form. The sonata form, and, as its
simpler prototype, the *Lied*, with its repetitions etc., are, literally speaking,
"in his blood," everything is, in the last analysis, somehow related to
them, linked up with them. Poet and composer find in him no comfortable halfway house. That is the reason why he could not become a
lyricist like Schubert or a music-dramatist like Wagner—not because he
was less, but because he was more of a musician, because he was
more exclusivley a musician; because the postulate of pure music affected
him more strongly, more inexorably. The musician in him felt inhibited,
not inspired by a text: he would not allow the textual form of a word
to dictate to him what form his music should take. Thus Beethoven becomes completely himself only when he is free to follow exclusively the
inherent demands of music.

That is the reason why he attempted in most cases to resolve a given
text into separate phases which he then tackled purely from the point of
view of music, for instance the individual numbers of *Fidelio*, starting

with the wonderful quartet—a most profound inspiration on a trifling occasion—and then the movements of the *Missa solemnis*, which can be described in this connection as a symphony with words.

This undoubtedly applies to all the works in which Beethoven set words to music. In the ninth symphony, when after three purely instrumental movements Beethoven suddenly resorted to words, the explanation can be found in a nonmusical, literary impulse . . . [But there is] a purely musical explanation even for this.

It is particularly important to clear the matter up, as ideas about this last movement have tended to be extremely confused ever since Wagner's somewhat arbitrary attempts to interpret it. We find, first of all, that in this instance, as in all others, Beethoven approaches his text purely as a musician. Already Wagner noticed that the music does not fit the words, but that the words were, not very happily, subsequently fitted to the melody. What really happened was that Beethoven was searching for suitable words to illustrate what he as a musician wanted to say, following the inner sense of the preceding movements—the whole composition— and to complete the work as a whole, and that he happened to find these words in Schiller, with his tendency to embrace the abstract and the ideal. A more realistic poet would perhaps have given preference to one definite manifestation of joy rather than to the idea of joy. But the latter suited Beethoven's purpose exactly: he was not to be nailed down by details of the text nor was he to be restrained in his freedom of musical expression. Thus he culled a few stanzas only from Schiller's poem and incorporated them in his music with repetitions *ad lib.*

Considered purely from the point of view of form, this last movement is cyclic in construction like the adagio which precedes it, or the final movement of the *Eroica*, or hundreds of similar movements by Beethoven: it is a set of variations on a grand scale. Admittedly, the individual variations would seem to have been adapted to the requirements of the text, and there is also a second subject which is heard later in a fugato passage together with the first subject, but the musical character of a set of variations albeit on a grand scale, is preserved to the very end.

For a composer like Beethoven, in whose works something "happens," a process of "becoming" is manifested, the last movements must have presented the greatest and hardest problems, since it was in them that the last, the decisive word was spoken. Beethoven attempted to attack this problem in a great many different ways. He could release the tension which had been mounting in the other movements by means of a finale full of high spirits and *joie de vivre*—a method in which Haydn had preceded him. There are many such finales, dating especially from his middle period. Then there are finales in which ecstatic merriment is given a diabolical twist, as for example the final movements of the quartets in C minor and C sharp minor, or the finale, again in a minor

key, of the *Appassionata*. It seems that he had at first intended to write
such a finale for the "ninth"; as we know from his scrapbooks, he later
used the theme of this finale to similar purpose in the string quartet in A
minor, Opus 132. Or again, there are finales which manifest a kind of humorous mastery of the world and which appear to be superficial although
they are in fact profound. Such final movements are difficult for the man
in the street to understand. Thus the last movement of the great trio in B
flat major, which may appear inferior to the wonderful adagio which precedes it, in reality represents a liberation, a progression into lighter,
purer air. Then there are rondos, as exemplified for the first time in
the *Sonata Pathétique*, in which the tension of the other movements
is relieved in epic and elegiac strains. With Beethoven, the possibilities of
each final synthesis are as varied as the works themselves.

What prompted him, in the "ninth," to choose a text, to use the human
voice, was nothing more than an urge born of the preceding movements,
i.e., of purely musical elements after all. It was the *theme* of this last
movement which brought with it everything else, the text, the human
voice, and the cycle form. This archetype of all themes, an invention of
the *musician* alone in Beethoven, could never be the explanation or
illustration of a definite text. On the contrary, it is rather the poem
which gives the impression of being an interpretation of the theme. And
in the same way we must consider the use of the human voice as nothing
more than the natural "instrumentation" of this ageless melody.

The way he uses this "instrument," the way the human voice is
introduced as such, yet musically motivated, reveals Beethoven's genius in
all its glory. Any other composer would probably have started with
the recitative and would then have embarked upon the choral movement.
Not so Beethoven, who, recognizing nothing but musical necessity within
his work, uses the following method of development: first, the adagio is
spun out into the infinite. It seems as if he would never be satisfied,
as if he could never stop. This sharpens the contrast with the mordant
opening of the last movement and the instrumental recitatives which
follow, and thereby invests the latter with a peculiar eloquence and
firmness. Already at this point one gets the feeling of being present at
the finale of all finales. This also fully explains the need for a retrospective examination of the preceding movements, which was subsequently often imitated and which might easily have seemed somewhat
artificial. At first, the instruments have the field, then at last, a consummation much to be desired, the theme of joy is heard, played at first,
unison, by the basses, in its most primitive form, as it were. It is then
developed in several variations until Beethoven, after a preliminary
conclusion in the dominant chord—as in a sonata movement—returns to
the beginning: a repetition, so to speak, of the first part. It is not until
this stage has been reached that everything which the instruments have

played so far, i.e., recitatives as well as the theme of joy, the former in an abbreviated form—is repeated, with the addition of the human voice; a *recapitulation* on a higher plane, as it were, an explanation, a glorification of something already there. In this movement, the human voice is nothing more than an additional instrument in the choir of instruments. It is the musical law of *intensification through repetition*—within the limits imposed by the symmetry of the whole—which is applied here on a large scale and which permeates the whole of this music, even in the smallest details.

Just compare with this the childlike, naïve manner in which Liszt seeks to motivate the introduction of the chorus in his *Faust* symphony. Beethoven succeeds in doing exactly the reverse, in making something as apparently illogical as the introduction from without of a recitative and choral movement into a purely orchestral work appear completely natural, convincing and artistically necessary. There is hardly any other example in the history of music which demonstrates so clearly the possibilities of purely abstract music, or offers more convincing proof that it is the musician and the musician alone who is at work therein. Beethoven's virtue lies not in the "idea" as such but in his power to turn this idea so completely into *music*.

People have always felt that Beethoven achieves a particular kind of definiteness of expression. This exactitude derives from his urge to say whatever he has to say in the shortest and simplest way possible. He is characterized by a particular determination and—a glance at his compositions reveals it—by an extraordinary ability to *simplify*. His surviving notebooks offer abundant evidence of this. We find, for example, that the assurance and simplicity of his thematic construction were not a natural gift, but an achievement. The original form of most of his themes, and frequently of the most beautiful, was more complex than the final form, not, as in the case of other composers, firmly established from the outset, or, as in the case of most modern composers, simpler and more primitive. His creative mind proceeded from chaos to form, towards a conscious simplification, and not, like that of the moderns, into deliberate complexities. It is this characteristic above all which distinguishes Beethoven so clearly from all others, predecessors as well as successors.

There is a further factor which operates in the development, the destiny of these themes, and which I have already referred to as the *logic of spiritual evolution*. The laws of development, of transition from one mood to another, the feeling for what themes, what moods, will blend together to make a new whole, the feeling for the proper sequence of the movements of a work—all represent a kind of spiritual logic which is the essence of the impression Beethoven's music has made on the world. For this logic is *human* in the real and profound meaning of the word. It is at the root of both artistic considerations and human emotions, and it is understood always, at all times. It would of course be rewarding to examine how and why and to what extent spiritual and musical logic coincide in this case; it would be the first step toward answering the far from idle question why a Beethoven symphony is better than so many inferior modern works. The discussion of purely musical forms on the one hand or simple descriptions of the processes of the soul on the other, get us nowhere, for what actually matters is that the spiritual should be perceived in terms of the musical and the latter in terms of the spiritual, that both should be considered *one* and indivisible, so that the very attempt to divide them is a fatal mistake. When prominent musicians disapprove of Beethoven because of the "literary" content of his works, it is to a large extent such misinterpretations which are to blame.

It is the determination to be simple, the musical logic of development which brings about that particular kind of definiteness of expression which strikes the sensitive listener again and again in Beethoven's music. And it is this definiteness which although, as I said before, it is of a purely musical nature, misleads people again and again into looking for more than music and into reading all kinds of things into the score.

Only someone for whom the language of music pure and simple does not suffice would want to interpret Beethoven's exactitude naturalistically in terms of underlying dramas or actual poetry which could be said to have inspired him to composition. Such a person would not know how infinite is the range of music's capacity to express definite meaning to anyone who will only surrender to her language, who can be prevailed upon to speak and understand it. But quite apart from all this, Beethoven has, to put it bluntly, given us neither cause nor right to treat his work in such a manner and to read into it arbitrarily things with which it has nothing whatever to do.

The ideas which his works are meant to embody are a different matter. Thus, Wagner is, to some extent, justified in calling the seventh symphony an "apotheosis of the dance." This has something to do with the curious firmness of Beethoven's musical language mentioned above, with his power of construction, with his particular ability to formulate clearly the essential nature of every work, to render it complete in itself, to *isolate* it. In this sense, almost every one of Beethoven's works represents an idea which could be put into words. But this, as I have said before, is of little importance. Let who will delight in putting these "ideas" into barren words, in impaling the content of something boundlessly alive on the point of an interpretation, like a butterfly on a pin. I personally prefer to stick to the works themselves.—WILHELM FURTWÄNGLER

Bruno Walter

This definite turn toward the supremacy of the work of art in my musical development was completed as I came to understand—in the years of my adolescence—the symphonic literature and the quartets of Beethoven.

From the psychological point of view, it is not so difficult to understand that stage in a young musician's development when the compositions he plays serve merely as a springboard for the testing of his own wings. He cannot have reached the musical or spiritual maturity needed for probing the depth of a work of art; he is yet lacking in the knowledge and experience that could make him appreciate it in its details, let alone in its entirety. What is more natural than that musical talent should first show itself as a delight in making music?[1] In music-making, the youthful temperament and enthusiasm of the young musician, his song-bird joy and rhythmic fire, find full vent; in music-making, the young, striving soul, sustained and uplifted by the element of music, finds its liberation from everyday life—the ego becomes aware of itself and its powers.

When, after years of slow maturing, we have come to understand the work of music as a revelation of creative inspiration; when the composer and his work have become the *dominating* factor in our inner life; when we have put ourselves at the *service* of this "other one" and his work—will the voice of our soul then go from our music-making? The answer is an emphatic "no." If a pianist, in Beethoven's E flat major concerto, wishes to put himself fully at the service of Beethoven's genius in his rendering of this dithyrambic work, this does not imply an act of servile self-negation. On the contrary, he will only be successful in his endeavor if he freely unfolds his own self, to the limits of its capacity. In bringing to life the fire, the grace, the melancholy, the passion of the composer's work, what can he call upon but his own fire, his own grace, melancholy and passion? Greatness is needed for understanding and expressing greatness; tenderness and passion must be his who would perceive and represent another's tenderness and passion; none but a fiery apostle can promulgate the fire of the prophet. In short, it is only the great reproductive artist who is able to penetrate and proclaim the work of a great creative artist.

Thus, the ideal musical interpreter will be one who is wholly taken

[1] Translator's note: the original has "Musizierlust an sich."

up with the work, wholly in line with it, but who, at the same time, conjures up the full force of his personality. Yet though I may fully understand Beethoven's *Hammerklavier* Sonata, having appreciated its musical meaning, its form, and the emotional depth of each single feature, it does not follow from this that I can play it now in Beethoven's style, giving full due to its Promethean stature. Our incessant struggle with the countless details may have taken us toward Beethoven time and again; we may have become at home in the sphere of this particular work, yet all this amounts to no more than the preconditions of an authentic interpretation.

Beethoven's human personality stands clearly before our eyes; it impresses us decisively as that of a world-conqueror in the realm of the spirit. In his tearing-up of the *Eroica's* dedication to Napoleon we recognize the same tempestuous force that informs his musical idiom, and the *Heiligenstädter Testament* seems to us like a Beethoven Adagio in words; nearly everything, in fact, that is known to us of his personal character and conduct—his human relationships, his letters, the reports of his friends, the conversation-books, his profound wish for self-improvement—all these show his mighty, inspired, Promethean soul, instinct with all that is sublime as it speaks to us with overwhelming expressive power in his music.—BRUNO WALTER

Pablo Casals[1]

"A unanimous admiration has never been granted to Rameau, Bach, Mozart, Schubert, Wagner, Debussy and many other composers who have endowed music with discoveries more fertile and more original or positive than Beethoven has; however, this unanimity has sprung to life quite effortlessly round his name. For some years now, important musicians have shown signs of surprise at this anomaly, and hope that posterity will value with more precision and justice the contribution of a great musician whose character has been unwittingly misrepresented in literature. It is striking to realize that, in fact, Beethoven owes his dictatorship more to poets and novelists than to musicians." (Emile Vuillermoz.)[2]

Why use this word "dictatorship"? The immense radiance of Beethoven may have momentarily outshone the glory of other masters. This

---

[1] The following few pages are from the book: *Conversations with Casals*, by J. Ma. Corredor (translated from the French by André Mangeot, E. P. Dutton and Co., New York, 1957). All of the comments in italics are by M. Corredor or are otherwise identified in the text; all of those in regular print are by Casals himself.—Editor.
[2] All quotations from Vuillermoz are from his book, *Histoire de la Musique*.

sort of thing has always happened. But time has always given to everyone the glory he deserves. As for the musicians' attitude toward Beethoven, what should we say about Schubert, who is so close to him? And of the devotion of Schumann and Liszt? And the "unswerving" veneration of Wagner? I don't understand why such opinions should be reproduced. In any case, the greatness of Beethoven does not lie in the amount of discoveries he made in music but in the significance and transcendency of his message. In my opinion, anything that has been said—truly or falsely—about him will not diminish the radiance of the light such a mind has brought us, and it will always be looked upon as one of the most glorious gifts humanity has received.

"... *The abyss that separates the commonplace passages which abound in the nine symphonies from the sublime thoughts that we find everywhere in the sonatas and the string quartets.*" (Emile Vuillermoz.)

All geniuses, in the course of their lives, have been through a process of development which is influenced by their personal experience. But in all genius, the germ is the thing to observe: and with Beethoven, perhaps more than with other great composers, this germ appears already in the first *Opus*. That is the most important fact to notice, as against analyzing the process, which inevitably bears the marks of all stages every composer must go through.

It has been said that in the first Trios and Sonatas, the real Beethoven is already there.

Yes, the early Opuses already carry the germ of the *Ninth Symphony* and of the *Missa Solemnis*.

Opus 1 is the delicious Trio in E♭ major *which you played with Istomin and Fuchs this year* (1953) *in the Abbey of St. Michel de Cuxa?*

Yes, but Beethoven had written it when he was twenty-five. One can imagine the attempts and the gropings which must have preceded it, until he reached the mastery we already witness in this work.

Do you accept the famous division of Beethoven's works into "three manners"?

Yes, as long as we only wish to classify the period of some of his works, but not in order to draw irrelevant conclusions.

Would you say that the compositions of the third period are deeper and "musically superior" to the others?

Deeper, yes. The Beethoven of the later years seems to hover in a mysterious and sublime sphere. In any case, I would not dare to say that, purely as "works of art," the later works are superior to the early ones, not even to the earliest ones. One cannot fail to see that the Opus 1 is a masterpiece in the fullest meaning of the word.

Debussy criticized Beethoven for "describing" instead of "suggesting" or "insinuating," which, according to him, is the real role of music as an art.

One can "describe" or "suggest." What really matters is the result, not the method.

In one of the early string quartets of Beethoven we find the title Malinconia. *Do you think that Beethoven might have been the first to describe in music this melancholy which became a sort of disease among artists affected by* le mal du siècle?

As I pointed out to you before, we find that Bach has "described" all manner of feelings, including melancholy. And I think one could say the same thing about Mozart.

And what about the romantic attitude to nature, not as scenery outside the artist, but as an element in which he is absorbed? Beethoven, who wrote "Nobody has loved nature as I have," may have been the beginner of this movement.

It also depends how we consider nature as an inspiration in music. Who can say precisely how certain Italian composers of the XVIIth century reacted to nature, or Bach, or Handel, and so many others? In music, it is more difficult than in literature to establish neat divisions between one tendency and another, for instance between classicism and romanticism. Of course the pathos of Beethoven emphasizes certain aspects, but to go further and assert that these aspects have their musical origin in him is a big step which I am not ready to take.

Do you think that the quality of pathos in Beethoven comes from the "concentration of his soul"?

But with Mozart we also find, in spite of certain appearances, a "concentrated soul."

Arthur Honegger says: "What always puzzles the masses is that the great composer was deaf. One cannot deny that a great deal of the admiration devoted to Beethoven is due to his infirmity. To tell the truth, once we forget the tragic side of this situation, the fact remains that, as a creator, he could never hear the performance of his work, which must have raised many technical difficulties for him. However, I am tempted to say that this affliction forced him to 'wall' himself in, and helped him to concentrate with all his genius, and, in so doing to avoid the 'insipidity' and 'banalities' of those days."[1]

This deafness naturally affected Beethoven's character. However, I would say that the great strength of his mind already protected him from the usual banalities of life, which surrounded him just as they do each one of us.

How do you see Beethoven as a man?

Just as he appears in the documents we have about him, the testimony of his contemporaries and the descriptions of his biographers. I have not got a personal picture of him in my mind. Although I can say that I have seen Beethoven and have spoken to him . . . in a dream, of course!

[1] Arthur Honegger: *Je suis compositeur.* (Editions du Conquistador. Paris.)

It was the Beethoven of the last period, a man stricken by a great sorrow, but a very serene sorrow.

When writers, not musicians, speak of Beethoven . . .

It all depends how they set about it. For instance, I very much like the biography by Edouard Herriot. On the other hand, without wishing to depreciate the value and the interest of Romain Rolland's writing, I fear that, when he sometimes gets mixed up with very technical questions, he generally shows that he is not qualified for it.

It has been said that in Fidelio *the composer appears more like a poet than a lyrical author for the stage.*

Yes, everyone seems to think that Beethoven did not feel at ease with the stage. It may be true. Everyone to his own opinion. But can anyone deny the unforgettable impression *Fidelio* makes on the listener?

Wagner recounts in Mein Leben *that after the final rehearsal of the Ninth Symphony in Dresden in 1849, Bakunin said to him "that if all music were to be destroyed in the coming universal conflagration, we ought at the risk of our lives to unite to preserve this symphony."*

It does indeed deserve to survive eternally, but perhaps Bakunin was mainly thinking of the *Hymn of Brotherhood*, in the last movement.

Seid umschlungen, Millionen!—and then, when we hear this call in our own times—and think of the hydrogen bomb . . . ! In spite of all gruesome predictions and dangers we must not lose our faith. I have always believed the day would come when the *Ode to Joy* would be sung by all the peoples of the earth. I inscribed this thought in the Book of the League of Nations at Geneva.

Vincent d'Indy has said that Beethoven's Sonatas are dominated by the search for an idea. On the other hand, Furtwängler, having asserted that Beethoven is neither a poet, nor a moralist, nor a philosopher, but only a musician, goes on to say: "It appears that Beethoven, more than any other musician, tends to answer the question put by his ideas in the most purely musical form possible. . . . He does not go half-way to meet the poet. And that is why he is not lyrical like Schubert, or a dramatic musician like Wagner. If he appears to be less willing to reconcile words and music, it is not because he is less of a musician, but because he is more so, more exclusively a musician."[1]

First of all, I think that nobody can be "more exclusively a musician" than Schubert is. That Beethoven has answered his ideas by elaborating purely musical forms seems to be quite evident. But I must say that I don't see very clearly what Furtwängler means with all this—perhaps his words are a bit exaggerated. Otherwise, how could we explain the character of supreme exaltation we find in the *Hymn of Brotherhood* in the *Ninth Symphony* so intimately adapted to the central idea of Schiller's text? I only give this as an example.

---

[1] All the quotations from Furtwängler are extracted from his book, *Entretiens sur la Musique*.

Curiously enough Furtwängler says about the finale of the Ninth Symphony: "*This theme—a theme par excellence, a theme of the highest type, the discovery of a great musician if ever there was one, this theme could not be in any way conceived in order to comment or expound one particular text. Just the opposite: it looks as if it were the poem which expounds the theme.*"

This theme becomes the musical climax (exclusively musical) of this symphony, but I cannot agree with anyone who says that it was not inspired by the *Ode to Joy*. When I hear it, I get an impression which is almost religious, a sort of feeling of fraternity, and it penetrates me like a glorious musical rendering of the poetical humanitarianism of Schiller.

"*With Beethoven great discoveries, especially the invention of themes and of details, are numerous. But that is not what his genius is made of, and those who see traces of hard work almost everywhere are not far from the truth. But his intuition goes much deeper, and that, in his best works, allows him to find a grouping of themes, made to complement each other by some inevitable law.*" (Wilhelm Furtwängler.)

Supposing Beethoven had one quality only; for instance, that of inventing great themes, but was lacking in the one Furtwängler talks about, he would not be the great composer he is. However, we find him complete because he possesses these two qualities among many others. As for the themes, it is true that we can find in his notebooks all the transformations they underwent, which show the difficulties he encountered before these themes finally took shape. If we take the slow movement of the *Eroica Symphony*, we shall see how many phases it went through before its completion. Nothing of the kind happened with Mozart or Schubert, whose themes emerged entire and complete in themselves, at least, so it seems to me.

Beethoven, I feel sure, had to fight with his material, and his works did not reach perfection until they had undergone many transformations. These transformations sometimes consisted of changing one note only, as we see in the initial theme of the *Ninth Symphony* (which is in my possession) where the previously modified note corresponds with a similar chord, and where this transformation simply gives a different rhythmical aspect to the final version.

"*In Bach we find that the whole piece with all its developments exists implicitly in the theme. In fact, Bach never wanders away from the material of his principal theme, even in a fugue where there are countersubjects, the style remains essentially monothematic. But in Beethoven, though the need for development in any theme is just as urgent, the way to it is not rigorously planned, as it is with Bach. The reason is that, with Beethoven, the development does not rest exclusively on the first theme. He has many, and through their contrast and interpenetration, the development proceeds on different lines.*" (Furtwängler.)

Yes! That is what we find in Bach and in Beethoven. The latter has felt the necessity of mixing up different themes. It can be compared to a tree-trunk from which start so many ramifications. And sometimes we find Beethoven producing all of a sudden a completely unexpected theme. One is tempted to ask, "Where does it come from?" With Bach we find that, the requirements of musical expression being different, he does not proceed on the same lines. As we said before, Bach goes right down to the bottom of the initial theme, and exploits it deeply. Is the Beethoven form an innovation? Of course it is, but he achieves it simply by saying what he has to say without veil or artifice.—J. M. CORREDOR

A Summing Up

In [the outline] of Beethoven's spiritual development we have regarded him chiefly as an explorer. What we may call his emotional nature was sensitive, discriminating, and profound, and his circumstances brought him an intimate acquaintance with the chief characteristics of life. His realization of the character of life was not hindered by insensitiveness, as was Wagner's, nor by religion, as was Bach's. There was nothing in this man, either natural or acquired, to blunt his perceptions. And he was not merely sensitive; he was not merely a reflecting mirror. His experiences took root and grew. An inner life of quite extraordinary intensity was in process of development till the very end. Other artists, of those few whose spirits were both sensitive and free, seem to have passed through similar stages of development. But perhaps even Shakespeare never reached that final stage of illumination that is expressed in some of Beethoven's late music. The other steps of the journey he knew, but Shakespeare never wrote his C sharp minor quartet. It is possible, indeed, that Beethoven's late music is unique, not only in music, but in the whole of art.

Although we have regarded Beethoven's music from its philosophic aspect, it is not for the purpose of deducing a philosophy from it. Beethoven's greatest music has meaning in the sense that it is not a mere pattern of sounds, but possesses a spiritual content; nevertheless, it does not in any sense express a philosophy. It expresses certain primary experiences as organized in the mind of this particular artist. But this organization of experience is utterly different from the organization of experience presented in a philosophy. It is an organization to which the

criteria of logical coherence do not in the least apply. Beethoven's profoundest attitude toward life, as expressed in his music, owes nothing
to the mediation of his intelligence. The synthesis of his experience
that is achieved by a great artist proceeds according to laws of which we
know almost nothing, but purely intellectual formulation plays a very
small part in it. If Beethoven reached the state, as we believe he did,
where he achieved the "submission" he felt to be so necessary, it was
not through any process of reasoning. And his realization of the necessity
of submission could not have been reached by any such process. As a
crude analogy we may suggest that there are spiritual appetites, as
there are bodily ones, necessary for development but which, like the
sexual appetite, make their appearance only at a certain stage of growth.
Comparatively few men, even among artists, manifest a true spiritual
growth. Their attitude toward life is relatively fixed; it may be exemplified
with more richness and subtlety as they mature, but it does not develop.
Such a transition, as we find from Beethoven's "second" to his "third"
period, where nothing is abandoned and yet where everything is changed,
is extremely rare. Beethoven, therefore, although he preached no philosophy, is of philosophical importance because he adds one to the very few
cases that exist of a genuine spiritual development. Such cases, it might
be said, do nothing to help the development of mankind. Beethoven's
music illustrates the development, but throws no light on the process
by which it came about. But such revelations have a strangely haunting
quality. We may be unable to earn for ourselves the capacity to utter
the prayer of thanksgiving of the A minor quartet, or to reach the state of
final serenity of the fugue of the C sharp minor quartet, but we can
henceforth take but little account of attitudes toward life that leave no
room for these experiences, attitudes which deny them or explain them
away. And our conviction that these experiences are valuable, even to us,
is reinforced by the whole bulk of Beethoven's work. If they stood alone
these superhuman utterances might seem to us those of an oracle who
was hardly a man. But we know, from the rest of his music, that
Beethoven was a man who experienced all that we can experience, who
suffered all that we can suffer. If, in the end, he seems to reach a state
"above the battle" we also know that no man ever knew more bitterly
what the battle is.—J. W. N. SULLIVAN

After an intervening century, it is especially appropriate to recall the
speech made by Grillparzer at Beethoven's grave. "He was an artist, and
what he was, was he through his art alone." Only that part of the life
of Beethoven which can be heard in the concert-room matters to us now,
and properly to appreciate it is to set in a diminishing perspective the
occurrence and opinions which caught the attention of contemporaries.
Unlovable and yet—since we are at a safe distance—in such need of

love that it is hard to read of him without affection; speechless and clumsy, yet with an unforced grandeur of aspiration which preserves him from ridicule; ungrateful, loutish, untruthful; by no means exempt from snobbery and a harsh self-righteousness, yet built to a scale so large that these qualities are relegated to a province of him—that province which comprises the whole life of more ordinary people—we can watch him without either awe or repulsion. Like the slow building of coral, his barren, ugly life of every day sufficed to carry forward an invisible process of creation.

The simplicity which all who knew him remarked in him, that simplicity which shows itself even in the forms of his misanthropy, allowed room for his greatness. It is, perhaps, essential to such greatness that he should have been so little of a clever man. When he rose at five in the morning, and bawled and stamped over his music, and kicked the desk in contrapuntal rhythms, we need not suppose that his conscious mind was struggling to express a concept of Giulietta Guicciardi or a personified Freedom; we need not pretend to explore very far his conscious processes of thought. He was trying to obey an instinct which demanded certain effects—effects which, once found, realized, sometimes perhaps even prompted, the emotion to which they afterwards were linked. The apparent discrepancy, then, between all that Beethoven seemed to *be* and all that we know he has *done* becomes less when we remember that the conscious mind of a creator works chiefly as a powerhouse to feed the unconscious—or perhaps it would be a better simile to call it a mechanism for collecting, storing, and later transcribing, impressions the significance of which is never wholly perceived until they are stabilized in a work of art.

His contemporaries were quick to perceive the paradox that a life such as Beethoven's has to be reconciled with music both lucid and noble. They accepted the sense of liberation in his manner of writing; they recognized the difference in range between his own work and that of his ablest forerunners, such as Bach[1] or Mozart or Haydn. After his death they went so far as to canonize his technical procedures and to identify the dimensions of his music with the ideal. Thus, his symphonies became, for the better part of a century, the unquestioned model for all symphonies; to rival Beethoven on his own ground became the hallmark of an elevated musical gift; and Vienna itself, as the home of Beethoven, acquired a position not unlike that of Rome in the religious world. In the persons of Brahms and Mahler an apostolic succession had to be assured until the Empire was swept away and the Vienna school disintegrated in America.

[1] It is a mistake to assume that Bach was a private discovery of Mendelssohn. As average a musician as Cramer was a devoted admirer of his music; and a Dr. Müller, who met Beethoven in 1820, "ventured" in a subsequent letter to compare him to Bach.

The extent to which Beethoven influenced the entire nineteenth century can be gauged by the welcome, not unmixed with surprise, given to the classical revivalism which succeeded it. A large public, nourished on the symphonic shapes and colors which derive from Beethoven, discovered—largely through the unexpected prompting of Strauss and of Stravinsky—that Handel and Mozart and Haydn offer examples of musical thought as rich, and possibilities of expression not less varied. This discovery, after the vast inflation of Beethoven's manner which filled the following century, was refreshing; it was also bewildering to those who hitherto had set his work entire in an aesthetic category of its own.

In consequence, it became fashionable, between the wars, to admire especially that part of Beethoven's music in which he gave a special subtlety to universal emotions without losing the sense of their breadth—in particular, the quartets. To ears accustomed to the sensuous scoring of the Russians, to the astringency of Central Europe, to French delicacy and Spanish rhythm, the symphonies inevitably lost their original air of powerful innovation. The quartets, however, by the nature of their medium, have proved timeless. They strain the resources of chamber music no less than the most arduous work of the present day; the listener, once used to the dynamic range of a quartet, has been jaded by no subsequent extension of technical resources. And so, as the symphonies recede, little by little, in critical estimation, the chamber music—and not the quartets only—are generally accepted as the supreme examples of Beethoven's art: a judgment which is unlikely to be revised by those whose canons are aesthetic rather than historical.

Herr Bekker has pointed out that of all very great composers Beethoven wrote the least. At the time of his death, of which he had no prescience, he was only beginning to satisfy himself that he had mastered his material. In a sense, therefore, his end is more tragic than that of Mozart or Schubert, young as they were, for he had set himself a more difficult aim than they, and was finding his way out of a hampering obscurity when he died. This obscurity is the harder to penetrate in that it arises less from complexity of emotion than from the personal nature of that emotion. Beethoven speaks from his own heart; his forerunners had applied their gifts to the common condition of humanity. Our greater familiarity with subjective art may make us unduly impatient of his solutions; we are aware of a struggle, yet unconvinced that the conflicting forces have been properly assessed. Nevertheless, it is impossible not to perceive the intensity of his struggle even though, like the cloud-figures of the Brocken, the reflection we now see is capriciously distorted by its distance from the original. Above all, Beethoven has changed the course of European music by inventing what today is called a tune: that is, a combination of cadence and surprise, which can be extended or varied at will to conclude, in terms of musical logic, a recognizable emotional situation. The tunes of the earlier masters have not the same autobiographical flavor; they are cooler, more dispassionate statements, polite, less entire, less authoritative. And the best of Beethoven's music has succeeded in finding a tune, and applying to it a resourcefulness, appropriate to any emotional complex which can be expressed in musical notation.

It may be objected that much of what Beethoven had to say is now commonplace or antiquated. The concept of personal nobility—the concept which inspired the subtlest Romantic art—is out of fashion, the concept of man as the central product of the universe—a doctrine which alone makes Romanticism intelligible—has few defenders; the world of 1820 has been reproved or overlaid or simply put aside by five generations each more doctrinaire than the last. Beethoven was himself too little of an intellectual to codify his own intentions; nevertheless, he could not wholly escape the metaphysical preoccupations of his own time. He is the Chateaubriand of music, in his romantic mood: occasionally absurd, occasionally irritating, never negligible. And, in addition, he employs with more humanity the extraordinary additional dimension which belongs to music alone: a dimension which escapes such labels as classical or romantic, Dionysiac or Apollonian.

Although he paid small attention to the forms of religion, he was passionately interested in those expressions of ethical conduct by which the early nineteenth century hoped to reconcile Reason with the divine. We know that he wished to impregnate his music with high moral purposes—an attitude which reflected a general insistence in his time upon the importance of the individual. He saw himself as a regenerative force. His private world had much in it that was noble in a wider sense even than the Goethean; it was warmer, more approachable. And at the same time he possessed an unequaled power of suggesting grandeur: a power which might be applied, as in the overture *Die Weihe des Hauses*, to an occasion as intimate as the opening of a small theater, with a majesty which would not appear forced at the dedication of an imperial city.

There is no likelihood, therefore, that the clearer light in which his personal life can now be viewed will interpose an unnecessary distraction between his admirers and his music. The legends which have often surrounded him do not easily bear investigation. He cannot easily be pitied for his courage in face of constant adversity, exalted for his sturdy independence, wondered at for the endurance with which he supported an unendurable family, or exonerated from the weight of his nephew's misdemeanors. His complaints may appear, on the contrary, extravagant, his independence be called rudeness outright, and his family may be conceived to have suffered more at his hands than he at theirs. But these evidences of human weakness, if they obtrude upon his

music at all, only give it a sharper poignancy; so that the almost unquestioned position of Beethoven at the summit of musical creation
can be ascribed to a general recognition of his power to erect the
somber fragments of human fallibility into a due monument. It tran-
scends and compensates us all.—ALAN PRYCE-JONES

Throughout this book[1] Beethoven has functioned as a versatile emancipator. We have seen him, by sheer personal magnetism, force of will,
and intensity of genius, liberate the art of music from the long-standing
indignity of being carried on by lackeys. We have seen him establish
the composer's vocation upon a professional basis. No longer, thanks to
Beethoven, would a musical genius sup, like Mozart, at the servants'
table or, like that unhappy lad, be kicked from the hall or discharged at a
moment's notice. The poor boy from Bonn was the first composer to
attain the dignity of seeing his symphonies printed in score.[2]
We have seen Beethoven deliver the music of his day from the
ignominious role of obsequious hanger-on of the fashionable world and
make it a universal thing—a materialization of the utmost range of the
human mind and spirit, omitting none of the peaks and abysses. We
have followed this imperious figure as he emancipated personality in
music, detonating in his scores such a profound charge of thought and
passionate emotion that the world still vibrates with the shock.
In this heroic campaign Beethoven did not scorn the most apparently
trivial details. A factor in the triumphant emergence of personality in
music was his minute and painstaking labor in developing nuance, through
the extension and invention of dynamic symbols and other marks of
expression.
He took Continental music from the salon to the concert hall; from
the castle to the cottage, and made it the most democratic thing in the
aesthetic world.

Through Beethoven melody has become emancipated from the influence of fashion and fluctuating taste, and elevated to an eternally
valid type of pure humanity.—RICHARD WAGNER.

To him we owe the absolute emancipation of instrumental music
from the trammels of polite artistic society . . . his hand . . . gained
for us the full measure of spiritual democracy which is our artistic
heritage to-day.—ERNEST WALKER.

The sum of his message was freedom, artistic freedom, political
freedom, personal freedom of will, of art, of faith, freedom of the individual in all the aspects of life.—PAUL BEKKER.

Freedom above all.—BEETHOVEN.

[1] Robert Schauffler, Beethoven—the Man Who Freed Music.
[2] Hermann Kretzschmar, Gesammelte Aufsätze über Musik.

He loosed this already grown-up art from the incongruous nursery and gave it a rightful place—for the first time on equal terms—among its adult brethren. For this act Richard Wagner paid him tribute:

> Through these last, and to us still unknown works of our wondrous master [Beethoven's posthumous quartets], of all others, the power of musical expression has taken a direction from which the music of earlier periods was often bound to hold deliberately aloof; I will here call that direction *the tenderly and deliberately passionate,* through whose expression music has first raised herself to an equal height with the poetry and painting of the greatest periods of the past. While with this expression Dante, Shakespeare, Calderon, and Goethe, like the great masters of painting in Italy and the Netherlands, took fee of every portrayable object in the world and man; and while it was this that first enabled them to paint the world and man: in music there had ruled an axiom which openly degraded her as a branch of Art, an axiom borrowed from the purely physical pleasure, the purely sensuous entertainment to be found in her.[1]

Beethoven liberated form, not from law, but from the specious compulsions of superficial and modish laws. He did much to free musical forms from slavery to the clogging conventions of formalism, and to give them that profound inner necessity through which they have ever since carried conviction. Nor was he wrecked on the reef of amorphism, which has meant destruction to so many romanticists.

As a practical harmonist he broke ground for the skyscraper of twentieth-century piano harmony. Philipp Emanuel Bach's innovation, the monodic style, had been used by Haydn and Mozart in their stand against the old polyphony. Beethoven's personal genius assimilated and hallmarked the contributions of these men and created a new harmonic, or chordal, technique for keyboard instruments. What was tentative, experimental in Hayden developed into Beethoven's characteristic idiom.[2]

He also freed modulation, brushing aside numerous hampering rules and enriching his harmonic scheme to match the liberty he had won in other departments.

This first great nature lover among composers took the art out of the study, purged it of whatever smell of the lamp still clung to it, and gave it the run of meadow and forest.

He freed music from that cloistered outlook which ignored the march of events in the outside world of action, as Palestrina, Bach, and Haydn had ignored them.

By his choice of texts he presented vocal music with the freedom of the world of great literature—a pioneer accomplishment.

[1] In his report to King Ludwig II of Bavaria upon the establishment of a German music school in Munich.

[2] As early as the *finale* of the F minor sonata (Opus 2, No. 1) the *Largo e mesto* of the D major (Opus 10, No. 3) and the introduction of the *Pathetique* (Opus 13).

Through the accidental circumstance that the B minor Mass of Bach was not published until years after Beethoven's *Missa,* our hero became the Luther among composers, extricating the Mass from the bonds of convention and dogma.

He released the dramatic overture from subservience to that hybrid thing, opera; and the concerto orchestra from its abject servility as a mere accompanist to the solo part.

More than any previous composer, he rid music of the exhibitionistic taint of virtuosity for virtuosity's sake, and the reproach of composing to the order of outer compulsion rather than from inner necessity.

His ingenuity helped to throw open to the piano and the orchestra a new world of richness and sonority. The accident of his deafness freed the art in another way, by decreeing a divorce between composer and virtuoso and smashing the harmful old convention that the creative musician must necessarily fritter away his energies in interpretive work.

Perhaps his supreme achievement as emancipator was the exertion of a more potent influence than that of his greatest predecessors toward freeing music from the shackles of literature, whose servant it was in the beginning. By pouring into music a wealth of suggestive factors which made it so much more opulent and self-contained than ever before, he made it easier for the imagination of the ordinary listener at length to escape from the weakening incubus of cliché programs and, under the stimulus of this powerfully independent art, to fashion its own poetic interpretations.

Beethoven did more than any other composer has ever done toward realizing that utopian dream of the day when "all men shall be poets." It was scarcely his fault that mistaken inferences drawn from the *Pastoral* symphony, and from the regrettable *finale* of the *Choral* (which, too late, he himself regretted), should have led to a new enslavement of music by the poetic idea. Happily our own day is witnessing a fresh revolt from this degradation. The true lover of music must rejoice that, from the time when centenary thoughts of the Master commenced to hold the minds of all musicians, the world currents of thought and inclination seemed to begin setting away from the compromise relativities of opera and program music toward the pure absolutism of Bach, Brahms, Franck, and Beethoven.

Beethoven found the art of music narrowed to the pastime of a special class. He made it broadly human. He left it superhuman. Of course he was far from being the only man who ever freed music. In many ages and lands the art has been enslaved and has found its liberators. But the most potent of all these was Beethoven.

A century after his death, why does Beethoven stand as the central— if not the chief—figure in music?

For one thing, because he was perhaps an even greater master of construction than the men who made the frieze of the Parthenon, *Macbeth*, the Sistine frescoes, the B minor Mass, and Chartres Cathedral.

By forcing himself to sketch the plan of a movement before he had its subjects more than dimly in mind, he brought into music an architectonic idea hitherto foreign to it. This is the way masters of the other arts often work. The novelist and dramatist frequently start with the plot and build up their architectural plan before the characters take on life or the setting emerges. The painter finds it natural to determine his color scheme and emotional outline before he knows exactly what figures are to appear in his fresco. The sculptor blocks out the important bony planes of his bust before focusing on details of features or drapery.

For a composer this way of working requires more concentrated imagination than for any other artist. But it is capable of accomplishing inestimable results. When Beethoven adapted to music this commonplace method of the other arts he performed a creative exploit of the first importance.[1]

We have seen how he took the charming, graceful, polished forms handed down to him by Haydn and Mozart, purified them of their superficial formalism, filled them instead with his own generous and fiery spirit, and made them "internal as well as external."[2] "His emotions," writes Mr. H. L. Mencken, "at their highest flight were almost godlike; he gave music a sort of Alpine grandeur."

In sonata-form movements we have watched him make a clean sweep of the star-play of "brilliant passages," the "dish-clatter" of bridgework, and the cut-and-dried sort of development in which the hearer knew all too well what was coming next because it advanced and retreated like certain armies in the late war, "according to a prearranged plan." We have followed his iconoclastic progress as he remodeled the anticlimactic "cracker-box" type of recapitulation which vainly tried to raise two laughs with the same story. And we have watched him replace it with a new and unpredictable version of the exposition. We have marveled as he took the ancient coda, which brought the old-fashioned movement to a close as briefly and formally as the word "finis," and made of it a glorious and significant thing that sometimes rivaled all the rest of the structure in size, interest, and splendor. This coda exploit was much as though he had found a cathedral consisting of nothing but a large entrance portal, a nave, and a bricked-up transept, in the east side of which there was a tiny door for egress. It was as though he had converted this door into a tremendous breach and had then completed the cathedral with an apse generous and radiant as the choir of Beauvais.

[1] For a most readable discussion of this subject see Newman, *The Unconscious Beethoven*, p. 115 ff.
[2] See Sir Hubert H. Parry's article: "Form," *Grove's Dictionary*, 3d ed.

We have seen Beethoven growing all his life progressively farther from the rococo procedure described by Sir Hubert H. Parry:

> Prior to Beethoven, the development of a long work was based upon antitheses of distinct tunes and concrete lumps of subject representing separate organisms, either merely in juxtaposition, or loosely connected by more or less empty passages.[1]

But the Master progressively changed all this. Until, in the last sonatas and quartets:

> the material is so continuous and unified that we are barely conscious of the passage from one theme to another. Sometimes the structure is so closely knit that even the searching eye of an analyst is defied.[2]

This, however, was by no means all that Beethoven did to form. He began with sonatas as long as the Mozart symphonies; went on to make symphonies twice as long as these; and finally in the *Hammerklavier* and the C sharp minor, lengthened the sonata and the quartet to correspond. Taking a cue from the suite of Bach's day, he increased the prescribed number of quartet movements to six or seven. In a word, he regenerated the formalism of sonata-form and made it a thing of enhanced beauty, vitality, and expressiveness.

Meanwhile he carried his audience along with him; for by some fortunate chance this man appeared at just the moment when music lovers had begun to find their way about in the neatly demarcated sonata-form of rococo days and sighed for more difficulties to conquer.

[We] may follow in detail the development of Beethoven's skill in the use of that interlocking thematic device we have called the germ-motive, by which he, first of composers, brought about complete inter-movement unity in long works.

This development of intermovement liaison had important results. It led to such unified one-movement sonatas as Liszt's B minor, and to that suppression of pauses between different sections of symphonies which, combined with the influence of the *Pastoral*, ended in the one-movement symphonic poem.

In Part II, chapters LV and LVI,[3] will be found studies of Beethoven's equally remarkable use of what we have called source-motives which lent thematic unity to his life work.

Beethoven changed for the better almost every form he touched. Even such a trivial and crystallized affair as the rondo he diversified,

---

[1] Article: "Sonata," *Grove's Dictionary*, 3d ed.
[2] Grace, *Beethoven*, p. 214.
[3] Schauffler, Robert. *"Beethoven—the Man Who Freed Music."* A study of those chapters is highly recommended for students interested in the interdependence of themes and motives in Beethoven's creative output.—Editor.

made more spacious, and endowed with elasticity, bringing it closer to sonata-form.

But he was not quite so successful with the strict fugue. He experimented at combining this with other forms. These experiments were seldom entirely happy, because the foreign matter introduced for relief tended to injure the fugue's essential oneness and make it too diffuse. Yet, after all, this originality was sometimes justified by magnificently satisfying examples, such as the finales of the third Rasoumowsky quartet and of the A flat sonata, the *Et vitam venturi* from the *Missa*, and supremely by the perfect opening of the C sharp minor quartet.

Of all Beethoven's concrete contributions to the art of music three were most original and powerful. There was (1) the first movement of titanic and elemental struggle (*Eroica, Serioso* quartet, Fifth, *Choral*).

There was (2) the scherzo of tumultuous humor and Dionysiac exultation or of elfin wit (*Eroica*, first Rasoumowsky, *Hammerklavier, Choral*). He did not invent the name scherzo. Haydn first quickened the minuet and called it by this attractive name. But Beethoven took what was handed him; broadened, deepened, elevated, and generally rebuilt it physically, intellectually, and emotionally into one of his most brilliantly original creations.

There was (3) the ethereal slow movement of mystic exaltation (*Choral*, B flat trio, twelfth, thirteenth, and fifteenth quartets, *Benedictus* of *Missa*, and C minor sonata, Opus 111). His supreme adagios in variation form decidedly outnumber those in song form.

> Beethoven's treatment of the variation-form is singularly interesting: it may be briefly described as a gradual advance back to the methods of Bach . . . in [his] colossal "Goldberg" variations (founded solely on the bass of the theme), which reaches its climax, in Beethoven's works, in the late pianoforte variations on a waltz of Diabelli. In this final aspect of the variation-form the merely melodic connection is secondary or indeed frequently non-existent: harmony and structure are the chief essential points, and though these may be altered to almost any extent, yet there is always, so to speak, the same intellectual thread running through the whole; and in place of the old rigid and merely decorative ideal, we have an ideal of unity in diversity, of the same subject presented in continually shifting and new lights.[1]

Beethoven was elementally original. Whenever the spirit moved him he could squeeze blood out of bricks. And he made rubies of the blood, and platinum of the residue of the bricks, and organized these products into miracles of design that would have put Benvenuto Cellini to shame. He could find laughter, beauty, and wonder in his own blaze of farcical fury over the loss of a groschen. (And he was capable of real fury, as

[1] Ernest Walker, *Beethoven*, 1920, p. 159.

well, on such an original provocation.) He could make an evolutionary epic—or the crack of doomsday—out of the peep of a small bird which was all but inaudible to his deaf ears.

Mr. John Middleton Murry's statement about the simple originality of Jesus might apply, almost word for word, to Beethoven.

> His qualities were all new: his quickness of apprehension, his profound simplicity of speech, his astonishing power of revealing an abysm of meaning through a transparent phrase—these appear before us in a combination so harmonious that we take them, as it were, for granted. They seem natural; and they are natural. Nothing is so new as a new naturalness, none so difficult to apprehend. A new simplicity is the most baffling of all human achievements, and the most perdurable.[1]

One reason why the musical embodiment of Beethoven's emotions was more original than that of his predecessors was this: He thought more deeply than they, and his music represented that deeper thought sublimated into feeling.

This music was an unprecedented thing under the sun. In spite of its liberal use of borrowed material, it differed astonishingly from other music. The contrast was almost as sharp as if a winged man had suddenly begun beating his majestic pinions and flashing his irised mail above the stupefied picnickers in the Viennese Prater.

> It was not merely [writes Mr. W. J. Turner] that music had been more formal in shape, more restricted in content, but that nobody before Beethoven had lived in his music, had imaged his life so fully in music. Earlier composers, Monteverde, Palestrina, Bach, Handel and Mozart, no doubt lived to some extent in their music. But we do not get from it the same impression of personality.[2]

A strong factor in Beethoven's originality was his dramatic power. This was best shown when unhandicapped by librettos, in overtures like *Egmont, Coriolanus,* and those named *Leonore.* The Master could condense more drama into four notes and a pause than Lord Tennyson could get into four acts, a prologue, and an epilogue. He could imply the momentousness of true dramatic suspense and conflict not only by the opposition of *mf* to *ff* and of *sf* to an abruptly following *mp,* but by the contrast with each other of phrases, subjects, sections, movements, and whole works within a group.

In these ways he was a tremendous innovator. And his dramatic sense even extended beyond nuance to a remarkable use of the symbols of literary expression. For example, in a letter to Schindler, 1823, he referred to his next of kin in these terms: "my brother?!"

The unexpectedness of Beethoven—even at the fiftieth repetition

[1] *Jesus, Man of Genius,* 1926, pp. 162–63.
[2] *Beethoven,* 1927, p. 31.

—is one of the major clues to his power over us. For he is so extremely un-
forseeable, yet after all so inevitable, that we more easily forget how his
music goes than in the case of other composers. He tricks us, artfully
holds us in harrowing suspense. By implication he strews between the
lines of his staves the impalpable largesse of wisdom, of delicate allusion
and sheer loveliness, for us to ferret out as we may. He tickles our
curiosity by offering two alternative solutions equally plausible, only to
settle on a third, undreamed-of but utterly convincing. He mocks our
tender emotion by drumming on the keys with the shaft of his ruthless
quill and the flat of his great paw. When we embark with him on some
foaming tide of Gargantuan fun he leaves us abruptly in the lurch.

> And our sincerest laughter
> With some pain is fraught.

He is always surprising, perennially unpredictable. A chief reason why
he charms us so completely is that almost every musical expedition on
which he allows us to accompany him turns into a hidden treasure hunt—
in the right spot.

He left [declares Dr. Dyson] thirty-two piano sonatas and nine
symphonies, yet the more intimately they are known the less can one
hazard even a guess as to what the thirty-third sonata or the tenth
symphony would be like. They would be Beethoven, and that is but
the statement of a formal enigma. How many movements they
would have, and which would be which; what would be the psychological mood of any or all of them either in detail or as a whole; whether
the theme would be slight and the handling sublime; whether there
would be an orgy of rhythm or a feast of melody, or both; whether
they would follow an old form or invent a new one; all these are
matters on which nothing intelligible can be said. He would state,
in some new and surprising way, ideas which so soon as they were
grasped would seem to be as inevitable as they were unaccountable.
We talk somewhat glibly of sonata-form and attach it to the name of
Beethoven. There never was a greater deception. It is no doubt possible to extract from his movements two themes and a coda, and to
say that here is, or might be, or should be, a double bar, and so forth.
But it is often equally possible to extract three or four or five themes,
though what will be their order of importance is beyond anyone to
lay down. . . . The late sonatas and quartets are admitted to be
beyond formal classification. He was descended in a measure from
Haydn and Mozart, but it is none the less true that the moment we
recognize his models we lose him. The things he himself said were
just those that had no place in his inherited architecture. Beethoven
is the creative iconoclast.[1]

He had that infectious intensity, that almost superhuman vitality characteristic of the great. His canvases suggest as profuse a lavishness of life

[1] *The New Music*, 1923, pp. 121–22.

as those of Rubens and Rembrandt, of Balzac and Dante and Shakespeare.
Yet they are never centrifugal. They reveal instead the economy and concentration of a New Testament parable.

Whatever he may have sometimes been as a man, when it came to music
Beethoven was nearly always big. It was not his way to let the notes hide
the melody or the details conceal the essentials. What artist of smaller
caliber could have stood like a colossus with one foot in classicism and one
in romanticism, taking the best of each and fusing them into that higher
thing which we have called "Beethovenism"?

Ever since he scrawled those memorable words beneath Moscheles's
piano score of *Fidelio*, Beethoven's "Man, help thyself!" spirit has been
a growing inspiration to humanity. Since the Great War a strong movement has actually started in Germany and Austria toward a modern
religion of strength and self-dependence, with Beethoven as its founder.

But even if he should fail as a prophet and the founder of a new
religious order, he is already recognized as a potent physician. There
is in his music something for everybody, everywhere, always. He is the
healer, friend, and consoler[1] of humanity. If we are sad, tired, agitated,
dull, wakeful, blue, bored, fainthearted, oppressed by ugliness; if we suffer
from a torpid imagination or from having the world too much with us,
we may find in his music a richer variety of effective antidotes than in
that of any other composer.[2] And, having found, we may echo that
closing line of Miss Millay's sonnet: *On Hearing a Symphony of Beethoven:*

> Music my rampart, and my only one.

After taking a Beethoven cure one understands why this man was the
chief consoler and fortifier of the Central Powers in the Great War and of
those Allies who were so large-minded as not to let national bitterness
taint the world of beauty. One is not surprised to learn that the Bol-
shevists adopted Beethoven's as the official music of their movement. And
one grasps more fully the truth in that remark of his to Bettina: "He
who truly understands my music must thereby go free of all the misery
which others bear about with them." Would that the poor physician had
been able to heal himself!

As a healer he will be found 99 per cent Jekyll and 1 per cent Hyde.
Like the ideal man of medicine, this man almost never spared himself.
With incredible faithfulness and courage he kept pouring out his force

---

[1] Readers of Proust's great novel will recall that, on the death of the hero's grandmother, her sisters telegraphed the single word "Beethoven." What piece did they have
in mind? Was it the *Cavatina*, or the slow movement of the *Pathétique*, "*Apassionata*,"
second Rasoumowsky, "*Archduke*," or *Choral*? (*Le Côté de Guermantes*, Vol. II, p.
34.)
[2] See chapter, "The Musical Pharmacy," in *The Musical Amateur*, 1911, and "Directions" and musical recipes in *The Poetry Cure with Music and Pictures*, 1927; both by
the author.

through his pen until the music was as good as it could be made. As Voltaire said of another artist, "He labored at every new work as if he had his reputation still to make." The mass of sketches for the C sharp minor quartet alone is staggering to contemplate, especially when one notices the amount of splendid material he set down and then rejected as not good enough. His six false starts on the fourth movement alone make a thrilling object lesson on the conscientious idealism of genius and on the steadfastness and desperation of effort which often goes to the making of immortal things.

Naturally no man's work can be all best; otherwise there would be none of those contrasts on which the very nature of the superlative depends. His personal life was a succession of trough and crest, and his work more or less followed suit. One might graphically show the comparative quality of the nine symphonies by some such arrangement of type as this:

$$1 \quad 2 \quad 3 \quad 4 \quad 5 \quad 6 \quad 7 \quad 8 \quad 9$$

Viewing his whole life work in the large, one can roughly discern something of the same periodicity, though in largo time, which one sees in the presto agitato ups and downs of his relations with his much-enduring friends. Though his works were not written in the strict order of their opus numbers, these numbers nevertheless form a chronological sequence roughly correct enough for a bird's-eye view. Of Beethoven's first one hundred numbered works (with the single exception of the glorious Opus 60's) the successive groups of ten, taken as wholes, oscillate from weaker to stronger and back to weaker. The groups beginning with Opus 10, 30, 50, 70, and 90 all contain better music than those beginning with Opus 1, 20, 40, and 80.

After the Napoleonic Wars a new generation arose which preferred to Beethoven the more easily comprehended music of Italy. The German Master was partially shelved as *vieux jeu*, only to regain his popularity after some years. A century later, in the United States, a similar thing happened to him. During the Great War the "Hun" Beethoven was taboo. And even after peace came the fashion-worshiping youngsters regarded him as a fossil. But before the centenary of his death he was again in high favor. The Beethovens can afford to disregard the fluctuations of fashion and to say, as the Master remarked when told that his work did not please: "It will please someday." Such a person is not for a day "but for all time." He is not for a nation but for all people. To him might better be applied the words of the Chevalier de Boufflers about Voltaire: "This man is too great to be contained in the bounds of his country; he is a gift from nature to the whole earth."—ROBERT HAVEN SCHAUFFLER

BIBLIOGRAPHY

ALBINI, EUGENIO. "Beethoven e le sui Cinque Sonate per Violoncello," *Revista Musicale Italiana*, Vo. XXX, No. 2. Turin: Fratelli Bocca, 1923.

ALDRICH, RICHARD. "George Thomson, Publisher," *Musical Quarterly*, April 1927.

ALTMANN, LUDWIG (ed.). *Beethoven's Works for Organ*. London: Hinrichsen, 1962.

ALTMANN, WILHELM (ed.). *Beethoven: String Quintet Opus 4*, Edition Eulenburg No. 214. London: Ernst Eulenburg, Ltd., 1937   (1)

————. "Beethoven: String Quartet in F Major," from *The Piano Sonata in E Major, Opus 14, No. 1*, Edition Eulenburg. Leipzig: Ernst Eulenburg, 1911.   (2)

————. Preface to *Beethoven: String Quintet, Opus 104*, Edition Eulenburg. No. 215. London: Ernst Eulenburg, Ltd., 1937   (3)

ANDERSON, EMILY (ed. and tr.). *The Letters of Beethoven*, Vols. I, II, and III. London: Macmillan & Co., Ltd., 1961.

APEL, WILLI. *Masters of the Keyboard*. Cambridge, Massachusetts: Harvard University Press, 1965.

APTHORP, WILLIAM FOSTER. On *The Analytical Concert Guide* by Louis Biancolli and William S. Mann (eds.). New York: Doubleday & Co., Inc., 1951.

ARANYI, YELLI D'. "The Violin Sonata," *Music and Letters*. April 1927.

AUER, LEOPOLD. *Violin Master Works and Their Interpretation*. New York and Boston: C. Fischer, Inc., 1925.

BARFORD, PHILIP T. "Beethoven's Last Sonata." In *Music and Letters*. Vol. XXXV, No. 4, October 1954.

BARZUN, JACQUES (ed.). *Pleasures of Music*. New York: Viking Press, 1951.

BENNETT, S. W. Jacket notes for Vanguard 71124.   (1)

————. Jacket notes for Vanguard VRS-1101.   (2)

BENTLEY, ERIC (ed.). *Shaw on Music*. New York: Doubleday & Co., Inc., 1955.

BERLIOZ, HECTOR. *A Critical Study of Beethoven's Nine Symphonies.* Translated by Edwin Evans. London: William Reeves, 1958.

BLAXLAND, J. H. "An Unknown Canzonetta by Beethoven," *Zeitschrift fur Musikwissenschaft,* Vol. XIV. Leipzig, 1931.

BLOM, ERIC. *Beethoven's Pianoforte Sonatas Discussed.* New York: De Capo Press, 1968.   (1)

———. Jacket notes for Angel COLH-66   (2)

BOROWSKY, FELIX. In *The Analytical Concert Guide* by Louis Biancolli and William S. Mann (eds.). New York: Doubleday & Co., Inc., 1951.

BROCKWAY, WALLACE. Jacket notes for RCA Victor LM-2420.

BURK, JOHN N. *The Life and Works of Beethoven.* New York: Random House, 1943.   (1)

———. Program notes for Boston Symphony Orchestra.   (2)

BUSONI, FERRUCCIO BENVENUTO. *Letters to His Wife.* Translated by Rosamond Ley. London: E. Arnold & Co., 1938.

CANBY, EDWARD TATNALL. Jacket notes for Nonesuch H-1025.

CARPENTER, CHARLES K. "Disease—or Defamation?" *Annals of Otology, Rhinology and Laryngology,* Vol. XLV, No. 4, December, 1936.

CARSE, ADAM. *The Orchestra from Beethoven to Berlioz.* New York: Broude Brothers, 1949.

CAWTHORNE, TERENCE. "The Influence of Deafness on the Creative Instinct," *Transactions of the American Laryngological, Rhinological and Otological Society, Inc.,* 1960.

CHITZ, ARTHUR. "Une oeuvre inconnue de Beethoven pour mandoline et piano," S.I.M. *Revue Musicale,* Vol. VIII, No. 12. Paris.

COBBETT, WALTER WILLSON (com. and ed.). *Cobbett's Cyclopedic Survey of Chamber Music,* Second Edition, Vols. I, II, and III. London: Oxford University Press, 1963.

COCKSHOOT, JOHN V. *The Fugue in Beethoven's Piano Music.* London: Routledge & Kegan Paul, 1959.

CORREDOR, J. MA. *Conversations with Casals.* Translated by André Mangeot. New York: E. P. Dutton & Co., Inc., 1958.

COURCY, G. I. C. DE. *Paganini the Genoese,* Vol. I. Norman, Oklahoma: University of Oklahoma Press, 1957.

CURTISS, MINA. *Bizet and His World.* New York: Alfred A. Knopf, 1958.

CZERNY, CARL. "Erinnerungen aus meinem Leben," *Musical Quarterly.* New York: G. Schirmer, July 1956.

DEBUSSY, CLAUDE. "Monsieur Croche the Dilettante Hater," *Three Classics in the Aesthetics of Music.* New York: Dover Publications, 1962.

Decca DL9543, Unsigned jacket notes.

DENT, EDWARD J. "The Choral Fantasia," *Music and Letters.* April 1927.

DEUTSCH, OTTO ERICH. Piano Edition of "*XII Deutsche Tanze mit Koda.*" Vienna: Edition Strache, No. 24, 1929.

DORIAN, FREDERICK. *The Musical Workshop*. New York: Harper & Brothers, 1947.

DOUEL, MARTIAL. "Beethoven's Adelaïde," *Musical Quarterly*. New York: G. Schirmer, April 1927.

DOWNES, EDWARD. Program notes for the New York Philharmonic, 1966.

DUKAS, PAUL. In *Composers on Music*. Edited by Sam Morgenstern. New York: Pantheon Books, Inc., 1956.

EDWARDS, BATEMAN. In *The Analytical Concert Guide*, by Louis Biancolli and William S. Mann (eds.). New York: Doubleday & Co., Inc., 1951.

FERGUSON, DONALD N. *Masterworks of the Orchestral Repertoire*. Minneapolis, Minnesota: University of Minnesota Press, 1954.　　(1)
———. *Music as Metaphor: The Elements of Expression*. Minneapolis, Minnesota: University of Minnesota Press, 1960.　　(2)
———. *Image and Structure in Chamber Music*. Minneapolis, Minnesota: University of Minnesota Press, 1964.　　(3)

FINKELSTEIN, SIDNEY. Jacket notes for Vanguard VRS-429.

FISCHER, EDWIN. *Beethoven's Pianoforte Sonatas*. London: Faber and Faber, 1959.

FISKE, ROGER. In *Chamber Music*. Edited by Alec Robertson. Baltimore: Penguin Books, 1957.

FORBES, ELLIOT (ed.). *Thayer's Life of Beethoven*, Vols. I and II. Princeton: Princeton University Press, 1964.

FRIMMEL, THEODOR. *Ludwig van Beethoven*. Berlin: Schlesische Verlagsanstalt, 1922.　　(1)
———. *Beethoven Handbuch*. Leipzig: Breitkopf & Härtel, 1926　　(2)

FURTWÄNGLER, WILHELM, *Concerning Music*. Translated by L. J. Lawrence. London, New York: Boosey & Hawkes, 1953.

GODDARD, SCOTT. "Beethoven and Goethe," *Music and Letters*. London: April 1927.

GOTTSCHALK, LOUIS MOREAU. *Notes of a Pianist*. Edited by Jeanne Behrend. New York: Alfred A. Knopf, 1964.

HARBREICH, HARRY. Jacket notes for Vox SVBX-545.　　(1)
———. Jacket notes for Vox FBX-53.　　(2)

HALE, PHILIP. Program notes for Boston Symphony Orchestra.　　(1)
———. In *The Analytical Concert Guide*, Louis Biancolli and William S. Mann (eds.). New York: Doubleday & Company, Inc., 1951.　　(2)

HALL, JAMES HUSST. *The Art Song*. Norman, Oklahoma: University of Oklahoma Press, 1953.

HAMBURGER, PHILIP. Jacket notes for Angel 35719.

HANSLICK, EDUARD. *Music Criticisms 1846–99*. Translated by Henry Pleasants. Baltimore: Penguin Books, 1950.

HERBST, KURT. "Beethovens Opferliedkompositionen," *Neues Beethoven-Jahrbuch*, Vol. V.

HERRIOT, EDOUARD. *The Life and Times of Beethoven.* Translated by A. I. Mitchell and W. J. Mitchell. New York: Macmillan Company, 1935.

HERTZMANN, ERICH. "The Newly Discovered Autograph of Beethoven's Rondo a Capriccio, Opus 129," *Musical Quarterly*, Vol. XXXIII.

HESS, WILLY. "Beethoven e lo Spielühr," *Ricordiana.* Milan: anno 3, n. 5, May 1927. (1)

———. Preface to first printed edition of "*No, non turbati.*" Wiesbaden: Bruchnerverlag, 1948. (2)

———. Das Singspiel "Die schone Schusterin." Jahrgang: Beethoven Jahrbuch, Jahrgang 1959/60. (3)

———. Preface to "*Szene aus Vestas feuer.*" Wiesbaden: Brucknerverlag, 1953. (4)

———. "Tarpeja." Jahrgang: Beethoven Jahrbuch, 1961/4. (5)

———. "Beethoven's Last Composition," *Music and Letters*, Vol. XXXIII. London: 1952. (6)

———. "Neues zu Beethovens Zapfenstreiche." *Schweizer Musikzeitung*, October 1, 1937. (7)

———. "Die Urauführing eines Beethovenschen Meisterwerk im Jahr 1939." Neues Beethoven Jahrbuch, Vol. IX, 1939. (8)

HITZIG, WILHELM. "Beethoven's Chorlieder mit Klavierbegleitung: Das Hochzeitslied für Nanni Giannastasio del Rio." Mainz: Neue Zeitschrift für Musik, Jahrgang 118, Heft 3, March 1957.

HOFFMANN, E. T. A. "Beethoven's Instrumental Music," *Musical Quarterly*, Vol. III, No. 1, January 1917. Translated by Arthur Ware Locke. (1)

———. *Musikalische Schriften.* Koln am Rhine: A. vom Ende's Verlag, 1899. (2)

HUFSTADER, ALICE ANDERSON. "Beethoven's Irische Lieder: Sources and Problems." *Musical Quarterly*, Vol. XLV, No. 3, July 1959.

INDY, VINCENT D'. *Beethoven: A Critical Biography.* Boston: Boston Music Company, 1911 (1)

———. In *Cobbett's Cyclopedic Survey of Chamber Music.* Walter Cobbett, comp. and ed. Second Edition, Vol. I. London: Oxford University Press, 1963. (2)

IVES, CHARLES. In *Three Classics in the Aesthetics of Music.* New York: Dover Publications, Inc., 1962.

KASTENDIECK, MILES. Program notes for Little Orchestra Society, New York, season 1949–50.

KAUFMAN, SCHIMA. *Mendelssohn.* New York: Tudor Publishing Company, 1934.

KERMAN, JOSEPH. *The Beethoven Quartets.* New York: Alfred A. Knopf, 1967.

KINSKY, GEORG. *Das Werk Beethovens.* Edited by Hans Halm. Munich: G. Henle Verlag, 1955.

———. *Katalog der Musik-historisches Museum von Wilhelm Heyer in Coln.* Coln: J. P. Bachem, 1916.

KLAUWELL, OTTO. "Ludwig van Beethoven und die Variationen-form," *Studien und Erinnerung.* Langesalza: Hermann Beyer und Söhne, 1906.

KOBBE, GUSTAV. *Complete Opera Book.* New York and London: Putnam's, 1919.

KOLODIN, IRVING. Jacket notes for Decca 9555.

KREHBIEL, H. E. Historical and critical notes, in *Schirmer's Library of Musical Classics,* Vol. 618, "Beethoven: Six Songs for High Voice." New York: G. Shirmer, Inc., 1902.   (1)

———. Preface to Schirmer Edition of Opus 98. New York: G. Schirmer, Inc., 1902.   (2)

LATHAM, PETER. In *The Music Masters,* by A. L. Bacharach (ed.). Dublin, London: Maurice Fridberg, 1948.

LEICHTENTRITT, HUGO. Analytical notes to *The Complete Pianoforte Sonatas of Beethoven.* New York: Hugo Leichtentritt, 1936.

LEVINSON, ANDRE. "Le Ballet de Prométhée: Beethoven et Vigano," *La Revue Musicale,* Numero special, annee 8, tome 3, no. 6. Paris: 1924.

MACARDLE, D. W. "Beethoven and Haydn," *Monthly Musical Record,* Vol. 89, No. 966. London: November–December, 1959.

MANDYCZEWSKI, EUSEBIUS. "Beethovens Rondo in B für Pianoforte und Orchester." Sämmebände der Internationalen Musik-Gesellschaft, Erste Jahrgang (1900), pp. 295–306.

MANN, ALFRED. *The Study of Fugue.* New Brunswick: Rutgers University Press, 1958.

MANN, THOMAS. *Doctor Faustus.* Translated by H. T. Lowe-Porter. New York: Alfred A. Knopf, 1965.

MANN, WILLIAM S. Jacket notes for Angel 35509.   (1)

———. Jacket notes for Angel 35843.   (2)

MAREK, GEORGE R. *Beethoven: Biography of a Genius.* New York: Funk & Wagnalls, 1969.

MAREN, JUAN. Preface to his edition of WoO 5.

MASON, DANIEL GREGORY. *Beethoven and His Forerunners.* New York: Macmillan Company, 1904.   (1)

———. *The Quartets of Beethoven.* New York: Oxford University Press, 1947.   (2)

MENDELSSOHN-BARTHOLDY, FELIX. *Letters.* Edited by G. Selden-Goth. New York: Pantheon Books, Inc., 1945.

MEYER, LEONARD B. *Emotion and Meaning in Music.* Chicago: University of Chicago Press, 1956.

MIDGLEY, SAMUEL. *Handbook to Beethoven's Sonatas for Violin and Piano.* London: Breitkopf & Härtel, 1911.

MILNE, A. FORBES. "Beethoven—The Pianoforte Sonatas, II," In *The Musical Pilgrim*, by Arthur Somervell (ed.). London: Oxford University Press, 1925.

MISCH, LUDWIG. *Beethoven Studies.* Norman, Oklahoma: University of Oklahoma Press, 1953.

MORGENSTERN, SAM (ed.). *Composers on Music.* New York: Pantheon Books, Inc., 1956.

MOSER, HUGO. *Das Deutsche Lied seit Mozart*, Vol. I. Berlin and Zurich: Atlantis Verlag, 1937.

NEWMAN, ERNEST. *The Unconscious Beethoven.* New York: Alfred A. Knopf, 1930.

NEWMAN, WILLIAM S. *The Sonata in the Classic Era.* Chapel Hill: University of North Carolina Press, 1963.

NEWMARCH, ROSA (ed.). *Modest Tchaikovsky.* New York: John Lane Company, 1906.

NIECKS, FREDERICK. "Beethoven's Sonatas for Pianoforte and Violin," *Monthly Musical Record*, Vol. XX, No. 236 and No. 237. London: August 1890 and September 1890. (1)

——. "Beethoven's Piano Variations," *Monthly Musical Record*, Vol. XIX, No. 218, February, 1889; No. 219, March 1889; and No. 220, April 1889. (2)

NOHL, F. "A New Composition of Beethoven," *Monthly Musical Record.* London: February 1, 1882.

NOHL, LUDWIG. "The Tenth Symphony," In *Beethoven's Symphonies: Their Idealized Meaning*, by Ernst Van Elterlein. London: William Reeves, 1893.

NOTTEBOHM, GUSTAV. *Zweite Beethoveniana.* Leipzig: Verlag von J. Rieterbiedermann, 1887.

POLLAK, GUSTAV. *Franz Grillparzer and the Austrian Drama.* New York: Dodd, Mead and Co., 1907.

PROD'HOMME, J.-G. *La Jeunesse de Beethoven.* Paris: Librairie Delagrave, 1927. (1)

——. "Un Lied et une Sonate de Beethoven—Le 'Wachtelschlag,' et le Sonate Opus 30, No. 3," *Revue de Musicologie*, Tome XI. Paris: Librairie Fischbacher, 1930. (2)

——. *Les Sonates pour Piano de Beethoven.* Paris: Librairie Delagrave, 1937. (3)

PRYCE-JONES, ALAN. *Beethoven.* London: Gerald Duckworth & Co., 1957.

RABE, JULIUS. "Antonio Salieri—Beethovens Lärare," *Svensk Tidskrift för Musikforskning.* arg 9, 1927.

RIES, FERDINAND. *Biographisches Notizen über Ludwig van Beethoven.* Edited by Franz Wegeler and Ferdinand Ries. Doblenz, 1838.

RIEZLER, WALTER. *Beethoven.* New York: E. P. Dutton & Co., 1938.

ROBERTSON, ALEC (ed.). *Chamber Music.* Baltimore: Penguin Books, 1957.

ROLLAND, ROMAIN. *Beethoven.* Translated by B. Constance Hull. London: Kegan Paul, Trench, Trubner and Co., Ltd., 1924. (1)

——. *Beethoven the Creator.* Translated by Ernest Newman. New York: Dover Publications, 1964. Unabridged republication of English translation first published by Victor Gollancz, Ltd., 1929. (2)

SAINT-SAËNS, CAMILLE. In *Composers on Music.* Sam Morgenstern (ed.). New York: Pantheon Books, Inc., 1956.

SANDELEWSKI, WIAROSLAW. Jacket notes for Auditorium Records AUD104.

SCHAUFFLER, ROBERT HAVEN. *Beethoven: the Man Who Freed Music,* Vol. II. New York: Doubleday, Doran & Company, Inc., 1929.

SCHENK, JOHANN. *Autobiography.* Quoted in *Forgotten Musicians,* by Paul Nettl. New York: Philosophic Library, 1951.

SCHIEDERMAIR, LUDWIG. *Der Junge Beethoven.* Leipzig: Quelle & Meyer, 1925.

SCHINDLER, ANTON FELIX. *Beethoven as I Knew Him.* Edited by Donald W. MacArdle; translated by Constance S. Jolly. Chapel Hill: University of North Carolina Press, 1966.

SCHMID, ERNST FRITZ. "Joseph Haydn und die Flotenühr," *Zeitschrift für Musikwissenschaft.* Leipzig: January 1932. Vol. XIV.

SCHMITZ, ARNOLD. *Beethoven Unbekannte Skissen und Entwürfe.* Bonn: Verlag des Beethovenhauses, 1924.

SCHONBERG, HAROLD C. *The Great Pianists.* New York: Simon & Schuster, 1963.

SCHUMANN, KARL. Jacket notes for DGG S138993/5.

SCHUMANN, ROBERT. *On Music and Musicians.* Edited by Konrad Wolff, translated by Paul Rosenfeld. New York: Pantheon Books, Inc., 1946.

SCHWARZ, BORIS. "Beethoven and the French Violin School," *Musical Quarterly,* Vol. XLIV, No. 4. October 1958.

SCOTT, MARION M. *Beethoven.* London: J. M. Dent & Sons, Ltd., 1934.

SEYFRIED, IGNATIUS VON (ed. & tr. by Henry Hugh Pierson). Appendix to Louis van Beethoven's Studies in Thorough-bass, Counterpoint and the Art of Scientific Composition. Schuberth & Co.: Leipzig, 1853.

SHEDLOCK, J. S. Preface to *Selection of Studies,* by Cramer. London: Augener & Co., 1893. (1)

——. "Beethoven and His Coypists," *Monthly Musical Record.* August 2, 1915. (2)

SHEPHERD, ARTHUR. *The Quartets of Ludwig van Beethoven*. Program notes for the Cleveland Quartet, Cleveland, Ohio, 1935.

SLONIMSKY, NICOLAS. *Lexicon of Musical Invective*. Second edition. New York: Coleman-Ross Company, Inc., 1965.

SONNECK, O. G. *Beethoven: Impressions by His Contemporaries*. New York: G. Schirmer, Inc., 1926.   (1)

———. (Translator and Editor) *Beethoven Letters in America*. New York: The Beethoven Association, 1927.   (2)

SPECHT, RICHARD. *Beethoven as He Lived*. Translated by Alfred Kalisch. London: Macmillan and Co., Ltd., 1933.

STEIN, FRITZ. "*Duett mit zwei obligaten Augenglasern: Sonatensatz fur Viola und Violoncello,*" notes. Leipzig: C. F. Peters, 1952.

STEVENS, DENIS. In *Chamber Music*. Alec Robertson (ed.). Baltimore: Penguin Books, 1957.

STRAVINSKY, IGOR, AND ROBERT CRAFT. *Conversations with Stravinsky*. New York: Doubleday & Co., Inc., 1959.

SULLIVAN, J. W. N. *Beethoven: His Spiritual Development*. New York: Vintage Books, 1960.

SZIGETI, JOSEPH. *The Ten Beethoven Sonatas for Piano and Violin*. Urbana, Illinois: American String Teachers Association, 1965.   (1)

———. *A Violinist's Notebook*. London: Gerald Duckworth & Co., Ltd., 1964.   (2)

THAYER, ALEXANDER WHEELOCK. *Chronologiches Verzeichniss der Werke Ludwig van Beethovens*. Berlin: F. Schneider, 1865.

———. *The Life of Ludwig van Beethoven*, Vols. I, II, III. Edited and translated by Henry Edward Krehbiel. New York: Beethoven Association, 1921.

THORPE, DAY. Jacket notes for Counterpoint/Esoteric 553.

TOCH, ERNST. *The Shaping Forces in Music*. New York: Criterion Music Corp., 1958.

TOVEY, DONALD FRANCIS. *Beethoven*. Edited by Hubert J. Foss. London: Oxford University Press, 1944. Oxford Paperbacks, 1965.   (1)

———. *Essays in Musical Analysis, Vol. I: Symphonies*. London: Oxford University Press, 1935.   (2)

———. *Essays in Musical Analysis, Vol. II: Symphonies, Variations and Orchestral Polyphony*. London: Oxford University Press, 1935.   (3)

———. *Essays in Musical Analysis, Vol. III: Concertos*. London: Oxford University Press, 1936.   (4)

———. *Essays in Musical Analysis, Vol. IV: Illustrative Music*. London: Oxford University Press, 1937.   (5)

———. *Essays in Musical Analysis, Vol. V: Vocal Music*. London: Oxford University Press, 1937.   (6)

——. *Essays in Musical Analysis, Vol. VI: Supplementary Essays, Glossary and Index.* London: Oxford University Press, 1939.　　(7)

——. *Essays in Musical Analysis: Chamber Music.* London: Oxford University Press, 1944.　　(8)

——. *A Companion to Beethoven's Pianoforte Sonatas.* London: Associated Board of the Royal Music Schools, 1931.　　(9)

——. *Musical Articles from the Encyclopaedia Britannica.* Edited by Hubert J. Foss. London: Oxford University Press, 1944.　　(10)

——. "Some Aspects of Beethoven's Art Forms," *Music and Letters.* London: April 1927.　　(11)

——. *The Main Stream of Music and Other Essays.* Oxford: Oxford University Press, 1949.　　(12)

——. Program notes for Reid Orchestral Series. February 10, 1923. (13)

Toye, Francis. *Rossini, A Study in Tragi-comedy.* New York: W. W. Norton & Co., Inc., 1963.

Turnabout TV 34162, jacket notes.

Turnabout TV 4059, jacket notes.

Turner, W. J. *Beethoven: The Search for Reality.* London: Ernest Benn, Ltd., 1927.

Ulrich, Homer. *Chamber Music.* New York and London: Columbia University Press, 1948.

Unger, Max. "The Immortal Beloved," *Musical Quarterly*, Vol. XIII, No. 2, April 1927.　　(1)

——. "Zu Beethovens letzten Tanzen," *Zeitschrift für Musik*, February 1938.　　(2)

——. *Ein Faust Opernplan Beethovens und Goethe.* Regensburg: Bosse, 1952.　　(3)

Vallas, Leon. *The Theories of Claude Debussy.* Translated by Maire O'Brien. London: Oxford University Press, 1929.

Vallat, George. *Alexandre Boucher et son temps.* Paris: Maison Quantin, 1890.

Vaughan Williams, Ralph. *Some Thoughts on Beethoven's Choral Symphony.* London: Oxford University Press, 1953. Reprinted 1959.

Veinus, Abraham. Jacket notes for Vanguard VRS1033.

Vogel, Alexander. *Beethoven: Sextet, Opus 81b.* Edition Eulenberg. London: Ernst Eulenburg, Inc.

Waack, Carl. "Beethoven's F Major String Quartet, Opus 18, No. 1, in Its Original Version," *Die Musik*, Vol. 12, March 2, 1904.

Wagner, Richard. *Richard Wagner's Prose Works*, Vol. I: "The Art-Work of the Future." Second Edition. Translated by William Ashton Ellis. London: Kegan Paul, Trench, Trubner & Co., Ltd., 1895.

——. *Richard Wagner's Prose Works,* Vol. II: Opera and Drama. Vol. III: The Theatre. Vol. IV: Art and Politics. Vol. V: Actors and Singers. Vol. VI: Religion and Art. Vol. VII: In Paris and Dresden. Vol. VIII: Posthumous, etc. Translated by William Ashton Ellis. London: Kegan Paul, Trench, Trubner & Co., Ltd., 1899.

WALTER, BRUNO. *Of Music and Music-Making.* Translated by Paul Hamburger. New York: W. W. Norton & Company, Inc., 1957.

WARRACK, JOHN. "Chamber Works with Wind Instruments (from 1700)." In *Chamber Music,* by Alec Robertson (ed.). Baltimore: Penguin Books, 1957.

WEGELER, FRANZ AND FERDINAND RIES (eds.). *Biographisches Notizen uber Ludwig van Beethoven.* Coblenz: 1838.

WEINSTOCK, HERBERT. Program notes for Little Orchestra Society, New York.

WERNER, JACK (ed.). *Classical Discoveries.* London: Elkin and Co., Ltd., 1960.

WESTERBY, HERBERT. *Beethoven and His Piano Works.* London: William Reeves, Bookseller. Limited. Undated.

WESTMINSTER S-9008. Unsigned jacket notes.

YEOMANS, WILLIAM. "Beethoven's Diabelli Variations," *Monthly Musical Record,* Vol. 89, No. 991. January–February 1959.